# The Blackwell Companion
# to the New Testament

# Blackwell Companions to Religion

The Blackwell *Companions to Religion* series presents a collection of the most recent scholarship and knowledge about world religions. Each volume draws together newly commissioned essays by distinguished authors in the field, and is presented in a style which is accessible to undergraduate students, as well as scholars and the interested general reader. These volumes approach the subject in a creative and forward-thinking style, providing a forum in which leading scholars in the field can make their views and research available to a wider audience.

## Published

**The Blackwell Companion to Judaism**
Edited by Jacob Neusner and Alan J. Avery-Peck

**The Blackwell Companion to Sociology of Religion**
Edited by Richard K. Fenn

**The Blackwell Companion to the Hebrew Bible**
Edited by Leo G. Perdue

**The Blackwell Companion to Postmodern Theology**
Edited by Graham Ward

**The Blackwell Companion to Hinduism**
Edited by Gavin Flood

**The Blackwell Companion to Political Theology**
Edited by Peter Scott and William T. Cavanaugh

**The Blackwell Companion to Protestantism**
Edited by Alister E. McGrath and Darren C. Marks

**The Blackwell Companion to Modern Theology**
Edited by Gareth Jones

**The Blackwell Companion to Christian Ethics**
Edited by Stanley Hauerwas and Samuel Wells

**The Blackwell Companion to Religious Ethics**
Edited by William Schweiker

**The Blackwell Companion to Christian Spirituality**
Edited by Arthur Holder

**The Blackwell Companion to the Study of Religion**
Edited by Robert A. Segal

**The Blackwell Companion to the Qur'ān**
Edited by Andrew Rippin

**The Blackwell Companion to Contemporary Islamic Thought**
Edited by Ibrahim M. Abu-Rabi'

**The Blackwell Companion to the Bible and Culture**
Edited by John F. A. Sawyer

**The Blackwell Companion to Catholicism**
Edited by James J. Buckley, Frederick Christian Bauerschmidt, and Trent Pomplun

**The Blackwell Companion to Eastern Christianity**
Edited by Ken Parry

**The Blackwell Companion to the Theologians**
Edited by Ian S. Markham

**The Blackwell Companion to the Bible in English Literature**
Edited by Rebecca Lemon, Emma Mason, John Roberts, and Christopher Rowland

**The Blackwell Companion to Nineteenth-Century Theology**
Edited by David Fergusson

**The Blackwell Companion to the New Testament**
Edited by David E. Aune

## Forthcoming

**The Blackwell Companion to Jesus**
Edited by Delbert Burkett

**The Blackwell Companion to Religion in America**
Edited by Philip Goff

**The Blackwell Companion to African Religions**
Edited by Elias Bongmba

**The Blackwell Companion to Christian Mysticism**
Edited by Julia A. Lamm

**The Blackwell Companion to Pastoral Theology**
Edited by Bonnie Miller McLemore

**The Blackwell Companion to Religion and Violence**
Edited by Andrew Murphy

**The Blackwell Companion to Chinese Religions**
Edited by Randall Nadeau

**The Blackwell Companion to Buddhism**
Edited by Mario Poceski

THE BLACKWELL COMPANION TO
# THE NEW TESTAMENT
EDITED BY David E. Aune

Written by more than forty scholars from
a variety of Christian denominations, this
Companion is a detailed introduction to New
Testament study. The contributors represent an
international scope and a wide field of expertise.
The early chapters consider the historical,
social, and cultural contexts in which the New
Testament was produced, and examine relevant
linguistic and textual issues. Later chapters treat
the twenty-seven books and letters of the New
Testament systematically, each chapter beginning
with a review of current issues and concluding
with an annotated bibliography.

Distinctive features include a unified treatment
of Luke and Acts, articles on the canonical
Gospels, and a discussion of the apocryphal New
Testament. Taken as a whole, the Companion
can be used as a text for courses on the New
Testament, or as a reference work for more
advanced students.

WILEY-
BLACKWELL

## Editor

DAVID E. AUNE is the Walter Professor of New
Testament & Christian Origins at the University
of Notre Dame. He has been a Fulbright Professor
at the University of Trondheim, Norway, has held
an Alexander von Humboldt Research Prize at
the University of Tübingen, Germany, and was
the Annual Professor at the Albright Institute of
Archaeological Research in Jerusalem. He is the
author of several books, including *The Westminster
Dictionary of the Literature and Rhetoric of the
New Testament and Early Christian Literature*
(2003) and *Revelation* (3 vols., 1997–8).

Cover image: Christ the Redeemer, Source of Life, *c.*1393–94,
Byzantine. Umjetnicka Gallerija, Skopje, Macedonia / Lauros /
Giraudon / The Bridgeman Art Library.

Cover design by Nicki Averill

WILEY-
BLACKWELL

# The Blackwell Companion to the New Testament

*Edited by*

David E. Aune

WILEY-BLACKWELL

A John Wiley & Sons, Ltd., Publication

This edition first published 2010
© 2010 Blackwell Publishing Ltd except for editorial material and organization
© David E. Aune

Blackwell Publishing was acquired by John Wiley & Sons in February 2007. Blackwell's publishing program has been merged with Wiley's global Scientific, Technical, and Medical business to form Wiley-Blackwell.

*Registered Office*
John Wiley & Sons Ltd, The Atrium, Southern Gate, Chichester, West Sussex, PO19 8SQ, United Kingdom

*Editorial Offices*
350 Main Street, Malden, MA 02148-5020, USA
9600 Garsington Road, Oxford, OX4 2DQ, UK
The Atrium, Southern Gate, Chichester, West Sussex, PO19 8SQ, UK

For details of our global editorial offices, for customer services, and for information about how to apply for permission to reuse the copyright material in this book please see our website at www.wiley.com/wiley-blackwell.

*Library of Congress Cataloging-in-Publication Data*

The Blackwell companion to the New Testament / edited by David E. Aune.
     p. cm. – (The Blackwell companions to religion)
  Includes bibliographical references and index.
  ISBN 978-1-4051-0825-6 (hardcover : alk. paper)
1. Bible. N.T.–Introductions.   I. Aune, David Edward.
  BS2330.3.B53 2010
  225.6–dc22
                2009033116

A catalogue record for this book is available from the British Library.

Set in 10 on 13 pt Photina by Toppan Best-set Premedia Limited

01   2010

Dedicated to the memory of three friends who died during 2009

PROFESSOR MARTIN HENGEL
(July 2)

RABBI PROFESSOR MICHAEL J. SINGER
(January 10)

PROFESSOR GRAHAM M. STANTION
(July 19)


"Precious in the sight of the Lord is the death of his saints"
(Psalm 116:15)

# Contents

# Contributors

**Dale C. Allison, Jr.** is Errett M. Grable Professor of New Testament Exegesis and Early Christianity at Pittsburgh Theological Seminary (Pittsburgh, Pennsylvania). His most recent books include *The Historical Christ and the Theological Jesus* (2009), *The Historical Jesus in Context* (edited with Amy-Jill Levine and John Dominic Crossan, 2006), *The Love That's Sleeping: The Art and Spirituality of George Harrison* (2006), *The Luminous Dusk* (2006), *Resurrecting Jesus: The Earliest Christian Tradition and its Interpreters* (2005), and *Studies in Matthew: Interpretations Past and Present* (2005).

**David E. Aune** is Walter Professor of New Testament and Christian Origins at the University of Notre Dame (Notre Dame, Indiana). He was elected a fellow in the Norwegian Royal Society of Sciences and Letters (Det Kongelige Norske Videnskabers Selskab) in 2000 and a fellow in the Norwegian Academy of Science and Letters (Det Norske Videnskaps-Akademi) in 2009. His most recent books include *Reading Religions in the Ancient World: Essays Presented to Robert McQueen Grant on his 90th Birthday* (edited with Robin Darling Young, 2007), *Apocalypticism, Prophecy, and Magic in Early Christianity: Collected Essays* (2006), *Rereading Paul Together: Protestant and Catholic Perspectives on Justification* (edited, 2006), *The Westminster Dictionary of New Testament & Early Christian Literature & Rhetoric* (2003), and a three-volume commentary on Revelation (1997–8).

**David L. Barr** is Professor of Religion at Wright State University (Dayton, Ohio). He is the author of *New Testament Story: An Introduction*, 4th edition (2009), *Tales of the End: A Narrative Commentary on the Book of Revelation* (1998), and (with James V. Panoch, Rodney Allen, and Robert Spivey), *The Bible Reader's Guide* (1970) and (with James V. Panoch) *Religion Goes To School: A Practical Handbook for Teachers* (1968). He has edited *The Reality of Apocalypse: Rhetoric and Politics in the Book of Revelation* (2006) and *Reading the Book of Revelation: A Resource for Students* (2003). He has also edited, with Linda Bennett Elder and Elizabeth Struthers Malbon, *Biblical and Humane: A Festschrift for John Priest* (1996) and, with Nicholas Piediscalzi, *The Bible in American Education* (1982).

**Jouette M. Bassler** is Professor of New Testament Emerita at Perkins School of Theology, Southern Methodist University (Dallas, Texas). She is the author of *Navigating Paul: An Introduction to Key Theological Concepts* (2007), *1 Timothy, 2 Timothy, Titus* (1996), and *God & Mammon: Asking for Money in the New Testament* (1991) and was an associate editor of *The HarperCollins Study Bible: New Revised Standard Version Including the Apocryphal/Deuterocanonical Books* (1993, revised edition 2006).

**Leslie Baynes** is Assistant Professor, Department of Religious Studies at Missouri State University (Springfield, Missouri). She is the author of *The Heavenly Book Motif in Judeo-Christian Apocalypses 200 BCE–200 CE* (2010).

**Karl Donfried** is Elizabeth A. Woodson Professor Emeritus of Religion and Biblical Literature at Smith College (Northampton, Maine). He is the author of *Who Owns the Bible? Toward a Recovery of a Christian Hermeneutic* (2006), and editor of *The Romans Debate: Expanded and Revised Edition* (first edition 1991; revised edition 2001).

**Dennis C. Duling** is Professor Emeritus, Department of Religious Studies and Theology at Canisius College (Buffalo, New York). He is the author and reviser, after the death of Norman Perrin, the author of the first edition, of *The New Testament: Proclamation, Parenesis, Myth and History* (2nd edition 1982; 3rd edition 1994; 4th edition 2003).

**John Fotopoulos** is Associate Professor of Theology at St. Mary's College (Notre Dame, Indiana). His most recent publications include *The New Testament and Early Christian Literature in Greco-Roman Context: Studies in Honor of David E. Aune* (edited, 2006), *Food Offered to Idols in Roman Corinth: A Social-Rhetorical Reconsideration of 1 Corinthians 8:1–11:1* (2003), translated in modern Greek as *Τα Θυσιαστήρια Δείνα στη Ρομαϊκη Κόρινθο. Μια Κοινονικο-Ρητορική Ανάλυσι του Α' Κορ. 8:1–11:1* (2006).

**Brian Han Gregg** is Assistant Professor of Biblical Studies at Sioux Falls University (Sioux Falls, South Dakota). He is the author of  *The Historical Jesus and the Final Judgment Sayings in Q* (2006).

**Paul A. Hartog** is Professor of New Testament at Faith Baptist Theological Seminary. He is the author of *Polycarp and the New Testament* (2002).

**Petra Heldt** teaches at Jerusalem University College and the Rothberg International School of Hebrew University (Jerusalem). She is the author of "Patristik," in Wolfgang Pauly (ed.), *Geschichte der christlichen Theologie* (2008), pp. 35–64, and of several articles on patristic subjects in *The New Interpreter's Dictionary of the Bible* (2008).

**Paul A. Holloway** is Associate Professor of New Testament in the School of Theology, the University of the South (Sewanee, Tennessee). He is the author of *Coping with Prejudice: 1 Peter in Social Psychological Perspective* (2009), *Consolation in Philippians: Philosophical Sources and Rhetorical Strategy* (2001) and is currently working on the Hermeneia commentary on Philippians.

**Michael W. Holmes** is University Professor of Biblical Studies and Early Christianity and Chair of the Department of Biblical and Theological Studies, Bethel University (St. Paul, Minnesota). He has edited and translated *The Apostolic Fathers: Greek Texts and English Translations* (3rd edition 2007) and *The Apostolic Fathers in English* (3rd edition 2006), both after the earlier version of J. B. Lightfoot and J. R. Harmer. He has edited, with Bart D. Ehrman, *The Text of the New Testament in Contemporary Research: Essays on the Status Quaestionis* (1995), and has edited, with Bart D. Ehrman and Gordon Fee, *The Text of the Fourth Gospel in the Writings of Origen*, vol. 1: *Introduction, Text, and Apparatus* (1992). He is the author of *1 and 2 Thessalonians: The NIV Application Commentary* (1998).

**Craig R. Koester** is Professor of New Testament at Luther Seminary (St. Paul, Minnesota). He is the author of *The Word of Life: A Theology of John's Gospel* (2008), *Symbolism in the Fourth Gospel: Meaning, Mystery, Community* (2003), *Hebrews: A New Translation with Introduction and Commentary* (2001), *Revelation and the End of All Things* (2001), *The Resurrection of Jesus in the Gospel of John* (1995), *A Beginner's Guide to Reading the Bible* (1991), and *The Dwelling of God: The Tabernacle in the Old Testament, Intertestamental Jewish Literature, and the New Testament* (1989). He has edited, with Reimund Bieringer, *The Resurrection of Jesus in the Gospel of John* (2008).

**Edgar Krentz** is Christ Seminary–Seminex Professor of New Testament Emeritus, Lutheran School of Theology at Chicago. He is the author of *The New Testament: History of Interpretation* (2004), *Galatians, Philippians, Philemon, 1 Thessalonians*, with John Koenig and Donald H. Juel (1985), *The Historical-Critical Method* (1975), and *Biblical Studies Today* (1960), and, with Arthur A. Vogel, *Easter* (1980).

**Amy-Jill Levine** is E. Rhodes and Leona B. Carpenter Professor of New Testament Studies, Vanderbilt University Divinity School, Vanderbilt University. She is the author of *The Misunderstood Jew: The Church and the Scandal of the Jewish Jesus* (2006) and *The Social and Ethnic Dimensions of Matthean Social History: "Go Nowhere among the Gentiles..." (Matt. 10:5b)* (1988). She has edited, with Maria Mayo Robbins, *A Feminist Companion to Patristic Literature* (2008), *A Feminist Companion to the New Testament Apocrypha* (2006), *A Feminist Companion to Mariology* (2005), and *A Feminist Companion to the Catholic Epistles and Hebrews* (2004). With Marianne Blickenstaff she has edited *A Feminist Companion to Paul* (2004), *A Feminist Companion to John* (2003), *A Feminist Companion to the Deutero-Pauline Epistles* (2003), and *A Feminist Companion to Mark* (2001). She has also edited *A Feminist Companion to Luke* (2002) and *"Women Like This": New Perspectives on Jewish Women in the Greco-Roman World* (1991). With Dale Allison and John Dominic Crossan, she has edited *The Historical Jesus in Context* (2006) and with Ernest Frerichs and Jacob Neusner she has edited *Religious Writings and Religious Systems: Systemic Analysis of Holy Books in Christianity, Islam, Buddhism, Greco-Roman Religions, Ancient Israel, and Judaism* (1989).

**John R. Levison** is Professor of New Testament at the School of Theology, Seattle Pacific University. He is the author of *Texts in Transition: The Greek Life of Adam and Eve* (2000), *Of Two Minds: Ecstasy and Inspired Interpretation in the New Testament World* (1999), *The Spirit in First Century Judaism* (1997), and *Portraits of Adam in Early Judaism: From Sirach to 2 Baruch* (1988). He is the editor, with Joseph Feldman, of *Josephus' Contra Apionem: Studies in its Character and Context with a Latin Concordance to the Portion Missing in Greek* (1996) and, with Priscilla Pope-Levison, of *Return to Babel: Global Perspectives on the Bible* (1999) and *Jesus in Global Contexts* (1992).

**Margaret Y. MacDonald** is Professor of Religious Studies at St. Francis Xavier University (Antigonish, Nova Scotia). She is the author (with Carolyn Osiek and Janet Tulloch) of *A Woman's Place: House Churches in Earliest Christianity* (2006), *Colossians and Ephesians* (2000), *Early Christian Women and Pagan Opinion: The Power of the Hysterical Woman* (1996), and *The Pauline Churches: A Socio-Historical Study of Institutionalization in the Pauline and Deutero-Pauline Writings* (1988). She is currently at work on a book projected entitled *Children and Childhood in Early Christian House Churches: The Significance and Impact of Household Codes.*

**Troy W. Martin** is Professor of New Testament at St. Xavier University (Chicago, Illinois). He is the author of *Metaphor and Composition in 1 Peter* (1992), *By Philosophy and Empty Deceit: Colossians as Response to a Cynic Critique* (1996), and, with Avis Clendenen, *Forgiveness: Finding Freedom through Reconciliation* (2002).

**C. Thomas McCollough** is Nelson D. and Mary McDowell Rodes Professor of Religion in the Department of Religion, Centre College (Danville, Kentucky). He has edited, with Douglas R. Edwards, *Archaeology and the Galilee: Text and Context in the Graeco-Roman and Byzantine Periods* (1997). Since 1985 he has been the assistant director of the archaeological excavations in Sepphoris, Israel, and in 2002 became the assistant director for the archaeological excavations of Khirbet Kana, Israel. He is working on a book project entitled *Ancient Christian Commentary of the Book of Daniel.*

**Kevin B. McCruden** is Assistant Professor of Religious Studies at Gonzaga University. He is the author of *Solidarity Perfected: Beneficent Christology in the Epistle to the Hebrews* (2008) and is editing (with Eric Mason) a collection of essays entitled *Interpreting Hebrews: Classic Sources and Contemporary Directions.*

**Mark D. Nanos** teaches at Rockhurst University (Kansas City, Kansas). He is the author of *The Irony of Galatians: Paul's Letter in First-Century Context* (2002) and *The Mystery of Romans: The Jewish Context of Paul's Letter* (1996). He is the editor of *The Galatians Debate: Contemporary Issues in Rhetorical and Historical Interpretation* (2002).

**Judith Newman** is Associate Professor of Hebrew Bible and Early Judaism, Emmanuel College of Victoria University in the University of Toronto. She is the author, with

Pieter van der Horst, of *Early Jewish Prayers in Greek* (2008), *Praying by the Book: The Scripturalization of Prayer in Second Temple Judaism* (1999), and is the editor, with Hindy Najman, of *The Idea of Biblical Interpretation: Essays in Honor of James L. Kugel* (2003).

**Jerome Neyrey** is Professor of New Testament Emeritus in the Department of Theology, University of Notre Dame (Notre Dame, Indiana). He is the author or editor of eighteen books, most recently *Give God the Glory: Ancient Prayer and Worship in Cultural Perspective* (2007), *The Gospel of John* (2007), *Render to God: New Testament Understandings of the Divine* (2004), *Honor and Shame in the Gospel of Matthew* (1998), and *Christ is Community: The Christologies of the New Testament* (1985). He has edited, with Bruce J. Malina, *Portraits of Paul: An Archaeology of Ancient Personality* (1996) and *Calling Jesus Names: The Social Value of Labels in Matthew* (1988), and, with Eric Stewart, *The Social World of the New Testament: Insights and Models* (2008).

**John Painter** is Professor of Theology at St. Mark's School of Theology, Charles Sturt University (Australia). He is the author of *Just James: The Brother of Jesus in History and Tradition* (1997; 2nd edition 2004), *1, 2, and 3 John* (2002), *Mark's Gospel: Worlds in Conflict* (1997), *The Quest for the Messiah: The History, Literature, and Theology of the Johannine Community* (1991; 2nd edition 1993), *Theology as Hermeneutics: Rudolf Bultmann's Interpretation of the History of Jesus* (1987), and *John Witness and Theologian* (1975; 2nd edition 1979; 3rd edition 1986). He has edited, with Alan Culpepper and Fernando Segovia, *Word, Theology, and Community in John* (2002).

**Ronald A. Piper** is Professor of Christian Origins and Vice-Principal at the University of St. Andrews (Scotland). He has served as the Secretary of the British New Testament Society, as an officer of the Studiorum Novi Testamenti Societas, as Convenor of the Q Seminar of the Society of Biblical Literature and as a Fellow of the Center for Theological Inquiry (Princeton, New Jersey). He is the author of *Wisdom in the Q-Tradition: The Aphoristic Teaching of Jesus* (1989) and (with Philip Esler) of *Lazarus, Mary and Martha: Social-Scientific Approaches to the Gospel of John* (2006). He is the editor of *The Gospel behind the Gospels: Current Studies on Q* (1995).

**Christophe Rico** is Assistant Professor at the École Biblique et Archéologique Française de Jérusalem and Visiting Professor at the Hebrew University of Jerusalem. He is the author of *Polis: Parler le grec ancien comme une langue vivante* (2009) and numerous articles focusing on linguistic issues.

**Vernon K. Robbins** was appointed Winship Distinguished Research Professor in the Department and Graduate Division of Religion, Emory University (Atlanta, Georgia), in 2001 and Professor Extraordinary at the University of Stellenbosch, South Africa in 2006. He is the author of *The Invention of Christian Discourse* (2009), *Sea Voyages and Beyond* (2009), *Exploring the Texture of Texts: A Guide to Socio-Rhetorical Interpretation* (1996), *The Tapestry of Early Christian Discourse: Rhetoric, Society and Ideology* (1996), *New Boundaries in Old Territory: Form and Social Rhetoric in Mark*

(1994), *Jesus the Teacher: A Socio-Rhetorical Interpretation of Mark* (1984, 2009), and, with Burton L. Mack, *Patterns of Persuasion in the Gospels* (1989, 2009). A Festschrift advancing his approach appeared in 2003, edited by David B. Gowler, L. Gregory Bloomquist, and Duane F. Watson: *Fabrics of Discourse: Essays in Honor of Vernon K. Robbins.*

**Calvin J. Roetzel** is the Sundet Professor of New Testament in the Department of Classical and Near Eastern Studies, College of Liberal Arts, University of Minnesota (Minneapolis). He is the author of *2 Corinthians* (2007), *Paul: A Jew on the Margins* (2003), *The Letters of Paul: Conversations in Context* (4th edition, 1998), *Paul: The Man and the Myth* (1998), *The World That Shaped the New Testament* (1985; revised edition 2002), and *Judgement in the Community: A Study of the Relationship between Eschatology and Ecclesiology in Paul* (1972).

**Jens Schröter** is Professor of New Testament Exegesis, Theology and New Testament Apocrypha, Faculty of Theology at the Humboldt University (Berlin, Germany). He is the author of *Jesus von Nazaret: Jude aus Galiläa, Retter der Welt* (2006, 2nd edition 2009), *Von Jesus zum Neuen Testament. Studien zur urchristlichen Theologiegeschichte und zur Entstehung des neutestamentlichen Kanons* (2007), *Das Abendmahl: Frühchristliche Deutungen und Impulse für die Gegenwart* (2006), *Jesus und die Anfänge der Christologie. Methodologische und exegetische Studien zu den Ursprüngen des christlichen Glaubens* (2001), *Erinnerung an Jesu Worte: Studien zur Rezeption der Logienüberlieferung in Markus Q und Thomas* (1997), and *Der versöhnte Versöhner: Paulus als unentbehrlicher Mittler im Heilsvorgang zwischen Gott und Gemeinde nach 2 Kor 2,14–7,4* (1993).

**Todd D. Still** is Associate Professor of Christian Scriptures at George W. Truett Theological Seminary, Baylor University (Waco, Texas). He is co-editor, with David G. Horrell, of *After the First Urban Christians: The Social-Scientific Study of Pauline Christianity Twenty-Five Years Later* (2009), and editor of *Jesus and Paul Reconnected: Fresh Pathways into an Old Debate* (2007). He is the author of "Colossians" in *The Expositor's Bible Commentary* (2006) and *Conflict at Thessalonica: A Pauline Church and its Neighbours* (1999).

**Richard P. Thompson** is Professor of New Testament and Chair of the Department of Religion, School of Theology and Christian Ministries, Northwest Nazarene University (Nampa, Idaho). He is the author of *Keeping the Church in its Place: The Church as Narrative Character in the Book of Acts* (2006).

**Thomas H. Tobin, SJ** is Professor of New Testament in the Theology Department at Loyola University Chicago. He is the author of *Paul's Rhetoric in its Contexts: The Argument of Romans* (2004), *The Spirituality of Paul* (1987, reprinted 2008), *On the Nature of the World and the Soul by Timaios of Locri: Text, Translation and Notes* (1985), and *The Creation of Man: Philo and the History of Interpretation* 1983), and the editor, with Harold W. Attridge and John J. Collins, of *Of Scribes and Scrolls: Studies on the*

*Hebrew Bible, Intertestamental Judaism, and Christian Origins Presented to John Strugnell on the Occasion of his Sixtieth Birthday* (1990).

**Patricia Walters** is Coordinator, Department of Religious Studies at Rockford College (Rockford, Illinois). She is the author of *The Assumed Authorial Unity of Luke and Acts* (2009).

**Duane F. Watson** is Professor of New Testament Studies in the School of Theology, Malone University (Canton, Ohio). He is the author of *The Rhetoric of the New Testament: A Bibliographic Survey* (2006), *Rhetorical Criticism of the Bible: A Comprehensive Bibliography with Notes on History and Method* (with Allan J. Hauser, 1994), *Invention, Arrangement, and Style: Rhetorical Criticism of Jude and 2 Peter* (1988), and the editor of *The History of Biblical Interpretation*, volume 1: *The Ancient Period* (with Alan J. Hauser, 2003), *Fabrics of Discourse: Essays in Honor or Vernon K. Robbins* (with David B. Gowler and L. Gregory Bloomquist, 2003), *The Intertexture of Apocalyptic Discourse in the New Testament* (2002), and *Persuasive Artistry: Studies in New Testament Rhetoric in Honor of George A. Kennedy* (1991).

# Introduction

## David E. Aune

The *Blackwell Companion to the New Testament* (*BCNT*), in preparation for several years, is one of the most comprehensive introductions to the literature of the New Testament currently available. The *BCNT* contains thirty-eight articles written by thirty-four New Testament scholars, women and men representing the best of Protestant, Catholic, and Jewish scholarship. While most of the contributors are from the United States, thus giving the book a distinctive American slant, some contributors are from Canada (two), Australia (one), the United Kingdom (one), Germany (one), and Israel (two). Despite the diverse religious and theological orientations and commitments of these contributors, all share the common secular methodological playing field of the historical-critical method, thus providing an overall unity to the volume.

As a collection of the classical and foundational texts of the Christian faith, the New Testament occupies a central, though not identical, role in all forms of Christianity. Those who keep track of religious statistics tell us that there are currently more than 4,200 religions in the world, and one of these religions, Christianity, consists of more than 33,000 denominations and groups. Since most of these groups presumably regard the New Testament as a foundational religious text, it is certainly striking how a single collection of twenty-seven writings could serve as a foundational text for so many variations of Christianity. The basic explanation centers on the fact that each socio-religious group that calls itself "Christian" has a particular shared understanding of who Jesus was and/or is and how "salvation" (which can be defined in many ways, but always refers to a particular perception of what it is that humans lack) was made possible by God through him. The basic religious or theological convictions shared by these groups (which can be very small or very large and complex) read the New Testament in such a way that it provides authorization for their belief systems. This largely unconscious way of manipulating a text provides divine authorization for the belief system that is read into it. Read in this way, the New Testament functions as a mirror for reflecting the image of whoever looks into it. The historical-critical method, on the other hand, focuses on the goal of reading a text to determine what it meant originally within the historical and social contexts within which the text arose. Thus while the purpose of historical criticism is to read a text as objectively as possible, complete objectivity is not finally attainable, though that is always the ideal goal of the method.

Students of the New Testament are aware that biblical scholarship is constantly in process of change and development (though laypeople often assume that everything worth knowing about the Bible surely must have been discovered many years ago). The first-century setting in which the New Testament is read is regularly augmented by new discoveries. One source of new knowledge is the discovery of ancient manuscripts from time to time, shedding new light on the cultural and religious context of early Christianity (the Dead Sea Scrolls, which began to be discovered near the Dead Sea in 1947, are perhaps the most striking example of such discoveries; more recently the Coptic Gnostic *Gospel of Judas* was discovered in the 1970s and first translated in 2006). Another source of new knowledge is archaeological excavations and explorations, which gradually expand our knowledge of the material culture of the ancient Mediterranean world. The Jewish city of Sepphoris in Galilee (a few miles from Nazareth, the hometown of Jesus) and Herod's port at Caesarea Maritima have been excavated in the last twenty years and the long-sought tomb of Herod the Great was finally discovered in 2007 at the Herodion, a fortress-palace few miles south of Jerusalem in the Judean hills, by a team led by Israeli archaeologist Ehud Netzer.

The *BCNT* contains twenty-one essays on individual books of the New Testament or groups of related books. The canonical New Testament itself contains twenty-seven separate compositions, including four biography-like works (the four gospels attributed to Matthew, Mark, Luke and John), one history-like work (the Acts of the Apostles, originally the second volume of the Gospel of Luke), twenty-one letters (thirteen attributed to Paul; the seven Catholic epistles, and Hebrews), some of these are letter-essays (e.g., Romans) and others are homilies framed like letters (Hebrews), or simply included with other letters (1 John) and one imaginative apocalyptic work (the Apocalypse of John). All of these texts came into existence from ca. 50 CE to ca. 125 CE, and reflect important aspects of the beginnings of Christianity.

## The Settings, Language, Text, and Canons of the New Testament

The first three essays in the *BCNT* provide a basic orientation to the major social and cultural settings within which early Christianity arose. The first two, "The World of Roman Hellenism" and "The World of Early Judaism," provide an brief overview of the two critical settings within which books of the New Testament were written and within which they must also be read and interpreted. Despite appearances, these two social and cultural complexes are not separable in any but an analytic sense. Jews in Palestine were influenced by Hellenism since the late fourth century BCE, when Alexander the Great moved through the Middle East conquering everything and everyone in his path.[1] Since the two essays on early Judaism and Greco-Roman culture are relatively short and even oversimplified, the bibliographies attached to them will provide further avenues for exploring the complexities that can only be dealt with in longer and more nuanced treatments of New Testament backgrounds. Since archaeology is a very specialized discipline, Tom McCollough, a seasoned archaeologist who has worked primarily in Israel, has provided an overview of the relevance of archaeological discoveries in Israel and the Greco-Roman world for understanding the New Testament.

The next three essays deal with three critical aspects of New Testament study, two internal and one external. In "The Greek of the New Testament," French linguist Christophe Rico discusses aspects of the Greek language used by the authors of the New Testament, providing a good introduction to a comparatively recent linguistic development in the study of the Greek language: verbal aspect. Next, the problem of determining the oldest text of each New Testament writing after many centuries of the kind of errors that beset copying manuscripts by hand is surveyed in "Reconstructing the Text of the New Testament" by seasoned textual critic Michael W. Holmes. Finally, Leslie Baynes discusses problems and theories relating to how the books of the New Testament were collected and invested with divine authority through the long ecclesiastical sorting process called "canonization." The title of her essay, "The *Canons* of the New Testament" (my emphasis), uses the plural form of "canon" since various segments of the early church had canons of the New Testament that were not in complete agreement with canons from other regions.

## Interpretive Methods

The seven essays that follow deal with some of the more important methodological approaches to New Testament interpretation. These essays have no common structure because of the distinctive history and features of each method, so each contributor has devised an outline appropriate for the subject. The first two essays, "Historical Criticism" and "Literary Criticism," written by the editor, deal with the two most basic modern methods of reading the New Testament: historical criticism and literary criticism. Both are umbrella terms for a variety of methods that are either "historical" or "literary" in orientation. Historical criticism, though it has roots in the ancient world, developed during the Enlightenment (often as a way of undercutting dogmatic beliefs of the church), brackets or rejects all the figurative methods of reading the Bible that were current in the Middle Ages, and insists on focusing on recovering the original meaning of a given text, in part by reading it in its historical context. During the nineteenth century, "Literary Criticism" practiced by biblical scholars primarily referred to what is now called source criticism: discerning the documents out of which a biblical author fashioned his work, but blossomed during the last third of the twentieth century as biblical scholars adapted the ever-changing and developing critical approaches of secular literary scholars. The next methodological essay on "Form Criticism," also written by the editor, deals with a method that began in the early part of the twentieth century in Germany and has been subject to much criticism recently, tries to deal with the fact that much of the Bible began in the form of oral tradition that was eventually reduced to writing. Form criticism therefore tries to isolate and identify oral forms that were transformed into written texts.

The next critical method presented is "Feminist Criticism" by the Jewish New Testament scholar Amy-Jill Levine, who has specialized in feminist criticism, an approach that developed during the last third of the twentieth century. Feminist criticism, actually a reading strategy, recognizes the ideological character of ancient texts like the New Testament; ideological in the specific sense that issues like gender, race, class, and ethnicity (to mention a very few of the categories used for social oppression) touched on in the New Testament are social constructs that need to be recognized for what they are.

"Rhetorical Criticism" by Duane F. Watson reflects another interpretive method that became an important tool particularly for the study of the New Testament letters beginning in the late 1970s. Rhetorical criticism was the central interpretive method for the 1979 commentary on Galatians by Hans Dieter Betz,[2] a work that has had wide influence methodologically on New Testament scholarship, and it was also presented as a method applicable to many parts of the New Testament by an important scholar in classical rhetoric, George A. Kennedy, in 1984.[3]

"Social Science Criticism and the New Testament" by Jerome H. Neyrey, a veteran New Testament scholar who has made numerous contributions to social science criticism, provides an introduction to the use of sociological and anthropological models in the study of ancient Christianity. Early Christianity arose in the eastern Mediterranean world nearly two millennia ago in a social, economic, political, and cultural context very different from the modern Western world. The use of modern socio-anthropological models in the study of modern non-Western peoples has provided surprising insights into the meaning of values that determined ancient perception and behavior (e.g. honor and shame, patron–client relationships, purity and pollution).

Vernon K. Robbins, the New Testament scholar who originated and who has continued to refine "Socio-Rhetorical Criticism" has contributed the article on that method. The hyphenated designation of the method indicates that it combines rhetorical criticism with social science criticism, with those two methodological complexes providing a matrix for socio-rhetorical interpretation, which is actually a holistic combination of methods and approaches to reading and interpreting texts that Robbins describes as an "interpretive analytic," namely "a multi-dimensional approach to texts guided by a multidimensional hermeneutic." This method has apparently become the focus of a series of commentaries called the "Socio-Rhetorical Commentary," with seven volumes by Ben Witherington III and one by David deSilva. In fact, Witherington has hijacked the term "socio-rhetorical" for a project that has very little in common with what Robbins describes as "socio-rhetorical commentary" in the BCNT essay.

## Introducing the Gospels and Related Texts: Mark, Matthew, Luke–Acts, and Johannine Literature

Since the second century the four canonical gospels have occupied a place of special honor in the church. In many traditions the congregation stands when the Gospels are read. The first mention of a collection of four gospels was made by Irenaeus of Lyons (d. ca. 202 CE) about 180 CE (Against Heresies, 3.11.8), though the fourfold gospel was probably in existence by 150 CE. While Luke is one of the synoptic gospels, its position in the New Testament is complicated by the fact that it was written as the first part of a two-volume work; the second volume is the Acts of the Apostles. They are treated together in the BCNT, which would probably have pleased the author. The

Gospel of John is quite different from the synoptic gospels (90 percent of the material in John is unique to that gospel) and unlike them has been traditionally associated with a collection of letters (1, 2, and 3 John).

## Introducing the gospels

In the interests of promoting uniform coverage of Mark, Matthew, Luke–Acts, and Johannine literature, the structure of each of these works was pre-programmed, so that each article on the gospels has a common structure. However, each contributor had the freedom to modify the structure of their essay if the particular character of the biblical material they covered required it. It is somewhat unusual to treat Luke–Acts as a single extended composition as we do in the *BCNT*, since Luke and Acts are almost always treated separately in introductions to the New Testament as well as in commentaries. However, since the author originally wrote one composition in two parts, it seems completely appropriate to honor his intentions by treating it as a unity. Further, rather than treat the Gospel of John in isolation, it is discussed, along with 1, 2, and 3 John, under the rubric of "Johannine literature," since the early church regarded all four works as the products of John the apostle, even though the Gospel of John was originally anonymous, and the Johannine letters contains the name "John" only in later superscriptions. 1 John was originally anonymous, while 2 and 3 John claim to have been written by "the Elder," without attaching an actual name to that title.

   Each of these four essays (Mark, Matthew, Luke–Acts, Johannine literature) contains the following stereotypical elements, though not always in the precise order given here: (1) Major Issues and Directions in Recent Study (to orient the reader to the recent history of scholarship); (2) Date and Place of Writing (to enable the reader to situate each gospel in the most likely temporal and spatial setting); (3) Textual Problems (to call attention to modern attempts to reconstruct the earliest possible text); (4) Genre (to situate each gospel in the history of ancient literature, a problematic issue since the genre of the gospels is a highly disputed subject); (5) Author and Setting (to call attention to the problem of "authorship," i.e., while all of the canonical gospels were originally anonymous, if the names of authors later affixed to the text are incorrect, they are examples of secondary pseudepigraphy; if correct, however, they are instances of secondary orthonymity); (6) Occasion (the cluster of possible or probable reasons why the text was written in the first place); (7) Literary and Composition Analysis (how the organization of the text helps the reader to better understand its meaning); (8) Sources and Intertextuality (focusing on the previously existing texts that the author quotes or alludes to, such as the Old Testament, and the way in which the author's work reacts to earlier texts and ideas); and (9) Annotated Bibliography (a list of the more helpful recent secondary sources that the reader can use to explore various issues of particular interests with regard to each of the gospels).

   Important aspects of the first three gospels are introduced by three essays dealing with particular issues important for understanding them. Dale Allison provides an overview of "The Problem of the Historical Jesus," a complicated subject that centers in the issue of authenticity: how can one determine which of the sayings and deeds of

Jesus narrated in the synoptic gospels are authentically derived from Jesus, which are the creations of the early church, and which are combinations of the two? Beyond this methodological obstacle course lies the problem of reconstructing a convincing narrative that puts all the authentic fragments of tradition together into a coherent whole.

"The Synoptic Problem" is discussed in some detail by Patricia Walters. The three synoptic gospels (here the term "synoptic," meaning "see together," refers to the fact that Matthew, Mark, and Luke can be arranged in parallel columns in gospel harmonies revealing many similarities and differences between them). Although it is evident that the first three gospels have some kind of literary relationship, just who copied from whom is a problem that has been "solved" in a number of different ways.

The last of the three articles that introduce the synoptic gospels in various ways is the essay on "Q: The Sayings Source" by Ronald A. Piper. One of the widespread solutions of the synoptic problem is the Two Source theory, i.e., that Matthew and Luke are dependent on Mark and that the non-Markan parallels between Matthew and Luke are the result of the fact that Matthew and Luke independently made use of a written or oral text consisting largely of sayings of Jesus called the "sayings source," often referred to as "Q" (from the German word *Quelle*, meaning "source").

### The Gospel of Mark

In "The Gospel of Mark," Jens Schröter provides an insightful introduction to the earliest and shortest of the four gospels. Since it was widely recognized that Mark was the earliest of the gospels in late nineteenth-century scholarship, it was for that reason considered the most historically reliable. That bubble burst with the demonstration by William Wrede in 1901 that the Markan motif of the messianic secret was already an unhistorical theological interpretation that tried to make sense of the traditions of the words and deeds of Jesus. Beginning at this point, Schröter shows how the study of Mark led to a series of insights during the course of the twentieth century, such as the movement from the earlier form-critical view that Mark was just a collector of traditions to the redactional critical view that Mark was actually a creative author with a coherent style. Schröter maintains that in the near term it will be necessary to take the narrative character of Mark more seriously in an approach that recognizes that the authors use of creative memory made the past relevant to the present. As Schröter observes, "history ought to be conceived as a creative act of remembering the past for the purpose of establishing identity in the present." In the area of Markan Christology, Schröter argues for the close relationship of the titles "Son of God" (comprehensible to both Jewish and pagan readers) and "Christ" to "Son of Man." At the narrative level, the messianic secret functions to emphasize the contrast between Jesus' growing reputation and his desire not to become known merely because of his powerful deeds. These are a few highlights from Schröter's informative discussion of aspects of Mark.

### The Gospel of Matthew

Dennis Duling provides an overview of the major historical and interpretive issues surrounding the Gospel of Matthew, the most influential of the four gospels in the history of the church. Like the other canonical gospels, Matthew was originally anonymous, and it remains a matter of speculation why the name of a rather obscure disciple of Jesus was placed in the superscription identifying the author. In Matthew the dominant image of Jesus is that of teacher, and Duling shows how the structure of the book reinforces this impression. Matthew has also been regarded as the most Jewish of the gospels, and this is borne out in part by the "formula quotations" that the author uses to cite a passage from the Old Testament and then to show how it was fulfilled in the life of Jesus (displayed in a chart in the essay). Duling provides expert guidance through the many issues and problems confronting readers of Matthew.

### Luke–Acts: The Gospel of Luke and the Acts of the Apostles

Luke–Acts (i.e., the Gospel of Luke and the Acts of the Apostles) constitutes the largest segment of the New Testament written by a single author (27 percent of the whole), though both works were originally anonymous. Though originally written as two volumes of a single work addressed to Theophilus (Acts 1:1 refers to the first book), they became separated, presumably when Luke was made part of the collection of four gospels by the mid-second century CE. Richard P. Thompson's essay on Luke–Acts provides a balanced entrée into the major issues and problems that surround the study of this significant work. One of the many issues that is still being debated is the genre of Luke–Acts. Because of the similarities between Luke 1:1–4 and introductions to Hellenistic historical works and a number of chronological synchronisms between local history and Roman history, "Luke" (the conventional name for this author since the time of Irenaeus in the late second century CE) has frequently been regarded as a self-conscious historian. If Luke is a historian, he is of course an ancient rather than a modern one and should be held to ancient rather than modern standards, as Thompson rightly insists. In the mold of the historical works in the Hebrew Bible, Luke sees the will of God as the driving force in the history he narrates. The problem of genre also involves deciding whether Luke–Acts belongs to a single genre in two books or whether Luke and Acts belong to two different literary genres (for example, is the Gospel of Luke an ancient biography?).

The Gospel of Luke covers the period from the birth of John the Baptist and Jesus through the ascension of Jesus (an event mentioned only in Luke–Acts and the longer ending that was added to Mark by the mid-second century, Mark 16:9–20). Acts begins by repeating the story of the ascension, which he relates in a strikingly different version, and continues with the story of the growth and expansion of the early church in Judea and Samaria and finally through the missionary activity of Peter and especially Paul, concluding with Paul's arrest in Jerusalem, his incarceration in Caesarea Maritima, and his trip to Rome by ship escorted by Roman soldiers. It ends rather uncertainly with Paul under house arrest in Rome awaiting trial. Acts is the earliest record we have of the growth of earliest Christianity, and since he writes with a theological agenda (e.g., he depicts Paul as a model Jew; the death of Jesus is exemplary rather than redemptive), scholars have debated the accuracy of virtually everything he reports. It seems clear, however, that Luke–Acts was intentionally written as apologetic historiography, i.e., the author was defending Christianity from its many detractors.

## Johannine Literature

John Painter contributed the essay on "Johannine Literature," which here consists of four writings, the gospel and the three letters attributed to John, though traditionally a fifth work, the Apocalypse of John, has been included in the Corpus Johanneum. Since the Apocalypse is the only one of the five works in this "collection" that actually claims to have been written by "John," it might seem odd that it is excluded from "Johannine literature." However, the style and language of the Apocalypse make it certain that this author was not the author of the other four writings in Johannine literature, so it has been treated separately. Further, since the Johannine letters have a different literary form than the gospels, the structure for the essay on those works necessarily varies from the default structure of the articles on Mark, Matthew, and Luke–Acts.

The Gospel of John, despite its apparent simplicity (first-year students in New Testament Greek often read selections from this gospel), is actually a very profound and complex composition. Though the gospels and letters of John share common theological motifs and a common worldview, it is difficult place "the Johannine community" who produced them (some argue) in relationship to other phases of early Christianity in the late first to early second century CE. Since the Jesus of the Fourth Gospel speaks with the same vocabulary and style as the narrator, the problem of reconstructing sayings and deeds of the historical Jesus from John is problematic, but has recently become the focus of some Johannine scholars.[4] It has long been recognized that John preserves some historical features not found in the synoptic gospels, such as the fact that Jesus traveled with some frequency from Galilee to Jerusalem and the probability of a three-year ministry of Jesus, and also refers to some archaeological features such as the Pool of Bethzatha (Bethesda) mentioned in John 5:2 that was discovered in 1871 near the Crusader church of St. Anne in the old city of Jerusalem just north of the Temple Mount. The issue of the historicity of aspects of John's narrative provokes the question of the source of Johannine tradition; much of it is similar to traditions preserved in the synoptic gospels, but scholars are agreed that John was not dependent on the synoptics but on sources behind them. There are many other issues and problems in the study of the Gospel of John, and John Painter proves to be a good guide through the underbrush.

The Johannine letters are actually a multi-genre collection, since 1 John is not really a letter (it lacks the typical epistolary opening and closing) so much as a homily, while 2 and 3 John are very similar to typical Greco-Roman letters. Some of the major issues confronting the reader of these letters include the order in which they were written, the nature and relationships of the house-churches reflected in these letters, and the problem of the disagreements and schisms in the communities reflected in these letters. Since 1 John is the longest and most historically and theologically significant of the three, Painter has provided the reader with a careful otline of its content.

## The Pauline Letters: Genuine and Pseudepigraphal

*Introduction*

The *BCNT* includes eleven essays on New Testament letters and a group of letters (the Pastorals) that are written under the name of Paul. While seven of the letters attributed to Paul are almost universally accepted as authentic (Romans, 1 and 2 Corinthians, Galatians, Philippians, 1 Thessalonians, Philemon), four are just as widely judged to be pseudepigraphal, i.e., written by unknown authors under Paul's name: Ephesians and the Pastorals (1 and 2 Timothy and Titus). Two letters are more problematic, with some scholars rejecting their authenticity, while others accept them as genuinely Pauline: Colossians and 2 Thessalonians. Essays on these letters are arranged in the *BCNT* in canonical order, with the exception that the essays on the letters that are certainly pseudepigraphal (Ephesians and the Pastorals) are located at the end of the series of essays on letters attributed to Paul.

Because of the importance of the Pauline letters (Luke–Acts and the Pauline letters constitute more than half of the New Testament) the eleven essays on the New Testament letters that are written under the name of Paul are introduced by an article on "Paul and his Letters" by Jouette M. Bassler. This essay consists of six sections surveying the most important general issues necessary for understanding Paul the apostle, evangelist, community-founder, theologian, and letter-writer: (1) Major Issues and Directions in the Recent Study of Paul: the main issues include the problem of determine the coherent center of Paul's theology, the influence of Greco-Roman rhetoric on Paul the letter-writer, social scientific approaches to the Pauline letters, and the development of feminist interpretation; (2) Paul between Judaism and Hellenism: Bassler argues that understanding Paul against the exclusive background of either Judaism or Hellenism is no longer viable; the socio-cultural background of Paul is much more complex than that either/or suggests; (3) The Collection and Influence of Paul's Letters: just how Paul's letters, written to individual Christian communities throughout the ancient Mediterranean world, were eventually collected continues to be a debated issue; (4) Pauline Chronology: one of the perennial problems in the study of Paul involves reconstructing the sequence of Paul's letters, reconstructing the sequence of events in Paul's life and the problem of dating Paul's letters and events in Paul's life; (5) Pauline Letters and Pauline Pseudepigrapha: while the actual Pauline authorship of seven letters is widely accepted (Romans, 1 and 2 Corinthians, Galatians, Philippians, 1 Thessalonians, Philemon), four letters are just as widely considered pseudepigraphal (Ephesians and the Pastorals, i.e., 1 and 2 Timothy and Titus), while the authorship of two letters is more ambiguous, regarded by some as authentic and by others as inauthentic: Colossians and 2 Thessalonians; (6) Annotated Bibliography, followed by bibliographical items cited in the essay.

The eleven essays on individual letters written under the name of Paul and the one group of three letters (1 and 2 Timothy and Titus) all follow a similar programmatic outline, though there is a certain amount of flexibility in that this structure is sometimes augmented (e.g., the topic of historical and archaeological setting in the case of 1 Corinthians, or of reception in the second century and church organization in the case of the Pastorals) and otherwise modified depending on the character and distinctive features of specific letters. The outline for most of these letters includes the following sequence of topics: (1) Major Issues and Directions in Recent Study; (2) Date and Place of Writing; (3) Purpose; (4) Language and Style; (5) Intertextuality; (6) Unity; (7) Constituent Literary Forms; (8) Genre; (9) Epistolary Analysis; (10) Rhetorical Analysis.

### The four longer letters

In the Corpus Paulinum, the four longest and most influential letters are Romans, 1 and 2 Corinthians, and Galatians. In the essay by Thomas H. Tobin, SJ, "Paul's Letter to the Romans" (the longest of all Paul's letters), the author, who has written a monograph on Paul's rhetorical argumentation in Romans,[5] covers the basic issues but adds sections on Paul and the Roman Christian community and on issues and arguments in Romans. Identifying just who the Christians in Rome are has been a perennial problem in research on Romans, and the issues and arguments in Romans, a continuation of the rhetorical analysis found earlier in the essay, constitutes a major contribution of this article.

"1 Corinthians" was contributed by John Fotopoulos, who spends much of each summer in Argos, a city on the Greek Peloponnesus, a short distance from the site of ancient Corinth. In a section of his essay entitled "Historical and Archaeological Setting" he has used his knowledge of the archaeology of Corinth not only to sketch the social, political, and cultural context of Roman Corinth during the first century CE, but also to solve some problems relating to the controversy over meat offered to idols found in 1 Corinthians 8:1–10:22.

Calvin J. Roetzel, the author of the essay on 2 Corinthians, has abandoned the common structure of most of the essays on the New Testament epistolary literature to focus on a reconstruction of the six letters that he argues were brought together in the final redaction of 2 Corinthians. Many of the specific topics found in the common outline are dealt with in various parts of his reconstruction of the sources of 2 Corinthians.

The essay on Galatians by Jewish New Testament scholar Mark Nanos reflects his distinctive solution for identifying the addressees of that letter and the "influencers" who were affecting them. After reviewing other solutions, Nanos proposes that all are Galatians, including Jewish subgroups that are recognizable by their positive attitude toward the meaning of Jesus for their lives. These Jewish subgroups also have Gentile members who assume that they have full standing in the Jewish community. Conflict was introduced by the influence of other Jewish synagogue communities who did not have a positive attitude toward the significance of Jesus.

### The shorter Pauline letters

There are five shorter Pauline letters, three of which are widely considered genuine (Philippians, 1 Thessalonians, Philemon), while the authenticity of two is disputed

(Colossians, 2 Thessalonians). Each of them, whether authentic or pseudepigraphal, makes a special contribution to our knowledge of the Pauline mission and provides insight into the varied communities that he founded or decisively influenced throughout the eastern Mediterranean world. One challenge lurking in the background is the extent to which these letters can be coordinated with the narrative of Paul's missionary journeys and ministry in the eastern Mediterranean theater.

"Philippians," contributed by Paul Hartog, is a letter written by Paul to a city in Macedonia which had become a Roman colony located on the Via Egnatia, a major Roman road. Among the central issues for the study of Philippians is the question of unity: was it originally a single letter or a combination of two or three letters? The unity question is closely tied to the epistolary and rhetorical analyses of the letter. Another major focus for the study of this letter is the magnificent Christ-hymn in Philippians 2:5–11, which narrates the story of the incarnation by beginning with the preincarnate existence of Jesus "in the form of God," through his incarnation, death, exaltation, and supremacy of his name and authority over all creation.

Troy Martin and Todd Still have co-authored the essay on Colossians, a letter that remains at the center of a lively debate over the issue of authenticity. Another central issue of the Colossians debate is the puzzling nature of the "Colossian philosophy" that the author opposes: a type of Jewish, Christian, or Gnostic syncreticism? None of the above? Another topic of perennial interest in the study of Colossians is its relationship to Ephesians. If the unknown author of Ephesians used Colossians in the composition of the former that in itself becomes an argument for the authenticity of Colossians. Like Philippians, Colossians contains a magnificent Christ-hymn that many scholars think the author has quoted from earlier Christian liturgical usage and a number of other possible liturgical fragments.

There are two essays on the Thessalonian letters: "1 Thessalonians" by Karl P. Donfried and "2 Thessalonians" by Edgar Krentz. 1 Thessalonians is the earliest Pauline letter and, indeed, the earliest written text to emerge from the nascent religious movement that later became known as Christianity (Acts 11:26; 26:28; 1 Pet. 4:16). Long in the shadow of the longer "doctrinal" letters, Romans and Galatians, 1 Thessalonians has recently been recognized for the valuable early witness it is to the early development of an important phase of early Christianity and for the evidence it contains relating to the beginnings of the Christian mission. Theologically, the strong emphasis on the imminent *parousia* (return of Christ) is striking with no counterpart in any of the later Pauline letters. In his essay on 2 Thessalonians, Krenz argues in a very even-handed and convincing way that 2 Thessalonians is pseudepigraphal. Since the non-authenticity of the letter would affect all aspects of its study (e.g., is the "destination" actually the "Thessalonians"?), the entire article deals with many aspects of the pseudepigraphal character of the letter. Krenz has been very influential in the United States for his carefully reasoned arguments for the non-authenticity of 2 Thessalonians, circulated in a paper originally given at the Thessalonians Seminar of Society of Biblical Literature in 1983, entitled "A Stone That Will Not Fit: The Non-Pauline Authorship of 2 Thessalonians." Finally, "Philemon," the essay by John Levison on the shortest of the Pauline letters, provides a competent exploration of the slavery issue, the central subject of this letter.

## Pauline pseudepigrapha: Ephesians and the Pastorals

"Ephesians," written by Margaret Y. MacDonald, is in many ways one of the more puzzling of the letters written in the Pauline tradition. While framed as a letter, Ephesians does not refer to any specific issues that might have been of concern to a local community and indeed even the address to the Ephesians is a later addition to the letter. One of the many puzzles surrounding Ephesians is its literary relationship to Colossians. Another puzzle is the purpose of the letter, if indeed it could be said to have a single purpose. MacDonald provides a balanced introduction to all of these issues as well as many others that challenge the readers of this beautiful composition.

The essay titled "The Pastoral Letters: 1 and 2 Timothy and Titus," by the editor, deals with a very special group of letters in the Pauline tradition. A rare example of a closely related group of pseudepigraphal letters, the Pastorals were written by a single author in an early second-century context that is difficult to reconstruct. The "heresy" combated in the Pastorals seems an impossible mélange of heterogeneous features and is probably an artificial construct. From the standpoint of the development of early Christianity in the early second century, the Pastorals reflect an organizational development that can be placed midway between the Acts of the Apostles and the Letters of Ignatius of Antioch.

## The Catholic Epistles and Hebrews

The term "Catholic [Universal] Epistles" or "General Epistles" is a label based on the fact that four of the letters in this group (James, 1 and 2 Peter, Jude) are not addressed to particular Christian communities, but to a much more general audience; they are virtually "open letters." James, for example, is addressed "to the twelve tribes dispersed throughout the world" (James 1:1) and Jude is addressed "to those whom God has called, who live in the love of God the Father and are kept safe for the coming of Jesus Christ" (Jude 1:1). Four of the seven Catholic epistles (James, 1 and 2 Peter, Jude) and Hebrews are discussed next (1, 2, and 3 John are already included in Painter's essay on "Johannine Literature"). These four Catholic epistles are widely regarded by critical scholarship as pseudepigraphal, but that does not really diminish their significance as witnesses to different trends in thought and practice that characterized turn-of-the-century Christianity. In the essay on the letter of James by Paul Holloway, the author competently reviews all the major issues confronting the study of James. Theologically, James has often been regarded as having a position in opposition to Paul's emphasis on justification by faith, an issue thoroughly explored by Holloway. James is also striking for its many apparent allusions to the sayings of Jesus, an issue that has recently been investigated from several perspectives.

The essay on 1 Peter by Brian Han Gregg explores the major issues surrounding this letter, which is written in a relatively high register of Greek when compared to the other writings of the New Testament (Hebrew and Luke–Acts are strong competitors in this regard). While 1 Peter was accepted as authentically Petrine throughout the early church, whether or not it is a pseudepigraph has been a major issue in modern research, though most critical scholars, including Gregg, regard it as pseudepigraphal. 1 Peter has a number of important themes, including a strong emphasis on suffering and persecution, which probably reflects pagan opposition in the region where 1 Peter arose, among which Rome and Roman Asia are strong possibilities. Two other related themes, baptism and the new birth, together with supporting language and imagery, have led some scholars to understand 1 Peter as a baptismal homily. 1 Peter is an eloquent document of late first-century Christianity and has recently been the subject of a number of fine commentaries, referred to by Gregg.

Kevin McCruden has contributed an essay on 2 Peter and Jude, two relatively short pseudonymous letters that, like Colossians and Ephesians, have a literary and thematic relationship; for that reason they have been treated in tandem. The two authors share the view that a communal crisis is under way, caused by false teachers from within or without. The problem of literary dependency is not straightforward; some argue that Jude was dependent on 2 Peter, while others (including McCruden) maintain the more likely view that 2 Peter was dependent on Jude. The path to canonization for 2 Peter was slow and painful, in part because many in the early church regarded it as pseudonymous. 2 Peter has the form of a testament of the "Apostle Peter" framed as a letter, in which the author looks forward to his coming death and reflects strong Jewish as well as strong Hellenistic influences; the author has his feet in both cultural worlds, and his Greek vocabulary reflects a preference for uncommon and unusual words which he uses in a florid style. In his discussion of Jude, McCruden argues suggestively for a Roman provenance for the letter rather than the more common proposal of a Palestinian provenance.

The essay on Hebrews, an anonymous homily (the author designates it as a "word of exhortation" in 13:22), written in the highest register of Greek found in the New Testament (including several periodic sentences and the occasional use of prose rhythm), was contributed by Craig R. Koester, author of the *Anchor Bible Commentary on Hebrews* (2001). Koester regards Hebrews as written to persuade an early Christian community experiencing discouragement and decline to remain faithful to God, Christ, and the Christian community. Like many other New Testament writings, it is difficult to reconstruct the basic facts about Hebrews (author, date, purpose, destination, and so on). Koester convincingly puts the production of Hebrews between 60 and 90 CE; the epistolary ending mentions Timothy, an associate of Paul in the 50s, and Hebrews itself was used in *1 Clement*, written from Rome ca. 90 CE. The metaphorical Christology of Hebrews is complex, highly developed, and quite unlike the ways of conceptualizing the significance of Jesus for salvation found in Paul and other New Testament writings. One important metaphor for Jesus in Hebrews is that of a priest who enters into the Holy of Holies of the Tabernacle to sacrifice himself for others. Koester provides a rich and rewarding exploration of this magnificent letter-homily.

### From the Apocalypse of John to the New Testament Apocrypha

The last book in the present arrangement of the New Testament is the Apocalypse of John, discussed in an essay by David L. Barr, a scholar who has specialized in that work.

In the New Testament the Apocalypse is in a class by itself as the only freestanding apocalypse. In the Old Testament, Daniel is technically the only apocalypse, but it is actually only the second half (Dan. 7–12) that merits that designation. Several pseudepigraphal apocalypses were produced in the early church from the second through the fourth centuries CE, such as the Apocalypse of Peter and the Apocalypse of Paul. Yet the Apocalypse of John is unique among extant early Jewish and early Christian apocalypses in that it is framed as a letter. Barr has tended to focus on the application of narrative criticism to the Apocalypse, a method usually applied only to the gospels and Acts. Barr regards the Apocalypse as a narrative text, and in this he is certainly standing on solid ground. In analyzing the plot of the Apocalypse he proposes that it consists of three interrelated stories, but maintains that this is just one of many possible approaches.

Finally, it seemed appropriate to provide some indication of important aspects of early Christian literature that arose after many of the books of the New Testament were written. Petra Heldt, a Patristics scholar from Jerusalem, Israel, has provided the last article on "New Testament Apocrypha." In this phrase the term "apocrypha" connotes "noncanonical," while "New Testament" implies that such works imitate the genres found in the New Testament canon. We therefore have apocryphal gospels (e.g., the *Gospel of the Hebrews*, the *Gospel of the Ebionites*), apocryphal acts (e.g., the *Acts of Paul and Thecla*), apocryphal letters (a small pseudepigraphal collection of letters purportedly exchanged by Paul and Seneca) and apocryphal apocalypses (e.g., the *Apocalypse of Peter*). Many of these works may have arisen as early as the late first century (e.g. the *Gospel of Thomas*) and continued to be produced through the fourth century and beyond. Until recently works categorized as New Testament apocrypha were almost ignored as slavishly imitative, fictional, and heretical. More recently, however, they have been regarded as valuable for the light they shed on the values and beliefs of ordinary Christians during the second through the fourth centuries and later. Heldt provides an expert overview of the issues involved in the reading and study of these early Christian works, with a concluding bibliography for further guidance.

## Notes

1    The classic work on this subject is Martin Hengel, *Judaism and Hellenism: Studies in their Encounter in Palestine during the Early Hellenistic Period* (Philadelphia: Fortress Press, 1974); see also Martin Hengel with Christoph Markschies, *The "Hellenization" of Judaea in the First Century after Christ* (London: SCM Press, 1990).
2    Hans Dieter Betz, *Galatians: A Commentary on Paul's Letter to the Churches in Galatia*, Hermeneia (Philadelphia: Fortress Press, 1979).
3    George A. Kennedy, *New Testament Interpretation through Rhetorical Criticism* (Chapel Hill: University of North Carolina, 1984).
4    Paul N. Anderson, *The Fourth Gospel and the Quest for Jesus: Modern Foundations Reconsidered* (London and New York: T. & T. Clark, 2006).
5    Thomas H. Tobin, SJ, *Paul's Rhetoric in its Contexts: The Argument of Romans* (Peabody, MA: Hendrickson, 2004).

# CHAPTER 1

# The World of Roman Hellenism

## David E. Aune

## Introduction

The movement that later came to be known as Christianity began ca. 26 CE with the public appearance of Jesus ben Joseph of Nazareth, a rural Jewish prophet and teacher in the Galilee, a relatively small region in the Jewish territories located in the eastern Mediterranean region. Though Jesus was executed in Jerusalem by the Roman authorities ca. 29 CE, by the end of the first century CE, conventicles of the followers of Jesus were to be found in urban centers throughout the Mediterranean world. In 313 CE, Constantine the Great (272–337 CE) issued the Edict of Milan that mandated religious toleration throughout the Roman empire, canceling the penalties associated with the profession of Christianity that had been the basis for the persecution and execution of Christians and officially restoring the property that had been confiscated from them. By the end of the fourth century, despite its humble origins, Christianity had become the dominant religion of the Roman empire.

Palestine, the cradle of Christianity, was a region that had been a pawn in the power politics of Near Eastern and Levantine kingdoms for nearly two millennia and in consequence suffered domination by a series of both eastern and western empires. As a reform movement, nascent "Christianity" has been profoundly influenced by the traditions of rural Galilean Judaism. Judaism itself had begun to experience various degrees of Hellenization as early as the fourth century BCE (Hengel 1974). The Roman empire, which eventually took over all the Hellenistic monarchies founded by Alexander's successors by 31 BCE, ironically became a military and administrative vehicle for continuing the spread of Hellenistic language and culture, making the term "Roman Hellenism" an appropriate political and cultural designation for the centuries following the Roman victory at the battle of Actium in 31 BCE.

## What is Hellenization?

Early Judaism and early Christianity were profoundly but unevenly influenced by Hellenistic culture, evident in the adoption of Greek language, Greek names, Greek institutions, and Greek literary and rhetorical forms and styles of writing and speaking (Aune 1987). While early Jewish Christianity experienced various degrees of Hellenization, converts to the new religious movement from the eastern Mediterranean were part of the culture of Roman Hellenism and required socialization into a faith with a strong Jewish cultural orientation and heritage.

The term "Hellenism" itself is a modern designation for the dominance of Greek language and culture over non-Greek societies in the ancient world, particularly during the three centuries following Alexander the Great (356–323 BCE) to the triumph of Rome, in the person of Octavian, over Ptolemaic Egypt, the last of the Hellenistic kingdoms, in the Battle of Actium. This period was first labeled "Hellenistic" by the nineteenth-century German historian J. G. Droysen (1877–8), author of an innovative history of Alexander the Great. According to Droysen the entire epoch was characterized by the meeting and combination of Greek with Near Eastern and Eastern cultures which together paved the way for Christianity. One of the most striking uses of the Greek term ἑλληνισμός occurs in 2 Maccabees 4:13, where it is paired with ἀλλοφυλισμός:

> There was such an extreme of *Hellenization* [ἑλληνισμός] and increase in the *adoption of foreign ways* [ἀλλοφυλισμός] because of the surpassing wickedness of Jason, who was ungodly and no true high priest, that the priests were no longer intent upon their service at the altar.

ἑλληνισμός, "Hellenism" or "the Greek way of life," is a one-word summary of Greek social and cultural identity, while ἀλλοφυλισμός has a more general meaning, "the adoption of foreign customs." Both terms are used pejoratively in 2 Maccabees 4:13 and are antithetical to Ἰουδαϊσμός, "Judeanism" or "the Judean way of life," i.e., Jewish religious and cultural identity (2 Macc. 2:21; 8:1; 14:38), which was thought by Jews to be threatened by both ἑλληνισμός and ἀλλοφυλισμός. The related term ἑλληνιστής ("Hellenist") occurs in Acts 6:1 (cf. 9:29; 11:20), where the terms "Hellenists" and "Hebrews" are used antithetically, apparently referring to Greek-speaking Jews from the Diaspora in contrast to Aramaic-speaking Palestinian Jews, without any suggestion of a negative attitude toward cultural assimilation like that found in 2 Maccabees 4:13.

Though Greeks had contact with other eastern Mediterranean cultures long before the formation of the Greco-Macedonian kingdom in 356 BCE, these contacts were sporadic and occurred largely in the context of trade and military operations. An incidental feature of the program of conquest begun by Philip II (382–336 BCE), and expanded by his son and successor Alexander the Great (356–323 BCE), was the use of Hellenism became a medium for unifying a vast and disparate empire, the result of the introduction and spread of Greek language and cultural institutions. Though the polymath Plutarch of Chaeronea (46–120 CE) was convinced that Alexander consciously used it as a tool for providing social and cultural unity for new areas of conquest, this was an anachronistic perspective based on the strikingly perduring Hellenistic character of Levantine and Near Eastern cities in the centuries following Alexander's conquest. These cities originated as military colonies which were populated with soldiers and civilians from the Greek world who, despite their humble origins became a cultural elite who regarded their language and way of life as superior to those of the "barbarians," i.e., the indigenous population. The Greek institutions that were part of each of the thirty or so "city-states" founded by Alexander typically included an acropolis, walls, an agora (a large public space that served as the center of commerce, local administration, and social and religious activities), temples, a theater, and a gymnasium (Pausanias 10.4.1). The gymnasium, a center for athletic exercise and training, traditionally done in the nude (from the Greek word *gymnos*, "naked"), was a symbol of Greek culture that often violated the attitudes toward the human body found in most Near Eastern cultures. The construction of a gymnasium in Jerusalem was extremely controversial (1 Macc. 1:14; 2 Macc. 4:9).

Predictably, native populations reacted to Hellenism in one of two ways. Those natives interested in upward social mobility in colonial society and government and who aspired to positions in Greek colonial administrations adapted to the changed conditions by their pragmatic acceptance of the superiority of Greek language and culture and the inferiority of their own. The Greeks themselves regarded their language and culture as superior to those of all other people, a conviction that was accepted at least for pragmatic reasons by upwardly mobile natives. For others, particularly those in rural areas, Hellenism constituted a culture shock which they considered a threat to their traditional way of life and values and which they resisted in a variety of overt and covert ways (Eddy 1961). These antithetical reactions are dramatized in the two accounts of the conflict between Seleucid Greeks and Palestinian Jews in 2 and 4 Maccabees, where we are told of a Hellenizing party in Judea (centering in the priestly families who ran Judaea as a temple-state) alongside a group who preferred to die rather than to violate ancestral Jewish religious traditions. There were also several less insidious features of Hellenism which were absorbed by non-Greeks in a variety of subtle ways, including the Greek language, constitutional forms, personal and place names, literary styles and genres, and architecture.

## The Political Framework of Roman Hellenism

### 1   The Hellenistic period (323–31 BCE)

The successful military campaigns of Alexander the Great in the second half of the fourth century BCE continued the expansion of the Macedonian empire begun by Philip II as far east as India and fundamentally changed the political and cultural character of both the Mediterranean world and the Near East. The Greek empire of Alexander also spelled the end of the Greek *polis* or city-state as an independent social and cultural entity. Alexander's unexpected death at the height of his career at the young age of 33 ignited a complex power struggle among those later called Alexander's *Epigonoi* or "heirs." Alexander's death was the end of an era marked also by the death of his private tutor Aristotle (384–322 BCE), one of the greatest and most influential and innovative of Greek philosophers. Upon Alexander's death, Perdiccas, one of his generals, became the guardian and regent of the empire, since the child who would be briefly designated Alexander IV was being carried by Alexander's wife Roxanne when he died. The so-called "Partition of Babylon" was an agreement brokered by Perdiccas to divide Alexander's empire up into various satrapies entrusted to men who belonged to Alexander's inner circle. The murder of all the members of Alexander's family was just one sordid chapter in the internecine conflicts between Alexander's would-be successors.

After several years of jockeying for power, following the battle of Ipsus in 301 BCE, three major Hellenistic kingdoms emerged, each named after its Greco-Macedonian founder. Antigonus I Monophthalmus ("one-eyed"), ca. 382–301 BCE, ruled over the Antigonid dynasty in Macedonia, Greece, and parts of Asia Minor, which finally capitulated to Rome at the battle of Pydna in 146 BCE. Seleucus I Nicator (358–281 BCE) had consolidated his control over Mesopotamia with the help of Ptolemy I Soter, the ruler of Egypt by 312 BCE, which became the date of the founding of the Seleucid dynasty. The largest of the Hellenistic kingdoms, the Seleucid empire included Asia Minor, Syria, and Mesopotamia. The Seleucid empire was also the most culturally and linguistically diverse of all the Hellenistic empires because it dominated an enormous geographical area. The Seleucid empire fell to Rome in 64 BCE. Ptolemy I Soter (367–282 BCE), who became satrap over Egypt in 323 BCE, founded the Ptolemaic dynasty that ruled over Egypt and Libya. The Ptolemies controlled Palestine until 198 BCE, exercising an iron-clad control over the local population for the purpose of maximizing taxation. Control of the high priesthood of the Jewish temple-state was a central instrument in the domination of the region. Alexandria, the capital of Ptolemaic Egypt, was also the home of a large Jewish population. Under the instigation of Ptolemy II Philadelphus (309–246 BCE, reigned 281–246 BCE), the translation of the Hebrew Bible into Greek began ca. 270 and was perhaps completed a century later. The story of this translation, with some legendary embellishment, is narrated in a pseudepigraphon called the *Letter of Aristeas*, written during the second century BCE. One indicator of Hellenization among the Jews of Egypt is the fact that the vast majority of surviving papyri and inscriptions written by Egyptian Jews are written in Greek (Haelst 1976; Horbury and Noy 1992). Ptolemaic Egypt was the Hellenistic monarchy that survived longest. Cleopatra VII, the last of the Ptolemaic rulers, committed suicide after she and Mark Antony were defeated by Octavian at the battle of Actium in 31 BCE.

The three main Hellenistic kingdoms were rivals with each other and with smaller Hellenistic kingdoms throughout most of their existence and these conflicts resulted in the frequent geographical reconfiguration of the boundaries of each empire. From 320 to 200 BCE, Ptolemaic Egypt dominated Syria and Palestine and was in constant conflict with the Seleucids over this region. It was also during the third century BCE that Greek replaced Aramaic as the lingua franca of the region. At the battle of Paneas in northern Galilee in 200 BCE, the Seleucid king Antiochus III the Great (241–187 BCE) took control of Palestine from the Ptolemies. The Seleucid kingdom, with its center of government in Syria, maintained control of Palestine until 142 BCE. The Seleucid empire was greatly expanded under Antiochus III, but his expansionist policies were halted by a series of catastrophic defeats at the hand of the Romans, beginning with the battle of Magnesia in 190 BCE.

Religious conflict was introduced to Palestine by Antiochus IV Epiphanes (215–164 BCE), who consciously made Hellenism a tool for uniting his vast empire with a focus on the introduction of Greek cults and the prohibition of native religious practices (1 Macc. 1:41–50). Antiochus began his Hellenizing policy in Palestine by appointing the

Hellenophile Jason, of the Oniad priestly family, to the high priesthood in 174 BCE. Jason embarked on a program of Hellenization by constructing a gymnasium in Jerusalem. Jason was ousted from his position in 172 BCE when a rival for the post, Menelaus, bribed Antiochus and was appointed high priest. In 167 BCE Antiochus had his troops occupy the Antonia, a fortress connected to the northwest corner of the Temple Mount. Antiochus then erected an altar to Zeus Olympios over the altar of burnt offering in the Jerusalem temple offering sacrifices on the twenty-fifth day of each month beginning with 25 Chislev 167 (1 Macc. 1:41–61; 2 Macc. 6:1–6). This act of sacrilege is remembered in Jewish apocalyptic literature as "the abomination that makes desolate" (Dan. 11:31; 12:11; Matt. 24:28). Antiochus also ordered the destruction of Torah scrolls and forbad the rite of circumcision.

This program of religious repression led to the Hasmonean rebellion led by Mattathias, a priest who lived in Modein. When a representative of Antiochus was sent to Modein to force Jews to sacrifice on a pagan altar, Mattathias refused to do so and killed both a fellow Jew who was about to sacrifice and the king's officer as well. The Jewish festival of Hanukkah ("dedication") had its origin as a commemoration of the retaking of Jerusalem and the Temple by the Jewish military leader Judas Maccabeus on 25 Kislev 165 BCE.

## 2    The Roman period (31 BCE–476 CE)

Even before the existence of the Greco-Macedonian empire under Philip II and Alexander the Great, Rome had been gradually expanding her influence in Italy and the western Mediterranean. By the middle of the third century BCE, Rome had taken political control of the Italian peninsula. After decisively winning a series of three wars with Carthage, a Phoenician colony in North Africa founded in the eighth century BCE and the chief economic competitor of Rome in the western Mediterranean, Rome gained undisputed control of the entire western Mediterranean. The three wars that Rome waged against Carthage were called the First Punic War (264–241 BCE), the Second Punic War (218–201 BCE), and the Third Punic War (149–146 BCE). The end of the Third Punic War was marked by the complete destruction of Carthage in 146 BCE, when Carthaginian territory was turned into the Roman province of Africa.

While Rome was expanding in Italy and the western Mediterranean in the third and second centuries BCE, she was also drawn into an expansionist policy in the eastern Mediterranean. By the conclusion of three Macedonian wars that Rome fought, first against Philip V of Macedon (214–205 and 200–197 BCE) and then Perseus of Macedon (171–168 BCE), Rome was largely in control of Macedonia and Greece. Following the second Macedonian war, Rome invaded Greece and defeated Antiochus III (241–187 BCE, ruler of the Seleucid empire at Thermopylae in 191 BCE. Finally, after putting down local revolts in Macedonia and Greece, both regions were turned into Roman provinces ruled directly from Rome. Corinth, which had participated in a revolt, was destroyed in 146 BCE by the Roman general Luciue. Mummius as part of a program of intimidation. In 44 BCE, Corinth was refounded as a Roman colony.

From 133 to 27 BCE, the republic, founded in 509 BCE with the expulsion of the last Etruscan king, began to decline as the result of the coming to power of a series of political and military strong men, such as Gaius Marius (157–86 BCE), who was elected consul seven times during his career, L. Cornelius Sulla (138–78 BCE), who marched on Rome in 88 BCE and established himself as dictator in 82 or 81 BCE and had 1,500 or more aristocrats proscribed, resulting in their murder, and Gnaeus Pompey (106–48 BCE), who conquered Palestine in 63 BCE and later came into conflict with Julius Caesar. The rise of strong populists culminated in that of Julius Caesar (100–44 BCE), who began a Roman civil war in 49 BCE, and thereafter was declared dictator for life, which ended with his assassination. This period (133–27 BCE) was marked by a conflict between the *optimates* and the *populares*, i.e., between those backing the senatorial aristocracy and supportive of an aristocratic oligarchy and those who sought dictatorial powers using their popularity with the masses as a power base. Octavian, an adopted son of Julius Caesar, came to power by defeating Mark Antony and his lover Cleopatra VII in 31 BCE at the sea battle of Actium. By 27 BCE, the republican form of government was in shambles, and Octavian, who took the name Augustus, became *princeps*, or the first man, and, assuming the autocratic powers granted to him by a puppet senate, ruled Rome from 27 BCE to 14 CE.

Augustus was an enlightened ruler who was careful to give the appearance of constitutionality to the powers granted him by the senate. The tribunician power (*tribunicia potestas*), granted to Augustus in 23 BCE, became the foundation of his principate, giving him the right to convene the senate and to veto any of its legislation; it also gave him personal inviolability (*sacrosanctitas*).

Under a series of emperors succeeding Augustus, including Tiberius (14–37 CE), the mad autocrat Gaius Caligula (37–41 CE), Claudius (41–54 CE), and Nero (54–8 CE), the Romans controlled all of the regions surrounding the Mediterranean sea, which they called mare nostrum ("our lake"). Roman military prowess, in combination with Roman roadbuilding and within the framework of political domination, ensured that the culture that the Greeks had introduced into the eastern Mediterranean was furthered by the Romans.

## Literature and Rhetoric

During the Hellenistic period a conscious attempt was made by Greek intellectuals to identify and preserve the most important literary works of the past. One major center for this scholarly activity was the Mouseion (a Greek word meaning "house of the Muses," the origin of the English word "museum") in Alexandria, a research institution for the promotion of scholarship in all fields that included conference rooms, lecture rooms, a reading room, observatories, a zoo, a park, and a place for eating meals in addition to a library. The Mouseion was founded at the beginning of the third century BCE by Ptolemy I Soter and expanded by his son Ptolemy II Philadelphus. Zenodotus of Ephesus became the first head of the library in 284 BCE and became the father of textual criticism by his work on the original texts of the *Iliad* and *Odyssey* as well as other classic Greek texts. He was succeeded by Apollonius of Rhodes, chiefly known as the author of the *Argonautica*. Eratosthenes of Cyrene succeeded Apollonius ca. 247

BCE. Lavishly funded by the Ptolemies, the Mouseion funded visiting scholars from all over the Mediterranean world, providing for their families as well, giving them high salaries, free meals, no taxes, good lodgings, and servants (Pfeiffer 1968: 1.97). At its height, the library contained between 400,000 and 700,000 papyrus rolls, including literary and scientific works. The Mouseion was partly destroyed in 48 BCE during the siege of Alexandria by Julius Caesar, after which it was moved to a temple called the Serapeum, where it remained until ca. 391 CE.

Aristophanes of Byzantium (257–180 CE), a famous grammarian and librarian at the Mouseion, apparently drew up a list of authors which were called *egkrithentes* ("accepted" or "approved"), i.e., "classics." In the late eighteenth century, this list of approved books was called the "canon" (Pfeiffer 1968: 1.207). The main evidence for this so-called "Alexandrian canon" is found in Quintilian (1.4.3, 10.1.53–72). The list was expanded at various periods. The ten literary categories included the following (the number of literary works in each category is shown in parentheses) (Aune 2003: 29–30): epic poets (5), iambic poets (3), lyric poets (9), tragic poets (5), comic poets (13), elegiac poets (4), orators (10), historians (9), philosophers (5), poetic pleiade (7). As an example of two of these lists, the five epic poets included Homer, Hesiod, Peisander, Panyasis, and Antichaus, while the five philosophers included Plato, Xenophon, Aeschines, Aristotle, and Theophrastus. The works on these lists were intended to serve as models of style and composition. The existence of the Alexandrian canon had both positive and negative effects on ancient literature. The works of "approved" authors were read in schools and by the educated; they were copied, recopied, and commented upon, and thus preserved for posterity. The works of "unapproved" authors, however, were neglected and eventually lost to posterity, though this was also the fate of many approved authors.

Despite the fact that the upper classes in the Greco-Roman world were highly literate and in possession of scores of stunning classics from the literarily creative periods of both Greek and Roman culture, on balance oral culture was a pervasive feature of the Mediterranean world in the first few centuries CE that had roots in classical Greece. Rhetoric, or persuasive speaking, was a crucially important skill in the ancient world. The Greek city-state, with its occasional democratic institutions, needed members of the assembly who could persuade others about important matters of policy. Complex legal systems required people who had need of the court system either to argue their case for themselves or hire someone who could do a better job. Much of the great literature that became canonized in Alexandria was available, not primarily through libraries (which were few and far between), but through oral interpretation in public places. Some of these great works, like the Herodotus' *History of the Persian Wars*, was written with the intention of oral presentation. Certainly the great tragedies and comedies written by the Greek playwrights were not closet dramas intended for private reading, but rather for presentation on the stage.

Following Aristotle, rhetorical theorists divided rhetoric into three types according to the institutional context and the intended effect on the hearers. Judicial rhetoric, the rhetoric of the law courts, was intended to persuade a jury about what events had occurred in the past. Deliberative rhetoric, the rhetoric primarily appropriate in the political assembly, was designed to persuade members who had the responsibility of voting on various issues about which course of action they should pursue in the future. Finally, epideictic or display rhetoric, was intended for providing enjoyment in the present by celebrating common social values, such as when a deceased person's virtues were extolled in a eulogy.

While the three types of rhetoric formulated by Aristotle lived on through the rest of antiquity and beyond into the medieval and modern world, they essentially preserve ways of coping rhetorically within the three primary institutions of the ancient city-state of the early fourth century BCE. When the assemblies of the city-state lost their governing power when their cities were subordinated to larger empires, deliberative rhetoric became attenuated into a rhetorical exercise with no real usefulness in the real world. Nevertheless, since the ancients virtually always read written texts aloud, authors consciously or unconsciously wrote in a kind of oral style since they knew their works would be read aloud. This is probably true, for example, of the letters of Paul. One can see Paul in one's mind's eye pacing back and forth as he dictates letters to his beloved communities, finally grabbing the pen from the secretary to scribble (Gal. 6:11): "See with what large letters I am writing to you with my own hand!"

## Religion

The political and cultural unity imposed on the Levant and the Near East by the Greeks and then on the whole Mediterranean world by the Romans resulted in a period of creativity and change in the areas of religion and philosophy. Previously isolated ethnic cultural traditions came into increasing contact with each other often through military conquest but also through trade and commerce, and influenced each other in a number of ways. Cults in the Hellenistic world tended to focus on myth and ritual to the virtual exclusion of theology and ethics, whereas in the modern West religion is thought to consist of belief and myth systems as well as ritual and ethics. For the most part, theology and ethics were the primary concern of philosophical schools.

"Religion" for the ancients was not a separable component of culture, but rather an integral set of ideas and practices that permeated all aspects of life and thought. Unlike the modern West, neither the Greeks nor the Romans had a word for "religion" in the modern sense. In 1962 the Harvard historian of religion Wilfred Cantwell Smith argued that "religion" was a Western invention that first appeared on the scene at the beginning of the eighteenth century. In a similar vein, the French anthropologist Daniel Dubuisson argued that "religion," regarded as a discrete concept or distinct domain, is a Western construct invented by scholars in the nineteenth century.

What modern scholars call "religion" in the ancient world was embedded in Greek and Roman culture to such an extent that it is impossible to separate various social and cultural components from each other. Neither the Greeks nor the Romans had a religious identity that could be distinguished from their Greek or Roman identity as citizens or as members of families, clans, and tribes. As applied to the ancient world, then, "religion" is a third-order category applied to certain first-order discourse about features of

ancient cultic life available to us in Greco-Roman literature, papyri, inscriptions, iconography, and material remains. These primarily literary sources, often reinforced by
the material remains of temples, altars, and the artistic depiction of cultic scenes on bas-
reliefs and painted vases, provide access to first-order discourse about ancient beliefs
expressed through prayers, hymns, oracles, festivals, rituals, and myths.[1]

Several distinct forms of "religion" and religious traditions flourished in the Hellenistic
world: (1) state cults, (2) domestic cults, (3) ruler cults, and (4) mystery cults.

## 1   Greek state cults

The Greek world consisted of hundreds of city-states in the Greek peninsula, the islands
of the Aegean Sea, and the west coast of Asia Minor, as well as in the western
Mediterranean in Sicily and in Magna Graecia in Italy. These city-states or *poleis* were
independent both politically and culturally from the late eighth century BCE (when
many of them were founded) through the mid-fourth century BCE. The independence
of these city-states was gradually compromised, first by compulsory membership in
leagues of cities dominated by particularly powerful cities, such as the Delian league of
ca. 150 city-states formed in the fifth century BCE to deal with the Persian threat, but
increasingly dominated by Athens. In the mid-fourth century BCE, many Greek city-
states became subject to the expanding Greco-Macedonian empire, first under Philip II
of Macedon (382–336 BCE) and then under Alexander the Great. Under the various
Hellenistic kingdoms that were carved out of Alexander's empire in the late fourth
century, despite the loss of political independence, the traditional state cults of the
Greek cities continued to flourish into the first few centuries CE within the framework
of the Roman empire. Since the primary function of state cults had been to ensure
national prosperity by promoting peace with the gods, the subjugation of cities to larger
political units meant that the quest for prosperity had to be pursued at a higher level.

The cultural unity of the Greek people was fostered by several important pan-
Hellenic institutions, including oracles and games. Herodotus (1.46) lists six oracles
that were consulted by Croesus, king of Lydia, including Delphi, Abae in Phocia, Dodona,
Amphiaraos, Trophonios, and Branchidae in Asia Minor. These oracles were consulted
by emissaries from the many city-states that dotted the Greek world as well as individuals searching for divine guidance. The many healing oracles of Asklepios, of which the
most famous were the sanctuaries at Cos (the center of a medical school) and Epidauros.
These healing oracles were consulted by individuals with various types of illness, who
typically underwent the process of incubation or sleeping in a temple of Asklepios.
Athletic contests or games held regularly after the middle of the fifth century BCE, the
major games included the Olympian (held every four years in August or September),
Pythian (held every four years on the third year of the Olympiad in late August in honor
of Apollo of Delphi), Nemean (held every second and fourth year in each Olympiad), and
Isthmian (held near Corinth in honor of Poseidon on alternate years in April or May).
Typical athletic events, including chariot racing, boxing, wrestling, sprinting, javelin
throwing and archery, drew participants from all over the Greek world and were made
possible in part by the temporary cessation of hostilities during the game in the event

that any the Greek cities were at war with each other. Major sacrifices and processions were the primary cultic features of such athletic celebrations.

The twelve Olympian gods became the most pervasive pan-Hellenic institution in the Greek world. The canonical list of twelve deities consists of Zeus, Hera, Poseidon, Hades, Apollo, Artemis, Hephaestus, Athena, Ares, Aphrodite, Hermes, and Hestia. This list exhibits variations, however, for the earth deities Demeter and Dionysus, intentionally omitted from the *Iliad* and *Odyssey* of Homer, are sometimes included on the list in place of Hades and Hestia. The many deities worshiped in the city-states of the Greek world were eventually identified with one or another of the Olympian gods and given epithets to distinguish them from deities of the same name worshipped elsewhere. Hesiod, a sixth-century BCE poet, wrote the *Theogony*, dealing with the origins of the gods and their genealogical relationships. The Olympic deities were still influential during the Roman period and are frequently mentioned in the Acts of the Apostles. For example, conflict between those who proclaimed the gospel and the worshipers of Artemis of Ephesus, an Olympian deity worshiped in the famous Artemision, is narrated in Acts 19:23–41. In Acts 14:8–20, Barnabas and Paul are mistakenly identified with Zeus and Hermes, and the local priest of Zeus attempted to offer sacrifice to them.

The Greeks recognized three categories of deity, the Olympian gods, associated with the sky (e.g., Zeus, Hera, Apollo, Poseidon), the chthonic or earth deities, associated with the earth (e.g., Demeter, Dionysos, Trophonios), and heroes, cults devoted to the powerful dead who occupied an intermediate position between gods and mortals (e.g., Herakles, Hippolytus). The Greek conception of deity is strikingly different from that of the Jews. For Greeks generally, the gods were immanent and active in the world, rather than transcendent and passive. While the God of the Jews is considered the creator of all that exists, for Greeks the cosmos is eternal and the gods originated in time. While Judaism conceives of God as omniscient and omnipresent, the gods of the Greeks are more powerful and wiser than humans, but can only be in one place at a time. From the eighth century BCE on, Greeks began to depict their gods in both painting and sculpture as ideal human beings: male gods are typically depicted as handsome and muscular, while female gods are presented as both beautiful and shapely.

Greek religion tended to focus on sacrifice, prayer, processions, and festivals, and each city-state typically had its own distinctive religious calendar. Greek sacrifice, performed both publicly and privately, centered on the slaughter of certain kinds of domestic animals, parts of which were burned on an altar and parts of which were eaten by those offering the sacrifice. Sacrificial protocol involved the knowledge of what kind of animal each deity required (e.g., Athena preferred cows, while Demeter preferred pigs). A further distinction was made between the sacrificial protocol for sky deities and earth deities. Sacrifices to sky deities (Zeus, Athena, Poseidon, etc.) were made during the daytime on raised altars with light-colored animals whose throats were slit so that the blood would spurt toward the sky. Sacrifices to earth deities (Demeter, Dionysos, etc.) were made on a low altar or in a pit, with a preference for dark-colored animals whose throats were slit so that the blood spurted downward. Sacrifices were typically accompanied by prayer and a procession of ivy-wreathed worshipers in the company of a flute-player. Divination was regularly used just before the sacrifice to determine whether or not it was propitious to offer a particular victim to a particular deity at a particular time.

Reciprocity is a pervasive feature of Greek society that also plays an important role in the Greek conception of prayer (Aune 2001: 23–42). In Greek culture, every gift or service rendered to someone else placed a moral obligation on the recipient for an equivalent counter-gift or counter-service. Prayer is closely linked with sacrifice because the gift of the victim to the deity obligates the deity to respond to the worshiper in an appropriate manner. The prayer accompanying the sacrifice is typically formulated to indicate what the worshiper would like in return for the sacrificial gift. Plato (*Politicus*, 290c; LCL trans.) expresses this cultic dynamic: "The priests, according to law and custom, know how to give the gods, by means of sacrifices, the gifts that please them from us and by prayers to ask for us the gain of good things from them." A regular feature of the structure of ancient Greek prayers was a section detailing the reasons why a particular divinity should respond favorably to a request. A clear example of this practice is found in *Iliad*, 1.39–42:

> Smintheus [an epithet of Apollo], if ever it pleased your heart that I built your temple, if ever it pleased you that I burned all the rich thigh pieces of bulls, or goats, then bring to pass this wish I pray for: Let your arrows make the Danaans [i.e., Greeks] pay for my tears shed.

Two other common reasons are included in prayers that tell the god why he or she should answer the prayer: (1) because the god or goddess had done so in the past, and (2) because it lies within his or her competence to do so.

Religious festivals were a central part of public religious observances in the Greek world. Athens, the Greek city about which most is known, celebrated ca. 120 festivals each year (Parke 1977). One of the more prominent and popular festivals in Athens was the Panathenaia in honor of Athena held on the twenty-eighth day of Hekatombaion, the first month of the Athenian year, commemorated as the birth day of the goddess (Parke 1977: 33–50). A central feature of the festival was the ritual presentation of a enormous and colorful new *peplos* (outer garment), which was woven and decorated each year by a group of young girls from aristocratic families. The garment was brought to the Parthenon on a cart built to look like a ship, where it was hung on the mast like a sail. From the mid-fifth century on, it was placed on the thirty-foot high statue of Athena sculpted by Pheidias. The Panathenaia procession is depicted in bas-relief on the disputed Elgin marbles, originally part of the architecture of the Parthenon, but which since the early nineteenth century have been held by the British Museum in London.

## 2   Greek domestic cults

In the ancient Greek world, the home of the extended family (οἶκος) was the center for a private cult that focused on the hearth, the tomb, and the domestic shrine. The male head of the family functioned as an absolute authority and as the priest of the domestic cult. The center of the home was the hearth (ἑστία; the goddess Hestia, invoked first in all domestic prayers, was the personification of the hearth), which also functioned as the domestic altar, but was also where the household cooking was done. The hearth fire was not allowed to go out until it was ceremonially extinguished and relit on a specified day each year. The hearth was the focus of several rites of passage (newborns several days old were carried around the hearth; brides were integrated into the family gathered around the hearth). The gods of the household consisted of sky deities, earth deities, and deified ancestors. Prayers to the household gods were pronounced every morning and evening, accompanied by a libation of wine poured into the fire before every meal. Two altars, one to Zeus Herkeios ("Zeus of the courtyard"), located in the courtyard and Zeus Ctesios ("Zeus who guards possessions"), who functioned as the protector of the household gods, were located in the house.

### 3   Hellenistic and Roman ruler cults

Ruler cults first developed in Greek world when the Greco-Macedonian empire began to expand into the Levant and the Near East and previously independent Greek city-states were subjected to external rule, first by Greco-Macedonian dynasties and eventually by the Romans. The Ionian cities of western Asia Minor had proclaimed the divinity of Alexander the Great when he liberated them during his campaign against the Persians. Among the mainland Greeks, however, only the league of Corinth voted divine honors to Alexander in 324 BCE, shortly before his death. Elsewhere, Alexander requested and received divine honors and in response provided various benefits for those cities which participated. After Ptolemy I died (ca. 280 BCE), his son and successor Ptolemy II arranged for the formal deification of his father and his mother as "savior gods." Ptolemy II and his wife Arsinoe were deified ca. 270 CE, and thereafter each successor to the Ptolemaic throne was deified upon accession.

While the Hellenistic ruler cults focused on living rulers, in Rome the ruler cult focused on deceased emperors who were deified by vote of the senate after death. Julius Caesar was posthumously deified by the senate in 42 BCE, arranged in part by Octavian his adopted son who took the title *divi filius*, "son of the god [Julius]" as a strategy for legitimating his intention to rule Rome. Many of the emperors beginning with Augustus were posthumously deified in emulation of the legend of the *apotheosis* or deification of Romulus, the legendary founder of Rome. In the eastern Mediterranean, however, particularly in Roman Asia, cults in honor of living emperors were instituted in various cities (e.g. Pergamum and Ephesus), who regarded the right to celebrate cults to living emperors as a great honor. Toward the end of the first century and beginning of the second century CE, Christians who were arrested were often required to sacrifice to the emperor to prove that they had renounced their beliefs.

### 4   Hellenistic mystery religions

The phrase "mystery religion" (based on the Greek words μύστης, which means "initiant," and μυστήριον, which means "ritual of initiation") were quasi-public cults that were voluntary and required initiation. In this respect, it was markedly different from the state and domestic cults of the Greek world, in which citizenship and membership in a family were the basic requirements for participation. Since the rituals of these cults were secret (like the masonic rituals of the modern West), the term μυστήριον came to connote "*secret* rites of initiation." While many mystery cults moved into the

Mediterranean region from further east during the Hellenistic era (the period of their greatest popularity was the first through the third centuries CE), the oldest of all mystery cults was indigenous to Greece: the Eleusinian mysteries, which had their cult center in Eleusis in Attica. The more prominent mystery cults from the Greek world, in addition to the Eleusinian mysteries are the Great Gods of Samothrace and the mysteries of Dionysos. The more prominent mysteries that moved into the Greek world from the Levantine countries include the mysteries of Mithras, the mysteries of Isis, and the mysteries of Magna Mater.

While very little is known about the inner workings of the mystery cults, their ritual programs had three primary features: (1) δρώμενα ("things acted out"), some kind of dramatization of the myth upon which the cult was based; (2) λεγώμενα ("things spoken"), the oral presentation of the myth on which the cult was based; (3) δεικνύμενα ("things shown"), the ritual presentation of symbolic objects to the one being initiated. Following the experience of a ritual initiation, new members of the cult became convinced that they would enjoy salvation, both in this life (i.e., health, prosperity, safety) as well as in the life to come. Sophocles, in a saying preserved by Plutarch (*How to Study Poetry*, 22f.) emphasizes the salvific benefits of initiation: "Twice blessed are those who go to Hades after beholding these rites. For them alone is there life there; for all others only evil."

Until the last third of the twentieth century, mystery religions were thought to be inspired by the annual decay and restoration of vegetation, symbolizing death and resurrection in the human world. In part this is the result of the comparison of the mystery religions with Christianity, which has a central focus on the death and resurrection of Jesus as the salvific event appropriated by individual Christians in baptism. Scholars associated with Göttingen-centered German history of religions school, active at the beginning of the twentieth century, argued that the Pauline understanding of the Lord's Supper and dying and rising with Christ in baptism had antecedents in the mystery religions. Scholarship during the second half of the twentieth century disclosed the widespread diversity that characterized Hellenistic mystery religions together with the fact that a dying and rising god was rarely a central mythic symbol. Even the phrase "mystery religions" itself is inappropriate, since they were in no way exclusive and were in fact special forms of larger contexts of religious practice (Burkert 1987: 10).

A prime example of the death–resurrection pattern in the mysteries is found in the Eleusinian mysteries, which celebrated the symbolic death of Persephone, the daughter of Demeter, who had been seized by Hades, the god of the underworld, and made his queen. After fruitlessly searching for her daughter for nine days, according to the myth (recounted in the Homeric *Hymn to Demeter*), after finally appealing to Zeus, who sent Hermes as his emissary to Hades, Persephone was returned to her mother Demeter on the condition that she spend one-third of every year in the Underworld with Hades. Demeter's name means "earth mother," while Persephone apparently represents grain; two-thirds of the year in Greece constitute the rainy season, while for one-third of the year conditions are dry and vegetation is dormant. Initiation into the Eleusinian mysteries was a two-stage process. The first stage involved initiation into the Lesser Mysteries (celebrated annually in Athens during the month Anthesterion), and, after the interval of at least one year, the second stage consisted of initiation into the Greater

Mysteries (which were held during the Athenian month Boedromion). The second stage began from Athens, with a sacrifice of pigs to Demeter, followed by a procession to the Telesterion ("hall of initiation") at Eleusis in western Attica, not far from the isthmus of Corinth, where the initiation ritual was held.

# Philosophy

## 1  Introduction

In the ancient world, the pursuit of philosophy achieved its classical expression in the thought of Plato and Aristotle during the late fifth through the late fourth centuries BCE, both of whom have profoundly affected Western thought. While the three most important Hellenistic schools of philosophy will be discussed in some detail below, there were many other philosophical traditions in play in the Hellenistic and Roman world. Cynicism, revived during the Roman period, is not treated here for two simple reasons: (1) it was not a "philosophy" in the ordinary sense of the word, with no school with successive leaders; (2) very little is known about the Cynics, who seem not to have had a system of teachings like the other philosophical schools, so much as a far-out lifestyle. Platonism continued to be influential, but had been transformed into what is now labeled Middle Platonism, which began in the late second century BCE (with the activities of Antiochus of Ascalon, 130–68 BCE) and lasted until the late second century CE with the work of Numenius of Apamea, who was a Neopythagorean concerned to trace Platonic doctrine back to Pythagoras.

In the Hellenistic and Roman periods, however, the most influential philosophical schools were Stoicism, Epicureanism, and Skepticism (or Pyrrhonism), all of which had their origins in the Hellenistic period. All of the philosophical schools were shut down by order of the Christian emperor Justinian I in 529 CE. Despite the diversity of their respective philosophical systems, all three schools shared several basic perspectives. (1) Founded during a period of Mediterranean history in which individuals and their societies were frequently subject to external forces over which they had no control, all three schools focused on the inner life of the mind over which individuals could exert control. (2) Further, while classical philosophical schools typically had three separate but related concerns – physics, logic and ethics – the three major Hellenistic philosophies placed a primary emphasis on ethics centering on living a life of virtue. (3) All three schools could agree with the Epicurean definition of philosophy (Sextus Empricus *Adversus mathematicos*, 11.169; LCL trans.): "philosophy is an activity which secures the happy life by arguments and discussions." (4) Finally, all three schools made wide use of a medical model: the philosopher functioned like a compassionate physician whose task was to diagnose human suffering experienced by individuals in order to provide the appropriate philosophical therapy, enabling them to recover and lead a flourishing life (Nussbaum 1994: 13–47). Cicero (*Tusculan Disputations*, 3.3.6) provides a typical example of the widespread use of this metaphor:

> Assuredly there is an art of healing the soul – I mean philosophy, whose aid must be sought not, as in bodily diseases, outside ourselves, and we must use our utmost endeavour, with all our resources and strength, to have the power to be ourselves our own physicians.

For Hellenistic philosophers, then, philosophy was a way of life rather than a theoretical discipline.


## 2   Stoicism

Stoicism is based on the Greek word *stoa*, meaning "colonnade" in the phrase *stoa poikile*, "painted colonnade," a structure overlooking the agora in Athens where the school was begun ca. 300 BCE by Zeno of Citium (334–262 BCE). Stoicism was an important philosophical tradition that had an 800-year history and became the most influential philosophy for the educated in the Roman empire. The focus of this brief description of Stoic ethics largely centers on Stoicism during the early Roman empire, a period that coincided with the rise of Christianity. Among the more prominent philosophers of late Stoicism, whose writings survive, is Epictetus (ca. 55–135 CE), a slave who became a noted Stoic philosopher. The oral lectures of Epictetus were transcribed by an auditor, Arrian of Nicomedia (ca. 86–after 146 CE). Other important Stoics of the early empire include Seneca, Arius Didymus (fl. late first century BCE and early first century CE), and the philosopher-emperor Marcus Aurelius (121–80 CE; emperor 161–80 CE).

An important feature of Stoic physics is the view that God and the material universe are essentially identical (Seneca, *Epistulae morales*, 92.30). Just as the soul pervades the human body and is endowed with reason (the faculty allowing humans to think, plan and speak), so God is identified with the divine λόγος ("Reason") or νοῦς ("Mind"), that pervades the cosmos and is also found in gods and in human beings. Note that Plato had earlier divided the soul into rational and irrational elements and that the presence of an irrational or emotional element in the soul was introduced into Stoicism by the Stoic philosopher Poseidonius (135–51 BCE), who accepted Plato's teaching on this subject, arguing that the irrational part of the soul should be subjected to the rational part. For Stoics, the cosmos consists of two substances; matter is a passive substance, while universal reason (or God) is the active substance which acts upon matter. Stoics were both materialists (rejecting any dualism of matter and spirit) as well as determinists. For them the cosmos consisted of material objects which interacted in accordance with unchanging laws that they designated as fate or providence. The human person with a rational soul and a physical body is a microcosm of the universe, which itself is a rationally organized structure. Human beings are ruled by fate or providence and cannot control external events; they can only accept them (or reject them at their peril). In the Stoic view, living in accordance with reason means living in harmony with the divine order of the universe.

Ancient philosophers thought that emotions were *cognitive*, e.g., fear is the expectation of impending evil. The Stoics maintained that all the passions or emotions were both unwanted and harmful, and held the extreme view that all passions should be eradicated. Aristotle and the Peripatetics, on the other hand, maintained that most emotions are useful in moderation and even essential for achieving the flourishing life. The Stoics had a generally intellectualist approach to understanding human emotions, maintaining that they were based on decisions made in the ἡγεμονικόν ("governing principle" or "self"), thought to be located in the heart, which was the center of rationality in human beings. The governing principle processes external appearances (φαντασίαι) that present themselves through the five senses. Stoics thought that they had the option of accepting or rejecting sense impressions or appearances about the world. They formulated three ways in which a sense impression could be accepted as true (Burnyeat 1983: 11): (1) δόξα ("opinion"), a weak and fallible belief; (2) κατάληψις ("cognition"), infallible belief; (3) ἐπιστήμη ("understanding"), the type of cognitive belief of the wise man, irreversible even by reason.

The Stoics maintained that there were four basic categories of the passions or emotions, which were the basis of all other emotions: pleasure, distress, appetite, and fear (the subtypes of each generic emotion are elaborated in Diogenes Laertius 7.111–14). The Stoic view that anyone can attain freedom from the emotions makes it necessary that they be considered voluntary. Further, each emotion involves at least two distinct value judgments separated in time. The first judgment determines whether something either good or bad is at hand and the second judgment decides that it is appropriate to react (Sorabji 2000: 29). Zeno argued that all emotions were harmful and originated in a conscious disobedience to reason, e.g., people in an emotional state often recognize that it is inappropriate to do what they are doing, but continue to do it anyway (Sorabji 2000: 55, 60). Chrysippus (280–208 BCE), a student and successor of Zeno, who expanded and modified the basic doctrines of Stoicism, argued that all emotions were not the result of *disobeying* reason, but were rather *mistakes* of reason, i.e., evaluative judgments. By the beginning of the first century CE there were, then, two different conceptions of the emotions: one understood them as the result of disobedience to reason and the other understood them as the result of mistakes of reason (following Sorabji 2000).

Seneca (4 BCE–64 CE) analyzed the emotions to determine the extent to which they were voluntary or involuntary. He argued that there were mental "first movements," i.e., expansions or contractions of the soul or what we would call physiological responses to various types of external stimuli. Using anger as an example of a negative emotion, Seneca proposed three stages of anger, with the first stage consisting of an involuntary component and the second and third stages consisting of voluntary components that harmonized the two different conceptions of emotion proposed by Zeno (disobedience to reason) and Chrysippus (mistakes of reason): (1) The first movement or agitation of the mind is involuntary, i.e., prior to the judgments characterizing stages (2) and (3), and cannot be considered an emotion (Sorabji 2000: 69–70; Seneca, *On Anger*, 2.2.1–2.4.2). (2) In the second stage, reason accepts the appearance of injustice, which is linked to the propriety of taking vengeance on the perpetrator (a mistaken judgment of moral reason). (3) In the third stage, one's emotions are carried away and anger is expressed, i.e., one disobeys the erroneous judgment of reason (Sorabji 2000: 61; Seneca, *On Anger*, 2.4.1).

When the governing principle is not allowed to rule a person's life through the exercise of self-control (ἐγκράτεια), harmful and destructive passions or emotions arise. The goal of philosophy is to learn what does not conform to reason and to nature and to reject it, a process that requires training, i.e., the examination of one's own judgments and behavior to determine how they have departed from universal reason.

The greatest good is happiness or the flourishing life, which can be attained through virtue, which consists in living according to reason, which is the same as living according to nature, for nature is the criterion of the rational and everything contrary to nature is considered irrational (Seneca, *Epistulae morales*, 5.4). The passions or emotions are always considered bad. An important term in Stoic ethics is ἀπάθεια ("freedom from passions or emotions"), i.e., a life unencumbered by human passions or emotions. Individuals are responsible, however, for their own actions, which can be controlled by examination and self-discipline. An example of such self-examination and reflection is expressed by Marcus Aurelius (*Meditations*, 2.1; LCL trans. [with modifications]):

> Say to yourself at daybreak: I shall come across the busybody, the thankless, the overbearing, the treacherous, the envious, the unneighborly. All this has happened to them because they do not know good from evil. But I, in that I have comprehended the nature of the Good that is beautiful, and the nature of Evil that it is ugly, and the nature of the wrongdoer himself that it is similar to me, not as sharing the same blood and seed but of intelligence and a portion of the Divine, can neither be injured by any of them – for no one can involve me in what is debasing – nor can I be angry with my kinsman and hate him.

Early Stoics traditionally attributed virtue in the proper sense only to the ideal sage, considering everyone as foolish (Seneca, *Epistulae morales*, 75.8). Later Stoics rejected the absolute dichotomy between the sage and fools and spoke of making progress toward virtue. Seneca, for example, outlines several stages characterizing those making progress in virtue (*Epistulae morales*, 75; cf. Ware 2008: 270–1): (1) The highest stage consists of those who have rid themselves of all passions and vices, and though they are approaching perfect wisdom are not yet truly wise. (2) The second stage consists of those who have abandoned only the greatest passions, but who may fall back into these vices. (3) The lowest stage consists of those who have escaped many great vices, but have not yet conquered others.

## 3   Epicureanism

Epicureanism was founded by Epicurus (341–270 BCE) about 307 BCE and was widely known as "the Garden" because Epicurus taught philosophy in the confines of his home and walled garden in Athens, where he and his followers lived a very private, simple, and frugal life. Epicurus himself was a prolific author who wrote more than 300 rolls, reportedly without citing earlier writers (Diogenes Laertius, 10.26). The five works which have survived include three letters: *Epistle to Herodotus* (Diogenes Laertius, 10.35–83), *Epistle to Pythocles* (Diogenes Laertius, 10.83–116), and *Epistle to Menoeceus* (Diogenes Laertius, 10.122–35; perhaps not genuine), a collection of maxims called the *Kyriai Doxai* or "Principle Doctrines," consisting of extracts from the teaching of Epicurus probably compiled by his disciples (Diogenes Laertius, 10.135–54), a set of eighty-one maxims preserved in a Vatican manuscript and carbonized fragments of Epicurus' thirty-seven-book work entitled *On Nature*, discovered in the Villa of the Papyri at Herculaneum, like Pompeii, a city destroyed during the eruption of Vesuvius in 79 CE. One of the most famous ancient exponents of Epicurean thought in the Roman world was Lucretius, who wrote *De rerum natura* ("On the Nature of Things"), a Latin poem containing a masterful poetic compendium of the basic theories and arguments of Epicureanism. Another representative of Epicureanism during the Roman period is Philodemus of Gadara (ca. 110–40 BCE), some thirty-six of whose works were discovered in the form of carbonized scrolls excavated in the eighteenth century in the Villa of the Papyri in Herculaneum. Another important second-century CE representative of Epicurean thought is Diogenes of Oenoanda, who carved a summary of Epicurean philosophy on a portico wall in Oenoanda in Lycia. Originally ca. 25,000 words long, about one-third of the inscription survives and is an important witness to Epicurean philosophy.

Epicurus thought that the primary purpose of philosophy was to enable people to live happy and pleasant lives, and therefore he focused on moral philosophy. The pleasant life, however, has moral entailments; according to *Kyriai doxai*, 5 (Diogenes Laertius, 10.140; LCL trans.): "It is impossible to live a pleasant life without living wisely and well and justly, and it is impossible to live wisely and well and justly without living pleasantly." The most important means for living a happy life is the acquisition of friends (*Kyriai doxai*, 27). Justice is based on an informal social contract (συνθήκη) which prevents one person from being harmed by another (*Kyriai doxai*, 31–7). Epicurus attributed the basic causes of human unhappiness to mistaken beliefs about the gods (Epicurus, *Ep. Pythocles*, 123–4), the destiny of the soul, and the things in life that are thought valuable, and his teaching centered on discrediting such mistaken beliefs and replacing them with what he considered to be true beliefs (Long 1986: 14). Epicureans are hedonists in the sense that they considered pleasure as the primary goal of life: "We call pleasure the beginning and end of a blessed life" (Epicurus, *Ep. Menoeceus*, 128). However, it is more accurate to characterize the greatest good for Epicureans as "the absence of pain in the body and of trouble in the soul" (*Ep. Menoeceus*, 131; cf. 137), but Epicurus also maintained that pains of the mind are worse than pains of the body (*Ep. Menoeceus*, 137). While pleasure is the beginning and end of the happy life, a distinction must be made between pleasures, with a preference for those that entail the least amount of pain. To seek more pleasure than one already has is to spoil the pleasure one has with the pain of unsatisfied desire. The ideal form of life is ἀταραξία ("imperturbability") and the best way to achieve it is through philosophy.

Like the Stoics (their primary philosophical antagonists), Epicureans were materialists, dependent on a modified account of the atomic theory of Democritus (460–370 BCE). Epicurus posited that all events and all substances perceived by the senses are temporary compounds of inanimate atoms or indivisible bodies (Lucretius, 2.865–990), which have infinite shapes, and empty space (Lucretius, 1.426; Epicurus, *Ep. Herodotus*, 39–40), making theories of supernatural causation unnecessary. Change is brought about by the rearrangement of these changeless atoms. Atoms move downward at a constant rate and sometimes collide because they swerve from their path (a modification of Democritus; see Annas 1992: 175–88). This element of unpredictability in the cosmos is the basis for rejecting all forms of determinism and teleology (*Ep. Menoeceus*, 133–4), providing the basis for the exercise of free will (Lucretius, 2.256–60). Both creation and the eternality of the cosmos, widely held postulates of Platonism and Aristotelianism, were rejected by Epicureans. In the Epicurean view, the body is the container or vessel of the soul, and the soul is in the body as scent is in perfume. The soul is composed of several kinds of very smooth and round atoms (Lucretius, 3.177–230), which disperse upon death, so that anxiety about death is rendered unnecessary, since there is no afterlife and no possibility of feeling (*Kyriai doxai*, 2; Lucretius, 3.830–69). The knowledge that the soul is dissolved upon death makes mortal life itself more enjoyable since there can be no desire for immortality (*Ep. Menoeceus*, 124–7). The soul is diffused throughout the body, with the rational element in the chest (the region of the emotions) and the irrational element everywhere else in the body (Annas 1992: 144–7).

Epicurus' theory of knowledge is based on the reliability of sense perception (Diogenes Laertius, 10.32), for the atoms of which all things are compounded give off εἴδωλα ("films" or "effluences"), which convey impressions to the senses and then to the mind. While such appearances are never false, mistaken judgments about them may occur through the formation of δόξαι ("opinions") by the mind. For Epicurus, the emotions are complex kinds of feelings based on two kinds of perceptions: pleasure and pain which are the two basic kinds of πάθη, "passions" or "emotions" (Diogenes Laertius, 10.34).

While the gods exist, they are composed of atoms and void like everything else in the cosmos. Their existence is known because their atomic structure gives off fine "films" or "images" that are perceived directly by the mind, not the senses (*Kyriai doxai*, 1). The gods live far from the earth, have no concern for the human world or the cosmos, but live untroubled lives of eternal happiness (*Kyriai doxai*, 1); as such they provide an ideal model for Epicurean communities. Because of this, Epicurus regarded prayer and sacrifice as unnecessary and he also rejected all forms of divination (*Ep. Menoeceus*, 134).

Sorabji (2000: 343–417) traces the Stoic legacy of the cognitive nature of the emotions on the Christian conception of temptation found in such early Christian writers as Origen, Evagrius, and Augustine. According to Sorabji, the Stoic theory of how to avoid agitation (involuntary first movements or contractions did not yet constitute an emotion, make it theoretically possible to stop the emotion from forming) was transformed by certain early Christian authors as a way of avoiding temptation. For Origen, the Stoic involuntary first movements became bad thoughts, blurring the sharp Stoic distinction between first movements (which are involuntary and not emotions), and the emotions proper (for which a person is completely responsible). Evagrius formulated eight types of bad thoughts (Stoics' first movements in a Christian disguise) that only became sin if they were allowed to linger.

## 4   Skepticism

There were two main streams of Hellenistic Skepticism. One can be traced back to an enigmatic character named Pyrrhon of Elis (ca. 360–270 BCE), while the other is the introduction of skepticism into the Academy (the philosophical school founded by Plato), by Arcesilaus (ca. 316–241 BCE), the founder of the New Academy, which lasted until it was weakened by Philo of Larissa (ca. 159–84 BCE) a later head of the Academy. The most important Skeptic philosopher who compiled some important philosophical works is Sextus Empiricus (ca. 200 CE), a Greek physician who represents an attempt to return to the Pyrrhonian origins of Skepticism. Sextus wrote two compendia covering 500 years of skeptical argumentation, which are the most important primary extant sources for the history and arguments of Hellenistic Skepticism – *Outlines of Pyrrhonism* and *Adversus mathematicos* (the latter was originally two separate works, one in books 1–6 and the other in books 7–11). The most important discussion of the skeptical phase of the Academy is represented by Marcus Tullius Cicero's *Academica* (Cicero studied under Philo of Larissa, the head of the New Academy, after he had come to Rome in 87 BCE).

There are two distinguishing characteristics features of Hellenistic Skepticism. The first and most important of these is "its radical conviction that to suspend assent and to resign oneself to ignorance is not a bleak expedient but, on the contrary, a highly desirable intellectual achievement" (Sedley 1983: 10). The second feature is the methodical collection of arguments against the possibility of knowledge.

The term "Skeptic" is based on the word σκεπτικός, meaning "inquirer," which first appears in the second century CE in the works of Sextus Empiricus as an alternate designation for "Pyrrhonist" (Sedley 1983: 20). Sextus uses "inquirer" in opposition to δογματικός, meaning "dogmatist" or more appropriately "doctrinaire thinker" (Sedley 1983: 21), an umbrella term for all philosophical schools who claimed to know something about reality. Why did Sextus prefer the term "inquirer" to designate the skeptical philosopher in opposition to the dogmatist? Ordinarily one thinks of an inquirer as someone who is open-minded and who seeks (and might eventually find) the truth. Apparently, the use of "inquirer" suggests that the Skeptic is one who is not hampered by doctrinal presuppositions, while the antithetical position is that of the dogmatist, who thinks he or she has already discovered the truth, e.g. Aristotle, the Stoics, and the Epicureans (Sextus Empiricus, 1.2–3). Sextus begins *Outlines of Pyrrhonism* with a definition of Skepticism:

> Skepticism is an ability or mental attitude, which opposes appearances to judgments in any way whatsoever, with the result that, owing to the equal and opposite force [ἰσοσθένειαν] of the objects and reasons thus opposed, we are brought firstly to a suspension of judgment [ἐποχή] and next to a state of tranquility [ἀταραξία]. (1.8; LCL trans. with modifications)

In this brief statement, Sextus emphasizes the goal of Skepticism, namely a kind of peace of mind represented by the frequent use of the term ἀταραξία (borrowed from Pyrrhon by Epicurus). The means to that goal is ἐποχή, "suspension of judgment," and the reason for suspending judgment is ἰσοσθένεια, i.e., the equal and opposite force of the arguments, which cancel each other out, making the acceptance of either of the opposed arguments impossible. This view is attributed to Arcesilaus by Cicero (*Academica*, 1.45; LCL trans.):

> His [Arcesilaus'] practice was consistent with this theory – he led most of his hearers to accept it by arguing against the opinions of men, so that when equally weighty reasons were found on opposite sides of the same subject, it was easier to withhold assent from either side.

Pyrrhon of Elis, who wrote nothing, was an older contemporary of Arcesilaus, who is often (and probably incorrectly) considered the founder of Skepticism (Burnyeat 1983: 14). He studied with Anaxarchus, a Democratean philosopher (a tradition that denied the possibility of knowledge), who was a student of Diogenes of Smyrna, who in turn studied with Metrodorus of Chio, who famously claimed (alluding to Socrates) that he knew nothing, not even the fact that he knew nothing (Cicero, *Academia*, 2.73; Diogenes Laertius, 9.10.58). It appears that Pyrrhon's major contribution to later Skepticism was as a model of someone who lived without beliefs (Burnyeat 1983: 15).

Arcesilaus, a younger contemporary of Zeno and Epicurus, introduced methodological Skepticism to the Academy when he became its head ca. 273 BCE. He regarded himself as a true Platonist and heir of Socrates, based on his reading of the earlier dialogues of Plato, though it appears that he smuggled in Pyrrhon's philosophy (the elimination of all belief) without explicit acknowledgment (Burnyeat 1983: 15–16). The innovation of Arcesilaus was to regard the equal force of opposing arguments, not only as a rhetorical exercise (found frequently, for example, in Plato), but as leading to a suspension of judgment and of belief (Burnyeat 1983: 11). For Skeptics, the disease that prevents people from living a happy and tranquil (ἀταραξία) life is any kind of belief or commitment. A basic motto of Skepticism is "to every argument, let an equal argument be opposed" (Sextus Empiricus, *Outlines of Pyrrhonism*, 1.204; my trans.).

According to Arcesilaus the goal (τέλος) of life is ἐποχή, "suspension of judgment," which is accompanied by ἀταραξία, "tranquility" (Sextus Empiricus, *Outlines of Pyrrhonism*, 1.232). Pyrrhon is also said to have maintained that the end was suspension of judgment, which brings along tranquility as its shadow (Diogenes Laertius, 9.107).

Aenesidemus, a member of the New Academy of which Philo of Larissa was head in the first century BCE, criticized the dogmatic tendencies of the New Academy under Philo after leaving to found his own more rigorous Skeptical school in which the hardline views of Pyrrhon were revived. This Pyrrhonist movement prevailed from the first cent. BCE through the end of the second cent. CE with Sextus Empiricus, whose primary source was the lost works of Aenesidemus, but who pays very little attention to Pyrrhon. The chief contribution of Aenesidemus was the formulation of ten methods of suspension of judgment (Sextus *Outlines of Pyrrhonism* 1.31–163; Diogenes Laertius 9.79–88).

## Note

1  According to this schema, second-order discourse about ancient "religion" consists of the gathering and arrangement of data by natives, based on first-order discourse through description, definition, classification and is concerned about what participants in ancient cults say about what they are doing and what they believe about what they are doing.

## Annotated Bibliography

Annas, Julia E. *Hellenistic Philosophy of Mind*. Berkeley, Los Angeles and London: University of California Press, 1992.
Aune, David E. *The New Testament in its Literary Environment*. Philadelphia: Westminster, 1987. The similarities and differences between Greco-Roman and early Jewish literary styles, forms, and genres are discussed.

Aune, David E. "Prayer in the Greco-Roman World." Pp. 23–42 in *Into God's Presence: Prayer in the New Testament*. Edited by Richard N. Longenecker. Grand Rapids: Eerdmans, 2001. An overview of the ideology of Greek prayer and the various prayer forms used in the Greek world.

Aune, David E. *The Westminster Dictionary of New Testament & Early Christian Literature & Rhetoric*. Louisville and London: Westminster John Knox Press, 2003.

Aune, David E. "The Problem of the Passions in Cynicism." Pp. 48–66 in *Passions and Moral Progress in Greco-Roman Thought*. Edited by John T. Fitzgerald. London and New York: Routledge, 2008.

Bonhöffer, Adolf. *Epiktet und das Neue Testament*. Giessen: Alfred Töpelmann, 1911.

Branham, R. Bracht and Marie-Odile Goulet-Cazé (eds.). *The Cynics: The Cynic Movement in Antiquity and its Legacy*. Berkeley, Los Angeles, and London: University of California Press, 1996.

Burkert, Walter. *Ancient Mystery Cults*. Cambridge, MA: Harvard University Press, 1987. An enlightened treatment of the mystery religions by one of the greatest living scholars of ancient Greek religion.

Burnyeat, Myles (ed.). *The Skeptical Tradition*. Berkeley, Los Angeles, and London: University of California Press, 1983.

Couissin, Pierre. "The Stoicism of the New Academy." Pp. 31–63 in Burnyeat 1983. An important but neglected article originally published in French in 1926 and first translated into English in the Burnyeat volume.

DeWitt, Norman W. *St. Paul and Epicurus*. Minneapolis: University of Minnesota Press, 1954. A respected classical scholar finds similarities between Paul and Epicurus by atomizing the Pauline letters and highlighting phrases that have some parallel in the writings of Epicurus, with completely unsatisfactory results.

Droysen, J. G. *Geschichte des Hellenismus*. 3 vols. 2nd edn. Tübingen: Mohr Siebeck, 1877–8. An important historical work by the scholar who gave Hellenism its name.

Dubuisson, Daniel. *The Western Construction of Religion: Myths, Knowledge and Ideology*. Trans. William Sayers. Baltimore: Johns Hopkins University Press, 2003.

Eddy, Samuel K. *The King is Dead: Studies in the Near Eastern Resistance to Hellenism 334–31 B.C.* Lincoln: University of Nebraska Press, 1961.

Engberg-Petersen, Troels. *Paul and the Stoics*. Edinburgh: T. & T. Clark, 2000.

Fitzgerald, John J., Dirk Obbink, and Glenn S. Holland (eds.). *Philodemus and the New Testament World*. Leiden: E. J. Brill, 2004. A not entirely successful attempt to relate the thought of the Epicurean philosopher Philodemus of Gadara to the world of the New Testament (in part 3).

Fitzgerald, John T. (ed.). *Passions and Moral Progress in Greco-Roman Thought*. London and New York: Routledge, 2008.

Glad, Clarence. *Paul and Philodemus: Adaptability in Epicurean and Early Christian Psychagogy*. NovTSupp 81. Leiden: E. J. Brill, 1995. Based on an examination of ancient educational theory, Glad focuses on several Pauline passages dealing with his own adaptability (e.g. "I have become all things to all people" in 1 Cor. 9:22). The central Pauline texts he examines includes 1 Cor. 9:19–23, Rom. 14:1–15:14, 1 Cor. 8:1–13 and 1 Cor. 10:24–11:1, making comparisons with philosophical notions of friendship, therapeutic speech, and moral transformation, placing Paul closer to the Epicurean psychagogy than to other philosophical traditions.

Hadas, Moses. *Hellenistic Culture: Fusion and Diffusion*. New York: Norton, 1959.

Haelst, Joseph van. *Catalogue des papyrus littéraires juifs et chrétiens*. Paris: Publications de la Sorbonne, 1976. An exhaustive list of extant Jewish and Christian papyri, primarily from Egypt.

Hengel, Martin. *Judaism and Hellenism*. 2 vols. Trans. John Bowden. Philadelphia: Fortress, 1974. The single most important study of the interaction between Judaism and Hellenism in the third and second centuries BCE, arguing that the Judaism of Palestine during this period was as thoroughly Hellenized as the Judaism of the Diaspora. This point is disputed by L. H. Feldman, "Hengel's *Judaism and Hellenism* in Retrospect," *Journal of Biblical Literature* 96 (1977), 371–82.

Horbury, William and David Noy. *Jewish Inscriptions of Graeco-Roman Egypt*. Cambridge: Cambridge University Press, 1992. This collection contains all known Jewish inscriptions from Greek and Roman Egypt.

Jeffers, James S. *The Greco-Roman World of the New Testament Era: Exploring the Background of Early Christianity*. Downers Grove: InterVarsity, 1999.

Leipoldt, Johannes and Walter Grundmann (eds.). *Umwelt des Urchristentums*. Berlin: Evangelische Verlagsanstalt, 1965.

Long, A. A. *Hellenistic Philosophy: Stoics, Epicureans, Sceptics*. 2nd edn. Berkeley and Los Angeles: University of California Press, 1986. One of the best short introductions to the three most important Hellenistic philosophical schools.

Long, A. A. and D. N. Sedley. *The Hellenistic Philosophers*. 2 vols. Cambridge: Cambridge University Press, 1987. Volume 1 contains the English translations of primary sources with commentary, while volume 2 contains the Greek and Latin texts from which the translations were made.

Malherbe, A. J. *Paul and the Popular Philosophers*. Minneapolis: Fortress Press, 1987.

Malherbe, A. J. *Paul and the Thessalonians: The Philosophic Tradition of Pastoral Care*. Philadelphia: Fortress Press, 1987.

Millar, Fergus. *The Roman Near East: 31 BC–AD 337*. Cambridge, MA: Harvard University Press, 1993.

Nussbaum, Martha C. *The Therapy of Desire: Theory and Practice in Hellenistic Ethics*. Princeton: Princeton University Press, 1994. The author focuses on a practical aspect of Hellenistic philosophy, namely its understanding of the role of philosophy in human life, under the medical model of diagnosing the ills of the mind and offering therapy through philosophical argument and discussion.

Parke, H. W. *Festivals of the Athenians*. New York: Cornell University Press, 1977. A discussion of what was known about Athenian religious festivals at the time of writing.

Pfeiffer, Rudolf. *History of Classical Scholarship: From the Beginnings to the End of the Hellenistic Age*. Oxford: Clarendon Press, 1968.

Roetzel, Calvin. J. *The World That Shaped the New Testament*. Revised edition. Atlanta: John Knox, 2002. A brief but reliable synthesis of the political, socio-economic, and religious setting of early Christianity.

Sedley, David. "The Motivation of Greek Skepticism." Pp. 9–29 in Burnyeat 1983.

Smith, Wilfred Cantwell. *The Meaning and End of Religion*. London: Macmillan; New York: American Library, 1962.

Sorabji, Richard. *Emotion and Peace of Mind: From Stoic Agitation to Christian Temptation*. Oxford: Oxford University Press, 2000. A comprehensive discussion of the role of emotions from Plato and Aristotle, through the major Stoic philosophers to early Christianity.

Walbank, F. W. *The Hellenistic World*. Cambridge, MA: Harvard University Press, 1981.

Ware, James. "Moral Progress and Divine Power in Seneca and Paul." Pp. 267–83 in Fitzgerald 2008.

Zangenberg, Jürgen, Harold Attridge, and Dale B. Martin (eds.). *Religion, Ethnicity, and Identity in Ancient Galilee: A Region in Transition*. Tübingen: Mohr Siebeck, 2007.

# CHAPTER 2
# The World of Early Judaism

## Judith H. Newman

## Introduction

The six centuries between the exile of the Israelites to Babylon in 586 BCE and the destruction of the Jewish temple in Jerusalem by the Romans in 70 CE are important in understanding not only the origins of Judaism but also the roots of Christianity. Jesus was a Jew, as were his first followers. Before there was a collection of writings to call the "New Testament," these Jews revered an older collection of writings as scripture, the Hebrew Bible, though they may have known it best in an Aramaic or Greek translation. Yet their Judaism was not, as many Christians assume, simply the religion of the Old Testament. The Judaism they practiced was rooted in the Old Testament, but formed over centuries after the kingdoms of Israel and Judah had come to an end. This time span is referred to as Second Temple Judaism in reference to the second temple in Jerusalem rebuilt on the site of Solomon's first temple in ca. 515 BCE, which stood until the Romans destroyed it in 70 CE. Rich and varied Jewish communities throughout the ancient Near East produced a broad spectrum of Jewish literature with which most people are unacquainted because most of these works did not become part of the Bible. The Hebrew Bible came into being during these centuries, not all at once, but gradually. So for example, the prologue to the book of Ecclesiasticus, written in 132 BCE, mentions "the Law and the Prophets, and the other books of our ancestors."

During the Second Temple period, Judaism developed distinctive features that have continued to characterize subsequent forms of Judaism: monotheism, the study of scripture and its interpretation as a central religious act; the observance of Jewish law; and prayer as a mandated part of worship. Aside from these commonalities, Jewish communities reflected a diversity of practices and beliefs explainable in part by geography. Early Judaism is distinguished from its ancestor in ancient Israel by the fact that Jews lived both inside Syria–Palestine itself and in a diaspora throughout the ancient Near East. Except for a brief period of political independence of less than a century (140–63 BCE), the Jews lived under foreign domination. First the Persian, then the Hellenistic (Greek), then the Roman empires held sway. Thus the story of early Judaism cannot be told without considering the political history through these centuries alongside social and cultural currents in Palestine and abroad.

## Judahite Exile and Jewish Return under the Persians (586–334 BCE)

Life in the small nations of Israel and Judah was perilous, caught in a geographic cross-roads between large empires battling for territory and influence. The story of early Judaism begins with the end of Israelite independence in 586 BCE when King Nebuchadnezzar of the great Babylonian empire conquered the southern kingdom of Judah and its capital Jerusalem. He deported the royal house of David and the upper echelon of Jerusalem society to Egypt and Babylon.

The destruction of Jerusalem was a major disruption in the history of Israel with far-reaching effects. The theological issues raised by the exile were profound. Institutions central to life in the southern kingdom and the relationship to God they assumed were gone. Two covenants between God and Israel seemed to have been broken. The first was the covenant made with Israel through Moses at Sinai (Exod. 19–24), promising the Israelites possession of the land of Canaan if the people were obedient to God's commandments. God had also made a two-pronged eternal promise to David (2 Sam. 7). God assured that David's descendants would always sit on the throne as the Lord's anointed (messiah). The second part was the election of Jerusalem as the site of the temple where God would dwell. The first temple is built by King Solomon, son of David, in the tenth century BCE and its daily sacrificial system had been in continuous operation for over 400 years. Male Israelites had been expected to make pilgrimage to the temple three times a year on the major feasts of Passover, Weeks, and Booths. The end of the Davidic dynasty and the destruction of the temple were thus the loss of major unifying institutions among the people.

Jewish literature from the exilic period addresses the crisis of exile and return in various ways. Chapters 40–55 of Isaiah were written on the cusp of the return from exile. In 539 BCE, Cyrus king of Persia conquered the Babylonian empire and issued an edict allowing the Jews to return to their homeland. The return from the exile is described as a new Exodus and a new creation, in which God is again redeeming Israel from its enslavement to re-create them as a people, a miracle witnessed by "the eyes of all the nations" (Isa. 52: 10). Isaiah lauds Cyrus as the anointed one (messiah) of the Lord (Isa. 45:1). The affirmation of a foreigner rather than an Israelite king of the Davidic lineage as Israel's messiah must have been shocking to those who had a memory of life as it was in pre-exilic Israel. From the perspective of the book of Isaiah, foreigners could play a positive role in God's plan for the Jews. The latter chapters of Isaiah offer a universal picture of divine salvation.

Not all of the post-exilic literature shares this perspective. The books of Ezra and Nehemiah are the chief source of information for Jewish life in Palestine during the Persian period. The Jews returned to Yahud, a Persian satrapy comprising Jerusalem and its neighboring territory. The Persians allowed the Jews to follow their ancestral laws. In addition, Cyrus pledged to use treasury funds to rebuild the temple in Jerusalem (Ezra 1:2–4). Only a small percentage of the exiles returned. Ezra's claim of 42,360

(Ezra 2:64) is probably exaggerated. Ezra, described as a priest-scribe, and Nehemiah, a cupbearer to the Persian king who would become governor, were two Jews who elected to return to the land, both with imperial support.

The dates and sequence for Ezra and Nehemiah's respective returns to Jerusalem are disputed, but the interests of the book's author are clear. The divine promise concerning Davidic kingship is not a central concern. Although the first leaders after the return are Zerubbabel, a Davidic descendant, and Joshua the high priest, leadership is soon taken over by a high priest alone. The books are written from the perspective of those who returned as a beleaguered minority in the land struggling to maintain the marks of their distinctive community. A major concern of Ezra–Nehemiah is maintaining the cohesiveness of the Jewish people. Ezra–Nehemiah depicts only those Judeans exiled to Babylon as true Jews who must not intermarry with others who are considered impure and a threat because of their false worship. The population in the land included those Israelites who had not gone into exile, as well as Samaritans, Edomites, Moabites, Ammonites, and Arabs. Nehemiah 8–10 depicts the efforts of Ezra to reform the community. They observe the feast of Booths according to the prescriptions found in the "Torah of Moses"; Ezra leads the people in a community confession; and they sign a covenant pledging to obey the prescriptions of the Torah particularly in refraining from intermarriage, observing the Sabbath, and supporting the temple.

Ezra–Nehemiah does not represent the full spectrum of early post-exilic Judaism, but a form of Jewish practice in which the Mosaic covenant at Sinai held a privileged position over the Davidic covenant. The prophetic books Haggai and Zechariah 1–8 also bear witness to the period of return and the dashed hopes of those who had wanted a swift restoration of the Davidic monarchy and a rebuilding of the temple. They focus on Zerubbabel, the Davidic descendant, never mentioning Ezra or Nehemiah. A climactic event in the lives of those who returned was the rebuilding and ultimate rededication of the Jerusalem temple ca. 515 BCE, which allowed sacrificial worship to be reinstituted and a renewal of the three great pilgrimage festivals.

The continued presence of Jews outside the land is indicated by Jewish names that appear in Babylonian documents of the fifth century BCE. Jews in Babylon had adopted the Aramaic language, the lingua franca of the western part of the Babylonian empire. No longer were all Jews fluent in Hebrew, necessitating translations of the sacred texts into Aramaic, known as targums (Neh. 8:7–8). Details of life in the Egyptian diaspora during this period are sparse, but there is no indication that any significant population of Egyptian Jews returned in the sixth century. Archaeological evidence from the late fifth and early fourth centuries BCE provides evidence of a Jewish military colony in Upper Egypt on the island of Elephantine which continued inhabited through the Greek period. The Elephantine Papyri, a collection of Aramaic letters, indicate that the Jewish community that lived on the island and in the adjacent city Syene had a temple founded in the sixth century. There the Jews worshiped the God Yahu, a form of the personal name for Israel's God Yahweh, as well as other gods. While cognizant and respectful of Jerusalem's temple, the Elephantine Jews seem to have practiced a more syncretistic form of Judaism than that suggested by the portrayal of the Ezra–Nehemiah community.

Little is known about life in exile except for brief mentions in the books of Ezekiel and Jeremiah and the sparse archaeological evidence, but Jewish literature of the exilic and early post-exilic period makes clear that life in exile forced a reexamination of central political and religious institutions. In this corporate soul-searching can be seen the origins of Judaism. Just as the people named "Israel" was born outside the land in the wilderness when God made the Sinai covenant with the Hebrew slaves newly liberated from Egypt, so too, early Judaism was born outside the land, in the Babylonian wilderness and other lands of the Diaspora where Israelites had settled. Three distinctive religious practices developed in exile that served to keep the community together with or without a king. They are all portable, not contingent on possessing land or a temple. The practice of circumcision as a sign of the relationship between God and Israel came to have a central place. Observance of the Sabbath, a "temple in time," a way to mark holy time rather than the holy space of a physical temple, takes on heightened importance. The Sabbath is also primarily a domestic practice not dependent on a public venue nor on the specialized skills of a priest. A third, and preeminent, feature of Judaism is the study and interpretation of the Torah and observance of its ordinances. The exile was a time of retrieval and consolidation of Israel's written traditions. During the exile, it is thought that a group of priests added to and edited the traditions that became the Pentateuch, the first five books of the Bible. These books, the Torah, would become the most important part of the Hebrew Bible, or Christian Old Testament. The Pentateuch is a first witness to the fledgling Israelite movement under the leadership of Moses, analogous in certain respects to the way in with the New Testament gospels serve as a first witness to the leadership of Jesus and the community of his first followers.

Though Jewish literature was written by a small, literate, elite minority, most Jews likely shared their views to some extent. The most distinctive feature of early Jewish literature, common to all works, was the pervasive presence of the scriptural world. New works were written using scriptural language and symbolism, without the sense of historical distance between "then" and "now" that has come to characterize modern Western interaction with scripture. While Jewish authors were influenced by their surrounding cultures to adopt new genres of literature, such as apocalypses, testaments, letters, and novellas, they never left "ancient Israel" behind. The New Testament writings, written primarily by Jews, share this actualizing tendency toward scripture, in which scripture is immediately relevant because it reveals the divine will for creation and humanity.

## The Hellenistic Period (332–63 BCE)

### Alexander the Great and his successors (the Diadochoi)

The power of Persia waned in the middle of the fourth century BCE and a new empire in the west ascended to conquer Asia. Alexander III, better known as Alexander the Great, soon changed the context of life for Jews in Palestine and the Diaspora. His father Philip II was king of Macedon to the north of Greece, a brilliant solder who succeeded in conquering and unifying the Greek city-states. Philip had intended to launch a campaign against Persia in order to staunch Darius III's encroachment on the Peloponnesus.

Philip's assassination in 336 BCE paved the way for his son to succeed him and lead the combined armies of the Macedonians and the Greeks toward the west.

The Persian armies under the command of Darius himself were defeated at Issus in Asia Minor in November 333. Alexander moved down the coast of Syria–Palestine, taking the cities of Damascus, Sidon, Tyre, and Jerusalem in turn. Alexander continued toward Egypt unopposed, where it is said he was welcomed as a god. In 332, he laid the foundations for Alexandria, the city on the western edge of the Nile delta that would become its capital during the Hellenistic period. The next year he continued his march again toward the major cities of the Persian empire, Babylon, Susa, and Persepolis. His troops followed him as far as India, before they finally refused to go any farther, thus ending his eastward campaign. In ten years, he had captured territory which encompassed what are now the modern nations of Turkey, Syria, Lebanon, Israel, Palestine, Jordan, Egypt, Iraq, Iran, Afghanistan, and Pakistan.

The treatment of the Jews under the comparatively lenient Persian policy would change dramatically during the centuries of Greek rule in Syria–Palestine. Alexander had been tutored by Aristotle for three years, and reputedly had a great love of Homer and of Greek culture generally, which he presumed was superior to all others. He established Greek cities throughout the region soon populated by immigrant Macedonians and Greeks, which led to an orientalized Greek culture especially among the native urban elites. The Hellenization of the western Mediterranean region would only accelerate, so that even during the Roman period, Greek culture reigned supreme. Greek dress, Greek architecture, Greek philosophy, Greek mores, and especially the adoption of Greek language, would influence the Jews profoundly during the next 600 years as part of the cultural milieu in which they lived.

### Ptolemaic sovereignty in Palestine (305–198 BCE)

Alexander's rapid conquest of Asia had left him little time for consolidation in order to ensure smooth administrative functioning of the regions newly under his control. His death in 323 at the young age of 33 led to a major power struggle among his generals, the Diadochi ("successors"). Eventually, two rulers emerged to lead significant parts of the old empire. Seleucus I (305–281 BCE) became king over Babylon and western Asia. Seleucus founded the capital city of the empire, Antioch in northwest Syria. Antioch would grow to become a major city, third in size only to Rome and Alexandria and with a sizeable Jewish population. Egypt and neighboring areas came under the rule of Ptolemy I, a Macedonian general. Ptolemy made Alexandria the capital of Egypt. The city prospered and became the cultural and educational center of the Hellenistic world, with a renowned royal library that contained 400,000 volumes. Jews had been living in Egypt since the beginning of the Babylonian exile and there was likely a Jewish presence in Alexandria from its founding. The city's reputation as a cultural center contributed to the apocryphal legend in the late third century BCE, *The Letter of Aristeas*. The *Letter*, written by a Jewish author for apologetic reasons, recounts the story of Ptolemy II's sponsorship of the translation of the Torah into Greek for his library. Seventy two Jewish scholars were summoned for the task; therefore, the translation was called the Septuagint. Whether or not the tale is historically accurate, many of the books of the Hebrew Bible were translated into Greek during the third century. The Hellenistic Jewish culture that produced the Septuagint was part of the larger Hellenized Greco-Roman culture out of which Christianity emerged, which explains why the New Testament itself was written in Greek.

*Seleucid hegemony in Palestine and the rise of the Maccabees (198–63 BCE)*

From 323 to 200 BCE much of Palestine was in Ptolemaic possession, but the Seleucid Greek rulers in Syria also longed for control. During the third century BCE, the region was a battleground between the two. The works of Josephus, a first-century Jewish historian, and the books of 1 and 2 Maccabees provide primary sources for reconstructing events of this time. Although these works are undoubtedly tendentious, a sequence of historical events can be tentatively reconstructed from them. In 198 BCE, the Seleucid dynasty won control of Jerusalem and Judea. While at first accommodating to the Jewish population, a decided shift in the Seleucid posture occurred during the reign of Antiochus IV "Epiphanes," who gained the throne in 175. Antiochus interfered with the customary hereditary appointment of the Jewish high priest, and appointed his own choices. These new high priests transformed Jerusalem into a Hellenistic city-state, complete with Greek gymnasium. They relaxed adherence to Jewish law and offered Jewish males Antiochian (Greek) citizenship. The Jews of Jerusalem were divided in their response to Hellenistic culture.

The attempts of Antiochus IV to conquer Ptolemaic Egypt brought him through the region. On one of his campaigns, in 169, he stormed Jerusalem, killing many recalcitrant Jews and plundering the temple. Soon thereafter, the king proscribed Torah study, observance of the Sabbath, and circumcision, all central marks of Jewish identity. Two years later, in 167 BCE, as a response to continuing rebellion among the Jewish population, Antiochus put an end to the daily sacrifices and desecrated the temple by instituting foreign sacrifice. His motivation was likely political rather than opposition to Jewish beliefs. As a result of such severe restrictions on Jewish practice, rebellion fomented, led by Mattathias, the patriarch of the priestly Hasmonean family, and his five sons. The rebellion grew, and when Mattathias died, his son Judas Maccabeus continued to lead guerrilla forces against the Seleucids. He was successful in wresting Jerusalem from Syrian control and restoring the sanctity of Jewish worship in the temple in 164 BCE. This triumph is commemorated in Judaism as the rededication of the temple, the eight-day festival of Hanukkah.

The events that transpired in Jerusalem during the reign of Antiochus IV left a deep scar on Palestinian Judaism. One Jewish literary response to the tyranny and depredations of the Seleucids is contained in apocalyptic literature of Daniel 7–12. Apocalypses, from the Greek word for revelation, became a common literary form in the late Second Temple period. In an apocalypse, divine revelation about history or about the heavenly or cosmic realm is made to a righteous person, usually through a mediating angel. Apocalypses were typically written in highly symbolic language, with the explicit identity of historical figures masked. In the latter half of Daniel, Daniel has a series of dreams in which the predetermined future of world history is unveiled to him. "The transgression that makes desolate, and the giving over of the sanctuary and host to be trampled" (Dan. 8:13) are given a fixed duration, with restoration of the temple cult to follow. Historical apocalypses were written to console those who were suffering unjustly with the assurance that God would intervene on their behalf and that their enemies would be punished. Many other apocalypses were written during the Greco-Roman era, including parts of the books of 1 Enoch, 4 Ezra, and 2 Baruch. The New Testament book of Revelation is also an example of this genre.

After the restoration of the temple, the five sons of the Hasmonean Mattathias ruled in succession. The last of the five, Simon, gained independence in 140 BCE from their former Syrian overlords. His fellow Jews recognized the Hasmonean dynasty as the political and religious leadership. Judea was now a fully independent state. Simon became high priest, commander-in-chief, and ethnarch of the Jews, the first of five generations of Hasmoneans to lead the nation. John Hyrcanus followed him as high priest (134–104 BCE). As part of his successful campaign to gain control of Samaria to the north of Jerusalem, John Hyrcanus destroyed the temple of the Samaritan sect on Mount Gerizim, near Shechem, in 128 BCE. The origins of the Samaritans are obscure, but the schism in Judaism may date as early as the sixth century BCE. The Samaritans saw themselves as the legitimate descendants of the northern kingdom of Israel, which was destroyed by the Assyrians in 722 BCE. They are mentioned in Ezra–Nehemiah as antagonists of the returned exiles, so the animosity between Jews and Samaritans was deep and long-standing, a conflict that puts the New Testament parable of the "good Samaritan" in perspective.

John was succeeded by Alexander Jannaeus (103–76 BCE) who, according to 1 and 2 Maccabees, won a nasty reputation for his violent excesses, including the grisly crucifixion of 800 Jewish opponents along with their wives and children. In spite of their founding legend preserved in 1 and 2 Maccabees, subsequent history suggests that the Hasmoneans adopted Greek ways as well, Alexander's name itself indicating Hellenized acculturation. After Alexander's death, his wife Salome Alexandra became queen. When Alexandra died in 67 BCE, her two sons, Hyrcanus II and Aristobulus II, fought over succession. Their dispute would result in the end of the Hasmonean dynasty and of Jewish independence in Palestine.

One segment of Palestinian Jewish life during the Hasmonean and Roman periods is also illuminated by the Dead Sea Scrolls, the most significant manuscript find in Syria–Palestine, and the related archaeological site at Qumran on the shores of the Dead Sea that was inhabited during the first century BCE until its destruction by the Romans in 70 CE. The Dead Sea Scrolls are thought to have been the library of the community that lived at Qumran. Scholars divide the scrolls into three categories: biblical manuscripts; non-biblical texts that were used by other Jewish groups, some of which are known to us because later Christians preserved them, such as the book of *Jubilees*; and "sectarian" texts deriving from the Qumran community itself. Fragments representing all the books that would later comprise the Hebrew Bible except for Esther were found at Qumran. Yet it is important to remember that the Bible was still in formation, and the Qumran community itself seems to have considered certain books as having scriptural status that never entered the canon.

The writings peculiar to the sectarian group itself provide a picture of a unique community of Jews. Among these writings are prescriptive "Rules" of the community (*The Damascus Document* and *The Rule of the Community*), representing a genre otherwise unknown in early Judaism that is closest to the early Christian church teaching documents, the *Didache* and the *Apostolic Constitutions*. The sectarians are generally understood to be a group of Essenes, one of three Jewish groups mentioned by Josephus (*War*, 2.119–66). The Essenes who lived at Qumran were ascetic males who had communal property and observed strict purity laws in all aspects of their life. Their literature also indicates that they had a strong disagreement with the Jerusalem authorities. The group may have started as a reaction to the Hellenizing high priests of the early Hasmonean period, because a "wicked priest" is regularly mentioned in the sectarian documents. The Qumran group believed that they were living in the end of days, and they expected a cataclysmic battle between the "sons of light" and the "sons of darkness." Although the composition and beliefs of the community surely evolved in the course of its years of existence, at some point, a "teacher of righteousness" played a central role in leading the group in nightly study of scripture, interpreting its mysteries for the present. The *Rule of the Community* depicts the group (the Yahad) as the true Israel living in a new covenant with God and anticipating the arrival of two messiahs, one a descendant of the house of David, the other a priestly messiah. Their messianism and their belief that the end of the world was imminent reveal similarities with the early Christian movement. The Qumran group itself, however, seems not to have survived the Roman response to the Jewish revolt in 70 CE, though its literary legacy lives on through this uniquely important archaeological discovery.

## Rome Controls Palestine (63 BCE–70 CE)

The Roman republic's direct involvement on the Palestinian stage occurred as a result of the dispute between the Hasmonean heirs, Hyrcanus and Aristobulus. The Roman general Pompey was in the region as part of his eastern campaign to unseat the Seleucid monarchy, and both sons appealed to him to settle their dispute. Pompey initially sided with Aristobulus, but then, angered at the defiant behavior of his followers, was impelled to wrest Jerusalem from his control. In 63 BCE, when Pompey entered Jerusalem to install Hyrcanus, the history of Judaism would take a new turn. The era of Judean independence under the Hasmoneans was over; Rome was their new master.

Rome would soon be distracted by its own civil war (49–31 BCE) resulting from the struggle between Pompey and Julius Caesar. The Parthians, a people from the eastern side of the Euphrates, used this instability as an opportunity to overrun Judea and seize Jerusalem in 40 BCE. Hyrcanus was taken into exile to Babylon and his nephew, a Parthian partisan, was put in his place. Rome thus sought a new ruler who could counter the threat. Herod, an Idumean, who had been a strong overseer of Galilee, proved the best choice. The Roman senate gave Herod the title "king of the Jews." Backed with Roman troops, Herod ousted the Parthians and killed the last of Hasmonean rulers. "Herod the Great" would reign with an iron fist for four decades (40–4 BCE). He is remembered as much for his massive building projects as for his ruthlessness. He

built a series of fortresses in Palestine, among them Masada and Herodiom. He reno-
vated the temple in Jerusalem, refitting it with "Herodian stone," massive blocks that
can still be seen in the remaining Western Wall. While Herod ruled Palestine, the
Roman republic became the Roman empire. A pivotal point was the naval battle of
Actium in 31 BCE, when Octavius (later Caesar Augustus) defeated Antony and
Cleopatra and became ruler of the empire, whose reach extended from western Europe
and the northwestern African coastal region to the entire Mediterranean basin.

After Herod's death in 4 BCE, the Romans had a difficult time maintaining peace in
Palestine. None of his three sons proved as strong a ruler as their father. Herod Antipas,
known from the New Testament as the Herod who killed John the Baptist, was the most
successful, and governed for over forty years (4 BCE–39 CE). Rome put Palestine under
direct rule and from 6 to 66 CE, the Jews were governed by a succession of prefects and
governors. The Jewish community itself was riven by various factions and their rival-
ries. Jesus of Nazareth was born during this turbulent era. The names of three main
groups are well known: the Pharisees, the Sadducees, and the Essenes, mentioned
above in connection with the Dead Sea Scrolls. These groups are not mentioned in other
Jewish literature before the first century CE. What we know about the Pharisees and
the Sadducees derives from a reconstructed portrait gleaned from their depiction in the
New Testament, later rabbinic literature, and the writings of Josephus. Josephus
describes the Pharisees as popular with the common people. They believed in the resurrection of the dead, the immortality of the soul, and the role of fate along with free will
in shaping the course of human events. They developed and adhered to a body of interpretation alongside the written Torah. The Sadducees, a name derived from Zadok, one
of King David's two chief priests, were a priestly group of some wealth. They are
depicted as the most accommodationist with Rome. Josephus describes their philosophy
in contrast to the Pharisees. They did not believe in the resurrection of the dead,
believed that fate played no role in determining events, and they opposed the traditions
of the Pharisees. Aside from these larger Jewish groups, a number of smaller popular
Jewish movements arose, led by self-proclaimed prophets or messiahs. The climate in
Palestine was one of social unrest and resistance, with a strong dose of class tension.
Josephus mentions a Jewish false prophet named Theudas who led a group of followers
to the Jordan, claiming he could part it in two. The Roman governor at the time, Fadus,
had him beheaded. Josephus also discusses the phenomenon of social banditry, in
which the poor peasantry took out their frustration against the inequities of society by
robbing the wealthy. One Jewish group had the name "Sicarii" after the *sica*, or dagger
that they carried with the violent aim of assassination and kidnapping members of the
Jewish upper classes. The stronghold of Herodian Masada by the Dead Sea became their
base, and they would be the last holdouts against Rome, finally committing suicide
rather than submit to the Romans.

The situation in Palestine spiraled steadily downward in the 60s. A culminating
event was the decision in 66 CE to stop offering sacrifices in the temple on behalf of
Rome. These sacrifices had in effect functioned as a substitute for Jewish participation
in the imperial cult, which was forbidden by Jewish law, and proved the loyalty of the
Jews to the Roman empire. Yet another group developed as a result of the revolt against
Rome in 66–70 CE. These were the Zealots, a nationalistic movement that advocated

violent overthrow of the Roman oppressors. The next four years were a bloody open revolt in which the Jews not only faced the wrath of the Romans, but also contended with their own internecine struggles.

In 70 CE the Roman general Titus besieged Jerusalem with his army. Though Jewish combatants tried to oppose him, he smashed Jerusalem's walls with battering rams and destroyed the temple. Titus's triumph in Jerusalem would be celebrated in the Arch of Vespasian in Rome, which displays the triumphal procession by the Romans holding the table of showbread and the seven-branched menorah from the temple. For the Jews, it was a tragedy. The conquest of Jerusalem by the Romans was as devastating to Jewish civilization as the Babylonian exile and would ultimately be the catalyst that would transform Judaism permanently. Within decades, the Jews in Palestine and the diaspora Jewish communities would learn again how to live without a temple and without political sovereignty over a land while preserving the identity and cohesion of a far-flung people. The era of classical Judaism had begun, the age during which the law code of the Mishnah and its two great commentaries, the Babylonian and Palestinian Talmuds, would provide a way to preserve Jewish life and culture far into the future.

## Annotated Bibliography

Barclay, John M. G. *Jews in the Mediterranean Diaspora*. Berkeley: University of California Press, 1996. A multi-faceted survey of Jewish life in the Diaspora which incorporates a sociological assessment of the degree of Jewish assimilation to their varied geographical and cultural environments.

Collins, John J. *The Apocalyptic Imagination: An Introduction to Jewish Apocalyptic Literature*. Grand Rapids: Eerdmans, 1998. An excellent introduction to the origins and development of apocalyptic literature and thought seen as lying in continuity with earlier Israelite literature rather than strictly a Persian import.

Collins, John J. *Between Athens and Jerusalem: Jewish Identity in the Hellenistic Diaspora*. 2nd edn. Grand Rapids: Eerdmans, 2000. An examination of Hellenistic Jewish literature as a unique font from which the wellspring of Western culture arose.

Freedman, David Noel (ed.). *The Anchor Bible Dictionary*. 6 vols. Doubleday: New York, 1992. A comprehensive resource for a host of topics related to the Bible.

Goodman, Martin (ed.). *Jews in a Graeco-Roman World*. Oxford: Clarendon Press, 1998. A collection of sixteen studies by historians and classicists on social, cultural, and religious aspects of the encounter between Judaism and Hellenism.

Grabbe, Lester L. *A History of the Jews and Judaism in the Second Temple Period*: vol. 1: *Yehud: A History of the Persian Province of Judah*. New York: T. & T. Clark, 2004. The first of four volumes treating the history of the Second Temple period from a positivist perspective, treating comprehensively archaeological, epigraphic, and literary sources.

Gruen, Erich S. *Heritage and Hellenism: The Reinvention of Jewish Tradition*. Berkeley: University of California Press, 1998. A treatment of the question how Jewish authors reconceived their traditions of practice and thought through the use of new literary and philosophical idioms occasioned by the encounter with Hellenism.

Kugel, James L. *The Bible as It Was*. Cambridge, MA: Harvard University Press, 1997. An elegantly written introduction to early Jewish and Christian biblical interpretation of the first five books of the Hebrew Bible with excerpts from ancient sources organized according to interpretive motifs.

Murphy, Frederick J. *Early Judaism: The Exile to the Time of Jesus.* Peabody: Hendrickson, 2002. A well-written introduction to the period and its literature.

Nickelsburg, George W.E. *Jewish Literature between the Bible and the Mishnah.* 2nd edn. Philadelphia: Fortress Press, 2005. A comprehensive introduction to much of the Jewish literature dating from the sixth century BCE to the third century CE setting it in its historical context.

Rajak, Tessa. *Josephus: The Historian and his Society.* Philadelphia: Fortress Press, 1983. An assessment of Josephus' account of the Jewish revolt against Rome that situates the author in the context of both his Jewish values and Greco-Roman culture.

VanderKam, James C. *An Introduction to Early Judaism.* Grand Rapids: Eerdmans: 2001. A clearly written, judicious, and concise treatment of early Judaism, its literature, history, beliefs, and practices.

VanderKam, James C. and Peter Flint. *The Meaning of the Dead Sea Scrolls.* New York: HarperCollins, 2002. An account of the discovery, range, and significance of the Dead Sea Scrolls for understanding early Judaism and Christian origins.

CHAPTER 3

# The Archaeological Setting

## C. Thomas McCollough

### The Rise of New Testament Archaeology

Long before the development of archaeology as a scientific endeavor there was an archaeological interest in the New Testament. By the second century, Christians traveled to the Holy Land to investigate ('ιστορία) the places (τόποι) associated with the deeds and words of Jesus. This curiosity about the places related to the life of Christ gave way to the first "excavation" when Helena, the mother of the emperor Constantine, journeyed to Jerusalem in 326 CE. Guided by local Christians and Jews and a divine revelation, Helena located the site of the crucifixion and, using a crew of soldiers and others, dug deeply and discovered the three crosses. The culminating work of this earliest phase of New Testament "archaeology" was produced by Eusebius of Caesarea around the year 331 CE. Eusebius authored a book of biblical geography that included a topography of ancient Judea, a plan of Jerusalem and the temple, and a list of place names in the Bible with descriptions of the location and history of the places. The latter, entitled *Onomasticon*, is all that remains of this project, which was important in the Christianization of Palestine and the long history of Christian pilgrims streaming to the Holy Land.

By the nineteenth century the discipline of archaeology had evolved, but its place in the study of the New Testament had changed little. Archaeology's contribution continued to be limited to largely apologetic endeavors. The founding document of the Palestine Exploration Society, written in 1870, describes its task as the "illustration and defense of the Bible." Suspicions about any serious role for archaeology in the study of the text were further reinforced with the collapse of the first "search for the historical Jesus" and the powerful influence of Rudolf Bultmann and his colleagues' view of the text as fundamentally theological in nature. To be sure, archaeology found ways to demonstrate its value, by providing finds that could be used to illumine the text (e.g., the Pilate inscription from Caesarea Maritima and the first-century boat from the shores of the Sea of Galilee) and by recovering ancient texts such as the Dead Sea Scrolls and the Nag Hammadi library (Crossan and Reed 2001). But it would not be until the latter part of the twentieth century that the data retrieved from archaeological excavations would be a true dialogue partner with the text and be used to advance the critical study of the New Testament.

The gradual transformation of the role of archaeology in New Testament studies may be traced to the emergence of concerns about the social teachings and social history of the text in the 1920s. Shirley Jackson Case, among others, drew attention to the importance of the social world of first-century Roman Palestine and Galilee, particularly for New Testament studies. While it was several decades before social world concerns really took root in the field, the latter part of the twentieth century saw a flurry of interest, and archaeological evidence took on an ever-expanding role in efforts at social reconstruction. Archaeology brought to light the houses, streets, religious structures, boats, and domestic wares of Roman Palestine and the Mediterranean basin, and efforts to reconstruct the setting went on independently of the text itself. Archaeology no longer offered discrete remnants of the ancient world but a working reconstruction of the social, economic, and religious world to which the text referred as well as the world inhabited by the authors of the text. As Eric Meyers pointed out, "Archaeological materials ... avoid the pitfalls of just doing straight history or political history and get one pointed more in the direction of social-historical reconstruction ... as a major building block for contextual study, archaeology is the *sine qua non* of both good historical and good exegetical work" (2003: 163).

## Archaeological Setting of the Gospel Narratives

One can follow the expanded and more consequential role of archaeology for the New Testament by first examining three ways in which the archaeological materials have been applied to the gospel narratives. The first is the way in which the archaeological record has brought to light the urban and rural texture of first-century Galilee and sparked discussions about the impact of a newly urbanized landscape on Jesus and his message and the Jesus movement. The second is archaeology's contribution to the critical question of religious and cultural landscape of Galilee in the first century. To what extent was Galilee "Hellenized" and what sort of religious groups or movements could one expect to encounter in that time and place? The third issue relates to the relationship of Galilee to Jerusalem and how the archaeology of Jerusalem might help one appreciate religious and political authority in Roman Palestine.

### The landscape of lower Galilee in the first century CE

The excavations of the Herodian cities of Sepphoris and Tiberius have created an archaeological setting for the gospel narratives that is far more complex than had been previously imagined. Although neither city is mentioned directly in the gospel accounts, their location in the heart of lower Galilee (Sepphoris a few miles north of Nazareth and Tiberius a few miles south of Capernaum) has rightly brought them into the study of the gospels and the historical Jesus. As the excavations pulled back the soil from these urban centers, it became clear that the first-century inhabitants of lower Galilee were confronted by the monumental architecture of a Roman *polis* along with the economic and social realities that cities manifest. Herod Antipas chose Sepphoris as the center for his administration of Galilee, and by the time of Jesus its population has been estimated at 10,000 to 15,000. Antipas went on to build a "port city" on the Sea of Galilee and name it for the Roman emperor Tiberius. In each case, the excavations have brought to life architecture typical of a Roman city, including theaters, paved roads, and a basilica. The largely agrarian, village-centered culture of lower Galilee was slowly transformed by the presence of these urban, commercial centers, and the consequence of that transformation on Jesus and the Jesus movement is now an important part of the study of the New Testament. How did the residents of the village of Nazareth respond to Sepphoris? One reading of the evidence has followed the paradigm that arose out of the work of Moses Finley, wherein the ancient city is largely parasitic on the countryside. (Finley 1977). In this case, the building of the city signaled the onset of economic exploitation and hardship and led to the rise of individuals and movements which offered alternative visions and values. Ramsay MacMullen has perhaps best characterized these hostile relations between city and village: "Economic ties between urban and rural centers ... are not friendly. The worlds regard each other as, on the one side, clumsy, brutish, ignorant, uncivilized; on the other side, as baffling, extortionate, arrogant" (MacMullen 1974: 15). Such a setting can be seen as fostering Jesus' critique of wealth, social stratification, and landholding. As Sean Freyne (2002: 175) noted,

> In terms of the kingdom of God which he [Jesus] proclaimed, it was the πτωχοί that he blessed. These are not the poor simply, but rather they are those who have lost their status or had it removed from them through loss of property, and are, therefore, destitute. At the same time he castigated the rich and called on them to share their goods with the needy, thereby radically challenging the social norms of honour, power and patronage as these operated at centres such as Sepphoris.

In a similar vein, Richard Horsley (1996) sees the arrival of the cities as disruptive not so much in socioeconomic terms but in terms of tension (and in time overt hostility) between an established agrarian society (that consisted largely of descendants of Israelites) and an intrusive urban elite (that was largely associated with Herodians and Judeans). Jesus' sayings and parables that reflect disquiet with issues such as debt, taxation, and land division, as well as sayings that counterpoise the kingdom of God with the corrupt kingdom constructed by the Romans, would be seen against this background (Reed 2000).

An alternative reading of the evidence argues for a more symbiotic relationship between city and village. This approach finds that the arrival of the cities offered markets and employment for villagers and provided a connection between lower Galilee and the markets of the region. (Edwards 1992). The excavations at Sepphoris have revealed large underground silos (presumably for storage) and unearthed a lead weight referring to *agoranomoi* or market inspectors – both of which suggest the city was acting as a market as well as an administrative center (Meyers, Netzer, and Meyers 1992). Moreover, as James Strange has argued, the interface between village and "urban overlay" was facilitated by Galilee's earlier exposure to Hellenism (Strange 1992). In this regard, one would note that in the sayings and parables of Jesus there are as many urban as rural images. Finally, the positive interaction of city and village would help account for the eventual urbanization of the early Christian movement (Overman 1988). In whichever direction one follows the analysis, it becomes clear that the archaeological excavations of the Herodian cities of lower Galilee are an important factor for understanding Jesus and the Jesus movement, and may provide critical clues in the exegesis of the gospels' sayings and parables.

### Religious and cultural identity

The important question of the ethnic and/or religious identities that would be found in Roman Palestine and in particular in Galilee in the first century is being addressed by archaeological excavations. Who were the inhabitants of the villages and newly con-structed Herodian cities of Galilee? While a conclusive answer to this question is not yet possible (in part awaiting more extensive excavations of villages), the excavations have allowed a tentative mapping that suggests that Sepphoris and the area surround-ing it was inhabited by Jews whose Jewish practices show points of continuity with the Judaism practiced in Judea. The recovery of stone vessels (suggesting compliance with Levitical purity laws), in domestic *miqva'ot* (ritual baths), the absence of pork in the analysis of bones, and the use of ossuaries for secondary burial all point to the connec-tion with the Judea and have for some even suggested a line of descent (perhaps Hasmonean colonists) from inhabitants of Judea/Jerusalem (Chancey 2002). Indicators of Jewish population centers also have been recovered from upper Galilee and the western shore of the Sea of Galilee. These areas were not sealed off from the non-Jewish (non-Samaritan) population, nor were they insulated from the pervasive influence of Hellenization. The Roman road system and the busy port of Caesarea Maritima ensured contact with the larger population, and traces of pagan cultic sites and pagan religious iconography are sprinkled through the archaeological record of first-century Palestine. As Joseph Geiger commented,

> local cults, still very much in their original guise, or beneath a thin or thicker veneer of interpretatio Graeca, like those of Marnas-Zeus at Gaza, Greek cults proper like that of Dionysius at Scythopolis, Roman cults, headed by the cults of the Emperors, chiefly in the four Palestinian cities named after them [e.g., Caesarea Philippi, Tiberius], and the influx of the so-called oriental religions, evidenced for instance by the Mithraeum at Caesarea, made up the complexity of what we refer to, for a lack of a better term, as paganism. (1998: 5)

While the archaeological evidence for extensive influence of Hellenism is largely from the excavations in Jerusalem, the arrival of the Herodian cities along with trade ensured that "Hellenism was integrated into the daily life of most Galileans ... Was Galilee Jewish? Yes! Was Galilee Hellenistic? Yes!" (Moreland 2003: 148).

One striking omission in the archaeological record of first-century Galilee to date is the presence of synagogues. That the gospels are replete with references to synagogues makes this gap even more mysterious. The solution has been to regard the references in the text as pointing to gathering places of a more generic sort (e.g., courtyards, private homes) rather than structures that have a specific role in the practice of Judaism. The ongoing excavations at Khirbet Qana have identified a building dated to the first

century with architectural elements associated with structures that have been identified as synagogues, e.g., the "synagogue" at Gamla (Edwards 2002). Until that building
is fully excavated and identified with greater certainty as a synagogue, New Testament
studies have been forced by the archaeological record to read the text and approach
the historical Jesus with this archaeological datum in mind.

## Jerusalem in the first century CE

The archaeological record of early Roman Jerusalem is scant. Herod the Great's massive
contributions to the city are to be seen not only in the foundation stones of walls. These
foundation stones are indeed impressive and suggestive of the monumental landscape
created by Herod. For example, Herod significantly expanded the size of the platform
surrounding the temple by filling in the valley to the north, as well as a portion of the
Tyropoeon Valley to the west, and by constructing a series of vaults along the southern
slope to support the platform above. Herod then surrounded the whole platform area,
the Temple Mount, with a retaining wall. The lowest course of this retaining wall has
been exposed, and is fashioned from stones that measure up to 40 feet long, 10 feet
high, and 14 feet thick, and weigh 500 tons. Architectural remnants of entrances onto
the Temple Mount (e.g., Robinson's arch) are also visible and reinforce the sense of an
immense architectural statement.

Archaeological excavations in the area of Jerusalem now known as the Jewish
Quarter have exposed a portion of a domestic area overlooking the Temple Mount. The
houses are remarkable for their large size, beauty, and evidence of wealth. One of the
houses (the "Palatial Mansion") was over 6,000 feet square and had many of the features of the luxurious villas exposed at Pompeii and Herculaneum. Frescoes covered
the walls and ornate mosaics decorated the floors, and among the ceramic and glass
remains were refined imported wares. The Jerusalem that Jesus encountered was one
that architecturally privileged the temple, expressed the power and benefits of Roman
occupation, betrayed the impact of Hellenization, and made evident social stratification
as a result of wealth and prestige.

One final aspect of the Jerusalem period where archaeology has provided some
insight is the death and burial of Jesus. The crucifixion of Jesus was consistent with the
practice of the Roman empire in its response to crimes perpetrated by peasants, slaves,
servants, and bandits. The Jewish historian Josephus reports that the Romans crucified
thousands in the area around Jerusalem in the early decades of the first century CE.
One who had been crucified would not normally receive a decent burial: the bodies
would be left to be eaten by animals or simply cast aside as further punishment and
humiliation. Accordingly, we are not surprised that we have found only one skeleton
with evidence of crucifixion. In fact, that we have recovered this one example from the
first century is remarkable. In 1968, several rock-hewn tombs were located in a northern suburb of Jerusalem. Five ossuaries (boxes for secondary burial) were found, and
in one the skeletal remains of two men and a child. The ankle bone of one of the men
had been pierced by a nail that had been driven into a wood plank. The nail had bent,
and thus when the man was taken from the wooden cross, the wood had broken off

and so the nail and wood accompanied the man in his burial. The man's legs had not been broken and his wrists showed no signs of being punctured, suggesting that his arms had been tied to the cross and that he suffered a slow and agonizing death as the diaphragm eventually collapsed and death came by asphyxiation. This archaeological discovery not only lends dramatic testimony to the horror of crucifixion, it also offers an example of the possibility of the burial of a crucified individual.

In terms of the place of Jesus' burial, the recovery of what was believed to be the tomb of Jesus was the goal of the first "archaeological excavation." Did the diggers employed by Constantine in fact uncover the tomb of Christ? We will never be certain that this was the true tomb, but we can speak of a range of credibility. In these terms, the evidence suggests that it is a reasonably credible claim that the Church of the Holy Sepulcher was constructed around the tomb of Jesus. The tomb is of typical construction for the first century. The ground in the area of Jerusalem is very rocky and thus tombs cut into the soft stone of the hills surrounding Jerusalem were preferred. The tomb identified as that used to bury Jesus was one of several cut into the face of an outcrop of limestone in an area that stood outside the wall of the city in the time of Jesus and had earlier served as a quarry. As was typical of these rock-cut tombs, it has a shelf cut into the side with an arch-shaped ceiling (known as an *arcosolium*) upon which the body would be laid. This area was brought within the walls of the city by 135 CE, and any bodies contained therein would have been buried elsewhere. When the Roman emperor Hadrian responded to the second Jewish revolt (132–5 CE) by expelling Jews from the city of Jerusalem and transforming it into a pagan city (renamed Aelia Capitolina), he filled in the area of the tomb and built a temple dedicated to Venus.

Beyond offering some sense of the setting for the gospels' narratives of Jesus' time in Jerusalem, the archaeological record has also spoken to the question of the extent of contact between Jewish parties or groups primarily associated with Jerusalem and Judea (e.g., the Pharisees) and Galilee. At this point, the material evidence reinforces Ze'ev Safrai's observation, "Basically, each of the major regions of Eretz-Israel – Judaea, Peraea, Galilee and Samaria – were separate units ... there was hardly any travel between the various regions" (1994: 269). As noted, there is reason to suspect that some Jews of Galilee were descended from Judean families, but the virtual absence of any ceramic or numismatic evidence from Judea in Galilee in the first century suggests little movement between the regions. Such archaeological data have important consequences for the way in which one treats the text's frequent reference to the presence of Pharisees in Galilee as well as the importance of Sadducees for Galilean affairs.

## Archaeological Settings for Paul and Other New Testament Authors

With the exception of Paul, discussions of an archaeological setting for the authors of the New Testament texts are invariably tentative as we are not certain of identity or provenance. That being said, it remains useful to postulate archaeological settings as part of an ongoing engagement with the text. It is a widely shared assumption of biblical scholarship that the authors of the New Testament are at once shaped by and attempt to give shape to their social and historical context. Archaeological excavations provide the data that define the contours of that context. As several scholars have shown, reading the text with possible archaeological settings of the author in mind can bring to light textual references and theological tendencies, and offer exegetical insights.

There are two contexts that provide possible archaeological settings. The first is the cities of western Asia Minor and Greece. These urban centers are obviously important for a discussion of Paul (and deutero-Pauline epistles) and likely have a bearing on the gospels of Mark and Luke, the Johannine writings, as well as the Acts of the Apostles and several of the pastoral epistles. The second is Galilee and in particular lower Galilee. The authors of the sayings source Q as well as the Gospel of Matthew can at least tentatively be located in this context.

## Cities of western Asia Minor and Greece

New Testament research, and in particular Pauline studies, have been well served by the excavations of the Greco-Roman cities of western Asia Minor and Greece. These cities, especially those of Asia Minor, create a setting that is in some ways strikingly different from Galilee in Roman Palestine. Beginning with the rule of Augustus, the cities of Asia Minor entered a period of reconstruction and prosperity that created a setting dense with the monumental structures typical of a Roman *polis* and a population that was diverse and in many cities socially and economically mobile. These cities enjoyed and indeed celebrated their assimilation into the empire. On the occasion of Augustus' birthday in 9 BCE, the *Koinon* (Provincial Assembly) of Asia set forth a proclamation honoring the emperor as the "divine Caesar" and as Savior (*Soter*). In the urban centers of Asia Minor, Paul encountered a world where "the sayings of Jesus matter little and the kingdom of God is not a central metaphor ... Politically, this is a world of cities, integrated urban centers benefiting sufficiently from their status to offer little encouragement to the growth of true political dissension" (Schütz 1982: 13).

The extensive architectural remains from the excavations at Corinth are indicative. Corinth had been destroyed by the Roman general Lucius Mummius in 146 BCE and refounded as a Roman colony by Julius Caesar in 46 BCE. The citizens of the new colony were drawn primarily from the population of freedmen as well as veterans. The city that Paul worked in was thus populated by men and women that were beginning something new and in a "foreign" setting. As Theissen (1982: 100) observed,

> Corinthian citizens were not only on the rise socially; the city had also experienced a rapid economic upturn, as excavations confirm. The oldest houses are still quite simply built, while later structures are laid out more handsomely. It is at just this time, in the first century, that the Corinthians are busily engaged in construction, donating buildings and amenities. Of twenty-seven instances testified to by inscriptions, seventeen fall into the short period between Augustus and Nero. Since in most instances the donor cannot be shown to come from outside Corinth, it may be assumed that local citizens took responsibility for such municipal benefactions. The Christian Erastus probably distinguished himself in just such manner.

The city was marked by social mobility, cultural heterogeneity, and economic prosperity. The result was that the city of Corinth proved to be far more receptive to the "new wisdom" Paul brought from the East than the more tradition-bound, socially stable cities like Athens, and it produced Christian congregations infused with social and economic potential for conflict.

Excavations in the domestic areas have produced a structure that makes evident how such conflict could have played out. A house, known as the Roman villa at Anaploga, has been excavated and securely dated to the first century. It included an atrium that measured 5 x 6 meters and a *triclinium* (dining-room) of 5.5 x 7.5 meters. It is a house such as this that would likely have served as the meeting place for the Christian community in Corinth. Using Murphy-O'Connor's figure of fifty as the base number for the size of the Christian community in first-century Corinth (Murphy-O'Connor 1983), it would mean that if "the whole church" (1 Cor. 14:23) gathered in the house, only a few could have been hosted in the *triclinium* (the room with the most prestige and where the best food would be offered), while others had to wait in the atrium. Paul's concern for divisions within the community and the tensions and arguments that resulted may reflect such an archaeological setting.

Corinth was a city marked by religious pluralism. The excavations of Corinth have brought to light a number of temples devoted to a host of deities (e.g., the Temple of Apollo) as well as several cultic sites related to mystery religions (e.g., the Sanctuary of Demeter). In addition, the excavations exposed an extensive complex associated with Asclepius, the god of healing. Among other interesting and relevant features of this complex was a large courtyard bordered by small dining-rooms. The dining-rooms could be used for purely social affairs, but more often they were used in conjunction with an event connected to the worship of Asclepius. Newly converted Christians invited to such affairs were invariably confronted with the question of eating meat dedicated or offered to idols. This is a concern that Paul addresses at some length in 1 Corinthians 8–10.

It is safe to presume that Corinth included a substantial and visible Jewish presence. The Jews living in the Diaspora in the first century numbered between 5 and 6 million, and besides the New Testament references we have Philo, who singles out Corinth (along with Argos) in his list of regions of the Diaspora. Architectural verification of the Jewish presence in the first century remains elusive, however. A lintel stone inscribed with the phrase "Synagogue of the Hebrews" was found, but it dates to a later period and because it was in destruction debris it cannot with certainty be tied with a synagogue location. The book of Acts makes several references to Paul visiting synagogues in the cities of Asia Minor. The recovery of inscriptions with the term "god-fearer" from the excavations at Sardis as well as Aphrodisias are important archaeological realia for the book of Acts references to Gentiles who were drawn to the practice of Judaism and to whom Paul made a special appeal (e.g., Acts 13:16).

One final aspect of this archeological setting that deserves mention is the nature and arrangement of domestic and public space. While population figures for ancient cities are highly speculative, the numbers for Corinth run as high as 300,000. Although population size is disputed (most place it lower than 300,000), there is little dispute in characterizing the city as densely populated (the estimates for Corinth run as high as 200 per acre). Given that as much as one-fourth of the city was devoted to public space, "the bulk of the population had typically to put up with the most uncomfortable crowding at home, made tolerable by the attractive spaciousness of the public facilities" (MacMullen 1974: 63). This very crowded domestic space was typically divided into sectors or quarters depending on country of origin (*ethnos*) or one's trade or craft practice. Among other consequences of such a situation was the ease and rapid facilitation of contacts within the city.

In the end, Paul proved eminently capable of meeting the challenges of and taking full advantage of the city as an archaeological context for his work and message (Meeks 1983: 9):

> Paul was a city person. The city breathes through his language ...When Paul constructs a metaphor of olive trees or gardens ... the Greek is fluent and evokes schoolroom more than farm; he seems more at home with the clichés of Greek rhetoric, drawn from gymnasium, stadium, or workshop. Moreover, Paul was among those who depended on the city for their livelihood ... When Paul rhetorically catalogs the places where he has suffered danger, he divides the world into city, wilderness, and sea (2 Cor. 11:26). His world does not include the *chōra*, the productive countryside; outside the city there is nothing – *erēmia*.

## Galilee

Inquiries about the archaeological setting of the sayings source Q have produced a diverse set of options. Q and the community behind the text have been located in Syria, Palestine, and, more specifically, in Galilee, and even more narrowly in the cities of Sepphoris or Tiberius or the region around Capernaum on the northern shore of the Sea of Galilee (Reed 2000: 170). As we have no external evidence to establish the locale of the community, we are dependent on internal or textual clues. In this regard, the region around Capernaum appears to be the best option, as place names as well as spatial imagery argue for this area of Galilee. While Q is rich in agricultural imagery, there are enough indicators of an awareness of an urban presence to suggest a scribal perspective that is acutely aware of the imposition of Herodian cities. Agricultural items associated with cities appear (e.g., granaries, Q 3:17) and there is often an urban perspective on agrarian practices. More importantly, the juxtaposition of urban and rural has a significant impact on the theological message of Q. Indeed, as Reed (2000: 193, 195) notes,

> a general dissatisfaction with urbanization can be seen in the recurring theme in Q of "going out" as the first step to belief ... the need to flee the city and apprehension of civilized life is complemented ... by an appreciation of nature as the arena for divine disclosure ... This perspective fits the cultural developments of Galilee in the first century C.E., when Galilee was urbanized with the building of Sepphoris and Tiberius in its midst, which led to social distress and tensions.

Q sets forth a vision of the kingdom of God that puts in stark opposition a community shaped by and following the message of Jesus and that formed by Herodian rule in Galilee.

As in the case of Q, so also for the Gospel of Matthew there is no consensus about the author's provenance. The two options that are favored are Antioch in Syria and one of the two cities of lower Galilee (Tiberius or Sepphoris). There are sound arguments for both locations, but in either case the archaeological setting is one in which the community is confronted by and the author responds to the architecture and values of imperial Roman occupation. As several scholars of the Gospel of Matthew have noted, the text offers a response to an urban context in which the elite are privileged, the social order is fragmented, and the impoverished are ignored. In response, the gospel offers an alternative reality that values inclusiveness, equality, and mercy. Moreover, it is a gospel that challenges the message of world sovereignty that imperial architecture expressed so boldly by proclaiming that the world belongs to God and not Rome or Jupiter.

## Annotated Bibliography

Chancey, Mark A. *The Myth of a Gentile Galilee*. Cambridge: Cambridge University Press, 2002. Using archaeological and literary resources, the author makes a strong case that the overwhelming majority of Galileans in the first century CE were Jews.

Crossan, John Dominic and Jonathan Reed. *Excavating Jesus: Beneath the Stones, Behind the Texts*. San Francisco: HarperSanFrancisco, 2001. A New Testament scholar (Crossan) and an archaeologist (Reed) join forces for a full treatment of the literary and archaeological materials that bear upon the question of the historical Jesus. The illustrations are excellent and effectively employed.

Edwards, Douglas R. "The Socio-Economic and Cultural Ethos of Lower Galilee: Exploring the Archaeological and Literary Evidence." Pp. 53–73 in *The Galilee in Late Antiquity*. Edited by L. I. Levine. New York: Jewish Theological Seminary, 1992. Using an analysis of pottery distribution in early Roman Galilee and other archaeological resources, the author argues for a symbiotic relationship between urban and rural inhabitants in the time of Jesus.

Edwards, Douglas R. "Khirbet Qana: From Jewish Village to Christian Pilgrim Site." Pp. 101–32 in *The Roman And Byzantine Near East*, vol. 3. Edited by J. H. Humphrey. Journal of Roman Archaeology Supplement Series, 49. Portsmouth, RI: Journal of Roman Archaeology, 2002. The author is the director of the excavations at Khirbet Qana (Cana of the Galilee) and he summarizes the results of the excavations from 1998 to 2001.

Finley, Moses I. "The Ancient City: From Fustel de Coulanges to Max Weber and Beyond." *Comparative Studies in Society and History* 19 (1977), 305–32. The author makes use of the work of Max Weber to conclude that the ancient city was fundamentally a center for consumption and ultimately parasitical on the surrounding countryside.

Freyne, Sean. "Archaeology and the Historical Jesus." Pp. 160–82 in *Galilee and Gospel: Collected Essays*. Leiden: E. J. Brill, 2002. The author offers a very clear synthesis of the archaeological evidence and concludes that, as it stands, the evidence paints a portrait of Galilee as predominantly Jewish in character with strong links to Judean Jewish practices.

Geiger, Joseph. "Aspects of Palestinian Paganism in Late Antiquity." Pp. 3–17 in *Sharing the Sacred: Religious Contacts and Conflicts in the Holy Land First-Fifteenth Century*. Edited by A. Kofski and G. G. Stroumsa. Jerusalem: Yad Izhak Ben Zvi, 1998. The article is a useful cataloging of the evidence for the persistence of paganism in Roman Palestine.

Horsley, Richard. *Archaeology, History and Society in Galilee: The Social Context of Jesus and the Rabbis*. Valley Forge, PA: Trinity Press International, 1996. A study of first-century CE Galilee which argues that the population of Galilee was primarily agrarian and of Israelite descent and offered active opposition to the new urban centers populated by elites who had ties to Judea and Jerusalem.

MacMullen, Ramsey. *Roman Social Relations 50 B.C. to A.D. 284.* New Haven: Yale University Press, 1974. The author, a noted social historian, brings together an impressive array of evidence to recreate the social relations in the early Roman empire. The work is especially helpful for understanding rural–urban relationships.

Meeks, Wayne. *The First Urban Christians: The Social World of Paul.* New Haven: Yale University Press, 1983. A noted scholar of Pauline literature shows how useful social world research can be for interpreting work of the apostle Paul.

Meyers, Eric. "Teaching Second Temple Judaism in Light of Archaeology." Pp. 151–63 in *Text and Artifact: Integrating Archaeology in Biblical Studies Teaching.* Edited by Milton C. Moreland. Atlanta: Society of Biblical Literature, 2003. The author is a long-time advocate of the importance of archaeology for the study of the Bible as well as early rabbinic literature. This article is a brief study highlighting examples of data drawn from archaeology that are relevant for understanding the social context and resultant literature from the Second Temple period.

Meyers, Eric, Ehud Netzer, and Carol Meyers. *Sepphoris.* Winona Lake: Eisenbrauns, 1992. The authors directed the excavations of Sepphoris on behalf of Duke University and the Hebrew University beginning in 1985. The book utilizes primarily the results of those excavations to offer a brief overview of what we now know of this ancient city in lower Galilee in the Roman and Byzantine periods.

Moreland, Milton C. "Archaeology in New Testament Courses." Pp. 133–49 in *Text and Artifact: Integrating Archaeology in Biblical Studies Teaching.* Edited by Milton C. Moreland. Atlanta: Society of Biblical Literature, 2003. The author, a New Testament scholar and archaeologist, draws upon his own experience of using archaeology in New Testament courses to offer a helpful survey of resources and useful insights on how different readings of the archaeological evidence can be drawn into classroom discussions.

Murphy-O'Connor, Jerome. *St. Paul's Corinth: Texts and Archaeology.* Wilmington, DE: Michael Glazier, 1983. A collection of Greek and Latin inscriptions, literary texts, and archaeological data that bring to life Corinth as Paul probably encountered it.

Overman, J. Andrew. "Who Were the First Urban Christians? Urbanization in Galilee in the First Century." Pp. 160–8 in Society of Biblical Literature Seminar Papers, 1988. Edited by David Lull. Atlanta: Scholars Press, 1988. The article stresses the importance of the urbanization of Galilee as creating a context in which the inhabitants (including followers of Jesus) would be more likely exposed to the religio-philosophical ideas of the Greco-Roman world.

Reed, Jonathan. *Archaeology and the Galilean Jesus: A Reexamination of the Evidence.* Harrisburg, PA: Trinity Press International, 2000. A clear and accessible discussion of the archaeology and its impact on efforts at recovering the historical Jesus. The book offers one of the few real efforts at tackling such important questions as population numbers while also offering intriguing observations on the way in which archaeology can shed light on such familiar texts as the Lord's Prayer and the parable of the Tenants and the Vineyard.

Safrai, Ze'ev. *The Economy of Roman Palestine.* London: Routledge, 1994. This book is the starting point for all efforts at unpacking the economic realities of Roman Palestine.

Schütz, John H. "Introduction." Pp. 1–23 in *The Social Setting of Pauline Christianity: Essays on Corinth by Gerd Theissen.* Edited and translated by John Schütz. Philadelphia: Fortress Press, 1982. The author of this introduction was also the translator of this very important work in social world studies of Paul. The introduction is not only a helpful point of entry into the work of Theissen but also a useful synthesis of the evidence from Corinth and its bearing on Paul's work and thought.

Strange, James F. "Some Implications of Archaeology for New Testament Studies." Pp. 23–59 in *What Has Archaeology To Do with Faith?* Edited by J. H. Charlesworth and W. P. Weaver. Philadelphia: Trinity Press International, 1992. The author is a seasoned archaeologist and offers a sensible perspective on the possibilities and limits of archaeology for the study of the New Testament.

Theissen, Gerd. *The Social Setting of Pauline Christianity: Essays on Corinth,* ed. and trans. John Schütz. Philadelphia: Fortress Press, 1982. This German scholar has been one of the most insightful and prolific contributors to the study of the social world of early Christianity. The essays in this collection contain important discussions of method as well as influential applications of that method to the situation in Corinth.

# CHAPTER 4
# New Testament Greek

## Christophe Rico

In this short overview of the Greek language of the New Testament we will focus on those topics that are of greatest importance for the average reader, that is, those with important implications for translating the New Testament into English. I will thus consider some aspects of New Testament Greek from the specific point of view of translation. In order to achieve this objective I will begin with the context of New Testament Greek, continue with some difficult syntactical issues (word order, system of prepositions), and conclude with the controversial field of verbal aspect.

## The Space–Time Context

How can the language in which the New Testament was written be defined? Most Greek lexicons present, in a single volume, all the Greek words that have been used from the texts of Homer up to the beginning of the Byzantine period. This widespread synchronic practice leads to a false conception of ancient Greek, far removed from reality. We might be tempted to think of it as a static language remaining unchanged with respect to space and time, spanning more than a thousand years and found in many geographical locations without any noticeable linguistic changes. The truth is quite different. The term "ancient Greek" can refer throughout antiquity to any of the various stages, each of them very different from each other, that this language passed through during this period of time.

But what kind of Greek is found in the New Testament? Two parameters allow us to answer this question: the *geographical region* (which defines the limits of a *topolect*, the specific kind of language that is only spoken in a particular region) and the *chronological period* (which defines the limits of a *chronolect*, the specific kind of language that is only spoken in a particular period). Chronologically the language of the New Testament differs from classical Greek (fifth to fourth centuries BCE) and early Koine (third to first centuries BCE) as well as from late Koine (fourth to fifth centuries CE). New Testament Greek belongs to middle Koine (first to third centuries CE). Within the framework of this chronolect, the Greek of the New Testament belongs to a specific topolect, that of

**Table 4.1**

| Near Eastern topolect | Other topolects |
| --- | --- |
| – | Athenian Classical Greek (fifth to fourth centuries BCE) |
| Early Semitized Koine (e.g., LXX, letter of Aristeus, third to first centuries BCE) | Early Koine (third to first centuries BCE) |
| Middle Semitized Koine (e.g., New Testament, first century CE; Justin Martyr, second century CE) | Middle Koine (first to third centuries CE) |
| – | Late Koine (fourth to fifth centuries CE) |

Near Eastern Greek, which was under the influence of Semitic languages. We could thus call it *semitized Koine*, because its Aramaic and Hebrew substratum distinguishes it from the Greek spoken in the first century CE anywhere else, such as in Greece itself, as indicated by the Greek of Plutarch of Chaeronea (46–120 CE).

Thus New Testament Greek belongs both to the Near Eastern topolect and to the early Christian era chronolect. Within this specific context, we could further distinguish different language levels (the popular Greek of Mark, the cultured Greek of Hebrews) and *idiolects* (the specific kind of language that is only spoken or written by a person, such as the gospel and letters of John, Luke–Acts, and so on). Table 4.1 summarizes the primary relevant chronological periods and geographical areas of ancient Greek.

## New Testament Greek and its Linguistic Context

In order to understand the language of the New Testament, special attention must be paid to the context. This is a relatively easy task for any living language, but it proves rather difficult for an ancient language like New Testament Greek. If the translator of a modern English play is bilingual, she can work on a text whose syntactic rules and vocabulary she fully controls. The text might cause some problems of interpretation, but those difficulties will not arise for the translator because of a lack of knowledge of the original language of the play. If the translator gets stuck in a difficult passage she can always check the linguistic sense by consulting a native English speaker. Therefore the real problem will not be that of understanding the text, but of translating it. The New Testament translator, however, confronts a language she has never heard. In fact, the translator will never have a complete knowledge of its rules and vocabulary since all her linguistic competence comes from studying and reading rather than from experiencing the living language itself. If she cannot make up her mind among several possible explanations of an obscure idiom, no biblical speaker will be available to help clear things up. Even for the really difficult passages, no dictionary will provide the definitive answer since lexicons do not base their information on the linguistic sense of speakers living during the biblical times, but rather on the research of learned people who have never heard live New Testament Greek spoken.

Koine Greek ceased being a living language a very long time ago. Linguistic evolution has constantly and profoundly modified that language up to the present time. The difference between modern Greek and New Testament Koine Greek could be compared to the difference between modern English and the language of a tenth-century poem like *Beowulf*. Therefore the competence of a modern Greek speaker will not necessarily shed any light on the linguistic difficulties of the New Testament. Strange as it may seem, the competence of a modern speaker might even prove deceptive, leading a translator to fill her version of a New Testament passage with nuances that have very little to do with New Testament Greek. From the point of view of linguistics, the original language of the New Testament, much more than biblical Hebrew, is definitely a dead language.

This being the case, what tools are at a translator's disposal if, in spite of everything, she attempts to translate the New Testament into a modern language? Let us suppose that an interpreter comes across a difficult Greek word or phrase. Being unable to discuss the point with a native speaker, she could certainly scan a large collection of Koine writings that provide an adequate sample of contextualized meanings of this word or idiom. In order to further define this meaning, the translator will have to examine its original context to determine the chronological period and geographical area to which the instance of the word belongs. It would be unsound to clarify the meaning of some uncommon words of biblical Greek through instances of the words in different topolects or chronolects, taken from the same language (Greek), but without taking into account the chronological or geographical distance. Toward the beginning of the Christian era we can single out the Near Eastern Greek topolect from all other contemporary regional kinds of Greek for its semitisms, its idioms, and even its specific use of verbal tenses. The texts that may help clarify the most difficult biblical words are to be found either in the Greek Bible (LXX and New Testament), in the writings of native authors from the Near East (Justin Martyr, the *Didache*, Greek intertestamental literature, the translation of Theodotion, etc.), or in the papyri texts (Moulton's dictionary provides us with a large number of examples).

Then a biblical translator might examine the main ancient versions of the Bible. For New Testament texts the most interesting translations are those directly made from the original Greek, especially if these versions come from cultural environments that were in close contact with Hellenism throughout antiquity. This is precisely the case with the Latin and Syriac versions. Furthermore ancient translations into those two languages share another characteristic in that they are the result of a historical evolution. Each new Latin or Syriac version has been translated taking into account the previous one, the new one being a revision rather than a translation *a novo*. Thus the most recent translations are the result of a specific tradition. This historical development resulted in translations of a high quality, namely the *Peshitta* in Syriac for the East and the Vulgate in Latin for the West. The first Latin version (*Vetus Latina*) is already the result of many revisions throughout the second, third and fourth centuries. The New Testament Vulgate itself (late fourth to early fifth century) comes from a revision of the *Vetus Latina*. As for the *Peshitta* (fifth century), it is derived from a revision of the *Vetus Syra* (third century), which in turn draws most of its inspiration from the text of the *Diatessaron* (second century).

As a consequence a modern translator would be ill advised to choose an interpretation for a particular passage that has been dismissed by all the Latin and Syriac
versions throughout antiquity. I will give an example related to Greek syntax. In John
8:26, the Greek text (ταῦτα λαλῶ εἰς τὸν κόσμον) is usually translated as "and I
declare to the world" (RSV) or "and I speak to the world those things" (KJV). However
the Vulgate has "and I declare those things *in the world*" (*haec loquor in mundo*).
Examining different instances of λαλῶ ("to declare") in the New Testament (as well as
in other writings belonging to the Near Eastern Koine topolect) gives us the explanation for the difference. This verb requires that the phrase mentioning the interlocutor
either be in the dative case (cf. Rom. 3:19) or begin with the prepositions μετά (with
genitive case, cf. John 4:27) or πρός (with the accusative, cf. Luke 1:19). As for the
preposition εἰς, it is never followed by a mention of the interlocutor if the verb of the
sentence is λαλῶ. It therefore seems impossible to understand εἰς τὸν κόσμον as an
indirect object mentioning the people one is speaking with ("declaring *to the world*").
On the contrary, the prepositional phrase amounts here to an adverbial complement
("declaring *in the world*") as given in Jerome's translation. As the meaning of the verb
λαλῶ does not indicate any movement, the adverbial complement beginning with εἰς
cannot express any direction ("[going] to the world") but rather an expanding movement: "[declaring] *in* the world" or "*throughout* the world." Such an interpretation of
verse John 8:26 is even more compelling when one notices that the three main ancient
Syriac versions (the *Sinaitic Syriac*, the *Harkleian version*, and the *Peshitta*) unanimously
translate εἰς τὸν κόσμον as *b'lm'* ("in the world"), therefore agreeing with the Vulgate
translation.

There is one final point that a New Testament translator should take into account,
and that is the explanations of how to understand the biblical texts given by the Church
Fathers. Here again it would seem ill advised to adopt, as a primary translation of a
biblical verse, a meaning that has been excluded by the whole of patristic tradition.
Something very similar occurs in classical Greek literature. In order to get at the
meaning of obscure words that even third-century BCE readers hardly understood, a
modern translator of the *Iliad* must take into account the ancient scholia of Homer.
This is because they may be based upon a genuine tradition and may give the correct
solution to many obscurities in the original text. In a similar way, a biblical translator
will find in the writings of the Church Fathers an actualization of sacred scripture
echoing the early reading context of the Bible.

By way of example, in his *Commentary to the Letter to the Galatians* (PG 61, 631), St.
John Chrysostom explains in the following way a *hapax legomenon* (a word
occurring just once) in the New Testament which appears in Galatians 1:18,
Ἔπειτα μετὰ ἔτη τρία ἀνῆλθον εἰς Ἱεροσόλυμα ἱστορῆσαι Κηφᾶν. Its usual translation is given as: "then after three years I went up to Jerusalem *to visit Cephas*" or
"*to see Peter*":

> Paul says that [he went up to Jerusalem] in order to ἱστορῆσαι Peter, that is not only to
> *see* him but also to ἱστορῆσαι him. This is the very word used by people who *stare at* huge
> and magnificent cities. This is why Paul thought it worth while going up to Jerusalem for
> the unique purpose of seeing this man.

## Word Order

Word order is a characteristic of semitized Koine for which we lack the kind of valuable information that one usually gets only from consulting native speakers. And yet this aspect of language is of paramount importance in Greek, producing a rich variety of semantic nuances in a text. Word order actually gives to each sentence its specific weight and significance.

As in any language each kind of grammatical clause in semitized Koine implies a usual (or neutral) word order. Any change with respect to this usual order conveys a particular stress on the part of the clause affected by the change. To a large extent the order of the words in a sentence allows us to characterize the style of a New Testament text. Accordingly, accurately translating word order amounts in many cases to translating the stress of the text.

I will give the example of John 1:6: ἐγένετο ἄνθρωπος ἀπεσταλμένος παρὰ Θεοῦ, "There was / a man / sent from God" (RSV). This sentence displays a very normal word order for semitized Koine: *past tense copular verb* (ἐγένετο) – *subject* (ἄνθρωπος) – *predicate or apposition* (ἀπεσταλμένος παρὰ Θεοῦ). In contrast, a word order such as *predicate – past tense copular verb – subject* is seldom found in the New Testament. Therefore such an order would certainly have sounded exceptional to a Koine-speaking person owing to the extraordinary force of the uncommon first-place predicate. This is precisely what happens in John 1:1: καὶ Θεός (predicate: "and God") ἦν (past tense copular verb: "was") ὁ Λόγος (subject: "the Word") where the utterly unusual position of Θεός stresses the importance that is given to this word. This emphasis given by the Greek word order is easily lost in translation, for example: "and the Word was God" (RSV).

For both of the verses just mentioned, the Vulgate translation closely follows the original word order: *Fuit homo missus a Deo* (1:6); *et Deus erat Verbum* (1:1). Being based, like Greek, upon case endings, a Latin sentence is capable of tremendous flexibility. This is the reason why, without straining the genuine Latin character in any way, St. Jerome was able, as a general rule for his translation, to follow a close rendering of the Greek word order. This particular tendency of the Vulgate reflects a deep understanding of the implications conveyed by the precise position of a word in a text of sacred scripture. St. Jerome says, [in] *Scripturis Sanctis* [...] *et verborum ordo mysterium est:* "In Sacred Scripture, even word order encompasses a mystery" (*Epistles*, 57.5). This shows the richness of the Vulgate version, which preserves the specific significance of the style of each Greek text.

Unfortunately what the nature of the Latin language enabled St. Jerome to do is not possible for the translator into most Western languages. For instance, in English, the meaning changes according to word order ("the cat eats the mouse" means quite the opposite to "the mouse eats the cat"). Therefore, unless the translator decides to produce an odd syntax with respect to modern English grammar, Jerome's rule needs some serious modification.

Most translations of John 1:1 and 1:6 into English display in both cases a neutral word order from the stylistic point of view ("and the Word was God"; "There was a man sent from God"), as if those two sentences carried a similar weight in the original language. However, contrary to the natural Greek rythm of the clause in John 1:6, the syntax of John 1:1 stresses the deep significance of the predicate. A translator should thus find a way to reflect in a vernacular language the profound meaning of the original clause structure. Failing to notice this simple fact, many modern translators follow a literal principle (translating the words without translating the stylistic stress of the sentence). Thus they provide us with a flat rendering of the verse ("and the Word was God") instead of giving a special force to the predicate. "God he was, the Word" or, "the Word was really God," would have been much more appropriate. An example like this proves that a literal rendering may be deceptive. On the pretext of fidelity one may end up betraying the original text by not taking into account the variation in meaning given by the word order and style.

## The Prepositional System

Since 1919, the year F. Regard published his *Contribution à l'étude des prépositions dans la langue du Nouveau Testament*, no new monograph on the Koine prepositional system has so far been published. Despite some unavoidable gaps, this book is still the reference point for this subject. Thus the following remarks on the usage of some New Testament prepositions which have a spatial meaning are inspired by the work of this French scholar.

A Greek preposition demands that its complement be either in the genitive, dative, or accusative case. With a preposition that has a spatial meaning the case expresses either the presence or absence of movement. Thus the dative implies *a fixed and clear position* (absence of movement), e.g., Matthew 2:2: εἴδομεν γὰρ αὐτοῦ τὸν ἀστέρα ἐν τῇ ἀνατολῇ, "for we have seen his star *in the East*."

As for the genitive it alludes to *the origin*, to *a movement coming from a specific point*, e.g., Matthew 28:2: ἄγγελος γὰρ Κυρίου καταβὰς ἐξ οὐρανοῦ καὶ προσελθὼν ἀπεκύλισεν τὸν λίθον: "for an angel of the Lord descended *from heaven* and came and rolled back the stone."

Finally the accusative means either a direction or an expanding movement. Thus, in Matthew 10:6, the preposition πρός, followed by accusative indicates the direction in which the disciples of Jesus should go: πορεύεσθε δὲ μᾶλλον πρὸς τὰ πρόβατα

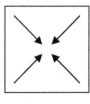

Accusative                    Dative                    Genitive

**Figure 4.1**

τὰ ἀπολωλότα οἴκου Ἰσραήλ, "go rather *to the lost sheep of the house of Israel.*" These three situations are shown in Figure 4.1.

Prepositions correspond to two types of spatial relationship, either internal or external.

## 1    Internal

ἐν is always followed by the dative. This preposition points to the existence of an internal relationship, that is to the presence of someone or something within an object or area. In any case, no movement is suggested, e.g., Matthew 2:2: εἴδομεν γὰρ αὐτοῦ τὸν ἀστέρα ἐν τῇ ἀνατολῇ: "for we have seen his own star *in the East.*"

ἐξ is followed by the genitive. It refers to a movement which begins inside a specific area or object, e.g., Matthew 28:2: ἄγγελος γὰρ Κυρίου καταβὰς ἐξ οὐρανοῦ: "for an angel of the Lord descended *from heaven.*"

εἰς is followed by the accusative. This preposition usually indicates a movement toward a place which one enters, e.g., Matthew 2:12: δι᾽ ἄλλης ὁδοῦ ἀνεχώρησαν εἰς τὴν χώραν αὐτῶν: "it was by another way that they came back *to their own country.*" However, in some instances εἰς may refer to the virtual spreading of the surface which is the framework of an action. This is especially the case whenever the preposition follows a verb whose meaning does not imply any movement toward a specific place, e.g., John 8:6: ὁ δὲ Ἰησοῦς ... κάτω κύψας τῷ δακτύλῳ κατέγραφεν εἰς τὴν γῆν: "But Jesus ... wrote with his own finger *on the ground.*" In this particular example the ground is seen as a surface that expands in our mind and whose limits are unclear, being referred to as a mere framework for the action of writing. Hence the use of εἰς τὴν γῆν instead of ἐν τῇ γῇ.

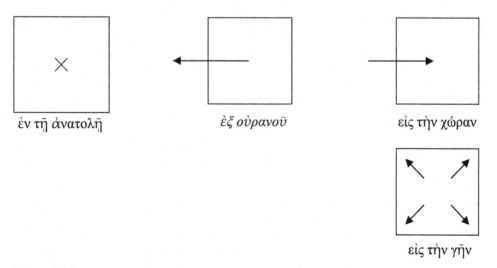

ἐν τῇ ἀνατολῇ          ἐξ οὐρανοῦ          εἰς τὴν χώραν

εἰς τὴν γῆν

**Figure 4.2**

## 2   External

Two main kinds of relationship can be identified: proximity and parallelism.

### 2.1   Proximity

*With the dative case.* We find πρός followed by the dative case to mark a fixed position whenever the reference is to a place or an object, e.g., John 20: 11: Μαρία δὲ εἱστήκει πρὸς τῷ μνημείῳ ἔξω κλαίουσα: "But Mary stood weeping *beside the tomb.*" If instead the reference is to a person, the preposition παρά is used. For instance, John 1:39: καὶ παρ᾽ αὐτῷ ἔμειναν τὴν ἡμέραν ἐκείνην: "and it was *beside him* that they stayed throughout the day." Notice the emphatic position of the adverbial complement.

*With the genitive case.* ἀπό, followed by the genitive case, is usually employed to mark a movement coming from close proximity to a person, object, or place, e.g., Luke 4:1: Ἰησοῦς δὲ πλήρης Πνεύματος Ἁγίου ὑπέστρεψεν ἀπὸ τοῦ Ἰορδάνου: "Jesus, full of the Holy Spirit, returned *from the Jordan.*" Less often the preposition παρά can also be used, but with a slightly different meaning. It indicates the movement coming from a close proximity to someone and implies a personal relationship with that person, e.g., John 9:33: εἰ μὴ ἦν οὗτος παρὰ Θεοῦ οὐκ ἠδύνατο ποιεῖν οὐδέν: "If this man were not *from God*, he could do nothing."

*With the accusative case.* The preposition πρός followed by the accusative case implies a directional movement leading close to a person, object, or place, e.g., Matthew 10:6: πορεύεσθε δὲ μᾶλλον πρὸς τὰ πρόβατα τὰ ἀπολωλότα οἴκου Ἰσραήλ, "but go rather *to the lost sheep of the house of Israel.*"

### 2.2   Parallelism

The parallel position is expressed with the preposition παρά, followed by the accusative. This parallelism usually implies a real physical *movement*, e.g., Matthew 4:18: περιπατῶν δὲ παρὰ τὴν θάλασσαν τῆς Γαλιλαίας εἶδεν δύο ἀδελφούς: "As he walked *by the sea of Galilee*, he saw two brothers." However, the preposition παρά followed by the accusative may mark no physical movement, referring instead to a fixed position along a place. This parallel position can be considered as a line that expands in our mind, hence the use of the accusative instead of the dative, e.g., Luke 8:12: οἱ δὲ παρὰ τὴν ὁδόν εἰσιν οἱ ἀκούσαντες, εἶτα ἔρχεται ὁ διάβολος καὶ αἴρει τὸν λόγον ἀπὸ τῆς καρδίας αὐτῶν: "The ones *along the path* are those who have heard, then the devil comes and takes away the word from their hearts." These relationships can be expressed in Figure 4.3.

## Verbal Aspect and Tense

Today verbal aspect is one of the most controversial topics in New Testament linguistics, so much so that a non-specialist reader could easily get lost among the many conflicting opinions on the subject. However, there is general agreement on some

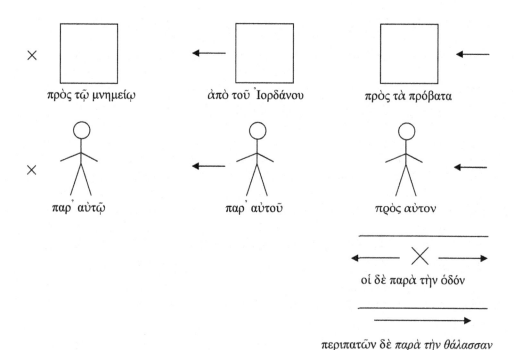

πρὸς τῷ μνημείῳ          ἀπὸ τοῦ Ἰορδάνου          πρὸς τὰ πρόβατα

παρ᾽ αὐτῷ          παρ᾽ αὐτοῦ          πρὸς αὐτον

οἱ δὲ παρὰ τὴν ὁδόν

περιπατῶν δὲ παρὰ τὴν θάλασσαν

**Figure 4.3**

specific points. I will describe them in order and give relevant examples when necessary.

Verbal aspect refers to the dynamic of the verbal event, either to its unfolding or to its performance. Some linguists (David Cohen) consider this characteristic to be an objective feature of the verbal action, whereas other scholars (McKay 1994: 27; Porter 1989; Fanning 1990) attribute it to the subjective point of view of the speaker about this action. However, both schools agree that verbal aspect as such constitutes a feature that is completely different from time or chronology.

Thus the present infinitive, λαλεῖν, expresses the act of "speaking" or "talking" as an event in progress, without taking into account its beginning or end. The verbal aspect here appears to be *non-limiting*. A "non-limiting" action is one that is considered as it is proceeding and whose two defining boundaries (beginning and end) are not taken into consideration. Thus in Matthew 12:22, καὶ ἐθεράπευσεν αὐτόν, ὥστε τὸν κωφὸν λαλεῖν ("And he healed him, so that the dumb man *spoke*") the act of speaking is seen as an ongoing event. The dumb man who was healed became able to speak for the rest of his life. The non-limiting aspect of λαλεῖν is even clearer in Acts 4:20: οὐ δυνάμεθα γὰρ ἡμεῖς ἃ εἴδαμεν καὶ ἠκούσαμεν μὴ λαλεῖν: "for we cannot but *speak* [*on and on*] of what we have seen and heard."

In Greek the verbal aspect of the present infinitive, λαλεῖν is contrasted with the aorist infinitive, λαλῆσαι, which expresses the action of "speaking," either as a simple fact, or as an act which is not in progress. Thus the aspect of λαλῆσαι is *limiting*. "Limiting aspect" implies that the defining boundaries of an action have been crossed, either referring it to the beginning of the action (if the meaning of the verb form is *ingressive*), "to start talking," or to the end of the action (if it is *terminative*), "to stop talking." It may also refer to both the beginning and the end. Then λαλῆσαι will express the simple fact of "talking" or "having talked," without considering the unfolding of the action.

Thus in Mark 16:19 the action of "speaking" is *terminative*: ὁ μὲν οὖν Κύριος Ἰησοῦς μετὰ τὸ λαλῆσαι αὐτοῖς ἀνελήμφθη εἰς τὸν οὐρανόν: "So then the Lord Jesus, once he *had finished speaking* to them, was taken up into heaven." On the other hand λαλῆσαι in Luke 1:20 expresses only the fact of "talking" as such, without taking into consideration its unfolding: καὶ ἰδοὺ ἔσῃ σιωπῶν καὶ μὴ δυνάμενος λαλῆσαι ἄχρι ἧς ἡμέρας γένηται ταῦτα: "And behold, you will be silent and unable *to speak* until the day that these things come to pass."

At first sight all these nuances may seem to be of very little significance. However, they can have very serious exegetical consequences. This can be illustrated by comparing the two texts of the Our Father as found in Matthew and Luke:

> Luke 11:3: τὸν ἄρτον ἡμῶν τὸν ἐπιούσιον δίδου [present imperative] ἡμῖν τὸ καθ' ἡμέραν: "*Give* us every day our *daily* bread" (here the Vulgate translates ἐπιούσιον as *cotidianum*).

> Matthew 6:11: τὸν ἄρτον ἡμῶν τὸν ἐπιούσιον δός [aorist imperative] ἡμῖν σήμερον: "*Give* us today our *sublime* bread" (here the Vulgate translates ἐπιούσιον as *supersubstantialem*).

In the text of Luke the present imperative (δίδου) points to a frequently made request, without considering any limit to the possible repetition of the act. As such this verb is followed by τὸ καθ' ἡμέραν ("every day"). Thus the use of δίδου in this sentence leads us to analyze the adjective ἐπιούσιον (an extremely rare occurrence in Greek) as a derivative of [ἡ] ἐπιοῦσα [ἡμέρα: "[the day] coming after." The word, ἐπιοῦσα is the present participle of the verb ἔπειμι, "to come after." The reader will thus understand: "give us every day enough bread to be able to get to the day after," that is: "give us the bread for every day," "the daily bread."

On the other hand in Matthew the imperative aorist of the verb, δός, "to give," rather suggests a one-time request, which is then highlighted by the adverb, σήμερον: "today." Hence, from the context of the whole sentence, quite a different interpretation ἐπιούσιον arises naturally. In this case this very uncommon Greek adjective will be considered as being a derivative of the phrase, ἐπὶ οὐσίαν, which means both "above the substance" and "[living] on means of subsistence." This gives us two different and complementary meanings that overlap. We can understand, the "bread for one's own subsistence," and "the transcendent (or sublime) Bread." The latter meaning points the reader toward a eucharistic interpretation.

However, not every verbal form necessarily conveys an aspect-value. For a particular language to have verbal aspects, this linguistic category has to appear in the verbal system with a specific grammatical form. This is the case in Greek for the non-limiting present infinitive, λαλεῖν, as opposed to the limiting aorist infinitive, λαλῆσαι. It is thus important to distinguish *verbal aspect* from *Aktionsart* ("kind of action"). In contrast to aspect, *Aktionsart* is a category that can be defined through lexical oppositions such as *do* in English with respect to *undo*, or λαμβάνειν ("to take") in Greek as opposed to ἀπολαμβάνειν ("receive").

In New Testament Greek we find aspectual opposition with respect to three verbal stems: aorist (-λυσ/θ-: λῦσαι), present (-λυ-: λυεῖν) and perfect (-λελυ-: λελυκέναι). From each one of these verbal stems is derived a series of modal oppositions, namely imperative, infinitive, subjunctive, and indicative. The optative mode can be omitted since its use in the New Testament amounts to no more than a surviving category of classical Greek. Aspectual opposition behaves differently in the indicative mood from the other moods. Hence they need to be analyzed separately.

### Aspectual meaning of aorist and present in the imperative, infinitive and subjunctive moods

Let us consider John 10:38 εἰ δὲ ποιῶ, κἂν ἐμοὶ μὴ πιστεύητε τοῦς ἔργοις πιστεύετε, ἵνα γνῶτε [aorist subjunctive] καὶ γινώσκητε [present subjunctive] ὅτι ἐν ἐμοὶ ὁ Πατὴρ κἀγὼ ἐν τῷ Πατρί: "But if I do them, even though you do not believe me, believe the works, *that you may realize and understand* that the Father is in me and I am in the Father." This verse contains a striking opposition between two different subjunctive forms of the same Greek verb γινώσκω, "to know," "to understand." The aorist γνῶτε, "realize," conveys an ingressive meaning and expresses a sudden intellectual awareness. By contrast, the present γινώσκητε, "understand," implies a non-limiting aspect and expresses an ongoing reflection. In order to translate the complete meaning of these two Greek words we need to use two different verbs in English.

In spite of the profound disagreement on aspect theory, both traditional grammars and recent research on the Greek New Testament verb admit that imperative, infinitive, and subjunctive moods indicate aspect and never suggest any chronological information regarding the event which is described by the verb. Another point of general agreement among scholars is the precise aspectual meaning conveyed by present and aorist stems. The present indicates that the event is viewed as an act in progress, as an event which is not yet completed. On the other hand the aorist implies that the action is viewed as an already performed event and is understood as a whole. Nigel Turner (1963: 59) sums up the classical opinion of New Testament grammars in the following way. A present stem usually expresses a "linear action" whereas an aorist stem points to a "momentary or punctiliar action." Recent linguistic research has confirmed these long-held opinions. In spite of slight differences in the wording, the definitions given by most modern scholars are roughly equivalent. McKay distinguishes between *imperfective* (present stem) "which expresses an activity as in process" and *aorist* "which expresses [an activity] as a whole action or simple event" (1994: 27). According to Porter (1989: 91), when the speaker uses the *imperfective* (present stem), he describes the action "immersed within it as ... an event in progress." In his opinion, the *imperfective* is opposed to the *perfective* (aorist stem) where the event is seen "in its immediacy ... in its entirety as a single and complete whole." Finally Fanning (1990: 103) views the *present* aspect as a situation which is described in its "development or progress ... in regard to its internal make-up, without beginning or end in view." The *aorist* aspect, on the contrary, shows the action "in summary, viewed as a whole from the outside, without regard for the internal make-up of the occurrence" (Fanning 1990: 97).

### Aspectual meaning of the perfect stem, regardless of mood

We find less agreement among scholars with respect to the aspectual meaning of the perfect stem. According to Porter (1989: 91), who refers to it as "stative," this verbal stem describes the event "as a condition or state of affairs in existence," without referring at all to its performance or completion. Most scholars, however, hold a different view. They prefer to think that the perfect stem expresses a completed event whose relevance is taken into consideration at the time of reference in a narrative or discourse. Thus Turner (1963: 69) stresses that the New Testament perfect is often "a true resultative perfect denoting a past action of which the results still vividly survive." For instance, in a text reporting a conversation, a verb in the perfect stem not only expresses past action but also links this action to the present situation of the dialogue. Thus this verbal stem means "fulfilment in the present of a process begun in the past or else the contemplation of an event having taken place in the past" (Turner 1963: 81). McKay points to the fact that this verbal stem "expresses the state consequent upon an action" (1994: 27) and Fanning concludes that "the Perfect in New Testament Greek is a complex verbal category denoting, in its basic sense, a state which results from a prior occurrence" (1990: 119).

Following the opinion of David Cohen, the aspectual meaning of the New Testament perfect can be summarized in a simple way. This verbal stem stresses the *incidence*, that is, the actuality of a performed act in a reference situation. Whenever it is used with the perfect stem, the Greek verb will express a past action which is taken into consideration regarding the situation which the speaker is now referring to.

In the passage about the Transfiguration found in Luke there is a striking example of the opposition between the aorist and the perfect of the same verb. According to the text of the third gospel, Peter, James, and John were heavy with sleep (Luke 9:32): διαγρηγορήσαντες δὲ εἶδον ["to see": aorist indicative] τὴν δόξαν αὐτοῦ καὶ καὶ τοὺς δύο ἄνδρας τοὺς συνεστῶτας αὐτῷ: "But they kept awake, and they *saw* his glory and the two men who stood with him." However, at the end of the passage (9:36), we have: καὶ αὐτοὶ ἐσίγησαν καὶ οὐδενὶ ἀπήγγειλαν ἐν ἐκείναις ταῖς ἡμέραις οὐδὲν ἐν ἑώρακαν ["to see": perfect indicative]: "And [the disciples] kept silence and told no one in those days anything of *what they had been able to see."*

From the aspectual point of view the first verb, which is in the aorist tense, amounts to little more than recording, within the narrative, the actual performance of an action: seeing the Lord's glory. The second use of the verb in the perfect, however, expresses the relevance of this act with respect to the situation being referred to: "in those days." The opposition of aspect of these different verb tenses conveys a specific significance. It suggests the importance of a unique experience (ἑώρακαν), whose secret the disciples had to carry for a long time.

*Aspectual meaning of the aorist and present indicative*

One of the most discussed areas of verbal aspect is the meaning of indicative tenses. Whereas all scholars agree that the perfect stem conveys an aspectual meaning even in the indicative mood, the situation is not so clear with the other verbal stems. Traditional grammars have always proposed that aorist and present indicative have no aspectual meaning whatsoever and that they only express time, past or present. Nevertheless some scholars reject this opinion. According to McKay (1994: 39), the so-called temporal meaning of the indicative is caused only by the context. Porter's view (1989: 75–109) is very similar, for he thinks that Greek verbs always express aspect even in the indicative. However, many linguists hold a different view on this verbal mood. According to this more common opinion, the indicative has a capacity for expressing time which is independent from the context (cf. Fanning 1990; Silva 1993; and Schmidt 1993).

There is a danger in these views which attempt to offer a unified theory about verbal aspect in Koine Greek. They run the risk of not taking into consideration the possibility of having a different aspectual system with respect to each idiolect. The study of each text of the New Testament shows, for instance, that what we can say about the Greek of Matthew does not necessarily apply to that of John. As a general rule it can be said that the indicative in New Testament Greek expresses chronological time rather than aspect, though there are many exceptions to this general rule. Even within any one text of the New Testament the indicative mood can take on opposite functions that change from one passage to another, that is to say, to have an aspectual meaning rather than a temporal meaning. This is quite frequent, for example, whenever an author relies on a source which was written in a Semitic language or shows a clear Semitic influence.

To take a case in point, the aorist and present indicatives in the Gospel of Luke do not always have one and the same value. In most of the dialogues these two tenses express chronological time. Thus the aorist indicative implies a past event which is understood as a completed action. On the other hand, the present indicative refers to an act which is simultaneous with the moment of speech. This is what happens in Luke 15:21: Πάτηρ ἥμαρτον [aorist indicative] εἰς τὸν οὐρανὸν καὶ ἐνώπιόν σου, οὐκέτι εἰμὶ [present indicative] ἄξιος κληθῆναι υἱός σου: "Father, *I have sinned* against Heaven and before you: *I am no longer* worthy to be called your son." The verb in the aorist tense (ἥμαρτον) refers to a past action which is seen as a completed unit. The second verb in the present (οὐκέτι εἰμὶ) indicates an action that is simultaneous with the moment of the dialogue, and this is why it appears in the present tense.

Nevertheless, in some other dialogues reported in the third gospel the evangelist applies verbal tenses in a very different way. In the opening sentence of the Magnificat (Luke 1:46–7) there is a clear aspectual opposition between two indicatives (present and aorist): Μεγαλύνει [present indicative] ἡ ψυχή μου τὸν Κύριον καὶ ἠγαλλίασεν τὸ πνεῦμα μου ἐπὶ τῷ Θεῷ τῷ σωτῆρί μου: "My soul *magnifies* the Lord, and my spirit *starts rejoicing* (ἠγαλλίασεν: aorist indicative) in God my Saviour."

Since these two actions are simultaneous, the opposition between aorist and present has nothing to do with chronology. The action of μεγαλύνει ("to magnify") refers to an event in progress. At the same time the act of ἠγαλλίασεν ("to rejoice") indicates an event affected by a limiting aspect. This ingressive aorist expresses the sudden occurrence of extreme happiness, as caused by God who "has regarded the low estate of his handmaiden" (Luke 1:48).

In another passage of this same gospel we find a series of present indicatives that indicate the *non-limiting* aspect. In this case the event is not seen as simultaneous with the moment of speech, but rather as about to happen in the very near future. This occurs in Luke 3:9: ἤδη δὲ καὶ ἡ ἀξίνη πρὸς τὸν ῥίζαν τῶν δένδρων κεῖται πᾶν οὖν δένδρον μὴ ποιοῦν καρπὸν καλὸν ἐκκόπτεται ["to be cut down": present indicative] καὶ εἰς πῦρ βάλλεται ["to be thrown": present indicative]: "Even now the axe is laid to the root of the trees; every tree therefore that does not bear good fruit *is about to be cut down and thrown* into the fire."

These two exceptions, taken from Luke 1:46–7 and 3:9, serve to show that we must be careful not to follow blindly the general rule that the opposition between present indicative and aorist indicative is only one of time. In the particular case of the idiolect present in the gospel and the letters of John we find a frequent aspectual function with respect to the present and aorist indicative. For example, in John 15:6 we have: ἐὰν μή τις μένῃ [present subjunctive] ἐν ἐμοί, ἐβλήθη [aorist indicative] ἔξω ὡς τὸ κλῆμα καὶ ἐξηράνθη [aorist indicative], καὶ συνάγουσιν [present indicative] αὐτὰ καὶ εἰς τὸ πῦρ βάλλουσιν [present indicative] καὶ καίεται [present indicative]: "If a man does not abide in me, *he is suddenly cast forth* [ἐβλήθη] as a branch, *he suddenly withers* [ἐξηράνθη], the branches *being gathered* [συνάγουσιν] and *thrown* [βάλλουσιν] into the fire where they *slowly burn* [καίεται]." The translation that I have given intends to reflect the aspectual contrast of this verse. The aorist indicatives ἐβλήθη and ἐξηράνθη, which express a transforming action (the sudden occurrence of a new state: "he is suddenly cast forth," "he suddenly withers"), are in strong opposition to the present indicatives συνάγουσιν, βάλλουσιν and καίεται, which suggest a non-limiting event ("being gathered," "being thrown," "they slowly burn").

## Conclusions

The translator of a dead language first of all needs to have a profound knowledge of its linguistic system in order to be able to reflect in his translation all the rich nuances enshrined in the original text. To achieve this goal with respect to sacred scripture, he must base his translation on the Koine Greek texts, the ancient Syriac and Latin versions, and the commentaries of the Church Fathers. This short survey of some of the most controversial points of the New Testament language shows that some semantic nuances, seemingly trivial at first sight, have serious consequences with respect to exegesis. To find the accurate translation that reflects the precise meaning of a New Testament text is the daunting challenge of the translator. The importance of biblical linguistics is paramount for this endeavour.

## Annotated Bibliography

### Dictionaries

Chantraine, P. *Dictionnaire étymologique de la langue grecque. Histoire des mots.* New, updated, edn. Paris: Klincksieck, 1999. An excellent etymological dictionary.

Liddell, H. G. and R. Scott. *A Greek–English Lexicon.* 9th edn. (frequently reprinted). Oxford: Clarendon Press, 1940. with Liddell, H. G., R. Scott, H. S. Jones, and R. McKenzie. *Greek-English Lexicon: Revised Supplement.* Oxford: Clarendon Press, 1996. This is the main reference for classical Greek.

Moulton, J. H. and G. Milligan. *The Vocabulary of the Greek Testament Illustrated from the Papyri and Other Non-Literary Sources.* London: Hodder & Stoughton, 1914–29. This remains the most inspiring dictionary for the vocabulary of the New Testament.

### Grammars and methods

Moulton, J. H. *A Grammar of New Testament Greek.* Edinburgh: T. & T. Clark, 1906–76. The most important reference grammar. The first volume, *Prolegomena* (1906; 3rd edn. 1908, subsequently reprinted) is a general introduction to the Greek of the New Testament and it deals mainly with the nouns, adjectives, pronouns, prepositions and verbal system of Koine Greek. The second volume, *Accidence and Word-Formation* (1919, ed. W. F. Howard), is a study on the morphology of the New Testament language. The third volume, *Syntax*, by N. Turner (1963), includes two books, namely on analytical syntax and synthetic syntax. Finally, the fourth volume, *Style*, by N. Turner (1976), deals with the stylistic aspects of each New Testament text.

For those who wish to learn New Testament Greek, a new method is now available in Christophe Rico, *Polis. Parler le grec ancien comme une langue vivante.* Paris: Cerf, 2009.

### Prepositional systems

Regard, P. F. *Contribution à l'étude des prépositions dans la langue du Nouveau Testament.* Paris: Ernest Leroux, 1919. This book, written by a disciple of F. de Saussure, gives many biblical examples and offers a general theory on the evolution of the prepositional system, from classical Greek up to New Testament Koine, including the LXX.

### Verbal aspect

Cohen, David. *L'aspect verbal.* Paris: Presses Universitaires de France, 1989. In spite of its high level of abstraction, this represents, in my opinion, the most profound study on verbal aspect that has ever been written. It examines this linguistic area from a very broad perspective, comparing many languages, most of them either Indo-European or Semitic. Cohen studies the evolution of some languages for which we have evidence, spanning more than 3,000 years (Greek, Ancient Egyptian, Aramaic), and describes the main trends in the history of aspectual systems. This approach permits him to propose some general rules that may be considered linguistic universals. For this reason David Cohen's contribution to the study of verbal aspect can be considered unique.

Fanning, Buist. *Verbal Aspect in New Testament Greek*. Oxford: Clarendon Press, 1990. The non-specialist will enjoy reading this book. Its arguments are both clear and convincing.

Two other important works are:

McKay, Kenneth. *A New Syntax of the Verb in New Testament Greek*. New York: Peter Lang, 1994.

Porter, Stanley. *Verbal Aspect in the Greek of the New Testament with Reference to Tense and Mood*. New York: Peter Lang, 1989.

## Other references cited in the text

Schmidt, Daryl. "Verbal Aspect in Greek: Two Approaches." Pp. 63–73 in *Biblical Greek Language and Linguistics: Open Questions on Current Research*. Edited by Stanley E. Porter and Donald A. Carson. Journal for the Study of the New Testament Supplement Series, 80. Sheffield: JSOT Press, 1993.

Silva, Moisés. "A Response to Fanning and Porter on Verbal Aspect." Pp. 74–82 in *Biblical Greek Language and Linguistics: Open Questions on Current Research*. Edited by Stanley E. Porter and Donald A. Carson. Journal for the Study of the New Testament Supplement Series, 80. Sheffield: JSOT Press, 1993.

# CHAPTER 5

# Reconstructing the Text of the New Testament

Michael W. Holmes

## Defining Textual Criticism

In an age when copy machines, computers, and the internet make it easy to transmit or share perfect copies of almost anything (documents, music, or images), it is difficult to imagine just how challenging it was to reproduce a book in earlier times. Prior to the development of printing, for example, one first had to locate a copy of the book, get its owner's permission to copy it, and then make (or have made, if one were wealthy enough) a copy of it by hand (hence books produced in this way are called manuscripts, from the Latin *manus*, hand). Copying was a slow, labor-intensive, and not inexpensive procedure; it was also easily affected by all the vagaries of the human body and mind. Thus no two copies of a book were ever identical, and no copy perfectly reproduced the model from which it was made.

This explains why all surviving manuscripts (MSS) of the New Testament differ from one another, sometimes in rather striking ways. For example, among the surviving MSS of the New Testament, the last (sixteenth) chapter of the Gospel of Mark is found in at least nine different forms. The episode involving Jesus and an adulterous woman, most often present as John 7:53–8:11, is instead in some MSS placed after John 21:25, John 7:25, or Luke 21:38 – and is absent from the earliest surviving MSS. Other instances may involve a single verse (such as the presence or absence of John 6:4, or Acts 8:37), or more often a short phrase or a single word (for example, in Mark 1:41, did Jesus feel "pity" or "anger"?).

None of these differences would matter, of course, if the "master copy" of a book (often referred to as the "original" or "autograph") were available: we could then set aside the copies and consult the master copy to determine what the author wrote (or dictated, as was often the case). But no master copy of any classical, biblical, or early church writing has survived. These two facts – that no master copy survives, and that all existing copies differ from one another – indicate why the text of a document must be reconstructed before we can begin to study it.

The process of reconstructing the text is known as *textual criticism*: the art and science of recovering the original wording of a document. It is a necessary and foundational step in the study of any ancient document (and even some relatively modern ones, such as Shakespeare's plays). The definition just given indicates the traditional goal of textual criticism: reconstructing the "original text" of a document. In recent years this goal has become the subject of considerable discussion (arising in part from the recognition of the difficulty of defining what is meant by "original"). Proposed redefinitions of the goal include "the recovery of the earliest surviving form of the text" or "the form the text had when released from the author's control." In addition, a second goal has emerged: the study of the different variant forms of the text for the insights they offer into the history of the churches and the people that transmitted the text (see further Epp 2007; Parker 1997).

For both goals the basic procedure is the same: (1) collect and organize the evidence; (2) compare the MSS with one another to determine where there are variations in the text (the different forms of a text found at any particular point in the MSS are called "variant readings" or "textual variants"); and (3) evaluate and assess the significance of the evidence. With respect to the first goal, step (3) will seek to determine, at each point of variation, which one of the competing variant readings is the source of the other readings and therefore most likely the "original" or "earliest recoverable" form of the text. With respect to the second goal, step (3) will seek to discover why and/or how each individual variant arose in the course of copying the text and to uncover whatever insight the different surviving forms of the text offer into the time and cultural context in which they created or transmitted.

## Causes of Error in the Transmission of the New Testament

The format of ancient books, the mechanics of the copying process, and the foibles of scribes made it easy to make mistakes when copying a book. Books were written in letters of one size in *scriptio continua* (i.e., LIKETHISWITHNOBREAKSORSPACESATALLBE-TWEENWORDS), and with minimal punctuation or other aids for a reader. Page layout varied from one wide column per page to several narrow ones. Under such circumstances it was easy to lose one's place while copying, and a frequent consequence was the omission or duplication of material (depending on whether one's eye skipped forward or back).

The activity of copying involves at least three steps: reading the text, remembering it in one's mind, and writing it down. At any or all of these stages mistakes could occur, such as misreading the text (or hearing it incorrectly, if copying was being done from dictation), inadvertently rearranging the word order, unconsciously substituting a more familiar word or phrase for a less common or unusual one, or simply writing it down incorrectly.

As for the copyist, fatigue, lack of attention, poor eyesight or hearing, physical discomfort, or simple stupidity could all contribute to the commission of errors while copying. The physical conditions in which copying took place also had an effect: one scribe reported that it was snowing heavily, his inkwell was frozen, and his hand was numb, while complaints about the physical discomfort of copying for hours at a time are not uncommon (see further Metzger 1992: 186–206).

Not all alterations of the text were inadvertent or accidental. Copyists would some-times change the text deliberately while copying it, usually thinking that they were correcting it as they did so. Harmonization to another passage (such as modifying the Lukan form of the Lord's Prayer to match the more familiar wording of the Matthean form) could happen deliberately as well as accidentally. As standards of Greek grammar, style, and syntax changed, a scribe might "update" a text to conform to current prac-tice, or substitute a more literary term for a colloquial one. If a copyist spotted what she or he thought was a mistake in the document being copied, the copyist might attempt to fix it – but might only substitute a new mistake for an existing one, compound the problem, or even replace the correct text with something different. As well, the text was sometimes deliberately altered for doctrinal reasons – either to prevent a text from being misinterpreted, or to ensure that the text actually said what everyone "knew" it was supposed to mean. The "orthodox" and "heretics" alike leveled this charge against one another, and the surviving evidence indicates there was some truth to the claim of tampering with the text by both sides (Ehrman 1993).

These, then, are some of the causes for error in the transmission of the New Testament text. Let us now turn to the resources available from which to reconstruct it.

## Resources for Reconstructing the Text

Due to the accidents of history, many classical or patristic texts survive today in only a few late copies or, in extreme cases, only a single, now destroyed, copy. In sharp contrast, the text of the New Testament survives in thousands of copies in several ancient languages. In addition, nearly the whole New Testament can be reconstructed on the basis of quotations by ancient writers. For ease of reference scholars have grouped these sources under three headings: Greek manuscripts, ancient versions, and patristic citations.

### 1   Greek manuscripts

Greek manuscripts are categorized (somewhat arbitrarily) on the basis of writing mate-rial, style, or format. First are the *papyri*, manuscripts written on papyrus, an ancient paper-like writing material. These MSS (designated by a Old English thorn (Þ) plus a superscript Arabic numeral, e.g., $Þ^{46}$), include some of the oldest surviving copies of the New Testament. As of mid-2009 the remains of about 124 papyri were known, most of which are extremely fragmentary. Some of the better-preserved and more important witnesses in this category include $Þ^{45}$ (third century; substantial parts of the gospels and Acts), $Þ^{46}$ (ca. 200 CE; Pauline epistles), $Þ^{66}$ (ca. 200 CE; large parts of John), $Þ^{72}$ (third/fourth centuries; parts of 1 and 2 Peter, Jude), and $Þ^{75}$ (early third century; over half of Luke and John).

Continuous-text Greek MSS written on material other than papyrus (usually parch-ment, though after the twelfth century increasingly on paper) are subdivided on the basis of writing style. *Majuscules* (more often called uncials) are MSS written in a formal literary style of unconnected capital letters. They were initially designated by letters of the alphabet; when these proved insufficient, the Greek and then Hebrew alphabets were used. Because of the resulting confusion, numbers prefixed with a zero (e.g., 01, 02) were eventually assigned to these MSS. Today only the most famous of the majuscules/uncials continue to be known by their original letters; these include the famous Codex Sinaiticus (ℵ/01; mid-fourth century), Alexandrinus (A/02; early fifth century), Vaticanus (B/03; mid-fourth century), Bezae (D/05; fifth century), and Washingtonianus (W/032; fourth/fifth century). As of mid-2009, 318 official numbers had been assigned, representing (once the number is reduced to reflect multiple numbers assigned to parts of the same MS) about 275 MSS.

*Minuscules* are MSS written in a smaller cursive style that was developed in the eighth or ninth century; it was faster to write and more space-efficient than the majuscule style. Minuscule MSS are identified by a simple Arabic numeral; the official list includes about 2,900 entries. Some of the more significant minuscules include groups or "families" headed by 1 and 13 (symbols: $f^1$ and $f^{13}$), and manuscripts 28, 33, 81, 323, 565, 614, 700, 892, 1241, 1424, 1739, and 2495.

In the final category of Greek witnesses are *lectionaries*, books containing selections from scripture for use in worship and other services. Over 2,400 lectionary MSS are known to exist today.

In all, something over 5,700 witnesses to the Greek New Testament are extant today. Many (if not most) of these, it should be noted, are fragmentary or incomplete, with some fragments being no larger than a credit card. Only three majuscules (ℵ/01, A/02, and C/04) and fifty-six minuscules contain the entire New Testament; another two majuscules and 147 minuscules lack only Revelation. In terms of content, the gospels are found in just over 2,300 MSS, the Acts and Catholic letters in about 655, the Pauline letters in about 780, and Revelation in about 290. With regard to date, over 65 percent are from the eleventh through fourteenth centuries, while fewer than 2.5 percent are from the first five centuries.

## 2   Ancient versions

As Christianity spread into regions where Greek was not understood, the need arose for translations of the New Testament. By about 180 CE the process of translating the New Testament into Latin, Syriac, and Coptic was under way. The Latin eventually developed into at least two major forms, the Old Latin or Itala, and the Vulgate (of which over 8,000 MSS are known), while the Syriac and Coptic exist in a number of versions and dialects. Later translations include Armenian, Georgian, Ethiopic, Gothic, and Old Church Slavonic. In several instances these translations were the first literary work in that particular language, and occasionally, as in the case of the Gothic, an alphabet first had to be created.

Because the roots of some of these early versions pre-date the vast majority of the Greek MSS, they are valuable historical witnesses to the transmission of the New Testament text, particularly regarding the form of the text in various regions or provinces. Limitations, however, in the ability of these languages to represent aspects of Greek grammar and syntax (for example Latin has no definite article) restrict their value at some points (see further Metzger 1977).

### 3  Patristic citations

Early Christian writers frequently quoted the New Testament in their writings and sermons, often at length, and many wrote commentaries on it. Together these constitute another important source of information about the New Testament text. Their particular value lies in the help they provide in dating and localizing variations in the text, because we usually know when and where a writer lived. Like the translated versions, however, their value is sometimes limited, in this case by a tendency to cite from memory or adapt a quotation to its context. Thus it can be difficult to determine if a reading represents a genuine variant or merely the author's adaptation of the text. Nevertheless these citations represent an important additional source of information.

The sheer volume of the information available to the New Testament textual critic makes it practically certain that the original form has been preserved somewhere among the surviving witnesses – a notable contrast to the textual criticism of the Old Testament, classical, and patristic texts, where textual emendation (the proposal of a reading or text form not found in any known witness) is routinely necessary. Nonetheless, even in the New Testament it is occasionally necessary to consider the possibility that the original form can only be recovered by means of textual emendation (possible instances include Acts 16:12 or 1 Corinthians 6:5).

## Classification and Genealogical Relationships of MSS

The large number of surviving witnesses – and the resulting very large volume of information they can (potentially) supply – means that textual questions can at times become quite technical and difficult. To be sure, computer applications have reduced some of the drudgery involved. Even so, simply gathering all the evidence for a particular problem, not to mention analyzing and evaluating it, can be a formidable challenge.

The phenomenon of *genealogical relationships* and the classification of MSS into certain broad textual traditions (text-types) do, however, alleviate the problem significantly. The concept of genealogy builds on the circumstance that under normal conditions, every MS copied from a distinctive model will itself exhibit most (perhaps even all) of the elements or characteristics that make the model copy distinctive. Because all the copies made from the same model will share these distinctive elements by virtue of their common parentage, they may be said to be genetically related, or to have a genealogical relationship. Now in the case of the New Testament, as it was being copied throughout the Roman empire, distinctive variations arose which (a) are found relatively consistently in some MSS and (b) do not, except by occasional sheer coincidence, occur in the same way or pattern in other MSS. On the basis of these shared distinctive variations (or particular patterns of variation) it is possible to group most (but certainly not all) MSS into one of three broad textual traditions: the Alexandrian, the Western, and the Byzantine. Each of these textual traditions can be identified on the basis of a significant degree of agreement between certain MSS with regard to (1) a set of distinctive variations specific to that textual tradition, and (2) an identifiable pattern of variation (even if individual readings may be shared with other traditions), and each has a distinctive character and history.

One of the three main textual traditions is known as the Alexandrian (after the city in Egypt, famous for its scholarship), so named because many of the MSS most characteristic of this tradition have some connection with Egypt. At one time this textual tradition was considered to be a carefully edited, late third-century revision or edition of the New Testament, the product of Alexandrian classical scholarship applied to the New Testament. But twentieth-century discoveries, especially of early papyrus MSS such as $\mathfrak{P}^{75}$ and $\mathfrak{P}^{46}$, have demonstrated that this textual tradition was already in existence well before the end of the second century AD. Thus it appears to represent the result of a carefully controlled and supervised process of copying and transmission. Primary representatives include $\mathfrak{P}^{46}$, $\mathfrak{P}^{66}$, $\mathfrak{P}^{75}$, $\aleph$, B, and Origen; secondary witnesses include the MSS C L W 33 892 1739, and later Alexandrian fathers like Didymus.

The "Western" textual tradition (so labeled because its first known representatives came from the western part of the Roman empire), is equally as old as the Alexandrian (if not perhaps even a bit older). It is widely attested geographically; major witnesses derive from North Africa, Italy, Gaul, Syria, and Egypt. But it lacks the homogeneity and consistency of relationships characteristic of the other two major textual traditions. It appears to represent a tradition of uncontrolled copying, editing, and translation: it exhibits harmonistic tendencies, paraphrasing and substitution of synonyms, additions (sometimes quite long), and a small but theologically significant group of omissions. Major representatives include Codex Bezae (D/05); $\mathfrak{P}^{45}$ $\aleph$ W in the gospels (all in part only), D/06 F G in the Pauline epistles, the Old Latin and Old Syriac versions, and Tatian, Irenaeus, Cyprian, and Tertullian among patristic writers.

The Byzantine textual tradition (also known as the Koine, Syrian, or Majority text) comprises the third major grouping; it includes about 90 percent of all known MSS. While scattered individual Byzantine readings are known to be ancient, the Byzantine textual tradition as such – that is, as an identifiable pattern of distinctive variants and agreements – first appears only in the mid-fourth century among a group of fathers associated with Antioch. It is the largest and latest of the three major text-types, and, in view of the secondary character of many of its distinctive readings, also the least valuable for recovering the original text (but still very important for tracing the history of the transmission of the text).

## Procedures and Methods for Reconstructing the Text

### 1  Numbers or weight?

Once the variant readings have been identified at a particular place in the text, and support for each of the surviving MSS, versions, and citations has been determined, how might one go about making a decision between competing variants?

One approach would be to count the number of witnesses supporting each option, and adopt the one with the most support. But the phenomenon of genealogical relationship mentioned earlier must be taken into account: if a large number of MSS turn out to be descendants of a single MS (or textual tradition), they add nothing to the weight or value of that one MS.

As an illustration, think in terms of a hypothetical small town whose church acquires a manuscript of the Gospel of Mark – one whose text of Mark 1:41 reads "Jesus felt anger." The MS is placed in the church, and soon three copies are made of it – call them A, B, and C. Copies A and B repeat exactly the wording of the church's text ("Jesus felt anger"). But the person making copy C wrote "Jesus felt pity." Copy A is given to a church in the next town over, and copy B is given to the person who reads the scripture on Sundays, to keep at home. Meanwhile copy C ends up in the library of a small monastery nearby, where it in turn gets copied several times – call them $C^{copy1}$, $C^{copy2}$, etc., up to $C^{copy10}$. Then disaster strikes: the church catches fire, and its manuscript is destroyed in the ensuing blaze.

Years pass, and a textual critic comes along and wants to reconstruct the text of the lost church manuscript. He locates thirteen surviving descendants of that lost copy – A, B, C, and the ten copies of C. When he compares them with one another, he learns that at Mark 1:41, two of the MSS (A and B) read "Jesus felt anger" and eleven read "Jesus felt pity." On a purely numerical basis, the support for the "pity" variant (eleven MSS) is clearly superior to the support for the "anger" variant (two MSS). But the raw numbers are misleading: because ten of the surviving MSS ($C^{copy1}$ through $C^{copy10}$) are copies of C, they add nothing to the weight of evidence, which is really two to one in favor of "anger" (A + B *vs.* C).

The point of this example is to illustrate a key principle of textual criticism: *it is not enough simply to count MSS, but rather the evidence they present must be weighed and evaluated.* Rather than simply counting manuscripts, one must first determine whether an MS is an independent witness – as in the case of A, B, and C – or only a secondary descendant of an independent witness (as in the case of the ten copies of C).

Applied in general terms to the reconstruction of the New Testament, this means that for the most part textual critics are usually dealing not so much with a collection of several hundred or more independent MSS, but more often with three textual traditions, whose evidence must be evaluated and not merely counted. This means, more specifically, that even though the Byzantine textual tradition includes approximately 90 percent of all surviving MSS, when the MSS are weighed rather than merely counted, these 90 percent generally count as one textual tradition, alongside the Western and the Alexandrian.

Another reason why it is necessary to weigh rather than count MSS has to do with a limitation of the genealogical principle just discussed. If each MS was in fact copied directly from another, with no interfering factors, it would be possible, at least in theory, to reconstruct one giant family tree of manuscript relationships and to trace one's way back through the branches to a single ancestor. But except for certain small subgroups of MSS (e.g., "Family 1" or "Family 13"), it has not been possible to reconstruct a stemma for the textual tradition as a whole. This is due in part to (1) the relatively large number of MSS involved, but even more so to (2) the widespread presence of mixture (or "cross-pollination" or contamination) within the textual tradition. That is, not all MSS were copied from a single model: sometimes a scribe might work from two models, following now one and then the other. The result would be, in genetic terms, a cross-pollinated copy. Thus the lines of descent of a particular MS often may be said to be mixed or contaminated. In such circumstances, genealogical analysis, other than in the most general sense (as when dealing with broad textual traditions), becomes very difficult.

In practical terms what this means is that at any given point even the most generally reliable MS or group of MSS may be wrong, due to the influence of contamination; conversely (at least in theory) even an MS of very poor quality may occasionally preserve a true reading. These circumstances reinforce the point made above: it is not enough simply to count MSS, or even textual traditions, but rather the evidence they present must be weighed and evaluated on a variant-by-variant basis.

## 2    Weighing the evidence

In a sense, textual criticism involves the *reversal* of the process of corruption described above. That is, the textual critic seeks to understand the transmission process and the causes and effects of corruption that produced imperfect copies from the originals in order to reverse the process and thus work back from these surviving imperfect copies to reconstruct the lost originals. In many respects it is comparable to a detective solving a crime: one begins with the evidence, analyzes it, and then seeks to uncover the explanation that makes the best sense of all the evidence.

The classical method of textual criticism relied heavily on a genealogical approach that attempted to construct a "family tree" of surviving MSS in order to identify a "best manuscript" to follow in reconstructing the text of a document. But in the case of the New Testament this approach doesn't work, due primarily to the problem of "cross-pollination" discussed above.

Instead, today nearly all New Testament textual critics utilize an approach that has come to be known as *reasoned eclecticism*. This approach seeks to apply to the New Testament, on a passage-by-passage basis, all the evidence, tools, and criteria available for the task at hand in an effort to reconstruct the text. No one rule or principle can be applied nor any one MS (no matter how reliable) or group of MSS (no matter how large) followed in a mechanical or across-the-board fashion; each variation unit must be approached on its own merits and as possibly unique. Depending upon the circumstances and evidence in any given instance of variation, a reasoned eclecticism applies an appropriate combination of internal and external considerations, evaluating the character of the variants in light of the manuscript evidence and vice versa, in order to obtain a balanced view of the matter (see further Holmes 2002). This is the method and approach most widely practiced today and that lies behind, for example, recent translations such as the NRSV, REB, NASB, and NIV.

Differences in results obtained by the use of this method often reflect the differing views of the history of the text employed in conjunction with it. For example, Westcott and Hort (followed by the UBS and NA editorial committees) view the Byzantine tradition as dependent on the Alexandrian and/or Western traditions (and therefore incapable of independently preserving an original reading), while Robinson views the Alexandrian and Western as dependent on the Byzantine tradition (and therefore views neither as capable of independently preserving an original reading), whereas Zuntz (followed by Holmes) is persuaded that any one of the three main textual traditions is capable of independently preserving original readings (with the Alexandrian doing so far more often than the other two).

The primary current alternative to reasoned eclecticism is the "thoroughgoing eclecticism" espoused primarily by G. D. Kilpatrick and J. K. Elliott. This approach essentially considers only internal evidence when making textual decisions. Convinced that virtually all textual variation arose in the second century, prior to the time of the earliest surviving manuscripts, they therefore view manuscripts simply as carriers of variants, and not as evidence to be weighed in the process of reaching textual decisions.

## Evaluating Variant Readings: The Method in Practice

Reasoned eclecticism seeks to follow one fundamental guideline that governs all other considerations: *the variant most likely to be original is the one that best accounts for the existence of the others*. That is, when confronted with two or more variant readings at some point in the text, it asks, "Which one best explains, in terms of *both* external and internal evidence, the origin or the existence of the others?" The variant that can best account for *all* the evidence is most likely to represent the original reading of the text.

To be sure, within the framework established by this fundamental guideline several factors must be taken into consideration. Exactly which ones ought to be considered and how much weight is to be given to each depends upon the particular facts and circumstances in any given case. It may be helpful, therefore, to list the basic criteria for evaluating variant readings along with the various considerations that must be taken into account. We will then give an example of their application and use.

### 1  External evidence

There are four basic factors to consider when evaluating external evidence (i.e., the evidence provided by the MSS and other witnesses themselves). These are: (1) the relative date of the evidence (Does the earlier evidence support one variant more than the others? Are some variants without any early support?); (2) the geographic distribution of the evidence (generally, the broader the geographic distribution of the supporting witnesses the higher the probability that the variant may be original); (3) the genealogical relationships among the MSS (Do the MSS supporting a variant represent a variety of textual traditions, or are they all from a single one?); and (4) the relative quality of the witnesses (some MSS preserve original readings more often than others, and thus, when all other factors are even, may carry more weight).

### 2  Internal evidence

Two categories of internal evidence need to be considered: *transcriptional* (having to do with the habits and practices of scribes) and *intrinsic* (having to do with the author's style and vocabulary).

With regard to evaluating transcriptional factors, it is a matter of asking whether any of the readings may be the result of scribal slips, errors, or alterations in the copying process. In addition to the causes of error discussed above, one must take into account scribal tendencies to smooth over or resolve difficulties rather than create them, to harmonize passages, and to add rather than omit material. Any variant which appears to be due to one or more of these causes is always suspect.

As for intrinsic factors, the aim is to evaluate readings in light of what an author is most likely to have written. Relevant factors include the author's vocabulary and style, the flow of thought and logic of the immediate context (here interpretation may be decisive for the textual decision), congruence with the author's ideas or teachings, whether traditional material is being utilized, and, in the gospels, the Aramaic background of Jesus' teachings.

Obviously not all these factors will apply in every case, of course, and it is not uncommon for two or more of them to conflict. This is why none of them can be applied or followed in a mechanical fashion and why the fundamental guideline must always be kept in mind when evaluating the various kinds of evidence: the variant most likely to be original is the one that best accounts for, in terms of both external and internal considerations, the origin of the others.

## An Example of Reconstructing the Text

At Colossians 2:2, one finds a startling number of variant readings after the phrase "knowledge of the mystery":

1   "of God of Christ" ($\mathfrak{P}^{46}$; B/03; Clement of Alexandria; Hilary)
2   "of God" (three majuscules, a few minuscules)
3   "of the Christ" (minuscule 1739 + a few other witnesses)
4   "of God who is Christ" (D/06; Augustine; a few others)
5   "of God who is in Christ" (minuscule 33 and Ambrosiaster)
6   "of God the Father of Christ" (ℵ/01; 048)
7   "of God the Father of the Christ" (A/02; C/04; a few other witnesses)
8   "of the God and Father of the Christ" (a few majuscules + a few minuscules)
9   "of God the Father and of the Christ" (one majuscule + a few other witnesses)
10  "of the God and Father and of the Christ" (the Byzantine textual tradition of MSS)

The application of the basic guideline given above – *the variant most likely to be original is the one that best accounts for the existence of the others* – is helpful in making some sense of this welter of options. Variants 6–10 clearly share a common basic structure. Within this group, 8 and 9 have very slim manuscript support (and are probably expanded versions of 7), and may be set aside. The difference between 6 and 7 (whether "the" precedes "Christ") is a matter of a single letter in Greek; both readings are supported by relatively early manuscripts. Version 10 has the support of the large majority of MSS, but in this instance they are all relatively late. Theoretically, one can view 8, 9, and 10 as expansions of 6/7, or 6/7, 8, and 9 as shortened versions of 10. Given that descriptions of God tended to grow rather than shrink, and that the earliest evidence supports 6/7 rather than 10, the shorter version (6 or 7) is more likely to be the source of the rest than the alternative.

As for variants 1–5, 1 is quite ambiguous: it could mean "of God Christ," "of God, that is, of Christ," "of God's Christ," or "of God: Christ" (the first two identify God and Christ, while the last two specify Christ as the content of the mystery). Options 2, 3, 4, and 5 (which all have relatively slender external support) all are explainable either as attempts to clarify 1 and/or (in the case of 2 or 3) accidental scribal error, and so may be set aside as secondary.

So the profusion of variants may quickly be reduced to two main options, 1 and 6/7. Which of these two best explains the origin of the other one? If 6/7 were original, it is hard to see how options 1–5 would ever have arisen: 6/7 is clear, easily understandable, and hardly in need of clarification. But if 1 were original, then 6 – like options 2–5 – appears to be yet another "clarification" of 1's obscurity. Moreover, the external support for 1 (very early Alexandrian) is strengthened when one adds to it the support for options 2–5 (which, as clarifications of 1, indirectly witness to the existence of 1). So 1, which has good early and broad external manuscript support, and in terms of internal considerations best accounts for the existence of all the other variants, therefore may be judged to be the earliest form of the text (cf. NIV, NASB, NRSV).

To this point, the discussion of this complex set of variants has focused on the first goal of textual criticism: recovering the earliest form of the text. One may also consider all the variants in light of the second goal: to understand better how the text was transmitted by those who read and copied it. In this case, the many variants offer an example of the general tendency of those who transmitted it to clarify its meaning and (perhaps under the influence of liturgical expressions) expand the descriptions of God in the scriptures.

## Annotated Bibliography

Aland, Kurt and Barbara Aland. *The Text of the New Testament. An Introduction to the Critical Editions and to the Theory and Practice of Modern Textual Criticism*. 2nd edn., revised and enlarged. Leiden/Grand Rapids: Brill/Eerdmans, 1989. A major introduction to all aspects of the subject by two of the discipline's most influential experts.

Elliott, J. K. "The Case for Thoroughgoing Eclecticism." Pp. 101–24 in *Rethinking New Testament Textual Criticism*. Edited by D. A. Black. Grand Rapids: Baker, 2002. A clear presentation of the theory of "thoroughgoing eclecticism" by the leading proponent of the method.

Finegan, Jack. *Encountering New Testament Manuscripts: A Working Introduction to Textual Criticism*. Grand Rapids: Eerdmans, 1974. A "hands on" (using photographs of actual manuscripts) introduction to the basics of textual criticism.

Holmes, Michael W. "The Case for Reasoned Eclecticism." Pp. 77–100 in *Rethinking New Testament Textual Criticism*. Edited by D. A. Black. Grand Rapids: Baker, 2002. A leading statement of the theory of and reasons for the approach known as "reasoned eclecticism."

Metzger, Bruce M. *The Text of the New Testament: Its Transmission, Corruption, and Restoration*. 3rd, enlarged, edn. New York: Oxford University Press, 1992; 4th edn. with Bart D. Ehrman, 2005. A major introduction to all aspects of the subject that includes the best (and widely influential) introduction to the practice of textual criticism.

Omanson, Roger L. *A Textual Guide to the Greek New Testament*. Stuttgart: Deutsche Bibel-gesellschaft, 2006. An adaptation of Bruce M. Metzger, *A Textual Commentary on the Greek New Testament*, 2nd edn.: *A Companion Volume to the United Bible Societies' Greek New Testament* (Stuttgart: Deutsche Bibelgesellschaft/United Bible Societies, 1994) that makes the wealth of information available in the latter accessible to a wider audience.

Parker, D. C. *An Introduction to New Testament Manuscripts and their Texts*. Cambridge: Cambridge University Press, 2008. Not an "introduction" in the usual sense, this is an indispensable and invaluable guidebook to current projects, resources, approaches, and debates within the discipline.

Robinson, Maurice. "The Case for Byzantine Priority." Pp. 125–39 in *Interpreting the New Testament: Essays on Methods and Issues*. Edited by D. A. Black and D. S. Dockery. Nashville: Broadman & Holman, 2001. An accessible statement by the leading proponent of the approach.

## For Further Reading

Birdsall, J. Neville. "The New Testament Text." Pp. 308–77 in *The Cambridge History of the Bible*. Vol. 1: *From the Beginnings to Jerome*. Edited by P. R. Ackroyd and C. F. Evans. Cambridge: Cambridge University Press, 1970. Especially valuable for its century-by-century survey of the transmission of the New Testament text.

Birdsall, J. Neville. "The Recent History of New Testament Textual Criticism (from Westcott and Hort, 1881, to the present)." Pp. 99–197 in *Aufstieg und Niedergang der römischen Welt*, 2.26.1. Edited by H. Temporini and W. Haase. Berlin and New York: De Gruyter, 1992. A magisterial survey of an important century of research.

Birdsall, J. Neville. *Collected Papers in Greek and Georgian Textual Criticism*. Texts and Studies 3rd series, 3. Piscataway, NJ: Gorgias Press, 2006. Chapters 1, 2, 5, and 9 are especially impor-tant with regard to methodology.

Colwell, Ernest C. *Studies in Methodology in Textual Criticism of the New Testament*. Leiden: Brill, 1969. A foundational collection of essays by premier practitioner and theoretician; an important critic of Westcott and Hort.

Ehrman, Bart D. *The Orthodox Corruption of Scripture: The Effect of Early Christological Controversies on the Text of the New Testament*. New York: Oxford University Press, 1993. Demonstrates that (and how) the transmitters of the New Testament text made sure its meaning was clear to its readers.

Ehrman, Bart D. and Michael W. Holmes. *The Text of the New Testament in Contemporary Research: Essays on the Status Quaestionis*. Studies and Documents, 46. Grand Rapids: Eerdmans, 1995; 2nd rev. edn., 2010. An authoritative set of essays setting out the present state of the question on a very wide range of topics and issues.

Elliott, Keith and Ian Moir. *Manuscripts and the Text of the New Testament: An Introduction for English Readers*. Edinburgh: T. &. T. Clark, 1995. A fine short introduction to the topic.

Epp, Eldon J. "It's All About Variants: A Variant-Conscious Approach to New Testament Textual Criticism." *Harvard Theological Review* 100 (2007), 275–308. Proposes both a new format for presenting variant readings and a "unified" definition of New Testament textual criticism that combines the two goals discussed above.

Epp, Eldon J. *Perspectives on New Testament Textual Criticism: Collected Essays, 1962–2004*. Supplements to *Novum Testamentum*, 116. Leiden and Boston: Brill, 2005. A foundational collection of essays for understanding many contemporary issues and debates.

Holmes, Michael W. "Textual Criticism." Pp. 4–73 in *Interpreting the New Testament: Essays on Methods and Issues*. Edited by D. A. Black and D. S. Dockery. Nashville: Broadman & Holman, 2001. A basic introduction that includes a brief history of New Testament textual criticism.

Holmes, Michael W. "The *Text of the Epistles* Sixty Years After: An Assessment of Günther Zuntz's Contribution to Text-Critical Methodology and History." Pp. 107–31 in *Transmission and Reception: New Testament Text-Critical and Exegetical Studies*. Edited by J. Childers and D. C. Parker. Texts and Studies, 3rd series, 4. Piscataway, NJ: Gorgias Press, 2006. Highlights the significance of Zuntz for contemporary textual criticism.

Holmes, Michael W. "The Text of P46: Evidence of the Earliest 'Commentary' on Romans?" Pp. 189–206 in *New Testament Manuscripts: Their Text and their World*. Edited by Tobias Nicklas. Leiden: Brill, 2006. An investigation of an important aspect of the early transmission of the New Testament text.

Kilpatrick, G. D. *The Principles and Practice of New Testament Textual Criticism: Collected Essays of G. D. Kilpatrick*. Edited by J. K. Elliott. BETL, 96. Louvain: Louvain University Press, 1990. Collected essays by the leading proponent of "thoroughgoing" eclecticism.

Metzger, Bruce M. *The Early Versions of the New Testament: Their Origin, Transmission, and Limitations*. Oxford: Clarendon Press, 1977. An outstanding and thorough survey of the subject; updated by the relevant chapters in Ehrman and Holmes.

Metzger, Bruce M. *Manuscripts of the Greek Bible: An Introduction to Palaeography*. New York: Oxford University Press, 1981. A foundational introduction to the topic.

Parker, D. C. *The Living Text of the Gospels*. Cambridge: Cambridge University Press, 1997. An important discussion of variations in the text by a major advocate of the second goal of textual criticism discussed above.

Reynolds, L. D. and N. G. Wilson, *Scribes and Scholars: A Guide to the Transmission of Greek and Latin Literature*. 2nd edn. Oxford: Clarendon Press, 1974. A magisterial survey by two leading classical scholars.

Westcott, B. F. and F. J. A. Hort. *The New Testament in the Original Greek*, [ii] *Introduction* [and] *Appendix*. Cambridge: Macmillan, 1881; 2nd edn. 1896. Hort's carefully reasoned statement of the fundamental principles upon which he and Westcott built their landmark edition of the Greek New Testament is still required reading for all New Testament textual critics.

Zuntz, Günther. *The Text of the Epistles: A Disquisition upon the Corpus Paulinum*. London: The British Academy, 1953. An outstanding exposition of "reasoned eclecticism" in both theory and practice by a classicist who turned his attention to the New Testament; offers a major corrective to Westcott and Hort's view of the history of the transmission of the New Testament text.

CHAPTER 6

# The Canons of the New Testament

## Leslie Baynes

At one point in the novel *The Da Vinci Code*, a character named Teabing declares: "The Bible did not arrive by fax from heaven ... the Bible is a product of *man* ... the Bible did not fall magically from the clouds." Regardless of the dubious historical value of *The Da Vinci Code* (Ehrman 2004), the book is correct on this one point, at least: the Bible did not fall from heaven. The process by which twenty-seven disparate Greek books written by many different authors became the New Testament as we know it was long and tortuous, and many aspects of it remain unclear. The best place to start in beginning to understand it is with basic definitions.

The word "canon" comes from the Greek *kanon*, a straight, inflexible rod. The root is a Mediterranean word that appears in Hebrew as *qaneh*, "reed." Because such a rod could be used for measurement, the term became synonymous with a measuring stick or ruler. When it was used to "measure" abstractions, "canon" took on the meaning of a rule or a norm. It is in this sense that it appears in Galatians 6:16: "As for those who will follow this rule [*kanon*], peace be upon them." This passage and 1 Corinthians 10:13, 15, 16 comprise its total usage in the New Testament. In the second century proto-orthodox Church Fathers began to write of the "rule of faith (or truth)" (*kanon tēs pisteōs* or *kanon tēs alētheias*) as the norm or measurement of emerging orthodoxy in the face of competing interpretations of Christianity (cf. Irenaeus, *Against Heresies*, 3.4.1–2; Clement of Alexandria, *Miscellanies*, 4.15; Tertullian, *Prescription Against Heresies*, 12–13). The word could also signify a list, but its first known use to designate a specific list of authoritative Christian books appears relatively late, in Athanasius' *Decrees of the Synod of Nicaea* (written shortly after 350 CE), where he declares that the *Shepherd of Hermas* is not "in the canon" (*mē on ek tou kanonos*) (Metzger 289–93). It is in fact Athanasius himself, who, in his thirty-ninth festal letter (367 CE), compiled the first canon list that contains the twenty-seven books of our own New Testament, no more and no less, though he does not list them in their modern order. Just because such a list was in existence at this time, however, does not mean that the New Testament canon was closed; that is, that everyone in Christendom accepted only those books. Athanasius did not speak for the universal church, and diversity in the lists and in other documents continued after 367, particularly regarding the book of Revelation and some of the Catholic epistles.

Just as the term "canon" could have multiple meanings in the ancient world, so too have modern scholars understood the concept in diverse ways. These variations in understanding influence their determination of what makes a canon a canon, and clarifying what one means by it is an important starting point in any discussion of the term. An example of this is the debate between two early giants of canon research, Theodor Zahn (1838–1933) and Adolf von Harnack (1851–1930). Through an examination of citations in the Church Fathers, Zahn determined that he could say "without anachronism" that there was a New Testament by the end of the first century (Barton 1998: 3). Harnack disagreed, arguing that there was a real difference between a simple knowledge and/or citation of a book that would later be a part of the New Testament and "citing it as an authority," "regarding it as 'Scripture'," and "assigning it a place in a restricted, official 'canon'" (Barton 1998: 4). Harnack's critique of Zahn laid the foundation for all later investigations of the New Testament canon, eliciting questions that have not been completely resolved to this day: for instance, how can one tell when ancient authors regarded a text as an authority? Is regarding a text as an authority the same thing as regarding it as scripture? When and how did early Christians develop "canon consciousness"? In other words, regarding the emergence of the New Testament canon, we may ask, "What did they know, and when did they know it?"

One place to go to begin answering these questions is to ancient canon lists, most of which date to the fourth century and later. However, as with other areas of study concerning the early church, while we possess much raw information, its full interpretation and contextualization is often elusive. Nowhere is this more evident than regarding the canon list that some allege to be the earliest, the so-called Muratorian fragment, which has been one of the most contentious objects in canon studies. An inquiry into the content of and controversies surrounding the fragment can illustrate, at least *in nuce*, many aspects of the development and academic study of the New Testament canon.

Published by Ludovico Antonio Muratori in 1740, the Muratorian fragment first attracted attention because of its barbarous Latin. The most disputed point about it since the mid-twentieth century, however, concerns its date. Prior to that time, there was general consensus that its reference to the *Shepherd of Hermas* dated the original composition of the Muratorian fragment to the mid- to late second century. While discussing the acceptability of reading the *Shepherd* publicly in church, the author of the canon notes that "Hermas wrote the *Shepherd* very recently, in our times, in the city of Rome, while bishop Pius, his brother, was occupying the chair of the church of the city of Rome." Pius was bishop of Rome from approximately 140 to 154 CE. If the canon were indeed written shortly after his episcopate, postulating a late second-century date for it would be appropriate. Muratori himself dated it to about 196, but B. F. Westcott argued that it could have been produced as early as 170. Therefore Westcott could write, based in large part upon the evidence in the Muratorian fragment, that "from the close of the second century the history of the Canon is simple, and its proof clear" (Westcott 1980: 6).

Although scholarly readers tussled over virtually every aspect of the Muratorian fragment, its date was generally not disputed in any serious way until 1973, when Albert Sundberg published a paper that challenged the second-century dating of the fragment. He was followed most notably by G. M. Hahneman in 1992. Both argued that the canon dated not to the second but to the fourth century, and not to Rome, but to the eastern empire. One of the central points of their argumentation hinged upon the difficult Latin of the text, especially in the section having to do with the *Shepherd*. The Sundberg–Hahneman hypothesis has not won overwhelming support (Verheyden 2003: 498), but, regardless of the number of scholars who accepted the later date, Sundberg and Hahneman's proposals did have the effect of problematizing the application of the fragment to any reconstruction of the development of the Christian canon; any subsequent mention of the fragment had to be qualified in some way to take their work into account. More recently, however, Joseph Verheyden, in a sizeable essay, refutes Sundberg and Hahneman, arguing persuasively that the earlier consensus about the fragment was correct: it is early and western rather than late and eastern. Thus he brings the debate full circle.

If the Muratorian fragment does indeed date to the second century, what aspects of the development of the New Testament canon might it help illuminate? Unfortunately, simply by virtue of accepting an early date for this particular manuscript, one may still disagree with Westcott's assertion that the history of the canon is simple and clear. The Muratorian fragment is not the only canon list in antiquity, and these lists demonstrate considerable diversity in content and order of books to the end of the fourth century and beyond. Furthermore, canon lists are not the only evidence to take into consideration when charting the development that produced the current twenty-seven-book canon of the New Testament. Many other texts from the Church Fathers give us indispensable information as well.

One does not have to accept an early date for the Muratorian canon in order to find it helpful in coming to an understanding of the process of canonization in the early church, however. As a matter of fact, whatever its date, it touches upon almost every issue that arises when one investigates that process. For the remainder of this essay, therefore, I will use a standard English translation of the Muratorian canon (Metzger 1987: 305–7) as a launching pad for further discussion of New Testament canon development as a whole. We will begin with the gospels, then move to the letters of Paul, the Catholic epistles, and the book of Revelation. Along the way we will compare and contrast various canon lists, examine testimony from the early church, discuss criteria for canonicity, and evaluate the possible influence of Gnosticism, Marcionism, and other groups upon the development of the New Testament canon.

The Muratorian fragment begins in mid-sentence with what is apparently a description of the Gospel of Mark, which presumably follows Matthew in the list. The first full sentence talks about the Gospel of Luke. The anonymous author of the fragment admits that Luke, "the well-known physician," had never seen Jesus in the flesh, but that Luke was a companion of Paul. Thus arises one of the first and most important criteria of canonicity for proto-orthodox Christians: who wrote the work under consideration? What authority did he possess to transmit traditions reliably? Was he an apostle or someone connected with an apostle? The closer a putative author was to being an eyewitness of Jesus' ministry, the better the chances of his book being acknowledged. For example, although Luke was not an associate of Jesus, he was at least a companion of Paul, himself an apostle after the fact. A long-standing tradition of authorship passed down through reliable sources seemed in most cases to be proof enough for the Fathers. A prime example of this tradition is the testimony of Papias (d. ca. 130), "the hearer of John, who was a companion of Polycarp and one of the ancients," and the first witness available to us who describes the genesis of the gospels of Mark (whom Papias claimed was the companion of Peter) and Matthew (Eusebius, *Ecclesiastical History*, 3.39.14– 16). We have no direct evidence that the early church ever challenged the gospels' attributions to Matthew, Mark, Luke, and John, but it did question the authorship of other books that eventually made up the New Testament, including Hebrews and the Revelation of John, as we will see.

Closely related to the criterion of authority or apostolicity is the criterion of ortho- doxy. Even if a document claimed apostolic authorship, if it did not cohere to the emerg- ing "rule [*kanon*] of truth/faith," it could not have been written by the putative author in the eyes of the proto-orthodox Fathers. Remarks of Eusebius of Caesarea (d. ca. 340) reflect this concern. Eusebius writes that:

> [we have distinguished] between those writings which, according to the tradition of the Church, are true and genuine and recognized, from the others which differ from them in that they are not canonical [*endiathēkous*], but disputed, yet nevertheless are known to most churchmen. [And this we have done] in order that we might be able to know both these same writings and also those which the heretics put forward under the name of the apostles; including for instance, such books as the Gospel of Peter, of Thomas, of Matthias ... Moreover, the character of the style also is far removed from apostolic usage, and the thought and purport of their contents are completely out of harmony with true orthodoxy and clearly show that they are the forgeries of heretics. (*Ecclesiastical History*, 3.25.6–7)

The books named in early canon lists were in competition with other documents produced by various factions in the early church. What were these factions? The most formidable was Gnosticism, represented above in Eusebius' list by the *Gospel of Thomas*. Full-fledged Gnosticism arose in the second century, and apologists such as Irenaeus and Tertullian combated it vociferously and at great length. A complex, multifaceted system, Gnosticism was the greatest theological threat to proto-orthodoxy in the second century. Since what we know as "traditional" Christianity ultimately prevailed, it is sometimes hard to remember that the Gnostics, too, saw themselves as legitimate Christians. Gnostics postulated that the God who created the physical world was evil, that all creation was evil, and that all bodies were evil. Thus Tertullian, in outlining his *kanon* of faith, wrote that "there is one only God, and that He is none other than the Creator of the world, who produced all things out of nothing through His own Word," that Jesus was made flesh in Mary's womb, and that he was truly resurrected from the dead, all of which points Gnostics rejected (*Prescription against Heretics*, 13). Gnostic writers were prolific and apparently persuasive, and they wrote many works that they called gospels, including the gospels of Thomas, Philip, and Mary, among others.

How many gospels may have been in circulation in the early church? Dan Brown's popular novel, *The Da Vinci Code*, claims that there were over eighty, and that Constantine (d. 337) was the final arbiter of which ones "made it into the canon." Both of these claim are incorrect. In an analysis of all available data, Charles Hedrick has hypothesized that there are thirty-four ancient gospels that we can identify in some way or another, either because we possess the text itself (i.e., the gospels of Matthew or Thomas), evidence of the source of an existing gospel (i.e., Q), or quotations from or titles of gospels that have otherwise vanished (i.e., the *Gospel of Basilides*). Proto-orthodox Christians clung to only four gospels, however, and none of our canon lists attests anything different (but see Gamble 1985: 34–5). Why these four and no more? Writing around 180 CE, 150 years before Constantine, Irenaeus of Lyons, our earliest source to discuss the issue, offers a lovely and poetic flight of fantasy about the four gospels that tells us nothing historical. "It is not possible that the Gospels can be either more or fewer in number than they are," he writes, "because there are four corners of the earth, four principal winds, four beasts before the throne of God in the book of Revelation, and four covenants that God made with humanity" (*Against Heresies*, 3.11.8). Origen, too (d. ca. 254), writes that the four gospels are "the only indisputable ones in the Church of God under heaven" (as recorded by Eusebius, *Ecclesiastical History*, 6.25.4). Eusebius doesn't even bother to name them individually; he simply calls them "the holy quaternion of the gospels" (*Ecclesiastical History*, 3.25.1).

It seems that a collection of four separate and distinct gospels first appeared in the western part of the empire (Lyons, Rome) and gradually was accepted as the norm in the east (as attested by Origen and Eusebius). In Syria, however, it was a different story. There not a collection but a harmonization of the four gospels was immensely popular. Around 170 CE, the Syrian Christian Tatian produced the *Diatessaron*, a word translated literally as "through the four" (gospels), which interwove the accounts of Matthew, Mark, Luke, and John, as well as some material that does not appear in any of them, into a continuous narrative. The *Diatessaron* simultaneously attests the importance of the four gospels in this region of the church and demonstrates quite a different mode of holding them authoritative than, for instance, Irenaeus did when he highlighted them individually.

The production and popularity of the *Diatessaron* is not surprising, for the early church certainly recognized differences in structure, chronology, and content between the gospels. Indeed, the original meaning of the word "gospel" was not "written document," even less "documents," but an oral proclamation, the "good news" of Jesus Christ. Thus Irenaeus, even while poetically extolling the beauty and fitness of the church's four different written gospels, writes that Jesus the Word "has given us the Gospel under four aspects, but bound together by one Spirit" (*Against Heresies*, 3.11.8). The Muratorian canon echoes this language in its discussion of John, the gospel that differs so greatly from the other three: "Though various elements may be taught in the individual books of the Gospels, nonetheless this makes no difference to the faith of believers, since by the one sovereign Spirit all things have been declared in all." Appearances to the contrary, these texts claimed that, regardless of the diversity of the four gospels, the Spirit guaranteed unity in their essentials.

To summarize the main points regarding the gospels: as many as thirty-four gospels circulated in the early church, but four, no more and no less, were accepted for use in the church, in the west by the mid- to late second century and slightly later in the east. Proto-orthodox Christians distinguished among the many gospels in circulation based on their perceived apostolic authorship (i.e., Matthew or John) or because their authors purported close connections to the apostles (i.e., Mark and Luke), and because the accepted gospels were consistent with the *kanon*, or rule of faith, in fighting against competing forms of Christianity, particularly Gnosticism.

After the gospels, the Muratorian fragment mentions Acts, written by Luke, who was, according to the author of the fragment, an eyewitness to the events narrated therein. Luke compiled the Acts of the Apostles "for the most excellent Theophilus" (Luke 1:3; cf. Acts 1:1). Always and everywhere the early church rightly recognizes the same person who wrote the Gospel of Luke as the author of Acts (cf. Origen in Eusebius, *Ecclesiastical History*, 6.15.14), but the two books never appear as a pair in any of the canon lists or ancient manuscripts. The position of Acts varies in canon lists and codices, sometimes appearing after the gospels, sometimes after the epistles of Paul, and sometimes at or near the end of the lists (Gamble 2002: 591–7).

Next in the Muratorian canon are the letters of Paul. It may be that Paul's writings were the first Christian documents to be regarded as "scripture," as 2 Peter suggests:

> Therefore, beloved, while you are waiting for these things, strive to be found by him at peace, without spot or blemish; and regard the patience of our Lord as salvation. So also our beloved brother Paul wrote to you according to the wisdom given him, speaking of this as he does in all his letters. There are some things in them hard to understand, which the ignorant and unstable twist to their own destruction, as they do the other scriptures [*graphai*]. (2 Pet. 3:14–15)

*Graphai* is the word the gospels and Paul use for "the scriptures," i.e., the Hebrew scriptures, when they quote them as authorities. 2 Peter was written at the beginning of the second century, probably around 120, and so it is very likely that sufficient time had passed by then to reckon Paul's works as "scripture" alongside more traditional authorities.

The letters of Paul are the earliest Christian documents that have survived, and they may also be the earliest Christian documents gathered and promulgated as a group. "The canon is in the main a collection of collections," writes Harry Gamble (2002: 275), and we have already seen that by the end of the second century the four gospels were appropriated as a group. We cannot specify what Pauline letters the author of 2 Peter had in mind at the beginning of the second century, but within several decades after he wrote, a figure emerges who had a sharply delineated list of his own: Marcion.

In the eyes of proto-orthodox Christians, Marcion and his followers were a formidable threat. Why? Marcion (d. ca. 160) believed that there were two gods, the god of the Jews and the god of Jesus. The former was an illegitimate tyrant fixated upon the law, while the latter was a god of love. Marcion rejected the Hebrew scriptures and embraced Paul, with his vexed treatment of the "works of the law," as the true expositor of the Christian God. Luke's gospel to the Gentiles (purged of its Jewish bits), was the only gospel in Marcion's list of approved scriptures. Irenaeus (*Against Heresies*, 3.11.7), writes that Marcion "circumcised" the Gospel of Luke, a finely ironical choice of words under the circumstances. Similarly, Marcion selected only those letters of Paul that undergirded his theological beliefs, submitting them, too, to a de-Judaizing scalpel. He had ten, in this order: Galatians, 1 and 2 Corinthians, Romans, 1 and 2 Thessalonians, Laodiceans (= Ephesians), Colossians (with Philemon?), and Philippians (Gamble 2002: 283).

Since Marcion was the first to draw up a "closed canon," so to speak, his influence and his possible impact on the canonical process of proto-orthodox Christianity is an important topic to consider. Early in the twentieth century, Adolf von Harnack argued that Marcion was the *sine qua non* of the New Testament canon, the one without whom it would not exist, but this opinion now finds few proponents (i.e., Miller 2004). At this point in time, many who study the New Testament canon agree that Marcion was an important figure in the ongoing process, but not the one who sparked it (Barton 1997, 2002; Gamble 2002: 284). As Barton writes,

> Marcion's concern was to *exclude* books that he disapproved of from his "canon." He was not assembling a collection of Christian books, but making a (very restricted) selection from the corpus of texts which already existed and which must already have been recognized as sacred by many in the church – otherwise he would not have needed to insist on abolishing them. (Barton 2002: 343)

It is important to note that Barton does not argue that there was a universally acknowledged, closed canon by the middle of the second century, but simply that certain books were probably "recognized as sacred by many in the church" at that time. Marcion was a step along the way in the canonical process, neither its beginning nor its end.

Collections of Paul's letters may have appeared long before Marcion, perhaps even during Paul's lifetime. David Trobisch argues that "Paul himself collected and gathered some of his own letters" (Trobisch 1994: vii), specifically 1 and 2 Corinthians, Romans, and Galatians, in order to articulate his own agenda regarding the Gentiles in opposition to the apostolic "pillars" of the Jerusalem church. An intriguing thesis in many ways, Trobisch's work is problematic and has not attracted widespread support (Gamble 2002: 285).

The Muratorian fragment insists that Paul wrote to only seven churches by name (the Corinthians, Ephesians, Philippians, Colossians, Galatians, Thessalonians, and Romans). The author of the fragment grants that Paul did write to the Corinthians and Thessalonians twice, "yet it is clearly recognizable that there is one Church spread throughout the whole extent of the earth. For John also, in the Apocalypse, though he writes to seven churches, nonetheless speaks to all." This insistence that Paul writes to seven churches only, on the analogy of the seven letters to the seven churches in Revelation 2–3, may support the Sundberg–Hahneman argument that the fragment is late, for the author seems to be trying his utmost to squeeze the letters of Paul into a pre-existing schema of seven. He runs into further difficulties when he has to add Paul's personal letters to Philemon, Timothy, and Titus to the mix. They, though addressed to individuals, "are held sacred in the esteem in the Church catholic for the regulation of ecclesiastical discipline," he writes. In other words, although Paul wrote these letters to individuals, they are applicable to a larger ecclesiastical context.

Just as the early collaters of the gospels had to grapple with the problems of plurality (Why four? Why not just one? Does a collection of multiple gospels imply that any one of them by itself is insufficient?), so too the Christians who collected the letters of Paul had to deal with the problem of particularity. Paul's letters were occasional; he wrote to specific churches about specific issues at specific times. Because of this, later communities who revered Paul's letters could not ignore certain questions: What do the epistles that Paul wrote to Corinth, to Philippi, to Rome, and so on, have to say to the larger church? What relevance do they have? The Muratorian fragment demonstrates one response to those difficulties – though writing to many churches, Paul in fact writes to the church universal. Other canon lists escape the problems inherent in the Muratorian canon's sevenfold scheme by referring to Paul's letters as a set of fourteen, which is of course double seven. This is spelled out explicitly in the canon of Amphilochius (d. after 394): "Paul having written to the churches twice seven epistles ...." A grouping of fourteen letters of Paul appears in the canons of Cyril of Alexandria (ca. 350), the Synod of Laodicea (ca. 363), Athanasius (367), Gregory of Nazianzus (ca. 329–89), and the list approved by the Apostolic Canons (ca. 380). To make Paul's letters add up to fourteen, however, Hebrews must be counted as one of them.

"The relation of Hebrews to Paul and his letters is an old chestnut," Harry Gamble observes (2002: 284). It appears in $\mathfrak{P}^{46}$, the earliest extant manuscript of Paul's letters, between Romans and 1 Corinthians. The author of the Muratorian canon either did not know of it or purposely and without explanation omitted it. Origen spent a fair amount of time musing over its style and content, comparing and contrasting it with acknowledged letters of Paul. He concludes,

> If I gave my opinion, I should say that the thoughts are those of the apostle, but the style and composition belong to some one who remembered the apostle's teachings and wrote down ... what had been said by his teacher. Therefore, if any church holds that this Epistle is by Paul, let it be commended for this also. For it is not without reason that the men of old time have handed it down as Paul's. But who wrote the Epistle, in truth, God knows. (Eusebius, Ecclesiastical History, 6.25.13)

Origen's ambivalent attitude about Hebrews foreshadows later reactions to the book. The Cheltenham canon (ca. 360) notes only thirteen letters of Paul; presumably Hebrews is the odd one out. The canon of Amphilochius of Iconium (ca. 394) lists it last of Paul's letters, and notes that "some say the one to the Hebrews is spurious, not saying well, for the grace is genuine." The letter to the Hebrews, then, presents a test case for the criterion of apostolicity.

To summarize the main points regarding the letters of Paul: by the first quarter of the second century, at least, an undefined collection of Paul's letters was recognized as "scripture" (2 Peter 3:14–15). Marcion's selection of ten letters is the first known designation of a group of Pauline letters as a "canon," though Marcion may have been dependent in some way on earlier collections, perhaps even one put together by Paul himself (Trobisch 1994). Proto-orthodox Christians tended to group Paul's letters into sets of seven or fourteen, with Hebrews acting as something of a wild card in those numerical schemas.

The so-called Catholic epistles were first called so by Eusebius in the fourth century: "Such is the story of James, whose is said to be the first of the Epistles called Catholic. It is to be observed that its authenticity is denied, since few of the ancients quote it, as is also the case with the seven called Catholic; nevertheless we know that these letters have been used publicly with the rest in most churches" (Ecclesiastical History, 2.23.25). There are several points worthy of note regarding these texts. First, compared to the other collections in the New Testament (the gospels and Paul), representatives of the

Catholic or general epistles experience the most difficulty being accepted in the church. Second, as Eusebius notes, often the Catholic epistles, like the Pauline, appear explicitly as a group of seven. The third introduces another criterion of canonicity in the early church: usage. Even if, according to Eusebius, the Catholic epistles are not "authentic," they are nonetheless important enough to some churches to be used for public reading (cf. the status of the *Shepherd of Hermas* in the Muratorian canon). Eusebius admits that, whatever his judgment about their authenticity, the Catholic epistles were indeed being read publicly.

The Catholic epistles as they appear in the modern New Testament are indeed seven: James, 1 and 2 Peter, 1, 2, and 3 John, and Jude. Of these, 1 Peter and 1 John seem to be the most well known and utilized in the second and third centuries (Gamble 2002: 287), but their "sequels," 2 Peter and 2 and 3 John, were not. Papias quoted from 1 Peter and 1 John (Eusebius, *Ecclesiastical History*, 3.39.17), and they are the only two of the Catholic epistles that Eusebius does not place in the "disputed" section of his canon list (*Ecclesiastical History*, 3.25.2–3). Origen believed that the apostle Peter wrote the first letter that appears in his name, "and possibly also a second, but this is disputed." In fact, Origen's acknowledgment of the existence of 2 Peter is the first time it is mentioned at all in the early church. Second, Peter itself is the first document to use the book of Jude, as 2 Peter 2:1–22 incorporates Jude 4–16. Origen also believed that John wrote "an epistle of a very few lines; and, it may be, a second and a third, for not all say these are genuine." The Muratorian canon does not mention James and 1–2 Peter, but it does accept two (unspecified) Johannine epistles and Jude. Some canon lists of the fourth century, however, instead of listing the epistles individually, include them only as a set of seven; for instance, the canons of Cyril of Jerusalem, Athanasius, and Amphilochius (which mentions "seven" but notes that several are disputed), and the canon approved by the Synod of Laodicea.

It is notable that the Muratorian canon lists the Wisdom of Solomon immediately following the Catholic epistles of Jude and the two letters of John (cf. the canon of Epiphanius). Wisdom, written in the first century BCE, usually appears in the "Writings" division of the Septuagint. Just as the disparate group known as the "Writings" was the third and last division of the Jewish scriptures to come together, and the rabbis contested the authority of certain of its books (i.e., Esther and Ecclesiastes) into the second century CE at least, so the collection of seven Catholic epistles is the last of the three major divisions of the New Testament to cohere and is the most disputed.

But while the Catholic epistles are the last *collection* in the New Testament, they do not include the Revelation/Apocalypse of John, the final book in the modern canon. This book has had a notoriously checkered history of reception, especially in the east, in part because of the ways some of its readers have interpreted it. The Muratorian canon accepted both it and the Apocalypse of Peter, though it noted that the latter should not be read in church (cf. the criterion of usage). Other writers, however, were not quite so sanguine about it. Eusebius demonstrates the general ambivalence regarding Revelation's status when he places it initially, "if it seems right," in the category of recognized books in his canon, and then immediately turns around and places it in his list of spurious books, again "if it seem right" because it is "rejected by some" (*Ecclesiastical History*, 3.25.2, 4).

Elsewhere Eusebius offers a wealth of information about the reception of the book. One of the primary problems with it was the dubious use that objectionable groups made of it. First were the followers of Cerinthus, who preached a future physical reign of Christ on earth, a kingdom allegedly characterized by sensual pleasure and revelry. Indeed, opponents of his followers claimed that Cerinthus himself had authored the Apocalypse since it served so well to propagate his ideas (*Ecclesiastical History*, 7.25.2–3). Then there were the Montanists, a popular charismatic and prophetic group. Their use of the Revelation of John led a certain Gaius, an opponent of Montanism, to reject it for its "garish imagery and millenarianism" (Metzger 1987: 104–5). Other opponents of Montanism, the so-called "Alogoi," not only rejected the Apocalypse, but also defamed it by attributing it to the aforementioned and reviled Cerinthus (Epiphanius, *Haer.*, 51.3). The criterion of apostolicity could be a double-edged sword.

On the whole the church of the west accepted the Apocalypse more readily than the church in the east. Even today some non-Chalcedonian Christians reject it, and although it is included in the canon of the present-day Orthodox Church, it is read not at all in its lectionary cycle. For the Orthodox, as in the early church, the authority of a book is proportional to its public reading in the liturgy (again, the criterion of usage; see Prokurat 1994). The situation is similar in the Roman Catholic Church. Although the Apocalypse found a sure place for itself in the west through the allegorizing herme-neutics of Augustine, and it was named unequivocally in the canon list of the Council of Trent (1546), it is read rarely in the Roman Catholic Church – only seven times in the three-year cycle of Sunday readings, appropriately enough considering the signifi-cance of the number seven in the Apocalypse.

In conclusion, the New Testament certainly did not fall from heaven. The canon of the New Testament grew in fits and starts over a period of several hundred years. No one person or group in the early church wrote or gathered its various books with a mind to a finished product, a point that is sometimes hard to grasp in hindsight. Even after many churches shared the same list of authoritative books, some diversity still existed based on local preferences. Apostolicity, orthodoxy, and usage in the church were the main criteria by which different groups evaluated the books that would ulti-mately comprise the New Testament. To the best of our knowledge, the gospels were the first to be recognized as a closed collection (four and no more), while dissension continued rather longer regarding a few of the letters of Paul (particularly concerning his authorship of Hebrews), some of the Catholic epistles, and the book of Revelation. While the New Testament canon is now closed, discussion about its origins and signifi-cance shows no signs of abating.

## Annotated Bibliography

Auwers, J. M., and H. J. de Jonge (eds.). *The Biblical Canons*. Bibliotheca Ephemeridum Theologicarum Lovaniensium 163. Leuven: Leuven University Press, 2003. A valuable collection of essays from the fiftieth Colloquium Biblicum Lovaniense (2001) on the Jewish and Christian canons; for more advanced students.

Barton, John. *Making the Christian Bible*. London: Darton, Longman and Todd, 1997.

Barton, John. "Marcion Revisited." Pp. 341–54 in *The Canon Debate*. Edited by Lee M. McDonald and James A. Sanders. Peabody: Hendrickson, 2002.

Barton, John. *Holy Writings, Sacred Text: The Canon in Early Christianity*. Louisville: Westminster John Knox Press, 1998. An excellent resource for the history of the modern academic debate about the development of the New Testament canon.

Ehrman, Bart. *Truth and Fiction in The Da Vinci Code*. Oxford: Oxford University Press, 2004. Ehrman offers non-tendentious corrections of the novel; he focuses on the history and litera- ture of the early church, including the development of the New Testament canon. For a general audience.

Gamble, Harry Y. *The New Testament Canon: Its Making and Meaning*. Guides to Biblical Scholarship. New Testament Series. Philadelphia: Fortress Press, 1985. A clear, concise treatment of the development of the canon; an excellent general introduction to the issues for beginners by a respected expert in the field.

Gamble, Harry Y. "The New Testament Canon: Recent Research and the Status Quaestionis." Pp. 267–94 in *The Canon Debate*. Edited by Lee Martin McDonald and James A. Sanders. Hendrickson: Peabody, MA, 2002. Updating of Gamble's ongoing work in studies of the New Testament canon.

Hedrick, Charles. "The Thirty-Four Gospels: Diversity and Division among the Earliest Christians." *Bible Review* 18 (2002), 20–31, 46–7. Surveys all available evidence to determine that early Christians wrote thirty-four gospels.

Hengel, Martin. *The Four Gospels and the One Gospel of Jesus Christ: An Investigation of the Collection and Origin of the Canonical Gospels*. Harrisburg, PA: Trinity Press International, 2000. Hengel argues that the gospels never circulated without their superscriptions (i.e., "the gospel according to Matthew").

McDonald, Lee M. and James A. Sanders (eds.). *The Canon Debate*. Peabody: Hendrickson, 2002. A voluminous and indispensable collection of essays on virtually every aspect of the Jewish and Christian canons.

Metzger, Bruce M. *The Canon of the New Testament*. Oxford: Clarendon Press, 1987. The standard scholarly introduction to the topic; a classic in the field of canon studies.

Miller, John W. *How the Bible Came to Be: Exploring the Narrative and Message*. New York: Paulist Press, 2004. Miller follows von Harnack in arguing that Marcion was the catalyst for the formation of the New Testament canon.

Prokurat, Michael. "Orthodox Interpretation of Scripture." In *The Bible in the Churches: How Various Christians Interpret the Scriptures*. 2nd edn. Edited by Kenneth Hagen. Marquette Studies in Theology, 4. Milwaukee: Marquette University Press, 1994.

Trobisch, David. *Paul's Letter Collection: Tracing the Origins*. Minneapolis: Fortress Press, 1994. An intriguing but problematic argument for the case that Paul gathered and published a collection of his own letters during his lifetime.

Trobisch, David. *The First Edition of the New Testament*. Oxford: Oxford University Press, 2000. Trobisch argues that a "final redaction" or canonical edition of the New Testament existed by the end of the second century.

Verheyden, J. "The Canon Muratori: A Matter of Dispute." Pp. 487–556 in *The Biblical Canons*. Edited by J. M. Auwers and H. J. de Jonge. Bibliotheca Ephemeridum Theologicarum Lovaniensium, 63. Leuven: Leuven University Press, 2003. Against Sundberg and Hahneman, Verheyden argues that the Muratorian canon is early (late second century) and western.

Westcott, B. F. *A General Survey of the History of the Canon of the New Testament*. 6th edn. London: Macmillan, 1880; repr. Grand Rapids: Baker Book House, 1980. Early classic of canon research; still valuable if read in conjunction with more recent works.

# CHAPTER 7
# Historical Criticism

## David E. Aune

## Introduction

"Historical criticism" and the "historical-critical method" are phrases widely used as umbrella terms for a group of related methods and approaches employed by mainstream Protestant, Catholic, and Jewish biblical scholars for interpreting the Bible (these methods include source criticism, form criticism, redaction criticism, social science criticism, etc.). Even though biblical scholars from various religious perspectives have distinctive faith commitments, the "objective" nature of historical criticism (i.e., critical scholars can agree on the basic elements of the method) enables them to have meaningful dialogue about the interpretation of biblical texts in ecumenical contexts (Collins 2005: 10).

The adjective "historical" has two different meanings often conveyed by two metaphors: (1) the text can be regarded as a *mirror* in the sense that it reflects the historical and cultural setting in which the biblical text originated, and (2) the text can be regarded as a *window* in the sense that it provides interpretive textual access to people, places, and events in the ancient world, making it both possible and necessary to judge the truth or falsity of the historical claims made in the text. The term "criticism" or "critical" (derived from the Greek verb *krinein*, "to decide, judge, evaluate"), refers to the use of independent reason in investigating the origins, text, composition, history, content, and claims of books of the Bible and to the ability to make informed decisions about authenticity and inauthenticity, truth and falsehood. In modern English usage, the term "criticism" has unfortunately taken on largely negative connotations, so that for many the phrase "historical criticism" is incorrectly understood as playing a primarily negative role in the interpretation of scripture. In reality, historical criticism plays a positive role as a tool for providing access to the meaning of ancient texts written in ancient languages.

There are several alternative designations for historical criticism. The phrase "higher criticism" (a paired opposite to "lower criticism" or "textual criticism") is a synonym for historical criticism that was in vogue from the eighteenth through the early twentieth centuries (the *Journal of Higher Criticism*, with its intentionally nostalgic title, briefly revived the phrase during the short period of its existence from 1994 to 2003).

The "historical-grammatical method" (or "grammatical-historical method") is a theologically sanitized form of the historical-critical method (the absence of "critical" or "criticism" is intentional), that varies wildly depending on who describes it. A kind of minimal definition was proposed by Gerald Sheppard (1974: 10) as

> an approach that presupposes a relatively conservative assessment in matters of author-ship and redaction history of biblical books, such that an exegesis can on critical grounds be *content to operate grammatically and historically only with the present text.*

This definition, however, only partially describes the scope of the historical-grammatical method, a designation widely used among contemporary Evangelicals as a conscious alternative to historical criticism (Martin 1977). On the other hand a maximal description of the method is proposed in fifteen points by Missouri Synod Lutheran Raymond Surburg (1974), and includes the following (reformulated and synthesized with some omissions): (1) The Bible, in its present canonical form, in the original languages and in its literal meaning, is the Word of God in entirely in the original autographs. (2) The Bible is the supreme authority in all theological matters. (3) The Bible is both a unity in the sense that God is the ultimate author and it is also inerrant containing no contradictions. The context for every passage of scripture is the entire Bible, so that one passage can be used to interpret other passages (the *analogia scriptura*) and the Christological interpretation of the Old Testament by the New Testament is warranted. (4) Since the Holy Spirit is the true interpreter of scripture every interpreter needs the enlightenment of the Spirit of God. Basically, Surburg's list does not describe an interpretive method so much as a synthesis of doctrines about the Bible that the author believes must be honored in the interpretive process. Midway between Sheppard and Surburg is the description of the method proposed by William Tolar (2002: 21–38), who includes no theological claims about the Bible. He does comment on the importance of the method (2002: 21): "No element of interpretation is more important to an accurate understanding of the Bible than is the grammatical-historical method. It is the *sine qua non* for any valid understanding of God's Word." Tolar divides the method logically into two components, "the grammatical principle," which uses a knowledge of language to understand the biblical text (2002: 21–9) and "the historical principle," focusing on such issues as the importance of finding out all that can be known about the author and audience and the social context of both as well as geography and topography (2002: 29–37). Under "the grammatical principle," Tolar only discusses the literal meaning of the text in the context of distinguishing literal from figurative language (2002: 25–7). By comparing these three accounts of the grammatical-historical method, it becomes obvious that there is very little agreement on just what the method includes, except that it clearly excludes more conventional approaches to historical criticism.

Finally, another label for historical criticism is "biblical criticism," which is sometimes used as an umbrella term for all scholarly approaches to the Bible, but for John Barton is a more accurate designation for the method of "historical criticism" (Barton 2007: 1, 39, 58). The adjective "historical" in "historical criticism" is misleading, he argues, since most biblical scholars are primarily concerned with literary and theological dimensions of the biblical text, not with the historical method *per se*. Further, the adjective "historical" connotes reductionism and skepticism. While, Barton admits, the application of historical criticism to the biblical texts has enabled scholars to reconstruct the history of Israel, the life and teachings of Jesus, and the history of the early church, reconstructing history is a very small part of the historical-critical method that is not significant enough to be considered part of the essence of "historical criticism." Barton generally underplays the historical concerns of "historical criticism," and his use of the term "biblical criticism" is inherently problematic, since it implies that there is a special type of criticism appropriate only for the Bible.

The opening sentence of this essay used the phrase "historical-critical *method*." Many scholars regard historical criticism as a method analogous to the scientific method, aided by the breadth of the German word *Wissenschaft*. While the phrase *wissenschaftliche Methode* means "scientific method," *Wissenschaft* is also used to mean "research" and "scholarship." The 1993 Pontifical Biblical Commission document "The Interpretation of the Bible in the Church" says of historical criticism (Béchard 2002: 251): "It is a critical method, because in each of its steps (from textual criticism to redaction criticism) it operates with the help of scientific criteria that seek to be as objective as possible." However, there are a number of scholars who maintain that historical criticism is more an art than a science and that it is not appropriate to categorize it as a "method" (Barr 2000: 32–58). John Barton (2007: 58), for example, argues that "biblical criticism" (his term for "historical criticism") is not a method, since texts are understood by an intuitive appropriation of the combination of words that constitute them. While the scientific character of historical criticism has been exaggerated, the term "method" is still appropriate in the general sense of "a way, technique or process for doing something" (see Merriam-Webster's *New Collegiate Dictionary*, 10th edn., 2001).

Historical criticism ideally approaches the literature of an earlier period without subjecting it to the values of the present (Frye 1957: 24), i.e., by refusing the temptation to read one's own ideas into the text (Barton 2007: 49).

The Bible is only one of the many ancient texts that have been subjected to the historical-critical method since it began to take on some of its modern contours in the seventeenth century. The problems involved in interpreting ancient texts did not become clear until the Enlightenment, when the distance between the biblical interpreter and the biblical text began to be more fully understood and appreciated. The Bible, in all its complexity, was written in ancient languages within the context of a variety of ancient Near Eastern and Mediterranean cultures. The task of historical criticism was to bridge this gap in order to understand ancient texts in their own terms. The first major conflict between the new morality of historical knowledge and traditional Christian belief was the problem of whether the Bible should be subject to the same methodological rules used to examine other written texts. The issue of whether the Bible should be regarded as unique or like any other book remains a central point of contention between conservative and liberal biblical scholarship. The central role of the Bible in both Christianity and Judaism has made the issue of historical criticism a particularly sensitive and volatile issue, particularly when it is used to distinguish true from false claims in scripture. Harrisville and Sundberg (2002: 4–5) regard the conflict between historical criticism and the dogmatic tradition of the church as essentially "a war between two worldviews of faith: the worldview of modern critical awareness originating in the Enlightenment and the inherited Augustinian worldview of the Western church."[1]

## The Emergence of Historical Criticism

While historical criticism is widely thought to have had its beginnings in the Renaissance, Reformation, and Enlightenment, critical and historical reasoning was an important part of the work of some of ancient Greek historians (particularly Thucydides and Polybius), and a certain level of critical thinking is evident in the work of some early Christian scholars (e.g., Origen). Nevertheless, it is true to say that historical criticism became increasingly dominant among European and American intellectuals and academics following the Enlightenment, which centered in the eighteenth century. The Renaissance in Europe spanned the fourteenth through the seventeenth centuries, and Renaissance humanists concerned with language and literature emphasized the *recursus ad fontes*, "back to the sources," by which they meant the renewed study of Greek and Latin classics, and in the case of Christian humanists, the Hebrew and Greek texts of the Old and New Testaments (e.g., Erasmus of Rotterdam, the Hebraist Johannes Reuchlin, and his grand-nephew Melanchthon). The Renaissance humanist Lorenzo Valla (1407–57), a Latinist, proved to be a pioneer of historical criticism by demonstrating that the so-called *Donation of Constantine* or *Constitutum Constantini* was a forgery. An imperial edict supposedly issued in the fourth century CE by the Emperor Constantine I (272–337), the *Constitutum Constantini* granted Sylvester I (314–36), the bishop of Rome, and his successors dominion over the western Roman empire and Palestine, a gift for curing the emperor of leprosy and baptizing him. Through his extensive knowledge of Latin, i.e., the fact that some Latin words varied in meaning over time (e.g., *retro*, "back, behind," had come to mean "still" or "again" by the eighth century), Valla demonstrated the *Donation* was a forgery originating ca. 755 CE. Valla's manuscript circulated privately after it was completed in 1440, but first published posthumously in 1517 (by the mid-sixteenth century, Valla's book had been placed on the Index of prohibited books). While the Protestant Reformers were not full-fledged practitioners of historical criticism (which began to take serious shape in the seventeenth century), some of them were Christian humanists, who shared the Renaissance emphasis on the *via moderna* (in contrast with the scholastic emphasis on the *via antiqua*), focusing on the original Greek and Latin classics, in particular the original Hebrew and Greek texts of the Bible.

The Enlightenment was a watershed for the development of historical criticism. The typical perspective of pre-Enlightenment "historiography" was an unquestioning acceptance of what texts claimed (*in dubio pro traditio*). Hence the "historian's" task was to compile and synthesize the testimony of so-called authorities or eyewitnesses, which were assumed to be reliable. The perspective of post-Enlightenment historiography was radically different since historians interrogated their sources and asked how the claims made in them could either be validated or discredited. During the eighteenth and nineteenth centuries, the frequent discovery of documentary errors, frauds, and forgeries underscored both the necessity of the autonomy of the historian and his or her skeptical attitude toward received reports.

The development of historical criticism reached its high point during the late nineteenth century, coincident with the development of critical historiography in Germany. Objective historiography was a nineteenth-century ideal, associated with the name of Leopold von Ranke (1795–1886), the father of modern historiography, who coined the phrase "wie es eigentlich gewesen ist" ("as it actually was"). Since that time, completely objective historical knowledge has increasingly been recognized as an impossible goal, nevertheless historians must consciously reflect on their subjective presuppositions and perspectives with the purpose of minimizing their influence on the sources of historical inquiry.

## The Tasks of Historical Criticism

### The literal meaning of the text

A central goal of historical criticism in biblical interpretation has been to establish the literal sense of the text. This involves giving attention to semantics (the study of meaning in communication) at various levels, i.e., the meaning of words, phrases, sentences, constituent textual units of various sizes, and even entire books (Barton 2007: 57), though the interpretive problems increase with the size of the text under examination. While it is relatively easy for scholars to agree over the meaning of a particular Greek word (particularly given the modern advances made in Greek lexicography), it is more difficult to find agreement on the meaning of an entire biblical book. Determining the meanings of particular words is itself a historical exercise, since words have particular meanings in the historical and cultural settings within which texts are composed, and the analysis of textual units and entire works involves the study of genres (an aspect of comparative literature), which are semantic social conventions providing meaning for units discourse (Aune 1987a, 1987b). Thus important aspects of historical criticism involve philology as well as comparative literature.

The literal sense generally enjoyed pride of place among the four senses of scripture that became popular by the medieval period, i.e., the literal, allegorical, moral, and anagogical senses (de Lubac 1998–2000). In the sections entitled "The Meaning of Inspired Scripture," and "The Interpretation of the Bible in the Church" (Béchard 2002: 279–84), Béchard discusses three senses of scripture, the literal, spiritual, and *sensus plenior* or "fuller sense," while Joseph A. Fitzmyer, SJ (2008: 86–100) discusses these three senses, but adds a fourth that he calls "the accommodated sense" in an article in which the literal sense essentially trumps the others. The literal sense became increasingly important during the early medieval period, as modeled by the role of scripture in the theology of the "Angelic Doctor" Thomas Aquinas (1225–74). The Protestant Reformers, including Luther, Melanchthon, Calvin, and Bucer, used the phrase *sensus literalis* to indicate the full Christian significance of scripture, a corollary of their emphasis on *sola scriptura* (the primacy of scripture over the church and its tradition-laden interpretation of scripture). The traditional assumption in Christian exegesis is that, since the Bible is the Word of God, the literal sense is theologically true. "The Interpretation of the Bible in the Church" maintains that "The literal sense of Scripture is that which has been expressed directly by the inspired human authors" (Béchard 2002: 280).

But what is meant by "literal sense"? Historical criticism often understands biblical texts literally, but does not always take them to be literally true (Barton 2007: 95). One minor example is the widespread critical view that 1 Timothy is a pseudo-Pauline letter, even though the text opens with "Paul, apostle of Christ Jesus according to the command of God our savior and Christ Jesus out hope" (1 Tim. 1:1). While the text clearly indicates that it was written by Paul, critical scholars do not accept this claim as true. Another example is the statement found in Revelation 22:20: "The one who testifies to these things [i.e., the exalted Jesus] says: 'Yes, I am coming soon! Amen, come Lord Jesus.'" While it is clear that this text predicts the imminent return of Jesus, it is obvious that this statement, written ca. 90 CE, cannot be true. While the literal sense of scripture is widely accepted as the goal of historical criticism, some biblical critics have preferred other designations such as the "original sense" or the "plain sense." However, determining the "original sense" of a text becomes problematic in works that have been compiled from earlier documents (like the gospels of Matthew and Luke), which may in turn be based on oral traditions. Barton (2007: 101) argues for the propriety of using the phrase the "plain sense," since biblical criticism is primarily a semantic and literary operation only indirectly concerned with the original, the intended, or the literal meaning.

### Authorial intention

Biblical scholars who practice historical criticism frequently maintain that the literal or plain meaning of the biblical text is identical with the intention of the author, or (alternatively) that the biblical text should be read and understood as it would have been by its first readers. Some texts provide clues to the purpose of the authors in composing them. Luke 1:1–4, for example, is similar to introductions to ancient historical works in which the author comments on previous works on which he is dependent, on his own efforts to get the story right, and on the usefulness of the work for Theophilus, apparently the author's patron: "that you may know the truth concerning the things of which you have been informed" (Luke 1:4). Analogously, John 20:30–1 provides an overview of the author's intention in writing his work:

> Now Jesus did many other signs in the presence of the disciples, which are not written in this book; but these are written that you may believe that Jesus is the Christ, the Son of God, and that believing you may have life in his name.

However, even when authors attempt to tell their readers what they're trying to accomplish, the literary work itself is almost always more complex and has more depth than even the authors realize. In practical terms authorial intention is embodied in the text itself and the hermeneutical challenge is to understand the meaning of the text. According to Umberto Eco, the *intentio operis* ("the intention of the work"), is not an exploration of the author's mind, but asking how the assertions of the text cohere with each other to make a comprehensible whole (Barton 2007: 105–6). Biblical texts are typically more complex than conventional literature in that they took shape over many years and by using many written and oral sources, so that in many instances (the Pentateuch and the Psalms are two good examples) the notion of an "author" is not appropriate. Even in the New Testament the notion of authorship is often complex. For instance, critical scholars typically maintain that the Christ hymn in Philippians 2:5–11 is an earlier Christian text inserted by Paul into its present paraenetic context. Is the "original meaning" of Philippians 2:5–11 the meaning intended by its unknown Christian author(s) or is it the meaning of the text in its present literary setting? Many of the sayings and stories of Jesus in the synoptic gospels were transmitted by oral tradition before being reduced to writing and incorporated into written texts. How useful is the notion of authorship when these traditions are subject to various degrees of transformation?

In the mid-twentieth century the widespread emphasis on authorial intention in biblical scholarship bumped heads with the so-called "intentional fallacy" (Wimsatt and Beardsley 1946), a crucial tenet of the New Criticism, a formalist literary critical movement in the US and UK from the 1920s through the 1960s. The New Criticism rejected all forms of *extrinsic criticism* (e.g., historical, biographical, and sociological approaches to understanding a literary work), in favor of *intrinsic criticism*, considering the literary work as an autonomous and unified object in itself. Wimsatt and Beardsley did not claim that there is no relationship between a text and the author's intentions in writing that text, but rather that an author's stated intentions have no validity in determining the meaning or value of a text. The validity of the "intentional fallacy" continued to be held by reader-response critics following the decline of the New Criticism in the 1960s, but for a different reason. Reader-response critics argue that the notion of a reading of a text sanctioned by the author improperly restricts the sovereign freedom of the reader.

## Issues of "introduction"

Texts for beginning courses on the New Testament taught in colleges, universities, and seminaries usually belong to the genre called "introductions to the New Testament," and try to answer the who, what, when, where, and why kinds of questions about the New Testament (the *Blackwell Companion to the New Testament* belongs to this genre). These texts deal with a menu of literary and historical issues including authorship and authenticity, audience, integrity (i.e., whether the text is a unity or a composite work), date and place of composition, occasion and purpose of writing, content, structure, style, and genre (Fitzmyer 2008: 63–4). In addition, Fitzmyer adds textual criticism, the attempt to reconstruct the oldest and most reliable text of the Old and New Testaments. What is missing (depending on one's perspective) is any direct engagement with the religious claims of the New Testament, generally regarded as outside the limits of historical criticism. The recent appearance of *theological* introductions to the Old or New Testaments, a relatively new subgenre of the more conventional introductions, represents an attempt to remedy this situation (e.g., Holladay 2005). Unlike Fitzmyer, Barton (2007: 3) maintains that since the aim of biblical criticism is understanding, it is only accidentally concerned with the issues of "introduction" or history, which are not part of the essence of the critical approach. Barton is simply wrong in this judgment, and for at least two reasons. First, his quest for the "essence" of biblical criticism wrongly assumes that it is something objectively "out there" to be described and analyzed. Historical criticism has evolved since the seventeenth century and has become a congeries of approaches to understanding that texts and aspects of that critical task are sometimes mutually contradictory. Second, while it is true that introductory matters are not central to the goal of understanding texts, they are certainly essential steps in realizing that goal.

### Other historical–critical approaches

Fitzmyer briefly discusses a number of approaches to the biblical text that are not themselves part of historical criticism, but are refinements of historical criticism (Fitzmyer 2008: 64–6). These include literary criticism, source criticism, form criticism, and redaction criticism. Missing from Fitzmyer's description of historical criticism is any mention of social science criticism (see Chapter 12, "Social Science Criticism of the New Testament," in this volume). Though the gap between the agrarian, pre-industrial world in which the New Testament was written and the modern world in which New Testament readers live is typically measured historically, it must also be measured socially. According to Malina and Rohrbaugh (1992: 2), "Such social distance includes radical differences in social structures, social roles, values, and general cultural features." Some of these include patron–client relations and the core values of honor and shame.

## Is the Historical-Critical Method Neutral?

Joseph A. Fitzmyer, SJ, a staunch defender of the historical-critical method, maintains that the method itself is neutral, but can be used with presuppositions of various sorts that are not really part of the method itself (Fitzmyer 2008: 66–9). He thus agrees with the perspective articulated in the Pontifical Biblical Commission's "The Interpretation of the Bible in the Church" (Béchard 2002: 251): the historical-critical method "operates with the help of scientific criteria that seek to be as objective as possible" and it can be used without presuppositions, i.e., a philosophical system (Béchard 2002: 252–3):

> It is a method which, when used in an objective manner, implies of itself no a priori. If its use is accompanied by a priori principles, that is not something pertaining to the method itself, but to certain hermeneutical choices which govern the interpretation and can be tendentious.

Fitzmyer laments the fact that early in its development, historical criticism was seriously infected with rationalistic presuppositions by such New Testament scholars such as

Reimarus, Baur, Strauss, and Renan, who sought to free the study of the New Testament from the influence of Christian dogma (here Fitzmyer apparently uses the term "rationalism" in the sense of "reliance on reason as the basis for establishing religious truth"). In the early twentieth century, he continues, Rudolf Bultmann also used historical criticism with presuppositions, including a Lutheran conception of kerygmatic theology, Strauss's mythical interpretation of the gospels and Heidegger's existentialist philosophical and theological presuppositions that proved not to be universally acceptable.

On the other hand, maintains Fitzmyer, modern Christians make appropriate use of the presuppositions of Christian faith in their use of the historical-critical method in exegesis. For Fitzmyer, the goal of exegesis is the discovery of the religious and theological meaning of the text, i.e., the meaning intended by the inspired writer. The presupposition, argues Fitzmyer (2008: 69),

> consists of elements of faith or belief: that the text being critically interpreted contains God's Word set forth in human words of long ago; that it has been composed under the guidance of the Spirit and has authority for the people of the Jewish-Christian heritage; that it is part of a restricted collection of authoritative writings (part of a canon); that it has been given by God for the edification and salvation of his people; and that it is properly expounded only in relation to the Tradition that has grown out of it within the communal faith-life of that people.

Indeed, the use of such faith presuppositions makes historical criticism a "properly oriented" method of biblical interpretation in which none of the constituent elements is an end in itself, but together they focus on the task of disclosing the literal sense of the Bible intended by the inspired writer (Fitzmyer 2008: 69). Fitzmyer also speaks of Christian presuppositions as a "plus," which actually seems more appropriate than the term "presupposition." The term "plus" is appropriate for Fitzmyer's project simply because his use of historical criticism has two distinct stages, the first based on reason and the second based on faith (reminiscent of the collocation of faith and reason in Aquinas). Fitzmyer divides the exegetical task (the goal of which is to uncover the literal sense of the text in its final form), into three progressive stages: (1) the textual meaning, (2) the contextual meaning, and (3) the relational meaning, i.e., biblical theology (Fitzmyer 2008: 68–9). It is only after this rational procedure is completed that the true goal of exegesis is reached (Fitzmyer 2008: 69):

> The combination of the textual, contextual, and relational meanings of a passage leads to the discovery of its religious and theological meaning – to its meaning as the Word of God couched in ancient human language.

While Fitzmyer maintains that historical criticism is (or properly ought to be) ideologically neutral, it appears that at this first methodological stage he considers the Bible "like any other book" (Jowett 1860). In another article, Fitzmyer makes this statement about the historical-critical method: "The historical-critical method, when used in biblical interpretation, has as its goal the ascertaining of the literal sense of the written Word of God" (Fitzmyer 2008: 78). Thus while he regards the historical-critical method as both essential and neutral, he applies it to the Bible which he presupposes is the Word of God, though bracketing out that understanding until the task of historical criticism is completed.

Though John Barton does not list in his bibliography the article by Fitzmyer, a portion of which was summarized above, his critical approach to the Bible is very similar. For Barton, biblical criticism contains three central features (Barton 2007: 58, 171): (1) attention to semantics (the meaning of words, phrase, chapters, whole books), i.e., establishing the plain meaning of the text; (2) awareness of genre; and (3) bracketing out questions of truth. Only after carrying out these three steps is it appropriate to ask whether what the text means is true (Barton 2007: 171). "Bracketing out" means that texts have to be allowed to answer their own questions and only then to answer ours (Barton 2007: 179).

## Separating Truth from Falsehood

Another largely unmentioned aspect of Fitzmyer's account of the historical-critical method (in addition to social-scientific criticism) is that aspect of the method that separates truth from falsehood in ancient texts (an operation that is obviously genre-dependent). Fitzmyer (2008: 64) touches on this issue obliquely: when discussing "introductory questions," he mentions "the authenticity of the writing (e.g., did Paul write the Epistle to the Ephesians?)." This involves judging whether or not the claim made in the epistolary opening is true or false. He touches on the problem of distinguishing truth from falsehood more directly a few pages later (Fitzmyer 2008: 66):

> Furthermore, we have learned through this method [historical criticism] that not everything narrated in the past tense necessarily corresponds to ancient reality, and that not everything put on the lips of Jesus of Nazareth by the evangelists was necessarily uttered by him.

These two references sound very much like a presupposition of historical criticism, namely that by use of critical reason a scholar is able to decide whether or not a claim made by a biblical text is true or false and not have that conclusion overridden (for example) by a prior notion about the character and implications of the inspiration of the Bible. In another essay, "Concerning the Interpretation of the Bible in the Church" (Fitzmyer 2008: 64–75), Fitzmyer argues forcefully against Philip Davies (1995), who distinguishes between confessional and nonconfessional approaches to the Bible and expresses a preference for the latter.

Historical criticism does much more than simply try to understand biblical texts in their historical context; it is also a formal method for *evaluating the truth or falsity of claims made explicitly or implicitly in the biblical texts*. Using the canons of independent critical reason, historical critics do not take their sources at face value but interrogate them, much as witnesses in modern courtrooms are subject to cross-examination to determine whether or not their testimony is true and holds up under scrutiny. In the modern world, such things as forged wills, forged signatures on legal documents and financial instruments, forged checks, and fake alibis need to be exposed to the light of truth so justice may prevail and innocent people are not made to suffer. Analogously, historical critics ask whether the person to whom the authorship of a particular biblical book is ascribed is in fact the actual author of that work. In antiquity, many literary works were ascribed to people who could not possibly have written them and they must therefore be judged as pseudepigraphs or forgeries. No one, for example, accepts the claim that the *Apocalypse of Adam* was actually written by the first man, nor that *1 Enoch* was written by the mysterious figure described in Genesis 5:18–24. Nor does anyone accept the authenticity of many other documents ascribed to ancient Israelite worthies such as the *Apocalypse of Abraham* or *4 Ezra*. Similarly, critical New Testament scholars reject the authenticity of some of the letters attributed to Paul, particularly Ephesians and the three pastoral letters (1 and 2 Timothy, Titus), as well as many of the Catholic letters (1 and 2 Peter, James, and Jude). Form criticism has taught us that many of the sayings and stories of Jesus preserved in the synoptic gospels have been modified in the course of transmission and some have even been created at some stage in the process.

The arguments against regarding certain of Paul's letters as actually having been written by Paul and the problem of the authenticity of the Jesus material in the gospels are not simply academic issues for many New Testament scholars, but a challenge to their theological views of the truth, accuracy, and authority of scripture, and it is this use of historical criticism that has been most controversial (and has been rejected by those who use the "grammatical-historical method" discussed above on p. 102). The use of historical criticism, i.e., independent critical reasoning, often clashes with traditional beliefs that Christians have about the New Testament.

Ernst Troeltsch (1865–1923), a professor of systematic theology at Heidelberg (1893–1914) and Berlin (1914–23), was a scholar whose academic interests centered in the relation between faith and history and who was particularly concerned with that aspect of the historical method that distinguished truth from falsehood. Troeltsch proposed three essential principles of historical criticism (Troeltsch 1912–25: II, 729–53; see also Harvey 1966: 14–15; Krentz 1975: 55–72): (1) The *principle of criticism* or methodological skepticism maintains that judgments about the past cannot simply be classified as true or false, for there is no such thing as historical certainty; all historical claims can only be assigned greater or lesser degrees of probability. (2) The *principle of analogy* maintains that all events of the past are analogous to those of the present, i.e., present experience becomes the criterion for what is probable in the past. This suggests that if miracles do not occur today, neither did they occur in biblical times, i.e., there is no possibility of divine causation in the natural order. (3) The *principle of correlation* holds that all historical events are so related and interdependent that no change in the historical nexus of events can occur without radically affecting a change in all that surrounds it. Historical events must be understood in terms of a chain of cause and effect so that supernatural intervention cannot be used as a principle of historical explanation. This means that the occurrence of a genuinely unique event (or a miraculous event) is excluded by definition and further that history is a unity in the sense that it consists of a closed continuum of events linked by cause and effect.

Particularly with its caveat against supernatural intervention in the historical process, the principles of historical criticism as formulated by Troeltsch have frequently been seen as reductionistic, skeptical, and rationalistic and therefore in conflict with traditional Christian faith. A series of responses to the radical historical criticism of Troeltsch and others have been forthcoming. The historian R. G. Collingwood (1946) maintained that historical events are unique and that the explanatory models useful for prediction in science do not apply to history. Richard R. Niebuhr (1957) made a series of points against the kind of historical criticism advocated by Troeltsch: (1) The metaphysical assumptions of Bultmann and other radical New Testament critics destroys genuine theological thinking. (2) Historical thinking requires an openness to the uniqueness and novelty of past events. (3) If the resurrection is what it appears to be, then it destroys the principle of analogy. Alan Richardson (1964), a New Testament scholar, argues that "There is no *scientific* presupposition of historical method which requires historians to rule out the possibility of divine action in history" and that it is "positivistic philosophy, not historical method, which decrees that the resurrection of Christ cannot be regarded as an historical event" (p. 153).

These reactions against the critical views of Troeltsch are completely understandable, particularly when it is not only the authenticity of a Pauline letter, or the authenticity of a saying of Jesus in the gospels that is involved, but the truth of the resurrection of Jesus Christ. The principle of the morality of historical knowledge advocated by Harvey (1966), maintains that historical criticism is not a tool to be applied when it is useful and then discarded or replaced by other methods. Rather, historical criticism is an article of modern critical orthodoxy which must be embraced as true. This absolutist position of Harvey is vulnerable, particularly in light of developments during the late twentieth century in the philosophy of science, from which we have learned that no method for understanding reality is free from the subjectivities of the individual and the society who make use of them. Thus the objectivity that Harvey sought to affirm in the historical-critical method must now be seen as illusory. Historical critics generally practice a reasonable objectivity, primarily in the sense that they try to focus on what the text actually says, rather than read alien meanings into it. Historical criticism remains a contested method, though in many ways it has shown its practical utility during the last two centuries.

## Note

1 By "Augustinian worldview," Harrisville and Sundberg mean the view that human beings are fallen and can only establish a right relationship to God through the intervention of divine grace and ultimate truth is Christian doctrine that comes from God through the Bible and the church to the individual Christian (the authority of the church has primacy over individual faith (2002: 26–7).

## Annotated Bibliography

Aune, David E. (ed.). *Greco-Roman Literature and the New Testament: Selected Forms and Genres.* Atlanta: Scholars Press, 1987a. A discussion of various ancient literary genres and how they influence early Christian literary production.

Aune, David E. *The New Testament in Its Literary Environment*. Philadelphia: Westminster, 1987b. A detailed discussion of each of the major and minor genres in the New Testament in light of comparable genres in Judaism and the Greco-Roman world.

Barr, James. *History and Ideology in the Old Testament*. Oxford: Oxford University Press, 2000. Basically a series of lectures on the state of the art of scholarship on the Hebrew Bible at the end of the twentieth century. In chapter 3 Barr mounts a counteroffensive against the attacks mounted by the postmodernist rejection of historical criticism, addressing several supposedly erroneous criticisms: (1) that historical criticism claims to be the sole possessor of objectivity, (2) that all historical criticism is obsessed with the original meaning, and (3) that historical criticism is a product of rationalism and the Enlightenment (rather, it continues Reformation principles).

Barton, John. *The Nature of Biblical Criticism*. Louisville and London: Westminster John Knox Press, 2007. An important work by a noted Old Testament scholar who argues that "biblical criticism" (his preferred term for "historical criticism") is a positive enterprise that, when properly carried out, has positive benefits for the church.

Béchard, Dean (ed. and trans.). *The Scripture Documents: An Anthology of Official Catholic Teachings*. Collegeville: Liturgical Press, 2002.

Collingwood, R. G. *The Idea of History*. Oxford: Clarendon Press, 1946. After Collingwood's death in 1943, this book was compiled by one of his students, T. M. Knox. Collingwood was a noted historian and archaeologist, and this book became a major inspiration for English work in the area of philosophy of history.

Collins, John J. *The Bible after Babel: Historical Criticism in a Postmodern Age*. Grand Rapids: Eerdmans, 2005. Writing in the context of postmodernism and various ideological perspectives, Collins argues that historical criticism is necessary in providing a foundation in biblical scholarship, if the latter is to make a contribution to both scholarship and the various faith communities that take the Bible seriously.

Davies, Philip. *Whose Bible Is It Anyway?* Sheffield: Sheffield Academic Press, 1995. 2nd edn.: London and New York: T. & T. Clark International, 2004.

Fitzmyer, SJ, Joseph A. "Historical Criticism: Its Role in Biblical Interpretation and Church Life." *Theological Studies* 50 (1989), 244–59.

Fitzmyer, SJ, Joseph A. *The Interpretation of Scripture: In Defense of the Historical-Critical Method*. New York and Mahwah: Paulist Press, 2008. This book is a collection of articles by Fitzmyer, perhaps the premier Roman Catholic New Testament scholar in the United States and staunch defender of the historical-critical method. Some of articles used here include "Historical Criticism: Its Role in Biblical Interpretation and Church Life," pp. 59–73 (originally published in 1989), "Concerning the Interpretation of the Bible in the Church," pp. 74–85 (originally published in 1999), and "The Senses of Scripture," pp. 86–100 (a combination of two articles, one published in 1995 and the other in 1996–7).

Frye, Northrop. *Anatomy of Criticism: Four Essays*. Princeton: Princeton University Press, 1957. Frye (1912–91), a Canadian, was one of the most distinguished literary critics and literary theorists of the twentieth century. In the opening pages of *Anatomy of Criticism*, Frye describes the work as a "synoptic view of the scope, theory, principles, and techniques of literary criticism" (p. 3).

Harrisville, Roy A. and Walter Sundberg. *The Bible in Modern Culture: Baruch Spinoza to Brevard Childs*. 2nd edn. Grand Rapids: Eerdmans, 2002. The authors, whose purpose is to write a "confessionally critical" history of modern biblical criticism, have an ambiguous attitude toward historical criticism: it has been immensely useful, but it is largely responsible for the increasing gap between biblical studies and the life of the church. The book focuses on analytical assessments of some key figures in the history of historical criticism (Spinoza,

Reimarus, Schleiermacher, Strauss, Baur, von Hoffmann, Troeltsch, Schlatter, Machen, Bultmann, Käsemann, Ricoeur, and Childs), putting them in historical context and evaluating their influence.

Harvey, Van. *The Historian and the Believer: The Morality of Historical Knowledge and Christian Belief.* New York: Macmillan, 1966. Harvey argues in detail that theology has failed to deal seriously with the challenge of the modern historical method.

Holladay, Carl. *A Critical Introduction to the New Testament: Interpreting the Message and Meaning of Jesus Christ.* Nashville: Abingdon, 2005. The intended title of this text was "A Theological Introduction to the New Testament," but the publishers insisted on a more conventional title that included the word "critical." The subtitle conveys the theological concerns of the author.

Jowett, Benjamin. "On the Interpretation of Scripture." In *Essays and Reviews.* London: Longman, Green, Longman & Roberts, 1860. A famous essay in which Jowett, a famous English classicist and rationalist, argues that the Bible ought to be interpreted like classical texts. Jowett advocates the principle of progressive revelation, which continues to the present day.

Krentz, Edgar. *The Historical-Critical Method.* London: SPCK, 1975. A short (eighty-eight-page) overview of the rise of historical criticism, its goals and techniques, its presuppositions and achievements, and its relation to theological discussion since 1945.

Linnemann, Eta. *Historical Criticism of the Bible: Method or Ideology.* Trans. Robert W. Yarbrough. Grand Rapids: Baker Book House, 1990. Linnemann, formerly a Bultmannian, was converted to a form of Protestant fundamentalism and thereafter rejected her work as a critical New Testament scholar.

Lubac, Henri de. *Medieval Exegesis: The Four Senses of Scripture.* 2 vols. Grand Rapids: Eerdmans, 1998–2000.

Maier, Gerhard. *The End of the Historical-Critical Method.* St. Louis: Concordia Publishing House, 1977. Maier argues that historical criticism is a method unsuitable for dealing with its subject, i.e., the Bible or divine revelation. Maier assumes that the entire Bible is divine revelation (a view that cannot be supported with arguments but only accepted by faith) and any method that attempts to distinguish the Word of God from scripture is doomed to failure. As an alternative he proposes an "historical-biblical" method that is conformed to the demands of divine revelation. Maier's book is severely criticized by Stuhlmacher 1977.

Malina, B. J. and R. Rohrbaugh. *Social-Science Commentary on the Synoptic Gospels.* Minneapolis: Fortress Press, 1992. A commentary focusing on the social and cultural values and customs that characterized the ancient Mediterranean world and how knowledge of such values and customs plays an essential role in interpreting the gospels.

Martin, Ralph P. "Approaches to New Testament Exegesis." Pp. 220–51 in *New Testament Interpretation: Essays on Principles and Methods.* Edited by I. H. Marshal. Exeter: Paternoster, 1977. In favoring the term "grammatico-historical method, Martin saw it in contrast to the more conventional historical-critical method, which typically was understood to have unsavory presuppositions.

Niebuhr, Richard R. *Resurrection and Historical Reason: A Study of Theological Method.* New York: Scribner's, 1957. For Niebuhr, the believer does not see different facts than the non-believer, but rather sees different meanings in them. The resurrection faith is the "right understanding" of what Niebuhr calls the "memory-image" of Jesus.

Plantinga, Alvin. "Two (or More) Kinds of Scripture Scholarship." Pp. 374–421 in *Warranted Christian Belief.* New York: Oxford University Press, 2000. A Reformed philosopher and theologian who works out of Calvin's emphasis on *autopistos*, convinced that the authority of scripture is not based on the church or on rational argumentation but is "self-convincing" (i.e., the source of true belief is scripture combined with the internal instigation of the Holy Spirit).

Prior, Joseph G. *The Historical Critical Method in Catholic Exegesis*. Serie Teologia, 50. Rome: Gregorian University Press, 1999. Prior, in this doctoral dissertation, characterizes the use of historical criticism in Catholic interpretation of scripture as "necessary but limited." The purpose of historical criticism is to uncover the literal sense of the text because the text is historically conditioned. However, the historical-critical method is limited, and Catholic exegetes are bound to go beyond it to discover the spiritual sense of the text.

Richardson, Alan. *History Sacred and Profane*. Philadelphia: Westminster, 1964. A New Testament scholar, the author has written an apologetic work on aspects of the philosophy of history, distinguishing the modern conception of history from the biblical conception of history, i.e., *Heilsgeschichte* (the "sacred history" of the title). The author argues that "the miraculous" can happen as part of ordinary history.

Sandys-Wunch, John. *What Have They Done to the Bible? A History of Modern Biblical Interpretation*. Collegeville: Liturgical Press, 2005. A competent survey of the rise of historical criticism beginning with the Reformation and ending in last quarter of the nineteenth century.

Sheppard, Gerald. "Canon Criticism: The Proposal of Brevard Childs and an Assessment for Evangelical Hermeneutics." *Studia Biblica et Theologica* 4 (1974), 3–17.

Stuhlmacher, Peter. *Historical Criticism and Theological Interpretation of Scripture: Towards a Hermeneutics of Consent*. Philadelphia: Fortress Press, 1977. Stuhlmacher attempts to move along the boundaries of kerygmatic theology, pietism, and biblically based Lutheranism to preserve the valid insights of historical criticism for the theological task of the church. He points to modern Catholic exegesis as a model for doing historical criticism with theological concern. Stuhlmacher severely criticizes Maier (1977) and then proposes his own program called a "hermeneutics of consent."

Surburg, Raymond F. "Presuppositions of the Historical-Grammatical Method as Employed by Historic Lutheranism." *Springfielder* 38 (1974), 278–88.

Tolar, William B. "The Grammatical-Historical Method." Pp. 21–38 in *Biblical Hermeneutics: A Comprehensive Introduction to Interpreting Scripture*. Edited by Bruce Corley, Steve Lemke, and Grant Lovejoy. 2nd edn. Nashville: Broadman & Holman, 2002.

Troeltsch, Ernst. *Gesammelte Schriften*. 4 vols. Tübingen: Mohr Siebeck, 1912–25. Volume 2 (pp. 729–53) contains his famous article "Über historische und dogmatische Methode."

Wimsatt, William K. and Monroe C. Beardsley, "The Intentional Fallacy." *Sewanee Review* 54 (1946), pp. 468–88. Revised and republished on pp. 3–18 of Wimsatt's *The Verbal Icon: Studies in the Meaning of Poetry*. Lexington: University of Kentucky Press, 1954. An important article in which the authors, proponents of the New Criticism, argue that the autonomy of the literary work is such that even the stated intentions of the author cannot be taken as normative in the task of interpretation.

CHAPTER 8

# Literary Criticism

## David E. Aune

## Introduction

"Literary criticism" refers to the careful reading, study, critical evaluation, and interpretation of literary texts. Literary criticism is frequently based on literary theory (or poetics), involving the systematic reflection on the principles, methods and goals of literary criticism, though sometimes the terms are used interchangeably, as in M. A. R. Habib's book *Modern Literary Criticism and Theory: A History* (2008). Literary criticism in the West has had a long and complex history, beginning with the work of Plato and Aristotle in the fourth century BCE (see Kennedy 1989; Blamires 1991; Habib 2005), though literary theory was not a major concern of scholars until early in the twentieth century.

In 1881, the phrase "higher criticism" was first used in English as a translation of the German phrase *die höhere Kritik* by William Robert Smith (Smith 1881: 105). While the origins of the German phrase are obscure, it goes back at least to the eighteenth century. After its introduction to English-speaking biblical scholarship by Smith, its usage spread quickly. From 1890 to 1914, dozens of books appeared in English using the phrase "higher criticism" in their titles; some in order to explain it to a wider audience, others condemning it. Higher criticism (used over against "lower criticism" which was essentially textual criticism) as traditionally practiced included what is now associated with literary criticism and historical criticism. Before the mid-twentieth century, however, the "literary criticism" practiced by biblical scholars was largely limited to what we would call "source criticism": it involved analyzing books of the Bible for the purpose of identifying and reconstructing portions of earlier texts that had been incorporated into them by the final author-editors.

During the 1970s, influenced by secular literary scholarship, biblical scholars began to use the phrase "literary criticism" in quite a different sense, one more aligned with secular literary criticism: as an umbrella term for the various critical theories and methods developed by secular literary critics that were borrowed and often modified by biblical scholars to fit the demands of biblical interpretation. In Germany, however, biblical scholarship still largely restricts *Literarkritik* ("literary criticism") to source criticism, as it has for the past two centuries. Beginning with the late 1960s through the early 1980s a number of literary-critical methods began to have an impact on New Testament scholarship. What New Testament scholars came to call "narrative criticism," a modified and eclectic type of literary criticism dependent on aspects of the New Criticism, the Chicago school of criticism and narratology, was introduced to the guild by the analyses of Mark by David Rhoads and Donald Mitchie (1982) and of John by Alan Culpepper (1983). French structuralism was introduced to New Testament scholarship somewhat earlier by Daniel Patte (1976) and Daniel and Aline Patte (1978). Somewhat later studies using deconstructionism were introduced by Stephen Moore (1989, 1992), and reader-response criticism by Robert Fowler (1991).

## Is the New Testament "Literature"?

From a historical perspective, the New Testament is a random collection of narrative and expository texts written by a small group of individuals, some named, some unnamed, and some writing under pseudonyms, from the lower tiers of ancient society who were part of a movement later designated "Christianity." None of the authors who contributed to what later became the New Testament wrote with the intention of creating an aesthetic work (Keefer 2008: 3), but all wrote with an ideological agenda. The Greek language and style of most New Testament authors would have been regarded as pedestrian by the educated native speakers of Greek in the first century CE, a time when there was a great gulf fixed between popular literature and literature produced by the educated elite. Scholars of the late nineteenth and early twentieth centuries agreed that "literature," in the proper sense of the term, was an inappropriate designation for the works preserved in the New Testament. Using a dyadic model, the language, style, subject matter, and oral style of the books of the New Testament were categorized as *Kleinliteratur* ("popular literature"), while the literature produced by members of the educated upper class was regarded as *Hochliteratur* ("cultivated literature"). Karl Ludwig Schmidt (1981: 66–7) argued that since the gospels, as well as the oral traditions of which they were constituted, were "unliterary," the written gospels could not be expected to conform to such ancient literary genres as biography or history.

While literary critics from the late nineteenth through the mid-twentieth centuries argued that "literature" could be distinguished from other written texts because of certain intrinsic aesthetic qualities, since the mid-twentieth century it has been increasingly maintained that written texts are "literature" because they have been separated from their original communication setting, making them susceptible to new and different lines of interpretation and because they exhibit enduring values for particular communities. Current ideas of what actually constitutes "literary" exhibit great diversity (Castle 2007: 5–9). Stanley Fish, a reader-response critic, puts the matter just right (1980: 10): "Literature, I argue, is a conventional category. What will, at any time, be recognized as literature is a function of a communal decision as to what will count as literature."

The central and authoritative role that the Christian Bible has played in Christianity throughout its fractious history is the primary reason why books of the Bible are widely regarded today as literature, a role it continues to play in secular public universities in the United States, either in departments of English as courses in "the Bible as literature" or in departments of religious studies, where it is included as part of a history of religions curriculum. Luther's German translation of the Bible (the New Testament appeared in 1522; the entire Bible with the Apocrypha in 1534) and the English Authorized Version of 1611 (the so-called "King James Version") were each influential in shaping spoken and written German and English respectively during the centuries after their appearance. The Bible, particularly narrative portions, became a cultural treasure, functioning as a perennial source of inspiration for Western artists and writers to the end of the nineteenth century and beyond (see Jeffrey 1992).

While it is therefore appropriate to regard the New Testament as literature for sociological reasons, the authors and author-editors of the books of the New Testament were for the most part not writing a literary form of Greek (avoiding, among other things, prose rhythm) and were not consciously creating belles-lettres. However, according to Northrop Frye (1982: 62), the Bible "is as literary as it can be without actually being literature." Keefer (2008: 4) goes even further: "Even if the New Testament authors did not envision themselves as rivals of Virgil, they ended up creating literature nonetheless." While modern literary theory is primarily focused on poetry and fiction, the New Testament is largely comprised of didactic narratives, some with similarities to biography (the four gospels), one with history-like qualities (the Acts of the Apostles), and one with the mythic character of science fiction (the Apocalypse of John). According to Wellek and Warren (1977: 20–8), only self-consciously imaginative literature is the proper object of literary criticism. This is a dated view. It is not as easy to distinguish between fiction and nonfiction as it once was (Eagleton 1996: 1–2). One underlying issue in the application of critical theory, largely concerned with interpreting fiction, to New Testament narratives is that while for the most part the gospels and Acts convey the intention of interpreting people and events of the actual past, i.e., they are referential texts (nonfiction); they make use of selection, composition, rhetoric, and imagination (Merenlahti 2002: 9).

Apart from the gospels, Acts, and the Apocalypse, most of the books of the New Testament have the character of letters or letter-essays (some of which are written by real authors addressing real audiences, while others are pseudonymous works addressing imaginary audiences), which have a primarily expository character and were written in popular Koine Greek prose with no literary intentions (Hebrews is a striking exception, though it is an essay or homily rather than a letter). While secular literary critics have many thousands of poetic and fictional works to read, New Testament scholars have just six narrative texts (the four gospels, Acts, and the Apocalypse of John) and a very few quasi-poetic fragments embedded in narrative and epistolary works (e.g., John 1:1–18; Phil. 2:5–11; Col. 1:15–20; 1 Tim. 3:16). While English literary texts outnumber the critics, New Testament literary critics decidedly outnumber the very limited pool of biblical narrative texts. Again, while literary scholars might specialize in Shakespeare or Milton, New Testament scholars, including those who use narrative criticism, typically specialize in particular works, such as Mark or John.

## "The Bible as Literature"

Often missing from accounts of the influence of literary criticism on biblical scholarship is the phenomenon of "the Bible as literature," i.e., perennially popular courses taught in English and literature departments of high schools, colleges, and universities throughout the UK and the United States that focus on the literary qualities of scripture (Norton 1993: II, 262–300; Ryken and Longman 1993: 49–68). The first one to use the phrase "the Bible as literature" was Matthew Arnold (1822–88), the English poet and cultural critic whose daytime job was as Her Majesty's Inspector of Schools (Norton 1993: II, 272–6). Arnold was concerned that the Bible in the form of the Authorized Version of 1611 often did not make sense and so revised Isaiah 40–66 for use in elementary schools. The most influential popularizer behind the Bible-as-literature movement in the United States was Richard Green Moulton (Norton 1993: II, 276–85). Moulton (1849–1924), a very successful university extension lecturer for Cambridge University, was appointed Professor of Literature in English at the University of Chicago in 1892 (the year after the university was founded). Moulton was a prolific author who wrote many popular works on the Bible as literature, including *The Modern Reader's Bible: A Series of Works from the Sacred Scriptures Presented in Modern Literary Form* (the first of twenty-one volumes was published in 1895), *The Bible as Literature* (a collection of essays published in 1899), and *A Short Introduction to the Literature of the Bible* (1901). Moulton emphasized "literary morphology," arguing that the Bible contained epics, lyrics, dramas, essays, sonnets, philosophical works, and histories, and also focused on the phenomenon of parallelism at the level of individual verses and clusters of verses, though he tended to ignore or downplay such matters as authorship, imagery, style, and subject matter.

While courses in "the Bible as literature" in secondary schools and colleges in the United States began to increase toward the end of the nineteenth century and became particularly popular in the 1960s, the offering of such courses was sometimes a strategy for smuggling in religious and theological values in order to get around constitutional restrictions. The United States Supreme Court prohibited Bible-reading and prayer in public schools in 1963 as a violation of rights guaranteed by the First and Fourteenth Amendments. A specific instance of strategies to get around this ruling is the recent law passed in 2007 by the Texas State Legislature mandating elective courses in the Bible as literature in high schools beginning in 2009–10 (House Bill 2871). Throughout the twentieth and into the twenty-first centuries, a steady stream of texts often bearing the generic title "The Bible as Literature" (as both the title or subtitle) were published to serve as texts for such courses.

There are several distinctive features of "the Bible as literature" courses: (1) they are most often taught in departments of English; (2) they include both Old and New Testaments as a literary unity; and (3) they are typically taught by those trained in literary criticism and theory, but who have no formal training in biblical studies or biblical languages and consequently they focus exclusively on the English text of the Bible, with the Authorized Version or King James Version as the preferred translation because of its widely recognized literary qualities (Norton 1993: I, 301–48 disagrees at length, speaking of "AVolatry"). The cursory bibliography listed above of texts designed for such courses indicates that they have been taught throughout the twentieth and into the twenty-first centuries and no signs of a decline in interest are apparent. It should be observed that the Bible-as-literature movement is much older than the rise of narrative criticism of New Testament (discussed below), and the two trends have separate genealogies.

Leland Ryken, a professor of English at Wheaton College since 1968 and an evangelical spokesman for the Bible-as-literature movement in the United States, maintains that a literary approach to the Bible consists of consists of recreating experience rather than producing logical arguments (Ryken 1987: 23):

> [The literary approach to the Bible] resists the impulse to reduce literary texts to abstract propositions or to move beyond the text to the history behind it. This means a willingness to accept the text on its own terms and to concentrate on reliving the experiences that are presented. A literary approach assumes that much of the meaning is communicated by means of characters, events and images.

Further, the fact that literature embodies an experience means that the entire poem or the entire story is the meaning (Ryken 1990: 9). In addition to experiential content, literature is also characterized by its techniques and forms, particularly literary genres (Ryken 1990: 10–11). For Ryken (1990: 11), a discourse becomes literary when the author employs metaphor, simile, allusion, pun, paradox, and irony (these are the essence of poetry). He estimates that 80 percent of the Bible qualifies as "literature."

## Modern Trends in Anglo-American Literary Criticism and Theory

*Introduction*

Literary criticism incorporates all methodologically reflective methods of reading and understanding literary texts, and is constantly in the process of developing, inventing, and changing. A recent guide to literary theory discusses fifteen types of literary theory, with each approach exhibiting its own diversity (Castle 2007: vii): cultural studies, deconstruction, ethnic studies, feminist theory, gender and sexuality, Marxist theory, narrative theory, New Criticism, New Historicism, postcolonial studies, postmodernism, poststructuralism, psychoanalysis, reader-response theory, structuralism, and formalism. A recent revised guide to literary approaches to the Gospel of Mark (Anderson and Moore 2008) contains articles on seven methods, most of them aspects of literary criticism: narrative criticism, reader-response criticism, deconstructive criticism, feminist criticism, social criticism, cultural studies, and postcolonial criticism. The limited size of this introductory essay, together with the limitations of the author, mean that just a few of these critical methods can be surveyed: three formalist approaches to literature (i.e., an analysis of the inherent properties of texts): New Criticism, the Chicago school of criticism and narratology, and finally reader-response criticism, a postmodern approach.

## The New Criticism

The New Criticism, a type of formalist literary criticism (i.e., the focus of attention is on literary form) that peaked in Anglo-American criticism from the 1920s through the early 1960s, continued to be influential into the 1970s and 1980s through those trained by exponents of this approach. Important representatives of the New Criticism include I. A. Richards (1893–1979), Robert Penn Warren (1905–89), T. S. Eliot (1888–1965) and Cleanth Brooks (1906–94). The New Criticism was a *text-centered* approach to reading poetry (in contrast to *author-centered* and *reader-centered* approaches) in reaction against a prevailing critical tendency through the nineteenth and early twentieth centuries to emphasize the importance of understanding the historical and social circumstances and politics of the era in which a work of literature arose, its philosophical or theological milieu, or the experiences and frame of mind of its author, as necessary steps for understanding the meaning of a literary work.

Focusing on the historical causes of literature, argued Wellek and Warren (1977: 73–4), runs the risk of reducing literature to a particular aspect of one of those causes. The New Critics rejected all forms of historical scholarship in the study of literature (labeled "extrinsic criticism" by Wellek and Warren 1977), focusing exclusively on *intrinsic criticism* through close textual analysis. New Critics, who tended to focus on poetic texts, treated literary works as autonomous and internally unified organisms, unconnected to the original author and the original readers. A literary work is united from beginning to end in a certain way and its meaning can be found in the complex interrelationship between its parts (i.e., in allusions, images, rhythms, sounds, etc.).

Several key concepts were central for many practitioners of the New Criticism (who also exhibited some variety) including the emphasis on the *close reading* of texts, the notion of *ambiguity* or *overdetermination*, the *intentional fallacy*, and the *affective fallacy*.

(1) The emphasis on the *close reading* of a text involves the careful reading of a literary text, paying close attention to words and their meanings, syntax, sentence structure, imagery, the themes that are treated, the way the narrative unfolds, and the view of the world created by the text; Cleanth Brooks, for example, emphasized "the interior life of a poem" (Leitch 2001: 1350–3). These can be reduced to four levels of focus: linguistic, semantic, structural, and conceptual. The notion of close reading has been widely adopted in many subsequent developments of literary-critical theory, though the notion has often been expanded to include the cultural element, i.e., the relationship of the text to its broader context.

(2) The principle of *ambiguity* or *overdetermination* recognized the fact that a literary text can exhibit multiple yet simultaneous meanings. The term "overdetermination" was adapted by I. A. Richards (from Sigmund Freud) to refer to this phenomenon of a surplus of meaning, also influential in some subsequent hermeneutical theory (Ricoeur 1976).

(3) The *intentional fallacy* is the principle that the author's intention in writing has no significant connection to determining the meaning of the work (Wimsatt and Beardsley 1946). Wimsatt and Beardsley did not claim that there is no relationship between a text and the author's intentions in writing that text, but rather that an author's stated intentions have no validity in determining the meaning or value of a

text (e.g., Aristotle's principle of "catharsis" as the effect of a tragedy on the audience). The intention of the author can only be known to the extent that it is realized in and inferred from the text itself. The intentional fallacy has been widely adopted by literary critics and theorists who no longer subscribe to the tenets of the New Criticism (Rosebury 1997: 16). Yet ruling out the author of discourse has been made problematic by speech-act theorists (e.g., John L. Austin and John R. Searle), who correlate the "illocutionary act" or "speech act" (i.e., by saying something we do something, e.g., "I now pronounce you man and wife") with the intention of the speaker (using the literary meanings, conventions, and rules of discourse), to produce understanding in the form of a recognition of that intention by the hearer.

(4) The New Criticism is also associated with the *affective fallacy* (another principle articulated by Wimsatt and Beardsley 1946), the view formulated in response to various forms of impressionistic criticism, namely that it is a mistake to confuse a literary work with the reader's emotional response to that work. The affective fallacy effectively ruled out the relevance of the reader, just as the intentional fallacy had ruled out the relevance of the author as salient interpretive factors.

### The Chicago school of criticism

One response to the New Criticism was the so-called "Chicago school of criticism" or "neo-Aristotelianism," associated with a group of scholars connected to the University of Chicago from the 1930s through the 1950s (and even later), "founded" by R. S. Crane (1886–1967); see Aune 2003: 317–18 and Schneider 1994. Like the New Criticism, the Chicago school advocated the abandonment of biographical and historical approaches to understanding literature as well as the issue of taste, focusing on the literary work as a rhetorical structure, i.e., they regarded the literary work as a communication between the writer and the reader. Aiming at total objectivity, exponents of the New Criticism tended to focus on such concerns as those discussed in Aristotle's *Poetics* as plot, character, and genre.

A preeminent critic associated with the "second generation" of the Chicago school was University of Chicago professor Wayne C. Booth (1921–2005), who wrote the widely influential book *The Rhetoric of Fiction* (originally published in 1961; second edition 1983), in which he introduced several influential concepts into the literary critical lexicon including "the implied author" (he also used the synonymous phrase "the inferred author") and "the unreliable narrator" (Booth 1983: 71–6, 157–8, 211–21). According to Booth (1983: 74–5), "The 'implied author' chooses, consciously or unconsciously, what we read; we infer him as an ideal, literary, created version of the real man; he is the sum of his own choices." When *The Rhetoric of Fiction* was first published in 1961, Booth accepted the validity of the "intentional fallacy" (in continuity with the New Criticism), yet adhered to the notion that literary works constituted intentionally structured normative worlds accessible to ethical criticism. The concept of the "implied author" enabled him to maintain that he could interpret and criticize the normative worlds of literary works without falling victim to the "intentional fallacy."

Despite the fact that the concept of "the implied author" originally proposed by Booth has become one eclectic feature of literary criticism generally, it has been subject to criticism, particularly by narratologists. Genette (1988: 137), for example, maintains that "narratology has no need to go beyond the narrative situation, and the two agents 'implied author' and 'implied reader' are clearly situated in that beyond." Mieke Bal (1981: 209), another prominent narratologist, argues that it would be better "to speak of the interpretation, or the overall meaning of the text" than of the implied author. Bal called the implied author a "remainder category, a kind of *passepartout* ("goes everywhere") that serves to clear away all the problematic remainders of a theory" (1981: 209).

## Narrative theory or narratology

Narratology or the structural analysis of narrative is (like the New Criticism and the Chicago school) one of several types of formalist theory. Narratology (the term *narratologie* was proposed by Todorov 1969: 10), is a type of structuralism that originated with the work of the Russian formalists of the 1920s, such as Vladimir Propp (1895–1970) and Roman Jacobson (1896–1982). One of the lasting insights of the structural approach to literature is the distinction made between story and discourse, i.e. the sequence of events that constitute the *story* does not necessarily coincide with the particular form of the narrative (*discourse*), i.e., there often tensions between the temporal order of the story and the actual structure of the narrative (Chatman 1978: 19; Castle 2007: 116–17). Influential narratologists include Roland Barthes (1915–80), Algirdas Greimas (1917–92), Gérard Genette (b. 1930), Seymour Chatman (b. 1928), and Mieke Bal (b. 1946).

Narratology is a descriptive method for discovering and describing the mechanics of narrative and as such is not a literary-critical method (Chatman 1978: 18) since it not concerned with judging whether a narrative is good or bad, whether it has a point or is pointless or whether it is characterized by unity or disunity. Though there are many contributions to narratology, it is instructive to focus on the work of Gérard Genette's *Narrative Discourse* (1988; originally published in French in 1972). Well-known narrative devices, such as the flashback, the omniscient narrator, and the third-person narrative, are the kinds of formal narrative features that narratologists are concerned with describing more systematically. Genette understands the term "narrative" in three senses (1988: 25–7): (1) the actual order of events in the text (i.e., plot); (2) the sequence in which those events actually occurred (i.e., story); and (3) the act of narrating itself. Each of the five chapters of *Narrative Discourse* discusses a main category of Genette's grammar of narrative discourse: (1) *Order*: the sequence of time as presented by the text, such as prolepsis ("anticipation"), analepsis ("flashback"), and anachrony (discordances between "story" and "plot"). (2) *Duration*: how the narrative shortens episodes, expands them, summarizes them, etc. (3) *Frequency*: whether an event in the story happens once and is narrated once, happens once but is narrated several times, happens several times but is narrated once, etc. (4) *Mood* involves both distance and perspective: (a) *distance*: is the story simply recounted by the narrator (diegesis) or it is presented as if narrated by someone else (mimesis)? (b) *Perspective* or point of view – does the author know more or less than the narrator, or the same as the narrator? – the narrative may be "non-focalized" (delivered by the omniscient narrator outside the actions) or "internally focalized" (recounted by one character from a specific or from varied perspectives or from the viewpoints of several characters). (5) *Voice* is the act of narrating itself; a narrator may be heterodiegetic (absent from his own narrative), homodiegetic (inside his narrative in first-person stories), or autodiegetic (the narrator is inside the narrative and is its principal character). While this is a cursory overview of Genette's analytical categories it does contain the rudiments of his program.

## Reader–response criticism

Reader-oriented criticism exhibits great variety, with its variant forms exhibiting neither a common methodology nor a common goal (Rabinowitz 1995: 375). Reader-response criticism focuses on the reader's experience of a literary work, unlike other forms of literary criticism that focus on the author ("authorial intention") or the literary work itself (e.g., New Criticism).

Reader-response criticism began in the 1960s and 1970s, just as the New Criticism was breathing its last. Types of reader-response criticism, which focuses on the reader rather than on the author or the text, began to flourish in the 1960s in both Germany and the United States through the work of such critics as the German scholar Wolfgang Iser (1978) and the American scholar Stanley Fish (1980). Reader-response critics range along a continuum from "individualists," such as the early Stanley Fish (who understand the individual reader as in control of the reading experience) and "uniformists," such as Wolfgang Iser (who emphasize the role of the text, and who understand the common features of readers as driven by the text). Reader-response approaches focus on precisely what the New Criticism sought to eliminate: the affective or subjective nature of criticism, arguing that the reader plays an active role in producing the meaning of a text. Reader-response criticism, then, is an umbrella term for a variety of reading strategies that leave behind "understanding" as signification, referentiality, and semantics for an emphasis on "experiencing what the text does to us in the process of reading" (Robert Fowler 1991: 55).

The collection of articles by Fish (1980), entitled *Is There a Text in This Class? The Authority of Interpretive Communities*, provides a nice entry into the author's evolving views on the role of the reader. In a retrospective introduction to his work, Fish (1980: 1) observes that in 1970 he was asking the question, "Is the reader or the text the source of meaning?" Fish was assuming the independence and stability of both the text and the reader, a stability that was central to formalistic approaches to texts (e.g., the New Criticism). Fish asked a new question, not "What does this text *mean*?" but "What does this text *do*?" Retaining a view of the text as a stable entity, at the same time he denied that the text contained a privileged meaning, giving the reader and the text joint responsibility for producing meaning. To avoid the objection that focusing on the reader was tantamount to abandoning the possibility of saying anything about a text that would be of general interest, Fish posited a level of experience that all people share, regardless of education or experience. Distinguishing something that was subjective and idiosyncratic from what was objective and shared, Fish favored suppressing what was subjective and idiosyncratic for a kind of reading response that everyone shares (Fish 1980: 5). Against the charge that emphasizing the reader results in anarchism and solipsism, Fish maintained that the text imposed restraints on the reader's imagination (still maintaining New Criticism's emphasis on the integrity of the text). Fish realized that the "units of sense" in text where readers "do things" are in fact not a property of the text but are the function of the interpretive model that readers unconsciously bring to a text (Fish 1980: 13). At this point, the notion of "interpretive communities" became central for the development of Fish's critical theory. He recognized that "it is interpretive communities, rather than either the text or the reader, that produce meanings and are responsible for the emergence of formal features" (Fish 1980: 14), signaling his abandonment of a subject–object dichotomy in the task of criticism. Meanings and texts produced by interpretive communities are not subjective because they are not the product of the idiosyncratic view of an individual, but rather are based on a public and conventional perspective. The reason for agreement and disagreement in interpretations became clear to Fish: competing interpretations of texts are thus based on the fact that they arise from different interpretive communities (Fish 1980: 15). He concludes: "In other words, there is no single way of reading that is correct or natural, only 'ways of reading' that are extensions of community perspectives" (Fish 1980: 16).

## Narrative Criticism

### Beginnings of narrative criticism

Narrative criticism, a phrase coined by Rhoads (1982: 112) but not used by secular literary critics, is an eclectic form of literary criticism that was developed by New Testament scholars in the 1970s and early 1980s as a synchronic literary method for interpreting the gospels. Seymour Chatman (1978) has what I hope he considers the honor of being the foster-father of narrative criticism, since his 1978 book *Story and Discourse* was formative in the development of narrative criticism as applied to Mark by Rhoads and Mitchie (1982), then Rhoads, Dewey, and Mitchie (1999) and then to John by Culpepper (1983). Though narrative criticism arose after the New Criticism had become *passé* in the early 1960s, it was nevertheless also indebted to the text-centered approach fostered by New Critics (i.e., the text as an independent narrative world), along with New Criticism's rejection of the relevance of biographical and historical factors in understanding the meaning of literary texts together with the *intentional fallacy* (Rhoads, Dewey, and Michie 1999: 269) and the *affective fallacy* (Chatman's own eclectic method was in part dependent on Booth 1961). The rise of reader-response criticism, which paradoxically found ready acceptance among biblical narrative critics (paradoxical because reader-oriented criticism rejects the assumptions of formalism), resulted in the rejection of New Criticism's affective fallacy, though the intentional fallacy continued to be maintained as valid.

During the 1960s and 1970s, particularly in the United States, some biblical scholars began to be critical of diachronic approaches to the study of New Testament that were more concerned with how a biblical text came into existence than with the text itself. The main concern of historical criticism and allied methods (source criticism, form criticism, redaction criticism) was on the written and oral sources that lay behind the gospels and how author-editors (i.e., "Mark," "John," "Luke," and "Matthew") assembled sources and edited them. Influenced particularly by the New Criticism, which had declined by the early 1960s, as well as by the work of narratologist Seymour Chatman (1978), some scholars began to emphasize a synchronic approach to the biblical text, preferring holistic over against atomistic analyses of biblical books, thus paying much closer attention to the narrative character of the gospels and Acts. This switch from an exclusively historical-philological approach to biblical narrative to a literary-critical approach has been regarded by some as a paradigm-shift in New Testament studies, particularly in American biblical scholarship (Ryken 1990: 3; Ryken and Longman 1993: 49).

One of the earliest calls for the use of literary criticism in the analysis of the gospels and Acts, as a complement to historical criticism, was William Beardslee (1970). Beardslee's little book was followed by the formation of the Seminar on Mark in the Society of Biblical Literature, from 1971 to 1980, some of whose members experimented with literary approaches to the Gospel of Mark (some of these included Joanna Dewey, Robert Fowler, Werner Kelber, Norman Perrin, Norman Petersen, and David Rhoads). Toward the end of the 1970s, Norman Petersen (1978), largely dependent on formalist criticism (i.e., he relies on René Wellek and Austin Warren, both of whom represented the New Criticism) as well as on the communications model of the Russian linguist and formalist critic and theorist Roman Jacobson, articulated a literary model for the historical criticism of biblical texts, making a distinction between illegitimate historicism and an appropriate mode of the historical criticism. Jacobson's model has the influential entailment that a literary text must be regarded as a self-enclosed narrative world that must be understood in its own terms and which may or may not refer to the real world (the central supposition of the New Criticism).

## Kermode on Mark (1979)

At the same time, Frank Kermode (b. 1919), a Shakespeare scholar who many regard as the greatest living English literary critic, gave a series of lectures in 1977–8 at Harvard University on the gospels, largely focusing on Mark, published in 1979 with the title *The Genesis of Secrecy: On the Interpretation of Narrative*. Combining British common-sense criticism with some features of French poststructural theory (Moore 1989: 122), Kermode styles himself as a critic (he does not pretend to be a theorist) who uses a secular approach to biblical studies, which is under the general control of a profession with some kind of "doctrinal adhesion" to "the ecclesiastical institution," while secular critics have none (1979: viii–ix). His focus is on the recalcitrance or "radiant obscurity" (1979: 42) of narrative, for which Mark provides a principal example as a narrative that both reveals and conceals (the parable theory of Mark

4:11–12 serves as a focus for this dialectic). He does not so much intend to offer an interpretation of Mark as to indicate "possibilities of interpretation which are not those of the professional" (1979: ix). He calls attention to the preference among interpreters for the latent "spiritual" readings to the manifest "carnal" readings (1979: 18), for virtually all interpreters come to a text expecting to discover something new. He focuses on parables as stories which are not taken at face value and which are emblematic of all narrative and are as open-ended as life itself (1979: 23–47). Kermode observes that there are powerful forces at work pushing readers to seek narrative coherence (1979: 53), leading to the discovery of occult plot designs (1979: 72). Mark is not a simple chronicle, he maintains, "but a history with a literary structure" (1979: 116–17) and fiction and history-writing have a close relationship, with no textual properties demarcating the one from the other (1979: 101–23). The temptation to read a plausible narrative like Mark as referring to the events it narrates is what he terms "the myth of transparency," i.e., ignoring what is written in favor of what it is written about, following Spinoza in distinguishing meaning from truth (1979: 118–19) a distinction Kermode considers characteristic of all modern interpretation (1979: 122). Taking a page from formalism, Kermode regards certain characters in Mark (Peter, Judas, and the young man in the shirt in Mark 14:51–2) as the developed plot functions of Denial, Betrayal, and Flight (1979: 84–92). He finds in Mark the schematic opposition of silence and proclamation as well as the existence of other related oppositions such as election and rebuke, clean and not clean, the things of God and the things of men (Kermode 1979: 140). Kermode is a critic, not a theorist, and the *Genesis of Secrecy* is itself emblematic of the recalcitrance of narrative. Kermode's book was widely reviewed by New Testament scholars, many of whom worried about his unstructured method and unsettling obscurity. For whatever complex reasons, Kermode's challenging discussion of Mark and the other gospels has had very little palpable influence on narrative criticism.

### Rhoads, Dewey, and Michie on Mark (1999)

Some years later, narrative criticism was applied to the Gospel of Mark in the slim but influential book on Mark by Rhoads and Michie (1982), with a second edition by David Rhoads, Joanna Dewey, and Donald Michie (1999), which takes account of changes in literary theory since 1982. The book reflects the influence of the formalist theories including the New Criticism (which had become *passé* nearly two decades before the first edition appeared). In this discussion the focus will be on the second edition of 1999.

Assuming the narrative coherence of the text (an assumption pointedly rejected by postmodernism), Rhoads and Mitchie (1982) discuss the story of Mark and the rhetorical techniques used to tell the story, including point of view, plot, character, setting, and style. Unlike many narrative critical treatments of the gospels and Acts that have appeared subsequently, Rhoads, Dewey, and Mitchie do not discuss in detail the critical theories that they have adopted to analyze the text of Mark. In that sense, it is a user-friendly analysis.

The basic purpose of the book is to introduce the Gospel of Mark *as story* and owes much to formalist types of literary theory, including the New Criticism and narratology.

The second edition also makes use of reader-response criticism, which is problematic in view of the theoretical tensions between formalism and reader-oriented approaches (narratology, for example, maintains the independence and integrity of the text, typically rejected by reader-response theories, and few reader-response critics would be as overly concerned as are the authors to "avoid reading our own ideas into a story" [1999: 148]). The authors maintain that there is no such thing as an "objective" or "legitimate" reading of Mark (1999: xi). The authors also claim to be influenced by a variety of other approaches, such as deconstructionist, feminist, and cultural interpretations. As in the first edition, the second edition emphasizes the coherence of Mark's narrative (1999: 3–4), a supposition that does not fit well with deconstructionist assumptions (mentioned in the introduction, but never to appear again). In view of Mark's unity, the gaps that exist in the story are regarded as intentional, due in part to the fact that it is an episodic text originally intended for oral performance. Mark is a version of historical events, in which the people, places, and events have coherence within that story world. Five key features are important for interpreting Mark (1999: 6–7): *narrator* (the voice and point of view of the storyteller reflecting the beliefs and values of the story); *setting* (the context within the story; the specific temporal and spatial contexts in which the events take place); *plot* (the order of the narrative, sequential relations, breakthroughs and the development and resolution of conflict); *characters* (actors in the story, their motives and drives, their changes and developments because of the action); and *rhetoric* (the ways an author uses the features of narrative to persuade readers to enter into and accept the world of the story).

The first section of the book (1999: 8–38) contains a fresh and lively translation of Mark; Peter, for example, is rendered "Rock" the English equivalent of the Greek alias *Petros*. Succeeding chapters are devoted to the narrator, the settings, the plot, the characters (Jesus, the authorities, the disciples, the people), and finally, the reader.

The "narrator" (1999: 39–62), of Mark is a third-person narrator who has "unlimited omniscience" and who guides the reader using narrative asides as a way of commenting on the story (e.g., Mark 13:14: "Let the public reader understand"). The narrator also provides privileged knowledge to the reader, as in 1:1, where he informs the reader that Jesus is "the anointed one, the Son of God." Under the rubric "point of view," the narrator controls the overarching point of view in the narrative; for example, Jesus is depicted as a reliable character who, viewed from within, is compassionate, loving, angry at oppression, and anguished over his impending death, while the narrator presents the authorities in an unfavorable light. The narrator's ideological point of view underlies the moral dilemma of either "thinking in God's terms" (which is good), or "thinking in human terms" (which is bad; 1999: 45). The narrator's style is characterized by brevity and economy, while the tempo imposed on the story is brisk (the term "immediately" occurs frequently). The narrative is episodic, with the episodes connected by overlapping patterns of repetition, two types of which are foreshadowing and retrospection (prolepsis and analepsis in Genette's categories). Mark also uses type-scenes (episodes with stereotypical features), episodes which are "sandwiched," i.e., one episode is framed by the beginning and end of another episode and episodes are arranged in concentric patterns and progressive episodes in series of three (1999: 51–5).

Turning to "the settings" of the story (1999: 63–72), Mark assumes a cosmic setting (God and angels, Satan and demons, clean and unclean animals, etc.), but this cosmic setting has somehow gone wrong and is in process of change, providing a context for divine–human conflict to drive the plot. The social setting (Israel occupied by the Romans) contributes an atmosphere of oppression and threat and is the context for the establishment of God's kingdom. The journey of Jesus is the setting for events described in the story, from the Jordan through Galilee to Gentile regions and then finally to Jerusalem, with the journey motif, with emphases on "going ahead" and "following" as a metaphor for the "way of God."

In discussing "the plot" (1999: 73–97), which like most plots involves conflict, the authors emphasize the cohesiveness of the actions in the story (1999: 73): "Mark's story is unified around one overall goal: Jesus struggles to establish the rule of God in the face of obstacles and opposition." Within this framework, three separate plot lines are represented by the conflicts between Jesus and three different sets of "characters": nonhuman forces (Jesus confronts Satan in the desert), the authorities (conflicts between this group and Jesus lead to his execution), and the disciples (miracles proliferate until Peter's confession that Jesus is the messiah). In Mark's plot, the human situation of Jesus and the disciples changes for the worse, yet Jesus himself is vindicated through the resurrection. God is the active "character" in Mark that drives the action of the plot and his rule challenges every other claim to power, beginning with Jesus' initial announcement of the arrival of the kingdom of God, which nevertheless remains hidden, until the kingdom will finally be revealed within a generation (i.e., after the destruction of Jerusalem) and resolve all conflicts by judgment and salvation.

There are four main characters or character-groups in Mark; Jesus the protagonist, the authorities as the antagonists, the disciples, and minor characters (1999: 98–136). The narrator does not develop full-blown characters, but his characterization is nevertheless rich by being minimally suggestive and he tends to regard characters as types that change very little. Mark's characters consistently embody one of two ways of thinking, God's terms or human terms. With regard to Jesus, a "round" character who is the central figure in the story, more and more is progressively revealed about who he really is, i.e., the one anointed by God and empowered by his spirit to establish his rule that will culminate in the restoration of all creation. Jesus has divine authority to challenge national institutions, has extraordinary trust in God, and yet renounces himself and gives his life for others, resulting in his execution and resurrection, signaled by the empty tomb that serves to place the emphasis in the story on the life of Jesus.

The authorities depicted in Mark have misunderstood God's authority (which they claim) in terms of domination rather than service, and in consequence have become "this adulterous and sinful generation." They are therefore willfully blind and deaf to the rule of God proclaimed by Jesus. The disciples, the twelve men that Jesus chooses to follow him, struggle with the dilemma of living on God's terms or human terms, and they are characterized as being fearful and lacking understanding, the opposite of faith, while at the same time they are devoted to Jesus and serve him. When they enter Jerusalem with Jesus, it seems that they might succeed in following Jesus, yet they fail him by fleeing to save their lives after his arrest. The reader is led to have ambivalent feelings about the disciples, whose fate is still open when the story concludes when the women at the tomb too fail because of fear.

After discussing all these primary narrative features, Rhoads, Dewey, and Michie include a chapter on "The Reader" (1999: 137–46) in which they ask what the reader is experiencing and how the reader is affected by that experience; in other words, they shift "from asking what the story means to asking what the story is doing to the reader in the course of reading" (1999: 137). They then introduce the notion of the ideal reader as a mirror-image of the narrator (a variant term for "the implied reader" introduced by Wolfgang Iser), concluding that "the story of Mark seeks to create ideal readers who will receive the rule of God with faith and have the courage to follow Jesus whatever the consequences" (1999: 138). Turning to the real first-century readers, they propose that Mark's rhetoric is intend to motivate real readers to become ideal readers and followers of Jesus.

### Culpepper on John (1983)

Another early and important contribution to the development of narrative criticism was Alan Culpepper's *Anatomy of the Fourth Gospel: A Study in Literary Design* (1983), with a foreword by Frank Kermode. The twenty-fifth anniversary of this publication was celebrated by a collection of essays edited by Tom Thatcher and Stephen D. Moore, *Anatomies of Narrative Criticism* (2008). The book proved useful to many in the guild because the author provided detailed discussions of each major narrative device. Culpepper pointedly avoids all of the typical concerns of historical criticism, but maintains that a literary approach to the Fourth Gospel can supplement them (1983: 11). In his analysis, Culpepper is primarily dependent on the communications model of Chatman (1978), ultimately derived from the model formulated by Roman Jacobson. The author discusses many of the features found in the structural analysis of narrative, dividing his book into chapters on narrator and point of view, narrative time, plot, characters, implicit commentary, and implied reader. Each chapter begins with a discussion of the literary theory and technical terms and concepts used in these approaches and then applies them to the narrative, often with striking results.

In the introduction to the chapter on "Narrator and Point of View," the author defines terms like "the real author" (not Culpepper's concern), "the implied author," a conception borrowed from Booth and rejected by Genette (unlike the narrator, the implied author has no voice and does not communicate with the reader, but is the sum of all the choices made by the real author in writing the narrative), and "the narrator" (the voice, or rhetorical device, that tells the story and speaks to the reader). Culpepper summarizes the function of the narrator in these words (1983: 17):

> In John, the narrator is the one who speaks in the prologue, tells the story, introduces the dialogue, provides explanations, translates terms, and tells us what various characters knew or did not know.

"Point of view" (based on proposals by Genette and Uspensky), is determined by whether the story is told by a main character within the story, or an omniscient author, or from the outside by someone assuming the role of observer. Based on the prologue in John 1:1–18, the narrator is omniscient, since he or she knows what occurred in the beginning when the Word was with God, as well as what Jesus is thinking. Culpepper argues that Jesus' point of view, found in the farewell discourse, "corresponds remarkably well with that of the narrator" (1983: 36). He goes on to maintain that (1983: 42–3):

> Actually, the author, who was probably informed by tradition handed down within the Johannine community, fashioned the character, Jesus, as he wrote and interpreted Jesus through both Jesus' dialogue and the narrator's interpretive comments.

The Paraclete and the Beloved Disciple may be idealized representations of the author (1983: 43–9).

In discussing narrative time (1983: 53–75) Culpepper, expressing dependence on Genette, distinguishes discourse (how it is told) from story (what is told). Under the headings of order, duration, and frequency (he has little to say about the last two), he discusses a few select examples. He uses two of Genette's temporal categories, analepsis (references to past events internal or external to the story) and prolepsis (anticipations of future events. One type of analepsis, found in John 6:70 ("Did I not choose you, the twelve ..."), is of an earlier event not mentioned. One type of prolepsis, in John 3:24 ("For John had not yet been put in prison"), anticipates an event that had not yet occurred in the story.

In discussing plot (1983: 79–98), Culpepper reviews several definitions and concludes that the central features of plot are "sequence, causality, unity, and affective power of a narrative" (1983: 80), though the term "unity" is absent from all the reviewed definitions. He argues that John does have a plot and describes it in these terms (1983: 88):

> In the face of opposition of cosmic proportions, his [Jesus'] task is to reveal the Father by bearing witness to the truth (which ultimately is personal rather than propositional) and take away the sin of the world.

Turning to characters (1983: 99–148), Culpepper first surveys conceptions of characterization then current in contemporary criticism. The two main options are considering characters as "autonomous beings" or agents with functions to be fulfilled. Accepting the first approach, he reviews E. M. Forster's well-known distinction between "flat" characters who are caricatures embodying single ideas or qualities from "round" characters" who are complex in motivation and temperament. The character of Jesus is static, and most characters in the Fourth Gospel represent ethical types. He then provides a survey of the features of the various "characters" in John, not all of whom are given an age or a physical description: Jesus and the Father, the disciples, the Jews, and minor characters. He concludes that the characters in the Fourth Gospel have two functions: (1) they serve to draw out Jesus' character by providing a series of individuals with whom he interacts, and (2) they represent alternative responses to Jesus with the attendant consequences.

Next, Culpepper turns to a discussion of implicit commentary or "silent" communication between author and reader (1983: 151–202), focusing on the occurrence of misunderstandings based on ambiguity, marking "insiders" off from "outsiders," which are eventually explained (all listed in 1983: 161–2); irony, directed not at the reader but rather the clumsy attempts of many of the characters to understand the enigma of Jesus (treated in detail by one of Culpepper's students, Paul Duke 1985); and symbolism (used to point to the transcendent mystery of Jesus). Finally, Culpepper discusses "the implied reader," a conception proposed by Wolfgang Iser (1983: 205–27). The author discusses the four types of audience embedded in every narrative text formulation proposed by Peter J. Rabinowitz (1983: 208): (1) the actual audience (the real reader, whether in the first century or today); (2) the authorial audience (the readers for whom the real author thinks he is writing); (3) the narrative audience (readers who suspend their disbelief and accept the story as a real historical account); and (4) the *ideal narrative audience*, the reader who "adopts the narrator's ideological point of view, penetrates his misunderstandings, appreciates the irony, and is moved to fresh appreciations of transcendent mystery through the gospel's symbolism."

## Major emphases of narrative criticism

There are four basic aspects of the approach of narrative criticism to the gospels (Merenlahti 2002: 18–19): (1) Narrative has a two-level structure in which aspects of form and content (the "how" and the "what") of narrative can be distinguished (borrowed from narratology). (2) Narrative criticism espouses the ideal of a distinctly *literary* approach that investigates the gospels as *literature*. (3) Narrative criticism regards the text as "a closed literary object whose form can be observed empirically." (4) Narrative criticism maintains that formal analysis reveals the literary value of a text which is based on the narrative unity of the text.

Narrative critics have shared the assumption that the gospels may be regarded as literature because they exemplify the qualities of literary unity and coherence, part of the traditional literary paradigm of what it is that characterizes literature in the proper sense of the term (Merenlahti 2002: 2). This single issue had three aspects, articulated by Merenlahti (2002: 3): "Are the gospels (1) unified enough to (2) be valued as literature, which would justify (3) a 'literary' approach?" The problem with this basic assumption is that the literary paradigm on which it is based, part of a traditional conception of what constitutes "literature," is open to serious doubt and in fact has few recent defenders.

Apart from the question of the literariness of the gospels, it remains true that the single most characteristic feature of narrative criticism has been the emphasis on the inherent unity of the gospel narratives. In his detailed review and critique of the rise and development of narrative criticism, Moore (1989) is particularly critical of the focus on narrative unity, an ideology that dominates the work of many narrative critics such as Tannehill (1986–90), whose two-volume narrative commentary on Luke–Acts is programmatically entitled *The Narrative Unity of Luke–Acts*. The emphasis on narrative unity is problematic because it is a concern distinctive of narrative critics with no real counterpart in secular literary criticism (Merenlahti and Hakola 1999). The use of deconstruction theory by New Testament scholars (of which Moore 1989 is an exponent) has joined forces with traditional historical criticism in recognizing the presence of aporias, contradictions and unevennesses in the texts of the gospels overlooked or ignored by narrative critics.

Concerned that traditional types of biblical criticism approach the text of the New Testament in a piecemeal and fragmentizing fashion, Rhoads argues for a holistic, text-oriented approach in which one would analyze "the close universe of the story-world" (Rhoads 1982: 413). This focus on the narratives of each of the gospels is aimed at integrating all the elements in each narrative into an overall construal of the whole narrative. To the extent that this is successful, the work can be regarded as an artistic success (Merenlahti and Hakola 1999: 15). This approach has obvious similarities with the New Criticism with its concentration on "the autonomous text."

Narrative criticism is a development within biblical scholarship which, though initially based on the theoretical studies of non-biblical literary critics (e.g., Chatman 1978, a structuralist or narratologist, and Booth 1961, a representative of the Chicago school), has incorporated a variety of insights from these critics which have evolved into an eclectic form of literary criticism with no direct counterpart in non-biblical literary criticism. Since the literary theory upon which narrative critics have drawn is primarily concerned with a poetics of fiction, to a certain extent, treating the gospels as fiction takes its cue from postmodernism, which blurs the difference between fiction and non-fiction (Merenlahti 2002: 10).

Narrative criticism exhibits great variety, in part because New Testament practitioners are rooted in a variety of theological contexts that in part determine how they construe the method. Resseguie (2005) deals with conventional narrative critical concerns such as rhetoric, setting, characterization, point of view, and plot. He parts company with those who espouse the intentional fallacy, however, by maintaining that a text guides readers to read it as the author intended (i.e., the typical concerns of reader-response criticism are marginalized).

## Annotated Bibliography

Ackerman, James S. with Jane Stouder Hawley. *On Teaching the Bible as Literature: A Guide to Selected Biblical Narratives for Secondary Schools*. Indiana: Indiana University Press, 1967. Ackerman has been a leader in the "Bible as literature" movement in the United States.

Ackerman, James S., Thayer S. Warshaw, and John Sweet (eds.). *The Bible as/in Literature*. 2nd edn. Glenview: Scott Foresman, 1995. One of the better texts used in American "Bible as literature" courses.

Adam, A. K. M. *What is Postmodern Biblical Criticism?* Minneapolis: Fortress Press, 1995. One of the best introductions to postmodern biblical criticism. An excellent introduction by a New Testament scholar committed to a postmodernist approach to the Bible.

Allen, Graham. *Intertextuality*. London and New York: Routledge, 2000. Readable introduction to a modern critical method not discussed in the preceding essay.

Alter, Robert and Frank Kermode (eds.). *The Literary Guide to the Bible*. Cambridge, MA: Harvard University Press, 1987. Rather than a "literary" guide to the books of the Bible, this edited work consists largely in conventional approaches to the study of the Bible, particularly historical criticism.

Anderson, Janice Capel and Stephen D. Moore (eds.). *Mark and Method: New Approaches in Biblical Studies*. 2nd edn. Minneapolis: Fortress Press, 2008. Collection of essays that showcases the newer literary approaches to the New Testament by two prominent New Testament deconstructionist critics.

Aune, David E. *The Westminster Dictionary of New Testament and Early Christian Literature and Rhetoric.* Louisville: Westminster John Knox, 2003. A reference work that focuses on ancient literary methods and genres, but which includes some emphasis on modern developments in New Testament studies as well.

Bal, Mieke. "The Laughing Mice: On Focalization." *Poetics Today* 2 (1981), 202–10.

Bal, Mieke. *Narratology: An Introduction to the Theory of Narrative.* 2nd edn. Toronto and Buffalo: University of Toronto Press, 1997. Important introduction to narratology by a prominent practitioner of the approach.

Bazerman, Charles. "Discursively Structured Activities." *Mind, Culture and Activity* 4 (1997), 296–308.

Beardslee, William A. *Literary Criticism of the New Testament.* Philadelphia: Fortress Press, 1970. Discusses the major forms in the New Testament, including gospels (religious stories centering on Jesus enabling the hearer-reader to be present at the saving acts), history, exemplified in Acts (linear portrayal because of God's purposes are open-ended), apocalypse (embodies a profound desire for the all-inclusive transformation of reality), as well as a discussion of the proverb.

Beebee, Thomas O. *The Ideology of Genre: A Comparative Study of Generic Instability.* University Park, PA: Pennsylvania State University Press, 1994. An important discussion of a new approach to genre criticism.

Blamires, Harry. *A History of Literary Criticism.* New York: St. Martin's Press, 1991. A work that provides an excellent overview of the history of literary criticism from its beginnings in the Greek world to the mid-twentieth century.

Booth, Wayne. *The Rhetoric of Fiction.* 2nd edn. Chicago: University of Chicago Press, 1983. The first edition appeared in 1961. An important work by a prominent member of the second general of the Chicago school of literary criticism that has influenced many developments in modern literary criticism.

*The Cambridge History of Literary Criticism.* 9 vols. Cambridge: Cambridge University Press, 1989–. The most authoritative and detailed work on the history of literary criticism now available. The first volume (Kennedy 1989) focuses on Classical literary criticism.

Carter, Warren. *John: Storyteller, Interpreter, Evangelist.* Peabody: Hendrickson, 2006. An introductory text that introduces the reader to the results of literary and historical criticism in analyzing the Fourth Gospel.

Castle, Gregory. *The Blackwell Guide to Literary Theory.* Oxford: Blackwell, 2007. A relatively short but excellent guide to the panoply of modern literary theories.

Chatman, Seymour. *Story and Discourse: Narrative Structure in Fiction and Film.* Ithaca, NY: Cornell University Press, 1978. An influential work by an American narratologist.

Cohen, Ralph. "History and Genre." *New Literary History* 17 (1986), 203–18.

Crane, R. S. "History versus Criticism in the Study of Literature." Vol. 2, pp. 3–24 in *The Idea of the Humanities and Other Essays Critical and Historical.* Chicago and London: The University of Chicago Press, 1967. A programmatic article by the "founder" of the Chicago school of literary criticism, originally published in 1934, urging literary critics to abandon historical and biographical approaches and the issue of taste in order to focus rather on the literary work as a rhetorically structured whole.

Culpepper, R. Alan. *Anatomy of the Fourth Gospel: A Study in Literary Design.* Philadelphia: Fortress Press, 1983. The first detailed application of narrative criticism to the Fourth Gospel using the work of narratologist Chatman (1978) as a template.

Day, Gary. *Literary Criticism: A New History.* Edinburgh: Edinburgh University Press, 2008.

Doty, William G. "The Concept of Genre in Literary Analysis." Pp. 413–48 in *The Society of Biblical Literature One-Hundred-Eighth Annual Meeting Book of Seminar Papers: Friday-Tuesday, 1–5 September 1972*. Edited by Lane C. McGaughy. 2 vols. Society of Biblical Literature, 1972. One of the first important contributions to the study of genre criticism by a New Testament scholar.

Duke, Paul. *Irony in the Fourth Gospel*. Atlanta: John Knox Press, 1985. An excellent work focusing on a literary device that pervades the Gospel of John by a student of Alan Culepper.

Eagleton, Terry. *Literary Theory: An Introduction*. 2nd edn. Oxford: Blackwell, 1996. Originally published in 1983, Eagleton's book has been one of the most influential introductions to the subject.

Fish, Stanley. *Is There a Text in This Class? The Authority of Interpretive Communities*. Cambridge, MA: Harvard University Press, 1980. An important collection of articles by a major representative of reader-response criticism, highlighting the development of his thought.

Fishelov, David. "Genre Theory and Family Resemblance – Revisited." *Poetics* 20 (1991), 123–38. A critique of the particular application of Wittgenstein's family resemblance theory that emphasizes the negative.

Fowler, Robert M. *Let the Reader Understand: Reader-Response Criticism and the Gospel of Mark*. Minneapolis: Fortress Press, 1991. Influential study of Mark by a New Testament scholar who introduced an approach to reader-response criticism to the guild.

Frow, John. *Genre*. London and New York: Routledge, 2006. A short but stunning book on the issue of genre that sorts through the many modern developments of genre criticism.

Frye, Northrop. *The Great Code: The Bible as Literature*. New York: Harcourt Brace Jovanovich, 1982. A classic work in which a prominent Canadian literary critic applies his craft to the Bible.

Genette, Gérard. *Narrative Discourse: An Essay on Method*. Ithaca: Cornell University Press, 1980. An influential work by one of the more prominent narratologists.

Genette, Gérard. *Narrative Discourse Revisited*. Ithaca, NY: Cornell University Press, 1988.

Genette, Gérard. *Paratexts: Thresholds of Interpretation*. Trans. Jane E. Lewin. Cambridge: Cambridge University Press, 1997. The author examines the structural packaging of literary works (advertising, titles, book jackets, layout, etc.).

Gymnich, Marion, Birgit Neumann, and Ansgar Nünning. *Gattungstheorie und Gattungsgeschichte*. Trier: Wissenschaftlicher Verlag, 2007. Up-to-date discussion of developments in German genre criticism by three German literary critics.

Habib, Rafey. *A History of Literary Criticism from Plato to the Present*. Malden, MA: Blackwell, 2005. Excellent overview of the entire history of literary criticism.

Habib, Rafey. *A History of Modern Literary Criticism and Theory*. Malden, MA: Blackwell, 2008. A competent presentation of twentieth-century developments in literary criticism and theory.

Hellholm, David. "The Problem of Apocalyptic Genre and the Apocalypse of John." *Early Christian Apocalypticism: Genre and Social Setting, Semeia* 36 (1986), 65–96. Using linguistic methods pioneered in Germany, Hellholm provides a generic analysis of the Apocalypse that finds significance in the most embedded textual unit (Rev. 21:5–8).

Iser, Wolfgang. *The Implied Reader: Patterns of Communication in Prose Fiction from Bunyan to Beckett*. Baltimore: Johns Hopkins University Press, 1974. English translation of a book published in 1972 in German.

Iser, Wolfgang. *The Act of Reading: A Theory of Aesthetic Response*. Baltimore: Johns Hopkins University Press, 1978.

Jeffrey, David Lyle (ed.). *A Dictionary of Biblical Tradition in English Literature*. Grand Rapids: Eerdmans, 1992. A large work that shows the widespread influence of the Bible on English literature from the eighteenth century on.

Keefer, Kyle. *The New Testament as Literature: A Very Short Introduction*. Oxford: Oxford University Press, 2008. A "very short" but excellent overview of modern developments in the literary study of the New Testament.

Kennedy, George A. *Classical Criticism. Vol. 1 of The Cambridge History of Literary Criticism*. Cambridge: Cambridge University Press, 1989.

Kermode, Frank. *The Genesis of Secrecy: On the Interpretation of Narrative*. Cambridge, MA: Harvard University Press, 1979. Kermode, regarded as the greatest living English literary critic, focuses his critical skills on the Gospel of Mark.

Leitch, Vincent B. (ed.). *The Norton Anthology of Theory and Criticism*. New York: W. W. Norton, 2001. An indispensable collection of articles and excerpts from the work of important literary critics and theorists.

Longenecker, Bruce W. (ed.). *Narrative Dynamics in Paul: A Critical Assessment*. Louisville: Westminster John Knox, 2002. A collection of essays that focuses on the application of narrative criticism to epistolary literature in the New Testament.

Longman, Tremper. *Literary Approaches to Biblical Interpretation*. Grand Rapids: Zondervan, 1987.

Malbon, E. S. and Edgar McKnight. *The New Literary Criticism of the New Testament*. Journal for the Study of the New Testament Supplementary Series, 109. Sheffield: JSOT Press, 1994. Competent introduction of modern literary critical methods to the New Testament guild.

McKnight, Edgar. *The Bible and the Reader: An Introduction to Literary Criticism*. Philadelphia: Fortress Press, 1985. Accessible introduction to the application of literary criticism to the Bible.

McKnight, Edgar. *Postmodern Use of the Bible: The Emergence of Reader-Oriented Criticism*. Nashville: Abingdon Press, 1988. One of a series of works by McKnight introducing modern literary theory to students of the New Testament.

Merenlahti, Petri. *Poetics for the Gospels? Rethinking Narrative Criticism*. London and New York: T. & T. Clark, 2002. A Finnish New Testament scholar critiques narrative criticism and provides steps for the development of a more sophisticated approach to New Testament literary criticism.

Merenlahti, Petri and Raimo Hakola. "Reconceiving Narrative Criticism." Pp. 13–48 in *Characterization in the Gospels: Reconceiving Narrative Criticism*. Edited by David Rhoads and Kari Syreeni. Journal for the Study of the New Testament Supplementary Series, 184. Sheffield: Sheffield Academic Press, 1999. A constructive critique of narrative criticism.

Moore, Stephen. *Literary Criticism and the Gospels: The Theoretical Challenge*. New Haven: Yale University Press, 1989. Perhaps the best description of how narrative criticism developed in New Testament studies by a poststructuralist New Testament critic.

Moore, Stephen. *Mark and Luke in Poststructuralist Perspectives: Jesus Begins to Write*. New Haven: Yale University Press, 1992. In this work and the next, the author introduces poststructuralism to students of the New Testament in a very competent way.

Moore, Stephen. *Poststructuralism and the New Testament: Derrida and Foucault at the Foot of the Cross*. Minneapolis: Fortress Press, 1994.

Moore, Stephen. "A Modest Manifesto for New Testament Literary Criticism: How to Interface with a Literary Studies Field that is Post-Literary, Post-Theoretical and Post-Methodological." *Biblical Interpretation* 15 (2007), 1–25. Moore discusses the more recent developments in literary theory and how they have begun to influence New Testament studies.

Moulton, Richard. *The Literary Study of the Bible: An Account of the Leading Forms of Literature Presented in the Sacred Writers, Intended for English Readers*. Boston: Heath, 1895. This book, along with the next two, were influential in their day and were written by the father of the "Bible as literature" movement in the USA and the UK.

Moulton, Richard. *A Short Introduction to the Literature of the Bible*. Boston: Heath, 1901.

Moulton, Richard. *The Modern Reader's Bible: The Books of the Bible with Three Books of the Apocrypha Presented in Modern English Form.* New York and London: Macmillan, 1907.

Neumann, Birgit and Ansgar Nünning. "Einleitung: Probleme, Aufgaben und Perspektiven der Gattungstheorie und Gattungsgeschichte." Pp. 1–28 in *Gattungstherie und Gattungsgeschichte.* Edited by Marion Gymnich, Birgit Neumann, and Ansgar Nünning. ELCH 28. Trier: Wissenschaftlicher Verlag, 2007. Excellent introductory article that nicely lays out the issues of genre criticism.

Norton, David. *A History of the Bible as Literature.* 2 vols. Cambridge: Cambridge University Press, 1993. This work surveys "literary" approaches to the Bible (from antiquity to 1700 in the first volume and from 1700 to the present in the second), but develops no criteria for defining what "the Bible as literature" means and so is not a "history" in any meaningful sense of the term.

Patte, Daniel. *What is Structural Exegesis?* Philadelphia: Fortress Press, 1976. This book and the next both introduce French structuralism to American students of the New Testament and try to relate structuralism to meaning (something structuralism is normally not concerned with).

Patte, Daniel and Aline Patte. *Structural Exegesis: From Theory to Practice.* Philadelphia: Fortress Press, 1978.

Petersen, Norman. *Literary Criticism for New Testament Critics.* Philadelphia: Fortress Press, 1978. The author uses an eclectic literary-critical method, though the core of his approach is heavily influenced by Roman Jacobson's communications model (i.e., a "message" must be successfully encoded by an author and successfully decoded by the recipients).

Petersen, Norman. " 'Literarkritik,' the New Literary Criticism and the Gospel of Mark." Vol. 2, pp. 935–48 in *The Four Gospels 1992: Festschrift Franz Neirynck.* Edited by Frans van Segbroeck. Three volumes. Louvain: Peeters, 1992.

Poland, Lynn M. *Literary Criticism and Biblical Hermeneutics: A Critique of Formalist Approaches.* Chicago: Scholars Press, 1985. The author uses the hermeneutical theory of Ricoeur to criticize and combine features of Bultmann's hermeneutical program with the concerns of formalism (in the form of American New Criticism) and focuses on how Dominic Crossan, Dan Via, and Hans Frei transform both Bultmann and formalism.

*The Postmodern Bible: The Bible and Culture Collective.* Edited by Elizabeth A. Castelli, Stephen D. Moore, Gary A. Phillips, and Regina M. Schwartz. New Haven: Yale University Press, 1995.

Powell, Mark Allan. *What is Narrative Criticism?* Minneapolis: Fortress Press, 1990. The best basic introduction to narrative criticism of the New Testament. A competent survey of narrative criticism for students of the New Testament.

Powell, Mark Allan, with Cecile G. Gray and Melissa C. Curtis. *The Bible and Modern Literary Criticism: A Critical Assessment and Annotated Bibliography.* New York, Westport, and London: Greenwood Press, 1992. Contains a valuable bibliography following a relatively short critical assessment.

Powell, Mark Allan. *Chasing the Eastern Star: Adventures in Biblical Reader-Response Criticism.* Louisville: Westminster John Knox Press, 2001. Excellent introduction to reader-response criticism by a New Testament scholar for students of the New Testament.

Rabinowitz, Peter J. "Other Reader-Oriented Theories." Pp. 375–403 in *From Formalism to Poststructuralism,* vol. 8 of *The Cambridge History of Literary Criticism.* Edited by Raman Selden. Cambridge: Cambridge University Press, 1995. Competent article surveys the great variety of reader-response theories.

Resseguie, James L. *Revelation Unsealed: A Narrative Critical Approach to John's Apocalypse.* Leiden: Brill, 1998.

Resseguie, James L. *Narrative Criticism of the New Testament.* Grand Rapids: Baker Academic, 2005. An introduction to narrative criticism for students of the New Testament.

Rhoads, David. "Narrative Criticism of the Gospel of Mark." *Journal of the American Academy of Religion* 50 (1982), 411–34. One of the first major contributions of Rhoads to the New Testament appropriation of formalist literary criticism and the first use of the phrase "narrative criticism."

Rhoads, David. "Narrative Criticism: Practices and Prospects." Pp. 264–85 in *Characterization and the Gospels: Reconceiving Narrative Criticism.* Edited by David Rhoads and Kari Syreeni. Journal for the Study of the New Testament Supplementary Series, 184. Sheffield: Sheffield Academic Press, 1999. Rhoads responds to various critiques of narrative criticism and emphasizes its adoption of reader-response theory.

Rhoads, David. *Reading Mark: Engaging the Gospel.* Minneapolis: Fortress Press, 2004. A collection of essays by Rhoads written between 1982 and 1999, the first of which is entitled "Narrative Criticism and the Gospel of Mark," which originally appeared with the same title in Rhoads 1982. Rhoads was a participant in the SBL Seminar on Mark, which ran from 1971 to 1980, and this paper was originally presented there in 1980.

Rhoads, David and Donald Michie. *Mark as Story: An Introduction to the Narrative of a Gospel.* Philadelphia: Fortress Press, 1982. The first introduction of narrative criticism to students of the New Testament that focuses on interpretation, but is light on theory.

Rhoads, David, Joanna Dewey, and Donald Michie. *Mark as Story: An Introduction to the Narrative of a Gospel.* 2nd edn. Minneapolis: Fortress Press, 1999. A revision of Rhoads and Michie 1982 that incorporates more recent developments in literary theory, such as reader-response criticism.

Ricoeur, Paul. *Interpretation Theory: Discourse and the Surplus of Meaning.* Fort Worth: Christian University Press, 1976. Important work on hermeneutics by a French philosopher who was deeply interested in the Bible.

Rosebury, Brian. "Irrecoverable Intentions and Literary Interpretation." *British Journal of Aesthetics* 37 (1997), 15–30.

Ryken, Leland. *The Literature of the Bible.* Grand Rapids: Zondervan, 1974. This and the following works by Ryken, an American Evangelical professor of English, focus on how to read the Bible as literature.

Ryken, Leland. *How to Read the Bible as Literature ... and Get More Out of It.* Grand Rapids: Zondervan, 1984.

Ryken, Leland. *Words of Light: A Literary Introduction to the Bible.* Grand Rapids: Baker Book House, 1987.

Ryken, Leland. "The Bible as Literature, Part I: 'Words of Delight': The Bible as Literature." *Bibliotheca Sacra* 147 (1990), 3–15.

Ryken, Leland and Tremper Longman III. *A Complete Literary Guide to the Bible.* Grand Rapids: Zondervan, 1993.

Schmidt, Karl Ludwig. "Die Stellung der Evangelien in der allgemeinen Literaturgeschichte." In *Neues Testament, Judentum, Kirche: Kleine Schriften.* Edited by Gerhard Sauter. Munich: Christian Kaiser, 1981. Reprint of a famous article by Schmidt in which he argues that the gospels are a type of folk literature rather than the kind of literature produced by the educated in the ancient world.

Schneider, Anna Dorothea. *Literarkritik und Bildungspolitik: R. S. Crane, the Chicago (Neo-Aristotelian) Critics und die University of Chicago.* Heidelberg: C. Winter, 1994. Perhaps the best analysis of the Chicago school of literary criticism available.

Scholes, Robert. *Semiotics and Interpretation.* New Haven: Yale University Press, 1982. A helpful introduction to semiotics by a critic who emphasizes a balanced consideration of the six elements in Roman Jacobson's communication theory (author, text, context, medium, codes, reader).

Seeley, David. *Deconstructing the New Testament*. Biblical Interpretation Series, 5. Leiden: Brill, 1994. This book is a reader-friendly "incognito" version of deconstruction theory applied to the four gospels and Paul, emphasizing the "fissures, disjunctions, breaks and seams" found in the text. The author has a very short section on methodology (pp. 3–8), and refers infrequently to the work of Derrida.

Smith, Stephen H. *A Lion with Wings: A Narrative-Critical Approach to Mark's Gospel*. Sheffield: Sheffield Academic Press, 1996.

Smith, William Robertson. *The Old Testament in the Jewish Church: Twelve Lectures on Biblical Criticism*. New York: D. Appleton, 1881.

Stibbe, Mark W. G. (ed.). *The Gospel of John as Literature: An Anthology of Twentieth-Century Perspectives*. Leiden: E. J. Brill, 1993. An anthology of essays, some of which date from the first half of the twentieth century.

Tannehill, Robert C. *The Narrative Unity of Luke–Acts: A Literary Interpretation*. Vol. 1: *The Gospel according to Luke* (1986); vol. 2: *The Acts of the Apostles* (1990). Philadelphia: Fortress Press. An early New Testament scholar who adopted a narrative critical approach to Luke–Acts in which he emphasizes the "unity" of the work and its value for narrative critics in general.

Thatcher, Tom and Stephen D. Moore (eds.). *Anatomies of Narrative Criticism: The Past, Present, and Future of the Fourth Gospel as Literature*. Atlanta: Society of Biblical Literature, 2008. A collection of essays celebrating the twenty-fifth anniversary of the publication of Culpepper 1983.

Todorov, Tzvetan. *Grammaire du "Décaméron."* The Hague: Mouton, 1969.

Todorov, Tzvetan. "The Origin of Genres." Pp. 193–209 in *Modern Genre Theory*. Edited by David Duff. Harlow: Peterson Education, 2000.

Tolbert, Mary Ann. *Sowing the Gospel: Mark's World in Literary Historical Perspective*. Philadelphia: Fortress Press, 1989. Tolbert proposes that the genre of Mark belongs to ancient popular literature, very similar to the ancient novel (e.g., the life of Apollonius). The author regards the two longer parables of the sower (Mark 4) and the vineyard (Mark 12) as keys to interpreting Mark – the first is a synopsis of Mark 1:11–10:54 and the second of Mark 11:1–16:8.

Tynyanov, Yury. "The Literary Fact." *Modern Genre Theory*. Pp. 29–49 in *Modern Genre Theory*. Edited by David Duff. Harlow: Pearson Education, 2000.

Via, Dan O. *The Parables: Their Literary and Existential Dimension*. Philadelphia: Fortress Press, 1967.

Waugh, Patricia (ed.). *The Oxford Guide to Literary Criticism and Theory*. New York: Oxford University Press, 2006.

Wellek, René and Austin Warren. *Theory of Literature*. 3rd edn. New York: Harcourt Brace Jovanovich, 1977. A widely used (in its day) introduction to literary theory by two major figures in the New Criticism.

Wilder, Amos N. *Early Christian Rhetoric*. Cambridge, MA: Harvard University Press, 1971. This popular text first appeared in 1949. The second edition appeared in 1959 and the third in 1977. A Harvard New Testament scholar (and brother of Thornton Wilder) who was deeply interested in literary approaches to the New Testament.

Wimsatt, William K. and Monroe C. Beardsley, "The Intentional Fallacy." *Sewanee Review* 54 (1946), 468–88. Revised and republished in Wimsatt, *The Verbal Icon: Studies in the Meaning of Poetry* (pp. 3–18). Lexington: University of Kentucky Press, 1954. The authors, proponents of the New Criticism, argue that the autonomy of the literary work is such that even the stated intentions of the author cannot be taken as normative in interpreting their works.

CHAPTER 9
# Form Criticism

David E. Aune

Form criticism, an English rendering of the German term *Formgeschichte*, literally "form history," is a critical method formulated to identify and analyze units of originally oral discourse that have been incorporated into ancient Israelite and early Christian written texts. New Testament scholars have applied the form-critical method primarily to the synoptic gospels and New Testament letters. The term *Formgeschichte* was introduced to New Testament scholarship through the title of an influential book on the subject published in 1919 by Martin Dibelius (1883–1947), *Die Formgeschichte des Evangeliums* ("The Form Criticism of the Gospel," translated into English from the second German edition as *From Tradition to Gospel* in 1934). Form critics typically analyzed the gospel texts in order to identify individual pericopes that may have had an oral origin, classifying them by form and assigning each form to a particular *Sitz im Leben* ("situation in life") in the early church.

## The History of Form Criticism

The development of form criticism as a method for analyzing the oral traditions that were incorporated into Old Testament narratives and poetry was first practiced by Hermann Gunkel (1862–1932), who applied the new form-critical method to the study of Genesis. Before the time of Gunkel, the Pentateuch had been subject to intense source-criticism analysis, from the Roman Catholic scholar Richard Simon (1638–1712) to the culminating work of Julius Wellhausen (1844–1918), who popularized the Graf–Wellhausen documentary hypothesis of the Pentateuch. For Gunkel, the earliest documentary sources of the Pentateuch (the "Yahwist" and "Elohist" documents) were not in themselves literary sources so much as collections of originally independent stories that changed during the long process of oral transmission. Gunkel classified the various stories or legends that he identified in Genesis on the basis of their purpose. He distinguished between four types of stories: (1) ethnological legends (fictitious stories explaining relationships between the Israelite tribes); (2) etymological legends (reflections on the origin and meaning of names); (3) ceremonial legends (stories explaining the origins of religious customs); and (4) geographical legends (legends explaining the origins of a locality, such as the Dead Sea).

The New Testament scholars who began applying form criticism to the synoptic gospels at the beginning of the twentieth century, independently of one another, in a series of monographs published between 1919 and 1921, include Martin Dibelius, Karl Ludwig Schmidt, Rudolf Bultmann, and Martin Albertz. Just as Gunkel accepted the prevailing nineteenth-century German view of source-critical analysis of the Pentateuch, so the early form critics accepted the prevailing German view of the source-critical theory of Synoptic origins, namely the two-source theory propounded by H. J. Holtzmann in 1863 (the two-source theory came to dominate English-speaking scholarship with the publication of B. H. Streeter's *The Four Gospels* in 1924). This theory maintained the priority of Mark as well as the view that both Matthew and Luke made independent literary use of the hypothetical Q document or sayings source. In the liberal quest for the most reliable documentary foundation for a life of Jesus, it was assumed that the earliest gospel, then recognized as Mark, preserved the most reliable portrait of the life and ministry of Jesus. However, William Wrede's monograph on the messianic secret of Mark, published in 1901, convinced the critical community in Germany that though Mark may have had reliable historical material available to him, he had overlaid this material with his own theological understanding of Jesus. Since source criticism was unable to identify any earlier written sources in Mark and Q, form criticism provided a new and exciting critical tool for identifying even earlier oral traditions that had been incorporated into Mark and Q.

## Presuppositions of Form Criticism

### Short units of oral tradition embedded in the gospels

One of the major assumptions of the early generation of form critics was that sayings of Jesus and narratives about Jesus circulated orally in relatively short isolated units or forms. Some of these oral units became parts of smaller collections, such as the collections of controversy stories in Mark 2:1–3:5 and 11:27–34 and the collection of parables in Mark 4:1–34 (Kuhn 1971; Telford 1992), i.e., what Klaus Berger (1987) designated *Sammelgattungen*. The major exception is the passion narrative, which is the longest pre-Markan block of tradition. Even though earlier practitioners of form criticism have been faulted for an inadequate conception of oral tradition, this is largely an anachronistic criticism, since both Bultmann and Dibelius were familiar with aspects of the state of folklore studies at the beginning of the twentieth century, when folklore studies were in their infancy. Both Dibelius and Bultmann, for example, were familiar with some of the ideas of the Danish folklore scholar Axel Olrik, published in a 1909 article in German entitled "Epische Gesetze der Volksdichtung," or "Epic Laws of Folk Narrative" (translated into English in 1965). Olrik (1864–1917) was a philologist and medievalist who worked primarily in the field of Scandinavian folklore and who proposed a set of diagnostic principles or "laws" to distinguish segments of originally oral performances preserved in written texts, precisely the task of form criticism as later practiced by Dibelius and Bultmann. Hermann Gunkel, the founder of Old Testament form criticism, read a copy of Olrik's lecture on the epic laws that he gave in Berlin in 1908. Gunkel corresponded with Olrik on the subject and refers to Olrik's epic laws in *Legends of Genesis* (1964; a translation of "Die Sagen der Genesis," the introduction to his commentary on Genesis, first published in 1901). The epic laws describe many characteristic features of fairy tales (see Olrik 1992: 41–61) such as the following: (1) The *law of three* indicates that narrative has a preference for three characters in the story (Cinderella and her two stepsisters; three blind mice, the three little pigs). (2) The *law of ascent*, by which Olrik means that the last occurrence of an event is decisive (baby bear discovers Goldilocks); (3) The use of actions rather than descriptions to illustrate a character's personality. (4) The *law of two to a scene*, i.e., folk narrative only reluctantly brings more than two characters on stage at one time (exemplified by the parable of the prodigal son in Luke 15:11–32).

The major exception to the oral circulation of the sayings and stories of Jesus in relatively short isolated units is the passion narrative, thought by many to have been a connected narrative that was put together comparatively early, antedating the composition of the Gospel of Mark. One bit of evidence pointing in this direction is found in Paul's introduction to his recital of the Eucharistic words of Jesus in 1 Cor. 11:23: "For I received from the Lord what I also handed on to you, that the Lord Jesus on the night when he was betrayed took a loaf of bread ...." Here it is evident that Paul knows not only the tradition of the Eucharistic words of Jesus (found with variations in Mark 14:22–5; Matthew 26:26–9; Luke 22:15–20), but that he is also aware of the narrative sequence in which the Eucharistic words were embedded. 1 Corinthians can be dated to 55 or 56 CE, some fifteen years before the composition of Mark.

### The artificiality of the framework of Jesus' life in the gospels

One of the corollaries of the view that the Jesus tradition originally circulated in relatively short oral units is that the framework of the life of Jesus in the gospels has no claim to historicity. K. L. Schmidt, who did not himself use the term "form criticism," argued that Mark was made up of short, originally independent episodes or *pericopae* that were linked together editorially by a variety of chronological and geographical bridge passages inserted by the evangelist with the intent of creating a connected narrative. The metaphor of pearls on a string has frequently been used of the discrete units of oral tradition that Mark had strung together on a chronological and geographical string. One of the implications of this view is that little or nothing has been preserved in Mark, Matthew, or Luke of the actual historical sequence of events in the life of Jesus of Nazareth, i.e., the synoptic gospels in their present form are not reliable sources for a biography of Jesus. In Schmidt's words (2002: v):

> The oldest Jesus tradition is "Pericope Tradition," that is, a tradition of individual scenes and individual sayings, which for the most part lack definite chronological and topographical identification within the community where they have been transmitted. Much of that which appears chronological and topographical is just the framework into which the individual pictures have been inserted.

Schmidt, Dibelius, and Bultmann all agreed that the primary role of the evangelists was that of collectors of traditions rather than authors (Dibelius 1934: 59):

> The composers of the Gospels, at any rate of the Synoptic Gospels, were not "authors" in the literary sense, but collectors; so the question is not what they knew about the facts, but what was known to those who gave the tradition its form. This form did not arise through writers', but through preachers' activities; not, therefore, in accordance with the wishes or efforts of individuals, but with the necessities of preaching, i.e., according to super-individual laws derived from the existence of the early Christian churches.

## Oral tradition and the written gospels as folk literature

The founders of form criticism, Karl Ludwig Schmidt, Martin Dibelius, and Rudolf Bultmann, categorized the oral traditions that were incorporated into the written gospels, as well as the gospels themselves, as *folk literature*, or to use the dichotomy made famous by Karl Ludwig Schmidt, *Kleinliteratur* rather than *Hochliteratur* (Schmidt 2002). Since the gospels, as well as the oral traditions of which they were constituted, were "unliterary," the written gospels could not be expected to conform to such ancient literary genres as biography or history. The founders of New Testament form criticism, Rudolf Bultmann and Martin Dibelius, independently developed taxonomies of oral forms preserved in the gospels based on analogous forms attested in both Jewish and Greco-Roman literature, but regarded the literary form of the gospels as without analogy. Bultmann argued that "while we need analogies for understanding the individual components of the Synoptic Tradition we do not need them for the Gospel as a whole" (Bultmann 1963: 373). He continues (1963: 373–4):

> The [literary] analogies that are to hand serve only to throw the uniqueness of the Gospel into still stronger relief. It has grown out of the imminent urge to development which lay in the tradition fashioned for various motives, and out of the Christ-myth and the Christ-cult of Hellenistic Christianity. It is thus an original creation of Christianity.

During the last quarter of the twentieth century it became clear to many scholars that the form-critical assumption of a dichotomy between *Kleinliteratur* and *Hochliteratur* was an artificial distinction that owed more to romantic notions of primitivity than to insights into comparative literature. Similarly, the notion that the gospels are *sui generis*, or a unique literary form, while still retained by a number of German New Testament scholars, has been widely rejected in English-speaking scholarship.

## Reconstructing the Sitz im Leben

Another assumption of form criticism is that the oral sayings and narratives arose in particular social contexts in the ministry of Jesus and the activities of the early church.

According to Bultmann (1963: 4), "The *Sitz im Leben* is not, however, an individual historical event, but a typical situation or occupation in the life of a community." The identification of the *Sitze im Leben* ("situations in life") of various units of tradition, however is based on a circular argument, as Bultmann himself admits (Bultmann 1963: 5): "The Forms of the literary tradition must be used to establish the influences operating in the life of the community, and the life of the community must be used to render the forms themselves intelligible."

Gunkel was the first to use the term *Sitz im Leben* ("situation in life") or *Sitz im Volkleben* ("situation in the life of a people"), as the setting within which literary types arose (see Byrskog 2007). By *Sitz im (Volk)leben*, Gunkel meant the roles played by particular groups of specialists, such as priests, wisdom teachers, and singers, who formulated laws, wisdom sayings, and songs. Form criticism further assumes that each individual oral form arose within and was determined by a particular social situation, or *Sitz im Leben*, either a situation in the life of Jesus (if all or part of the tradition can be traced back to Jesus), or else to a situation in the life of the early church. As the early Jesus movement expanded into the Roman world, form critics argued for a diachronic series of cultural and linguistic stages through which the Jesus tradition was transmitted. In order to do this they typically developed a model of the history of early Christianity that they correlated with the transmission and expansion of the oral tradition stemming from Jesus or which was attributed to Jesus in the early church. The first of these cultural-linguistic diachronic stages is the Aramaic-speaking Palestinian church, that is, those who were part of the original circle of disciples and followers of Jesus as well as those who were attracted to their post-Easter message that Jesus was the messiah. The second stage was Greek-speaking Hellenistic Judaism, i.e., Hellenistic Jews who were part of the Jesus movement living in Palestine as well as in Hellenistic Jewish settlements in the eastern theater of the Mediterranean world in cities like Antioch. The third stage was the Greek-speaking world of Hellenistic Gentiles, such as Pauline converts from paganism associated with Christian congregations in such Greco-Roman cities as Galatia, Thessaloniki, and Corinth. Finally, the fourth setting is that of each of the written gospels themselves, which served as final repositories for written forms of originally oral Jesus traditions.

### Early Christian creativity and the historical skepticism of form critics

Both Dibelius and Bultmann assumed that early Christians were adept at creating stories of Jesus to fit various situations in the life of the church. Since the early form critics were convinced that oral units of the Jesus tradition were preserved, modified, or created to fit the current needs of the church as reflected in the typically practical *Sitze im Leben* of the community, they assumed that there was little or no historical interest operative in the transmission and preservation of these traditions. A corollary of this is the assumption of many form critics, particularly Rudolf Bultmann, that the oral tradition behind the synoptic gospels, the sayings of Jesus, and narratives about Jesus cannot be trusted to represent what the historical Jesus really said and did. For Bultmann, it was primarily the needs and interests of the early church that shaped its conception of the ministry and message of Jesus, not a desire for reliable evidence of what the historical Jesus did and said. Bultmann expresses this assumption clearly in the opening paragraphs of *The History of the Synoptic Tradition* (1963: 1):

Mark is the work of an author who is steeped in the theology of the early Church, and who ordered and arranged the traditional material that he received in the light of the faith of the early Church – that was the result; and the task which follows for historical research is this: to separate the various strata in Mark and to determine which belonged to the original historical tradition and which derived from the work of the author.

For Bultmann, then (in the critical evaluation of Schwartz 2005: 48), "the memory of Jesus, thus, becomes little more than a repercussion of the church's search for legitimacy." Schwartz regards Bultmann's "theory of memory" (his label for form criticism), as characterized by "unmasking," that is, if the stories and sayings of Jesus can be connected with a function that they performed in the life of the early church, that in itself is enough to reveal that such Jesus traditions cannot have had a historical origin. However in the view of Schwartz, it is obvious that the one need not exclude the other (Schwartz 2005: 48). Bultmann saw the form-critical task as that of identifying fabrications in the Jesus tradition in order to peel them away to reveal the core of historical truth. Yet to do so with any confidence, he must already know the difference between the real and the fabricated Jesus, i.e., Bultmann's method assumes the very knowledge it seeks to discover (Schwartz 2005: 48). Bultmann's approach to the synoptic gospels is similar to that of Maurice Halbwachs (1877–1945), the founder of the field of social memory. Again according to Schwartz (2005: 49):

> Halbwachs advances a pejorative conception of collective memory, one that distrusts and works to undermine established beliefs. He assumes that memory, as opposed to history, is inauthentic, manipulative, shady, something to be overcome rather than accepted in its own right.

Schwartz argues the contrary, maintaining that the task of social memory scholarship is to appraise what we know of the past by considering relevant documents like the gospels as sources of information about early Christian popular beliefs, not to be concerned with their authenticity. For Schwartz (2005: 50),

> The Gospels are critical because they put us in touch with the way early Christians conceived Jesus' place in their world, and because without them our understanding of the social memory of this world would be more shallow.

## Identifying Oral Forms in the Gospels

When the first monographs applying form criticism to the gospels were published by Martin Dibelius in 1919 and Rudolf Bultmann in 1921, both scholars had devised different ways of classifying what they regarded as the various types of originally oral forms that had been embedded in the written gospels. Though both scholars introduced modifications into their classification systems with the second editions of their monographs (Dibelius in 1933 and Bultmann in 1931), their classification systems were far from complementary. Dibelius, for example, classified some miracle stories as "paradigms" and others as "tales." In the years that followed the second editions of these works scholars have tended to gravitate toward the more detailed system of Bultmann, which we follow in the present discussion (with some input from the conservative English form critic Vincent Taylor). Form criticism assumes that all types of human verbal communication are expressed in well-defined patterns, i.e., forms and genres, and that sentences are given meaning by the generic "package" that contains them. In communication situations, the intuitive recognition of the various genres of oral communication enables hearers to understand the meaning conveyed by the generic packaging of sentences.

### Pronouncement stories

For English-speaking scholars, Vincent Taylor's descriptive phrase "pronouncement story" has been preferred as the simplest and most appropriate designation for this form (see Tannehill 1981), though it is not strictly accurate to call this form a "story." Bultmann himself favored the transliterated Greek word *apophthegma* (anglicized as "apophthegm") meaning "a terse saying" (the plural form of which is *apophthegmata*), for what he described as short, pointed sayings that are ideal constructions rather than historical reports (1963: 11–69). Some New Testament scholars have preferred the ancient Greek rhetorical term *chreia*, "a brief sentence or maxim, often illustrating an anecdote" (see Robbins 1988). Bultmann proposed that apophthegms consisted of several subtypes: (1) conflict sayings, (2) scholastic dialogues, and (3) biographical apophthegms. The primary source of parallels for Bultmann is the body of rabbinic dialogues, which means for him that this material was formed in the Palestinian church, though the final sayings of Jesus found in all examples might have originated with the historical Jesus. In the following examples of these three types of apophthegms, the italicized portion calls attention to the focal saying of Jesus that characterizes this basic form.

An example of what Bultmann labels a *conflict saying* is found in Mark 2:23–8 (plucking grain on the Sabbath), which Bultmann considers to be a composition of the church, since it focuses on the behavior of the disciples rather than the behavior of Jesus; the concluding saying of Jesus is italicized (Bultmann 1963:16):

> One Sabbath he was going through the grainfields; and as they made their way his disciples began to pluck heads of grain. And the Pharisees said to him, "Look, why are they doing what is not lawful on the Sabbath?" And he said to them, "Have you never read what David did, when he was in need and was hungry, he and those who were with him: how he entered the house of God, when Abiathar was high priest, and ate the bread of the Presence, which it is not lawful for any but the priests to eat, and also gave it to those who were with him?" *And he said to them, "The Sabbath was made for man, not man for the Sabbath; so the Son of man is lord even of the Sabbath."*

Luke 12:13–14 is an example of the second subtype of apophthegm, the *scholastic dialogue* (Bultmann 1963: 23):

> One of the multitude said to him, "Teacher, bid my brother divide the inheritance with me." *But he said to him, "Man, who made me a judge or divider over you?"*

An example of Bultmann's third subtype, the *biographical apophthegm*, is found in Q, Luke 9:57–8, and Matthew 8:19–20, which Bultmann regards as an old proverb that tradition has turned into a saying of Jesus (Bultmann 1963: 28–9):

> As they were going along the road, a man said to him, "I will follow you wherever you go." *And Jesus said to him, "Foxes have holes, and birds of the air have nests; but the Son of man has nowhere to lay his head."*

## Dominical sayings

Bultmann distinguished five types of *Herrenworte* or "dominical sayings," all of which could have been independent elements in the tradition, and at least some of which consisted of originally Jewish material taken over by Christian tradition: (1) logia (i.e., proverbs or aphorisms), (2) prophetic and apocalyptic sayings, (3) legal sayings or church rules, and (4) I-sayings (mission statements of Jesus). These categories of forms are distinguished partly on the basis of the actual form, but largely on the basis of content. This way of classifying the sayings of Jesus is problematic because of the mixed criteria used for distinguishing the five subtypes. The five categories of dominical sayings have not been unanimously adopted by other form critics. Dibelius designated the same Synoptic sayings as *paradigmata*, "paradigms" or *Paränese*, "paraenesis" (Dibelius 1934: 37–69). Vincent Taylor lumped all such material together as "sayings of Jesus," omitting all subcategories (Taylor 1935: 88–100), while Dominic Crossan proposed a simple taxonomy of two types of sayings, parables and aphorisms (Crossan 1986: 22–130).

An example of a *logion* (or wisdom saying of Jesus) is found in Mark 3:24–5:

> If a kingdom is divided against itself, that kingdom cannot stand. And if a house is divided against itself, that house will not be able to stand.

An example of a prophetic or apocalyptic saying is found in Luke 7:22–3, a saying in which Bultmann finds such an "immediacy of eschatological consciousness" that he maintains could not have been taken over from Judaism (Bultmann 1963: 126):

> And he answered them, "Go and tell John what you have seen and heard: the blind receive their sight, the lame walk, lepers are cleansed, and the deaf hear, the dead are raised up, the poor have good news preached to them. And blessed is he who takes no offense at me."

For a *legal saying or church rule*, we can use the divorce saying in Matthew 5:31–2 as an example:

> It was also said, "Whoever divorces his wife, let him give her a certificate of divorce." But I say to you that every one who divorces his wife, except on the ground of unchastity, makes her an adulteress; and whoever marries a divorced woman commits adultery.

An example of an *I-saying* (involving mission statements by Jesus) is found in Luke 12:49–50:

> I came to cast fire upon the earth; and would that it were already kindled! I have a baptism
> to be baptized with; and how I am constrained until it is accomplished.

In this case, Bultmann regards verse 49 as probably an authentic saying of Jesus, but
not verse 50, which alludes to his death and so should be understood as a *vaticinium
ex eventu* (Bultmann 1963: 153–4).

### Similitudes and similar forms

Following earlier scholars like Adolf Jülicher (1857–1938), the author of a famous
book on the parables of Jesus (1910), Bultmann distinguished between the similitude
and the parable (Bultmann 1963: 174). A similitude uses a typical condition or recur-
rent event as the basis for comparison, while a parable makes use of a particular situation that is interesting. Mark 4:30–2 is an example of a similitude:

> And he said, "with what can we compare the kingdom of God, or what parable shall we
> use for it? It is like a grain of mustard seed, which, when sown upon the ground, is the
> smallest of all the seeds on earth; yet when it is sown it grows up and becomes the greatest
> of all shrubs, and puts forth large branches, so that the birds of the air can make nests in
> its shade."

As examples of parables proper we can simply mention such famous examples as the
good Samaritan (Luke 10:29–37) or the prodigal son (Luke 15:11–32).

### Miracle stories or novellas

Bultmann and Taylor preferred the term "miracle story," while Dibelius waffled between
the designations "paradigm" and "tale." There are several types of miracle stories,
including healing miracles (e.g., Mark 5:21–43, the woman with the issue of blood and
Jairus' daughter) and nature miracles (e.g., Mark 4:37–41, the stilling of the storm).
Miracle stories fall into three categories: healing miracles, exorcisms, and nature miracles. Dibelius describes miracle stories in terms of a threefold structure: (1) description
of the problem, (2) Jesus' action in solving the problem, and (3) the reaction of the
crowd. These three features are often evident in even very short miracle stories such as
Mark 1:30–1:

> Now Simon's mother-in-law was in bed with a fever, and they told him about her at once.
> He came and took her by the hand and lifted her up. Then the fever left her, and she began
> to serve them.

Bultmann (1963: 221–6) has a much more complex taxonomy consisting of a number
of motifs found in miracle stories (developed in greater detail by Theissen 1983: 47–
72), including the length of the sickness, the dreadful and dangerous character of the
disease, the ineffective treatment of physicians, doubt and contemptuous treatment of

the healer, etc. For Bultmann the tradition was enriched by miracle stories both in the oral and the written stages of the tradition, and some such stories are of Hellenistic origin (Bultmann 1963: 238–9).

The miracle stories of the gospels and Acts have been subject to a formalist analysis by Gerd Theissen (1983), who intends to advance the discussion of classical form criticism. Theissen deals with miracle stories as structured forms (a synchronic approach) as well as in terms of a tradition that undergoes redaction (a diachronic approach). Like Berger (his colleague at Heidelberg) he is not particularly concerned with oral transmission. Theissen (1983: 31), who does not think that miracle stories reproduce historical reality, regards them as symbolic narratives (Theissen 1983: 287): "Primitive Christian miracle stories are symbolic actions in which a new understanding of existence is opened up." In treating the miracle stories as symbolic actions, Theissen (1983: 231–302) explores the problem of *Sitz im Leben*, in terms of social location (town/country; upper-class/lower-class; east/west), function in the history of ancient religion, and existential function. In his synchronic treatment, Theissen finds in the Synoptic parables fields of seven "characters" (demon, sick person, companion, opponents, crowd, disciples, miracle-worker), thirty-three "motifs" in a systematic expansion of the motifs found in Bultmann (e.g., the coming of the miracle-worker, the appearance of the crowd, the appearance of the distressed person, etc.) and six "themes" (exorcism, healing, epiphanies, rescue miracles, gift miracles, rule miracles).

### Parables

The parables of Jesus have been defined variously. According to Dodd (1961: 16):

> The parable is a metaphor or simile drawn from nature of common life, arresting the hearer by its vividness or strangeness, and leaving the mind in sufficient doubt about its precise application to tease it into active thought.

Scott (1989: 8) defines a parable more concisely as a "*mashal* that employs a short narrative fiction to reference a transcendent symbol." Adolf Jülicher devised a threefold system for classifying the parables of Jesus which has proven extremely influential: (1) the similitude (*Gleichnis*), (2) the parable (*Parabel*), both comparisons, and (3) the example story (*Beispielerzählung*), containing an example to be imitated (found only in the Gospel of Luke). Various scholars have counted the number of parables in the gospels differently, primarily because it is often difficult to draw the line between extended figures of speech in the sayings of Jesus and full-blown parables. According to Aune (2003: 330–2), there are six parables in Mark, twenty-two in Matthew, fifteen in Luke without Synoptic parallels, with a total of twenty-eight parables in Luke including those with Synoptic parallels, and seventeen in the *Gospel of Thomas*. Bultmann (1963: 166–205), accepts the distinction between the similitude and the parable made by Jülicher, but argues that parables, for the most part, did not originate in a Hellenistic but in an Aramaic environment (Bultmann 1963: 166). In describing the features of the parable, Bultmann (1963: 187–92) is dependent on Axel Olrik in making the following observations: (1) only the necessary persons appear; (2) there are never more than three characters, typically two; (3) three characters reflects the "law of three" (e.g., the lender and his two debtors in Luke 7:41–2; the father and his two sons, Matthew 21:28–31); (4) the law of the single perspective; (5) feeling and motives are mentioned only when essential; (6) there is a complete lack of motivation in the description.

## Responses to Form Criticism

### General observations

Form criticism has typically shown little interest in the historical Jesus, since the units of oral tradition that have been incorporated into the written gospels are thought to have been either created by the early church or reshaped in response to the varied uses to which the Jesus traditions were subjected as they were given stereotypical form in the various *Sitze im Leben* in early Christian communities. With the renewed interest in the historical Jesus by the mid-twentieth century, New Testament scholars developed various criteria of authenticity to reconstruct the *ipsissima vox Jesu* ("the very voice of Jesus") embedded in the sayings and stories found in gospel tradition. Very few scholars, however, have pursued the problem of the means by which authentic Jesus traditions were preserved from the ministry of Jesus to the formation of the canonical gospels. Birger Gerhardsson, following rabbinic analogies, argued that Jesus traditions were memorized and transmitted by a special group within the early church charged with that task. More recently, Richard Bauckham has revived an ancient perspective (that of Papias of Hierapolis in the early second century CE) and argued that the gospels were the products of eyewitness testimony.

### Birger Gerhardsson

Birger Gerhardsson (1961, 1977) pounced on what he rightly perceived as a major weakness in the form-critical conception of the oral transmission of the Jesus tradition in early Christianity: it affirmed *that* oral tradition happened, but provided no account of *how* it happened, i.e., form critics neglected to formulate a theory of memory. Gerhardsson's work centered on a collection and analysis of what can be known of oral and written transmission in rabbinic Judaism from tannaitic and amoraic sources (ca. 70–500 CE), which he regarded as an appropriate historical analogy to the origin and transmission of Jesus traditions. One of Gerhardsson's primary purposes was to question the fundamental assumptions and methods of form criticism (Gerhardsson 1961:9–15).

He applied the rabbinic model to the more fragmentary evidence for the oral transmission of Jesus traditions in first-century Christianity, focusing on evidence in Acts and Paul. Gerhardsson argues that, like the rabbis, the disciples of Jesus and their successors carefully memorized and even took notes on the words and deeds of Jesus, which they then accurately transmitted in relatively unchanged form (Gerhardsson 1961: 335, 328–9). This deposit of tradition was preserved and transmitted by duly constituted authorities, the twelve apostles, originally headquartered in Jerusalem, who constituted a *collegium* with supreme doctrinal authority in the early church (conceptions influenced by the influx of Pharisees into the church), and were "bearers, not only of the tradition concerning Christ, but also of the correct interpretation of the Scriptures" (Gerhardsson 1961: 221 n.2, 230, 321). The publication of Gerhardsson's dissertation in 1961 was not well received by critical New Testament scholarship, but it has attracted increasing interest and favor in the last two decades. Jacob Neusner, who published a scathing review of Gerhardsson's published dissertation, has since become a strong supporter of Gerhardsson's approach and even wrote the introduction to the 1998 reprint of two of Gerhardsson's books.

Richard Bauckham's book (2006) focused on the memory of eyewitnesses or from those who had close contact with Jesus as an alternative to the form-critical theory of the oral transmission of Jesus traditions. Bauckham centers his discussion primarily on the gospels of Mark and John. Who are the eyewitnesses? In this group Bauckham includes the twelve (an official body of eyewitnesses who had both formulated and promulgated the main corpus of gospel tradition), several female disciples, some of whom experienced healing by Jesus, and various others. Bauckham accepts the ancient tradition that Mark incorporates the eyewitness testimony of Peter (a view recently emphasized by Samuel Byrskog, 2000: 71), who calls Peter "the primary eyewitness of them all"), while John was written by John the Elder, also an eyewitness of the ministry of Jesus. Bauckham uses modern studies of orality, particularly Jan Vansina, *Oral Tradition as History* (1985).

## Erhardt Güttgemanns

In 1970 (in a book translated into English in 1979), Erhardt Güttgemanns raised a number of criticisms of the form-critical method. One of Güttgemanns' primary concerns was the problem of using linguistic forms as a key for illuminating some underlying history, raising serious problems about the sociological assumptions of the appeal of form critics to a reconstructed *Sitz im Leben*. In recent studies on oral performance and writing, the smooth, linear transition between oral and written has proven to be impossible to validate. Bultmann, it must be remembered, saw no real difference or intention between oral and written tradition, since both were the products of *Kleinliteratur* (popular or folk literature); the gospels, in Güttgemanns' view, were wrongly assumed to be the final products of the process of collecting material that originated in oral processes, i.e., anthologies. Güttgemanns uses Gestalt theory to argue, contrary to both form and redaction criticism, that the gospels are greater than the sum of their parts. Güttgemanns points out that the analogy between rabbinic tradition and the Jesus tradition is problematic because the former is connected to a text and the interpretation of the text in a way that the Jesus tradition is not (1979: 213). For Güttgemanns, the gospel form must be treated as an autosemantic *Gestalt*, not as the development of its parts or even as the sum of its parts.

## Werner Kelber

In the light of modern studies of orality, particularly the work of Walter Ong, SJ (1982), Werner Kelber (1983) has followed Güttgemanns in making a sharp distinction between orality and textuality. Before an oral tradition is reduced to writing, he argues, there is no single oral version that can claim primacy or originality. Each oral performance of a tradition differs from all other performances of that tradition, so no single version can properly be regarded as the original version (a view of folktales held by modern folklore scholarship). The form-critical quest to recover the earliest form of a Jesus tradition is therefore a hopeless quest. Kelber regards the written version of oral tradition represented by the Gospel of Mark as a negative development, and also pits the written gospels against the earlier, unwritten forms as the product of a segment of the Christian community which was challenging the authority of the apostles as the guardians of the oral tradition. He sees the textuality of the gospels as creating a more rigid, fixed way of telling the story of Jesus than was permitted by oral tradition. Although traces of orality still appear in the gospels, especially Mark, the value of classic form criticism is greatly diminished for this approach.

## Klaus Berger

In his 1987 book on form criticism, Klaus Berger argues that one cannot reconstruct oral forms antecedent to written texts using literary methods (a view similar to Güttgemanns 1979). Like the English practitioners of form criticism (e.g., Vincent Taylor 1935), Berger maintains that issues such as historicity and authenticity are not directly relevant to the form-critical method. Berger emphasizes the linguistic form of a text (i.e., stylistic, syntactical, and structural features) much more than traditional form criticism. "Forms" (*Gattungen*) are groups of texts distinguished by common formal and material features arranged hierarchically. Since forms are conventions reflecting typical situations and functions within early Christianity, the role of exegesis is to distinguish between the conventional form and deviations reflecting the particular communication situation for which the form was used. Berger's discussion of New Testament forms is arranged in three categories, corresponding to the three rhetorical genera in antiquity, symbouleutic, epideictic, and dikanic rhetoric. Under symbouleutic forms, Berger includes twenty-seven forms including various types of paraenesis, vice and virtue catalogues, woes, domestic codes, and community rules. Under epideictic forms he includes forty forms, including acclamations, doxologies, hymns, reports of visions and auditions, travel reports, encomia, narratives of the suffering and rescue of the righteous, and so on. Finally, under dikanic forms, Berger includes just six forms, including apologetic texts and speeches of indictment and accusation.

## The Future of Form Criticism

Even though form criticism has itself undergone a lengthy period of criticism, the method appears to have survived the hazing process remarkably well. Form criticism has been accepted as a basic tool of critical scholarship, despite the fact that some of its premises remain rather shaky. Nevertheless, New Testament scholars, particularly in Germany, as well as many in the United States have found form criticism to be a fruitful method for achieving diachronic understanding of the gospel tradition. The use of the form-critical method in the study of Old Testament texts, however, though it has undergone some transformations over the years, is still regarded by many Old Testament scholars as a fruitful approach to the text (see Sweeney and Ben-Zvi 2003). However, since the keynote essay by James Muilenburg in 1969 , Old Testament scholarship too has tended to value synchronic approaches to the text (e.g., literary criticism) over diachronic approaches to the text such as source criticism and form criticism (see House 1992).

## Annotated Bibliography

Aune, David E. "Oral Tradition and the Aphorisms of Jesus." Pp. 211–65 in *Jesus and the Oral Gospel Tradition*. Edited by Henry Wansbrough. *Journal for the Study of the New Testament* Supplementary Series, 64. Sheffield: Sheffield Academic Press, 1991.

Aune, David E. *The Westminster Dictionary of New Testament and Early Christian Literature and Rhetoric*. Louisville and London: Westminster John Knox, 2003.

Bauckham, Richard. *Jesus and the Eyewitnesses: The Gospels as Eyewitness Testimony*. Grand Rapids: Eerdmans, 2006.

Berger, Klaus. *Einführung in die Formgeschichte*. Tübingen: Mohr Siebeck, 1987.

Bultmann, Rudolf. *The History of the Synoptic Tradition*. Trans. John Marsh. New York: Harper & Row, 1963.

Bultmann, Rudolf and Karl Kundsin. *Form Criticism: Two Essays on New Testament Research*. Trans. F. C. Grant. New York: Harper & Brothers, 1962.

Buss, M. J. *Biblical Form Criticism in its Context*. JSOT Supp. 274. Sheffield: Sheffield Academic Press, 1999. A comprehensive review of form criticism in ancient Judaism and early Christianity from 1875 (the work of Hermann Gunkel) to 1965.

Byrskog, Samuel. *Story as History – History as Story: The Gospel Tradition in the Context of Ancient Oral History*. WUNT 123. Tübingen: Mohr Siebeck, 2000. Byrskog, a student of Birger Gerhardsson and now his successor at the University of Lund, Sweden, explores ancient historiography through the lens of modern studies in oral history.

Byrskog, Samuel. "A Century with the *Sitz im Leben*: From Form-Critical Setting to Gospel Community and Beyond." *Zeitschrift für die neutestamentliche Wissenschaft* 98 (2007), 1–27.

Crossan, John Dominic. *Sayings Parallels: A Workbook for the Jesus Tradition*. Philadelphia: Fortress Press, 1986. An extremely useful workbook that contains canonical and noncanonical sayings of Jesus in a synoptic arrangement.

Dibelius, Martin. *From Tradition to Gospel*. Trans. B. L. Woolf. New York: Charles Scribner's Sons, 1934. Translation of *Die Formgeschichte des Evangeliums*. 6th edn. Tübingen: Mohr Siebeck, 1971. A classic statement of form criticism by one of its founding fathers.

Dodd, C. H. *The Parables of the Kingdom*. Rev. edn. New York: Charles Scribner's Sons, 1961.

Gerhardsson, Birger. *Memory and Manuscript: Oral Tradition and Written Transmission in Rabbinic Judaism and Early Christianity*. Uppsala: Gleerup, 1961. Gerhardsson 1961 and 1964 were reprinted as *Memory and Manuscript: Oral Tradition and Written Transmission in Rabbinic Judaism and Early Christianity; with, Tradition and Transmission in Early Christianity*. Grand Rapids: Eerdmans; Livinia: Dove Booksellers, 1998.

Gerhardsson, Birger. *Tradition and Transmission in Early Christianity*. Lund: C. W. K. Gleerup, 1964.

Gerhardsson, Birger. *The Origins of the Gospel Traditions*. Philadelphia: Fortress Press, 1977. A succinct overview of Gerhardsson's thesis that the sayings and stories of Jesus were preserved by a cadre of special traditionalists in the early church.

Gunkel, Hermann. *The Legends of Genesis: The Biblical Saga and History*. Trans. W. H. Carruth. New York: Schocken, 1964. A translation of the introduction to Gunkel's German commentary on Genesis, first published in 1901.

Güttgemanns, Erhardt. *Candid Questions Concerning Gospel Form Criticism: A Methodological Sketch of the Fundamental Problematics of Form and Redaction Criticism*. Trans. William G. Doty. Pittsburgh: Pickwick Press, 1979. A critic of form criticism who bases his argument on the naive use of language by form critics.

House, Paul R. (ed.). *Beyond Form Criticism: Essays in Old Testament Literary Criticism*. Winona Lake, IN: Eisenbrauns, 1992.

Hultgren, Arland. *Jesus and His Adversaries: The Form and Function of the Conflict Stories in the Synoptic Tradition*. Minneapolis: Augsburg Press, 1979. A relatively recent analysis of the conflict story in the gospels.

Hultgren, Arland J. *The Parables of Jesus: A Commentary*. Grand Rapids: Eerdmans, 2000. An ideal introduction to the study of the parables. The author is thoroughly familiar with the vast secondary literature on parables.

Jülicher, Adolf. *Die Gleichnisreden Jesu*. Tübingen: Mohr Siebeck, 1910. An influential analysis of the parables of Jesus in which the author argues for a single point to each parable and rejected the tendency to treat the parables as allegories with multiple points of comparison.

Kelber, Werner H. *The Oral and the Written Gospel: The Hermeneutics of Speaking and Writing in the Synoptic Tradition, Mark, Paul, and Q*. Philadelphia: Fortress Press, 1983. One of the first appropriations by a New Testament scholar of the implications of the modern distinction by scholars such as Walter Ong, SJ and Erdhardt Güttgemanns between orality and textuality.

Kuhn, Heinz-Wolfgang. *Ältere Sammlungen im Markusevangelium*. Göttingen: Vandenhoeck & Ruprecht, 1971.

McKnight, Edgar V. *What is Form Criticism?* Philadelphia: Fortress Press, 1969. Helpful introductory overview of the form-critical method.

Muilenburg, James. "Form Criticism and Beyond," *Journal of Biblical Literature* 88 (1969), 1–18. The "beyond" in the title refers to the application of rhetorical criticism to Old Testament texts, which the author regards as an important step to take in biblical interpretation beyond form criticism.

Olrik, Axel. "Epic Laws of Folk Narrative." Pp. 129–41 in *The Study of Folklore*. Edited by Alan Dundes. Englewood Cliffs, NJ: Prentice-Hall, 1965. A translation of "Epische Gesetze der Volksdichtung," *Zeitschrift für deutsches Altertum* 52 (1909), 1–12. This article by the Danish folklorist influenced the founders of biblical form criticism, including Herman Gunkel, Martin Dibelius, and Rudolf Bultmann.

Olrik, Axel. *Principles for Oral Narrative Research*. Trans. Kirsten Wolf and Jody Jensen. Bloomington and Indianapolis: Indiana University Press, 1992. The English translation of a posthumous work of Olrik in Danish, *Nogen Grundsætninger for Sagnforskning*, ed. Hans Ellekilde (Copenhagen: Det Schønberske Forlag, 1921).

Ong, Walter J. *Orality and Literacy: The Technologizing of the Word*. London and New York: Methuen, 1982. An important and influential work focusing on the social transformation involved in the development of print culture.

Palmer, Humphrey. *The Logic of Gospel Criticism: An Account of the Methods and Arguments Used by Textual, Documentary, Source, and Form Critics of the New Testament*. London: Macmillan; New York: St. Martin's Press, 1968. A critique of the major methods of New Testament criticism.

Robbins, Vernon K. "The Chreia." Pp. 1–23 in *Graeco-Roman Literature and the New Testament*. Edited by David E. Aune. SBL Sources for Biblical Study, 21. Atlanta: Scholars Press, 1988.

Schmidt, Karl Ludwig. *The Place of the Gospels in the General History of Literature*. Trans. Byron R. McCane. Columbia: University of South Carolina Press, 2002. Originally published in 1919 as "Die Stellung der Evangelien in der allgemeinen Literaturgeschichte," reprinted in *Neues Testament, Judentum, Kirche: Kleine Schriften*, ed. Gerhard Sauter (Munich: Christian Kaiser, 1981).

Schwartz, Barry. "Christian Origins: Historical Truth and Social Memory." Pp. 43–56 in *Memory, Tradition, and Text: Uses of the Past in Early Christianity*. Semeia Studies, 52. Atlanta: Society of Biblical Literature, 2005.

Scott, Bernard Brandon. *Hear Then the Parable: A Commentary on the Parables of Jesus*. Minneapolis: Fortress Press, 1989.

Streeter, B. H. *The Four Gospels: A Study of the Origins Treating of the Manuscript Traditions, Sources, Authorship, and Dates*. London: Macmillan, 1924. A classic British statement of the four-source theory.

Sweeney, Marvin and Ehud Ben-Zvi (eds.). *The Changing Face of Form Criticism for the Twenty-First Century*. Grand Rapids: Eerdmans, 2003.

Tannehill, Robert C. *Pronouncement Stories*. Semeia, 20. Chico, CA: Scholars Press, 1981.

Taylor, Vincent. *The Formation of the Gospel Tradition*. 2nd edn. London: Macmillan, 1935.

Telford, William R. "The Pre-Markan Tradition in Recent Research (1980–1990)." Vol. 2, pp. 693–723 in *The Four Gospels 1992: Festschrift Frans Neirynck*. Edited by Frans van Segbroeck. 3 vols. Leuven: University Press, 1992.

Theissen, Gerd. *Miracle Stories of the Early Christian Tradition*. Trans. Francis McDonagh. Philadelphia: Fortress Press, 1983. The German original appeared in 1974.

Vansina, Jan. *Oral Tradition as History*. Madison: University of Wisconsin Press, 1985.

CHAPTER 10
# Feminist Criticism

## Amy-Jill Levine

## What Is Feminist Criticism?

Feminist New Testament criticism is not a method but a reading strategy, a critical analysis that interrogates both biblical and extra-canonical texts as well as those who comment upon them, not only for their depictions of women and constructions of gender, but also for their ideological views of sexuality, race, class, ethnicity, practice, belief, and other categories of social oppression. Conceived as a corrective not only to so-called "objectivist" biblical studies (i.e., analyses that do not acknowledge their own biases) but also to the barriers women faced in both academy and church, New Testament feminist criticism is often unabashedly political. It seeks to enable women to locate their own places in Christian history, to argue for changes in ecclesial practice and doctrine, and to find personal inspiration. Feminist criticism provides for some practitioners a means of affirming all scripture while preventing misuse (e.g., using Colossians 3:18, Ephesians 5:22–4, or 1 Peter 3.1–6 to sanction spousal abuse). For others, its concern for the role of experience allows readers to develop their own canon within a canon or to include within their religious and historical resources non-canonical materials such as Nag Hammadi or New Testament apocryphal works. Still others have determined that the text is so riddled with kyriarchy – a term coined by Elisabeth Schüssler Fiorenza to replace "patriarchy" (with its focus on gender dualism) and to signal the socio-cultural, religious, and political system of elite male power which contributes to structures of dehumanization – that it cannot be redeemed.

Divergence also marks how feminist readers engage in interpretation. Some readers privilege relatively strict historical investigation; others take what might be called a hermeneutics of imagination: they adopt a more generous approach to historical investigation and so privilege the possible and the plausible, especially when it serves to enhance women's liberation. Nevertheless, both approaches recognize their own interested nature and consequently the contingencies of their conclusions. Feminists readers do not claim to speak for all women – essentializing arguments are strategically albeit rarely employed – rather, it encourages recognition that there is more than one way to read a text, and that what is 'good news' for some may be the old oppressive story for others.

Aware that men are socialized to identify with male characters while they do not typically identify with female characters – women have little difficulty identifying with the prodigal son whereas men do not typically identify with Mary and Martha; women identify with Jesus in his suffering but less often in his leadership role – the feminist reader may explore how gender impacts biblical interpretation. Refusing to stop with the observation of difference, feminist readers offer several means by which readers can avoid sinking under the weight of singular, hegemonic claims or find themselves floating off into space without an anchor of critical prudence. The point is less (or not) to win the debate, silence other readers, or offer the superior interpretation; it is rather to continue the conversation about the text and its readers.

Among questions feminist readers ask, the following are representative:

1   Can women's voices or lives be recovered from this text? Can the text's impact on women be determined? To what extent is the text prescriptive rather than descriptive, and to what extent does it suppress or reveal?

2   Through what mechanisms do women characters achieve their goals? Are they coded as deceitful or forthright, meek or strident, in positions of authority or subservience?

3   How are metaphors of female experiences – e.g., labor and parturition imagery, menstruation, female sexuality and desire – depicted, and to what ends? How do such depictions reinforce or challenge ideological constructs concerning gender?

4   Can the text be read "against the grain" in order to find "good news" for women? See Judith Fetterley, *The Resisting Reader: A Feminist Approach to American Fiction* (Bloomington: Indiana University Press, 1978).

5   How are pericopes titled and people labeled? Should Luke 7:36–70 be identified as "the woman who sinned" or "the woman who loved much"? Should the sin be identified as "prostitution"? What are the connotations of terms such as apostle, disciple, and teacher, and to what extent are they determined by gender-based considerations?

6   What are the implications of named vs. anonymous characters, and how can unidentified figures be recovered?

7   What are the political or, more broadly, ideological interests encoded in the text, and how might the application of the "hermeneutics of suspicion" (a strategy developed by Paul Ricoeur and introduced into feminist New Testament study primarily through the work of Elisabeth Schüssler Fiorenza) reveal such interests?

8   How does the social location of the reader impact interpretation?

## The History of Feminist Criticism

Although not using the term "feminist," nineteenth-century women began what has been considered the first wave of feminist New Testament study. Anna Julia Cooper,

Matilda Joslyn Gage, Angelina and Sarah Grimké, Elizabeth Cady Stanton, Sojourner Truth, Frances Willard, and other women, some of whom had formal training in biblical studies and all of whom had a commitment to Christianity, sought to reclaim women's contributions to Christian history and to correct what they correctly perceived to be inconsistencies in how texts were interpreted and translations were made, usually to the detriment of women.

Epitomizing this effort is Elizabeth Cady Stanton and the Revising Committee's *The Woman's Bible* (1895). Marking the diversity of "feminist" views even then, the twenty-eighth annual convention of the National American Woman's Suffrage Association (1896), by a vote of 53 to 41, repudiated the effort, despite the president Susan B. Anthony's pointed question: "Who can tell now whether Mrs Stanton's commentaries may not prove a great help to woman's emancipation?"

Despite this early work, the topic of women remained considered of little value in the academy. Popular books on women in the Bible appeared throughout the first part of the twentieth century; still occasionally cited is Edith Deen's comprehensive *All the Women of the Bible* (New York: Harper & Row, 1955). Only in the late 1960s and early 1970s, accompanying the women's liberation movement, did feminist biblical studies begin to impact divinity school and seminary education. With the concurrent development of departments of religious studies distinct from theologically focused programs, biblical studies came into closer contact with other disciplines, themselves also open to feminist concerns. What might be called the "second wave" (the feminist in me is wary of the label) of feminist New Testament studies began in the mid-1970s. One example of the second wave of such studies is the seminal – better, "ovarial" – publication of Letty Russell's edited collection, *The Liberating Word: A Guide to Nonsexist Interpretation of the Bible* (1975).

Concurrently, feminist biblical interpretation was also beginning in western Europe. For example, *Traditionen der Befreiung 2: Frauen in der Bibel* (Munich and Gelnhausen: Kaiser/Burckhardthaus-Laetare, 1980), edited by Willy Schottroff and Wolfgang Stegemann, contained essays by the feminists Luise Schottroff ("Frauen in der Nachfolge Jesu in neutestamentliche Zeit" [Women as Disciples of Jesus in New Testament Times]) and Elisabeth Schüssler Fiorenza ("Der Beitrag der Frauen zur urchristlichen Bewegung" [The Contribution of Women to the Early Christian Movement]); the latter, refused publication in a Festschrift for Rudolf Schnackenburg, outlines what would become the feminist-critical watershed volume, *In Memory of Her*.

Luke's Gospel became in those early years a feminist rallying point. Mounting an argument that to some extent confused quantity with quality and, whether knowingly or not, sometimes reflected Adolf von Harnack's view that Luke the Evangelist received some of his information from Philip's daughters (see Acts 21:8–9) and so had a particular interest in women's leadership, feminist readers hailed Luke as celebrating women's discipleship, self-determination, and leadership. The Magnificat (Luke 1:46–55) announces the triumph of the poor and the humble, and the annunciation (Luke 1:26–38) reveals heaven's dependence on female strength and fidelity; Mary's visit to Elizabeth bespeaks women's solidarity as well as testifying to a gynocentric alternative to the patriarchal systems of Rome and Jerusalem (Luke 1:39–45). The woman who anoints Jesus controls her own finances, as do the women who provide for him out of their means. Jesus releases Martha from gender-determined domestic responsibilities and the emotional anxiety that accompanies them, and he affirms her sister Mary's choice of intellectual and spiritual development. Women are prominent among those commanded to remember and enjoined to recount the story of Jesus' life and resurrection. Not only does the Gospel of Luke, compared to the other canonical gospels, have the most references to women, scholars have also argued that its author was a woman.

With the publication of Elaine Pagels' *The Gnostic Gospels* (New York: Vintage Books, 1979), feminist New Testament studies expanded beyond the canon. Some feminist critics claimed to find in Gnostic materials a positive view of women as well as evidence of women's leadership suppressed by the Great Church. The Gnostic Sophia became the recovery of a feminine element of divinity, and the apocryphal Acts were regarded as literature written by and for women. Interest in the Gnostic "Sophia" and the eventual equating of Jesus with Sophia in circles both academic and popular found the second wave of feminist New Testament studies ending on a positive, and positivistic note.

Much of this second wave of feminist New Testament study manifested particular ideological blinders. The participants, generally educated middle-class Christians, tended to universalize their own experiences and concerns. Echoing the period's dominant New Testament scholarship, they used rabbinic texts uncritically in order to show how Jesus or Paul offered something better than Judaism; worrisome statements were regarded as Paul's lapses to his "rabbinic" past or insertions by a *Jewish* Christian redactor. Texts were approached in a positivistic manner; Jesus was presumed to have established an egalitarian (the word was rarely if ever defined) community; Thecla provides a role model for today. Voices speaking from womanist, mujerista, lesbian, Asian, and other self-acknowledged identities challenged feminist readings particularly from the 1970s and early 1980s as promoting a white, Western, elitist agenda inattentive to the concerns of other groups generally identified by race and/or ethnicity. While it is incorrect to see womanist, mujerista, lesbian, etc. readings simply as subsets of feminism, the overlap remains in the concerns of all such reading strategies to acknowledge the import of the reader's social location.

As with their fore-sisters, so second wave of feminist New Testament scholars also faced external pressures. Their courage in challenging both academy and church is what permitted the next generations of feminist biblical critics to continue the work. On the one hand, those early feminist readers, like others interested in demonstrating how institutional religion had marginalized women's contributions even while perpetuating negative stereotypes about them, encountered academic ridicule and employment risk. Detractors of feminist readings whether academic or clerical did, and some still do, insist that all feminists – already the statement is problematic, for there is no feminist party line – are anti-Christian or anti-Bible. Then again, there are those who decry anyone who questions the historicity of biblical events, traditional interpretations of passages, or even the translation a particular church uses. Feminist criticism may receive comparably more negative reaction, but the reaction it did receive generally comported with the larger culture wars.

As the third wave took hold in the 1980s and 1990s, feminist New Testament studies manifested a growing engagement with theoretical matters, increasing recognition of the multiplicity of women's voices and the complexities of the texts and their social contexts, and a healthy self-critical ethos. Works appeared such as Elisabeth Schüssler Fiorenza's pioneering *In Memory of Her: A Feminist Theological Reconstruction of Christian Origins* (New York: Crossroad, 1983); Mary Ann Tolbert's edited collection *The Bible and Feminist Hermeneutics* (Semeia 28, 1983); and *Feminist Perspectives on Biblical Scholarship* (Chico, CA: Scholars Press, 1985), edited by Adela Yarbro Collins for the Society of Biblical Literature. Ironically, among the first sustained studies of women in the New Testament were those not of a self-identified feminist, but of Ben Witherington III. Although Witherington's works (e.g., *Women in the Ministry of Jesus* [SNTS MS 51; Cambridge: University Press, 1984]) have ranged from drawing feminist fire to a deliberate neglect, he is to no small extent responsible for reintroducing the New Testament's depiction of women to the academy.

Following Schüssler Fiorenza's introduction of Paul Ricoeur's "hermeneutics of suspicion" into feminist New Testament discourse, feminist readers began to question the received teachings of both church and academy. "Patriarchy" or "kyriarchy" were systemic evils to be named and then demolished, whether manifested in the text or by those who regarded the text as authoritative. Feminist readers queried the absence of stories of women from lectionaries; some advocated inclusive language for biblical translations and lectionary readings. Believing the New Testament accounts of women to represent "the tip of the iceberg," they were convinced that the texts could be read to recover contribution to the nascent movement as well as to identify how and why this story was suppressed.

Feminist New Testament studies accorded historical-critical attention to locating the lives of real women as well as positive female images in the early church and early Judaism. Those engaged in literary-critical work began to explore the negotiations women readers make in order to find an authoritative voice in an androcentric text. In both cases, the focus remained on material directly concerning or addressing women, from female characters to injunctions concerning women's lives.

Centering an early and optimistic reconstruction was the view that Jesus and his earliest companions created a "community of equals" or "woman church" (the terms are Schüssler Fiorenza's). References to the *Basileia* (a feminine noun) began to replace the androcentric English translation "kingdom." Select pericopes – for example the Samaritan woman (John 4); Mary and Martha of Bethany (Luke 10:28–32; John 11–12); Phoebe the deacon and Junia the apostle (Romans 16) – were adduced as evidence of women's leadership roles in the initial movement. Even more optimistically, Peter's mother-in-law, who rises from her sickbed to serve Jesus and his (male) followers, becomes exemplary of women's discipleship if not deaconate. The Syro-Phoenician/Canaanite woman (Mark 7:24–31a; Matt. 15:21–8) was seen the embodiment of the outcast and oppressed.

Since Jesus does not appear to be proactive on women's issues (he summons no woman to discipleship; he appoints no woman among the twelve; he commissions no woman to teach or preach publicly), and since Paul's silencing of women in 1 Corinthians 14:33b–36 is no clarion of women's liberation, a common liberationist approach was to highlight women's prominence: the Samaritan woman was hailed as the first successful evangelist; Mary of Bethany epitomized discipleship; and Mary Magdalene as first witness to the resurrection must have been a "leader" in the early church. Galatians 3:28, interpreted as making women equal to men (rather than as a call for the original male-coded androgyne), became the heart of Pauline thought: passages such as 1 Corinthians 14:36–7 were regarded either as aberrations, a recrudescence of his "rabbinic" past (the anachronism went unnoticed) or non-Pauline interpolations. The Pastorals were seen as capitulating to Roman social expectations in light of the delay of the *parousia*, and the Pastorals, as well as 1 Peter, seen as pseudepigraphical, were deemed of lesser value. Underlying these moves was yet another vestige of earlier biblical studies, that is, "early Catholic" (Frühkatholozismus) works are more easily dismissed than Paul's undisputed letters. A number of Christian feminists easily dismissed potentially oppressive statements as either case-specific or as interpolations and so of lesser value. The interpolation argument worked well for liberal readers, but the idea of dismissing any text created a problem for more conservative interpreters.

Pope John Paul II's 1988 *Mulieris dignitatem*, acknowledging "the manifestations of the feminine 'genius' which have appeared in the course of history" and which offers the hopeful anticipation of Galatians 3:28, the time when there is "no longer 'male or female'" but we are "all one in Christ Jesus" neatly epitomizes the quandary of second-wave New Testament feminism. The two points can be seen as mutually exclusive: if gender distinctions are erased, then the special role of women in the church risks erasure as well. Conversely, if gender distinctions are maintained, then hierarchical valuations may come in their wake; the separate-but-equal system may be theoretically nice, but it does not always work in practice.

That same year, Elisabeth Schüssler Fiorenza was elected president of the Society of Biblical Literature. Her presidential address, "The Ethics of Interpretation: Decentering Biblical Scholarship" (published in the *Journal of Biblical Literature* 107 [1988], pp. 3–17), brought feminist critiques to the center of the biblical studies guild.

By the 1990s, feminist biblical studies had its own niche in the academy. Major feminist collections began to reflect both a more diverse authorship and a less positivistic approach to the text. These included Elisabeth Schüssler Fiorenza's edited collections, *Searching the Scriptures* volumes 1 (1993) and 2 (1994), *The Women's Bible Commentary*, edited by Carol A. Newsom and Sharon H. Ringe (1992; expanded edition 1998), and Athalya Brenner's edited series, Feminist Companion to the Bible, with volume 1, on the Song of Songs, appearing in 1993. The New Testament sister series, edited by Amy-Jill Levine with Marianne Blickenstaff, did not begin appearing until 2001. Finally, 2000 witnessed the publication of Carol Meyers, Toni Craven, and Ross Shepard Kraemer (eds.), *Women in Scripture: A Dictionary of Named and Unnamed Women in the Hebrew Bible, the Apocryphal/ Deuterocanonical Books, and the New Testament*.

During this period, second-wave enthusiasm was checked by both external critique and internal re-evaluation. Epitomizing the shift is Mary Rose D'Angelo's 1990 *Journal of Biblical Literature* 109 (1990) essay, "Women in Luke–Acts: A Redactional View" (pp. 441–60). This article proposes that Luke's editing served to restrict women's public roles in conformity with Hellenistic moral views and so limit their prophetic ministry. Luke was no longer a feminist patron, but a patriarchal pawn. Other scholars began to suggest that the Virgin Mary is no self-actualized breaker of gender roles but a reassertion that a woman's value lies only in her procreative ability, and even that is negated by the gospel's preference for celibacy. The anointing woman of Luke 7 is so scandalously physical that this "sinner" – like all women – is less celebrated disciple than dangerous threat. Luke undercuts the authority of the women who support Jesus by describing them as erstwhile demoniacs; they receive no special commission as do the (healthy) male disciples, and they engage in no discussions with Jesus. Martha's *diakonia* is dismissed in favor of Mary's better portion: submissiveness, servility, and silence. At best, Luke becomes seen as offering a "Double Message" (the term is Turid Karlsen Seim's) to women. Thus, Witherington's conclusion that Luke reaffirms the maintenance of a gender-bifurcated system in which men have public authority came to be repeated by a number of feminist writers.

Finally, the late 1990s brought feminist New Testament studies into conversation with gay history and queer theory. For some readers who identified as feminist, the call for liberation did not – because of both particular interpretations of select biblical texts and particular socially conditioned values – extend to gay and lesbian, let alone bisexual and transgendered, individuals. With the publication of her *Love Between Women: Early Christian Responses to Female Homoeroticism* (Chicago and London: University of Chicago Press, 1996), Bernadette J. Brooten offered a correction to feminist interpreters who "have largely failed to include female homoeroticism as part of the history of women or as a subject for gender analysis" (p. 14).

Today, as feminist readers recognize the effects of our work and meet the criticisms of our analyses brought by feminists and non-feminists alike, our interpretive processes continue to mature and expand. Feminist readers are so diverse in terms of approach (literary, historical, sociological, text-critical, ideological, cross-cultural ...), focus (imagery, characterization, genre, plot, Christology, ethics, politics, polemic ...), hermeneutics (of suspicion, of recovery ...), identity (womanist, Latina, African, evangelical, lesbian, Jewish, Catholic, male, determined by age, health, education, class, physical condition ...) and conclusions – i.e., it is just like most biblical studies and indeed like most academic disciplines in the humanities and social sciences – that any single definition of what constitutes a 'feminist reading' is necessarily reified.

New voices contribute to new categories of analysis and new understandings of texts. South and East Asian, African, eastern European, Central and South American, Native American, African and Hispanic American readers, exploring the meaning developed between their own experiences and that of the text, provide new insight into ancient materials. The Syro-Phoenician woman becomes a model for women who resist discrimination where rituals, customs, and attitudes treat them as unclean or dangerous; her shouting after Jesus becomes the model for women's participation in political rallies; her concern for her daughter cries out in settings where girl children are aborted or killed; but her story must be resisted from a post-colonial perspective as encouraging women to submit their own ethnic and religious identities to the external group with the needed technology or medicine.

The recognition of this distinction between the academy and the church, between 'professional' and 'naive' readers, between those who study and those who clean (Mary and Martha come to mind) as well as of the need for crossing these boundaries and so facilitating discussion and critique, is at the forefront of much feminist thought in the twenty-first century. Through these tensions between liberation and constraint, gender-determined servitude and egalitarian discipleship, more integrative interpretations are developing.

The "double message" of Luke has now permeated much textual study. Applying the same "hermeneutics of suspicion" practiced so helpfully in light of the received interpretations of the guild to earlier feminist work, feminists today debate whether Jesus was "egalitarian" and even whether the word had any meaning in a first-century context. Telling is the subtitle of the first full-scale feminist study on the subject: Kathleen Corley's *Women and the Historical Jesus: Feminist Myths of Christian Origins* (Santa Rosa, CA: Polebridge Press, 2002).

Less concerned today about whether Paul is "good" or "bad" for women, feminist critics seek out women's voices in the epistles, comment on Paul's maternal imagery, and learn from his pastoral sensibilities. Ephesians 5 is recognized both as contributing to the abuse of women and, when the injunctions to men are considered, as promoting marital harmony by restricting the husband's role. While some readers continued to dismiss 1 Corinthians 14:33b–36 as an interpolation and continued to condemn the Pastorals, others from Evangelical perspectives insisted that such dismissal was an affront both to the canon and to the women who acknowledge the entire text as sacred. No longer is Gnostic thought the great liberator of women, and no longer can one so easily argue that the apocryphal Acts were stories told by and for women. Today as well, debate continues over Revelation: is it a call for steadfastness and hope in the presence of an oppressive empire, or is it a misogynistic fantasy depicted in the empire's terms?

Even Galatians 3:28 received some mitigating of its emblematic status: the erasure of gender roles was found to be not necessarily a liberating move for women, especially if it entailed abrogating sexuality, fasting to become "like men," and otherwise conforming to an androgynous model.

Feminist critics today are less likely to seek the historical heroine (Thecla and even Perpetua are usually relegated to the category of fiction; some feminist readers would look at all characters as constructs, with locating "real" women only an elusive dream) than they are to find sites for reflection. Where earlier readers had found feminine metaphors for the divine indicative of women's elevated roles in the communities preserving such teachings, today scholars advocate caution, for metaphors need not reflect women's experience or political actuality.

Today there is also less interest in making women figures into representatives of particular groups and more attention to characters' multiple identities and the text's multiple interpretive possibilities. For example, Jesus' rebuke of Martha can be regarded as a negation of women's ecclesial leadership if seen only in the context of Luke 10.38–42, but given that Luke elsewhere depicts Jesus' rebuking of hosts in the context of table fellowship, Martha can also be placed as in the same role as Pharisees or even male disciples. This recontextualization moves the interpretation of the pericope away from a focus on gender and toward a concern for appropriate leadership.

This new feminism addresses new categories of analysis. No longer focused just on *women per se*, feminist work today engages such questions as the construction of "fatherhood," the role of the household, and the configuration of the fictive family; the roles of patron and clients; the function of anonymity; the depiction of female illness; intertextual resonances (e.g., Herodias and Jezebel); the relationship between sexuality and violence; the relation between ethnicity and gender, and between gender and violence; depictions of slaves and children. Feminist readers mark texts not specifically addressed to women, but which have been read as oppressive to women (and others) by glorifying suffering and encouraging victimization instead of resistance, such as Mark 8:34 ("take up your cross"). Included in understanding the New Testament are not only the standard appeals to earlier Hebrew literature but also to Asclepius and Philostratus, archaeology and cross-cultural social modeling. Less frequent are blithe references to a unified Mediterranean cultural region, the categories of public and private, and the honor/shame model. New understandings of public and private spheres, marked by time as much as by place, complicate the contextualizing of the texts.

These more complex readings are complemented by New Testament feminism's return to engagement with theology. Progressing past the stark phrasing of "Can a male savior save women?" feminist critics seek new understandings of the cross, of the contextual nature of the call for self-denial, of the word of G-d in the context of suffering.

As we look to the future, not a few feminist readers find both encouragement and discouragement. The attention to gender substantially prompted by feminist studies has expanded to reflect upon the construction of masculinity; consequently, represen-tations of women threaten to be of interest only for what they indicate about men's position in society. Real women are, in this setting, of little or no interest at all. Rather than move to a post-feminist erasure of women, it is likely that feminist biblical studies will continue to show that understanding the performance of masculinity requires scrutiny not only of the feminization process, but of women's lives as well.

The rise of post-colonial feminist (whether the term is used or not) work opens both possibilities and problems. Critique "from above" remains difficult, and feminist writers have and may continue to find themselves in an unwanted competition for attention to particular forms of oppression (e.g., anti-Semitism, racism, homophobia). What is a substantive matter for one writer may be of no concern to another (see A.-J. Levine et al., "Roundtable Discussion: Anti-Judaism and Postcolonial Biblical Interpretation," *Journal of Feminist Studies in Religion* 20/1 [Spring 2004], pp. 91–132).

The good news is that, today, feminist approaches appear in prestigious journals and award-winning books; they are topics for sessions and major addresses at Society of Biblical Literature and Catholic Biblical Association meetings; they have found their way into growing numbers of classrooms and curricula, both confessional and secular. In some church and academic circles feminist readings are met with dismissal and disparagement, with labels ranging from "bad scholarship" to "heresy"; in other contexts, they are lumped together with studies reflecting the experiences and reading strategies of non-Western interpreters and then presented as alternatives to the way "we normally do things." Nevertheless they inexorably continue to challenge their detractors even as they to grow in sophistication and diversity.

## Annotated Bibliography

Levine, Amy-Jill with Marianne Blickenstaff (eds.). *The Feminist Companions to Mark, Matthew, Luke, John.* Vol. 1: Paul; vol. 2: *The Deutero-Pauline Writings, the Acts of the Apostles.* New York: Continuum, 2001–4.

Levine, Amy-Jill with Maria Mayo Robbins (eds.). *The Feminist Companions to the Catholic Epistles and Hebrews, Mariology, New Testament Apocrypha, Christian Apocalyptic Literature, Patristics, the Historical Jesus.* New York: Continuum, 2004– . These collections of new, revisited, and out-of-print essays from established scholars and those at the beginning of their careers, men and women, from Europe, South and East Asia, Australia, and the Americas introduce a variety of approaches and address, along with questions of gender and sexuality, issues of race, ethnicity, and class, social status, speech and silence, constructions of masculinity, post-colonial feminism, goddess imagery, the household, and women's roles and representations.

Meyers, Carol (gen. ed.), Toni Craven, and Ross S. Kraemer (assoc. eds.). *Women in Scripture: A Dictionary of Named and Unnamed Women in the Hebrew Bible, the Apocryphal/Deuterocanonical Books, and the New Testament.* New York: Houghton Mifflin, 2000. Following introductory essays on the Bible, feminist biblical scholarship, and naming practices, the 592-page volume identifies named, unnamed, and groups (e.g., "widows," "daughters") of women, deities, and personifications.

Newsom, Carol A. and Sharon H. Ringe (eds.). *Women's Bible Commentary.* Louisville: Westminster John Knox, 1992; expanded edn., 1998. The editors identify this volume as "the first comprehensive attempt to gather some of the fruits of feminist biblical scholarship on each book of the Bible in order to share it with the larger community of women who read the Bible" (p. xxi).

Schüssler Fiorenza, Elisabeth. *In Memory of Her: A Feminist Theological Reconstruction of Christian Origins.* New York: Crossroad, 1983. Following detailed discussion of feminist critical hermeneutics, method, and historical reconstruction, this ground-breaking study, ranging from "The Jesus Movement as Renewal Movement within Judaism" to the "Patriarchal Household of G-d and Ekklesia of Women" located at the end of the first Christian century, presents the "History of the Discipleship of Equals" (p. 97).

Schüssler Fiorenza, Elisabeth (ed.). *Searching the Scriptures.* Vol. 1: *A Feminist Introduction; Searching the Scriptures;* vol. 2: *A Feminist Commentary.* New York: Crossroad, 1993, 1994. "Seeks to indicate the ambivalent relationship that women as marginalized people have to the scriptures" (vol. I, p. x) through interpretive works of deconstruction and revisioning. Volume I explores interpretation from different socio-historical locations, offers various feminist "frames of meaning," rethinks critical methods, and locates feminist biblical scholarship in practice. Volume II, the commentary, "transgresses canonical boundaries by including essays on several Nag Hammadi documents, Deutero-canonical writings and Pseudepigrapha, martyrologies, and New Testament Apocrypha."

# CHAPTER 11
# Rhetorical Criticism

## Duane F. Watson

Rhetoric is the art of using spoken and written discourse according to accepted rules and techniques to inform, persuade, or motivate an audience according to the agenda of the speaker or writer. Rhetorical criticism of the New Testament is the analysis of the biblical books, in part or in whole, for conformity to or modification of rhetorical conventions for speaking and writing in the Greco-Roman period in which they were written and/or according to more modern conceptions of rhetoric and its functions. Rhetorical criticism tries to understand the biblical authors' messages, how they constructed and intended their texts to function, and how the hearers/readers were likely to have perceived and responded to the texts.

The following is an overview of the origins and history of rhetorical criticism of the New Testament; contemporary approaches using ancient rhetoric, modern rhetoric, or both; and the practice of the rhetorical criticism of the gospels, epistles, Acts of the Apostles, and Revelation.

## Origin and History of Rhetorical Criticism

Rhetorical criticism of the New Testament has many historical precedents. In his work *De Doctrina Christiana* (Book 4) St. Augustine (354–430 CE), a former professor of rhetoric, used rhetorical conventions from Cicero's *De Inventione* and *Orator* to analyze the Bible. He concluded that the rhetoric of the Bible was not that of paganism, but of another equally qualitative variety suited to its authors and the importance of the subject matter. Even so he found that Paul's letters upheld standards of classical rhetoric. The Venerable Bede, the English biblical scholar (ca. 673–735), analyzed figures and tropes in both Testaments in his *De schematibus et tropis*.

Some Reformers analyzed the Pauline epistles from a rhetorical perspective. Most prominent is Philip Melanchthon (1497–1560), a rhetorician in his own right like Augustine, who even published works on rhetoric itself. His rhetorical commentaries on Romans and Galatians use Greco-Roman conventions of invention, arrangement, and style, as well as more contemporary conventions of these. Desiderius Erasmus (ca. 1469–1536) gave us rhetorical analyses of 1 and 2 Corinthians in his *Paraphrasis in chias epistolas Pauli ad Corinthios.* John Calvin (1509–64) analyzes Romans rhetorically in his *In omnes D. Pauli Novi Testamenti Epistolas, atque etiā in Epistolā ad Hebraeos commentaria luculentissima.*

After the Reformation rhetorical analysis of the New Testament was minimal until the late eighteenth to early twentieth centuries when German scholars turned their attention to it. Notable here are Karl Ludwig Bauer's massive study of Paul's use of classical rhetoric, entitled *Rhetoricae Paullinae, vel. Quid oratorium sit in oratione Paulli* (1792) and Eduard Konig's encyclopedia of rhetorical features of the Bible, along with parallels in classical literature, entitled *Stilistik, Rhetorik, Poetik in Bezug auf die biblische Literatur* (1900), Johannes Weiss (1863–1914) wrote "Beitrage zur paulinischen Rhetorik" (1897) and *Die Aufgaben der neutestamentlichen Wissenschaft in dem Gegenwart* (1908), in which he evaluates the rhetoric of the Pauline epistles, especially in regard to parallelism, antithesis, and symmetry. Rudolf Bultmann, a doctoral student of Weiss, wrote a dissertation entitled *Der Stil der paulinischen Predigt und die kynisch-stoische Diatribe* (1910). He found features of the Cynic–Stoic diatribe in the Pauline epistles and concluded that Paul was functioning like a Cynic street preacher and his epistles were from a low level of rhetorical culture in which the Cynics dwelt. Notable too was a debate as to whether or not classical categories of rhetoric could be applied to the New Testament and, if so, to what extent. How much of Paul's rhetoric was due to the use of common figures like antithesis and repetition, and how much was due to Hellenistic and/or Jewish rhetoric, or a unique contribution of his own?

During most of the twentieth century rhetoric was not a part of the study of the New Testament. Rhetorical analysis of the New Testament focused mainly on style to the neglect of more central matters of invention and arrangement, and focused almost solely on the Pauline epistles. Contributing factors to this neglect were the loss of rhetorical study in the school curricula of the Western world and the assessment in Germany that Paul's letters were non-literary and thus not an appropriate subject for rhetorical analysis.

The last three decades have witnessed a major renewal of the use of rhetoric as a key tool for the interpretation of the New Testament. The works of Amos Wilder and Robert Funk helped ignite this renewal. In his book, *Early Christian Rhetoric* (1961), Wilder argued that literary forms and genres yield information about the social-historical setting and situation that produced them. In his book, *Language, Hermeneutic, and Word of God* (1966), Funk emphasized that letters are structured speech and rhetoric is a key to understanding both.

Bringing rhetorical criticism back into biblical studies in general was J. Muilenburg's presidential address to the Society of Biblical Literature in 1968. In addition to form criticism that sought the typical and representative, he encouraged biblical scholars to seek the unique, individual, and artistic in a text, that is, its rhetorical finesse. He saw his enterprise within the boundaries of literary criticism with an emphasis on stylistics. The reintroduction of rhetorical criticism to New Testament studies in particular is attributed to H. D. Betz's work on Galatians. He assumed that Paul's epistles were composed using classical categories of invention, arrangement, and style, and that these categories could aid interpretation. He classified Galatians as an "apologetic letter" that uses judicial rhetoric common to courts of law. His rhetorical analysis of Galatians is synthesized in his commentary, *Galatians: A Commentary on Paul's Letter to the Churches in Galatia* (1979). Betz began a new trend in commentary writing – rhetorical analysis of an entire epistle using Greco-Roman rhetoric. While Betz was working with Greco-Roman rhetoric, W. Wuellner was introducing more modern rhetoric into New Testament study. Working with Romans, he urged that the Pauline epistles should be approached primarily as argumentative and rhetorical.

## Contemporary Methodologies in Rhetorical Criticism of the New Testament

Rhetorical criticism of the New Testament is performed with a variety of methodologies. Some interpreters use only Greco-Roman rhetoric, some only modern rhetoric, and some various combinations of both. Within these three broad groupings there is further variety. Biblical texts are rhetorical and subject to analysis by the principles of both Greco-Roman and modern rhetoric. Both ancient and modern rhetoric are concerned with two interrelated areas of the text's discursive techniques and the how these techniques function to persuade readers to act as the writer wishes them to act. Both Greco-Roman and modern rhetoric are interested in the larger social context of communication that includes both the rhetor and audience and the effect of rhetoric upon both.

### Greco–Roman rhetoric

The Jewish rhetorical heritage is preserved in written sources (Old Testament texts especially), but did not leave a self-aware, much less systematic, treatment. However, Greco-Roman rhetoric is preserved not only in written sources (speeches, letters), but also in self-aware, systematic rhetorical handbooks. Among others these include Aristotle's *Ars Rhetorica*, Cicero's *De inventione* and *De oratore*, and Quintilian's *Institutio oratorio*. Knowledge of ancient Jewish and Greco-Roman rhetorical conventions helps the interpreter to understand how the New Testament texts functioned in their oral and written cultures.

Ancient rhetorical theory was discussed under the five main categories of invention, arrangement, style, memory, and delivery. The last two will not concern us. Invention begins with the stasis, the basis of the conflict or main question to be addressed. Then it continues to the determination of the species of rhetoric appropriate to the stasis: judicial, deliberative, or epideictic. These are the rhetoric of the courtroom, political forum, and public ceremony respectively. Judicial rhetoric pertains to accusation and defense with regard to past action, deliberative rhetoric concerns persuasion and dissuasion of thinking or courses of future action, and epideictic applies to praise or blame based on current communal values.

Invention primarily involves the creation of convincing proofs. Proofs can be inartificial or artificial, not created or created by the rhetor respectively. Inartificial proofs include previous judgments or documents. In the New Testament these proofs are usually eyewitness testimony and quotations of the Old Testament. Artificial proofs include *ethos* (authority or moral character of the speaker), *pathos* (emotion aroused for the speaker and against the opposition), and *logos* (propositions and supporting arguments). Proof from *logos* can be from induction or deduction, from example and argument respectively. Examples used in the New Testament are often taken from the Old Testament, Jewish tradition, and nature. Arguments in the New Testament are often enthymemes, a proposition with one supporting reason that is convincing to an audience. Schemes of elaboration of themes and arguments are also used in proof.

Arrangement is the ordering of the various components that, in their fullest form, are the *exordium* (introduction to the key points to be made), *narratio* (statement of the facts of the case), *partitio* (propositions to be developed), *probatio* (arguments and development of topics in support of the proposition), *refutatio* (refutation of the opposition), and *peroratio* (summary of points made and appeal to audience emotion). Style is fitting the language to the needs of invention and arrangement, and includes such things as figures of speech and thought. Important figures in the New Testament are antithesis, hyperbole, irony, metaphor, paronomasia, personification, and repetition.

In his book *New Testament Interpretation through Rhetorical Criticism*, the classicist G. A. Kennedy (1984) was the first to provide a methodology using Greco-Roman rhetoric to analyze New Testament texts. His methodology has been very influential and has these five interrelated steps: (1) Determine the rhetorical unit. The rhetorical unit can be either a well-defined pericope (e.g., Sermon on the Mount) or an entire book (e.g., Romans). These units should correspond to units in rhetorical handbooks, speeches, and letters of the classical period. (2) Define the rhetorical situation, that is, a situation in which the persons, events, and exigence necessitate a verbal response. (3) Determine the rhetorical problem or stasis and the species of rhetoric. (4) Analyze the invention, arrangement, and style in detail. (5) Evaluate the rhetorical effectiveness of the rhetorical unit in utilizing invention, arrangement, and style to address the rhetorical situation.

Using Greco-Roman rhetoric to analyze the New Testament assumes that the authors of the New Testament were familiar with the rhetoric of their time. This familiarity comes either from formal, secondary education in which rhetoric played a major role (mainly for the wealthy), and/or exposure to oral and written rhetorical practice that permeated Jewish and Hellenistic cultures. Rhetorical finesse is evident in the composition of the New Testament, whether consciously or unconsciously applied. New Testament texts are argumentative with a complex, interwoven structure. Biblical authors used invention, arrangement, and style to present the gospel to convince their audiences of the legitimacy of their claims.

Analyzing the New Testament using Greco-Roman rhetoric is a historical enterprise. It is using a discipline from the context of the New Testament to analyze its texts. Like historical- critical methodologies before it, rhetorical criticism is concerned with the situation of the authors of the New Testament texts and their audiences. The interpreter can glimpse the dynamics that created the text through analysis of the type of rhetoric, arguments, and strategies selected, especially as these are informed by other studies of the social, cultural, and ideological milieu of the first-century Mediterranean world.

This historical approach to rhetorical criticism has raised several questions: (1) To what extent did Greco-Roman rhetoric influence Jewish culture by the first century CE, and is this rhetoric rightly used in analyzing Jewish texts, particularly those from a specifically Palestinian context like several of the New Testament texts? (2) To what degree did rhetorical theory influence the epistolary genre (to be discussed further below)? (3) Does Greco-Roman rhetorical analysis ignore peculiar features of early Christian rhetoric?

### Modern rhetoric

For many interpreters, conducting rhetorical criticism using only Greco-Roman rhetorical conventions is too limited. They consider ancient rhetoric to be inadequate for modern hermeneutics because it does not address all theoretical, philosophical, and practical issues posed by speech. They deem modern rhetorical theory to be a more developed and sophisticated understanding of rhetoric and thus a better tool of interpretation.

Rhetorical criticism of the New Testament based on modern rhetoric can take three main approaches. First it can use Anglo-American theories of argumentation, continental theories of literary rhetoric, or American theories of rhetoric derived from social science hermeneutics. *The New Rhetoric* of Chaim Perelman and L. Olbrechts-Tyteca has been prominent in rhetorical criticism using modern rhetoric. Theirs is a philosophical assessment of argumentation in the tradition of Aristotle's *Ars Rhetorica*. Rhetoric is the art of increasing the adherence of the mind to the values and theses that the rhetor wishes the audience to reaffirm or accept for the first time. Speech is part of the historical and social situation that produce it and in which it was enacted. Rhetoric is a liaison between text and social context.

Rhetorical criticism using modern rhetoric is a philosophical reconceptualization of Greco-Roman rhetoric, a synchronic approach to argumentation. It is not as suited to historical concerns in interpreting New Testament texts as Greco-Roman rhetoric. However, modern rhetoric may go beyond historical questions without neglecting them altogether. It neither ignores the historical nature of a text nor does it solely depend upon it. It takes historical information into account, but rather than being descriptive it tries to understand the intention of the text and how values of the time are utilized in the argumentation. It is not trying to reconstruct the original situation, but rather to discover the argumentation of the text in its own right. It is looking at the social, cultural, and ideological values assumed in the premises, topics, and argumentation used.

## The Practice of Rhetorical Criticism

### The gospels

As mentioned above, recent rhetorical criticism in gospel study began with the approach of J. Muilenburg proposed in 1968. He urged the biblical field to move beyond form criticism with its atomistic approach and seek the larger literary patterns in the gospels. The method proposed defining the literary unit and observing *inclusio*, major themes, and points of climax. The macro- and micro-structures are then discovered by noting features like chiasm, parallelism, antithesis, repetition, and rhetorical questions. The interrelationship of the parts of a discourse informed the interpreter of the meaning of the text.

Kennedy applied his method to portions of the gospels, specifically the Sermon on the Mount (Matt. 5–7), the Sermon on the Plain (Luke 6:20–49), and the Farewell Discourse (John 13–17). He argued that the Sermon on the Mount is deliberative rhetoric because it provides the audience with advice on a manner of living that is advantageous to their future with God. The *exordium* (5:3–16) puts forward the Beatitudes. The *propositio* (5:17–20) presents the two propositions that the law and prophets are fulfilled (5:17) and the righteousness of the audience must exceed the righteousness of the scribes and Pharisees (5:18–20). *The probatio* (5:21–7:20) develops the first proposition by *ethos* and *pathos* (5:21–48) and the second by *logos* or enthymemes (6:1–7:20). The *peroratio* (7:21–7) both summarizes the points made (7:21–3) and appeals to emotion (7:24–7).

Although Kennedy's methodology is applicable to portions of the gospels, it does not work for the study of a gospel as a single rhetorical unit. This is due to limitations inherent in Greco-Roman rhetoric and the nature of the gospels as narrative. Greco-Roman rhetoric lacks a theory of narrative that discusses plot with issue, development, and resolution of the issue. This limitation led scholars to pursue other rhetorical avenues. It was discovered that the gospel writers used rhetorical imitation of traditional examples and narrative paradigms to construct their gospels. For example, portions of Luke's Gospel imitate Old Testament texts as well as holding up positive and negative examples for moral imitation.

One of the most fruitful avenues explored for analyzing the gospels as narrative was the *chreia* and an ancient pattern of argumentation. A *chreia* (plural *chreiai*) is a saying, a description of an action, or both that is concise, attributed to a person or group, appropriate to the situation it is used to address, and considered to improve life. Oral and written communication in the Greco-Roman world relied upon *chreiai*, especially for transmitting the words and deeds of kings, generals, and philosophers. An example of a *chreia* is: "Diogenes the philosopher, on being asked by someone how he could become famous, responded: 'By worrying as little as possible about fame.'"

*Chreiai* were the basis of many of the rhetorical exercises described in the *progymnasmata* (preliminary exercises), the rhetorical textbooks written from the first to the fifth centuries CE. *Progymnasmata* were a central part of the rhetorical instruction in the curricula of post-secondary education in the Roman empire. The *progymnasmata* taught students to elaborate the meaning of the saying or action in a *chreia* using long-established topics. The *progymnasma* most commonly used to interpret the New Testament is that of Aelius Theon of Alexandria, a contemporary of the New Testament (ca. 50–100 CE). His elaboration pattern for a *chreia* includes recitation of the *chreia* in similar words, inflection in all the numbers and cases of the language, appending commentary or positive statement, appending an objection or negative statement which is antithetical to the commentary, expansion or recitation at greater length, condensation or recitation in more concise form, and refutation and/or confirmation.

The role of *chreiai* in oral and written culture in the ancient Mediterranean provides insight into the formation and transmission of the sayings of Jesus through the gospel tradition, and the way in which the gospel writers used this tradition to construct their gospels. The words and deeds of Jesus were transmitted as *chreiai*, probably in both oral and written form. One example is: "Now after John was arrested, Jesus came to Galilee, proclaiming the good news of God and saying, 'The time is fulfilled, and the kingdom of God has come near; repent, and believe in the good news'" (Mark 1:14–15 NRSV). The gospel writers were able to use the progymnasmatic exercises to elaborate the *chreiai* of Jesus and the Jesus tradition according to rhetorical conventions to suit their polemical, theological, and literary needs. This is demonstrated by the fact that a *chreia* in one gospel is elaborated in its parallel account. For example, Mark 10:13–16 is an elaborated *chreia* that is found in a more condensed form in Matthew 19:13–15. The use of *chreiai* in the gospels strongly indicates that the gospel writers had some degree of rhetorical education.

*Chreiai* were manipulated and modified to be fitting responses to situations. They were crafted and not necessary historical reminiscences. Putting the sayings and actions of Jesus in *chreia* form provided some parameters for transmission in tradition, but some elaboration occurred both in the placement in *chreia* form and in the use of the *chreia* in the composition of the gospels. It was common to elaborate internal description, expand dialogues, and align the point of the *chreia* with the needs of the discourse. Rhetorical criticism of the gospels alerts the interpreter to distinguish between the rhetoric of the historical Jesus, the rhetoric of the Jesus tradition as represented by Q, and the rhetoric of the gospels. These are related, but not the same.

Besides rhetorical criticism of the gospels based upon Greco-Roman rhetoric, there are important studies based on modern rhetorical theory in combination with literary and narrative criticism as well as sociology. Literary criticism distinguishes between the content of the narrative (the story) and the form of the narrative (the rhetoric). The latter involves how the rhetorical devices create the desired effect on the reader. In literary criticism of the gospels the role of rhetoric in creating authority and challenging the audience to accept new insights and change behavior are emphasized.

An exciting new development is socio-rhetorical criticism, an interpretive analytic that creates dialogue between different disciplines and approaches to the gospels. It explores the inner texture, intertexture, social and cultural texture, ideological, and sacred texture of a gospel. Rhetoric, old and new, dialogues with many related fields. For example, one insight, gained from V. K. Robbins's work, *Jesus the Teacher* (1984), is that Mark creates a biography of Jesus that depicts him as a disciple-gathering teacher enacting a system of thought and action. Jesus is portrayed as a composite of biblical prophets and Greco-Roman philosopher-teachers. Thus Mark makes Jesus understandable and identifiable to first-century Mediterranean society.

### The epistles

There is strong debate about the extent to which Greco-Roman rhetorical theory influenced the epistolary genre in antiquity. This debate is naturally important for discerning the relationship between rhetoric and the epistles of the New Testament, particularly those of Paul. Some interpreters understand rhetoric to have only a secondary influence in the writing of the New Testament epistles – mainly matters of style. Other interpreters understand the New Testament epistles to be speeches in epistolary form to be read orally, and thus constructed according to matters of invention, arrangement, and style. There is much middle ground as well, with interpreters granting differing amounts of influence to epistolary and rhetorical concerns in the epistles.

In part this debate is fostered by the fact that epistolary and rhetorical theory developed separately in antiquity. The rhetoricians taught epistolary theory, but it was not integrated into rhetorical theory. Rhetorical handbooks rarely discuss the role of rhetoric in epistles. If they do, style is the focus. The first extant rhetorical handbook to discuss letter-writing is that of Julius Victor from the fourth century CE (*Ars Rhetorica*, 27 – *De Epistolis*). In turn, manuals for writing epistles do not discuss the role of rhetoric in epistles, but rather the types of epistles and the style appropriate to them.

There is overlap between epistolary and rhetorical theory in practice. To some extent, the three species of rhetoric – judicial, deliberative, and epideictic – can also be used to classify epistles. The large varieties of epistles naturally produced some functional parallels with all three species, but nothing close to complete conformity. It was not the needs of the argumentation that determined the inventional topics used in an epistle, but the type of epistle appropriate to the situation. *Ethos* and *pathos*, two types of proof by *logos*, occur naturally in letters. Rhetorical arrangement was not prescribed for epistles, but there are functional parallels between epistolary and rhetorical arrangement. The letter body opening, middle, and closing function like the *exordium, narratio-probatio,* and *peroratio* respectively. Stylistic concerns were shared by both rhetorical and epistolary theory.

The study of epistles indicates that rhetorical and epistolary instruction may not have been as separate as extant handbooks and manuals indicate. There is careful development of invention, arrangement, and style in epistles. By the first century BCE rhetoric had exerted a strong influence on epistolary composition so that epistles were understood as means of persuasion. For example, the epistles of Demosthenes (fourth century BCE) are written according to rhetorical conventions. Official letters were substitutes for speeches, and rhetoric played a great role in their composition. Rhetorical handbooks may not have discussed epistolary theory because their focus was upon speeches and the judicial rhetoric of the law court that are not appropriate to epistles, but rhetoric still appears to have influenced epistles.

All the epistles of the New Testament have been analyzed according to the conventions of invention, arrangement, and style as preserved in the ancient rhetorical handbooks. The undisputed Pauline epistles have been a particular focus. Since Paul's epistles were read to the house churches in order to persuade them, they functioned like speeches central to rhetorical practice. What rhetorical prowess does appear in Paul's epistles may derive from the conscious application of rhetorical theory or conscious or unconscious imitation of written sources or observed speeches. Although the debate continues, many Pauline scholars believe that Paul's use of epistles and rhetoric is the result of formal rhetorical training at the secondary level in which rhetoric played a major role. Paul's opponents noted that his speech was contemptible, but conceded that his letters were strong, which probably implies "rhetorically effective" (2 Cor.

10:10). Although Paul said that his preaching was not marked by the use of persuasive rhetoric (1 Cor. 1:17–2:5), he did not rule out rhetorical skill. He (and likely his opponents) was referring to Sophistic rhetoric that was more interested in structure and a show of rhetorical prowess than in the content of the speech. Paul refused to demonstrate rhetorical prowess with the usual stylistic flair and prescribed topics. Instead he was interested in the content of Jesus crucified (1 Cor. 2:1–5). The sophistication of Paul's boasting in 2 Corinthians 10–13, with its extensive parallels to Plutarch's *On Praising Oneself Inoffensively*, is a fine example of a rhetoric that seems clearly derived from formal education consciously applied.

Probably the most famous debate in rhetorical criticism of the Pauline epistles is the rhetorical classification and function of Galatians. Betz first classified it as judicial rhetoric – Paul is defending himself and his gospel against attack. Others argue that Galatians is deliberative rhetoric – Paul is persuading his readers to be true to his gospel and dissuading them from accepting the false gospel of the Judaizers. Still others see the first portion as judicial (1:6–4:11) and the second as deliberative rhetoric (4:12–6:18).

Modern conceptions of rhetoric also have been used to analyze Paul's epistles. In his *Abraham in Galatians* (1989), G. W. Hansen has used the New Rhetoric of Perelman and Olbrecht-Tyteca to analyze the argumentation of Galatians. Several arguments are identified. There is the argument by authority that Paul uses to claim that his apostleship has a divine commission (Gal. 1:1) and that his gospel is true and has no alternative versions (Gal. 1:6–9). There is also the argument by definition that defines the gospel by connecting it to other key topics like promise, faith, law, and works of the law. Another is the argument by dissociation of ideas that relies upon antithesis to exclude ideas to be dissociated from the gospel. Paul also uses the argument of the severance of the group and its members. As he discusses the Galatians and the Judaizers he continues to place them into separate groups. For instance, the Galatians are children of Hagar while the Judaizers are children of Sarah (Gal. 4:29). Finally there is the argument by sacrifice that stresses the value of something for which a sacrifice was made. Paul stresses the sacrifice of Christ on the cross as the basis for the value of the freedom in Christ that the sacrifice made possible (Gal. 1:4; 2:4, 20–1; 3:1, 13–14; 4:4; 5:1).

### The Acts of the Apostles and Revelation

Studies of the rhetoric of the Acts of the Apostles are naturally tied to the Gospel of Luke, to which it is closely tied. However, the change of genre from gospel to historiography also means a change of rhetorical approach, as a shift of genre typically does. Rhetorical criticism of Acts has focused upon the rhetoric of the speeches that comprise about a third of it. These speeches are written according to Greco-Roman rhetorical conventions. For example, Paul's defense speeches are good examples of judicial rhetoric (Acts 24:10–21; 26:1–23).

Rhetorical criticism has also focused on the purpose of Acts as apologetic speech. Acts can be understood as defending Christianity to Rome as law-abiding. In Acts, Roman officials never find Christianity in violation of the law. Acts can also be viewed as a defense to Paul's detractors that Paul's apostleship as authentic. Peter, whose apostleship was never in doubt, is contrasted with Paul. Whatever Peter does in chapters 1–12, Paul does in chapters 13–28.

The rhetoric of Revelation conforms the least of any New Testament book to Greco-Roman rhetorical conventions. But it is very rhetorical nonetheless. It is at once judicial (indictments and warnings), deliberative (calls for decision), and epideictic (liturgical and hymnic) rhetoric. It employs sacred language, metaphors, myths, and images to create a symbolic universe portraying the cosmic drama between good and evil. The audience is enabled to see their present economic ostracism and political oppression from Rome as part of this cosmic battle. They can see the broad span of God's plan and that, while the powers of Rome seem strong at the moment, Jesus is the victor and those remaining faithful to him will be victorious. The symbols evoke meaning and channel emotion to persuade the churches to modify their perspective and reaffirm their allegiance to Jesus, not the emperor, as Lord.

The rhetoric of Revelation is dramatic. It relies upon symbols and images that recur with a different mix of associations each time. For example, the beast from the sea has associations with the chaos monster Leviathan, the Roman empire as agent of evil, and the cult of emperor-worship and its idolatry (Rev. 13:1–8). Larger contrasts are key to the rhetoric of Revelation as well, such as the woman clothed with the sun representing the people of God (Rev. 12:1–6) who contrasts with the whore of Babylon representing the unrepentant sinners (Rev. 17:1–17). Numerical patterns based on 3 and 7 in particular structure the narrative, often functioning as amplification by repetition. For example, the three judgments by seven seals, trumpets, and bowls amplify the quantity and comprehensive nature of God's judgment.

## Conclusion

The Christian rhetoric of the New Testament challenged the dominant rhetorical theory and practice of the Greco-Roman world. It did not rely upon the same values and hierarchy of values in the invention of its arguments. To illustrate, Paul considered his weakness as strength worthy of boasting (2 Cor. 10–13), while his non-Christian neighbors would consider weakness unworthy and shameful. Rhetorical criticism shows us the way that biblical authors used rhetoric to shape their communities' values and perceptions. Finding the underlying values and assumptions of the argumentation that the authors assume they share with their churches gives us insight into the cultural, social, and ideological background of the early Christians. The rhetorical strategies used help us understand how the authors and audiences perceived themselves in relation to the broader culture.

## Annotated Bibliography

Anderson, R. Dean Jr. *Ancient Rhetorical Theory and Paul*. Rev. edn. Contributions to Biblical Exegesis and Theology, 18. Leuven: Peeters, 1999. Fine assessment of the use of rhetorical criticism of Paul's letters as currently practiced.

Aune, D. E. *The Westminster Dictionary of New Testament and Early Christian Literature and Rhetoric*. Louisville, KY: Westminster John Knox, 2003. Among many other subjects, a broad range of entries on early Christian literary genres, rhetorical forms, and rhetorical practice.

Betz, H. D. *Galatians: A Commentary on Paul's Letter to the Churches in Galatia*. Hermeneia. Philadelphia: Fortress Press, 1979. A rhetorical commentary that reintroduced Greco-Roman rhetoric into New Testament exegesis.

Hock, R. F. and E. N. O'Neil (eds.). *The Chreia in Ancient Rhetoric*, vol. 1: *The Progymnasmata*. Texts and Translations, 27. Graeco-Roman Religion Series, 9. Atlanta: Scholars Press, 1986. Includes the *chreiai* exercises of prominent *progymnasmata*.

Hock, R. F. and E. N. O'Neil (eds.). *The Chreia and Ancient Rhetoric: Classroom Exercises*. Writings from the Greco-Roman World, 2. Atlanta: Society of Biblical Literature, 2002. Primary source material for the *chreia* elaboration used in gospel studies.

Kennedy, G. A. *New Testament Interpretation through Rhetorical Criticism*. Chapel Hill: University of North Carolina Press, 1984. First work in biblical studies in modern times to introduce rhetorical criticism of the New Testament in a systematic way using Greco-Roman rhetoric.

Mack, B. L. *Rhetoric and the New Testament*. Minneapolis: Fortress Press, 1990. A solid introduction to New Testament rhetoric according to Greco-Roman rhetoric and the New Rhetoric.

Perelman, C. and L. Olbrechts-Tyteca. *The New Rhetoric: A Treatise on Argumentation*. Trans. J. Wilkinson and P. Weaver. Notre Dame: Notre Dame University Press, 1969. Classic work on the New Rhetoric used in rhetorical criticism of the New Testament.

Watson, D. F. *Rhetorical Criticism of the New Testament: A Bibliographic Survey*. Leiden: Deo Press, 2006. Thorough bibliography of the rhetorical criticism of the New Testament with introduction.

Witherington, B. *New Testament Rhetoric*. Eugene: Cascade Books, 2009. An introduction to the rhetoric of large portions of the New Testament with explicit discussion of its implications for interpretation.

# CHAPTER 12
# Social-Scientific Criticism

Jerome H. Neyrey, SJ

## The Emergence of Social-Scientific Criticism

*History*

We first find consideration of the Bible in terms of "social" issues in the nineteenth-century German study of religion, in which Max Weber and Ernst Troeltsch respectively theorized about the institutionalization of groups and the ideal types of groups which emerged, particularly "sects." Twentieth-century roots are found in the Chicago school under the guidance of Shirley Jackson Case and Shailer Matthews (see Funk 1976). Two recent networks of scholars, however, galvanized modern concerns with "social" matters. In 1972 one network began asking social questions of the New Testament in terms of "social history" and "social description." Simultaneously, another network asked social questions by means of cultural anthropology and sociology. The latter began formally employing cross-cultural, anthropological models for interpretation of the New Testament. Thus two parallel ways of considering New Testament documents in terms of "social" perspectives emerged with significantly different presuppositions, aims, and methods: forms of "social history" on the one hand, and "social-scientific" interpretation on the other (see Elliott 1993: 17–35).

*How is "social" being used?*

When scholars began using the term "social," as in "the social world of ...," "the social function of ...," or "the social description of ...," this represented a turn from theological investigation of authors and documents to the influences on the formation of their thinking and the effects they might have on a group (see Elliott 1990; 1–20; Malina 1996). One exponent of the "social" history/description branch of scholarship argues that "social" contains four elements: (1) *social description* of facts or the *realia* such as foodstuffs or occupations of the early Christians; (2) genuine *social history* which integrates "social description" with social and political history and theology; (3) *social organization* of early Christianity, i.e., the *social forces* which led to the rise of Christianity and its *social institutions*; and (4) *social world*, the creation of a world of meaning which provided a plausibility structure (Smith 1975).

Alternately, when other scholars use the term "social," they endeavor to interpret data by formal use of materials from the "social sciences," cultural anthropology and sociology. Inasmuch as they focus less on "history" and more on "meaning," they interpret by attending to what is common about groups: social systems of groups, institutions, values, economics, and modal personalities (Malina 2001: 19–22). The former mainly do "history," with a acute concern for an accurate telling of "social" conflicts, groups, and material culture. The latter, in contrast, are concerned with interpretation in light of the social system of cultural and political life of a given people. The use of "social," therefore, is more than a turning from individuals to groups, but especially the study of the cultural system using formal "social" models. The difference between the two usages of "social" noted above is no minor matter, for it replicates in biblical study the same distinction made between history and sociology,[1] that is, the study of what is particular and unique as opposed to what is common to and shared by individuals and groups.

## Representative figures

Let us put faces to these types of "social" criticism. First, Wayne Meeks claims to be doing "social description," by which he means "social history," as well as description of "social environment" (Meeks 1983). Most reviewers of his book *First Urban Christians* hailed it as the best social history to date of at least a part of early Christianity. It satisfied the general historical goal to "discern the texture of life in particular times and particular places," while at the same time it aimed to attend to "the collectivities to which they [the first urban Christians] belonged and to glimpse their lives through the typical occasions mirrored in the texts" (Meeks 1983: 1–2). Basically, better history. Not all readers agreed that *First Urban Christians* deserved such praise for its "social" matters (see Malina 1985; Elliott 1985). Although Meeks acknowledges sociologists and anthropologists in his bibliography, they have scant influence on his text; for he and other social historians are leery of models. His organizing frameworks were quite eclectic, not surprising in a pioneering work. Yet the most important of all social models was nowhere to be found, namely, what is a "city," not just the archaeological materials, but the social, economic, political, and cultural meaning of "city." To the uninitiated, his work seems revolutionary (which it is) and critically sound (for this type of social criticism). But let us consider what is absent from Meeks's "social" study.

An alternate theorist of "social-scientific" criticism, Bruce Malina, in *New Testament World* (Malina 2001) differs from Meeks in that he formally uses models from cultural anthropology as the heuristic guide for modern Western readers to interpret the non-Western world of Jesus and Paul.[2] He offers the rare scientific study of how we readers actually read, which emphasizes how modern readers must hear the ancient cultural meanings of "father" or "bride" or "honor" without imposing modern meanings on them.[3] His study urges modern readers to find their way into the institution of kinship, the pivotal values which structure perception and behavior (i.e., "honor and shame" and "purity and pollution"). Most importantly, he shows how modern individualists ("I did it my way!") differ from the group-oriented personality (see Malina and Neyrey 1996: esp. 1–18 and 153–201), the dominant mode in antiquity. Also included in *New Testament World* are studies of the perception of limited good and envy, the perennial spark which ignites feuding and controversy, as well as models of stages of group development. Unlike those of Meeks, Malina's models are not eclectic, but are the fundamental topics found in anthropology textbooks for interpreting cultures. These models, moreover, are derived especially from Middle Eastern and Mediterranean anthropology, with the aim that, with suitable adaptation to the antique world, they provide a superior window into the ancient world than ethnocentric Western "social history." Less history than Meeks, perhaps, but more accurate and complete "social" interpretation.

## Comparison and contrast

Table 12.1 may sharpen the differences between the two uses of "social" in contemporary criticism.

To understand more precisely each way of doing "social" criticism, let us sharpen the differences between them by attending to some the major elements in the table. First, both understand themselves as operating within the dominant paradigm, the historical-critical method. But socio-cultural interpretation argues that new tools belong in the interpreter's toolbox. Second, while all interpreters are eclectic in their choice of tools and questions, socio-cultural criticism differs from social history/description in that it argues for a systems approach, that is, a consideration of institutions (politics, kinship), values (honor and shame), economics, and types of person (group-oriented).[4] Third, they differ in terms of focus ("history" = diachronic attention to story and particularity; "interpretation" = synchronic attention to culture and meaning) and epistemology (former = immaculate perception; latter = perception only through models). Finally, the two differ radically over the use of models in interpretation, whether to be explicit in the use of them or whether to use them at all. Those who practice "social description" or "social history" tend to stress the incommensurability of cultures, especially the distance between modern and ancient cultures (Stowers 1985). Embedded in this judgment is a fear of ethnocentric anachronisms, which regularly occur when modern readers impose an alien system of social organization, meanings, and values on an ancient document. Hence, the formal use of social-science models, theories, or concepts is presumed to corrupt the reading process because of anachronism, for ironically "imposing" on it their data, often called a procrustean bed or cookie cutter. Hence, scientific interpretations are always suspect. Models and concepts for this group should only arise directly out of a document; one should not bring such notions to one's reading. Alternately, social-scientific critics argue that without formal and appropriate models, social histories blithely practice their own anachronism by presuming that our world must be like their world.

**Table 12.1**   Social description v. social science

| Social history – social description | Social-science interpretation |
|---|---|
| 1  Diachronic: focus on discrete historical slice of a history of a place, person or time | 1  Synchronic: an in-depth interpretation of typical patterns of institutions, culture, etc. |
| 2  Aim: to tell the story accurately | 2  Aim: to interpret the story accurately |
| 3  Emphasis: particularity of this place or time | 3  Emphasis: what is typical or common about this place or time |
| 4  Emic or native reporting trumps etic or sociological interpretation | 4  Emic or native reporting itself needs to be interpreted |
| 5  Epistemology: "immaculate perception"– modern Westerners can immediately understand the narrative. | 5  Epistemology: no "immaculate perception"– all perception is culturally conditioned; only with a model can an observer see |
| 6  Observer sees only what emic native says he sees: small canvas, fine detail | 6  Observer sees much more than emic native, because he sees more and at a more integrated vantage point: large canvas of the social system |
| 7  Focus: discrete data, which may or may not be related | 7  Focus: basic cultural system within which data have meaning |
| 8  Latent model operative, which is generally unaware of ethnocentrism or anachronism | 8  Explicit model which interprets in terms of cross-cultural materials adapted to be culturally appropriate to ancient world, not ours |
| 9  Models, if used, tend to be eclectic; weak sense of "system" of ancient life | 9  Models used are understood as part of larger social system |
| 10  "Social" = description, accuracy of story | 10  "Social" = interpretation, meaning of story |

## Models

Since the use of models lies at the heart of socio-cultural interpretation, we ask "What is a 'model'?" Malina defines a model as "an abstract, simplified representation of some real world object, event, or interaction constructed for the purpose of understanding, control, or prediction" – in short, a type of abstraction which seeks what is common instead of what is unique and distinctive.[5] Why models? Precisely because modern readers attempt to understand a literature and culture far removed from them, they need reliable tools to make perception possible at all. Euro-American tourists arriving in Damascus, Cairo, Riyadh, or Baghdad immediately suffer culture shock. Hence, the US State Department publishes books and pamphlets about the countries and cultures to which diplomats and troops travel. This is why the US government commissioned Ruth Benedict's *The Chrysanthemum and the Sword* to facilitate understanding of

Japanese culture by the US occupying army. Cultural models are not optional, but essential tools for seeing and understanding.

Those who employ formal models, theories, and concepts from the social sciences maintain that every reader or interpreter is inescapably using some model of social relationships or some implicit conception of how the world works. The simple fact that all human beings practice forms of abstraction to chunk data together indicates that every historian or interpreter of the ancient world brings some type of abstraction to his or her reading.[6] There is no "immaculate perception." But do readers know what models they bring? Have they any clues to the alternate culture, which is both most assuredly in the ancient document and just as assuredly not familiar to the modern reader? In response to anti-model criticism, it has to be claimed that there are two types of scholars: (1) those who use models and do not know or admit this, and (2) those who use models consciously and critically (Elliott 1993: 42). How curious, then, is Meek's statement on the need for models:

> The difficulty is that without interpretation [i.e., theory] there are no facts. Every observation entails a point of view, a set of connections. The pure empiricist would drown in meaningless impressions. Even so simple a task as translating a sentence from an ancient language into our own requires some sense of the social matrices of both the original utterance and ourselves ... To collect facts without any theory too often means to substitute for theory our putative common sense. Making that substitution modernizes no less than does the scientist who follows his theory, for our common sense, too, is a cultural artifact. (Meeks 1983: 5)

## What Theory? What Models?

What new tools for social-scientific criticism belong in the scholar's toolbox? The following models come from standard anthropological textbooks and represent the basic items that must be known to read another cultural world, especially the ancient one.

### Institutions

An institution is a system of interrelated behaviors, relationships, roles, and exchanges created in response to persistent social needs. Although we know many institutions (educational, financial, religious, etc.), the ancient world revolved around two, namely, kinship/family and politics. Aristotle said that "There are two divisions of philosophy, the practical and the theoretical. The practical part includes ethics and politics, and in the latter not only the doctrine of the state (*polis*) but also that of the household (*oikia*) is sketched" (Diogenes Laertius, 5.28). Ancient social elites understood the institution of politics, inasmuch as this entailed relationship with Caesar and Rome. But the 90 percent of the peasant and artisan non-elite population focused its attention and energy around the family. While all peoples in antiquity belonged to both of these institutions, their involvement in each differed. As regards politics, non-elites all paid taxes to the *polis* or empire – "Render to Caesar the things that are Caesar's" – and often performed corvée labor for Caesar's legions. The elite few belonged to local assemblies which deliberated and decided on political matters. But the institution of kinship was for all peoples at all times more significant than politics.

Biblical characters are only occasionally interested in the world of politics, such as when someone like Jesus is acclaimed "king" or when Israelites confess "We have no king but Caesar." Jesus' discourse on the "kingdom of God" surely recognizes this institution, since he speaks of an alternative kingdom to that of Herod or Caesar. Only when people pay taxes to Caesar or to the temple do they typically contact the institution of politics.

"Family," however, deserves closer attention. The family was one's complete locus of nurture and social support: here one was raised, fed, clothed, socialized, married, cared for in illness, and buried. Since there was no health system, no social security, and no retirement benefits, the family provided all. Although we moderns use the words "family" and "marriage," we understand them to refer to social realities totally foreign to those of the ancients. An appropriate cultural model of "family" would ask: (1) What did marriage mean (union of two families)? (2) What was marriage like (patrilocal residence)? (3) Who inherited (primogeniture)? (4) Who constituted the family (extended family of elders and residential, married sons)? (5) How were marriage partners selected (endogamous usually)? (6) What was the cultural significance of the roles of father and mother, firstborn male, other sons? Table 12.2 compares and contrasts how family in ancient Israel radically differs in structure, purpose, and functioning from that in contemporary USA. Hence, any passage in the New Testament which talks about "family" must take into account all the data included in this table, or risk utterly misunderstanding that ancient institution.

**Table 12.2**    The concept of "Family"

| Variables | First-century Palestine | Twentieth-century USA |
|---|---|---|
| 1 Family form | Endogamous community (multigenerational) | Absolute nuclear (dual-generational) |
| 2 Spousal choice | Controlled by custom and parents | Free choice by couple |
| 3 Marriage strategy | Endogamous (ideal) | Exogamous (by law) |
| 4 Marriage arrangement | Betrothal: families negotiation | Engagement: individual's commitment |
| 5 Wedding endowment | Formal: dowry, indirect dowry, and bridewealth | Informal: family gifts |
| 6 Postmarital residence | Patrilocal: with groom's parents | Neolocal: new household |
| 7 Cohabitation of married sons with parents | Yes | No |
| 8 Economic function of marriage | Producing and consuming unit | Consuming unit |
| 9 Inheritance distribution | Eldest son: double Other sons: single Daughters: dowries | No inheritance rules |

*Source*: Based on Hanson and Oakman 1998: 22.

## Honor and shame

The premier value that drove the behavior of the ancients and for which they competed intensely was "honor." "Honor" means respect, praise, fame, admiration, and the like. Aristotle provides a succinct description view of this social value ((*Rhetoric*, 1.5.9; emphasis added):

> *Fame* means being respected by everybody, or having some quality that is desired by all men ... *Honor* is the token of a man's being famous for doing good ... The constituents of honor are: sacrifices; commemoration, in verse or prose; privileges; grants of land; front seats at civic celebrations; state burial; statues; public maintenance.

As regards the sources of honor, it may be either ascribed or achieved. First, honor is *ascribed* to someone by birth (son of David, Levitical priesthood), adoption, laying on of hands or commissioning. Jesus' genealogies ascribe honor to him as stemming from the houses of Abraham and David; he also enjoys ascribed honor as God's agent at his baptism (Mark 1:9–11); Jesus himself ascribes honor to the "twelve." Pontius Pilate is Caesar's agent for Palestine. Alternately, people *achieve* honor by prowess or, e.g., military, athletic, aesthetic prowess, and by benefaction. Thus runners win crowns for their races; generals earn triumphs; benefactors are awarded special seats, statues, and meals (see Danker 1982).

*Honor claims acknowledged.*    Although all honorable deeds are done in public, they do not produce honor until others acknowledge them. For example, Jesus often experiences a "schism"; while many acknowledge his worth and status and so honor him, his rivals refuse to honor his good deeds (see Matt. 9:32–4; Luke 13:16–17; John 7:12). This acknowledgment may be verbal, as in Jesus' case, or more substantive, as Aristotle stated above in his list the tangible markers of honor: "the constituents of honor are. ..."

## Honor and rhetoric

Among the three species of rhetoric, honor and shame are coterminous with epideictic, that is the rhetoric of honor and shame. This third type of rhetoric flourished in funeral orations for Athens' fallen warriors, in *bioi*, and in hymns to the gods; but it touches New Testament documents first in letters of praise and blame (e.g., 1 Cor. 11:2 and 17) and in doxologies and prayers in them. But two exercises in the *progymnasmata*, the *chreia* and the encomium, express the dynamic of honor and shame most vividly. *Chreiai* are small stories in which a sage or philosopher is challenged by someone, denying him honor and respect. He responds, sometimes with just an action or a word or both. It has been shown that the ubiquitous challenging of Jesus when he is out of doors is narrated in just such a form, in which Jesus' clever response both defends and even increases his honor (Neyrey 1998b). The encomium, a narrative of praise, draws on the criteria which the ancients considered basically honorable: origins (noble *polis* or bloodlines), birth (celebrated by prophecy or celestial phenomena = divine favor), nurture and training (education or discipline learned), deeds of the soul (virtue, especially prudence, justice, fortitude, and temperance), and noble death with posthumous honors (Neyrey 1994a). Paul often appeals to the encomium as part of his apologetic argument (Gal. 1:12–2:14; 2 Cor. 11:22–33; Phil. 3:4–6); but all the gospels promote the honor of Jesus by attention to his (noble) birth, parents, nurture, and deeds according to the instructions found in the encomium (Neyrey 1998a).

### Purity and pollution

Let us not reduce this topic to a study of Leviticus, kosher foods, and Sabbath observance, because "purity and pollution" requires us to reconstruct an elaborate worldview, not just of Israel but also of the Mediterranean world. Put simply, something is "clean" or "pure" when in its proper place. A farmer's dung-covered boots are not "unclean" in the field, but only when he wears them in the house. A bottle of beer graces a cookout, where it is "pure" because in place, but becomes "unclean" when consumed during the Sunday church service. The same object, but "clean" or "unclean" depending on its context. Hence, one must know the code or cultural context that makes something clean or unclean, that is, the implicit "maps" of where persons, places, times, and things "belong."

*Israel's purity system in creation and temple.*   We find the code to Israel's maps both in Genesis 1 and in the temple system. God himself created maps by "separating" and "dividing": (1) *place* (wet/dry), (2) *times* (light/dark, day/night, sun/moon), (3) *things* (sea creatures, air creatures and land creatures; trees with seeds in them), and (4) *persons* (Adam and Eve). This prayer sums up Israel's sense of order and purity based on God's map-making (Havdalah prayer on Sabbath):

> Blessed are you, Lord our God, king of the world, who divides between holy and profane, between light and darkness, between Israel and the peoples, between the seventh day and the six days of work. Blessed are you, Lord, who divides between sacred and profane.

The ordered universe of Genesis 1 is replicated in the temple, which enjoys comparable "maps": (1) *time* (full liturgical calendar), (2) *things* (system of offerings, vessels, garments), (3) *places* (Mount Zion, courts), and (4) *persons* (priests and Levites). Pilgrims need visit Jerusalem's temple only once to see all of these maps laid out clearly and enforced: (1) *place*: a holy mount, with restricted places for females, Gentiles, Israelite males, Levites, priests, and high priest; (2) corresponding to these places are *persons*: females in their court, Gentiles in theirs, Israelites around the altar, priests at the altar, and the high priest in the Holy of Holies; (3) *time*: worship and offerings occur daily (morning and evening), weekly, monthly, annually, and on special feasts such as Yom Kippur, Tabernacles, Dedication, Passover, Pentecost, etc.; (4) *things*: appropriate vestments for priests, appropriate, i.e., "unblemished," offerings and sacrifices, as well as vessels and other tools needed. Thus many label Jesus' actions in the temple as "unclean" (Mark 11:15–19) or charge Paul with violating the system by bringing a Gentile into the temple (Acts 21:27–31). Thus, there was such a code which put everything and person in its proper place; hence all of Jesus' touching of unclean people, eating with sinners, not washing before meals, not keeping the strict Sabbath indicate in the eyes of those who enforce the maps that Jesus is frightfully "out of place."

*Purity and body.*    "Clean" and "unclean" also apply to the physical human body. The argument goes that where control is strong in the social body (boundaries, ports/ cities of entrance and exit), so there will be comparable control of the physical body (boundaries: hair, skin, clothing; orifices: eyes, ears, mouth, and genitals). *Surfaces*: the Torah was concerned about clothing, that is, that men wear men's clothing and women wear women's (Deut. 22:5), that it be made of only one stuff, either wool or flax, but not both. Flaking skin, boils, and "leprosy" suggest uncleannesses of bodily surfaces. *Orifices*: eyes should not look in lust or envy; mouths should eat only kosher foods and speak only true speech; ears should not itch for novel gossip. Genitals, too, are controlled as to marriage partners (endogamous marriages; degrees of consanguinity), when husbands and wives may have intercourse (i.e., not during menstruation), and which animals may breed (no hybrids, Deut. 22:10).

*Too much or too little.*    What makes a body "clean" or "unclean"? As we saw above, bodily orifices which are not controlled allow matter which is "out of place" to enter or exit. Moreover, a body which is "clean" must not have "too much" or "too little." Only priests with whole bodies may serve at the altar. Philo merely paraphrases Leviticus 21:18–21 when he speaks of the need for bodily wholeness for priests: "It is ordained that the priest should be perfectly sound throughout, without any bodily deformity. No part, that is, must be lacking or have been mutilated, nor on the other hand redundant, whether the excrescence be congenital or an after-growth due to disease. Nor must the skin have been changed into a leprous state or into malignant tatters or warts or any other eruptive growth" (*Special Laws*, 1.80).[7]

One must know this code accurately to interpret Jesus' healings of "unclean" people. He touches dead bodies and lepers, puts his fingers in mouths and smears his spittle on the tongues and eyes of others. Unclean people in turn touch him, such as a menstruating woman or the sick lying in the street. Moreover, he eats with sinners and eats food not tithed; he does not wash his hands before meals. It can be said that he is in constant contact with the "unclean" of his world; but contrary to the popular notion of "contagion," he is not rendered unclean as a result; rather, he makes the unclean "whole" or pure again. He acts as the unique person authorized to deal with such persons, "limit breakers" whom society authorizes to cross lines, such as physicians with the contagious sick, police with criminals, psychiatrists with the mentally ill, and the like.

### Group–oriented personality

Ancient peoples were strongly group-oriented, not modern individualists. We know them primarily in terms of tribes, clans, parents, and husbands: "There was a certain man of Ramathaim, a Zuphite from the hill country of Ephraim, whose name was Elkanah son of Jeroham son of Elihu son of Tohu son of Zuph, an Ephraimite" (1 Sam. 1:1; see Josh. 7:16–18). Moreover, they may be identified as part of a religious or political party, a Sadducee, a Pharisee, a Zealot. Their social status is often signaled by note of their father's trade ("son of a carpenter") or their position in temple or palace or some other status label. In short, they are known in terms of stereotypes. Virgil uses such a perspective when in the *Aeneid* he identifies the Greek traitor: "If you know one, you know them all." Group-oriented persons, moreover, are socialized from birth to know the ways and customs of their group and to live up to these expectations; the "common good" outweighs personal desires. Such persons constantly seek to know what others think about them or expect of them, so as to know what they should do. Failure to live up to the group's expectations results in "shame" (see "Honor and Shame").

### Ancient economics: exchange and reciprocity

Our greatest risk of anachronism arises when we consider economics in antiquity. US culture is totally driven by the pursuit of wealth, either wages, benefits, capital, or stock. Along with its super-rich, it also has a strong middle class, owning property and earning good wages. Jesus' world was utterly different. A few elites controlled most of the wealth, basically land; they employed retainers to keep their books, police their properties, and collect their taxes. There was no middle class, as we know it. Most of the population was rural and so tied to land and agriculture; they were severely burdened by taxes. Displaced farmers migrated to cities as artisans, but few made anything of any value; and life was much crueler in cities than in the countryside. At society's bottom lived beggars, cripples and blind people, prostitutes, and other untouchables huddled around the cities, who had no financial support whatsoever. Most of the wealth, then, was in the control or possession of the top few, the elite. Yet whatever wealth could be grown in the rural areas was also heavily taxed by local rulers, Herods and Caesars. This rare remark narrates how much taxation Demetrius forwent, also indicating how much previously he took: "I free you and exempt all the Jews from payment of tribute and salt tax and crown levies, and instead of collecting the third of the grain and the half of the fruit of the trees that I should receive, I release them from this day" (1 Macc. 10:29–30). Moreover, Roman taxation of Palestine was both systematic and crushing, with the result that debt became the economic cancer of the day: ruinous taxes, bad harvests, and loans to stay afloat eventually led to debt, foreclosure, and then loss of peasant land. It is no minor matter for Jesus to pray in the Our Father "give us daily bread ... forgive us our debts." On top of this taxation were endless tolls paid here and there as crops and produce were brought to some sort of market; and then, of course, there was the "tithe" for support of the temple.

## Other Models and Concepts, Briefly Described

What other models? This brief sketch of "social-scientific criticism" cannot go into any depth about other valid and valuable models, but only list them and indicate their salient points.

### City and countryside

Except for Rome, Alexandria, and Antioch, most "cities" held ca. 25,000–30,000 inhabitants; cities were the storehouses and fortresses of the elites, although some artisans were allowed within. Villages and towns existed in a dependency relationship with the city, who provided safety and market. They were often called the "daughters" of such-and-such a city, who extracted steep taxes from them. Only 10 percent of the population lived in the crowded, dirty cities; the rest lived in agricultural settings.[8]

## Illness and healing

Scientific medicine speaks of "curing" "disease," whereas in antiquity the appropriate nomenclature was "illness" and "healing." Without microscopes, there can be no scientific identification of bacteria or viruses; hence the taxonomy of illness in antiquity included notions of source (personal: who did this to me? God or spirit aggression) and classification according to purity notions.

## Rites and ceremonies

Victor Turner distinguished two types of rituals: "I consider the term 'ritual' to be more fittingly applied to forms of religious behavior associated with social *transitions*, while the term 'ceremony' has a closer bearing on religious behavior associated with religious *states* ... Ritual is transformative, ceremony confirmatory" (Turner 1967: 95; emphasis added).

Transformations include baptism, repentance and belief, marriage, laying on of hands, healings, dying and the like; ceremony describes meals, festivals, anniversaries, paying taxes or making contributions to Jerusalem, and the like (see Neyrey 1995; see Table 12.3).

## Social location

Class conflict infected Hellenistic and Judean society both horizontally and vertically. Elites competed for wealth and power and non-elites competed with elites for status and

**Table 12.3**   Rituals and ceremonies

| Rituals: status transformation | | Ceremonies: confirmation | |
|---|---|---|---|
| 1 | Frequency: irregular pauses | 1 | Frequency: regular pauses |
| 2 | Schedule/calendar: unpredictable, when needed | 2 | Schedule/calendar: predictable, planned |
| 3 | Temporal focus: from present to future: change | 3 | Temporal focus: from past to present: re-presentation |
| 4 | Presided over by: professionals: "limit breakers" and authorized line crossers | 4 | Presided over by: officials and guardians of institutions |
| 5 | Purpose: change status elevation or status degradation | 5 | Purpose: confirmation of roles and statuses in group or institution |

subsistence. To locate persons and groups relative to others in their world, one needs a model of social stratification, such as Lenski provides (see Rohrbaugh 1993; Duling 1992).

## Gender–divided world

The ancient world was completely and thoroughly gender-divided. There were different virtues and behaviors expected of males and females; they "belonged" in different spaces, used different tools, performed different tasks (Neyrey 1994b). Male praise is "honor," but female worth is "shame." Females sensitive to their reputation (sexual, of course) "have shame"; were they unconcerned, they would be "shame-less." But both male and female are concerned with reputation, whether "honor" (for him) or "shame" (for her).

## Et cetera

Social-scientific criticism would also invite use of materials about the social configuration of space ("territoriality"), patron–client relations, gossip, conflict theory, gift and reciprocity, recruitment, witchcraft accusations, and the evil eye.

## Notes

1   Invaluable here is the argument of Peter Burke (Burke 1993: 1–43).
2   Along with his *New Testament World*, Malina has argued his case repeatedly in articles – see e.g. Malina 1982 and 1983.
3   "Reading Theory," the important epistemological and philosophical basis for "social" study is completely neglected by "social historians"; but see Malina 1991b; see also Elliott 1986.
4   There is no debate over what tools social-scientific critics need: see Burke 1993: 44–104; John Elliott (1993) provides a most comprehensive itemization of these topics, concepts, and questions.
5   On models, see Carney 1975: 1–43; Malina 1982: 231–8; Malina 2001: 17–25; and Burke 1993: 21–33.
6   See n. 4 above.
7   Numerous are the narratives of Antiochus mutilating the ear of Hyrcanus, thus forestalling his ever serving as high priest (Josephus, *Antiquities*, 14.366–7; Wars, 1.269–70).
8   For what it was like to live in an ancient city, see Stark 1991.

## Annotated Bibliography

What are some of the most important resources? All of the books noted below have elaborate bibliographies to aid scholars in their searches for appropriate materials. In particular, we recommend Elliott 1993, Neyrey 1999, and Malina 2001.

## Surveys

As mentioned, Bruce Malina's student guide (Malina 2001), provides a student-friendly, system-atic approach to most of the major topics and models of this type of criticism. For professors and graduate students, John H. Elliott's *What is Social-Scientific Criticism?* (Elliott 1993) is indispen-sable; see also Jerome Neyrey's *The Social World of Luke–Acts* (Neyrey 1999), in which thirteen social models are used to interpret Luke and Acts. Richard Rohrbaugh's *The Social Sciences and New Testament Interpretation* (Rohrbaugh 1996) provides an accommodating reader's guide to ten major social models and topics. Comparably Douglas Oakman and K. C. Hanson's *Palestine in the Time of Jesus* (1998) brings many neglected social models to bear on creating the right reading scenario for the New Testament world..

## Monographs

On reciprocity, see Moxnes 1988 and Oakman 1986. On patron–client relations, see Eisenstadt and Roniger 1984 for cross-cultural models. On ancient personality, see Malina and Neyrey 1996. On honor and shame, see Neyrey 1998a. On ancient social values, see Pilch and Malina 1998. On illness and healing, see Pilch 2000.

## Commentaries

On the synoptic gospels and John, see Malina and Rohrbaugh 2003 and Malina and Rohrbaugh 1998; on Romans, see Esler 2003; on 1 Peter, see Elliott 2000, and on 2 Peter and Jude, see Neyrey 1993; on Revelation, see Malina and Pilch 2000.

## References

Burke, Peter. *History and Social Theory*. 2nd edn. Ithaca, NY: Cornell University Press, 1993.
Carney, Thomas. *The Shape of the Past: Models and Antiquity*. Lawrence, KS: Coronado Press, 1975.
Danker, Frederick W. *Benefactor. Epigraphic Study of a Graeco-Roman and New Testament Semantic Field*. St. Louis: Clayton Publishing House, 1982.
Duling, Dennis. "Matthew's Plurisignificant 'Son of David' in Social Science Perspective: Kinship, Kingship, Magic and Miracle." *Biblical Theology Bulletin* 22 (1992), 99–116.
Eisenstadt, S. N. and L. Roniger. *Patrons, Clients and Friends: Interpersonal Relations and the Structure of Trust in Society*. Cambridge and New York: Cambridge University Press, 1984.
Elliott, John H. Review of Wayne A. Meeks, *First Urban Christians. Religious Studies Review* 11 (1985), 329–35.
Elliott, John H. "Social-Scientific Criticism of the New Testament: More on Methods and Models." *Semeia* 35 (1986), 1–33.
Elliott, John H. *Home for the Homeless*. Rev. edn. Minneapolis, MN: Fortress Press, 1990.
Elliott, John H. *What is Social-Scientific Criticism?* Minneapolis, MN: Fortress Press, 1993.
Elliott, John H. *1 Peter: A New Translation with Introduction and Commentary*. AB 37B. New York: Doubleday, 2000.

Esler, Philip. *Conflict and Identity in Romans*. Minneapolis: Fortress Press, 2003.

Funk, Robert W. "The Watershed of the American Biblical Tradition: The Chicago School, First Phase, 1892–1920." *Journal of Biblical Literature* 95 (1976), 4–22.

Malina, Bruce J. "The Social Sciences and Biblical Interpretation." *Interpretation* 36 (1982), 229–42.

Malina, Bruce J. "Why Interpret the Bible with the Social Sciences?" *American Baptist Quarterly* 2 (1983), 119–33.

Malina, Bruce J. Review of Wayne A. Meeks, *First Urban Christians*. *Journal of Biblical Literature* 104 (1985), 346–9.

Malina, Bruce J. "Interpretation: Reading, Abduction, Metaphor." Pp. 253–66 in *The Bible and the Politics of Exegesis*. Edited by David Jobbing, Peggy Day, and Gerald Sheppard. Cleveland, OH: Pilgrim Press, 1991a.

Malina, Bruce J. "Reading Theory Perspective: Reading Luke–Acts." Pp. 1–23 in *The Social World of Luke–Acts. Models for Interpretation*. Edited by Jerome Neyrey. Peabody: Hendrickson, 1991b.

Malina, Bruce. "Rhetorical Criticism and Social-Scientific Criticism: Why Won't Romanticism Leave Us Alone?" Pp. 73–9 in *Rhetoric, Scripture and Theology*. Edited by Stanley Porter and Thomas Olbricht. Sheffield: Sheffield Academic Press, 1996.

Malina, Bruce J. *The New Testament World. Insights from Cultural Anthropology*. 3rd edn. Louisville, KY: Westminster John Knox, 2001.

Malina, Bruce J. and Jerome H. Neyrey, *Portraits of Paul: An Archeology of Ancient Personality*. Louisville: Westminster John Knox, 1996.

Malina, Bruce and John Pilch. *Social-Science Commentary on the Book of Revelation*. Minneapolis: Fortress Press, 2000.

Malina, Bruce and Richard Rohrbaugh. *Social-Science Commentary on the Gospel of John*. Minneapolis: Fortress Press, 1998.

Malina, Bruce and Richard Rohrbaugh. *Social Science Commentary on the Synoptic Gospels*. 2nd edn. Minneapolis: Fortress Press, 2003.

Meeks, Wayne A. *The First Urban Christians*. New Haven: Yale University Press, 1983.

Moxnes, Halvor. *The Economy of the Kingdom*. Philadelphia: Fortress Press, 1988.

Neyrey, Jerome. *2 Peter, Jude*. AB 37C. New York: Doubleday, 1993.

Neyrey, Jerome H. "Josephus' *Vita* and the Encomium: A Native Model of Personality." *Journal for the Study of Judaism* 25 (1994a), 177–206.

Neyrey, Jerome H. " 'What's Wrong with This Picture?' John 4, Cultural Stereotypes of Women, and Public and Private Space." *Biblical Theology Bulletin* 24 (1994b), 77–91.

Neyrey, Jerome H. "The Footwashing in John 13:6–11; Transformation Ritual or Ceremony?" Pp. 198–213 in *The Social World of the First Christians: Essays in Honor of Wayne A. Meeks*. Edited by L. Michael White and O. Larry Yarbrough. Minneapolis, MN: Fortress Press, 1995.

Neyrey, Jerome H. *Honor and Shame in the Gospel of Matthew*. Louisville, KY: Westminster John Knox, 1998a.

Neyrey, Jerome H. "Questions, Chreiai, and Challenges to Honor: The Interface of Rhetoric and Culture in Mark's Gospel." *Catholic Biblical Quarterly* 60 (1998b), 657–81.

Neyrey, Jerome. *The Social World of Luke–Acts: Models for Interpretation*. Peabody: Hendrickson, 1999.

Oakman, Douglas. *Jesus and the Economic Questions of his Day*. Lewiston: Mellon Press, 1986.

Oakman, Douglas and K. C. Hanson. *Palestine in the Time of Jesus*. Minneapolis: Fortress Press, 1998.

Pilch, John. *Healing in the New Testament: Insights from Medical and Mediterranean Anthropology*. Minneapolis: Fortress Press, 2000.

Pilch, John and Bruce Malina. *Handbook of Biblical Social Values*. 2nd edn. Peabody: Hendrickson, 1998.

Rohrbaugh, Richard L. "The Social Location of the Gospel of Mark." *Biblical Theology Bulletin* 23 (1993), 114–27.

Rohrbaugh, Richard (ed.). *The Social Sciences and New Testament Interpretation*. Peabody: Hendrickson, 1996.

Smith, Jonathan Z. "The Social Description of Early Christianity." *Religious Studies Review* 1 (1975), 19–25.

Stark, Rodney. "Antioch as the Social Situation for Matthew's Gospel." Pp. 189–210 in *Social History of the Matthean Community: Cross-Disciplinary Approaches*. Edited by David Balch. Minneapolis, MN: Fortress Press, 1991.

Stowers, Stanley K. "The Social Sciences and the Study of Early Christianity." Vol. 5, pp. 149–81 in *Approaches to Ancient Judaism*. Edited by William Green. Atlanta: Scholars Press, 1985.

Turner, Victor. *The Forest of Symbols: Aspects of Ndembu Ritual*. Ithaca, NY: Cornell University Press, 1967.

CHAPTER 13

# Socio-Rhetorical Interpretation

## Vernon K. Robbins

Emerging in the 1970s, socio-rhetorical interpretation received its name in 1984 with an integration of rhetorical, anthropological, and social-psychological insights in a study of the Gospel of Mark. During the 1980s, ancient *progymnasmata* manuals guided the development of rhetorical strategies to interpret elaborated argumentation in Christian and Greco-Roman literature. During the 1990s, investigation of inner texture, intertexture, social and cultural texture, ideological texture, and sacred texture moved the approach into an interpretive analytic. Currently, incorporation of conceptual blending, cognitive theory, and cultural geography theory are guiding interpretation of the blending in early Christian literature of six rhetorolects – prophetic, apocalyptic, wisdom, precreation, priestly, and miracle – in the context of religious mantic (divine communication), philosophical, and ritual discourse in the Mediterranean world.

## Introduction

Socio-rhetorical interpretation is a multi-dimensional approach to texts (Robbins 1996a, 1996b, 2009a; Porter and Olbricht 1997: 24–52; Tate 2006) guided by a multi-dimensional hermeneutic (Robbins 1998a, 2004, 2005a; Detweiler and Robbins 1991; Porter and Stamps 2002: 48–60). Rather than being one more method for interpreting texts, socio-rhetorical interpretation is an interpretive analytic – an approach that evaluates and reorients its strategies as it engages in multi-faceted dialogue with the texts and other phenomena that come within its purview (Robbins 1996a: 11–13; Porter and Olbricht 1997: 25–33). This means that it invites methods and methodological results into the environment of its activities, but those methods and results are always under scrutiny. Using insights from sociolinguistics, semiotics, rhetoric, ethnography, literary studies, social sciences, cognitive science, and ideological studies, socio-rhetorical interpretation enacts an interactive interpretive analytic that juxtaposes and interrelates phenomena by drawing and redrawing boundaries of analysis and interpretation (Lawson and McCauley 1990: 22–31). The approach uses a transmodern philosophical position of relationism to interrelate ancient, modern and postmodern systems of thought with one another (Robbins 2005a). Cognitive theory concerning conceptual blending (Fauconnier and Turner 2002; Oakley 1998, 1999, 2009; Coulson and Oakley 2000; Robbins 2007, 2008) and culture geography theory concerning places and spaces (Gunn and McNutt 2002) guide socio-rhetorical interpretation of pictorial scenes (rhetography) and argumentation (rhetology) that discourse evokes through the ears and eyes of hearers and readers.

Socio-rhetorical interpretation began to emerge after 1975, with a goal of integrating rhetorical and anthropological modes of interpretation (Gowler 1994; Robbins 1992a: xix–xliv). An additional feature of socio-rhetorical interpretation is its special interest in the orality of texts (Robbins 1989a, 1993a, 1996a: 106–8, 121–4, 1996b: 40–62, 1994b, 2009a: 9–14, 60–61, 283–6). Bernard Brandon Scott and Margaret E. Dean have developed this aspect of the approach into a special area of investigation with its own strategies of analysis and interpretation (Scott and Dean 1993, 1994; Dean 1996a, 1996b, 1998). During the 1990s, socio-rhetorical criticism featured analysis and interpretation of multiple textures of texts (Robbins 1994c, 1996a, 1996b). Five textures have been central to the interpretive activity: inner texture, intertexture, social and cultural texture, ideological texture, and sacred texture (Robbins 1996b; Gowler 2000; Tate 2006). A wide range of socio-rhetorical studies using textural strategies emerged during the 1990s. The seven "Pepperdine" rhetoric conferences, initiated and nurtured by Thomas H. Olbricht, played an important role in advances in rhetorical biblical study from 1992 to 2002 (Robbins 2005c),[1] and socio-rhetorical interpretation has benefited and grown in the context of these conferences and the volumes that have emerged from them. The SBL section on "Rhetoric and the New Testament" played a special role during the 1990s in nurturing socio-rhetorical interpretation of apocalyptic (Carey and Bloomquist 1999; Watson 2002) and miracle discourse (Watson 2010) in the New Testament. L. Gregory Bloomquist, Chair of the SBL section from 2002 through 2008, published a series of essays developing various aspects of socio-rhetorical interpretation.[2] Duane F. Watson, a former Chair of the SBL Section, and H. J. Bernard Combrink have written programmatic essays on the challenges and benefits of writing socio-rhetorical commentary (Porter and Stamps 2002: 129–57; Combrink 2002). During 1999–2003, the Studiorum Novi Testamenti Societas provided the context for a Socio-Rhetorical Interpretation Seminar that met at annual meetings in South Africa (Pretoria), Israel (Tel Aviv), Canada (Montreal), Great Britain (Durham), and Germany (Bonn). Since 2004, David A. DeSilva has chaired the SBL Rhetoric of Religious Antiquity Seminar in the context of his own production of integrated multi-textural applications of socio-rhetorical interpretation.[3] Progress is under way currently for production of socio-rhetorical commentaries in a series entitled "Rhetoric of Religious Antiquity."[4]

## Initial Socio-Rhetorical Studies

Socio-rhetorical interpretation began with analysis and interpretation of social and cultural dynamics in written works. The first sustained socio-rhetorical study was an analysis of the relation of the we-passages in Acts to ancient Mediterranean sea voyages

(Robbins 1975, 1976, 1978). As Robbins observed in a later study: "This study in 1975 revealed that traveling in a boat on the sea with other people created a social environment that made it natural for some authors in antiquity to use first-person plural 'we' for literary accounts of sea voyages" (Robbins 1992a: xix). This common social environment became a well-known cultural phenomenon in Mediterranean literature. In 1999–2000, Dennis R. MacDonald emphasized that the cultural intertexture of the sea voyages in Acts goes back to Homer's *Odyssey* and Marianne Palmer Bonz expanded the epic nature of Paul's sailing to Rome to include Virgil's *Aeneid* (MacDonald 1999; Bonz 2000. Cf. Talbert and Hayes 1995; Alexander 1995). Other interpreters have focused so intently either on the historical intertexture of the sea voyages in Acts or on literary coherence in Acts itself that they have missed the broader social and cultural intertexture of the sea-voyage accounts (Robbins 2009b).[5] Robbins' 1975 study was an initial interpretation of social and cultural intertexture among the sea voyages in Acts and other Mediterranean accounts of sea voyages (Robbins 1996a: 108–18, 1996b: 58–63).

The second sustained socio-rhetorical analysis concerned the teaching-learning cycle in the Gospel of Mark. The first steps of this analysis appeared in studies of Jesus' calling of his disciples and of repetitive-progressive summoning in the Gospel of Mark (Robbins 1981, 1982). The full-scale study of these phenomena in Mark, which appeared in 1984, appealed to the works of Kenneth Burke and the ancient rhetorical treatises entitled *progymnasmata* (Kennedy 2003; Hock and O'Neil 1986; Hock and O'Neil 2002) for analysis of rhetorical repetition and progression (Robbins 1984, 1992a). It also appealed to the works of Clifford Geertz, William Bascom, Roger D. Abrahams, Roger M. Keesing, Theodore R. Sarbin, and Vernon L. Allen for social, cultural, and social-psychological analysis. This study revealed evidence of a Mediterranean teaching-learning cycle the Gospel of Mark reconfigures as it tells the story of Jesus' life and death. Subsequent studies have built on the analysis and interpretation in this book.[6]

In the midst of various socio-rhetorical studies between 1981 and 1991 (Robbins 1981, 1982, 1985a, 1987a, 1987b, 1991a, 1991b, 1991c), specific discussions of rhetorical interpretation and specific strategies of analysis using insights from classical rhetorical treatises on the *chreia* and its elaboration appeared.[7] Willi Braun completed a Ph.D. dissertation that included a substantive socio-rhetorical analysis and interpretation of Luke 14, and it appeared in the Society for New Testament Studies monograph series in 1995 (Braun 1993, 1995). David B. Gowler, who had independently developed a socio-narratological approach to New Testament literature (Gowler 1989, 1991, 1993; Gowler, Bloomquist, and Watson 2003: 89–125), wrote a programmatic essay on the development of socio-rhetorical interpretation showing the manner in which it developed out of literary, rhetorical, social, and cultural studies during the 1970s and 1980s (Gowler 1994). These studies were precursors to the organization of socio-rhetorical interpretation on the basis of multiple textures of signification, meanings, and meaning effects in texts. David Hester Amador included a full-length critical assessment of socio-rhetorical interpretation in this earlier form (Amador 1999). Amador perceived the approach during this earlier phase to be driven by disciplinary strategies and goals, rather than being truly interdisciplinary or multi-disciplinary in its approach.

## Expansion beyond Biblical Literature

A major feature of socio-rhetorical interpretation since its inception has been its reach beyond biblical literature. Usually the literature outside the Bible was included for the purpose of intertextural analysis of biblical texts (Robbins 1975, 1978, 1982, 1991d). These interests led to analysis and interpretation in *Jesus the Teacher* (1984, 1992a) of the *Dialogues* of Plato, Xenophon's *Memorabilia*, sections of Flavius Josephus and Philo Judaeus, rabbinic literature, Philostratus' *Life of Apollonius*,[8] and the *Discourses* of Dio Chrysostom.[9] Half a decade later, it led to the publication of over 1,500 biblical, Greco-Roman, early Christian, rabbinic, and Muslim pronouncement stories and a volume of essays on rhetorical analysis of some of them (Robbins 1989b, 1993b).

During the 1990s, socio-rhetorical interpretation moved into a wider and wider range of sacred texts. One of the reasons is that socio-rhetorical interpretation features a constellation of interests that naturally moves an interpreter into programmatic analysis and interpretation of literatures of various kinds in various cultures, both on their own terms and in their own contexts. Another reason, however, was that inter-preters from various areas of specialty began to apply socio-rhetorical analysis and interpretation in their own fields of study. Jack N. Lightstone published a socio-rhetor-ical investigation of portions of the Babylonian Talmud (Lightstone 1994), followed by portions of the Mishnah, Tosefta, and Semahot (Lightstone 2002). Martin Oosthuizen produced a multiple texture socio-rhetorical interpretation of Deuteronomy 15:1–18 (Oosthuizen 1997). Gordon D. Newby began to use socio-rhetorical strategies of inter-pretation on portions of the Qur'an (Newby 1998). Thomas J. Bell produced a full-scale socio-rhetorical study of two medieval "sequences" attributed to Peter Abelard (Bell 1999). H. J. Bernard Combrink wrote socio-rhetorical essays interpreting religious traditions and biblical interpretation in South Africa (Combrink 1998, 1999, 2007), and Robbins wrote an essay on participation in African biblical interpretation (Robbins 2001). Patrick Gray analyzed the social rhetoric of sinfulness and punishment in the *Apocalypse of Peter* (Gray 2001). In turn, Robbins extended his socio-rhetorical studies into the Coptic *Gospel of Thomas* (Robbins 1987b, 1997, 1998b, 2006), portions of the *Book of Mormon* (Robbins 1995), the Mishnah (Lightstone 2002: 201–16), and the *Apocalypse of Paul* (Robbins 2003). During the 1990s, Robbins and Newby teamed with Laurie L. Patton in Emory College and Graduate School courses in "interactive" socio-rhetorical interpretation of Jewish, Christian, Muslim, Hindu, and Buddhist sacred texts (Patton, Robbins, and Newby 2009). At the beginning of the twenty-first century, R. Kevin Jaques used socio-rhetorical strategies of interpretation in his Ph.D. dissertation on Islamic law (Jaques 2001) and Stuart Young produced as a senior honors thesis a socio-rhetorical study of African American slave songs (Young 2002). During the early 2000s, Robbins and Newby worked as a team on socio-rhetorical interpretation of the relation of the Qur'an and the Bible (Robbins and Newby 2003; Gowler, Bloomquist, and Watson 2003: 333–54), and Robbins started a special investigation of gospel tradi-tions in the Qur'an (Robbins 2005b). Socio-rhetorical interpretation has continually moved beyond biblical studies into other disciplines and traditions. This is a natural result of its interdisciplinary and intercultural base and focus, and one can expect an even greater extension of this approach into other fields in the coming years.

## Discerning Multiple Textures in Sacred Texts

The paperback edition of Robbins' *Jesus the Teacher* contained an introduction that launched the organization of socio-rhetorical strategies of analysis and interpretation according to inner texture, intertexture, social and cultural texture, and ideological texture (Robbins 1992a: xix–xliv). Robbins' initial display of a multi-textural approach occurred in an essay on the "Woman who Anointed Jesus," written for the purpose of inviting multiple authors into interpretation and discussion of the multiple versions of the story in the gospels (Robbins 1992c). Robbins published his first programmatic multi-textural study in an essay on Mary, Elizabeth, and the Magnificat in Luke (Robbins 1994c). Wesley H. Wachob produced the first full-length Ph.D. dissertation containing multi-textural socio-rhetorical analysis, working in detail on James 2:1–13, and this study appeared in the Society for New Testament Studies monograph series (Wachob 1993, 1999; also Watson 2002: 165–85; Gowler, Bloomquist, and Watson 2003: 264–80). Subsequently, many insights in this work were incorporated into Luke Timothy Johnson's commentary on the epistle of James (Johnson 1995), and Wachob and Johnson co-authored a socio-rhetorical essay on sayings of Jesus in James (Wachob and Johnson 1999). Russell B. Sisson produced the second multi-textural Ph.D. dissertation on a New Testament text, working on 1 Corinthians 9, and subsequently he has produced socio-rhetorical essays on the Sermon on the Mount and Philippians (Sisson 1994, 1997; Gowler, Bloomquist, and Watson 2003: 242–63). To display a full textural approach to New Testament texts, Robbins produced *The Tapestry of Early Christian Discourse*, exploring 1 Corinthians 9 from the perspective of inner texture, intertexture, social and cultural texture, and ideological texture (Robbins 1996a).[10] Then Mark 15 served as the sample text throughout *Exploring the Texture of Texts*, in which Robbins added a chapter on sacred texture (Robbins 1996b: 120–31).[11]

The entire textural mode of interpretation, as it exists at present, is available in an interactive mode on the web.[12] H. J. B. Combrink wrote essays probing the Gospel of Matthew from a rhetorical perspective that was moving toward social-rhetorical analysis and interpretation (Combrink 1992, 1993). During this period of time, Robbins produced additional socio-rhetorical studies of various kinds (Porter and Olbricht 1993: 443–63; Robbins 1994a, 1995). In addition to the Ph.D. dissertations of Braun, Wachob and Sisson, four additional socio-rhetorical dissertations were produced by 1997 (Huie-Jolly 1994; Adams 1994; Hendricks 1995; Ascough 1997). Then two more full-scale multi-textural dissertations were written by H. Stephen Brown on two second-century Christian martyr texts and by Thomas J. Bell on two medieval musical sequences attributed to Peter Abelard (Brown 1999; Bell 1999). Also, Jon Ma. Asgeirsson produced a series of studies on the *Gospel of Thomas* that contain significant socio-rhetorical dimensions (Asgeirsson 1997, 1998a, 1998b, 2002). During the 1990s, other people also produced studies that contained significant use of socio-rhetorical strategies of analysis and interpretation.[13] The beginning of the twenty-first century exhibits an increasing rate of socio-rhetorical studies appearing on multiple continents.[14]

## The Emergence of Multiple Rhetorolects in Early Christianity

By 1996, socio-rhetorical analysis and interpretation began to exhibit significantly different textures for different kinds of early Christian discourse. For example, early Christian miracle discourse has a different texture than wisdom or apocalyptic discourse. In addition, early Christian prophetic discourse is different from precreation discourse. In this context, Robbins defined and described six kinds of discourse in the New Testament as "rhetorolects" (Robbins 1996c). According to the essay, "A rhetorolect is a form of language variety or discourse identifiable on the basis of a distinctive configuration of themes, topics, reasonings, and argumentations" (Robbins 1996c: 356). Each rhetorolect blends with the other rhetorolects during the first seven decades of the emergence of early Christian discourse. This raises a challenge for interpreters to describe the texture of each rhetorolect and to explain and display the manner in which each rhetorolect blends with the other rhetorolects during the emergence of Christian discourse as an identifiable phenomenon in the Mediterranean world.

Robbins' move to analysis of rhetorolects had actually started with his papers at the 1992 Heidelberg conference and the 1993 annual *Exegetiska dagen* at the University of Uppsala, where he investigated different kinds of culture in relation to different kinds of discourse (Porter and Olbricht 1993: 443–63; Robbins 1994d). This means that attention to multiple textures in early Christian discourse began to emerge prior to the publication of the books that presented the multi-textural approach in 1996. However, Robbins actually launched the multiple discourse approach in a paper on the dialectical nature of six kinds of early Christian rhetorolects at the second annual South African Rhetorical Conference in 1996 at the University of Stellenbosch (Robbins 1996c). The names that have gradually evolved for these six rhetorolects are: prophetic, apocalyptic, wisdom, precreation, priestly, and miracle.[15] In 1996, Robbins also published an article on the game-like nature of the wisdom discourse in the epistle of James, using insights from the anthropologist Bradd Shore (Robbins 1996d; Shore 1996). As Robbins began to analyze different modes of early Christian discourse more intensively, socio-rhetorical analysis of enthymemes became a more prominent feature of the approach (Porter and Olbricht 1997: 33–40). The result was a conclusion that enthymemes work with social, cultural, ideological, and theological topics and values, using some topics and values as a context for reconfiguring others.

Beginning in 1998, Robbins' analysis and interpretation of enthymemes began to display rule, case, and result, rather than simply major premise, minor premise, and conclusion (Robbins 1998b, 1998c, 2006). The purpose was to invite a discussion concerning the relation of deductive, inductive, and abductive reasoning in early Christian argumentation. Robbins argued that the unusual sequence of argumentation in Luke 11:4 and 11:13 is abductive in a context where enthymematic networks about praying to God to be forgiven merge with a context where one forgives others, and where God's giving of the Holy Spirit appears in a context where God is being presented as a father who gives food and other basic needs to people (Robbins 1998c: 210–14). In addition, Robbins proposed that there were a series of instances of abductive reasoning in the *Gospel of Thomas* (Robbins 1998b: 346–7, 356–86, 2006). L. G. Bloomquist, in a context of careful exploration of C. S. Peirce's statements about abduction, has concluded that only in a few instances might one be able to detect abductive reasoning in New Testament texts (Porter and Stamps 2002: 61–96). Rather, he suggests, "What Peirce calls deduction, as the tracing out of necessary and probable consequences of certain original hypotheses that were held, seems widely present in the New Testament argumentation and, in fact, appears to be the primary argumentative form" (Porter and Stamps 2002: 85). D. E. Aune has objected to any discussion of abduction in relation to enthymemes in the New Testament, asserting that "Enthymemes, like syllogisms, are *always deductive* ..." (Aune 2003: 315). Aune does not discuss Bloomquist's essay, nor does he cite Robbins' essay on the *Gospel of Thomas* nor Richard L. Lanigan's discussion of abduction and the enthymeme in his 1995 essay (Lanigan 1995), on which Robbins' analysis was initially based. Socio-rhetorical analysis and interpretation of enthymemes is still in its early stages, and it appears that it may be the center of some considerable debate. Jeffrey Walker has published an important analysis and interpretation of the "lyric enthymeme" in the writings of Pindar, Alcaeus, Sappho, and Solon (Walker 2000). This study promises to contribute substantively to the discussion, since it contains enthymematic interpretation of quite lengthy sections of text that people have not regularly considered to be rhetorically argumentative (Walker 2000: 154–273).

As the twentieth century was drawing to a close, Robbins turned to apocalyptic discourse and produced an essay on Mark 13 that contains a significant amount of socio-rhetorical analysis of its enthymematic texture in a context that interprets the passage as transferring holiness from the Jerusalem temple to the bodies of Jesus' disciples (Carey and Bloomquist 1999: 95–121). Bloomquist also has produced socio-rhetorical studies of apocalyptic discourse.[16] Newby, who began socio-rhetorical analysis in the Qur'an in 1997, also has produced essays on apocalyptic discourse in Surahs 2, 10, and 18 of the Qur'an (Newby 1998; Gowler, Bloomquist, and Watson 2003: 333–54). Thus apocalyptic rhetorolect, which blends extended sequences of vivid, graphic images with emphatic assertions about God's actions, became the testing ground for rhetorical analysis and interpretation that moved beyond semi-philosophically oriented wisdom rhetorolect grounded in God's created order to a rhetorolect grounded in God's ability to act as an omnipotent emperor who can destroy all evil in the universe and transport all holy souls to an environment of well-being.

By the time of the Lund Rhetoric Conference in 2000, it was becoming evident that different ways of "elaborating" *topoi* held the key for describing each rhetorolect on its own terms and in relation to the other rhetorolects in early Christian discourse. Robbins' socio-rhetorical essay for the Lund conference worked programmatically with enthymematic argumentative elaboration in the six rhetorolects that are perceived to be central to first-century Christian discourse (Eriksson, Olbricht, and Übelacker 2002: 27–65). In the context of writing a socio-rhetorical study of the intertexture of apocalyptic discourse in Mark for the 1999 SBLNT Rhetoric session, Robbins began to distinguish between narrative-descriptive and argumentative-enthymematic elaboration,[17] and to work with their relation to one another in each rhetorolect. Since 2000, Robbins has considered narrative description to be "rhetography" which is picturesque or pictorial expression (Robbins 2008; Jeal 2008; DeSilva 2008). In turn, Robbins considers argumentative enthymeme to be "rhetology," which is argumentative expression. Narrative begins by creating a verbal picture or pictograph (Oakley 1999: 110–11). Elaboration of one verbal picture by means of additional pictures in a sequence (rhetography) creates a graphic story. Argumentation, in contrast, begins by asserting a thesis (logos). Elaboration of a thesis through some combination of rationale, opposite, contrary, analogy, example, citation of authoritative testimony, and/or conclusion creates an argument (rhetology). Each early Christian rhetorolect has its own way of blending rhetography (pictorial narration) and rhetology (argumentation).

The essay on the intertexture of apocalyptic discourse in Mark, mentioned above, focused primarily on enthymematic argumentation. Virtually every instance identified as a "case" features pictorial narration. In addition, it is characteristic of apocalyptic discourse to create both "Rules" and "results" through pictorial narration. This means that the enthymematic argumentation (rhetology) of apocalyptic discourse unfolds through pictorial narration (rhetography). The essay states many of these things only implicitly, however, as it attempts to exhibit the sequential rhetology (enthymematic argumentation) of Markan apocalyptic discourse through different sequences of Rule, Case, and Result, and through different manifestations of Rule, Case, and Result.[18] Both the 1999 SBL essay and the 2000 Lund essay explicitly attempt to negotiate multiple early Christian rhetorolects in a context of analysis and interpretation of enthymematic argumentation. H. J. B. Combrink contributed to this subsequently in an investigation of the enthymematic nature of prophetic rhetorolect in Matthew 23 (Gowler, Bloomquist, and Watson 2003: 1–35).

## Cultural Geography and Conceptual Blending in Rhetorolects

In the context of analysis and interpretation of the different modes of argumentation in the six major early Christian rhetorolects, reasoning associated with particular social, cultural, and religious locations began to emerge as highly significant. This has led more and more to analysis of social, cultural, and ideological places in socio-rhetorical interpretation. It became obvious, first of all, that a major characteristic of early Christian discourse emerges from the patterns with which it creates enthymematic argumentation out of pictorial narration and reasoning related to people's bodies, households, villages, synagogues, cities, temples, kingdoms, empires, geophysical world, and cosmos. In other words, the cognitions and reasonings were emerging from "lived experiences" in specific places in the first-century Mediterranean world. This has led to the use of "critical spatiality theory" in socio-rhetorical interpretation (Berquist 2002, 2007). This area of study, located in the field of cultural geography studies, builds in particular on writings by Henri Lefebvre (1991 [1974]), Robert D. Sack (1986, 1997), Pierre Bourdieu (1989), Edward W. Soja (1989, 1993, 1996), and Stephen Toulmin (1990). James W. Flanagan was especially instrumental in bringing critical spatiality theory into biblical study (Flanagan 1999; Gunn and McNutt 2002). In 1991, Robbins used Robert D. Sack's *Human Territoriality* for socio-rhetorical analysis of "images of empire" in Acts (Robbins 1991b) and T. F. Carney's *The Shape of the Past* (1975) for the social location of the implied author of Luke–Acts (Robbins 1991a). Jerome H. Neyrey has applied strategies for interpreting the social location of the implied author to Jude and 2 Peter (Neyrey 1993: 32–42, 128–42), Luke's social location of Paul (Neyrey 1996), the Gospel of John (Neyrey 2002a, 2002b), and to Paul's writings (Gowler, Bloomquist, and Watson 2003: 126–64). Paul Elbert (2006) has applied pictorial narrative strategies to suggest how Luke's use of examples and appropriate cultural intertextuality serves to clarify Paul's discursive Spirit-language. Since 2000, Roland Boer has written an important study on "the production of space" in 1 Samuel 1–2 (Boer 2009), Claudia V. Camp an important essay on "storied space" in Sirach (Gunn and McNutt 2002: 64–80), Victor H. Matthews an important discussion of physical, imagined, and "lived" space in ancient Israel (Matthews 2003), Thomas B. Dozeman an essay on Ezra–Nehemiah (Dozeman 2003), and Bart B. Bruehler a study of social-spatial functions in Luke 18:35–19:48 (Bruehler 2007).

Socio-rhetorical interpretation is using critical spatiality theory together with cognitive theory about conceptual blending to analyze and interpret the nature of early Christian discourse (Robbins 2007). Here the foundational work is Gilles Fauconnier and Mark Turner's *The Way We Think: Conceptual Blending and the Mind's Hidden Complexities.*[19] Robert von Thaden has produced the first full socio-rhetorical study of a New Testament text using conceptual blending theory (von Thaden 2007). The merger of conceptual blending theory with critical spatiality theory is clarifying the relation of social places to cultural, ideological, and religious spaces in the six major early Christian rhetorolects. According to Fauconnier and Turner: "Conceptual integration always involves a blended space and at least two inputs and a generic space" (Fauconnier and Turner 2002: xv, 279). Socio-rhetorical analysis and interpretation of rhetorolects begins, therefore, with a perception that places and spaces are related to conceptual blending in multiple ways. Sensory-aesthetic experiences of the body in various places create the contexts in which people interpret the places they experience as cultural, ideological, and religious spaces. In New Testament discourse, the most prominent places for "remembered" and "imagined" experiences of the body are: household, village, city, synagogue, kingdom, temple, geophysical world, and cosmos. Desert, road, sea, and mountain are four of the most prominent geophysical places in early Christian memory. People's interpretations in the ongoing context of their sensory-aesthetic experiences are the "spaces of blending" in which they lead their daily lives. In this context, socio-rhetorical analysis is revealing that different blends of "cultural geography" distinguish early Christian rhetorolects from one another.

In the context of the three major streams of mythical, philosophical, and ritual Mediterranean religious discourse described by the Roman writer Varro ca. 45 BCE (Rives 2007: 21–3), first-century Christianity produced localized versions of mantic (divine communication), philosophical, and ritual religious discourse. First-century emerging Christian rhetorolects were "localizations" within these three major streams of Mediterranean religious discourse. Emerging Christian prophetic and apocalyptic rhetorolects were localizations of Mediterranean mantic (divine communication) discourse (Beech 2007), with an emphasis on the oracular in prophetic and the visual in apocalyptic rhetorolect. Emerging Christian wisdom and precreation rhetorolects were localizations of Mediterranean philosophical discourse, with an emphasis on moral philosophy based on the visible world in wisdom and speculative philosophy based on the invisible in precreation rhetorolect. Emerging Christian priestly and miracle rhetorolects were localizations of Mediterranean ritual discourse, with an emphasis on sacrifice and mystery in priestly and on healing in miracle rhetorolect.

Early Christian prophetic rhetorolect was a localization of Mediterranean oracular mantic discourse that blends the speech and action of a prophet's body with the concept of a "kingdom of God" that has political boundaries on the earth. The reasoning in the rhetorolect presupposes that the prophet has received a divine message about God's will. The prophet speaks and acts on the basis of this message in a context of significant resistance, and often explicit rejection and persecution. In the space of blending, God functions as heavenly king over his righteous kingdom on earth. The goal of prophetic rhetorolect is to confront religious and political leaders who act on the basis of human greed, pride, and power rather than God's justice, righteousness, and mercy for all people in God's kingdom on the earth.

Early Christian apocalyptic rhetorolect was a localization of Mediterranean visual mantic discourse that blends human experiences of the emperor and his imperial army with God's heavenly temple city, which can only be occupied by holy, undefiled people. In the space of blending, God functions as a heavenly emperor who gives commands to emissaries to destroy all the evil in the universe and to create a cosmic environment where holy bodies experience perfect well-being in the presence of God. Apocalyptic rhetorolect, then, features destruction of evil and construction of a cosmic environment of perfect well-being. The goal of this blending is to call people into action and thought guided by perfect holiness. The presupposition of the rhetorolect is that only perfect holiness and righteousness can bring a person into the presence of God, who destroys all evil and gathers all holiness together in his presence. Apocalyptic redemption, therefore, means the presence of all of God's holy beings in a realm where God's holiness and righteousness are completely and eternally present.

Early Christian wisdom rhetorolect was a localization of Mediterranean moral philosophical discourse based on the visible world that blends human experiences of the household, one's interpersonal body, and the geophysical world with God's cosmos. In this conceptual blending, God functions as heavenly father over God's children in the world, whose bodies are to produce goodness and righteousness through the medium of God's wisdom, which is understood as God's light in the world. In this context, wisdom rhetorolect emphasizes "fruitfulness" (productivity and reproductivity). The goal of wisdom rhetorolect is to create people who produce good, righteous action, thought, will, and speech with the aid of God's wisdom.

Early Christian precreation rhetorolect was a localization of Mediterranean speculative philosophical discourse based on the invisible that blends human experiences of an emperor (like the Roman emperor) and his household with the cosmos, with the presupposition that God has an eternal status as a loving heavenly emperor with a household populated by loving people. The result of this blending is the presence of the loving emperor father God in God's heavenly household before all time and continually throughout God's "non-time." God's son existed with God during "non-time" before time began with the creation of the world. This "eternal" son does what his father asks him to do, and heirs and friends of the eternal emperor and his eternal son receive eternal benefits from their relation to this eternal household. In the space of blending, God functions as heavenly emperor father who possesses eternal blessings he will give to people as a result of his love for the world and the people in it. People may enter into this love by believing, honoring, and worshiping not only God but also his eternal son and members and friends whom God sends out with a message of eternal blessings. Precreation rhetorolect, then, features love that is the source of all things in the world and the means by which people may enter into God's eternal love. In this rhetorolect, God's light is love that provides the possibility for entering into eternal love, rather than being limited to light that is the basis for the production and reproduction of goodness and righteousness. The goal of the blending in precreation rhetorolect is to guide people toward community that is formed through God's love, which reflects the eternal intimacy present in God's precreation household.

Early Christian priestly rhetorolect was a localization of Mediterranean sacrificial and mystery ritual discourse that blends human experiences in a temple with a concept of temple city and God's cosmos. Reasoning in priestly rhetorolect presupposes that ritual actions benefit God in a manner that activates divine benefits for humans on earth. In the space of blending, people make sacrifices by giving up things that give them well-being in the form of giving them to God. Things like food, possessions, and money, but also things like comfort and honor, may be given up to God. Some of these things may be given to God by giving them to other people on earth, or by allowing other people to take things like honor or fame away without protest. The greatest sacrifice people can offer to God, of course, is their entire life. Usually, in contrast, a person gives up only certain highly valued things in life. Much, though not all, early Christian priestly rhetorolect somehow relates to Jesus' death on the cross and the mystery that accompanies its benefits to humans and the world. Priestly rhetorolect features beneficial exchange between God and humans in a context of human sacrificial action that regularly is ritualized. The goal of the conceptual blending is to create people who are willing to give up things they highly value in exchange for special divine benefits that come to them, because these sacrifices are perceived to benefit God as well as humans. In other words, sacrificial actions by humans create an environment in which God acts redemptively among humans in the world.

Early Christian miracle rhetorolect was a localization of Mediterranean healing ritual discourse with a primary focus on human bodies afflicted with paralysis, malfunction, or disease. In this context, a malfunctioning body becomes a site of social geography. Miracle rhetorolect features a bodily agent of God's power who renews and restores life, producing forms of new creation that oppose powers of affliction, disruption, and death. The location of importance for early Christian miracle rhetorolect, therefore, is a ritualized space of relation between an afflicted body and a bodily agent of God's power. In this rhetorolect, there is no focus on any particular social, cultural, political, or religious "place" on earth. A bodily agent of God's power, wherever it may be, is a "location" where God can function as a miraculous renewer of life. A major goal of miracle rhetorolect is to effect renewal within people that moves them toward speech and action that produces communities that care for the well-being of one another.

The inclusion of conceptual blending theory and cultural geography theory in socio-rhetorical interpretation allows an interpreter to construct a topology of spaces in early Christian rhetorolects and to interpret the rhetorical power of the blending of spaces in these rhetorolects. Since each of the rhetorolects presents social, cultural, and ideologi-

SOCIO-RHETORICAL INTERPRETATION     203

cal language, story-telling and argumentation that evoke specific pictures, emotions, cognitions, and reasonings, each rhetorolect made vital contributions to an emerging culture of Christian discourse during the first century. Since many of the social places present in early Christian discourse (such as household, village, places of sacred ritual, city, etc.) continue to exist to the present day in some kind of reconfigured form, early Christian discourse continually functions anew in places believers perceive to be similar in social, cultural, and religious function. Some believers locate their thinking primarily in one rhetorolect at a time, blending aspects of other rhetorolects into this one rhetorolect for very specific purposes. Other believers locate their thinking in a particular blend of multiple rhetorolects, inviting specific aspects of other rhetorolects in implicit, subtle, and nuanced ways. These variations produce a dynamic conceptual, cognitive, and verbal system of Christian discourse that is highly adaptive to multiple contexts and cultures.

Dynamic blending of the six early Christian rhetorolects created a richly variegated culture of early Christian discourse by the end of the first century. Believers blended each rhetorolect dynamically with the other rhetorolects either by blending multiple rhetorolects into one dominant rhetorolect or by blending particular rhetorolects together in a particularly forceful manner. The dynamics of these blendings throughout the verbal culture of early Christianity produced a continually increasing combination of cognitions, reasonings, picturings, and argumentations. This interactive process continued in Christian discourse throughout the centuries, and it continues in our present day.

## Socio-Rhetorical Commentary in Six Steps

At present, interpreters have developed six steps for writing socio-rhetorical commentary that incorporates insights concerning rhetography and rhetology, textures of discourse, modes of elaboration, and multiple rhetorolects in biblical discourse.

### Step I:   Describe the rhetography (visual imagery, scene construction) in the discourse

Interpreters begin socio-rhetorical commentary with a description of the blending of rhetorolects that occurs through the sequence of pictures the discourse evokes. This beginning point is motivated by insights both from conceptual blending theory and from rhetorical interpretation of early Christian discourse. Todd Oakley, a conceptual blending theorist working with rhetorical interpretation, asserts that: "At the most basic levels of intelligent behavior, scene construction is fundamental" (Oakley 1999: 110). For this reason, spoken or written discourse begins its persuasive work by creating a sequence of pictures in the mind. Averil Cameron, after discussing the multiple rhetorics in early Christian discourse in a chapter entitled "How Many Rhetorics?", discussed the pictorial nature of early Christian discourse in two succeeding chapters entitled "Showing and Telling" and "Stories People Want" (Cameron 1991: 15–119). Currently, socio-rhetorical interpreters focus especially on the rhetography in prophetic, apocalyptic, wisdom, precreation, priestly, and miracle rhetorolects to present an initial interpretation of the blending of rhetorolects in biblical tradition during the first Christian century. As an aid to this first step in socio-rhetorical commentary, interpreters produce an initial "blending outline," like the following outline for 2 Peter 1:1–11:

I.  *Introductory blending of prophetic, priestly, wisdom, miracle, and apocalyptic Christian rhetorolects*

**Step 1 Prophetic**
Peter adopts a prophetic role with his hearers

1:1 Simon Peter, a servant and apostle of Jesus Christ, To those who have obtained a faith of equal standing with ours in the righteousness of our God and Savior Jesus Christ:

| **Step 2** | **Wisdom** |
| **Blended priestly rhetorolect** | A priestly blessing based on wisdom from God |

1:2 May grace and peace be multiplied to you in the knowledge of God and of Jesus our Lord.

| **Step 3** | **Wisdom** | **Prophetic** |
| **Blended miracle** | God's miraculous power through God's wisdom calls |
| **rhetorolect** | the speaker and hearers to prophetic responsibility |

1:3 His divine power has granted to us all things that pertain to life and godliness, through the knowledge of him who called us to his own glory and excellence,

| **Step 4** | **Apocalyptic** |
| **Blended prophetic rhetorolect** | Prophetic speech guides the hearers to escape from corruption at the end of time |

1:4 by which he has granted to us his precious and very great promises, that through these you may escape from the corruption that is in the world because of passion, and become partakers of the divine nature.

II.  *Blending wisdom with priestly, prophetic, and apocalyptic*

**Step 1 Wisdom**
Wisdom paraenesis

1:5 For this very reason make every effort to supplement your faith with virtue, and virtue with knowledge, [6] and knowledge with self-control, and self-control with steadfastness, and steadfastness with godliness, [7] and godliness with brotherly affection, and brotherly affection with love. [8] For if these things are yours and abound, they keep you from being ineffective or unfruitful in the knowledge of our Lord Jesus Christ.

| **Step 2** | **Priestly** |
| **Blended wisdom rhetorolect** | Wisdom rationale grounded in priestly reasoning |

1:9 For whoever lacks these things is blind and shortsighted and has forgotten that he was cleansed from his old sins.

| **Step 3** | **Prophetic** | **Apocalyptic** |
| **Blended wisdom** | Paraenetic wisdom conclusion directed toward prophetic |
| **rhetorolect** | life that leads to entrance into God's eternal kingdom |

1:10 Therefore, brethren, be the more zealous to confirm your call and election, for if you do this you will never fall; [11] so there will be richly provided for you an entrance into the eternal kingdom of our Lord and Savior Jesus Christ.

This blending outline reveals a sequence of pictures in which Peter functions as prophet, priest, sage, agent of God's power, and apocalyptic seer. In turn, his hearers are members of God's kingdom on earth, recipients of priestly holiness, possessors of wisdom from God, benefactors of God's miraculous powers, and visionaries of God's eternal kingdom.

After Step 1, socio-rhetorical commentators exercise the freedom to present Steps 2–5 in whatever order they wish and blended in whatever manner they wish. The essential feature is explicit analysis and interpretation of all four textures of the text.

*Step 2: Analyze and interpret the inner texture of the rhetography and rhetology in the discourse*

Using guidelines from Robbins 1996a: 44–95 and Robbins 1996b: 7–39 as an initial frame of reference, socio-rhetorical commentators analyze and interpret the relation of rhetography and rhetology in the elaboration of the discourse. The initial frame of reference calls attention to repetitive, progressive, narrational, opening-middle-closing, argumentative, and sensory-aesthetic rhetorical strategies in discourse (Gowler, Bloomquist, and Watson 2003: 1–28, 97–102, 246–8, 282–96). These strategies activate and correlate two traditions of inquiry that often are separated: the "image tradition of inquiry" and the "logic tradition of inquiry" (Coulson and Oakley 2000: 193, based on Galison 1997: 19–31). The goal of this "double mode" of "inner texture" inquiry is to locate patterns that integrate and correlate rhetography and rhetology in the discourse. This is a double mode of inquiry, since patterns are likely to call attention both to images and to logical assertions in the discourse. Underlying the strategies of analysis and interpretation is a presupposition that humans "elaborate blends by treating them as simulations and running them imaginatively according to the principles that have been established for the blend ... Part of the power of blending is that there are always many different possible lines of elaboration, and elaboration can go on indefinitely" (Fauconnier and Turner 2002: 48–9).

### Step 3:   Analyze and interpret the intertexture of the rhetography and rhetology in the discourse

Using guidelines from Robbins 1996a: 96–143 and 1996b: 40–70 as an initial frame of reference, socio-rhetorical commentators analyze and interpret various aspects of oral-scribal, cultural, social, and historical intertexture from the perspective of both rhetography and rhetology (Gowler, Bloomquist, and Watson 2003: 28–30, 103–5, 248–51, 264–80, 296–302, 333–54). These procedures of analysis and interpretation presuppose that humans blend images and reasonings by recruiting great ranges of "background meaning" to create richer patterns through processes of "pattern completion" (Fauconnier and Turner 2002: 48). In this context, memory functions as "a complex and dynamic process of constructing a complex scene and marshaling our learned capacity to order successive changes" (Oakley 1999: 109).

### Step 4:   Analyze and interpret the social and cultural texture of the rhetography and rhetology in the discourse

Using guidelines from Robbins 1996a: 144–91 and Robbins 1996b: 71–94 as an initial frame of reference, socio-rhetorical commentators analyze and interpret various aspects of social and cultural texture (specific topics, common social and cultural topics, and final cultural categories) from the perspective of both rhetography and rhetology (Gowler, Bloomquist, and Watson 2003: 30–4, 36–63, 126–64, 252–61, 277–8). Using insights from cultural geography studies that have been refined through critical spatiality theory, socio-rhetorical commentators identify and interpret the relation of socially experienced places (firstspace) to socially and culturally imagined spaces (secondspace) and spaces of daily living and blending (Gunn and McNutt 2002: 14–50, 64–80; Dozeman 2003: 455). At present, this analysis and interpretation keeps prophetic, apocalyptic, wisdom, precreation, priestly, and miracle rhetorolect in Mediterranean discourse in the forefront as an overall frame of reference.

### Step 5:   Analyze and interpret the ideological texture of the rhetography and rhetology in the discourse

Using guidelines from Robbins 1996a: 192–236 and Robbins 1996b: 95–119, socio-rhetorical commentators analyze and interpret various aspects of ideology (individual locations, relation to groups, modes of intellectual discourse, and spheres of ideology) from the perspective of both rhetography and rhetology (Gowler, Bloomquist, and Watson 2003: 34–5, 64–125, 165–241, 252–63, 279–80, 317–32). In this context, places and spaces are understood to be politically charged as places of domination, marginalization, and/or resistance (Gunn and McNutt 2002: 30–80).

*Step 6:  Analyze and interpret the rhetorical force of the rhetography and rhetology as emergent Christian discourse*

After presenting analysis and interpretation on the basis of Steps 2–5, socio-rhetorical commentators explain the rhetorical force of the emerging Christian discourse in the Mediterranean world. Using insights into the reconfiguration of concepts of deity, holy person, spirit being, human redemption, human commitment, religious community, and ethics (Robbins 1996b: 120–31), socio-rhetorical commentators analyze and interpret how rhetorolects blend rhetography and rhetology into newly configured Mediterranean discourse. This step in socio-rhetorical commentary emerges from the observation that "if ever there was a case of the construction of reality through text, such a case is provided by early Christianity. Out of the framework of Judaism, and living as they did in the Roman Empire and in the context of Greek philosophy, pagan practice, and contemporary social ideas, Christians built themselves a new world" (Cameron 1991: 21). Socio-rhetorical commentary further presupposes that "the very multiplicity of Christian discourse, what one might call its elasticity, while of course from the Church's point of view needing to be restrained and delimited, in fact constituted an enormous advantage in practical terms, especially in the early stages. No account of Christian development can work if it fails to take this sufficiently into account" (Cameron 1991: 9).

## Conclusion

Socio-rhetorical interpretation began in the 1970s with an attempt to explain special characteristics of language in the accounts of voyaging on the sea in Acts and Jesus' calling, gathering, teaching, and sending out of disciples in the gospels. In both instances, the goal was to understand the language of New Testament literature in the context of Mediterranean literature, both religious and non-religious. Also, the goal was to understand the use of language in relation to social, cultural, ideological, and religious environments and relationships in the Mediterranean world. During the 1980s, the rhetorical treatises entitled *Progymnasmata* (*Preliminary Exercises*) played a major role in the interpretation of abbreviation, expansion, addition, rebuttal, commendation, and elaboration in biblical and Mediterranean literature before and during the time of the emergence of early Christianity. During the 1990s, socio-rhetorical interpretation identified multiple textures of texts for the purpose of reading and re-reading them in ways that activated a wide range of literary, rhetorical, historical, social, cultural, ideological, and religions "webs of signification" in texts. This led to a display of strategies of interpretation for five textures of texts: inner texture, intertexture, social and cultural texture, ideological texture, and sacred texture. During the last half of the 1990s, socio-rhetorical interpretation gradually moved toward analysis of different rhetorolects in early Christian discourse. Gradually, six early Christian rhetorolects have appeared: prophetic, apocalyptic, wisdom, precreation, priestly, and miracle. Having initially gravitated toward wisdom rhetorolect during the 1980s and early 1990s, socio-rhetorical interpreters focused specifically on apocalyptic and miracle rhetorolect during the last half of the 1990s. A Festschrift appeared in 2003 that reviewed many of the developments in socio-rhetorical interpretation and featured contributions to the approach from various angles (Gowler, Bloomquist, and Watson 2003). Socio-rhetorical interpreters still face major challenges of analyzing and inter- preting precreation, priestly and prophetic rhetorolect in early Christian writings. In addition, they face the challenge of writing programmatic commentary that displays the manifold ways in which early Christian writings blend early Christian rhetorolects together. Work is under way to display this kind of socio-rhetorical commentary in a forthcoming series entitled Rhetoric of Religious Antiquity.[20]

## Notes

1   Porter and Olbricht 1993, 1996, 1997; Porter and Stamps 1999, 2002; Eriksson, Olbricht, and Übelacker 2002; Olbricht and Eriksson 2005.
2   Porter and Olbricht 1997: 200–31; Carey and Bloomquist 1999: 181–203; Porter and Stamps 1999: 173–209; Porter and Stamps 2002: 61–96; Eriksson, Olbricht, and Überlacker 2002: 157–73; Bloomquist 1999, 2002; Watson 2002: 45–68; Gowler, Bloomquist, and Watson 2003: 165–93.
3   DeSilva 1995a, 1995b, 1996, 1997, 1998a, 1998b, 1999a, 1999b, 1999c, 2000, 2004, 2006; Carey and Bloomquist 1999: 123–39; Watson 2002: 215–41; Gowler, Bloomquist, and Watson 2003: 303–16.
4   See online: <http://www.deopublishing.com/rhetoricofreligiousantiquity.htm>.
5   e.g., Cadbury 1956; Fitzmyer 1985: 35–53, 1989: 16–22; Hengel 1980: 66–7; Hemer 1985; Porter 1994; Gilchrist 1996; and. Barrett 1998.
6   Sawicki 1988, 1994: 51–76; Melbourne 1988; Beavis 1989; Robbins 1990a = Robbins 1994a: 219–42; Dillon 1995.
7   Robbins and Patton 1980; Robbins 1985b, 1988a, 1990b, 1991b, 1993b: vii–xvii, 3–31, 95–115; Mack and Robbins 1989.
8   Robbins 1984 and 1992a: Plato, 87–94, 136–47; Xenophon, 54, 60–8, 86, 126–8, 172–3, 206–9; Josephus and Philo, 94–101, 134–5; rabbinic literature, 101–5; Philostratus, 105–8, 147–55, 208–9.
9   Robbins 1984 and 1992a: 189–91, 1992b.
10  Sisson 1994 was an important resource for the socio-rhetorical interpretation of 1 Corinthians 9 in Robbins 1996a.
11  Brown 1994: I, 873–7, 1461–2, in which Brown used and expanded earlier work by Robbins (Robbins 1988b, 1992b), and contributed to the socio-rhetorical interpretation of Mark 15 throughout Robbins 1996b.
12  <http://www.religion.emory.edu/faculty/robbins/SRI/defns/index>.
13  Blount 1993; Czachesz 1995; Hester 1992; Huie-Jolly 1997; Jensen 1992; Penner 1996, 1999; 2004; Arnal 1997; Braun 1997; Batten 1998; van den Heever 1998; Porter and Stamps 2002: 297–334; Cottril 1999; Kloppenborg 1999, 2000: 166–213, 409–44; Gowler, Bloomquist, and Watson 2003: 64–88; Park 1999.
14  Theissen 2001; Lee 2001; Nel 2002; Megbelayin 2002; Gowler, Bloomquist, and Watson 2003; Jeal 2005a, 2005b, 2008; Long 2005.
15  The names "oppositional, suffering-death-resurrection and cosmic" in the 1996 essay grad- ually have changed to "prophetic, priestly and precreation respectively."

16   Carey and Bloomquist 1999: 181–203; Porter and Stamps 1999: 173–209. Also see DeSilva
     1998b, 1999c; Watson 2002: 215–41; Gowler, Bloomquist, and Watson 2003: 303–16.
17   Watson 2002: 11–44. The origin of Robbins' awareness of this distinction lies in Wuellner
     1978: 467.
18   In Watson 2002: 11–44: contrary Rule (25), contrary Case (29, 32, 33, 39), contrary
     Result (29), exhortative Result (20, 31), petitionary Result (39).
19   The use of Fauconnier and Turner 2002 for socio-rhetorical commentary is the result of an
     email by L. G. Bloomquist on Dec. 4, 2002, which called attention to the relation of con-
     ceptual blending theory to early Christian blending of rhetorolects, which was a topic of
     discussion at the Rhetoric of Religious Antiquity meetings prior to the AAR/SBL sessions at
     Toronto in November 2002.
20   <http://www.deopublishing.com/rhetoricofreligiousantiquity.htm>.

## Bibliography

Adams, E. "Constructing the World: An Exegetical and Socio-Rhetorical Analysis of Paul's Uses
     of *kosmos* and *ktisis*." Ph.D. diss., University of Glasgow, 1994.
Alexander, L. C. "'In Journeyings Often': Voyaging in the Acts of the Apostles and in Greek
     Romance." Pp. 17–49 in *Luke's Literary Achievement: Collected Essays*. Edited by C. M.
     Tuckett. *Journal for the Study of the New Testament* Supplementary Series, 116. Sheffield:
     Sheffield Academic Press, 1995.
Amador, J. D. H. "Academic Constraints in Rhetorical Criticism of the New Testament: An
     Introduction to a Rhetoric of Power." *Journal for the Study of the New Testament* Supplementary
     Series, 174. Sheffield: Sheffield Academic Press, 1999.
Arnal, W. E. "Gendered Couplets in Q and Legal Formulations: From Rhetoric to Social History."
     *Journal of Biblical Literature* 116 (1997), 75–94.
Ascough, R. S. "Voluntary Associations and Community Formation: Paul's Macedonian
     Communities in Context." Ph.D. diss., University of St. Michael's College, 1997.
Ascough, R. S. "Paul's Macedonian Associations: The Social Context of Philippians and 1
     Thessalonians." Wissenschaftliche Untersuchungen zum Neuen Testament 2.161.
     Tübingen: Mohr Siebeck 2003.
Asgeirsson, M. "Arguments and Audience(s) in the Gospel of Thomas (Part I)." *Society for Biblical
     Literature Seminar Papers* 36 (1997), 47–85.
Asgeirsson, M. "Arguments and Audience(s) in the Gospel of Thomas (Part II)." *Society for Biblical
     Literature Seminar Papers* 37 (1998a), 325–42.
Asgeirsson, M. "Doublets and Strata: Towards a Rhetorical Approach to the Gospel of Thomas."
     Ph.D. diss., Claremont Graduate University, 1998b.
Asgeirsson, M. "The *Chria* as Principle and Source for Learning Literary Composition." In
     *Alexander's Revenge: Hellenistic Culture through the Centuries*. Edited by J. M. Asgeirsson and
     N. van Deusen. Rekjavik: University of Iceland Press, 2002.
Aune, D. E. "Use and Abuse of the Enthymeme in New Testament Scholarship." *New Testament
     Studies* 49 (2003), 299–320.
Barrett, C. K. *A Critical and Exegetical Commentary on the Acts of the Apostles*. Vol. 2. ICCONT.
     Edinburgh: T. & T. Clark, 1998.
Batten, A. J. "Patience Breeds Wisdom: Q 6:40 in Context." *Catholic Biblical Quarterly* 60 (1998),
     641–56.
Beavis, M. N. *Mark's Audience: The Literary and Social Setting of Mark 4.11–12. Journal for the Study
     of the New Testament* Supplementary Series, 33. Sheffield: JSOT Press, 1989.

Beech, T. "A Socio-Rhetorical Analysis of the Development and Function of the Noah-Flood Narrative in *Sybilline Oracles* 1–2." Ph.D. diss., St. Paul University, Ottawa, 2007.

Bell, T. J. "The Paraclete Abbey Bridal Tapestry: A Socio-Rhetorical Analysis of Peter Abelard's Sequences *Virgines castae* and *Epithalamica*." Ph.D. diss., Emory University, 1999. [= *Peter Abelard after Marriage: The Spiritual Direction of Heloise and Her Nuns Through Liturgical Song*. Cistercian Studies, 211. Kalamazoo, MI: Cistercian Publications, 2007.]

Berquist, J. L. "Critical Spatiality and the Construction of the Ancient World." Pp. 14–29 in *"Imagining" Biblical Worlds: Studies in Spatial, Social and Historical Constructs in Honor of James W. Flanagan*. Edited by David M. Gunn and Paula M. McNutt. *Journal for the Study of the Old Testament* Supp., 359. Sheffield: Sheffield Academic Press, 2002.

Berquist, J. L. "Introduction: Critical Spatiality and the Uses of Theory." Pp. 1–12 in *Constructions of Space I: Theory, Geography, and Narrative*. Edited by J. L. Berquist and C. V. Camp. New York and London: T. & T. Clark, 2007.

Bloomquist, L. G. "Patristic Reception of a Lukan Healing Account: A Contribution to a Socio-Rhetorical Response to Willi Braun's *Feasting and Social Rhetoric in Luke 14*." (Society for New Testament Studies Monograph Series, 85, Cambridge: Cambridge University Press, 1995.) Pp. 105–34 in *Healing in Religion and Society: From Hippocrates to the Puritans*. Edited by S. Muir and J. K. Coyle. Studies in Religion and Society, 43. Lewiston: Edwin Mellen Press, 1999.

Bloomquist, L. G. "First Century Models of Bodily Healing and their Socio-Rhetorical Transformation in Some New Testament Synoptic Gospel Traditions." *Queen: A Journal of Rhetoric and Power*, Special Issue (2002), 1–28. <http://www.ars-rhetorica.net/Queen/VolumeSpecialIssue/Articles/Bloomquist.html>.

Blount, B. K. "A Socio-Rhetorical Analysis of Simon of Cyrene: Mark 15:21 and its Parallels." *Semeia* 64 (1993), 171–98.

Boer, R. "Henri Lefebvre: The Production of Space in 1 Samuel." Pp. 1–24 in *Constructions of Space II: The Biblical City and Other Imagined Spaces*. Edited by C. V. Camp and J. L. Berquist. London: T. & T. Clark, 2009.

Bonz, M. P. *The Past as Legacy:Luke–Acts as Ancient Epic*. Minneapolis: Fortress Press, 2000.

Bourdieu, P. "Social Space and Symbolic Power." *Sociological Theory* 7 (1989), 14–25.

Braun, W. "The Use of Mediterranean Banquet Traditions in Luke 14:1–14." Ph.D. diss., University of Toronto, 1993.

Braun, W. *Feasting and Social Rhetoric in Luke 14*. Society for New Testament Studies Monograph Series, 85. Cambridge: Cambridge University Press, 1995.

Braun, W. "Social-Rhetorical Interests: Context." Pp. 93–5 in *Whose Historical Jesus?* Edited by W. E. Arnal. Studies in Christianity and Judaism, 7. Waterloo: Wilfrid Laurier Press, 1997.

Brown, H. S. "The Martyrs on Trial: A Socio-Rhetorical Analysis of Second Century Christian Court Narrative." Ph.D. diss., Temple University, 1999.

Brown, Raymond E. *The Death of the Messiah: From Gethsemane to the Grave*. New York: Doubleday, 1994.

Bruehler, B. B. "The Public, the Political, and the Private: The Literary and Social-Spatial Functions of Luke 18:35–19:48." Ph.D. diss., Emory University, 2007.

Cadbury, H. J. "We and I Passages in Luke–Acts." *New Testament Studies* 3 (1956), 128–32.

Cameron, Averil. *Christianity and the Rhetoric of Empire: The Development of Christian Discourse*. Berkley, Los Angeles, and London: University of California Press, 1991.

Carey, G. and L. G. Bloomquist (eds.). *Vision and Persuasion: Rhetorical Dimensions of Apocalyptic Discourse*. St. Louis, MO: Chalice Press, 1999.

Carney, T. F. *The Shape of the Past: Models and Antiquity*, Lawrence, KS: Coronado Press, 1975.

Combrink, H. J. B. "Reference and Rhetoric in the Gospel of Matthew." *Scriptura* 40 (1992), 1–17.

Combrink, H. J. B. " 'n Retoriese benadering tot die Nuwe Testament." *Skrif en Kerk* 14/2 (1993), 146–62.

Combrink, H. J. B. "The Rhetoric of the Church in the Transition from the Old to the New South Africa: Socio-Rhetorical Criticism and Ecclesiastical Rhetoric." *Neot* 32 (1998), 289–307.

Combrink, H. J. B. "The Challenge of Making and Redrawing Boundaries: A Perspective on Socio-Rhetorical Criticism." *Nederduitse Gereformeerde Teologiese Tydskrif* 40 (1999), 18–30.

Combrink, H. J. B. "The Challenges and Opportunities of a Socio-Rhetorical Commentary." *Scriptura* 79 (2002), 106–21.

Combrink, H. J. B. "The Contribution of Socio-Rhetorical Interpretation to the Reformed Interpretation of Scripture." Pp. 91–106 in *Reformed Theology: Identity and Ecumenicity II: Biblical Interpretation in the Reformed Tradition*. Edited by W. M. J. Alston and M. Welker. Grand Rapids, MI: Eerdmans, 2007.

Cottrill, J. M. "A Christological Contradistinction in the Gospel of Matthew." Master's thesis, Garrett-Evangelical Theological Seminary, 1999.

Coulson, Seana and Todd V. Oakley. "Blending Basics." *Cognitive Linguistics* 11/3–4 (2000), 175–96.

Czachesz, I. "Socio-Rhetorical Exegesis of Acts 9:1–30." *Communio Viatorum* (Praha) 37 (1995), 5–32.

Dean, M. E. "The Grammar of Sound in Greek Texts: Toward a Method for Mapping the Echoes of Speech in Writing." *Australian Biblical Review* 44 (1996a), 53–70.

Dean, M. E. "Elements of a Sound Map." Unpublished paper presented to the Bible in Ancient and Modern Media Group, SBL, November, 1996b.

Dean, M. E. Textured Criticism, *Journal for the Study of the New Testament* 70 (1998), 95–115.

DeSilva, D. A. *Despising Shame: The Social Function of the Rhetoric of Honor and Dishonor in the Epistle to the Hebrews*. Society of Biblical Literature Dissertation Series, 152. Atlanta: Scholars Press, 1995a. Rev. edn. 2008: *Despising Shame: Honor Discourse and Community Maintenance in the Epistle to the Hebrews*. Studia Biblica, 21. Atlanta: SBL.

DeSilva, D. A. "The Noble Contest: Honor, Shame, and the Rhetorical Strategy of 4 Maccabees." *Journal for the Study of the Pseudepigrapha* 13 (1995b), 31–57.

DeSilva, D. A. "The Wisdom of Ben Sira: Honor, Shame, and the Maintenance of the Values of a Minority Culture." *Catholic Biblical Quarterly* 58 (1996), 433–55.

DeSilva, D. A. "Investigating Honor Discourse: Guidelines from Classical Rhetoricians." *Society for Biblical Literature Seminar Papers* 36 (1997), 491–525.

DeSilva, D. A. "Honor Discourse and the Rhetorical Strategy of the Apocalypse of John." *Journal for the Study of the New Testament* 71 (1998a), 79–110.

DeSilva, D. A. "The Persuasive Strategy of the Apocalypse: A Socio-Rhetorical Investigation of Revelation 14:6–13." *Society for Biblical Literature Seminar Papers* 37 (1998b), 785–806.

DeSilva, D. A. *The Hope of Glory: Honor Discourse and the New Testament*. Collegeville, MN: Liturgical Press, 1999a.

DeSilva, D. A. "Hebrews 6:4–8: A Socio-Rhetorical Investigation. Part I/Part II." *Tyndale Bulletin* (1999b), 50/1: 33–57; 50/2: 225–35.

DeSilva, D. A. "A Socio-Rhetorical Investigation of Revelation 14:6–13: A Call to Act Justly toward the Just and Judging God." *Bulletin for Biblical Research* 9 (1999c), 65–117.

DeSilva, D. A. *Perseverance in Gratitude: A Socio-Rhetorical Commentary on the Epistle "to the Hebrews."* Grand Rapids, MI: Eerdmans, 2000.

DeSilva, D. A. *An Introduction to the New Testament: Contexts, Methods and Ministry Formation*. Downers Grove, IL: InterVarsity Press; Leicester: Apollos, 2004.

DeSilva, D. A. "The Invention and Argumentative Function of Priestly Discourse in the Epistle to the Hebrews." *Bulletin for Biblical Research* 16 (2006), 295–323.

DeSilva, D. A. "Seeing Things John's Way: Rhetography and Conceptual Blending in Revelation 14:6–13." *Bulletin for Biblical Research* 18 (2008), 271–98.

Detweiler, R. and V. K. Robbins. "From New Criticism and the New Hermeneutic to Poststructuralism: Twentieth Century Hermeneutics." Pp. 225–80 in *Reading the Text: Biblical Criticism and Literary Theory.* Edited by S. Prickett. Oxford: Basil Blackwell, 1991.

Dillon, J. T. *Jesus As a Teacher: A Multidisciplinary Case Study,* Lanham, MD: International Scholars Publications, 1995.

Dozeman, T. B. "Geography and History in Herodotus and in Ezra-Nehemiah." *Journal of Biblical Literature* 122 (2003), 449–66.

Elbert, P. "Possible Literary Links Between Luke–Acts and Pauline Letters Regarding Spirit-Language." Pp. 226–54 in *Intertextuality in the New Testament: Explorations of Theory and Practice.* Edited by T. L. Brodie, D. R. MacDonald, and S. E. Porter. New Testament Monographs, 16. Sheffield: Sheffield-Phoenix Press, 2006.

Eriksson, A., T. H. Olbricht, and Übelacker (eds.). *Rhetorical Argumentation in Biblical Texts: Essays from the Lund 2000 Conference.* Emory Studies in Early Christianity, 8. Harrisburg, PA: Trinity Press International, 2002.

Fauconnier, Gilles and Mark Turner. *The Way We Think: Conceptual Blending and the Mind's Hidden Complexities.* New York: Basic Books, 2002.

Fitzmyer, J. A. *The Gospel According to Luke X–XXIV.* AB 28A. New York: Doubleday, 1985.

Fitzmyer, J. A. *Luke the Theologian: Aspects of his Teaching.* New York: Paulist, 1989.

Flanagan, J. W. "Ancient Perceptions of Space/Perceptions of Ancient Space." *Semeia* 87 (1999), 15–43.

Galison, P. *Image and Logic: A Material Culture of Microphysics.* Chicago: University of Chicago Press, 1997.

Gilchrist, J. M. "The Historicity of Paul's Shipwreck." *Journal for the Study of the New Testament* 61 (1996), 29–51.

Gowler, D. B. "Characterization in Luke: A Socio-Narratological Approach." *Biblical Theology Bulletin* 19/2 (1989), 54–62.

Gowler, D. B. *Host, Guest, Enemy and Friend: Portraits of the Pharisees in Luke and Acts.* Emory Studies in Early Christianity, 1. New York: Peter Lang, 1991.

Gowler, D. B. "Hospitality and Characterization in Luke 11:37–54: A Socio-Narratological Approach." *Semeia* 64 (1993), 213–51.

Gowler, D. B. "The Development of Socio-Rhetorical Criticism." Pp 1–35 in Robbins, *New Boundaries in Old Territory: Forms and Social Rhetoric in Mark.* Edited by D. B. Gowler. Emory Studies in Early Christianity, 3. New York: Peter Lang, 1994. <http://userwww.service.emory.edu/%7Edgowler/chapter.htm>.

Gowler, D. B. "Heteroglossic Trends in Biblical Studies: Polyphonic Dialogues or Clanging Cymbals?" *Review & Expositor* 97 (2000), 443–66.

Gowler, D. B., L. G. Bloomquist, and D. F. Watson (eds.). *Fabrics of Discourse: Essays in Honor of Vernon K. Robbins.* Harrisburg, London, and New York: Trinity Press International, 2003.

Gray, P. "Abortion, Infanticide, and the Social Rhetoric of the *Apocalypse of Peter.*" *Journal of Early Christian Studies* 9 (2001), 313–37.

Gunn, David M. and Paula M. McNutt. *"Imagining" Biblical Worlds: Studies in Spatial, Social and Historical Constructs in Honor of James W. Flanagan. Journal for the Study of the Old Testament* Supp., 359. Sheffield: Sheffield Academic Press. 2002.

Hemer, C. J. "First Person Narrative in Acts 27–28." *Tyndale Bulletin* 36 (1985), 79–109.

Hendricks, Jr., O. M. "A Discourse of Domination: A Socio-Rhetorical Study of the Meaning of 'Ioudaios' in the Fourth Gospel." Ph.D. diss., Princeton University, 1995.

Hengel, M. *Acts and the History of Earliest Christianity*, Philadelphia: Fortress Press, 1980.

Hester, J. D. "Socio-Rhetorical Criticism and the Parable of the Tenants." *Journal for the Study of the New Testament* 45 (1992), 27–57.

Hock, R. F. and E. N. O'Neil. *The Chreia in Ancient Rhetoric, vol. 1: The Progymnasmata*, Atlanta: Scholars Press, 1986.

Hock, R. F. and E. N. O'Neil. *The Chreia and Ancient Rhetoric: Classroom Exercises*, Atlanta: SBL, 2002.

Huie-Jolly, M. R. "The Son Enthroned in Conflict: A Socio-Rhetorical Analysis of John 5.17–23." Ph.D. diss., University of Otago, New Zealand, 1994.

Huie-Jolly, M. R. "Like Father, Like Son, Absolute Case, Mythic Authority: Constructing Ideology in John 5:17–23." *Society for Biblical Literature Seminar Papers* 36 (1997), 567–95.

Jaques, R. K. "A Muslim History of Islamic Law: Ibn Qadi Shuhbah's Tabaqat al-fuqaha' al-Shafi'iyah (The Generations of the Shafi'i Jurists)." Ph.D. diss., Emory University, 2001.

Jeal, R. R. "Melody, Imagery and Memory in the Moral Persuasion of Paul." Pp. 160–78 in *Rhetoric, Ethic, and Moral Persuasion in Biblical Discourse: Essays from the 2002 Heidelberg Conference*. Edited by T. H. Olbricht and A. Eriksson. Emory Studies in Early Christianity, 11. New York and London: T. & T. Clark International, 2005a.

Jeal, R. R. "Clothes Make the (Wo)Man." *Scriptura* 90 (2005b), 685–99.

Jeal, R. R. "Blending Two Arts: Rhetorical Words, Rhetorical Pictures and Social Formation in the Letter to Philemon." *Sino-Christian Studies* 5 (2008), 9–38.

Jensen, J. S. "Retorisk kritik: Om en ny vej I evangelieforskningen" [Rhetorical Criticism: On a New Way in Gospel Research]. *Dansk teologisk tidsskrift* 55 (1992), 262–79.

Johnson, L. T. *The Letter of James*, AB 37A, New York: Doubleday, 1995.

Kennedy, G. A. *Progymnasmata: Greek Textbooks of Prose Composition and Rhetoric*. Atlanta: SBL, 2003.

Kloppenborg, J. S. "Patronage Avoidance in James." *Hervormde Teologiese Studies* 55/4 (1999), 755–94.

Kloppenborg, J. S. "The Q Document and the Q People" and "Social Characterizations in Theological Perspective." Pp. 166–213 and 409–44 in *Excavating Q: The History and Setting of the Sayings Gospel*. Minneapolis: Fortress Press, 2000.

Lanigan, R. L. 1995 "From Enthymeme to Abduction: The Classical Law of Logic and the Postmodern Rule of Rhetoric." Pp. 49–70 in *Recovering Pragmatism's Voice: The Classical Tradition, Rorty, and the Philosophy of Communication*. Edited by L. Langsdorf and A. R. Smith. Albany, NY: SUNY Press, 1995.

Lawson, E. T. and R. N. McCauley. *Rethinking Religion: Connecting Cognition and Culture*. Cambridge: Cambridge University Press, 1990.

Lee, C. W. "The Pauline Concept of the Law in Romans 7: A Socio-Rhetorical Approach." D.Th. diss., University of Stellenbosch, 2001.

Lefebvre, H. *The Production of Space*. Oxford: Blackwell, 1991 [1974].

Lightstone, J. N. *The Rhetoric of the Babylonian Talmud: Its Social Meaning and Context*. Studies in Christianity and Judaism/Études sur le christianisme et le judaïsme, 6. Waterloo: Wilfrid Laurier University Press for the Canadian Corporation for Studies in Religion/Corporation Canadienne des Sciences Religieuses, 1994.

Lightstone, J. N. *Mishnah and the Social Formation of the Early Rabbinic Guild: A Socio-Rhetorical Approach*. Studies in Christianity and Judaism/Études sur le christianisme et le judaïsme, 11. Waterloo: Wilfrid Laurier University Press for the Canadian Corporation for Studies in Religion/Corporation Canadienne des Sciences Religieuses, 2002.

Long, F. J. "From Epicheiremes to Exhortation: A Pauline Method for Moral Persuasion in 1 Thessalonians." Pp. 179–95 in *Rhetoric, Ethic, and Moral Persuasion in Biblical Discourse:*

*Essays from the 2002 Heidelberg Conference*. Edited by T. H. Olbricht and A. Eriksson. Emory Studies in Early Christianity, 11. New York and London: T. & T. Clark International, 2005.

MacDonald, D. R. "The Shipwrecks of Odysseus and Paul." *New Testament Studies* 45 (1999), 88–107

Mack, B. L. and V. K. Robbins. *Patterns of Persuasion in the Gospels*. Sonoma, CA: Polebridge, 1989; repr. 2008, Eugene, OR: Wipf & Stock.

Matthews, V. H. "Physical Space, Imagined Space, and 'Lived Space' in Ancient Israel." *Biblical Theology Bulletin* 33 (2003), 12–20.

Megbelayin, O. J. "A Socio-Rhetorical Analysis of the Lukan Narrative of the Last Supper." Ph.D. diss., St. Paul University, Ottawa, Canada, 2002.

Melbourne, B. L. *Slow to Understand: The Disciples in Synoptic Perspective*. Lanham, New York, and London: University Press of America, 1988.

Nel, M. J. "Vergifnis en versoening in Matteus (Forgiveness and Reconciliation in Matthew)." D.Th. diss., University of Stellenbosch, 2002.

Newby, G. D. "Quranic Texture: A Review of Vernon Robbins's *The Tapestry of Early Christian Discourse* and *Exploring the Texture of Texts*." *Journal for the Study of the New Testament* 70 (1998), 93–100.

Neyrey, J. H. *2 Peter, Jude*. Anchor Bible, 37C. New York: Doubleday, 1993.

Neyrey, J. H. "Luke's Social Location of Paul: Cultural Anthropology and the Status of Paul in Acts." Pp. 251–79 in *History, Literature, and Society in the Book of Acts*. Edited by B. Witherington III. Cambridge: Cambridge University Press, 1996.

Neyrey, J. H. "Spaces and Places, Whence and Whither, Homes and Rooms: 'Territoriality' in the Fourth Gospel." *Biblical Theology Bulletin* 32 (2002a), 60–74.

Neyrey, J. H. "Spaced Out in John: Territoriality in the Fourth Gospel." *Hervormde Teologiese Studies* 58 (2002b), 633–63.

Oakley, Todd V. "Conceptual Blending, Narrative Discourse, and Rhetoric." *Cognitive Linguistics* 9/4 (1998), 321–60.

Oakley, Todd V. "The Human Rhetorical Potential." *Written Communication* 16/1 (1999), 93–128.

Oakley, Todd V. *From Attention to Meaning: Explorations in Semiotics, Linguistics, and Rhetoric*. European Semiotics: Language Cognition and Cultures Series, 8. Bern: Peter Lang, 2009.

Olbricht, T. H. and A. Eriksson (eds.). *Rhetoric, Ethic, and Moral Persuasion in Biblical Discourse: Essays from the 2002 Heidelberg Conference*. Emory Studies in Early Christianity, 11. New York and London: T. & T. Clark International, 2005.

Oosthuizen, M. J. "Deuteronomy 15:1–18 in Socio-Rhetorical Perspective." Pp. 64–91 in *Zeitschrift für Altorientalische und Biblische Rechtsgeschichte 3*. Edited by Eckart Otto with assistance from von Klaus Baltzer et al. Wiesbaden: Harrassowitz Verlag, 1997. <http://www.religion.emory.edu/faculty/robbins/studies/OosthuizenDeut.pdf>.

Park, J.-S. "The Shepherd Discourse in John 10: A Rhetorical Interpretation." D.Th. diss., University of Stellenbosch, 1999.

Patton, L. L., V. K. Robbins, and G. D. Newby. "Comparative Sacred Texts and Interactive Reading: Another Alternative to the 'World Religions' Class." *Teaching Theology and Religion* 12/1 (2009), 37–49.

Penner, T. C. "Narrative as Persuasion: Epideictic Rhetoric and Scribal Amplification in the Stephen Episode in Acts." *Society for Biblical Literature Seminar Papers* 35 (1996), 352–67.

Penner, T. C. "James in Contemporary Research." *Currents in Research: Biblical Studies* 7 (1999), 257–308.

Penner, T. C. *In Praise of Christian Origins: Stephen and the Hellenists in Lukan Apologetic Historiography.* Emory Studies in Early Christianity, 10. New York and London: T. & T. Clark International, 2004.

Porter, S. E. "The 'We' Passages." Pp. 545–74 in *The Book of Acts in its First Century Setting*, vol. 2: *The Book of Acts in its Graeco-Roman Setting.* Edited by D. W. J. Gill and C. Gempf. Grand Rapids: Eerdmans, 1994

Porter, S. E. and T. H. Olbricht. *Rhetoric and the New Testament: Essays from the 1992 Heidelberg Conference. Journal for the Study of the New Testament* Supplementary Series, 90. Sheffield: Sheffield Academic Press, 1993.

Porter, S. E. and T. H. Olbricht. *Rhetoric, Scripture and Theology: Essays from the 1994 Pretoria Conference. Journal for the Study of the New Testament* Supplementary Series, 131. Sheffield: Sheffield Academic Press, 1996.

Porter, S. E. and T. H. Olbricht (eds.). *The Rhetorical Analysis of Scripture: Essays from the 1995 London Conference. Journal for the Study of the New Testament* Supplementary Series, 146. Sheffield: Sheffield Academic Press, 1997.

Porter, S. E. and D. L. Stamps (eds.). *The Rhetorical Interpretation of Scripture: Essays from the 1996 Malibu Conference. Journal for the Study of the New Testament* Supplementary Series, 180. Sheffield: Sheffield Academic Press, 1999.

Porter, S. E. and D. L. Stamps (eds.). *Rhetorical Criticism and the Bible. Journal for the Study of the New Testament* Supplementary Series, 195. Sheffield: Academic Press, 2002.

Rives, J. B. "Religion in the Roman Empire." Oxford: Blackwell Publishing, 2007.

Robbins, V. K. "The We-Passages in Acts and Ancient Sea Voyages." *Biblical Research* 20 (1975), 5–18.

Robbins, V. K. "By Land and By Sea: A Study in Acts 13–28." *Society for Biblical Literature Seminar Papers* 15 (1976), 381–96.

Robbins, V. K. "By Land and By Sea: The We-Passages and Ancient Sea Voyages." Pp. 215–42 in *Perspectives on Luke-Acts.* Edited by C. H. Talbert. Perspectives in Religious Studies, Special Studies Series, 5. Macon, GA: Mercer University Press; Edinburgh: T. & T. Clark, 1978.

Robbins, V. K. "Summons and Outline in Mark: The Three-Step Progression." *Novum Testamentum* 23 (1981), 97–114. [= Pp. 119–35 in Robbins 1994a = Pp. 103–20 in *The Composition of Mark's Gospel: Selected Studies from Novum Testamentum.* Edited by D. E. Orton. Brill's Readers in Biblical Studies, 3. Leiden: Brill, 1999.]

Robbins, V. K. "Mark I.14–20: An Interpretation at the Intersection of Jewish and Graeco-Roman Traditions." *New Testament Studies* 28 (1982), 220–36. [= Robbins 1994a: 137–54.]

Robbins, V. K. *Jesus the Teacher: A Socio-Rhetorical Interpretation of Mark*, Philadelphia: Fortress Press, 1984.

Robbins, V. K. "Pragmatic Relations as a Criterion for Authentic Sayings." *Forum* 1/3 (1985a), 35–63.

Robbins, V. K. "Picking Up the Fragments: From Crossan's Analysis to Rhetorical Analysis." *Forum* 1/2 (1985b), 31–64.

Robbins, V. K. "The Woman who Touched Jesus' Garment: Socio-Rhetorical Analysis of the Synoptic Accounts." *New Testament Studies* 33 (1987a), 502–15. [= Robbins 1994a: 185–200.]

Robbins, V. K. "Rhetorical Argument about Lamps and Light in Early Christian Gospels." Pp. 177–95 in *Context, Festskrift til Peder Johan Borgen.* Edited by P. W. Böckman and R. E. Kristiansen. Relieff, 24. Universitetet i Trondheim: Tapir, 1987b. [= Robbins 1994a: 201–17.]

Robbins, V. K. "The Chreia." Pp. 1–23 in *Greco-Roman Literature and the New Testament.* Edited by D. E. Aune. Atlanta: Scholars Press, 1988a.

Robbins, V. K. "The Crucifixion and the Speech of Jesus." *Forum* 4/1 (1988b), 33–46.

Robbins, V. K. "Foxes, Birds, Burials & Furrows." Pp. 70–4 in *Patterns of Persuasion in the Gospels*. Edited by B. L. Mack and V. K. Robbins. Sonoma, CA: Polebridge, 1989a.

Robbins, V. K. (ed.) *Ancient Quotes and Anecdotes: From Crib to Crypt*. Sonoma, CA: Polebridge, 1989b.

Robbins, V. K. "Interpreting the Gospel of Mark as a Jewish Document in a Graeco-Roman World." Pp. 47–72 in *New Perspectives on Ancient Judaism*. Edited by P. V. M. Flesher. Lanham, New York, and London: University Press of America, 1990a. [= Robbins 1994a: 219–42.]

Robbins, V. K. "A Socio-Rhetorical Response: Contexts of Interaction and Forms of Exhortation." *Semeia* 50 (1990b), 261–71.

Robbins, V. K. "The Social Location of the Implied Author of Luke–Acts." Pp. 305–32 in *The Social World of Luke–Acts: Models for Interpretation*. Edited by J. H. Neyrey. Peabody, MA: Hendrickson, 1991a.

Robbins, V. K. "Luke–Acts: A Mixed Population Seeks a Home in the Roman Empire." Pp. 202–21 in *Images of Empire*. Edited by L. Alexander. Sheffield: JSOT Press, 1991b.

Robbins, V. K. "Beelzebub Controversy in Mark and Luke: Rhetorical and Social Analysis." *Forum* 7/3–4 (1991c), 261–77.

Robbins, V. K. "Writing as a Rhetorical Act in Plutarch and the Gospels." Pp. 157–86 in *Persuasive Artistry: Studies in New Testament Rhetoric in Honor of George A. Kennedy*. Edited by D. F. Watson. Sheffield: JSOT Press, 1991d.

Robbins, V. K. *Jesus the Teacher: A Socio-Rhetorical Interpretation of Mark*. Pbk. edn. Minneapolis: Fortress Press, 1992a; repr. 2009: Fortress Press, *ex libris*.

Robbins, V. K. "The Reversed Contextualization of Psalm 22 in the Markan Crucifixion: A Socio-Rhetorical Analysis." Pp. 1161–83 in *The Four Gospels 1992. Festschrift Frans Neirynck*. Vol. 2. Edited by F. van Segbroeck, C. M. Tuckett, G. Van Belle, and J. Verheyden. Bibliotheca Ephemeridum Theologicarum Lovaniensium, 100. Leuven: Leuven University Press, 1992b.

Robbins, V. K. "Using a Socio-Rhetorical Poetics to Develop a Unified Method: The Woman Who Anointed Jesus as a Test Case." *Society for Biblical Literature Seminar Papers* 31 (1992c), 302–19.

Robbins, V. K. "Progymnastic Rhetorical Composition and Pre-Gospel Traditions: A New Approach." Pp. 116–31 in *The Synoptic Gospels: Source Criticism and the New Literary Criticism*. Edited by C. Focant. Bibliotheca Ephemeridum Theologicarum Lovaniensium, 110. Leuven: Leuven University Press, 1993a.

Robbins, V. K. (ed.). *The Rhetoric of Pronouncement*. Semeia, 64. Atlanta: Scholars Press, 1993b.

Robbins, V. K. *New Boundaries in Old Territory: Forms and Social Rhetoric in Mark*. Edited by D. B. Gowler. Emory Studies in Early Christianity, 3. New York: Peter Lang, 1994a.

Robbins, V. K. "Oral, Rhetorical, and Literary Cultures: A Response." *Semeia* 65 (1994b), 75–91.

Robbins, V. K. "Socio-Rhetorical Criticism: Mary, Elizabeth, and the Magnificat as a Test Case." Pp. 164–209 in *The New Literary Criticism and the New Testament*. Edited by E. S. Malbon and E. V. McKnight. Sheffield: Sheffield Academic Press, 1994c.

Robbins, V. K. "Interpreting Miracle Culture and Parable Culture in Mark 4–11." *Svensk Exegetisk Årsbok* 59 (1994d), 59–81.

Robbins, V. K. "Divine Dialogue and the Lord's Prayer: Socio-Rhetorical Interpretation of Sacred Texts." *Dialogue* 28 (1995), 117–46.

Robbins, V. K. *The Tapestry of Early Christian Discourse: Rhetoric, Society and Ideology*. London: Routledge, 1996a.

Robbins, V. K. *Exploring the Texture of Texts: A Guide to Socio-Rhetorical Interpretation*. Valley Forge, PA: Trinity Press International, 1996b.

Robbins, V. K. "The Dialectical Nature of Early Christian Discourse." *Scriptura* 59 (1996c), 353–62. <http://www.religion.emory.edu/faculty/robbins/dialect/dialect353.html>.

Robbins, V. K. "Making Christian Culture in the Epistle of James." *Scriptura* 59 (1996d), 341–51. <http://www.religion.emory.edu/faculty/robbins/James/James341.html>.

Robbins, V. K. "Rhetorical Composition and Sources in the Gospel of Thomas." Pp. 86–114 in *Society for Biblical Literature Seminar Papers 1997*. Missoula: Society of Biblical Literature, 1997.

Robbins, V. K. "Socio-Rhetorical Hermeneutics and Commentary." Pp. 284–97 in *ΕΠΙ ΤΟ ΑΨΤΟ: Essays in honour of Petr Pokorny on his Sixty-Fifth Birthday*. Edited by J. Mrazek, S. Brodsky, and R. Dvorakova. Praha-Trebenice: Mlyn Publishers, 1998a. <http://www.religion.emory.edu/faculty/robbins/commentary/commentary284.html>.

Robbins, V. K. 1998b "Enthymemic Texture in the Gospel of Thomas." Pp. 343–66 in *Society for Biblical Literature Seminar Papers 1998*. Missoula: Society of Biblical Literature, 1998b.

Robbins, V. K. "From Enthymeme to Theology in Luke 11:1–13." Pp. 191–214 in *Literary Studies in Luke–Acts: A Collection of Essays in Honor of Joseph B. Tyson*. Edited by R. P. Thompson and T. E. Phillips. Macon, GA: Mercer University Press, 1998c.

Robbins, V. K. "Why Participate in African Biblical Interpretation?" Pp. 275–91 in *Interpreting the New Testament in Africa*. Edited by M. N. Getui, T. S. Maluleke, and J. Ukpong. Nairobi, Kenya: Acton Publishers, 2001. <http://www.religion.emory.edu/faculty/robbins/Africa/africa10.htm>.

Robbins, V. K. "The Legacy of 2 Corinthians 12:2–4 in the *Apocalypse of Paul*." Pp. 25–339 in *Paul and the Corinthians: Studies on a Community in Conflict*. Edited by T. J. Burke and J. K. Elliott. Supplements to *Novum Testamentum*, 109. Leiden/Boston: Brill, 2003.

Robbins, V. K. "Where is Wuellner's Anti-Hermeneutical Hermeneutic Taking Us? From Scheiermacher to Thistleton and Beyond." Pp. 105–25 in *Rhetorics and Hermeneutics: Wilhelm Wuellner and His Influence*. Edited by J. D. Hester and D. Hester. Emory Studies in Early Christianity, 9. New York and London: T. & T. Clark International, 2004.

Robbins, V. K. "The Rhetorical Full-Turn in Biblical Interpretation and its Relevance for Feminist Hermeneutics." Pp. 109–27 in *Her Master's Tools? Feminist and Postcolonial Engagements of Historical-Critical Discourse*. Edited by C. Vander Stichele and T. Penner. Global Perspectives on Biblical Scholarship, 9. Atlanta: SBL, 2005a.

Robbins, V. K. "Lukan and Johannine Tradition in the Qur'an: A Story of (and Program for) *Auslegungsgeschichte* and *Wirkungsgeschichte*." Pp. 336–68 in *Moving Beyond New Testament Theology? Essays in Conversation with Heikki Räisänen*. Edited by T. Penner and C. Vander Stichele. Helsinki: Finnish Exegetical Society; Göttingen: Vandenhoeck & Ruprecht, 2005b.

Robbins, V. K. "From Heidelberg to Heidelberg: Rhetorical Interpretation of the Bible at the Seven 'Pepperdine' Conferences from 1992–2002." Pp. 335–77 in *Rhetoric, Ethic, and Moral Persuasion in Biblical Discourse:Essays from the 2002 Heidelberg Conference*. Edited by T. H. Olbricht and A. Eriksson. Emory Studies in Early Christianity, 11. New York and London: T. & T. Clark International, 2005c.

Robbins, V. K. "Enthymeme and Picture in the Gospel of Thomas." Pp. 175–207 in *Thomasine Traditions in Antiquity: The Social and Cultural World of the Gospel of Thomas*. Edited by J. Ma. Asgeirson, A. DeConick, and R. Uro. Nag Hammadi and Manichaean Studies, 59. Leiden and Boston: Brill, 2006.

Robbins, V. K. "Conceptual Blending and Early Christian Imagination." Pp. 161–95 in *Explaining Christian Origins and Early Judaism: Contributions from Cognitive and Social Science*. Edited by

P. Luomanen, I. Pyysiäinen, and R. Uro. Biblical Interpretation Series, 89. Leiden and Boston: Brill, 2007.

Robbins, V. K. "Rhetography: A New Way of Seeing the Familiar Text." Pp. 91–106 in *Words Well Spoken: George Kennedy's Rhetoric of the New Testament*. Edited by C. C. Black and D. F. Watson. Studies in Rhetoric and Religion, 8. Waco, TX: Baylor University Press, 2008.

Robbins, V. K. *The Invention of Christian Discourse*. Vol 1. Rhetoric of Religious Antiquity, 1. Blandford Forum: Deo Publishing, 2009a.

Robbins, V. K. *Sea Voyages and Beyond*. Emory Studies in Early Christianity, 14. Blandford Forum: Deo Publishing, 2009b.

Robbins, V. K. and G. D. Newby. "A Prolegomenon to the Relation of the Qur'an and the Bible." Pp. 23–42 in *Bible and Qur'an: Essays in Scriptural Intertextuality*. Edited by J. Reeves. Symposium Series. Atlanta: Society of Biblical Literature, 2003.

Robbins, V. K. and J. H. Patton. "Rhetoric and Biblical Criticism." *Quarterly Journal of Speech* 66 (1980), 327–37.

Sack, R. D. *Human Territoriality: Its Theory and History*, Cambridge: Cambridge University, 1986.

Sack, R. D. *Homo Geographicus: A Framework for Action, Awareness, and Moral Concern*, Baltimore: Johns Hopkins University Press, 1997.

Sawicki, M. *The Gospel in History: Portrait of a Teaching Church*, Mahwah, NJ: Paulist, 1988.

Sawicki, M. *Seeing the Lord: Resurrection and Early Christian Practices*. Minneapolis: Fortress Press, 1994.

Scott, B. B. and M. E. Dean "A Sound Map of Mark 7:1–23." Unpublished paper presented for the Rhetoric and New Testament Section, SBL Annual meeting, 1994.

Scott, B. B. and M. E. Dean "A Sound Map of the Sermon on the Mount." *Society for Biblical Literature Seminar Papers* 32 (1993), 672–725; repr. in *Treasures Old and New: Recent Contributions to Matthean Studies*. Edited by D. Bauer and M. A. Powell. Atlanta: Scholars Press, 1995.

Shore, B. "Culture in Mind: Cognition, Culture, and the Problem of Meaning." New York: Oxford University Press, 1996.

Sisson, R. B. "The Apostle as Athlete: A Socio-Rhetorical Interpretation of 1 Corinthians 9." Ph.D. diss., Emory University, 1994.

Sisson, R. B. "Voices of Authority in the Sermon on the Mount." *Society for Biblical Literature Seminar Papers* 36 (1997), 551–66.

Soja, E. W. *Postmodern Geography: The Reassertion of Space in Critical Social Theory*, New York: Verso, 1989.

Soja, E. W. "Postmodern Geographies and the Critique of Historicism." Pp. 113–36 in *Postmodern Contentions: Epochs, Politics, Space*. Edited by J. P. Jones III, W. Natter, and T. R. Schatzki. New York: Guildford, 1993.

Soja, E. W. *Thirdspace: Journeys to Los Angeles and Other Real-and-Imagined Places*, Oxford: Blackwell, 1996.

Talbert, C. H. and J. H. Hayes. "A Theology of Sea Storms in Luke–Acts." *Society for Biblical Literature Seminar Papers* 34 (1995), 321–36.

Tate, W. R. "Socio-Rhetorical Criticism." Pp. 342–46 in *Interpreting the Bible: A Handbook of Terms and Methods*. Peabody, MA: Hendrickson, 2006.

Theissen, G. 2001. *Gospel Writing and Church Politics: A Socio-Rhetorical Approach*. Chuen King Lecture Series, 3. Hong Kong: Theology Division, Chung Chi College, Chinese University of Hong Kong.

Toulmin, S. *Cosmopolis: The Hidden Agenda of Modernity*, Chicago: University of Chicago Press, 1990.

van den Heever, G. A. "Finding Data in Unexpected Places (Or: From Text Linguistics to Socio-Rhetoric). A Socio-Rhetorical Reading of John's Gospel." *Society for Biblical Literature Seminar Papers* 37/2 (1998), 649–76.

von Thaden, R. "Fleeing *Porneia*: 1 Corinthians 6:12–7:7 and the Reconfiguration of Traditions." Ph.D. diss., Emory University, 2007.

Wachob, W. H. " 'The Rich in Faith' and 'The Poor in Spirit': The Socio-Rhetorical Function of a Saying of Jesus in the Epistle of James." Ph.D. diss., Emory University, 1993.

Wachob, W. H. *The Voice of Jesus and the Social Rhetoric of James*. Society for New Testament Studies Monograph Series, 106. Cambridge: Cambridge University Press, 1999.

Wachob, W. H. and L. T. Johnson. "The Sayings of Jesus in the Epistle of James." Pp. 430–50 in *Authenticating the Words of Jesus*. Edited by B. Chilton and C. A. Evans. *Nederlands Theologisch Tijdschrift* Series, 28. Leiden: Brill, 1999.

Walker, J. *Rhetoric and Poetics in Antiquity*. New York: Oxford University Press, 2000.

Watson, D. F. (ed.). *The Intertexture of Apocalyptic Discourse in the New Testament*. Symposium Series, 14. Atlanta: Society of Biblical Literature, 2002.

Watson, D. F. *The Role of Miracle Discourse in the Argumentation of the New Testament*. Symposium Series. Atlanta: Society of Biblical Literature, 2010.

Wuellner, W. H. "Toposforschung und Torahinterpretation bei Paulus und Jesus." *New Testament Studies* 24 (1978), 463–83.

Young, S. " 'My Lord's Coming Again': Biblical Interpretation through Slave Songs." B.A. Senior Honors Thesis, Emory University, 2002. <http://www.religion.emory.edu/faculty/robbins/Pdfs/YoungThesis.pdf>.

CHAPTER 14

# The Problem of
# the Historical Jesus

## Dale C. Allison, Jr.

Origen, the third-century Christian apologist and theologian, candidly confessed that "to try and substantiate almost any story as historical fact, even if it is true, and to produce complete certainty about it, is one of the most difficult tasks and in some cases is impossible" (*Contra Celsus*, 1.42). This unfortunate fact is why the historical Jesus is indeed a problem, and why he will always be so.

Until the last two or three centuries, Christians assumed that the four canonical gospels, because divinely inspired and written by eyewitnesses or their compatriots, are excellent records of what Jesus of Nazareth said and did. Modern criticism, however, having concluded not only that no gospel is likely to be directly from an eyewitnesses, but further that the four different stories are often in disagreement with each other, has dismantled the old certainties of faith and generated a host of difficult historical questions. The upshot is that the gospels are, today, a battleground of arguments, with numerous scholars defending their divers reconstructions of Jesus and attacking those of others. Generalizations about the current state of scholarship are increasingly dubious, and for the foreseeable future no consensus is in sight.

## The History of the Quest

The Protestant Reformers, in rejecting Roman Catholic legends of the saints, introduced a critical attitude toward sacred stories, and the growing secularism that followed the later wars of religion and the Enlightenment fostered disbelief in miracles. Critical examination of the gospels became inevitable, and by the eighteenth century the modern quest was under way.

The most important of the early critics was Hermann Samuel Reimarus (1694–1768), a one-time German pastor much influenced in his views by the English deists. Unable to believe in miracles, he compiled objections to the Bible, including the gospels. Reimarus was one of the first – the third-century CE Greek philosopher Porphyry anticipated him in this, as did the British deist, Thomas Morgan (d. 1743) – to distinguish between what Jesus himself said and what his disciples said he said. To his followers alone Reimarus attributed belief in the Second Coming and Jesus' atoning death. He also argued that Jesus' kingdom was basically political, a sort of Jewish replacement for the Roman empire, and that his tomb was empty because the disciples stole the body. As Reimarus was rhetorically adroit, and as many of his rationalistic arguments had substance, his work generated support as well as the predictable opposition.

The next phase in research saw the proliferation of the so-called liberal lives of Jesus in Germany throughout the nineteenth century. Agreeing with Reimarus that miracles do not happen, but dissenting from much of his skepticism regarding the historicity of the gospels, the authors of these liberal lives tended not to dispute the events in the gospels but rather their supernatural explanations. Instead, however, of invoking deliberate deception, these critics thought in terms of misperception. Jesus did not walk on the water; he only appeared to do so when disciples on a boat saw him afar off on the shore or a sandbar. Jesus did not raise anyone from the dead; rather, the recovery from comas of some he prayed over led to that erroneous belief. Jesus survived crucifixion and revived in the cool of his tomb; but his disciples, who were rather simple and superstitious, thought he had died and come back to life.

This school of thought lost its popularity in the middle of the nineteenth century for several reasons, chief among them being the critical work of the German historian and theologian, David Friedrich Strauss (1808–74), who disparaged the liberal lives no less than the conservative harmonists. Like the liberals, he disbelieved in miracles. Unlike the liberals, he believed the gospel narratives to be thoroughly unreliable, and he dismissed John entirely. He considered the texts, although not Jesus himself, to be mythological, mostly the product of reflection upon the Old Testament narratives. Illustrative is the transfiguration, which according to Strauss was concocted out of the very similar transfiguration of Moses in Exodus 24 and 34. Again, the feeding of the five thousand was modeled upon 2 Kings 4:42–4, as the striking similarities show. Strauss was able to pile up parallel after parallel and establish on a critical footing the intertextual nature of the gospels. In doing this he was, from one point of view, just following Tertullian and Eusebius, Church Fathers who had also observed the parallels between the Testaments. Those earlier defenders of the faith were pursuing apologetical ends: the coincidences demonstrated the hand of God in history. Strauss was pursuing polemical ends: the parallels proved the fictional character of the tradition.

Some after Strauss argued that he had not gone far enough, that Jesus was not a historical figure who attracted myths but was rather a myth himself, no more real than Zeus. The future was not, however, with such radicalism, which could never really explain Paul or Josephus' two references to Jesus. Far more lasting in their influence were Johannes Weiss (1863–1914) and Albert Schweitzer (1875–1965), two German scholars who, more trusting of the synoptics than Strauss, argued that the historical Jesus was all about eschatology. He was an apocalyptic visionary, which is why his ethics are so unrealistic. They are not for everyday life but are instead an "interim ethic," an ethic of perfection designed for a world about to go out of existence. When Jesus said that the kingdom was at hand, he was announcing the imminence of the new world or utopian order. His expectations were not fulfilled in Easter or Pentecost or the destruction of the temple in 70 CE.

Most scholars since Schweitzer would concede that he and Weiss, whether right or wrong in their conclusions about Jesus himself, largely set the agenda for much of the twentieth century. There is agreement that many of the traditions about Jesus are full of eschatological themes, and that the texts themselves assume a near end. The debate has been to what extent the relevant texts go back to Jesus and whether a more or less literal interpretation of them is correct. Schweitzer himself tried to force a choice between eschatology and historicity. That is, he urged that, if the synoptics are reliable, then we must accept that Jesus was an eschatological prophet. If, to the contrary, Jesus was not an eschatological prophet, then the synoptics are unreliable guides and we should resign ourselves to skepticism.

Joachim Jeremias (1900–79) of the Georg-August University of Göttingen was probably the most important player after Schweitzer implicitly to accept his basic analysis. Jeremias thought that, with the exception of the miracle stories, the synoptics are relatively reliable, and he agreed with Schweitzer that Jesus believed in a near consummation, expected his death to inaugurate the great tribulation, and hoped for his own resurrection as part of the general resurrection of the dead.

Not all accepted Schweitzer's dichotomy. While Rudolf Bultmann (1884–1976), for instance, believed that Jesus was indeed an eschatological prophet, he was far more skeptical about the historicity of the synoptics than Schweitzer. Bultmann's views lie somewhere between Strauss' skepticism and Schweitzer's confidence. A form critic, Bultmann sought to isolate, classify, and evaluate the components of the Jesus tradition. Given that the order of events varies from gospel to gospel and that there is usually no logical connection between adjacent episodes, we cannot, Bultmann concluded, know the true order of events. And since the church contributed as much to the sayings attributed to Jesus as did Jesus himself, it is no longer possible to write a biography of Jesus, only to sketch an outline of his teachings within a rather bare narrative.

Another significant scholar who rejected Schweitzer's dichotomy was C. H. Dodd (1884–1973). Although he accepted the basic synoptic portrait (with the exception of Mark 13 and its parallels, which he thought misrepresented Jesus), he disagreed with Schweitzer regarding eschatology. Dodd famously urged that Jesus had a "realized eschatology" (Dodd 1960). That is, the kingdom of God, Jesus' name for the transcendent order in which there is no before or after, had manifested itself in the crisis of his ministry. Further, Jesus expected vindication after death, which he variously spoke of as resurrection, the coming of the Son of Man, and the rebuilding of the temple. But the church came to long for the future coming of the Son of Man, now conceived of as Jesus' return. In this way eschatology ceased to be realized. The change of outlook was such that the church eventually, and according to Dodd regrettably, made Revelation its canonical finale.

Probably the most prominent of recent scholars to reject Schweitzer's dichotomy is John Dominic Crossan (b. 1934). He has argued that while much of the material Schweitzer used in his reconstruction comes from the church, we can still know a great deal about Jesus. For Crossan, Jesus was indeed utopian, but what he envisaged was not the standard catastrophe found in some of the Jewish apocalypses. Jesus was instead a Jewish peasant whose revolutionary social program is best preserved in aphorisms and parables. These depict a Cynic-like sage who welcomed outcasts as equals. The common eschatological scenario of resurrection, last judgment, heaven, and hell and its attendant violence do not make an appearance. Crossan freely acknowledges that a great many sayings in the Jesus tradition state and presuppose eschatological expectations that contradict his reconstruction; he simply regards these as misrepresentations, as in effect apocryphal.

Many now affirm that we have been, for the last two or three decades, witnessing a so-called "third quest" of the historical Jesus. The assumption is that contemporary activity can be clearly distinguished from previous activities (the so-called "first quest" of the nineteenth century and the so-called "new quest" in the middle of the twentieth century). My own view is that there is some chronological snobbery, an exaggerated sense of contemporary self-importance, behind this assumption, or rather presumption, as well as much ignorance of the extent to which the present is indebted to and a continuation of the past. In any case, different writers have created lists of features that supposedly differentiate current work from its predecessors. William R. Telford (1994) has, not uncritically, inventoried some of these lists, and he finds that it is now not uncommon to affirm the following: (a) Scholars today have a historical rather than a theological orientation. (b) More attention is now paid to broader questions, such as Jesus' social identity and relationship to Judaism, less to the authenticity of single pericopae. (c) Confidence that we can give a reasonably comprehensive account of Jesus' ministry has increased. (d) There is a reaction against a perceived over-emphasis on the tradition-critical analysis of gospel material, especially the sayings attributed to Jesus. (e) Currently many are less enamored of the criterion of dissimilarity, which christens as authentic items in the tradition that cannot be traced either to Judaism or early Christianity. (f) Contemporary researchers emphasize placing Jesus in a wider context. (g) An interdisciplinary openness and a special interest in the social sciences characterize current studies.

There is more than a little to query in this list. Generalization (a) holds for some. Certainly a smaller percentage of New Testament academics is in the service of the church than in times past. As for writers on Jesus in particular, E. P. Sanders (1985, 1993) does not wear his theological convictions, whatever they may or may not be, on his sleeve, and John Meier (1991–2009) has been trying to write about Jesus with minimal interference from his Catholic convictions. And yet it is at the same time true that neither scholar is in this obviously representative. Marcus Borg (1987) and N. T. Wright (1996), for example, are forthright about their theological interests, which largely drive their projects, as they freely acknowledge. It is, furthermore, evident that some we might think of as having no theological agenda are partly motivated by an animus against traditional Christian doctrine, which is in reality just another sort of theological agenda. The trite truth is that nobody is, has been, or can be wholly free of philosophical biases or theological interests when examining the origins of Christianity, so the alleged lack thereof is no criterion for distinguishing any period.

Generalization (b) is also problematic. Certainly great attention is being paid to Jesus' place within Judaism. But this emphasis is part and parcel of a much larger tendency to attempt to interpret all of earliest Christianity as a Jewish phenomenon. Thus Paul's Jewish context and character are also highlighted by present scholarship. In addition, the focus upon Jesus the Jew marks not a new beginning but only an intensification of a line of investigation that can be traced back ultimately to the works of such as John

Lightfoot (1602–75) and Johann Salomo Semler (1725–91) as well as some of the deistic critics of Christianity, such as Lord Bolingbroke; such investigation was then carried forward by later Jewish and Christian scholars such as Adolf Schlatter (1852–1938), Gustav Dalman (1855–1941), Joseph Klausner (1874–1958), and Joachim Jeremias (1900–79). They were all, in one way or another, trying to find Jesus by looking for Judaism. We may regard their use of Jewish sources as less sophisticated than our own; and Christian scholars may further, with the guilt of the Holocaust hanging over our heads and the modern spirit of relativism urging us not to reckon one religion better than another, see more continuity with Judaism whereas our predecessors saw less. Yet we are not walking down a new path but rather just going further down the old one.

That there is increased confidence in our ability to give a reasonably comprehensive account of Jesus' ministry, point (c), is not at all obvious. On the one hand, this generalization does not clearly encompass the voting of the Jesus Seminar (see below), a group of influential scholars, many of whose members have a relatively skeptical take on the tradition. On the other hand, there is nothing new about comprehensive accounts of Jesus' ministry, as remembrance of Jeremias (1971) and Dodd (1971), neither a second-stringer on the sidelines of New Testament studies, suffices to establish.

With respect to (d), the generalization that there is less faith in tradition-historical analysis certainly holds for my own work (Allison 1998) as well as that of Sanders (1985, 1993) and Wright (1996). Yet many important scholars still reconstruct Jesus by primarily engaging in more or less conventional tradition-historical analysis. Both Meier (1991–2009) and John Dominic Crossan (1991), for example, do so, albeit with very different results.

Regarding (e), perhaps skepticism regarding the criterion of dissimilarity has increased of late. One hopes so. Yet critiques of this criterion have existed for some time; they are hardly confined to the most recent phase of scholarship (see Hooker 1971). Furthermore, there are important scholars, such as Meier (1991–2009), who nonetheless continue to use this criterion.

Point (f) seems to be largely a variation of (b), and as already indicated, it is not just recent scholars who have brought to the fore Jesus' relationship to Judaism. Anyone who doubts this should read John Lightfoot on Matthew and Mark or the rabbinic commentary of August Wünsche (1838–1913) on the gospels or Wilhelm Bousset's *Jesus* (1906) or the studies of Gustav Dalman on the gospels or Joseph Klausner's *Jesus of Nazareth* (1925). The effort to understand Jesus within the wider historical and religious context of ancient Judaism is nothing new, and assertions to the contrary ungraciously ignore our debts to our predecessors. The major differences between now and then are that today, because of archaeological discoveries, including the Dead Sea Scrolls, as well as critical advances in the study of the pseudepigrapha and rabbinic literature, we know a lot more about Jesus' environment; and we are more inclined, for various reasons, to construct with our new knowledge fairer presentations of early Judaism.

Perhaps the most justified of the various generalizations is (g), for there is indeed an interdisciplinary openness among many. My own work, for instance, interprets Jesus with the aid of parallels from millenarian movements (Allison 1998), and Crossan (1991) uses data from studies of peasants and of Mediterranean society to fill out his reconstruction. One must keep in mind, however, that many important scholars, including Meier (1991–2009), Sanders (1985, 1993), and Wright (1996), continue to work on Jesus without calling upon much interdisciplinary assistance.

If lists purporting to characterize current research are not very illuminating, indeed seem partly contrived, this is largely due to the overwhelming diversity among contemporary scholars and their reconstructions. Contemporary work has no characteristic method. It has no body of shared conclusions. And it has no common set of historiographical or theological presuppositions. Differences in opinion about Jesus have become as common as differences in taste. So summary generalizations about it do not persuade. Those who continue to speak of the third quest and justify themselves by delineating its distinctive features are engaging in a quaint, antiquated activity that needs to be deconstructed. There has been no radical disjunction in the history of the discipline; one thing has just led to another. Furthermore, if the truth be told, positions staked out as new are sometimes recovery operations, or at least far less innovative than they are made to appear. The natural temptation is to magnify our own contributions. Schweitzer (2001) downplayed the extent to which scholars before him had found troubling eschatological convictions in Jesus; this allowed him to turn Johannes Weiss into his forerunner, his very own John the Baptist, and to make himself out to be the fulfillment of Weiss' promise. Similarly in our own day, N. T. Wright (1996), in forwarding his metaphorical interpretation of eschatological language, which finds Jesus' prophecies realized in subsequent events, somehow fails to parade his lengthy pedigree, which includes not just Dodd (1961) but a host of Church Fathers.

Although hunting for broad agreements in the methods or conclusions of contemporary scholars is not the most profitable of undertakings, and although we are less original than we sometimes imagine, this does not mean that there is nothing new under the sun. For one thing, there is the increase, much remarked upon, in the number of books of articles on the historical Jesus. If the fact is obvious, its meaning is less so. Sometimes this increase is spoken of as though it is due to fresh ideas or new discoveries. The truth, however, is that it is even more a product of current economic and educational realities. There just happen to be, for reasons that have nothing to do with historical Jesus research, more New Testament scholars and publishers of what those scholars produce than in the past. This is why books on Paul have also multiplied of late. So too have books on Hebrews, and even books on James and Jude, not to mention Festschrifts. The guild is much larger than in the past, more young scholars are seeking tenure in a publish-or-perish world than in the past, and there are many more publishers and journals – including now the *Journal for the Study of the Historical Jesus* – than in the past, so there are naturally more books and articles on Jesus, as on everything else, than in the past.

One other recent development merits remark. This is the advent and prominence of the Jesus Seminar, co-founded by Crossan and Robert Funk (1926–2005). The Seminar is a loosely affiliated group of fewer than 100 scholars who began, in the 1980s, meeting twice a year to discuss and vote upon questions concerning the historical Jesus. The upshot of their work, published in Funk and Hoover (1993) and elsewhere, is that approximately 18 percent of the sayings attributed to Jesus in the synoptics go back to him or represent something that he said. Among their other conclusions, which have generated much controversy, are these: only one saying in John reflects something Jesus said (John 4:44); Jesus did not consider himself to be messiah or Son of Man; he said little or nothing about resurrection and judgment; he was a laconic sage known for pithy one-liners and parables; he did not keep kosher; and he did not much cite or refer to scripture. A major achievement of the Seminar, whose conclusions represent only one group of scholars, has been to bring contemporary critical work to public notice.

The Seminar has also been helpful in successfully contributing to breaking down further the canonical barrier. While there have been exceptions, scholars have traditionally reconstructed Jesus solely with pieces from the synoptics and John. There are, however, many extra-canonical traditions about Jesus also – in the apostolic fathers, in the apocryphal gospels, and in the collection known as the Nag Hammadi library. From a historical point of view, there is no a priori reason why the canonical record should be privileged. One may indeed decide, after studying the evidence, that the canonical records are in fact the oldest and most helpful; this is in fact the conclusion of Meier (1991–2009) and Sanders (1985, 1993). But most members of the Seminar have found reasons to believe that the *Gospel of Thomas*, at least sometimes, contains traditions independent of the NT writings. Those of us who agree will necessarily need to include *Thomas* in the potential pile of data about Jesus.

## The Problem of the Criteria of Authenticity

How should one decide what goes back to Jesus and what does not? Early in the twentieth century, many mistakenly imagined that source criticism would allow the recovery of history. If Mark was a source of Matthew and Luke, and if Matthew and Luke also used a lost collection of sayings (scholars dub this "Q"), then perhaps, it was hoped, one could find Jesus by concentrating on the earliest sources, Q (insofar as it can be reconstructed) and Mark. Later skepticism, however, gradually abraded this sort of confidence, which overlooked the extent to which the early church shaped even Mark and Q and their traditions. Given this, most scholars have changed strategies. The upshot has been the invention and employment of so-called "criteria of authenticity," tests by which we can allegedly fish dominical items out of the sea of traditions.

The standard criteria appeal to common sense. For instance, that a tradition should not be thought authentic unless it coheres with traditions otherwise regarded as genuine – the criterion of consistency – seems self-evident. Again, that we may feel confident in assigning a unit to Jesus if it is dissimilar to characteristic emphases both of ancient Judaism and of the early church – the criterion variously known as dissimilarity or distinctiveness or double discontinuity or dual irreducibility – has an initial plausibility. So too does the criterion of embarrassment, according to which a fact or saying is original if there is evidence that it embarrassed early Christians. And who would challenge the criterion of multiple attestation, according to which the more widely attested a complex is in independent sources, the more likely it is to have originated with Jesus? This is just the old rule of journalism, that each fact should be attested by at least two witnesses.

Reflection, however, foments doubts. Coherence, for example, is a very subjective notion. Two things that fit together for one exegete may seem irreconcilable to another. Some have thought that if Jesus taught his disciples to love their enemy because God loves everyone, including the wicked, then it is unlikely that he also taught anything much about hell, despite abundant testimony in the tradition to the contrary. One understands the point and sympathizes with the sentiment. Yet what is the justification for assuming that Jesus, who was no systematic theologian or critical philosopher, must have been, to our way of thinking, consistent – especially when Q, Matthew, and Luke are, in this matter, also to our eyes inconsistent? One can always, as should be obvious in this age of deconstructionism, find tensions or contradictions between two texts. Romans and Galatians say different things about the law, but Paul wrote them both. The apostle, who was surely a more orderly thinker than Jesus, said some things that do not obviously go together. Consistency is in the eye of the beholder; and Jesus, who lived in a very different time and place, may not have beheld what we behold.

The criterion of dissimilarity, which like our commercials implicitly equates new with improved, is no less troublesome than the criterion of consistency. As others have often remarked, it can at best tell us what was distinctive, not what was characteristic, of Jesus. Because Jesus lived and moved and had his being within the Jewish tradition, the criterion is not a net that catches fish of every kind: it can find only things that Jesus did not take from elsewhere. All too often, however, dissimilarity has been misused as a means of separating the authentic from the unauthentic, that is, a way of eliminating items from the corpus of authentic materials. The result is a Jesus cut off from both his Jewish predecessors and his Christian followers. Beyond this, we just do not know enough about first-century Judaism or early Christianity to make the criterion reliable. Why pretend to prove a negative?

There is also the striking fact that those who profess allegiance to the criterion of dissimilarity often ignore its dictates. Surely most scholars have attributed the gist of Matthew 5:38–48 (= Luke 6:27–36), which exhorts disciples to turn the other cheek and to love their enemy, to Jesus himself; indeed, modern pictures of Jesus often make out this instruction to be characteristic of him. Yet the parallels in Christian sources are extensive (see Rom. 12:14, 17, 21; 1 Thess. 5:15; *Didache*, 1:3–5; *1 Clement*, 13:2; and Polycarp, *Philippians*, 2:2–3); and the Talmud supplies this close parallel, in *b. Šabbat* 88b and *b. Gittin* 36b: "Our rabbis taught: Those who are insulted but do not inflict them, who hear themselves being reviled and do not answer back, who perform [religious precepts] out of love and rejoice in chastisement, of them the Scripture says, 'And they who love him are as the sun when he goes forth in his might [to shine upon all]'" (Judg. 5:31). It would seem that the criterion of dissimilarity should prohibit us from assigning Matthew 5:38–48 (= Luke 6:27–36) to Jesus. Few, however, feel that this can be correct.

The criterion of embarrassment is more promising. Certainly historians in other fields have often reasoned according to its logic – as when scholars of Islam have affirmed that the so-called "Satanic verses" rest upon a historical episode because Muslims did not invent a story in which Mohammed mentions the names of three goddesses. And yet there is a problem. We must face the surprising fact that all of the supposedly embarrassing facts or words are found in the Jesus tradition itself. This means that they were not sufficiently disconcerting to be expurgated. This hints at the pluralism of the early church, and it suggests that what may have flustered some may have left others unperturbed.

Even the principle of multiple attestation is worrisome. The more frequently a complex is attested, the more congenial, one naturally infers, it was to early Christians.

But the more congenial a complex was to early Christians, surely the less likely it is, for the critical, skeptical historian, that Jesus composed it. Conversely, the less congenial a tradition, the more likely its origin with Jesus and the less likely its multiple attestation. Here the criterion of multiple attestation is in a tug-of-war with the criterion of dissimilarity: they pull the same unit in opposite directions.

Whether or not one shares my skepticism that the criteria of dissimilarity, coherence, embarrassment, and multiple attestation do not prove equal to their task, it is certain that they have not led us into the promised land of scholarly consensus. If they were designed to overcome subjectivity and bring order to our discipline, then they have failed.

Recently, Theissen and Winter (2002), also unhappy with the conventional criteria, especially dissimilarity, have formulated what they call the criterion of historical plausibility, which comes down to this: "What Jesus intended and said must be compatible with the Judaism of the first half of the first century in Galilee"; "What Jesus intended and did must be recognizable as that of an individual figure within the framework of the Judaism of that time"; "Those elements within the Jesus tradition that contrast with the interests of the early Christian sources, but are handed on in their tradition, can claim varying degrees of historical plausibility" (Theissen and Winter 2002: 211).

Although it would be foolhardy to disagree with these assertions, heeding them will not reduce the diversity that haunts the field, for the criterion remains most malleable. The synoptics contain very little that cannot be made to fit within first-century Galilean Judaism, about which, despite the relevant extant texts and ongoing archaeological discoveries, we still know so little. Again, one can hardly object to favoring traditions that contrast with the interests of early Christian sources, but how much help is this, given how little we really know, if we are honest, about the early church? In the end, the criterion of historical plausibility, like a trap in a forest that catches only the occasional passerby, works on just some items. No one would deny that a reconstructed Jesus should be plausible within his Galilean environment and not look too much like a Christian. Yet recognizing this is not going to enable us to peer across the darkness of two thousand years and discern if he did or did not speak about a coming Son of Man, or whether the pigs really did run over the cliff.

## A Proposal on Method

When we look back upon our encounters with others, our most vivid and reliable memories are often not precise but general. I may, for instance, not remember exactly what you said to me last year, but I may recall approximately what you said, or retain what we call a general impression. It is like vaguely recollecting the approximate shape, size, and contents of a room one was in many years ago – a room which has, in the mind's eye, lost all color and detail. After our short-term memories have become long-term memories they suffer progressive abbreviation. I am not sure I remember a single sentence that either of my beloved grandparents on my father's side ever said to me. But I nonetheless know and cherish the sorts of the things that they said to me.

All of this matters for study of the Jesus tradition because it goes against universal human experience to suppose that early Christians, let us say, accurately recorded many of Jesus' words but somehow came away with false general impressions of him. If the tradents of the Jesus tradition got the big picture or the larger patterns wrong then they also got the details – that is, the sentences – wrong. It is precarious to urge that we can find the truth about Jesus on the basis of a few dozen sayings deemed to be authentic if those sayings are interpreted contrary to the general impressions conveyed by the early tradition in its entirety. If Jesus was, for example, either a violent revolutionary or a secular sage, then the tradition about him is so misleading that we cannot use it for investigation of the pre-Easter period – and so we cannot know that Jesus was either a violent revolutionary or a secular sage. Here skepticism devours itself.

What is the alternative to skepticism? The early Jesus tradition is, to state the obvious, not a collection of totally disparate and wholly unrelated materials. On the contrary, certain themes and motifs and rhetorical strategies are consistently attested over a wide range of material. And surely it is in these themes and motifs and rhetorical strategies, if it is anywhere, that we are likely to have an accurate memory. Indeed, several of these themes and motifs and strategies are sufficiently well attested that we have a choice to make. Either they tend to preserve pre-Easter memories or they do not. In the former case we may know enough to begin our attempts at authenticating individual items: the general might help us with the particular. But in the latter case our questing for Jesus is not just interminable but probably pointless and we should consider surrendering to ignorance. If the tradition is so misleading in its broad features, then we can hardly make much of its details.

Consider, as illustration, the proposition that Jesus and his disciples saw his ministry as effecting the defeat of Satan and demonic spirits. This conviction is reflected in sundry sources and in divers genres – parables, apocalyptic declarations, stories of exorcism, etc.:

1   The temptation story, in which Jesus bests the Devil: Mark 1:12–13; Matthew 4:1–11 (= Luke 4:1–13 [Q])
2   Stories of successful exorcism: Mark 1:21–8; 5:1–20; 7:24–30; 9:14–20; Matthew 12:22–3 (= Luke 11:14 [Q]); Matthew 9:32–4; cf. the passing notices of successful exorcisms in Mark 1:32, 34, 39; 3:22; Matthew 8:16; Luke 13:32
3   Jesus' authorization of disciples to cast out demons: Mark 3:15; 6:7; cf. 6:13; Matthew 7:22; Luke 10:19–20
4   Saying about Satan being divided: Mark 3:23–7; Matthew 12:25–7 = Luke 11:17–19 (Q)
5   Parable of binding the strong man: Mark 3:28; Matthew 12:29 (= Luke 11:21–2 [Q]); *Gospel of Thomas* 35
6   Story of someone other than a disciple casting out demons in Jesus' name: Mark 9:38–41
7   Declaration that Jesus casts out demons by the finger/Spirit of God: Matthew 12:28 (= Luke 11:20 [Q])
8   Report of Jesus' vision of Satan falling like lightning from heaven: Luke 10:18
9   Announcement that the ruler of the world has been driven out; John 12:31; 16:11 (cf. 14:30)

One infers from all this material not only that Jesus was an exorcist but also that his ministry in its entirety was seen, by Jesus himself as well as by others, as a conflict with Satan, which Jesus was winning. This holds whatever one makes of the individual units, at least some of which (for example, the temptation story) are difficult to think of as historical. What counts is not the isolated units but the patterns they weave, the larger images they form. Indeed, even if one were, against good sense, to doubt the truth of every individual story and saying just listed and count them all creations of the community, one might still reasonably retain a certain faith in the whole of them taken together and suppose that the recurring motif tells us something about Jesus' ministry. One can draw an analogy here with medical experiments. Taken by itself, even perfectly devised double-blind, randomized trials count for little. What counts is replication. And in areas where matters are particularly controverted, what finally counts is meta-analysis, the evaluation of large collections of results from numerous individual studies, including those with possible design flaws. What instills conviction is the tendency of the whole, not any one experiment or piece of evidence.

The motif of victory over Satan is only one of a number of themes and motifs that recur in the sources. Others are God as a caring father; the requirement to love, serve, and forgive others; special regard for the unfortunate; the dangers of wealth; extraordinary requests and difficult demands; conflict with religious authorities; disciples as students and assistants; and Jesus as miracle-worker.

It is not naive or precritical to urge that we should probably regard all of these as being rooted in the teaching and ministry of Jesus. Either the tradition instructs us that Jesus spoke often about God as a father, showed special regard for unfortunates, and had disciples who followed him around, or the tradition is so corrupt that it is not a useful source for Jesus and the quest for him is hopeless. I admit that this conclusion is contained in my premise, which is that memory, if anywhere, must be in the larger patterns; but then nothing but this premise allows research to proceed.

If the isolation of major, recurring themes and motifs is where the reconstruction of Jesus ought naturally to begin, if it is to begin anywhere at all, the next step is to correlate those themes and motifs with whatever circumstances about his life can be recovered, which includes his rough dates (ca. 7/5 BCE – 30/33 CE), his baptism by John the Baptist, his choosing of twelve disciples, his (last or only?) journey from Galilee to Jerusalem, his protest in the temple there, his arrest and condemnation at the hands of the Romans, and his crucifixion. By setting the major recurring themes and motifs within the framework of what we otherwise know about Jesus, we can begin to get a fair picture of who he was. Only after that is accomplished should one undertake the difficult and often impossible task of trying to decide which individual units may go back to things Jesus probably said or what individual stories come close to something that really happened.

## Eschatology

In addition to the several themes and motifs introduced above, the following also appear regularly in the tradition:

1   The kingdom of God
2   Future reward for the righteous
3   Future judgment for the wicked
4   Suffering/persecution for the saints
5   Present and coming victory over evil powers
6   A sense that something new is both here and at hand

These items, taken together, strongly suggest a Jesus with strong eschatological expectations. The relevant texts envisage the advent, after suffering and persecution, of a great judgment followed by a utopia, the kingdom of God, when the dead will come back to life and Israel will be restored. Then the poor will become rich, the first will become last, and the last will become first. We have here the standard pattern of Jewish messianism, which is also found in millennial movements world-wide – a time of tribulation followed by eschatological reward and punishment.

My own conclusion, then, is that those, such as Weiss and Schweitzer, who have thought that Jesus was an eschatological prophet were near the truth. This conclusion, which does not depend upon a critical analysis of particular sayings, is buttressed by additional observations, three of which may be briefly noticed here:

(1)   Passages from a wide variety of sources show us that many early followers of Jesus believed the eschatological climax to be near (for example, Acts 3:19–21; Rom. 13:11; Heb. 10:37; Jas. 5:8; 1 Pet. 4:17; Rev. 22:20). We also know that, in the pre-Easter period, Jesus himself was closely associated with John the Baptist, whose public speech, if the synoptics are any guide at all, featured frequent allusion to the eschatological judgment, conceived as imminent (see Matthew = Luke Q 3:7–17, Q). Indeed, Jesus submitted to the baptism of John. Obviously, then, there must have been significant ideological continuity between the two men. So, as many have observed again and again over the last one hundred years, to reconstruct a Jesus who did not have a strong eschatological or apocalyptic orientation entails discontinuity not only between him and people who took themselves to be furthering his cause but also between him and the Baptist, that is, discontinuity with the movement out of which he came as well as with the movement that came forth from him.

(2)   The canonical gospels, traditions in Acts, and the letters of Paul are united in relating that at least several pre-Easter followers of Jesus, soon after his crucifixion, declared that "God [had] raised Jesus from the dead" (cf. Mark 16:6; Acts 2:24; Rom. 10:9; 1 Thess. 1:10) or vindicated him by "the resurrection of the dead ones" (Acts 4:2; cf. Rom. 1:4). Their combined testimony on this matter is not doubted by anyone, so we may ask why people made this claim, why they affirmed the occurrence of an event – resurrection of the dead – otherwise associated with the end of the age. The best explanation is that several influential individuals came to their post-Easter experiences, whatever they were, with certain categories and expectations antecedently fixed, that they already, because of Jesus' teaching, envisaged the general resurrection to be imminent. This is why "resurrection" was for many the chief category by which to interpret Jesus' vindication.

(3)    The apocalyptic writings of Judaism put us in touch with a type of eschatology that was well known in Jesus' time and place. Not only did the sacred collection itself contain apocalyptic materials – for example, Isaiah 24–7, Daniel, Zechariah 9–14 – but portions of *1 Enoch*, some of the Jewish *Sibylline Oracles*, and the *Testament of Moses* were in circulation in Jesus' day; and the decades after Jesus saw the appearance of *4 Ezra*, *2 Baruch*, and the *Apocalypse of Abraham*. His time was also when the Dead Sea Scrolls, so many of which are charged with apocalyptic expectation, were presumably being composed or copied and studied. The point, reinforced by Josephus' remarks on the general popularity of the apocalyptic book of Daniel (*Antiquities* 10.268), is simply that the sort of eschatology Weiss and Schweitzer attributed to Jesus was indeed flourishing in Jesus' day. We can make the inference from the New Testament itself. For in the words of Barnabas Lindars (1976: 62):

> the rapid expansion of Christianity would really be inexplicable except against the background of a widespread feeling amongst Jews of the day that they were living in the End Time. For it is ... only because of the pre-understanding of the Bible in this eschatological sense, attested not only in Qumran and apocalyptic, but also to some extent in rabbinic sources, that the church's application of the whole range of Old Testament to Jesus could be felt to be a plausible undertaking and find acceptance.

The point is this: to propose that Jesus thought the end to be near is just to say that he believed what many others in his time and place believed.

## Objections

Despite the observations just made, the apocalyptic interpretation of Jesus has inevitably had its opponents. Recently, moreover, some have imagined that Schweitzer's descendants are beleaguered on every side; a few have even gone so far as to claim that the old consensus of an apocalyptic-like Jesus has disintegrated. How one counts heads on an issue such as this escapes me; but what matters in any case are the arguments. Of the several reasons commonly forwarded for divorcing Jesus from an eschatological or apocalyptic worldview, I shall briefly review two.

(1)    The ethical exhortations of Jesus do not regularly refer to a near end as their sanction. They rather seem to be independent of such an expectation, as their employment throughout Christian history has made manifest. Jesus commands people to love their enemies because God loves them, not because the world is winding down. He enjoins his hearers to love the Lord their God and their neighbor because the scripture decrees it, not because the judgment is at hand.

What is the force of such observations? There has been much confusion here, due in large measure to widespread dislike of Schweitzer's notion of an "interim ethic," which does stand in need of qualification. The nearness of the end does not in and of itself generate moral imperatives. I know a man who, fearing no retribution after death, claims that he would sin in new ways if he thought he had little time left, because he then would not have to suffer the consequences. The imminence of the end may be an effective way of concentrating the mind, but it does not generate a moral tradition. So how one responds to the anticipated end depends on the tradition within which one already stands. In Judaism that tradition has always been Torah. This is why the Jewish apocalypses typically do not offer unheard-of exhortations but instead seek to get people to do what they already know they should be doing but are not. The Jesus tradition is similar. Its moral imperatives have an eschatological context, but few of them were created by or for that context. Nor was there any reason to court boredom by belaboring the obvious and appending to every injunction, "The end is near." At the same time, preachers who believe in a near end will be especially fond of those elements in their tradition that emphasize the transience of things. This is one reason the Jesus tradition picks up ascetic-like elements (see for instance Matt. 10:9–10 [= Luke 10:4 (Q)]; Matt. 19:12; and Mark 9:43–8) and teachings about the fleeting nature of wealth (Matt 6:19–21 [= Luke 12:33–4 (Q)]; Mark 10:21, 23; etc.).

(2)   Several recent scholars have decided that an early version of Q contained no future Son of Man sayings, and that much of the eschatological pathos present in the Q known to Matthew and Luke was a secondary development (so Kloppenborg 1987). If accepted, this result would be consistent with the theory that the Christian tradition, without help from Jesus, was responsible for the strong eschatological character of so much in the gospels.

Many would, however, hesitate to put much confidence in the hypothetical compositional history of the hypothetical document Q. Others would offer alternative histories that do not eliminate a strong eschatological element from the earliest stratum. For the sake of argument, however, what follows if one grants that the first level of Q was indeed empty of eschatological feeling? Very little. One can readily imagine that the initial compiler of Q had interests different from the compilers of later, expanded editions. But why those first interests, as opposed to later interests, would alone favor the preservation of authentic sayings is unclear. If we were envisaging a documentary history that spanned generations, then an earlier contributor would certainly be in a privileged position. Q, however, was opened and closed within, at most, a thirty- year period. One might accordingly even suppose that the enlarged Q, by virtue of additional, authentic material, resulted in a fuller and less distorted impression of the historical Jesus. Is arguing that the first stratum of Q alone gives us an accurate picture of what Jesus did or did not say about eschatological matters really any more persuasive than urging that the first biography written about, let us say, Abraham Lincoln, must be more reliable than all of those that came later? Should we, because we learn of Jesus' crucifixion not from Q but from other sources, perhaps entertain the notion that Jesus was not crucified? Obviously Q leaves much out of account, even much of importance, which it must have known. Q's silences may indeed be omissions, and the sayings source need not be a full-length mirror of any individual's or community's convictions.

In the end, the case for an apocalyptic Jesus persuades. The kingdom of God was the central theme of Jesus' proclamation, and he conceived of that kingdom as eschatological in the proper sense of that word.

## Coda

Having said this, a note of caution should be appended. While eschatology counts for much, it does not count for everything. It is true that vast portions of the tradition relate themselves directly or indirectly to eschatology. But when Schweitzer promoted "thoroughgoing eschatology," he eschewed prudence, as have I in some of my own writings on this matter. The historical Jesus cannot be captured by an eschatological reductionism, a sort of epiphenomenalism which views everything in the original tradition as caused by his eschatological convictions. Jesus was not a monomaniac. Nor was he an eschatological machine who produced only eschatological products. Much in his teaching was eschatological, but not everything was. Much was colored by eschatology, but there is more to things than color. Most of his ethical imperatives, as already observed, cannot be reduced to eschatology, even though their eschatological context gave them an added urgency. The same is true of several of the major themes and motifs of his ministry, including his depiction of God as a caring father, his demand that people love, serve, and forgive others, and his special regard for the unfortunate. Good sense forbids reducing the complex to the simple, the many to the one.

## Annotated Bibliography

Allison, Dale C., Jr. *Jesus of Nazareth: Millenarian Prophet*. Minneapolis: Fortress, 1998. An attempt to apply cross-cultural millenarian materials to the Jesus tradition.

Borg, Marcus. *Jesus: A New Vision*. San Francisco: Harper & Row, 1987. Best-selling volume by a well-known member of the Jesus Seminar.

Crossan, John Dominic. *The Historical Jesus: The Life of a Mediterranean Jewish Peasant*. San Francisco: Harper & Row, 1991. The most discussed of recent books on Jesus.

Dodd, C. H. *The Parables of Jesus*. Rev. edn. New York: Charles Scribner's Sons, 1961. An important discussion of the parables that consistently interprets them in terms of "realized eschatology."

Dodd, C. H. *The Founder of Christianity*. London: Collins, 1971. A summing up by a major British scholar.

Funk, Robert W., Roy Hoover, and the Jesus Seminar. *The Five Gospels: The Search for the Authentic Words of Jesus*. New York: Macmillan, 1993. The results of the Jesus Seminar's voting on the words of Jesus.

Hooker, Morna. "Christology and Methodology." *New Testament Studies* 17 (1971), 48–87. A persuasive critique of the criterion of dissimilarity.

Jeremias, Joachim. *New Testament Theology*, vol. 1: *The Proclamation of Jesus*. New York: Charles Scribner's Sons, 1971. A systematic presentation of the teaching of Jesus by one of the most influential of twentieth-century questers.

Klausner, Joseph. *Jesus of Nazareth: His Life, Times, and Teachings*. New York: Macmillan, 1925. An overview by a famous Jewish scholar still worth reading.

Kloppenborg, John S. *The Formation of Q: Trajectories in Early Christian Wisdom Traditions*. Philadelphia: Fortress, 1987. Perhaps the most influential of recent books on Q.

Lindars, Barnabas. "The Place of the Old Testament in the Formation of New Testament Theology." *New Testament Studies* 23 (1976), 59–66. Extract on page 232 © Cambridge University Press. Reprinted with permission.

Meier, John P. *A Marginal Jew*. 4 vols. New York: Doubleday, 1991–2009. A detailed and comprehensive discussion of all the major issues and topics by a Roman Catholic scholar. A fifth volume is planned.

Sanders, E. P. *Jesus and Judaism*. Philadelphia: Fortress Press, 1985. An attempt to understand Jesus within his Jewish context that starts with events and facts rather than sayings.

Sanders, E. P. *The Historical Figure of Jesus*. London: Penguin, 1993. A more popular and in some ways broader presentation than *Jesus and Judaism*.

Schweitzer, Albert. *The Quest of the Historical Jesus*. 1st complete edn. Minneapolis: Fortress Press, 2001. The classic review of the eighteenth and nineteenth centuries that ends with Schweitzer's own eschatological interpretation.

Strauss, David Friedrich. *The Life of Jesus Critically Examined*. Philadelphia: Fortress Press, 1972. The most important nineteenth-century book on Jesus.

Telford, William R. "Major Trends and Interpretive Issues in the Study of Jesus." Pp. 33–74 in *Studying the Historical Jesus: Evaluations of the Current State of Research*. Edited by Bruce Chilton and Craig A. Evans. Leiden and New York/Cologne: E. J. Brill, 1994.

Theissen, Gerd and Annette Merz. *The Historical Jesus: A Comprehensive Guide*. Minneapolis: Fortress Press, 1998. The best contemporary introduction to all facets of the discussion.

Theissen, Gerd and Dagmar Winter. *The Quest for the Plausible Jesus: The Question of Criteria*. Louisville and London: Westminster John Knox, 2002. An overview of the critical criteria of authenticity.

Wright, N. T. *Jesus and the Victory of God*. Philadelphia: Fortress Press, 1996.

CHAPTER 15

# The Synoptic Problem

## Patricia Walters

## Introduction

Rarely does a topic in New Testament studies affect so many aspects of critical scholarship as the aptly named "synoptic problem." An intriguing compositional quandary, *the synoptic problem is grounded in the proposition that a literary interdependence exists among the first three books of the New Testament canon*: the gospels of Matthew, Mark, and Luke, also called the "synoptic" gospels. Coined by Johann Jakob Griesbach in the first edition of his Greek New Testament (1774), the term "synopsis" refers to placing gospel texts in parallel columns for ease of analysis (Griesbach, 1776; see also Kümmel 1972: 74f.). On the one hand, *that* a literary relationship exists is today seldom questioned. Indeed, striking content and linguistic parallels among the synoptic gospels have been observed since antiquity. On the other hand, explaining precisely *how* the relationship is configured continues to pique scholarly imagination and, in so doing, requires the mapping, analysis, and evaluation of a massive constellation of data. For any particular *solution* to the synoptic problem, evidence is usually offered in support of two central issues: first, determining the earliest gospel and, second, identifying the various directions of literary dependence, both of which, taken together, should give solid coherence to the labyrinthine set of agreements and disagreements in the three gospels' content, style, and arrangement. Because scholarly contributions to the synoptic problem continue to accrue at a breathtaking rate, this essay necessarily highlights ideas and areas enjoying currency within the broad spectrum of literature on this subject. To organize the ever-increasing amount of research, this essay treats the synoptic problem in four parts: (1) a survey of its historical roots; (2) the broad contours of the problem with examples; (3) three prevailing solutions to the synoptic problem including the evidence for and against them; and (4) the major issues and directions in recent study.

## Historical Roots of the Synoptic Problem[1]

In the early second century, Papias, the bishop of Hierapolis, promulgated a compositional theory, held for centuries, namely, that Matthew, Mark, and Luke were composed independently. Unfortunately, only fragments of his writings are preserved in Eusebius of Caesarea's *Ecclesiastical History* (ca. 263–ca. 339 CE), in which he claims the author of Mark wrote down all the remembrances of Peter accurately and fully, but not in order, because Peter "randomized" his teachings as the occasion demanded (Eusebius, *Ecclesiastical History*, 3.39.14–15). The Petrine "improvisational" ordering implies that not only does Mark lack a definite completeness (Dungan 1999: 19ff.) but also, more significantly, Papias' version of Mark may not be our canonical Mark but rather an earlier, or later, version. Why? Because, from his extant fragments, we know Papias knew the gospels of Mark *and* Matthew; we also know the Markan arrangement of contents roughly *parallels* that of Matthew; hence, if the remembrances were recorded out of order in Mark as Papias says, it appears logical he may have had access to a different version of Mark. In the case of Matthew, Papias claims the author wrote down the *logia* of Jesus in the Ἑβραΐδι διαλέκτῳ, "in the Hebrew language" (Eusebius, *Ecclesiastical History*, 3.39.16). Open to question is whether Ἑβραΐδι διαλέκτῳ means Matthean material was originally composed in Hebrew or whether the gospel was written in a Hebraic "manner of expression." A majority of scholars privilege the latter, that is, a Torah-like compositional style. Papias identifies no details of Markan or Matthean order, and none of his extant fragments mentions Luke at all.

Papias' influence notwithstanding, the historical roots of the synoptic problem as it is known today may be traced to other early Christian texts. In order to reconcile content disparities, Christian theologians began to harmonize the gospel texts. In the mid-second century, Tatian, Justin Martyr's student, crafted a Syriac four-gospel harmonization, the *Diatessaron*, which merged Matthew, Mark, Luke, and John into one seamless text, used widely in Christian worship. Harmonization produced a coherent view of Jesus' life and message; nevertheless, the search to resolve discrepancies was under way. In the third century, Origen of Alexandria, a brilliant systematic theologian, resolved apparent gospel discrepancies by proposing they must be understood on two levels, literally and spiritually (Origen, *Commentary on John* [*Commentarii in evangelium Joannis*]; see Dungan 1999: 78ff.). If a story's literal meaning baffled, its spiritual meaning did not. In short, even though the evangelists sometimes depicted Jesus' motivations differently, each wrote spiritual truth. In the fourth century, as intent as Origen to explain differences, Eusebius of Caesarea supplied an ingenious method of studying parallel gospel accounts. Recasting the earlier work of Ammonius of Alexandria (ca. 220 CE), Eusebius first coded all gospel pericopes with a number and then constructed ten tables of gospel parallels by listing their numerical codes in adjacent columns: one table for parallels in all four gospels, three tables for parallels in three gospels, five tables for parallels in two gospels, and one table for pericopes particular to each gospel. Thus, parallel accounts could be studied while the gospels themselves remained intact. As a testament to their enduring quality, Eusebius' numerical codes and ten tables are still published in the Nestle–Aland *Novum Testamentum Graece* in the twenty-seventh edition on pages 84*ff.

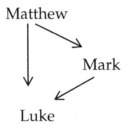

**Figure 15.1**

### The Influence of Augustine

In the fifth century, in what must be considered a masterstroke of textual and theological harmonization, Augustine wrote *On the Consensus of the Evangelists* (*De Consensu Evangelistarum*). Building on the work of earlier exegetes, Augustine drafted an immensely influential document that reconciled the literal and spiritual truth of the gospels. In particular, Augustine's understanding of compositional order matched their canonical sequence: Matthew first, then Mark, then Luke, and finally John (*De Consensu*, 1.3–4). Figure 15.1 shows the direction of compositional dependence in what is now known as the Augustinian hypothesis. Indeed, compositional order according to canonical sequence informed scholars for centuries to come.

To recapitulate, early harmonizations and exegetical methods clearly served a theology of unified spiritual Truth, thereby ably explaining discrepancies in the synoptic gospels' content, arrangement, and style.

### The Influence of Historical Criticism

Emerging in the Enlightenment, particularly in German universities, historical criticism marked a dramatic shift in focus from the prevailing theologically unified interpretations of the gospels toward "free investigation" of them via scientific, historical analysis (Kümmel 1970: 62–3). Johann Salomo Semler, for example, an early historical critic who published an influential work in 1771–5, has been quoted thusly (Kümmel 1970: 63):

> Holy Scripture and the Word of God are clearly to be distinguished, for we know the difference. ... Let us suppose, for instance, that the whole story of the woman taken in adultery in John 8 were lacking, as it is lacking in many ancient copies and translations of large parts of the Church: a piece of so-called Holy Scripture would then be lacking, but the Word of God would be lacking in nothing whatever, for it is and remains unchangeable, despite all these accidental and continuous changes in a document whose copyists, it must be admitted, enjoyed no divine aid ... Every intelligent person, if he is fortunate enough to take his own mental powers seriously, is free – yes, it is his very duty – to pass judgment on these matters without any fear of men ... The only proof that

completely satisfies an upright reader is the inner conviction brought about by the truths that confront him in this Holy Scripture ... the witness of the Holy Spirit in the soul of the reader.

An epistemological fissure, as it were, in the unity of historical and theological inter-pretation began to appear and indeed expand. As an umbrella term, "historical criti-cism" covers not only the scientific analysis of ancient manuscripts (text criticism) and transmission history, but also the evangelists' received oral tradition (See Chapter 9, "Form Criticism" in this volume), their editorial activity (redaction criticism), and their written sources, if any (source criticism). The problem of sources, then, especially in regard to the synoptic problem, touches each of these scientific methods.

In 1774–6, Johann Jakob Griesbach (1745–1812), a German scholar at the University of Jena, published a synopsis of the gospels of Matthew, Mark, and Luke (*Synopsis Evangeliorum Matthaei Marci et Lucae*) in which he placed the texts in three adjacent columns, placing parallel accounts side by side while keeping the order of each gospel generally in tact. Contemporary use of the term "synopsis" and "synoptic," in fact, derives from Griesbach's work. In 1789, Griesbach published his theory of com-positional interdependence in *A Demonstration that the Whole of the Gospel of Mark was Extracted from the Commentaries of Matthew and Luke* (*Commentatio qua Marci Evangelium totum e Matthaei et Lucae commenariis decerptum esse monstratur*). Shown in Figure 15.2, the Griesbach hypothesis postulates that Matthew was written first, then Luke, and finally Mark, whose author copied from Matthew and Luke when they agreed and copied one or the other when they disagreed. The Griesbach hypothesis remained virtu-ally unchallenged until the next century.

In the early to middle nineteenth century, synoptic gospel research by such German critics as Christian Gottlob Wilke and Christian Hermann Weise introduced and devel-oped the proposal of Markan priority, that is, that Mark is the earliest gospel; later, Heinrich Julius Holtzmann, building on their work, argued most convincingly for not only Markan priority but also a hypothetical second source to account for the "dou-blets" (over 230 parallel verses found in Matthew and Luke but not Mark), formulating what would become known as the Two-Document hypothesis (see below). By now, *both* Matthean and Markan priority had been proposed for the synoptic gospels, and so began intensive research in Germany and elsewhere for a solution to the synoptic problem.

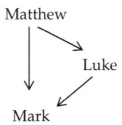

**Figure 15.2**

## Broad Contours of the Synoptic Problem

As implied above, most scholars who agree that Matthew, Mark, and Luke exhibit an overall coherence readily admit they contain notable disparities. With respect to coherence, Table 15.1 shows the relative order of shared material in the three gospels, which clearly begins where Mark begins and ends where Mark ends. Beyond the framework shared with Mark, both Matthew and Luke begin their gospels with an infancy narrative and end them with a set of resurrection appearances. For discussion of the ending appended at a later date to Mark (Mark 16:9–20), which contains resurrection appearances, see Chapter 17, "The Gospel of Mark," in this volume.

By drilling down through the shared framework to inspect individual pericopes or complexes of pericopes, it is evident the three gospels contain a substantial number of similar or identical verses in pericopes or sets of pericopes, arranged in comparable order and appropriately called the *triple tradition*. Furthermore, it is evident that Matthew and Luke contain some 230 similar or identical verses not found in Mark, and, fittingly they are known as the *double tradition*. While the triple tradition material maintains relatively the same order, the double tradition does not. That is to say, despite several major exceptions (see Neirynck 1990), the sequence of shared material in Matthew, Mark, and Luke is generally maintained throughout,[2] but the sequence of double tradition material in Matthew rarely follows that in Luke (see Neirynck 1990). As shown in the examples in Table 15.2, although disparities in the triple tradition occur, they are minimal; likewise, parallels in the double tradition indicate a solid literary link. Studying a synopsis, especially its index of parallels, reveals the details of both parallels and disparities in order, content, and style; fine synopses include Sparks, *A Synopsis of the Gospels* (1964) and Aland, *Synopsis of the Four Gospels* (1982) in English; and Aland, *Synopsis Quattuor Evangeliorum* (1996) and Huck, *Synopsis of the First Three Gospels* (1963) in Greek.

Regarding the contours of the synoptic problem, then, any solution needs to account for both agreements and disagreements in the overall shared framework, individual pericopes or complexes of pericopes, and intra-pericope content. Most investigators of the synoptic problem readily admit that today no solution explains all the data to

**Table 15.1** General order of the synoptic gospels

|  | Matthew | Mark | Luke |
| --- | --- | --- | --- |
| Infancy narrative | 1:1–2:23 |  | 1:5–2:52; 3:23–38 |
| Precursory events | 3:1–4:11 | 1:1–13 | 3:1–22; 4:1–13 |
| Jesus' days in Galilee | 4:12–18:35 | 1:14–9:50 | 4:14–9:50 |
| Journey to Jerusalem | 19:1–20:34 | 10:1–52 | 9:51–19:27 |
| Jesus' days in Jerusalem | 21:1–25:46 | 11:1–13:37 | 19:28–21:38 |
| Passion and death | 26:1–27:66 | 14:1–15:47 | 22:1–23:56 |
| The empty tomb | 28:1–8 | 16:1–8 | 24:1–12 |
| Resurrection appearances | 28:9–20 |  | 24:13–52 |

**Table 15.2**   Examples of the triple and double traditions

| Matthew | Mark | Luke |
|---|---|---|

**TRIPLE TRADITION examples (with disparities underlined; cf. Aland1982: 83, 115)**

| 9:15b | 2:20 | 5:35 |
|---|---|---|
| The days will come, when the bridegroom is taken away from them, and then they will fast. | The days will come, when the bridegroom is taken away from them, and then they will fast in <u>that day</u>. | The days will come, when the bridegroom is taken away from them, and then they will fast in <u>those days</u>. |
| 13:12 | 4:25 | 8:18b |
| For to him who has will more be given, and <u>he will have abundance</u>; <u>but</u> from him who has not, even what he has will be taken away. | For to him who has will more be given; and from him who has not, even what he has will be taken away. | ... for to him who has will more be given, and from him who has not, even what <u>he thinks that</u> he has will be taken away |

**DOUBLE TRADITION examples (with parallels in italics; Aland1982: 62, 187)**

| 7:12 | 6:31 |
|---|---|
| So whatever *you wish that men would do to you, do so to them*; for this is the law and the prophets. | And as *you wish that men would do to you, do so to them* |
| 5:25–6 | 12:58–9 |
| Make friends quickly *with your accuser*, while you are going with him to court, *lest* your accuser hand *you* over *to the judge, and the judge to the* guard, and *you* be put *in prison*; truly, *I say to you, you will never get out till you have paid the* last *penny*. | As you go *with your accuser* before the magistrate, make an effort to settle with him on the way, *lest* he drag *you to the judge, and the judge* hand you over *to the* officer, and the officer put *you in prison. I* tell *you, you will never get out till you have paid the* very *last* copper. |

everyone's satisfaction; every solution remains imperfect to a degree. While true, this fact supplies the necessary impetus for many to continue searching. J. A. Fitzmyer summarizes the grand shortcoming this way (Fitzmyer 1981: 63):

[The synoptic problem is] a problem that has thus far failed to find a fully satisfying solution. The main reason for this failure is the absence of adequate data for judgment about it. Extrinsic, historically trustworthy data about the composition of these Gospels are totally lacking, and the complexity of the traditions embedded in them, the evangelists' editorial redaction of them, and their free composition bedevil all attempts to analyze objectively the intrinsic data with critical literary methods.

It is fitting to ask what arguments must be furnished by any viable solution to explain sufficiently the two rudiments mentioned above: the earliest gospel and the direction of literary dependence.

## The Problem of Priority: Which Gospel Came First?

Given their literary interdependence, the logical question is which came first, Matthew, Mark, or Luke? The earliest, having "priority," would then serve as a *source* for one or both of the others. Even though in theory the priority of any of them is possible, current research focuses most heavily on Mark, and, to a lesser extent, Matthew. Markan priority means that Mark serves as a source for either Matthew or Luke or both; conversely, Matthean priority means that Matthew functions as a source for Mark or Luke or both. How is that determined? What arguments support the claim? For the most part, it is solution-specific; see "Prevailing solutions to the synoptic problem" below. Although it sounds simple, the "priority" concept belies underlying complexity due to the number and import of the exceptions found in any solution. In brief, to answer or account for the exceptions, either non-extant or hypothetical sources have been variously proposed; examples include an ur-Mark (a pre-canonical Mark, sometimes called proto-Mark), a deutero-Mark (a post-canonical Mark), a pre-Matthean translated Aramaic sayings source, the source Q (see Chapter 16, "Q: The Sayings Source," in this volume). A further caveat: in describing the three prevailing solutions, two proposing Markan priority and one Matthean, it is a challenge to use vocabulary not favoring one solution over another; this essay attempts to avoid as much bias as possible and still convey the synoptic problem's pith.

## Direction of Dependence

Determining priority first naturally narrows the number of possible configurations vis-à-vis how the gospels interconnect. More specifically, with respect to the other two, do they use the earliest gospel as a source *independently*, or does one use *both* the earliest *and* the other? Again the answer is solution-specific. Shown in Figure 15.3, if the earliest gospel is denoted by A and the other two by B and B', five possible solutions or configurations of literary dependence exist. While each is possible, the first three exhibit the most plausibility in light of the strictly linear relationship of the last two.

### Prevailing Solutions to the Synoptic Problem

After traversal of a brief history and summary of the synoptic problem, it is fitting to become acquainted with three solutions currently in vogue, namely, the Two-Document

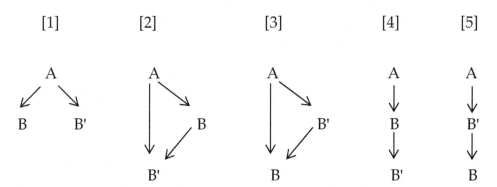

**Figure 15.3**

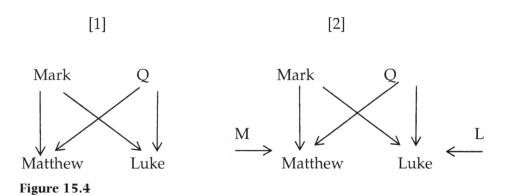

**Figure 15.4**

hypothesis, the Farrer–Goulder hypothesis, and the Neo-Griesbach hypothesis (sometimes called the Two-Gospel hypothesis).

### The Two–Document hypothesis

Historically, as noted, the Two-Document hypothesis, also called the Two-Source hypothesis or theory, emerged from biblical analysis in nineteenth-century Germany; it is today the most widely accepted solution. In the Two-Document hypothesis, three propositions obtain: first, the priority of Mark, making it a source for Matthew and Luke; second, also a source for Matthew and Luke, a hypothetical "sayings" source, whose moniker, Q, probably derives from *Quelle*, German for "source;" and third, the *independent* composition of Matthew and Luke (see Chapter 16 in this volume).

Markan priority anchors the Two-Document hypothesis, shown in Figure 15.4[1].[3] In 1924, British scholar Burnett Hillman Streeter published *The Four Gospels: A Study of Origins*, laying out five arguments for Markan priority: (1) Matthew contains about 90 percent of Mark and Luke over 50 percent in similar or identical language; (2) triple tradition material in an average section is seen almost identically in Matthew and Luke, either in both or alternatively; (3) the relative order of Markan material is supported by Matthew and Luke, and where either diverges from Mark, the other agrees with it; (4) the Greek of Mark is more primitive, and thus, appears to be earlier than that of Matthew and Luke; and (5) the distribution of Markan material in Matthew and Luke points to Mark as a single written document used by the authors of Matthew and Luke. Moreover, in addition to Mark and Q, suggests Streeter, material peculiar to each may indicate an earlier tradition. To wit, known as M or Special M, examples of Matthew-only text include the parable of weeds among wheat (Matt. 13:24–30), the unforgiving servant (18:23–35), and workers in the vineyard (20:1–16). Likewise, named L or Special L, examples of Luke-only material include the parable of the good Samaritan (Luke 10:29–37), the prodigal son (15:11–32), and the dishonest steward (16:1–13). Thus, if one considers M and L, or some parts of them, to be documentary sources, Streeter's concept of a "Four-Source" hypothesis also applies, as shown in Figure 15.4[2].

## Evidence against the Two–Document hypothesis

The Two-Document hypothesis has an Achilles' heel. If evidence existed that contraindicates the independence of Matthew and Luke, then the need for Q would disappear since the double tradition – roughly 230 verses common to Matthew and Luke – could logically be explained by the author of either Matthew or Luke simply copying the other. Numerous minor agreements between Matthew and Luke against Mark present such a challenge to the independence of Matthew and Luke. Although no consensus exists as to the precise number, Frans Neirynck (1974) compiled a cumulative list of over 700 minor agreements. The minor agreements are categorized as positive – identical or nearly identical agreements between Matthew and Luke in phrasing, grammar, syntax, or vocabulary – or negative – the identical absence of Markan material. A minor agreement example that is difficult to explain occurs in Mark 14:65, Matthew 26:67–68, and Luke 23:63–5, in the words shouted by those who held Jesus after his arrest. Matthew, Mark, and Luke all attest the imperative "Prophesy" followed in Matthew by "to us, Christ!" but only Matthew and Luke attest the next sentence, an identical sarcastic question, "Who is it that struck you?" If Matthew and Luke wrote independently, how is possible to explain this identical question at the identical location? Sometimes it is suggested the authors of Matthew and Luke copied from a version of Mark other than canonical Mark – either an earlier one (ur-Mark or proto-Mark) or a later one (deutero-Mark). According to these hypotheses, the earlier or later version of Mark was used by Matthew and Luke, not our canonical Mark, contained the question, "Who is it that struck you?" and thus the minor agreement is explained. A second example is the group of minor agreements, two negative and two positive, in Mark 5:27, Matthew 9:20, and Luke 8:44, the story of the woman with the hemorrhage who comes up behind Jesus and touches his garment. Absent from both Matthew and Luke are the Markan clause, "she had heard the things about Jesus" and the phrase, "in the crowd." Present in both Matthew and Luke but not Mark is a prefix on the Greek participle "coming up (to)" to describe the woman's approach to Jesus. More significantly, present in Matthew and Luke but not Mark is the word "fringe" to identify what the

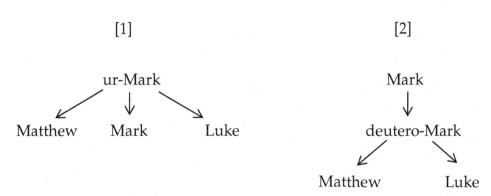

**Figure 15.5**

woman touches; Mark attests the more generic word "garment." Does this group of two negative and two positive minor agreements in such a small segment of text suggest coincidental but independent editing? Or does it point to a different version of Mark copied by the authors of Matthew and Luke?

The ur-Mark or deutero-Mark concept attractively accounts for the minor agreements of Matthew and Luke against Mark (Burkett, 2004; Sanders and Davies 1989: 73f.). Figure 15.5[1] shows how an *earlier* version of canonical Mark, ur-Mark, can be a source for not only Matthew and Luke but also canonical Mark. Consider, for instance, Jesus' saying in Matthew 12:8, Mark 2:28, and Luke 6:5, "the Son of Humanity is Lord of the Sabbath." In Mark, immediately preceding and paired with it is the saying, "the Sabbath was made for humanity, and not humanity for the Sabbath" (Mark 2:27), a saying absent from Matthew and Luke. Did Matthew and Luke independently decide to omit it or did they copy from an earlier version of Mark that did not have it? Conversely, shown in Figure 15.5[2], another possibility suggests the authors of Matthew and Luke copied from a version of Mark *later* than canonical Mark, namely, deutero-Mark. In the same example, the editor of deutero-Mark would have "improved" canonical Mark by deleting the saying, "the Sabbath was made for humanity, and not humanity for the Sabbath," and thus the authors of Matthew and Luke could not be aware of it since they used (the earlier) canonical Mark. Albert Fuchs, in his five-volume *Spuren von Deuteromarkus* (2004, 2007), has devoted extensive study to deutero-Mark to account for the minor agreements of Matthew and Luke against canonical Mark. While attractive, the ur-Mark or deutero-Mark theory adds a distinct level of complexity to any solution.

In addition to the minor agreements problem are the so-called "Mark-Q" overlaps, an embarrassment to the Two-Document hypothesis that raises questions about the independence of Matthew and Luke (Stein 1987). For example, the parable of the mustard seed is found in the triple tradition (Matt. 13:31–2; Mark 4:30–2; Luke 13:18–19). In Mark, however, it is preceded by and paired with a parable unique to Mark, the seed growing secretly (Mark 4:26–9); in Matthew and Luke, it is followed by and paired with the parable of the yeast (Matt. 13:33; Luke 13:20–1). Thus it is suggested the mustard seed parable was paired with the yeast parable in Q, resulting in an overlap with the mustard seed parable in Mark. Likewise, analysis of the Beelzebul controversy in Matthew 12:24–32, Mark 3:23–30, and Luke 11:15–22 shows seeming overlaps between Mark and "Q." Although problematic to the Two-Document hypothesis, "Mark-Q" overlaps do explain certain minor agreements of Matthew and Luke against Mark.

Advocates of the Two-Document hypothesis admit the difficulty in accounting for minor agreements between Matthew and Luke but often understand them as coincidences of independent redaction, evidence of textual corruption (Streeter 1930: 306ff.), or instances of overlapping oral tradition (Stein 1987: 113ff.). Challengers of the Two-Document hypothesis quickly point out that the sheer number of minor agreements militates against the Two-Document hypothesis as a viable solution to the synoptic problem.

### The Farrer–Goulder hypothesis, or Mark without Q

In 1955, Austin Farrer proposed a solution to the synoptic problem, built on Markan priority but without the need for Q (Farrer 1955). Shown in Figure 15.6, Farrer's hypothesis is that, if the author of Luke copied from both Mark and Matthew, Q is dispensable. This hypothesis was taken up and furthered by Farrer's student, Michael Goulder; hence, it is often called the Farrer–Goulder hypothesis.

Questions about Lukan primitivity arise again. If Matthew was written before Luke, how is apparent Lukan primitivity explained, and indeed, primitivity that alternates between Matthew and Luke? In the Beatitudes (Matthew 5:2–12; Luke 6:20–3), for example, there has been almost unanimous agreement that Luke 6:20b ("Blessed are the poor") is more primitive than Matthew 5:3a ("Blessed are the poor in spirit"). The addition of "in spirit" by Matthew's author is usually said to dovetail neatly with the Matthean theological agenda. Mark Goodacre, an adherent of the Farrar–Goulder hypothesis, however, replies by arguing that Lukan primitivity in this case is simply presumed by scholars (2001: 133ff.). He offers an equally plausible idea: the *removal* of "in spirit" by Luke's author neatly dovetails with the Lukan theological agenda of attending to the poor and destitute. Goodacre argues Lukan secondarity should not be dismissed in light of equally plausible arguments for Matthean primitivity. Problematic for the Farrar–Goulder hypothesis are the dissimilarities in the Matthean and Lukan infancy and resurrection narratives. Both infancy narratives (Matt. 1–2; Luke 1–2) contain certain themes intrinsic to the story, for example, (1) Jesus' parents are named

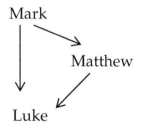

**Figure 15.6**

Mary and Joseph; (2) Jesus was born in the city of Bethlehem; and (3) the family ends up living in Nazareth. If Matthew served as a source for Luke, the striking differences must also be explained, for instance, (1) in Matthew, Mary and Joseph appear to live in Bethlehem already but in Luke, they travel there; (2) in Matthew, an angel speaks to Joseph but in Luke, he speaks to Mary; (3) in Matthew, Gentile Magi come to worship Jesus but in Luke, Jewish shepherds; and (4) in Matthew, the family from Bethlehem flees to Egypt only to end up settling in Nazareth, but in Luke, the family does not travel to Egypt, rather it returns home to Nazareth. Disparities outweigh similarities in the distinctive resurrection appearances in Matthew and Luke as well (Matt. 28:9–10, 16–20; Luke 24:13–53).

### The Neo–Griesbach hypothesis

The Neo-Griesbach hypothesis, also called the Two-Gospel hypothesis, is a revival of the eighteenth-century proposal by Johann Jakob Griesbach shown in Figure 15.2. Because of an emphasis on the literary relationship between Matthew and Mark, Griesbach's theory left the Matthew–Luke relationship somewhat open-ended. In the twentieth century, a revival of the Griesbach hypothesis, most notably by William Farmer in *The Synoptic Problem: A Critical Analysis* (1976), addressed this situation. Based on Matthean priority as well as Luke's dependence on Matthew and Mark's dependence on Matthew and Luke, the Neo-Griesbach hypothesis requires no Q sayings source since the double tradition is accounted for by Luke's author copying from Matthew. The author of Mark then copied material from Matthew and Luke when they agreed, but copied from one or the other or neither when they disagreed. As a result, Matthew and Luke do not generally agree with each other against Mark.

### Evidence against the Neo–Griesbach hypothesis

The Neo-Griesbach hypothesis faces major challenges of a qualitative rather than quantitative nature (Tuckett 1983). Since Mark would be an abridgement of Matthew and Luke, the Neo-Griesbach hypothesis must explain the omission of germane material from Matthew and Luke. Why would the author of Mark omit the Lord's Prayer (Matt. 6:9–13; Luke 11:2–4) or key sayings from the Matthean Sermon on the Mount (Matt. 5–7) or Lukan parables such as the good Samaritan (Luke 10:30–7) or the prodigal son (Luke 15:11–32)? The Markan abridgement also requires a puzzling dissection of the Matthean sermons. Further, the Neo-Griesbach hypothesis must adequately explain passages in which Luke is considered more primitive than Matthew. Due in part to the starkness of its structure and language, for instance, the Lord's Prayer in Luke (Luke 11:2–4) is usually considered more primitive than that in Matthew (Matt. 6:9–13). Since the Neo-Griesbach hypothesis requires Matthean priority, how does it explain the occurrences of seeming primary material in Luke? Even in Griesbach's time, supporters of his theory questioned these instances of apparent Lukan primitivity.

## Major Issues and Directions in Recent Study

Noted at the beginning of this essay, synoptic problem research has recently experienced a surge in the number of publications that offer new theories as well as fresh perspectives on and reassessments of existing ones. As a result, the Two-Document hypothesis, whose supremacy was at one time almost incontrovertible, is now more regularly called into question. Coming out are fresh perspectives on the *Gospel of Thomas* (see below) and the *Marcionite Gospel* (Klinghardt 2008) as they relate to the synoptic problem. Furthermore, forthcoming is a volume of significant essays presented by a group of specialists at the Oxford Conference on the Synoptic Problem in 2008; for a summary of these papers on topics such as the Farrer–Goulder hypothesis, the *Gospel of Thomas*, the Griesbach hypothesis, the minor agreements, synopses, and the Two-Document hypothesis, see Batovici 2009.

Mark Goodacre, a noted synoptic problem scholar, suggests those who actually study or write about the synoptic problem are quite evenly divided on their allegiance to the Two-Document hypothesis, whereas those whose scholarly focus lies elsewhere adopt "a kind of blithe confidence, almost a complacency over the correctness of the Two-Source Theory" (Goodacre 2001: 24).

Solutions other than the Two-Document hypothesis, the Farrer–Goulder hypothesis, and the Neo-Griesbach hypothesis have so far garnered only minor support, but that may not hold for the future. The Boismard hypothesis is fascinating as the most technically complex solution proposed so far. A Multi-Source theory from Delbert Burkett (2004) proposes a two-tiered set of "proto-Mark" sources. Finally, Matthean posteriority is explored by Ronald V. Huggins (1992).

### The Boismard hypothesis

The Boismard hypothesis attests to the principle that the greater the number of problems solved, the greater the complexity of the solution (Benoit and Boismard 1972). The Boismard solution, shown in Figure 15.7, proposes a Palestinian proto-gospel (A), a Gentile–Christian revision of it (B), and an early independent document, perhaps from Palestine (C) as well as the Q sayings source, an "interim Matthew" (dependent on A and Q), an "interim Mark" (dependent on A, B, and C), and a "proto-Luke" (dependent on "interim Matthew," B, C, and Q). Canonical Matthew is thus dependent on "interim Mark" and "interim Matthew." Canonical Mark is at least dependent on "interim Mark" with perhaps a link to "interim Matthew." Canonical Luke is dependent on "interim Mark" and "proto-Luke."

Its complexity notwithstanding, the Boismard solution accounts for all problematic circumstances so far identified. Because it posits at least six hypothetical documents in addition to the Q sayings source, to trace the directions of literary dependence along this array of trajectories means the adoption of support for evidence yet to be discovered.

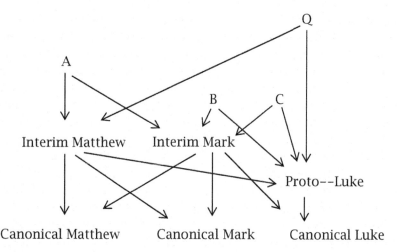

**Figure 15.7**

*A new Multi-Source theory*

A new Multi-Source theory argued by Delbert Burkett (2004) derives from a careful analysis of key redactional elements in Mark, Matthew, and Luke. Arguing that none of the synoptic gospels could have been the source for the others, Burkett's hypothesis understands a "proto-Mark" source, edited into "proto-Mark A" and "proto-Mark B," which in turn along with Q served as a source for canonical Matthew and Luke, respectively. Both "proto-Mark A" and "proto-Mark B" served as a source for canonical Mark as well as K, which is simply Markan redaction and material peculiar to Mark. Although complex, due to the rigor of Burkett's arguments, this theory deserves attention and exploration.

*A Matthean posteriority hypothesis*

Ronald V. Huggins (1992) explores the theory of Matthean posteriority built on a configuration of Markan priority, Lukan dependence on Mark, and Matthean dependence on Luke and Mark. Not often addressed, this configuration offers answers to major problems. The need for Q or other hypothetical documents is eliminated and the minor agreements and problems with Lukan dependence on Matthew are explained. Like Burkett's new Multi-Source theory, Matthean posteriority deserves further attention.

## Concluding Observations

No solution to the synoptic problem has yet been accepted as the *opinio communis*. On the one hand, the Two-Document hypothesis, the Farrer–Goulder hypothesis, and the Neo-Griesbach hypothesis in their contrasting ways explain *almost* all literary

interdependencies among the synoptic gospels. The Two-Document hypothesis operates effectively at the level of generality but less successfully explains the numerous
minor agreements between Matthew and Luke. The Farrer–Goulder hypothesis dispenses with the need for a hypothetical document, Q, but must answer the question of
apparent alternating primitivity in Matthew and Luke. The Neo-Griesbach hypothesis
does not sufficiently explain the rationale behind the literary license and editorial judgment exercised by the author of Mark, although it solves the synoptic problem at a
purely technical level. On the other hand, complex solutions require a multi-tiered
framework of hypothetical documents to account for all the evidence. To many who
observe current developments in synoptic problem research, a solution seems farther
away than ever. The trend toward complexity shows dissatisfaction with the simpler
yet imperfect solutions. Skepticism of complex solutions, however, leads to the conclusion there may be no recoverable solution. Until scholars agree that recoverability is
impossible or a solution obtains permanent, unquestioned acceptance, fresh approaches
and improvements to existing solutions must and will continue to be sought.

## Notes

1   This section owes much to the synoptic problem history found in Dungan 1999 as well as
Kümmel 1972.
2   Exceptions occurring within the triple tradition tend to follow a three-part pattern (Stein
1987: 34–7; Sanders and Davies 1989: 88ff.). First, when Matthew's gospel diverges from
the parallel sequence, Mark and Luke still agree. In Matthew 4:23, for instance, the summary
of Jesus' teaching in Galilee shows up out of relative order when compared to Mark 1:39 and
Luke 4:44; or, in Matthew 10:1–4 the selection of the twelve appears out of order when
viewed against Mark 3:13–19 and Luke 6:12–16. Second, when Luke's gospel diverges from
the parallel sequence, Mark and Matthew still agree. In Luke 4:16–30, for example, the rejection of Jesus at Nazareth is out of relative order when compared to Matthew 13:53–8 and
Mark 6:1–6a. Third, as a rule Mark's gospel does not diverge at all.
3   Evidence of "Markan priority" is sometimes considered biased toward the solution it supports.
Occasionally preferred is the concept that Mark stands in the "middle" between Matthew and
Luke. "Middle" Mark suggests a more objective, less biased assessment of the evidence; thus,
in the Two-Document hypothesis, the "middle" position of Mark translates to Markan prior-
ity, whereas in the Neo-Griesbach hypothesis, the "middle" position of Mark translates to
Markan posteriority. See Goodacre 2001: 50ff.

## Annotated Bibliography

Aland, K. *Synopsis of the Four Gospels: English Edition*. United Bible Societies, 1982. Using the
Revised Standard Version, 2nd edn., this English synopsis provides a valuable index (pp.
341–55) of all gospel pericopes and their parallels placed in adjacent columns for ease of
viewing.
Aland, K. *Synopsis Quattuor Evangeliorum*. 15th edn. Stuttgart: Deutsche Bibelgesellschaft, 1996.
Using the *Novum Testamentum Graece*, 27th edn., this Greek synopsis provides a valuable
index (*Conspectus locorum parallelorum evangeliorum*) of all gospel pericopes and their

parallels placed in adjacent columns. Pericope descriptions are given in German, Latin, and English.

Batovici, D. "The Oxford Conference on the Synoptic Problem." *Currents in Biblical Research* 7 (2009). 245–71. Summaries of all the essays presented at the conference by a group of specialists on the synoptic problem; topics include the Farrer–Goulder hypothesis, the *Gospel of Thomas*, the Griesbach hypothesis, the minor agreements, synopses, and the Two-Document hypothesis.

Benoit, P. and M.-É. Boismard. *Synopse des quatre Évangiles en Français avec parallèles des apocrypes et des pères*. Vol. 2. Paris: Les Éditions du Cerf, 1972. This classic Boismard text argues the complex theory of a multi-tiered set of hypothetical documents used as sources for the canonical gospels. Due to the intricacy of its dependencies, this theory is recognized as the example *par excellence* of complexity.

Burkett, D. *Rethinking the Gospel Sources: From Proto-Mark to Mark*. New York: T. & T. Clark International, 2004. Burkett proposes a new Multi-Source theory based on an impressive analysis of key redactional elements in Mark, Matthew, and Luke. Arguing that none of the synoptic gospels could have been the source for the others, Burkett's hypothesis understands a proto-Mark source edited into "proto-Mark A" and "proto-Mark B," which in turn along with Q served as a source for canonical Matthew and Luke, respectively.

Carlson, Stephen C. <http://www.hypotyposeis.org/synoptic-problem/ and http://www.mind-spring.com/~scarlson/synopt/catalog.htm>. Web resources for the synoptic problem.

Dungan, D. L. *A History of the Synoptic Problem: The Canon, the Text, the Composition, and the Interpretation of the Gospels*. Anchor Bible Reference Library. New York: Doubleday, 1999. This volume is a valuable, comprehensive treatment of the historical roots and development of the synoptic problem, beginning in the first century and traversing subsequent centuries. An adherent of the Neo-Griesbach hypothesis, Dungan engages the reader in the history of the synoptic problem within its religious, political, and economic contexts.

Farmer, W. R. *The Synoptic Problem: A Critical Analysis*. New York: Macmillan, 1964; repr. Western North Carolina Press, Dillsboro, NC, 1976. This classic text revives the eighteenth-century Griesbach hypothesis. Farmer argues for Matthean priority, Lukan dependence on Matthew, and Markan posteriority. Technically a complete solution to the synoptic problem, this theory must face qualitative questions about the omission of so much germane material from Matthew and Luke.

Farrer, A. M. "On Dispensing with Q." Pp. 55–88 in *Studies in the Gospels: Essays in the Memory of R. H. Lightfoot*. Edited by D. Nineham. Oxford: Basil Blackwell, 1955. This classic essay by Farrer initiated study into a solution to the synoptic problem that retains Markan priority but dispenses with "Q."

Fitzmyer, J. A. *The Gospel According to Luke (I–IX)*. Anchor Bible vol. 28. New York: Doubleday, 1981. A definitive commentary on the Luke, it is a classic and reliable text for the study of the third gospel.

Foster, P. "Is It Possible to Dispense with Q?" *Novum Testamentum* 45 (2003), 313–26. A valuable assessment of the Farrer–Goulder hypothesis, this article highlights the questions that must be asked of any solution that challenges the Two-Document hypothesis. Given a judicious evaluation is the Ronald V. Huggins' theory of Matthean posteriority.

Fuchs, A. *Spuren von Deuteromarkus*. Five volumes. Münster: Lit Verlag, 2004, 2007. Technically sound and comprehensive, this work shows that all minor agreements are explained by an editor of our canonical Mark, whose redacted version of Mark (deutero-Mark) was used by the authors of Matthew and Luke.

Goodacre, M. ⟨http://www.ntgateway.com/⟩. Web resource for the synoptic problem; also "NTGateway" may be followed on Twitter.com.

Goodacre, M. *The Synoptic Problem: A Way Through the Maze*. London: Sheffield Academic Press, 2001. Goodacre gives both the beginner and advanced student of the synoptic problem an accessible means by which to understand it. An adherent of the Farrer–Goulder hypothesis, Goodacre argues for its viability in lieu of the Two-Document hypothesis and others.

Goulder, M. D. *Luke: A New Paradigm*. *Journal for the Study of the New Testament* Supplementary Series, 20. Sheffield: Sheffield Academic Press, 1989. A student of Austin Farrer, Michael Goulder took up the hypothesis of his teacher and argues for Markan priority without the necessity of a Q sayings source. In fact, Goulder argues that Q, M, and L did not exist at all.

Griesbach, J. J. *Synopsis Evangeliorum Matthäi Marci et Lucae una cum iis Joannis pericopis quae omnino cum caeterorum Evangelistarum narrationibus conferendae sunt ... J. J. Griesbach*. [A Synopsis of the Gospels of Matthew, Mark, and Luke, Together with those Pericopes in which all the Evangelists Can Be Compared as to their Narratives. The Text Edited by J. J. Griesbach]. 2nd edn. Halle, 1776.

Griesbach, J. J. *Marci Evangelium totum e Matthaei et Lucae commentariis decerptum esse monstratur*. Jena: Stranckmann, 1789–90.

Hawkins, J. C. *Horae Synopticae: Contributions to the Study of the Synoptic Problem*. 2nd edn. Oxford: Clarendon Press, 1909. Still used today, this classic volume is a comprehensive compilation and analysis of stylistic features characteristic of Matthew, Mark, and Luke as well as their interrelationships.

Huck, A. *Synopsis of the First Three Gospels*. 9th edn. Revised by Hans Lietzmann. Oxford: Basil Blackwell, 1935; repr. 1963. A high-quality Greek synopsis, whose English edition was translated by F. L. Cross.

Huggins, R. V. "Matthean Posteriority: A Preliminary Proposal." *Novum Testamentum* 34 (1992), 1–22. In a novel configuration theory of synoptic gospel interdependence, this article argues for Matthean dependence primarily on Mark but secondarily on Luke. Lukan material is always more primitive than Matthean.

Klinghardt, M. "The Marcionite Gospel and the Synoptic Problem: A New Suggestion." *Novum Testamentum* 50 (2008), 1–27. The inclusion of the Marcionite gospel in the solution to the synoptic problem avoids problems inherent in the Two-Document hypothesis or the Farrer–Goulder hypothesis as treated by Mark Goodacre.

Kloppenborg Verbin, J. S. *Excavating Q: The History and Setting of the Sayings Gospel*. Edinburgh: T. & T. Clark, 2000. This volume contains an excellent overview of the synoptic problem. Cohering with the Two-Document hypothesis, the Kloppenborg discussion of the synoptic problem is recommended for its comprehensive quality.

Kümmel, W. G. *Das Neue Testament: Geschichte der Erforschung seiner Probleme*. Freiburg: Karl Alber, 1970. [*The New Testament: The History of the Investigation of its Problems*. Trans. S. McLean Gilmour and Howard C. Kee. Nashville: Abingdon Press, 1972.] A most comprehensive historical treatment of New Testament issues, including significant portions of quoted primary criticism.

Neirynck, F. *The Minor Agreements of Matthew and Luke Against Mark, with a Cumulative List*. Bibliotheca Ephemeridum Theologicarum Lovaniensium, 37. Leuven: Leuven University Press, 1974. This important volume records the cumulative total of over 700 negative and positive minor agreements of Matthew and Luke against Mark, compiled from the works of over thirty-five scholars. A section on stylistic features of agreement in Matthew and Luke against Mark concludes the volume.

Neirynck, F. "Synoptic Problem." *The New Jerome Biblical Commentary*. Edited by R. E. Brown, J. A. Fitzmyer, and R. F. Murphy. Engelwood Cliffs, NJ: Prentice-Hall, 1990. An adherent of the Two-Document hypothesis, Neirynck lays out a description of the synoptic problem in a succinct manner. This reference is recommended as a valuable source for comprehensive, precise explanations of synoptic gospel interrelationships.

Sanders, E. P. and M. Davies. *Studying the Synoptic Gospels*. London: SCM Press, 1989. Sanders and Davies offer one of the most objective descriptions of the synoptic problem. Built on and developed from numerous pertinent examples, this treatment gives the beginner or advanced scholar a good foundation in both simple and complex theories.

Sparks, H. F. D. *A Synopsis of the Gospels: The Synoptic Gospels with the Johannine Parallels*. Philadelphia: Fortress Press, 1964. An English synopsis, this volume provides comprehensive details of the triple and double tradition.

Stein, R. *The Synoptic Problem: An Introduction*. Grand Rapids: Baker Book House, 1987. In this thorough and clearly written volume, Stein explores the contours of the synoptic problem. He uses numerous well-placed examples and a developed approach to argue for the merits of the Two-Document hypothesis.

Streeter, B. H. *The Four Gospels: A Study of Origins*. London: Macmillan, 1930. In this classic text Streeter outlines the now famous arguments for Markan priority in the Two-Document hypothesis, which he argues is really a "Four-Source" hypothesis when M and L are included. Streeter also discusses the existence of proto-Luke.

Tuckett, C. M. *The Revival of the Griesbach Hypothesis: An Analysis and Appraisal*. Cambridge: Cambridge University Press, 1983.

Tuckett, C. M. s.v. "Synoptic Problem." *The Anchor Bible Dictionary*. Vol. 6. New York: Doubleday, 1992. Tuckett's article offers an introduction to the synoptic problem and provides a well-honed argument for the Two-Document hypothesis.

CHAPTER 16

# Q: The Sayings Source

Ronald A. Piper

## Major Issues and Directions in Recent Study of Q

Modern scholarship of the New Testament gospels has long reckoned with the possibility that prior to our written gospels (and even contemporaneous with them) other traditions about Jesus might have circulated amongst early Christ-followers. Some of these traditions may have been gathered into collections, but, if so, the fact that they have not been preserved means that they are effectively lost to us. They therefore become topics of speculation, and this has been particularly evident in source criticism of the canonical gospels. According to the Two-Document hypothesis, which has had a dominant (but not unchallenged) position in source criticism during the previous century, the earliest gospel was Mark. Matthew and Luke were both believed independently to have used Mark, accounting for much material that seems to be in common to Mark, Matthew, and Luke. Matthew and Luke, however, also share Jesus-traditions that are not found in Mark. An example of this material common to Matthew and Luke is the longer version of Jesus' temptation by Satan in Luke 4:1–13/Matthew 4:1–11 (cited hereafter as Q 4:1–13 whereby a Q text is identified by its Lukan location). This example happens to comprise both narrative and teaching material, but most of the traditions that Matthew and Luke share (which they do not derive from Mark) are *sayings* of Jesus with little narrative. So, complementary to a belief in the priority of Mark, the Two-Document hypothesis proposed that Matthew and Luke had independent access to another common source, a "lost" *sayings source* labeled "Q" (from the German word *Quelle*, meaning "source").

If such a source for traditions of Jesus' sayings did exist, then it would have considerable significance. Not only might it be important for understanding the source of many of the shared traditions found in Matthew and Luke that cannot be found in Mark, but also such a source *behind* the gospels of Matthew and Luke would have been placed closer *in time* to the historical Jesus than these gospels themselves. Would the reconstruction of this source therefore bring us also closer *in substance* to the historical Jesus than the canonical gospels that followed?

Many issues have characterized discussion of Q in the last century. Could such a collection of sayings of Jesus, with relatively little narrative content, have really existed as a "source"? Because the reconstructions of Q generally lack any narrative of Jesus' death and resurrection in particular, is it thinkable that such a source would have had currency in the early church? Are there other, and better, explanations for how Matthew and Luke might have come to share non-Markan traditions about Jesus? While, on the one hand, the recent publication of a critical text of Q by the International Q Project has given a sense of "reality" to Q as a *document*, on the other hand growing interest in ancient orality has raised the question of whether in fact we are not really dealing with clusters of traditions that circulated and grew in an oral culture and should not be considered in a documentary way at all.

Behind such debates are found other concerns. J. S. Kloppenborg, *The Formation of Q* (1987), presented a powerful case for Q having a compositional history as a document. At the earliest stage of Q there was a collection of six "wisdom" speeches that were sapiential in their mode of argument. This then expanded into a set of sayings that was more polemical and hostile in nature, particularly in its stance towards Israel. Then a final stage of redaction occurred, adding a more biographical element to the collection, with stories such as the Q temptation narrative, referred to earlier. Although Kloppenborg himself did not assert that the early sapiential strand was truest to the historical Jesus, other scholars such as Burton Mack (1993) and J. Dominic Crossan (1991) did pursue such an argument. This has had great influence on recent study of the historical Jesus, and particularly for those who argue that Jesus preached a message of the kingdom that was free of apocalyptic ideas, a kingdom that was primarily for the "present." This, it has been suggested, is precisely what one finds in the earliest stratum of Q before it became mixed with eschatological pronouncements of impending judgment.

Such views have not gone unopposed, but Q tends to remain at the heart of the controversy. In contrast to a view of Jesus as an (admittedly controversial) teacher of wisdom, R. Horsley (1991, 1999), for example, has argued for a more eschatologically oriented Jesus and also for a view of Q that gives greater recognition to a mixing of sapiential and eschatological ideas even in the earliest clusters of Q traditions, which may have been oral in any case. For Horsley the heart of the Q message focuses upon a prophetic call to local renewal, as part of a socio-economic opposition to the ruling elite, and he locates this early message of resistance in (perhaps largely oral) clusters of "Q" sayings. For some other scholars, any multi-layered compositional theory of a document Q, such as that of Kloppenborg, has another consequence. It interposes editors with particular interests between the historical Jesus and the final form of Q. Jens Schröter, for one, suggests that such compositional documentary theories give insufficient recognition to the *accurate* recollection of Jesus' teaching in the largely oral culture. Thus the ramifications of the debates about the composition and documentary character of Q are widespread.

If there did exist a document Q, gathered and edited at one or more stages and reflecting certain identifiable concerns, then one also has to consider the possible existence of "Q people" associated with this process. It is unlikely that such a process of compilation existed in a vacuum. This in turn raises questions about the social location of such "Q people." W. Arnal (2001) argues that *village scribes* may have been responsible for the composition of Q, due in part to a negative evaluation of urban areas and institutions. While Q seems to represent "low" rather than "high" culture, it nevertheless required a compiler with some scribal skill. Thus the result of a documentary interpretation of Q is increasingly to attempt to reconstruct the social, geographical, and cultural setting of the "Q people." But even those less committed to a documentary theory of Q, such as Horsley, are often interested in this. As described above, for Horsley the social context is almost the key to his theory.

## Date and Place of Composition

Because the source Q is a hypothetical construction, it will be no surprise to find that ideas about its provenance are fluid. Yet the same is true for many New Testament writings that have been preserved. Whatever Q's origins, the hypothesis requires that Q was available to the writers of Matthew and Luke in the immediate post-70 period of the first century CE. Most Q scholars in fact now date Q between 40 and 70 CE, and C. Tuckett (1999) has argued that it is unwise to try to be more precise than this. B. H. Streeter (1924) located Q in Antioch around 50 CE, significantly earlier even than Mark. Because Matthew is also often located in Antioch, some decades later, Q might have been easily available to the author of this gospel. Locating Luke geographically is more difficult, but in view of Luke's self-avowed active research into sources of Jesus-traditions (Luke 1:1–4) his precise location may be of less relevance. Some scholars believe that Q was actually known to Mark, even though not much used by Mark, and if so then it must pre-date Mark. Yet it is probably preferable, and certainly more cautious, to argue that Mark may have shared a few traditions with Q, but without knowing the final form of Q. In this case, it is not necessary (on these grounds) that the *final* form of Q is placed much earlier than 70 CE.

Are there other grounds relevant to dating or location? G. Theissen (1991) has argued that the details of the Q temptation story, believed by Kloppenborg to have been one of the latest stories to be incorporated into Q, allude to the crisis created by Caligula in the early 40s. In addition he finds Q close to the ideology of Paul at several points, and also believes that Q depicts a mission to Israel that is early. Myllykoski (1996) and Kloppenborg have both challenged Theissen's arguments, however. Indeed, an increasing number of Q scholars have begun to believe that the *final* formulation of Q was very near the time of the first Jewish revolt, coming to a climax with the fall of Jerusalem in 70 CE. Kloppenborg finds the most decisive indications of this in the sayings about the abandonment of the temple in Q 13:34–5. These might have arisen any time from the early 60s to the early 70s. Because Kloppenborg believes, however, that other traditions were added to Q after Q 13:34–5, he is inclined to date the *final* form of Q slightly after the event of 70 CE. Those who judge Q to have gone through several stages of compilation must allow for some spread in the dating between the earliest and latest parts of Q. A date in the early 60s or earlier for the bulk of the Q traditions can help to explain the lack of clear evidence of concern about the Jewish war in much of the Q material, while a final form around or after 70 CE can explain traditions that seem to reflect knowledge of this event. Other arguments also come into play. A. Jacobson (1992) notes that the significant theme of the deuteronomistic tradition of the fate of the prophets is minor in later New Testament writings. Therefore its prominence in many Q sayings (see below) is likely to be evidence of an early stage of thinking for these sayings, which, he argues, is reflected also in the relatively undeveloped Christology of much of Q.

From this brief discussion, it is clear that the tendency of Q scholars to view Q either as a composition occurring in discrete stages or as a gradually accumulating compilation means that a determination of Q's dating must account for a process extending over several decades. The date of the "final" form of Q is very dependent upon which traditions are believed – whether on compositional grounds or on the basis of their content – to be latest. Assumptions about the proximity of Q 13:34–5 to the events of 70 CE have been crucial to such a judgment.

The fall of Jerusalem in 70 CE to the Roman siege has been less critical for delimiting the *geographical* origins of Q. Discussions about location have tended to be conducted on a broader front, taking into account the kind of social context presupposed in many of the Q sayings, references to places, inherent assumptions about audience, attitudes towards temple and Torah, and the like. J. Reed, W. Arnal and others (including Kloppenborg) have proposed a Galilean setting on the basis of how the sayings in Q cohere with what we believe that we know of the situation in first-century Galilee. The presumption of an Israelite context is common virtually to all the traditions of Q. Even the sayings often considered the latest, the sayings of the temptation story, explicitly appeal to the Torah. Reed (in Kloppenborg 1995) has argued that the second layer of material in Q centers around three Galilean towns: Capernaum, Chorazin, and Bethsaida. This, combined with a negative attitude to the hierocratic features of Jerusalem, is taken to support a social location in Galilee. There are in fact few actual mentions of Jerusalem in Q. More precisely, the failure to mention significant urban centers at all – even in Galilee (Tiberias, Sepphoris) – combined with a suspicion expressed in Q of urban institutions such as marketplaces, prisons, and law courts, directs the attention of several scholars to the *villages* of lower Galilee. Such a perspective complements the theory of Arnal regarding the composition of Q by village scribes, and the arguments of Horsley (among others) for a bias towards "low" culture and local renewal. In many circles, the coherence detected between Q and social conditions of Galilee in the mid-first century CE have resulted in a shift from earlier suggestions of an Antiochene origin for Q. A high confidence in any precise location is of course impossible. A recent attempt has been made by Larry Hurtado (2003) to argue that the most likely provenance for Q may be the "Hellenists," a group of Jewish Christians who spoke in Greek. A consequence of such a theory would be to widen the readership for Q well beyond Galilee.

Still focusing for a moment on Galilee, however, a rather different understanding of the Q tradents (the bearers of the Q traditions) has been suggested by some scholars. L. Vaage (1994), B. Mack (1993), and F. G. Downing (1992) have likened early Q tradents to an itinerant Cynic-like movement. Cynics displayed provocative counter-cultural attitudes and behaviors, and these three scholars have found important parallels between Cynics and the early aphoristic or sapiential sayings in Q. This theory has been strongly resisted, however, by several other scholars. H. D. Betz (1994) has raised doubts about whether Cynics were present at all in Galilee in the first century. Others, such as C. Tuckett (1989), have attacked the alleged parallels with Cynicism on the basis of content and dating. Because Cynics were normally associated with urban centers, which represent most strikingly the culture that the Cynics seek to subvert,

Jesus' apparent avoidance of cities in the Q tradition is considered by some scholars to be a significant difference from Cynic practices. At stake in this discussion are matters that go well beyond the location of the Q people. Can a Cynic Jesus still be a Jewish Jesus? How far removed were the earliest Christ-followers from the ideological soil of Jewish views about God and God's kingdom?

## Purpose

Such questions also lead to a consideration of the purpose(s) underlying the collection of the Jesus traditions in Q. Because Q is not a narrative account and because it also appears to lack a narrative of the death and resurrection stories of Jesus, Q does not really "tell the story of Jesus" like the canonical gospels. On most reconstructions, Q is an extended collection of sayings ascribed to Jesus, many of which may have originally been isolated sayings. To discover the purpose(s) for creating a compilation with the characteristics of Q requires some recognition of Q's distinctive genre, some analysis of the principles of the arrangement of the material, and some investigation of the main themes of the material and their coherence. Furthermore, if Q was composed in clearly defined stages, then one has to reckon with the possibility that different motives or purposes are to be associated with the different compositional layers.

Some of the earliest Q scholars, such as Harnack (1908), simply understood Q as an early attempt by Christ-followers to gather sayings that originated with the historical Jesus. Its usefulness, as a document mostly composed of teaching rather than narrative, was probably to provide a kind of guide for living. It was not long, however, before other aspects of Q became points of focus, such as the purportedly distinctive Christologies reflected in Q and how far these unlocked the purpose(s) of Q. A decisive step was taken by J. M. Robinson (1971), who observed that the genre of Q was akin to wisdom collections that had antecedents in works such as *Ahikar* and *Sirach* and successors in works such as the *Gospel of Thomas*, *Pistis Sophia*, and the *Sentences of Sextus*. Not only did Jesus' teaching in Q fall on a trajectory of "sayings of the sages," but also Jesus' message was understood in Q in a rather distinctive way, as the message of divine Sophia.

But what exactly was that message? Kloppenborg has argued that a key issue is to identify what has *salvific* value in Q. Because this hypothetical source seems to lack a narrative of Jesus' death and resurrection and to contain little evidence of a passion kerygma, what exactly is "saving" for those whom Q addresses? If much of Q is sapiential in nature, then is "knowledge" in some sense salvific for Q, placing it on a trajectory leading to full-blown Gnosticism? Yet Q seems less to promote an *esoteric* message than an announcement that God's kingdom requires attitudes of radical trust in God's care. Kloppenborg (2000: 392) writes that in the formative stage of Q "the kingdom sayings ... are connected with exhortations to a countercultural lifestyle that includes love of enemies, nonretaliation, debt forgiveness, and a willingness to expose oneself to danger, all undergirded by appeals to the superabundant care of a provident God." Kloppenborg argues, against much earlier German scholarship, that the Christology of Q is subservient to this purpose, even at the later redactional stage where Son of Man statements are more evident but "remain embedded in a broader strategy of defending the ethos of the Q group and threatening those who are seen as opponents" (2000: 392). In these later layers of Q the judgment against "this generation" comes to the fore (probably in response to the rejection of the message of the early Christ-followers by neighboring Jews), and apocalyptic tendencies accordingly become more evident as part of the defensive stance of the Q group.

There are of course many refinements and variations of such a theory. On the one hand, working from a similar stratification theory for Q, those like Mack and Vaage who support the Cynic hypothesis tend to emphasize how similar both the mission speech in Q and the subversive nature of the "sapiential" sayings are to the alternative reality advocated by Cynics, whose dominant concern was to subvert the current cultural and social order. Jesus was not to be interpreted so much as a figure standing within the epic of Israelite history but rather as a figure with a more general counter-cultural agenda. Only at later stages did Mack see Q being transformed, through secondary myth-making, into a people concerned with the prophetic and deuteronomistic history of Israel and its future apocalyptic hopes. Thus for him there seems to be not only a substantial change in purpose but also a significant change of ethos in the later stages of Q.

On the other hand, for those who are more critical of Kloppenborg's stratification theory, again the purposes of Q receive different emphasis. Migaku Sato, for example, has argued (based on a different redactional analysis of Q from that of Kloppenborg) that Q is modeled on prophetic books and is largely prophetic in nature. The effect is to put greater emphasis throughout Q on issues of how Q may be "divine speech." Such tendencies are also revealed, it is argued, in the association of Jesus with John the Baptist, the significance of the Son of Man sayings, and the pronouncement of judgment against "this generation." Horsley too is inclined, as we have seen, to see prophetic and sapiential strands as mixed closely together from the start, with the result that the purpose of Q is throughout to declare a prophetic message of renewal of local Jewish communities against the interests of the ruling elite. Whilst this could be said to be "counter-cultural," it is tied closely to conditions of first-century Jewish life in Palestine. Yet, contrary to Horsley, there remain significant clusters of sayings within Q in which prophetic themes are largely absent and in which the sanction for instruction is rarely an explicit reference to God or to eschatological judgment (as argued by R. Piper).

For those who are doubtful about the documentary nature of Q at all, "the purpose of Q" looks different again. J. P. Meier, for example, questions whether a coherent theology can be reconstructed, despite the efforts of scholars such as Kloppenborg to demonstrate both consistent rhetorical patterns and a broad set of consistent themes in Q. If no coherent theology can be reconstructed, and if no particular group of tradents can be identified with the collection and transmission of the Q material, then it is virtually impossible to discern a "purpose" for Q. It is simply a disparate collection of early sayings attributed to Jesus. Perhaps Q represents simply attempts to preserve the memory of what Jesus taught, whether orally or in written form. While this is attractive to many scholars, the ultimate question will be whether it does justice to the evidence for the selection and arrangement of the Q material. If a persuasive case can be made for the theological coherence of the Q traditions (preference for certain Christological understandings of Jesus, particularly understandings of the death and vindication of Jesus, distinctive and recurring aspects of Jesus' kingdom message and mission instructions, a distinctive motif of Jesus in relation to Sophia/Wisdom) in a way that sets Q apart from other gospel traditions, then questions about purpose or communicative intention become harder to escape. We shall return to this shortly.

## Literary Genre

At first glance, Q might appear to be a loose collection of sayings attributed to Jesus, including some sayings with brief descriptive settings (*chriae*), but with little overall narrative framing and with only a few narrative accounts (in addition to the Q temptation story in Q 4:1–13, note also the healing of the centurion's servant in Q 7:1–10). As mentioned earlier, reconstructions of Q tend in particular to lack any passion narrative describing the death of Jesus. Thus the reconstruction of Q looks rather unlike any of the canonical gospels and has frequently been described as the "sayings source" or as a "sayings collection."

Underlying the larger collection "Q," several sub-collections of sayings with a particular rhetorical formulation have been identified (see Zeller 1977, Piper 1989; Kloppenborg 2000; Kirk 1998). Examples include the collected sayings on asking and receiving in Q 11:9–13 and on anxiety about material subsistence in Q 12:22–31. These include gnomic sayings and admonitions, motive clauses, and rhetorical questions, arranged as carefully formulated arguments similar to patterns typical of the "instruction" genre of the ancient Near East. The use of such argumentation and sayings drawn from everyday life persuades an audience in a way very different from (for example) prophetic threat or announcement.

These collections are, however, embedded in a larger body of material. The genre of this larger whole is more difficult to align with other instances of literature known from the period. As it stands, Q shows evidence of some limited narrative framing, which Kloppenborg (as we have seen) attributes to the secondary, redactional stage of Q when the instructions were supplemented with other sayings of a more prophetic nature. The description of genre for Q as a whole that is preferred by Kloppenborg is that of an "expanded instruction," although he also shows interest in F. Gerald Downing's arguments that "final" Q resembles *bios* literature (analogous to *Demonax*) in several respects, despite its limited interest in recording the deeds of Jesus. It is certainly true that the final formulation of Q represents a complex genre in which collections of instruction are either embedded in or were the formative stage for the growth of a larger work. Whether this is a step towards a primitive biography or simply an expanded instruction is still a matter of discussion. Other scholars like Horsley believe the genre of Q was a mixed one from the start and was not achieved developmentally. Less likely is Sato's judgment that Q was modeled upon prophetic books. There are no declarations "Thus says Yahweh" in Q. Even recognition of a theological appraisal of Jesus as in the line of the prophets is not sufficient to define the genre of Q as modeled on prophetic books.

Occasionally modern Q scholars will refer to "the Sayings *Gospel* Q." This is not an attempt, however, to suggest that Q is of the same genre as the canonical gospels, which have a strong narrative sequence and are marked biographical elements. Indeed, "gospel" is barely a proper literary category or genre in any case, for many works were called "gospels" in early Christianity that have no distinct literary features in common. The Gospel of Luke is very different from the *Gospel of Thomas* or the *Gospel of Truth*. Those who prefer to refer to Q as a sayings gospel therefore primarily do so as a serious way of depicting it as a source of the sayings and deeds of Jesus that is able to stand on its own and to make "a theological claim."

## Literary and Compositional Analysis

It will be clear from the preceding sections that diverse views exist regarding the literary unity of Q and the stages of its composition. As Arland Jacobson (1992: 61) notes, because "we are dealing with traditional sayings material rather than free composition by an author, we might expect to find the kind of miscellaneous assortment of sayings that one often finds in sayings collections rather than a high degree of literary unity." Nevertheless, Jacobson himself does argue for an underlying unity in Q expressed through genre, vocabulary, themes, and redactional traits.

B. H. Streeter (1911) observed long ago that Q at the very least must have had a fixed sequence for its sayings. Even though Matthew and Luke regularly disagree about where they locate a Q saying in their respective gospels after the first few pericopes (as, for example, the Lord's Prayer appears in Matthew's Sermon on the Mount whereas in Luke it appears several chapters after the sermon), a high proportion of Q sayings are placed in the same *relative* order in Matthew and Luke. Even if it is possible that such a sequence could have been preserved in oral memory, it was not a wholly *fluid* oral memory. It must have been as firmly fixed in orality as in a written document. This then allows one to consider composition and unity.

Discussion of the literary unity of Q may be focused on either the final formulation of Q or on proposed earlier layers of composition. On the theory of Kloppenborg, it is in large part the perceived literary coherence of the formulation of the instructional material in Q that enables him to isolate this material and identify it as the formative stratum of Q. For the formative instructional material, this has been primarily done on formal grounds rather than upon identification of particular motifs or theological themes, even though there is a tendency to label his formative stratum as "sapiential" in contrast with the later redaction in which "polemical" material – such as prophecy or eschatological announcements of judgment – is more prominent. Unity is therefore identified within a *layer* of Q, even though other Q material from later stages might be quite different. Some have questioned whether all of the sayings that Kloppenborg attributes to this early layer are indeed of the type he suggests (particularly in the case of the mission sayings in Q 10:2–16), but he argues that these sayings are closer to the early stage of Q than to later stages (see below).

Several scholars, such as Lührmann (1969), Kloppenborg, and Jacobson, have found the redactional layer of Q (which is Kloppenborg's second layer) characterized by a dominant concern with the announcement of judgment, perhaps reflecting rejection of the early mission of the Q tradents by their neighboring Jews. Furthermore, the announcement of judgment against "this generation" is formulated quite specifically. It places "this generation" in a long line of those in Israel who rejected God's true messengers, the prophets, throughout Israel's history (the deuteronomistic tradition of the fate of the prophets). Even more distinctively, at times it also depicts God's true messengers as having been sent by "Sophia," or "Wisdom" (cf. Q 11:49–51, Q 7:35), thereby uniting the deuteronomistic tradition with the motif of Wisdom as the sender of the prophets. Interestingly, the motif of a personified Wisdom is not found in the collections of sapiential instruction in Q, but this may be an instance in which an early interest in wisdom admonitions developed into a perspective that associated personified Wisdom with the source of Jesus' message. The theme of opposition is of course much more pronounced in the non-instructional material, which includes the announcements of judgment by John the Baptist, the attack upon Jesus by his opponents in the Beelzebul controversy, and the eschatological woes announced against the Galilean towns and in the so-called Q apocalypse (Q 17:20ff.).

The final formulation of Q may include still further additions.

Despite the attractiveness of Kloppenborg's formulation, several scholars have serious reservations about a clear stratification of Q and too clear-cut a move from instruction to polemic. In addition to Horsley, who has been mentioned earlier, J. Schröter (1997), A. Kirk (1998), and J. D. G. Dunn (2003) have questioned the theory of compositional layers for Q. For example, Dunn suggests that whilst various clusters of Q sayings may have been used in Q communities for a variety of different purposes when they gathered, there is nothing to suggest that these clusters have not been pulled together in a *single* compositional act into what we consider to be "Q."

When taken as whole, how far does Q demonstrate a coherence of perspective? Supporters of Q have often argued that Q is not entirely a "grab bag" of traditions about Jesus. The absence of narrative relating to the death of Jesus is particularly noteworthy. An understanding of the death and vindication of Jesus is present in Q, but the death is not presented as a "sacrifice," or in redemptive or sacramental language as in some other early Christian literature. The dominant understanding in Q is that Jesus' death is in the line of the fate of the prophets, in contrast to the presence of this as a relatively minor motif in other early Christian writings. Similarly the Christology of Q makes only limited use of "Son"/"Son of God" Christology (mainly in the temptation narrative, considered late by many scholars, and in Q 10:23–4). These features have been claimed to show that the material in Q is truly "distinctive," namely that Q is identifiable as a source with interests that mark it off from the two gospels in which its material is now found. More difficult to determine is whether hostility to "this generation"/"Israel" and an occasionally favorable presentation of Gentiles might signify that a mission to Gentiles is in view in Q (favored by Lührmann [1969] and Uro [1987], and opposed by Jacobson and Horsley). If not, then this too would set Q apart from other early Christian literature in which validation of a mission among the Gentiles is frequently an important theme. Whilst this emphasis on the "peculiarity" of the perspective of Q is frequently seen as enhancing Q's identification as a real source, Hurtado (2003) has recently argued that there is no necessary connection between the two. One can accept, he argues, a form of the Q hypothesis without necessarily suggesting that it differs much from other early Christian belief. He seeks to challenge the distinctiveness of the theological and social perspectives in Q while still adhering to a form of the Q hypothesis.

## Language and Style

If many of the sayings found in Q were in fact traditional, with some going back to Jesus himself, then it is not improbable to think of some of these sayings having originally been uttered in Aramaic. Moreover, it is reported that the early churchman Papias wrote that Matthew collected "the *logia* [sayings]" in the Hebrew language. These two factors have spawned an ongoing discussion of the original language of Q.

Yet one has to proceed carefully. The Gospel of Luke, and most probably the Gospel of Matthew, were originally composed in Greek. Q is defined as a source for these two gospels, so was the language of the "source Q" (by which we mean the formulation of Q known to Matthew and Luke) Greek or Aramaic? There may well be sayings in Q that were originally composed in Aramaic, but, if so, were they still in Aramaic when the traditions were used by Matthew and Luke? To make the matter even more complex, was there an early version of Q that was Aramaic, even if the "final" formulation of Q was translated into Greek prior to use by the writers of Matthew and Luke? Or indeed were there two distinct sources with one in Greek and one in Aramaic, as argued by Bussmann (1929)?

These questions were of particular interest in early studies of Q, but have received some renewed attention due to a recent study by Maurice Casey (2002). Casey has sought to argue that, with respect to Q, Matthew and Luke used two different Greek translations of an underlying Aramaic source, parts of which were very early. His analysis is based upon detailed study of some particular passages, where he argues that the differences in the wordings in Matthew and Luke for a given pericope derive from different translational decisions. From these observations he also seeks to reconstruct the underlying Aramaic source. As M. Black noted earlier (in 1967), these possible translation variants are the strongest evidence for thinking of an Aramaic *Vorlage* for Q. Even though few scholars have yet had the opportunity to react to the detail of Casey's work, for some decades Q scholars have sought to understand most differences in the wording of Matthew and Luke for Q sayings in terms of the editorial and theological interests of one or both of the evangelists. If this is so, then it is difficult to assert that the differences in the two gospels *must* be due to translational variants in their sources.

In addition, there have been some arguments that have sought positively to favor Q as a Greek source. The number of instances in which there is exact verbal correspondence between Matthew and Luke has often been noted. This argument is strengthened if the verbal correspondence includes some very unusual Greek expressions, where it is difficult to believe that such a Greek word or phrase occurred naturally to two independent translators of an Aramaic original. N. Turner (1969) has further argued that the Greek of Q (as known from Matthew and Luke's versions) betrays few of the expected characteristics of Greek that has been translated from a Semitic language. While some scholars would like to believe Q had an Aramaic formulation on the grounds that this would put the source closer to the historical Jesus, most Q scholars up to now have reflected the view expressed by Tuckett that even if it cannot be proven that Q was available to the evangelists as a Greek document, it is certainly more likely that this was so than theories of the Aramaic nature of such a source.

## Sources and Intertextuality

In so far as Q is itself a hypothetical source, it may seem that an exploration of the sources of Q only compounds hypotheses. By reference to "sources" one normally means identifiable collections or compositions of material that existed prior to Q and which were taken up for full or partial incorporation into Q. It is difficult to identify sources in this sense. Earlier collections of sayings have more commonly been understood as early stages in the composition of Q itself rather than distinct sources used by the compilers of Q. The origins of the individual traditions that are incorporated into Q are very difficult to trace with any confidence, and in many cases the key question is whether they can be considered traditions stemming from Jesus himself. The criteria used to determine the authenticity of Jesus traditions have been the subject of considerable debate in their own right.

The Q tradents were, however, also inheritors of the traditions and texts of Israel. Despite the harshness of some of the Q sayings accusing "this generation" of killing God's true messengers, the encounter appears to be amongst those who share a Jewish heritage. There is no radical questioning of the Jewish law in Q. On the contrary, the sayings in Q 16:17–18 not only affirm the law's validity, but also seem to take a quite conservative attitude towards its interpretation. While some direct citations of scriptures are found in Q, more frequently appeal is made by allusion or reference to the epic history of Israel. For example, Q 11:29–32 refers explicitly to the story of Nineveh's repentance at the preaching of Jonah and of the coming of the Queen of the South to hear Solomon. In Q 17:26–30 examples are drawn from the days of Noah and the days of Lot. Furthermore, the key tradition of the fate of the prophets (cf. Q 11:49–51) draws upon a perspective of the epic history of Israel that is not confined to a single allusion. Even in the less polemical parts of Q, one can find occasional references to this history, as in the example of Solomon's glory cited in Q 12:27.

Direct scriptural citations are rare in Q. The most significant example appears in the Q temptation narrative, where citations from the LXX Deuteronomy 6–8 are used by Jesus in response to the Devil's testings (although the Devil cites from Psalm 91). Jacobson (1992: 88) suggests that certain Q scribes may thereby intend to present Jesus as "the faithful son who stands in contrast to the faithless generation addressed by Moses in Deuteronomy 6–8." This may also fit a wider interest, already noted, in deuteronomistic traditions. More contested is whether texts such as Luke 10:25–8 (the double commandment; cf. Deuteronomy 6:5 and Leviticus 19:18) and Luke 4:18 (citing Isaiah 61) were originally part of Q.

The allusion to Isaiah 61 is particularly interesting in view of the significance of this text for Christological development in the New Testament. In Q, Isaiah 61 appears to be applied to Jesus with respect to his activity in "preaching the good news to the poor" in Q 7:22. The various activities attributed to Jesus in this text probably allude to a small collection of texts drawn from the LXX version of Isaiah 61:1; 29:18–19; and 35:5–6. More debated is whether Isaiah 61:1–2 has also influenced the Q beatitudes in Q 6:20–1. If similar influence is found here, then it must be very significant that at the initial articulation of Jesus' message in the Q Sermon on the Mount, the words of Isaiah are employed and that texts from the prophet Isaiah are again used to vindicate

Jesus' ministry in Q 7. In addition, Tuckett has argued that Luke 4:18 might be another indicator of such a distinctive feature of Q's Christology, but (as noted above) not all scholars are convinced that this saying was found in Q.

The use of citations from the scriptures to assign "roles," however, is also evidenced in Q. Q appears to desert the LXX for another version of texts from Malachi 3:1 and Exodus 23:20 in Q 7:27 to describe the role of John (the Baptist). The distinctive use of the "the coming one" as a description of Jesus is present in the reference to "the one who comes" in Q 13:35b. This is an unusual direct citation of LXX Psalm 117:26.

## Arguments against the Existence of Q

Scholars who believe in the existence of Q do so not because of any external evidence of such a source but rather because they believe that this hypothesis is easier to accept than the major alternative hypotheses used to explain the observable phenomenon of non-Markan traditions shared by Matthew and Luke. Scholars who reject the existence of Q often point to weaknesses of the Q hypothesis, but ultimately this is not enough. Every hypothesis has weaknesses, and there is no solution to the synoptic problem that does not involve hypotheses. In the end, those who reject Q have to find a more plausible hypothesis to explain the phenomena that the Q hypothesis seeks to explain.

Generally speaking, the Q hypothesis occupies the middle ground between two main alternatives. On the one hand, there are scholars, like Michael Goulder, who argue that hypothetical sources should be postulated only when absolutely necessary. So, if it is possible to explain the similarities of Matthew and Luke (for their non-Markan traditions) without recourse to any unknown sources, then we should do so. Goulder (1989) does in fact try to apply Ockham's razor by suggesting that Luke made direct use of Matthew. In other words, the similarities of Matthew and Luke are due to the direct dependence of one gospel (Luke) upon the other gospel (Matthew). Goulder therefore accepts the task of having to explain why all the differences in the contexts observed for these shared non-Markan traditions in the two gospels are due to Luke rearranging Matthew's order of material, according to various principles. The differences in wording also have to be due to Luke altering Matthew's wording, and Luke's version of these traditions must therefore always be secondary to Matthew's. Where did Matthew obtain all of these non-Markan traditions in the first place? On the whole, according to Goulder, they are Matthew's own composition; it is not necessary to postulate any unknown source(s), although occasionally Goulder appeals to oral tradition as an additional "source." This hypothesis – that Mark was the first canonical gospel, that Matthew used Mark and little else in the way of sources, and that Luke used Mark and Matthew – provides a clear alternative to Q. Whether it is a more plausible alternative continues to be a matter of debate, but it has been recently championed by Mark Goodacre in his recent work, *The Case Against Q* (2002). There is another group of scholars who rely upon Luke's use of Matthew to explain the shared material, but who argue that Matthew was the *first* gospel written rather than Mark. For his part, Goulder defended Markan priority against advocates of the Augustinian and Griesbach hypotheses, but the latter has had a number of modern followers (including H.-H. Stoldt, D. L.

Dungan, W.R. Farmer, T. R. W. Longstaff, D. B. Peabody, and A. J. McNicol; see Chapter 15, "The Synoptic Problem," in this volume).

On the other hand, there are scholars who argue against Q for reasons completely contrary to those of Goulder. The Q hypothesis, they assert, is not too complex (by introducing unnecessarily a hypothetical source); rather, the Q hypothesis is too simple. One must reckon with the existence of *many* lost sources in order to explain synoptic relationships. Indeed, it is arguable that our canonical New Testament represents only a fraction of what must have been written by early Christians, a great deal of which has been lost. So, the argument goes, there is no *a priori* reason to oppose the idea of lost sources and probably every reason to expect that many other sources of Jesus-traditions circulated and that some of our existing gospels had earlier (now lost) versions. If the Q hypothesis struggles to explain some of the features of shared non-Markan traditions in Matthew and Luke, it is because there were other variant traditions available to the evangelists. Any peculiar difference between a common tradition in Matthew and Luke, in principle, could be attributed to yet one more (lost) hypothetical source. Relying upon a *single* hypothetical source to explain the phenomena is both ultimately unsuccessful and inherently unlikely (see, for example, Sanders and Davies 1989). One might consider radical proponents of oral tradition hypotheses to be a variation on such a position. Oral traditions and appeal to the collective memory of traditions in effect posit a kind of "multiple source" model. In response, those who support the "relatively simple" Q hypothesis argue that the detectable relative sequence of common non-Markan traditions found in Matthew and Luke and the distinctive theological emphases of these traditions are more consistent with a single common source than with a diverse set of sources.

Having recognized that the case against Q ultimately has to be coupled with the proposal of a more plausible alternative hypothesis, one must nevertheless give some attention to a few of those areas where scholars have suggested that the Q hypothesis itself is flawed. These may be briefly summarized as follows.

1   In Markan material where Q influence is not generally posited (such as the passion narrative), one sometimes finds "minor agreements" of Matthew and Luke against Mark. If such agreements can occur without the influence of Q, then is Q necessary to explain the other agreements and does this not drive us towards some other hypothesis, such as direct use of Matthew by Luke? The more numerous such "minor agreements" outside the boundaries of Q are, the more telling the case against Q. In response, advocates of the Q hypothesis tend to explain these "minor agreements against Mark" in a variety of ways. In some cases, they could be due to independent (but coincidentally similar) attempts by Matthew and Luke to alter something difficult in Mark. In other cases, they could be due to the result of early corruptions of the texts of Matthew or Luke by later scribes who tried to harmonize the gospels. Some Q scholars would even widen the normal boundaries of Q in order to incorporate such instances within the Q hypothesis. The debate hinges upon the persuasiveness of each of these defensive explanations and the number of instances that remain inexplicable by Q supporters.

2   Differing reconstructions of the extent of Q, alluded to above, have also been seen to be a weakness of the Q hypothesis. Because Q is a hypothetical source, the boundaries of which sayings might have been included in Q and which might have been excluded are inevitably unclear. Recently, the International Q Project has published a reconstruction of Q based upon a "minimal Q" (*The Critical Edition of Q*; see Robinson et al. 2000). This work has also sought critically to assess the most likely wording and order of Q passages. While this may begin to create a greater consensus about the extent of Q, it sometimes serves to articulate the degree of uncertainty. Thus it will be unlikely to end debate.

3   Contrary to Q adherents who appeal to distinctive theological themes that characterize Q, Goodacre (2002: 70) has argued that "Q" is no more than a "'Luke pleasing' re-working of Matthew's non-Markan material." In other words, the theory that Luke directly used Matthew is as adequate to explain the characteristics of this shared material, when isolated, as any theory of a distinctive hypothetical source. If there is a theological coherence to the Q material, it is allegedly because the material coheres with Lukan theology.

4   Earlier criticism of the Q hypothesis sometimes focused on the implausibility of a sayings source of the kind represented by Q, partly based on the absence of analogous examples. The *Gospel of Thomas* and numerous other sayings collections from the ancient Near East, however, demonstrate that there is no *a priori* objection that can be raised to the genre of Q. A more recent criticism based upon the genre and structure of Q, however, has been formulated by Goodacre. He notes that Q reveals narrative properties from the John the Baptist sayings in Q 3 up to Q 7:35 (the sayings about Jesus and John the Baptist), but thereafter the narrative features fall away. Thus parallels in genre sometimes drawn between Q and the *Gospel of Thomas* fail to do justice to Q's difference from the *Gospel of Thomas*, because the *Gospel of Thomas completely* lacks narrative structure. Furthermore, Goodacre argues that even if Q were on a trajectory towards a biographical genre, it is still difficult to explain the uneven nature of the narrative elements in Q on the basis of the Q hypothesis. He argues that it is easier to appreciate on the theory that Luke used Matthew, because the narrative elements in their shared non-Markan material appear where Matthew is known to have reworked the narrative of Mark (Matthew 3–11), and they bear purportedly Matthean characteristics, but these elements do not appear in the parts of Matthew used by Luke where Matthew is indistinguishable from Mark (Matthew 12–25).

5   The absence of reference to the events of the death and resurrection of Jesus has also been sometimes offered as a criticism of the Q hypothesis, on the basis that such an omission would be unthinkable for an early Christian document about Jesus. Q proponents have been at pains to stress that such a presupposition is applied with difficulty to a collection of sayings material. Moreover, several texts show how Q was aware of Jesus' fate and interpreted that fate in terms of "the fate of all of God's envoys and the righteous" (Kloppenborg 2000: 373). This might have led naturally to an expectation of Jesus' vindication, although for Q this is more clearly expressed in terms of his role in future

judgment than by direct reference to Jesus' resurrection. Ultimately this debate hinges upon the extent of diversity that scholars attribute to early kerygmatic formulations, and how far such diversity is "unthinkable."

Throughout the preceding discussion, it has been shown that the Q hypothesis continues to be a fertile area for debate. As indicated at the start of this essay, however, it is not just a debate over points of detail with little real significance. A great deal of relevance to our understanding of Jesus and earliest Christianity rests upon the hypothesis that one adopts for depicting that relationship between the gospels of Matthew and Luke.

## Annotated Bibliography

Allison, Dale C. *The Jesus Tradition in Q*. Harrisburg, PA: Trinity Press International, 1997. The author sets out a distinctive thesis on the composition of Q, based on the identification of various "sayings groups." He argues that several of these sayings groups were formulated and transmitted by wandering and wonder-working missionaries.
Arnal, W. E. *Jesus and the Village Scribes*. Minneapolis: Fortress Press, 2001. The author argues strongly against Theissen's thesis of wandering radicals as the earliest transmitters of the Jesus tradition. He maintains that the formation of Q is the product of Galilean village-based scribes, working in the context of a socio-economic crisis in Galilee under the Romans.
Betz, H. D. "Jesus and the Cynics: Survey and Analysis of a Hypothesis." *Journal of Religion* 74 (1994), 453–75 A careful analysis of the "Jesus as Cynic" hypothesis and of the purported parallels between the sayings of Q and Cynic traditions. Betz argues that further investigations of the Cynic hypothesis need to be more nuanced and aware of the complexities.
Bussmann, Wilhelm. *Synoptische Studien*. Vol. 2: *Zur Redenquelle*. Halle (Saale): Buchhandlung des Waisenhauses, 1929.
Casey, M. *An Aramaic Approach to Q: Sources for the Gospels of Matthew and Luke*. Cambridge: Cambridge University Press, 2002. The author argues for a complex model of Q and challenges the conventional model of Q being a single Greek document. Various early Aramaic sources are postulated as lying behind Q.
Catchpole, D. R. *The Quest for Q*. Edinburgh: T. & T. Clark, 1993. A collection of important and detailed studies of themes in Q, preceded by a careful defense of the Q hypothesis against recent criticisms.
Crossan, J. D. *The Historical Jesus: The Life of a Mediterranean Jewish Peasant*. San Francisco: Harper, 1991. Landmark study of the historical Jesus, developing the hypothesis that Jesus was a radical social revolutionary, a "peasant Jewish Cynic," and that Jesus' message about God's brokerless kingdom was ethical and sapiential rather than apocalyptic. This view, he argues, is confirmed by the earliest stratum in Q.
Downing, F. Gerald. *Cynics and Christian Origins*. Edinburgh: T. & T. Clark, 1992. A study that develops the hypothesis that Jesus and the early church are heavily indebted to popular Cynic thought, in contrast to interpretations that stress Jewish apocalyptic eschatology as formative for Christianity.
Dunn, J. D. G. *Jesus Remembered. Christianity in the Making*. Vol. 1. Grand Rapids and Cambridge: Wm. B. Eerdmans, 2003. As part of this wide-ranging study of Christian origins, Dunn emphasizes the impact made by *oral* tradition upon the sayings of Jesus (hence the title of

this volume), and this affects his understanding of Q. He questions attempts to describe a "Q community" with markedly different stages in its development.

Goodacre, M. *The Case Against Q: Studies in Markan Priority and the Synoptic Problem*. Harrisburg, PA: Trinity Press International, 2002. Goodacre, as the effective successor of Goulder, sets out the most recent and comprehensive attack on the Q hypothesis. Goodacre accepts Markan priority, but dispenses with Q in favor of Luke's use of Matthew.

Goulder, M. *Luke: A New Paradigm*. Sheffield: Sheffield Academic Press, 1989. The author painstakingly attempts to demonstrate how Luke's Gospel was formulated on the basis of Luke's use of Matthew and Mark as sources (rather than Q and Mark).

Goulder, M. "Is Q a Juggernaut?" *Journal of Biblical Literature* 115 (1996), 667–81. Goulder here attempts to defend his view that the seeming success of the Q hypothesis owes more to the momentum of Q studies than to rational argument.

Harnack, A. von. *The Sayings of Jesus: The Second Source of St. Matthew and St. Luke*. London: Williams & Norgate; New York: G. P. Putnam's Sons, 1908. One of the early studies of the sayings source "Q" by a noted liberal Protestant scholar.

Horsley, R. A. "Q and Jesus: Assumptions, Approaches and Analyses." Pp. 175–209 in *Early Christianity, Q and Jesus*. Edited by J. S. Kloppenborg and L. E. Vaage. Semeia, 55. Atlanta: Scholar's Press, 1991. Horsley, whilst a proponent of Q, is critical of the stratification of Q into sapiential and prophetic strands set forth by Kloppenborg. He develops the model of Q as composed of clusters of sayings with particular purposes. Purportedly sapiential clusters are, he argues, in context popular covenantal teaching seeking the renewal of the people of Israel, based in local communities.

Horsley, R. A. and J. A Draper. *Whoever Hears You Hears Me: Prophets, Performance, and Tradition in Q*. Harrisburg, PA: Trinity Press International, 1999. In furtherance of the attack on the stratification of Q into sapiential and prophetic strands, Horsley and Draper argue that Q is an "orally derived" text, that it seeks renewal of the social order (but not embedded in itinerant radicalism), and that the Q material is permeated more by prophetic than wisdom emphases.

Hurtado, L. W. *Lord Jesus Christ: Devotion to Jesus in Earliest Christianity*. Grand Rapids and Cambridge: Wm. B. Eerdmans, 2003. An important and wide-ranging study of Christian origins that considers Q possibly to have been composed by Hellenist believers and to have been carefully designed to display certain thematic concerns. It also shows evidence of scribal arrangement.

Jacobson, A. D. *The First Gospel: An Introduction to Q*. Sonoma, CA: Polebridge, 1992. An excellent introduction to the Q hypothesis and to much recent work on Q. He argues Q was a "gospel" in its own right with a distinctive and coherent theology.

Kirk, A. *The Composition of the Sayings Source: Genre, Synchrony and Wisdom Redaction in Q*. Leiden: E. J. Brill, 1998. Kirk, a student of Kloppenborg, questions Kloppenborg's theory of compositional layers in Q and sets forth an alternative hypothesis. He compares Q with ancient parenetic texts and argues that Q is comprehensible as an integral document.

Kloppenborg, J. S. *The Formation of Q: Trajectories in Ancient Wisdom Collections*. Philadelphia: Fortress, 1987. The seminal study proposing the stratification of Q, which has spawned much recent work on Q and the historical Jesus. In this he sets out the case for the distinction between the formative stratum of Q as (sapiential) "instruction" and a redactional stratum concerned with the announcement of judgment on "this generation."

Kloppenborg, J. S. (ed.). *Conflict and Invention: Literary, Rhetorical and Social Studies on the Sayings Gospel Q*. Valley Forge, PA: Trinity Press International, 1995. An important collection of studies by a variety of Q scholars, including J. Reid, R. Horsley, R. Piper, L. Vaage, S. Carruth, R. C. Douglas, W. Cotter, P. Hartin, and W. Arnal.

Kloppenborg Verbin, J. S. *Excavating Q: The History and Setting of the Sayings Gospel*. Edinburgh: T. & T. Clark, 2000. Kloppenborg's most recent and most comprehensive magisterial discussion of the origins, theology, and social location of Q. It analyses and reflects upon most current debate about Q.

Lindemann, A. (ed.). *The Sayings Source Q and the Historical Jesus*. Leuven: Leuven University Press/Peeters, 2001. An important collection of essays deriving from a variety of scholars at a colloquium in Leuven in 2000, dealing with Q and its significance for recent study of the historical Jesus. A variety of viewpoints is represented.

Lührmann, Dieter. *Die Redaktion der Logienquelle*. Wissenschaftliche Monographien zum Alten und Neuen Testament, 33. Neukirchen-Vluyn: Neukirchener Verlag, 1969.

Mack, B. L. *The Lost Gospel: The Book of Q and Christian Origins*. San Francisco: HarperCollins, 1993. A stimulating articulation of how the stratification of Q proposed by Kloppenborg can lead to an understanding of the origins and development of Christianity, beginning with Jesus as a Cynic-like teacher of wisdom in the earliest stratum in Q and tracing the incorporation of Jewish apocalyptic and messianic thought into the Jesus tradition as part of early Christian "mythmaking."

Meier, J. P. *A Marginal Jew: Rethinking the Historical Jesus*, vol. 2: *Mentor, Message and Miracles*. New York, London, and Toronto: Doubleday, 1994. Part of the multi-volume study of the historical Jesus. Amongst other things, this volume sets forth Meier's understanding of Q as a loose collection of Jesus traditions, or "grab bag," in contrast to compositional analyses of Q.

Myllykoski, M. "The Social History of Q and the Jewish War." Pp. 143–99 in *Symbols and Strata: Essays on the Sayings Gospel Q*. Edited by R. Uro. Helsinki: Finnish Exegetical Society; Göttingen: Vandenhoeck & Ruprecht, 1996. An essay that finds the setting of the redactional stage of Q located in the socio-political events in Palestine during 30–70 CE, culminating in a final composition of Q ca. 75 CE.

Piper, R. A. *Wisdom in the Q-Traditions: The Aphoristic Teaching of Jesus*. Cambridge: Cambridge University Press, 1989. A study of the sapiential traditions in Q, arguing that a set of discernible "aphoristic collections" with a common design suggests that wisdom modes of expression were a significant and characteristic feature of parts of the sayings source. No comprehensive compositional theory extending beyond these clusters is proposed, however.

Piper, R. A. (ed.). *The Gospel Behind the Gospels: Current Studies on Q*. Leiden: E. J. Brill, 1995. An edited collection of several important Q studies, preceded by an introduction on the state of research on Q. Contributors include C. Tuckett, F. Neirynck, J. Lambrecht, D. Lührmann, W. Cotter, M. Sato, P. Hoffmann, L. Vaage, R. Uro, J.M. Robinson, J. Kloppenborg, B. McLean, L. Schottroff, and A. Jacobson.

Robinson, J. M. "The Q Trajectory: Between John and Matthew via Jesus." Pp. 173–94 in *The Future of Early Christianity*. Edited by B. A. Pearson. Minneapolis: Fortress Press, 1991. In this essay, Robinson challenges the model of unbroken apocalypticism extending from John to Paul by suggesting a nuanced Q trajectory between John and Matthew, where one finds a "major sapiential deviation and a re-apocalypticizing."

Robinson, J. M., P. Hoffmann, and J. S. Kloppenborg. *The Critical Edition of Q: Synopsis*. Leuven: Peeters, 2000. The fruit of many scholars' work (as part of the International Q Project) to reconstruct a critical text of Q in Greek and in English. Included are indications of the level of certainty associated with some of the decisions about the earliest wording and order of the Q sayings.

Robinson, J. M. and H. Koester. *Trajectories through Early Christianity*. Philadelphia: Fortress Press, 1971 [1964]. A significant collection of essays by Robinson and Koester, including the seminal essays by Robinson on "Logoi Sophon: On the Gattung of Q" and by Koester on

"Gnomai Diaphoroi: The Origin and Nature of Diversification in the History of Earliest Christianity" and "One Jesus and Four Primitive Gospels."

Sanders, E. P. and M. Davies. *Studying the Synoptic Gospels*. London: SCM Press; Philadelphia: Trinity Press International, 1989. An introduction to careful study of the synoptic gospels, including support for the likelihood of multiple sources and versions lying behind the synoptic gospels. The Q hypothesis is considered to have erred by simplifying too much the complexity of source relationships, and this is why there are weaknesses in the explanation offered by the Q hypothesis for several synoptic phenomena.

Sato, M. *Q und Prophetie. Studien Zur Gattungs- und Traditionsgeschichte der Quelle Q*. Tübingen: Mohr Siebeck, 1988. In contrast to those who argue for an early sapiential layer of composition of Q, Sato attempts to argue that Q is permeated throughout with a prophetic orientation.

Schröter, J. *Erinnerung an Jesu Worte. Studien zur Rezeption der Logienüberlieferung in Markus, Q und Thomas*. Neukirchen-Vluyn: Neukirchener, 1997. An analysis of how the Jesus tradition has been "remembered," which argues for a single compositional stage for Q and for a continuity between oral transmission and written transmission of the sayings.

Streeter, B. H. "On the Original Order of Q." Pp. 141–64 in *Oxford Studies in the Synoptic Problem*. Edited by W. Sanday. Oxford: Clarendon Press, 1911. An article in which Streeter sets out an argument for Q having a fixed order, even though Matthew and Luke regularly situate Q sayings in different contexts in their gospels.

Streeter, B. H. *The Four Gospels: A Study of Origins, Treating of the Manuscript Tradition, Sources, Authorship, and Dates*. London: Macmillan, 1924. An early and significant discussion of the sources for the synoptic gospels, supporting a four-source hypothesis (including Q).

Theissen, G. *The Gospels in Context: Social and Political History in the Synoptic Tradition*. Minneapolis: Fortress Press, 1991. Theissen argues for a Palestinian origin for Q, for the collected sayings being primarily the traditions of itinerant (not community-based) charismatics, and for a dating of Q near the time of the Caligula crisis.

Tuckett, C. M. "A Cynic Q?" *Biblica* 70 (1989), 349–76. An article in which Tuckett attacks the views of those who have argued for a Cynic Q.

Tuckett, C. M. *Q and the History of Early Christianity: Studies on Q*. Edinburgh: T. & T. Clark, 1996. A detailed study where Tuckett analyses characteristic features of Q, including a possible theology of Q and social context for the Q Christians. Major themes of Q are insightfully examined.

Turner, Nigel. "Q in Recent Thought," *Expository Times* 80 (1969) 324–8.

Uro, Risto. *Sheep among the Wolves: A Study of the Mission Instructions of Q*. Annales Academiae Scientiarum Fennicae Dissertationes Humanarum Litterarum. Helsinki: Suomalainen Tiedeakatemia, 1987.

Vaage, L. E. *Galilean Upstarts: Jesus' First Followers According to Q*. Valley Forge, PA: Trinity Press International, 1994. A provocative study in which it is argued that Q derives from wandering Galileans that look very much like Cynics who conducted a form of popular resistance to the conventions.

Zeller, Dieter. *Die weisheitliche Mahnsprüche bei den Synoptikern*. Forschung zur Bibel, 17. Würzburg: Echter, 1977.

# CHAPTER 17
# The Gospel of Mark

Jens Schröter

## Major Issues and Directions in Recent Study

The Gospel of Mark presumably represents the oldest extant narrative about Jesus. Normally, methodological and historical questions arising in the exegesis of the synoptic gospels are first discussed in connection with scholarship on the Gospel of Mark. In this regard, the question as to how Mark interprets the actions and fate of Jesus is of fundamental significance.

During the reorientation of research on Jesus at the beginning of the twentieth century, William Wrede (1859–1906) pointed out that the literary level of Mark must be distinguished from the historical level of the reported events. Wrede's theory of the so-called "messianic secret" became influential in the understanding of the Gospel of Mark: there was a difference between Jesus' own self-understanding and the early Christian confession of his status as the messiah, since Jesus presumably did not understand himself as the messiah (although Wrede later mitigated this assumption). In order to explain this discrepancy, according to Wrede, early Christianity developed the theory that Jesus consciously concealed his messianic status during his earthly ministry. Mark found this theory already present in the material he assembled and made it into the basis of his entire narrative.

In a thoroughgoing analysis of the composition of Mark, Karl Ludwig Schmidt (1963 [1919]) then demonstrated that Mark was not interested in depicting the factual development of Jesus' public ministry, but rather assembled previously existing traditions chronologically and geographically into a coherent narrative. Taking up this insight, the form-critical scholarship inaugurated by Martin Dibelius (1883–1947) and Rudolf Bultmann (1884–1976) concentrated on understanding these traditions more precisely and determined how they fit into the history of early Christianity. The contribution of the author of the Gospel of Mark was thus essentially seen as that of the collection, composition, and interpretation of previously existing material. Rudolf Bultmann viewed the theological achievement of the author to be found in the connection of the story of Jesus to the *kerygma* ("proclamation") of the Hellenistic congregations. Following Wrede, he concluded that only through this connection were the reports of

Jesus' actions and teachings anchored in the theology of early Christianity. The assumption, still widespread in the nineteenth century, that the Gospel of Mark presents a basically accurate report of Jesus' activity and impact was thereby shattered.

In more recent scholarship the use of methods derived from literary and narrative criticism resulted once again in a reorientation. Decisive in this regard was the insight that the interpretation of Jesus' actions and fate in the Gospel of Mark can only be achieved by analyzing the gospel's compositional and narrative structures. Redaction criticism had already drawn attention to the interpretive role of the author, the guiding principle of which was the distinction between tradition and redaction. The result of this distinction was that the intention of the author was ascertained primarily from the redaction of previously existing traditions. In contrast, in their analysis of Mark as a consciously arranged work with its own perspective, narratological approaches have their starting point beyond this tradition/redaction distinction. Thus, narrative structures, the framework of space and time, and the development of the characters are all seen as important for the interpretation of the text. The older view, in which the traditions about Jesus were simply collected and provided a meaning from without, was thus corrected. It was replaced by the insight that the interpretation of the events surrounding Jesus' life and work lies in the composition of the narrative itself and does not come to it from without.

Of major importance is the realization that the Gospel of Mark creates its own narrative world through the composition of the different episodes. The reader is introduced into this world and learns its locales and characters from the perspective of the narrator. At the outset the reader is informed that Jesus is the Son of God and that John the Baptist is his precursor who was announced in the Hebrew scriptures. The reader gets glimpses into significant events during which Jesus is alone or almost alone, such as his baptism, the transfiguration, and the prayer in the garden of Gethsemane (14:32–42). The reader receives explanations of details pertaining to Jewish customs or to the meaning of particular concepts (among other things) which underscore the basic significance of Jesus' work (3:23–7; 4:11–12; 7:19), and is also able to assess the different characters through the way they are portrayed. The reader is also introduced to themes which are important for understanding the story being narrated and is enabled to recognize the standpoint of the author, in matters such as the significance of the twelve (3:13–19; 6:6–13) or the nature of Jesus' proclamation (4:33–4). The author looks beyond the ending of the narrative (2:20, 8:38, 9:1, 13:1–37; 14:62), he assesses the characters (1:22; 2:6; 3:6; 4:41; 6:52), and he makes known through the summaries in 1:32–4 and 4:33f. that he is reporting exemplary episodes from Jesus' ministry.

In structurally oriented studies, this approach – also labeled "synchronic" – has been from time to time understood in such a way that only the text world of Mark's Gospel is seen to bear any significance for its interpretation, while historical and tradition-historical questions fade into the background. It was, however, rightly objected that compositional and tradition-historical aspects must be treated together in order to interpret the Markan account of Jesus appropriately. It is indisputable that the Gospel of Mark has preserved memories of places, people, and circumstances related to Jesus' activity, such as his actions in Galilee and Jerusalem, the names and vocations of disciples, or the Jewish groups to which Jesus' opponents belonged. Mark is based, moreover, upon previously existing traditions, in which these memories had in part already taken the form of small episodes, such as in the healing scenes or the disputes with opponents. Nonetheless, the arrangement of this information and these traditions into a narrative of the actions and fate of Jesus represents the product of an independent, creative author, who in this way expresses the significance of the Jesus-event for the first time in narrative form.

The narratological approach is supported by recent scholarship on orality as well as by observations regarding the style of Mark's Gospel. Earlier form criticism considered the relationship of pre-synoptic oral traditions to their written form to be essentially one of continuity and thus deemed it possible to retrieve oral traditions by means of literary criticism and, with the help of the sociological category of the *Sitz im Leben* or "setting in life," to fit them into the history of early Christianity. More recent scholarship has effectively called this view into question. It became clear that one cannot begin with the assumption that oral traditions preserve a stable wording, and consequently the oral forms of a tradition in the pre-textual phase cannot be reconstructed. As a comparison of parallel traditions in the synoptic gospels demonstrates, the passing on of traditions about Jesus was not oriented towards preserving an exact wording – an observation additionally supported by the parallels found in noncanonical texts.

Furthermore, the Gospel of Mark is characterized by a largely coherent style, which shows that the redacted traditions were also integrated into the narrative with respect to language and style. This is more readily observed in narrative passages than in the sayings of Jesus, in which stylistic features such antithetical parallelism or conditional relative clauses occasionally appear and can possibly be traced back to oral traditions (cf., e.g., Mark 2:17; 4:25; 8:35; 10:11). On the whole, however, it should be kept in mind that Mark in large part edited his material and arranged it into a narrative with its own linguistic profile.

In regard to the classification of the older traditions, it ought finally to be pointed out that they are only with great difficulty assigned a place in early Christian history, if one prescinds from considering their redaction into the Markan narrative. The determination of different genres in their hypothetical settings (the so-called *Sitz im Leben*), which was proposed by form criticism to that end, does not in most cases make possible any clear conclusion regarding use in a pre-textual phase. The *chreiai*, parables, conflict narratives, or healing stories found in the Gospel of Mark could in principle serve any number of different purposes – mission, paraenesis, preservation of the historic memory of Jesus' ministry. A clear context of use is therefore not ascertainable by means of assigning genres.

If the literary Jesus-narrative accordingly takes the place of earlier usage contexts, then the question concerning the historical value of the Markan account also appears in a new light. It is certainly accurate to say that the form of several episodes from the synoptic tradition can be traced back to their function in the circles of those who transmitted them. Thus, for instance, the *chreiai* concerning the disciples (Mark 1:16–20) or the disputes about the forgiveness of sins (2:1–12), keeping the Sabbath (2:23–8; 3:1–6), or not following purity codes (7:1–20) might in any case have the additional function of establishing norms. Likewise, one should note that Mark distinguishes between his own time and narrated time. Preserving the memory of Jesus' life – which is clearly narrated with a view towards the Markan community's own time – is therefore an important function of the Markan account. This is apparent, for example, in the fact that Mark reports numerous details pertaining to people as well as geographical, political, and cultural circumstances, all of which imbue the gospel with the character of a historical narrative. Mark also has a historical interest in the person of Jesus, but only because his own time becomes understandable in light of the narrative of Jesus.

If then, on the one hand, the scholarship from the first half of the twentieth century rightly emphasized that the Gospel of Mark cannot be viewed positivistically as a reflection of Jesus' actual actions and fate, it nonetheless inadequately described the relationship between pre-synoptic tradition and the composition of the gospel. The narratological approach, on the other hand, has sometimes not sufficiently emphasized Mark's relationship to previously existing traditions and to Jesus' life. In both scholarly camps, moreover, the significance of the Gospel of Mark as a historical narrative has been underestimated.

In the future, therefore, it will be necessary to give greater attention to the fact that the Gospel of Mark must be interpreted as a narrative which makes the story of Jesus' life fruitful for the (narrative's) present by means of creative memory. The basis of such an interpretation must be a concept of history which neither adheres to the idea of a "reconstruction of the past" nor annuls the relationship to the events of Jesus' life and death by means of a strictly redaction-critical exegesis. Rather, history ought to be conceived as a creative act of remembering the past for the purpose of establishing identity in the present. Without a doubt, the author of the Gospel of Mark had his own time in view when he wrote his account about Jesus. However, he solves the problems of the present in such a way that he simultaneously looks back at Jesus' history and forward towards its fulfillment. His narrative accordingly represents an interpretation of his own time which functions by reaching back to the time of the earthly Jesus and looking forward to Jesus' return in judgment.

The Gospel of Mark's Christology must be described against this background as a narrative or implicit concept. While for a long time the so-called *Hoheitstitel* or "regal titles" were a focal point of research, more recently it has been established that the interpretation of the figure of Jesus emerges from the narrative, within which the various designations of royalty, so important for Mark, gain their significance. As their use in Jewish texts shows, these titles are not to be understood as concepts with a strictly defined meaning, but rather they receive their specific interpretation through their integration into the Markan narrative.

The interrelationship of the titles, which are essential to interpreting the figure of Jesus, can be clarified by examining the passage in 8:27–9:13, itself central to the Markan account. On the basis of Jesus' actions, which have been hitherto recounted, Peter answers Jesus' question about who the disciples consider him to be with the confession that Jesus is the anointed one (the Christ). The subsequent proclamation by Jesus, that the Son of Man will suffer, die, and then rise after three days (8:31–3), makes clear that Peter's recognition of Jesus' identity is only provisional. Thereupon in 8:38 the coming of the Son of Man in judgment is announced. In the following episode (9:1–13) Jesus, on a mountain in front of the three disciples, is declared by God himself to be the Son.

The composition of the scene illustrates that the title "Christ" possesses only limited explanatory value for Mark. Jesus is only correctly understood when he is recognized as the Son of God working in the Spirit, and when the way he must go in life, which is linked with his self-identification as the Son of Man, is grasped. In his baptism Jesus receives the Spirit of God, by whose power he immediately begins to set up the reign of God against that of Satan. His identity as the Son of God is accordingly recognized by the demons. By contrast, people around him wonder about the source of his power, with his opponents even attributed it to Beelzebul (3:22). As the Son of Man, Jesus has the power to forgive sins and to interpret the commandment regarding the Sabbath (2:10, 28). His divine sonship is again explicitly confirmed in light of the predicted suffering of the Son of Man (9:7). Jesus' identifications as the Son of God and as the Son of Man are thus closely related to each other, a fact also shown by the mention of God as the Father of the Son of Man in 8:38. The title "Son of God" thereby ensures the divine legitimation of Jesus, whereas the expression "Son of Man," which Jesus himself regularly uses, describes the path he must follow, one which leads through suffering, death, and resurrection to his elevation at the right hand of God. Only on this condition can Jesus be called the Christ: he must be understood as the one called the Son by God and as the Son of Man who sits at God's right hand. On the other hand, Mark resists a conception of the Christ which is oriented towards Davidic lineage (12:35–7). The close relationship of the titles "Son of God" and "Christ" to the expression "Son of Man" also becomes evident in the hearing before the high priest in 14:61–2, when Jesus answers the question as to whether he is the Christ, the Son of the Most High, affirmatively and then proceeds to announce the coming of the Son of Man. When, upon seeing Jesus' death, the centurion under the cross proclaims that he was the Son of God (15:39), then this is, according to the understanding set forth in the Gospel of Mark, the beginning of the correct recognition of who Jesus is.

The expression "Son of God," which Mark employs in a way comprehensible to both Jewish and pagan readers (especially in the story of the transfiguration), as well as the titles "Son of Man," "Christ," and "Son of David," differ from their use in other (mostly Jewish) texts. By their integration into the story of Jesus, they are provided with new content.

The analysis of the Gospel of Mark as narrative leads finally to the differentiation of the characteristics summarized by Wrede under the concept of the "messianic secret." If the notion of an "unmessianic" activity on the part of Jesus is already problematic, then the announcement of the imminent reign of God, the so-called "parable theory" developed in Mark 4:11–12, the occasional commands to be silent placed upon the disciples and those who have been healed, as well as the disciples' lack of understanding reveal themselves to be independent narrative strategies. The reign of God comes about through Jesus' activity, although inconspicuously and recognizably only to the initiated. The commands to keep silence are not intended to be part of a thoroughgoing effort to keep Jesus' power secret, but rather in certain places they reinforce the contrast between the spread of his reputation and his own wish not to become known only because of his mighty deeds. Finally, the disciples' lack of understanding serves to illustrate, by the example of those closest to Jesus, how difficult it is to understand Jesus' way and message correctly.

To read the Gospel of Mark as narrative thus entails identifying the various strategies, characters, and aspects of Jesus' activity and impact. In this way a complex picture emerges of a narrative about Jesus as God's representative and whose ministry marks the advent of the reign of God.

## Date and Place of Composition

The oldest external attestation of the Gospel of Mark is its mention by Papias (ca. 125 CE in Eusebius, *Ecclesiastical History*, 3.39.15). According to Papias, Mark recorded from memory the words and deeds of the Lord as they were transmitted and interpreted in the teachings of Peter (similarly Irenaeus, *Against Heresies*, 3.1.1, 3.10.6; Tertullian, *Against Marcion*, 4.5). In accordance with the Two-Source theory, which is today the widely accepted solution to the question of the synoptic gospels, the Gospel of Mark is dated prior to Matthew and Luke.

Support for the Two-Source theory (i.e., that Matthew and Luke are literarily dependent on Mark and Q) as a solution to the synoptic problem is primarily found in the observation that the order of episodes in Matthew and Luke are largely in agreement at those points where they also agree with Mark (see Chapter 15, "The Synoptic Problem," in this volume). The easiest explanation for this is that Matthew and Luke took over a previously existing narrative and expanded it. Mark is temporally and materially closer to this older composition and therefore presumably represents the oldest extant narrative about Jesus. However, this is not to say – and it is also highly improbable – that Matthew and Luke knew the Gospel of Mark in the form which can be reconstructed from the extant manuscripts. Evidence to the contrary is found, for example, in the so-called minor agreements, in which Matthew and Luke are in agreement over against Mark, but which can only partially be explained as mutually independent revisions of an identical text of Mark. Further evidence is possibly found in the fact that Luke is missing Mark 6:45–8:26. Presumably, then, Matthew and Luke used different versions of Mark than are attested in the extant manuscripts.

These external clues initially help situate Mark's date of composition in the last decades of the first century C.E. The destruction of the Jerusalem temple predicted in 13:2 as well as the establishment of an "abomination of desolation" prophesied in 13:14 (cf. Dan. 9:27; 11:31; 12:11; 1 Macc. 1:54; cf. also 1 Macc. 6:7; 2 Macc. 6:2) constitute internal evidence from the Gospel of Mark itself. Against the background of the events predicted – that is, reported – in Daniel and 1 and 2 Maccabees, it is often assumed that an older draft forms the basis of Jesus' speech in Mark 13, which can be linked to the intention of the Roman emperor Gaius Caligula (12–41 CE) to have his own image set up as a statue of Zeus in the Jerusalem temple. However, because this plan was never carried out, but instead was averted through delaying tactics and finally by the emperor's death, the presumed source most likely originated prior to Caligula's death.

It remains an open question whether one can with much probability assume the existence of such an early source from the events surrounding the crisis initiated by Caligula. At any rate, clear literary evidence for this theory is hard to find in Mark 13. Nonetheless, it is clear that the impending destruction of the temple is an event contemporaneous with the composition of Mark. The gospel can consequently be dated either immediately before or after 70 CE, depending upon whether 13:2 is judged to be a *vaticinium ex eventu* ("prophecy after the event") or a genuine prophecy made in the face of the war which had already broken out. The prophesied establishment of a "sacrilege of desolation" should be understood, in connection with the apocalyptic events announced by Jesus in Mark 13, as a prediction of Jerusalem's destruction by an arising adversary (cf. the masculine participle ἑστηκότα, "standing" in 13:14). The fact that no concrete circumstances surrounding the seizure of Jerusalem appear in Mark 13 (in contrast to Luke 21:20) might suggest that the Gospel of Mark had already been written before the destruction of the city. The years 68/69 CE seem the most plausible time of origin.

It is more difficult, however, to answer the question regarding Mark's *place of origin*. Early church tradition holds it to be Rome (Clement of Alexandria in Eusebius, *Ecclesiastical History*, 6.14.6), a solution which has been proposed well into the period of modern scholarship. Advocates of this view since Clement have pointed to the link between Mark and Peter attested to in 1 Peter 5:13 and by Papias, a link which, coupled with the mention of Peter's stay in Rome, could provide a clue to the gospel's location. Nevertheless, it is improbable that the Gospel of Mark can be traced back to the public teachings of Peter, and Peter's stay in Rome has not been factually established. Critical scholarship on the Gospel of Mark has shown, rather, that the redacted traditions derive from the previously existing oral, and possibly also written, traditions about Jesus, and much less likely from the public teachings of Peter. Even the occasional Latinisms found in the Gospel of Mark (e.g., μόδιον, "basket" in 4:21; λεγιών, "legion" in 5:9; κῆνσον, "taxes" in 12:14; δηνάριον, "denarius" in 12:15; κοδράντης, "quadrans" in 12:42; πραιτώριον, "praetorium" in 15:16) offer little evidence for an origin in Rome, since they represent common expressions from Roman coinage and military affairs, knowledge of which can be presupposed in other cities and regions of the Roman empire.

By contrast, the explanations of Jewish rituals (7:3–4; 14:2; 15:42), acquaintance with which the author apparently could not assume among his readers, could be used as internal clues to the gospel's place of origin. The translation of Aramaic expressions such as Βοανηργές (*Boanerges*, i.e., "sons of thunder") in 3:16, ταλιθα κουμ (*talitha koum*, i.e., "little girl, get up") in 5:41, κορβᾶν (*korban*, i.e., "an offering to God") in 7:11, or εφαθα (*ephatha*, i.e., "be opened") in 7:34, show that the audience, who spoke Greek and did not know Aramaic, would need such explanations. Those for whom Mark was written, therefore, consisted at least in part of Gentile Christians who were unacquainted with the relevant Jewish practices and expressions.

However, it appears less certain whether one can infer an ignorance of Palestinian geography from Mark 5:1 and 7:31, as is often assumed. The χώρα τῶν Γερασηνῶν ("region of the Gerasenes") mentioned in 5:1 could refer to territory belonging to Gerasa, on the eastern shore of Lake Genesaret, and does not necessarily have to indicate the Gerasa which is situated approximately 30 miles farther southeast (Mark calls the territory belonging to a city ὅρια ("boundaries") in 7:24, 31, not χώρα ("district, region"), and in 8:27 he speaks of the κῶμαι Καισαρείας τῆς Φιλίππου ("villages of Caesarea Philippi"). In 7:31 the northwestern area in which Jesus operated is summarily described by the route from Tyre via Sidon, whereby the detail ἀνὰ μέσον τῶν ὁρίων Δεκαπόλεως ("through the region of the Decapolis") is probably accurate, since Jesus is in fact located in the Decapolis on the eastern shore of the sea.

Although the traditions redacted by Mark indicate in these and other cases – such as the synagogue in Capernaum, Peter's house, the names and careers of Jesus' disciples who are called in 1:16–20, and Jesus' provenance in Nazareth – a thorough knowledge of the area in which Jesus operated – this area cannot immediately be taken to be the Gospel of Mark's place of origin. Because Mark is apparently dealing with a predominantly Gentile Christian audience, because the authority of Peter plays a role, and because the similarities to early Christian Christological terms and concepts are of a general nature (εὐαγγελίον, "gospel" and the identification of Jesus as χριστός, "Christ or messiah") and υἱὸς θεοῦ, "son of God"), the place of origin is probably, rather, a region which had absorbed the influence of pre-Pauline development and then developed it further independent of Paul. If one considers additionally that the events announced in Mark 13, the destruction of Jerusalem and the temple, are current events for the gospel's readers, a location in Syria or Palestine suggests itself more readily than one in Asia Minor or Rome.

## Textual Issues and Problems

The oldest textual attestation of the Gospel of Mark is $\mathfrak{P}^{45}$, a papyrus from the third century that contains part of Mark 4:36–12:28. The uncial manuscripts Sinaiticus and Vaticanus provide evidence for the complete text from the fourth century, as do Alexandrinus and (with a few gaps) Ephraem Syri Rescriptus and Freerianus, albeit from a somewhat later date. External evidence extends back to an earlier date than does attestation of the text itself.

The textual history of the concluding section of the Gospel of Mark is significant from the perspective of textual criticism. In the codices Sinaiticus and Vaticanus, the minuscule 304 from the twelfth century, as well as in Syriac, Georgian, and Armenian translations and at least one Sahidic manuscript, the Gospel of Mark ends in 16:8 with the women fleeing in fright from the empty tomb. This evidence is also supported by statements in Eusebius and Jerome. The Latin Codex Bobiensis (fourth/fifth century) contains the so-called shorter ending, which speaks of how the women told "those around Peter" all that had been commanded them and how through them Jesus sent out the holy and imperishable message of eternal life from east to west.

The overwhelming majority of manuscripts present the so-called longer ending of Mark (16:9–20). This ending contains reports of appearances of the resurrected Jesus to Mary Magdalene, two disciples, and then the eleven, and the commissioning of the disciples to proclaim the gospel, as well as an account of Jesus' ascension. Several copyists in fact make clear through textual critical marks or marginal notes that they know about the problematic nature of this passage. In additional manuscripts (112; 099; L; Y), the two endings of the Gospel of Mark are combined, and Codex W contains the so-called Freer-Logion between verses 14 and 15b, a dialogue between the resurrected Jesus and his disciples.

The most plausible explanation for these findings is that the Gospel of Mark, which originally ended in 16:8, was later expanded around the traditions of the resurrected Jesus and likewise strove to rectify the problems at the end in 16:8 – namely, that out of fear the women do not follow the heavenly messenger's command.

A further problem, from the point of view of textual criticism, lies in the ambiguous attestation of υἱὸς θεοῦ ("son of God") in 1:1. The expression was inserted into Codex Sinaiticus by a later hand and is missing from Q (the sayings source). Codex Alexandrinus contains it, as does Codex Bezae. Consideration of the textual history could suggest that there was a later addition that, at the very beginning of the gospel, inserted as a title of Jesus that has great importance for the Gospel of Mark. However, it is also possible that the shorter text indicates an alignment with the customary expression εὐαγγελίον Ἰησοῦ Χριστοῦ ("gospel of Jesus Christ"). In the end, the issue cannot be decided with absolute certainty.

Finally, in this context one ought to mention the so-called "secret gospel of Mark" discovered by Morton Smith. In concerns two passages that have come down to us in Clement of Alexandria. They are found, respectively, between Mark 10:34 and 35 and between 10:45 and 46, and they tell of a young man whom Jesus raises from the dead. The young man then spends the night in Jesus' company and is introduced by the latter to the secret of the kingdom of God. In the latter passage Jesus meets the young man's sister as well as Salome, but he does not initiate them into the secret. Theories based on the hypothesis of a version of Mark that is older than the canonical one have, for good reason, not gained wide acceptance. Probably there were later additions made to the Gospel of Mark which resulted in a version that was used, according to Clement, by the Carpocratians, a Gnostic sect.

## Literary Genre

At the time the Gospel of Mark was written, there was no literary genre category of "gospel." This first develops in the second century CE, when Justin uses the plural εὐαγγελίαι ("gospels") as a label for narratives about Jesus. He understands them as ἀπομνημονεύματα, or "memorabilia," that is, writings preserving the memory of Jesus. The term "gospel," in the sense of a category of literary genre for texts which report on the life of Jesus, is thus a specifically Christian genre category whose use cannot be assumed in the first century CE.

The phrase εὐαγγελίον Ἰησοῦ Χριστοῦ ("gospel of Jesus Christ") in Mark 1:1 is, accordingly, not a designation of the literary type of what follows, but rather the description of its content. The further use of the term "gospel" in Mark also illustrates this when it is employed to characterize Jesus' teaching (1:14–15), as well as when the whole of the events surrounding Jesus become the content of the εὐαγγελίον (8:35; cf. 8:38; 13:10; 14:9). Mark adopts this term, which had already been used before him for the message of Christ (e.g. Rom. 1:1, 16; 1 Cor. 15:1), and applies it to the narration of Jesus' actions and fate. Consequently, one cannot determine the genre by employing the concept of εὐαγγελίον.

The similarity between the Mark and ancient biography has been noted quite often. The Gospel of Mark clearly focuses upon the actions and the fate of a single individual, whence it already possesses the features of biography. There is a wide variety of biographies from antiquity. Greco-Roman accounts often arranged the material transpiring between birth and death, occurrences which are generally (though not always) reported, thematically rather than chronologically, and they were more heavily oriented towards bringing out typical rather than individual traits. The depiction of Jesus in Mark relates to this insofar as there also the interest is not in a chronological organization, but rather in exhibiting typical features and the cultural content of Jesus' actions and influence. Of course, here Mark is interested exclusively in Jesus' public ministry as well as in the circumstances that led to his death, and not in providing personal details or a portrait of Jesus' character. Furthermore, there is an identifiable historiographical interest, as Mark traces Jesus' appearance back to God's decision to establish his lordship on earth and to bring salvation to the Gentiles.

In order to describe the genre of the gospel, one must take into account the readily available biographical accounts of prophets and kings in Israelite-Jewish writings. This explains why Mark began with the appearance of John the Baptist and the related integration of Jesus into the history of Israel. It likewise explains the declaration of Jesus as the Son of God (if that reading in Mark 1:1 was original) and Mark's concentration on Jesus' function as the one commissioned by God. Hence, the Markan depiction of Jesus tells the story of God working through him and thereby represents theological writing of history in biographical form.

## Author and Setting

As with the other gospels, the author of the Gospel of Mark is nowhere named in the text, and unlike in Luke 1:1–4 and Acts 1:1–2, he also does not enter the picture through the use of the first person singular. The attribution to an author with the name Mark, found as an *inscriptio* or *subscriptio* in the manuscripts, is first attested in Papias, who, according to Eusebius, *Ecclesiastical History*, 3.39.7, 14, had based it on information from a certain Aristion or the presbyter John. The early church tradition (according to Eusebius, Papias already does so himself: *Ecclesiastical History*, 3.15.2; 3.39.17; Clement, *Hypotyposes*, 6, in Eusebius, *Ecclesiastical History*, 3.15.2; Origen, *Commentary on Matthew* in Eusebius, *Ecclesiastical History*, 6.25.5; Jerome, *On Illustrious Men*, 8), by identifying the author with the Mark mentioned in 1 Peter 5:13 and traces the Gospel of Mark back to the public teachings of Peter (thus in addition to Papias, who describes Mark as ἑρμηνευτής ["interpreter"] of Peter, see especially the legendary tale in Clement, *Commentary on 1 Peter 5:13*). However, church tradition mentions no connection to the Mark belonging to the circle around Paul (mentioned in Col. 4:10; 2 Tim. 4:11; Philem. 24), nor to the John Mark mentioned in Acts 12:12, 25 and 15:37–9.

These reports provide no information about the identity of the author; rather, they represent later attempts to provide the Gospel of Mark with apostolic authority. Similarly, the occasional effort to identify the author with the fleeing youth from Mark 14:51–2 remains ultimately an unprovable hypothesis. Even if one operates according to the assumption that the text was only later attributed to "Mark," the question still arises as to why the gospel was not – as would have seemed more likely – attributed directly to the authority of Peter. While the possibility therefore cannot be excluded that the name "Mark" attached itself very early to the gospel, any further clues as to the author's identity can only be taken from the text itself.

The composer of the text appears as an "implicit author" who presents the events surrounding the actions and fate of Jesus in a traditional narrative style. For this reason, it makes little sense to doubt that Greek was his native language. In two places the author steps out of the narrative in order to address his readers directly: in 7:2–3 he explains the Jewish custom of washing hands before eating, and in 13:14 he indicates the explicit meaning of the expression "abomination of desolation" and the related interpretation of the situation which he has narrated. From this one can conclude that he wrote for Gentile Christians who were affected by the destruction of Jerusalem and the temple, events interpreted in Mark 13.

The author is evidently acquainted with both Jewish and early Christian traditions. He often makes reference to the scriptures of Israel. He knows of the group of the twelve as an institution created by Jesus, and he later refers to the events surrounding the actions and fate of Jesus as an example in order to make them useful for interpreting his own time. The actions and impact of Jesus are thereby given an orientation beyond Israel to the Gentiles as well. This is already indicated by the explanation of Jewish customs as well as by the programmatic removal of the boundaries between pure and impure (7:15). Jesus' activity in the Gentile regions, in the Decapolis, and in the district of Tyre and Sidon (7:24, 31) point in this direction. The double narrative of the multiplication of loaves in 6:30–44 and 8:1–9 is presumably related to Jesus' activity among Jews and Gentiles. The commission in 13:10 to proclaim the gospel to all nations corresponds to this orientation beyond Israel.

Whether, therefore, the author of Mark was himself a Gentile Christian cannot be determined with any certainty. In any case, he stands in close proximity to these early Christian ideas which lent support to a coexistence between Gentile and Jewish Christians. From the perspective of the history of theology, Mark thus stands within a trajectory that in the New Testament was above all advanced in areas under Pauline influence. The concept of "gospel" as well as the statement regarding the abolition of pure and impure (cf. Rom. 14:14) point in this direction. Of course there remain clear differences from Paul, which indicate that any similarities are the result of links in the tradition, rather than of a direct literary relationship.

## Occasion

The Gospel of Mark emerges from a situation in which conflict has arisen over Jesus' identity and over the coming of God's reign which Jesus had proclaimed. The readers are confronted with the fact that people will persecute and hate them on account of Jesus' name (4:17; 13:13) and that they will be set before Gentile and Jewish courts and rulers. The act of following Jesus is described as one involving suffering (8:34–7), even martyrdom (8:35; 10:39; 13:12).

The events mentioned in Mark 13 represent the concrete background of the gospel. The war between the Jews and the Romans in Palestine apparently also affected Christians, although the Gospel of Mark indicates that it considers the Christians as already separated from the Jewish community. In this way a situation arose in which the followers of Jesus, both Jewish and Gentile, encountered hostility. They had to expect

persecution from their Jewish compatriots and were at the same time beset by the puni-
tive measures of the Gentile rulers. Amid this strife Mark exhorts his readers through
the narrative of Jesus to remain steadfast in discipleship and not to doubt Jesus' legitimacy. He responds to the challenge of his time with his narrative about the reign of
God, which has dawned in a way barely visible. One must therefore pay all the more
attention to it in order to be counted among the saved at the end of time (4:3–9). The
way of Jesus thereby becomes the model of how to endure suffering and death. To adhere
to Jesus and his words means not to lose sight of the future salvation even amid adversity
and temptation. Mark refers in this respect to the returning Son of Man who will gather
up his elect, yet who will be ashamed of those who were ashamed of him (13:27; 8:38).

Mark thus narrates the story of Jesus during a situation of besieged faith in order to
fortify his readers and to enjoin steadfastness in discipleship. At the same time, he preserves the memory of Jesus, which now ran the risk of fading into oblivion some forty
years after his execution and after the generation of eyewitnesses had died off. He
assembles a story that explains how a community has emerged from the activity of
Jesus, a community which no longer lives within Judaism, but rather orients itself
towards the way of Jesus, the Son of God.

## Literary and Compositional Analysis

The Gospel of Mark's literary character emerges from its place in the early Christian
tradition. Previously existing traditions are redacted in the narrative in various ways.
Among these earlier traditions there were possibly also smaller collections. The narrative account therefore possesses an episodic character inasmuch as the individual
scenes are often put together from a thematic point of view and among themselves are
only loosely connected.

Mark 1:1 serves as the heading and 1:2–15 as the prologue of the narrative. Mark
depicts here how John the Baptist prepares the way for the coming of Jesus, and how
Jesus is recognized as the Son of God in his baptism. In 1:14–15 Mark introduces Jesus'
activity in Galilee in summary fashion. The clearest break in the narrative occurs after
8:26, when Jesus' public activity in Galilee and the surrounding region has ended. Here
Peter's confession possesses explicit significance and introduces the following section,
in which the suffering of Jesus and his followers comes to the fore.

### The advent of the reign of God (1:16–8:26)

The first part of the gospel can be subdivided into the sections 1:16–4:34 and 4:35–
8:26. With Jesus' speech concerning the kingdom of God, Mark concludes a section in
which the activity of Jesus in Galilee, as well as the various reactions thereto, have been
described and which then ends with the parable about the mystery of the reign of God.

Jesus' activity begins with the first disciples in 1:16–20. They accompany him to
Capernaum (1:21) and go with him into the synagogue there and into the house of
Simon and Andrew. This house is presumably the one which is mentioned in 2:1; 3:20;

7:17; and 9:33, where there are similar references to the house in Capernaum. The first disciples whom Jesus calls are also the first ones named in the list of the twelve in 3:14–19. Furthermore, the geographic reference in Mark 1:16 παρὰ τὴν θάλασσαν τῆς Γαλιλαίας ("along the sea of Galilee") indicates the area in which Jesus will now most often be active.

Quite a few historical details regarding places and individuals are indicated in the episode marking the beginning of Jesus' activity. At the same time, the scene is clearly styled as a call narrative reminiscent of Elijah's calling of Elisha (1 Kings 19:19–21). Comparable elements are, above all, the call to discipleship and the leaving of the father. Mark has formed the call of Jesus' disciples according to the model of a prophetic call in Israel's scriptures.

The following scenes take place in Capernaum and depict the first day of Jesus' activity, first of all in the synagogue, then in the house of Simon and Andrew. With respect to language, the scenes are strung together by means of the paratactic καί ("and"), as is often the case in Mark. The plot is enlivened and spurred on by the word εὐθύς ("immediately"), which is typical of Mark, in 1:21, 23, 29, 30. Finally, the regular shifting of verb tenses and the copious use of the historical present characterizes the Markan narrative style. The historical present occurs in 1:21, where Jesus' entry into Capernaum is recounted by means of a verb in the present tense which opens up the scene. What follows is narrated in the imperfect (1:21–2: ἐδίδασκεν, "he was teaching," ἐξεπλήσσοντο, "they were amazed," ἦν διδάσκων, "he was teaching"), while the event in 1:23–8 is narrated in the aorist. Verses 21–2 thus set the context into which the event narrated from 1:23 onward is placed. One can trace a similar movement in the next episode: the action progresses in the aorist (verse 29: ἦλθον, "they came"), the situation is initially described by means of an imperfect verb (verse 30: κατέκειτο, "was lying down"), and the historical present draws attention to the action that follows.

Jesus appears as one teaching in the synagogue whose instruction amazes the people on account of his authority. Here the confrontation with the scribes, who for Mark are Jesus' main opponents, takes place for the first time. Jesus' teaching itself, however, is not reported. Rather, the author recounts the expulsion of an unclean spirit, an event which is the occasion for much amazement on the part of the people at Jesus' "new teaching with authority" (1:27). It becomes clear, then, that Mark assimilates Jesus' teaching to his mighty actions: the authority over the unclean spirit offers proof that Jesus' activity is that which frees human beings from the power of the demons and brings about the kingdom of God. That this is Mark's primary concern already becomes apparent in the first scene of Jesus' public ministry: through Jesus' mighty deeds and exorcisms the power of the unclean spirits is broken, people are healed of sicknesses, and Jesus establishes his own circle of followers through his call to discipleship.

Finally, a further characteristic of the Markan narrative is evident in these initial scenes. On the one hand, Mark narrates some episodes broadly and vividly. The scene in the synagogue in 1:21–8 is depicted in a very lively and detailed way: there is a sharp exchange of words between the unclean spirit and Jesus, the spirit shakes the man back and forth, and the people are astonished. But then Mark can also briefly summarize activities with succinct observations and overviews, such as in 1:32–4, where Jesus' healing ministry is described in summary fashion without details or individual episodes.

In the following complex of disputes, Jesus is explicitly introduced as the Son of Man who acts with divine authority. The healing narrative in 2:1–12 is characterized by the insertion in verses 5b–10 of a discussion with the scribes about Jesus' authority to forgive sins. Only afterwards, in verse 10c, does the healing narrative resume where it left off in verse 5b and come to its anticipated conclusion. The healing narrative thus helps Mark bring out the significance of Jesus' ministry: Jesus assumes functions which otherwise belong only to God. This claim compels the scribes to accuse him of blasphemy, an accusation which then recurs in the healing in 14:62. It is this claim which ultimately leads to Jesus' condemnation and execution. It is consistent, then, that the Pharisees and the Herodians conspire to kill Jesus at the end of this complex (3:6): the decision to kill Jesus arises from his appearance in the name and with the authority of God, an appearance which becomes such an offense to Jesus' opponents that they seek to eliminate him.

In the subsequent section the theme of the relationship to Jesus comes to the fore. After the summary in which Jesus' ministry is described as already known beyond the region of Galilee, Jesus forms the group of the twelve (3:13–19), whereupon the controversy concerning the pact with Beelzebub immediately follows (3:20–35). At the end of this section it is clear: there are different reactions to Jesus' activity, and different circles around him, beginning from the closest circle of the twelve to those who hear the Word of God, carry it out, and are thus the "true relatives" of Jesus (3:31–5), all the way to those who reject him (his family according to the flesh), those who consider him to be in league with Beelzebub (the scribes), and even those who want to kill him (the Pharisees and Herodians).

In 3:20–35 there appears one of the "sandwich arrangements" or "intercalations," which are typical of Mark. Doubling phenomena are found regularly in Mark: one already occurred in 2:5 and 2:10, where in both verses the expression λέγει τῷ παραλυτικῷ ("he said to the paralytic") is used. A comparable phenomenon can be observed in 3:20–35, when Mark connects two episodes in sandwich fashion: accusation of the family – accusation of the scribes – reaction of Jesus to both of these accusations (3:23–7, 28–30) – reaction to the accusation of the family. In the episode 3:31–5 Mark consciously plays with the expressions ἔξω ("outside") and οἱ περὶ αὐτῶν ("those around him"), which are used ambiguously: outside and inside are not only descriptions of physical location; at the same time, they indicate the proximity to and distance from Jesus. This is also the theme of the parables in 4:1–34.

Within the series of parables one can distinguish different narrative layers. In 4:1–2, 10 and 33–4, the narrator intervenes and addresses the audience with observations on the situation: in 4:1–2 the parable speech is introduced, and in verse 10 a new situation begins (Jesus is alone with those περὶ αὐτῶν, "around him" and with the twelve, who ask him about the parables), and in verse 33 the speech concludes with the indication that Jesus taught by many parables. In addition, the narrator intervenes in Jesus' speech by using the introductions καὶ ἔλεγεν ("and he said") or καὶ ἔλεγεν αὐτῷ ("and he said to them") whereby each time he leads into the next narrative unit.

In regard to content, the narrator makes clear that he is concerned with a definite type of parable which is linked to his specific interpretation of why Jesus teaches with them. This emerges from the transition: Jesus teaches the crowd καθὼς ἠδύναντο ἀκούειν ("just as they were able to hear"). This ability to hear is thematized within the parable discourse itself: verse 12 states that the teaching in parables is for "those outside" (οἱ ἔξω), in order that they, though hearing, may not understand. Contrariwise, for those around Jesus the μυστήριον τῆς βασιλείας ("the mystery of the kingdom") is explained in the parables. The concluding observations of the passage likewise refer to this in that in verse 34 Jesus is said to have explained everything to his disciples when he was alone with them. The parable discourse thus distinguishes a circle of those who remain outside from those in the inner circle of Jesus. Only the one who opens him or herself to Jesus' teaching via the kingdom of God's distinct mode of operation belongs to the inner circle. Lacking understanding, everyone else remains outside.

Besides this external narrative framework there are within the speech of Jesus, first, his previously mentioned discourse *about* the parables (verses 10–12); second, the speeches which occur in parable form (4:3–8, 26–9, 30–2, and 21–5); third, the interpretation of the first parable in verses 13–20. Within the speech a systematic program becomes evident through which Mark develops his conception of the advent of the kingdom of God. Here Mark has edited older material. With regard to the sayings in verses 21–5 as well as the parable of the mustard seed in verses 30–2, one can demonstrate this with the help of parallels in the Q-source. No independent source is attested for the other two parables. Nonetheless, Mark is evidently relying on older traditions. The parables are held together by the "seed" imagery, which portrays the reign of God as a power which is growing.

The intention of the parable discourse is to instruct the disciples in the mystery of God's reign (verse 11). More precisely, this means calling them to hear Jesus' proclamation in the right way. This is the theme of the first parable. It begins with ἀκούετε ("hear!") and concludes with the call to listen in verse 9. The theme of the parable is the sowing of the kingdom of God through Jesus' preaching, which in the case of most people falls on infertile ground, while only in the case of a few does it fall upon fertile soil. In the interpretation of this parable, the theme of ἀκούειν ("hearing") is especially emphasized. The parable and its interpretation are so closely related to each other in terms of language that theories concerning a separation of form tradition and subsequent interpretation cannot be based upon linguistic arguments. The ὁ σπείρων ("the sower") in verse 3 is formulated with a view towards its employment again in verse 14 (ὁ σπείρων τὸν λόγον σπείρει, "the sower sows the word"). Likewise, the exhortation to hear is strongly emphasized in both passages. The second group of hearers possesses special significance in the parable and in the interpretation (4:5–6, 16–17). Finally, in the case of the last group of hearers, the plural (ἄλλα, "others") is used, to which the particularly bountiful yield in the interpretation corresponds.

The parable thus intends to say: only for a few does the λόγος, "message" (i.e., the proclamation of the reign of God) bear fruit, and therefore it is especially important to hear it in the right way and bring forth a good harvest. Practically speaking, it is significant that the first parable is interpreted as an example. This fact indicates that the parables can only be properly understood if one recognizes the unique structure of Jesus' proclamation, the true meaning of which is not readily apparent. The parable thus also implies that the meaning of Jesus' preaching remains closed to many ("those outside"). For this reason it is important that the mystery of the reign of God is entrusted to the disciples.

The sayings in 4:21–5 draw attention to the connection between the concealed beginning and the disclosed end, whereupon is indicated once again the significance of correct hearing, which is decisive for the final judgment (verses 24–5). In this context the theme of right hearing reoccurs (verses 23–4).

The last two parables (verses 26–9, 30–2) point towards the interval of time in which the kingdom of God grows, in Jesus' absence and without his assistance, until the judgment comes. The parable of the mustard seed also underscores the connection between a small, inconspicuous beginning and a great end.

In this way the parable discourse elucidates the manner in which the reign of God operates: the mystery is that the kingdom, although hidden, nonetheless dawns in the action of Jesus. This inconspicuousness notwithstanding, one should not let oneself grow restless, but rather should belong to the "inner circle" and thus, at the end, to those who are saved.

In the second section of this first part of the gospel (4:35–8:26), Jesus' mighty deeds in Gentile and Jewish areas as well as the relationship between Jews and Gentiles are the focal point. Immediately following the parable discourse this becomes apparent in the narrative of the calming of the storm. To this narrative are then attached the story of the exorcism of the demoniac at Gennesaret and the healing of the hemorrhaging woman, which is itself encapsulated in the narrative about the raising of Jairus' daughter from the dead. The two miracles whereby Jesus feeds the multitudes (6:30–44; 8:1–10), the healing of the Syrophoenician woman, and finally, the healing of the blind man in 8:22–6 should also to be mentioned. This part of the gospel illustrates how the reign of God comes about: it takes place in Jesus' healings and in the communal meals with his followers. The two feedings of the multitude already anticipate the last supper (compare 6:41; 8:6 with 14:22).

The calming of the storm, which is reported immediately following Jesus' parable discourse, ends with his disciples asking after his identity (4:41). It soon becomes clear that despite the instruction regarding the mystery of the kingdom of God given to the disciples just beforehand, they immediately fall into doubt again. This shows a tendency in the Gospel of Mark to portray the disciples as those who, when faced with Jesus' incomprehensible way, continually doubt, lack faith, and do not understand. Thus in 8:18 the disciples are even put on the same plane as those about whom it was said in 4:12 that they have eyes but do not see and ears but do not hear. This critical tendency also finds expression in the confession of Peter, when he reproaches Jesus for the latter's predicted suffering, and in the passion narrative, where Peter denies Jesus, and all the disciples flee. This critical tendency has even led to the assumption that Mark has a fundamentally negative view of the disciples. However, this view is both extreme and unlikely because the disciples are always the ones who form the most intimate circle around Jesus, accompany him during his ministry, are initiated into the mystery of the reign of God, and are sent out with the commission to continue his work. The narrative function of the disciples is therefore one of identification figures who serve as examples of the community of Jesus' followers. At the same time, it becomes clear, in their regard, that discipleship is always jeopardized by failure and denial. Nonetheless, the twelve constitute the "focal point" of Jesus' followers, beyond whom there is then a definite circle of disciples. Indeed, the whole nation is confronted with the call to discipleship. Mark thus develops a conception of discipleship that has its origin in the group of twelve formed by Jesus himself and then is opened up into the post-Easter situation. In this way, the term ἀκολουθεῖν ("to follow") in Mark can, on the one hand, indicate the factual following behind Jesus; so for instance in 1:18 in alternation with ἔρχεσθαι ὀπίσω αὐτοῦ ("to come/go after him") in verse 20; 2.14 (a statement made to Levi) and can then, in a further sense, be related to belonging to the community of Jesus' followers (8:34–10:28).

The problem of Jesus' identity climaxes in this section of the gospel. Following the calming of the storm, the disciples are amazed at Jesus' authority, and they consequently ask who he is. In 6:2 the residents of Nazareth are astounded – just as were those of Capernaum in 1 2:27 – at his teaching. And in 6:14–16 Herod, wondering who this one is whose name has become known, considers him to be John the Baptist raised from the dead. This question is finally taken up at the beginning of the next complex in 8:27, when Jesus asks his disciples who they think he is, and this inquiry receives the same answers as those already suggested in 6:14–15 (John the Baptist, Elijah, one of the prophets). Jesus' identity has been at issue since the beginning of his ministry; it is that question which the Gospel of Mark seeks to answer.

Just as the narrative in 4:35–41 plays a programmatic part in the construction of the Gospel of Mark, so also does the narrative in 7:31–7, but in a different way. The healing of a deaf man in the Decapolis is narrated here, and the passage concludes with the cry of the crowd (7:37): "He has done everything well; he even makes the deaf to hear and the mute to speak." By appealing to prophetic words, this confession interprets Jesus' healings as the action of God at the end of time. Furthermore, it refers not only to this particular healing narrative, but also looks back at the whole of the stories of Jesus' healing in Gentile areas.

With respect to the history of scholarship, here one ought to point out that a contrast between the miracle stories and the chronology of Mark has often been asserted. This culminated in the view that Mark only took up the miracle stories in order to correct them by means of the passion tradition. Jesus' mighty deeds in Mark, however, are proof of the advent of God's reign. Through the commands to keep silent and the passion narrative, they are governed by a particular presupposition: the way of the Son of God must be understood as the way of the Son of Man and may not be interpreted apart from this. This way leads through suffering and death to resurrection and a seat at God's right hand. Jesus' mighty deeds serve to confirm the fact that the kingdom of God actually has come about in the actions of Jesus. They are then, of course, situated in the context of the path Jesus must follow.

### Prediction of suffering and discipleship (8:27–10:45)

A decisive shift in theme marks this section of the gospel, inasmuch as the focal point becomes the question as to how the authority of the Son of Man, or of the Son of God working in the Spirit – an authority which was described in the first part of the gospel

– relates to the necessity of his suffering. This section is given structure by the three passion predictions, which are linked closely with the theme of discipleship. The discussion of the disciples' own crosses follows immediately upon the first passion prediction (8:34–7); the teaching about the first and the last follows the second prediction (9:33–7); and the teaching that the one who wishes to be first must become the servant of all follows the third (10:33–4). Jesus' way of tribulation thus becomes the paradigm for the community of his followers. The statement about the Son of Man, who gives his life as a ransom for all (10:45), is therefore given programmatic pride of place at the end. Discipleship is given concrete form in the children, the rich man, and the words of Peter, namely, that they have left everything behind in order to follow Jesus.

The Markan themes of Jesus' identity and the nature of discipleship are given further treatment in light of Jesus' way of suffering, which lies at the core of this part of the gospel. Jesus' way is described in the first part of the gospel as that through which the kingdom of God comes about, an event that expresses itself concretely in the healing of the sick and the exorcism of the possessed. The section beginning in 8:27 commences once again with the theme of Jesus' identity. What is new is that this time Jesus asks the disciples who he is. He himself thereby provokes – as he does similarly in 12:35–7 with respect to the question concerning the Davidic lineage of the Christ – continued clarification of the question of his identity. The passage in 8:34–9:1 is thus of central importance, because on the one hand it brings into view the path Jesus must follow all the way up to his death, and at the same time links this way with the theme of discipleship. Accordingly, the recognition of the necessity of suffering implies that Jesus' followers can also become disciples who suffer. What is essential is not the desire to preserve one's earthly life and in the process to lose one's life in eternity, since for the latter there is no replacement. The motivation for discipleship, even in suffering and persecution, is effected with a view toward the end of time: the life which matters at the end of time is squandered if one seeks to save one's earthly life and is for this reason ashamed of Jesus, the Son of Man, and his teachings. This will be made manifest when the Son of Man returns. Here, for the first time, the function of the Son of Man as the apocalyptic judge appears.

On the whole, this section underscores a close connection between Jesus' own way and what discipleship looks like. The interpretation of Jesus' death which thereby emerges implies that it is a necessary part of the divine plan of salvation, a model for the disciples, and the inauguration of a universal offer of salvation by God. The ἀντὶ πολλῶν ("for many") from 10:45 is to be understood in this sense. Jesus began by healing the sick and unclean. This event of liberation, the establishment of God's kingdom, continues in time through the promulgation of the gospel until Jesus' return. For this reason, his death is a ransom for many.

The other place in which Jesus' death is spoken of in a comparable manner is in the word over the cup in 14:24. There Jesus speaks of the covenant, which is sealed by the blood and "for many." This can also be related to the kingdom of God which comes about through Jesus and which applies to all, as especially the healings and exorcisms outside of Galilee have indicated. However, Mark does not make a specific connection between Jesus' death and the removal of sins. Human beings are liberated from their sins because Jesus forgives them their trespasses and heals them (2:5, 10) and establishes the kingdom of God, and because this establishment continues also after his death until he returns.

### The events in Jerusalem (11:1–16:8)

In the third part of Mark, the clash with the Jewish authorities – including a criticism of the temple – a glimpse of the end of time and the return of the Son of Man (Mark 13), and the events surrounding the passion (Mark 14–16) form the focal points. Jesus is henceforth located in the place where the animosity towards him coalesces and where, moreover, the events announced in the passion predictions will occur. The narrative thus reaches its dramatic climax in this third part. Jesus arrives in Jerusalem, where he has been headed since Mark 10. His arrival there has already been referred to explicitly in the third passion prediction, but it has also been hinted at in passages such as 3:22 (the scribes come down from Jerusalem to Galilee).

The section begins with Jesus' entry into Jerusalem, where he is greeted by the crowd as the one who will establish "the kingdom of our father David." This entry narrative is structured, by means of various motifs, as the entry of the expected Davidic ruler. First there is a donkey, upon which, according to Zechariah 9:9 (cf. Gen. 49:11), the apocalyptic King of Peace will ride. In Matthew 21:5, this verse of scripture is cited explicitly. There is also the reception by the crowd who greet Jesus as a king in Jerusalem. But Jesus will only fulfill the expectations of the people in a certain way. He will not establish the Davidic monarchy, and to that extent it becomes evident that the crowd has an understanding of Jesus' identity and reign that needs correcting. The reign of God proclaimed by Jesus is not identical to the anticipated Davidic reign; rather, it possesses a unique dynamic insofar as it entails the suffering, death, resurrection, and return at the end of time of all those who belong to it. This thematic is henceforth brought to its conclusion.

The events of Mark 11 are arranged according to a three-day scheme, in which Jesus criticizes the temple, to which he opposes his own form of relationship to God by his exhortation to faith in God and to prayer. By linking the pericopes of the fruitless fig tree, the cleansing of the temple, and the collection of sayings about faith and the proper way to pray, Mark orients his readers towards a relationship with God marked by faith and prayer, a relationship which at the same time stands in opposition to the Jerusalem temple.

The parable of the vintner in 12:1–9 as well as the ensuing discussions about the resurrection of the dead, the greatest commandment, and the questions regarding the Davidic lineage of the messiah, reveal Jesus to be the one who disputes with the scribes about Israel's scriptures. Here the conflict with the Jewish authorities, which has already been touched upon in 3:6, becomes more acute. The question of Jesus' authority arises again (11:18, 27–33), since it suggests an authority that at once surpasses that of the high priests and the scribes and calls it into question. For this reason, as in 3:6, the intention of Jesus' opponents to kill him appears once again (11:18). It is thus the authority with which Jesus comes onto the scene that leads his Jewish adversaries to seek to eliminate him, because they see their own authority thereby called into question. Jesus himself thematizes this in the parable of the wicked tenants who lease the vineyard, kill the servants, and finally also kill the son sent to them by the owner, so that the vineyard may belong to them. The consequence of their action, however, is that God will take the vineyard "Israel" away from the high priests, the elders, and the scribes and give it to others (12:9). The conflict with the Israelite authorities intensifies and paves the way for the events of the passion.

As seen in Mark 4, where the question arose about the reign of God in the face of the different reactions to Jesus, the intensifying animosity toward Jesus leads now to the question about the relation of Jesus' fate to the kingdom of God. Mark develops an answer to this question in chapter 13. The speech concerning the end of time corresponds to the parable discourse in Mark 4, inasmuch as it focuses attention henceforth upon the span of time stretching until the Son of Man returns. From a literary point of view, it distinguishes itself from the latter in that it contains no interruptions – up until 13:4 – by which the narrator might insert himself. The speech has an apocalyptic character in that it brings into view the time until the end, announces horrifying events, and, by the reference to the "abomination of desolation" (verse 14), adopts an expression which in an esoteric way points toward the unique significance of the impending events.

As 13:1–2 make clear, the speech is formulated in light of the destruction of the Jerusalem temple, an event which has either already occurred or is expected in the immediate future. In the Gospel of Mark the events – which, concretely speaking, have to do with a Roman intervention on account of Jewish rebellion – are interpreted by means of such apocalyptic motifs as the great distress before the end (verses 14–20), the cutting short of days (verse 20), and false messiahs. The delimitation of the time horizon by the returning Son of Man shows, moreover, that the events surrounding Jesus possess a meaning for Mark which is relevant for history all the way to its end.

The Markan passion narrative is a coherent report that, literarily speaking, is distinct from the rest of the gospel account. The episodic narration is set aside in favor of a continuous report in which the individual scenes build upon one another. The question regarding pre-Markan traditions, when it comes to the passion narrative, is typically understood as involving a pre-Markan passion narrative as a whole, since in the individual scenes are found hardly any starting points for inquiries into the tradition history.

Another question concerns the reliability of the basic historical events, such as the fact of Jesus' execution and the individual features of his trial, such as the condemnation by the Roman governor in Judea and the Roman death penalty of crucifixion. They can certainly be viewed as historically reliable. It is more difficult to judge the involvement of the Sanhedrin, because it did not actually possess any capital jurisdiction and consequently could not impose the death penalty. Here there is a clear tendency to emphasize Jewish guilt for Jesus' death.

The passion narrative begins in Mark 14:1–9 with the account of the anointing at Bethany, wherein the theme of the Markan Christology becomes evident: Jesus will die as the anointed one. Furthermore, the Last Supper tradition deserves special attention. Mark adopts the words of Jesus, which interpret the bread and the wine with respect to his body and blood, from a previously existing tradition (cf. 1 Cor. 11:23–5). The difference from Paul (and Luke 22:19–20) consists in the fact that the blood is described as the spilled blood of the covenant, whereas Paul and Luke label the cup as the new covenant. The reference from the Hebrew Bible is Exodus 24:8 (LXX), where the expression "blood of the covenant" also appears. In Paul and Luke, however, mention of the new covenant is an allusion to Jeremiah 38:31 (LXX). The dominant motif of the Last Supper narrative seems therefore to have been the sealing of the covenant. Mark also depicts the Last Supper as a Passover meal; Matthew and Luke follow him in this regard. Apart from the question of historicity, it is clear that this context provides an interpretive framework for Mark.

The narrative of the empty tomb and the reference to Galilee (which appears already in 14:28) points the audience in the direction of Galilee. Unlike Luke, where the history of Christianity originates with the appearance of the risen Jesus in and around Jerusalem, Mark orients his readers towards Galilee as the place to which Jesus will precede his disciples and where they will see him.

## Sources and Intertexuality

In multiple ways, the Gospel of Mark stands within the tradition history of early Christianity. It adopts the titles Christ, Son of God, Son of David, and Son of Man from the tradition just as it does the expression "gospel" and the tradition of the twelve. If one adheres to the Two-Source theory, then it further turns out that besides Mark there existed a second early collection of Jesus traditions (Q). Presumably Mark did not have before him a written form of this source. Nonetheless, one can identify in a few places traditions which pre-dated Mark and Q. Among them are for example the appearance of John the Baptist and his announcement of Jesus (Mark 1:4–8; Q 3.7–9, 16–17), the temptation of Jesus (Mark 1:12–13; Q 4.1–13), the controversy regarding Beelzebub (Mark 3:23–7; Q 11.14–20), the parable of the mustard seed (Mark 4:30–2; Q 13.18f.), the sending out of the disciples (Mark 6:7–13; Q 10.2–16), the sayings concerning the hiddenness of God's kingdom (Mark 4:22; Q 12.2), and the sayings concerning the disciples' cross (Mark 8:34–5; Q 14.26f., 17.33). These texts suggest that Mark and Q both shared in a common sphere of tradition. They therefore make possible a glimpse into a pre-Markan layer of the tradition.

To other pre-Markan traditions belong the previously mentioned traditions of the last supper, the saying regarding clean and unclean (cf. Rom. 14:14) or the one concerning divorce (Mark 10:11f.; cf. 1 Cor. 10:7, 10f.). In these cases the pre-Markan tradition is established by analogies in Paul.

It cannot be clarified any further whether Mark had any written sources. Even if written collections of traditions about Jesus should lie behind individual parts of Mark's Gospel, only in Mark do we find the first narrative about Jesus. In scholarship concerning this issue, Jesus' speech in Mark 13 and the passion narrative play a significant role. In both cases there is the possibility that Mark could have redacted written sources. One can in fact observe places which suggest the existence of previously existing texts, even if their concrete written form can no longer be reconstructed.

In addition, Mark appeals to the Hebrew scriptures in order to interpret Jesus' ministry. The appearance of John the Baptist is already interpreted as the fulfillment of prophetic predictions, and in the baptism story an allusion is made to Psalm 2:7. When the coming of the Son of Man is announced in 13:26 and 14:62, there is a reference to Daniel 7:13–14. And when, in the parable discourse in 4:12, those who do not understand are said to be made obdurate, this is based on a passage from the Old Testament (Isa. 6:9–10; cf. the reference to Jer. 5:21 in 8:18). In the dispute over divorce, Jesus quotes Genesis 1:27 in connection with Mark 2:24; and in the dialogue with the rich man in 10:19 he quotes the second tablet of the Decalogue. Scriptural quotations and allusions then increase in the passion narrative, where Psalms 22 and 27, as well as Zechariah 13:7, are employed in order to interpret the events.

Mark presupposes a reader who is informed about Jesus' activity and fate, who is acquainted with early Christian understanding of Jesus as the Son of God and the Christ, and who also possesses knowledge of the Hebrew scriptures. In his account of Jesus, Mark illustrates to the reader how these traditions join together to form a narrative which imbues Jesus' actions and fate with a specific meaning. He shows how the Hebrew scriptures, as well as the early Christian confessions, are themselves opened up, if one reads them in light of the story of Jesus.

## Bibliography

Breytenbach, Cilliers. *Nachfolge und Zukunftserwartung nach Markus. Eine methodenkritische Studie.* AThANT 71. Zurich, 1984.

Bultmann, Rudolf. *The History of the Synoptic Tradition.* Trans. John Marsh. New York, 1963.

Cancik, Hubert (ed.). *Markus-Philologie.* Wissenschaftliche Untersuchungen zum Neuen Testament, 33. Tübingen 1984.

Capel Anderson, Janice and Stephen D. Moore (eds.). *Mark and Method: New Approaches in Biblical Studies.* Minneapolis, 1992.

Danove, Paul L. *The Rhetoric of the Characterization of God, Jesus, and Jesus' Disciples in the Gospel of Mark. Journal for the Study of the New Testament* Supplementary Series, 290. New York, 2005.

Dibelius, Martin. *From Tradition to Gospel.* Trans. B. L. Woolf. New York: Charles Scribner's Sons, 1934. [Translation of *Die Formgeschichte des Evangeliums.* 6th edn. Tübingen, 1971.]

Donahue, John R. and Daniel J. Harrington. *The Gospel of Mark.* Sacra Pagina Series 2. Collegeville, 2002.

Dormeyer, Detlev. *Das Markusevangelium.* Darmstadt, 2005.

Dormeyer, Detlev *Das Markusevangelium als Idealbiographie von Jesus Christus, dem Nazarener.* Stuttgarter Bibelstudien, 43. Stuttgart, 1999; 2nd rev. edn. 2002.

Dschulnigg, Peter. *Sprache, Redaktion und Intention des Markusevangeliums.* Stuttgarter biblische Beiträge, 11. Stuttgart, 1984.

Du Toit, David S. *Der abwesende Herr. Strategien im Markusevangelium zu Bewältigung der Abwesenheit des Auferstandenen.* Wissenschaftliche Monographien zum Alten und Neuen Testament, 111. Neukirchen, 2006.

Eckey, Wilfried. *Das Markusevangelium. Orientierung am Weg Jesu. Ein Kommentar.* Neukirchen-Vluyn, 1998.

Edwards, J. "Markan Sandwiches: The Significance of Interpolations in Markan Narratives." *Novum Testamentum* 31 (1989), 193–216.

Elliott, J. Keith (ed.). *The Language and Style of the Gospel of Mark*. New Testament Studies, 71. Leiden, 1993.

Focant, Camille. *L'Évangile selon Marc.. Commentaire biblique*, Nouveau Testament 2. Paris, 2005.

Fowler, Robert M. *Let the Reader Understand. Reader-Response Criticism and the Gospel of Mark.* Minneapolis, 1991.

France, Richard T. *The Gospel of Mark. A Commentary on the Greek Text*. New International Greek Testament Commentary. Grand Rapids, 2002.

Gundry, Robert H. *Mark: A Commentary on His Apology for the Cross*. Grand Rapids, 1993.

Guttenberger, Gudrun. *Die Gottesvorstellung im Markusevangelium*. Beihefte zur Zeitschrift für die neutestamentliche Wissenschaft, 123. Berlin and New York, 2004.

Hahn, Ferdinand (ed.). *Der Erzähler des Evangeliums: Methodische Neuansätze in der Markusforschung.* Stuttgarter Bibelstudien, 118/19. Stuttgart, 1985.

Iersel, Bas M.F. van. *Mark. A Reader-Response Commentary. Journal for the Study of the New Testament* Supplementary Series, 164. Sheffield, 1998.

Kelber, Werner. *Mark's Story of Jesus*. Philadelphia, 1974.

Kingsbury, Jack T. *The Christology of Mark's Gospel*. Philadelphia, 1983.

Lane, William L. *The Gospel According to Mark: The English Text with Introduction, Exposition and Notes*. New International Commentary on the New Testament. Grand Rapids, 1999.

Lohmeyer, Ernst. *Das Markusevangelium*. KEK, I/2. Göttingen, 1968.

Lührmann, Dieter. *Das Markusevangelium*. Handbuch zum Neuen Testament, 3. Tübingen, 1987.

Marcus, Joel. *Mark 1–8: A New Translation with Introduction and Commentary*. AB 27. New York, 2000.

Marxsen, Willi. *Der Evangelist Markus. Studien zur Redaktionsgeschichte des Evangeliums.* Forschungen zur Religion und Literatur des Alten und Neuen Testaments, 67 [= NS 49]. Göttingen, 1956; 2nd edn. 1959.

Miller, Susan. *Women in Mark's Gospel. Journal for the Study of the New Testament* Supplementary Series, 259. London, 2004.

Moloney, Francis J. *Mark: Storyteller, Interpreter, Evangelist*. Peabody, MA, 2004.

Neirynck, Frans. *Duality in Mark*. Bibliotheca Ephemeridum Theologicarum Lovaniensium, 31. Leuven, 1972; rev. edn. 1988.

Räisänen, Heikki. *The "Messianic Secret" in Mark*. Trans. Christopher Tuckett. Edinburgh, 1990.

Reinbold, Wolfgang. *Der älteste Bericht über den Tod Jesu*. Beihefte zur Zeitschrift für die neutestamentliche Wissenschaft, 69. Berlin and New York, 1994.

Reiser, Marius. *Syntax und Stil des Markusevangliums*. Wissenschaftliche Untersuchungen zum Neuen Testament, II/11. Tübingen, 1984.

Rhoads, David and Donald Michie. *Mark as Story: An Introduction to the Narrative of a Gospel.* Philadelphia, 1982; 2nd edn. 1999.

Robbins, Vernon K. *Jesus the Teacher: A Socio-Rhteorical Interpretation of Mark*. Philadelphia, 1984.

Roskam, Hendrika Nicoline. *The Purpose of the Gospel of Mark in its Historical and Social Context.* Supplements to *Novum Testamentum*, 114. Leiden, 2004.

Sabbe, Maurits (ed.). *L'Évangile selon Marc.*. Bibliotheca Ephemeridum Theologicarum Lovaniensium, 34. Leuven, 1974.

Schmidt, Karl Ludwig. *Der Rahmen der Geschichte Jesu. Literarische Untersuchungen zur ältesten Jesusüberlieferung*. Darmstadt, 1963. [Originally published 1919.]

Smith, Morton. *Clement of Alexandria and a Secret Gospel of Mark*. Cambridge, MA, 1973.

Söding, Thomas (ed.). *Der Evangelist als Theologe. Studien zum Markusevangelium*. Stuttgarter Bibelstudien, 163. Stuttgart, 1995.

Taylor, Vincent. *The Gospel According to St. Mark*. London, 1953.

Taylor Shiner, Whitney. *Proclaiming the Gospel: First-Century Performance of Mark.* Harrisburg, 2003.

Telford, William R. *The Theology of the Gospel of Mark.* Cambridge, 1999.

Wrede, William. *The Messianic Secret.* Trans. J. C. G. Greig. Cambridge. [Originally published in German, 1901.]

Yarbro Collins, Adela. "From noble death to crucified Messiah." *New Testament Studies* 40 (1994), 481–503.

CHAPTER 18

# The Gospel of Matthew

## Dennis C. Duling

## Major Issues and Directions in Recent Study

Historically the Gospel of Matthew has been one of the most influential books in the Christian version of the Bible. It contains familiar material to Christians, including an account of the Virgin Birth; ethical teachings in Jesus' Sermon on the Mount; the Lord's Prayer ("Our Father"); the Last Supper; missionary instructions; distinctive parables; church law, discipline, and conduct; references to baptism, including a Trinitarian-sounding baptismal formula; and an attribution of authority to Peter so important that it eventually became the key biblical passage for defending the primacy of the bishop of Rome in the third century CE. From the second to the eighteenth centuries Matthew was believed to have been composed about a decade after the middle of the first century by a Galilean toll collector and disciple of Jesus named Matthew. So important were the putative author and the content of this gospel that it was placed first in ancient scrolls of the four gospels and, when the New Testament canon was finally formed and the gospels placed first, it became the first book in the New Testament.

Scholarly study of Matthew beginning in the eighteenth century has led to a very different theory of its origins. The critical consensus is that Matthew was not composed by Jesus' disciple Matthew within three decades after Jesus' death, but rather by an unknown scribe near the end of the first century, one who had at his disposal a variety of oral traditions and written sources about Jesus. This perspective means that Matthew is a highly interpreted source for the life of Jesus and modern scholars resort to a variety of critical methods to interpret it.

The newest directions in contemporary critical scholarship shift the focus to Matthew's revision of sources and literary composition on the one hand and to its historical, political, and cultural settings on the other. Isolating Matthew's sources allows access to how the ancient author interpreted them in a particular historical and social context. Some modern literary analysts shift the focus to the final form of the story, stressing matters such as plot, characters, and point of view, or, if they are interested in ancient forms, to genre. Historical questions have been given impetus by the discovery of the Nag Hammadi texts and the Dead Sea Scrolls, sources that offer rich comparative material for a variety of Matthean passages, especially Jesus' interpretation of the Torah. Recent social-historical, social-scientific, and feminist interpretations also open up many new avenues of interpretation.

Several key issues in recent scholarship are worth noting. The first, primarily historical and literary, is the question whether the gospel is really "Christian" in the usual sense of the term. A number of scholars now hold that it is a "Jewish" document that represents a "sectarian" community of those who believed that Jesus was a messiah and who opposed those who did not, especially the Pharisees. Understanding the gospel as "Jewish" – in this essay, "Israelite" (in conformity with Matthean language) – has its own problems, for example, determining what "Jewishness" was in the late first century CE. The importance of this issue cannot be underestimated, given worldwide ethnic tensions, especially post-Holocaust Jewish–Christian–Muslim relations.

The second issue concerns social relations in the gospel. Examples are problems related to the politically powerful few and powerless many, rich and poor, large institutions in tension with marginal groups and persons, styles of leadership, family relations, gender dynamics, marriage and divorce, insiders in conflict with outsiders, internal conflicts and community organization, the law and religious questions, ethnic prejudices, and political tensions with Rome. Perspectives on these social relations and others help to understand the author, the community or communities in and for which Matthew was written, and related historical questions. One example will suffice.

Those who live in modern western democracies normally think of social strata in terms of three major classes, a smaller upper class, a very large middle class, and a smaller lower class, with some gradations between. In contrast, advanced agrarian societies – the ancient Roman empire is a major example – have a tiny, wealthy, ruling elite supported by an official cult, a military establishment, and government bureaucracy ("retainers"). Below them are the vast ruled masses consisting mainly of poorer rural peasants, but also a few merchants, artisans, and at the very bottom "expendables," such as bandits, beggars, and prostitutes. In short, there are two major classes, not three; there is no real middle class. This social ranking is relatively static, that is, fixed by birth. Upward social mobility is virtually negligible with the exception of military advancement, voluntary associations, and certain marriage alliances. By careful observation it is possible to see this vertical social stratification in Matthew: Caesar; prefects/procurators; kings and client kings; priestly aristocracy; lay aristocracy; priests; elders; merchants; retainers (toll collectors; military personnel, Roman centurions, temple police); scribes; "ruler (of the synagogue)"; artisans and fisherfolk; slaves; peasants; the urban poor; the unclean; crowds; day laborers; tenant farmers; expendables and the destitute (the blind, lame, and dumb; paralytics, epileptics, demoniacs, and lepers; a man with withered hand; bandits; thieves). There are also herders, which is a different social structure.

For the Christian churches that have preserved the gospel as sacred and normative, these directions in Matthean study have given it a new relevance, especially in the area of understanding religious beliefs, social relations, and ethical norms.

## Date and Place of Writing

About 185 CE a "Church Father" named Irenaeus, bishop of Lyons, Gaul (modern France), claimed that Matthew was written in Hebrew by Jesus' disciple Matthew at the time Peter and Paul were in Rome (*Against Heresies*, 3.1.1), which by modern calculations would have been in the late 50s or early 60s. In the fifth century CE another Church Father, Jerome, naturally deduced that Hebrew Matthew was written in Judea (*On Illustrious Men*, 3). Modern scholars have doubts about Irenaeus' and Jerome's views. Their alternative theories are based on four kinds of evidence: (1) earliest references to the gospel by early church writers; (2) references within the gospel story to datable historical events; (3) the gospel writer's use of sources; and (4) a plausible social-historical context. These need to be noted.

The earliest surviving manuscripts of Matthew are ancient Greek papyri from Egypt dating from about 200 CE (see "Textual Problems" below), but other evidence by Church Fathers puts the date earlier. About 110 CE, Ignatius, bishop of Antioch, Syria, cited a distinctly Matthean phrase, "that all righteousness might be fulfilled by him" (Matt. 3:15; Ignatius, *To the Smyrnaeans*, 1.1). Most scholars think that this reference was derived from Matthew itself (see also Matt. 15:13 in *To the Philadelphians*, 3.1). Some scholars have argued that the author of 1 Peter in the New Testament, writing perhaps as early as 90–100 CE, also knew Matthew (1 Pet. 2:12 [Matt. 5:16]; 1 Pet. 3:14 [Matt. 5:10]); however, the allusions in 1 Peter might have come from oral tradition, not the written gospel. In short, the latest possible date for composition (*terminus ad quem*) is usually fixed at about 110 CE.

The earliest possible date (*terminus a quo*) for Matthew is sometime after 70 CE. Mark 13:14 refers to the "desolating sacrilege" set up where it ought not to be, and this gospel is usually dated about 70 CE. Matthew 24:15–16 interprets the Markan words (see "Sources and Intertextuality") as *someone standing in the holy place* and identifies their scriptural source as "the prophet Daniel" (Dan. 9:27; 11:31; 12:11; cf. 1 Macc. 1:54). Most scholars think that these words allude to the Roman general Titus who not only ravaged Jerusalem, but destroyed the temple in 70 CE, an event commemorated by the Arch of Titus in the Roman Forum. Titus subsequently became emperor (79–81 CE) and it is very likely that an allegorical comment in Matthew 22:7 – a "king"/"emperor" destroyed "their [the Israelites'] city" – refers to the destruction of Jerusalem in 70 CE. The range of possibility is 70 to 110 CE. Most scholars prefer a date for Matthew midway between, about 80–90 CE, allowing some years after Mark. This time period is strongly supported by an internal analysis of Matthew and other known historical events (see "Occasion" and "Literary and Composition Analysis").

The gospel's place of origin is uncertain. As noted, fifth-century Jerome settled on Judea. Modern scholars favor some urban area with a mixed ethnic/religious population because the gospel is written in Greek and yet has a strong Semitic flavor and represents an Israelite-oriented Christ-believing community (see "Literary and Composition Analysis"). Jerusalem, Caesarea Maritima, Alexandria (Egypt), and Edessa (Syria), have been proposed, but have not won much favor. Two passages in the gospel say that Galilee and Judea lay "beyond [west of] the Jordan" (Matt. 19:1; 4:15), which suggests some place *east* of the Jordan river, possibly Pella where, according to a church tradition Christ believers of Jerusalem migrated just before the revolt against Rome in 66 CE (Eusebius, *Ecclesiastical History*, 3.5; the tradition is sometimes contested). Others have argued for some location in Galilee or southern Syria. The most common suggestion, however, is Antioch in Syria. It was a large Hellenistic city, had a mixed ethnic population, including many Israelites, and became a center of early church missionary activity. This theory has the added advantage that the earliest likely reference to the written gospel, as stated previously, comes from Ignatius of Antioch about 110 CE.

## Textual Problems and Language

In the late second century Irenaeus thought that the original language of Matthew was Hebrew and this view persisted in the Church Fathers. A Hebrew version of Matthew exists, and one modern scholar speculates that its origin was ancient (Howard 1995). However, other scholars judge it to be medieval (e.g., Petersen 1989) and it is generally accepted that the original language of Matthew was Greek, not Hebrew (or Aramaic), despite the gospel's strong Semitic flavor.

The best and earliest Greek papyri of the New Testament, Papyrus 66 ($\mathfrak{P}^{66}$) and Papyrus 75 ($\mathfrak{P}^{75}$), both from the late second or early third century CE, unfortunately do not contain Matthew. Twenty-four Greek papyrus fragments that do contain Matthew date from about 200 to 800 CE. This group includes the "Magdalen Papyrus" ($\mathfrak{P}^{64}$ [plus $\mathfrak{P}^{67}$ and $\mathfrak{P}^{4}$]) which contains three Matthew fragments (26:7–8 + 31; 26:10 + 32–3; 26:14–15 + 22–3). Early papyrologists dated the fragments to about 200 CE. Carston Thiede has attempted to redate them to the late first century CE (Thiede 1995), but other papyrologists support the earlier view (e.g., Elliott 1996; Head 1995; Parker 1996; Peterson 1995). The most valuable of the remaining manuscripts that contain Matthew are the uncials (block capital letter manuscripts) Codex Sinaiticus (or $\aleph$) and Codex Vaticanus (B), both dated to the fourth century CE, and some Coptic translations in the Sahidic and Boharic dialects. They are considered to be from the best manuscripts called the Alexandrian Text Type which had its origins some time in the early second century.

Bruce Metzger's *A Textual Commentary on the Greek New Testament* (2002 [1971]) lists 216 noteworthy textual variants in the Greek text of Matthew, most of them copyists' errors. The following example is an important exception.

The familiar doxology "for yours is the kingdom and the power and the glory forever" which in some churches is prayed at the end of the Lord's Prayer (Matt. 6:13) has several variations in the manuscripts. Moreover, the manuscripts are relatively late. Unfortunately, the twenty-four surviving papyri fragments do not contain this section of Matthew. The early important uncial manuscripts Sinaiticus and Vaticanus have the prayer but not the concluding doxology. Other early manuscripts of less reliable text types, the Western Text (especially Codex Claromontanus, or D) and the pre-Caesarean Text Type ($f^1$), as well as early Church Fathers, who comment on the Lord's Prayer, do not have the doxology, either. Thus, the overwhelming manuscript evidence is that the Lord's Prayer in Matthew never ended with the doxology. Text critics think that it was added to the prayer, perhaps from early Christian liturgies, and may ultimately have gone back to a similar doxology in 1 Chronicles 29:11–13 (especially verse 11). Later manuscripts of Jerome's late fourth-/early fifth-century Latin Vulgate conform in this instance to the best early manuscripts. Consequently, the Roman Catholic liturgy of the Mass which is based on the Vulgate is probably textually accurate when it omits the doxology immediately after the Our Father (it is recited slightly later).

## Literary Genre

The modern English word "gospel" is derived from Old English *godspell*, "good news," which translates Latin *evangelium* or Greek *euangelion*, both of which in turn are possible translations of biblical Hebrew *basrah*. In sixth-century BCE Israel the verb *basar* (Greek *euangelizesthai*) was used "to proclaim" or "to announce" by God's messenger peace, good news, and the reign of God (Isa. 52:7; cf. Isa. 40:9). Centuries later in 9 BCE a Greek inscription from Asia Minor (western Turkey), the "Calendar Inscription of Priene," in describing the emperor Augustus with honor-laden titles ("savior," greatest of all "benefactors," and "god"), referred to the "good news" (*euangelion*) that was heralded as a new era of peace. Thus, in both the Hebrew and Greek languages the term "gospel" meant oral proclamation of good news about a deity's gift of salvation. Not surprisingly, New Testament references to *euangelion*, especially Paul's statements about Jesus' death and resurrection, can have this meaning.

No book called "gospel" has survived outside the New Testament. Furthermore, the ancient titles of the gospels in the manuscripts ("superscriptions") were simply "According to Matthew," "According to Mark," and so on, *without* the term "gospel." To be sure, the first verse of the Gospel of Mark says, "The beginning of *the gospel* of Jesus Christ ..." (1:1). However, "gospel" in this verse probably did not originally refer to the whole book. In any case, such a verse does not appear in the other three canonical gospels. Thus, it is possible that these books were not called "gospel" until the latter half of second century CE.

The name itself does not solve the problem of the genre. Various candidates for a predecessor or prototype of the gospel genre include:

1   Ancient biographies or *bioi* ("lives"), that is, tales about the remarkable exploits of gods, heroes, and heroines. Problem: surviving *bioi* are longer and some details do not conform to the New Testament gospels.
2   *Aretalogy*, a story of a hero who has "virtue" (Greek *aretē*), teaches, works miracles, and is martyred. Problem: no ancient text is called by this modern name.
3   *Greek tragedy* (complication, crisis, resolution). Problem: a debating, miracle-working Galilean does not quite fit the tragedy form.
4   *Tragicomedy*, a "hopeful" tragedy. Problem: same as 3.
5   Hellenistic *"romance"* novel, which combines history with myth. Problem: its strange and fanciful elements are not like stories in the gospels.
6   *Martyrology*, story of a brave person's martyrdom. Problem: it has a very different tone.

7   *Midrash*, narrative commentary of Israelite sacred scripture. Problem: it is too narrow to fit the New Testament gospels.

8   *Church lectionary*, or readings for the church calendar. Problem: it is very difficult to demonstrate lectionary elements in the gospels.

9   *Parable*. Parables have a mysterious element and are open to various interpretations. Problem: the gospels are too long and the outcome is implied in advance.

10  *Apocalyptic myth*, which transfers paradise into the future, with impending social and cosmic disruption. Problem: while apocalyptic themes are very important in the gospels, at least in Mark and Matthew, they are combined with non-apocalyptic features and their protagonist is a recent historical figure.

11  *Prophet biography* combined with *office biography*. Problem: looks promising, but has not yet won support.

None of these suggested genres is *totally* satisfactory. In Matthew "gospel" refers to what Jesus *says* (e.g., 4:23; 9:35), not the whole narrative. Nonetheless, genres are never totally new or pure; communication requires some sort of understandable genre (Stanton 1992: 54–5). The most satisfactory view among scholars at present is that Matthew is a subgenre of the ancient Greco-Roman biography, or *bios* (Shuler 1982; Aune 1988a, 1988b; Burridge 2004: 218–19; Neyrey 1998: 91). Aune defines it thus (1988b: 107):

> Greco-Roman biography is a type of independent literary composition which typically focused on the character, achievements and lasting significance of a memorable and exemplary individual from birth to death, emphasizing his public career.

Matthew fits this genre definition. It also has a popular literary style, a chronologically ordered narrative, a plot much like Greek tragedy, and the inclusion of oral and literary forms (Aune 1988a: 47–54). It praises its hero (*encomium*) and functions as religious propaganda, as a model for insiders of the lower social strata in the Christ Movement.

## Author and Setting

The earliest surviving tradition about Matthew comes from Papias of Hierapolis in Asia Minor (modern Turkey) about 125–50 CE. His views were preserved by the early Christian historian, Eusebius of Caesarea (ca. 260–ca. 339 CE), generally held by modern scholars to be fairly trustworthy. The "Papias tradition" says, "Then Matthew put together [text variant "wrote"] the sayings [*logia*] in Matthew the Hebrew [*Hebraiois*] dialect [*dialectō*] and each one translated [*hērmēneusen*] them as he was able" (Eusebius, *Ecclesiastical History*, 3.39.16). By "Matthew" it is very likely that Papias had in mind Jesus' disciple (Mark 3:18; Matt. 10:3; Luke 6:15; Acts 1:13). In Matthew – and only in Matthew – "Matthew" is identified as "the toll collector" (Matt. 10:3: *telōnēs*), the one previously said to have been sitting at the "toll booth" (Matt. 9:9: *telōnion*) near Capernaum (the northwest corner of the Lake of Galilee). The parallels in Mark 2:14

and Luke 5:27 call this toll collector "Levi," not Matthew, but Levi is not in the disciple lists. Modern scholars usually interpret the Papias tradition to mean that Papias thought that Jesus' disciple Matthew the toll collector had assembled a collection of Jesus' sayings in Hebrew (or Aramaic, cf. John 20:16) and then others translated them (Irenaeus, *Against Heresies*, 31.1–2; Eusebius, *Ecclesiastical History*, 3.24.5).

If this interpretation of Papias is correct, there are several historical problems. First, modern specialists in language hold that the author of Matthew wrote in Greek, not Hebrew or Aramaic. Second, most scholars accept the Two-Source theory (see Chapter 15, "The Synoptic Problem," in this volume). This theory requires that the author of Matthew knew and used Greek versions of Mark and Greek Q as sources. Third, the gospel *contains* sayings and sayings collections, but is itself not a collection of sayings such as Proverbs or the *Gospel of Thomas*. In short, Papias' description does not correspond well with the New Testament.

Nonetheless, by the second half of the second century CE the Papias tradition had become normative: Jesus' disciple Matthew was thought to be the gospel's author and "According to Matthew" as a superscription found its way into the manuscripts. Why Matthew and not some other person? It is impossible to be certain, but there are excellent possibilities. The author surely wanted apostolic authority for his story, and the disciple Matthew fits. This disciple/apostle was most likely honored in the circles where the gospel was written. The name "Matthew" is more prominent in this gospel (Matt. 9:9; 10:3) than the other gospels. In Hebrew Matthew means "gift of Yah(weh)" and a feature of the narrative is that God graciously accepts "toll collectors and sinners." Again, Torah teacher is a dominant image of Jesus in the gospel and in Greek *mathētēs* means "learner," that is, "disciple," and the command *mathete* means "learn!" Thus, the name *Matthias* might have suggested a learned disciple. Whatever the reason – some combination is possible – second-century Christ believers attributed this gospel to Jesus' disciple, the Capernaum toll collector. Papias undoubtedly meant this person.

Although the Papias description does not precisely describe Matthew, much can be said about the unknown author of Matthew on the basis of internal analysis. The author wrote very good Greek. This Greek betrays the influence of Semitic languages (see "Literary Composition and Analysis" below), implying that the author was an Israelite ethnically and religiously. Internal analysis also suggests that the author had intimate familiarity with technical legal issues of Torah that were debated in his day. Internal analysis further indicates that there are many inconsistencies, paradoxes, and tensions in the story. Thus, it is likely that the author (and probably the community in and for which he wrote) stood on the boundary between traditional and non-traditional Israelite values. Finally, the author was male. Consider, for example, certain ethnic, purity, and especially gender issues. The Matthean Jesus accepts women among his followers (27:55–6), is willing to transgress the purity code by touching a woman with a flow of blood (9:20–2 [Mark 5:25–34]), heals a synagogue leader's daughter (9:18–19, 23–6 [Mark 5:21–5, 35–42]) and the daughter of a Canaanite woman because of the mother's great faith (15:21–8 [Mark 7:24–30]), and says that a woman at Bethany will be remembered for anointing Jesus (26:6–13 [Mark 14:3–9]). Nevertheless, the male Jesus and his male disciples seem to control the dramatic action. An illustration is the warning to *men* about the lusty eye (5:26).

Again, the author was most probably an ethnic Israelite male scribe from some Hellenistic city, possibly Antioch of Syria.

The impression that the author was an urban Israelite male scribe is reinforced by the scribal image of Jesus in the gospel. Jesus' scholarly attack on the Pharisees and the(ir) scribes can be vicious. Six times the author of Matthew has him say, "Woe to you, scribes and Pharisees, hypocrites!" (23:13, 15, 23, 25, 27, 29). Jesus adds, "Woe to you blind guides" (23:16) and "... you ... outwardly appear righteous to men, but within you are full of hypocrisy and iniquity" (23:28). However, the writer is not always consistent in his view of Jesus' attacks. On the one hand the Pharisees are said to be quite correct: "The scribes and the Pharisees sit on Moses' seat; so practice and observe whatever they tell you" (Matt. 23:2–3). On the other hand they are said to interpret the details of the Torah incorrectly (e.g., 15:6). On the one hand the Pharisees are said to observe Torah laws very carefully (6:1–18); on the other hand, they are condemned for not practicing what they teach (23:2b). On the one hand Jesus forbids using Pharisaic titles such as "rabbi," "father," and "instructor" (Matt. 23:8–10). On the other, there appear to be clearly defined leadership roles: "prophets" (10:41; 23:34) and warnings against "false prophets" (7:15–23; cf. 24:11–12, 23–4; cf. *Didache*, 11–13); Matthean "scribes" like the author (13:52; 23:34); "wise men" (23:34); and "righteous men" (10:41–2; 13:17; 23:29).

It should be observed in this connection that there is a more positive image of the disciples in Matthew than in his Markan source. Peter is given authority, probably teaching authority (16:17–19). In contrast to Mark, at times the disciples are credited with having understanding (e.g., 13:51; cf. the omission in 14:32 [Mark 6:52] and 17:23 [9:32]), even if they are labeled "men of little faith" (6:30; 8:26; 14:31; 16:8). Indeed, the resurrected Jesus sends them out as dependable missionaries to baptize all the peoples of the world (28:19).

The sharpened conflicts between the Pharisees and Jesus in Matthew suggest that the gospel emerged in relation to the growing authority of the Pharisees in the late first century CE. That, plus echoes of Palestinian traditions, the author's facility with Semitic and Greek languages, his knowledge of the Torah and Prophets, and his five-book structure (see "Structure") – all suggest that the author may have been a Jesus-believing Israelite scribe "trained ["discipled"] for the Kingdom," thus, "like a master of a household who brings out of his treasure what is new and what is old" (13:52). He stands on the boundary between the old order and the new order (Duling 1993; Senior 1999).

## Occasion

The major historical event in the Mediterranean region in the first century was the Jewish Revolt against Rome (66–73 CE). The war resulted in the Roman destruction of the city of Jerusalem and its sacred temple in 70 CE, as already noted. The temple, despite priestly abuses, symbolized traditional Israelites' cultural, political, economic, social, and religious life and values. Romans would have viewed Christ believers as members of a messianic sect of Israel and from time to time as potentially suspect. Eusebius of Caesarea, claiming as his source second-century Hegesippus, says that the

Roman emperor Domitian (81–96 CE) interviewed Jesus' relatives who were descended from David, found them to be poor peasants incapable of insurrection, and released them, whereupon they continued to lead the church (Eusebius, *Ecclesiastical History*, 3.19–20).

This empire context is important for Matthew, which was written in the post-war years (Riches and Sim 2005). The Romans were imperialists. They had a self-defined ethnocentric identity supported by an imperial ideology illustrated by a sentence taken from a longer inscription at the Emperor Augustus' tomb in Rome (the *Res Gestae Divi Augusti*): "These are the deeds performed by the deified Augustus, by which he subjected the entire world to the power [*imperio*] of the Roman people [*populi Romani*]." The term translated "power" is the Latin word *imperium*, which can also be translated "empire," and which has roots in the Roman army. In short, the divine Augustus, mediator of the gods, is said to have universal rule over the empire on behalf of the elect Roman "people" (*populi*). This ideology is clearly a Roman theology.

The Greek equivalents of the two Latin terms from the inscription are *basileia*, which is usually translated "kingdom," but can also mean "empire," and *ethnos*, which is usually translated "nation," but should usually be translated "people." Modern readings have usually viewed Matthew as relatively neutral about Roman politics, indeed to a certain extent pro-Roman or pacifist. Illustrations are the portraits of the Roman Pontius Pilate and his wife who, in contrast to the Israelite leaders and the people, think that Jesus is innocent (27:19, 24). However, while it is possible to suggest that Pilate's wife is positively portrayed – she responds to a dream message and recognizes Jesus as a "righteous man" – Pilate himself is indecisive and vacillating and in the end yields to the crowd (Weaver in Riches and Sim 2005). In general, a political reading suggests that Jesus' proclamation of God's *basileia* is an alternative to the Roman *basileia*: the true empire is the empire of *God*, not Caesar, and his true mediator is his messiah Jesus, not the emperor. The political implications of this reading are enormous.

Narrowing down to Palestine in the late first century CE, three of the four major Israelite parties mentioned by the ancient historian Josephus did not survive the war with Rome. The aristocratic Sadducees whose power centered in the temple gradually disappeared. Their priestly rivals, the sectarian Essenes living along the shore of the Dead Sea, were overrun by the Romans. The rebellious "fourth philosophy" and related groups were finally defeated when the Romans defeated the Sicarii at the siege of Masada along the Dead Sea. That left the Pharisees.

During the war, a prominent Pharisee named Rabbi Johanan ben Zakkai received permission from Rome to establish a school at Yavneh (Greek Jamnia) in Judea not far from the Mediterranean coast. From this center the Pharisees sought to extend their authority in the years following the war. They copied, interpreted, and attempted to punctiliously adhere to Torah regulations in everyday life, especially in the area of ritual purity. Their special concerns were rules about kosher food, strict observance of the Sabbath, festivals, prayer, fasting, almsgiving, payment of tithes, swearing oaths, and lawful and unlawful divorce. Their concrete applications built "a fence around the Torah," that is, offered specific rules to help the pious avoid violating general commands. Their interpretations led to an elaborate oral tradition which, they claimed, came from Moses himself. Legal experts – rabbis and scribes – committed the laws and their interpretations to memory, some of which was eventually codified as the Mishnah about 200 CE. Sometime in the late first or early second century CE the Pharisees also inserted into the synagogue prayers the "Prayer Against the Heretics" which was meant to condemn deviants, including members of messianic sects, and ban them from the synagogues (cf. John 9:22, 34; 12:42; 16:2a). They also began the process of establishing the Hebrew canon. Assembling sacred books and the correct interpretation of them were two impulses for the eventual formation of "rabbinic Judaism."

As noted, attitudes toward the emergent Pharisees in Matthew are openly hostile and include the sevenfold hypocrisy charge (23:13–31) and scattered references to "*their* synagogues" (4:23; 9:35; cf. 10:7; 28:20) and "*their* scribes" (7:29). Such references illustrate intensified conflict between the Pharisees in the Matthean communities in the late first century. Antagonism between Pharisees and Matthean Christ believers raises an important question: were the Matthean groups still part of the house of Israel or had there been a "parting of the ways"? Several scholars have recently argued that the conflict was not a conflict between "Pharisaic *Judaism*" and "Matthean *Christianity*," but between two rival "*Jewish* sects," one that believed that Jesus was the messiah and one that did not (e.g., Overman 1990; Saldarini 1994). From this perspective, Matthew is an *Israelite* writer living in an *Israelite* community.

An alternative reading is that these Jesus messianists were further along in the process of separating from the house of Israel, at least as led by the Pharisees. To be sure, Jesus' own mission had been to "the lost sheep of the house of Israel" (10:5; 15:24); however, polemic against the Pharisees combined with opposition from the Jerusalem leaders in the execution of Jesus leads to this comment: "Then the people as a whole answered, 'His blood be on us and on our children!' " (27:25).

In addition to conflict with Israelites, there is openness to non-Israelites in Matthew. While the disciples do not teach during the course of Jesus' life, the author's transfer of teaching authority to Peter (16:17–19) anticipates the final gospel scene where all eleven disciples are given authority to teach converts from all *ethnē* ("peoples") what Jesus commanded (28:19). This move toward non-Israelites is anticipated in passages such as Jesus' descent from Abraham and the four women (1:1, 3, 5, 6), Galilee as the land of the Gentiles (4:15), the healing of the centurion's servant (8:5–13), and the healing of the Canaanite woman's daughter (15:21–8). The suggestion has been made that the final commission to the disciples was really about a mission to Israelites of the Diaspora (Jackson 2000), but the more likely interpretation is that "all *ethnē*" refers to both Israelites and non-Israelites (recently, Stanton 1995; Davies and Allison 1988–97). Some scholars have called this a "third race." At the very least, the Matthean group stands on the boundary "between Israel and non-Israel," which is one social-scientific definition of marginality (Duling 1993, 2002).

Another dimension of conflict in Matthew is internal. Jesus tells parables illustrating that there will be good and bad persons (13:24–30; 22:1–14; 25:1–13) and "righteous" and "unrighteous" persons in the Matthean communities (13:41; 16:28) until the Day of Judgment. In the parable of the wedding garment, Jesus warns that "many are called, but few are chosen" (22:11–14).

In sum, political readings of Matthew suggest that its author was a scribe trained for *God's* empire, not the Roman empire. Divine imperialism is set against Roman imperialism. The author also wrote his story to legitimate various Christ-believing communities in conflict with the Pharisees in a particular region of the Roman empire. He may have been offering teachers a way of instructing large numbers of mostly uneducated, illiterate new believers drawn from *all* the "peoples." At the same time, there is clear evidence of internal conflict. Such an occasion fits an ethnically mixed group in a large city, perhaps Antioch, about 80–90 CE.

## Literary Composition and Analysis

The Greek of Matthew is a more polished Semitic Greek than one finds in Mark. The Matthean author's language has been affected also by the Greek translation of Hebrew sacred texts, sometimes characterized as "synagogue Greek" (Luz 1989: 49–73). Certainly the author displays a number of linguistic features that indicate Semitic influence. There are Hebrew and Aramaic idioms and parallel sentences typical of Hebrew poetry (*parallelismus membrorum*). Themes occur that are developed through the narrative. The writer likes certain numbers and numerical groupings. Doubling and the number two occur very frequently: two disciples (21:1); two brothers (1:2; 4:2, 18, 21; 6:24; 20:21, 24); two masters (6:24); two demoniacs (8:28); two men and two women (24:40, 41); two sons (20:21; 21:28); two witnesses (18:16; 19, 20); two robbers (27:38); two great commandments (22:40); two tunics (10:10); two sparrows (10:29); two fish (14:17, 19); two hands and two feet (18:8); two eyes (18:9); two talents (25:15, 17, 22). He duplicates significant words in a section, such as "angel of the Lord" (1:18–2:23) or "righteousness" (5–7). There are also different accounts of essentially the same story, or "doublets," such as two accounts of two blind men (9:27–31; 20:29–34). He likes the number three, as well: three days (12:40; 15:32; 26:61; 27:40) and three nights (12:40); three measures of wheat (13:33); three booths (17:4); three denials (26:34).

Numbers also influence the organization of sections. There are two sets of three antitheses (5:21–48); three religious practices (6:1–18); three kinds of destruction (moths, rust, and thieves, 6:19–24); and three warnings (7:12). There are four parables about the church (21:28–22:11), seven parables (13) and seven "woes" (23). The author often collects together materials around a common theme (e.g., ten miracles [8–9]; three parables that deal with the relationship of Israel to the "church" [21:28–22:14]; seven woes against Pharisees [23]; see the five discourses discussed below). The style of Matthew is often very tightly focused and appears to be designed for teaching.

Other examples of tight construction appear. Modern scholars call one such construction "framing" or "inclusion," that is, beginning and concluding sections with verses that are the same or similar and that summarize the intervening content. One of the best examples is the section Matthew 4:23–9:35. The author introduces this section with a teaching/preaching and healing summary sentence (4:23). He constructs the Sermon on the Mount (Matt. 5–7) and then clusters together ten miracle stories (Matt. 8–9). Indeed, he duplicates a couple of stories (doublets), apparently to arrive at the number ten. As Moses received the Torah on a mountain, so Jesus teaches the new Torah on a mountain (and he sits to teach, like teachers of Torah!); and as

Moses performed ten miracles in Egypt (the plagues), so Jesus performs ten miracles in Galilee. Jesus is the new Moses (Allison 1993). This alternation of teaching by, and narrative about, Jesus is typical of the gospel. Finally, he concludes the five chapters with virtually the same summary sentence that opened them (9:35; see 4:23). In other words, he frames the two sections with summary formulae. An outline of this section looks like this:

4:23: summary introduction:
    "And *he* went about all *Galilee*,
    *teaching* in their synagogues and
    *preaching* the gospel of the kingdom, and
    *healing* every disease and every infirmity *among the people*."
5–7: teaching and preaching (The Sermon on the Mount)
8–9: healing (a cluster or ten miracles)
9:35: summary conclusion:
    And *Jesus* went about all *the cities and villages*,
    *teaching* in their synagogues and
    *preaching* the gospel of the kingdom, and
    *healing* every disease and every infirmity.

Given the tight structure of this section, one might think that the rest of the gospel is very tightly structured. Did its author have a plan?

At least three major observations have been made. First, the overall spatial plan follows Mark: Galilee – Caesarea Philippi – Jerusalem – but it is prefaced with a genealogy and infancy story (1–2) and concluded with a post-resurrection appearance (28:16–20). In the intervening sections, some of the author's most distinctive changes are found in the first half of the gospel. Not only does he preface his narrative with an infancy story, he becomes structurally innovative in chapters 5–13, as the teaching/preaching and healing section just discussed shows. The result is that the gospel is rather carefully and tightly structured in the first thirteen chapters. However, he follows Mark more closely from 14:1 to the end, as he had in chapters 3–4. Did the author experience "literary fatigue" in the latter half of the gospel (Gundry 1994: 10; Goodacre 1998)?

A second major structural observation also takes account of the Markan geographical framework, but attempts to demonstrate how the author centers his arrangement around five major discourses. He expanded two Markan speeches (Mark 4 = Matthew 13; Mark 13 = Matthew 24–5), but added three more developed mostly from Q and Special M (Matt. 5–7; Matt. 10; Matt. 18). Each of these five discourses ends with a formula, "when Jesus [had] finished these sayings," as in Figure 18.1.

Building on the influential work of B. W. Bacon (1930), C. H. Lohr (1961) put forth a gospel outline based on the five speeches (Figure 18.2). This balanced structure is a giant "chiasm" or "ring structure" (A, B, C, D, E, F, G, F′, E′, D′, C′, B′, A′). It alternates six narrative segments (italics) with five discourses (boldface) and frames or brackets the whole by a Prologue and an Epilogue. The construction is balanced, that is, discourses 1 and 5 (C, C′) are longer, discourses 2 and 4 (E, E′) are somewhat shorter and about the same length, and the parables chapter, chapter 13, is in the center.

| Matthew | Subject of Discourse | | Formula Ending |
|---|---|---|---|
| 5:1-7:27 | Sermon on the mount | 7:28: | And when Jesus finished these sayings |
| 10:5-42 | Missionary discourse | 11:1 | And when Jesus had finished instructing his twelve disciples |
| 13:1-52 | Teaching in parables | 13:53 | And when Jesus had finished these parables |
| 18:1-35 | Community regulations | 19:1: | Now when Jesus finished these sayings |
| 24:3-25:46 | Apocalyptic discourse | 26:1 | When Jesus had finished all these sayings |

**Figure 18.1**

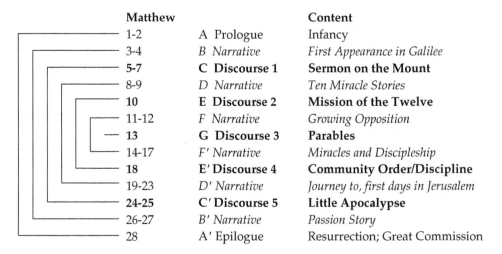

| Matthew | | Content |
|---|---|---|
| 1-2 | A Prologue | Infancy |
| 3-4 | B Narrative | First Appearance in Galilee |
| 5-7 | C Discourse 1 | Sermon on the Mount |
| 8-9 | D Narrative | Ten Miracle Stories |
| 10 | E Discourse 2 | Mission of the Twelve |
| 11-12 | F Narrative | Growing Opposition |
| 13 | G Discourse 3 | Parables |
| 14-17 | F' Narrative | Miracles and Discipleship |
| 18 | E' Discourse 4 | Community Order/Discipline |
| 19-23 | D' Narrative | Journey to, first days in Jerusalem |
| 24-25 | C' Discourse 5 | Little Apocalypse |
| 26-27 | B' Narrative | Passion Story |
| 28 | A' Epilogue | Resurrection; Great Commission |

**Figure 18.2**

Organization around five books is surely not accidental. As B. W. Bacon realized long ago (1930), perhaps it hints at the five books of the Torah (the Pentateuch) believed by first-century Israelites to have been written by Moses. For Matthew, the new revelation fulfills, yet supersedes, the old. Perhaps Jesus was being interpreted as the new Moses: as Moses taught (and wrote) a five-book Torah – "the book of Moses" – so Jesus taught a new five-book Torah. This structure corresponds to several covert Moses themes in the narrative, for example, murder of male infants (2:16–18), exodus from Egypt (2:13–15), revelation on a mountain (5–7), and ten miracles (8–9). It reinforces the dominant Matthean image of Jesus as teacher.

Not all scholars are content with the five-book hypothesis. First, it seems a little too neat. Second, the structure is not as carefully constructed when the author picks up the Markan outline in chapter 14. While these two objections seem to cancel out each other, a third and related complication is that Matthew 11 and 23, which fall in the narrative sections, are actually more discourse than narrative. Fourth, there are also

| I | 1:1-4:16 | The Person of Jesus Messiah, Son of God |
| II | 4:17-16:20 | The Proclamation of Jesus Messiah |
| III | 16:21-28:20 | The Suffering, Death, and Resurrection of Jesus Messiah |

**Figure 18.3**

minor speeches in supposed narrative sections (e.g., 12:25–45; 21:18–22:14). Finally, since the author has no hesitation to think of Jesus as the Davidic messiah Son of David/ Son of God, why is the notion of Jesus as the new Moses not more explicit?

Problems such as these have led to other structural hypotheses. Taking account of another formula, "from that time on, Jesus began ... ," which occurs twice (4:17; 16:21), the gospel can be divided into three sections (Krentz 1964; Kingsbury 1989: 1–37; see Figure 18.3). This structure highlights an exalted view of Jesus (Christology) in Matthew, as well as the thesis that the author develops a continuous, unified story. This division also has problems. The twofold "from that time on Jesus began ..." is not nearly as pronounced as the speech-ending formula of the five-discourse structure. Also, it plays down what seems to be a clear break between the infancy (chs. 1–2) and beginning of the adult years (chs. 3–4), which is marked in 3:1 by a time reference, "In those days. ..."

Other scholars argue that it is impossible to find a careful structure in the gospel; it is the connected narrative – the whole story itself – that counts. Some go further and say that the analysis of authors' intentions, sources, outlines, historical contexts, social contexts, and the like is not the best way to think about the gospel; one does not truly understand the text as a window on the past, but as a mirror, or mirrors, that reflect on each other and ultimately on the interpreter's own self. It is thus impossible to discover what the original author of Matthew intended ("the intentional fallacy") or the first readers or hearers expected ("the affective fallacy"). "Narrative critics," for example, interpret the story as it unfolds – beginning, middle, and end (see Chapter 8, "Literary Criticism," in this volume). They may search for the "point of view" of the story, but it is attributed not to the actual author, whose views one cannot know, but to an "implied author" reconstructed out of the story. It is also possible to analyze "characters" (character types), the roles they take, the plot (conflict and its resolution), and the development of individual scenes. Some narrative critics also discover a fictional storyteller called the "narrator" (comparable to the "voice-over" narrator in films) or the "narratee," a fictional, imaginary hearer of the "narrator's" voice. Narrators can be either "reliable," that is, accurately represent the beliefs, values, and norms of the "implied author" (whether the actual author or not) or "unreliable," that is, represent beliefs, values, and norms that are called into question.

Traditional historical, social-historical, and social-scientific critics look through the text as a window to the past ("the world behind the text"); new literary critics and narrative critics shift to the text itself ("the world within the text"); reader-response critics shift to what the reader (or hearer) brings to the text (the world "in front of the text").

Various individual factors – the reader's family, place of origin, experiences, gender, race, ethnicity, and the like – affect how one interprets the text. Some would even say that a text lies dormant until a reader picks it up and reads it; thus, the reader "creates" meaning in the process of reading. Some critics talk about an "interaction" between reader and text.

Yet, some recent literary critics contend that there must be *some* correspondence between implied authors/speakers and readers/hearers and real readers/hearers, especially in ancient texts that are not meant to be modern fiction. Writers/speakers and readers/hearers share a "contract" and must be "considerate" of each other. After all, the first real writers/speakers and first readers/hearers shared the same cultural context and without something in common communication would have been impossible. Thus, it is all the more important for modern readers to find a way to be considerate of ancient writers.

How does contemporary literary criticism affect the interpretation of Matthew in particular? Possibilities abound. The narrative text is the *whole* Matthean narrative. Its implied author and implied readers, in contrast to most modern fiction, overlap with a real ancient author and real ancient readers. The story has a hidden, unnoticed, thus unidentified, "narrator" who sees all and knows all, that is, who can transport readers/hearers from Jesus scene to Jesus scene. If the narrator gains the confidence of readers and convinces them that his "point of view" is "right," he by implication represents the divine point of view – God's will (Matt. 16:23) – as is also shown by the formula quotations. The major characters in the narrative are the protagonist Jesus, his followers/disciples, and his opponents, the religious leaders. The major conflict is between Jesus and the religious leaders. Jesus is the messianic king from the line of David, the Son of God, and an authoritative teacher/preacher and miracle-worker like Moses. Jesus' disciples/followers are those of "little faith" who nonetheless will ultimately teach and carry on his mission. His opponents are the Evil One and his army of demons as well as the Israelite leaders. In the passion story the leaders are joined by anonymous crowds. The plot is driven by conflict and resolution. Thus, Jesus has both supernatural and natural opponents, the Evil One and his army of demons on the one hand and the Pharisees and Sadducees on the other. It is the classic conflict between good and evil. Jesus appears to lose the final battle, but ultimately wins it because he does not give in to temptation, defeats demon possession and disease by his healing and exorcism, has power over nature, and his death ironically leads to his victory in the resurrection. He is the Son of Man who will come at the End with his angels on the clouds of heaven with power and glory to judge the world. Considerate readers read correctly – or hear correctly – if they identify with the forces of good. As such they do not get the perspective of the Israelite leaders, primarily the Pharisees, but God himself.

The narrative flow is, of course, interrupted by the five discourses. The trustworthy narrator helps the readers/listeners to identify with the protagonist and his authoritative teaching. In the first speech (Matt. 5–7), the narrator transports the readers/listeners to a mountain top somewhere in Galilee (Matt. 5:1). There Jesus, like Moses, interprets the "law and the prophets" (5:17–20) to his disciples and the crowds and offers his special prayer (6:9–13). His second speech (10) provides a model for the dedicated missionary, the third (13) offers parables that emphasize especially the choice of

1. Introduction: Jesus, the new Moses and Son of God, 1:1-4:22

        1:1-2:23        Prologue: The Infancy Story

        3:1-4:22        Narrative: John and Jesus in Galilee

2. The Message of Jesus to Israel in Galilee, 4:23-13:58

        4:23-7:29        *Discourse 1*: Sermon on the Mount

        8:1-9:38        Narrative: Ten Miracles

        10:1-11:1        *Discourse 2*: The Missionary Discourse

        11:2-12:50        Narrative: Growing Opposition of Leaders

        13:1-52        *Discourse 3*: Parables Speech to Israel and disciples

3. Transition: The Message of Jesus to his Disciples in Galilee and his journey on the Way to

        Jerusalem, 14:1-20:34

        14:1-17:27        Narrative: Miracles, Confession, Transfiguration, and Discipleship

        18:1-18:35        *Discourse 4*: Community Order and Discipline

        19:1-20:34        Narrative: Households and Discipleship

3. Jesus' Activity in Jerusalem, 21:1-25:46

        21:1-23:39        Narrative: The Final Clash between Jesus and the Jewish Leaders

        24:1-25:46        *Discourse 5*: The Apocalyptic Discourse

4. Jesus' Passion in Jerusalem and the return to Galilee, 26:1-28:20

        26:1-27:66        Narrative: Passion Story

        28:1-20        Epilogue: The Resurrection and Great Commission

**Figure 18.4**

God for his followers, the fourth (18) the order of the church, and the last (24–5) his teaching about the End.

A compromise view that combines an outline with the five speeches alternating with narratives, thus the Moses theme, is shown in Figure 18.4.

## Sources and Intertextuality

By the second century CE, it was believed that the gospels were written by those apostles whose names were being inserted in gospel manuscripts as titles ("superscriptions"). Moreover, the sequence of the gospels in the four-gospel manuscripts and eventually the New Testament itself was considered to have been the order in which they had been written – Matthew, Mark, Luke, and John. With respect to sources, it was thought that each canonical gospel writer knew and used the gospel(s) that preceded it.

That theory did not survive modern source criticism, which began in the late eighteenth century. This criticism accepts that Matthew, Mark, and Luke share Greek wording and overall sequence, indicating that they have some literary relationship, as the ancients realized. However, most modern scholars solve this "synoptic problem" by arguing that the earliest gospel was Mark (the "Markan Priority"), not Matthew, and that the authors of Matthew and Luke used Mark as a source, independently copying it (or some version close to it), and independently interpreting it (see Chapter 15, "The Synoptic Problem," in this volume). This solution requires that the same or very similar wording in passages common to Matthew and Luke but *not* in Mark – about 235 verses, most of which are sayings attributed to Jesus – must be explained. How can the Matthean and Lukan gospels have the same or similar wording if their respective authors did not know the other gospel? Usually scholars posit a lost gospel called "Q" (German *Quelle*, "source"; or Q after P [= Peter, traditional source of Mark]) or today "the Q gospel." Passages found *only* in Matthew and Luke are then called "Special M" and "Special L." This theory means that the author of Matthew had at least three main sources: Mark, Q, and "Special M." These sources were undoubtedly supplemented by oral tradition.

The Two-Document hypothesis or Two-Source theory (Four-Document or Four-Source if Special M and Special L are included), is not universally held. One important reason is that in a few passages where Matthew, Mark, and Luke have the same or similar material, Matthew agrees with the Gospel of Luke *against* Mark (the "minor agreements"). How can this be if the author of Luke did not know Matthew or vice versa? Two main alternative theories have arisen. The first is that the author of Luke did in fact know Matthew – Q becomes unnecessary – and the Markan author knew and shortened both Matthew and Luke. In this Two-Gospel hypothesis (the "Griesbach theory," after a nineteenth-century theorist), Matthew is the source of the other two. Since Matthew is first, how its author used and revised Mark and Q as his two main sources disappears (Farmer 1964).

A second theory builds on the Markan Priority. Its proponents suggests that that Mark came first, the author of Matthew used Mark, and then the Lukan author knew and used the Gospel of Mark and Matthew as sources. Matthean interpretation can proceed by observing the Matthean author's use and interpretation of Mark alone; again, Q becomes unnecessary. This view is sometimes termed the "Farrar hypothesis" (Farrer 1955; Goodacre 2001).

Two-Source theorists usually respond to the Two-Gospel theorists by asking whether it is reasonable that the author of Mark would have lengthened many passages shared by all three – Markan passages are often longer – while at the same time omitting such key passages as the infancy and Virgin Birth, the Sermon on the Mount, and the like. They ask why there are there no *major* agreements against Mark and then proceed to explain the "minor agreements" by either overlap in sources or chance changes. Difficulties with the Farrar hypothesis include the problem of accounting for so much of Matthew's extra material and the attempt to explain Lukan redaction of Matthew.

Despite its flaws, the Two-Source theory is still held by the majority of scholars, and for Matthew that means that the author of Matthew knew, used, reorganized, and revised Mark, Q, and Special M.

Other sources in Matthew involve sacred texts, or what would become scripture. Matthew contains some forty-one quotations, twenty found only in this gospel. Most distinctive are what scholars call "formula quotations" or "fulfillment quotations," that is, scriptural quotations introduced by a formulaic expression such as "all this took place to fulfill what the Lord had spoken by the prophet X." There are fourteen instances of this special kind of formula, thirteen in which a scriptural text is cited. With two exceptions (2:5–6; 13:14–15), the formula quotations function like footnotes, that is, explanatory commentary directed to the reader. They inform the reader that a particular teaching or event is the fulfillment of God's will and thus they give divine warrants. Figure 18.5 gives a list of the formula quotations. A striking fact is that while most of

| Matthew | Scriptures | Incident from the Life of Jesus |
|---------|-----------|-------------------------------|
| 1:22-23 | Isa 7:14 | The virgin birth |
| (2:5b-6) | Mic 5:1(2); 2 Sam 5:2 | The birth in Bethlehem |
| 2:15b | Hos 11:1 | The flight to Egypt |
| 2:17-18 | Jer 31:15 | The massacre of the innocents |
| 2:23b | Unknown (Isa 11:1?) | Jesus dwells in Nazareth |
| 3:3 | Isa 40:3 | John the Baptist |
| 4:14-16 | Isa 9:1-2 | Jesus moves to Capernaum in Galilee |
| 8:17 | Isa 53:4 | The healing ministry of Jesus |
| 12:17-21 | Isa 42:1-4 | The healing ministry of Jesus |
| 13:14-15 | Isa 6:9-10 | Jesus' reason for parables |
| 13:35 | Ps 78:2 | Jesus' teaching in parables |
| 21:4-5 | Isa 62:11; Zech 9:9 | Jesus' entry into Jerusalem |
| 26:56 | No specific text quoted | Jesus taken captive |
| 27:9-10 | Zech 11:12-13; Jer 18:1-13; 32:6-15 | The fate of Judas |

**Figure 18.5**

the quotations in this gospel are from the Greek Septuagint, these formula quotations are mostly *not* from any known version of the Septuagint. This suggests that they might have come from a special scriptural collection or they might have been translated from Hebrew into Greek by the author.

## Annotated Bibliography

### Research surveys

Capel Anderson, J. "Life on the Mississippi: New Currents in Matthaean Scholarship, 1983–93." *Currents in Research: Biblical Studies* 3 (1995), 169–218. Surveys innovative Matthean studies, especially in the USA.

Davies, W. D. and D. C. Allison. *The Gospel According to Matthew*. International Critical Commentary. 3 vols. Edinburgh: T. & T. Clark, 1988–97. Volume 1, *Matthew I–VII*, pp. xii–xlvii, has an extensive bibliography. The introduction (pp. 1–148), contains critical issues from a technical perspective. Volume 3, *Matthew: A Retrospect*, "Epilogue," is an excellent overview.

Luz, U. *Matthew: A Commentary*. Trans. W. C. Linss. Minneapolis: Fortress Press, 1989–2005. Excellent, more technical, overview from a leading German scholar.

Senior, D. *What Are They Saying About Matthew?* 2nd edn. New York: Paulist, 1996. Surveys select recent Matthean studies; introductory.

Stanton, G. N. "The Origin and Purpose of Matthew's Gospel: Matthean Scholarship from 1945–1980." *Aufstieg und Niedergang der römischen Welt*, II.25.3, 1890–1951 (1985). Almost a half-century history of ground-breaking Matthew studies.

### Historically influential studies

Bacon, B. W. *Studies in Matthew*. New York: Holt, Reinhart, & Winston, 1930. Develops the five-book, Moses-oriented view of Matthew.

Bornkamm, G., G. Barth, and H. J. Held. *Tradition and Interpretation in Matthew*, Philadelphia: Westminster Press, 1963. First redaction critical studies.

Davies, W. D. *The Setting of the Sermon on the Mount*. Cambridge: Cambridge University Press, 1964. Specialized study related to the discovery of the Dead Sea Scrolls.

Goulder, M. D. *Midrash and Lection in Matthew*. London: SPCK, 1974. Innovative theory that the order of Matthew follows the early church lectionary.

Kilpatrick, G. D. *The Origins of the Gospel According to Matthew* Oxford: Clarendon Press, 1966. Excellent historical studies.

Stanton, G. (ed.). *The Interpretation of Matthew*. Edinburgh: T. & T. Clark, 1995. Recent work on a variety of topics, including structure and community.

### Sources and intertextuality

Farmer, W. R. *Synoptic Problem*. New York: Macmillan, 1964; repr. 1976 Western North Carolina Press. Foremost proponent of the Two-Document (Griesbach) hypothesis.

Farrer, A. M. "On Dispensing with Q." Pp. 55–88 in *Studies in the Gospels: Essays in Memory of R. H. Lightfoot*. Edited by D. E. Nineham. Oxford: Basil Blackwell, 1955. Repr. in *The Two-Source Hypothesis*. Macon: Mercer University Press, 1985, pp. 321–56. Basis of the Farrar hypothesis.

Goodacre, M. S. *The Synoptic Problem: A Way Through the Maze*. Sheffield: Sheffield Academic Press, 2001. Defends the Farrar hypothesis.

Gundry, R. H. *The Use of the Old Testament in St. Matthew's Gospel. With Special Reference to the Messianic Hope*. Leiden: E. J. Brill, 1975. Meticulous historical-critical scholarship.

Klein, R. H. *The Synoptic Problem. An Introduction*. Grand Rapids: Baker Book House, 1987. Excellent survey, defends the Two(Four)-Source hypothesis.

Orchard, J. B. and T. R. W. Longstaff (eds.). *J. J. Griesbach: Synoptic and Text-Critical Studies, 1776–1976*. Cambridge: Cambridge University Press, 1978.

Stendahl, K. *The School of St. Matthew*. Lund: Gleerup, 1968. A classic, technical, multi-linguistic study of biblical quotations in Matthew.

## Recent commentaries / annotations

Boring, M. E. "Matthew." In *New Interpreter's Bible*. Nashville: Abingdon Press, 1994.

Davies, W. D., and D. C. Allison. *A Critical and Exegetical Commentary on the Gospel According to Saint Matthew*. New International Critical Commentary. 3 vols. Edinburgh: T. & T. Clark, 1988–97.

Duling, D. C. *The Gospel According to Matthew in The HarperCollins Study Bible: New Revised Standard Version with the Apocryphal/Deuterocanonical Books*. San Francisco: HarperCollins, 1993.

Garland, D. E. *Reading Matthew: A Literary and Theological Commentary on the First Gospel*. New York: Crossroad, 1993.

Gundry, R. H. *Matthew A Commentary on his Handbook for a Mixed Church under Persecution*. 2nd edn. Grand Rapids: Eerdmans, 1994.

Hare, D. R. A. *Matthew*. Louisville: John Knox, 1993. Interpretation.

Harrington, D. J. *Gospel of Matthew*. Sacra Pagina. Collegeville: Liturgical Press, 1991.

Luz, U. *Matthew: A Commentary*. Trans. W. C. Linss. 3 vols. Minneapolis: Augsburg, 1989–2005.

Malina, B. J and R. Rohrbaugh. *Social-Scientific Commentary on the Synoptic Gospels*. Minneapolis: Fortress Press, 1992.

Overman, J. A. *Church and Community in Crisis: The Gospel According to Matthew*. The New Testament in Context. Valley Forge: Trinity International Press, 1996.

Patte, D. *The Gospel According to Matthew: A Structural Commentary on Matthew's Faith*. Philadelphia: Fortress Press, 1987.

Senior, D. *Matthew*, Interpreting Biblical Texts. Nashville: Abingdon Press, 1998.

## Genre

Aune, D. E. *The New Testament in its Literary Environment*. Philadelphia: Westminster, 1988a.

Aune, D. E. "Greco-Roman Biography." Pp. 107–26 in *Greco-Roman Literature and the New Testament: Selected Forms and Genres*. Edited by D. E. Aune. SBL Sources for Biblical Study 21. Atlanta: Scholars Press, 1988b.

Burridge, R. A. *What Are the Gospels? A Comparison with Graeco-Roman Biography*. 2nd edn. Grand Rapids: Eerdmans, 2004.

Frickenschmidt, D. *Evangelium als Biographie. Die vier Evangelien im Rahmen antiker Erzählkunst*. Tübingen and Basel: Francke Verlag, 1997.

Shuler, P. L. *A Genre for the Gospels: The Biographical Character of Matthew*. Philadelphia: Fortress Press, 1982.

Talbert, C. H. *What Is a Gospel? The Genre of the Canonical Gospels*. Philadelphia: Fortress Press, 1977.

## Recent studies

Allison, D. C. *The New Moses: A Matthean Typology*. Minneapolis: Fortress Press, 1993.

Aune, D. E. (ed.). *The Gospel of Matthew in Current Study. Studies in Honor of William G Thompson*. Grand Rapids: Eerdmans, 2001. Articles by R. S. Ascough, D. E. Aune, W. Cotter, D. J. Harrington, J. D. Kingsbury, A.-J. Levine, A. J. Saldarini, D. Senior, G. N. Stanton, T. H. Tobin, and E. M. Wainwright.

Balch, D. L. (ed.). *Social History of the Matthean Community: Cross-Disciplinary Approaches*. Minneapolis: Fortress Press, 1991. Essays from a symposium of early social-historical studies on Matthew.

Bauer, D. R. and M. A. Powell (eds.). *Treasures Old and New: Recent Contributions to Matthean Studies*. Atlanta: Scholars Press, 1996. Literary-critical studies from the Society of Biblical Literature.

Capel Anderson, J. *Matthew's Narrative Web Over, and Over, and Over Again*. Sheffield: JSOT Press, 1994.

Carter, W. C. *Matthew and the Margins: A Sociopolitical and Religious Reading*. Marynoll: Orbis Books, 2000. Combines literary, social-historical, and religious interests.

Duling, D. C. "The Matthean Brotherhood and Marginal Scribal Leadership." Pp. 159–82 in *Modelling Early Christianity: Social-Scientific Studies of the New Testament in its Context*. Edited by Philip Esler. London: Routledge, 1995.

Duling, D. C. "Matthew as a Marginal Scribe in an Advanced Agrarian Society." *Hervormde Teologiese Studies* 58 (2002), 520–75. Combines marginality theory with historical and archaeological work on scribes.

Goodacre, Mark. "Fatigue in the Synoptics," *New Testament Studies* 44 (1998), 45–58.

Jackson, G. S. "Are the 'Nations' Present in Matthew?" *Hervormde Teologiese Studies* 56 (2000), 935–48. Views *ethnē* (28:19) as Diaspora Jews.

Horsley, R. A. *The Liberation of Christmas: The Infancy Narratives in Social Context*. New York: Crossroad, 1989. Ground-breaking social-historical and political analysis.

Kingsbury, J. *Matthew as Story*. 2nd edn. Philadelphia: Fortress Press, 1988. Narrative-critical approach to Matthew.

Kingsbury, J. *Matthew. Structure, Christology, Kingdom*. Philadelphia: Fortress Press, 1989. Study originally published in 1975 that analyzes Matthew in three divisions.

Krentz, E. M. "Extent of Matthew's Prologue: Toward the Structure of the First Gospel." *Journal of Biblical Literature* 83 (1964), 409–14. Develops a threefold division of Matthew.

Levine, A.-J., with M. Bickerstaff (eds.). *A Feminist Companion to Matthew*. Sheffield: Sheffield Academic Press, 2001. Essays by Levine, J. Capel Anderson, J. Sheffield, C. Deutsch, G. R. O'Day, E. M. Wainwright, S. Humphries-Brooks, A. J. Saldarini, M.-E. Rosenblatt, T. R. W. Longstaff, and C. Osiek. Excellent feminist scholarship.

Lohr, C. H. "Oral Techniques in the Gospel of Matthew." *Catholic Biblical Quarterly* 23 (1961), 403–35. Develops chiastic structure based on Bacon.

Luz, U. *The Theology of the Gospel of Matthew.* Cambridge: Cambridge University Press, 1995. Excellent discussion by a Swiss scholar.

Malina, B. J. and J. H. Neyrey. *Calling Jesus Names: The Social Value of Labels in Matthew.* Sonoma: Polebridge Press, 1988. Ground-breaking social-scientific work based on labeling theory.

Neyrey, J. H. *Honor and Shame in the Gospel of Matthew.* Louisville: Westminster John Knox Press, 1998. Social-scientific study based on Mediterranean anthropology and Greco-Roman literature.

Orton, D. E. *The Understanding Scribe: Matthew and the Apocalyptic Ideal.* Sheffield: Sheffield Academic Press, 1989. Basic historical background.

Overman, J. A. *Matthew's Gospel and Formative Judaism: The Social World of the Matthean Community.* Minneapolis: Fortress Press, 1990. One of the first to use the social sciences and argue that the gospel is Israelite.

Riches, J. and D. C. Sim (eds.). *The Gospel of Matthew in its Roman Imperial Context.* London: T. & T. Clark, 2005. Ground-breaking socio-political studies by J. Riches, P. F. Esler, J. S. McLaren, D. C. Duling, P. Oakes, D. C. Sim, D. J. Weaver, and W. Carter.

Saldarini, A. J. *Matthew's Christian-Jewish Community.* Chicago: University of Chicago Press, 1994. Highly praised work on the Matthean group as Israelite.

Senior, D. "Between Two Worlds: Gentile and Jewish Christians in Matthew's Gospel." *Catholic Biblical Quarterly* 61 (1999), 1–23.

Sim, D. C. *Apocalyptic Eschatology in the Gospel of Matthew.* Cambridge: Cambridge University Press, 1996. Important study that builds on Matthew as "Jewish."

Stanton, G. N. *A Gospel for a New People: Studies in Matthew.* Edinburgh: T. & T. Clark, 1992. Studies by a leading British scholar.

Wainwright, E. M. *Towards a Feminist Critical Reading of the Gospel According to Matthew.* Berlin and New York: Walter De Gruyter, 1991.

*Manuscripts and textual criticism*

Elliott, J. K. "Review of the Jesus Papyrus and Eyewitness to Jesus." *Novum Testamentum* 38 (1996), 393–9.

Elliott, J. K. "Six New Papyri of Matthew's Gospel." *Novum Testamentum* 41 (1999), 105–7.

Head, P. M. "The Date of the Magdalen Papyrus of Matthew (P Magd Gr 17 = Þ64): A Response to CP Thiede." *Tyndale Bulletin* 46 (1995), 251–85.

Metzger, B. M. *A Textual Commentary on the Greek New Testament.* 2nd edn. Stuttgart: Deutsche Bibelgesellschaft, 2002.

Parker, D. C. "Was Matthew Written before 50 CE? The Magdalen Papyrus of Matthew." *Expository Times* 107 (1996), 40–3.

Peterson, S. "Matthew Fragment." First Century Judaism Discussion Forum (May 24, 1995), accessed April 20, 2005. ⟨http://ccat.sas.upenn.edu/~petersig/thiede.txt.final.reply⟩.

Skeats, T. C. "The Oldest Manuscript of the Four Gospels?" *New Testament Studies* 43 (1997), 1–34.

Thiede, C. P. "Papyrus Magdalen Greek 17 (Gregory-Aland [P]64): A Reappraisal." *Zeitschrift für Papyrologie und Epigraphik* 105 (1995) 13–20 (and plate IX); *Tyndale Bulletin* 46 (1995), 29–42.

## Language

Howard, G. *The Gospel According to a Primitive Hebrew Text.* 2nd edn. Macon: Mercer University Press, 1995.

Petersen, W. L. Review of G. Howard, *The Gospel According to A Primitive Hebrew Text. Journal of Biblical Literature* 108 (1989), 722–6.

# CHAPTER 19

# Luke–Acts: The Gospel of Luke and the Acts of the Apostles

## Richard P. Thompson

## Introduction

The use of the title "Luke–Acts" reflects the contemporary scholarly consensus that the Gospel of Luke and the Acts of the Apostles were originally a single literary work in two volumes. It is recognized that there are no extant ancient manuscripts or canonical lists that combine or connect the two books together. Nonetheless, since Henry Cadbury's proposal (1927) regarding the singularity of these two works in both composition and message, Luke–Acts has become a commonplace expression that assumes the unity of these two biblical books.

There is little external evidence to prove that these two books were written as two companion volumes of a larger work by a single author. However, there is also little evidence demonstrating the separation of these two volumes in the canonical process. On the one hand, these two texts deal with divergent material that is reflected in their respective canonical placement: the Gospel of Luke depicts the life of Jesus, whereas the Acts of the Apostles deals with the early church and, most noteworthy, the characters of Peter (Acts 1–12) and Paul (Acts 13–28). The similarities between the Gospel of Luke and the other synoptic gospels suggest that these three gospels be placed together, whereas the significant role of Paul in the Acts of the Apostles provides a useful historical outline of the early church within which to place the Pauline corpus.

On the other hand, the differences in content do not overshadow the literary links between the Lukan Gospel and Acts. Both books identify a "Theophilus" as the recipient. The book of Acts reminds this addressee about the author's "first book" regarding Jesus (Acts 1:1), which seems to be a clear reference to the Lukan Gospel. The considerable overlap between the ending of Luke and the beginning of Acts joins the books together: the promise of the Father (Luke 24:48; Acts 1:4), the description of Jesus' followers as "witnesses" and the role of "power" that would come upon them (Luke 24:48; Acts 1:8), and the distinctly Lukan inclusion of Jesus' ascension to heaven (Luke 24:51; Acts 1:9–11), just to name a few. In addition, there are numerous instances where the narrative depictions of characters and journeys in Acts mirror what the reader finds in the gospel narrative. One may account for these similarities by arguing that the author of Acts imitated the style and features of the Gospel of Luke. However, the majority of scholars believe that the scarcity of external evidence for linking these two books together is overcome by the plethora of internal (or literary) evidence for doing so (contra Parsons and Pervo 1993).

Approaching Luke–Acts as a single work rather than two separate works has significant ramifications for biblical study in general. Rather than reading the Gospel of Luke as only one voice among the evangelists and reading the Acts of the Apostles as an introduction to Paul's letters, Luke–Acts becomes the largest single contribution to the New Testament that comprises 27 percent of the entire collection. Thus, the Lukan contribution to the writings and thought of the New Testament has increasingly become the focus of scholarly attention.

## Major Issues and Directions in Recent Study

The increased scholarly attention on aspects of Luke–Acts has generally focused in one of four areas: historical issues, theology, social-scientific matters, and literary or narrative features. To be sure, many of the discussions have not been confined merely to one of these areas. Nonetheless, there are significant issues that have been explored in these various directions in the recent study of Luke–Acts.

### Historical issues

One of the significant questions in the recent study of Luke–Acts has to do with Luke's role as a historian. While this includes the question of genre, this issue also involves the author's ability to deal accurately with historical details of persons and events as a historian. The historical data in the book of Acts have been compared to the related data contained in the writings of Paul. It is widely recognized that the Lukan materials do not correlate well with the Pauline materials on a number of substantive issues. For instance, scholars have long debated over the possible yet problematic correlation between the Jerusalem council of Acts 15 and the encounter between Peter and Paul in Galatians 2. Also, the author of Acts seems reticent to describe Paul as an apostle, whereas Paul does not hesitate to use that term as a self-designation. In addition, there is the peculiar silence in Acts regarding the collection for the Jerusalem church that is mentioned in several of Paul's letters (Gal. 2:10; 1 Cor. 16:1–4; 2 Cor. 8–9; Rom 15:25–8). Finally, the characterization of Paul in Acts seems to be that of a loyal Jew who faithfully followed the Jewish law, whereas Paul's self-description in letters such as Galatians suggests that Paul was no longer a follower of Jewish law.

Typically, scholars assumed *a priori* that Paul's writings should be granted favored status on historical matters over Acts, due to the first-person perspectives that those letters reflect (Knox 1987). However, such assumptions fail to recognize that first-person perspective alone does not ensure historical accuracy in Paul's letters nor account for Paul's own rhetorical purposes. A number of scholars have given considerable attention to Luke as a Greco-Roman historian (Plümacher 1972; Sterling 1992).

The prologue of the Gospel of Luke (especially 1:3) hints about the historical character of the author's work following the tradition of the Greek historian Thucydides (see, e.g., Thucydides, 1.22.2): he investigated the details, he did his work "carefully" (*akribōs*), and he offered an "orderly" or "sequential" (*kathexēs*) account. To be sure, these hints about the nature of Luke–Acts do not solve all the puzzling aspects of the work, most noteworthy among them being the sometimes entertaining, dramatic, and humorous qualities of the work and the occasional questions about possible historical inaccuracies (e.g., the census at the beginning of Quirinius' governorship in Luke 2). Some aspects of the work point to specific issues regarding genre (see below). Others, such as matters of historical precision, may reflect the nature of historical forms of writing in the ancient world, where orality tended to accentuate event over detail, and thus facilitate the creative role of the author in shaping the narrative in purposeful ways.

One feature of the book of Acts that has stimulated considerable attention with regard to historical matters is the prominent role of speeches within that book. Just as Thucydides (1.22) openly described his role in re-creating the speeches of characters depicted in his historical work, one discovers the Lukan author's hand in the various speeches in Acts through shared themes and emphases. Often these speeches do not fit the specific historical context in which they were reportedly spoken, but they do seem to accentuate or contribute to the overall work. These speeches, therefore, must be interpreted on multiple levels, acknowledging both the hand of the historian in the written form of the speech and the role of the different speeches in the larger purposes of the whole work.

Although in Lukan studies discussions regarding historical accuracy and speeches have generally focused on the Acts of the Apostles, such questions have not been absent from the study of the Gospel of Luke. Nonetheless, one finds that attention to such questions centers on the problem of the historical Jesus within gospel studies (see Chapter 14, "The Problem of the Historical Jesus," in this volume). While there is little doubt that Luke saw himself in the role of a historian, the purposes and perspective of each evangelist, not to mention the faith perspective(s) of the oral tradition that they utilized, shaped different renditions of the story of Jesus. Thus, while the contemporary version of the quest for the historical Jesus encounters difficulties in reconstructing an "objective" account of Jesus' life and teachings from any or all of the Christian gospels (both canonical and non-canonical), one must also consider the nature of the Greco-Roman historical text and both the assumptions and expectations that such a text carried with it. In other words, one must evaluate Luke's work as a historian based on ancient standards, not contemporary ones.

### Theology

Luke's work as a historian does not preclude him from shaping the narrative in theological ways. While Luke went about his theological task much differently and perhaps less systematically than what one finds in, for instance, Paul's letter to the Romans, there is little doubt that Luke offers something like a "theological history" in which God functions as the primary mover behind the narrated historical events and persons. Throughout Luke–Acts, what orients the scenes and their arrangement is the will and purposes of the God of Israel (see Shepherd 1994). Luke's theological perspective, however, stands out among the other evangelists because he includes not only the story of Jesus as God's messiah but also the story of the earliest Christians. That is to say, the addition of the second volume of Acts creates something much different from the other gospels. Some have suggested this addition reflects the influence of the delay of the *parousia* (or Second Coming of Jesus), so that Luke relinquished the view that Christians were living in the last days in favor of a salvation-historical understanding of the Jesus-event as the midpoint between the time of Israel and the time of the church (Conzelmann 1961). Others have understood Luke to see a time of God's promise followed by a pro-tracted time of fulfillment. Such interpretations of Luke's theological schema, however, often reflect contemporary theological concerns as much as they reflect the perspective of the narrative of Luke–Acts. Nonetheless, two aspects of the theology in Luke–Acts have provoked more intensive scholarly scrutiny: salvation and the place of believing Gentiles in relation to Israel or the people of God, and the portrayal of Jewish people and Judaism in Luke–Acts.

An essential element in Luke's theology is the universality of salvation, including both Jews and non-Jews as part of the one people of God. The view that the Lukan materials emphasize more positively the inclusion of Gentiles, not only in comparison with the other gospels but also in the subsequent narrative of the earliest Christians in Acts, is widely held. However, Luke borrows images and vocabulary from the Septuagint to depict the Christian movement in ways that suggest continuity with Israel. For instance, in Peter's Pentecost speech, the quotation from the prophet Joel offers an interpretation of the Pentecost phenomena as God's fulfillment to Israel. In addition, the use of the term *ekklēsia* (typically translated "church" in the New Testament) appropriated the concept of the assembly of Israel as God's people already found in the Septuagint. Thus, on the one hand there is the theme of continuity, with the God of the Jewish people at the center of the action. Jervell (1972) has rightly noted the elements of Luke–Acts that affirm such issues of continuity and the success of the Christian message among the Jewish people. On the other hand, this same God also steers the believers to non-Jews like the godfearer Cornelius (Acts 10) and the Antiochians in Syria (Acts 11) before spreading throughout the eastern part of the Mediterranean world. The scholarly debate has tended to emphasize either the success of the Jewish mission or the success of the Gentile mission in Luke–Acts, with the latter stressing the Lukan emphasis on the replacement of Israel by the church. An issue raised throughout the narrative of Luke–Acts pertains to the relation of Jesus to the heritage and legacy of Israel as the people of God. Related to this question is the matter of the respective roles of the Jewish people and the church from the Lukan perspective. Does Luke portray the church as Israel's replacement apart from the historic Jewish people? Does Luke present Israel and the church continuing as distinct "peoples"? Does Luke offer a narrative refinement of the theological understanding of Israel, from an exclusively Jewish orientation to an orientation that includes both Jewish and non-Jewish believers in the resurrection of Jesus? Such questions continue to provoke vigorous debate (Moessner 1999).

Closely related to the increased emphasis on the Lukan understanding of the univer-sality of salvation is the portrayal of Jewish people and Judaism in Luke–Acts. Significant attention has been given to the different ways that Luke describes the Jewish people more generally, Jewish individuals and smaller groups of individuals, and Judaism as both a religion and cultural system (Tyson 1988). There is a general consensus among scholars that the portrayal of Jewish persons and customs tends to be negative. Both the harshness of the accusations by Peter against the inhabitants of Jerusalem ("this man [Jesus] ... you killed," Acts 2:23) and the ongoing role of "the Jews" as opponents of Paul in the latter half of Acts accentuate and contribute to this negative portrayal. Such evidence contrasts with the inclusion of Gentiles into the realm of God's salvation. Some scholars such as Sanders (1987) conclude that the Lukan perspective regarding the Jewish people is extremely negative due to a crisis in Luke's church over the inclusion of Gentiles which the Jewish Christians opposed. Sanders contends that this Jewish opposition led to the division between Judaism and Christianity, with the result that the Gentile church replaced Israel as the people of God. More than a few scholars have asked if the Lukan perspective should be considered anti-Semitic. Others, among them Tyson (1992), evaluate the evidence from a literary perspective and conclude rightly that the image is mixed, albeit more negative than positive. Still others, most notably Jervell (1996), conclude that the negative images of Jews and Judaism in Luke–Acts are confined to the unbelieving Jews and that Israel was actually divided over the gospel message. Jervell's contribution to the discussion accentuates the fact that Paul's mission was not to the Gentiles in Acts but mostly to the Jews, and that Gentiles received salvation in contexts where Jewish persons did as well.

## Social–scientific criticism

Some of the theological inquiries into the Lukan materials are also related to social and cultural issues (see Chapter 12, "Social-Scientific Criticism," in this volume). A narrative that depicts the inclusion of both Jews and non-Jews together raises complex questions, some theological in nature and others social and cultural. In a Greco-Roman context where political and religious practices were intricately intertwined, the lack of place for the Christians was no insignificant matter. The recent appropriation of interpretive methods that draw from the social sciences such as sociology, cultural anthropology, and psychology has provided fruitful results. Esler (1987) contends that the theology of Luke–Acts reflects a response to the political and social pressures that were facing the Christian community to which Luke wrote. Thus, Esler applies sociological and anthropological theory and models to the analysis of Luke–Acts and concludes that political legitimation was at the heart of the author's purposes. Moxnes (1988) also probes Lukan theology, but he explores the social world of Luke–Acts with particular attention to the role of social conflict, purity issues, and economic relations. An important collection edited by Neyrey (1991) offers fruitful studies of the Lukan materials that seek to interpret these texts in light of the different social values (such as honor and shame), worldviews, and social structures of the first-century Mediterranean world. In other words, social-scientific approaches to Luke–Acts have opened wide a window to the complexities of the social world in which these texts were written and were to be read and engaged. In addition, these approaches continue to highlight the

324    RICHARD P. THOMPSON

social codes, values, conventions, expectations, and practices that these texts sometimes assume and sometimes challenge.

### Literary or narrative features

Perhaps the area of greatest scholarly interest in Luke–Acts in recent years has been
the study of these texts using literary or narrative approaches (see Chapter 8, "Literary
Criticism," in this volume). In fact, the development of literary-critical approaches to
the study of biblical texts has seen the greatest scholarly activity in the Lukan materials.
Tannehill's two-volume work (1986, 1990) set the initial standard for literary
approaches and their interpretive value by exploring Luke–Acts holistically as a narrative unity. Such approaches have applied both contemporary and ancient literary
theory to the study and interpretation of both the Gospel of Luke and the Acts of the
Apostles. These kinds of studies are concerned with not only what the text says but
why things are stated or described as they are and how these texts might function for
the original audience who heard them. Rather than focusing only on historical-critical
concerns such as the historical influences behind the text of Luke–Acts, such interpretations have focused increasingly on textual features and cues of the narrative world
as shaped by the Lukan author, as well as on the role of the interpreter in making
appropriate connections and conclusions. On the one hand, interpretations have found
in Luke–Acts such narrative features as plot, narrative placement and sequence, characterization, and the role of specific themes and scenes, exploring how these features
contribute to the rhetorical and functional purposes of this work. On the other hand,
such approaches also consider the role of the interpreter (either the hearing audience
or the reader) in the process of connecting together different elements of the narrative
and evaluating the characters, actions, and plot in light of the narrative progression.
Among the abundance of literary studies on Luke–Acts have been those on characters
such as Paul (Lentz 1993; Porter 2001), Philip (Spencer 1992), the Pharisees (Gowler
1991; Darr 1992), and God (Brawley 1990), as well as on the narrative role of such
diverse narrative features as sinners (Neale 1991), possessions (Johnson 1977), and
meal scenes (Heil 1999).

## The Genre of Luke–Acts

The question of genre is important due to the unstated assumptions and expectations
that accompany any conventional literary work.

The difficulties in determining the genre of Luke–Acts are compounded when these
texts are regarded as a two-volume work rather than two distinct works (Parsons and
Pervo 1993). If one views the Gospel of Luke as a separate literary work, then the
debates regarding the possibility of the uniquely Christian genre "gospel" may apply
here as well (see the discussion on genre in Chapters 17, "The Gospel of Mark," and
18, "The Gospel of Matthew," in this volume). That is, one possibility is that the Lukan
Gospel follows the literary pattern laid out by the Gospel of Mark, which alone uses the

term "gospel" in its introduction of the text. The problem with the notion of a gospel genre is that there is no indication that such a genre truly existed in the first century, since the term "gospel" was used rather loosely as a designation for both canonical and noncanonical gospels. In addition, if one assumes the unity of Luke–Acts, the insistence that the Gospel of Luke should be categorized as belonging to the gospel genre ignores the second volume.

A more likely possibility from the ancient world is that the Gospel of Luke (as well as the other New Testament gospels) followed the literary conventions of the Greco-Roman biography, which typically focused on significant personages, including rulers and philosophers. Because there were different kinds of biographical literature in the ancient world, scholars have increasingly recognized that the early Christian gospels themselves (both canonical and non-canonical) may not follow any one specific generic pattern. However, what are noteworthy are the similarities between the canonical gospels like the Gospel of Luke and Hellenistic biography in focusing the reader's attention on the life, influence, and character of the central figure (Burridge 1992). Such biographical works often described the person's incredible birth, deeds, and teachings. Such features compare favorably with the New Testament gospels, including the Gospel of Luke. While this argument often does not deal with Luke–Acts combined as a literary work (e.g., Burridge 1992), Talbert (1974) contends that the book of Acts falls within the scope of the biography since such works often described the legacy of the subject in ways reminiscent of that subject in both the subsequent lives and teachings of followers.

While the genre of Greco-Roman biography correlates with some prominent features of Luke–Acts, the identification of the two-volume Lukan work as biography tends to account for more features characteristic of the Gospel of Luke than of the Acts of the Apostles. The fact that the Lukan narrative moves well beyond the story of Jesus and treats not only the followers of Jesus but also the people of Israel suggests that this text moves beyond the scope of the biographical genre. In addition, the categorization of Luke–Acts as biography ignores some of the textual indicators that the author composed this work as one shaped by the broader Greco-Roman historiographical tradition that included the ancient biography but was not limited only to the emphases and features of that specific literary form. First, the preface to the Lukan Gospel corresponds with the prefaces found in other historiographical texts of that era in a number of ways. The author's description of his investigatory work and consultation of a variety of sources in preparation for the work's composition parallels statements by Herodotus (1.1) and Thucydides (1.20.3, 1.22.2). He describes his work as "careful" or "accurate" (akribōs), a theme found not only in Thucydides (1.22.2) but also in Polybius (1.14.6, 16.20.8, 34.4.2), Dionysius of Halicarnassus (Roman Antiquities, 1.1.2, 1.5.4, 1.6.3), Josephus (Jewish War, 1.2, 6, 9), and Lucian (How to Write History, 7, 24, 39–44). The description of Luke's work as an "orderly" or "sequential" (kathexēs) account correlates with emphases found in other historians regarding their role in the arrangement of the historical work into a unified account (e.g., see Polybius, 1.3.4, 1.4.2–3). Second, Luke links the stories about Jesus and the church both to the larger story of Israel and to the even larger story of human history by alluding to Old Testament events and persons as well as by offering references to contemporary events and persons in the Greco-Roman world.

One additional suggestion that has been proposed recently regarding the genre of Luke–Acts has been that Luke–Acts or at least Acts belongs to the genre of historical fiction. According to Pervo (1987), the popular novel of the first and second centuries provides a better model for assessing the generic qualities of the book of Acts. Pervo suggests that both Luke's inabilities as a historian and his extraordinary abilities as a creative writer indicate that the author wrote to edify and speak to his audience by offering a pleasing and entertaining work. To be sure, this proposal suffers from its inability to account for the relationship between the Lukan Gospel and Acts as well as the obvious demarcations in the preface to the work that distinctly point to the Greco-Roman historiographical tradition with its emphasis on truthfulness. Nonetheless, Pervo usefully highlights the creative aspect of the Lukan composition and how such dramatic and entertaining features contribute to the effectiveness of that work.

When one compares the features of Luke–Acts with other literary genres of the first century, these biblical materials correlate best with the broad category of Greco-Roman historiography. However, when dealing with generic issues, one must recognize the influence of the historiographical tradition on a wide range of literature, including both biographical texts and historical novels. At the same time, features in these and other types of literature were typically imported into historiography, as the author sought to compose a work in effective ways (Aune 1987).

## Purpose and Occasion

Closely related to the issue of genre regarding Luke–Acts are the purpose and occasion for the work, since different genres have potentially different functions and purposes. In other words, one must consider what kind of history Luke–Acts is and the possible purposes that may have informed its composition. Thus, the question of the purpose of Luke–Acts demands careful assessment not only of genre but also of the author's point of view, narrative plot and progression, characters, and emphases.

The dominant view in Lukan studies is that Luke–Acts was written as apologetic literature or, in this case, apologetic historiography. In other words, the Lukan materials were composed to provide justification, explanation, and defense for various aspects of the Christian movement. This broad apologetic purpose corresponds with the final part of the preface in Luke 1: "so that you may know the truth concerning the things about which you have been instructed" (1:4; NRSV). If one understands apologetic literature in this general way, then such a work could have envisaged a broad audience, such as Roman government officials or the inhabitants of the Roman empire generally, or with a smaller, more focused audience in mind, such as the Christian movement. An apology of the former kind might have purposes and an audience *outside* the context of the earliest Christian believers, so that an apologetic work may assist the church more *indirectly* with possible *external* pressures and tensions regarding her place within the Roman empire. An apology of the latter kind might have purposes and an audience *inside* the context of those earliest Christian believers, so that such a work may assist the church more *directly* with possible *internal* issues and tensions regarding her identity and place within the will and purposes of the God of Israel.

Some have argued that Luke–Acts functions as an apology for the Christian movement or church within the broader context of the Roman empire. From this point of view, such a work might have conveyed to Roman officials and others that the Christian movement need not be feared as a subversive movement and perhaps that the Christians should be granted the same religious freedom as Jews. On the one hand, Luke composed the Christian story in ways that depict key characters as friendly to the Romans. Joseph and Mary obey a governmental edict and go to his hometown as required (Luke 2:1–5). While Luke depicts Jesus dying by Roman crucifixion, a Roman centurion gives verbal witness to Jesus' innocence (23:47). The followers of Jesus are repeatedly arrested without just cause, imprisoned improperly (Acts 16:35–9), and even ruled to be innocent of any violation of Roman law (18:14–16; 19:35–41; 26:30–2). On the other hand, the author often presents Roman officials as treating the Christians as though they are actually a small group within Judaism (18:12–16; 19:35–41). Thus, this portrayal may indicate an attempt to establish the roots of the Christian movement within the soil of Judaism. The strength of such views of the purpose of Luke–Acts lies in the attempts to interpret these narrative materials within the broader contexts of the Roman world. However, such views typically fail to account for Luke's negative portrayals of Roman officials.

The majority of scholars have understood Luke–Acts as a form of apologetic literature within the Christian movement or church itself. Some, like Maddox (1982) and Walaskay (1983), interpret the evidence to suggest that the purpose of Luke–Acts was to encourage Christians to view Roman officials and the empire more openly. Esler (1987) argues that Luke provided legitimation for those Roman officials within the Christian church who needed reassurance that faith in the one crucified by Rome was not incompatible with an allegiance to Rome. Others, such as Jervell (1972), suggest that the characterization of Paul and the long section narrating legal proceedings against him indicate that Acts functioned as an apology and defense for Paul and his teaching, perhaps because a vocal Jewish minority within the Christian movement saw him as an apostate Jew.

As important as these possibilities are for understanding the purpose of Luke–Acts, other kinds of evidence for understanding that purpose are found in both volumes of this work. For instance, the author declares that his literary account would supplement the instruction that the recipient had received about "the happenings that have been fulfilled among us" (1:1) with "stability" or "security" (*asphaleia*; Luke 1:4). In addition, throughout Luke–Acts there is growing incongruity between the saving activity of God and the people of Israel. At the heart of the narrative is the inclusion of Gentiles into the realm of God's purposes that is progressively developed in Acts, particularly with the ministry of Paul. Accompanying the developing role of the Gentiles within the purposes of God is an emergent tension due to opposition to, and ultimately rejection of, those divine purposes on the part of non-believing Jews. Thus, these growing tensions that are both depicted in Luke–Acts and also arise in the reading of the narrative may say something specific about this apologetic purpose of providing stability and certainty. If the Jewish people were the recipients of God's promises and called to be the people of God, then the inclusion of Gentiles raises questions about God, the place of the Jewish people in God's purposes, the understanding of what it means to be the people of God or Israel, and the legitimacy of the place of Gentiles with regard to that understanding about Israel.

Such apologetic concerns naturally lead to the question about the general occasion to which Luke–Acts was addressed. This question is not easily answered, as the diversity of scholarly opinion attests, because narrative texts do not directly address specific situations or occasions as a letter does. However, some tentative conclusions about general contextual issues may be offered, based on inferences from the narrative itself. The dominant view that has governed Lukan studies for decades is that Luke–Acts was addressed to predominantly Gentile Christians (e.g., Conzelmann 1961). This view is based in part on the success of Paul's mission in Acts among the Gentiles and also on the corresponding failure of his mission among Jews. Luke–Acts, therefore, serves to legitimize the role of Gentiles in the Christian movement in two distinct ways: (1) by including the story of Jesus within the larger story of God's purposes and promises to Israel, and (2) by demonstrating how their inclusion is part of that larger story of God's saving activity in history. However, the assumption of a Gentile Christian audience does not adequately account for other emphases of Luke–Acts, most notably the ongoing conflict between Jews and Gentiles and the distinctly Jewish characterization of Paul and his ministry. Jervell (1996) and Brawley (1987) contend that Luke–Acts may have been directed toward Jewish Christians who were in tension with Gentile believers. These questions have made it necessary to reexamine past assumptions in light of Lukan narrative cues, making it possible to understand Luke–Acts as directed to both Jewish and Gentile believers.

While there is a lack of consensus about the occasion to which Luke addressed his work, the narrative does imply some things about the audience. On the one hand, the narrative assumes that the audience not only knew the Greek language but also was familiar with Greek and Roman coinage and geography. The author also assumes that the audience shares his Christian perspective. On the other hand, the narrative also assumes that the audience was familiar with aspects of Judaism mentioned with no explanation: the Sabbath followed by the first day of the week, religious practices and institutions, significant figures of Jewish history, and the Septuagint (Luke employs numerous allusions to the wording and stories of this Greek translation of the Jewish scriptures). Such assumed familiarity suggests that any member of the implied audience would have been either a person similar to the "godfearers" depicted in Luke–Acts as devout Gentiles who were attracted to Jewish worship and ethics (see, e.g., Luke 7:1–10; Acts 10) or perhaps a Diaspora Jew (see Tyson 1992).

These possibilities regarding the purpose, occasion, and setting for Luke–Acts provide an adequate context to consider the identity and role of the twice-stated recipient of this work, Theophilus. The name, which means "friend or lover of God," appears in extant Greek writings and inscriptions and was used by both Jews and Gentiles. It is unclear, however, whether the Lukan author referred to an actual person by that name, an unnamed Christian, using "Theophilus" as a fictitious name to hide the person's identity, or any anonymous Christian reader as a wordplay on the name. The prefatory remarks to the gospel, which dedicate the work to "most excellent Theophilus", and the later address in the opening of Acts, "O Theophilus," are often cited as indications that this may have been an actual person, perhaps even one who was socially prominent. Many suggestions regarding his identity have been proposed, for example, that he was a patron who financially underwrote much of the cost of writing Luke–Acts or that he was a prominent leader among those for whom Luke wrote. However, more likely is the possibility that the name "Theophilus" refers generally to a broader audience or group of Christians who would gladly receive this narrative about God and God's people as "those who love God."

## Authorship

Like the other New Testament gospels, Luke–Acts is an anonymous work, with the author concealed behind the narrative. To be sure, the author often addresses the audience directly through summary statements and sections, but then he slips out of view as the story resumes. Most of what is known about the author is limited to hints that the narrative offers. While many would like to discover who the real author is, only the "implied author," constructed from those textual hints and cues about the author's knowledge, perspective, background, can be known. We can conclude, for example, that the author had considerable literary skill, revealed by his dramatic storytelling and extensive use of the Septuagint (particularly the Torah). Allusions to various biblical stories and vocabulary suggest that the author had a deep knowledge of the Jewish scriptures. While it has been long assumed that the author of Luke–Acts was a Gentile, this familiarity with the Jewish scriptures tempers any confidence one might have in such a presupposition.

Perhaps the most significant element of Luke–Acts that has influenced attempts to discover the real author is the use of the first person plural pronoun "we" in seemingly random sections of Acts 16–28. While the author uses the third person throughout the narrative (with the exception of the historical prefaces in Luke 1:1–4 and Acts 1:1–2) to Acts 16:9, suddenly the first person plural appears: "Immediately *we* sought to depart to Macedonia, because we were in agreement that God had called *us* to proclaim the good news to them" (Acts 16:10; emphasis added). This first-person narration continues through verse 17 and then vanishes, only to appear and then disappear again in 20:5–15, 21:1–18, and 27:1–28:16. Some have attributed this phenomenon to the source that "Luke" was using at the time. However, it would seem strange that this author, who had polished literary skills and typically rewrote other sources in his own style, failed to change the first person plural of his source to the third person. Another possibility is that this shift in narrative style indicates that the author was himself a participant in the events he narrates. This, too, is not unproblematic, since Acts often conflicts with information in the letters of Paul. One would assume that someone who was with Paul would have been better informed about such matters. A third solution is that the shift in narration may be a literary device, either to provide a more vivid narrative or to indicate that Paul, the author, and the audience all share a common perspective in the early development of the church.

The traditional view about the authorship of Luke–Acts has understood the "we" passages in Acts as an indication that the author was one of Paul's co-workers. According to early church tradition from the latter part of the second century, Luke the physician and co-worker of Paul wrote both the Gospel of Luke as well as the book of Acts. Irenaeus cited these "we" passages as evidence for the claim that this author was Paul's associate and for the validity of the Lukan authorship of the gospel (*Against Heresies*, 3.14.1–2). The oldest extant manuscript of the Gospel of Luke, Þ⁷⁵, which dates to ca. 175–225 CE, contains the earliest surviving textual evidence for the title "The Gospel According to Luke." The New Testament, however, provides little information about this Luke. In Philemon 24 Luke's name is part of a list of Paul's "fellow workers." Colossians 4:14 identifies Luke as "the beloved physician." Finally, the letter of 2 Timothy (probably written later by one of Paul's companions) merely mentions that "only Luke is with me" (2 Tim. 4:11).

The paucity of information about Luke and his connection with the third gospel means that caution is required when drawing conclusions about authorship. On the one hand, more traditional attempts to defend the physician Luke as the author of Luke–Acts, by insisting that the writing style and perspective of the narrative reflected the work of a medical doctor, tend to misinterpret both the textual details as well as the entire work (Cadbury 1920). On the other hand, while the differences between the portrait of Paul in Acts and what Paul reveals about himself in his letters must be considered, one must also entertain the possibility that both the time lapse between the Pauline letters and Acts as well as the different rhetorical purposes of the authors may be partially to blame. It is certainly possible that Luke–Acts was written by the same Luke who served with Paul for a time, but it is also possible to argue that the "we" passages cannot be linked with any specific person. Thus, while most scholars still refer to the author of Luke–Acts as Luke for the sake of convenience, the mystery about his precise identity remains unsolved. Fortunately, interpreting the narrative of Luke–Acts does not depend on solving the problem of authorship.

## Date and Place of Writing

In recent years the scholarly debates over the possible date for the composition of Luke–Acts have waned. However, there are a number of literary and historical details that provide some parameters that have guided such considerations. Since the book of Acts ends with Paul under Roman house arrest (in the early 60s), that date serves as the *terminus a quo* (i.e., the earliest possible date) for the composition of Acts. In addition, if the author's mention of his use of "other accounts" (Luke 1:1) refers to other gospels, such as the Gospel of Mark, as the Two-Source hypothesis contends, then one must date Luke–Acts after the composition of Mark, generally dated to the mid- or late 60s. From the time of Jerome (ca. 340–420 CE) on, many have argued Luke–Acts was written in the short span between Paul's house arrest and his death. This dating for Luke–Acts has continued to have adherents for the following reasons: (1) the abrupt ending of Acts that mentions nothing about Paul's acquittal and later death; (2) no mention is made of Nero's persecution in 64 CE or the destruction of Jerusalem in 70 CE; and (3) there is no indication that the author knew any of Paul's letters, which were probably collected no earlier than 90 CE. However, currently the dominant view is that Luke–Acts was written after the destruction of Jerusalem in the year 70, probably in the early 80s. This is suggested in part by passages in the Gospel of Luke where the words of Jesus apparently allude to the fate of Jerusalem (13:35a; 19:43–4; 21:20–4; 23:28–31). A date in the early 80s precedes the time when Paul's letters were collected and gained wide circulation and therefore accounts for the fact that the author gives no indication that he knew any of Paul's letters. While dating Luke–Acts to the early 80s does not solve the problem of the abrupt ending of Acts, such a date does not demand a historical explanation for the ending, that may have a literary or rhetorical explanation.

While there is a general consensus about the date of the composition of Luke–Acts in the early 80s, another hypothesis about dating that been recently revived is that Acts was written well into the second century. Knox (1942) proposed that Acts was written in response to the heretic Marcion of Sinope (born ca. 110 CE and founded a heretical sect in Rome in 142 CE), and Tyson (2006) proposes a similar theory for both Luke and Acts. According to this view, Luke–Acts was written to recover Paul from Marcionite teachings and distortions and must therefore have been written no earlier than the mid-140s. Pervo (2006) argues that Acts was written somewhat earlier, i.e., during the first quarter of the second century. While his proposal creates problems for the assumed unity of Luke–Acts, it does help to explain the problematic differences between Luke and Acts as well as their canonical separation (Parsons and Pervo 1993). In addition, these alternative proposals for dating Luke and/or Acts help to explain the differences between the Lukan portrayal of Paul in Acts and the self-portrayal of Paul in his letters.

The place where Luke–Acts was written is even more difficult to assess than the date of writing, the identity of the author, or even the identity of the audience. Since the author remains hidden behind the narrative, there is little information about the identity of the author or where he wrote his work. Scholars agree only that Luke–Acts was not written in Palestine because of the author's imprecise geographical information about the region.

Although there are few solid conclusions about the specific historical context to which or within which Luke–Acts was written, one must realize that the nature of these ancient narrative texts does not make such precision possible. These narratives do not directly reflect the specific circumstances of the author or any intended audience. Rather, Luke–Acts offers the audience a narrative world, to which they are called and within which they are to witness persons and events narrated by the author. In order to read and interpret the Gospel of Luke and the Acts of the Apostles, one must account for the historical particulars of that Lukan narrative world, which will presumably share many of the same things that comprised the actual world of Luke's original audience but which cannot be presumed to be a mirror of that audience's specific context. Thus, the interpretation of Luke–Acts does not ultimately depend on precise reconstruction of those historical contexts. Instead, those interpretations of Luke–Acts that shed light on that particular narrative world may also uncover new possible understandings about such historical matters.

## Textual Problems

The various translations of the Bible and their readers are indebted to the meticulous labors of textual critics who have analyzed thousands of papyrus scraps and the later and more complete parchment texts containing portions of New Testament texts. Like all other New Testament books, the critical form of the Greek version of Luke–Acts has been scrutinized and improved by textual criticism. Most variations in readings are of minor importance and frequently originated through errors of the eye when copied by hand by ancient scribes. However, in the case of Luke–Acts, it is noteworthy that there are significant differences between two major textual traditions, commonly designated the Alexandrian and Western traditions. Texts of the Alexandrian tradition include parchment copies of both Luke and Acts from as early as the fourth century and the oldest papyrus text of Luke's Gospel, $\mathfrak{P}^{75}$, from ca. 175–225 CE. Texts of the Western tradition include parchment copies of Luke and Acts from as early as the sixth century, as well as papyrus fragments and citations from early patristic writers such as Tertullian, Cyprian, and Augustine that go back as early as the third century. In particular, two major differences between these textual traditions stand out in the case of Luke–Acts: Western texts have eight textual omissions present in the Alexandrian texts of Luke 22–4, but Western texts also exhibit a version of Acts that is approximately 10 percent longer than that found in the Alexandrian texts. In other words, the tendencies behind textual transmission seem to go in opposite directions for the two volumes of Luke–Acts. On the one hand, the omissions from Luke's Gospel in the Western texts of portions (22:19b–20; 24:3b, 6a, 12, 36b, 40, 51b, 52a) raise questions about why these passages were omitted. B. F. Westcott and F. J. A. Hort (1881) labeled these omissions "Western non-interpolations." On the other hand, the Western versions of Acts include additions to the Alexandrian textual tradition – additions that amplify some stories and tend to accentuate the Jewish rejection and the role of the Holy Spirit in ways that are stylistically different from the rest of Acts.

The complexities of these text-critical issues are reflected in the differences the scholarly assessment of the value of these two text traditions. Some scholars, notably Boismard and Lamouille in their extensive work on the text of Acts (1984), propose that the two versions of Acts may indicate that Luke revised the original work after a few years. Strange (1992) theorizes that Luke died before finishing Acts, leaving a work with notations that others later edited, one edition with notes and one without. Presently most scholars accept the Alexandrian textual tradition as the more authentic one, and these texts shape the Greek texts used in critical scholarship and translation, while the Western texts betray a tendency to revise the text of Acts by adding phrases and sentences to the Acts narrative. The problem, however, is that this same argument would favor the Western textual tradition in the Gospel of Luke (Parsons 1986). The debate continues (Delobel 1999).

## Sources and Intertextuality

The Lukan preface offers a number of general indications about the sources for his "orderly account" (Luke 1:3) that the author dedicated to Theophilus. First, because the author did not categorize himself as one of the eyewitnesses or the "servants of the message" (1:2), he was indebted to these others for whatever information that he possessed. Second, the author was aware of other "narrations" (*diēgēsis*) of what had occurred among the believers (1:1) – a description that would probably include writings about Jesus like those labeled as "gospels." Third, the author described his work as careful investigation, which suggests that he probably consulted these sources during the composition process. In addition to these indications from the preface, one may presume that Luke was privy to the teachings and stories that were part of Christian oral tradition. Careful study of Luke–Acts also suggests the existence of other sources that the author may have used at various stages and in various ways throughout the process of composition.

The consensus in Lukan studies is that there were three sources for the Gospel of Luke: the Gospel of Mark, a written source "Q" (from the German *Quelle* meaning "source"), and a third source for uniquely Lukan materials, typically designated "Special L" or just "L." This understanding of the sources used by Luke is based on the "Two-Document hypothesis" (see Chapter 15, "The Synoptic Problem," in this volume). This hypothesis proposes an explanation for the similarities and differences between the three synoptic gospels, called the "synoptic problem." Luke's use of Mark is apparent in a number of ways. First, substantial portions of Luke's narrative are very similar to those found in Mark and suggest some kind of literary dependence, since more than half of Mark's narrative is found in Luke. Second, Luke has appropriated much (but not all) of Mark's narrative sequence in chapters 3–9 and 19–24. The parts where the Luke's narrative is substantially different include chapters 1–2, most of the section dealing with Jesus' journey to Jerusalem (9:51–19:27), and the end of Luke (24:13–53) (see Fitzmyer 1981). Third, points of clarification and explanation that Luke includes in addition to the material found in Mark suggest that he has edited the text of Mark to suit his own literary style and structure. In other words, the comparison of the Greek texts of these two gospels suggests the likelihood that Mark was one of those "narrations" (1:1) available for Luke to consult and appropriate in the composition of his own work. Both the preface to the Gospel of Luke and the comparative study of the synoptic gospels suggest that the author appropriated other sources besides the Gospel of Mark in the composition of Luke. Evidence for another source may be seen in the remarkable (often verbatim) parallels between Luke and Matthew amounting to ca. 230 verses, most of which were not found in Mark. Interestingly, although Luke and Matthew each place segments of this material in different contexts, there is a general agreement in the sequence of the material that the two gospels share. While some who maintain the priority of Matthew argue that this evidence points to Luke's use of Matthew (Peabody 1998), most scholars agree with the hypothesis that these similarities point to a written source "Q" containing sayings and teachings of Jesus. The major obstacle to the "Q" hypothesis is the fact that "Q" exists only in parallels between Matthew and Luke and not independently. Nonetheless, this evidence still indicates the Lukan use of a second source other than Mark's Gospel.

In addition to the two sources mentioned above which account for nearly two-thirds of the materials included in the Gospel of Luke, there are other passages in Luke found in no other gospel that have been given the collective designation "Special L" or simply "L." Among these are the birth and infancy stories of chapters 1–2, the programmatic scene of Jesus in the synagogue of Nazareth (4:16–30), the familiar parables of the good Samaritan (10:29–37) and the prodigal son (15:11–32), the story of Zacchaeus (19:1–10), and the appearance of the risen Jesus to the two disciples on the road to Emmaus

(24:13–35). Nothing about these uniquely Lukan texts indicates whether they came from one or multiple sources (although the latter is more probable). Nothing about these texts indicates whether they were derived from written sources, oral sources, or both, although it is commonly thought that the source for much of the information in the first two chapters may have been Mary the mother of Jesus herself. There is no evidence to indicate the extent to which these passages reflect the author's own hand in composition, although they are similar to the style and tendencies of other edited portions. Thus, one should not assume that "L" was derived from a single source, whether literary or oral.

In addition to the question about sources of Luke, there are also questions about sources used in the composition of Acts. Unlike the similarities between the synoptic gospels indicating literary dependency, there are no similar texts parallel to Acts that can suggest the existence of specific sources. Many have argued that the "we" passages reflect one source that Luke used in compiling Acts, but other more plausible explanations mentioned above make such an argument less than convincing. While one may plausibly assume that Luke had sources for Acts, there has been no success in defining what those sources might be, a fact due in part to the author's tendency to rewrite his sources in his own style and vocabulary (Dupont 1964). Some have attempted to distinguish a "Jerusalem source" and an "Antioch source," since those two cities are central loci for the action in Acts; Jerusalem in the first half of Acts, and Antioch in the second half. A minority view holds that Paul's letters were available to Luke, but this fails to deal adequately with the problem of the *differences* between Acts and the Pauline letters. However, Walker (1998) suggests that Luke may have known and used Galatians, though he *reverses* the roles and views of Paul and Peter. Other parts of Acts, such as the accusations against Paul in chapter 21, may even reflect what Paul says in Galatians, rather than what Luke narrates about Paul elsewhere in Acts. Nonetheless, the issue about the sources of Acts lacks any definitive conclusions.

Nevertheless, there is widespread awareness of an important additional source for the composition of Luke–Acts: the Septuagint. While it might be argued that Luke borrowed stylistic features and ways of telling a good story from a variety of sources, it is clear that he was particularly dependent on the Septuagint in shaping the narrative of Luke–Acts (see Evans and Sanders 1993; Litwak 2005). The intertextual relationship between Luke–Acts and the Septuagint is evident in two distinct ways. First, Luke inserts scriptural quotations at strategic narrative points, such as Jesus' reading from the scroll of Isaiah at the Nazarene synagogue (Luke 4:18–19), Jesus' final words from the cross (quoting Psalm 31:5; 30:6 in the Septuagint), Peter's explanation of the Pentecost phenomenon (Acts 2:17–21), and numerous instances in Acts when Jesus is proclaimed as the Christ (e.g., 2:25–8; 3:22–3; 4:11). Second, Luke's vocabulary and telling of particular stories not infrequently allude to particular stories and themes in the Jewish scriptures. For instance, the story of Zechariah and Elizabeth (Luke 1:5–25) is reminiscent of the Abraham and Sarah story, and Luke links the incident about Ananias and Sapphira with the story of Achan's sin in Joshua 7. In other words, one discovers scriptural echoes throughout Luke–Acts, where the narrative alludes to the story of Israel – its vocabulary, stories, and theology – found in the Jewish scriptures both to tell the stories of Jesus and the church as well as to reinterpret the story of Israel.

Thus, Luke uses these and many other intertextual associations in Luke–Acts so that these stories of Jesus and his followers are understood as part of the continuing story of God's salvific purposes as told in the scriptures.

## Literary and Composition Analysis

Luke used various oral and written sources, including the Septuagint, that function *inter*textually by contributing to the reading and interpretation of Luke–Acts. There are also *intra*textual features that shape and structure the work. Part of Luke's literary repertoire includes narrative summaries, speeches, and mirroring of events and characters, all of which facilitate the interpretation of his narrative by his readers. Luke's narrative summaries, which appear more frequently in Acts (e.g., Acts 2:42–7; 4:32–7; 5:12–16) than in the gospel, not only link scenes together but provide the audience with more explicit commentary than can be accomplished through narrative alone. The speeches in Luke–Acts, including both those of reliable Christian characters (like Peter, Stephen, and Paul) in Acts as well as Jesus' teachings in Luke, provide Luke's audience with an interpretive perspective for understanding surrounding passages as well as for the larger work. Luke's tendency to depict narrative events and characters in ways that mirror one another encourages the audience to draw conclusions based on these associations. Thus, the descriptions of Jesus performing miracles in Luke and the Apostles and others doing the same thing in Acts (e.g., Acts 3:1–10; 5:12–16; 14:8–11), link the story of Jesus with the ongoing story of the church. The Cornelius event of Acts 10 is reminiscent of the faith-filled centurion of Luke 7:1–10. In these and numerous other instances, Luke guides the audience in distinct ways that serve the overall narrative objectives.

There are a number of other narrative features that provide more general means of guidance in understanding the organization and structure of Luke–Acts. Among these are Luke's distinctive use of geography and his use of similar scenes to structure the narrative rhetorically. First, Luke uses different geographical features such as Jerusalem and the journey motif to structure Luke–Acts. Jerusalem functions as a center for much of Luke's narrative. The Gospel of Luke begins at the temple in Jerusalem (Luke 1:5–25), returns there twice (2:22–38, 41–51), becomes the destination of the journey of Jesus that stretches over more than a third of the gospel (9:51–19:27), and provides the setting for the culminating events of Jesus' passion, resurrection, and ascension (19:28–24:53). Acts begins where the gospel ends – in Jerusalem – and depicts the fulfillment of God's promises to Israel there in the first seven chapters (e.g., Acts 2:14–40). The spread of the Christian message to other parts of the world begins with the scattering of believers from Jerusalem due to Jewish persecution (8:1–3), confirming Jesus' last words that his followers would be his "witnesses in Jerusalem, and in all Judea and Samaria, and to the end of the earth" (1:8). Significantly, the narrative action returns to Jerusalem at strategic points: the introduction of the converted Saul to the Jerusalem leaders (9:26–30), questions about salvation and Gentiles (11:1–18; 15:1–35; 21:17–26), and the legal proceedings against Paul (21:27–23:30). These examples indicate that Jerusalem is not merely a *geographical* center for most of Luke–Acts but also a *theological* center. The role of Jerusalem grounds Luke's story of Jesus and the story of the church, including the inclusion of Gentiles, within the story of God's dealings with Israel. However, the fact that the narrative does not end in Jerusalem suggests a shift in that narrative and in the theological role of Jerusalem (Parsons 1998).

Another geographical element, the journey motif, also has a theological function in Luke–Acts. The prominent portion of the gospel that contains a large percentage of uniquely Lukan materials is organized as a journey of Jesus from Galilee to Jerusalem (9:51–19:27). In Acts, Luke depicts the spread of the Christian message as believers traveled from Jerusalem to the surrounding regions and then to the rest of the Mediterranean world, with particular attention given to the travels of figures like Philip (8:4–40) and Paul (13:4–14:28; 15:36–18:22; 18:23–21:16). Thus, by structuring the narrative with the journey motif along with the centering role of Jerusalem for much of the narrative, Luke identifies the Christian movement with the purposes of God.

Second, Luke arranges similar scenes through Luke and Acts to structure smaller sections of the narrative for a rhetorical purpose. For instance, the meal scene or the scene of table fellowship throughout Luke–Acts functions to highlight significant narrative themes and developments as well as to contrast different elements within that narrative (Heil 1999). In the Gospel of Luke, two similar scenes, in which Jesus enters the home of a tax collector (Luke 5:27–32; 19:1–10), create an *inclusio* framing the heart of the central narrative. Hostile responses to Jesus' association and table fellowship with "outsiders" reflect the ancient context, where meals were a microcosm of the web of social and religious markers and boundaries that were part of the larger social system or worldview. These meal scenes became occasions of controversy because the complainants saw in Jesus' actions some form of boundary transgression, which threatened their identity and solidarity. Interestingly, within the larger section of Luke framed by these two scenes are three additional meal scenes, all of which treat Jesus' presence at a dinner in a Pharisee's home (7:36–50; 11:37–54; 14:1–24). In each case, Luke directs the focus of attention to issues involving purity and the type of people with whom one might associate by sharing table fellowship with them, thereby contrasting Pharisaic attitudes and actions with those of Jesus. These divergent elements in Luke's Gospel set the narrative "table" for two final meal scenes, when Jesus shares his table with a group of apostles, including his betrayer and those who jockey for positions of honor (22:7–30), and when Jesus breaks bread with two disciples (perhaps a husband and wife) who failed to recognize him (24:13–35). Such narrative and structural features in Luke provide the backdrop for numerous references to "breaking bread," table fellowship, and meals in Acts, including those scenes that raise either explicitly or implicitly the problematic issues of table fellowship among Jews and Gentiles that surfaced repeatedly in narrated meetings of the Jerusalem church in chapters 11, 15, and 21.

When reading Luke–Acts with an attentive eye for literary and structural features of the work, its possible purposes and objectives along with accompanying themes and emphases begin to emerge. Both the extensive intertextual connections between Luke–Acts and the Septuagint and the literary aspects of the work suggest that the Lukan theological understanding of the concept "people of God" is central to the plot and purposes. The Gospel of Luke begins and ends with declarations about how God is dealing with Israel (Luke 1:54–5; 24:44–9). Numerous connections with the Septuagint along with the narrative role of Jerusalem and the temple establish this story of divine activity in Jesus within the larger framework of God's dealing with his chosen people. From the beginning, Luke's portrayal of Jesus as God's prophet among God's people triggered results similar to the experiences of biblical prophets: there was division among the people over the divine message he delivered (e.g., Luke 4:14–30). While the Lukan Jesus embodies an understanding of God's people that offers salvation *today* to outsiders and the disenfranchised by eating with them and thus making *them* "clean," others like the Pharisees in Luke regard his actions as making *him* "unclean" and therefore an outsider. As Jesus journeys to Jerusalem (9:51–19:27), the words that he speaks to different groups function prophetically both to call together and form a people faithful to God as well as to provoke opposition and rejection. Even Jesus' words to one of the criminals crucified with him (23:43) epitomize the tension between radically different understandings of salvation and of the people of God. Thus, throughout the Gospel of Luke one finds God's visitation of the people in the person of Jesus depicted in ways that challenge the expectations and values of that day. This Lukan theme of reversal affirms the inclusion of all whom society and religion have deemed "outsiders": the poor, the leper, the outcast, the sinner, the Samaritan, even the Gentile.

While the Acts of the Apostles similarly reflects the activity of God from beginning to end, the narrative takes a different turn. The importance of Pentecost early in Acts demonstrates the faithfulness of God, whose actions through the resurrection of Jesus and the outpouring of the Spirit fulfilled the divine promises to Israel. Luke's portrayal of the apostles (most notably Peter) and other believers in Acts 1–7 focuses on the proclamation of what God has done and the divine presence through the Holy Spirit that has created the unanimity and extraordinary communal dynamics among the believers. In many ways, the Lukan image of the apostles resembles the prophetic Jesus of Luke's Gospel, and with similar results. The antithetical depictions of the Jewish believers and the Jewish religious leaders in Acts are reminiscent of the division among the Jewish people who responded to Jesus in various ways in Luke. The persecution against Stephen and other believers mirrors the passion of Jesus. Nonetheless, the Lukan choice of the term *ekklēsia* ("church") to describe these believers appropriates the terminology of Israel or the people of God, thereby contrasting this group with the unrepentant Jews. With the focus on the spread of the Christian message and God's role in offering that message of salvation to Gentiles as well as Jews that begins in chapter 8, Luke continues to use the terminology of Israel to depict a new conception of the people of God – one that includes Jewish and Gentile believers. The fact that Luke inserts his accounts of the Jerusalem church wrestling over such questions suggests something about the problem, at least in Jewish circles, of affirming what God is doing in saving both Jews *and* Gentiles. On the one hand, the acknowledgment of God's activity among this "mixed" people might be at odds with Jewish customs regarding table fellowship with non-Jews. On the other hand, the acknowledgment of the priority of Jewish custom might conflict with the Lukan perspective regarding God's purposes and presence among the "mixed" people. Both the absence of Jerusalem the city and the Jerusalem believers at the end of Acts and the likely role of the Jewish believers in the seizure of Paul in the temple (cf. Acts 21:30 – "the whole city was aroused, and the people rushed together ... seizing Paul") imply the severity of this problem (Thompson 2005). Still, this incident creates the scenario for the rest of the Acts narrative. Scholars have long debated the reasons behind the extended narrative treatment of the imprisonment of Paul and the subsequent legal proceedings that followed. It may be that these narrated trials and hearings against Paul ultimately function in Acts, not as a means of defending Paul *per se*, but as a defense of what the narrative offers: an inclusive understanding of salvation and the people of God rooted in the story of the ongoing activity and presence of God.

## Annotated Bibliography

Bartholomew, C. G., J. B. Green, and A. C. Thiselton (eds.). *Reading Luke: Interpretation, Reflection, Formation*. Grand Rapids: Zondervan Publishing House, 2005. This particular collection of essays represents recent attempts to read and interpret biblical texts in new ways that take seriously the hermeneutical possibilities for the contemporary church reading these texts as scripture while also appropriating critical methods. These contributions to the study of the Gospel of Luke from a broad range of critical approaches model different ways to move from text to application.

Cadbury, H. J. *The Making of Luke–Acts*. New York: Macmillan, 1927; repr. Peabody: Hendrickson Publishers, 1999. Although now dated, this reprint of Henry Cadbury's classic work remains essential reading for those interested in significant contributions to Lukan studies. Here one finds Cadbury's groundbreaking notion regarding the unity of the Gospel of Luke and the Acts of the Apostles as Luke–Acts and his assessment of the Lukan author.

Conzelmann, H. *The Theology of St. Luke*. Philadelphia: Fortress Press, 1961. This is another work that may be deemed a classic within Lukan studies, due to its long shadow of influence. Many studies on Lukan theology begin or engage with some of the ideas first proposed by this redaction-critical study. While some of these ideas are now obsolete, there is still value in reading this work that significantly shaped the study of Luke–Acts.

Darr, J. A. *On Character Building: The Reader and the Rhetoric of Characterization in Luke–Acts*. Louisville: Westminster John Knox Press, 1992. This study provides a useful guide in interpreting characters within the Lukan writings. Darr explores aspects of characterization that account for the respective roles of text and reader. He examines three characters within Luke–Acts: John the Baptist, the Pharisees, and Herod the tetrarch.

Esler, P. F. *Community and Gospel in Luke–Acts: The Social and Political Motivations of Lucan Theology*. Cambridge: Cambridge University Press, 1987. Esler's appropriation of sociology and anthropology for the study of Lukan theology has long provided the standard for socioscientific studies in Luke–Acts. This monograph usefully recognizes that any study of the theology of the Luke writings will be contextual and must appropriate methodology that explores the social dynamics and realities of the Christian community to which these writings were addressed.

Fitzmyer, J. A. *Luke the Theologian: Aspects of his Teaching*. New York: Paulist Press, 1989. This work offers explorations of eight theological themes in Luke–Acts. While the background of this particular work is the author's two-volume Anchor Bible commentary on the Gospel of Luke and precedes his subsequent volume on Acts, this contribution from a leader in Lukan studies provides a useful introduction to the theological perspective reflected by the Lukan writings.

Green, J. B. *The Theology of the Gospel of Luke*. Cambridge: Cambridge University Press, 1995. This concise work from a leading contributor to Lukan studies seeks to articulate the theological perspective that resonates from the Gospel of Luke. Both the synthesis of contributions from various methodical approaches and the breadth of critical work on Green's part makes this volume a helpful introductory and summary of Lukan thought reflected in this particular gospel.

Jervell, J. *The Theology of the Acts of the Apostles*. Cambridge: Cambridge University Press, 1996. Like Green's work above, this particular volume succinctly articulates Lukan thought, this time as reflected in the Acts of the Apostles. Jervell's arguments regarding the success of the church's Jewish mission continue to stimulate vigorous debate about the purposes of Luke–Acts and about the Lukan perspectives toward Judaism and the Jewish people.

Klauck, H.-J. *Magic and Paganism in Early Christianity: The World of the Acts of the Apostles*. Edinburgh: T. & T. Clark, 2000. This is a concise work that focuses on portions of the book of Acts that depict the encounter between Christianity and paganism. While this contribution really ends up something like a commentary on these scenes and what may be perceived as the mission to the Gentiles, it also provides an accessible treatment of some difficult passages in Acts that have not received adequate treatment to date.

Levine, A.-J. (ed.). *A Feminist Companion to Luke*. Cleveland: Pilgrim Press, 2001. This collection brings together fourteen insightful essays dealing with different aspects of the Gospel of Luke pertaining to women. Given the common assumptions regarding the Lukan perspective toward women as well as the relative silence of feminine voices within biblical studies until recent decades, these studies offer fresh interpretations of key passages that either mention women or may be understood differently from a feminist perspective.

Maddox, R. *The Purpose of Luke–Acts*. Göttingen: Vandenhoeck & Ruprecht, 1982. This frequently cited contribution to Lukan studies offers the perspective that Luke–Acts was written to validate the faith of church that was becoming increasingly Gentile. Maddox argues that this church was experiencing both the Jewish rejection of Jesus and the gospel and the Roman challenges of a gospel about one who was executed by the Romans.

Marshall, I. H. and D. Peterson (eds.). *Witness to the Gospel: The Theology of Acts*. Grand Rapids: William B. Eerdmans, 1998. This collection of twenty-five essays explores a variety of major theological themes in Acts. Edited by I. H. Marshall, these essays provide a substantial contribution to the theology of Acts that takes seriously contemporary approaches to the Lukan writings.

Moessner, D. P. (ed.). *Jesus and the Heritage of Israel*. Harrisburg: Trinity Press International, 1999. A strong collection of respected Luke–Acts scholars, this work offers essays that examine Luke's writings to uncover the Lukan perspectives on Israel and Jesus' role with regard to Israel. The consensus among the contributors is that Luke–Acts claims that Jesus is Israel's heritage and legacy to the rest of the world. Some essays focus on the Lukan prologues and what they might suggest regarding how the work might function in its Greco-Roman context. Others explore the narrative and thematic issues in reading Acts in light of the Lukan Gospel, including how Acts affects and contributes to the Lukan rearticulation of the story of Israel.

Moxnes, H. *The Economy of the Kingdom: Social Conflict and Economic Relations in Luke's Gospel*. Philadelphia: Fortress Press, 1988. This particular work is illustrative of the prospects of social-scientific approaches to the study of Luke–Acts. As the author notes, the focus of this work is not the historical Jesus or the historical situation of Luke. Rather, this work explores the social world of the Gospel of Luke so that the interpreter may come to grips with the radical nature of the Lukan message as it would have been understood in that world.

Neyrey, J. H. (ed.). *The Social World of Luke–Acts: Models for Interpretation*. Peabody: Hendrickson Publishers, 1991. Like the previous work, this book also explores issues regarding the social world of Luke–Acts. This collection of thirteen essays draws from a variety of sociological, anthropological, and psychological theories to examine and interpret the Lukan writings in light of the ancient social values and structures in which and to which they were written.

Parsons, M. C. *Body and Character in Luke–Acts: The Subversion of Physiognomy in Early Christianity.* Grand Rapids: Baker Academic, 2006. This work explores how ancient understandings of the human body with regard to character may contribute to readings of passages where specific aspects of a person's body are included in the narrative. Parsons contends that the author of Luke and Acts intentionally subverts such understandings, thereby denying direct correlation between a person's physical appearance and moral character.

Parsons, M. C. and R. I. Pervo. *Rethinking the Unity of Luke and Acts.* Minneapolis: Fortress Press, 1993. This compact book reopens the question about the assumed unity of Luke–Acts as a single work. The authors contend that assumptions about common author do not imply generic, narrative, or theological unity. The issues raised by this study helpfully force the interpreter of Luke and Acts to clarify the ways in which one might and might not talk about the Lukan writings as a single, two-volume work.

Penner, T. And C. Vander Stichele (eds.). *Contextualizing Acts: Lukan Narrative and Greco-Roman Discourse.* Atlanta: Scholars Press, 2003. This collection of twelve essays offers suggestive ways of studying the book of Acts in ways that move beyond traditional approaches of interpretation and appropriate more recent developments in literary, discourse, cultural, and historical analyses. The contributors explore Acts both in light of its historical and literary context as well as in light of the ways in which this work may have shaped the identity and social location of the earliest Christians.

Pervo, R. I. *Profit with Delight: The Literary Genre of the Acts of the Apostles.* Philadelphia: Fortress Press, 1987. This monograph is both provocative and enjoyable to read. Pervo forcefully asserts the dramatic and entertaining aspects of Acts, identifying the work not as a work of history but as a popular work of historical fiction or as a historical novel. Whether or not one accepts Pervo's thesis, his emphasis on the creative side of the Acts narrative is an important addition to Lukan studies.

Pervo, R. I. *Dating Acts: Between the Evangelists and the Apologists.* Santa Rosa: Polebridge Press, 2006. Against the general consensus dating Acts in the 80s, Pervo argues here for a later date in the first quarter of the second century. Given recent developments in Lukan studies that are beginning to challenge traditional dating, Pervo offers arguments worth considering.

Phillips, T. E. (ed.). *Acts and Ethics.* Sheffield: Sheffield Phoenix Press, 2005. This recent publication is a collection of essays addressing the issue of ethics in Acts from a variety of perspectives. While this work does not exhaust nearly all the possibilities to this particular issue, the different critical approaches and methods offer helpful guides for further explorations in Acts and beyond.

Porter, S. E. *Paul in Acts.* Peabody: Hendrickson Publishers, 2001. After many shorter studies on Paul in Acts in the preceding two decades, this book draws from these predecessors but also offers new insights into aspects associated with Paul in this portion of Luke–Acts. Of note are Porter's assessment of the theology and perspective of the "we" passages of Acts and his study of Paul's arrest in Acts 21.

Reimer, I. R. *Women in the Acts of the Apostles: A Feminist Liberation Perspective.* Minneapolis: Fortress Press, 1995. This is a significant work that attempts to reconstruct the history of women in Acts while acknowledging the limits of a text such as Acts with an androcentric perspective. What stands out in her work are the overlooked questions that she raises about the role of these women in the Lukan stories. Her study does not come to the same conclusions as Seim's work (see below), as she identifies ordinary working women among those who spread the Christian message.

Seim, T. K. *Double Message: Patterns of Gender in Luke–Acts.* Edinburgh: T. & T. Clark, 1994. Coming out about the same time as Reimer's work, this important monograph also reexamines the assumptions regarding the Lukan perspective on women. Seim contends that there is a "double message" in Luke–Acts: one that preserves positive traditions about women and their roles in the Christian church, another that limits women's roles in the public proclamation and ministry of the church in Acts.

Tannehill, R. C. *The Narrative Unity of Luke–Acts: A Literary Interpretation*. 2 vols. Philadelphia and Minneapolis: Fortress Press, 1986–90. This two-volume work on Luke–Acts focuses on the Lukan understanding of God's purposes that unifies the entire Lukan work. The author emphasizes how all the major characters all share in a common mission directed and controlled by those divine purposes. All aspects of the Lukan writings are interpreted in ways that account for their contribution to the entire Lukan narrative.

Tyson, J. B. (ed.). *Luke–Acts and the Jewish People: Eight Critical Perspectives*. Minneapolis: Augsburg Publishing House, 1988. This small collection of essays offers a concise overview of the issues and difficulties in the interpretation of the place of the Jewish people and Judaism in Luke and Acts. While the discussion of these issues has moved beyond some of the arguments contained here, these essays still provoke the reader of Luke–Acts to examine the textual evidence on these matters again.

Tyson, J. B. *Images of Judaism in Luke–Acts*. Columbia: University of South Carolina Press, 1992. Continuing the conversation about the role and Lukan perspective of Judaism in Luke–Acts, Tyson offers a sequential narrative analysis of Judaism and Jewish persons in these writings. The author concludes that the Lukan writings include both positive and negative images of Judaism, which the interpreter must consider in the interpretation of these texts.

Tyson, J. B. *Marcion and Luke–Acts: A Defining Struggle*. Columbia: University of South Carolina Press, 2006. This recent work offers the hypothesis that Luke and Acts were written in response to Marcion and should therefore be dated well into the second century. The evidence cited in support of the argument makes an interesting and compelling case that should be considered in discussions about the dating and purpose of Luke–Acts.

## Works Cited

Aune, D. E. *The New Testament in Its Literary Environment*. Philadelphia: Westminster Press, 1987.

Boismard, M. É. and A. Lamouille. *Le Texte occidental des Actes des Apôtres: Reconstitution et réhabilitation*. Paris: Éditions Recherche sur les Civilisations, 1984. An important but somewhat eccentric study of the so-called Western Text of Acts.

Brawley, R. L. *Luke–Acts and the Jews: Conflict, Apology, and Conciliation*. Atlanta: Scholars Press, 1987.

Brawley, R. L. *Centering on God: Method and Message in Luke–Acts*. Louisville: Westminster John Knox Press, 1990.

Burridge, R. A. *What Are the Gospels? A Comparison with Graeco-Roman Biography*. Cambridge: Cambridge University Press, 1992. A monograph that argues that the canonical gospels are a type of Greco-Roman biography by an Anglican New Testament scholar with a strong educational background in classical philology.

Cadbury, H. J. *The Style and Method of St. Luke*. Cambridge, MA: Harvard University Press, 1920.

Cadbury, H. J. *The Making of Luke–Acts*. New York: Macmillan, 1927; reprinted Peabody: Hendrickson Publishers, 1999. One of the most important works on Luke–Acts produced by an American biblical scholar.

Conzelmann, H. *The Theology of St. Luke*. Philadelphia: Fortress Press, 1961. A classic study of redaction criticism of Luke–Acts.

Darr, J. A. *On Character Building: The Reader and the Rhetoric of Characterization in Luke–Acts*. Louisville: Westminster John Knox Press, 1992.

Delobel, J. "The Text of Luke–Acts: A Confrontation of Recent Theories." Pp. 83–107 in *The Unity of Luke-Acts*. Edited by J. Verheyden. Leuven: Leuven University Press, 1999.

Dupont, J. *The Sources of the Acts*. New York: Herder & Herder, 1964. A comprehensive study of the material used by Luke in writing Acts.

Esler, P. F. *Community and Gospel in Luke–Acts: The Social and Political Motivations of Lucan Theology*. Cambridge: Cambridge University Press, 1987. One of the earliest attempts to profile the community behind Luke–Acts.

Evans, C. A. and J. A. Sanders. *Luke and Scripture: The Function of Sacred Tradition in Luke–Acts*. Minneapolis: Fortress Press, 1993.

Fitzmyer, J. A. *The Gospel According to Luke: Introduction, Translation, and Notes*. 2 vols. Garden City, NY: Doubleday, 1981–5. One of the more important recent commentaries on the Gospel of Luke by a renowned Roman Catholic scholar.

Gowler, D. B. *Host, Guest, Enemy and Friend: Portraits of the Pharisees in Luke and Acts*. New York: Peter Lang, 1991.

Heil, J. P. *The Meal Scenes in Luke–Acts: An Audience-Oriented Approach*. Atlanta: Scholars Press, 1999.

Jervell, J. *Luke and the People of God: A New Look at Luke–Acts*. Minneapolis: Augsburg Publishing House, 1972.

Jervell, J. *The Theology of the Acts of the Apostles*. Cambridge: Cambridge University Press, 1996.

Johnson, L. T. *The Literary Function of Possessions in Luke–Acts*. Missoula: Scholars Press, 1977.

Knox, J. *Marcion and the New Testament: An Essay in the Early History of the Canon*. Chicago: University of Chicago Press, 1942. An exploration of the fact that Marcion included the Gospel of Luke (though without that title) in his "canon" of New Testament writings.

Knox, J. *Chapters in a Life of Paul*. Macon: Mercer University Press, 1987.

Lentz, J. C., Jr. *Luke's Portrait of Paul*. Cambridge: Cambridge University Press, 1993.

Litwak, K. D. *Echoes of Scripture in Luke–Acts: Telling the History of God's People Intertextually*. London: T. & T. Clark International, 2005.

Maddox, R. *The Purpose of Luke–Acts*. Göttingen: Vandenhoeck & Ruprecht, 1982. An attempt to explore the signals that Luke gives regarding his purpose in writing Luke–Acts.

Marshall, I. H. and D. Peterson (eds.). *Witness to the Gospel: The Theology of Acts*. Grand Rapids: William B. Eerdmans, 1998.

Moessner, D. P. (ed.). *Jesus and the Heritage of Israel*. Harrisburg: Trinity Press International, 1999. A collection of important essays on Luke–Acts by a scholar who has focused his work on that subject.

Moxnes, H. *The Economy of the Kingdom: Social Conflict and Economic Relations in Luke's Gospel*. Philadelphia: Fortress Press, 1988.

Neale, D. A. *None but the Sinners: Religious Categories in the Gospel of Luke*. Sheffield: JSOT Press, 1991.

Neyrey, J. H. (ed.). *The Social World of Luke–Acts: Models for Interpretation*. Peabody: Hendrickson Publishers, 1991. A basic work applying social-science criticism to Luke–Acts.

Parsons, M. C. "A Christological Tendency in $\mathfrak{P}^{75}$." *Journal of Biblical Literature* 105 (1986), 463–79.

Parsons, M. C. "The Place of Jerusalem on the Lukan Landscape: An Exercise in Symbolic Cartography." Pp. 155–71 in *Literary Studies in Luke–Acts: Essays in Honor of Joseph B. Tyson*. Edited by R. P. Thompson and T. E. Phillips. Macon: Mercer University Press, 1998.

Parsons, M. C. and R. I. Pervo. *Rethinking the Unity of Luke and Acts.* Minneapolis: Fortress Press, 1993. A study that reexamines the assumption that Luke–Acts is a work by a single author.

Peabody, D. B. "Luke's Sequential Use of the Sayings of Jesus from Matthew's Great Discourses: A Chapter in the Source-Critical Analysis of Luke on the Two-Gospel (Neo-Griesbach) Hypothesis." Pp. 37–58 in *Literary Studies in Luke–Acts: Essays in Honor of Joseph B. Tyson.* Edited by R. P. Thompson and T. E. Phillips. Macon: Mercer University Press, 1998.

Pervo, R. I. *Profit with Delight: The Literary Genre of the Acts of the Apostles.* Philadelphia: Fortress Press, 1987. A comparison of Acts with the ancient novel.

Pervo, R. I. *Dating Acts: Between the Evangelists and the Apologists.* Santa Rosa: Polebridge Press, 2006.

Plümacher, E. *Lukas als hellenisticher Schriftsteller: Studien zur Apostelgeschichte.* Göttingen: Vandenhoeck & Ruprecht, 1972. The best study of Acts as Hellenistic historiography.

Porter, S. E. *Paul in Acts.* Peabody: Hendrickson Publishers, 2001.

Sanders, J. T. *The Jews in Luke–Acts.* Philadelphia: Fortress Press, 1987.

Shepherd, W. H., Jr. *The Narrative Function of the Holy Spirit as a Character in Luke–Acts.* Atlanta: Scholars Press, 1994.

Spencer, F. S. *The Portrait of Philip in Acts: A Study of Roles and Relations.* Sheffield: JSOT Press, 1992.

Sterling, G. E. *Historiography and Self-Definition: Josephus, Luke–Acts and Apologetic Historiography.* Leiden: E. J. Brill, 1992.

Strange, W. A. *The Problem of the Text of Acts.* Cambridge: Cambridge University Press, 1992.

Talbert, C. H. *Literary Patterns, Theological Themes, and the Genre of Luke–Acts.* Missoula: Scholars Press, 1974.

Tannehill, R. C. *The Narrative Unity of Luke–Acts: A Literary Interpretation.* 2 vols. Philadelphia and Minneapolis: Fortress Press, 1986–90.

Thompson, R. P. " 'What Do You Think You Are Doing, Paul?' Synagogues, Accusations, and Ethics in Paul's Ministry in Acts 16–21." Pp. 64–78 in *Acts and Ethics.* Edited by T. E. Phillips. Sheffield: Sheffield Phoenix Press, 2005.

Tyson, J. B. (ed.). *Luke–Acts and the Jewish People: Eight Critical Perspectives.* Minneapolis: Augsburg Publishing House, 1988.

Tyson, J. B. *Images of Judaism in Luke–Acts.* Columbia: University of South Carolina Press, 1992.

Tyson, J. B. *Marcion and Luke–Acts: A Defining Struggle.* Columbia: University of South Carolina Press, 2006.

Walaskay, P. W. *"And So We Came to Rome": The Political Perspective of St. Luke.* Cambridge: Cambridge University Press, 1983.

Walker, W. O., Jr. "Acts and the Pauline Corpus Revisited: Peter's Speech at the Jerusalem Conference." In *Literary Studies in Luke–Acts: Essays in Honor of Joseph B. Tyson.* Edited by R. P Thompson and T. E. Phillips. Macon: Mercer University Press, 1998.

Westcott, B. F. and F. J. A. Hort. *The New Testament in the Original Greek.* Cambridge: Macmillan, 1881.

# CHAPTER 20

# Johannine Literature: The Gospel and Letters of John

## John Painter

## The Johannine Corpus

Since the time of Irenaeus (died ca. 202 CE), tradition has ascribed the authorship of the gospel and (three?) epistles of John to the apostle John, the son of Zebedee. Irenaeus reports a tradition going back to the Elders of Asia Minor, of whom he names Polycarp of Smyrna and Papias of Hierapolis. From these references the identification of the Beloved Disciple with John the son of Zebedee is made. While some scholars have suspected that Irenaeus was mistaken in making this identification, grounds for doing this are more related to the conviction that the apostle was not the author of all the books attributed to him by Irenaeus than to the early sources themselves. In ancient times (but some time after Irenaeus) the distinction between John the apostle and John the Elder was used to reject the apostolic authorship of Revelation. In modern times authors have been more likely to associate the apostle with Revelation than with the gospel and epistles (C. K. Barrett). Only in Revelation does the author name himself as John. 1 John neither identifies nor names the author. In 2 and 3 John the author identifies himself as "the Elder." This identification is peculiar because there were many elders. Such identification presupposes the use of a name with "elder," like "John the Elder." Some scholars see an identification of the author with the Beloved Disciple in the gospel. But the identity of the Beloved Disciple remains hidden behind this *nom de plume*. Thus these books, attributed by Irenaeus to one and the same author, fall into three groups: (1) strictly anonymous (1 John); (2) written by an unidentified elder (2 and 3 John) or Beloved Disciple (John); (3) written by an author who identifies himself simply as "John" but without specifying which John (Revelation). Nothing in any of these books specifically connects it with any of the others as the product of a common author. The nearest we get to this is the self-identification of the author of 2 and 3 John as the Elder. We might suppose that the Elder was known by those to whom these writings were addressed, though it is possible that an impressive title was used to give added authority to these writings.

Nevertheless, a common vocabulary, idiom, point of view, and worldview connect the gospel and epistles. In vocabulary, idiom, and point of view, 1 John stands close to the gospel, while 2 and 3 John stand together. At the same time 1 John is closer to 2

John than to 3 John. While there are connections between Revelation and the gospel and epistles, these are fewer and less impressive than the connections between the gospel and epistles. E. Schuessler Fiorenza argued that Revelation is closer to the Pauline corpus than the Johannine literature. It may be that genre accounts for some of the differences between these writings. At the same time, acceptance that the gospel and the Johannine epistles constitute the Johannine literature need not imply their common authorship. Many scholars think that the hands of more than one author are responsible for the gospel. This seems to be implied by John 21:24. There a group attests the truth of what was written in the book by another author. "This is the disciple who bears witness concerning these things and has written these things, and we know that his witness is true." This reference suggests that the Johannine literature is the product of a school, shaped by the vocabulary, idiom, point of view, and worldview of a single seminal teacher. The school attests the truth of the Johannine gospel. One or more of that group may be the author(s) of 1, 2, and 3 John.

## Changing Views of Authorship, Context, and Purpose

The evidence of Irenaeus makes a case for a Jewish author of the Johannine literature but implies that the form of Christianity represented by John was Christian and not distinctly Jewish. "John, the Lord's disciple, in Ephesus, going to bathe, and seeing Cerinthus in the place, leaped out of the bath without using it, adding, Let us fly, lest the very bath fall on us, where Cerinthus, the enemy of the truth, is" (Irenaeus, *Against Heresies*, 3.3.4). This implies that both John and Cerinthus frequented the Roman bathhouse. The adoption of the practice has cultural implications. It implies a loosing of connections with Judaism. The relationship between John and Polycarp also implies a form of Christianity that has settled into the Hellenistic reality of the Roman empire in Asia Minor.

Representative of this view in modern times is the work of Brooke Foss Westcott (1825–1901). Westcott produced the classic argument to establish that the author of the gospel was a Jew, a Jew of Palestine, an eyewitness, an apostle, St. John. But the gospel (and epistles) was written at a later stage in the church's life than the synoptic gospels. It was written in Asia, remote from the events it describes. It provides evidence that the gospel had spread beyond the limits of Judaism so that John's church was by no means Jewish but it reflects the reality of Christianity in Ephesus in the last decade of the first century CE. Westcott sees gospel and epistles addressed to the same situation of the church in the Roman empire.

Rudolf Bultmann also saw gospel and epistles against a common background. Gospel and epistles made use of the same revelation discourses source shaped by early oriental Gnostic influence. The evangelist historicized the source in his distinctively Christian interpretation. C. H. Dodd argued that the evangelist and the authors of the epistles interpreted the gospel in relation to the higher religion of Hellenism, which finds expression in the writings of Philo and the Poimandres Tractate of the Corpus Hermeticum. Like Westcott, Dodd and Bultmann understand the gospel and epistles to be independent of Judaism and universal in orientation. This involves the merging of Jewish and Hellenistic language and culture in the understanding of the gospel and "salvation."

The Johannine tradition was an expression of Christianity making its way in the Roman world. The approach of Bultmann and Dodd has its precursor in Robert Law's brilliant exposé, *The Tests of Life* (1909). His approach was given detailed exegetical expression in Rudolf Schnackenburg's *Die Johannesbriefe*, first published in 1953.

A departure from this approach is found in the work of J. A. T. Robinson (*Twelve New Testament Studies*, 1962, including essays published from 1947 through 1961). He saw the Johannine writings as expressions of Jewish Christianity originating in Judea but directed to Jews in the Diaspora. In adopting this view he was giving full weight to literary parallels between the Johannine writings and some of the Qumran texts. He recognizes that the texts from Qumran were written in Hebrew, appropriate to their origin in the Judean desert. The Johannine literature was penned in Hellenistic Greek, appropriate for texts addressed to the Diaspora. At the same time Robinson identifies different functions for the gospel and 1 John. The gospel was addressed to Diaspora Jews inviting them to believe in Jesus the messiah. 1 John was addressed to believing Jews to combat gnosticizing tendencies that continued to attract converts. In support of this view Robinson appeals not only to the evidence of 1 John itself, but also to Irenaeus, who refers to the conflict between Cerinthus and John. Robinson argues that Cerinthus was both Judaizer and gnosticizer. He concludes that the Johannine epistles were written for the same "Hellenistic Jewish community for which the gospel was written." But it is a form of Judaism in which a metaphysical dualism has distorted Johannine thought and the author of 1 John reasserts a Hebraic understanding of all key terms. He argues that 1 John can best be understood as providing "correctives to deductions drawn from the teaching of the fourth gospel by a Gnosticizing movement within Greek-speaking Diaspora Judaism."

Robinson's work was seminal for much work that followed in the twentieth century and beyond. With the impact of Qumran studies the Jewishness of the Johannine writings became the focus of more studies. J. L. Martyn interpreted the gospel as a document reflecting Jewish history at two levels. The evangelist was a Jew of the Diaspora who retold the story of Jesus in a way that reinterpreted the history of his own community in its struggle with the local synagogue. Raymond Brown's commentary (1966) also adopted this view. His theory of compositional stages of the gospel allowed for a phase beyond an intra-Jewish struggle and overlapped with the writing of the Johannine epistles. The epistles reveal an intra-Christian struggle involving a serious Christological conflict with ethical consequences. From the mid-1960s to the end of the twentieth century the paradigm, most widely represented by the work of Martyn and Brown, dominated the interpretation of the gospel and epistles of John. Towards the end of the twentieth century there were signs of serious dissent from this approach.

Quite early there were critiques of Martyn's use of the *birkat ha-minim* (blessing against the heretics) to explain the references to casting people out of the synagogue in John 9:22, 34, 12:42, and 16:2. It may well be that the eighteenth benediction cannot be dated or identified with a decision to remove from the synagogues Jews who believed in Jesus. All John presupposes is such a decision in the relevant region. Thus the debate over *birkat ha-minim* is a bit of a red herring. More serious in some ways is the critique of this position emerging from the United Kingdom from such scholars as Judith Lieu and Richard Bauckham, and from further afield by Terese Okure and Martin Hengel.

Since the publication of *The Second and Third Epistles of John* (1986), Judith Lieu has set out to overturn the common paradigm for the interpretation of the gospel and epistles of John. Intentionally this change was grounded in viewing the Johannine writings from the standpoint of 2 and 3 John. Lieu concludes that the gospel and epistles were written at the same time and in the same context to deal with the same issues. The context is Jewish and the issues focus on the confession of Jesus as the messiah. In both gospel and epistles, a schism lies in the past. What distinguishes the writings is not time, place, and issues but different authors. The gospel is a unity in spite of reflecting multiple hands in composition. Its complex dialectical theology is held together by its Christological focus in a way that distinguishes it from the epistles where the focus is centered on the community. The epistles draw on Johannine tradition and reflect a less able author or authors than the gospel though they draw on a common Johannine tradition. 2 and 3 John probably have a common author and follow in the same community-centered track as 1 John, which may have an independent author. Lieu's position on 1 John has been developed further in the work of one of her students. In *Keep Yourselves from Idols* (2002) Terry Griffith has argued that 1 John is to be interpreted in a Jewish context and is the product of a continuing debate between Jews and Jewish Christians over whether Jesus was the messiah, at a time when some Johannine Jewish Christians had reverted to Judaism.

A not dissimilar position was developed by Teresa Okure in her *The Johannine Approach to Mission* (1988). She too argues that the gospel is to be understood as a unity and that gospel and epistles were written about the same time to deal with the same crisis. But her work was dependent on the chronology of J. A. T. Robinson. Thus she argues that gospel and epistles were written by the same author, an eyewitness (the Beloved Disciple), before the destruction of Jerusalem, to a community of predominantly Jewish Christians in Palestine (Okure 1988: 235–81, especially 262, 268, 273–81). Yet she allows for a second edition of the gospel in Ephesus some thirty years later (Okure 1988: 279–81). A crisis arose because some within the community were not persuaded that the claims of Jesus' messiahship satisfied the criteria of the Jewish scriptures and traditions and were even more troubled by the Johannine claims concerning Jesus' ontological divine sonship (Okure 1988: 260, and see 247, 257–9). In this way she identifies conflicts within the gospel with the schism and controversy of 1 and 2 John (cf. John 6:41–2; 5:18; 8:56–9; 10:33–9; 1 John 4:2, 15; 5:1, 5; 2 John 7).

Martin Hengel's position has much in common with both Lieu and Okure. He sees gospel and epistles in a common Hellenistic Jewish Diaspora setting that was both Jewish and dualistic (1989: 44–5). He argues that Cerinthus was a Judeo-Christian dualist in such a synagogue setting and his teaching illuminates the Christological controversy of the Johannine epistles. He agrees with Okure against Lieu concerning the common authorship of the gospel and epistles. The evangelist (the Elder) was a Judean Jew who migrated to Ephesus before the Jewish War. There, at the end of the first century, the epistles were written. The gospel had long been in the process of composition. It was published soon after the death of the Elder, suitably edited by his pupils. When it was published the epistles were circulated with it (Hengel 1989: 59–63, 73, 105–6, 176–7 n.7). Given the view of common authorship, this presupposes that the epistles were written with full knowledge of the development of the gospel to that stage.

In this case, the priority of the epistles in publication does not rule out the influence of the tradition yet to be published in the gospel. Hengel's criticism of Brown is misleading because Brown argues that the author of 1 John and his opponents were aware of the Johannine tradition at some stage of its development, whether or not the gospel was yet complete or published. At the same time, Hengel also recognizes later strata of the gospel (including the Prologue, the prayer of consecration of John 17, and chapters 6 and 10) were added after the acute crisis that led to the writing of the letters (Hengel 1989: 61, and see also 95, 105).

According to Hengel, the breach with the synagogue was long past before that crisis. The crisis that provoked the writing of the epistles and the publication of the gospel was precipitated by the entry into the community of Cerinthus, whom Hengel thinks was a Hellenized Judeo-Christian, with a docetic Christology (Hengel 1989: 60–3). The gospel and epistles were addressed to the predominantly Gentile Johannine community where the false teaching had produced a crisis. "Now all this means that the gospel and letters, which primarily address the school, are not predominantly aimed at Jewish Christians but at Gentile Christians. The immediate controversy with the Jews has long ceased to be the main theme of the school" (Hengel 1989: 121). Although the schism was precipitated by a Jewish Christian (Cerinthus), the community itself is now dominantly Gentile. Here Hengel departs from his general agreement with Lieu and Okure. Much more than either of them he is willing to allow for the growth of the gospel and is prepared to delineate layers, even before the final redaction by the pupils of the Elder after his death. He notes, in agreement with Okure, that the gospel tradition was shaped in the teaching of the Elder (for Okure, the Beloved Disciple) which began in Judea before the Jewish War of 66–74 CE. The breach with the synagogue, also acknowledged by Lieu, long past by the time the gospel was written, nevertheless left its mark on the gospel. Against Okure and Lieu, Hengel argues that the crisis that called forth the gospel and epistles was the docetic teaching of Cerinthus (Hengel 1989: 59–63). Though Cerinthus is said to be a Judeo-Christian, his position is some distance from the Ebionite troublemakers proposed by Okure (1988: 260). Indeed, Hengel goes on to describe the problem in terms of

> a group of its members who, influenced by the view taken for granted among educated Greeks that a god was incapable of suffering, separated the man Jesus from the divine Logos, Son of God and Christ and radically devalued his significance for salvation. The three letters of John are fruits of the way in which the old school-head combated the threat. They, together with the gospel, were probably edited soon after his death by his pupils (or one of them) not long after 100 CE, and this editing appears to be the last visible action of the "school." (Hengel 1989: 81)

Hengel's attempt to harmonize two views is found in the suggestion that "Cerinthus was a Judeo-Christian teacher coming from outside with some popular philosophical learning of the kind widespread in the Greek-speaking synagogue" (Hengel 1989: 60). But the success of the intruder (Cerinthus) appears to be dependent on the predominantly Gentile Christian character of the Johannine school (Hengel 1989: 119–24).

Hengel's reconstruction recognizes the evangelist as a Judean Jewish Christian who came to Ephesus in the 60s. The gospel was shaped over a long period of time. The epistles were written in a predominantly Gentile Christian context and soon after the evangelist's death the gospel was edited and published with the epistles. There is here the potential to trace development from Jewish to predominantly Gentile contexts. In spite of this and a good deal more hypothetical reconstruction (Hengel 1989: 94–135 and notes), Hengel concludes (1989: 205 n.85):

> Nowadays we already have too many attempts to reconstruct a "history of the Johannine community". They are all doomed to failure, because we know nothing of a real history which even goes back to Palestine, and conjectures about it are idle.

Indeed, what is necessary is for Hengel to take seriously his own analysis of the Judean origin of the Elder, the breach from the synagogue, and the later layers of the gospel. Already in these observations there is room to say a good deal about the history of the Elder and those associated with him. For example, if the Prologue and John 17 were added to cope with the crises caused by the entry of Cerinthus into the community that suggests that the bulk of the gospel had already been shaped in response to other issues. Even if the breach from the synagogue lay in the distant past, the gospel suggests that the issue had been sufficiently traumatic to leave permanent marks on the gospel. Thus, although Hengel appears to postulate a common context for gospel and epistles his view of the long period of composition for the gospel makes allowance for the influence of other contexts in its shaping. Whereas Lieu saw different theologies in the gospel and epistles, Hengel hears in all the voice of one towering theologian, the Elder (1989: ix, 108, and see 96, 99, 104). Certainly I agree that the Prologue and John 17 represent late strata of the gospel, but I doubt that John 6 as a whole is late.

## Johannine Literature and History

### The literary objection to historical reconstruction

In the 1980s New Testament studies experienced a resurgence of literary interest producing what can be called the new literary criticism of the New Testament (see Chapter 8, "Literary Criticism," in this volume). At one level it was precipitated by the failure of historical-critical studies to produce secure and lasting conclusions. This situation led some scholars to reject historical-critical studies as obsolete. Some scholars embraced the new literary approaches without abandoning historical methods. Alan R. Culpepper (*Anatomy of the Fourth Gospel*, 1983) is a good example of a more inclusive approach. More recently, Francis J. Moloney's three-volume narrative *Commentary on John* (1993, 1996, 1998) explicitly sets out to combine historical methods with a literary narrative reading of the gospel. He features the role of the implied reader to track the process of the growth in understanding as a first reader of the gospel. The role of the implied reader provides some control over arbitrary readings. At the same time, recognition of textual complexity demands the use of a variety of different methods and approaches.

## Social and anthropological readings

The distinctive language of the Johannine gospel and epistles has long been recognized as an expression of a distinctive social reality. In 1968 Herbert Leroy published his *Rätsel und Misverständnis: Ein Beitrag zur Formgeschichte des Johannesevangeliums* ("Riddle and Misunderstanding: A Contribution to the Form Criticism of the Gospel of John") in which he analyzed pericopes in which an enigmatic saying of Jesus was misunderstood. Recognition of this led him to investigate the *Sitz im Leben* ("life situation") of the social group in which the form originated. He laid the foundation for recognizing the language of John as the language of a minority group, distinct from the larger society. In this way, the language of John came to be identified with what came to be described as a sect. Only insiders, members of the subgroup, would understand this language.

Wayne Meeks published an essay entitled "The Man from Heaven in Johannine Sectarianism" in 1972. In this groundbreaking essay he marshaled the evidence of the way Johannine language and imagery are used to construct a sectarian worldview. Bruce Malina, "The Gospel of John in Sociolinguistic Perspective" (1985), using linguistics and anthropology, came to similar conclusions. His work on John was taken further in collaboration with Richard L. Rohrbaugh, in their *Social Science Commentary on the Gospel of John* (1998). Like Leroy they focused on the language of the gospel. They drew attention to two features of that language: re-lexicalization and over-lexicalization. The former draws attention to the substitution of characteristically Johannine words for conventional terms while the latter notes that John uses multiple words of the same subject. These words may be identical in meaning or have overlapping meanings. Over-lexicalization is compatible with John's use of very limited vocabulary. Even with limited vocabulary he manages this overlapping use of words. Malina also draws on the evidence of modern subgroups that constitute a reaction to the dominant culture. These develop their characteristic language use, intelligible only to the subgroup. Malina names this "anti-language" because it is defined over against the language of the dominant culture. It is characterized by the same kind of re-lexicalization and over-lexicalization he identifies in John.

The social-science perspective is continued in the work of Jerome H. Neyrey, *An Ideology of Revolt* (1988). Neyrey's work begins with Meeks and his essay on Johannine sectarianism. But, as a member of the "Context Group" inspired by Bruce Malina, his work moved increasingly into the area of Mediterranean anthropology. Malina's application and exposition of this approach has become fruitful across the broad area of the New Testament, including the gospel and epistles of John.

David Rensberger has further illuminated Johannine sectarianism in his studies of the gospel (1988, 1998, 2002) and epistles (1997). Rensberger has drawn attention to the importance of dualism in the sectarian understanding. A dualistic perspective enabled the community to maintain its distinctive values in a mission to an inhospitable world. Rensberger identifies inherent dangers for a group that identifies itself with goodness and stigmatizes the world as the area of darkness, sin, and death.

*Jesus and the Jewish authorities*

John stands apart from the other gospels in the way the conflict between Jesus and the Jewish authorities is described during the ministry of Jesus. Each of the gospels portrays Jesus in conflict with the Jewish authorities. In the synoptic gospels two issues provoke reaction to Jesus, his failure to observe purity and Sabbath law. On the latter Jesus justifies his freedom to act by asserting, "The Sabbath was made for man not man for the Sabbath, therefore the Son of Man is Lord of the Sabbath" (Mark 2:27). In John purity is not an issue. In this gospel neither Jesus nor his disciples is charged with mixing with unclean people, or handling unclean objects, or eating with unwashed hands. The Sabbath certainly is the ground for objection and bitter controversy. The bitterness of the controversy arises from Johannine perspectives in the narrative. On the one hand the Jewish authorities make Sabbath observance the touchstone for the observance of the Mosaic law. Because of this the Jewish authorities set Jesus over against Moses. On the other hand, Jesus does not deny his failure to keep the Sabbath or justify his actions in acceptable terms. Instead he puts himself outside the boundaries where the law applies and identifies himself with God. "My Father is working until now and I am working" (John 5:17). The "now" in question here is the Sabbath on which the commandment forbids all manner of "work." The commandment applies to creatures, including humans. The Jewish authorities correctly understand Jesus' reference to "my Father" as a reference to God. The claim that God works on the Sabbath was neither novel nor controversial. That Jesus called God "my Father" in this context is both novel and controversial because Jesus uses the fact that God works on the Sabbath to justify his own work. The assertion puts Jesus on the side of God over against humanity. Technically the saying does not justify human contravention of Sabbath law. But John obviously assumes that Jesus had authority to relax Sabbath law because he instructed the man to pick up his bed and carry it off on the Sabbath (John 5:8–11). In this instance the interpretation of this action as a contravention of Sabbath law was not a tradition of the Elders, but a specific biblical application of the law (Jer. 17:21–2).

It is notable that, in John, the Sabbath issue is linked to the charge that Jesus made himself equal to God (John 5:18). Clearly, if equality is the right term to be used, the Jesus of John and the Jewish authorities understood equality in quite different ways (John 10:25, 29–31, 32–9). While they understood equality in terms of independence of God, Jesus understood equality as an expression of his dependence on the Father. This is reinforced by Jesus' formulaic references to God as "the Father who sent me" and his stress on *doing the will* of "him who sent me" (John 4:34).

## The Gospel of John and the Historical Jesus

The differences between John and the synoptics have led scholars to question the usefulness of John as a source for evidence of the historical Jesus. The most widely recognized criterion for recognizing historical tradition in John is the overlap with the synoptic tradition. The overlap suggests that John adds nothing to what we learn of Jesus from the synoptics. At the same time, even where John has tradition in common with the synoptics, there are differences in detail and in the placing of the tradition within the context of the ministry of Jesus. The placing of the temple incident is a case in point. John places the incident at the beginning of the ministry of Jesus (2:13–22) while Mark (followed by Matthew and Luke) places it at the end (Mark 11:15–19). Scholars generally attribute the Johannine placing to the evangelist's theological tendencies. But the synoptics must place the incident late because, according to their schema, Jesus visits Jerusalem only once, at the end of his ministry. Nevertheless, many scholars accept something like the Johannine chronology of Jesus' ministry, lasting something like three years and involving multiple visits to Jerusalem, rather than Mark's single-line plot leading from Galilee to Jerusalem in a space that could be measured by weeks rather than years. Consequently a case can be made for the recognition of useful historical tradition in John. The problem is to identify it and to establish its probable historical reliability.

## History and Theology in John

Recognition of historical tradition in John is placed alongside the recognition that John is written using a distinctive vocabulary and literary style. This distinctiveness overlaps the language of Jesus in his discourses and the language of the narrator, who not only narrates the story but also provides explanatory commentary on it to ensure that the reader does not miss the point. We may ask, "Does the Jesus of John speak with the voice of the evangelist?" Or, "Does the narrator speak in the idiom of Jesus?" Adding to this complexity, in his witness John (the Baptist) also speaks with the same voice (John 3:31–6).

It could be argued that both John (the Baptist) and the evangelist have been so influenced by Jesus that they each speak with his voice. But the absence of this voice from the synoptic tradition (Matt. 11:25–30, the so-called Johannine thunderbolt, will not bear the weight of this proposition) seriously undermines that hypothesis. Much more likely is the view that the Jesus of John speaks with the voice of the evangelist. While some of the idioms of the Jesus of the synoptics make rare appearances, like the references to the kingdom of God in John 3:3 and 5, the absence of such central vocabulary, and the synoptic parables, from John confirms that the voice of the evangelist dominates this gospel.

The dominant voice of the evangelist reminds us that there is no historical narrative that is not, at the same time, interpretation. But there are degrees of interpretation in balance with the events that are interpreted. John represents a higher level of interpretation than the synoptics. That need not mean that John is any more or less valid an interpretation of Jesus than the synoptics. But it seems likely that the synoptics retain something more like Greek versions of the words of Jesus than John does.

Two quite different approaches have attempted to deal with the distinctive character of John. Bultmann attributes the distinctive character of John to the influence of distinctive sources. Robert Fortna (1970) has picked up one aspect of Bultmann's hypothesis. His work seeks to establish the evangelist's use of a signs gospel. Fortna makes no attempt to account for the discourse material but argues that the narrative material is primary. Bultmann went further in arguing that John also made use of a distinctive discourse source.

An alternative to this view, adopted by C. K. Barrett, Michael Goulder, F. Neirynck, and the Leuven school, argues that John used one or more of the synoptics in writing his gospel. This is a return to the position prior to P. Gardner-Smith, whose work awakened C. H. Dodd to the task of demonstrating that John was dependent on synoptic-like tradition but not any of the synoptic gospels. That the tradition underlying John was synoptic-like was also the view of Barnabas Lindars. Whether John used the synoptics, or synoptic-like tradition, the transformation of this tradition in the gospel was the work of the evangelist. Johannine interpretation is reflected in the choice, arrangement, and new linguistic framework in which the Jesus tradition is expressed.

John's thoroughgoing interpretation of the tradition has a strong theological drive. One ground for this is the evangelist's theology of the incarnation. Because the divine Logos, through whom all creation has its being, became flesh and is known in Jesus of Nazareth, his life is a revelation of the Father. Consequently, his loving self-giving reveals the self-giving love of the Father, of God. Jesus' love for his own and for the world is emphasized in the farewell discourses (13:1–17, 34–5; 17:20–6). In John 3:16 the loving mission of Jesus is said to reveal God's love for the world. This argument is given fuller treatment in 1 John 4:7–21.

Second, there is a drive to continuing reinterpretation through the presence and activity of the Spirit of Truth in the life of the believing community (John 14:15–18, 26; 15: 26–7; 16:7–11 and especially 12–15). The belief that the risen Jesus continues to renew his teaching within the believing community through the inspiring presence of the Spirit of Truth is a distinctive and developed teaching of the Jesus of John. What made this drive so potent was the lengthy period over which the Johannine tradition developed before the finished gospel reached definitive form through publication. In this process, the memory of Jesus' life and death was transformed by the experience of the Spirit and the new perspective brought by Jesus' resurrection and glorification, all now understood in the light of scripture (2:22; 12:16; 14:26).

The last serious addition to the text of John (7:53–8:11) is first attested in manuscripts from the fifth century, though the addition could be earlier. It cannot have been part of the gospel as originally published. It interrupts the narrative of John 7 and 8 and is not found in the early manuscript tradition.

An earlier addition, attested uniformly by our manuscript tradition, is John 21. It is identified as an addition by a critical examination of the text: (1) John 20:30–1 reads like the original conclusion to the gospel. (2) Chapter 21 is distinguishable from John 1–20 on grounds of style, vocabulary, and content. (3) The "we" of John 21:24 implies that chapter 21 was added by hands other than that of the disciple who bore witness in John 1–20. (4) The evidence suggests that the perspective of John 21 is an extension of the Johannine tradition, but in a way unprepared for by John 1–20. There Peter and the Beloved Disciple were paired in several scenes, always to the advantage of the latter. In John 21 the presence of the Beloved Disciple is noted, but Peter plays the leading role, and the final scene portrays Peter with Jesus in a way that restores Peter after his threefold denial of Jesus. Jesus three times asks Peter if he loves him and Peter three times affirms his love. Three times, with varying words, Jesus charges Peter to exercise his charge in caring for Jesus' sheep. The sheep belong to Jesus, the true shepherd of the sheep, but Peter is charged with the responsibility of care for them. The perspective of John 21 presupposes the absence of Jesus so that Peter cares for his flock in his place. (5) The conclusion of John 21 also assumes the absence of the Beloved Disciple because, although the gospel is attributed to him, this conclusion is given in the voices of those who attest the veracity of what he wrote. What makes this necessary is the absence of the Beloved Disciple. The terms in which Peter discusses his fate with Jesus (John 21:20–3) suggest that the Beloved Disciple had died before the gospel was published with John 21.

John 21:20–4 suggests the evangelist lived until old age. Throughout his long life he reflected on the gospel tradition and developed his teaching. This process began in Judea but continued, after the Jewish War, somewhere in the Diaspora, perhaps in the vicinity of Ephesus. The tradition, even in the developed form we find in the gospel, manifests its Judean origin. But the Greek of the gospel is a consequence of its Diaspora context. The evangelist reflected on the gospel tradition and interpreted it to speak to the various changing situations until his death. The gospel makes the claim that the risen Jesus continues to speak through the inspired witness of those who knew him and whom the Spirit of Truth led into all truth. Even when the Beloved Disciple died, those who had been taught by him continued his work, as John 21 confirms. We may only guess what additions were made to John 1–20. It may be that they added the references to their teacher as the Beloved Disciple and the explanations of Jewish festivals and terms.

The gospel provides its own rationale for the reinterpretation and development of the Jesus tradition. The theological necessity came from the evangelist's understanding of the incarnation. Changing social situations created both the need and the opportunity for reinterpretation. The gospel teaches that the presence and activity of the Spirit Paraclete renewed the teaching of Jesus in these changing life situations.

## An Outline of the Gospel of John: Form and Content

In John form and content are intricately interwoven. The poetic character of the Prologue (1:1–18) is matched by the speech of Jesus in the long discourses (especially in chapters 14–17), reminding the reader that Jesus and the narrator (evangelist) speak in the same language and express the same point of view. The Prologue provides a powerful and dramatic opening to the gospel. It begins with words that unmistakably summon the reader to reflect on the opening of Genesis. Though drawing on Genesis John pushes back behind the act of creation to the being of the divine Logos with God in the beginning. John uses an interpretive tradition whereby God's act of speaking (Genesis 1) becomes the Word of God, understood as the Wisdom of God, the Torah (see Ps. 33:6; Prov. 1:29; 3:18, 19; 6:23; 8:22–3, 30, 31, 35; Wisd. 6:22; 7:14, 21–7, 29–30; 8:1; 9:1–2, 4, 9, 10; Ecclus. 24:8–12, 23; 1 Enoch 42:1–2). In this tradition both Wisdom and Torah are hypostasized or personified. John affirms the incarnation of the Logos in Jesus of Nazareth as the one who reveals the mind and heart of God. Expressed in this way John makes clear the loving purpose of God.

The Prologue also sets up the paradox of the world, created by God, in conflict with God who seeks to save the world. The dilemma is expressed in terms of the dominant symbolic structure of the gospel, the darkness of the world in conflict with the light of the divine Logos. The ethical self-revealing character of the light is implicit in the Prologue and explicit in the narrative exposition in the body of the gospel. The Prologue provides the reader with deep and incisive insights into the meaning of the story narrated by the gospel, privileging the reader in comparison to characters in the story.

## 1   The Prologue (1:1–18)

1:1–2: The divine Logos in relation to God.

1:3: Creation of all things by the divine Logos.

1:4–5: The life-giving light of the divine Logos shines in the darkness.

1:6–8: The foundational witness of John (the Baptist) to the true light *that all may believe through him*.

1:9–13: The historic coming of the true light of the Logos into the world, the rejection of it by the world, even his own people, but reception by the few who were given authority to become children of God.

1:14: Recapitulation of the incarnation of the Logos by those who received him. "We beheld his glory."

1:15–18: Recapitulation of the witness of John (1:15) merged with the witness of those who received the incarnate Logos (1:16–18).

## 2   The body of the gospel (1:19–20:31)

### I.   The quest for the messiah (1:19–51 and 2:1–11)

1:19–51: The quest for the messiah, the foundational witness, and the gathering of the disciples.

2:1–11: Bridge passage: the first sign and the belief of the disciples.

### II.   From Cana to Cana: signs of life and the response of belief (2:1–4:54)

2:1–11: The first (foundational) Cana sign and the belief of the disciples. The sign is a response to a re*quest* by the mother of Jesus and leads to the belief of the disciples. This bridge passage forms the climax of the gathering of the disciples (1:19–51) and opening the public ministry of Jesus. Jesus does not act without his disciples. The first Cana sign forms a signaled inclusio (see 2:1, 11 and 4:46, 54) with the second Cana sign of 4:46–54.

2:12: Jesus, his mother, brothers, and disciples in Capernaum. The surprise first mention of Jesus' brothers in a positive context with Jesus, his mother, and the disciples.

2:13–25: First Passover in Jerusalem.

2:13–22: The temple act and the disciples' understanding of the risen Jesus as the new temple. Belief based on the act of Jesus, scripture, and the resurrection of Jesus (2:22 and compare 12:16).

2:23–5: In Jerusalem many believe on the basis of the signs Jesus performed during Passover, but their belief is unreliable.

3:1–21: Nicodemus, an example of belief based on signs.

3:13–21: Jesus to Nicodemus or narrator to reader(s)?

3:22–36: Jesus and John (the Baptist).

3:22–6: The dispute caused by Jesus' return to Ainon where John is baptizing.

3:27–30: John's witness in response.

3:31–6: John to his disciples or narrator to reader(s)?

4:1–42: Jesus, the disciples, the Samaritan woman, and the Samaritans who believe through her witness.

4:43–5: The return to Galilee to a believing reception. Implied less than favorable reception in Jerusalem, Jesus' hometown!

4:46–54: The second Cana sign, again in response to a request (by the nobleman). The healing, at a distance, of the nobleman's son by Jesus' life-giving word, "Your son lives," the nobleman's belief in Jesus' word and subsequent belief in Jesus by the nobleman's entire household on the basis of the actual healing.

*III.   Signs of conflict (5:1–12:50)*   Jesus initiates two of the signs in this section (5:1–9a and 9:1–12) without any request for healing. Each of these leads into a controversy dialogue concluding with the rejection of Jesus by the Jewish authorities. These dialogues are developed on the basis of what looks like an afterthought indication that each of these signs was performed on the Sabbath (5:9b and 9:14). Thus the Jewish authorities assert that Jesus is a lawbreaker, opposed to Moses (5:9b–47 and 9:13–41). The charge against Jesus in 5:17, and the basis for it, are taken up again in John 10, in the dialogue that follows John 9 (see 10:30–9).

Second Passover in Galilee (6:4): Between John 5 and 9 Jesus performs a feeding sign (6:1–15). The sign is a response to the great crowd that has followed him, having seen the healing signs he has performed (6:2). The feeding sign stands apart from chapters 5 and 9 in that the crowd responds positively, if misguidedly to the feeding. But Jesus eludes their attempt to take him forcibly (*harpazein*) and make him king (see 6:15). The following scenes portray the crowd following Jesus across the sea to Capernaum. The subsequent dialogues suggest that the crowd is progressing to belief in Jesus. But Jesus presupposes their failure to believe in him (6:36–40) in response to his invitation (6:35). This is confirmed by the murmuring of the Jews – previously described as the crowd? – (6:41–59). Retrospectively this scene is set in the synagogue in Capernaum (6:59; compare the retrospective indication of Sabbath setting in 5:9 and 9:14). This is not a positive context in John. Worse is to come. Many of Jesus' disciples also turn away from him (6:60–71).

The feast of Tabernacles in Jerusalem (7:2): chapters 7–8 reintroduce the brothers of Jesus, this time less positively than in 2:12. They are, nonetheless, in the company of Jesus and his disciples. The situation (7:1) is a return to the hostility of 5:16–18.

Jesus returns to Jerusalem at the feast of Tabernacles and a game of hide and seek follows in which the Jewish authorities seek to arrest (kill, stone) Jesus (7:11, 25, 30, 44; 8:59), but he evades them and they fail to lay a hand on him.

The Sabbath-breaking sign of John 5 led to the healed man becoming an informer so that the Jews persecuted and sought to kill Jesus. The Sabbath-breaking sign of John 9 led to the blind man becoming a believer so that he was cast out of the synagogue and became a follower of Jesus. At the end of the chapter, Jesus has the better of a controversy with the Pharisees, and pronounces judgment on them: "Now because you say 'We see,' your sin remains" (9:39–41).

John 10 presupposes the continuation of the controversy from John 9 but the intensity of the conflict between Jesus and the Jews increases. With the assertion "I and the Father are one" Jesus provokes the charge of blasphemy and the consequent attempt by the Jews to stone him (10:30–3, 39). They accuse him, "you being a man make yourself God." This is a return to the situation of 5:16–18 where Jesus responded to the charge of Sabbath-breaking by claiming, "My Father is working until now and I am working." His words provoked the Jews to attempt to kill him, understanding that he was "making himself equal with God."

John 10:40 marks a return from Jerusalem to the place, on the other side of the Jordan, where John was baptizing, where he bore witness to Jesus. Thus 10:40–2 forms an inclusio with the opening narrative of the gospel in 1:19–34. The concluding summary notes that many were attracted to Jesus because they judged that John (the Baptist's) witness to Jesus was correct (10:40–2). John did no sign but his witness to the sign-performing Jesus was true. This provides a double basis for the concluding words, "many believed on him [Jesus] there" (10:42).

John 11–12 also combines the rejection of Jesus with popular belief in him, but John 12 concludes on a more negative note than 10:42. John 11 begins with the implied request from Mary and Martha to Jesus, asking him to come and heal their brother Lazarus. This, like the implied request of 2:3, and the explicit request of 4:47, 49, does not produce an immediate agreement by Jesus. Rather the plaintiffs must persist with their requests in the face of Jesus' apparent refusal to act. By the time Jesus goes to Bethany Lazarus has already been dead four days (11:39). The words of Martha to Jesus are filled with pathos. For the reader, who knows of Jesus' planned delay, the words may carry a strong sense of reproach. "Lord, if you had been here, my brother would not have died" (11:21). At a more straightforward level there is recognition that healing the sick person is one thing; to raise a dead person after four days is another, quite different from the common Jewish belief that the dead would be raised on the last day (11:24).

The words and situation are also suggestive of the time between the resurrection and Parousia of Jesus. The publication of John had to take account of the death of believers before the return of Jesus, including the death of the Beloved Disciple, 21:20–3. Had Jesus returned, these believers need not have died! Why was Jesus' return subject to such a delay? Aspects of this question are clearly in view in 21:20–3. Are they also reflected in the telling of the Lazarus story? The narrative of John 11 is powerful when read in this context (the death and burial of a believer, especially one in the prime of life).

As in each of the stories where Jesus' help is requested (2:1–11; 4:46–54), eventually Jesus complies with the request to act. The response to Jesus' act is belief: the belief of the disciples (2:11), of the nobleman and his household (4:50, 53), of Martha (11:27), and of many of the Jews (11:45). But there is also a sinister plot to kill Jesus in response to the popular belief in him and even a plot to kill Lazarus as well (11:46–53, and see also 12:9–11). As a consequence, Jesus can no longer move openly in Judea (11:54; compare 7:1; 8:59; 10:31, 39).

The third Passover approaches (12:1): John 12 begins with the anointing of Jesus followed by Jesus' entry into Jerusalem to popular acclaim but with Jesus providing premonitions of his death and its hidden meaning. The coming of Greeks requesting to see Jesus signals the coming of the hour for the plot of the Jewish authorities to arrest Jesus to succeed, but in a way quite different from what they suppose. It is the time for the exaltation of the Son of Man and the judgment of the world. That event is at once a manifestation of the power of darkness and the fulfillment of the purposes of God (12:27–36a). God is able to, and does, bring good out of evil. John 12 concludes with Jesus' withdrawal because, in spite of the many signs he had performed, they do not believe in him. Nevertheless the narrator tells the reader, even many of the rulers believe in him, but they fear the Pharisees and the threat of exclusion from the synagogue, so they do not confess their belief (12:36b–43).

Jesus' words then sum up this situation at the conclusion of his public ministry (12:44–50). He has come as the emissary of the Father, speaking only the words spoken to him by the Father. He came to save the world and those who believe in him are delivered from the power of darkness but those who do not believe will be judged on the last day by the word he has spoken to them (12:44–50). The narrative of John 12 ends on a more negative note (12:36b–43) than what was probably the earlier conclusion to this section (John 10:42). Nevertheless, the summary words of Jesus provide a more balanced conclusion, reflecting the continuing struggle between the light and the darkness before the judgment on the last day.

*IV.  The farewell of the messiah (13–17)*    The third Passover in Jerusalem: John 13–17 is often called the "farewell discourses." The scene is set at supper in Jerusalem before the feast of Passover. There Jesus washes the feet of his disciples both as a symbolic act of cleansing and as an example to them of service concretely demonstrating how to fulfill the command to love one another (13:34–5). At the supper Jesus exposes Judas as the betrayer, allowing him a last chance. But Judas goes out into the darkness bent on the betrayal of Jesus (13:30).

The supper is the specific context for the discourses. A clear demarcation of the end of the first discourse is given in 14:31, with Jesus' words, "Arise, let us be going from here!" But only in 18:1 does the narrator note, "Having said these words Jesus went out with his disciples ... ," presupposing that 18:1 once followed 14:31. This suggests that 13:31–14:31 is the original discourse and that 15:1–17:26 (later Johannine versions of the discourse) have been introduced subsequently without adjusting the relationship of 14:31 to 18:1. The Johannine editors (see 21:24) may have been anxious to preserve traditions from their revered teacher that had not already been incorporated in the gospel. On this assumption, the original discourse, dealing with the glorification of the Son of Man and his absence from his grieving disciples, is found in 13:31–14:31. The teaching about the coming of the Paraclete, Spirit of Truth is the response to the disciples' grief at the departure of Jesus (14:15–16, 26). The Paraclete, Spirit of Truth maintains the sense of Jesus' presence and renews his teaching. At least one other version of the discourse follows. A good case can be made for recognizing two plus the farewell prayer of John 17. The second version of the discourse is found in 15:1–16:4a. This version deals with the witness of the disciples before a hostile world, which is described in predominantly Jewish terms. How will the witness be continued in this hostile context? The presence of the Paraclete ensures an inspired witness to Jesus by those who were with him from the beginning. A third form of the discourse (in 16:4b–33) leaves behind any reference to the Jewish context. The world seems less threatening. Indeed. Jesus says, "I have conquered the world" and promises that the coming Paraclete will expose/reveal the sin of world, the righteousness of God, and the judgment of the world (16:7–11). Jesus promises that the Spirit of Truth will prepare believers for mission by leading them into all the truth found in the glorified Jesus (16:12–15).

John 17 is a prayer set just prior to the crisis of Jesus' arrest, trial, and execution. But it does not deal with this crisis in the life of Jesus as does Mark 14:32–42. The equivalent to Mark is John 12:27, but there Jesus quickly moves on to the prayer for glorification (12:28). John 17 commences with Jesus' prayer for glorification (17:1–5). The real substance of the prayer is focused on the disciples (17:6–26). The prayer, though addressed to the Father (17:1, 5, 11, 21 24, 25), is a model of teaching for the disciples in their mission to the world. In 17:6–26 Jesus' attention shifts from his own completed mission to his concern for the uncompleted mission of the disciples and those in the future who would believe through their witness. Jesus asks that they may be kept from the corrupting power of the world by the name and the word of God, which he has revealed and given to the disciples. There is no mention of the Spirit in this chapter. But the disciples are not kept from the world. They are kept in and for the world, kept in unity with the life-giving love of God.

*V. Passion and resurrection (18–20)*    John 18–19 narrate the betrayal and arrest of Jesus (18:1–11), Jesus before the high priest and the threefold denial of Peter (18:12–27), Jesus before Pilate (18:28–19:16a), the crucifixion and death of Jesus (19:16b–30), the piercing of Jesus' side, and the burial (19:31–42).

John 20 narrates the finding of the empty tomb by Mary Magdalene, her report to Simon Peter and the Beloved Disciple and their race to the tomb to view the evidence (20:1–10), the appearance of the risen Jesus to Mary Magdalene (20:11–18), the first appearance of Jesus to the disciples (apart from Thomas) to commission and empower them (20:19–23), the second appearance to the disciples (including Thomas) to provide evidence for those who doubt and to assert the blessedness of belief on the basis of believing testimony (20:24–9). The chapter concludes with what appears to be the statement of the purpose of the gospel (20:30–1). It asserts the plenitude of signs performed by Jesus. Those narrated in this book have been selected to lead readers to believe that Jesus is the Christ, the Son of God, and the purpose of this is that those who believe may have life, that is, eternal life (20:30–1).

## 3  Epilogue for publication (21)

After 20:30–1, John 21 looks like an epilogue, added to the gospel by members of the school at publication, some time after the death of the evangelist (21:20–4). Additions probably included references to the disciple Jesus loved, explanatory notes for non-Jewish readers, and additional material that the evangelist had gathered but had not included in the gospel. Chapter 21 tidies up unfinished issues raised by John 1–20. (1) It builds on the two earlier appearances of Jesus to the disciples in 20:19–23 and 24–9 and enumerates a third appearance to them in 21:14. (2) In so doing John reconciles the Jerusalem appearance tradition of John 20 with the implied Galilean tradition of Mark which finds full expression Matthew 28:16–20. (3) It also provides a context for the reinstatement of Peter after his disastrous threefold denial colorfully predicted and narrated in John 13:36–8; 18:15–18, 25–7. (4). The threefold questioning by Jesus and Peters threefold affirmation of love is followed by Jesus' threefold recommissioning of Peter to care for Jesus' sheep (20:15–19). (5) Even more pointed is Peter's questioning of Jesus about the role and fate of the Beloved Disciple. From chapter 13 until this point Peter has suffered by comparison with the Beloved Disciple. Now Peter, reinstated in his role of caring for Jesus' sheep, has his place alongside the Beloved Disciple. (6) The death of the Beloved Disciple is implied by the way his witness is attested, and by the way Jesus clarifies what he said about the Beloved Disciple. He did not say that the Beloved Disciple would not die (21:23). This, and the corporate testimony to the witness embodied in what the Beloved Disciple wrote, suggests that others published his work after his death.

## The Special Character of John

This gospel clearly stands out from the synoptics in a number of ways. The Prologue sets the beginning before creation with the divine Logos in the presence of God (the Father, 1:1, 18). Here already God and the Logos are implicitly understood as the Father and the Son so that, although the original reading of 1:18 probably refers to "the only begotten God who is in the bosom of the Father," the variants that read "only begotten Son" and "only begotten Son of God," are early and correct interpretations (see 3:16). The Prologue begins with the Logos in the presence of God (*pros ton theon*) and concludes with the only begotten God in the bosom of the Father. In between all things are created by the Logos, and the light of the Logos shines in the darkness of the world. The light of the Logos historically enters the world, is incarnate, and reveals God's glory, the glory of the only begotten from the Father, witnessed to by John (the Baptist), who bore testimony that all people may believe. The incarnate Logos is the revealer of the transcendent and invisible God. But the Prologue concludes with the affirmation that the Son has returned to the bosom of the Father. This rules out any paradoxical understanding that suggests that the Logos is at one and the same time in the bosom of the Father and present on earth. Rather, the Logos, who begins with God, proceeds in creation and incarnation before returning to the bosom of the Father (compare 17:5).

In the body of the gospel the incarnation of the Logos is spoken of in terms of the mission of the Son into the world, and God is spoken of as the Father who sent or gave the Son. Indeed, Jesus characteristically refers to God as "the Father who sent me" (4:34; 5:23, 24, 30, 37; 6:38, 39, 44; 7:16, (18), 28, 33; 8:16, 18, 26, 29; 9:4; 12:44, 45, 49; 13:20; 14:24, 26; 15:21; 16:5). The complexity of the Father–Son relationship is one of the keys to understanding John. The Father loves the Son and reveals everything to him (5:20) and gives all power to him (3:34–5). The Son loves the Father and does only what the Father wills (4:34; 10:17; 14:31; 15:9–10). For this reason, John understands the life and mission of Jesus as the revelation of the life and mission of God. In their obedience to the love command of Jesus (13:34–5) the disciples are to love one another and in so doing extend the mission of Jesus to the world (17:20–6).

The Prologue speaks of a man called John (the Baptist) as the foundational witness to the Logos made flesh, through whom all people come to believe (1:6–8, 15 and see 3:22–30; 5:33; 10:40–2). The narrative begins in 1:19 with the witness of John to the Jews and continues with his witness to two of his disciples (1:35). Through his witness these two become followers of Jesus and themselves become witnesses so that two other disciples are gathered. John is the foundational witness through whom all come to believe. John has a prominent role amongst the witnesses to Jesus. It is a feature of this gospel that, although God (the Father) initiated Jesus' mission, during his ministry Jesus often responds to the initiative of others. In Mark Jesus calls his disciples to follow him (1:16–20; 2:13–17). In John the disciples take the initiative which they maintain in bringing of others to Jesus (1:35–42). There is an emphasis on human initiative in the quest for life and the finding of it in Jesus the messiah.

John's understanding of Jesus the messiah develops from tradition much like what is found in the synoptics but develops the mission of Jesus in a distinctive presentation of the Father–Son relationship. Jesus also speaks of the work of the messiah in terms of the role of the Son of Man. His statements about the Son of Man find a parallel in "I" sayings in which Jesus speaks of his glorification and exaltation. References to his glorification and exaltation bring out the Johannine interpretation of the crucifixion by means of which the prince of this world is judged and cast out, and the revelation of God is made effective. Thus the ministry of Jesus is set in the context of the conflict between the light and the darkness. Jesus, as the light of the world, overcomes the darkness, enabling those who were imprisoned in the darkness to go free to walk in the life-giving light. The Jesus of John uses both light and bread as symbols of his life-giving work. Because the life of the Logos is the light (1:4), Jesus speak of himself as both the bread of life (6:35) and the light of the world (8:12; 9:5, the light of life).

In the sayings about the bread of life and the light of the world Jesus gives symbolic expression to his life-giving work in "I am" sayings (6:35; 8:12). There are other "I am" sayings. Jesus is "the door" to life (10:9), "the way" to the Father (14:6), "the good shepherd" who gives his life for the sheep (10:11), "the vine" that enlivens the branches (15:1), "the truth and the life" (14:6). All of these images express the way eternal life is found in Jesus the messiah.

The focus of this gospel is on eternal life, a theme that replaces the central motif of the kingdom of God in Mark. The characteristic parables of Jesus are also missing from John, though John 10:6 refers to 10:1–5 as "this *paroimian*," which we might translate as "this parable." But John does not use *parabole*, which is commonly found in the synoptics. On the analogy to John 10:1–5, we might say that John 15 is the explanation of the implied parable of the vine. In John 10, the parable is given in 10:1–5, the parable is identified in 10:6, and a twofold explanation is given in 10:7–18. Compare the parable of the soils (Mark 4:3–9) and the explanation (4:13–20). The theme of the Johannine parables is life.

In John 20:31 the evangelist expresses the purpose of the gospel. The purpose is that the reader may receive eternal life by coming to believe that Jesus is the messiah (see 1:41). John interprets messiahship in terms of the Father–Son relationship portrayed in the gospel. The life he brings has its source in God's love. That life is expressed in the love of Jesus for his disciples and in their love for one another. But the gospel makes clear that this is not a closed circuit of life. God's life, which has the character of self-giving love, has as its goal the inclusion of the world.

John 20:30–1 refers to the narrative selection of Jesus' *signs* recorded in this book. The selection expresses the purpose of the gospel to provide a narrative of life-giving signs to evoke belief in Jesus the messiah. Of the gospels, only John refers to certain of Jesus' works as signs. All of these signs are what we call miracles. The narrator characteristically describes them as "signs." Jesus uses the term only in 6:26 where he says that the crowd did not seek him because it saw signs. But his preferred reference to his activity is in terms of his "works." One reason is that this word enables him to identify his works with the Sabbath work of the Father (5:17).

Although the world is the creation of the Logos, it is the scene in which the struggle between the light and the darkness takes place. Jesus' signs of life are decisive windows into an understanding of the purpose of God in creation and redemption. They provide a basis for belief in Jesus as the one who reveals God's life-giving purpose for his creation. The signs enable the believer to experience eternal life in the midst of the darkness, to know the life-giving love of God in a world where hatred and death seem to reign.

The seven signs of Jesus (narrated in John 1–20) include three nature "miracles": the turning of water into wine, the multiplication of loaves and fishes, the stilling of a storm; three healing "miracles": the nobleman's son, a lame man, and a blind man; and the raising to life of a dead man (Lazarus). John 21 narrates the miraculous catch of 153 large fish. Other signs are referred to in summary statements.

The gospel presupposes that the effectiveness of Jesus' presence and teaching is continued through the coming of Paraclete, Spirit of Truth. See especially the distinctive Johannine teaching in 14:15–16, 25–6; 15:26–7; and 16:7–15. Thus through the Spirit-inspired transformation of memory the word of Jesus remains living and active within the believing community to renew and nurture the experience of the loving action of God in his mission to the world in the life of the believing community.

## Special Roles

Distinctive to John is the Logos, whose role in creation and revelation finds no counterpart in the other gospels (but compare the role of the Logos in Philo). Then there is the only John named in the gospel. He is the foundational witness to Jesus. His prophetic mission is totally subsumed into the function of witness to Jesus. Only in the Gospel of John is Andrew, Simon Peter's brother, named as one of the two disciples of John who take the initiative to follow Jesus. Eventually Andrew leads Peter to Jesus, having identified Jesus as the messiah. Andrew also has a named role in the feeding sign in 6:8. The unnamed "other disciple" might be identified as the Beloved Disciple, who is mentioned by this designation for the first time at the supper in John 13:23–4. This disciple has the better of Peter throughout the narrative of the following chapters until chapter 21 more or less reconciles their roles. If Philip is not the second of the two disciples, he alone of the first disciples is called by Jesus. Philip (like Andrew) finds another person (Nathanael) and brings him to Jesus (1:43–51). He also has a named role in the feeding sign (6:5, 7). Philip and Andrew bring the request of the Greeks to see Jesus to him (12:21–2). Their parallel roles suggest that he might be the second disciple of 1:37–40. The coming of Nathanael is the occasion for Jesus' first and enigmatic Son of Man saying (1:51).

Though not as prominent as in the synoptics, Peter plays a leading role amongst the disciples. But in John 13–20 it is a role secondary to that of the Beloved Disciple. The role of Judas as betrayer is featured in John as in the synoptics. The Evangelist always identifies him as the betrayer, from the first mention of his name in 6:70–1 (and see 12:4–6; 13:2, 21, 26–30). In John Jesus refers to Judas as a devil (6:70–1). According to the narrative, at the last meal of Jesus with his disciples, the Devil has already put it into the heart of Judas to betray Jesus (13:2). Just when this happened is unclear, though the reference seems to suggest a recent event. At the same time, according to 13:26–7, only when Jesus gives the "morsel" to Judas does Satan enter him. The narrative suggests that Jesus' evaluation of Judas in 6:70–1 is retrospective. It is not to be understood that Jesus chose "a devil" to be one of his disciples. Rather, he chose twelve, and one of them turned out to be a devil. The narrative (12:1–8) provides some basis for the transition from chosen to devil. There Judas Iscariot, one of his disciples, who was about to betray him, objects to the waste of costly ointment in the anointing of Jesus. His motivation is shown to be theft. As treasurer he had the opportunity to steal from the communal resources. Only here in John is Judas called Judas Iscariot. In the other references he is called Judas son of Simon Iscariot.

The mother of Jesus and his brothers are not mentioned by name in John. The mother of Jesus is especially prominent, precipitating the first sign (2:1, 3). She is also mentioned, with the brothers and the disciples, in linking passage of 2:12. Thus, mother and brothers are early linked with the followers of Jesus in John. Jesus' mother is depicted as an ideal disciple, at the foot of the cross with the Beloved Disciple (19:25–7). The second mention of the brothers is again in the company of Jesus' followers (7:3–5), though the evangelist evaluates their suggestion as evidence that they did not yet believe in Jesus. But we should not assume that the brothers were not followers of Jesus at this stage. In 16:30–2, when the disciples affirm that they now know and believe, Jesus interjects, "Do you now believe? Behold the hour comes, and it has arrived, when you will all be scattered. ..." But that does not mean that the disciples were not followers of Jesus. Events are to show that they too were fallible followers.

Nicodemus first appears as an example of those who believe in Jesus on the basis of his signs (2:23–3:15). It is unclear where the narrative leaves Nicodemus. This episode is left open. He simply disappears and the discourse of Jesus continues to the reader and should probably be identified with the voice of the narrator in 3:16–21, although no change in speaker is indicated. Nicodemus reappears in 7:50–2. His earlier appearance is noted. He takes Jesus' side in a somewhat guarded fashion and is silenced by the question of his association with Jesus. Perhaps he is included in the reference to the many rulers who believe but for fear of the Pharisaic threat of excommunication from the synagogues do not confess their faith openly (12:42). The narrator's assessment of those who could "so easily" be silenced is harsh: "For they loved the praise (glory) of men rather that the praise of God" (12:43). Finally, Nicodemus is again mentioned, as the one who came to Jesus by night, in the account of the burial of Jesus (19:38–42). He is linked here with Joseph of Arimathea, who is described as a secret disciple of Jesus. This probably implies that Nicodemus is also a secret disciple (see 12:42). In the narrative of the burial, Joseph and Nicodemus do what the disciples do not dare to do. The irony of this is not lost on the reader and one can only suspect that the narrative intention is clear on this point also.

Through the narrative of the Samaritan woman (John 4) the gospel explores the relationship between Jews and Samaritans, and of Jesus to women, and allows Jesus to speak of the life-giving water that he gives. Jesus affirms the priority of Jewish worship only to override it by the eschatological call now to worship God in Spirit and Truth in a way that makes Jerusalem and its temple obsolete. The dialogue ends with the woman affirming that "when messiah comes he will tell us all things," and Jesus affirms "I am [the messiah] who speaks with you." The incident leads to the woman's tentative witness to the people of her town and their belief on the basis of her word, which leads to meeting Jesus and declaring "We have heard for ourselves and know that this is the savior of the world" (4:42). The principle of belief on the basis of witness is not over-ridden here though it does lead on to belief based on personal experience.

Two signs call for parallel treatment. In John 5 Jesus heals a long-term lame man and in John 9 he heals a man born blind. In each of these narratives only at the end of the end of the story is the reader told that the incident occurred on the Sabbath (5:9b; 9:14). Nevertheless, each story develops quite differently. In John 5 the once lame man blames the person who healed him for his work on the Sabbath. That person, unknown at the time, told him to take up his bed and walk. When he discovers Jesus' identity he becomes an informer, with the result that the Jews persecute Jesus. The remainder of the chapter is developed as a dispute between Jesus and the Jews in which Jesus calls on supporting witnesses.

The healed blind man of John 9 persists as a defender of Jesus' healing activity on the Sabbath. His conviction is first based on the nature of the signs performed by Jesus. He argues that Jesus is a prophet because, if he were not from God he could do nothing. It is the once blind man who bears the brunt of the attack and, as the strength of the attack increases, so the boldness of his faith grows. The incident closes with the man being cast out of the synagogue by "the Jews." Having been cast out, he is found by Jesus, who further reveals himself to the man, who believes and worships him. Jesus final words of judgment are spoken to the Pharisees.

Reference to the Jews in John is complex. On the one hand, Jesus and his disciples are Jews. At the same time, the opposition to Jesus is often said to come from the Jews.

In some instances the reference appears to be to the Jewish authorities, and some of these references are interchangeable with references to the Pharisees. There are other instances where the reference may be to Judeans. References to the Jews are complex and the specific nuance can only be drawn in the light of the specific context. The completed gospel seems to reflect the period when the believers had largely separated from the Jewish community, and this produced a language where Jew and believer were distinct. But the narrative demands recognition that in the story all of the main characters are Jewish. The result is a complex and somewhat confusing use of "Jewish" terminology.

## The Johannine Epistles

A strong case can be made for the dependence of the epistles on the tradition embodied in the gospel. Yet there are grounds for thinking that the gospel and the epistles have different authors. The author (or authors) of 1, 2, and 3 John was less able than the substantial author of the gospel who wrote more clearly, compellingly, and simply than the author(s) of 1, 2, and 3 John. The case for recognizing that 2 and 3 John have the same author is strengthened by the author's distinctive identification of himself as "the Elder." Common style and language in these short letters (245 and 219 words respectively) provide a strong basis for common authorship. 1 John stands apart from these typical Hellenistic letters. 1 John is not a letter and is much longer and more complex than the letters. Nevertheless it is stylistically and linguistically close to 2 John, less close to 3 John. While there is but slender evidence upon which to base a conclusion, it is likely that these three writings have a common author. Much of what separates 1 John from the two letters is bound up with their letter form. Given that 1 John is not a letter, the similarities look a lot stronger.

There is no precise evidence upon which to base a view of the chronological order of the writings. A good case can be made for accepting the canonical order, not because it is canonical, but because it makes sense. Earliest reference (Irenaeus) to 1 and 2 John treats them as if they were one composition. This suggests that 2 John might have been a covering letter for 1 John. The letter is addressed by the Elder to the Elect Lady and her children (2 John 1). This is a symbolic reference to a church and its members. It is an appropriate way to address a circular letter to a circle of local churches. The greeting at the conclusion comes from "the children of your Elect Sister." That this is the greeting from the church of the Elder seems clear. There is no greeting from the sister (the church), but only from the children (members of the church).

2 John picks up the two main issues of 1 John and, by way of introduction, summarizes them briefly. The first issue concerns the command to love one another (5–6). This is the ethical foundation of the argument in 1 John. It is inseparable from the second, the Christological foundation in the confession of Jesus Christ come in the flesh (7). 2 John adds to the teaching of 1 John the instruction that, if any one comes, not abiding by this teaching, they are not to be provided with hospitality. The mission progressed through the provision of hospitality, reserved for those who walked in the truth of the gospel according to the Elder. That there were those who saw things

differently is clear from the reference to "many deceivers." Anyone who would not make the true confession is dubbed "the deceiver and the Antichrist" (7). The Elder made his case against supporting the mission of such preachers.

3 John is addressed to the beloved Gaios. This appears to be a genuine letter from the Elder to an individual named Gaios. The Elder writes to commend Gaios for his support of the brothers. Evidently Gaios has provided them with hospitality in their mission and the Elder wishes to consolidate that practice. The reason for writing is probably given in the reference to Diotrephes. The Elder complains about his actions on a number of issues. Diotrephes rejected what the Elder wrote to the church. He also refused hospitality to the brothers and threatened exclude from the church anyone who provided hospitality for the brothers (9–10). Just who was Diotrephes and what was his role? He cannot be identified with any known person. But he was probably the head of a house church and a leader of significant influence in his locality. His rejection of what the Elder wrote and refusal of hospitality to those the Elder describes as brothers might place Diotrephes with the opposition. But the Elder does not criticize him in these terms. It seems more likely that Diotrephes was a local leader who refused to support visiting missionaries whether they came from the Elder or his opponents. The issue of hospitality binds 2 and 3 John together. Each letter deals with a different aspect of it. 2 John warns against the provision of hospitality to the opponents of the Elder while 3 John commends Gaios' support of missionaries from the Elder but complains about the opposition of Diotrephes. Gaios was probably head of a house church somewhere close to Diotrephes. The Elder feared that Gaios might become influenced by Diotrephes and recognized the strategic importance of Gaios, given the opposition of Diotrephes. Demetrios (12) is commended by the Elder, who appeals to a threefold testimony to him. He is probably the leader of the brothers and perhaps also the bearer of 3 John, which then functions as a letter of commendation.

The closing greetings in 2 and 3 John are quite similar (2 John 12–13 and 3 John 13–15). The main differences are that 3 John includes a closing blessing ("Peace be with you," 15a). But 2 John has an extended opening blessing (3). 2 John includes a final salutation (to the Elect Lady and her children) from the children of her elect sister. In 3 John the Elder passes on salutation to Gaios from "the friends" and directs Gaios to salute "the friends" by name. This is a new term (quite distinct from "brothers") and might take in a secular context. The friends in the Elder's locality salute Gaios. The Elder directs Gaios to salute by name the friends in his locality.

1 John contains the teaching of the Elder, developed over time, and put together in this form in response to the bitter schism referred to in 2:18–19. It was designed for use in a number of contexts. It was the author's message to the church in which he lived and worked and where he and his message needed no formal introduction. It was sent out to surrounding house churches, some, or all of which might have been founded by a mission spearheaded by the Elder. 2 John introduced 1 John to these house churches. 2 John was a circular letter addressed symbolically to individual house churches and their members.

The use of 2 John to introduce 1 John, followed by 3 John, suggests that a circle of house churches, spread over a distance of some days journey between churches, was affected by the schism. The distances between churches made it impossible for the Elder to move easily from one to another. But the network of house churches appears to belong to a local region, perhaps around Ephesus.

2 John addresses the reader personally and identifies the two main issues of the more detailed account in 1 John. The issues at the heart of the schism concern a refusal to confess Jesus Christ come in the flesh (4:2; 2 John 7) and failure to acknowledge the obligation to love the brother (one another). All of the issues dealt with in 1 John seem to be related to these two interrelated issues. The schism had left believers uncertain of their standing, uncertain of their faith. There was also the trauma caused by the rending of a community with all the pain and confusion that brings. 1 John addresses the trauma of the schism and its aftermath and sets out to heal, reaffirm, and reassure the believers. At the same time it sets out to undermine the position of the schismatics to ensure that their destabilizing influence is minimized. It does this by setting out a series of tests, which expose the false claims and provide assurance for those who abide in faith and love.

The Johannine epistles give us a window into the life of a network of early Christian communities at a time when they were no longer living in the shadow of Judaism. Certainly this reflects a time after the Jewish War. While the epistles reflect the Jewish origin of the early Christian movement, there is no evidence of dialogue or conflict with Judaism, as there is in the gospel. The house churches appear to have developed a tradition of settled leadership. The Elder may well have exercised authority in a particular church but also sought a sphere of influence in the house churches of the surrounding area. Just how far afield his authority was recognized is unclear. But he was writing to individuals and churches some distance from him. This is indicated by his closing greetings in 2 and 3 John. Expression of his unfulfilled desire to deal face to face with those to whom he writes would have been implausible had the addressees been but a short distance from him.

The epistles provide evidence of itinerant preachers and teachers. The churches in the surrounding area might have been established by such teachers. The Elder's expression of his desire to visit those to whom he wrote suggests that he was an itinerant as well as a leader settled in a particular church in the locality. Evidence of itinerant missionaries is found in the Elder's warning not to provide hospitality to any teachers who come with teaching at odds with his teaching. So there were wandering false teachers deceiving and leading astray those who received them. But the Elder commended those he describes as "the brothers," one of whom was Demetrios, who might have been their leader. Diotrephes and Gaios were probably leaders of neighboring house churches. The Elder sought to influence their policies on hospitality, which was so important for the success of his mission. He seems to have had some success with Gaios but was in a fairly tense struggle with Diotrephes. Diotrephes might have resented the Elder's interference in his sphere of authority. Alternatively, he might have given support to the opponents of the Elder, whose activity is evident in 1 and 2 John. The Elder dubbed them deceivers and Antichrists, showing the bitterness of the struggle. That he does not refer to Diotrephes in such terms casts doubt on any identification with the opponents. Rather Diotrephes appears to be resistant to the influence of itinerant missionaries and to the influence of the Elder in his settled sphere of influence. This problem is reflected in the *Didache* and probably helps to date the epistles in the late first or early second centuries.

The following outline of 1 John highlights the controversy and its effect on the believers. The position of the opponents had undermined the faith and assurance of believers. 1 John set out to refute the opponents' position and restore the confidence of the believers (5.13). The epistle first establishes the basis of its witness before setting out two broad-ranging tests (ethical and Christological) to refute what the opponents claimed, to establish what they denied, and to reassure the believers that they had eternal life.

## 1 Prologue, 1:1–5

The opening of the gospel resonates with Genesis 1, and the epistle builds on John 1:1, 14–16. 1 John speaks of what was from the beginning, what was with the Father. Through the incarnation of the Word, the witnesses had seen, heard, and touched the Word of life.

## 2 First presentation of the two tests (1:6–2:27)

I. The ethical (love) test and refutation of two series of false claims (1:6–2:17). Because God is light, walking in the light of God's love is the test of union with God. Six claims refuted on this basis: 1). Union with God, 1:6–7. Variant claims (claims 2 and 3) to be sinless (1:8–2:2). In the second series, false claims to know God, abide in him, and to be in the light are refuted (2:4–5, 6, 9–11).
II. Faith in Jesus Christ is the second test to the claim to have union with God (2:18–27).

## 3 Second presentation of the two tests (2:28–4:6)

I. The ethical (righteousness = love of the brothers) test of being born of God (2:28–3:24).
II. The Spirit of God confesses Jesus Christ come in the flesh (4:1–6).

## 4 Third presentation of the two tests (4:7–5:12)

I. Love based on faith in the revelation of love is the proof of knowing God and being born of God (4:7–21).
II. Faith in Jesus as the Christ is the foundation of love (5:1–12).

## 5 Conclusion (5:13–21)

I. Statement of the purpose of 1 John: to reestablish assurance and confidence, 5:13–15.

II. Prayer for those sinning, 5:16–17.
III. God and the problem of sin, 5:18–20.
IV. Final exhortation, 5:21.

## Annotated Bibliography

Barrett, C. K. *The Gospel of John and Judaism*. London: SPCK, 1975a. An exploration of the complex relationship of the gospel to Judaism.

Barrett, C. K. *Essays on John*. London: SPCK, 1975b. The essays in this volume supplement the commentary and its introduction. It focuses on significant issues in more detail than was possible in the commentary.

Barrett, C. K. *The Gospel According to St John*. 2nd edn. London: SPCK, 1978. This commentary on the Greek text was first published in 1955 and was significantly revised and updated in 1978. Since it was first published it has been the most useful and up to date commentary on the Greek text.

Beutler, Johannes. *Habt keine Angst, Die erste johanneische Abschiedsrede (Joh 14)*. Stuttgarter Bibelstudien, 116. Stuttgart: Verlag Katholisches Bibelwerk GMBH, 1984. An important thematic treatment of John 14 from the perspective of the recognition that it constitutes a first edition of the farewell discourse.

Beutler, Johannes. *Die Johannesbriefe*. Regensburger Neues Testament. Regensburg: Verlag Friedrich Pustet, 2000. A concise, contemporary, and careful treatment of the epistles by a leading German scholar.

Brown, R. E. *The Gospel according to John*. Anchor Bible, 29 and 29A. New York: Doubleday, 1966–70. Brown's two-volume commentary is the most detailed English-language treatment of the gospel from the second half of the twentieth century. It excels in its treatment of the scholarly literature and the development of a hypothesis of the literary stages of the gospel in the context of the history of the Johannine community.

Brown, R. E. *The Epistles of John*. Anchor Bible, 30. New York: Doubleday, 1982. The most detailed commentary in English updating Brown's views on the Johannine community and providing detailed commentary on the epistles from this perspective while providing a detailed critique of the literature on the epistles.

Bultmann, Rudolf. *Theology of the New Testament*. 2 vols. London: SCM, 1955. A profound treatment of the theology of the gospel and epistles is contained in the second volume.

Bultmann, Rudolf. *The Gospel of John*. Oxford: Basil Blackwell, 1971. Bultmann's brilliant commentary was fist published in German in 1941. Though it took thirty years for it to appear in English, this commentary reshaped the study of the gospel in the twentieth century and remains an important study of the gospel, though elements of his literary source theory no longer command widespread support.

Culpepper, R. Alan. *Anatomy of the Fourth Gospel*. Philadelphia: Fortress, 1983. A pioneering treatment of the gospel making use of the literary theory of Seymour Chatman. Culpepper introduces a wide-ranging study of the gospel making use of a complex literary approach.

Culpepper, R. Alan. *The Gospel and Letters of John*. Nashville: Abingdon, 1998. A reliable and concise treatment of the gospel and epistles.

Dodd, C. H. *The Johannine Epistles*. London: Hodder & Stoughton, 1946. In this concise treatment Dodd provided a brilliant interpretation of the epistles and a readable, interesting, and persuasive fashion. The commentary holds up well after sixty years.

Dodd, C. H. *The Interpretation of the Fourth Gospel*. Cambridge: Cambridge University Press, 1953. Dodd's treatment of the context in which the gospel was written takes account of both the Jewish and Greek perspectives. This leads to a profound interpretation of the leading ideas of the gospel which students of the gospel need to reckon with.

Dodd, C. H. *Historical Tradition and the Fourth Gospel*. Cambridge: Cambridge University Press, 1963. Developing a short summary in his *Interpretation of the Fourth Gospel*, Dodd builds a case for John's independence of the synoptics while recognizing the use of synoptic-like material. This study has shaped subsequent work on John's relationship to the synoptics.

Fortna, R. T. *The Gospel of Signs*. Cambridge: Cambridge University Press, 1970. Fortna is the leading exponent of Bultmann's signs source hypothesis in English scholarship and has broadened and deepened Bultmann's approach.

Fortna, R. T. *The Fourth Gospel and its Predecessor*. Philadelphia: Fortress Press, 1988. Fortna deepens and nuances his treatment of the signs gospel while demonstrating the way the evangelist, making use of redaction critical methods, developed and used this primitive gospel. His aim is to elucidate the theology of the gospel.

Gardner-Smith, P. *Saint John and the Synoptic Gospels*. Cambridge: Cambridge University Press, 1938. Gardner-Smith's work is now seen as a decisive turning point leading to the reassertion of the independence of John from the synoptics. Dodd acknowledges the influence of Gardner-Smith's work in the shaping of his position in *Historical Tradition*.

Hengel, Martin. *The Johannine Question*. London: SCM, 1989. Hengel's treatment of the traditions concerning John in the early church led to his reassessment of the conclusions of much modern scholarship concerning authorship, purpose, and the relationship of gospel and epistles. The English edition appeared before an expanded German edition.

Keener, Craig S. *The Gospel of John: A Commentary*. 2 vols. Peabody, MA: Hendrickson, 2003. A detailed commentary, featuring the ancient literary sources relevant to the composition and interpretation of the gospel.

Kysar, Robert D. *The Fourth Evangelist and his Gospel*. Minneapolis: Augsburg, 1975. The best summary of modern research on John up to 1975.

Kysar, Robert D. *John*. Minneapolis: Augsburg, 1986. A concise and reliable commentary on the gospel, emphasizing its unique style, approach, and theology.

Law, Robert. *The Tests of Life*. Edinburgh: T. & T. Clark, 1909. A pioneering work on 1 John, which has influenced scholarship for the past century, as can be see in the commentaries of A. E. Brooke, C. H. Dodd, R. Schnackenburg, R. E. Brown, J. Painter.

Leroy, H. *Rätsel und Missverständnis: Ein Beitrag zur Formgeschichte des Johannesevangeliums*. Bonner biblische Beiträge 30. Bonn: Peter Hanstein, 1968. A pioneering work on riddle and misunderstanding in John. It continues to bear fruit in modern literary studies.

Lieu, Judith. *The Second and Third Epistles of John*. Edinburgh: T. & T. Clark, 1986. An important study of the Johannine literature from the standpoint of the two short epistles, 2, and 3 John. Lieu argues that these short epistles provide crucial social data that illuminates the epistles and that enables the reader to place and understand the epistles more accurately than is otherwise possible.

Lieu, Judith. *The Theology of the Johannine Epistles*. Cambridge: Cambridge University Press, 1991. Lieu provides a reading of the theology of the epistles from the perspective of her approach of giving precedence to the light shed by 2 and 3 John.

Lieu, Judith. *I, II, and III John: A Commentary*. The New Testament Library. Louisville and London: Westminster John Knox Press, 2008. A detailed commentary based on Dr. Lieu's approach.

Lincoln, Andrew T. *The Gospel According to Saint John*. Black's New Testament Commentary. London and New York: Continuum/Hendrickson, 2005. A succinct and readable commentary illuminating the gospel from a literary perspective.

Lindars, B. *Behind the Fourth Gospel*. London: SPCK, 1971. Lindars deals with the development of the fourth gospel, outlining his view of the oral and written sources used by the evangelist.

Lindars, B. *The Gospel of John*. New Century Bible. London: Marshall Morgan & Scott, 1972. Lindar's commentary makes use of his composition theory, paying careful attention to the completed gospel.

Malina, Bruce J. and Richard L. Rohrbaugh. *Social-Science Commentary on the Gospel of John*. Minneapolis: Fortress Press, 1998. Leading members of the Context Group demonstrate their method and approach in this commentary on John.

Martyn, J. L. *History and Theology in the Fourth Gospel*. Nashville: Abingdon, 1968; 2nd edn. 1979. Martyn's modern classic has now appeared in a third edition introduced by Moody Smith. Martyn's theory of John as a two-level drama telling the story of Jesus and the story of the Johannine community around the last decade of the first century has been widely influential though it has been subject to a widening challenge. Martyn's approach is complemented by Brown's interpretation of the development of the gospel and reconstruction of Johannine history.

Meeks, Wayne. *The Prophet-King*. Leiden: Brill, 1967. An important essay on Mosaic tradition and its bearing on the interpretation of John.

Meeks, Wayne. "The Man from Heaven in Johannine Sectarianism." *Journal of Biblical Literature* 91 (1972), 44–72. An important socio-historical reading of John.

Moloney, F. J. *The Gospel of John*. Sacra Pagina, 4. Collegeville, MN: Liturgical Press, 1998. The first full-scale narrative critical commentary on John from the perspective of the implied reader.

Neirynck, F. "John and the Synoptics: 1975–1990." Pp. 3–62 in *John and the Synoptics*. Edited by Adelbert Denaux. Bibliotheca Ephemeridum Theologicarum Lovaniensium, 101. Leuven: Leuven University Press, 1992. An important survey of scholarship developed to support the case for John's dependence on the synoptics.

Neyrey, J. H. *An Ideology of Revolt*. Philadelphia: Fortress Press, 1988. An anthropological reading of John from a member of the Context Group.

Neyrey, J. H. *The Gospel of John*, The New Cambridge Bible Commentary. Cambridge and New York: Cambridge University Press, 2007. The commentary illuminates the text using insights from Mediterranean anthropology, its values and worldview.

Okure, Teresa. *The Johannine Approach to Mission*. Tübingen: Mohr Siebeck, 1988. An important study of the theme of mission in John set in the context of a defense of Johannine authorship and early dating.

Painter, John. *John Witness and Theologian*. London: SPCK, 1975; 2nd edn. 1979; 3rd edn. Melbourne: Beacon Hill Books, 1986. A succinct treatment of the major themes and motifs of the gospel and 1 John.

Painter, John. *The Quest for the Messiah*, Edinburgh: T. & T. Clark, 1991; 2nd edn. 1993. A detailed treatment of the gospel taking account of evidence of development in which the widespread quest for the messiah gives way to rejection, which leads to the reinterpretation of messiahship.

Painter, John. *1, 2, and 3 John*. Sacra Pagina, 18. Collegeville MN: Liturgical Press, 2002. A recent detailed commentary on the epistles giving priority to the text of the epistles while taking account of the history of interpretation.

Rensberger, David. *Johannine Faith and Liberating Community*. Philadelphia: Westminster, 1988. Rensberger understands the Johannine community as an alternative community challenging the beliefs and values of the world, and interprets the gospel from this perspective.

Rensberger, David. *1 John, 2 John, 3 John*. Abingdon New Testament Commentaries, Nashville: Abingdon, 1997. A concise reliable commentary on the epistles.

Rensberger, David. "Sectarianism and theological Interpretation in John." Pp. 139–56 in *"What is John?"* vol. 2: *Literary and Social Readings of the Fourth Gospel*. Society of Biblical Literature Symposium Series, 7. Edited by Fernando F. Segovia. Atlanta: Scholars Press, 1998.

Rensberger, David. "Spirituality and Christology in Johannine Sectarianism." Pp. 173–88 in *Word, Theology, and Community in John*. Edited by John Painter, R. Alan Culpepper, and Fernando F. Segovia. St. Louis: Chalice Press, 2002.

Robinson, J. A. T. *Twelve New Testament Studies*. London: SCM, 1962. Seminal essays which have helped to shape contemporary Johannine studies in recognizing the Jewishness of John. Robinson was already heading in the direction of the early date of John.

Schnackenburg, Rudolf. *The Johannine Epistles: A Commentary*. New York: Cross Road, 1992. For a long period the German edition, first published in 1953, was the most important modern commentary on the epistles. English-language commentaries were dependent on it although it did not appear in English until 1992.

Schuessler Fiorenza, E. "The Quest for the Johannine School: The Apocalypse and the Fourth Gospel." *New Testament Studies* 23 (1976–7), 402–27. Fiorenza argues that Revelation is closer to the Pauline school than to John.

Smith, D. Moody. *First, Second, and Third John*. Louisville: John Knox, 1990. Interpretation. A clear and reliable commentary written with the needs of preachers clearly in mind.

Smith, D. Moody. *John*. Abingdon New Testament Commentaries. Nashville: Abingdon, 1999. A concise but solid commentary on John. Moody Smith exhibits all of his strengths in concise, clear, and compelling treatment of the text of John.

# CHAPTER 21
# Paul and his Letters

## Jouette M. Bassler

## Major Issues and Directions in the Recent Study of Paul

Recent study of Paul can be fairly described as energetic and, at times, contentious, for there has been a disintegration of old consensuses, an emergence of new paradigms, and a proliferation of methodological approaches. Whether the issue is the nature of Paul's theology, the rhetoric of his letters, social analysis of his churches, or feminist, ideological, postcolonial, or cultural critiques of his message, Pauline scholarship is currently in a state of rich intellectual ferment. The one thing it is not, is boring.

### Theological issues

The most fundamental theological issue of all – the nature, even the very existence, of something that can be called Paul's theology – has been called into question, especially by the work of the Society of Biblical Literature's Pauline Theology Group (1986–95). Earlier scholars had no qualms about producing accounts of his theology, organized around the categories of systematic or dogmatic theology (Bultmann 1951; Whiteley 1966; Fitzmyer 1967). These, however, have been critically appraised as artificial harmonizations that create the impression of a coherent theological vision only by careful selectivity from Paul's diverse statements. Indeed, when the theological tensions in Paul's comments are taken seriously, he does not appear to be a coherent or systematic thinker at all (Räisänen 1986b; Sanders 1983). What he says, for example, about the role of the law seems to be highly contingent on the problem he is wrestling with. In different contingencies Paul gives different, contradictory answers, to the consternation of many who study his theology. Beker's proposal (1980) that Paul's theology is characterized by both a coherent center and contingent interpretations offered a popular explanation. This construal recognizes the fluidity of Paul's expression and the dynamic quality of his theology, while retaining the notion of a constant center at the core of his thought (see, e.g., Dunn 1998). Yet problems remain. Since the only data available in the letters are contingent expressions, the coherent center must be reconstructed. It is not clear, though, just what constitutes this center. Is it an integrated set of beliefs or convictions (so Wright 1991)? Or does the gospel or the story of God's acts of redemption lie at the center of Paul's thought (so Hays 1991; Longenecker 2002)?

There is a new tendency to focus on Paul's activity as a theologian and to regard his theology as emergent rather than fixed. Some retain the concept of a central core but argue that Paul's acts of contingent interpretation affected his core beliefs, so that they too evolved (Kraftchick 1993; Roetzel 1993). Others locate the gospel at the center and define his theology as the outcome (not the core) of his reflections (Meyer 1997; Furnish 1997). For them, Paul's theology is understood as always contingent and, because contingencies changed, always a work in progress, theology in the making.

Beyond these questions concerning Paul's theology as a conceptual whole, individual aspects of his thought are also being vigorously debated. With the publication of Sanders' *Paul and Palestinian Judaism* (1977), a long-standing consensus was shattered. It had long been held that Paul's attacks on works of the law (e.g., Gal. 2:15–3:5; Rom. 3:20–31) were directed against the view that salvation could be earned by strict obedience to the deeds prescribed by Jewish law (legalism). What Sanders found in the Jewish sources was quite a different pattern of religion, in which works did not earn salvation but maintained good status within a covenant defined by grace – the grace of election, forgiveness, and atonement. If that is the case (and not all agree), then either Paul is misrepresenting Judaism in his attack (a view some hold: Watson 1986; Räisänen 1986a), or the focus of Paul's objections has been misunderstood. To correct this misunderstanding, a "New Perspective" on Paul has emerged, not completely displacing the older legalistic interpretation (see, e.g., Westerholm 1988; Gathercole 2002) but sharing the stage with it. According to this new perspective, Paul's critique of works of the law was directed against the view that such works were badges of national privilege, boundary markers between those in and out of covenant relationship with God (Dunn 1983). At stake in this debate is whether Paul's primary concern was the individualistic issue of earning salvation or the corporate issue of limiting God's favor to a single group, and scholars are deeply divided in their opinions.

A second theological issue that continues to resist a scholarly consensus is the correct translation and meaning of the phrase traditionally rendered "faith in Jesus Christ" (Rom. 3:22, 26; Gal. 2:16, 20;3:22; Phil. 3:9). In this rendering the phrase signifies a person's obedient trust in God's act in Christ, which is the condition for salvation. The Greek phrase, however, can also be translated "faith (or faithfulness) of Jesus Christ," and a significant number of scholars now argue that it is more naturally and appropriately rendered this way. (The same grammatical construction, for example, is found in Romans 4:12, which can only be understood as a reference to the faithfulness of Abraham, and in Romans 3:3, which is undeniably a reference to the faithfulness of God.) This translation gives greater significance to the life of Jesus, during which he manifested faithful obedience to and trust in God, including faithful acceptance of his death on the cross (Rom. 5:12–21; Phil. 2:5–8). Followers partake of this faith by their participation in Christ, whereby his faithfulness becomes their faithfulness as they are being conformed to Christ (Gal. 2:19–20; Phil. 3:8–9).

Defenders of the traditional view point to passages in the deutero-Pauline letters (those written in Paul's name probably after his death) which contain clear references to faith in Christ (1 Tim. 3:13; 2 Tim. 1:13; 3:15). They also argue that since Paul expresses the concept of believing in Christ in other places using different language (Rom. 10:14; Gal. 2:16; Phil. 1:29), it is reasonable to assume that the debated phrase expresses the same thought. Opponents, however, note that these other expressions can also be understood as expressions of participation (believing *into* Christ). The theological implications of this dispute are considerable, but no grammatical or exegetical arguments have proved decisive. Though the discussion continues, resolution of the issue does not seem to be in prospect (Hays 1997; Dunn 1997; Achtemeier 1997).

### Rhetorical issues

Not all scholars have been asking about what Paul said. Some are asking instead about how Paul said it, that is, about his modes of argumentation. Early work on this question involved assessing Paul's letters according to the conventions of Greco-Roman rhetoric (see Chapter 11, "Rhetorical Criticism," in this volume). The approach was primarily descriptive as the letters were categorized according to their dominant type of rhetoric, their contents labeled according to the formal structure of a speech, and the presence or absence of classical rhetorical devices debated (Betz 1979; Wuellner 1976). The endeavor helped to situate Paul more firmly in the oral culture of his world and to focus attention on the strategy, not just the content, of his letters. But the emphasis on labeling had a stultifying effect on outsiders to the discipline. As historical rhetorical criticism gained maturity and adherents, though, it became less concerned with demonstrating the presence of rhetorical features in the letters and gave more attention to using those features to illuminate Paul's message and method. The results have been impressive and anything but stultifying. Mitchell (1993), for example, uses rhetorical criticism to confirm the thematic and compositional unity of 1 Corinthians; Martin's research (1990) reveals how radical Paul's rhetorical strategy was in that letter; and Given (2001) draws the surprisingly postmodern conclusion that the apostle's rhetoric was often deliberately ambiguous and deceptive. In the wake of such studies, the impact of the discipline has grown, even though some critics continue to express reservations about its underlying assumptions (Anderson 1996; Kern 1998).

   Some of the more radical developments in this field have been influenced by the "New Rhetoric" of Perelman and Olbrechts-Tyteca (1969), which explores rhetoric, not in terms of ancient conventions, but in terms of its persuasive intent. Correspondingly, the focus shifts from the author's skill in employing classical rhetorical devices to the effect of language on its audience. To gain the full persuasive impact of Paul's argument, that audience must be carefully defined, not simply in terms of its theological positions but more specifically in terms of its concrete social character and location. Indeed, careful attention to the range of responses that Paul's argument could elicit from various social groups is leading to insightful reconstructions of his intended readers. Wire (1990), for example, has drawn a richly nuanced picture of the women in the church of Corinth from her analysis of the rhetoric of 1 Corinthians.

   This interest in the persuasive power of Paul's arguments is moving in several other directions as well. Since the new rhetoric explores how a text attempts to shape an audience's attitudes, it exposes the ideology – the system of beliefs, assumptions, and values that define and serve Paul's worldview – embedded in Paul's letters and so contributes to the ideological criticism of them (Robbins 1996). Moreover, recognition of the fact that Paul's rhetoric is used to promote an ideology – in short, for propagandistic purposes – allows and (some claim) even requires ethical evaluation of it (Schüssler Fiorenza 1987; Bible and Culture Collective 1995). Finally, since part of Paul's persuasive technique is to present himself in the text in a way that promotes the desired response, modern rhetorical criticism also exposes – and exposes to critique – dynamics of power and authority at work in the text (Castelli 1991; Kittredge 1998; Polaski 1999).

Rhetorical criticism is seen by its proponents as a correction or alternative to theological inquiry, but it also serves to enhance that inquiry, especially insofar as it clarifies the social contingency of Paul's theologizing and provides a new perspective from which to evaluate charges of theological inconsistency.

## Social analysis

Discontent with the way Paul's theology was usually studied as if it existed in a hermetically sealed environment of pure ideas has fueled another development as well. In the 1970s there emerged an interest in exploring social aspects of Pauline Christianity (see Chapter 12, "Social-Science Criticism," in this volume). Early on these studies took two different directions. One uses the data and methods of historiography to develop a "thick" or "microscopic" description of the texture of life in the cities and households where Paul's house churches took root (Meeks 1983). Another uses the models and theories of the social sciences to reconstruct the patterns of social interaction that existed in and around Paul's churches (Neyrey 1986; Malina 1981). Each method has come under criticism (usually from practitioners of the other) – the first for failing to recognize and acknowledge the models implicitly governing the selection and interpretation of data, the second for interpreting the first-century Greco-Roman world through models based on modern societies. Yet singly, in combination, and enhanced by rhetorical studies, both methods are producing richly textured descriptions of the lives of the women (Kraemer and D'Angelo 1999; Gardner 1986; Treggiari 1991), slaves (Martin 1990), and families (Moxnes 1997; Osiek and Balch 1997) that populated Paul's churches, and of the cultural systems of patronage (Chow 1992), kinship, honor, shame, and purity (DeSilva 2000) that shaped their experience of the gospel. It is not only the understanding of Pauline Christianity that is benefiting from these studies, but the understanding of Paul's theology as well. As one social historian has observed, and as many theologians now recognize, "[t]o analyze theological language from the point of view of theology alone is to distort its significance for any real social group, theologians included" (Martin 1990: xiv).

Some of the complexity of this study, which is as complex as society itself, is indicated by the hyphenated subcategories that populate the field: socio-cultural, socio-economic, socio-rhetorical, social-psychological, socio-linguistic, and socio-political. Though all are active and productive areas of inquiry, one that characterizes particularly well the evolving multidisciplinary and postmodern quality of current scholarship is socio-political criticism. This field emerged as the recognition that the Roman empire was not just the political background of Paul's activity, but often the foreground of his message. His gospel of Jesus Christ was also a message against the empire (Georgi 1991; Elliott 1994). Read against imperial propaganda, Paul's proclamation of a savior from heaven (Phil. 3:20), before whom every knee would bend (Phil. 2:9–11) and by whom every ruler, authority, and power would be destroyed (1 Cor. 15:24), has a decidedly political thrust. Romans 13 and its message of submission to the empire is exceptional. Throughout Paul's letters can be heard an insistent undercurrent against imperial power, politics, and cult (Horsley 1997, 2000).

Interest in the political aspects of Paul's message has expanded to include the political aspects of interpretation, and the field now embraces postcolonial and ideological criticism, and has natural affinities with cultural readings as well. Under the rubric of postcolonialism, non-Western scholars inquire into the way Western interpretations of Paul contribute to an imperialistic view of other people and religions and seek alternative readings of these letters (Kwok 1995; Sugirtharajah 1998). Ideological criticism is a broader category for exposing and destabilizing the social and political agendas of texts and interpretations. Both are natural partners with the growing number of cultural readings of the Bible, which are self-consciously made from the particular social and cultural positions of their authors and make no claim to neutral objectivity. Recent readings of Paul from, for example, the positions of a Jewish talmudist (Boyarin 1994), African American scholars (Blount 2001; Callahan 1997), womanist scholars (Weems 1991), and feminist scholars (Schüssler Fiorenza 1994) challenge the notion of singular meaning and expose the limitations and biases of putative neutral readings.

Not all, of course, are comfortable with these destabilizing developments in Pauline studies. Nevertheless, they have had the salutary effect of jolting scholarship out of familiar terrain and exposing the text and its interpreters to new questions and fresh perspectives.

*Feminist interpretation*

Feminist scholars have been actively engaged in all the major scholarly developments, contributing their insights and perspectives especially to studies of Paul's rhetoric, to social descriptions of his churches, to ideological critiques of his arguments, and to cultural readings of his letters (see Chapter 10, "Feminist Criticism," in this volume). One particular development, however, warrants special treatment because of its historical importance. Galatians 3:28 ("There is no longer Jew or Greek, there is no longer slave or free, there is no longer male and female; for all of you are one in Christ Jesus.") has long functioned as the key to overturning a pervasive perception of Paul as a misogynist. This perception was based primarily on the household and church codes of Ephesians 5:22–6:4, Colossians 3:18–4:1, 1 Timothy 2:11–15, and Titus 2:1–10, which relegate women to silent roles and subordinate status. In opposition to these codes, which are found in letters of disputed authorship (see below), Galatians 3:28 presents Paul's own view as one in which the hierarchical gender differences of society (and ethnic and class differences as well) seem to be dissolved. Thus this text became the basis for a revisionary interpretation of early Christianity, and the Pauline churches in particular, as a community of equals within the wider patriarchal culture (Schüssler Fiorenza 1983). Yet this interpretation has recently been challenged by scholars who claim that the text in question announces, not gender equality, but an end to sexual differentiation for all those who are "in Christ." All are subsumed into a masculine identity (Moxnes 1989; Fatum 1991; Martin 1995: 231–2). If this interpretation is correct, Galatians 3:28 would have promoted, not an early egalitarian community where women (as women) were equal to men, but a celibate community in which the female sex was devalued even as women regendered in Christ assumed roles of authority within the church.

## Paul between Judaism and Hellenism

Paul was a Jew, a "Hebrew born of Hebrews" (Phil. 3:5). Yet according to Acts, he was from the deeply Hellenized city of Tarsus. His letters show that he was immersed in Jewish scripture, but he wrote and spoke in Greek. Moreover, his understanding of his call to apostolic ministry was very specifically a call to bring the message of the Jewish messiah to the Gentiles of the Roman empire. Small wonder, then, that the question of the relative importance of Judaism and Hellenism in Paul's thought and practice has been repeatedly asked. Finding an answer to that question – finding even the appropriate way to frame the question – has, however, proved to be remarkably difficult. Several issues complicate the inquiry. First there is the issue of definitions. To what do the terms "Hellenism" and "Judaism" refer? The second and related issue concerns the way presuppositions have guided the research. A brief survey of the history of the investigation illustrates the impact that definitions and presuppositions have had – and continue to have – on framing the questions and shaping the answers that have emerged. (For more fulsome surveys, see Meeks 2001; Martin 2001; and P. S. Alexander 2001.)

### A brief history of the debate

The Judaism–Hellenism question first emerged in nineteenth-century Germany, and it did so in a form that was to control the debate for years to come. The question was posed dualistically – *either* Judaism *or* Hellenism. The categories were assumed to be self-contained and mutually exclusive, and they were defined in ahistorical, value-laden terms, "code words for complex sets of ideas masquerading as historical entities" (Meeks 2001: 19). Thus, for example, in some of the earliest discussions "Judaism" was defined in terms colored not only by German anti-Semitism but also by the anti-Catholicism that had infused Reformation readings of Paul. In that time and place, "Judaism" stood for narrow ethnic particularity, legalism, and ritualism; while "Hellenism" represented universality, freedom, and rationalism. Paul, not surprisingly, was identified with the latter. Later the values changed. "Rabbinic Judaism" retained the negative connotation of legalism, but "Judaism" (now defined as apocalyptic or prophetic Judaism) came to represent the positive values of covenant, universalism, revelation, freedom, purity, and simplicity. In this framework "Hellenism" denoted what was foreign or pagan, what was complex, philosophical, and doctrinal. Here Paul was identified with the "good" Judaism. Until the mid-twentieth century, ideology, not history, defined the terms and predetermined the results of the debate. However Hellenism and Judaism were defined (and they were defined in ways that reflected the definer's culture and presuppositions), Paul was identified with the "good" side.

In the mid-twentieth century, however, some things changed. The Holocaust brought forcibly home to scholars the ideological bias of interpretations of Paul's Jewishness. Post-war scholarship could not continue on the old trajectory. Furthermore, research in the newly developed or newly energized fields of Judaic studies and Roman history provided historical concreteness to the terms "Judaism" and "Hellenism." Finally, the multicultural, postmodern emphasis of North American scholarship in the late twentieth and early twenty-first centuries nurtured an appreciation for the diversity, complexity, and ambiguity of the emerging picture.

One result of these developments was that the understanding of Judaism and Hellenism as distinct, separate entities with clearly defined boundaries was discarded. The actual Judaism of Paul's day was not only characterized by great diversity (some argue that one should speak of a plurality of Judaisms rather than a singular entity), but all forms of Judaism were already Hellenized, influenced to some degree by the culture of the Greco-Roman world. And Hellenism, the culture of the eastern Mediterranean world from the time of Alexander the Great to the decline of the Roman empire, was itself influenced by oriental civilizations, including Judaism. In fact, Hellenism came to be defined not primarily as a reference to the Greekness of the culture of the eastern empire, but as a reference to its syncretism, its blending of elements from all its constitutive components.

In light of this revised understanding of the cultural realities designated by "Judaism" and "Hellenism," it no longer made sense to pose the issue in dualistic terms, as if either Hellenism or Judaism defined Paul. Paul, like everyone else in his world, was a mixture of elements, and in that sense he was typically Hellenistic. Researchers therefore began to ask the Judaism–Hellenism question in a radically different way.

### The Judaism–Hellenism debate reframed

Though it is no longer valid or useful to use the terms "Jewish" or "Hellenistic" in any summary fashion to define Paul, it remains valid and useful to compare elements of Paul's letters with cultural practices that had distinctly Jewish roots or distinctly Greek ones (Engberg-Pedersen 2001). What is to be avoided, however, are any a priori assumptions that a given element or passage can be fully illuminated by comparison with material drawn exclusively from one or the other source. With the understanding that Hellenistic culture was a fusion of elements, and that Paul was a man of that complex culture and not uniquely isolated from it, scholars now cast the interpretive net broadly to locate appropriate comparative material. Not surprisingly, a complicated picture emerges.

Paul, for example, drew frequently and heavily upon Jewish traditions and Jewish scriptures in his letters. He also repeatedly distanced himself and his churches from non-Jewish aspects of his culture (1 Cor. 6:9–11; 2 Cor. 6:14–7:1). Yet at the same time it is evident that he used Hellenistic rhetorical techniques and frequently drew upon topics (e.g., autonomy, free will) characteristic of the philosophical schools. Furthermore, the model of the Hellenistic philosophical school seems to shed more light on the structure and practices of the Pauline congregations than the temple-oriented synagogues of his day (L. Alexander 2001; Stowers 2001).

In light of this complexity, the earlier impulse to place a single label on Paul has largely vanished. It sometimes subtly returns, however, in assertions of a hierarchy of importance: Hellenistic influences do not emerge in Paul's thought, it is claimed, at places that really matter, that is, at the core of his theology (Barclay 1996). Such an assertion rests, however, on presuppositions about what really matters for Paul (theology, for example, and not ethics). It further assumes that what Paul says can be neatly severed from the way Paul says it. Moreover, upon closer evaluation (and wider net-casting) many of Paul's theological statements appear to have far more complex roots than is usually assumed.

It is generally agreed, for example, that the basic structure of Paul's worldview belongs to Jewish apocalypticism, with its emphasis on cosmological dualism and eschatological consummation. Yet it can be shown that "Jewish apocalypticism is itself a particular version of certain basic ideas in the Hellenistic world at large, Jewish as well as non-Jewish" (Tronier 2001: 167). Similarly, Paul's anthropology has tradition-ally been regarded as essentially monistic (that is, presuming an indissoluble unity of the inner and outer person), a view which was further regarded as quintessentially Jewish. Yet such an understanding is problematic in several ways. First, Hellenistic views of human nature were varied and included both monistic and dualistic concep-tions. Secondly, various strands of Judaism reflect various views of the nature of the human person. And finally, Paul himself shows no consistency, drawing on monistic views at some points of his argument (e.g., Rom. 7) and dualistic views at other points (2 Cor. 4:16–5:10) (Aune 1994, 2001).

Even Paul's views of Christ and of God seem to have been influenced at significant points by Greek ideas. Paul's presentation of himself as becoming "all things to all people" (1 Cor. 9:22) is, as one scholar has noted, "quintessentially Hellenistic" (Mitchell 2001: 198). It reflects among other things a Greco-Roman preoccupation with the importance of adaptability or condescension for successful moral instruction and guid-ance. Yet Paul takes the concept in theological directions as well (as did other Hellenistic Jews). He presents his adaptability as modeled on that of Christ (1 Cor. 10:33–11:1; Rom. 15:1–3) and even presumes God's accommodation in dealing with Jews and Gentiles (Rom. 11) (Stowers 1994). A Hellenistic moral commonplace seems to have shaped Paul's vision of at least one aspect of divine nature.

Though Paul's core beliefs derive from a Jewish matrix (see, e.g., Sanders 1996), recognition of Hellenistic elements in them not only makes Paul more comprehensible as a person of his Hellenistic culture, it also helps explain how Christianity developed so rapidly among Gentiles. Paul's thought, even at significant theological points, had roots deep enough in Hellenistic concepts that "the Greeks, had they set their minds to it, [would not] have found the Christian gospel all that difficult to grasp" (P. S. Alexander 2001: 80).

# The Collection and Influence of Paul's Letters

The presence of the Pauline letters in the New Testament canon presents something of a puzzle. The letters are quite obviously directed to the specific needs and concrete circumstances of particular congregations, yet rather quickly they were collected and read as relevant to many congregations. Just how and why this came to pass is not at all clear, and to account for it a number of theories have been put forward. These can be divided into three basic lines of interpretation. (For more detailed surveys and critiques, see Gamble 1985 and Lovering 1988.)

## Collection theories

One line of interpretation posits that a period of neglect followed the initial reception of the letters. They were deemed relevant for the moment and then forgotten. Sometime around the end of the first century they were rescued from this obscurity by a devoted follower of Paul, who painstakingly collected the surviving letters and gathered them into a corpus, which was then circulated among the churches. Various individuals have been identified as the collector, and different events have been suggested as the decisive factor in prompting the collection. Often a key component of this hypothesis is the claim that Ephesians was composed by the collector to serve as a "cover letter" to introduce the major themes of the collection. Details differ, but a common feature of this line of interpretation is the idea of a dramatic rescue of Paul's letters from oblivion by a bold act that created the "first edition" of the collection of Pauline letters.

The fact that Acts makes no mention of any Pauline letters lends some support to this thesis, for this can be taken to imply that the author of Acts was unaware of the existence of any letters. Yet other factors speak strongly against the thesis. Apart from the silence of Acts (which can be explained on other grounds), the assumption of the letters' rapid descent into oblivion has no external support. Moreover, the variety of the collections (different letters in different sequences) that are indicated in early literature is difficult to reconcile with a definitive first edition. The Ephesians component of this hypothesis is also flawed, for that letter does not provide a summary introduction to the content of the rest of the letters, nor does it ever appear at the head of any collection. For these reasons, few scholars have embraced the "rescue" theory.

A second approach locates the collecting activity, not with a single individual, but within a "Pauline school." This school comprised a group of Paul's disciples, who were committed to Paul's mission and sought to perpetuate and expand his influence and authority after his death by collecting and broadly circulating his letters. It is usually assumed that the group gathered copies of the letters from various Pauline churches in order to form the collection, but it has also been suggested that they worked from copies that Paul had retained for himself (Gamble 1995). Such a school would also have been responsible for editing the letters for more general use and for composing new letters to bring Paul's teachings to bear on new situations. This activity would have been understood not so much as a rescue operation than as a continuation of Paul's own practice.

This proposal has the advantage of offering a single explanation and context for three types of activities known to have taken place around Paul's letters: their collection, their editing, and the creation of new letters in Paul's name. Its primary weakness is that is presumes the existence of an entity – a "Pauline school" – for which there is no clear evidence. Paul certainly had co-workers in the mission field and even co-authors of his letters. There is, however, no trace of an institution as cohesive, geographically centered, or organized as the word "school" and its suggested activities implies.

The third theory proposes a more nebulous and haphazard process than the first two, but for that very reason it may cohere better with the circumstances of the early churches. Often dubbed the "snowball" hypothesis, it proposes that collections of Paul's letters emerged, not by design, but fortuitously and gradually and in several different places as churches exchanged letters in their possession. The various collections would, on this hypothesis, initially have differed in content and arrangement, but through the process of exchange they would have "inched toward uniformity" (Lovering 1988: 278). Such a theory rests on the assumption that Paul's letters were not neglected or forgotten after their initial reception, or treasured only within a school, but were valued and sought out by the churches that Paul had founded.

The actual circumstances of the collection are, at this point, beyond recovery and were at any rate probably more complex than a single theory can comprehend. Individuals, perhaps former colleagues of Paul, certainly had a role. Certain events may have served as catalysts at various points. But a process of gradual development seems to flow most naturally from procedures initiated by Paul himself and is further indicated by some of the later letters in the collection.

Paul's letter to the Galatians, for example, was intended for all the churches in the region (Gal. 1:2). Those multiple addressees could have been reached either by sending enough copies with the carrier for all the churches or by sending a single letter with the expectation that each church would make its own copy (Gamble 1995). Either way, a sort of circulation of the letter would have been envisioned. Likewise, the letter to the Romans was intended for a number of house churches in the city (Rom. 16), and the letter, or multiple copies of it, was probably circulated among them. Colossians depicts a slightly different procedure: the church there was explicitly instructed to exchange letters with the church in Laodicea (Col. 4:16). Since the authorship of Colossians is disputed (see below) we cannot be certain that this directive came from Paul. If it did not, however, it certainly indicates that a follower of Paul wished to encourage an exchange of letters and assumed that the request would not be regarded as highly unusual. Finally, 2 Thessalonians warns that unauthorized letters were already circulating in Paul's name (2 Thess. 2:2; 3:17), though the possibility of pseudonymous authorship of this letter raises questions about the context and purpose of such a warning.

Evidence of another sort derives from some ancient copies of Romans and 1 Corinthians that lack the name of the specific communities (Rome, Corinth) to which the letters were addressed. (The same is true for the letter to the Ephesians, but that involves a different set of issues related to its pseudonymity [see below].) Deletion of the names of the addressees can only have been done to promote the use of the letters in other communities, but it is impossible to determine when the omissions were made. There are good grounds, however, for assuming that they occurred early, for once the conviction arose in the second century that "what Paul said to one he said to all" (Tertullian, *Against Marcion*, 5.17), there would have been little incentive to remove references to the original addressees.

## The influence of Paul's letters

Not surprisingly, views about the early influence of Paul's letters fall into two camps that are roughly comparable to the views about the collection. Some deny any influence in "mainstream" Christianity until after the middle of the second century; others affirm a steady and growing stream of influence from the start. The first view has long been dominant. In some versions it asserts not only widespread neglect of Paul's letters after their initial reception, but also suspicion or hostility toward them because of their appropriation by heretical groups. The decisive moment, according to this view, came in the mid-second century when Marcion, a church teacher excommunicated in Rome for his unorthodox views, embraced ten Pauline letters and an edited version of the Gospel of Luke as the normative canon for the churches he established. So strong was this Marcionite movement, and so close were its ties to Paul, that the orthodox church was faced with the choice of either abandoning Paul to that movement or claiming him for their own canon. The church chose the latter route, but, it is argued, it did so more out of anti-Marcionite sentiment than because of a real understanding and appreciation of Paul's thought.

This "backlash hypothesis" (Rensberger 1981: 45) was based to a large extent on the relative paucity of citations from Paul's letters during the second century, a silence that was interpreted as evidence of hostility. Careful attention to the sorts of literature produced in this period and to the aims of this literature yields a different picture. It is true that Paul is infrequently cited before the end of the second century. There is little reason, however, to expect him to be cited before his letters reached normative status, or to be cited in literature focused on Jesus or written for outsiders who would have no knowledge of Paul. Moreover, the early creation and circulation of letters in Paul's name (see below) and narratives about Paul (Acts of the Apostles, *The Acts of Paul*) provide clear evidence of high regard for the apostle (in some circles at least) in the late first and early second centuries.

Moreover, though citations of Paul are rare, they are not completely absent from the literature of this period. Writings that focus on ethical admonitions to Christian groups do refer to Paul (*1 Clement*; Polycarp, *Philippians*) or use language derived from Paul or from traditions shared with Paul (*Epistle of Barnabas*). Christians undergoing persecution – Ignatius, Polycarp, the martyrs of Lyons – seem to have had a particular affinity for Paul's writings, and the Gnostic teachers Basilides and Valentinus cite him frequently. Rarely, however, do these early writers attempt to explicate or understand Paul. Rather his words and his authority are used primarily in support of the authors' own separate concerns. In none of these writings, except those from Jewish-Christian groups, is there any trace of hostility toward Paul.

The overall pattern is one of a gradually increasing number of appeals to Paul as his letters became more widely known and highly valued. Paul may not have been prominent in the writings of the late first and early second centuries, but he was not marginal or marginalized. Marcion, by focusing so intently on Paul as the primary basis for his theology and as the primary authority for his churches, probably speeded the growth of Paul's influence in orthodox churches, but the process, it seems, was already in motion before Marcion came on the scene (Rensberger 1981; Lindemann 1979).

After Marcion, Paul became a significant influence on second- and third-century writers. They were, however, not concerned to explore or explain Paul's theological statements, but they found him a helpful and increasingly authoritative resource for dealing with the issues of their own times. And though in using Paul they did not focus on what has been viewed since the Reformation as the heart of his theology – justification by grace through faith – they did not misuse Paul. The ideas they were promoting – the continuity of God's saving acts through history (Irenaeus), the role of the Spirit as the sign and seal of the new age (Tertullian), and the importance of free will over fate for final salvation (Augustine) – were certainly true to Paul's own thought. And by developing these ideas in dialogue with Paul they clearly came under the influence of his thought (Babcock 1990).

## Pauline Chronology

Most writings on Paul provide a tabular chronology of his life and letters as an aid to readers. Such lists of dates and events suggest a high level of scholarly certitude that is quite at odds with the reality of the situation. In fact, this topic is plagued by methodological controversies, huge gaps in the historical record, apparent contradictions, and, as a consequence, widely divergent proposals. (For a survey of these difficulties, see Hurd 1983.) Hardly an item on the chronological list enjoys consensus status among scholars. To sort out this complex situation, three issues in the debate can and should be distinguished, for they rely on different methods, rest on different data, and therefore have different – and independent – degrees of reliability. These issues are the relative order of Paul's letters, the relative order of events in his life, and the absolute dating of these letters and events.

### The sequence of the letters

Establishing the correct sequence of Paul's letters is of crucial importance for identifying any patterns of development in Paul's thought (see above). Yet the task is fraught with almost insurmountable difficulties. There is no external evidence: Acts does not mention Paul's letters, and the letters themselves are not dated. One must rely largely on references within the letters to events that suggest a logical sequence. This task is complicated, however, by the likelihood that several letters in the collection (most notably 2 Corinthians and Philippians) are composite documents created out of several different pieces of correspondence written at different times. Moreover, there are few unambiguous cross-references within the letters and even these objective internal clues establish only a partial sequence. Fleshing out the sequence of the full roster of letters requires a more subjective approach, usually in the form of assumptions about the way Paul's thought would have developed. This, however, is circular: it assumes what the sequence is supposed to reveal. And, of course, different assumptions lead to different results. Moreover, this approach ignores the possibility that the circumstances of the letters could affect the way Paul expresses himself as much as – or more than – any coherent or consistent development in his thought. The prospects are not encouraging.

One event that does establish the rudiments of a sequence is the collection of money that Paul undertook for the relief of the church in Jerusalem (Gal. 2:10). References in other letters to the progress of this collection establish a clear sequence. 1 Corinthians 16:1–4 mentions the inauguration of the collection in Corinth; 2 Corinthians 8–9 describes a midpoint in the activity when interest there was flagging; and in Romans 15:25–6 Paul refers to his imminent departure for Jerusalem with the completed collection. Thus the sequence 1 Corinthians – 2 Corinthians (chapters 1–9 if the letter is composite) – Romans seems secure. It is very likely on other grounds that 1 Thessalonians was the earliest letter in the corpus, for it reflects a time when believers still assumed that Christ would return before any of them died (4:13–18).

Beyond this framework, though, there is no consensus regarding the placement of the remaining letters in the sequence. (For a survey of proposals, see Jewett 1979; Knox 1990; Roetzel 1998.) Some assume that the theology of Philippians requires that it be placed between 1 and 2 Corinthians. Others link a portion of Philippians (assuming it is a composite letter) with the earliest letters because it contains no evidence of the problem with Judaizers that (presumably) emerged later. Yet others place it among the last of Paul's letters because it contains no references to the (presumably completed) collection. Arguments based on similarly subjective criteria have been presented for locating Galatians before 1 Thessalonians, just after 1 Thessalonians, just before Romans, or just after it. The placement of 2 Thessalonians and Colossians also varies greatly, depending on the assumptions made about the authorship of these letters (see below).

## The sequence of events

Paul's letters contain some information about events in Paul's apostolic ministry, but not enough to construct a complete sequence. Acts provides a much more fulsome account, but scholars are deeply divided about the historical reliability of this document. Some express great confidence in its account and use it to establish the basic chronological framework of events, which is then supplemented with information from the letters (Moody 1989); others are utterly skeptical and avoid the use of Acts altogether (Riddle 1940). Most fall somewhere between these two poles, giving primary weight to data in the letters but using Acts cautiously to supplement that data (Knox 1987). Various criteria have been invoked to identify reliable information in Acts – a connection with "primitive" sources (Knox 1990; Lüdemann 1984) or restricting attention to "incidental chronological details" that do not reflect the theological concerns of the book (Jewett 1979). These judgments are, however, highly subjective and result in widely different chronologies.

One issue of particular importance here is the location of the Apostolic Council within the sequence of events. Did this meeting in Jerusalem with other leaders of the church come early or late in Paul's apostolic career? Finding the answer to this question is important for assessing the significance of that meeting for Paul's ministry, but a clear answer is not forthcoming. The primary problem is that Acts reports five trips to Jerusalem, while Paul's letters indicate only three, and the two accounts can be harmonized in different ways.

Paul's description of events leading up to the Council seems remarkably precise, providing the most detailed chronological data we find in his letters (Gal. 1:16–2:10). He reports his conversion, a three-year stay in Arabia and Damascus, his first return visit to Jerusalem, a departure for the regions of Syria and Cilicia, active proclamation of the faith, and after fourteen years (counting from his conversion or from his first visit to Jerusalem?) a second visit to Jerusalem to meet with the Jerusalem leaders (the Apostolic Council). All seems fairly straightforward until one turns to Acts to confirm or clarify these events, and then serious problems emerge. Paul, for example, is insistent ("before God, I do not lie!" – Gal. 1:20) that he met with the Jerusalem apostles only *once* before the Council. Acts reports *two* prior meetings (9:26–30; 11:27–30), assuming – as most do – that the meeting described in Acts 15 is the same one that Paul refers to in Galatians 2. Paul's account suggests rather strongly that the fourteen years between the two meetings were spent in Syria and Cilicia (Gal. 1:21–4). Acts describes a lengthy mission trip to Cyprus and Asia Minor during that period (Acts 13–14).

The attempts to reconcile these and other discrepancies are as diverse as they are creative. (For a survey of various proposals, see Jewett 1979.) The problem of the extra pre-Council Jerusalem visit in Acts is sometimes resolved by identifying the visit recorded in Acts 11 with the Council, even though that account has little in common with Paul's description of events in Galatians 2. The fourth Jerusalem visit, reported in Acts 18, has also been identified as the occasion of the Council, and the visits described in chapters 11 and 15 attributed to Luke's creative hand. In this way the five visits in Acts are reconciled with Paul's three, and the seventeen "silent" years before the meeting are filled with missionary activity. Tenuous confirmation of this is claimed in Paul's terse reference to "proclaiming the faith" during this period, under the assumption that this proclamation was not limited to the two regions, Syria and Cilicia, that Paul mentions by name (Alexander 1993).

Such harmonizations of Acts and the letters strain the credulity of many scholars. Even assuming the merit of this approach, the number and variety of the proposals erode confidence that a consensus chronology can easily be achieved.

## The dating of letters and events

The prospect of getting absolute dates to anchor the chronology is raised by references in the letters and Acts to known and presumably datable persons and events. In 2 Corinthians 11:32, for example, Paul relates a dramatic escape from Damascus during the reign of King Aretas, a period which can be dated between 37 and 40 CE. If this escape coincides with Paul's first trip to Jerusalem after his conversion (Gal. 2:17–18), it provides a reasonably fixed point for dating that conversion (three years earlier) and the Council meeting that occurred some years afterward. The length of Aretas' reign and the various ways of construing the three- and fourteen-year periods (as consecutive or concurrent periods, as including only full years or reckoning partial years in the tally) preclude certainty, but one reasonable reconstruction that has emerged from this data is the following:

33/34 CE    Conversion
37 CE       First Jerusalem visit
48 CE       Second Jerusalem visit/Apostolic Council (concurrent reckoning of the two time periods)
or, 51 CE   Second Jerusalem visit/Apostolic Council (consecutive reckoning of the two periods)

This is, however, far from a consensus position. Some insist that the Council must be dated before Herod's death in 44 CE, for according to Acts 12 this king disrupted and dispersed the Jerusalem leadership of the church. That moves Paul's first Jerusalem visit to 33 CE (assuming the eleven-year period) and his conversion three years earlier (Betz 1992).

Acts contains many more references to known persons and events, but most of these yield too broad a range of possible dates to be useful. One, however, seems to provide an opportunity for more precision. Acts 18:1–18 refers to Paul's hearing before the proconsul Gallio in Corinth, and an inscription allows Gallio's time in office to be dated about 51–2 CE. If the account of Paul before Gallio is historically reliable, and if it has been reliably placed in the narrative of Paul's missions, then it can serve as a fixed point from which other dates can be calculated. Working forward and back from this event, using known distances and seasonal restrictions on sea routes to calculate travel times, some scholars have devised remarkably precise chronologies that provide not only the year but often the season and occasionally even the month and the day of events in Paul's life (Jewett 1979; Lüdemann 1984). But the assumption on which such calculations rest – the historical reliability of Acts 18 – is questionable and the "firm" date that serves as the anchor – the duration of Gallio's proconsulship – may be uselessly broad, for a range of 49–54 CE instead of 51–2 has also been vigorously argued (Slingerland 1991).

The confident results of chronological studies are meager: a sequence for four of the letters; a couple of reasonable dates in the 40s or early 50s for the Apostolic Council. Paul's conversion was probably in the early 30s. His death is not mentioned in Acts or (of course) in his letters, though it is assumed to have occurred in Rome during Nero's persecution of Christians there in 64 CE. For the rest, it may be best to confess an honest "We don't know."

## Pauline Letters and Pauline Pseudepigrapha

Thirteen letters in the New Testament canon bear Paul's name as the author, claims that were for centuries accepted without question. However, with the rise of critical scholarship in the late eighteenth century, their authorship came under closer scrutiny. At some point in the early history of the debate, the authenticity of every letter in the Pauline corpus was challenged, but by the last decades of the nineteenth century only six were still seriously debated. Today the authorship of the same six letters – 2 Thessalonians, Colossians, Ephesians, 1 and 2 Timothy, and Titus – continues to be a source of controversy. (For a history of this debate, see Guthrie 1965.)

The central issues of the debate concern the vocabulary and style of the disputed letters, their historical settings, and their theology. For two letters – 2 Thessalonians and Colossians – the deviance from the undisputed letters is modest and scholarly opinion is deeply divided. The remaining four differ more widely and are generally, though not unanimously, deemed pseudepigraphical – that is, writings that make false claims of authorship.

The issue of the authorship of these letters is of paramount importance, for the contours of Paul's thought and the trajectory of its development are profoundly affected by the inclusion of any of them among the authentic letters. Moreover, the presence of pseudonymous writings in the canon is incompatible with some doctrines of inspiration and raises serious concerns for those holding such views.

## The case for pseudepigraphy

Second Thessalonians straddles the divide between the undisputed and the disputed letters. It is omitted without comment or argument from many treatments of Pauline pseudepigrapha (Donelson 1986, 1996; Meade 1987); and many commentaries, including the Anchor Bible Commentary (Malherbe 2000), treat it as genuine. Yet many other writings, including the *Anchor Bible Dictionary*, assume pseudonymous authorship (Krentz 1992). Clearly the evidence is ambiguous.

Questions about the authorship of 2 Thessalonians rest primarily on two interrelated issues. First, the letter seems very close in language and structure to 1 Thessalonians. This suggests either that they were both written at about the same time while the words were still fresh in Paul's mind or that one served as the literary template for the other, indicating a different author. Secondly, there are significant theological differences in the two letters, especially in the eschatological views that they promote. It is not that the theology of 2 Thessalonians is incompatible with views found in the undisputed letters. What is problematic is the presence of strikingly different theological emphases in letters written to the same church at about the same time. In 1 Thessalonians 4:13–18, for example, Paul encourages the community with the message of the nearness of the Lord's return. In 2 Thessalonians 2:1–12, however, he (or someone writing in his name) argues against an imminent expectation. The first letter anticipates the sudden arrival of the day of the Lord "like a thief in the night" with no warning signs. The second lists a series of events (signs) that will herald that day. There are, additionally, perceived differences in style (2 Thessalonians is more wooden) and tone (2 Thessalonians is more impersonal).

These differences have been reconciled with Pauline authorship in several ways. Some minimize the similarities in language and structure, eliminating the need to posit nearly simultaneous composition. This allows for the passage of several months to account for the changed circumstances. Alternatively, it is claimed that the letters were written at the same time but intended for different groups in the church, thus accounting for different emphases and tone. It has also been suggested that the canonical order is wrong: if 2 Thessalonians was written first, there is a more natural progression of circumstance, tone, and eschatology.

Each of these proposals has some merit, but the counterarguments are also strong. The letters' similarities are difficult to ignore, and there is no indication that different groups are addressed. The canonical order also seems to be correct, for Paul's careful rehearsal of his contact with the church in 1 Thessalonians 2:1–3:5 does not mention an earlier letter. The best explanation, many argue, is that 2 Thessalonians is pseudonymous, written in Paul's name to correct an eschatological error that had developed in that church.

As this brief summary indicates, the judgments about similarities in language and structure and differences in tone and style are very subjective. Moreover, while the theological position of 2 Thessalonians is unusual for Paul, it is not beyond the possible parameters of his thought, especially if it was written in response to a theological crisis. One other aspect of the letter complicates the situation. In 2 Thessalonians 2:2 the author warns against "a letter, as though from us, to the effect that the day of the Lord is already arrived." If the letter is genuine, this means that very early in Paul's career letters were being written and sent in his name, but without his approval. To many scholars, that seems unlikely. On the other hand, if 2 Thessalonians is not by Paul, it presents the irony of one pseudonymous letter warning against the danger of another. That too seems unlikely. The result is that neither position has won the day.

The case for the pseudonymity of Colossians is only slightly stronger (Barclay 1997). The vocabulary differs somewhat from that of the undisputed letters, but no more than can be explained in terms of a new set of issues that Paul was confronting. The style seems unusual for Paul, with long, loose sentences and many repetitious phrases. (This is most obvious in the Greek, where 1:3–8 is a single sentence, as is 1:9–11 and, most notably, 1:12–20.) Yet Paul was a versatile writer, and even computer-aided statistical analyses of the style are inconclusive (Newmann 1990). The letter itself is Pauline in its general structure and content, with greetings that closely (but not too closely) match those of Philemon 23–4. The nature of the error that the letter attacks (Col. 2:8, 16–23) is difficult to reconstruct with precision, but it is not impossible to reconcile it with developments that were plausible in Paul's lifetime. It is in the area of theology, though, that the most significant questions about authorship are raised.

Christ's cosmic role and divine nature are emphasized in ways barely anticipated in the undisputed letters (see 1:15–20; 2:9–10; cf. 1 Cor. 8:6; Phil. 2:6–11). Colossians proclaims the present status of believers in terms that are usually reserved in the undisputed letters for their resurrection (2:9–14; cf. Rom. 6:5). The church is depicted as a cosmic entity (2:19; 4:15) instead of a local gathering of believers. Paul himself is described in striking terms as the one who completes what is lacking in Christ's affliction (1:24). Finally, the exhortations to wives and slaves to be subordinate seem to sit uncomfortably with the admonitions of 1 Corinthians 7 and Philemon. The question here is not whether the theology of Colossians agrees with that of the undisputed letters. It does not. Rather, the question is whether it would have been possible, in certain circumstances, for Paul's theology to have developed in this direction. On that issue, scholars are divided.

The remaining four letters – Ephesians, 1 and 2 Timothy, and Titus – are much more readily and widely identified as pseudepigrapha. Ephesians resembles Colossians in many ways, so many, in fact, that the question of literary borrowing is often raised (cf. Eph. 6:21–2 and Col. 4:7). Yet in matters of style, historical circumstances, and theology, the differences with the undisputed letters are more pronounced for Ephesians. In addition, the earliest manuscripts lack any reference to specific addressees, reading simply "to the saints who are also faithful in Christ Jesus" (Eph. 1:1, NRSV textual note), and Marcion seems to know this letter as addressed to the Laodiceans. This can be taken as evidence that the document was conceived as an "open letter," in which case it certainly does not conform to Paul's known practice of addressing specific situations in specific locations. The pastoral letters differ dramatically from the other letters in style, vocabulary, and especially theology. Moreover, they reflect a level of church organization – deacons, presbyters, bishops, enrolled widows – unknown in the churches of Paul's day. They are also absent from some early canon lists. There are a number of plausible interpretations of this absence, but one possibility is that they were unknown at the time the lists were made.

So strong are the arguments for non-Pauline authorship of Ephesians, 1 and 2 Timothy, and Titus that pseudonymity is often presented as a "foregone conclusion" (Meade 1987: 118; see also Donelson 1986). Yet not all are willing to accept that conclusion, for the problems that this conclusion generates outweigh for them the evidence in its favor.

### The problem of canonical pseudepigrapha

Though it is recognized that pseudepigraphy was common in the ancient world (Rist 1972; Metzger 1972), finding it in the Pauline corpus raises a number of troubling questions for those accepting the canon as inspired truth. Since false attribution of authorship seems incompatible with inspiration and truth, some conservative scholars have defined the issue as a stark choice: if a document is pseudepigraphical it cannot be canonical, and if it is canonical it cannot be pseudepigraphical. Thus the Pauline authorship of all letters attributed to the apostle is vigorously defended on dogmatic grounds (see Guthrie 1965; Ellis 1992).

Others accept the evidence for pseudepigraphy but distinguish between innocent and culpable forms of this practice. Some use psychological arguments to absolve the authors of canonical pseudepigrapha of any intent to deceive and describe the attribution of the letters to Paul as a transparent literary fiction (see the survey in Meade 1987: 4–12). Pseudepigraphy, they claim, was a familiar phenomenon and the authors of these letters intended and expected them to be recognized as such. Alternatively, modesty has been suggested as the motivating factor. Recognizing that Paul – or the Holy Spirit (Aland 1965) – was the source of their ideas, the canonical pseudepigraphers were too modest to present them under their own names. Appealing as they are, such arguments attribute motives to the authors for which there is no hard evidence.

Yet others reframe the definition of canonical pseudepigraphy to distinguish it from forgery. One approach is to attribute the letters to Paul's secretaries, under the assumption that these scribes were given unusual freedom by the apostle to compose the letters in their own words (Ellis 1999). This accounts for differences in style and vocabulary but provides a less satisfactory explanation of the differences in theological content and historical context. Another approach finds an explanation in the literary milieu of Judaism and early Christianity. There, it is argued, attributing one's work to a religious figure of the past was a way of actualizing that tradition after the founder was gone. Pseudonymity, then, was an assertion of the letter's authoritative tradition, not a statement of its authorship (Meade 1987). It remains a question, though, whether early readers of the letters would have made this distinction.

Most who accept the pseudonymity of some or all of the disputed letters link their creation with disputes in the early church. In the struggles for the hearts, minds, and souls of believers, various heretical groups appealed to Paul. So the writers of the pseudepigrapha responded by doing the same. In this context, the pseudepigrapha can be regarded as a "noble falsehood," the end of which (a victory for emergent orthodoxy) justified the means.

With the exception of the secretary hypothesis, all these attempts to explain and defend canonical pseudepigrapha meet with the objection that the early church was rigorous in its efforts to identify and exclude from the emergent canon any works of dubious authorship. Yet the earliest evidence for this is from the mid- to late second century. A more fluid situation seems to have existed at the beginning of that century before the concept and contents of the Christian canon were relatively fixed (Meade 1987). At that time, before the letters were authoritative enough to be quoted and interpreted for a new situation, writing letters that brought elements of Paul's thought to bear on that situation may have been an acceptable option in the circles that produced them.

Reconstruction of the mechanics of the production and distribution of the pseudepigrapha poses quite a different problem. They were written by people who esteemed Paul highly and, at least for 2 Thessalonians, Colossians, and Ephesians, understood him well. They were written for communities who also esteemed him highly, for otherwise their attribution to Paul would serve no purpose. But how, assuming they were intended to pass as Pauline, did they enter circulation? If they were sent shortly after Paul's death, their acceptance as genuine poses no problem. But most show clear signs of later composition. On the hypothesis that the letters grew slowly into a collection as they were shared among congregations, it is easy to imagine a late pseudonymous letter arousing no suspicion when it was initially added to the growing corpus. But assuming continued circulation of the collection, how did it retain its credibility when the community to which it was ostensibly addressed, but which had never received it during Paul's lifetime, learned of its existence? Ephesians might have been accepted as an unknown circular letter, and the appearance of the pastoral letters, because they were addressed to individuals and not congregations, would not have raised questions. But for Colossians and 2 Thessalonians, the problem of the mechanics of their propagation as pseudepigraphs strengthens somewhat the argument that they were not.

## Annotated Bibliography

Aune D. E. (ed.). *Rereading Paul Together: Protestant and Catholic Perspectives on Justification.* Grand Rapids: Baker Academic, 2006. A vigorous and thoughtful ecumenical dialogue.

Babcock, W. S. (ed.). *Paul and the Legacies of Paul.* Dallas: Southern Methodist University Press, 1990. A wide-ranging collection of essays exploring the influence of Paul on the early history of Christianity.

Crossan, J. D. and J. L. Reed. *In Search of Paul: How Jesus's Apostle Opposed Rome's Empire with God's Kingdom: A New Vision of Paul's Words and World.* New York: HarperCollins, 2004. The lengthy subtitles indicate the focus of this interesting and provocative study.

Engberg-Pedersen, T. (ed.). *Paul Beyond the Judaism/Hellenism Divide.* Louisville: Westminster John Knox Press, 2001. An excellent collection of essays on the interplay of Jewish, Greek, and Roman elements in Paul's thought and practice.

Gamble, H. Y. *Books and Readers in the Early Church: A History of Early Christian Texts.* New Haven: Yale University Press, 1995. This wide-ranging study illuminates many aspects of the collection and circulation of the Pauline letters.

Jewett, R. *Romans: A Commentary.* Hermeneia. Minnesota: Fortress Press, 2007. An excellent commentary that brings the most recent developments in Pauline scholarship to bear on one of Paul's most challenging letters.

Johnson, E. E. and D. M. Hay (eds.). *Pauline Theology*, vol. 4: *Looking Back, Pressing On.* Society of Biblical Literature Symposium Series, 4. Atlanta: Scholars Press, 1997. This fine collection of essays reflects the ongoing debate over the appropriate definition of Pauline theology and some of its constituent components.

Knox, J. *Chapters in a Life of Paul.* Rev. edn. Macon: Mercer University Press, 1987. A lucid, methodologically rigorous proposal for establishing the chronology of Paul's life by using the epistles as the primary source of reliable data; originally published in 1950.

Martin, D. B. *The Corinthian Body.* New Haven: Yale University Press, 1995. An intriguing analysis of 1 Corinthians in terms of ancient ideologies of the human body, it sets the argument of the letter firmly within the conceptual possibilities provided by Greco-Roman culture.

Meade, D. G. *Pseudonymity and Canon: An Investigation into the Relationship of Authorship and Authority in Jewish and Earliest Christian Tradition.* Grand Rapids: William B. Eerdmans, 1987. A careful exploration of literary and theological aspects of New Testament pseudonymity against the backdrop of Jewish religious pseudepigrapha.

Roetzel, C. J. *Paul – A Jew on the Margins.* Louisville: Westminster John Knox Press, 2003. A collection of essays that explores the impact of Paul's complex relationship to his cultural and religious environments on his thought.

Sanders, E. P. *Paul and Palestinian Judaism: A Comparison of Patterns of Religion.* Philadelphia: Fortress Press, 1977. This carefully documented study directly challenged the long-dominant hypothesis that the Judaism of Paul's day was defined by legalism, the need to earn salvation by obedience to the law.

Watson, F. *Paul and the Hermeneutics of Faith.* London: T. & T. Clark International, 2004. An important, erudite, and provocative study of the way Paul read scripture.

Wire, A. C. *The Corinthian Women Prophets: A Reconstruction through Paul's Rhetoric.* Minneapolis: Fortress Press, 1990. A creative and provocative reconstruction of the lives and theology of women prophets in Corinth, using the tools of the "new rhetoric."

## References

Achtemeier, P. J. "Apropos the Faith of/in Christ: A Response to Hays and Dunn." Pp. 82–92 in *Pauline Theology*, vol. 4: *Looking Back, Pressing On*. Edited by E. E. Johnson and D. M. Hay. Society of Biblical Literature Symposium Series, 4. Atlanta: Scholars Press, 1997.

Aland, K. "The Problem of Anonymity and Pseudonymity in Christian Literature of the First Two Centuries." Pp. 1–13 in *The Authorship and Integrity of the New Testament*. No editor. Theological Collections, 4. London: SPCK, 1965.

Alexander, L. C. A. "Chronology of Paul." Pp. 115–23 in *Dictionary of Paul and his Letters*. Edited by G. F. Hawthorne and R. P. Martin. Downers Grove: InterVarsity Press, 1993.

Alexander, L. "IPSE DIXIT: Citation of Authority in Paul and in the Jewish and Hellenistic Schools." Pp. 103–27 in *Paul Beyond the Judaism/Hellenism Divide*. Edited by T. Engberg-Pedersen. Louisville: Westminster John Knox Press, 2001.

Alexander, P. S. "Hellenism and Hellenization as Problematic Historiographical Categories." Pp. 63–80 in *Paul Beyond the Judaism/Hellenism Divide*. Edited by T. Engberg-Pedersen. Louisville: Westminster John Knox Press, 2001.

Anderson, R. D., Jr. *Ancient Rhetorical Theory and Paul*. Contributions to Biblical Exegesis and Theology 18. Revised edition. Kampen: Kok Pharos, 1999.

Aune, D. E. "Human Nature and Ethics in Hellenistic Philosophical Traditions and Paul: Some Issues and Problems." Pp. 291–312 in *Paul in his Hellenistic Context*. Edited by T. Engberg-Pedersen. Studies of the New Testament and its World. Edinburgh: T. & T. Clark, 1994.

Aune, D. E. "Anthropological Duality in the Eschatology of 2 Cor. 4:16–5:10." Pp. 215–39 in *Paul Beyond the Judaism/Hellenism Divide*. Edited by T. Engberg-Pedersen. Louisville: Westminster John Knox Press, 2001.

Babcock, W. S. (ed.). *Paul and the Legacies of Paul*. Dallas: Southern Methodist University Press, 1990.

Barclay, J. M. G. *Jews in the Mediterranean Diaspora: From Alexander to Trajan (323 BCE–117 CE)*. Edinburgh: T. & T. Clark, 1996.

Barclay, J. M. G. *Colossians and Philemon*. New Testament Guides. Sheffield: Sheffield Academic Press, 1997.

Bassler, J. M. (ed.). *Pauline Theology*, vol. 1: *Thessalonians, Philippians, Galatians, Philemon*. Minneapolis: Fortress Press, 1991.

Beker, J. C. *Paul the Apostle: The Triumph of God in Life and Thought*. Philadelphia: Fortress Press, 1980.

Betz, H. D. *Galatians: A Commentary on Paul's Letter to the Churches in Galatia*. Hermeneia. Philadelphia: Fortress Press, 1979.

Betz, H. D. "Paul." Pp. 186–201 in *Anchor Bible Dictionary* 5. Edited by D. N. Freedman. New York: Doubleday, 1992.

Bible and Culture Collective. "Rhetorical Criticism." Pp. 149–86 in *The Postmodern Bible*. New Haven: Yale University Press, 1995.

Blount, B. K. *Then the Whisper Put on Flesh: New Testament Ethics in an African American Context*. Nashville: Abingdon Press, 2001.

Boyarin, D. *A Radical Jew: Paul and the Politics of Identity*. Contraversions, 1. Berkeley: University of California Press, 1994.

Bultmann, R. *Theology of the New Testament*. Vol. 1. New York: Scribner's, 1951.

Callahan, A. D. *The Embassy of Onesimus: The Letter of Paul to Philemon*. Valley Forge: Trinity Press International, 1997.

Castelli, E. *Imitating Paul: A Discourse of Power*. Literary Currents in Biblical Interpretation. Louisville: Westminster John Knox Press, 1991.

Chow, J. K. *Patronage and Power: A Study of Social Networks in Corinth*. JSNT Supp. 75. Sheffield: Sheffield Academic Press, 1992.

DeSilva, D. A. *Honor, Patronage, Kinship and Purity: Unlocking New Testament Culture*. Downers Grove: InterVarsity Press, 2000.

Donelson, L. R. *Pseudepigraphy and Ethical Argument in the Pastoral Epistles*. Hermeneutische Untersuchungen zur Theologie, 22. Tübingen: Mohr Siebeck, 1986.

Donelson, L. R. *Colossians, Ephesians, First and Second Timothy, and Titus*. Westminster Bible Companion. Louisville: Westminster John Knox Press, 1996.

Dunn, J. D. G. "The New Perspective on Paul." *Bulletin of the John Rylands Library* 65 (1983), 95–122.

Dunn, J. D. G. "Once More, PISTIS CRISTOU." Pp. 61–81 in *Pauline Theology*, vol. 4: *Looking Back, Pressing On*. Edited by E. E. Johnson and D. M. Hay. Society of Biblical Literature Symposium Series, 4. Atlanta: Scholars Press, 1997.

Dunn, J. D. G. *The Theology of Paul the Apostle*. Grand Rapids: William B. Eerdmans, 1998.

Elliott, N. *Liberating Paul: The Justice of God and the Politics of the Apostle*. Maryknoll: Orbis Books, 1994.

Ellis, E. E. "Pseudonymity and Canonicity of New Testament Documents." Pp. 212–24 in *Worship, Theology and Ministry in the Early Church: Essays in Honor of Ralph P. Martin*. Edited by M. J. Wilkins and T. Paige. JSNT Supp. 87. Sheffield: Sheffield Academic Press, 1992.

Ellis, E. E. *The Making of the New Testament Documents*. Biblical Interpretation Series, 39. Leiden: Brill, 1999.

Engberg-Pedersen, T. "Introduction: Paul beyond the Judaism/Hellenism Divide." Pp. 1–16 in *Paul Beyond the Judaism/Hellenism Divide*. Edited by T. Engberg-Pedersen. Louisville: Westminster John Knox Press, 2001.

Fatum, L. "Image of God and Glory of Man: Women in the Pauline Congregations." Pp. 56–137 in *Image of God and Gender Models in Judaeo-Christian Tradition*. Edited by K. E. Børresen. Oslo: Solum Forlag, 1991.

Fitzmyer, J. A. *Pauline Theology: A Brief Sketch*. Englewood Cliffs: Prentice-Hall, 1967.

Furnish, V. P. "Where is 'the Truth' in Paul's Gospel? A Response to Paul W. Meyer." Pp. 161–77 in *Pauline Theology*, vol. 4: *Looking Back, Pressing On*. Edited by E. E. Johnson. and D. M. Hay. Society of Biblical Literature Symposium Series, 4. Atlanta: Scholars Press, 1997.

Gamble, H. Y. *The New Testament Canon: Its Making and Meaning*. Philadelphia: Fortress Press, 1985.

Gamble, H. Y. *Books and Readers in the Early Church: A History of Early Christian Texts*. New Haven: Yale University Press, 1995.

Gardner, J. F. *Women in Roman Law and Society*. London: Croom Helm, 1986.

Gathercole, S. J. *Where Is Boasting? Early Jewish Soteriology and Paul's Response in Romans 1–5*. Grand Rapids: William B. Eerdmans, 2002.

Georgi, D. *Theocracy in Paul's Praxis and Theology*. Minneapolis: Fortress Press, 1991.

Given, M. D. *Paul's True Rhetoric: Ambiguity, Cunning, and Deception in Greece and Rome*. Emory Studies in Early Christianity, 7. Harrisville: Trinity Press International, 2001.

Guthrie, D. "The Development of the Idea of Canonical Pseudepigrapha in New Testament Criticism." Pp. 14–39 in *The Authorship and Integrity of the New Testament*. No editor. Theological Collections, 4. London: SPCK, 1965.

Hay, D. M. (ed.). *Pauline Theology*, vol. 2: *1 & 2 Corinthians*. Minneapolis: Fortress Press, 1993.

Hay, D. M. and E. E. Johnson (eds.). *Pauline Theology*, vol. 3: *Romans*. Minneapolis: Fortress Press, 1995.

Hays, R. B. "Crucified with Christ: A Synthesis of the Theology of 1 and 2 Thessalonians, Philemon, Philippians, and Galatians." Pp. 227–46 in *Pauline Theology, vol. 1: Thessalonians, Philippians, Galatians, Philemon.* Edited by J. M. Bassler. Minneapolis: Fortress Press, 1991.

Hays, R. B. "PISTIS and Pauline Christology: What is at Stake?" Pp. 35–60 in *Pauline Theology, vol. 4: Looking Back, Pressing On.* Edited by E. E. Johnson and D. M. Hay. Society for Biblical Literature Symposium Series, 4. Atlanta: Scholars Press, 1997.

Horsley, R. A. (ed.). *Paul and Empire: Religion and Power in Roman Imperial Society.* Harrisburg: Trinity Press International, 1997.

Horsley, R. A. (ed.). *Paul and Politics: Ekklesia, Israel, Imperium, Interpretation.* Harrisburg: Trinity Press International, 2000.

Hurd, J. C., Jr. *The Origin of 1 Corinthians.* Rev. edn. Macon: Mercer University Press, 1983.

Jewett, R. *A Chronology of Paul's Life.* Philadelphia: Fortress Press, 1979.

Johnson, E. E. and D. M. Hay (eds.). *Pauline Theology, vol. 4: Looking Back, Pressing On.* Society for Biblical Literature Symposium Series, 4. Atlanta: Scholars Press, 1997.

Kern, P. *Rhetoric and Galatians: Assessing an Approach to Paul's Epistle.* Society for New Testament Studies Monograph Series, 101. Cambridge: Cambridge University Press, 1998.

Kittredge, C. B. *Community and Authority: The Rhetoric of Obedience in the Pauline Tradition.* Harvard Theological Studies, 45. Harrisburg: Trinity Press International, 1998.

Knox, J. *Chapters in a Life of Paul.* Rev. edn. Macon: Mercer University Press, 1987. (Originally published 1950.)

Knox, J. "On the Pauline Chronology: Buck-Taylor-Hurd Revisited." Pp. 258–74 in *The Conversation Continues: Studies in Paul and John in Honor of J. Louis Martyn.* Edited by R. T. Fortna and B. R. Gaventa. Nashville: Abingdon Press, 1990.

Kraemer, R. S. and M. R. d'Angelo (eds.). *Women and Christian Origins.* Oxford: Oxford University Press, 1999.

Kraftchick, S. J. "Seeking a More Fluid Model: A Response to Jouette M. Bassler." Pp. 18–34 in *Pauline Theology, vol. 2: 1 & 2 Corinthians.* Edited by D. M. Hay. Minneapolis: Fortress Press, 1993.

Krentz, E. M. "Thessalonians, First and Second Epistles to the." Pp. 517–23 in *Anchor Bible Dictionary 6.* Edited by D. N. Freedman. New York: Doubleday, 1992.

Kwok, P. L. *Discovering the Bible in the Non-Biblical World.* The Bible and Liberation Series. Maryknoll: Orbis Books, 1995.

Lindemann, A. *Paulus im ältesten Christentum: Das Bild des Apostels und die Rezeption der paulinischen Theologie in der frühchristlichen Literatur bis Marcion.* Beiträge zur historischen Theologie, 58. Tübingen: J. C. B. Mohr (Paul Siebeck), 1979.

Longenecker, B. W. (ed.). *Narrative Dynamics in Paul: A Critical Assessment.* Louisville: Westminster John Knox Press, 2002.

Lovering, E. H, Jr. "The Collection, Redaction, and Early Circulation of the Corpus Paulinum." Ph.D. diss., Southern Methodist University, 1988.

Lüdemann, G. *Paul, Apostle to the Gentiles: Studies in Chronology.* Philadelphia: Fortress Press, 1984.

Malherbe, A. J. *The Letters to the Thessalonians.* Anchor Bible, 32B. New York: Doubleday, 2000.

Malina, B. L. *The New Testament World: Insights from Cultural Anthropology.* Atlanta: John Knox Press, 1981.

Martin, D. B. *Slavery as Salvation: The Metaphor of Slavery in Pauline Christianity.* New Haven: Yale University Press, 1990.

Martin, D. B. *The Corinthian Body.* New Haven: Yale University Press, 1995.

Martin, D. B. "Paul and the Judaism/Hellenism Dichotomy: Toward a Social History of the Question." Pp. 29–61 in *Paul Beyond the Judaism/Hellenism Divide*. Edited by T. Engberg-Pedersen. Louisville: Westminster John Knox Press, 2001.

Meade, D. G. *Pseudonymity and Canon: An Investigation into the Relationship of Authorship and Authority in Jewish and Earliest Christian Tradition*. Grand Rapids: William B. Eerdmans, 1987.

Meeks, W. A. *The First Urban Christians: The Social World of the Apostle Paul*. New Haven: Yale University Press, 1983.

Meeks, W. A. "Judaism, Hellenism, and the Birth of Christianity." Pp. 17–27 in *Paul Beyond the Judaism/Hellenism Divide*. Edited by T. Engberg-Pedersen. Louisville: Westminster John Knox Press, 2001.

Metzger, B. M. "Literary Forgeries and Canonical Pseudepigrapha." *Journal of Biblical Literature* 91 (1972), 3–24.

Meyer, P. W. "Pauline Theology: A Proposal for a Pause in its Pursuit." Pp. 140–60 in *Pauline Theology, vol. 4: Looking Back, Pressing On*. Edited by E. E. Johnson and D. M. Hay. Society for Biblical Literature Symposium Series, 4. Atlanta: Scholars Press, 1997.

Mitchell, M. M. *Paul and the Rhetoric of Reconciliation: An Exegetical Investigation of the Language and Composition of 1 Corinthians*. Louisville: Westminster John Knox, 1993.

Mitchell, M. M. "Pauline Accommodation and 'Condescension' (συγκατάβασισ): 1 Cor. 9:19–23 and the History of Influence." Pp. 197–214 in *Paul Beyond the Judaism/Hellenism Divide*. Edited by T. Engberg-Pedersen. Louisville: Westminster John Knox Press, 2001.

Moo, D. "*Paul and the Law in the Last Ten Years*." Scottish Journal of Theology 40 (1987), 287–307.

Moody, D. "A New Chronology for the Life and Letters of Paul." Pp. 223–40 in *Chronos, Kairos, Christos: Nativity and Chronological Studies Presented to Jack Finegan*. Edited by J. Vardaman and E. M. Yamauchi. Winona Lake: Eisenbrauns, 1989.

Moxnes, H. "*Social Integration and the Problem of Gender in St. Paul's Letters*." Studia Theologica 43 (1989), 99–113.

Moxnes, H. (ed.). *Constructing Early Christian Families: Family as Social Reality and Metaphor*. London: Routledge, 1997.

Newmann, K. J. *The Authenticity of the Pauline Epistles in the Light of Stylostatistical Analysis*. Society of Biblical Literature Dissertation Series, 120. Atlanta: Scholars Press, 1990.

Neyrey, J. H. "Body Language in 1 Corinthians: The Use of Anthropological Models for Understanding Paul and his Opponents." *Semeia* 35 (1986), 129–70.

Neyrey, J. H. *Paul, In Other Words: A Cultural Reading of his Letters*. Louisville: Westminster John Knox Press, 1990.

Osiek, C. and D. L. Balch. *Families in the New Testament World: Households and House Churches*. The Family, Religion, and Culture Series. Louisville: Westminster John Knox Press, 1997.

Perelman, C. and L. Olbrechts-Tyteca. *The New Rhetoric: A Treatise on Argumentation*. Notre Dame: University of Notre Dame Press, 1969.

Polaski, S. H. *Paul and the Discourse of Power*. The Biblical Seminar 62: Gender, Culture, Theory, 8. Sheffield: Sheffield Academic Press, 1999.

Räisänen, H. "Legalism and Salvation by the Law: Paul's Portrayal of the Jewish Religion as a Historical and Theological Problem." Pp. 25–54 in *The Torah and Christ: Essays in German and English on the Problem of the Law in Early Christianity*. Helsinki: Finnish Exegetical Society, 1986a.

Räisänen, H. *Paul and the Law*. Philadelphia: Fortress Press, 1986b.

Rensberger, D. K "As the Apostle Teaches: The Development of the Use of Paul's Letters in Second-Century Christianity." Ph.D. diss., Yale University, 1981.

Riddle, D. W. *Paul: Man of Conflict*. Nashville: Cokesbury, 1940.

Rist, M. "Pseudepigraphy and the Early Christians." Pp. 75–91 in *Studies in New Testament and Early Christian Literature: Essays in Honor of Allen P. Wikgren*. Edited by D. E. Aune. Supplements to *Novum Testamentum*, 33. Leiden: Brill, 1972.

Robbins, V. K. *The Tapestry of Early Christian Discourse: Rhetoric, Society and Ideology*. London: Routledge, 1996.

Roetzel, C. J. "The Grammar of Election in Four Pauline Letters." Pp. 211–33 in *Pauline Theology*, vol. 2: *1 & 2 Corinthians*. Edited by D. M. Hay. Minneapolis: Fortress Press, 1993.

Roetzel, C. J. *Paul: The Man and the Myth*. Studies on Personalities of the New Testament. Columbia: University of South Carolina Press, 1998.

Sanders, E. P. *Paul and Palestinian Judaism: A Comparison of Patterns of Religion*. Philadelphia: Fortress Press, 1977.

Sanders, E. P. *Paul, the Law, and the Jewish People*. Philadelphia: Fortress Press, 1983.

Sanders, E. P. "Paul." Pp. 112–29 in *Early Christian Thought in Its Jewish Context*. Edited by J. Barclay and J. Sweet. Cambridge: Cambridge University Press, 1996.

Schüssler Fiorenza, E. *In Memory of Her: A Feminist Theological Reconstruction of Christian Origins*. New York: Crossroad, 1983.

Schüssler Fiorenza, E. "Rhetorical Situation and Historical Reconstruction in 1 Corinthians." *New Testament Studies* 33 (1987), 386–403.

Schüssler Fiorenza, E. (ed.). *Searching the Scriptures*, vol. 2: *A Feminist Commentary*. New York: Crossroad, 1994.

Slingerland, D. "Acts 18:1–18, the Gallio Inscription, and Absolute Pauline Chronology." *Journal of Biblical Literature* 110 (1991), 439–49.

Stowers, S. K. *A Rereading of Romans: Justice, Jews, and Gentiles*. New Haven: Yale University Press, 1994.

Stowers, S. K. "Does Pauline Christianity Resemble a Hellenistic Philosophy?" Pp. 81–102 in *Paul Beyond the Judaism/Hellenism Divide*. Edited by T. Engberg-Pedersen. Louisville: Westminster John Knox Press, 2001.

Sugirtharajah, R. S. (ed.). *The Postcolonial Bible*. Sheffield: Sheffield Academic Press, 1998.

Treggiari, S. *Roman Marriage: Iusti Coniuges from the Time of Cicero to the Time of Ulpian*. Oxford: Clarendon Press, 1991.

Tronier, H. "The Corinthian Correspondence between Philosophical Idealism and Apocalypticism." Pp. 165–96 in *Paul Beyond the Judaism/Hellenism Divide*. Edited by T. Engberg-Pedersen. Louisville: Westminster John Knox Press, 2001.

Watson, F. *Paul, Judaism and the Gentiles: A Sociological Approach*. Society for New Testament Studies Monograph Series, 56. Cambridge: Cambridge University Press, 1986.

Weems, R. J. "Reading her Way through the Struggle: African American Women and the Bible." Pp. 57–77 in *Stony the Road We Trod: African American Biblical Interpretation*. Edited by C. H. Felder. Minneapolis: Fortress Press, 1991.

Westerholm, S. *Israel's Law and the Church's Faith: Paul and His Recent Interpreters*. Grand Rapids: William B. Eerdmans, 1988.

Whiteley, D. E. H. *The Theology of St. Paul*. Philadelphia: Fortress Press, 1966.

Wire, A. C. *The Corinthian Women Prophets: A Reconstruction through Paul's Rhetoric*. Minneapolis: Fortress Press, 1990.

Wright, N. T. "Putting Paul Together Again: Toward a Synthesis of Pauline Theology." Pp. 183–211 in *Pauline Theology*, vol. 1: *Thessalonians, Philippians, Galatians, Philemon*. Edited by J. M. Bassler. Minneapolis: Fortress Press, 1991.

Wuellner, W. "Paul's Rhetoric of Argumentation in Romans: An Alternative to the Donfried-Karris Debate over Romans." *Catholic Biblical Quarterly* 38 (1976), 330–51.

CHAPTER 22

# Paul's Letter to the Romans

Thomas H. Tobin, SJ

## Major Issues and Directions in Recent Study

Romans is Paul's longest and most complex letter. Romans has always attracted great interest from interpreters. Since the Reformation, Romans has served as a battle-ground between Roman Catholics and Lutherans, Calvinists, and other Protestant denominations. In recent years, however, a number of commentaries have appeared that have tried to move beyond the Reformation debates and take on a more ecumeni-cal viewpoint (e.g. Wilckens 1978; Dunn 1988; Fitzmyer 1993; Byrne 1996; Moo 1996; Keck 2005). In addition, the discussion has broadened to include important contributions from Jewish scholars (e.g. Segal 1990; Nanos 1996). At times these discussions have concentrated on the interpretation of Romans itself. At other times the discussion of Romans has been part of broader considerations of all of Paul's letters. Three other areas among many should also be highlighted. First, there has been a great deal of interest of the relationship of Romans to various aspects of the larger Greco-Roman world. This has especially involved the relationship of Romans to Greco-Roman rhetoric. The interest in this area has been at two levels. The first level is that of the letter taken as a whole. Various suggestions have been made at this level: a "testament," a letter essay, an epideictic speech or, more particularly, a protreptic discourse that exposes error and points to truth, an ambassadorial letter, a letter of self-recommendation, a letter of friendship, or a diatribe (Aune 1991: 287–8). The second has been at the level of particular passages in Romans. The argument at this level is the extent to which Paul does or does not make use of more limited rhetorical devices in smaller parts of Romans. More recently discussion has been extended also to include Paul's familiarity with other Greco-Roman literary and philosophical motifs and viewpoints, including some knowledge of Stoic philosophy (Engberg-Pedersen 2000: 179–292).

A second area of interest has been in trying to locate Romans in the particular situ-ation in which Paul wrote it (Esler 2003). This has involved the question of how much Paul and the Roman Christian community knew of each other, whether very little or a good deal, and the makeup of the Roman Christian community. The study of the latter has been greatly aided recently by Peter Lampe's *From Paul to Valentinus: Christians at Rome in the First Two Centuries* (2003).

A third area of interest has been the relationship of Paul's views in Romans to the Judaism of his time. From the work of E. P. Sanders (1977, 1992) and others, it has become clearer in recent years how complex a reality Judaism was in the first century CE. It has also become clear that, however one thinks of Paul's relationship to the issue of the continued observance of the Mosaic law by believers in Christ, Paul always saw himself as a believing Jew and participant in the traditions of Judaism. What remains in dispute is what that means more specifically. For example, did Paul think that observance of the Mosaic law as a whole was no longer required of believers in Christ? Or was it no longer required of Gentile believers but still required of Jewish believers? Or were only the dietary and purity regulations no longer required but the observance of the ethical commandments was still required? All of these issues are still very much disputed (see Dunn 2001).

## Date and Place of Writing

Paul wrote Romans from the city of Corinth. In 16:1–2 Paul writes a recommendation to the Roman Christians for Phoebe, a deaconess of the church in Cenchreae, the eastern port for Corinth. Phoebe was a prominent Christian in Cenchreae. In 16:2 Paul refers to her as a "patroness" of many in the community and of Paul himself. She was probably the one who brought Paul's letter to Rome. Paul also mentions that a certain Gaius, who was Paul's host and host of the whole church, sends greetings to the Roman Christians (Rom. 16:23). This Gaius is almost certainly the same Gaius whom Paul mentioned in 1 Corinthians 1:14 as one of the few Corinthian Christians whom he himself baptized. Another Christian Paul mentions in Romans 16:23 as sending greetings to Rome is Erastus, whom Paul describes as the "treasurer of the city." Like Gaius he was a prominent Corinthian Christian (see also Acts 19:22; 2 Tim 4:20). This evidence taken together makes it virtually certain that Paul wrote Romans from Corinth. There is more dispute, however, about the dating of the letter. The dispute ranges, however, only over a three-year period, from early 55 to early 58 CE and depends on how one reconstructs the chronology of Paul's journeys preceding this stay in Corinth. Dating Romans to the winter of 56/57 CE makes best sense of the chronology of Paul's journeys from the end of a previous stay in Corinth in the summer of 52 CE, his roughly three-year stay in Ephesus between the middle of 53 and the middle of 56 CE, his journey through Macedonia in the latter part of 56 CE to his arrival again in Corinth toward the end of 56 CE. On the basis of this chronology, Paul would have written Romans during his final three-month stay in Corinth during the winter of 56/57 CE.

## Language and Style

Paul wrote to the Roman Christians in Greek. Even in the first century, Greek was the predominant language of a considerable part of Rome's inhabitants and perhaps even the predominant language of Rome (Fitzmyer 1993: 89). It was certainly the language of both Roman Jews and Roman Christians. The Greek that Paul wrote in was known as Koine, that is the pan-Hellenic form of Greek that developed and became widespread in the course of the Hellenistic period. Paul's Greek shows he had a good Hellenistic education and was familiar with the language and style of the popular philosophers and rhetoricians of his day. Paul's Greek style is more that of an orator than of a writer. Paul dictated the letter orally (Rom. 16:22) and expected that the Roman Christians would hear the letter rather than read it. He makes extensive use especially of rhetorical techniques associated with the diatribe (see below). His Greek is also affected by the language of the Septuagint. This is reflected, for example, in placing the verb first in many sentences (Fitzmyer 1993: 90). Although Paul's Greek is inferior to that of the Gospel of Luke or the letter to the Hebrews, he often expresses himself with rhetorical power (for example, Rom. 8:31–9).

## Intertextuality

A characteristic of Romans is the extent to which it takes up themes and phrases from Paul's earlier letters (see the list in Fitzmyer 1993: 71–3). The importance of these references to earlier letters for Paul's arguments in Romans varies. The two most important letters for understanding Romans are Galatians and 1 Corinthians. In the course of Romans 1:16–11:36, Paul substantially revises several of the central positions he took in Galatians, especially the relationship of faith in Christ to the practice of the Mosaic law, the basis of Christian ethical behavior, and the future fate of the Jewish people as a whole. Paul's arguments in Romans often stand in significant contrast to those he made in Galatians. In Romans 12:1–15:7, Paul makes extensive use especially of 1 Corinthians 8–10, 12–14. But his use of 1 Corinthians is quite different from his use of Galatians. Here there is continuity rather than contrast. In Romans 12:1–15:7 Paul uses what he wrote in 1 Corinthians and applies it to analogous situations.

Paul also uses the Jewish scriptures in Romans to a much greater extent than he does in his other letters, and almost always in their Septuagint form. Paul quotes the Jewish scriptures about sixty times in Romans. In addition, the Jewish scriptures play a much more important role than they do in his other letters. The arguments Paul makes in substantial sections of Romans depend for their force on his interpretations of the Jewish scriptures (Rom. 2:1–3:20; 4:1–25; 7:1–25; 8:31–11:36).

## Unity of Romans

Although almost all scholars agree that Romans is a literary unity and not a composite of several letters or letter fragments, the textual tradition of Romans is complex. As early as the second century the text of Romans seems to have existed in several forms: (1) Romans 1–14; (2) Romans 1–15; (3) Romans 1–16. These three forms are reflected in the various places where the doxology of Romans 16:25–7 is found in different manuscripts. The fourteen-chapter version of Romans is clearly secondary and may reflect a shortened form circulated by Marcion or his followers in the second century.

Some have suggested that the fifteen-chapter and the sixteen- chapter versions go back to Paul himself. Paul sent the fifteen-chapter version to Rome and then added chapter 16 to the letter and sent it to Ephesus. The reason for this suggestion is that several names mentioned in the greetings in Romans 16:3–16 (Prisca and Aquila, Epaenetus, Andronicus and Junia) are associated with Ephesus. Harry Gamble (1977), however, has shown that Romans 1:1–16:24 is probably the earliest version of the text of Romans and the one Paul sent to Rome.

## Epistolary Analysis

Romans 1:1–15 and 15:14–16:24 clearly form the letter framework of Romans. Paul begins with an address and greeting to the Roman Christian community (1:1–7). This is followed by a thanksgiving (1:8–10). Both these elements, although expanded somewhat, were standard ways in which Paul began his letters. In Romans 1:11–15, Paul explains to the Roman Christians his longstanding desire to come to Rome. Since Paul had not founded the community and so had no authority over it, he first tries to gain an attentive and benevolent hearing from the community. In 15:14–16:24, Paul returns to the letter framework. He first takes up again the reasons why he has not previously traveled to Rome and why he now wants to come to Rome on his way to Spain (15:14–21). He has completed his work of preaching Christ to the Gentiles of the eastern Mediterranean and now wants to travel by way of Rome to Spain to preach the gospel there. He then goes on to explain his travel plans more specifically (15:22–33). In Romans 16 Paul concludes the letter with a recommendation for Phoebe who was bringing the letter to Rome, an elaborate list of greetings to various Roman Christians and the house churches to which they belong, and a concluding benediction. Although more elaborate than usual, Romans 16 basically follows the pattern Paul usually used to conclude his letters.

## Rhetorical Analysis

An analysis of the body of the letter (Rom. 1:16–15:13) is more complex. There is a consensus, however, on two points. First, Paul intended Romans 1:16–15:13 to be taken as a whole. This is because the beginning and the end of the body of the letter are framed by an inclusion. In 1:16–17 Paul states the basic proposition or thesis of 1:16–15:13 by claiming that the gospel is the power of God to everyone who has faith, to the Jew first and also the Greek (i.e., Gentiles). In 15:7–13 he restates this proposition about the centrality of Christ for both Jews and Gentiles and concludes the arguments he has made in the course of the letter. Second, Romans 12:1–15:7 forms a distinct *exhortatory* or *paraenetic* section of the letter. This section is similar to exhortatory sections found in several of Paul's other letters (1 Thess. 4:1–2; 5:12–22; Gal. 5:1–6:10; Phil. 1:17–2:18).

There are, however, significant differences in how interpreters understand the structure of Romans 1:16–11:36. Rather than seeing the structure of this section of the letter based on theological themes, it makes more sense to look for literary cues in

Romans which would have guided Paul's Roman Christian audience in understanding his arguments.

As one reads Romans 1:16–11:36, one cannot but be struck by differences in style between different sections of the text. Some sections read like expositions or explanations of a topic. Their tone is calm and not explicitly argumentative. Romans 1:18–32; 3:21–6; 5:1–21; and 8:1–30 are of this sort. Other sections of Romans, however, are quite argumentative or polemical in style. Romans 2:1–3:20, 3:27–4:25, 6:1–7:25, and 8:31–11:36 are of this sort. These sections are marked by rhetorical devices that create a much livelier, more engaged, and argumentative tone.

These devices include the frequent use of rhetorical questions, apostrophes (addresses to imaginary interlocutors) (2:1–11, 17–29; 9:20–9; 11:11–24); dialogues with imaginary interlocutors (3:1–10; 3:27–4:2); refutations of objections and false conclusions (3:1–9, 27–31; 4:1–2; 6:1–3, 15–16; 7:7, 13–14; 9:14–15, 19–20; 11:1, 19); speeches-in-character (7:7–25; 10:6–8); comparisons of various sorts (2:6–10, 12–16; 6:4–11, 6:15–23; 7:1–6; 8:5–17; 9:30–3; 11:17–24); and examples (4:1–25; 9:6–9, 10–15, 16–18). The style of these passages is also enlivened by the frequent use of phrases such as "What then?" (3:9; 6:15; 11:7); "What then shall we say?" (3:5; 4:1; 6:1; 7:7; 8:31; 9:14, 30); "Certainly not!" (3:4, 6, 31; 6:2, 15; 7:7, 13; 9:14, 30); and "O man!" (2:1, 3; 9:20). These literary devices and phrases are almost completely missing from Romans 1:18–32, 3:21–6, 5:1–21, and 8:1–30. These expository and argumentative passages in Romans are distinct from one another in two other important ways. First, with the exception of Romans 1:18–32, the three other expository sections have in common that they draw on and develop traditional cultic language and imagery about Christ's death as a sacrifice (3:24–5; 5:8–9; 8:3). Even Romans 1:18–32 is a fairly traditional and uncontroversial piece of Hellenistic Jewish critique of pagan religion. All four expository sections, then, have in common that they appeal to traditional viewpoints Paul and his Roman Christian audience have in common. Second, none of the expository sections ever quotes from the Jewish scriptures. The argumentative sections of the letter, however, are marked, for the most part, by Paul's extensive use of the Jewish scriptures. In addition, each of the more argumentative sections takes off from some aspect of the preceding expository section. In Romans 2:1 Paul begins by drawing a conclusion from Romans 1:18–32, "Therefore you have no excuse, whoever you are when you judge another." In Romans 3:27 he begins with "What then becomes of boasting?" referring back to Romans 3:21–6. In Romans 6:1 he begins with "What shall we say then?" referring back to what he wrote in Romans 5:1–21. Finally, in Romans 8:31 Paul begins with "What then shall we say to this?" referring back to Romans 8:1–30. Similarly, Romans 3:21–26, 5:1–21, and 8:1–30 (the second, third, and fourth expository sections) each moves beyond the previous argumentative section to a new stage in his argument. On the basis of this analysis, the structure of Romans 1:16–15:13 looks like this:

1:16–17 (Proposition)
(1)  1:18–3:20
    a.  1:18–32 (expository)
    b.  2:1–3:20 (argumentative)

(2)    3:21–5
    a.    3:21–6 (expository)
    b.    3:27–4:25 (argumentative)
(3)    5:1–7:25
    a.    5:1–21 (expository)
    b.    6:1–7:25 (argumentative)
(4)    8:1–11:36
    a.    8:1–30 (expository)
    b.    8:31–11:36 (argumentative)
(5)    12:1–15:7 (exhortatory/paraenetic)
5:8–13 (Conclusion)

## Constituent Literary Forms (Diatribe)

Romans 12:1–15:7 is clearly an exhortation. The genre of Romans 1:16–11:36, however is more complex. But establishing the genre of this section of Romans is important for the interpretation of Romans because it establishes the interpretive framework within which Paul wrote most of the letter and within which his Roman Christian audience would have heard it. The issue of genre is obviously complex, both today and in the Greco-Roman world. Genre is probably best understood, however, as sets of publicly shared conventions and expectations. Literary and rhetorical genres in the Greco-Roman world especially had to do with conventions and expectations. A genre was the fairly stable clustering of different conventions such that they formed a commonly recognized pattern. These patterns then informed the ways in which authors composed and readers and hearers understood these compositions.

Within this context Romans 1:16–11:36 is best understood as a diatribe. In modern English the word "diatribe" usually refers to bitter or abusive speech or writing. This modern use needs to be distinguished from the way the word was used in the Greco-Roman world. In Greek, the word "diatribe" had a range of meanings. It could mean "pastime" or "amusement," or in a negative sense "waste of time." It could also refer to study or even a school of philosophy. The range of meanings that interests us, however, is "classroom instruction" or "school discourse," usually of an ethical-religious nature. The classroom or school in question was the philosophical school rather than a primary or secondary school. Diatribes were discourses or instructions of a more popular sort in which there was a strong dialogical or "Socratic" component. They were not, however, actual dialogues. The purpose of diatribes was not simply to impart knowledge but to transform students, to point out error and to cure it (Stowers 1981: 76).

The discourses of Teles (fl. ca. 235 BCE), Musonius Rufus (ca. 30–100 CE), Musonius' pupil Epictetus (ca. 55–135 CE), and some of the discourses of Dio of Prusa (ca. 45–112 CE) and Plutarch of Chaeronea (before 50 CE to after 120 CE) are examples of diatribes. The most helpful author for understanding Romans as a diatribe is Epictetus. Most of his discourses have a good deal in common. These common elements establish the conventions and expectations that make the diatribe recognizable. These common elements are especially apparent in the rhetorical techniques Epictetus used. These techniques establish and maintain the lively, dialogical style of the diatribes. They include rhetorical questions with which Epictetus' diatribes are filled. They also include apostrophes (addresses to imaginary interlocutors) (Epictetus, *Discourses*, 1.6.23–8, 37–8, 40–3, 2.8.9–14, 3.24.75–7, 78–83),1 dialogues with imaginary interlocutors (e.g. *Discourses*, 1.6.3–7, 1.7.6–9, 2.22.7–12, 19–22, 3.22.26–44), objections and false conclusions (e.g. *Discourses*, 1.2.34–5, 1.6.30–2), speeches-in-character (e.g. *Discourses*, 1.4.28–9, 1.9.12–16, 1.26.5–7, 3.24.68–70, 97–102), comparisons (e.g. *Discourses*, 1.6.12–22, 23–4, 2.8.15–23; 2.11.2, 3.22.3–8, 14–18), and examples (e.g. *Discourses*, 1.2.2, 8–11, 12–18, 19–24, 25, 32, 1.6.32–6, 1.9.22–6, 2.22.57–8, 78–80, 90–2). Several phrases occur frequently which also contribute to the lively, dialogical flavor of the diatribes: "O man!"; "What then ...?"; and "Not at all!" Epictetus also frequently uses quotations, mostly from Homer, as authorities to support arguments he is making (*Discourses*, 1.12.3, 1.24.16, 2.1.13, 3.1.38–9, 4.4.34, 4.8.32).

Through the use of these devices Epictetus created lively exchanges between himself and imaginary interlocutors or addressees. In these exchanges, Epictetus was trying to point out some failing or misunderstanding on the part of these imaginary interlocutors or addressees. He was also trying to persuade them about how properly to live their lives in accord with nature. In neither case, however, was he directly addressing his actual audience. Rather he was addressing them only indirectly. Because Epictetus was not directly accusing his audience of the faults and failings he was talking about, the audience could more easily identify themselves with him in both what he was censuring and what he was advocating. Structurally most of Epictetus' diatribes began with a statement of the proposition, the position he was going to argue. After that, however, there was a good deal of fluidity to their structure. The extent to which he used the rhetorical devices varied. Sometimes a diatribe was made up almost entirely of them. But sometimes Epictetus' discourses also included expository passages. These passages usually functioned to clarify and support the other arguments he was making. They served as a less controversial explanation or foundation for the other arguments. Examples of diatribes which made use of such expository passages are *Discourses*, 1.2, 1.4, 1.6, 1.12–1.27, 2.1, 2.10, 2.11, 3.24. When one turns to Romans 1:16–11:36, there are obvious similarities. The most obvious is Paul's frequent use of many of the same rhetorical devices found in the diatribe. Romans 2:1–3:20, 3:27–4:25, 6:1–7:25, and 8:31–11:36 are all marked by the lively, argumentative, dialogical style of the diatribe. These devices include such things as rhetorical questions, apostrophes, dialogues with imaginary interlocutors, refutations of objections and false conclusions, speeches-in-character, comparisons of various sorts, and examples. This style is also enlivened by the frequent use of phrases such as "What then?" in Romans 3:9; 6:15; and 11:7; "What then shall we say?" in 3:5; 4:1; 6:1; 7:7; 8:31; and 9:14, 30; "Certainly not!" in 3:4, 6, 31; 6:2, 15; 7:7, 13; and 9:14, 30; and "O man!" in 2:1, 3 and 9:20. While Paul made use of some of these devices in his other letters, the variety and frequency of their use in Romans is much greater than in his other letters. As in Epictetus' diatribes, Paul's use of these devices in Romans creates the same kind of indirection that allows for his Roman audience to identify more easily with what he was both censuring and advocating.

But the similarities also go beyond the use of rhetorical devices in several significant ways. First, as was the case with almost all of the diatribes of Epictetus, Paul begins his arguments by stating his basic proposition (Rom. 1:16–17). In addition, Paul makes use of a number of quotations from the Jewish scriptures both as a basis of and as a support for his arguments in Romans 1:16–11:36. This is similar to, although not identical with, the citations of authority, especially of Homer, used by Epictetus in his discourses. In addition, like several of Epictetus' diatribes, Romans 1:16–11:36 alternates between expository passages and longer, more argumentative passages. Like the diatribes of Epictetus, these calmer, more expository passages in Romans are also much shorter than the longer and more argumentative ones. The expository sections in both Epictetus and Romans 1:16–11:36 serve similar functions by serving as the basis and the support of the other more argumentative sections. Taken together, the similarities between Romans 1:16–11:36 and some of Epictetus' discourses indicate that Paul's Roman audience would have understood this central section of Romans as a diatribe and that Paul himself was intentionally using the conventions of the diatribe as he wrote this section of the letter.

## Paul and the Roman Christian Community

To understand Romans one must understand the origins and viewpoints of the Roman Christian community. In the late 30s or early 40s of the first century, Jewish believers in Jesus from Jerusalem or Palestine came to Rome. There they won over to belief in Jesus as the Christ some Roman Jews as well as some sympathetic Gentiles associated with the Jewish community. All of this took place within the Roman Jewish community. By the end of the 40s, however, serious conflict developed within the community over belief in Jesus. This led to the expulsion of both Jewish and Gentile believers in Jesus from the Roman Jewish community. The number of these believers must have been large enough that the disturbances caused by their expulsion came to the attention of the Roman authorities. As a result, the emperor Claudius, in 49 CE, expelled from Rome at least some of those involved in these disturbances (Suetonius, *Claudius*, 25.4).

Obviously what distinguished Roman Christians from Roman Jews was the belief of the former in Jesus as the Christ. But in other significant ways, the beliefs and practices of both Jewish and Gentile members of the Roman Christian community remained in continuity with Roman Jewish beliefs and practices and they continued to see themselves as still connected with and as part of the Jewish way of life. This continuity was rooted first of all in Jewish monotheism, belief in one God and the rejection of all others. It also involved an emphasis on the superiority of the Mosaic law, specifically of its ethical aspects, over what they saw as the degrading ethical practices of the Greco-Roman world. This was especially the case in areas of sexual morality. For a minority of the community, it also involved continued observance of the Sabbath and, perhaps, other festivals, as well as the observance of some of the dietary laws. This aspect was a matter of controversy among the Roman Christians (Rom. 14:1–15:7). There was, however, no demand that male Gentile believers undergo circumcision, and there was no controversy over this. They would have found it difficult, even impossible, to understand how anyone could be a believer in Jesus without also accepting the continued observance of the ethical commandments of the Mosaic law. Any challenge to the sanctity of that law or to the observance of its ethical precepts would have appeared to them perverse. Paul and the Roman Christians certainly had a great deal in common. Both believed in Jewish monotheism, in Jesus as the messiah or Christ as the fulfillment of their Jewish hopes and expectations, in the authority of the Jewish scriptures, and in the equality of Jewish and Gentile members of the community. Neither believed that circumcision was now required to become full members of the community. But there were also significant differences. Rooted in his experience of the risen Lord, Paul was convinced of his call to preach the gospel to the Gentiles (Gal. 1:15–16) based on faith in Jesus as the Christ but without either circumcision or observance of the Mosaic law (Phil. 3: 4–11). Both Jewish and Gentile believers were to live their lives in love of neighbor guided by the Spirit in the practice of virtue (Gal. 5). These convictions embroiled Paul in controversies with the churches of Jerusalem, Antioch, and eventually with the Galatian community he himself had founded. The intensity of his controversy with the Galatians led Paul to so sharpen the contrasts between righteousness through faith and observance of the law so that it became difficult to see how the law or its observance could ever have been commanded by God (Gal. 3:1–14, 15–18). These same stark contrasts seemed even to exclude the Jewish people from ultimately receiving the inheritance promised to them by God in the scriptures (Gal. 3:26–4:11; 4:21–31).

The stark contrasts Paul drew must have seemed incomprehensible to most Roman Christians. His rejection of the value of observance of the Mosaic law must have seemed scandalous to them. His arguments in Galatians called into question not only the value of their observance of the law but also the value of the observance of the law by the Jewish people as a whole in the course of their history. His arguments even seemed to call into question the future of the Jewish people to which they were convinced they belonged. As the example of the Corinthian Christians showed, his views about how to live ethically through the guidance of the Spirit rather than by observance of the Mosaic law led predictably to confusion and disarray.

How was Paul going to deal with this situation? He not only risked losing their support for his mission to Spain; he also risked alienating himself and his communities from the important community in Rome in addition to the communities in Jerusalem and Antioch. Paul obviously needed and wanted to persuade the Roman Christians of the correctness of the gospel he preached. To do this he needed to persuade them that his gospel was indeed based on convictions they held in common and that it flowed from those same common convictions.

But he also needed to do this with integrity and without compromising his own basic convictions. It was not as simple as trying to convince the Roman Christians of the correctness of the views for which he had become so controversial. His own views were also changing. No doubt this was partly due to how these views were understood or, as he thought, misunderstood by the Roman Christians. But to a significant degree it was also due to the ways Paul himself was coming to rethink and revise significantly many of the earlier, polemical views he so forcefully argued in Galatians. Yet Paul is not simply defending his previous convictions in a less controversial manner. He is sorting out what these basic convictions really are, discarding some, revising others, and recasting all of them within a different framework.

## Issues and Arguments in Romans

The best way to get a sense of how Paul dealt with the issues at the heart of the Roman Christians' misgivings about him and his gospel is to look at the four major stages in his argument (Rom. 1:18–3:20; 3:21–4:25; 5:1–7:25; 8:1–11:3 6) (Tobin 2004). In each stage, Paul begins by appealing to beliefs or convictions he and the Roman Christians have in common. He then develops those beliefs or convictions in such a way as to support some central aspect of his gospel. Finally, he tries to show how the controversial aspects of his gospel should be acceptable to them and should not raise misgivings for them either about him or about his gospel. For the most part, he supports the controversial aspects of his gospel by appealing to the Jewish scriptures to show how the gospel he preaches is in continuity with the scriptures and with Jewish tradition. Finally, we also need to turn to the function of his exhortation in Romans 12:1–15:7.

In Romans 1:18–3:20, Paul argues for the equal sinfulness of Jews and Gentiles. He begins with the claim that the wrath of God is being revealed against *all* ungodliness and wickedness. Since God's invisible nature can be perceived from creation, human beings are without excuse for not recognizing God (Rom. 1:18–20). He then moves on to a quite conventional Hellenistic Jewish critique of Gentile religion and morality (Rom. 1:21–32). Both his initial claim and his subsequent critique would have found ready acceptance with the Roman Christians. Only in Romans 2:1–3:20 does Paul then argue more controversially that Jews as a group are as sinful as Gentiles. Paul seems well aware of how offensive this claim would have been to the Roman Christians. How could someone like Paul place Jews on the same level as Gentiles? If it were true, what good is either being a Jew or circumcision? For the Roman Christians the very value of the whole Jewish tradition would have been at issue. Because of this Paul argues his case first on the basis of a scriptural principle, God's impartiality (Rom. 2:1–11), and second on the basis of the Jewish scriptures (Rom. 3:10–18). More importantly, he goes out of his way to reaffirm the value both of circumcision and of being a Jew (Rom. 2:25–3:8). Circumcision is of value if one obeys the law. And Jews have been privileged because they have been entrusted with God's scriptures. He hoped that these traditional Jewish arguments would appeal to the Roman Christians and convince them that his views about the equal sinfulness of Jews and Gentiles were indeed rooted in Jewish tradition itself. In comparison to Galatians, Paul also fundamentally alters how he now frames the issue. He refers to Psalm 143:2 ("For no one will be made righteous before him") both in Romans 3:20 and earlier in Galatians 2:16. In Galatians 2:16 Paul's point was that it was *impossible* for anyone, whether Jew or Gentile, to be made righteous through observance of the law. His use of it at the end of Romans 2:1–3:20, however, serves a quite different purpose. No one is made righteous by God by observance of the law because Jews as a group are as sinful as Gentiles as a group, because scripture shows that, in the course of their history, they *in fact* have not observed the law (Rom. 3:10–18). In Romans 3:21–4:25 Paul moves to the next stage of his argument. He begins in Romans 3:21 by claiming that "now the righteousness of God has been manifested apart from the law, although the law and the prophets bear witness to it." In Romans 3:22–6 Paul draws on a traditional creedal formula he has in common with the Roman Christians. He then comments on it to show that this righteousness, which comes through the death of Christ, is now received through faith, and is for both Jews and Gentiles without distinction. In Romans 3:27–4:25, he then argues that, although this righteousness is both apart from the law and intended for both Jews and Gentiles alike, this does not annul the law. Rather, it upholds the law. In support of this, he uses the paradigm of Abraham. He argues on the basis of Genesis 12:3; 15:5–6; 17:5, 10–11; and 18:18 that as a group, Gentiles are sinful because of their foolish religious beliefs and depraved moral practices. Jews are sinful because in fact they have not observed the law. Abraham was made righteous by his faith in God and not by his observance of the law. In addition, through the promises made to him because of his faith, Abraham is the father of both Jews and Gentiles. The issues at stake in Romans 3:21–4:25 become clear when set against the backdrop of Paul's earlier arguments in Galatians. In Galatians, Paul starkly contrasted righteousness through faith with observance of the law. The contrast seemed to be a matter of principle. But in Romans 3:21–6 Paul does not contrast righteousness through faith with the law. Rather, righteousness takes place "apart from the Law." In addition, the contrast Paul does draw is not one in principle but a temporal one. The righteousness of God is *now* being manifested apart from the law. Paul clearly uses Abraham very differently from how he used him in Galatians. In Galatians 3:6–14 the promises to Abraham seemed to be intended for the Gentiles but not really for the Jews. These promises seemed to bypass the Jewish people and come directly to Christ (Gal. 3:15–18). In Romans 4:1–25, however, Paul emphasizes the role of Abraham as the father of both Jews and Gentiles. Paul's very different view of Abraham is shown most starkly in his radically different use of the phrase "and to your seed" from Genesis 12:7. In Galatians 3:16 Paul interpreted "seed" as a singular noun referring specifically to Christ and not to the Jewish people. In Romans 4:13–17, however, he interprets "seed" as a collective noun that includes both Jews and Gentiles. In Romans 5:1–7:25 Paul is primarily concerned with issues of how believers are to live their lives once they have been made righteous by faith. In Romans 5:1–21 Paul explains how righteousness through faith, apart from the law and its observance, is incompatible with sin. He does this first by appealing to the conviction he and the Roman Christians share that Christ's death was meant to reconcile sinners to God (Rom. 5:6–11). He then uses a comparison and contrast between Adam and Christ to show how sin is incompatible with the grace in which believers, both Jews and Gentiles alike, now stand (Rom. 5:12–21). In Romans 6:1–7:25 Paul significantly revises some of his earlier controversial views on ethics. The first part (Rom. 6:1–23) is based on a reinterpretation of baptism and its consequences. In baptism, by dying with Christ, believers also die to sin in order to live to God in Christ Jesus (6:1–14). Thus freed from sin they are now slaves to God through righteousness (6:15–23). In the second part (Rom. 7:1–25) Paul defends the holiness of the law itself and contrasts it with the weakness of human beings. He appeals especially in a speech-in-character to the difficulties he thought the Gentile Roman Christians experienced in their attempt to observe the ethical commandments of the law (Rom. 7:7–25).

In Romans 5–7, Paul struggles with two issues which troubled his relationship with the Roman Christians. The first is their deep misgivings about his view of ethics, expressed in Galatians 5:1–6:10, as freedom from the law and the practice of virtue guided by the Spirit. In Romans 6, Paul significantly revises his rhetoric about ethics. He emphasizes not freedom from the law but freedom from sin. In addition, he emphasizes for the first time that baptism is a dying with Christ to sin. The second issue is the Roman Christians' deep misgivings about Paul's earlier denigration of the value of the law. Romans 7 is the point at which Paul deals in detail with this vexing issue. It is the first time in any of his letters that he writes of the holiness of the law. On both issues Paul seems very aware that these problems were to a great extent of his own making and were largely caused by his own intemperate rhetoric in Galatians.

The final stage of Paul's argument (Rom. 8:1–11:36) is by far the longest and most complicated. It is concerned primarily with issues of eschatology. The first part (Rom. 8:1–30) is an explanation of the role of the Spirit in believers' lives. By walking according to the Spirit rather than according to the flesh, believers become sons of God and heirs destined for glory (Rom. 8:1–17). The Spirit also serves as the basis for an inclusive, universalizing eschatology (Rom. 8:18–30). The second and more argumentative part (Rom. 8:31–11:36) is an anguished series of arguments about the ultimate incorporation of the Jewish people in the mysterious plan of God. Paul develops these reflections in three stages. First, he reflects on God's original choice of Israel and God's extension of it the Gentiles (Rom. 9:6–29). He then deals with the present situation of Israel's unbelief in relation to Gentiles' belief (Rom. 9:30–10:21). Finally, he deals with the mystery of God's future plan in which there will be final salvation for both Israel and the Gentiles alike (Rom. 11:1–36).

This section is clearly the climax of Paul's argument. It also reflects the personal anguish that this issue came to cause Paul. On the one hand, he would not and could not give up his basic conviction that in Christ salvation was offered equally to Gentiles as well as to Jews. On the other hand, he realized that, even though most of his fellow Jews had not come to have faith in Christ, God's promises to Israel still could not fail. He also realized that some of his own rhetoric in Galatians (especially in 3:26–4:11 and 4:21–31) seemed to cast doubt on the trustworthiness of these promises. Above all, Paul struggles with the truth of the Roman Christians' accusation that, in his intense polemic in Galatians, he seemed really to exclude Jews from the inheritance promised to them by God in the scriptures.

This overview reveals some of the central issues that lay just below the surface of the letter. These issues can be grouped into three distinct but related clusters. The first issue clusters around the status and the value of the Mosaic law and its observance. Paul's views that believers are no longer obliged to obey the Mosaic law seem to devalue its observance even in the past. The second issue clusters around how believers are to live their lives in an ethical fashion. What are the consequences of no longer being obliged to observe the law? Can the consequences be anything but disastrous? The last issue clusters around the status of the Jewish people, Israel, and its relationship to the Gentiles. Do not Paul's views place Jews and Gentiles on the same level? Do they not lead to a devaluation of the Jewish people, its history, and even God's promises to Israel? Do they not consistently seem even to exclude the Jewish people from those promises?

Paul's responses to these issues were equally complex. In the light of objections from the Roman Christians to his earlier controversial views, Paul radically revised and even reversed some of the central arguments he made in Galatians. At the same time, however, there is also continuity in his basic convictions. He was still convinced and tried to convince the Roman Christians that, in Christ, righteousness is through faith apart from the observance of the Mosaic law and is meant equally for both Jews and Gentiles. These convictions were so rooted in his own experience that he would not and could not change them. His confrontation with the Roman Christians over these issues, however, forced him to rethink and sort out what his basic convictions really were and, perhaps as importantly, what they were not. This confrontation also forced him to reconsider whether, in the intensely polemical atmosphere of his controversy with the Galatians, he had in fact lost sight of some of his other basic convictions. More specifically, had he lost sight of the importance of the Jewish people and of God's promises to them?

This confrontation also led Paul to reconsider the framework within which he formulated his views. The interpretive framework of Romans differs radically from the framework of Galatians. While Galatians is dominated by stark contrasts that seem to allow of no resolution, Paul's interpretive framework in Romans is temporal and historical. The four major stages of his argument in Romans 1:16–11:36 are arranged in a temporal sequence. Paul begins with the equally sinful situation of Jews and Gentiles prior to the manifestation of God's righteousness and mercy in Christ (Rom. 1:18–3:20), then deals with that manifestation itself (Rom. 3:21–4:25) and its consequences (Rom. 5:1–7:25), and concludes with the salvation of both Jews and Gentiles together (Rom. 8:1–11:36). Paul also sets his struggle to understand the situation of his fellow Jews in Romans 9–11 within a temporal framework: past (9:6–29), present (9:30–10:21), and future (11:1–36).

Romans 12:1–15:7, the last part of the body of the letter, is an exhortation. The Roman Christians have already heard about what they thought were Paul's ethical perspectives and have been deeply suspicious of them. Paul tried to deal with some of these basic suspicions in Romans 5–7. But he was primarily concerned there with broad ethical dispositions. In 12:1–15:7, he turns more explicitly and specifically to ethical practice. The exhortation falls into two major parts. The first, 12:1–13:14, emphasizes the values of love, unity, and harmony both inside and outside the community. Paul draws heavily on Jewish wisdom instructions (12:1–21) and early Christian baptismal imagery (3:11–14). In the second part of the exhortation (14:1–15:7), Paul is concerned about resolving tensions between the "strong" and the "weak" members of the Roman Christian community. The tensions are primarily over the insistence by some members of the Roman Christian community (the "weak") on the observance of Jewish dietary laws (14:2–3, 6, 14–17, 20–1, 23) at community gatherings. Drawing on what he wrote in 1 Corinthians 8–10, Paul exhorts the "strong," who see no reason to observe the Jewish dietary regulations, to cede to the wishes of the "weak" for the sake of the unity and wellbeing of the community as a whole. The two parts of the exhortation are inseparable. The first part serves as the basis for the resolution of the tensions between the strong and the weak in the second part. Conversely, the second part shows how Paul is concretely the advocate of the values of love and harmony he emphasized in the first part.

It is not simply the contents of his ethical exhortation, however, that are important for Paul. Equally important is the portrait he presents of himself in Romans 12:1–15:7. In ancient rhetorical terms, Paul is concerned not simply about the arguments themselves (the *logos*) but also about the character (the *ethos*) of the person presenting them. For the Roman Christians, Paul does not simply hold controversial ethical views. He himself is controversial and a cause of division. For this reason, his ethical exhortation in Romans 12:1–15:7 is no less about who he is and what his character is than it is about what he is exhorting the Roman Christians to. One of Paul's goals in Romans 12:1–15:7 is to show how he is not the sower of dissension and division but an advocate of love, harmony, accommodation, and the common good of the whole community.

## Note

1    The lectures given by Epictetus were preserved in notes taken by his student Arrian of Nicomedia. These notes have been given the Latin title *Epicteti Dissertationes ab Arrianus digestae*, but the work is frequently referred to as Epictetus, *Dissertationes* or "Dissertations."

## Annotated Bibliography

Aune, David E. "Romans as a *Logos Protreptikos*." Pp. 278–96 in *The Romans Debate: Revised and Expanded Edition*. Edited by Karl P. Donfried. Peabody, MA: Hendrickson, 1991. A valuable essay on the rhetorical genre of Romans as a protreptic discourse.

Byrne, Brendan. *Romans*. Sacra Pagina, 6. Collegeville, MN: Liturgical Press, 1996. An insightful and accessible commentary on Romans.

Dunn, James D. G. *Romans*. 2 vols. Word Bible Commentaries. Dallas: Word, 1988. A fine, detailed commentary on Romans by a leading interpreter of Paul.

Dunn, James D. G. (ed.). *Paul and the Mosaic Law*. Grand Rapids, MI: Eerdmans, 2001. An important collection of essays on the various issues connected with the relationship of Paul to the observance of the Mosaic law.

Engberg-Pedersen, Troels. *Paul and the Stoics*. Louisville, KY: Westminster John Knox, 2000. A study of the relationship of Paul and his letters to the ethics of Stoic philosophy.

Esler, Philip F. *Conflict and Identity in Romans: The Social Setting of Paul's Letter*. Minneapolis: Augsburg Fortress, 2003. A fine commentary on Romans from a social-scientific perspective.

Fitzmyer, Joseph A. *Romans: A New Translation with Introduction and Commentary*. Anchor Bible 33. New York: Doubleday, 1993. A first-rate commentary on Romans. Especially helpful for its detailed references to other ancient literature.

Gamble, Harry Y. *A Textual History of the Letter to the Romans: A Study in Textual and Liberary Criticism*. Studies and Documents, 42. Grand Rapids, MI: Eerdmans, 1977. The most important study on the complicated issue of the Greek text of Romans.

Gaston, Lloyd. *Paul and the Torah*. Vancouver: University of British Columbia Press, 1987. A collection of the author's essays in which he argues that the inclusion of Gentiles does not mean the displacement of Israel or its law.

Hays, Richard B. *The Faith of Jesus Christ*. Society of Biblical Literature Dissertation Series 56. Chico, CA: Scholars Press, 1983. The most important study to argue for the interpretation of the Greek phrase *pistis Iesou Christou* as a subjective genitive ("the faith of Jesus Christ").

Keck, Leander E. *Romans*. Abingdon New Testament Commentaries. Nashville: Abingdon, 2005. A very good compact, critical commentary on Romans by a first-rate scholar on Paul.

Lampe, Peter. *From Paul to Valentinus: Christians at Rome in the First Two Centuries*. Minneapolis: Fortress, 2003. A monumental study of the evidence for Christianity in Rome in the first two centuries.

Moo, Douglas J. *The Epistle to the Romans*. New International Commentary on the New Testament. Grand Rapids, MI: Eerdmans, 1996. A fine commentary on Romans from an evangelical perspective.

Nanos, Mark D. *The Mystery of Romans: The Jewish Context of Paul's Letter*. Minneapolis: Fortress Press, 1996. An important study of Romans by a Jewish scholar who argues for the continued participation of Roman Christians in the Roman Jewish community.

Porter, Stanley E. "Paul of Tarsus and his Letters." Pp. 533–85 in *Handbook of Classical Rhetoric in the Hellenistic Period (330 BC–AD 400)*. Edited by Stanley E. Porter. Leiden: Brill, 1997. An important article that takes a critical view of claims that Paul made extensive use in Romans of ancient rhetoric.

Sanders, E. P. *Paul and Palestinian Judaism: A Comparison of Patterns of Religion*. Philadelphia: Fortress Press, 1977.

Sanders, E. P. *Judaism: Practice and Belief 63 BCE–66 CE*. Philadelphia: Trinity International, 1992.

Segal, Alan. *Paul the Convert: The Apostolate and Apostasy of Saul the Pharisee*. New Haven: Yale University Press, 1990. An important study of Paul by a Jewish scholar that tries to sort out the complex relationship of Paul to Judaism.

Stendahl, Krister. *Paul Among Jews and Gentiles*. Philadelphia: Fortress Press, 1976. A groundbreaking collection of essays on Paul that set the agenda for a good deal of subsequent scholarship on Paul.

Stowers, Stanley K. *The Diatribe and Paul's Letter to the Romans*. Society of Biblical Literature Dissertation Series 57. Chico, CA: Scholars Press, 1981. An important rhetorical study of Paul's use of the Greco-Roman diatribe.

Stowers, Stanley K. *A Rereading of Romans: Justice, Jews, and Gentiles*. New Haven: Yale University Press, 1994. An interpretation of Romans that emphasizes Paul's attempts to clarify for Gentile followers of Jesus their proper relation to the Mosaic law, Jews, and Judaism.

Tobin, Thomas H. *Paul's Rhetoric in its Contexts: The Argument of Romans*. Peabody, MA: Hendrickson, 2004. This book concentrates on Paul's arguments in Romans and sets them in their historical and rhetorical contexts in order to move beyond the theological debates rooted in the Reformation.

Wilckens, Ulrich. *Der Brief and die Romer*. 3 vols. Evangelisch-katholischer Kommentar zum Neuen Testament. Zurich: Benziger; Neukirchen-Vluyn: Neukirchener Verlag, 1978–92. Probably the best recent commentary on Romans in German.

# CHAPTER 23

# 1 Corinthians

## John Fotopoulos

## Major Issues in Recent Study

The recent publications on 1 Corinthians are quite numerous, making mastery of the material by any one scholar extremely difficult. Nevertheless, several major issues and directions present themselves in the letter's recent study. A central matter is the scholarly debate over the existence of factions in the Corinthian church. Some scholars hold that there were no factions in the Corinthian church, but rather that there was one unified body in conflict with Paul over various issues addressed in the letter (Hurd 1983; Fee 1987: 4–6). These scholars tend to see Paul's influence over the group slipping away as he attempts to reassert his apostolic authority to a unified church regarding various issues. Other scholars, taking cues from 1 Corinthians 1:12, have argued that there were two or more factions in the Corinthian church which held allegiance to particular leaders such as Paul, Apollos, Cephas, or Christ. In this respect, Mitchell's work has significantly influenced the question of actual divisions in the Corinthian assembly by examining the composition of 1 Corinthians using literary rhetorical analysis based on the rhetoric of Greco-Roman compositions (Mitchell 1991). By comparing the argumentation, vocabulary, style, and stock literary devices of Greco-Roman rhetorical speeches and handbooks with those of 1 Corinthians, Mitchell has convincingly demonstrated that 1 Corinthians is an example of deliberative rhetoric (rhetoric persuading or dissuading a future course of action) in which Paul attempts to persuade a factious community divided over numerous issues to unite in love. From 1 Corinthians 1:12, the impression is given that there were four factions in the Corinthian church centered around Paul, Apollos, Cephas, and Christ. However, 3:1–9 and 4:6 almost certainly give a more accurate picture of Corinthian factionalism, many scholars thus asserting that there were only two factions in the Corinthian assembly, one loyal to Paul and one loyal to Apollos. Consequently, the statements of 1:12 are generally interpreted as an example of *prosopopoiia* (impersonation) whereby Paul engages in an exaggerated caricature of the Corinthians' factional mindset (Mitchell 1991: 86). A related issue is the role of Apollos in the origin of the Corinthian Christian factions. Apollos was a missionary co-worker of Paul who visited Corinth some time after Paul's departure from the city in order to conduct ministry there (1 Cor. 3–4; Acts 18:18–19:1). Acts 18:24 reports that Apollos was an *aner logios*, a description which probably means that he was an eloquent orator or rhetorician. Paul indicates in 1 Corinthians 3:6 that Apollos did indeed continue Paul's apostolic work in Corinth, but it seems that Apollos used a different method of evangelization. In 1 Corinthians 2:1, Paul states that he consciously used an anti-sophistic evangelical strategy in Corinth, that is, he ministered to the Corinthians without the ornamental use of epideictic rhetoric which was extremely popular in the Greco-Roman world (see below). Apollos, however, seems to have used an epideictic evangelical strategy, much to the liking of the socially conscious, higher-status Corinthian Christians, but not to that of those lower-status members of the church loyal to Paul. Thus, Apollos' work and method of evangelization in Corinth is a likely cause of the Corinthian Christian divisions and the issues addressed in 1 Corinthians. It is interesting to note that the Corinthian Christian divisions associated with loyalties to different teachers (3:21; 4:6) mirror divisions commonly associated with followers loyal to various ancient Sophists of the Greco-Roman world (Pogoloff 1992). Despite the difficulties caused by the ministry of Apollos, Paul conveys that he and Apollos are God's fellow workers having no dispute (1 Cor. 3:8–9). Paul also states that he has urged Apollos to return to Corinth (1 Cor. 16:12), something which Apollos was not currently willing to do. The urging of Apollos' return to Corinth was probably to assist in correcting the situation that began with Apollos' ministry in the city.

Whether or not scholars believe that there were divisions in the Corinthian church, or whether or not Apollos played a causal role in the Corinthian problems, there are certainly numerous issues addressed in 1 Corinthians which must have some ideological, theological, or philosophical foundation. Thus, even if scholars do not identify the issues addressed in 1 Corinthians with a particular leader, attempts are still made to identify the sources which helped generate the Corinthian issues. Such range from the Corinthian Christians' interests in pagan social values (Witherington 1985; Martin 1995; Thiselton 2000), Gnosticism (Schmithals 1971), proto-Gnosticism (Conzelmann 1975), Hellenistic Judaism (Horsley 1978a, 1978b), an overly realized Christian eschatology (Fee 1987), the entrance of outside Judaizing agitators into the community loyal to Cephas (Baur 1831; Barrett 1963; Goulder 1998), or some combination thereof. Issues related to pagan social values (formal meals in pagan sanctuaries; the purchase of sacrificial food at the market; the desire for higher social status by boasting; the popular desire for rhetorical/oracular prowess; head-covering in worship; law suits; sexual relations) seem to be the primary source of the themes addressed in the letter, although many of these issues are also fueled by the overly realized eschatology of the Corinthian Christians (Thiselton 2000: 40). Such an overly realized eschatology gave the Corinthians an avenue to increased social status within their Christian subculture by providing them with valued spiritual gifts such as charismatic speech while it also allowed them to participate in the wider social relations of Roman Corinth without negative spiritual consequences.

Another important scholarly issue in the letter's interpretation is the historical occasion(s) of 1 Corinthians. What was the source or sources of Paul's information about the situation in Corinth? According to 1 Corinthians 7:1, the Corinthians had written a letter to Paul which addressed at least some of the issues present in 1 Corinthians.

Scholars are in general agreement that the Corinthians' letter to Paul asserted their positions on numerous disputed issues (Hurd 1983) and did not simply contain friendly questions seeking the counsel of the apostle. In addition to the written information available to him from the Corinthians' letter, this was probably supplemented by information conveyed by the apparent carriers of the Corinthians' letter, Stephanas, Fortunatus, and Achaicus (16:17–18). Paul also certainly had oral information about the situation in Corinth from "Chloe's people" regarding factions in the Corinthian church (1:11). Some scholars have argued that 1 Corinthians 1–4 contains material that Paul had learned of from the oral communication given by Chloe's people, while 1 Corinthians 5–16 contains material conveyed by the Stephanas delegation orally (5–6) and by letter (7–16) (de Boer 1994). There are also various issues addressed in 1 Corinthians 7:1 ff. which begin with the formula *peri de* ("and concerning"), a formula which has been used by scholars to identify the subjects that were raised in the Corinthians' letter to Paul (Hurd 1983: 61–74). However, Mitchell has shown that the use of *peri de* in Greek literature simply serves as a topic marker introducing a subject that is readily known to the author and the audience (Mitchell 1989: 234). *Peri de* does not indicate the source of the subject matter that Paul is addressing. Therefore, Mitchell has concluded that Paul's use of the *peri de* formula may or may not indicate subjects raised by the Corinthians' letter. Paul may also have become aware of some of these subjects through oral communication. Thus, although *peri de* does not reveal the sources of information about the Corinthian church that Paul addresses, *peri de does* indicate that these are subjects with which both the Corinthians and Paul were familiar "from some element of their shared experience" (Mitchell 1989: 256). Consequently, the historical occasions of 1 Corinthians are the Corinthians' letter to Paul as well as oral information that he had obtained from several sources. However, there is no simple way to identify the precise occasions or sources of the individual subjects in 1 Corinthians as they are treated by Paul since he freely arranged his letter as a cohesive argument without matching various sections of the epistle to the written and oral sources of information available to him.

## Date and Place of Composition

1 Corinthians was composed in Greek by Paul (and Sosthenes cf. 1:1, possibly Paul's scribe since Paul communicates largely in the first person singular) from the city of Ephesus (1 Cor. 16:8). Paul informs the Corinthians of his future travel plans at the end of the letter and mentions that he will stay in Ephesus until the Jewish festival of Pentecost because of the opportunities for fruitful missionary work that have arisen there. His reference to Pentecost leads scholars to believe that the letter was written in the spring, but Paul may simply be looking forward to future plans that are several months away. The date of 1 Corinthians' composition is more complex. Acts 18:12–17 reports that when Paul was in Corinth he was brought to a hearing at the tribunal (*bema*) of Gallio, who was the proconsul of Achaia. An essential piece of evidence which allows a suggested date for this event and for the letter's composition is the so-called Gallio inscription, more precisely described as the Delphi inscription containing the epistle of Claudius mentioning the proconsul L. Junius Gallio (Plassart 1967: 372–8; Oliver 1971: 239–40). The Gallio

inscription, along with a letter of Seneca the brother of Gallio which communicates that the proconsul did not serve his full term of office but abandoned his post because of a phony fever brought on by his dislike of Achaia (Seneca, *Moral Epistles*, 104.1) enable scholars to narrow the date of Gallio's proconsulship from July of 50 CE to June of 51 CE, or from July of 51 CE to June of 52 CE, with the latter date being more probable (Murphy-O'Connor 1983: 154–8; Lüdemann 1984: 163–4). Acts 18:11 states that while in Corinth Paul stayed there for eighteen months. This suggests a probable chronology for Paul's first visit to the city during 51–2 CE. However, although probable, this suggestion is not certain since it might be assumed that Paul had been somewhat active in the city before coming to the attention of Gallio. Nevertheless, a date earlier than 49 CE for Paul's arrival in Corinth seems untenable since Acts 18:2–3 reports that Aquila and Prisca (cf. 1 Cor. 16:19; Rom. 16:3) went to Corinth after Claudius' expulsion of the Jews from Rome (ca. 49 CE), after which time Paul reached the city. Moreover, the date of composition of 1 Corinthians depends on the historicity and duration of Paul's subsequent travels after his departure from Corinth to Ephesus, Caesarea, Jerusalem, Galatia, Phrygia, and return to Ephesus as recorded in Acts 18:18–19:1. During this period of Paul's travels Acts 18:24–19:1 reports that Apollos went to Corinth to minister to the Christians there. This event seems to have generated some of the issues addressed in 1 Corinthians and was clearly written after Apollos' return to Paul in Ephesus (16:12).

A final matter necessary to consider for the date of 1 Corinthians' composition is that the letter referred to as 1 Corinthians was not the first letter that Paul had written to the Corinthian church. In 1 Corinthians 5:9 Paul refers to a previous letter that he had written to the Corinthians (commonly designated as Corinthians A) which required further clarification. Paul's previous letter had given the Corinthians instructions prohibiting social relations with those who were sexually immoral, among other matters (Hurd 1983). The Corinthians had misinterpreted Paul's instructions as prohibiting social relations with pagans, something which they articulated in a reply letter to Paul (cf. 1 Cor. 7:1). Paul subsequently clarified the instructions of his previous letter in 1 Corinthians 5:9–13 by clearly prohibiting social relations with certain types of immoral Christians, but allowing continued social relations with pagans. Therefore, the date of 1 Corinthians' composition must consider Paul's travels after his departure from Corinth in 52 CE, his fruitful work in Ephesus, Apollos' visit to Corinth, departure, and meeting with Paul, Corinthians A, the Corinthians' reply letter to Paul, and oral reports about the Corinthian church which reached Paul through Stephanas, Fortunatus, and Achaicus (16:17–18) and Chloe's people (1 Cor. 1:11). Thus, scholars date 1 Corinthians from 53 CE to as late as 57 CE, with most opting for dates of 54, 55, or 56 CE (Barrett 1968: 5; Conzelmann 1975: 4–13; Fee 1987: 15; Schrage 1991–2001: I, 36; Witherington 1995: 73; Collins 1999: 24; Thiselton 2000: 32; Lindemann 2000: 17; Aune 2003: 113).

## Historical and Archaeological Setting

In the first century of the Common Era, Corinth was becoming one of the most prominent cities in the Roman empire. Corinth's commercial, imperial, athletic, and social importance had far surpassed that of Athens, the latter having become a tired academic city surviving on the reputation of its past glory. Corinth, however, was a bustling and competitive Roman colony that had been refounded in 44 BCE by Julius Caesar. Greek Corinth had been severely devastated in 146 BCE when it was a member of the Achaean League during a power struggle against Rome that resulted in war, the Romans being led in victory by L. Mummius. Some of the Corinthian Greeks were able to flee to neighboring cities, while those men who fought in the city were killed and the women and children were sold into slavery. Corinth itself was largely destroyed and laid in ruins for over a hundred years with only squatters living among the rubble (Cicero, *Tusculan Disputations*, 3.53; Williams 1987: 26). When Julius Caesar resettled the city, it was populated with freedmen and freedwomen from Italy, as well as with Roman veterans who had come to the city for the social and economic opportunities it offered (Strabo, 8.6.23c; Appian, *Roman History*, 8.136; Plutarch, *Julius Caesar*, 47.8). Unfortunately, the new colonists did not get by so easily and some resorted to grave-robbing, selling Greek Corinthian terracotta votive offerings and coveted Corinthian bronze vessels to an eager Roman clientele (Strabo, 8.6.23c). Despite the difficulties that the early colonists endured, Roman Corinth was a city that soon provided many diverse opportunities for its citizens, residents, and visitors.

When Corinth was refounded in 44 BCE, much of the devastated city needed to be rebuilt from scratch, although some of the existing Greek buildings and temples were modernized or rededicated in Roman style (Williams 1987: 32). The entire city was rebuilt on a Roman grid pattern known as centuriation and utilized Roman architecture and style (Engels 1990: 62; Romano 1993: 9–30). Roman influences did not cease with the city's infrastructure, but also permeated Corinth's system of government and law, and the predilections of its colonists. Roman Corinth was refounded in honor of Julius Caesar with the name Colonia Laus Julia Corinthiensis (Broneer 1941: 388–90), a prestigious Latin title which, according to Engels, avoided "the more common *–ius* or *–us* ethnic, which implies that the Italian colonists wished to distinguish themselves from the original Greek inhabitants of the city" (1990: 69). Of the extant inscriptions dedicated by Corinth's inhabitants from the period of Augustus to Nero, seventy-three are composed in Latin while only three are composed in Greek (Kent 1966: 18–19). However, these Latin inscriptions probably indicate more about the city's social elite and its governing bodies than they do about Corinth's urban masses (Meeks 1983: 47). Certainly the colonists of Roman Corinth and their descendants attempted to foster a sense of *Romanitas* as the city's cultural orientation (Winter 2001: 7–25), but Corinth was filled with people of diverse ethnic backgrounds such as Greeks, Jews, Syrians, Egyptians, Anatolians, and Phoenicians (Apuleius, *Metamorphoses*, 11.11; Wiseman 1979: 497; Engels 1990: 70–1) seeking socio-economic opportunities while Greece and its culture surrounded and penetrated the city. Ostraca and lead curse tablets from the first century CE – writings reflecting a greater cross-section of Corinthian society than public inscriptions dedicated by the social elite – are composed almost entirely in Greek (Bookidis and Fisher 1972: 304; Stroud 1973: 228; Winter 2001: 14). Thus, although Latin was the official language of the city, Greek was the lingua franca of the city's inhabitants (Kent 1966: 18; Engels 1990: 67–74). It should then come as no surprise that Paul's letters to the Corinthians were composed in Greek. Indeed, the mix of Roman and Greek cultures in Corinth makes the designation Greco-Roman truly appropriate for the city (Litfin 1994: 213; Witherington 1995: 8).

The location of Roman Corinth itself contributed both to its multi-ethnic character and to the socio-economic opportunities available there. Strabo writes, "Corinth is called 'wealthy' because of its commerce, since it is situated on the Isthmus and is master of two harbors, of which the one leads straight to Asia, and the other to Italy; and it makes easy the exchange of merchandise from both countries that are so far distant from each other" (Strabo, 8.6.20a). The Isthmus is a narrow stretch of land measuring six kilometers in width (Wiseman 1979: 441) which separates the Gulf of Corinth (Ionian Sea) and its harbor of Lechaion on the Saronic Gulf (Aegean Sea) and its harbor of Kenchreai. Ships carrying merchandise to Italy or Asia could avoid the treacherous and lengthy trip around Cape Malea at the southern tip of the Peloponnese (southern Greece) by docking at either of Corinth's two harbors. There they could unload their goods that could be carried by pack animals or slaves to waiting ships on the other side. This merchandise was subject to Corinthian taxation and generated a sizeable income for the city. In addition to merchandise, smaller ships could be hauled across the Isthmus on a paved, specially tracked roadway for carts called the *diolkos* (Engels 1990: 58–9). Corinth was also a vital crossroads for those traveling by land between the Peloponnesus and central Greece.

When describing the important socio-economic factors at Corinth, Strabo also notes that "the Isthmian Games, which were celebrated there, were wont to draw crowds of people" (Strabo, 8.6.20a.). As host of the Isthmian Games – a biennial pan-Hellenic festival dedicated to Poseidon held at Isthmia – Corinth provided various goods and services to tourists, sailors, athletes, merchants, government officials, and visitors of diverse socio-economic status (Engels 1990: 50–2). It is likely that Paul was in Corinth during the Isthmian Games held in the year 51 CE, a major event that would have provided him with a wide target audience for his gospel message and with opportunities to ply his trade as an artisan working on leather or canvas goods. Engels has convincingly argued that Roman Corinth was a service economy rather than a city that accumulated is revenue through the taxation, rents, and consumerism of its own people (1990: 43–65). Apuleius also remarks that Roman Corinth was extremely competitive in business dealings and in all matters generally (*Metamorphoses*, 10.35). It was this competitive economy that enabled freedman such as Cnaeus Babbius Philinus to rise in status to *aedile* (city manager), *pontifex* (priest), and *duovir* (magistrate), advertising his success with public inscriptions and buildings such as the Babbius Monument (Kent 1966: nos. 155, 241). One other such prominent public inscription that can be seen on-site today just north of the ancient theater is that of Erastus, an *aedile* of Corinth who laid the pavement for the theater at his own expense (Kent 1966: no. 232). Erastus' inscription is not only significant for its large-size letters of public self-promotion, but also because it seems quite probable that this is the same person referred to by Paul as the *oikonomos tēs poleōs* ("city treasurer," a suitable Greek translation of the Latin word *aedile*) and as such was a high-status member of the Corinthian Christian assembly (Rom. 16:23; Kent 1966: 100; Meeks 1983: 58–9; Murphy-O'Connor 1983: 38).

As visitors and residents such as Paul would enter the forum of Corinth on the city's main thoroughfare, the Lechaion Way (which was not paved with the stones that can be seen on-site today until after 77 CE), they would encounter several markets selling commercial goods and food products. One such market was the *macellum*, a meat market that also sold other foodstuffs such as fish, which Paul refers to in 1 Corinthians 10:25 in connection with the Corinthian Christian dispute over the consumption of sacrificial food. People would come to the forum to purchase pottery, fabric, leather, canvas, materials to repair ships and sails, and to get hot meals and wine at various snack shops and pubs. Corinth also had an abundance of freshwater springs that supplied the city with fountains and baths for drinking and bathing (Pausanias, *Description of Greece*, 2.3.5). Corinth's bronze goods, the fine quality of which was supposedly generated by the unique properties of water drawn from the Peirene spring (Pausanias *Description of Greece*, 2.3.3), were widely exported during Corinth's Greek period. Although Corinth's bronze goods are often referred to in New Testament commentators' exegesis of the "noisy gong" and "clanging cymbal" of 1 Corinthians 13:1, there is little evidence that Roman Corinth produced such high-quality bronze or exported it (Wiseman 1969: 64–106; Pemberton 1981: 101–11; Witherington 1995: 9–10). The forum also housed the administrative and legal edifices of the Roman Corinthian government, including that of the south stoa, *bouleuterion* (council chambers), and the *bema* (tribunal), where Paul reportedly had a judicial hearing before the proconsul Gallio (cf. Acts 18.12–17). People spending time in Corinth could also find various forms of entertainment near the forum, such as an assortment of dramas or oratorical performances held at the city's 15,000 person capacity theater.

Corinth's service economy also catered to the religious proclivities of its visitors and residents. According to Pausanias, the forum was also the location of the majority of the city's temples. Here visitors could worship various deities of their choosing at their respective temples or shrines such as Tyche, Hermes, Venus, or Sarapis. Prominent temples associated with Roman imperial rule could also be seen, such as the Temple of Octavia – identified by most scholars as Temple E (Fotopoulos 2003: 135–9) – which was built overlooking the Roman forum as a sign of imperial rule, and the Temple of Apollo – identified by most scholars as the Archaic Temple because of its seven Doric columns which still stand erect (Fotopoulos 2003: 142). Located just outside of the ancient city center approximately 500 meters from the forum was the Asklepieion of Corinth. This sanctuary provided greenery, a freshwater spring, and a shaded colonnade that made it an environment conducive to healings and the prescriptions given by the god Asklepios to visitors who underwent the rite of incubation in the *abaton* building (dormitory) of the complex. Hundreds of terracotta votive offerings depicting human body parts dedicated by healed devotees of Asklepios found at the Asklepieion are frequently mentioned by New Testament scholars as a possible source of Paul's body imagery in 1 Corinthians 12:12–31 (Lanci 1997). However, these votive offerings date from the fifth and fourth centuries BCE (Roebuck 1951: 113), whereas no such Corinthian votives have yet been discovered from the sanctuary's Roman period. The Asklepieion also had three dining rooms that provided a luxurious environment for people to recline at formal meals serving sacrificial food to celebrate the healing activities of Asklepios – a plausible context for Paul's instructions concerning formal sacrificial food consumption in an "idol's temple" (1 Cor. 8:1–10:22; Fotopoulos 2003).

South and upward from the forum stands the Acrocorinth, the summit and citadel of Roman Corinth which is 575 meters high (Murphy-O'Connor 1983: 59). The Acrocorinth was sacred to the goddess Aphrodite, who had a small temple on the site from the fifth century BCE which remained until its destruction in the fourth or fifth century of the Common Era (Blegen 1936: 21). Greek Corinth's reputation for sexual opportunities with prostitutes who were under the patronage of Aphrodite is a fact well accepted by scholars. "Not for every man is the voyage to Corinth," was a clever saying that originally conveyed the commercial risks that awaited the city's visitors, but later referred to the sexual risks associated with visiting Corinth (Strabo, 8.6.20c; Murphy-O'Connor 1983: 56–8). Indeed, Corinth's reputation for sexual pleasure associated with the patronage of Aphrodite was well known, even in the city's Roman period. Strabo, in a passage frequently quoted in study Bibles, modern travel books on Greece, and older commentaries on 1 Corinthians, makes reference to the presence of a thousand sacred prostitutes at the Temple of Aphrodite on Acrocorinth during the city's Greek period (Strabo, 8.6.20C). However, the existence of a thousand sacred prostitutes present at the Temple of Aphrodite during the time of Paul's sojourn in Corinth has been correctly rejected by Conzelmann (1969: 247–61) and Murphy-O'Connor (1983: 57) as a pre-146 BCE phenomenon, if such a phenomenon ever truly existed at all in Corinth. Despite this, Roman Corinth did still enjoy a reputation for sexual promiscuity and prostitution, some of which seems to have been associated with Aphrodite and her patronage of the city. This reputation for sexual opportunity was advertised on the city's coinage, with several coins depicting the cult statue of Aphrodite perched on the Acrocorinth, naked from the waist up and armed with a shield (Head 1963). The allure of Aphrodite's sexual pleasures was one more kind of popular service attracting visitors and catering to people engaged in various pursuits in the city.

## Purpose

The purpose of 1 Corinthians is to unite a factious Corinthian church that is divided over numerous issues addressed in the letter. Although the various issues addressed in 1 Corinthians seem to have no immediate relationship to one another, the common thread linking them is the divisions which these issues have generated in the Corinthian church. Thus, Paul addresses the signs, attitudes, and expressions of factionalism such as boasting, arrogance, loyalty to various leaders, and claims to be wise, spiritually gifted, theologically knowledgeable, and strong. Paul attempts to unite the Corinthians by urging them to do what is in their best interest or common advantage (*sympherein*, cf. 6:12; 7:35; 10:23; 10:33; 12:7), a stock term used in Greek deliberative speeches urging concord (Mitchell 1991: 25–39). In this way, Paul carefully crafts his arguments as part of an overall reconciliatory strategy by appealing to the best interests of both Corinthian factions. The Corinthians' overly realized eschatology which empowers them to engage in various spiritual activities (tongues; prophecy) and bodily practices (sexual immorality; sexual abstinence) with supposed impunity must also be corrected by Paul, who does so by communicating the imminence of future judgment and the bodily resurrection of Christians.

## Language and Style

Paul's Greek is a kind of elevated Koine mixed with Septuagintisms (Conzelmann 1975: 5) and various New Testament *hapax legomena*, or Greek words that occur just once (Robertson and Plummer 1911: xlix–lii). It seems clear from Paul's greeting with his own hand (16:21) that he has not physically written the letter himself, but has dictated the letter to an amanuensis (scribe). This is also supported by the presence of several parenthetical remarks that seem to have been added by Paul after he had already dictated his initial thoughts. In 1:14–15, for example, Paul states that he baptized no one in the community except for Crispus and Gaius, parenthetically adding that he also baptized Stephanas' household. Because Paul is dictating 1 Corinthians as though it is a speech, he has also devised the rhetorical *invention* (the development of arguments and use of literary *topoi*, or commonplaces), the *disposition* (the arrangement and order of the discourse), and the *elocution* (the style with terms and phrases). He employs various rhetorical figures of style such as a dialogical objection in the form of *prosopopoiia* (speech in character) in 10:29–30 with the additional rhetorical figure of an ellipse in the form of an omission of the speaker's identity (Fotopoulos 2003: 246–7). Watson (1989) has correctly identified the euphonic character of 10:31, which displays several rhetorical techniques such as *polysyndeton* (the successive use of a connective conjunction – *eite*), *epiphora* (the last word of two successive clauses is repeated – *poiete*), and *homoeoptoton* (two words or more present together in the same case with the same endings – *esthiete, pinete, poiete*). Smit (1997) notes that 10:31 also displays *homoeoteleuton* (the correspondence in the ending of two or more clauses or sentences – the sevenfold *-te* of *eite esthiete, eite pinete, eite poieite ... poieite*), and *homoiokatarkton* (the repetition of consonants together in the same clause – *pinete, poieite, panta, poieite*). Diatribe, an oral-literary, dialogical style, is also used by Paul in 15:29–41 with characteristic features of it present in imaginary opponents, hypothetical questions and objections, and false conclusions (Aune 2003: 128). Collins (1999: 14–16) has highlighted Paul's use of chiasm on the macro-level as an important stylistic feature present throughout 1 Corinthians. He argues that when Paul treats issues in the letter he characteristically presents a general consideration (A), engages in a digression (B), then offers a further reflection specifying the general reflection and addressing the issue at hand (A'). However, Collins' thesis is questionable for numerous reasons, especially because it is not clear that Paul is digressing at many points in the letter and because Paul's listeners would have had serious difficulty recognizing chiasm at such an extended macro-level. On the other hand, Paul did utilize chiasms as a stylistic feature on the micro-level such as in 7:22 ("For whoever was called in the Lord as a slave [A] is a freed person belonging to the Lord [B], just as whoever was free when called [B'] is a slave of Christ [A']").

## Intertextuality

1 Corinthians was written in light of a network of previous relationships, ideas, letters, and texts presupposed by Paul. The apostle had founded the Christian assembly in Corinth and had converted many of its members. Thus, Paul's teaching in Corinth

establishes a prior set of codes and conventions upon which 1 Corinthians is built. Eriksson has shown that a significant amount of Paul's argumentation in 1 Corinthians is based on earlier Pauline traditions which the apostle taught the Corinthian Christian assembly while in the city and then used in his letter as rhetorical proofs (Eriksson 1998). Before the composition of 1 Corinthians, there were several important communications between Paul and the Corinthians which are essential to consider for a coherent interpretation of the letter. As we have seen it is known from 5:9 that Paul had written a previous letter to the Corinthians (Corinthians A). This previous letter dealt with a host of issues, including that of sexual relations and social interaction with pagans, and subsequently elicited a written response from the Corinthians in a letter to Paul (cf. 7:1). The Corinthians' letter does not seem to have been a cordial request for further advice from Paul, but rather asserted the views of the dominant Corinthian party, the Strong. There is a scholarly consensus that in several verses Paul quotes Corinthian positions or slogans that formed a part of their letter to him. Thus, portions of the Corinthians' letter are embedded within 1 Corinthians and Paul uses these quotations to refute their assertions and to argue his positions. In 7:1b Paul clearly quotes a Corinthian position by introducing it with the *peri de* (the "now concerning" formula) and then referring to the matters about which the Corinthians wrote (" 'It is good for a man not to touch a woman' "). This quotation is then refuted with Paul's position that is first introduced by an adversative *de* ("But [*de*] because of sexual immoralities, each man should have his own wife and each woman should have her own husband"). Other probable Corinthian quotations in the letter appear in 6:12a; 6:12c; 6:13a–b; 6:18b; 8:1b; 8:4b–c; 8:5a; 8:6; 8:8a; 8:8b (without the double *oute*, "neither"), 10:23a; and 10:23c, some of these appearing with quotation marks in various English translations of the Bible to identify them as positions of the Corinthians. The Corinthians' letter to Paul was also supplemented by oral reports arriving with Chloe's people and with the possible carriers of the letter, Stephanas, Fortunatus, and Achaicus. These intertexts remind the modern reader that the focal text of 1 Corinthians must be read in light of the previous communication between Paul and the Corinthians. Moreover, Corinthians A, the Corinthians' letter to Paul, and 1 Corinthians are part of an intertextual relationship that continues with several personal visits to Corinth made by Paul and his envoys Timothy and Titus, as well as with Paul's composition of two to six additional letters to the Corinthians which are embedded within 2 Corinthians.

Another dimension of intertextuality in 1 Corinthians is Paul's use of the Hebrew scriptures. Sometimes these uses are mere echoes or whispers, while at other times they are quotations, citations, and larger figurations that are utilized for Paul's argumentation (Hays 1989: 18–21). Frequently Paul's citations of the Hebrew scriptures are preceded by introductory formulas such as "it is written" (1:19) or "it is said" (6:16), while he can also quote texts with no introductory markers (2:16; 15:32). Moreover, Paul can use explicit scriptural figurations as he does in 10:1–13 where events of Exodus and Numbers are interpreted typologically for their eschatological application to the Corinthian Christian assembly (Hays 1989: 91–104). Robertson and Plummer note that in 1 Corinthians Paul quotes directly from the Hebrew scriptures about thirty times, the exact number being difficult to calculate since Paul sometimes conflates passages which he seems to be quoting from memory (1911: lii). The Hebrew scriptures most frequently used by Paul in the letter are Isaiah, Psalms, Deuteronomy, Genesis, Exodus, and Numbers. Paul commonly quotes from the Septuagint, although in some cases his quotations more closely resemble the Masoretic text, possibly because he knows a proto-Masoretic text type or because he consciously attempts to bring the Greek translation into conformity with the Hebrew. Finally, in 1 Corinthians 15:33 Paul cites a familiar Greek maxim from Menander's *Thais* which is used to characterize Corinthian thinking and behavior – a maxim that indicates Paul's familiarity with popular Hellenic culture rather than the depth of his Greek education.

## Literary Unity

The majority of scholars hold that the letter is a compositional unity, while a small minority of exegetes partition 1 Corinthians into various letters or letter fragments. These partition theories attempt to make sense of apparent contradictions within 1 Corinthians. In addition to the lack of manuscript support for such partition theories, no scholarly consensus exists among those advocating partition theories regarding the identity (embedded chapters and verses) or number of supposed letters or letter fragments within 1 Corinthians. Those scholars proposing various partition theories argue that there are as many as two to six letters or letter fragments embedded in 1 Corinthians (Weiss 1910; Schmithals 1971; Jewett 1978; Klauck 1984; Sellin 1991; Yeo 1995; Richter 1996), with many more letters or fragments alleged in 2 Corinthians. The work of J. C. Hurd and M. M. Mitchell, however, has effectively demonstrated the unity of 1 Corinthians and shown that the letter's apparent contradictions can be readily understood in light of its historical occasion and Paul's rhetorical strategy, in which he attempts to unite factions divided over various issues within the Corinthian church.

## Constituent Literary Forms

Within the framework of 1 Corinthians, there are several pre-Pauline constituent literary forms (relatively short literary units) that are embedded which presumably circulated in oral or written form before they were incorporated by Paul into his correspondence. However, the identification of these constituent forms is especially difficult since there is no generally accepted method for identifying these units or ascertaining if the pre-Pauline unit at Paul's disposal existed in oral or written form. Even more difficult is the identification of a constituent literary form's geographical, historical, and genetic situation of origin (*Sitz im Leben*) with which some past scholarship has been preoccupied. Despite these difficulties, there are several constituent literary forms evident in 1 Corinthians that appear to be pre-Pauline in origin, while being adapted to their present context in some cases by the apostle.

### Confessions (prayers and creedal statements)

The most obvious pre-Pauline constituent literary form is the Aramaic phrase *Marana tha*, which has been transliterated into Greek in 1 Corinthians 16:22, translated as "Our

Lord, come." This is a prayer for the imminent *parousia* (arrival) of Jesus (Conzelmann 1975: 301; Fee 1987: 838), echoed in *Didache* 10:6 (Aramaic transliterated into Greek) and in Revelation 22:20 (a Greek translation, "Come, Lord Jesus"), which may have been used generally or within the Lord's Supper as a prayer for Jesus' return from heaven (Eriksson 1998: 117). Another pre-Pauline phrase is the creedal statement "Jesus is Lord" appearing in 1 Corinthians 12:3 (parallels in 2 Cor. 4:5; Phil. 2:11; Rom. 10:9; Col. 2:6). Although the phrase lacks the clear introductory formula "confess," one scholarly criterion among twelve proposed for the identification of hymns by Stauffer (1955) and adopted by Aune (2003: 224) for creedal statements, hymns, and prayers, the phrase "Jesus is Lord" appears in Romans 10:9 and Philippians 2:11 with the "confess" formula, while the context of 1 Corinthians 12:3 indicates that the phrase is a Corinthian Christian confession of faith.. This creedal statement may have been used within the context of worship or specifically during baptism (Eriksson 1998: 112).

1 Corinthians 8:6 contains a creedal statement regarding the oneness of God the Father and the oneness of the Lord Jesus Christ. The original source of this confessional formula is not clear, with scholars arguing for it as pre-Pauline (Conzelmann 1975: 144; Schrage 1991–2001: II, 241) or Pauline (Dunn 1980: 182; Gardner 1994: 38). It is almost certain that the creedal statement "there is one God" has been drawn from the *Shema* of Deuteronomy 6:4, while it also seems likely that Paul himself had transmitted this creed to the Corinthian church while preaching in the city since the formula is also used by the apostle in Galatians 3:20 and Romans 3:30 (Eriksson 1998: 123).

Paul utilizes a pre-Pauline creedal statement or summary of the gospel in 15:3–5 that is introduced by an introductory formula explaining that he has received this unit from earlier tradition. 1 Corinthians 15:5–7 may also be a conflation of two originally separate creedal statements regarding witnesses to the risen Lord Jesus, one list headed by Cephas and the other by James (Aune 1987: 194).

## Hymns

Although Paul refers to the singing of hymns in Corinthian Christian worship (14:26), scholars are hard pressed to find examples of hymns present in 1 Corinthians. Some exegetes have identified 13:4–7 as a hymn to love (Robertson-Plummer 1911: 285–6; Héring 1962: 135) which is either Pauline (Robertson-Plummer 1911: 285) or non-Pauline (Titus 1959) in origin. However, close scrutiny of the passage indicates that this is not a hymn but a carefully crafted Pauline response to the Corinthians' particular factional behavior.

## Paraenetic forms

1 Corinthians 6:9–10 contains a stereotypical paraenetic form commonly referred to as a virtue and vice list, although this instance does not catalogue virtues but only vices as an offender list. This catalogue is an example of a polysyndetic offender list which is characterized by the connective particles *oute, ou,* and *ouch* ("neither," "nor"). Another

polysyndetic offender list appears in 1 Corinthians 5:10–11 and is characterized by the connective particle *ē* ("or") (Aune 1987: 194–5).

## Sayings of Jesus

Several sayings of the historical Jesus are cited or alluded to by Paul in 1 Corinthians. These sayings demonstrate that particular teachings of the historical Jesus were known by, important to, and used by Paul in his missionary activity. Paul refers four times to commands and words of the Lord (7:10–11; 9:14; 11:23–5; 14:37) that he uses as proofs for arguments regarding various issues. In 7:10–11 Paul makes it clear to the Corinthians that he is conveying a "command of the Lord" prohibiting divorce for wives and husbands. This command is a variant of Jesus' teaching on divorce recorded in Mark 10:9–12 (parallel in Matthew 19:9) and Q (parallels in Matthew 5:32 and Luke 16:18). In 1 Corinthians 9:14 Paul states a command of the Lord which demonstrates the propriety of compensation for those who proclaim the gospel. This is an allusion or a variant of Jesus' teaching to the seventy disciples recorded in Luke 10:7 (parallel in Matthew 10:10) that "the laborer deserves to be paid." The third instance of Jesus' teaching in 1 Corinthians appears in 11:23–5 where Paul cites the words of institution for the bread and the cup used by Jesus at the Last Supper. These words of Jesus were probably handed on to Paul as part of an early liturgical formula used within the eucharistic meal. It is interesting to note that Paul is aware of several historical details surrounding the Last Supper, such as its setting on the night when Jesus was betrayed, as well as that Jesus gave thanks and broke the bread before reciting the words of institution. The words of institution as cited by Paul differ slightly from the parallels recorded in Mark 14:22–4, Matthew 26:26–8, and Luke 22:19–20. The fourth and final instance of a command of the Lord at Paul's disposal appears in 1 Corinthians 14:37. However, this case seems to be a prophetic substantiation of Paul's prior instructions regarding tongues and prophecy in 1 Corinthians 14 rather than an allusion to a particular saying of the historical Jesus (Fee 1987: 711–12).

## Midrash

A final constituent literary form that has been commonly identified is that of midrash (a Jewish exegetical genre and method common in rabbinic Judaism) in 10:1–13 (Weiss 1910: 249–50; Meeks 1983). However, 10:1–13 lacks the formal features of midrash as it is narrowly defined but might be classified as midrashic, that is, not as a literary form but as an interpretive approach (Aune 2003: 302–5), having been composed by Paul for its context within 1 Corinthians as a rhetorical *exemplum* (example) from Israel's history (Fotopoulos 2003: 228–33). In this way, 10:1–13 also resembles an isolated or discontinuous *pesher* (a method of biblical interpretation at Qumran using only a few scriptural verses within a larger composition characterized by the text's eschatological fulfillment within the community) since Paul uses verses from several Hebrew scriptures which are fulfilled eschatologically by the Corinthian assembly in the context of difficulties with sacrificial food consumption.

## Literary Genre

1 Corinthians is clearly a letter serving as a substitute for Paul's personal presence and which exhibits the standard features of ancient Greek letters such as the opening formulas, letter body with transitional formulas and epistolary *topoi* and closing formulas (Aune 2003: 268–72; see "Epistolary Analysis" below). However, 1 Corinthians is far longer than the numerous documentary papyrus letters from Greco-Roman Egypt which are usually very short personal or business correspondences (White 1986). Furthermore, 1 Corinthians also exhibits rhetorical features typical of Greco-Roman deliberative speeches urging concord (Mitchell 1991; see "Rhetorical Analysis" below). In this way, 1 Corinthians is a fusion of epistolary and rhetorical theory (Mitchell 1991: 21–3; 186; Hester 2002). Thus, the literary genre of 1 Corinthians may be properly designated as a deliberative letter (Kennedy 1984: 87; Mitchell 1991: 20–64, 186–7; Schrage 1991–2001: I, 80; Collins 1999: 19).

## Epistolary Analysis

1 Corinthians exhibits the standard features of ancient Greek letters (opening formulas, body, closing formulas) with several typically Pauline conventions. The opening formulas of 1 Corinthians consist of an epistolary prescription in 1:1–3 and a prayer of thanksgiving in 1:4–9. This epistolary prescription contains a superscription (sender) – the apostle Paul (and Sosthenes, possibly Paul's scribe); an adscription (addressee) – the *ekklesia* (assembly/church) of God which is in Corinth and all those who call on the name of the Lord Jesus Christ in every place; and a salutation – grace to you and peace from God our Father and the Lord Jesus Christ. The prayer of thanksgiving praises God for the spiritual gifts of speech and knowledge with which the Corinthians have been enriched as they wait for the revealing of "our Lord Jesus Christ," prays that they will be blameless on the day of Jesus' return from heaven, and reminds the Corinthians that God has called them into *koinonia* ("communion," "fellowship," "partnership") with "his Son, Jesus Christ our Lord." In this way, Paul's thanksgiving serves to introduce several themes of the letter such as the spiritual gifts of speech and knowledge, imminent eschatology as a foil to the Corinthians' overly realized eschatology, and communion with the Lord Jesus to which factional behavior is antithetical. The thanksgiving also functions as a rhetorical *exordium* (introduction) attempting to secure the goodwill of the audience (Aune 1987: 186; see "Rhetorical Analysis" below). The body of the letter begins in 1:10, signaled by the internal transitional formula *parakalō* ("I appeal"; Bjerkelund 1967), and extends to 16:18. Although most scholars take for granted that the body of the letter extends only to 15:58, possibly because the next subjects treated by Paul are not theological in nature but include business (collection of money for Jerusalem [16:1–4], travel plans [16:5–12]) and concluding *paraenesis* (exhortation, 16:13–18), these subjects are clearly standard epistolary *topoi* belonging to the body of an ancient letter rather than to the closing formula (for such *topoi* and helpful sketches of the formal structure of Pauline letters, see Aune 1987: 188–91; Aune 2003: 268–72). Thus, the body of the letter (1:10–16:18) exhibits the standard epistolary *topoi* of business (16:1–

4), domestic events (5:1–6:11), letter-writing (4:14; 5:9; 7:1), and the reunion with addressees (4:18–21). Also present are autobiographical statements (9:1–27; 15:9), travel plans (16:5–12), and concluding *paraenesis* (16:13–18). Although 1 Corinthians does contain a small concluding *paraenesis* typical of Paul's letters, it is not confined to a section at the end but is woven throughout the composition. The closing formulas of 1 Corinthians contain standard letter features such as secondary greetings (16:19–20a), an autographed greeting (16:21), and a final wish of love (16:24). Typically Pauline conventions appear in the appeal to greet one another with a holy kiss (16:20b) and the grace benediction (16:23). Also present are a uniquely Pauline curse formula (16:22a, "Let anyone be accursed who has no love for the Lord"), followed by the pre-Pauline Aramaic prayer for the imminent arrival of Jesus (16:22b, *Marana tha*).

## Rhetorical Analysis

Although epistolary theory assists in identifying the standard letter features present in 1 Corinthians, it offers very little in regard to an analysis of Paul's argumentation since, as stated above, 1 Corinthians is far lengthier than the documentary papyrus letters from Greco-Roman Egypt. Rather, the argumentation of 1 Corinthians functions much like a Greco-Roman deliberative speech. Although the relationship between epistolary theory and rhetorical theory was not formalized in the first century CE, in practice the popular moralists of antiquity made frequent use of Greco-Roman rhetoric in literary letters. Thus, analyzing 1 Corinthians with the tools of ancient rhetoric and identifying the rhetorical structure of the composition facilitate a coherent interpretation of Paul's argumentation and the relationship between the various themes addressed within the letter. As a deliberative letter, the rhetorical structure of 1 Corinthians may be identified as follows: (1) 1:4–9, *exordium* (praise of audience seeking good reception); (2) 1:10, *propositio* (main thesis); (3) 1:11–17, *narratio* (facts which generate the discourse); (4) 1:18–16:12, *probatio* (proofs/arguments); (5) 16:13–24, *peroratio* (restatement of main thesis/final appeal). Within the *probatio* section (1:18–16:12), five subsections can be identified: (1) 1:18–4:21, which addresses Corinthian factionalism, demonstrates the need for Paul's instructions, and reestablishes Paul's anti-sophistic evangelical strategy and example of self renunciation; (2) 5:1–11:1, which addresses various divisive issues related to the Corinthians' pagan social environment such as sexual immorality, court battles, marriage, social status, and sacrificial food consumption; (3) 11:2–14:40, which addresses divisive issues related to Corinthian Christian worship such as the wearing of head coverings, abuses at the Lord's Supper, and the spiritual gifts of tongues and prophecy; (4) 15:1–58, which addresses divisions over the actual bodily resurrection of Christians at the future arrival (*parousia*) of Christ; (5) 16:1–12, which addresses issues related to the two leaders, Paul and Apollos, to whom the Corinthian factions are loyal, Paul's directions concerning the monetary collection for Jerusalem, the options available to Paul when he arrives in Corinth for sending the collection to Jerusalem, Paul's travel plans, the friendly Corinthian reception of Timothy as Paul's emissary, and Paul's urging of Apollos to visit Corinth which Apollos was presently unwilling to do.

## Annotated Bibliography

Barrett, C. K. *The First Epistle to the Corinthians.* Harper's New Testament Commentaries. New York: Harper & Row, 1968. A good, reliable commentary on 1 Corinthians by a renowned conservative scholar.

Bieringer, R. (ed.). *The Corinthian Correspondence.* Leuven: Leuven University Press, 1996. A collection of important papers stemming from the forty-third gathering of the Colloquium Biblicum Lovaniense addressing both 1 and 2 Corinthians.

Collins, R. F. *First Corinthians.* Sacra Pagina Series, 7. Collegeville: Liturgical Press, 1999. A solid commentary by a Roman Catholic exegete, Collins carefully approaches a range of subjects in his interpretation. However, his view that chiasmus as the macro-level serves as the interpretive key to the letter's coherence is highly questionable.

Conzelmann, H. *A Commentary on the First Epistle to the Corinthians.* Trans. J. W. Leitch. Hermeneia, 36. Philadelphia: Fortress Press, 1975. The English translation of the original German commentary published in 1969. This commentary contains many useful insights, although Conzelmann is sometimes content to accept contradictions in Paul's argumentation in 1 Corinthians without satisfactory explanation. Conzelmann posits that the Corinthians' beliefs as reconstructed from the letter allow for an appropriate description of them as proto-Gnostic.

de Boer, M. C. "The Composition of 1 Corinthians." *New Testament Studies* 40 (1994), 229–45. An influential article which has proposed that 1 Corinthians is a response to two historical occasions, that of oral information given by Chloe's people in 1 Corinthians 1–4 and that of material conveyed by the Stephanas delegation orally (1 Cor. 5–6) and by letter (1 Cor. 7–16).

Engels, D. W. *Roman Corinth: An Alternative Model for the Classical City.* Chicago: University of Chicago Press, 1990. A convincing study maintaining that Roman Corinth was a service-based economy rather than an economy based on the taxation, rents, and consumerism of its own people. Engels' book paints a vivid portrait of economic, political, social, and religious life in Roman Corinth, making it a foundational work for understanding the city and people which Paul addressed in 1 Corinthians.

Eriksson, A. *Traditions as Rhetorical Proof: Pauline Argumentation in 1 Corinthians.* Coniectanea Biblica New Testament Series, 29. Stockholm: Almqvist & Wiksell International, 1998. Eriksson demonstrates that Paul persuades the Corinthians with rhetorical arguments drawn from earlier traditions that he had taught them during his founding mission to Corinth.

Fee, G. D. X. *The First Epistle to the Corinthians.* New International Commentary on the New Testament. Grand Rapids: Eerdmans, 1998. An important commentary marked by the careful, erudite interpretation of a Pentecostal scholar. Fee understands Paul to be addressing a united Corinthian church whose issues have been generated by the Corinthians' over-realized eschatology. A standard work necessary for any collection on 1 Corinthians.

Fotopoulos, J. *Food Offered to Idols in Roman Corinth: A Social-Rhetorical Reconsideration of 1 Corinthians 8:1–11:1.* Wissenschaftliche Untersuchungen zum Neuen Testament 2. Reihe 151. Tübingen: Mohr Siebeck, 2003. A detailed social-rhetorical study of Paul's instructions regarding the consumption of sacrificial food in Roman Corinth. This study engages past scholarly reconstructions of the Corinthian idol-food dispute and conducts a comprehensive archeological investigation of temple dining facilities. By using rhetorical-critical methods, the author argues that Paul's instructions in 1 Corinthians 8:1–11:1 are a coherent prohibition of known idol-food consumption.

Goulder, M. D. *Paul and the Competing Mission in Corinth*. Peabody: Hendrickson, 1998. A modern revival of an unconvincing thesis first promoted by F. C. Baur in 1831 suggesting that Judaizing Christians loyal to Peter were at the root of the opposition to Paul which began in Corinth after Paul's departure.

Grosheide, F. W. *Commentary on the First Epistle to the Corinthians*. New International Commentary on the New Testament. Grand Rapids: Eerdmans, 1953. A somewhat dated but insightful commentary still filled with fresh, clear-headed perspectives.

Hurd, John Coolidge. *The Origins of 1 Corinthians*. Macon: Mercer University Press, 1983; repr. of 1965 edn. Hurd attempts to reconstruct the prior exchanges between Paul and the Corinthians in order to understand the content of the letter. By doing so, Hurd makes a very strong case for the literary integrity of 1 Corinthians although many of his proposed reconstructions of this prior exchange as well as his conclusions regarding Paul's instructions are unconvincing.

Lindemann, Andreas. *Der erste Korintherbrief*. Handbuch zum Neuen Testament, 9.1. Tübingen: Mohr Siebeck, 2000. A concise, solid German language commentary on 1 Corinthians by a very well respected scholar.

Martin, D. B. *The Corinthian Body*. New Haven: Yale University Press, 1995. Martin examines Greco-Roman conceptions of the body to illuminate the various issues present in 1 Corinthians. He argues that Paul and the lower-class members of the Corinthian assembly (the Weak) were more concerned with pollution of the physical and corporate bodies than were the higher-class members of the church (the Strong).

Meeks, W. A. *The First Urban Christians: The Social World of the Apostle Paul*. New Haven: Yale University Press, 1983. A ground-breaking work that greatly assists in understanding the social world of Paul and the first urban Christians with many insights on the Corinthian Christian assembly and Paul's Corinthian correspondence.

Mitchell, M. M. "Concerning *ΠERI ΔE* in 1 Corinthians." *Novum Testamentum* 31 (1989), 229–56. A very important article that examines the use of the topic marker *peri de* in Greek literature, the findings of which necessitate caution for reconstructing 1 Corinthians' historical occasion.

Mitchell, M. M. *Paul and the Rhetoric of Reconciliation: An Exegetical Investigation of the Language and Composition of 1 Corinthians*. Louisville: Westminster John Knox Press, 1991. Mitchell's masterful work has convincingly demonstrated 1 Corinthians' literary unity by connecting the various issues addressed in the letter to Corinthian factionalism. By her insightful use of rhetorical criticism, Mitchell shows that 1 Corinthians is a deliberative letter whereby Paul urges a divided church to do what is in its own best interest and to unite in love. This book is a must-read for those truly wanting to understand Paul's argumentation in 1 Corinthians.

Murphy-O'Connor, J. *St. Paul's Corinth: Texts and Archaeology*. Good News Studies, 6. Wilmington, Delaware: Michael Glazier, 1983. A convenient collection of literary and archaeological primary source material on Corinth available in English.

Robertson, A. and A. Plummer. *A Critical and Exegetical Commentary on the First Epistle of St. Paul to the Corinthians*. International Critical Commentary. New York: Scribner's, 1911. An older but still often referred to commentary that is one of the few to treat the characteristics, style, and language of 1 Corinthians.

Schmithals, Walter. *Gnosticism in Corinth: An Investigation of the Letters to the Corinthians*. Trans. J. E. Steely. 3rd edn. Nashville and New York: Abingdon Press, 1971. The third-edition English translation of his 1956 *Die Gnosis in Korinth* in which Schmithals proposes his elaborate partition theory for the letter and surveys the heretical theology of the Corinthian Gnostics.

Schrage, W. *Der erste Brief an die Korinther*. 4 vols. Evangelisch-katholischer Kommentar zum Neuen Testament. Neukirchen-Vluyn and Düsseldorf: Neukirchener and Benziger, 1991–2001. An extremely thorough German-language commentary dealing with all aspects of the letter in amazing detail and clarity.

Theissen, G. *The Social Setting of Pauline Christianity: Essays on Corinth*. Philadelphia: Fortress Press, 1982. An important collection of articles with four essays exploring the social matrix of Corinth and its importance for the issues raised in 1 Corinthians.

Thiselton, A. C. *The First Epistle to the Corinthians*. New International Greek Testament Commentary. Grand Rapids and Cambridge: Eerdmans/Paternoster Press, 2000. An exhaustive commentary taking advantage of nearly every publication available on 1 Corinthians until the year 2000, both ancient and modern. Thiselton conducts careful, detailed exegesis of the text while also highlighting issues of contemporary relevance.

Watson, D. F. "1 Corinthians 10:23–11:1 in the Light of Greco-Roman Rhetoric." *Journal of Biblical Literature* 108 (1989), 301–18.

Weiss, J. *Der erste Korintherbrief*. Meyer K. Göttingen: Vandenhoeck & Ruprecht, 1910. This influential German commentary was one of the first to advocate a detailed partition theory for 1 Corinthians and upon it many such later theories have been built.

Witherington III, B. *Conflict and Community in Corinth: A Socio-Rhetorical Commentary on 1 and 2 Corinthians*. Grand Rapids and Carlisle: Eerdmans/Paternoster Press, 1995. A user-friendly commentary that employs socio-rhetorical criticism to locate 1 Corinthians within the context of first-century Corinth. Witherington's book is especially appropriate for students, while also beneficial to scholars.

# References

Appian. *Historia romana*. Trans. H. White. 4 vols. Loeb Classical Library. London and New York: W. Heinemann and G. P. Putnam, 1912–13.

Aune, D. E. *The New Testament in its Literary Environment*. Library of Early Christianity, 8. Philadelphia: Westminster Press, 1987.

Aune, D. E. *The Westminster Dictionary of New Testament and Early Christian Literature and Rhetoric*. Louisville: Westminster John Knox, 2003.

Barrett, C. K. "Cephas and Corinth." Pp. 1–12 in O. Betz, M. Hengel, and P. Schmidt (eds.), *Abraham unser Vater: Festschrift für Otto Michel zum 60. Geburtstag*. Leiden: E. J. Brill, 1963.

Baur, F. C. "Die Christus Partei in der korinthischen Gemeinde." *Tübinger Zeitschrift für Theologie* 5 (1831), 61–206.

Bjerkelund, C. J. *Parakalo: Form, Funktion und Sinn der Parakalo-Sätze in den paulinischen Briefen*. Oslo: Universitetsforlaget, 1967.

Blegen, C. W., O. Broneer, R. Stillwell, and A. R. Bellinger. *Corinth: Results of Excavations Conducted by the American School of Classical Studies at Athens*, vol. 3, part 1: *Acrocorinth. Excavations in 1926*. Cambridge, MA: Harvard University Press, 1936.

Bookidis, N. and J. E. Fisher. "The Sanctuary of Demeter and Kore on Acrocorinth: Preliminary Report 4: 1969–1970," *Hesperia* 41 (1972), 283–331.

Broneer, O. "Colonia laus Julia Corinthiensis." *Hesperia* 10 (1941), 388–90.

Cicero. *Tusculanae Disputations*. Trans. J. E. King. Loeb Classical Library. London and New York: W. Heinemann and G. P. Putnam, 1927.

Collins, R. F. *First Corinthians*. Sacra Pagina, 7. Collegeville, MN: Liturgical Press, 1999.

Conzelmann, H. "Corinth und die Mädchen der Aphrodite. Zur Religiongeschichte der Stadt Korinth," *Nachrichten von der Akademie der Wissenschaften in Göttingen* 8 (1967), 247–61.

Conzelmann, H. *A Commentary on the First Epistle to the Corinthians*. Trans. J. W. Leitch. Hermeneia 36. Philadelphia: Fortress Press, 1975.

de Boer, M. C. "The Composition of 1 Corinthians," *New Testament Studies* 40 (1994), 229–45.

Dunn, J. D. G. *Christology in the Making: A New Testament Inquiry into the Origins of the Doctrine of the Incarnation*. Philadelphia: Westminster Press, 1980.

Engels, D. W. *Roman Corinth: An Alternative Model for the Classical City*. Chicago: University of Chicago Press, 1990.

Eriksson, A. *Traditions as Rhetorical Proof: Pauline Argumentation in 1 Corinthians*. Coniectanea biblica, New Testament, 29. Stockholm: Almqvist & Wiksell International, 1998.

Fee, G. D. *The First Epistle to the Corinthians*. New International Commentary on the New Testament. Grand Rapids: Eerdmans, 1987.

Fotopoulos, J. *Food Offered to Idols in Roman Corinth: A Social-Rhetorical Reconsideration of 1 Corinthians 8:1–11:1*. Wissenschaftliche Untersuchungen zum Neuen Testament, 2.151. Tübingen: Mohr Siebeck, 2003.

Gardner, P. D. *The Gifts of God and the Authentication of a Christian: An Exegetical Study of 1 Corinthians 8–11:1*. Lanham, MD: University Press of America, 1994.

Goulder, M. D. *Paul and the Competing Mission in Corinth*. Peabody, MA: Hendrickson, 1998.

Grosheide, F. W. *Commentary on the First Epistle to the Corinthians*. New International Commentary on the New Testament. Grand Rapids: Eerdmans, 1953.

Head, B. V. *Catalogue of Greek Coins. Corinth, Colonies of Corinth, etc*. Bologna: Arnaldo Forni, 1963.

Héring, J. *The First Epistle of Saint Paul to the Corinthians*. Trans. A. W. Heathcote and P. J. Allcock. London: Epworth, 1962.

Hester, J. D. "Rhetoric and the Composition of the Letters of Paul." Cited 4 February 2002, in the *Journal for the Study of Rhetorical Criticism of the New Testament*. ⟨http://newton.uor.edu/FacultyFolder/Hester/Journal/HesterComp.html⟩.

Horsley, R. A. "The Background of the Confessional Formula in 1 Cor 8:6." *Zeitschrift für die neutestamentliche Wissenschaft und die Kunde der älteren Kirche* 69 (1978a), 130–5.

Horsley, R. A. "Consciousness and Freedom among the Corinthians: 1 Corinthians 8–10." *Catholic Biblical Quarterly* 40 (1978b), 574–89.

Hurd, J. C. *The Origins of 1 Corinthians*. Macon, GA: Mercer University Press, 1983.

Jewett, R. "The Redaction of 1 Corinthians and the Trajectory of the Pauline School." *Journal of the American Academy of Religion*, supplement, 46 (1978), 571.

Kennedy, G. A. *New Testament Interpretation through Rhetorical Criticism*. Studies in Religion. Chapel Hill, NC: University of North Carolina Press, 1984.

Kent, J. H. *Corinth: Results of Excavations Conducted by the American School of Classical Studies at Athens*, vol. 3, part 3: *The Inscriptions. 1926–1950*. Princeton, NJ: American School of Classical Studies at Athens, 1966.

Klauck, H.-J. *1 Korintherbrief*. Die Neue Echter Bibel, 7. Würzburg: Echter, 1984.

Kugel, J. L. "Two Introductions to Midrash." Pp. 77–103 in G. H. Hartman and S. Budick (eds.), *Midrash and Literature*. New Haven: Yale University Press, 1986.

Lanci, J. R. *A New Temple for Corinth: Rhetorical and Archaeological Approaches to Pauline Imagery*. Leuven: Peter Lang, 1997.

Lindemann, Andreas. *Der erste Korintherbrief*. Handbuch zum Neuen Testament, 9.1. Tübingen: Mohr Siebeck, 2000.

Litfin, A. D. *St. Paul's Theology of Proclamation: An Investigation of 1 Cor. 1–4 in Light of Greco-Roman Rhetoric*. SNTS MS, 79. Cambridge: Cambridge University Press, 1994.

Lüdemann, G. *Paul, Apostle to the Gentiles: Studies in Chronology*. Trans. S. F. Jones. Philadelphia: Fortress Press, 1984.

Martin, D. B. *The Corinthian Body*. New Haven: Yale University Press, 1995.

Meeks, W. A. "'And rose up to play': Midrash and Paraenesis in 1 Corinthians 10:1–22." *Journal for the Study of the New Testament* 16 (1982), 64–78.

Meeks, W. A. *The First Urban Christians: The Social World of the Apostle Paul*. New Haven: Yale University Press, 1983.

Mitchell, M. M. "Concerning ΠΕΡΙ ΔΕ in 1 Corinthians." *Novum Testamentum* 31 (1989), 229–56.

Mitchell, M. M. *Paul and the Rhetoric of Reconciliation: An Exegetical Investigation of the Language and Composition of 1 Corinthians*. Louisville: Westminster John Knox Press, 1991.

Murphy-O'Connor, J. *St. Paul's Corinth: Texts and Archaeology*. Good News Studies, 6. Wilmington, DE: Michael Glazier, 1983.

Oliver, J. H. "The Epistle of Claudius which Mentions the Proconsul Junius Gallio," *Hesperia* 40 (1971), 239–40.

Pemberton, E. G. "The Attribution of Corinthian Bronzes," *Hesperia* 50 (1981), 101–11.

Plassart, A. "L'Inscription de Delphes mentionnent le proconsul Gallion." *Revue des études grecques* 80 (1967), 372–8.

Plutarch. *Caesars*. Trans. B. Perrin in *Plutarch's Lives*, vol. 7/11. Loeb Classical Library. London and New York: W. Heinemann and G. P. Putnam, 1914–26.

Pogoloff, S. M. *Logos and Sophia: The Rhetorical Situation of 1 Corinthians*. Atlanta: Scholars Press, 1992.

Richter, H.-F. "Anstößige Freiheit in Korinth: Zur Literarkritik der Korintherbriefe (1 Kor. 8, 1–13 und 11, 2–16)." Pp. 561–75 in R. Bieringer (ed.), *The Corinthian Correspondence*. Leuven: Leuven University Press, 1996.

Robertson, A. and A. Plummer. *A Critical and Exegetical Commentary on the First Epistle of St. Paul to the Corinthians*. International Critical Commentary. New York: Scribner's, 1911.

Roebuck, C. A. *Corinth: Results of Excavations Conducted by the American School of Classical Studies at Athens*, vol. 14: *The Asclepion and Lerna*. Princeton, NJ: American School of Classical Studies at Athens, 1951.

Romano, D. G. "Post-146 BC Land Use in Corinth and Planning of the Roman Colony of 44 BC." Pp. 9–30 in T. E. Gregory, *The Corinthia in the Roman Period*. Journal of Roman Archaeology Supplementary Series, 8. Ann Arbor, 1993.

Schmithals, W. *Gnosticism in Corinth: An Investigation of the Letters to the Corinthians*. Trans. J. E. Steely. 3rd edn. Nashville and New York: Abingdon Press, 1971.

Schrage, W. *Der erste Brief an die Korinther*. 4 vols. Evangelisch-katholischer Kommentar zum Neuen Testament. Neukirchen-Vluyn and Düsseldorf: Neukirchener Verlag and Benziger Verlag, 1991–2001.

Sellin, G. "In Korinther 5–6 und der 'Vorbrief' nach Korinth: Indizien für eine Mehrschichtigkeit von Kommunikationsakten im ersten Korintherbrief," *New Testament Studies* 37 (1991) 535–58.

Smit, J. "The Function of First Corinthians 10, 23–30: A Rhetorical Anticipation." *Biblica* 78 (1997), 377–88.

Stauffer, E. *New Testament Theology*. London: SCM Press, 1955.

Strabo. *Geographica*. Trans. H. L. Jones, based in part upon the unfinished version of J. R. S. Sterrett. 8 vols. Loeb Classical Library. London and New York: W. Heinemann and G. P. Putnam, 1917–32.

Stroud, R. "Curses from Corinth." *American Journal of Archaeology* 77 (1973), 228.

Thiselton, A. C. *The First Epistle to the Corinthians*. New International Greek Testament Commentary. Grand Rapids and Cambridge: Eerdmans/Paternoster Press, 2000.

Titus, E. L. "Did Paul Write 1 Corinthians 13?" *Journal of Bible and Religion* 27 (1959), 299–302.

Watson, D. F. "1 Corinthians 10:23–11:1 in the Light of Greco-Roman Rhetoric: The Role of Rhetorical Questions." *Journal of Biblical Literature* 108 (1989), 301–18.

Weiss, J. *Der erste Korintherbrief.* MeyerK. Göttingen: Vandenhoeck & Ruprecht, 1910.

White, J. L. *Light from Ancient Letters.* Philadelphia: Fortress Press, 1986.

Williams, C. K. "The Refounding of Corinth: Some Roman Religious Attitudes." Pp. 26–37 in *Roman Architecture in the Greek World.* Edited by S. Macready and F. H. Thompson. Society of Antiquaries of London Occasional Papers. London: Society of Antiquaries, 1987.

Willis, Wendell Lee. *Idol Meat in Corinth: The Pauline Argument in 1 Corinthians 8 and 10.* Chico, CA: Scholar's Press, 1985.

Winter, B. W. *After Paul Left Corinth: The Influence of Secular Ethics and Social Change.* Grand Rapids: Eerdmans, 2001.

Wiseman, J. "Excavations in Corinth, the Gymnasium Area, 1967–1968," *Hesperia* 38 (1969), 64–106.

Wiseman, J. "Corinth and Rome I: 228 BC–AD 267." Pp. 438–549 in *Aufstieg und Niedergang der römischen Welt.* Edited by H. Temporini and W. Haase. Vol. 7.1. Berlin: Walter de Gruyter, 1979.

Witherington III, B. *Conflict and Community in Corinth: A Socio-Rhetorical Commentary on 1 and 2 Corinthians.* Grand Rapids, MI and Carlisle: Eerdmans/Paternoster Press, 1995.

Yeo, K.-K. *Rhetorical Interaction in 1 Corinthians 8 and 10: A Formal Analysis with Preliminary Suggestions for a Chinese, Cross-Cultural Hermeneutic.* Biblical Interpretation Series, 9. Leiden: E. J. Brill, 1995.

# CHAPTER 24

# 2 Corinthians

Calvin J. Roetzel

## Introduction

2 Corinthians is a treasure hidden in a thorny thicket. It is so rich, so full of insight and wisdom, so poetic, so human, and so poignant. Yet literary, rhetorical, theological, chronological, textual, and hermeneutical brambles frustrate all efforts at easy access. From the second century to the present 2 Corinthians has offered its riches grudgingly if at all, and even then it has rewarded only the most careful and attentive inquiry. In the second century Marcion found here the authorization for his ditheism (2 Cor. 4:4). In the twenty-first century some conservative scholars find a charter here for an emphasis on individual salvation (5:17); others scholars see instead a focus on the corporate and social nature of salvation.

While Pauline specialists disagree about the letter's literary integrity, rhetorical strategy, complex chronology, and the ideological face of Paul's antagonists, the sharpest clashes have been theological ones. In the past decade, scholars have written ten commentaries on 2 Corinthians, an unprecedented output in so short a time, and while some are cautious and measured, others are driven by a conservative theological agenda. That exegesis should come with theological presuppositions should surprise no one, for so it has always been. And yet, sound exegesis requires a hermeneutic of humility, i.e. an eagerness to place the fruits of one's study under scholarly scrutiny and correction lest the letters simply become a reflection of our own theological face. The heightened sense of the ideological underbrush blocking access to this treasure further complicates the interpretive task. This cautionary tale is hardly intended to cause one to despair of ever finding a way through the exegetical briar-patch that this letter inhabits; rather, it only lifts up the challenge this book demands of its readers for hard, careful, critical, thoughtful, and meticulous study. This difficult and important work, I believe, will reward disciplined study now and then with reflected facets of light from the gems concealed that can only be savored and spur one on.

## The Setting of 2 Corinthians

The Corinthian letters offer the best record we have anywhere of an apostle's extended interaction with his churches. They tell of numerous letter exchanges, personal visits, challenges to Paul's apostleship from internal and external critics, and contrarieties threatening the future of Paul's Gentile mission. They name sixteen converts in Corinth, more than in any other except the Roman church (Theissen 1982: 94–5). They recite our earliest known eucharistic formula (1 Cor. 11:23–6), the earliest summary of the gospel Paul received and preached (1 Cor. 15:1–11), and the best accounts of how churches were founded (1 Cor. 3:6). They show how these circles were socially constructed, and how they struggled to translate the Jesus message to address everyday concerns with gender, hierarchy, money, sex, food, civil disputes, power, and religious ecstasy (1 Cor. 6:1–13:13). They reveal how Paul responded to challenges from internal and external critics (1 Cor. 4:1–21; 9:1–12; 2 Cor. 2:14–7:4 [minus 6:14–7:1] and 10–13). They offer the clearest account of the re-socialization of converts (1 Cor. 8:6), and they provide the best record of the accommodations required to negotiate a pluralistic religious setting populated by the cults of Asklepios, Apollo, Isis, Serapis, Demeter, Persephone, Tyche, Aphrodite, Dionysus, Poseidon, the emperor, and the God of Israel.

As the imperial capital of Achaia and as a richly diverse, bustling port city Corinth was a cosmopolitan urban area that was strategically located for launching a Gentile mission to Rome and beyond, and cosmopolitan enough to embrace a Jesus movement with ties to Palestine and Jerusalem, the symbolic center of the religion of Israel. Whether by accident or design, the choice of Corinth and environs as a mission center appears in retrospect to have been a brilliant stratagem by Paul.

## Paul's Mission to Corinth

In the late 40s CE Paul crossed over at the Hellespont from Asia Minor to Macedonia. His mission took him first to Philippi and then to Thessalonica, where he gathered small circles of converts to the Jesus cult. That missionary activity provoked such fierce resistance that the persecution and harassment of both Paul and his converts (1 Thess. 1:6–7) forced his flight from Macedonia for Achaia. Eventually he came to Corinth in "fear and much trembling" (1 Cor. 2:3), perhaps worried that he would suffer the same abuse and opposition he met in Macedonia (1 Thess. 2:2–3). According to Acts 18:11, his mission in Corinth, Cenchraea, and parts of Achaia stretched over eighteen months, In Corinth he assembled a motley collection of believers drawn mostly but not exclusively from the underclass – the poor, uneducated, "weak" and "despised" (1 Cor. 1:14), slaves and freed (7:21–4; 12:13). Exceptions were Crispus, allegedly a synagogue leader baptized by Paul (Acts 18:8), Erastus, the city treasurer, and Gaius, Paul's host (Rom. 16:23). Most of the converts were Gentile, though some may have been "god-fearers" who attended the synagogue and observed the law.

Aided by Timothy and Silvanus, and Aquila and Prisca, Jewish messianist fugitives from Rome, and Phoebe, a patron of the church in Cenchreae, Paul founded assemblies in house churches throughout the area. Through his preaching of the messiah Jesus and the ritual of baptism Paul initiated Gentile converts into the sacred story of Israel with all of its promises and assurances. The scriptures of Israel became the story of the converts. The promises, hopes, and expectations of these writings, he preached, were now coming to glorious fruition in the new age God was inaugurating through the life, death and resurrection of the messiah Jesus.

The life-giving power of the Spirit, enthusiastically received and celebrated in the house churches, gave palpable evidence of the arrival of God's eschatological rule and the triumph of righteousness. Thus the incorporation of the "holy ones" and the gift of the Spirit placed them at the epicenter of history's climactic, apocalyptic moment that was initiating dramatic, convulsive, revolutionary change. As Paul succinctly announced, "the forms of this world are passing away" (1 Cor. 7:31), and a "new creation" was now dawning (2 Cor. 5:17). As in Thessalonica Paul's preaching enjoyed success for a time, but eventually because of a public outcry he was haled before Gallio, the Roman proconsul (Acts 18:12f.) in the summer of 52 CE, and was either expelled or left Corinth voluntarily.

Before settling in Ephesus he may have visited the churches in Macedonia and Galatia, though the duration and scope of that itinerary are pure guesswork. Eventually he settled in Ephesus, his base of operations for some time. Acts (20:31) suggests that Paul was in Ephesus for three years, but since the ancients counted years with any part standing for the whole, three years could be anything from thirteen to thirty-six months. While he was there he wrote perhaps as many as six letters, received oral and written communication from the Corinthians, dispatched delegations, possibly suffered imprisonment, returned there after the short, painful, humiliating visit to Corinth, there launched an effort at reconciliation, there wrote letters to other churches, and from there later set out for Troas, and then Macedonia to meet Titus to learn of the outcome of his reconciling work. Given this period of extended contact it is probable that all of Paul's letters to Corinth (perhaps as many as seven) were written between 52 and 58. While we can hardly be certain where each and every letter was scribed, this extended correspondence began with a letter that pre-dated 1 Corinthians, now lost (1 Cor. 5:9). That epistle dates as early as 52, probably in Macedonia, and his last to the Corinthians was written from Macedonia as late as 57. Romans, the last letter we have of his, was written from Corinth itself (Rom. 16:23) in 58 before he set sail for Jerusalem with the collection for the poor among the saints.

## Major Issues and Directions in Recent Study

For over two centuries 2 Corinthians has been an exegetical minefield. Disputes about the literary integrity of the letter and the identity of the "super apostles" have dogged the steps of Pauline scholars up to the present day. It is those two issues that must frame the discussion below.

*Survey of hypotheses of partition*

While exegetical conundrums hide behind every bush and lurk in every dark corner of 2 Corinthians no issue is more contested than the literary integrity of the letter. Since our earliest manuscript evidence for 2 Corinthians comes from the third century ($\mathfrak{P}^{46}$), it sheds no light on the earlier literary history of the letter. It hardly surprises, therefore, that before 1758 the literary integrity of the letter was simply taken for granted. That was an auspicious year, however, for in that year Johann Salomo Semler published a commentary on 2 Corinthians that shattered the presumption that the canonical 2 Corinthians reliably represents its original literary shape (1758). The stitching across seams in the letter, Semler identified as an effort by a later hand to piece together distinctly different Pauline letter fragments. Semler's argument that 2 Corinthians contained parts of two letters was earth-shaking. It disturbed the orthodox synthesis on the perfection of the canon and set the course for the study of 2 Corinthians for the next two-plus centuries. His study sparked off a fierce debate, but once the genie was out of the bottle there was no putting it back, and ever since, his study has forced all serious students of 2 Corinthians to face the literary challenges posed by this letter.

Since the time of Semler, many scholars have tried valiantly to untangle this literary rats' nest. Many others have fought valiantly to defend the unity of the letter. But so far no theory of either unity or partition has won a consensus. Nevertheless, modern students of 2 Corinthians can simply not close their eyes to the import of this discussion for the interpretation of this letter. For convenience sake, let us attend to the four major literary theories that still dominate 2 Corinthians scholarship.

*The argument for literary unity*

From the time of Semler to the present conservative scholars have argued for the literary integrity of the letter by dismissing all theories of partition as "unprovable conjectures" (Kümmel 1975: 291). Even while recognizing the literary seams in the epistle, the gaps in narrative sequence, and the contradictions, many insist they can all be explained either by interruptions of Paul's dictation, or by psychological changes in Paul's mood, or by differences in purpose from one part to another. Conservatives side with Kümmel, arguing that the canonical version of 2 Corinthians was Paul's original epistle, and they tend to ignore the hypothetical nature of their construction even while repudiating the hypotheses of partition theorists (Kümmel 1975: 292).

Enormous challenges, however, face those who defend the unity of the letter. Serious scholars of 2 Corinthians must recognize and account for the abrupt shifts in tone in the letter (chapters 1–9 versus 10–13), the literary interruptions of Paul's travelogue (1:1–2:13; 7:5–16), the lumpish disruption of his train of thought in 6:14–7:1 with strongly non-Pauline language, the redundancy of his instructions on the offering in chapters 8 and 9, and the contradictory expressions of confidence and lack of confidence in the Corinthians (7:16 and 11:19–21; 12:20–1). These features dispose a majority of Pauline interpreters to read 2 Corinthians as a collection of letter fragments stitched together by a later hand.

Nevertheless, in the past two decades a number of scholars have appealed to rhetorical theory to buttress their argument for the unity of the letter.

While their applications are varied, their appeal to theories of classical rhetoric to support their arguments at least recognizes the hypothetical nature of any construction. Among those appealing to rhetorical theory are Matera (2003: 29 n.24), P. Barnett (1997), D. E. Garland (2000), J. Lambrecht (1994), J. W. McCant (1999), Young and Ford (1988), J. M. Scott (1998), and B. Witherington III (1995). Granted that Paul may have been influenced by the conventions of forensic rhetoric, scholars disagree on how those conventions apply to this letter (Thrall 1994–2000: I, 10–13), and differ dramatically on how substantial is their appeal. For example, the volume edited by Young and Ford is devoted entirely to the relevance of rhetorical theory for interpreting 2 Corinthians, Matera's recent commentary only superficially uses rhetorical theory to support his argument.

For the most part, however, these attempts falter when judged by more compelling arguments from rhetorical theory for the partition of the letter. Kennedy, for example, who is often invoked to support rhetorical arguments for the literary unity of 2 Corinthians, argued instead for the separation of 2 Corinthians 1–9 from 10–13 as a discrete and separate rhetorical unit (Kennedy 1984: 87–91). Buttressed by arguments from rhetorical theory, Betz makes a strong if not compelling case for separating 2 Corinthians 8 from 2 Corinthians 9 as separate rhetorical letters (1985). And finally, Danker cautions that even if rhetorical theory is used to argue that chapters 10–13 are the rhetorical climax of the letter as it now stands, that hardly proves that Paul so designed these chapters as a part of a single letter (1991: 280). A redactor steeped in the Hellenistic tradition could just as easily have constructed the present arrangement. These appeals to rhetoric that lead to starkly opposite conclusions at least raises a flag of caution about appealing to rhetorical theory to buttress an argument for the unity of the letter (Thrall 1994–2000: I, 10–13). The support of other historical-critical evidence must also be invoked.

### The two-letter hypothesis

A survey of the recent scholarship on 2 Corinthians reveals a debt accumulated over the past two centuries (Betz 1985: 3–36). Semler's groundbreaking work was the first to see in the canonical 2 Corinthians two separate letters. In 1870 Adolf Hausrath made a case for reading 2 Corinthians 10–13 as a separate letter. He erroneously thought that if he could solve the literary problem posed by the distinctive character of 2 Corinthians 10–13, the shape and message of the rest of the letter would fall into place. After Semler's breakthrough more than a century earlier (1758), his proposal was hardly novel or even revolutionary. Nevertheless, it set off a firestorm of criticism that he referred to as an exegetical war of "all against all" (Betz 1985: 12). His argument for the chronological priority of the "letter of tears" (10–13) sparked further study, and the attention he gave to the offering project treated in 2 Corinthians 8–9, and to Paul's apostolic rivals offered an advance.

Nevertheless, it remained for an English scholar working independently of German scholarship to develop a more carefully reasoned justification for the two-letter hypothesis. In 1900 J. H. Kennedy argued that chapters 10–13 were 2 Corinthians and chapters 1–9 were 3 Corinthians. After gaining some notoriety and the imprimatur of the esteemed scholar Kirsopp Lake, Kennedy's thesis gained in popularity, but then lost influence as English scholars facing a confusing array of partition theories grew skeptical of all such theories and sought instead to try to make sense of canonical 2 Corinthians as it stands rather than to engage in unfounded speculation (Betz 1985: 14). More recently, however, Kennedy's thesis has gained an advocate in Watson (1984, below).

The most influential advocates of the two-letter hypothesis are C. K. Barrett (1973) and Victor Paul Furnish (1984) who with characteristic care and caution offer a "simpler" solution to this literary puzzle. Following Weiss, both see the importance of 2 Corinthians 12:17f. for fixing the sequence of the letters. There we find a perfect tense and two aorists that doubtless refer to Paul's earlier commission of Titus and the brother to conclude the offering: "Did I take advantage of you through any of those whom I *sent* [*apestalka*, perfect] to you? I *urged* [*parekalesa*, aorist] Titus to go; and *sent* the brother with him ... [*sunapesteila*, aorist, my emphasis]." This retrospective view presumably recalls the commissioning of Titus and the two brothers mentioned in 8:6, 17f. The aorists in 2 Corinthians 8 are typically read as epistolary aorists behaving like the present tense (NRSV), but given the presence of the perfect tense and two aorists in 12:17 it is clear there that a past event is being recalled. If that be so, the conclusion is inevitable: chapter 8 was written *before* 2 Corinthians 12:17f.

Since Barrett and Furnish hold 1 Corinthians 8 to be an integral part of the earlier, larger literary unit (chapters 1–9), then it follows that chapters 10–13 came later as a separate letter. So interpreted, simple logic requires that the present order be understood as the true chronological order of the two letters. Even while agreeing on the broader outlines and sequence of the two letters, they disagree about the status of 6:14–7:1. Barrett accepts it as Pauline and integrated into the letter's argument (1973: 192–203); Furnish is more circumspect. He views the passage as enigmatic and of doubtful Pauline authorship and probably a later interpolation (1984: 383).

The advantage of this two-letter hypothesis is that assigning 1–9 and 10–13 to different letters accounts for the sharp change in tone, context, and subject matter between 9:15 and 10:1. Moreover, their conclusion that chapters 10–13, if a separate letter, was written after chapter 8 is sound. But since both scholars hold chapters 1–9 to be an earlier single letter, Paul's reference to the "letter of tears" in the past tense, "I *wrote* [*egrapsa*, aorist, my emphasis]" raises questions about its location. Both Barrett and Furnish are forced to the hypothesis that it is lost. Of the credible hypotheses dealing with the literary structure of the letter, this is surely the simplest, a not inconsiderable virtue.

The disadvantages of this hypothesis, however, are considerable. Their thesis requires that the "letter of tears" mentioned in and pre-dating 2:4 must be considered lost if 10–13 *follows* chapters 1–9. Moreover, if 10–13, with all of its acrimony and slashing rhetoric, is the last letter in the collection, how is one to account for the positive report Paul scribes shortly after in Romans 15:26–7? As he dictates Romans, Paul is in Corinth; the collection is ready; the delegation has gathered and he heaps praise on believers in Achaia, including those in Corinth. "They are," he says, "pleased to do this." That dramatic shift, while not impossible if 10–13 was written immediately prior to Paul's last Corinthian visit, is at the least improbable. The two-letter hypothesis must satisfactorily explain how the long excursus (apology) in 2:14–7:4 really fits in the suspense-filled travelogue about Paul's tortured mind and spirit as he awaits news from Titus on the outcome of a last-ditch effort at reconciliation (2:12–13; 7:5–16). It hardly helps to dismiss Paul's suspense-filled account of his travels and the anxiety he felt waiting for word from Titus as something other than a travelogue. Finally, in the minds of many the two-letter hypothesis fails to deal with the seeming independence of the two accounts of the offering in chapters 8 and 9. To many, these appear to be separate and independent accounts, perhaps from different letters. While no one of these challenges to the two-letter hypothesis is decisive in and of itself, the cumulative weight of all of them taken together seriously weakens the case for this thesis.

Following the lead of Kennedy mentioned above, Watson (1984), however, offers a convincing alternative to the thesis of Barrett and Furnish. By showing the exegetical links between Paul's description of the "painful letter" in 2:3–4 and the actual letter in 10–13, Watson offers important evidence for reading chapters 10–13 as the "letter of tears" that Barrett and Furnish must presume lost. By placing 10–13 in the prior position chronologically, Watson is able to set the more positive letter of reconciliation last (chapters 1–9), thus paving the way for the positive outcome Paul notes in Romans 15:26–7 and for expressions of confidence in and praise of the Corinthians. While psychological explanations alone are hardly compelling, psychological factors can hardly be discounted entirely. There is one small problem, however, with this thesis that is not really so small. If chapters 10–13 are placed in the prior position ahead of chapters 1–9, how does one explain the retrospective reference to 8:6f. in 12:27f. if, in fact, 8:6f. pre-dates 12:27f.? If 12:27f. refers to the Titus commission with the brothers in the past tense and chapter 8, the object of the reference, has not yet been written, there is a serious problem. Watson responds that 12:28 is referring to a visit prior to and different from that mentioned in 8:6 and which is mentioned nowhere else. The literary parallels between 12:28 and 8:6, however, insist that they are referring to the same event. So, while there is much in this hypothesis that is attractive, it falters when confronted by this challenge.

## The three-letter hypothesis

The three-letter hypothesis advanced by an impressive array of scholars has the advantage of dealing with one or more of the weaknesses of the two-letter hypothesis.

The most notable advocate of this position was the distinguished scholar Johannes Weiss, who in 1910 was working on his *Urchristentum* ("primitive Christianity") that was to be followed by a commentary on 2 Corinthians. The untimely death in 1914 of this revered teacher-scholar left his *Primitive Christianity* incomplete, and the commentary assigned to him was passed on to Hans Windisch. Nevertheless, Weiss offered the brilliant thesis that 2 Corinthians 8 was written soon after 1 Corinthians 16:1–4 and was separate and distinct from 2 Corinthians 9 (1959: I, 352–7). After this letter (chapter 8), came letter 2, the so-called "letter of tears" (2:14–7:4 [minus 6:14–7:1], 10–13), and finally came letter 3, the letter of reconciliation (2 Cor. 1:1–2:13; 7:5–16; 9). Had he lived to complete his commentary we can only speculate about the final shape of his letter partition theory, yet his argument for the priority of 2 Corinthians 8 was brilliant.

Hans Windisch (1924), the heir to Weiss's commentary, offered a careful, incisive, and still influential commentary on 2 Corinthians, and supported a variant of Weiss' three-letter hypothesis. Windisch also expressed doubts about the literary unity of chapters 1–7, viewed 10–13 as a fragment of a separate letter (though not the letter of "tears" mentioned in 2:4), and treated chapters 8 and 9 as parts of separate letters about the offering project. The chief advantage of the three-letter hypothesis is that it deals in separate and creative ways with the challenge posed by the redundant accounts of the offering in chapters 8 and 9. In the end we must credit Weiss for advancing the discussion significantly, and stimulating other plausible alternatives.

### The five-letter hypothesis

The legacy of Weiss lingered in the work of his students at Heidelberg, shaping the discussion of the literary shape of 2 Corinthians to this day. Rudolf Bultmann (1976), like other students who spent long evenings in Weiss' home, revered his mentor, and eventually wrote a commentary on 2 Corinthians that reflected Weiss' influence. While that commentary did little to move the discussion forward, his own student, Gunther Bornkamm (1971), offered a brilliant and innovative solution to the literary composition of 2 Corinthians. His influential five-letter hypothesis has remained to inform continued discussion of the literary integrity of the letter. Revising Weiss, he took 10–13 as the "letter of tears" (2:4) and held 2 Corinthians 2:14–7:4 (minus 6:14–7:1) to be Paul's first apology followed by the second in chapters 10–13, "the letter of tears." The letter of reconciliation followed (2 Cor. 1:1–2:13; 7:5–16). Chapter 8, that treated the offering, he held to be either a separate letter or an attachment to the letter of reconciliation. Chapter 9 was the final letter in the series. Weiss, however, had noted how the fact that 2 Corinthians 12:17f. refers to Titus' collection efforts first mentioned in 8:6 requires that chapter 8 precede 10–13. This observation exposes a major weakness of Bornkamm's construction that places the "letter of tears," 10–13, *before* the offering letter, chapter 8. Though contested, Bornkamm's thesis has profoundly influenced scholars like Hans Dieter Betz and Margaret M. Mitchell, and my own debt will become obvious. Moreover, his work has provoked vigorous reactions from conservative scholars who support a hypothesis of the literary unity of the letter.

Mitchell (2004: 307–38) has provided a sophisticated narrative framing of the letter fragments that has great promise. Following Weiss, her essay, a delicate interweaving of literary and historical reconstruction, convincingly secures the chronological priority of chapter 8 in the 2 Corinthians collection (Weiss 1959: I, 353). When the reference to Titus' commission to organize the offering in Corinth (12:17f.) is recognized as a retrospective one, the case for viewing chapter 8 as chronologically prior is compelling. And if it can be isolated as a letter, then it would follow on the heels of 1 Corinthians. Mitchell goes beyond Weiss in offering a strong historical and textual warrant for placing chapter 8 directly after 1 Corinthians 16:1–11. She finds in 2:14–7:4 (minus 6:14–7:1) Paul's first defense, in 10–13:20 the "letter of tears," or second defense, in

1:1–2:13, 7:5–16, and 13:11–13 Paul's reconciling letter, and in chapter 9 final instructions on the offering to all of the churches in Achaia.

The five-letter hypothesis has much in its favor. It accounts for the literary connection between 2:11–13 and 7:5–16; it recognizes the unity of the argument in 2:14–7:4; it allows for an argument that does not require the loss of either the "letters of tears" or an earlier commissioning of Titus; it locates 10:1–13:10, "the letter of tears," in a sequence of exchanges that allows reconciliation afterwards that leads to the offering success reported shortly after in Romans 15:24–9; finally it recognizes the difficulty of trying to support a congruent literary connection between chapters 8 and 9. In this regard, her thesis overcomes some of the weakness of that of Betz and Bornkamm who must locate chapters 8 and 9 as separate letters at the end of Paul's correspondence with Corinth. That placement leaves their construction open to the criticism of Weiss and others that 12:18 requires that the reference in chapter 8 to the collection mission of Titus and the brothers be earlier. It is precisely this issue that both Weiss and Mitchell address (Mitchell 2004: 307–38, ). Mitchell's thesis, however, is still a work in progress. What needs to be developed is a treatment of the role of the itinerant apostles in the doubts being raised about the integrity of Paul's ministry. Moreover, a sequel to Bornkamm's explanation of the redactional pre-history of the present letter and some explanation for the present arrangement of the letter fragments would be most welcome. Nevertheless, Mitchell's emphasis on tensions created by Paul's strategy in promoting the offering and their linkage with doubts about Paul's apostolic legitimacy in 1 Corinthians is convincing. In summary, one may outline Mitchell's thesis as follows:

1  2 Cor. 8 commends Titus and the brothers to the Corinthian church to complete the collection. Effort founders and word comes of Corinthian suspicions of Paul's conduct and fitness for ministry.

2  2 Cor. 2:14–7:4 (minus 6:14–7:1) responds to charges about Paul's fitness for apostolic ministry and his lack of divine authority. His trailing visit was a disaster. He left Corinth humiliated by the individual and hurt by the defecting church (2 Cor. 2:1; 7:9, 11f.).

3  2 Cor. 10:1–13:10 includes Paul's second, slashing defense of his apostolic claims and message. This "letter of tears" was hand-carried by Titus with the hope he could right the floundering mission and restore confidence in Paul.

4  2 Cor. 1:1–2:13; 7:5–16; and 13:11–13 offers a softer rhetoric of the reconciliation Titus effected.

5  2 Cor. 9 sets in motion the final stages of the offering. Addressed to *all* of the churches in Achaia, this letter envisions the great assembling of the collection from the churches of Achaia and Macedonia and their delegates for the pilgrimage to Jerusalem to deliver the offering.

6  Paul writes the Roman church from Corinth that the offering is ready, the delegation is chosen, and the journey to present the offering is about to begin Paul is quite anxious that the presentation may not go well (Rom. 15:26–32).

## Summary of Letter Partition Theories

*Selected proponents*

*Single–letter hypotheses*
> W. G. Kümmel (1975), N. A. Dahl (1977), B. Witherington III (1995), J. Lambrecht (1994), and F. Matera (2003). See Matera (2003: 29 n.24) for others, but exempt F. Danker, who was erroneously included.

*Two–letter hypotheses*
> 1    2 Cor. 1–8; Rom. 16; 2 Cor. 9 and 13:11–13 (first after 1 Cor.); 2 Cor. 10:1–13:10 (second) – Semler (1758).
> > 2 Cor. 10–13, "letter of tears," and 2 Cor. 1–9 – Hausrath (1870).
> > 2 Cor. 1–9 followed by 10–13; "letter of tears" lost – Furnish (1984) and Barrett (1968).
> 2    2 Cor.10–13 ("letter of tears") followed by 1–9 – J. H. Kennedy (1900) and Watson (1984).
> > See Thrall (1994–2000: I, 49) for other scholars holding this position.

*Three letters*
> 1    2 Cor. 1–8; 9; 10–13 – H. Windisch (1924), M. Thrall (1994–2000), Quesnel (2003). (1) 2 Cor. 8 (offering); (2) 2:14–7:1 minus 6:14–7:1; 10–13 ("letter of tears"); (3) 1:1–2:13; 7:5–16; 9 (letter of reconciliation) – Weiss (1910).
> 2    2 C.or. 10–13 ("letter of tears"); 1–8 (letter of reconciliation); 9 – F. Lang (1973). Also, 10–13:10 ("letter of tears"); 9; 1–8 – Héring (1958).

*Five letters*
> 1    2 Cor. 2:14–7:4; 10–13; 1:1–2:13; and 7:5–16 perhaps with chapter 8; 9. Bornkamm (1971).
> > Similarly, Georgi (1964) and Betz (1985) except 8 and 9 are seen as separate letters.
> > For other scholars holding one of these positions see Thrall (1994–2000: I, 48f.).
> 2    2 Cor. 8; 2:14–7:4; 10–13:10; 1:1–2:13; 7:5–16; 13:11–13 (reconciling letter); 9 (offering appeal to assemblies of Achaia) – Mitchell (2004).

## What Went Wrong at Corinth? Source(s) of the Conflict

While 2 Corinthians bristles with literary challenges, others face the reader as well. What or who was behind the Corinthian hostility toward, or suspicion and ridicule of, Paul? Who commissioned the "super apostles"? What was their gospel? Did they have allies? Did they represent a movement? Did Paul really understand the substance of their criticism?

More than fifty years ago (1957) a dissertation by Dieter Georgi named Paul's antag-onists and offered a verbal sketch of their profile. Drawing on the research of the great historian of religion Richard Reitzenstein, Georgi believed that the emphasis on the union with God of the mystery religions was the key that unlocked the deep secrets of the identity and the *modus operandi* of the "super apostles." Mediated through a Hellenized Diaspora Judaism that brought the great heroic figures like Moses, Abraham, and Elijah under a mystical nimbus, this mystical spirit then bled into the early Jesus movement shaping a *theios aner* (divine man) Christology. The incan-descent power of the miracle-working Jesus as a *theios aner*, it was believed, infused and transformed the apostles and early missionaries into miracle-working *theioi andres*, i.e. divine men incorporating all kinds of mystical and miraculous powers. Among them were rhetorical prowess and the powers of inspired exegesis. So manifested, these powers rose up to legitimate their apostolic claimants, to authenticate the power of their gospel, and to provide a legitimate ground for boasting in what God was doing through them. Moreover, their rhetorical skills and apostolic persona undercut those of the weakly and rhetorically unskilled Paul. According to Georgi, these anony-mous "super apostles" (2 Cor. 11:5; 13; 21–31) claimed the right to a financial support that appropriately affirmed their status as divine men. The challenge posed by these wandering "super apostles," Georgi claimed, completely differentiated 2 from 1 Corinthians.

As attractive and provocative as was Georgi's thesis, it was flawed. The neat history-of-religions trajectory Georgi drew between the mystery religions and the Diaspora synagogue rested on a very weak historical reed. The links he sought to forge between the Hellenized Diaspora synagogue and a divine-man Christology were easy to assert but impossible to prove. In spite of these blemishes, Georgi's thesis remains to this day to exert a profound influence on Pauline scholarship.

For the generation since Georgi's work most scholars have assumed that wholly different situations separate 1 from 2 Corinthians. In 1 Corinthians, a vicious critique of Paul was waged from within, while in 2 Corinthians the challenge to the legitimacy of Paul's gospel and his apostleship came from without through these divine men viewed as charismatic miracle-workers.

Except for Galatians, nowhere was the challenge to the legitimacy of Paul's apostle-ship more threatening than in parts of 2 Corinthians. The "holy ones" are suspicious of Paul's motives; they suspect him of dishonesty; they judge him inferior to the "super apostles." Compared to those of the rival apostles, Paul's credentials are notably defi-cient. He carries no letter(s) of recommendation that attest to his prowess as a charis-matic miracle-worker. He lacks the rhetorical skill they display in spontaneous, spirit-filled oratory. His weak bodily presence (2 Cor. 10:10) hardly radiated the glory they associated with spirit possession. His claim to financial self-sufficiency while simul-taneously raising money for the Jerusalem offering raised suspicions about his integrity and apostolic legitimacy.

But already in 1965 John C. Hurd Jr. placed this scholarly dogma under question. While not explicitly challenging Georgi's thesis, Hurd's study of *The Origin of 1 Corinthians* offered an implicit critique of the emerging scholarly orthodoxy that a totally different challenge inspired 2 Corinthians than provoked 1 Corinthians. Drawing especially on his comparison of 1 Corinthians 9 and 2 Corinthians 8 Hurd (1965: 202–6) saw continuities that until Mitchell were largely overlooked or ignored.

Mitchell has recently dealt a detailed, devastating blow to the scholarly orthodoxy that has made 2 Corinthians a focused response to the challenge brought by the itinerant rival apostles who were totally different from the intramural troublemakers in 1 Corinthians. Her observations are compelling, but what remains to be decided is the role the rival, itinerant apostles played in further inflaming suspicions of Paul and his gospel and questions they raised about his fitness for ministry that were already appearing in 1 Corinthians. Some level of continuity can be assumed between the two letters; however, there are discontinuities as well. And the recent, formidable challenge to Paul's ministry posed by the "super apostles" lingered to complicate and poison an already strained relationship between Paul and the church. In the discussion below, we shall attend to both internal and external challenges to Paul's ministry.

## A Proposed Order and Discourse of the Letter Fragments

A series of contacts between Paul and the Corinthians pre-dates the writing of any part of 2 Corinthians. In outline form let us view those contacts:

1   Paul's preaching in Corinth.
2   Hearing before Gallio and his departure.
3   Letter A written to the Corinthians (1 Cor. 5:9). Missing.
4   Corinthians write Paul (1 Cor. 7:1; letter lost) and send oral communication (16:17) about deteriorating situation in the church at Corinth.
5   Letter B: Paul writes 1 Corinthians responding to both oral and written communication perhaps from Macedonia.
6   Letter C: Paul writes third letter, 2 Corinthians 8, and dispatches it with a delegation led by Titus to complete the offering project.
7   Paul receives word of challenges to his ministry. Complex but spring from two interactive sources – itinerant rival apostles, and converts skeptical of his legitimacy, perhaps even questioning his honesty.
8   Letter D: Paul writes letter 4, 2 Corinthians 2:14–7:4 (minus 6:14–7:1) defending his ministry. Dispatches the letter.
9   Further troubling news prompts Paul to make brief "painful" visit to Corinth that is a disaster (2 Cor. 2:1–2). Paul retreats to Ephesus in disgrace.
10  Letter E: Paul writes the "letter of tears" (2 Cor. 10:1–13:10) and dispatches Titus with the letter in an attempt to effect a reconciliation.
11  Paul leaves Ephesus, perhaps by land, with plans to meet Titus in Troas. When Titus does not show, Paul crosses into Macedonia and there a rendezvous takes place. Titus brings news of reconciliation.
12  Letter F: Paul writes reconciling letter (2 Cor. 1:1–2:13, 7:5–16, 13:11–13) and dispatches Titus with the letter.
13  Letter G: Paul sends on ahead his final instructions on preparing the offering to all of the churches in Achaia (2 Cor. 9).

14    Paul travels to Corinth with a delegation from Macedonia. The offering complete, the delegation constituted, Paul writes Romans (15:25–9) of plans to lead the delegation to Jerusalem and then to visit Rome on his way to Spain.

## Letter C: 2 Corinthians 8

### Introduction

The linguistic ties between Paul's instructions about the offering in 1 Corinthians 16:1–11 and 2 Corinthians 8 suggest a direct literary sequence of the two passages. In 2 Corinthians 8:1, 4, 6, 7, and 19 *charis* alludes to the offering implicitly even when not directly denoting it. 1 Corinthians 16:3 has *charin humon* for "your gift ('grace')." The move from *logeia* ("collection") to *charis* (gift or "grace") parallels the shift from *charis* ("grace" or gift) to diakonia (ministry) of 2 Corinthians 8:4 (Mitchell: 2004: 20–2). When Paul's retrospective comment in 12:17f. regarding an earlier offering project in chapter 8 is added to these literary connections the argument for considering chapter 8 as an independent letter coming on the heels of 1 Corinthians is compelling. The long pre-history of the offering project need not be recited here (Gal. 2:1–2, 6–10), but its dedication to the "poor among the saints" in Jerusalem recalls the eschatological vision of Isaiah (2:1–5; 60:10–16). While presumably a significant number of the Jesus people in Jerusalem were desperately poor, it was the combination of their need, and the apocalyptic vision of the gathering of God's people there, that most likely gave the offering its symbolic power and moral imperative.

If the positing of this sequence is plausible then Paul would have composed and sent 2 Corinthians 8 with Titus, and two strangely anonymous brothers, one of whom was chosen by a democratic vote of the churches, to assist with readying the collection. Paul recognized the importance of giving the collection project transparency (8:20). Begun in Corinth the year before (2 Cor. 8:10), the offering must now be completed in readiness for the Jerusalem visit. But between Paul's dispatch of Titus and the "brothers" with this letter and the penning of 2 Corinthians 2:14–7:4 (minus 6:14–7:1) came news of setbacks for the offering project and disturbing news of attacks on Paul's ministry.

Chapter 8 falls into two parts – one appealing to the examples of the Macedonian church and the sacrifice of the Lord Jesus to urge the completion of the offering (8:1–15), and the other urging a welcome of Titus and the brothers by giving proof of "their love," i.e. by completing the project begun the year before (8:16–24).

A later hand removed the traditional salutation and thanksgiving to join chapter 8 to a broader narrative framework. The letter body begins with the disclosure formula "We want you to know [*gnōrizomen*], brothers and sisters about the grace of God that has been granted to the churches of Macedonia" (8:1; cf. 2 Cor. 1:8; 1 Cor. 1:8; Philem. 8–9; Gal. 1:11; 1 Thess. 2:1; and Phil. 1:12).

In a long, rambling, overloaded sentence Paul opens the body of the letter by lifting up the Macedonian converts (8:1–5) as models worthy of emulation. Even though dirt poor themselves, the Macedonians begged for the privilege of sharing in this grace. Their example, Paul claims, summons the Corinthians to complete their offering as an act of religious devotion (*diakonia*) and a shared participatory act (*koinonia*).

The introduction concludes with a reference to the commission of Titus (8:6) and a diplomatic encomium praising the Corinthians for their abundance "in everything" – faith, speech, knowledge, zeal, and love (8:6–7; note the formal parallel to 1 Cor. 1:5–7). Thus Paul forged a subtle link between their charismatic gifts sometimes on display (1 Cor. 12–13) and the offering as an earthy gesture of *charis*. To this praise Paul links a rich Christological formula (8:8–9) that speaks of Jesus' act of self-abnegation – who though rich for their sake became poor that they who were poor might become rich. Thus Paul bound the readers in a pact with Christ whose logical consequence was obvious. Trailing this Christological formula came the "advice" (*gnōmēn*) to complete the collection. Given the paucity of imperatives in this chapter (only one) Paul may be alive to the charge that he had earlier acted in an imperious, high-handed manner. Then the first part of the letter concludes by promoting a vital reciprocity between Corinthian and Jerusalem believers (8:13–15) and calling on Exodus 16:18 (LXX) almost verbatim to support his appeal.

In this second part of the letter, Paul commends his envoys to the congregation (8:16–23). He introduces Titus and the two anonymous "brothers" who are to assist, advise, and encourage the completion of the offering. Paul's commendation is based on his first-hand knowledge of the efforts in Macedonia of Titus (8:6), whom he portrays as a man of a divinely inspired, multivalent zeal (*spoudē*, 8:16) – i.e. earnest, serious, dedicated, conscientious, skilled, diligent, reliable, and of sound moral character (8:16). Titus' acceptance of this commission, confirms his suitability for this task (8:17). He mentions the *anonymous* "brother," "famous among all the churches for his preaching" (8:18, RSV), who was democratically chosen "by a showing of hands" (*cheirotonētheis*). As a delegate of the churches he would lend the process integrity and transparency. Obviously, Paul says this to telegraph his good will, and to deflect blame (8:19–21).

In 8:22 Paul commends a second anonymous "brother" briefly, and praises both "brothers" as representatives of the churches and Christ's glory. But by naming Titus as the leader of the delegation he takes the spotlight off the brothers, delegates of the churches, to focus it on Titus, his appointee, as a "partner" and "co-worker" on "your behalf" (8:23). This has all of the traits of a power move by Paul that may have later aggravated tensions between him and the Corinthians.

The conclusion of the letter (8:24) directs the church to welcome the delegation, give evidence of their love – a theme of the letter (8:7–8) – by giving it concrete expression. The proof of their love is twofold: a generous gift to the offering and a warm welcome of the commissioned delegation. Folded into this admonition is a return full circle to Paul's boast about the Corinthians (8:24b).

## Letter D: 2 Corinthians 2:14–7:4 (minus 6:14–7:1)

*Paul's first defense of his apostolic fitness*

After dispatching Titus and the two "brothers" Paul learns, perhaps from Titus himself, of Corinthian suspicions of and questions about his fitness for ministry. He also hears about the presence in Corinth of wandering charismatic preachers who have come with letters of recommendation from other churches and who are further aggravating an already inflamed situation. This letter reveals only fleeting glimpses of these intruders, thus making any sketch of their profile difficult. We cannot know if the outburst in 2 Corinthians 2:17 refers to Corinthian suspicions of Paul or Paul's ridicule of the itinerant rivals as "peddlers of God's word." Nevertheless, in 3:1 he does explicitly raise the specter of challengers arriving with "letters of recommendation" from other churches, perhaps even Pauline ones. That could not have been good news for Paul. Later in 5:12 Paul describes the *modus operandi* of these rivals: They "boast in outward appearance and not in the heart." They sow suspicions that Paul preaches an opaque or "veiled" gospel (4:3). While the exact nature of their claims is unclear, their collusion with internal critics fanned the flames of distrust and suspicion of Paul's ministry and his offering project. The heat of his response to these shadowy figures is tepid when compared with the flaming, vicious sarcasm later heaped on the "super apostles" in chapters 10–13. That fiery rejoinder, however, came after his short and disastrous "painful visit" to Corinth soon after this defense was written. Might that visit have given Paul a direct and painful experience of the threat they posed that at this stage was somewhat diffuse?

## Introduction: 2:14–3:6

While the conventions of the letter opening have been removed, a vestige of the thanksgiving may remain – the thanksgiving traditionally telegraphs the agenda of the letter to the reader. The letter begins, "To God be thanks ..." (2:14a) and prefigures a statement of the letter's central theme – Paul's defense of his fitness for ministry, his apostolic integrity, his fiscal trustworthiness, and his powerful status as *diakonos* – i.e. agent, servant, intermediary, or minister (2:14b–17). His self-portrayal as a herald of and participant in God's powerful, triumphal, apocalyptic victory procession contrasts starkly with the puny, physical persona that invited sneers and ridicule (2 Cor. 4:7–12; 6:4–10; 11:23–9).

The two evocative metaphors Paul employs in the opening contrast the humiliation and glory of his ministry. In the first Paul inserts himself into God's dramatic triumphal procession, a metaphor taken from the victory parade of a returning triumphant Roman commander. The metaphor invites an act of imagination. If Paul speaks of being an agent or herald of God's apocalyptic triumph, the metaphor of triumph and holy war collides dramatically with that his critics use, namely that he is a charlatan, a "huckster," hawking God's word for selfish gain (2:17). If, on the other hand, Paul's place in the procession is less noble, paraded in chains in shameful display as a pitiable captive, the metaphor assumes a profoundly ironic character that hides the secret of God's means of self-disclosure and a defense of his fitness for apostolic ministry.

The first metaphor, however, interacts with and is interpreted by a second. Paul's second metaphor interacts with and interprets the first. Here fragrance meets fragrance. Like incense rising to praise and thank the gods for salvation, for the victory proclaimed, the *Pax Romana* secured, the fragrance of Christ rising up from God's procession is being announced everywhere. But depending on one's social and political location the metaphor can signify quite different things. For those "being saved," i.e. victors, the fragrance is a token of life, but for those "perishing," i.e. victims, the fragrance reeked with the stench of carrion (2:16). This pregnant metaphor thus links Paul's own mortality with the death of Jesus and simultaneously with incipient life, and lays the groundwork for the defense of the "sufficiency" (*hikanos*) of his ministry that will follow.

### The body of the letter: 3:7–6:10

The contrasts drawn in 3:7–4:6 defend Paul's ministry; they stoutly assert, "we preach not ourselves but Christ Jesus our lord ..." (4:5). This section rings with a powerful description of Paul's ministerial self-understanding and the Christological and soteriological elements informing it. Throughout there is a clear apologetic aim, a defense and oft-times a polemic. In dispute was an interpretation of Exodus 34:29–35 that belittled Paul's ministerial competence. It radiated no blinding incandescent glory. Did critics view the evanescent divine glory reflected in Moses' face after his encounter with Yahweh as an authenticating sign of divine agency? Similarly, did Paul's bodily weakness and charismatic deficiency raise doubts about the authenticity of his divine commission? In response, Paul sought to relativize Moses' ministry of the old "covenant" with his "ministry of the new" (3:6), Moses' "ministry of death" (3:7) with his ministry of life-giving "spirit" (3:8), Moses' "ministry of condemnation" (3:9) with his own "ministry of righteousness" (3:9). (Please note, he does not repudiate Moses or the law.)

In 4:7–5:10 body language dealing with Paul's apostolic ministry and human mortality comes to the fore. Behind Paul's biting irony that "we have this treasure in clay pots" (4:7) lurk hostile questions: If Paul's ministry is so glorious why is his physical presence so pitiful? If his gospel is of God why is it given such a weak bodily presence? Here Paul defends his lack of physical gravitas by fixing on eternal, unseen verities (4:16–18). In 5:11–21 Paul highlights his "ministry of reconciliation" (5:19), giving it a substantial theological foundation. Finally, in 6:1–13 and 7:2–4 he offers a powerful, concluding speech of summation reminiscent of the concluding remarks of a defense attorney before a jury. He urges his hearers not to accept God's word in vain (6:1). He protests his innocence – giving no one occasion to find fault with his ministry (6:3). He flicks out a jab at his critics in a sentence dripping with irony. He "commends" himself negatively – in beatings, imprisonments, persecution, anguish, riots, labors, sleepless nights, and hunger (6:3–5) – and only then positively – in purity, patience, kindness, sincere love, and true speech (6:6–8). With sarcasm he recites accusations and replies – seen as deceivers but yet true, as dying, but miraculously alive, as punished but not dying, as destitute but "making many rich," as having nothing and yet having everything (6:9–10). He defends the honesty and openness of his speech (mouth) and begs the Corinthians to make room in their hearts for him (6:11–13; 7:2–3). And finally, in what probably just preceded the final "grace" that typically closes the letter, he offers a brief recapitulation: "We have wronged no one; we have corrupted no one; we have defrauded no one" (7:2, my translation), and that is followed by a conventional expression of confidence in the Corinthians and abounding joy in all of his tribulation (7:2–4). One can almost sense the hush settling over the hearers as the letter was read aloud to the congregation.

## Letter E: 2 Corinthians 10:1–13:10

### "The letter of tears" or Paul's second defense

An appeal for reconciliation and trust, a plea for an open-armed welcome of Paul and his co-workers, and a protestation of innocence ends the first apology (letter D). Paul's hopes for an open-armed reception were dashed, however, when he soon learned that the situation in Corinth was so dire that a personal visit to repair the damage was urgent. He set out for Corinth. However, his brief, "painful" visit (2:1) was a disaster. In a public confrontation, partisans of the "super apostles" (11:6–7) humiliated him, criticized his weak physical presence, his inept speech (10:10; 11:6; 12:7), and his cowardice (10:1). Publicly shamed and demeaned, Paul beat a hasty retreat (12:21; 13:2) to Ephesus. Then, from a safe distance, he wrote the "letter of tears" (later reported in 2:4) in defense. Simultaneously he dispatched Titus to attempt a rapprochement. Paul and Titus agreed to rendezvous in Troas (near ancient Troy), but, worried sick, Paul could not wait, and set sail for Macedonia, intercepting Titus there. The stakes were high. The legitimacy and future of Paul's Gentile mission were at stake. With the visit of Titus and the impassioned defense of his ministry (10–13) Paul sought to turn the tide, but the outcome was clearly in the balance.

In 10:1–18 Paul rehearses the charges against him "by some" (10:3). They mock him for his bravado from a safe distance, he who is so humble when he is present among them (10:2); they reckon that he walks "according to the flesh" (10:2). In 10:10 Paul recalls the antagonist's charges against him (singular "he who" not "they who" in NRSV): "his letters are weighty and strong, but his bodily presence is weak and his speech is despicable." Paul had opened the letter appealing to the Corinthians "in the meekness and gentleness of Christ" (10:1), but soon defines the contest with metaphors of warfare with its horror and devastation (10:3–6).

In 11:1–12:13 Paul brilliantly parodies himself as a fool. With withering sarcasm, dripping irony, and caustic parody Paul attempts to demolish the arguments of his antagonists. Where they glorify strength, he magnifies "weakness" (12:9, 10). Where they draw invidious comparisons between themselves and him, he refuses to be condemned by these comparisons (11:5, 13–15; 12:11–13). Where they glorify their rhetorical skills, he diminishes his (but not his "knowledge," 11:6). Where they accept pay for their ministry and fault Paul for refusing local support, Paul defends his refusal of financial support (11:7–12; 12:13).

In 12:14–13:10 Paul rushes to the end of the letter. He announces an impending threatening "apostolic *parousia*" and concludes with a "shotgun" parenesis. (Apparently 13:11–14 belongs to the letter of reconciliation that was to follow.)

# Letter F: 2 Corinthians 1:1–2:13, 7:5–16, 13:11–13

*Letter of reconciliation*

After Titus left Ephesus for Corinth with the "letter of tears" on his healing mission, Paul set out by land to rendezvous with him either in Troas or one of the mission cities in Macedonia. Out of his mind with worry, when Paul could wait no longer, he set sail for Macedonia hoping to intercept Titus with news from Corinth. To his profound relief he met Titus who brought the happy report of the Corinthian reconciliation with Paul and renewed trust in his ministry and gospel. Paul was obviously relieved, if not ecstatic. With the passing of the storm, Paul wrote the entire letter that we have in amended form (1:1–2:13; 7:5–16; 13:11–14). Later hands trimmed and inserted other letter fragments to form what we now have in the canon. Where the previous letter had ended with a stern warning: ""I write this ... in order that when I come I may not have to be severe in my use of the authority which the Lord has given me" (13:10). The tone of the letter of reconciliation, however, is totally other. It is full of generosity; it softens the earlier harsh rhetoric; it breathes collegiality, partnership, trust, and confidence; and finally, it ends with a warm benediction and grace. These softer, gentler tones are obvious in the outline following.

Although addressed to the Corinthian church the salutation includes "all the saints throughout Achaia" (1:1) as well, and concludes with the stereotypical "Grace to you and peace from God our father and the Lord Jesus Christ" (1:2). Instead of the thanksgiving stands a blessing, a wonder-full poem of praise to God for the consolation bestowed in distress (1:3–7) through which is affirmed a partnership with the believers in Corinth *and* Achaia. Exactly as the thanksgiving functions, this *berakah* articulates the theme of the letter.

To this blessing is attached a disclosure formula (1:8) with new information in it. Paul reveals how very close to death he came in Asia, and how his extremity occasioned their prayers, linking them once again in partnership (1:8–11). The contrast of this language of partnership (1:3–11) with the soft-toned defense of charges of fickleness and unreliability (1:15–24) and the painful recollection of his earlier disastrous visit (2:1) that sparked "the tearful letter" (2:1; 10–13) is so powerful that the letter almost pulses in one's hands. Nevertheless, through these painful recollections Paul's emphasis on partnership remains in effect (1:23–4). It soft-pedals his apostolic authority so boldly asserted only recently (1:24 vs. 13:10) and affirms a love that once seemed distant (2:4).

This same spirit of accommodation and reconciliation continues in 2:5–11 where the now more pastoral apostle urges the church to "forgive" and "console" the repentant offender who so berated him on his "painful visit" (2:7). Please note the recurring emphasis on consolation so necessary for healing a fractured relationship.

In 2:12–13 Paul recalls his agonizing and suspenseful trip probably from Ephesus to Troas and later Macedonia, desperately hoping for reassuring news from Titus on a reconciling mission to Corinth perhaps with the "letter of tears." Their separate journeys end happily when Titus brings word to Paul about the reconciliation of the Corinthians and their longing for Paul (7:5–7). Continuing with his earlier emphasis on consolation (1:3–4, 5–7, 8–11, 23) Paul rejoices over the consoling end to various afflictions (7:6–7).

In 7:8–12 Paul reflects on the "letter of tears." At one point, he regretted sending it (7:8–9), but given the "good grief" it produced that brought them to their senses, he no longer regrets having written it (7:8–12). The change in their attitude toward Paul that it produced – the "repentance unto salvation" it effected – has obviously generated a similar change in him. The crisis that so recently threatened their relationship has been resolved, and the theme of consolation with which the letter opened finds a poignant articulation in this restoration of confidence. Whereas he has so recently berated the Corinthians, he now is able to express "complete confidence" in them (7:16). Paul's relief is palpable, as his sickening worry (7:5–6) turns to joy and confidence (7:13–16), and enables him to end the letter with the warm benediction and grace in 13:11–13: "The grace of the Lord Jesus Christ, the love of God, and the communion of the Holy Spirit be with all of you."

## Letter G: 2 Corinthians 9:1–15

*Offering letter to churches in Achaia*

Now in Macedonia, and with the fury of the storm passed, Paul returns to his initial concern with and promotion of the offering effort (1 Cor. 16:1–4; 2 Cor. 8), In 2 Corinthians 9:1–18 he addresses all of the house churches in Achaia, urging them to ready their offering for presentation to the "poor among the saints" in Jerusalem. When we next hear from Paul he is in Corinth. The offering from the churches in Macedonia and Achaia is ready for delivery and delegates have been chosen to accompany the offering. With fear and trembling Paul heads to Jerusalem with the delegation commissioned to deliver the collection (Rom. 15:25–33). In 9:2–5 Paul introduces the "brothers" who will organize and encourage the collection effort, and in 9:2–14 he provides a theological rationale for the offering with a strong eschatological nuance. The letter concludes with a spontaneous cry of thanksgiving (9:15). The traditional expression of grace and closing is missing.

## An Appended Note

The way that 2 Corinthians 6:14–7:1 interrupts a discussion begun in 6:11–13 and is resumed in 7:2 urging the Corinthians to open their hearts to Paul and his co-workers has convinced many scholars that this is a non-Pauline interpolation or even an anti-Pauline interpolation (Furnish 1984: 360–8; Betz 1985: 88–108). Both the non-Pauline language and the non-Pauline viewpoints of the passage when combined with the lack of integration into its present context all argue against a Pauline provenance. For example, its urging of the addressees to separate themselves from unbelievers and all uncleanness flatly contradicts 1 Corinthians 7:12–16 and 14:21–4 that commends some accommodation with unbelievers, and hardly harmonizes with Paul's proscription against attending pagan temple ceremonies (1 Cor. 10). If cited by Paul but from another source, it seems to gainsay other instructions given to the Corinthians. Consequently, at best it would remain only tangentially Pauline in its emphasis and theology. It seems more likely that a later redactor inserted it perhaps to deal with fearful compromises with a dominant and imposing culture.

## Conclusion

Paul's extended correspondence with the Corinthians, his use of apostolic envoys, personal visits, and argument, gives us an excellent picture of how he dealt with crises in the Corinthian church. Paul not only defended himself against charges and suspicions raised by critics from within but also from those without from itinerant apostles and their followers. He also laid the groundwork for a gospel that provided a means of separating the true from the false, the true apostle from the huckster, the true witness from the imposter, the true from trifling speech, real from false strength, true wealth from the counterfeit coinage, and the true gospel from the glitzy rival focused on success and glory. He offered no escape from the harsh realities of this world but offered a new vision of those realities. And finally, he offered a ministry of the "new creation" that helped define true fitness for ministry, apostolic legitimacy, and the realization of a ministry of reconciliation when profound differences emerged.

### Selected Bibliography

Barnett, P. *The Second Epistle to the Corinthians*. Grand Rapids: Eerdmans, 1997.

Barrett, C. K. *A Commentary on the First Epistle to the Corinthians*. London: Adam & Charles Black, 1968.

Barrett, C. K. *A Commentary on the Second Epistle to the Corinthians*. Harper's New Testament Commentaries. New York: Harper & Row, 1973.

Betz, H. D. *2 Corinthians 8 and 9*. Hermeneia. Philadelphia: Fortress Press, 1985.

Bornkamm, G. "Die Vorgeschichte des sogenannten zweiten Korintherbriefes." Pp. 162–90 in *Gesammelte Aufsätze*. Beiträge zur evangelischen Theologie, theologische Abhandlungen, Band 48. Munich: Kaiser, 1971. Originally published as *Die Vorgeschichte des sogenannten zweiten Korintherbriefe*. Sitzungsberichte der Heidelberger Akademie der Wissenschaften, Philosophisch-Historische Klasse. Jahrgang 1961. 2. Abhandlung. Heidelberg: C. Winter, 1961. Abbreviated English rendition: "The History of the Origin of the So-Called Second Letter to the Corinthians," *New Testament Studies* 8 (1962), 258–63.

Bultmann, R. *The Second Letter to the Corinthians*. Trans. R. A. Harrisville. Minneapolis: Augsburg Publishing House, 1976.

Dahl, N. A. *Studies in Paul*. Minneapolis: Augsburg Publishing House, 1977.

Danker, F. W. "Paul's Debt to the *De Corona* of Demosthenes: A Study of Rhetorical Techniques in Second Corinthians." Pp. 268–80 in *Persuasive Artistry: Studies in New Testament Rhetoric in Honor of G. A. Kennedy*. Edited by D. F. Watson. Sheffield: Sheffield Academic Press, 1991.

Furnish, V. P. *II Corinthians: Translated with Introduction, Notes and Commentary*. Anchor Bible, 32A. Garden City, NY: Doubleday, 1984.

Garland, David. *2 Corinthians*. Nashville: B. & H. Publishing Group, 2000.

Georgi, D. *Die Gegner des Paulus im 2. Korintherbrief.* Wissenschaftliche Monographien zum Alten und Neuen Testament, 11. Neukirchen-Vluyn: Neukirchener Verlag, 1964. The author's doctoral dissertation at the University of Heidelberg, 1958.

Georgi, D. *The Opponents of Paul in Second Corinthians*. Philadelphia: Fortress Press, 1986.

Hausrath, A. *Der Vier-Kapitel-Brief des Paulus an die Korinther*. Heidelberg: Basserman, 1870.

Héring, J. *La Seconde Épitre de Saint Paul aux Corinthiens*. Neuchatel: Delachaux et Niestle, 1958.

Hurd, J. C., Jr. *The Origin of 1 Corinthians*. London: SPCK, 1965.

Käsemann, E. "Die Legitimität des Apostels. Eine Untersuch zu II Korinther 10–13," Zeitschrift für die neutestamentliche Wissenschaft 41 (1942), 33–71.

Kennedy, G. A. *New Testament Interpretation through Rhetorical Criticism*. Chapel Hill: University of North Carolina Press, 1984.

Kennedy, J. H. *The Second and Third Epistles of St. Paul to the Corinthians*. London: Methuen, 1900.

Kümmel, W. G. *Introduction to the New Testament*. Trans. H. C. Kee. Nashville: Abingdon, 1975.

Lambrecht, J. *Studies on 2 Corinthians*. Leuven: Leuven University Press, 1994.

Lang, Friedrich. *2. Korinther 5, 1–10 in der neueren Forschung*. Beiträge zur Geschichte der biblischen Exegese, 16. Tübingen: Mohr Siebeck, 1973.

Matera, F. J. *II Corinthians, A Commentary*. Louisville: Westminster John Knox, 2003.

McCant, J. W. *2 Corinthians*. Sheffield: Sheffield Academic Press, 1999.

Mitchell, M. M. "Paul's Letters to Corinth: The Interpretive Intertwining of Literary and Historical Reconstruction." Pp. 307–38 in *Urban Religion in Roman Corinth*. Edited by Daniel Schowalter and Steven J. Friesen. Cambridge, MA: Harvard University Press, 2004.

Murphy-O'Connor, J. *Paul, A Critical Life*. Oxford: Clarendon Press, 1996.

Murphy-O'Connor, J. *St. Paul's Corinth. Texts and Archeology*. Collegeville: Liturgical Press, 2002.

Quesnel, Michael B. *Conformation to the Death of Christ and the Hope of the Resurrection: An Exegetico-Theological Study of 2 Corinthians 4, 7–15 and Philippians 3, 7–11*. Rome: Editrice Pontificia Università, 2003.

Scott, J. M. *2 Corinthians*. Peabody: Hendrickson, 1998.

Semler, Johann Salomo. *Commentatio ad 2. Corinth*. Hallae Magdeurgicae: Hendel, 1758.

Thrall, M. E. *A Critical and Exegetical Commentary on the Second Epistle to the Corinthians*. International Critical Commentary on the Holy Scriptures of the Old and New Testaments. 2 vols. Edinburgh: T. & T. Clark, 1994–2000.

Theissen, G. *The Social Setting of Pauline Christianity. Essays on Corinth*. Edited and translated J. H. Schültz. Philadelphia: Fortress Press, 1982.

Watson, F. "2 Cor. x–xiii and Paul's Painful Letter to the Corinthians." Journal of Theological Studies 35 (1984), 324–46.

Weiss, J. *Der erste Korintherbrief*. Kritisch-exegetischer Kommentar über das Neue Testament, 7. Göttingen: Vandenhoeck & Ruprecht, 1910; repr. 1970.

Weiss, J. *Das Urchristentum*. Ed. R. Knopf. Göttingen: Vandenhoeck & Ruprecht, 1917. English translation: *Earliest Christianity*. 2 vols. Trans. F. C. Grant et al. New York: Harper & Brothers, 1959.

Windisch, H. *Der zweite Korintherbrief*. Kritisch-exegetischer Kommentar über das Neue Testament, 6. 9. Auflage. Göttingen: Vandenhoeck & Ruprecht, 1924.

Witherington, Ben. *Conflict and Community in Corinth: A Socio-Rhetorical Commentary on 1 and 2 Corinthians*. Grand Rapids: Eerdmans; Carlisle: Paternoster, 1995.

Young, F. M. and D. F. Ford. *Meaning and Truth in 2 Corinthians*. Grand Rapids: Eerdmans, 1988.

CHAPTER 25

# Galatians

Mark D. Nanos

## Major Issues and Directions in Recent Study

The role of Galatians in the history of Pauline interpretation can hardly be overstated. During the second century, Marcion placed it at the beginning of his canon of epistles. Although Tertullian opposed Marcion, he agreed with him that Galatians was "the primary epistle against Judaism" (*Adversus Marcionem*, 5.2.1). In the sixteenth century, Luther referred to Galatians affectionately as "my epistle," to which he considered himself betrothed. At the dawn of the historical-critical period, F. C. Baur argued that this text provided a perfect thesis for the application of Hegelian dialectic theory, since here Paul supposedly distinguished his so-called "law-free gospel" from the vestiges of Jewish religion, to which James and Peter, the rivals to emerging Pauline (Gentile) Christianity, were deemed to be enslaved.

Paul's rhetoric engages many issues of Jewish identity and behavior, often citing the Tanakh (i.e., Old Testament), making Galatians a natural focal point for any discussion of Paul and Judaism or Torah (law). Many if not all constructions of early Christian church history, including the study of its principal authorities (Paul, Peter, and James), and its major developments (Pauline and Jewish Christianity) depend upon interpretations of the autobiographical narratives of Galatians 1–2. Discussion of the incident at Antioch, where Paul relates his condemnation of Peter (2:11–21) – a text feared by Origen, Chrysostom, and Jerome to potentially undermine the united voice of the apostles if taken as real instead of a strategic pretension – has been a central text for "new perspective" and other interpreters seeking to challenge traditional views of Paul and Judaism (cf. Cummins, 2001; Dunn 2002; Esler 2002; Fredriksen 2002; Nanos 2002d; Zetterholm 2003). Furthermore, many interpreters suppose the writing of this letter to be in response to the influence of Paul's "opponents" upon the Galatian addressees. Although variously defined, it is the interpreter's identification of these supposed opponents that continues to guide historical-critical constructions of the situation of Paul's addressees.

Similarly, Galatians has always been important to Christian theological developments. In addition to such obvious candidates as the study of Paul and Torah (Jewish law), concepts of freedom, spirituality, and ethical responsibility, the development of the doctrine of justification by faith and other subjects depend upon how this letter is interpreted. For example, the contemporary debates about how to understand Paul's use of the Greek phrases *erga nomou* ("works of law") and *pistis christou* (subjective or objective genitive; that is, as the "faith*fulness of* Christ" or "faith *in* Christ"), center around statements made in Galatians. Because of the appeal to values such as freedom and equality, Galatians is also of special interest to feminist, post-colonial, Jewish–Christian relations, and other contemporary critics, and continues to appeal to a broad range of readers.

Since the 1970s, the employment of rhetorical analysis in the study of Galatians has been particularly noteworthy. There is a noticeable shift of methodology in some recent works toward the employment of "new rhetoric," along with a growing recognition of the role of epistolary analysis – emphasizing that this is a letter rather than an oration.

## Date and Location of Addressees

Paul does not indicate where this letter was written, or when. The location of the letter's recipients also eludes certainty. Hence, each theory advanced to date depends upon a complex web of assumptions and decisions. In addition to analysis of features of Galatians, decisions frequently depend upon interpretations of Acts and the way events described therein are understood to correspond with details in Galatians, sketches of Paul's missionary journeys and references to his collection project, and a variety of theological matters.

Paul addresses more than one community in Galatia (he writes "to the church*es* [*ekklēsiai*]"), which raises several questions from the start. How close were these communities to each other, and how intimately were they linked? Was he referring to the ethnic *territory* of the Celts (which includes Ancyra, Pessinus, and Tavium), and thus northern west-central Asia Minor (Anatolia/approximating modern Turkey), the so-called North Galatian theory? This view represents the traditional consensus and was not substantially challenged until the late nineteenth century, by William M. Ramsay (1997: 197–340). Many interpreters remain convinced of its probability (cf., Lightfoot 1981: 18–25; Moffatt 1918: 90–101; Mussner 1974: 3–9; Betz 1979: 5–7; Martyn 1997: 15–17; Esler 1998: 32–6). Or were the addressees in the Roman *province* of Galatia, which, after 25 BCE, included the ethnic territory, from which the provincial name was derived (Mitchell 1993: II, 4), extending south almost to the Mediterranean Sea (incorporating Pisidia, Lycaonia, and part of Phrygia)? This administrative region (so-called South Galatia, although incorporating the ethnic territory to the north) includes locations in which Acts reports Paul's activities along the Roman road, via Sebaste (e.g., 13:1–16:5; 18:23), for example, Pisidian Antioch, an important Roman colonial city with Jewish communities, and other cities with Roman as well as Jewish populations: Derbe, Lystra, and Iconium. Since the groundbreaking argument of Ramsay, this view has been developed extensively (cf. Hemer 1989; Mitchell 1993: II, 3–10; Scott 1995; Breytenbach 1996; Witulski 2000), and adopted by a growing list of commentators (e.g., Burton 1921: xxi–xliv; Fung 1953: 1–3; Bruce 1982: 3–18;

R. Longenecker 1990: lxi–lxxii; Matera 1992: 19–26; Williams 1997: 19–21; Witherington 1998: 2–8; Jervis 1999: 7–15).

One ostensible advantage of including the south to south-central areas provided for by the provincial theories lies in the ability to account more naturally for the Jewish identity and behavioral matters that arise in Paul's rhetoric without requiring the intrusion of outside interest groups lacking local ties. These matters might be expected to arise within local Jewish communities of the south/south-central Roman province if Christ-believing non-Jews were seeking to understand themselves to be equal co-participants in the people of God, children of Abraham apart from proselyte conversion, and thus no longer obliged to participate in local "pagan" rituals, for example, imperial cult (Martin 1996; Nanos 2002a: 257–71).

Concerning dating, those who argue for the ethnic territory usually date the letter to the mid- to late 50s, based upon their understanding of Acts 16:6 and 18:23, combined with reading Galatians 4:13 as a reference to Paul's earliest visit. They argue that Paul would not have founded communities in the north until his second or third journeys, and would have written even later. The issues of circumcision and Torah arise after Paul's departure due to the arrival of Jewish–Christian groups with Jerusalem- or Antioch-based connections, not as a result of local Galatian communal dynamics. Thus, the probable paucity of Jewish communities in the ethnic territory to account for Paul's rhetorical concerns is not considered an obstacle to this thesis. Provincial theories generally date the letter to the late 40s to mid-50s, noting correspondence with locations to which Paul traveled as described in Acts, facilitated by Roman roads available in the southern areas of the province (unattested for the northern territory until after 70 CE), among other factors. Decisions between these choices are also often linked to the interpreter's understanding of whether or not the Jerusalem meeting mentioned in 2:1–10 took place before the meeting described in Acts 15 (11:27–30 or 12:25), describes the same meeting, or refers to a later one (chapter 21) (see Francis and Sampley 1984: 67, 141, 175, 207, 223, for outlines of five possible ways to align the texts of Galatians 2 and Acts). Advocates of each position support their arguments by appeal to Paul's mention of surprise at the suddenness of the Galatians' consideration of the alternative message (Gal. 1:6: "I am *surprised* that you are *so quickly* ..."); however, as discussed below, expressions of suddenness are a stereotypical feature of letters feigning "surprise" (*thaumazô*). Hence, this rhetorical detail does not quantify the time between Paul's departure and the writing of this letter in the way often supposed.

The interpreter of Galatians is arguably best served at present by working from Paul's rhetoric without privileging a choice of location or date (several recent commentaries adopt this approach: Dunn 1993a: 5–7; Perkins 2001: 1–3; and some listed above relativize the importance of this decision for their interpretations). The letter could have been written to any number of places within west-central Asia Minor, and at virtually any time in Paul's ministry, beginning either fourteen or seventeen years after the revelation of Christ he relates in Galatians 1:15–16 (cf. 1:18: "after three years"; 2:1: "after fourteen years"), in other words, at any time after the mid- to late 40s.

More agreement exists about the make-up of the individuals targeted by Paul's remarks. Since he refers to them as "formerly idolaters" (4:8–9), seeks to instill confidence in their right to understand themselves to be children of Abraham without becoming proselytes (3:8–9, 14, 25–9), and to dissuade them from going any further toward engaging in the ritual process of proselyte conversion (5:2–12; 6:12–15), most interpreters understand the addressees to be non-Jews, Gentiles, representatives of the nations (*ethnoi*). That there may be Jewish people among the groups addressed, even disciples of Paul, is likely; nevertheless, Paul's message targets non-Jewish people within groups that have formed as a result of his proclamation of the gospel when among them. These non-Jews are often considered in Jewish communal terms to be or to have been so-called "God-fearers" or "righteous Gentiles" (cf. Davies 1984).

## Situation(s)

Paul's letter is in response to his perception of a situation among believers in his gospel, an exigence ("urgency of moment") that, from his perspective, compels this course of action. Analyzing his rhetorical approach thus provides a basis for offering a construction of the *rhetorical* situation or situations. The interpreter thereby hypothesizes the circumstances of the addressees from what he or she imagines Paul's point of view to have been when he wrote, including how his letter appears to the interpreter to have been designed to influence the addressees and their circumstances thereafter. While this process includes the analysis of all the historical information that can be mounted, it stops short of effectively hypothesizing the *historical* situation of the addressees (situations really, since the letter is written to more than one location and the context of the various recipients was surely multi-dimensional), unless it also seeks to account for the perceptions of other players involved, including those influencing the addressees. Then portraits of the historical as well as rhetorical situations among the addressees can be advanced.

Constructing the probable situations is no simple task. To date, most analyses of the situation(s) in Galatia articulate the interpreter's perception of the rhetorical point of view of Paul. The resulting interpretations are often internalized as programmatic, privileging Paul's perspective in spite of recognizing the polemical nature of his language. Usually, little if any interest is displayed in understanding the interests of the other parties involved – to construct and test hypotheses which account for their own probable points of view – least of all those of the influencers. Instead, ascertaining Christian theological truths from Galatians has been the traditional concern. Even descriptions and labels employed for the situations and players have inhibited the interpretive process, and not just in historical-critical terms. Because of the role of context – whether constructed or presumed – in determining the usage of language, such decisions predetermine interpretive conclusions, perpetuating long-held views, including prejudices, instead of testing them. In addition, another problem arises from lack of attention to the different circumstances suggested by rhetoric addressing an issue concerning the proposition of circumcision (proselyte conversion) for non-Jews, an issue of *identity* clearly in view in Galatians, rather than Torah observance for non-Jews (or Jews), a question of *behavior* for those who are circumcised (Jews and proselytes) that is not so clearly at issue. Since Paul's rhetorical strategy to dissuade the addressees from undertaking proselyte conversion entails the warning that they will thereafter be obliged to observe the whole Torah (5:3), this may imply that observation of Torah is not what the addressees have actually been encouraged to consider, and thus is not what Paul's letter seeks to oppose.

Most discussions about the letter's setting hinge on a supposed opposition to Paul surfacing in the area (see e.g., the essays in Nanos 2002b, esp. 321–433). Those considered responsible for developments provoking Paul's letter are referred to as "opponents," and judged to be opponents of the values most highly prized by Paul and the believer in his gospel, such as freedom, love, and grace. Their motives, methods, and theological message are disparagingly contrasted to those of Paul and the believer in his gospel. Challenges have been mounted to the "mirror-reading" methodology upon which such constructions depend – for example assuming that what Paul asserts or opposes responds directly to that of which he has been accused (Berger 1980; Lyons 1985; Mitternacht 1999: 38–49; Barclay 2002). Moreover, is it really likely that the ones whose influence Paul opposed stood against values such as freedom and Torah-oriented norms such as love of one's neighbor? Might not the addressees have been surprised and even baffled by the oppositional language in Paul's letter, not having thought of those influencing themselves as opponents but as advocates of their interests, as was Paul (Howard 1990: 9–11; Mitternacht 1999: 89–108; Nanos 2002a, 193–283)? In sum, although Paul opposes some person, group, or group's influence, and a message that implicitly challenges the basis of his message as he perceives the case to be, it is by no means clear *a priori* that anyone has opposed Paul, or if anyone has, to what degree that stance defines anyone's overall interests and identity.

Those influencing Paul's addressees are often called "judaizers," by which most interpreters mean that they promote Jewish values and identity for the addressees (an interest valued negatively by many interpreters who would, however, value Paul's role as a "missionary" positively; note, without the negative valence communicated by "mission*izer*" or "Christian*izer*"). The term "judaizer" translates a reflexive verb, however. Thus it technically refers to *non*-Jewish people who seek to adopt Jewish behavior or identity, being a synonym for "proselyte" (cf. Cohen 1999: 175–97). That is, the term "judaizer," if used, should refer to a non-Jew who chooses to be identified positively in Jewish terms, or to become a Jewish person.

Those whom Paul opposes are also generally described as "outsiders," and usually assumed to be Jewish believers in Christ from Jerusalem (or Antioch) engaged in a mission to undo Paul's work. This proposition is circular, since it requires drawing conclusions from the evidence in Galatians that should be under investigation itself: Paul nowhere states that these influencers are any less Galatian than the addressees, or that they have any association with the Jerusalem or Antioch churches. Paul does speak of events in Jerusalem and Antioch in the autobiographical narrative of chapter 2, and there are indeed interest groups in those places whose policies he also opposes. Nevertheless, the analogies to be drawn by the addressees in Galatia require knowledge about the identities of the players and situations among themselves that the later interpreter does not possess, and thus represent precisely the kinds of matters that should be investigated, not presupposed. Thus, while notions that the influencers have either arrived from outside of Galatia or were local Galatians should be considered and tested by the data available, it is not helpful to privilege a topic to be examined by labeling them "outsiders" or in other unknown location-oriented terms in the course of that investigation.

These influential people are also frequently labeled "troublemakers" and "agitators." Such monikers privilege Paul's polemical approach to their identity, but are counterproductive for historical investigation. They inhibit inquiry into the influencers' and addressees' points of view, and thus arguably also obstruct deeper probing of Paul's perspectives, including his choice of the rhetorical tactics, not least the employment of these descriptions and other assaults on the influencers' and addressees' motives. Is it not likely that those influencing Paul's addressees toward what they believe to be "good" for them would label Paul (at least after receipt of this letter!) a troublemaker or agitator? Nevertheless, interpreters would recognize this to be a relative judgment, and perhaps not a fair appraisal of Paul's person, role, or interests, evaluated on his own terms, or considered from the perspective of other interested parties, such as, perhaps, that of any addressees persuaded by his intervention. Thus, although Paul probably caused trouble for them – and intended to obstruct their influence – that is not the sole or even central purpose or identity to be concretized by the historical critic, even if it is what might have been most salient about him to those he opposed.

J. L. Martyn helpfully proposes the less value-laden description "teachers." I offer an alternative that eschews even the implied occupational dimension "teachers" retains, suggesting instead "influencers," since Paul presumes that they have influenced and are influencing his addressees. This label and description do not implicitly judge their motives and methods negatively vis-à-vis those attributed to Paul. Paul is an "influencer" too. He could hardly argue that his purpose in writing was not to dissuade the addressees from being influenced further by them, or to persuade the addressees to instead continue in the direction of his original influence. However, this label can imply that the influencers' primary identity is related to their involvement with the addressees in the matters of concern to Paul, which may not have been the case from *their* point of view, especially if the influencers are local Galatians instead of emissaries from elsewhere.

The most popular construction of the situation(s) – the major lines of which can be traced to the Church Fathers (e.g., Chrysostom, *Galatians*) – maintains that after Paul's departure emissaries from the Jerusalem apostles (or the Antioch churches in conjunction with them) have arrived in Galatia to challenge Paul's supposed "law-free gospel" with one that combines elements of Jewish tradition with belief in Jesus Christ. In some proposals, these emissaries are understood to *mis*represent the position of one or another of the Jerusalem apostles, or to act to some degree independent of them (cf. Howard 1990). These emissaries are often tied to interest groups Paul is understood to oppose in his other letters, and usually deemed to be specifically engaged in an anti-Paul mission. They seek to persuade, even to compel, Paul's Gentile converts to Christ to become proselytes (represented by the circumcision of males). Some interpreters understand them to seek observance of Jewish law, but others doubt that this is what they are concerned about, or teach. That is, they proclaim *another* gospel of Christ which includes circumcision and observance of certain Jewish laws (at least, the calendrical observances of 4:10), whereas Paul is understood to proclaim *the* gospel of Christ independent of, and (commonly understood to be) in opposition to Jewish identity and behavior.

In the emissaries' opposition to Paul, different accusations are imagined to have been made – ranging from hypocrisy to heresy, from surreptitious dependence upon the apostles who had been directly appointed by Jesus to inappropriate independence and deviation from them and their teaching – to which Paul's rhetoric is understood to respond defensively from the start: "Paul, an Apostle not from humans or through humans, but through Jesus Christ and God the Father" (1:1). The motives attributed to these emissaries range from a *benign* interest to complete Paul's work (Howard 1990), to an *expedient* concern to comply with the demands of Judean or local Jewish groups bringing pressure upon them (Jewett 2002; Harvey 2002), to a *rival* mission with a different gospel of Christ (Martyn 1997), to a *venomous* agenda to undermine Paul's accomplishments (Lüdemann 1989). They are variously understood to be trying to persuade or force the addressees to turn to the course proposed. Although certain interpreters maintain that some of the addressees have already undertaken the rite of circumcision, most interpret Paul's rhetoric to suggest that he fears they have to some degree begun to consider this other message as an advantage for themselves, but that they have not actually undertaken the rite. Paul's rhetorical approach suggests to most interpreters that he believes the situation can be put back on the course on which they had begun in response to his initial preaching (5:10), and thus, that at least his *target* recipients have not yet been circumcised.

There are several alternative constructions to discuss. Denying any involvement of Jewish Christian groups, in fact, virtually any Jewish contact, Christ-believing or not, J. Munck challenges the consensus view, especially F. C. Baur's way of construing a James/Peter (Jerusalem) versus Paul rivalry. Munck argues that Christ-believing Gentiles have on their own, because of their reading of scripture in combination with their former association with synagogues as "God-fearers," come to the conclusion that they should become circumcised, with the result that "these Judaizing Gentile Christians have been canvassing among the Galatians for their own particular conception of Christianity" (1959: 89, and see 87–134; see also Gaston 1987: 81, 90, 109, 221). Ironically, Munck observes that this "heresy" would not have been conceived apart from the positive portrait of Jerusalem Christianity that Paul espoused, which created a desire to emulate them, although in a way in which Paul disapproved. P. Richardson has modified this view to include pressure from local synagogues, and a desire to continue these previously developed relationships (1969: 90–7). Whereas Munck concentrates his analysis on the Antioch Incident when discussing the Galatian situation, in keeping with the methodological approaches of those Munck sought to debate, Richardson questions this decision. He notes that, although in Antioch a group's arrival from Jerusalem plays some role, the presence of such a group is not indicated in Galatia.

In a different way, A. E. Harvey challenges the consensus view by proposing that the pressure to become circumcised came from local synagogues, mediated by Christ-believing members who were also now attending the newly formed Pauline groups (2002; see also Dix 1953: 41–2; Winter 1994: 133–43). Paul regards the members of the Jewish synagogues responsible for this policy, and the members of his groups yielding to this pressure by seeking to persuade the others to comply – proselytes (Harvey writes of circumcised Gentiles) and Jews alike – as his opponents.

The consensus view, that the ones influencing Paul's addressees are somehow linked to the interests of James and the Jerusalem churches, is also the target of criticism by W. Schmithals. Drawing on arguments developed from the Corinthian correspondence (as had Baur), Schmithals proposes that the emissaries are Jewish or Jewish Christian Gnostics proposing circumcision as part of the process of gaining access to knowledge (1972: 16–64, 245–53).

The so-called two-front theory maintains that Paul's opposition consisted of two different groups (Lütgert 1919; Ropes 1929). On one side were legalists, Christian proselytes representing Jewish groups who opposed Paul's "law-free gospel" claims, which accounts for his rhetoric in chapters 3 and 4, and at various other places in the letter. On the other side was a group of libertine spiritualists galvanized in opposition to the influence of these "judaizers," having taken to extremes the implications of Paul's teaching of receipt of the Spirit apart from Jewish law, accounting for the rhetoric opposing antinomianism in chapters 5 and 6.

I propose that Paul founded groups within the Jewish communities of Galatia that were not yet identified separately as "Christian" groups, but as Jewish subgroups recognizable for their convictions about the meaning of Jesus Christ for themselves (Nanos 2002a, 2002c). The situational issues that arose were local, intra- and inter-Jewish. Everyone involved – except Paul! – was a Galatian, including those Paul opposed. The Gentile members of his subgroups have trusted Paul's message that because of their faith in Christ they now have full standing in these Jewish communities as fellow children of Abraham, and are not merely "guests" who have yet to make the transformation from pagan identity. During Paul's absence, in the course of communal integration, they have begun to run into resistance from representatives of the larger synagogue communities who do not share their convictions about the meaning of Jesus Christ, as well as from kin and fellow-citizens of their local (pagan) communities. The addressees find themselves between a rock and a hard place. On the one side, it is likely that Jewish communal leaders, such as those who are responsible to welcome and orient Gentile "guests" and "friends," would react in several ways to the claims being made by these Gentiles when they appeal to Paul's (Jewish) teaching. They may be expected to extend a welcoming hand to the degree that these Gentiles see themselves as friends and guests. To the extent that these Gentiles express an interest in full incorporation as members, they may be expected to invite them to begin the ritual process of proselyte conversion. Yet at the same time, if these Gentiles are claiming to have already gained that standing apart from proselyte conversion and are expressing expectations of attendant rights, then it is likely that their claims would be resisted, with alternatives offered at first, and eventually ultimatums.

On the other side, it is likely that the addressees' local pagan communal leaders, family members, and neighbors have a vested interest in the claims and behavior of these fellow-citizens. They would not likely accept these fellow-non-Jews' new disregard for the various communal and familial cult practices to which they are obliged, if they are appealing to a new identity (not Jewish proselytes, yet not idolaters) without precedent to legitimate such "scandalous" behavior. In response to this reaction – perhaps in anticipation of it – the (minority) Jewish communal leaders and facilitators of Gentile contacts and policies would be expected to challenge its legitimacy. They would seek to avoid suffering for the legitimacy claims of non-Jews who might be neglecting, for example, continued participation in familial, local, and imperial cult based upon transformations of identity they have not completed – not even begun – according to prevailing Jewish as well as non-Jewish communal norms. Hence Galatians 6:13, where Paul accuses the influencers of seeking to avoid "persecution for the cross of Christ." The "influencers," although not believers in Jesus Christ, do not seek to make these Gentiles abandon their confession of faith in Jesus Christ *per se*. They merely endeavor to confirm the status quo, in which they, as representatives of the minority Jewish communities, have a vested interest. That is, the addressees are not interested in abandoning or even compromising their faith in Christ, but they are rather "unsettled" by the reaction they have experienced, and are thus considering an option that seems to promise relief from intensified social identity dissonance and its attendant disadvantages. They now realize that if they decide (a) not to comply with prevailing Jewish communal norms for full membership by becoming proselytes, and also (b) to eschew idolatrous practices of the larger communities, such as the civic calendar (4:10), this will result in perpetual social status dissonance and marginality.

## Purpose(s) and Message(s)

The interpreter's understanding of the purposes and messages of Galatians are shaped by his or her construction(s) of the situations addressed, since they represent the interpreter's conceptualization of the author's response: what Paul is understood to want to accomplish. There is no extant evidence of the results of the letter's receipt, beyond the mere fact of its preservation, which can be explained variously apart from the copy or copies received in the several Galatian communities addressed.

The traditional and still prevailing views understand Galatians to be Paul's response to the accusations of Jerusalem- or Antioch-based opponents of his mission and message of good news in Christ. Within the "churches" he has established, Paul aims to challenge the accusations and undermine the influence of these intruders proclaiming a different gospel of Christ, one that includes circumcision and some degree of law-observance. He seeks thereby to dissuade the addressees from further consideration of the course of action they propose, and to persuade them to continue on the path he had proclaimed. The message can be broken down into two primary sections. The first, 1:1–5:12, contains a largely theological message, arguing against the components of Jewish identity and behavior contained in this other gospel, and for the law-free gospel which Paul had proclaimed among them. The second section, 5:13–6:10, concerns ethical matters, wherein Paul challenges any notion of antinomianism that might arise from his theological dismissal of the place and value of law for the Christ-believers (cf. Kraftchick 1985; Barclay 1988; Lategan 2002). For many critics, to the degree that his purpose is understood to be defensive, in reply to accusations, the rhetoric is understood to be forensic or judicial. When it is understood to be a call for new decisions and activities, it is considered deliberative. And when understood to seek a return to values already embraced, it is considered epideictic.

Although similarities with the consensus understandings of the purposes and messages of Galatians are many, some differences are notable. J. Munck emphasizes Paul's refutation of the misrepresentations of himself, arguing that his authority is not from the Jerusalem apostles and that he has not omitted the inclusion of circumcision in the gospel they gave him in order to avoid problems. Paul's authority is not from the Jerusalem apostles: they do not teach circumcision and law-observance any differently than he does. By explaining the nature of the movement of which the addressees have become a part, he expects them to understand that these people have no business "completing" his work in the way proposed (Munck 1959: 90). A. E. Harvey argues that rather than "answering the theological objections of his opponents," Paul's message should be understood "as awakening his correspondents from their theological thoughtlessness" (2002: 320–1). It is the addressees' consideration of compliance with local synagogue expectations arising from renewed contact, without recognition of the theological implications of the course of action proposed (circumcision and certain other Jewish observances), that Paul seeks to correct. W. Schmithals observes that Paul's message seeks to clarify that his apostleship is directly from God, not mediated. Paul argues this point because he does not know much about the Gnostics influencing his addressees, since he miscalculates that they are advocating circumcision, as if "judaizers." Paul supposes that they are interested in Torah observance, instead of merely appealing to Torah for tactical reasons; but they are actually interested in seeking the liberation of the *Pneuma* ("Spirit"). Because Paul misunderstands their oppositional comments about himself, he mistakenly develops a message based on traditional Jewish premises, which has led to misdiagnosis by interpreters ever since (Schmithals 1972: 18–19, 33–4, 38–46, 245–53). W. Lütgert and J. Ropes understand Paul to reprove the addressees for consideration of the views of the "judaizers," and, at the same time, to be seeking to repel the attacks of radical antinomian enthusiasts, who oppose both the "judaizers" as well as Paul, because his teaching retains the moral traditions of Jewish law. Paul calls his addressees to resist both of these groups.

Nanos (2002a) argues that Paul responds to news that some of his non-Jewish converts are considering proselyte conversion in order to gain social acceptance according to the prevailing norms, supposing that this can be accomplished without compromising their confession of Christ (see also Mitternacht 1999: 145–6, 318–20; 2002). Paul employs ironic rebuke in the manner of a parent seeking to dissuade teenagers seduced by peer pressure, by the desire "to be like everyone else." He thereby seeks to ensure that the addressees do not act upon this ostensible "*other* good news," which, from his perspective, undermines the claim of "*the* good news of Christ" by which these Gentiles have *already* become children of Abraham. For in Christ Jesus, Paul believes, the age to come – when Israel and all the (other) nations (whom these addressees, in part, represent) will together worship the One God of all humankind – has dawned. Thus, to become proselytes in order to gain standing as children of Abraham logically undermines the confession that the addressees are already such children, and denies the witness of the Spirit they have received. Paul's rhetoric implies confidence that they would wish to do no such thing. The instructions of chapters 5 and 6 represent a call to minority group solidarity in view of the resistance to majority group norms for which Paul has argued, rather than a hedge against antinomianism necessitated by anticipation of the logical implications of opposing compliance with Torah. If the addressees are successfully to "wait for the hope of righteousness" (5:5), that is, the confirmation of their standing as children of Abraham apart from becoming proselytes – which Paul's message claims for non-Jewish believers in Jesus Christ – they will need the support of each other. They must not strive for advanced standing according to the standards of the communal norms that they are called to resist. In this endeavor they are to imitate Paul, who is suffering similarly – albeit as a Torah-observant Jew – for his role in bringing them this non-conformist message (cf. Mitternacht 2002).

## Rhetorical Analysis

The employment of rhetorical analysis by Paul's interpreters can be traced back to the commentators of the fourth century (Fairweather 1994; Classen 2002; Cooper 2000); however, H. D. Betz's 1975 article ("Literary Composition"), followed by his 1979 *Galatians* commentary, initiated an unprecedented level of interest among contemporary scholars, exemplified by research on Galatians. Essays representing the various contemporary approaches and trends are collected in Nanos 2002b.

Betz's argument is based upon his understanding of Galatians as an "apologetic letter," in which Paul defends himself against the accusation of his opponents to his addressees, who serve as the jury. Although Betz's categorization of this text as an example of a letter exemplifying judicial (forensic) oration met with significant criticism from those who argue that it represents a different rhetorical genre, many critics nevertheless share his conviction that this text should be analyzed according to the theories and practices developed by Greco-Roman rhetoricians. For example, classicist G. Kennedy champions the classification of Galatians as deliberative rhetoric. He regards the letter not as a defense of Paul's authority *per se*, but expressing concern that the addressees believe in his gospel and act accordingly. The focus is not on judging Paul's past, but on the addressees deciding about their future. Where the element of exhortation, especially as expressed in 5:1–6:10, creates an obstacle to Betz's classification, since exhortation is not a part of judicial rhetoric in the ancient authorities he investigates, it is to be expected in deliberative oration, which exhorts and dissuades, appealing to the advantage the audience will experience for following the recommended course. Kennedy's argument is vulnerable to criticism as well, for Paul states that he is not disclosing something new, but calling the addressees to hold on to values already proclaimed in the face of competing claims (1:9, 13; 3:1; 4:12–20; 5:3, 7, 21), arguably the characteristic of epideictic rhetoric. Furthermore, it is not clear that in this letter Paul "preached the gospel of Christ" (Kennedy 1984:145), any more than, with Betz, that he "defended" it. Rather, Paul's approach arguably assumes that the addressees remain committed to Christ as previously proclaimed by Paul, on which basis he reveals to them how the conduct under consideration "surprisingly" represents allegiance to "another gospel" that undermines "the meaning of the death of Christ" for themselves. Paul expresses confidence that the addressees will not disregard the guidance offered in this letter, now that the issues are – "again" – made clear.

Recent commentators have often followed Kennedy's (and, e.g., R. Hall's and J. Smit's) lead (e.g., Matera 1992; Esler 1998; and esp. Witherington 1998), sometimes combining aspects of forensic rhetoric in their analyses, and epideictic as well, although the latter is less commonly argued. Several commentaries have eschewed the classical rhetorical approach (e.g., Dunn, 1993a: 20; Martyn, 1997: 20–3), and not a few interpreters have challenged the enterprise, especially to the degree that it fails to take into account later rhetorical theories, such as contemporary insights of the "new rhetoric" (Classen 2002; Kern 1998). These interpreters argue that interpretation should not be bound to demonstrating formal correspondence with rhetorical considerations likely to be available to Paul. Among other reasons offered, it is maintained that it is not possible to know to what degree Paul himself was informed by the sources now available to the interpreter, or sought to work within such formal rhetorical parameters. In addition, some interpreters now prefer to emphasize that, while functional and even formal aspects of these oral rhetorical theories may be identified in the letter, and can be helpful especially in outlining the letter, it is to epistolary theory that the interpreter should look for formal characteristics. Galatians is, after all, a letter, and correspondences with ancient letter types as well as examples are identifiable.

Rhetorical analysis has especially advanced new ways to outline Paul's argument, which is actually what H. D. Betz originally suggested the method would yield (1975). To date this analysis has arguably not, however, led to significant reevaluation of the traditional understanding of the situations, purposes, or messages of the letter. Hence caution in its practice is warranted, since it is possible to make a case for each classification, and against each, or to argue for various combinations thereof on the basis of the working hypotheses – or assumptions – with which the interpreter begins.

## Epistolary Analysis

In addition to the contemporary interest in rhetorical analysis of Galatians, interpreters have begun to investigate the implications of epistolary analysis. Traditionally it has been noted that the letter's frame, its formal opening (1:1–5) and closing summary features (6:11–18), correspond with examples from Paul's time. Galatians differs dramatically from Paul's other letters in that it offers no word of thanksgiving for the addressees in the opening; instead, a polemical statement of Paul's basis of authority greets the recipient, coupled with expressions of rebuke, and curse-wishes for those who would teach otherwise. Especially notable for epistolary analysis is the declaration of "surprise" (*thaumazô*) regarding the addressees' interest in "another gospel" in 1:6, an expression of ironic disapproval discussed in ancient handbooks (e.g., Pseudo-Demetrius, *Epistolary Types*; Pseudo-Libanius, *Epistolary Styles*; both available in Malherbe 1988). Such surprise is expressed often at the beginning or in the transition to the body of ancient letters.

In keeping with the syllogisms rehearsed in the handbooks, many papyrus letters from the time declare the failure of the recipient to have responded to earlier letters sent, or to take the action requested, for example: "I am very much surprised, my son, that till today I have not received any letter from you ..." (P. Oxy. 123.5; cf. Roberts 1991). This turn of phrase is ironic, in that it is not an expression of an author's failure to anticipate, but rather, in a Socratic sense, it constitutes a rebuke for inappropriate ideas or behavior by feigning ignorance, i.e., in this case surprise (Mullins 1972; White 1971; Dahl 2002; Roberts 1992; Nanos 2002a: 39–49). Paul appeals throughout the letter to the fact that he has instructed them in the direction to which this letter calls them to return (1:9, 13; 3:1; 4:13; 5:3, 21). Such letters of "ironic rebuke," which seek to check the actions regarded by the author as negligent or inappropriate, are written with the expectation of the addressees' sympathetic receipt, that is, presupposing that the recipient will be inclined to value the friendship or other social ties threatened by the writer's perception of a breach of conduct, and feel obliged to act accordingly.

G. W. Hansen categorized Galatians as a letter of rebuke-request, because following the rebuke beginning at 1:6, the first request in the letter is not made until 4:12, wherein the addressees are called to emulate Paul (Hansen 1989, 1994; see too R. Longenecker 1990). Mitternacht emphasizes that Paul's "petition" is to emulate him in choosing to suffer to uphold the principles of the gospel of Christ Paul proclaimed when these might conflict with the prevailing interpretations of tradition (2002). In the addressees' case, this means suffering the status dissonance that may result from making the claims the message of Christ makes apart from becoming proselytes.

If Galatians expresses ironic rebuke, then this should challenge the interpreter to look to the ironic level of many elements of the text that have traditionally been analyzed apart from this insight, including the identities of the players and the character of the situations implied by Paul's rhetoric, as well as the message itself (Nanos 2002a: 32–61 *passim*). In ironic letters the plain meaning of the text is different than it appears to be to the reader unaware of the ironic level. That would be evident to the original recipient who recognizes how either the delivery, the character of the speaker, or the nature of the subject are out of keeping with the words the author would choose if expressing him or herself sincerely (see Quintilian, *Institutio Oratoria*, 8.6.54). If Galatians is a letter of ironic rebuke, then the anticipation of the author likely accounts for many of the comments traditionally understood to reflect Paul's reaction or defense. For example, it is arguable whether those influencing the Galatian addressees are claiming their message to be a "Good News [Gospel] *of Christ*" – as supposed by the interpretive tradition on the basis of mirror-reading what Paul has written here about "another Good News" – rather than simply the traditional message of proselyte conversion. For the traditional message of proselyte conversion promises to resolve the identity dissonance raised for the non-Jewish believers in Paul's message without challenging their faith in Christ *per se* (and in this sense can be regarded as good news indeed). If proselyte conversion and not a message of Jesus Christ constitutes the influencers' message of good, doing so without opposition to the addressees' faith in Christ *per se* (from the influencers' point of view), then Paul may be introducing the comparison around the language of "good news" in order to undermine this "apparent" gain by exposing the "real" loss that would result.

Letters expressing stereotypical ironic surprise often also comment upon the *quickness* of the development, as does Paul in 1:6, without this suggesting that the development was sudden and unexpected *per se*. Likewise, such letters often seek to express the implied betrayal of friendship and lack of appreciation toward the author that they detect in the addressees' course – even if not recognized as such by the addressees beforehand – as part of a strategy to dissuade them from continuing that course

(4:12–20). The author polarizes two alternative options, with the one necessarily opposed to and subverting the other, when this level of incompatibility was not how things had been perceived by the recipients beforehand. Furthermore, these letters often suggest that the addressees must be undergoing manipulation by some outside person or force (such as alcohol) to even consider such an "oppositional" course of action from that which the author "expected" of them, which corresponds to Paul's analysis that the Galatians have been "unsettled" by the message of those influencing them (1:6–7; 5:7–12; 6:12), as well as by their exclusionary tactics (4:17), thus questioning whether they have fallen under the envious designs of an evil (envious) eye (3:1–5) (see Nanos 2002a: 49–56, 184–91, 279–83).

## Literary Structure and Outline

The Galatians discourse contains several literary units, although the breaks between them and their relative function are variously defined. The epistolary frame consists of the opening salutation in 1:1–5, and the closing summary and farewell greeting in 6:11–18. The transition to the body of the letter is arguably begun in 1:6, but it is less clear whether the next section begins with verse 10, 11, 12, or 13 (see Holmstrand 1997: 148–56).

From 1:13 to 2:21, Paul narrates historical incidents that he brings to bear upon the message for his addressees in Galatia (some suggest that at 2:15 Paul turns from recalling what he said to Peter, and through verse 21 explains instead the implications for the addressees, but see Holmstrand 1997: 157–65). The analogies they are expected to draw to their own situation are far from clear. The later interpreter does not know how the narrative details relate to what Paul – or anyone else, if anyone at all – has told them beforehand, the specifics of their situation in Galatia, or precisely how Paul may have planned for these units to have influenced them when read.

At 3:1, Paul begins a new unit wherein he challenges the addressees' current consideration of the alternate course on offer with rebuking interrogatives (cf. Cosgrove 1988).

Beginning with 3:6, and continuing through chapters 3 and 4 until 4:7, he introduces a narrative concerning the role of Abraham, Moses, and Christ, and the implications of each for the identity of the Gentile recipients, which may be regarded as an example of midrashic methodology.

At 4:8–11, Paul again directly challenges the addressees' ostensible current consideration of a path other than the one that he had set out when among them. In verse 12, Paul requests their emulation of his suffering, and appeals to past friendship and mutual trust through verse 20.

Then, after the rebuking question of verse 21, Paul again engages in narrative discourse, in this case in an allegory, from 4:22 to 5:1.

The statements of 4:31–5:1 answer the rebuking question posed in 4:21, and set up Paul's transition to another unit of discourse directly challenging the addressees' way of analyzing the options currently on offer, calling them to stay the course upon which they have begun in response to Paul's teaching. This instruction runs from 5:2 until the end of the body of the letter at 6:10, consisting of several sub-units emphasizing different topics (arguably 5:2–6, 7–12, 13–26; 6:1–10). It includes a call to continue faithful to Paul's gospel of Christ in the face of alternatives which implicitly undermine it until the hope of righteousness is realized (5:1–6); vilification of those influencing Paul's addressees otherwise (verses 7–12); and the call to mutuality among themselves in the face of resistance to their non-compliance. Paul assures the addressees that the ultimate Judge will legitimate faithfulness to this course (verses 13–6:10).

A summary of Paul's message and final greeting conclude the letter (6:11–18).

The letter thus consists of both situational units that directly address the recipients in their Galatian circumstances, and narrative units Paul introduces to support his situational arguments and instructions. Situational discourse units include Paul's opening greeting and transition to the body of the letter, which contain a strong statement expressing his disposition toward the situation of the addressees, and sets out his authority to do so (1:1–5, 6–12); rebuking comments for the addressees' supposed present deliberations in 3:1–5 and 4:8–11; an appeal to friendship in 4:12–20; and a call to remain faithful to the course upon which they began, arguably the theme of the letter (5:1–6). These appeals include vilification of those who might persuade them otherwise (1:8–9; 5:7–12; cf. 6:12–13), and a call to serve each other in love until the choice of this course has been finally legitimated beyond dispute, instead of engaging in efforts to mitigate the suffering that resisting the prevailing conventions might entail (5:13–6:10). The narrative discourse units include those wherein Paul refers either to his own past experiences, from his calling and early ministry outside of Judea (1:13–24), to his meeting in Jerusalem (2:1–10), and confrontation of Peter at Antioch (2:11–21); his midrashic treatments of the history of Israelite figures such as Abraham, Moses, and Jesus Christ (3:6–4:7); and the construction of an allegory developed around the theme of Abraham's two wives and their respective sons (4:21–5:1). The summary comments of 6:11–17 may also be considered situational, recapping the thrust of Paul's message in his own hand. The final verse, 6:18, expresses the letter's formal closing in a prayer.

## Bibliography

Barclay, John M. G. *Obeying the Truth: a Study of Paul's Ethics in Galatians*. Edinburgh: T. & T. Clark, 1988.

Barclay, John M. G. "Mirror-Reading a Polemical Letter: Galatians as a Test Case." Pp. 367–82 in *The Galatians Debate: Contemporary Issues in Rhetorical and Historical Interpretation*. Edited by Mark D. Nanos. Peabody: Hendrickson, 2002. [Originally published 1987.]

Baur, Ferdinand Christian. *Paul the Apostle of Jesus Christ: His Life and Works, his Epistles and Teachings: A Contribution to a Critical History of Primitive Christianity*. Trans. Allan Menzies from 2nd edn.; ed. Eduard Zeller. 2 vols. 1845. London: Williams & Norgate, 1873–5; repr. in one volume, Hendrickson, 2003.

Berger, Klaus. "Die impliziten Gegner. Methode des Erschließens von 'Gegnern' in neutestamentlichen Texten." Pp. 372–400 in *Kirche. Festschrift für Günther Bornkamm zum 75. Geburtstag*. Edited by D. Lührmann and G. Strecker. Tübingen: Mohr Siebeck, 1980.

Betz, Hans Dieter. *Galatians: A Commentary on Paul's Letter to the Churches in Galatia*. Hermeneia. Philadelphia: Fortress Press, 1979.

Betz, Hans Dieter. "The Literary Composition and Function of Paul's Letter to the Galatians." Pp. 3–28 in *The Galatians Debate: Contemporary Issues in Rhetorical and Historical Interpretation*. Edited by Mark D. Nanos. Peabody: Hendrickson, 2002. [Originally published in 1975.]

Botha, Pieter J. J. "Letter Writing and Oral Communication in Antiquity: Suggested Implications for the Interpretation of Paul's Letter to the Galatians." *Scriptura* 42 (1992), 17–34.

Breytenbach, Cilliers. *Paulus und Barnabas in der Provinz Galatien: Studien zu Apostelgeschichte 13f.;16, 6;18, 23 und den Adressaten des Galaterbriefes*. Arbeiten zur Geschichte des antiken Judentums und des Urchristentums, 38. Leiden and New York: Brill, 1996.

Brinsmead, Bernard Hungerford. *Galatians: Dialogical Response to Opponents*. Society of Biblical Literature Dissertation Series, 65. Chico: Scholars Press, 1982.

Bruce, F. F. *The Epistle to the Galatians: A Commentary on the Greek Text*. New International Greek Testament Commentary. Grand Rapids: Eerdmans, 1982.

Bryant, Robert A. *The Risen Crucified Christ in Galatians*. Society of Biblical Literature Dissertation Series, 185. Atlanta: Society of Biblical Literature, 2001.

Burton, Ernest De Witt. *A Critical and Exegetical Commentary on the Epistle to the Galatians*. International Critical Commentary, 48. Edinburgh: T. & T. Clark, 1921.

Chrysostom, St. "Homilies on Galatians." In *Chrysostom, Saint*. Edited by Philip Schaff. Select Library of Nicene and Post-Nicene Fathers, 13. Grand Rapids: Eerdmans, 1956.

Ciampa, Roy E. *The Presence and Function of Scripture in Galatians 1 and 2*. Wissenschaftliche Untersuchungen zum Neuen Testament, 2.102. Tübingen: Mohr Siebeck, 1998.

Classen, Carl Joachim. "St. Paul's Epistles and Ancient Greek and Roman Rhetoric." Pp. 95–113 in *The Galatians Debate: Contemporary Issues in Rhetorical and Historical Interpretation*. Edited by Mark D. Nanos. Peabody: Hendrickson, 2002. [Originally published, 2000.]

Cohen, Shaye J. D. *The Beginnings of Jewishness: Boundaries, Varieties, Uncertainties*. Hellenistic Culture and Society, 31. Berkeley: University of California Press, 1999.

Cooper, Stephen A. "*Narratio* and *Exhortatio* in Galatians According to Marius Victorinus Rhetor." *Zeitschrift für die neutestamentliche Wissenschaft* 91 (2000), 107–35.

Cosby, Michael R. "Galatians: Red-Hot Rhetoric." Pp. 296–309 in *Rhetorical Argumentation in Biblical Texts: Essays from the Lund 2000 Conference*. Edited by A. Eriksson et al. Emory Studies in Early Christianity. Harrisburg, PA: Trinity Press International, 2002.

Cosgrove, Charles H. *The Cross and the Spirit: A Study in the Argument and Theology of Galatians*. Louvain, Belgium and Macon: Peeters/Mercer, 1988.

Cronjé, J. Van W. "Defamiliarization in the Letter to the Galatians." Pp. 214–27 in *A South African Perspective on the New Testament*. Edited by J. H. Petzer and P. J. Hartin. Leiden: Brill, 1986.

Cummins, S. A. *Paul and the Crucified Christ in Antioch: Maccabean Martyrdom and Galatians 1 and 2*. Cambridge: Cambridge University Press, 2001.

Dahl, Nils. "Paul's Letter to the Galatians: Epistolary Genre, Content, and Structure." Pp. 117–42 in *The Galatians Debate: Contemporary Issues in Rhetorical and Historical Interpretation*. Edited by Mark D. Nanos. Peabody: Hendrickson, 2002.

Davies, W. D. "Galatians: A Commentary on Paul's Letter to the Churches in Galatia." Pp. 172–88 in *Jewish and Pauline Studies*. Philadelphia: Fortress Press, 1984.

Dix, Gregory. *Jew and Greek: A Study in the Primitive Church*. Westminster: Dacre Press, 1953.

Dunn, James D. G. *The Epistle to the Galatians*. Black's New Testament Commentaries. Peabody, MA: Hendrickson, 1993a.

Dunn, James D. G. *The Theology of Paul's Letter to the Galatians*. NT Theology. Cambridge and New York: Cambridge University Press, 1993b.

Dunn, James D. G. "The Incident at Antioch (Gal. 2:11–18)." Pp. 199–234 in *The Galatians Debate: Contemporary Issues in Rhetorical and Historical Interpretation*. Edited by Mark D. Nanos. Peabody: Hendrickson, 2002. [Originally published, 1983.]

Elliott, Susan M. *Cutting too Close for Comfort: Paul's Letter to the Galatians in its Anatolian Cultic Context. Journal for the Study of the New Testament* Supplementary Series, 248. London and New York: T. & T. Clark International, 2003.

Esler, Philip Francis. *Galatians.* New Testament Readings. London and New York: Routledge, 1998.

Esler, Philip Francis. "Making and Breaking an Agreement Mediterranean Style: A New Reading of Galatians 2:1–14." Pp. 261–81 in *The Galatians Debate: Contemporary Issues in Rhetorical and Historical Interpretation.* Edited by Mark D. Nanos. Peabody: Hendrickson, 2002. [Originally published, 1995.]

Fairweather, Janet. "The Epistle to the Galatians and Classical Rhetoric: Parts 1 and 2." *Tyndale Bulletin* 45 (1994), 1–38.

Fairweather, Janet. "The Epistle to the Galatians and Classical Rhetoric: Part 3." *Tyndale Bulletin* 45/2 (1994), 213–43.

Francis, Fred O. and J. Paul Sampley. *Pauline Parallels.* 2nd edn. Philadelphia: Fortress Press, 1984.

Fredriksen, Paula. "Judaism, The Circumcision of Gentiles, and Apocalyptic Hope: Another Look at Galatians 1 and 2." Pp. 235–60 in *The Galatians Debate: Contemporary Issues in Rhetorical and Historical Interpretation.* Edited by Mark D. Nanos. Peabody: Hendrickson, 2002. [Originally published 1991.]

Fung, Ronald Y. K. *The Epistle to the Galatians.* New International Commentary on the New Testament. Grand Rapids: Eerdmans, 1953.

Gaston, Lloyd. *Paul and the Torah.* Vancouver: University of British Columbia Press, 1987.

Hall, Robert G. "The Rhetorical Outline for Galatians: A Reconsideration." Pp. 29–38 in *The Galatians Debate: Contemporary Issues in Rhetorical and Historical Interpretation.* Edited by Mark D. Nanos. Peabody: Hendrickson, 2002. [Originally published, 1987.]

Hansen, G. Walter. *Abraham in Galatians: Epistolary and Rhetorical Contexts. Journal for the Study of the New Testament* Supplementary Series, 29. Sheffield: Sheffield Academic Press, 1989.

Hansen, G. Walter. *Galatians.* Downers Grove, IL: InterVarsity Press, 1994.

Hardin, Justin K. *Galatians and the Imperial Cult: A Critical Analysis of the First-Century Social Context of Paul's Letter.* Wissenschaftliche Untersuchungen zum Neuen Testament, 2.237. Tübingen: Mohr Siebeck, 2008.

Harvey, A. E. "The Opposition to Paul." Pp. 321–33 in *The Galatians Debate: Contemporary Issues in Rhetorical and Historical Interpretation.* Edited by Mark D. Nanos. Peabody: Hendrickson, 2002. [Originally published 1968.]

Hays, Richard B. *The Faith of Jesus Christ: An Investigation of the Narrative Substructure of Galatians 3:1–4:11.* 2nd edn. Grand Rapids: W. B. Eerdmans, 2002.

Heath, Malcolm. "John Chrysostom, Rhetoric and Galatians." *Biblical Interpretation* 12/4 (2004), 369–400.

Hemer, Colin J. "Galatia and the Galatians." Pp. 277–307 in *The Book of Acts in the Setting of Hellenistic History.* Edited by Conrad H. Gempf. Tübingen: Mohr Siebeck, 1989.

Hester, James D. "Epideictic Rhetoric and Persona in Galatians One and Two." Pp. 181–96 in *The Galatians Debate: Contemporary Issues in Rhetorical and Historical Interpretation.* Edited by Mark D. Nanos. Peabody: Hendrickson, 2002.

Hietanen, Mika. *Paul's Argumentation in Galatians: A Pragma-Dialectical Analysis of Galatians 3:1–5:12.* Library of New Testament studies 344. London: T. & T. Clark, 2007.

Holmstrand, Jonas. *Markers and Meaning in Paul: An Analysis of 1 Thessalonians, Philippians and Galatians.* Trans. Martin Taylor. Coniectanea biblica, New Testament Series, 28. Stockholm: Almqvist & Wiksell International, 1997.

Howard, George. *Paul: Crisis in Galatia: A Study in Early Christian Theology*. 2nd edn. Society for New Testament Studies Monograph Series, 35. Cambridge: Cambridge University Press, 1990.

Jervis, L. Ann. *Galatians*. New International Bible Commentary. Peabody, MA: Hendrickson/ Paternoster Press, 1999.

Jewett, Robert. "The Agitators and the Galatian Congregation." Pp. 334–47 in *The Galatians Debate: Contemporary Issues in Rhetorical and Historical Interpretation*. Edited by Mark D. Nanos. Peabody: Hendrickson, 2002. [Originally published, 1970–1.]

Kennedy, George Alexander. *New Testament Interpretation through Rhetorical Criticism*. Studies in Religion. Chapel Hill: University of North Carolina Press, 1984.

Kern, Philip H. *Rhetoric and Galatians: Assessing an Approach to Paul's Epistle*. Society for New Testament Studies Monograph Series, 101. Cambridge: Cambridge University Press, 1998.

Kraftchick, Steven John. "Ethos and Pathos Appeals in Galatians Five and Six: A Rhetorical Analysis." Ph.D. diss., Emory University, 1985.

Kraftchick, Steven John. "Why Do the Rhetoricians Rage?" Pp. 55–79 in *Text and Logos: The Humanistic Interpretation of the New Testament*. Edited by Theodore W. Jennings, Jr. Atlanta: Scholars Press, 1990.

Lategan, B. C. "The Argumentative Situation of Galatians." Pp. 383–95 in *The Galatians Debate: Contemporary Issues in Rhetorical and Historical Interpretation*. Edited by Mark D. Nanos. Peabody: Hendrickson, 2002. [Originally published, 1992.]

Le Cornu, Hilary and Joseph Shulam. *A Commentary on the Jewish Roots of Galatians*. Jerusalem: Academon, 2005.

Lightfoot, J. B. *St. Paul's Epistle to the Galatians*. Lynn: Hendrickson, 1981. [Originally published 1865.]

Longenecker, Bruce W. *The Triumph of Abraham's God: The Transformation of Identity in Galatians*. Nashville: Abingdon Press, 1998.

Longenecker, Richard N. *Galatians*. Word Biblical Commentary, 41. Dallas: Word Books, 1990.

Lüdemann, Gerd. *Opposition to Paul in Jewish Christianity*. Trans. M. Eugene Boring. Minneapolis: Fortress Press, 1989.

Lull, David John. *The Spirit in Galatia: Paul's Interpretation of Pneuma as Divine Power*. Society of Biblical Literature Dissertation Series, 49. Chico, CA: Scholars Press, 1980.

Lütgert, Wilhelm. *Gesetz und Geist: Eine Untersuchung zur Vorgeschichte des Galaterbriefes*. Beiträge zur Förderung christlicher Theologie, 22.6. Gütersloh: C. Bertelsmann, 1919.

Lyons, George. *Pauline Autobiography: Toward a New Understanding*. Society of Biblical Literature Dissertation Series, 73. Atlanta: Scholars Press, 1985.

Malherbe, Abraham J. *Ancient Epistolary Theorists*. Stuttgarter Bibelstudien, 19. Atlanta: Scholars Press, 1988.

Martin, Troy. "Pagan and Judeo-Christian Time-Keeping Schemes in Gal. 4:10 and Col. 2:16." *New Testament Studies* 42 (1996), 120–32.

Martyn, J. Louis. *Galatians: A New Translation with Introduction and Commentary*. Anchor Bible, 33. New York: Doubleday, 1997.

Matera, Frank J. *Galatians*. Sacra Pagina, 9. Collegeville: Liturgical Press, 1992.

Mitchell, Stephen. *Anatolia: Land, Men, and Gods in Asia Minor*. 2 vols. Oxford: Clarendon Press, 1993.

Mitternacht, Dieter. *Forum für Sprachlose: Eine kommunikationspsychologische und epistolar- rhetorische Untersuchung des Galaterbriefs*. Coniectanea biblica, New Testament Series, 30. Stockholm: Almqvist & Wiksell, 1999.

Mitternacht, Dieter. "Foolish Galatians? – A Recipient-Oriented Assessment of Paul's Letter." Pp. 408–33 in *The Galatians Debate: Contemporary Issues in Rhetorical and Historical Interpretation*. Edited by Mark D. Nanos. Peabody: Hendrickson, 2002.

Moffatt, J. *An Introduction to the Literature of the New Testament.* 3rd edn. Edinburgh: T. & T. Clark, 1918.

Morland, Kjell Arne. *The Rhetoric of Curse in Galatians: Paul Confronts Another Gospel.* Emory Studies in Early Christianity, 5. Atlanta: Scholars Press, 1995.

Muddiman, John. "The Anatomy of Galatians." Pp. 257–70 in *Crossing the Boundaries: Essays in Biblical Interpretation in Honour of Michael Goulder.* Edited by Stanley E. Porter et al. Leiden, New York, and Cologne: Brill, 1994.

Mullins, Terence Y. "Formulas in New Testament Epistles." *Journal of Biblical Literature* 91 (1972), 380–90.

Munck, Johannes. *Paul and the Salvation of Mankind.* Trans. Frank Clarke. Richmond, Virginia: John Knox Press, 1959.

Mussner, Franz. *Der Galaterbrief.* Herders theologischer Kommentar zum Neuen Testament, 9. Freiburg im Breisgau, Basel, and Vienna: Herder, 1974.

Nanos, Mark D. *The Irony of Galatians: Paul's Letter in First-Century Context.* Minneapolis: Fortress Press, 2002a.

Nanos, Mark D. (ed.). *The Galatians Debate: Contemporary Issues in Rhetorical and Historical Interpretation.* Peabody: Hendrickson, 2002b.

Nanos, Mark D. "The Inter- and Intra-Jewish Political Context of Paul's Letter to the Galatians." Pp. 396–407 in *The Galatians Debate: Contemporary Issues in Rhetorical and Historical Interpretation.* Edited by Mark D. Nanos. Peabody: Hendrickson, 2002c. [Originally published, 2000.]

Nanos, Mark D. "What Was at Stake in Peter's 'Eating with Gentiles' at Antioch?" Pp. 282–318 in *The Galatians Debate: Contemporary Issues in Rhetorical and Historical Interpretation.* Edited by Mark D. Nanos. Peabody: Hendrickson, 2002d.

Nanos, Mark D. "Intruding 'Spies' and 'Pseudo-Brethren': The Jewish Intra-Group Politics of Paul's Jerusalem Meeting (Gal 2:1–10)." Pp. 59–97 in *Paul and his Opponents.* Edited by S. E. Porter. Pauline Studies, 2. Leiden and Boston: Brill, 2005.

Oepke, Albrecht. *Der Brief des Paulus an die Galater.* 3rd edn. Theologischer Handkommentar zum Neuen Testament, 9. Berlin: Evangelische Verlagsanstalt, 1973.

O'Neill, J. C. *The Recovery of Paul's Letter to the Galatians.* London: SPCK, 1972.

Perkins, Pheme. *Abraham's Divided Children: Galatians and the Politics of Faith.* Harrisburg, PA: Trinity Press International, 2001.

Plumer, Eric Antone. *Augustine's Commentary on Galatians.* Oxford Early Christian Studies. Oxford: Oxford University Press, 2003.

Ramsay, William M. *Historical Commentary on Galatians.* Edited by Mark Wilson. Grand Rapids: Kregel Publications, 1997. [Originally published 1900.]

Richardson, Peter. *Israel in the Apostolic Church.* Society for New Testament Studies Monograph Series, 10. London: Cambridge University Press, 1969.

Riches, John Kenneth. *Galatians Through the Centuries.* Blackwell Bible Commentaries. Oxford: Blackwell, 2008.

Ridderbos, Herman N. *The Epistle of Paul to the Churches of Galatia.* New International Commentary on the New Testament. Grand Rapids: Eerdmans, 1953.

Roberts, J. H. "ΘΑΥΜΑΖΩ: An Expression of Perplexity in Some Examples from Papyri Letters." *Neotestamentica* 25 (1991), 109–21.

Roberts, J. H. "Paul's Expression of Perplexity in Galatians 1:6: The Force of Emotive Argumentation," *Neotestamentica* 26 (1992), 329–37.

Ropes, James Hardy. *The Singular Problem of the Epistle to the Galatians.* Harvard Theological Studies, 14. Cambridge, MA and London: Harvard University Press/Oxford University Press, 1929.

Schlier, Heinrich. *Der Brief an die Galater*. KEK. 7. Göttingen: Vandenhoeck & Ruprecht, 1971. [Originally published 1949.]

Schmithals, Walther. "The Heretics in Galatia." Pp. 13–64 in *Paul and the Gnostics*. Nashville and New York: Abingdon Press, 1972.

Scott, James M. *Paul and the Nations: The Old Testament and Jewish Background of Paul's Mission to the Nations with Special Reference to the Destination of Galatians*. Wissenschaftliche Untersuchungen zum Neuen Testament, 84. Tübingen: Mohr Siebeck, 1995.

Silva, Moisés. *Explorations in Exegetical Method: Galatians as a Test Case*. Grand Rapids: Baker Books, 1996.

Smit, Joop. "The Letter of Paul to the Galatians: A Deliberative Speech." Pp. 39–59 in *The Galatians Debate: Contemporary Issues in Rhetorical and Historical Interpretation*. Edited by Mark D. Nanos. Peabody: Hendrickson, 2002. [Originally published, 1989.]

Sullivan, Dale L. and Christian Anible. "*The Epideictic Dimension of Galatians as Formative Rhetoric: The Inscription of Early Christian Community*," Rhetorica 18/2 (2000), 117–45.

Tarazi, Paul Nadim. *Galatians: A Commentary*. Orthodox Biblical Studies. Crestwood, NY: St. Vladimir's Seminary Press, 1994.

Tolmie, D. F. *Persuading the Galatians: A Text-Centred Rhetorical Analysis of a Pauline Letter*. Wissenschaftliche Untersuchungen zum Neuen Testament, 2.190. Tübingen: Mohr Siebeck, 2005.

Tolmie, D. F. (ed.) *Exploring New Rhetorical Approaches to Galatians: Papers Presented at an International Conference, University of the Free State Bloemfontein, March 12–14, 2006*. Acta Theologica Supplementum, 9. Bloemfontein: Publications Office of the University of the Free State, 2007.

White, John L. "Introductory Formulae in the Body of the Pauline Letter." *Journal of Biblical Literature* 90 (1971), 91–7.

White, L. Michael. "Rhetoric and Reality in Galatians: Framing the Social Demands of Friendship." Pp. 307–46 in *Early Christianity and Classical Culture: Comparative Studies in Honor of Abraham J. Malherbe*. Edited by J. T. Fitzgerald et al. Supplements to Novum Testamentum 110. Leiden and Boston: Brill, 2003.

Wiley, Tatha. *Paul and the Gentile Women: Reframing Galatians*. New York: Continuum, 2005.

Williams, Sam K. *Galatians*. Abingdon New Testament Commentaries. Nashville: Abingdon Press, 1997.

Wilson, R. McL. "Gnostics in Galatia?" Pp. 358–67 in *Studia Evangelica*. Vol. 4. Edited by F. L. Cross. Berlin: Akademie, 1968.

Wilson, Todd A. *The Curse of the Law and the Crisis in Galatia: Reassessing the Purpose of Galatians*. Wissenschaftliche Untersuchungen zum Neuen Testament, 2.225. Tübingen: Mohr Siebeck, 2007.

Winter, Bruce W. *Seek the Welfare of the City: Christians as Benefactors and Citizens*. Grand Rapids and Carlisle: Eerdmans/Paternoster Press, 1994.

Witherington, Ben. *Grace in Galatia: A Commentary on St. Paul's Letter to the Galatians*. Grand Rapids: Eerdmans, 1998.

Witulski, Thomas. *Die Adressaten des Galaterbriefes: Untersuchungen zur Gemeinde von Antiochia ad Pisidiam*. Forschungen zur Religion und Literatur des Alten und Neuen Testaments 193. Göttingen: Vandenhoeck & Ruprecht, 2000.

Zetterholm, Magnus. *The Formation of Christianity in Antioch: A Social-scientific Approach to the Separation between Judaism and Christianity*. London and New York: Routledge, 2003.

CHAPTER 26
# Philippians

## Paul Hartog

## Major Issues and Directions in Recent Study

Four major issues have concerned much of Philippians scholarship during the last century: the question of the letter's unity, the place and date of composition, the so-called "Christ-hymn" of 2:6–11, and the nature of the opponents. More recently, however, many scholars have begun to concentrate on new avenues of investigation, including rhetorical analysis, literary analysis, and sociological analysis. Much of the sociological analysis has concentrated on Greco-Roman concepts of friendship, the sharing of finances, and the role of women in the Philippian community. Several major works have recently been published which re-examine the archaeological and historical evidence.

## Date and Place of Composition

Any view of the place of composition must take into account the following facts: (1) Paul was imprisoned yet free to evangelize (1:7, 12–17). (2) He was awaiting a trial that could end in either release or death (1:19–26; 2:17, 24). He desired to visit Philippi if acquitted (1:25–6; 2:24). (3) Others were extensively evangelizing around him in a hostile manner (1:14–17). (4) Timothy was with Paul (1:1; 2:19–23). (5) Intermediaries made several trips (perhaps four) between Paul and Philippi during his imprisonment, and more trips were planned (2:19–28; 4:18). (8) A *praetorium* and members of "Caesar's household" were both nearby (1:13; 4:22).

First, the traditional (second-century) location of Rome still has many defenders. Acts speaks of Paul being under "house arrest" in Rome for at least two years (Acts 28:16–31). During this time, he still had certain freedoms, including the liberty to receive visitors, send letters, and preach (Acts 28:31). The *praetorium* in Rome would naturally refer to the elite Praetorian Guard that was headquartered there. Rome was also the center of the imperial administration and of "Caesar's household." However, opposing scholars find it difficult to reconcile the number of communication trips implied in the letter with the geographical distance between Rome and Philippi (around

1,300 km). Also, Paul reported in Romans 15:23–8 that his eastern ministry was completed. (Yet compare his change of plans in 2 Corinthians 1:15–18.)

Second, Caesarea Maritima has been suggested as the place of composition. Acts relates that Paul was detained at Caesarea for at least two years (Acts 24:27). Acts specifically states that he was kept in Herod's *praetorium* in Caesarea, but he was allowed to visit with friends (Acts 23:35; 24:23). Paul's references to his "defense" (*apologia*) of the gospel in Philippians 1:7–17 can be reconciled easily with the accounts of Acts 24–7. If released, he could have visited Philippi on his planned trip westward (Phil. 2:24; cf. Rom. 15:20–8). Distance may still be a problem, however, since Caesarea is even further from Philippi than Rome is. Furthermore, Paul does not seem to have been in danger of execution while imprisoned in Caesarea (Acts 24:26; 25:27), since he could have appealed to Caesar as he did (Acts 25:7–11).

Third, many scholars have opted for Ephesus. Timothy was definitely with Paul in Ephesus, and Paul sent him from Ephesus to Macedonia (Acts 19:22; 20:4). Paul suffered difficulties in Ephesus, and some have inferred that he was actually imprisoned there (1 Cor. 15:32; 2 Cor. 1:8–10). An Ephesian (and therefore early) provenance would explain why Paul only mentions the founding of the Philippian church, and not his later visits (4:15–16). Perhaps the greatest strength of the Ephesian view lies in its close proximity to Philippi. The various trips of communication between Paul and the Philippians could have taken place relatively quickly. An Ephesian origin is especially convenient for those who espouse conflation theories of Philippians, since it would allow a series of letters to be sent in a short period of time. A weakness of the Ephesian view is the lack of direct evidence for an imprisonment in Ephesus (but see 2 Cor. 6:5; 11:23; 1 *Clement*, 5.6). Even if Paul had been imprisoned there, it is not clear that he would have been detained on a capital crime, hovering between life and death. If he feared judicial execution, he could have exercised his citizenry rights and appealed to Caesar (cf. Acts 16:37–9; 25:10). Moreover, opposing scholars argue that the proconsular headquarters in a senatorial province would not have been labeled a *praetorium*, and members of "Caesar's household" more likely would have been in nearby Pergamon. Furthermore, the Jerusalem fund was an important priority at the time of the suggested Ephesian composition. But Paul does not mention this fund in Philippians, although he accepted a gift for himself and engaged in other monetary discussions (4:10–20).

Several commentators have attempted to alleviate the problem of distance in relation to the traditional Roman (or Caesarean) imprisonment. They have reduced the number of necessary trips by arguing that Epaphroditus fell ill while traveling to Rome (2:30) and sent word back to Philippi while still in transit. Ephaphroditus may have simply assumed that the Philippians were worried about him without hearing this directly (2:26). Even if each trip between Philippi and Rome took several months, Paul was imprisoned in the capital long enough to accommodate the necessary duration.

The place of origin remains a question of probability rather than a certain conclusion. One wonders whether, in the absence of definitive contrary evidence, the traditional location of Rome demands a substitution. The references to the *praetorium* and "Caesar's household" seem to be mentioned for the effect they would have had on readers (Fee 1995: 34–7). Amazement at "the whole praetorium" hearing the gospel (1:13) better fits Rome and its large praetorian company. In any case, an Ephesian composition would date Philippians in the mid-50s; a Caesarean composition in the late 50s; and a Roman composition in the early 60s. If one adopts a partition theory of Philippians, it is possible to place the letters in different originating locales (Bormann 1995: 125–6).

## Historical and Archaeological Setting

Philippi was a leading town in the Roman province of Macedonia. A conservative estimate of its population in the first century CE would be fewer than 10,000 inhabitants, based upon the size of its theater (Pilhofer 1995: 74–6). Philippi was located along the Via Egnatia on a plateau near Mount Pangaion. The Egnatian Way angles south from Philippi a further 16 kilometers to the Aegean seaport of Neapolis. Colonizers from Thasos first settled this fertile region around 360 BCE and named the town Krenides ("Springs"). A few years later, Philip of Macedon took control of the city and named it for himself. In turn, the Romans conquered Macedonia in 168–7 BCE. In 42 BCE, the forces of Octavian (the later emperor Augustus) and Mark Antony triumphed over Brutus and Cassius in twin battles at Philippi. After the battle of Actium (31 BCE), Augustus refounded Philippi as a Roman colony (cf. Acts 16:12). He eventually renamed it Colonia Iulia Augusta Philippensis and settled it with legionary veterans. He also granted the city the *ius italicum* (the same rights under Roman law as an Italian city). Its citizens had various property and legal rights as well as an exemption from poll and land taxes. Philippi's appearance, architecture, constitution, and administration were modeled on the city of Rome, including the two chief magistrates (*stratēgoi*) and their attending lectors (*rhabdouchoi*) (cf. Acts 16:35, 38). The vast majority of surviving inscriptions are in Latin, and the aristocracy was largely Roman and Latin-speaking. Greek may have been the language of everyday life and commerce for many of the inhabitants, although some older Thracian elements remained.

The worship of the emperor was an important religious factor in the city. Several scholars have tied the imperial cult to hostility toward the church (see Perkins 1991; Telbe 1994). This background may explain the stress on Christ as *kurios* (2:9–11) and *sōtēr* (3:20), since these were common titles in the imperial cult. Philippi was also a center of the "folk religion" of Silvanus, of the local cult of Dionysus, and of the worship of the "Thracian Rider" (Pilhofer 1995). The only evidence found of a Jewish community in Philippi is a centuries-later tombstone that mentions a synagogue (Pilhofer 1995: 232). Acts 16 does not mention Paul visiting a *sunagōgē* ("synagogue"), the norm in Acts. Rather, he visited a group gathered on the Sabbath at a *proseuchē* ("place of prayer"), outside the city by a river (Acts 16:13; cf. Pilhofer 1995: 171–3).

Paul and his companions arrived in Philippi around 50 CE. According to Acts 16:12–40, they sailed from Troas to Neapolis and then journeyed to Philippi. Acts 16 is structured around three episodes. The first concerns Lydia, a purple-dye merchant from Thyatira. The second section concentrates on the exorcism of a slave girl with a spirit of divination. The third episode relates the conversion of a Philippian jailer. Following his release, Paul revealed his Roman citizenship and was ushered out of the city. He first bade farewell to the young Christian assembly that met in Lydia's house

(Acts 16:35–40). None of these episodes from Acts is mentioned in Philippians, although Paul does allude to his "struggle" in Philippi (Phil. 1:29–30; cf. 1 Thess. 2:2). Paul later returned to Philippi (Acts 20:1–6; cf. 1 Cor. 16:5; 2 Cor. 2:13; 7:5). In 2 Corinthians 8:1–5 and 11:9, he describes the "rich generosity" that arose from the "extreme poverty" of the Macedonian believers (presumably including the Philippians). In the second century, the Philippian church assisted Ignatius of Antioch on his way to martyrdom and corresponded with Polycarp of Smyrna (Polycarp, *Philippians*, 1, 3, 9, 13).

## Purpose

Views of the function of the letter have varied, including an attempt to provide encouragement in suffering, a reaffirmation of friendship, a call to progress in sanctification, a theological discourse on the person of Christ, or simply an exchange of news. The immediate impetus for this "occasional letter" was Epaphroditus' trip to Philippi. Paul sent the letter along with Epaphroditus, thereby proving the latter's return to health and commending his character so that the Philippians might rejoice (2:25–30). Paul used the occasion to describe his own affairs, including his imprisonment and the furtherance of the gospel (1:12–18). Paul commends Timothy and related his own desire to see the Philippians (2:19–24). He warns them of the dangers of false teaching (3:2–18) and internal disunity (2:1–4, 14; 4:2–3). He also thanks them for their generosity, recently sent through Epaphroditus (4:15–18).

Many commentators see "joy" as the theme of Philippians (1:4, 18, 25; 2:2, 17–18, 28–9; 3:1; 4:1, 4, 10). Yet humility is also a common theme (1:17; 2:3–11; 4:2, 8–9). Obedience and a lack of complaint may be further applications of humility (2:1–11 leads into 2:12–14). Unity (*koinōnia*) is a frequent topic as well (1:5, 7; 2:1; 3:10; 4:14–15). Phrases such as "having the same mind" recur, as do various *sun*-compound words. Another theme is the proper response to suffering. Paul discusses his own suffering (1:13–20), and he encourages the Philippians in their suffering (1:27–8). "Partnership" in the gospel of Christ (1:5) may be the overarching theme under which the sub-themes of unity, joy, humility, and suffering can be grouped. The relationship between the cause of the gospel and unity is especially prominent in the proposition of 1:27, where Paul exhorts them to "stand fast firm in one spirit, with one soul striving together for the faith of the gospel."

## Language and Style

The most engaging aspect of the style is its warm affection for the recipients. Philippians manifests a personal style and includes fifty-one first-person personal pronouns. Although Timothy is listed as a co-sender in 1:1, Paul himself obviously supplied the material (cf. the autobiographical section of 3:4–14). Paul probably intended Philippians to be read publicly in a Christian assembly (cf. 1 Thess. 5:27; Col. 4:16). Wordplay, assonance, alliteration, chiasmus, and repetition are found throughout Philippians. Such constructions were designed to be memorable in an oral culture. Overall, though, the style exudes a certain simplicity. Tropes and figures of speech, when they are found, do not occur merely for the sake of ornamentation.

As with many Greco-Roman letters, Philippians seeks to bridge the problem of distance. The letter was a substitute for face-to-face oral communication. Paul explicitly refers to the role of absence and presence (2:12). He recalls his presence among the Philippians (1:3–11), explains his current circumstances in his absence (1:12–26), calls upon them to live worthily in his absence (1:27–2:18), plans to send Timothy and Epaphroditus (2:19–30), addresses their issues (3:1–4:9), and thanks them for sharing with him in his absence (4:10–20).

## Intertextuality

In Paul's other letters, he commonly argues from the Old Testament to establish his own position, especially when he confronts some form of judaizing. All such citation is noticeably absent from Philippians, even in chapter 3 where the argument relies rather upon the personal example of Paul. Philippians never includes introductory formulae, such as "it is written." Although Philippians does not quote the Old Testament, the epistle does include some instances of allusions and echoes. For example, Philippians 2:7–11 seems to draw from Isaiah 45:23 (see also Isa. 49:3; 52:13; 53:12). Philippians 2:14–15 exhorts readers not to be complainers (perhaps an implicit comparison with the Israelites in their wanderings), but to be "lights" in the midst of a crooked and perverted generation (cf. Deut. 32:5; Dan. 12:3). Philippians 4:3 echoes Psalm 69:28 (cf. Exod. 32:32; Ezek. 13:9; Dan. 12:1); Philippians 2:17 and 4:18 echo Old Testament sacrificial language (cf. Gen. 8:21; Exod. 29:18; Ezek. 20:41). The assertion that "the Lord is near" in 4:5 is reminiscent of Old Testament phraseology (Ps. 145:18). Other reminiscences may perhaps occur in 1:11 (Prov. 11:30), 1:19 (Job 13:16), and 2:16 (Isa. 49:4; 65:23). According to some commentators, Paul's general lack of Old Testament references may be due to the primarily non-Jewish background of the Philippian Christians. Polycarp's letter to the Philippians is similarly limited in its use of the Old Testament.

## Unity

Many scholars have argued that Philippians is a combination of two or three letters. Most partition theories separate a "Letter of Thanks" (4:10–20) and a "Letter of Warning" (from 3:1b or 3:2 to 4:1 or 4:3 or 4:9) from the remainder. Although partition theories have varied greatly in detail, a representative form would divide the current text into three letters: Letter A, consisting of 4:10–20; Letter B, consisting of 1:1–3:1; 4:4–9; 4:21–3; and Letter C, consisting of 3:2–4:3.

Evidence for these theories includes the following: (1) A lack of clear logic in the overall structure of the letter's argument and organization. (2) The presence of travel plans in 2:19–30, rather than at the end of the letter. (3) An abrupt transition between 3:1 and 3:2 (or between 3:1a and 3:1b), followed by the change in style, tone, and subject matter of chapter 3. (4) The use of *to loipon* in 3:1 and 4:8 (often translated adverbially as "finally"). (5) The possible translation of *chairete* in 3:1 as a farewell. (6) The delay of the note of thanks until the end of the letter (4:10–20). This "thanks" would also be delayed in time, since the gift had been brought by Epaphroditus, who had since recovered from illness (2:26–7). (7) Polycarp's reference to the "letters" Paul had written to the Philippian church (*Philippians*, 3.2).

Those who argue for the unity of Philippians stress the following: (1) The variance and lack of consensus in partition theories (see the chart in Garland 1985: 155). Commentators have had some difficulty in explaining why a redactor would have arranged matters as they currently stand. (2) The inclusion of material similar to Philippians 2:19–30 in the middle of 1 Thessalonians (2:17–3:13) and 1 Corinthians (4:14–21). (3) Examples of abrupt transitions in other ancient letters. Such abruptness is not necessarily inconsistent with a personal, conversational style (Rom. 16:16–27; 1 Thess. 2:13–17). (4) The possible translation of *to loipon* as a transitional device ("well then, and so" or "in addition, furthermore") rather than as a closing formula ("finally"). (5) The translation of *chairete* as an exhortation ("rejoice in the Lord"), rather than a farewell. In fact, *chairete* is never used as a closing salutation in any extant letter (Alexander 1989). (6) The examples of other ancient letters that do not include the personal thanks at the beginning (Alexander 1989: 97–8). Some have argued that the postponement of thankfulness (4:10–20) is due to Paul's personal (autographic) writing of this section, his sensitivity about material support, the formation of an *inclusio* between 1:5 and 4:10–20, or the desire to keep the thanks as a rhetorical climax. In regard to the delay caused by Epaphroditus' sickness, he may have fallen ill already on his way to Paul. (7) Polycarp's reference could be a generalized plural or rhetorical statement about the "letter-writing" of Paul, an inference based upon Philippians 3:1, a supposition that the Thessalonian correspondence was also sent on to Philippi, or a possible reference to other genuine Pauline letters which have not survived (cf. 1 Cor. 5:9; Col. 4:16). (8) The lack of any external textual evidence for the various independent letters. The manuscript transmission is consistently unified.

Some studies have pointed to the themes and ideas that cut across all three supposed letters. For example, Christ's self-emptying in 2:5–11 parallels Paul's self-denial in 3:4–14. The examples of Timothy and Epaphroditus are sandwiched in between (2:19–30) and also include various verbal parallels. There are striking parallels of vocabulary and ideas between 2:6–11 and 3:20–1 (Garland 1985). The similar use of *phronein* cuts across the various letters (2:2, 5; 3:15; 4:2; see also 1:7; 3:19; 4:10). The reference to "striving together" for the gospel occurs in both 1:27 and 4:3. The themes of suffering, fellowship, co-sharing, and joy also traverse the letters. The thanksgiving of 1:3–11 anticipates topics from all three purported letters. Garland contends that an *inclusio* marks the section from 1:27 to 4:3. He identifies various verbal parallels between 1:27–30 and 3:20–4:3. Other recent studies have tried to use rhetorical criticism and discourse analysis to argue for the unity of the letter (Black 1995; Reed 1997; Watson 1988). It must be admitted that the new critical tools can be used to support assumed stances on both sides. Yet in the final analysis, "partition theories have turned out to raise more questions than they answer" (Bockmuehl 1997: 25). The epistle can be interpreted as a unified whole as it now stands.

## Constituent Literary Forms

Literary forms embedded within Philippians include a prayer of thanksgiving (1:3–11), commendations or travelogues (2:19–30), a possible traditional fragment in 3:20–1, a doxology (4:20), and a benediction (4:23). But the most examined form has been the so-called "Christ-hymn" of 2:6–11. Scholars have debated the original language, form, structure, function, authorship, and conceptual milieu of this passage. Most scholars agree that the passage reflects hymnody or lyrical poetry (or an encomium), due to its unusual language, rhythmical structure, and elevated style (cf. though Fee 1995: 40–3). Yet these scholars have disagreed how many strophes or couplets form the structure.

Various scholars have viewed the original background of the "hymn" as Adamic typology, Suffering Servant imagery, Hellenistic Jewish wisdom literature, Jewish sectarian literature, gospel tradition (Jesus' footwashing), or religious syncretism. One must emphasize that it currently stands within a Christian composition. The "tradition history" behind the text may answer other questions, but it cannot fully answer what Paul intended by inclusion (or even composition) of the material in the present passage. Some have suggested that the passage is an example of Adam–Christ typology rather than a reference to the pre-existence of Christ. The common view, however, is that the "hymn" refers to the pre-existent Christ. Debate surrounds the translation of such words as *morphē* and *harpagmos*. The term *morphē* may be understood as "condition/ status," rather than "outward appearance" or "ontological existence." The use of *harpagmos* may refer to the idea that Christ did not consider equality with God a matter of "grasping," a "booty," or (perhaps more likely) something to be exploited or used for one's own advantage.

Some have interpreted the "hymn" as an ethical/moral example, expounding an ideal of self-humiliation one should follow. Others have opted for a "soteriological" interpretation. Perhaps neither a simplistic moralizing of the passage nor a hypothesized "cosmic drama" is the best interpretation. The saving activity of God in Christ may serve as a paradigm of humbly renouncing legitimate status for the sake of others. Paul did not use specifically redemptive language to interpret the cross (or add such language to pre-existing material). Yet the inclusion of the climactic exaltation points beyond Jesus being a mere role model. The passage becomes both the basis and pattern of the paraenetic argument of the surrounding context (cf. 2:1–4).

## Genre

First, Holloway has asserted that Philippians is "first and foremost a letter of consolation" (*epistolē paramuthētikē*) (Holloway 2001: 2). Ancient practitioners of consolation sought to remove grief by means of rational argument and frank exhortation (even open rebuke). Yet Holloway stresses that this classification is more a matter of function and content rather than form. Thus, he acknowledges that Philippians might also be discussed as a "letter of friendship" or a "family letter," since such individuals had the duty to console one another.

Second, Alexander has compared Philippians with ancient "family letters." The purpose of these letters was to reinforce familial ties through exchanging news of personal welfare between the sender and his or her family. Alexander points to the common use of familial terms such as "brother" and "sister" in early Christian communities, which could even regard themselves as "families" or "households" (Alexander 1989: 99). Arguments for this categorization of Philippians include the parental imagery (2:15, 22) and the calls for imitation (Witherington 1994: 118–21). However, such calls for imitation are not necessarily indicative of family letters. Ancient epistolary theorists did not discuss this specific genre, and most extant examples come from the third century.

Third, others have categorized Philippians as a "letter of friendship" (*philikos typos*). Ancient epistolary theorists discussed such letters, and this type first appears in Pseudo-Demetrius' list of twenty-one types of letters (cf. also Pseudo-Libanius). The "friendly type" was a personal exchange of intimacies between two geographically distanced friends. Philippians is structured around the affairs of the sender (1:12–26), the affairs of the recipients (1:27–2:18; 3:1–4:9), a discussion of intermediates (2:19–30), and a discussion of partnership (4:10–20). The rhetoric of friendship in Philippians includes the desire to be together (cf. 1:7, 8; 4:1); the emphasis on unity, mutual affection, and *koinōnia* (1:5, 7; 2:1; 3:10; 4:14–15); the stress on being of one mind (cf. 1:27; 2:2), various *sun*-compounds; and perhaps even the discussion of common enemies (cf. 1:29–30). However, there are no known examples of one person sharing a letter of friendship with a collective group. Furthermore, Philippians lacks any of the expected *philia* terms.

Fee proposes that Philippians reflects the essential characteristics of both the letter of friendship and the letter of moral exhortation (Fee 1995: 12–14). Therefore, he labels Philippians as a "hortatory letter of friendship." According to Pseudo-Demetrius, the "letter of moral exhortation" was usually written within a "friendship" or a patron–client context. The author of a "letter of moral exhortation" would often appeal to examples, including his own. Such exemplary paradigms in Philippians include Christ (2:5–11) Timothy and Epaphroditus (2:19–30), and Paul himself (3:4–14). Even Paul's discussion of his personal affairs (1:12–26), which fits well within a "letter of friendship," also functions as a moral paradigm of righteous suffering (1:27–30). The language of "imitation" is found in 3:15, 17; 4:9. According to Fee, the normal two-way bond of Greco-Roman friendship has been transformed into a "three-way bond" involving Christ himself (Fee 1995: 13). This mixed form demonstrates that the exact categorization of Philippians (even as an *epistolē philikē*) is somewhat difficult, but the presence of friendship as a *topos* is clear.

## Epistolary Analysis

The letter opening begins with an address or epistolary prescript in 1:1–2. It states the senders and recipients and includes a greeting. As in Paul's other letters, the salutation is similar to the common first-century form ("A to B, greetings"), yet has been theologically modified ("grace be unto you and peace from God our Father and the Lord Jesus Christ"). The recipients are "in Christ Jesus" and are "in Philippi." A thanksgiving appears in 1:3–11. It includes a customary thanksgiving introduced by *euxaristō* (1:3–

8) and a prayer introduced by *proseuxomai* (1:9–11). The thanksgiving prepares the reader for various topics within the letter. It also engages in subtle exhortation and provides an eschatological reference to the discussion.

The phrase "But I want you to know" in 1:12 serves as a formal opening to the body of the letter. The body of Philippians runs from 1:12 to 4:20. As is common in Pauline letters, the body includes paraenesis (moral exhortation). In Philippians, the paraenesis is closely tied to the relationship between the writer and readers. The "travelogues" of 2:19–30 focus on his two associates, Timothy and Epaphroditus (with the exception of 2:24). The body draws to a close with a note of thanks (4:10–20), concluding with a doxology (4:20).

The letter closing (4:21–3) includes the exchange of greetings with third parties (4:21–2) and a benediction (4:23). The letter closing returns to the *pas/pantote* word group of the letter opening's thanksgiving (cf. 4:21–3 and 1:3–4), reiterated by the unifying phrase *tou pneumatos humōn*. Unlike many Greco-Roman letters, Philippians does not contain a closing wish for good health.

## Rhetorical Analysis

Questions remain concerning the proper application of rhetorical criticism to Philippians (and Paul's other epistles). Consideration must be given to Paul's background and training, the letter form, the non-elite audience, and the extent to which Paul followed contemporary rhetorical guidelines. Specifically, attempts to superimpose an ancient rhetorical grid like Quintilian's upon Philippians have produced varying results (Watson 1988; Bloomquist 1993; Witherington 1994). On a basic level, interpreters have disagreed whether Philippians exhibits deliberative or epideictic rhetoric (cf. Schenk's discussion of judicial rhetoric, 1984: ch. 3). The epistle may be composed of mixed rhetorical styles. Scholars have also disagreed about the rhetorical exigence (situation addressed).

Most practitioners agree on a few key points. First, the letter seeks to persuade through both *ethos* and *pathos*. *Ethos*, or credibility with the readers, is established through confirming Paul's character and ministry in prison. Paul also builds *ethos* through identification with his audience. The emotive phrases in 2:1–4 would have elicited *pathos*. The appeal in 3:2–21 would have aroused a negative reaction to the opponents. Second, Paul appeals to the Philippians' sense of "citizenship." They are to "live as citizens" (*politeuesthe*) in a worthy manner, since their citizenship (*politeuma*) is in heaven (1:27; 3:20). Third, Paul masterfully "implores" both Euodia and Syntyche toward unity in a manner that does not state a guilty party (4:2–3). Fourth, Philippians seems to use various forms of *inclusio*. (For example, 1:12–26 is marked off by the use of *prokopē*.)

An example of rhetorical analysis might include the following functional parallels: An *exordium* is found in 1:3–11 and a *narratio* in 1:12–26. The *argumentatio* begins with a *propositio* in 1:27–30 and is developed through a *probatio* in 2:1 and following, including the three *exempla* of Jesus, Timothy, and Epaphroditus. A *refutatio* occurs in 3:1–21, and a *peroratio* may be found in 4:1–20. (For alternative rhetorical structures, see Bloomquist 1993, Watson 1988, and Witherington 1994.)

## Theology

Paul proclaimed that God was at work in the Philippians (1:6; 2:13). He would supply their every need (4:19), including grace (1:2), peace (1:2), and mercy (2:27). God is worthy of worship (3:3), praise (1:11), and glory (2:11). The Holy Spirit is rarely mentioned in Philippians (1:19; 2:1; 3:3?).

Jesus Christ, the one who had "seized" Paul (3:12) is an all-encompassing central focus in Philippians. For Paul, Christ was life itself (1:21), and death would simply be a departure to be with Christ (1:23). Philippians stresses the supreme good of knowing Christ in an intimate way (3:7–8). Knowing him includes being conformed into the likeness of his death (3:10) as one presses on toward the prize (3:14). This intimate knowledge of Christ is balanced with language of Christ as sovereign ruler (2:9–11; 3:20–1). Of course, 2:6–11 has been fertile ground for centuries of Christological reflection.

Philippians also emphasizes eschatology, especially the believer's eschatological triumph. Paul was confident that God would continue a work in the Philippians until the "day of Christ Jesus" (1:6; cf. 1:10; 2:16). Paul presented himself as a paradigm of one who pursued the ultimate eschatological prize as he awaited the resurrection (3:11). He anticipates the coming of his Lord and Savior Jesus Christ and the changing of his own body (3:20–1). The ambiguous statement that "The Lord is near" in 4:5 could also be interpreted in an eschatological sense.

The noun "gospel" occurs more often in Philippians than in any of Paul's other epistles (1:5, 7, 12, 17, 27a, 27b; 2:22; 4:3, 15). Philippians testifies to the sure advance of the gospel, including Paul's own defense of the gospel (1:7). Paul states that true righteousness is not a righteousness of the law, but a righteousness that is of God by faith (3:9). Philippians begins and ends with grace (1:2 and 4:23). Full salvation lies in the future in "the day of Christ" (1:6, 10; 2:16).

Philippians also contains teachings concerning Christian living and church life. Philippians 1:1 refers to the "bishops and deacons" in the church at Philippi. The letter stresses Christian unity within the local congregation (1:27–30; 2:12–13). Christian charity involved sharing material goods (4:10–20), which could be referred to in sacrificial language (4:18). The theme of Christian sanctification fills Paul's opening prayer (1:9–11), the *propositio* (1:27), and the main body (2:1–4, 12, 15). Paul stresses continued progress (3:8–16), yet in constant dependence on God (1:6, 2:13; 1:19–20; 3:12; 4:13, 19).

## Opponents

A debate surrounds the nature of the opponents in Philippians. The opponents in 1:15–18 cannot be judaizers, since they are not anathematized for preaching "another Gospel" (cf. Gal. 1:6–9). The issue in Philippians 1:15–18 concerns motive more than message. They hoped to add to Paul's suffering and preached with envy, rivalry, and selfish partisanship. Paul rejoiced that Christ was still preached, in spite of their impure motives (1:18). Those who opposed the Philippians in 1:28 may have been pagan opponents (though see Silva 1988: 9). A pagan Gentile opposition lies behind 2:15.

In chapter 3, Paul castigates certain enemies as "dogs," "workers of iniquity," and "mutilators" who emphasized circumcision (3:2; cf. Paul's three responses in 3:3). These three labels are all inversions of Jewish boasts. For example, Jews used the term "dog" to refer to Gentiles in a derogatory manner. These enemies in 3:2–3 were probably Jewish Christian missionaries, although some believe they were non-Christian Jews (possibly from Thessalonica). One might fruitfully compare the judaizers elsewhere, as in Galatians, who sought to impose circumcision and obedience to the law on Gentile Christians. The label "workers of evil" may be understood as a critique of judaizing "missionary workers." (Some have even compared 3:1–21 with the so-called "charismatic missionaries" presupposed by 2 Corinthians 11.)

After a largely autobiographical section in 3:12–16, Paul continues a description of adversaries. (Some believe the opponents taught a form of perfectionism, based upon 3:12–16, but this is not necessary). The opponents in 3:17–19 are enemies of the cross of Christ who have set their mind on earthly things. Their end is destruction, their god is their belly, and their glory is in their shame (3:19). Some see a second group in this these verses, perhaps antinomians or gnosticizing libertines. Perhaps it is simpler to demonstrate how one group of adversaries could fit the evidence of both 3:1–3 and 3:17–19. For example, the reference to their "belly" may involve Jewish dietary laws, and their "shame" may be a reference to the mark of circumcision (Hawthorne 1983: xlvi–xlvii). Perhaps Paul is simply borrowing from Hellenistic Jewish polemics against pagans, and inverting it upon the judaizers (Perkins 1991). In any case, the opponents are described as self-centered, self-gratifying, and this-worldly (contrast 2:6–11).

## The Structure of Philippians

| | |
|---|---|
| 1:1–2 | Greeting |
| 1:3–11 | Thanksgiving and Prayer |
| 1:12–26 | Paul's Circumstances of Imprisonment and Ministry |
| 1:27–2:18 | Paul's Call for Like-Mindedness and Humility |
| 2:19–30 | Paul's Commendation of Timothy and Epaphroditus |
| 3:1–21 | Paul's Contrast of Himself and the Opponents |
| 4:1–9 | Paul's Plea for Unity and Rejoicing |
| 4:10–20 | Paul's Thanks for the Philippians and their Generosity |
| 4:21–3 | Farewell |

## Annotated Bibliography

Alexander, Loveday. "Hellenistic Letter-Forms and the Structure of Philippians." *Journal for the Study of the New Testament* 37 (1989), 87–101. Alexander argues for the unity of the epistle based upon epistolary analysis. She compares Philippians with ancient "family letters."

Black, David Alan. "The Discourse Structure of Philippians: A Study in Textlinguistics." *Novum Testamentum* 37 (1995), 16–49. Black defends the integrity and unity of Philippians through literary and rhetorical methods. The theme of the deliberative letter is a call to unity arising from the exigence found in 4:2–3.

Bloomquist, L. Gregory. *The Function of Suffering in Philippians. Journal for the Study of the New Testament* Supplementary Series, 78. Sheffield: Sheffield Academic Press, 1993. Part I surveys past study of the theme of suffering in Philippians. Part II applies modern analyses, such as epistolary and rhetorical criticism, to the letter. Part III combines the results of rhetorical study with an examination of the theme of suffering.

Bockmuehl, Markus. *The Epistle to the Philippians.* Black's New Testament Commentaries. Peabody: Hendrickson, 1997. Bockmuehl attempts to combine a classic "historical" exegesis with theological analysis. He seeks to join an "ecclesial stance of faith" with "considered critical judgement" (p. 43).

Bormann, Lukas. *Philippi: Stadt und Christengemeinde zur Zeit des Paulus.* Supplements to Novum Testamentum, 78. Leiden: Brill, 1995. The first part of this work investigates archaeological, numismatic, epigraphical, and literary sources related to Philippi. The second part examines Paul's relationship with the Philippians within their political, religious, and social context. Bormann emphasizes the dominant imperial cult and the resultant conflict with the Philippian Christians.

Fee, Gordon D. *Paul's Letter to the Philippians.* New International Commentary on the New Testament. Grand Rapids: Eerdmans, 1995. Fee writes for a twofold audience, both academic readers and parish ministers. Therefore, the commentary is scholarly yet accessible. Most technical discussions are consigned to the footnotes.

Garland, David E. "The Composition and Unity of Philippians: Some Neglected Literary Factors." *Novum Testamentum* 27 (1985), 141–73. Garland thoroughly examines partition theories and presents a case for the unity of the letter. His literary criticism seeks to demonstrate Paul's uses of *inclusio* and his cohesive argumentation from 1:27 to 4:3.

Hawthorne, Gerald F. *Philippians.* Word Biblical Commentary. Waco: Word, 1983. This commentary is a careful and judicious exposition of the Greek text. Hawthorne argues for a Caesarean place of composition, and he maintains that the opponents of chapter 3 were antagonistic Jews.

Holloway, Paul A. *Consolation in Philippians: Philosophical Sources and Rhetorical Strategy.* SNTS Monograph Series, 112. Cambridge: Cambridge University Press, 2001. Holloway places Philippians within ancient theories and literary practices of "consolation," and he seeks to demonstrate that the epistle has a unified overall strategy within such a context. Part II focuses on the exegesis of the consolatory *topoi* and arguments that Holloway finds in Philippians.

Hurtado, Larry W. "Jesus as Lordly Example in Philippians 2:5–11." Pp. 113–26 in *From Jesus to Paul: Studies in Honour of Francis Wright Beare.* Edited by P. Richardson and J. C. Hurd. Waterloo: Wilfrid Laurier University Press, 1984. Hurtado critiques the views of Käsemann and Martin concerning the so-called "Christ hymn." Hurtado focuses on an early Christian milieu of the language, and he presents the passage as a lordly example of service.

Martin, Ralph P. *A Hymn of Christ: Philippians 2:5–11 in Recent Interpretation and in the Setting of Early Christian Worship.* Downers Grove, IL: InterVarsity Press, 1997. This third edition includes a new preface and supplementary indexes. The new material updates readers on recent developments in the interpretation of the passage. Martin argues against an "ethical" view of the text and contends that Paul modifies a previously existing hymn to Christ.

Martin, Ralph P. and Brian J. Dodd (eds). *Where Christology Began.* Louisville: Westminster/John Knox, 1998. This collection of ten essays covers Philippians 2:5–11. The essays review the important works of Lohmeyer and Käsemann, examine the controversial interpretation of important terms in 2:6, investigate possible Adam–Christ typology, and discuss the role of ethics in the passage.

Mearns, Chris. "The Identity of Paul's Opponents at Philippi." *New Testament Studies* 33 (1987), 194–204. Through the use of a "mirror reading" of the repeated affirmations and denials in Philippians, Mearns seeks to reconstruct the opponents. Mearns concludes that they attached no central saving significance to the cross, and they espoused a confident "triumphalist" theology, a strongly realized eschatology, and a moral perfectionism through obedience to the Torah.

Müller, Ulrich B. *Der Brief des Paulus an die Philipper*. Theologischer Handkommentar zum Neuen Testament. Leipzig: Evangelische Verlaganstalt, 1993. This is a short but balanced commentary. Müller defends the literary unity of Philippians, but believes different situations are presupposed in chapters 1–2 and 3–4.

Oakes, Peter. *Philippians: From People to Letter*. SNTS Monograph Series, 110. Cambridge: Cambridge University Press, 2001. Oakes attempts to construct a model of the social make-up of the Christian community in Philippi. Based upon his modeling, he interprets Philippians as "a call for unity under economic suffering." Paul and Christ then serve as models in the midst of suffering, and Philippians 2:6–11 is "a carefully crafted piece of exhortation and encouragement, written specifically for the Philippian situation" (p. xiii).

O'Brien, Peter T. *The Epistle to the Philippians: A Commentary on the Greek Text*. New International Greek Testament Commentary. Grand Rapids: Eerdmans, 1991. O'Brien's work is a detailed and theological exposition of the Greek text. He covers virtually every exegetical problem in the letter and provides sound evidence for his own decisions.

Perkins, Pheme. "Philippians: Theology for the Heavenly Politeuma." Pp. 89–104 in *Pauline Theology*, vol. 1: *Thessalonians, Philippians, Galatians, Philemon*. Edited by Jouette M. Bassler. Minneapolis: Fortress Press, 1991. Perkins examines the apologetic context of Philippians (conflict with the imperial cult), the Christ hymn as governing metaphor (renouncing status), and the role of the exalted Lord and heavenly *politeuma*.

Pilhofer, Peter. Philippi, vol. 1: *Die erste christliche Gemeinde Europas*. Wissenschaftliche Untersuchungen zum Neuen Testament, 87. Tübingen: Mohr Siebeck, 1995. This volume discusses the epigraphy and archaeology of Philippi; examines its physical, political, and religious features in the first century; summarizes the city's history from Paul through Polycarp; and traces the history of the Philippian church. A second volume publishes inscriptions from Philippi.

Reed, Jeffrey T. *A Discourse Analysis of Philippians: Method and Rhetoric in the Debate over Literary Integrity*. Journal for the Study of the New Testament Supplementary Series, 136. Sheffield: Sheffield Academic Press, 1997. Reed's work is a technical, dense discourse analysis of the epistle. Reed argues for the unity of the letter by demonstrating that "semantic chains" span the disputed sections of Philippians. He also contends that personal hortatory letters did not necessarily have a single theme.

Reumann, John. "Philippians, Especially Chapter 4, as a 'Letter of Friendship': Observations on a Checkered History of Scholarship." Pp. 83–106 in *Friendship, Flattery, and Frankness of Speech: Studies on Friendship in the New Testament World*. Edited by John T. Fitzgerald. Supplements to Novum Testamentum, 82. Leiden: Brill, 1996. Reumann surveys the patristic and recent discussion of friendship in Philippians and the possible classification of the epistle as a "letter of friendship." Reumann concludes that the influence of the friendship *topos* on Philippians is better supported than its literary categorization as an *epistolē philikē*.

Schenk, Wolfgang. *Die Philipperbriefe des Paulus: Kommentar*. Stuttgart: Kohlhammer, 1984. Schenk's commentary is not a traditional verse-by-verse commentary, but an eleven-part application of "textlinguistic" methodology to Philippians. He argues for a compilation hypothesis based upon various epistolary and rhetorical considerations.

Silva, Moisés. *Philippians*. Baker Exegetical Commentary on the New Testament. Grand Rapids: Baker, 1988; 2nd edn. 2005. Silva's commentary traces the flow of the larger argument of Philippians through its individual units. The volume's goal of "uncluttered exposition" tends to limit its direct interaction with wider scholarship (p. xv). Silva argues that the twin truths of divine sovereignty and human responsibility are central to Philippians.

Stowers, Stanley K. "Friends and Enemies in the Politics of Heaven: Reading Theology in Philippians." Pp. 105–21 in *Pauline Theology*, vol. 1: *Thessalonians, Philippians, Galatians, Philemon*. Edited by Jouette M. Bassler. Minneapolis: Fortress Press, 1991. Stowers views Philippians as a hortatory letter of friendship. The fundamental "architecture" of the letter is a series of models, most often contrasting Paul and his opponents. Christ is spoken of as both sovereign ruler and friend.

Telbe, Mikael. "The Sociological Factors behind Phil. 3:1–11 and the Conflict at Philippi." *Journal for the Study of the New Testament* 55 (1994), 97–121. Telbe concludes that Paul's argument was shaped by the ongoing conflict between the church and Roman society in Philippi. Paul was worried that church members would have been tempted to take on Jewish "identity markers" for the sake of social protection.

Watson, D. F. "A Rhetorical Analysis of Philippians and its Implications for the Unity Question." *Novum Testamentum* 30 (1988), 57–88. Watson contends that Philippians was "organized and written according to the principles of Greco-Roman rhetoric" (p. 57). If our current letter is made up of letter fragments, extensive redaction must have created the rhetorically unified whole, but the supposition of integrity is the easier solution.

White, L. Michael. "Morality between Two Worlds: A Paradigm of Friendship in Philippians." Pp. 201–15 in *Greeks, Romans and Christians: Essays in Honor of Abraham J. Malherbe*. Edited by D. L. Balch, E. Ferguson, and W. A. Meeks. Minneapolis: Fortress, 1990. White interprets the epistle as a friendly hortatory letter that adapts the Hellenistic emphasis on the moral virtues of *philia*. The "hymn" of 2:6–11 is then interpreted as a paradigm of selfless love, the supreme virtue of friendship.

Wick, Peter. *Der Philipperbrief: Der formale Aufbau des Briefs als Schlüssel zum Verständnis seines Inhalts*. Beiträge zur Wissenschaft des Alten und Neuen Testaments, 7.15. Stuttgart: Kohlhammer, 1994. Wick ascertains ten blocks of material in Philippians, with the first five paralleling the last five. He considers Philippians 2:5–11 to be the center of the epistle, to have a paraenetic function, and to be written by Paul himself. *Koinōnia*, which includes having the same mind, mutual service, and rejoicing, is the primary theme. Wick argues for the unity of Philippians and a Roman origin.

Witherington, Ben III. *Friendship and Finances in Philippi: The Letter of Paul to the Philippians*. New Testament in Context Series. Valley Forge: Trinity Press International, 1994. This short commentary stresses insights from the social sciences and a study of Greco-Roman rhetoric.

CHAPTER 27

# Colossians

## Troy W. Martin and Todd D. Still

This precious gem of the Pauline corpus is one of the so-called "prison epistles" of Paul. It provides a wealth of issues for reflection and assessment and continues to be a rich resource for understanding both ancient and contemporary Christianity.

## Major Issues and Directions in Recent Study

In his survey of Colossian scholarship, Schenk (1987: 3327–54) presents the question of authorship and the identification of the opponents as the two major issues in this scholarship prior to 1985. Along with a few additional issues, scholars continue to examine the authorship and opponents of the letter.

The authenticity of Colossians no longer enjoys a consensus among scholars. Brown (1997: 610) estimates that "about 60 percent of critical scholarship holds that Paul did not write the letter." Since Mayerhoff (1838) first questioned Pauline authorship for the entire letter, notable scholars have lined up on both sides of the debate (Percy 1946: 6–7). When comparing Colossians to Paul's undisputed letters, interpreters recognize (considerable) variations. Differences in style, diction, syntax (Bujard 1973), and theology fuel this ongoing debate as scholars examining the same data reach differing conclusions. Several scholars adopt mediating positions between the two poles of affirming or denying Pauline authorship. A few posit an original authentic letter that a later editor revised and supplemented (Holtzmann 1872: 148–93, 325–30; Sanders 1966: 45; Schmithals 1998: 170). The later expansion of an original Colossians effectively explains the non-Pauline features of the canonical Colossians without requiring the personal references in the letter to be pseudonymous (Schmithals 1998: 155). Others propose a letter written by a secretary of Paul such as Timothy (Schweizer 1976: 13–14; 1982: 23–4; Dunn 1996: 38; Hay 2000: 24) or Epaphras (Lähnemann 1971: 181–2), to which letter Paul gave his approval and added a few personal touches. Still others conceive of an authentic letter of Paul that nevertheless relies on non-Pauline traditional materials (Cannon 1983: 229). Even though this contentious debate is nowhere near an end, an increasing number of scholars deny the authenticity of

Colossians in the face of staunch defenders of Pauline authorship (O'Brien 1982: xli–lxix; Wright 1986: 31–4; Barth and Blanke 1994: 125). Perhaps the careful presentation of the data in synoptic form (Reuter 1997) and the precise analysis of the data by computer-based stylometry will provide new momentum to this debate. Indeed, some recent stylometric analyses refute older investigations of style and affirm Pauline authorship, but the results are still not completely conclusive (Barclay 1997: 31–3). The importance of this debate transcends historical curiosities and has striking consequences for Pauline theology. Accepting the authenticity of Colossians requires a significant expansion and reassessment of Paul's thought as determined solely on the basis of the seven undisputed letters. If Colossians were pseudonymous, on the other hand, it becomes an even more important witness to the way the early church appropriated Pauline theology (Merklein 1987: 409–47).

Since Lightfoot first raised the issue in 1875, the description and identification of the Colossian philosophy has become a central issue in Colossians studies (Francis and Meeks 1975; Hübner 2003: 263). Rather than a convergence of opinion, scholars offer an increasing variety of proposals (Gunther 1973: 3–4). These numerous proposals fall into five distinct categories of Jewish Gnosticism, Gnostic Judaism, mystical Judaism, Hellenistic syncretism, and Hellenistic philosophy (DeMaris 1994: 38–9). With few exceptions (Attridge 1994: 481–98; Hay 2000: 112; Wilson 2005: 57), recent scholars have abandoned the first two categories and surrendered attempts to link the philosophy to Gnosticism. Several recent scholars identify the philosophy as some form of Judaism (Wright 1986: 27), especially mystical Judaism (Evans 1982: 204; O'Brien 1982: xxxviii; Sappington 1991: 19–22; Dunn 1995: 154; Smith 2006). Others view the philosophy as some form of Hellenistic syncretism. The various mixtures are diverse and encompass a Hellenistic Jewish syncretism (Lincoln 2000: 567), Christian ascetic visionaries (Sumney 1993: 386), and a Christian syncretism composed of Phrygian folk religion including magic, Jewish cultic observances, as well as pagan mystery cult initiation (Arnold 1995: 228–44). Still others designate the philosophy as one of the known philosophical schools such as Pythagoreanism (Schweizer 1982: 132–3), Middle Platonism (DeMaris 1994: 17), or Cynicism (Martin 1996a: 205–6). Arguably, the Scythian perspective in Colossians 3:11 provides an important textual clue for the identity of these philosophers (Martin 1995b: 249–61; 1999: 256–64). Nevertheless, the increasing variety of proposals has engendered a skepticism that questions whether there were even any false teachers at Colossae (Hooker 1973: 315–31) or whether an identification of the Colossian philosophy is even possible (Barclay 1997: 53–4; Hübner 2003: 263).

Scholars generally agree that the text of Colossians rather than external parallels must provide the primary data for identifying the opponents. In particular, Colossians 2:16–23 forms the crux of the discussion. Colossians 2:16–17 is crucial for determining whether the opponents or the Christians practice the eating, drinking, and calendrical observances (Martin 1995a: 249–55; 1996a: 116–34). Colossians 2:18 is important for determining whether those opposed are insiders (Barclay 1997: 39), outsiders (Barth and Blanke 1994: 21–2; Martin 1996a: 140–1), or both (Standhartinger 1999: 193). Despite translation difficulties, many scholars understand this verse to hold the key to the identification of the philosophy (Dibelius 1975: 83–4; Francis 1975: 163). For example, Arnold (1995: 123) translates, "Let no one condemn you by insisting on ascetic practices and invoking angels because he 'entered the things he had seen.' " His translation renders the genitive ἀγγέλλων as objective rather than as subjective (Francis 1975: 164) or as a genitive of source (Martin 1996b: 168). Further, Arnold renders the participle θέλων ("insisting on") as a Semitic construction (Martin 1996a: 137), the perfect verb ἑόρακεν as a past tense ("entered"), and the present participle ἐμβατεύων as a pluperfect tense ("had seen"). Arnold's external parallels determine his translation rather than the rules of translation, and such imprecise renderings drive the increasing variety of proposals regarding the Colossian philosophy (Martin 1996a: 14).

Aside from the two consuming issues of authorship and the philosophy, other issues also occupy Colossian scholars. Discussions of cosmology in the letter focus on the meaning of the *stoicheia tou kosmou* in 2:8 and 20. In spite of the overwhelming lexical evidence that this phrase refers to the elements of earth, water, air, and fire (Blinzler 1961: 429–42; Schweizer 1988: 456–64; Rusam 1992: 119–25; cf. Martyn 1997: 393–406), some still hold to the principal interpretation of elemental teaching (Moule 1957: 91–2; Carr 1981: 75–6; Sappington 1991: 169), first principles (DeMaris 1994: 73–87), or the law and the flesh as the basic forces in the world (Bandstra 1964: 68–72). Even allowing the meager and controversial evidence for the personal interpretation of the term *stoicheia* as elemental spirits (Arnold 1995: 176–83), the evidence is lacking that this term limited by *tou kosmou* conveys a personal meaning (Schweizer 1982: 128).

In addition to cosmology, scholars show interest in the Christology, eschatology, ecclesiology, and soteriology of the letter (Barclay 1997: 25–8; cf. Still 2004). Colossians also continues to be a source for Christian ethical reflection (Meeks 1993; 1996; Bevere 2003; Héring 2007). In particular, the Christ-hymn in Colossians 1:15–20 provides a central text not only for contemplating theological issues (Pizzuto 2006) but also for developing a Christian ecological position (Clifford 1994: 1–26; Davis 2000: 275). Several scholars respond to the ethical problem of subordination in the household code in Colossians 3:18–4:1 by emphasizing the immediate context of equitableness (Standhartinger 2000: 129) or the broader scriptural context of equality (McGuire 1990: 72–85). The investigation of all these major issues in Colossians studies shows no signs of abating.

## Date and Place of Composition

Discussions of the date and place of composition depend upon attribution of authorship. Scholars affirming Pauline authorship place the writing of the letter in Ephesus (Martin 1974: 26–32; Schweizer 1976: 15), Caesarea (Reicke 1970: 277–82), or Rome (O'Brien 1982: xiii; Barth and Blanke 1994: 126–34). An Ephesian imprisonment requires a date of 53–55 CE, a Caesarean imprisonment 56 CE, and a Roman imprisonment the late 50s or early 60s (Donelson 1996: 10). Scholars denying Pauline authorship sometimes still prefer Ephesus as the place of writing because the supposed Pauline school was located there (Pokorný 1991: 18). Recent arguments for the decentralization of this school, however, increase the difficulty of identifying the place of composition for those rejecting the authenticity of the letter (Müller 1988: 325). These scholars usually date the letter in the 70s, 80s, or 90s because of its relationship with Ephesians.

## Relation to Ephesians

"The similarities between Colossians and Ephesians are much closer than between any other two letters in the Pauline corpus" (Muddiman 2001: 7; cf. similarly MacDonald 2000: 4). With few contemporary exceptions (e.g. Best 1997: 72–4, 96; 1998), Pauline interpreters tend to explain the similarities in vocabulary, structure, content, and style by positing the priority of Colossians (see Polhill 1973). Scholars who stand on either side of the authorship debate embrace this interpretive presupposition. Consequently, comparative study between the two letters is typically relegated to works on Ephesians (note esp. Mitton 1976 and Lincoln 1990).

The closest connections between the two epistles occur in their respective salutations (Col. 1:1–2//Eph. 1:1–2) and conclusions (Col. 4:7–8//Eph. 6:21–2; cf. also Col. 1:25//Eph. 3:2; Col. 1:26//Eph. 3:9; Col. 1:14//Eph. 1:7; Col. 2:19//Eph. 4:16). Their conclusions correspond precisely over a stretch of twenty-nine consecutive words. In addition to exact verbal parallels, "of the 1,570 words in Colossians, 34 percent reappear in Ephesians, and conversely 26.5 percent of the 2,411 words in Ephesians are paralleled in Colossians" (Lincoln 1990: xlviii; on the language of Colossians with respect to Ephesians and other Pauline and New Testament literature, see esp. Lohse 1971: 84–91).

In addition to vocabulary, the letters are similar in their structure, content, and style. Colossians and Ephesians proceed along similar lines (see Lincoln 1990: xlvi–lii) with comparative modes of expression (see "Language and Style" below) and share a number of terms, concepts, and concerns (e.g. Christ as "head" of his body the "church" [Col. 1:18; 2:19; Eph. 1:22; 4:15–16; 5:23], "fullness" [Col. 1:19; 2:9; Eph. 1:10, 23; 3:19; 4:13], "mystery" [Col. 1:26–7; 2:2; 4:3; Eph. 1:9; 3:3; 4, 9; 5:32; 6:19], "reconciliation" [Col. 1:20, 21–2; Eph. 2:16], baptism [Col. 2:12; 3:1; Eph. 2:4–7], and both Christian conduct in general [Col. 3:1–4:6; Eph. 4:1–6:20] and Christian household relations in particular [Col. 3:18–4:1; Eph. 5:21–6:9] [see Furnish 2:536]). However, differences between the epistles have not been lost on scholars. In addition to more subtle lexical and theological differences, Colossians is more occasional, includes more Pauline personnel, and makes sparse use of scripture (see Furnish 2:536–7; MacDonald 2000: 5–6; cf. Beetham 2008). Nevertheless, it is their similarities that have captured scholarly imagination and received the lion's share of academic attention. On the relation between Colossians and Philemon, see Knox (1959) and conversely Lohse (1971: 175–7). For the argument that Colossians is similar to authentic Pauline letters because it is dependent upon them, see Sanders (1966: 28–45) and Leppä (2003).

Those scholars affirming Paul as the author of both Colossians and Ephesians are inclined to explain the letters' (dis)similarities with recourse to situational exigencies and apostolic flexibility (e.g., Bruce 1984: 28–32). Interpreters who regard Colossians as authentic and Ephesians as pseudonymous tend to view the latter as fashioned upon the former (so Kümmel 1975: 357–63). In addition to prioritizing Colossians, those who regard both letters to be inauthentic are disposed to see Colossians as beyond the Pauline pale in both in content and style (see Furnish 1:1092–5).

## Historical and Archaeological Setting

A number of scholars who regard Colossians as pseudonymous view the mention of Colossae in Colossians 1:2 as a literary fiction and thus regard the city itself as immaterial to the interpretation of the epistle. Some within this interpretive group have posited that Laodicea (see Col. 2:1; 4:13, 15–16; cf. Rev. 1:11; 3:14), a city located some ten miles northwest of Colossae, was the actual destination of the letter addressed to the Colossians (so, e.g., Lindemann 1981; Pokorný 1991: 21; Furnish 1:1095; Lincoln 2000: 580; contrast Reicke 1973: 432). It is thought that such a theory is necessitated by the Roman historian Tacitus' (ca. 55–ca. 117 CE) report that Laodicea was devastated by an earthquake in 60–1 CE (*Annals*, 14.27.1). By inferring from this passage in Tacitus that Colossae was also crippled by this disaster and subsequently ceased to be a population center and by following Tacitus' claim that Laodicea recovered rapidly from this tragedy, interpreters find additional support for this hypothesis.

It should be noted, however, that Tacitus does not explicitly state that the earthquake also affected Colossae, perhaps because of Colossae's lesser importance in the first century CE in comparison with both Laodicea and Hierapolis (note Col. 4:13), a city located some fifteen miles north-northwest of Colossae (see Arnold 1:1089). The church historian Eusebius (265–340 CE) records that an earthquake, most likely the same one to which Tacitus refers, occurred in 63–4 CE and laid waste not only Laodicea but also Colossae and Hieropolis (*Chronicle*, 1.21–2; see further Lightfoot 1995 [1875]: 37–40). In any event, whether suddenly in the early to mid-60s or gradually over the course of three or four centuries CE, the city of Colossae eventually devolved into the unoccupied, unexcavated tell it is today as its inhabitants moved to the neighboring town of Chonae, modern Honaz (see Bruce 1984: 5).

Whether one regards ancient Colossae as peripheral or integral to the interpretation of Colossians, a student of the letter is confronted with the unfortunate lack of data regarding the city. The ancient site of Colossae was discovered by the explorer W. J. Hamilton in 1835. There was a time when Colossae was an important and perhaps the principal city of the Lycus river valley. Herodotus (7.30; ca. 480–ca. 425 BCE) described Colossae as "a great city of Phrygia," and Xenophon (*Anabasis*, 1.2.6; ca. 430–ca. 355 BCE) spoke of it as "a populous city, prosperous and great." During the Roman imperial period, this once famous and well-to-do city (so Pliny, *Historia Naturalis*, 5.145; cf. Diodorus Siculus, 14.80.8; Strabo, 12.8.13) known for the purple hue of its wool (Pliny, *Historia Naturalis*, 21.51; Strabo, 12.18.16) faded from glory before inconspicuously disappearing from history. Prior to its demise, Colossae not only experienced relative prosperity due to its textile industries and strategic location on a major trade route, it also, according to numismatic evidence, was marked by religious diversity (for Colossian coins, see Head 1906: 154–7). Certain interpreters of Colossians show particular interest in the sizeable Jewish population in the territory of Phrygia to which Colossae belonged (relevant primary sources include Josephus, *Antiquities*, 12.3.4; Cicero, *Pro Flacco*, 28.68) and speculate about how interaction with Colossian Jews may have shaped the congregation and the Pauline letter addressed to it (Dunn 1996: 21–2, 29–35; Garland 1998: 29; esp. Smith 2006).

## Purpose

Articulations of the purpose of Colossians vary widely among scholars. Some emphasize the entextualized purpose of responding to the opponents (O'Brien 1982: xxx; Barclay 1997: 37) or challenging the readers to continue in their relationship with the Lord (Cannon 1983: 175; Olbricht 1996: 312). Others emphasize the implied purpose of the pseudonymous author as furnishing a comprehensive summary of Paul's gospel (Hay 2000: 31; cf. Sumney 2008: 8), supporting the apostolic witness (Pokorný 1991: 14–17), affirming and confirming new converts (Wilson 1997), or encouraging the growth of the implied recipients by presenting the worldview and judgments of the fictive author in the particular situation created by the text (Standhartinger 1999: 59, 175–6). Still others emphasize the timeless message of the letter in explaining how the world actually works if Jesus is Lord (Donelson 1996: 10).

## Language and Style

Thirty-four words found in Colossians appear nowhere else in the New Testament. An additional twenty-eight words contained in Colossians are not utilized in the undisputed Pauline letters. Colossians shares an additional ten words in common only with Ephesians. Furthermore, Colossians and Ephesians contain fifteen words used elsewhere in the New Testament but not found in the seven undisputed Paulines. Taken together, one encounters no fewer than eighty-seven words in Colossians not encountered in those epistles adjudged as assuredly Paul's (for the details, see Lohse 1971: 85–6). Although this is a striking number of terms relative to the letter's size, interpreters point to a number of mitigating factors which should caution against drawing hasty conclusions about the letter's authenticity based solely upon its vocabulary. Altogether, this unique vocabulary accounts for roughly 5.5 percent of the epistle, which is some 1,570 words in length, and may arise from the specific situation and subjects addressed within the letter (see, e.g., O'Brien 1982: xliii). Almost all scholars would concur that in and of itself "vocabulary usage (or non-usage) is an inadequate criterion" for determining whether Paul did or did not write Colossians (Barclay 1997: 30).

Following the detailed analysis of W. Bujard (1973; cf. Kiley 1986: 51–9), Pauline interpreters often suggest that the style of Colossians (and Ephesians) is different than Romans, 1–2 Corinthians, Galatians, Philippians, 1 Thessalonians, and Philemon. Specifically, some note that, in contrast to Paul's undisputed letters, Colossians contains long, complex sentences employing participial phrases and relative clauses and making abundant use of synonyms and appositional phrases. As a result, these scholars maintain that the style of Colossians is "wordy and tautologous" (Furnish 1:1093). In addition to mentioning stylistic elements they regard as incongruent with Paul, these interpreters also posit that the letter lacks stylistic features typical of Paul, for example, conjunctions, articular infinitives, and logically developed, rhetorically robust argumentation.

While no critical interpreter of Colossians would deny that there are stylistic differences between the letter and the undisputed epistles of Paul, scholars differ in the conclusions they draw from such data. A number of exegetes regard the un-Pauline style of Colossians to be the decisive sign that the letter is post-Pauline (most notably Bujard 1973 and those who think his arguments are compelling). However, other scholars – including some who consider Colossians to be pseudonymous (e.g. Lohse 1971: 91, 180–1) – remain reluctant to assign the letter to the category of Pauline pseudepigrapha solely on the basis of its demonstrably variable style (so Barclay 1997: 33). These interpreters contend that contextual factors (so Percy 1946), traditional materials (see Cannon 1983), and/or scribal influence (e.g., Murphy-O'Connor 1997) adequately explain the stylistic variation between Colossians and Paul's other letters. Even though conversations pertaining to Colossians' style vis-à-vis other Pauline letters are likely to continue, one can wonder with legitimate skepticism if the debate will ever move beyond perspectival impasses. Consequently, those seeking to ascertain who wrote Colossians will need to continue considering both the style and the content of the letter.

## Intertextuality

Colossians contains no explicit quotations and few allusions to the Old Testament (see, however, esp. Beetham 2008). The most distinct Old Testament echoes occur in Colossians 3. The claim that Christ is "seated at the right hand of God" (3:1) clearly alludes to Psalm 110:1, the most frequent intertext in the New Testament (see, e.g., Hay 1973). Additionally, talk of a new nature's "being renewed in knowledge according to the image of its creator" in 3:10 is "an unavoidable allusion to Gen. 1:26f." (Wolter 1993: 180). Furthermore, the call for slaves to fear the Lord (3:22) and the assertion that there is no partiality (with God [3:25]) cohere with Old Testament texts such as Deuteronomy 10:20, Proverbs 1:7; 3:7, and Ecclesiastes 5:7 in the first instance (cf. Sir. 1:11–30; 2:7–9) and Deuteronomy 10:17 in the second (cf. Sir. 35:15). Interestingly, 2 Chronicles 19:7 conjoins fear of the Lord on the one hand with the Lord's impartiality on the other.

Connections to the Old Testament also occur at other points in the epistle. For example, the contrast between light and darkness found in 1:12–13 recurs in the Old Testament (e.g. Gen. 1:4; Isa. 42:16; Amos 5:18, 20; Eccles. 2:13; Lam. 3:2), even if the pairing is employed with different nuances and for other purposes. Furthermore, some scholars suggest that particular terms utilized within 1:12–14 (esp. "inheritance," "saints," "delivered," "transferred," and "redemption") are chosen so as "to evoke a whole world of imagery relating to Israel's exodus from Egypt and her entry into the promised land" (so Wright 1986: 60–3; cf. Caird 1976: 171–4). Interpreters (see, e.g., Burney 1925–6) also note how Colossians' description of Christ as "the firstborn of all creation" and "the beginning" is parallel to Proverbs' depiction of wisdom in 8:22–31 (cf. Sir. 24:9). Further links between Colossians and the Old Testament appear in chapter 2 of the letter which mentions (un)circumcision (2:11, 13; cf., e.g., Gen. 17:10–4) as well as "food and drink," "festival(s)," "new moon(s)," and "sabbath(s)" (2:16; cf., e.g., Ezek. 45:17).

Presuming the pseudonymous origin of Colossians, many interpreters (e.g. Lohse 1971: 175–7) posit the epistle's literary dependence upon Philemon with special respect to named Pauline workers (cf. Col. 1:1; 4:9–12, 14, 17 with Philem. 2, 10, 23–4). Presuming the authenticity of Colossians, others explain this overlap by histori-cal congruence as opposed to literary dependence (so, e.g., O'Brien 1982: 269). A few propose that Colossians is not only dependent upon Philemon but also upon Romans, 1 and 2 Corinthians, Galatians, and 1 Thessalonians (Sanders 1966; Leppä 2003). This hypothesis, however, has not won widespread approval among Pauline interpreters (considered and rejected by, among others, Lohse 1971: 182 n.15; Barclay 1997: 24; Thurston 1995: 5–6; cf. Furnish 1:1094). On the presumed dependence of Colossians upon Ephesians, see "Relation to Ephesians" above. On the reception of and allusion to Colossians by the early church, see Abbott (1897: l–li).

## Literary Unity

Lacking the standard indications of composite sources such as inconsistencies, repeti-tions, and stylistic differences, Colossians is usually considered to be a single literary unit (Mullins 1984: 292). Nevertheless, some attempt to identify an original letter sup-plemented by a later editor (Holtzmann 1872: 325–30; Bowen 1924: 177–82; Munro 1972: 446). A recent proponent of this view designates the following as belonging to the original letter: 1:1–5a, 7–9a, 10a, 24–7; 2:1–2a, 4–5, 16, 20–1, 22b; 3:3–4, 12–14a, 15a, 16–17; 4:2–18 (Schmithals 1998: 170). The problem with such source-critical work is the lack of consistent, objective criteria to make such determinations (Bowen 1924: 177–82), and the majority of scholars maintain the unity of Colossians while allowing for the use of preformed traditional materials such as the Christ-hymn in Colossians 1:15–20 (Käsemann 1982: 166–7; Stettler 2000: 100), the *Haustafel* ("household table") in 3:18–4:1 (Crouch 1972; Standhartinger 2000: 117–30), and the vice and virtue lists in 3:5–12 (Cannon 1983: 51).

## Constituent Literary Forms

In addition to the largely formulaic epistolary opening and closing of Colossians (on which see, e.g., Wilson 1997: 230–1, 252–4 and the bibliographical materials he notes), scholars identify a number of other formal features in the letter. These forms are comparatively minor and do not factor significantly into the scholarly discussion of Colossians. Some observe a strong trace of formal material at the conclusion of the thanksgiving in 1:12–14. Although interpreters do not energetically embrace the argument that the whole of 1:12–20 is best viewed in the context of a baptismal liturgy (so Käsemann 1982: 136–68), they nevertheless label 1:12–14 as "traditional" or "liturgical" (so, e.g., Lohse 1971: 40 n.63). The same is true with respect to 2:13–15. Although scholars frequently regard 2:9–15 as confessional material into which the author taps (e.g., Furnish 1:1090), they are not generally persuaded by the proposal that a baptismal hymn lies behind this passage (as argued by Schille 1965: 31–7). Some think that a formulaic, kerygmatic expression underlies the "then"/"now" antithesis that appears in 1:21–2 (see Tachau 1972; cf. 3:7–8). Additionally, some view Colossians

2:1, 4 as an example of the literary form known as "disclosure" in which the writer in a personal and intentional fashion draws upon previous discussion and anticipates subsequent instruction (as noted by Wilson 1997: 240).

There is widespread agreement among scholars that three portions of Colossians bear the marks of traditional materials that have been preserved through the utilization of standard literary forms, namely, 1:15–20, 3:5–17 (esp. verses 5, 8, 12), and 3:18–4:1 (see, e.g., Aune 1987: 192–6). Interpreters typically regard 1:15–20 as an early Christian "hymn" and divide it into at least two strophes (1:15–18a and 1:18b–20 respectively). While most, although by no means all (see esp. Wright 1990), exegetes regard the passage as a pre-formed piece that the author incorporated into Colossians, there is considerable debate regarding whether and to what extent the writer redacted the "hymn" as well as whether and to what extent 1:15–20 coheres with the theological vision articulated elsewhere in the epistle (for the details, consult Fowl 1990: 103–54 and esp. Stettler 2000). Lists of virtues and vices, like the fivefold listings set forth in 3:5, 8, and 12, are frequently found in Greco-Roman, non-canonical Jewish, and early Christian (including the New Testament) literature (see Fitzgerald 6:857–9). Debate continues regarding the origin of New Testament virtue/vice lists like those found in Colossians and the precise relation of such lists to the recipients' life-setting (see esp. Bevere 2003: 182–224). Lastly, it is now commonly thought that the *Haustafel* of 3:18–4:1 is the earliest Christian codification of a then current discussion in (Hellenistic) Jewish and Greco-Roman (philosophical) circles regarding familial roles and responsibilities (see Lincoln 1999 and Standhartinger 2000). Questions such as why the codes were incorporated, albeit modified, into Colossians in the first place (see Bevere 2003: 239–54) and how, if at all, they might be appropriated in contexts far different than that of ancient Colossae (note, e.g., Meeks 1996) continue to exercise contemporary New Testament interpreters.

## Literary Genre

Scholars classify Colossians as a refutation, an apology, a dialogue, and a pastoral essay (Barth and Blanke 1994: 42–3). One recent scholar points to the striking structural similarities between Colossians and antique farewell speeches as well as Jewish testaments, and posits that Colossians is a *Himmelsbrief* ("heavenly letter") meant to comfort and console Christians shaken by Paul's death (Standhartinger 1999: 193). However, the dominant tendency has been to describe Colossians as a polemical writing because of the opposition to the opponents in 2:8–23. Nevertheless, recent studies reveal an increasing trend to identify Colossians as a paraenetic letter (Furnish 1:1090; Wilson 1997; Lincoln 2000: 560).

## Epistolary Analysis

Epistolary analyses of Colossians proceed along the lines of the standard conventions of a Pauline letter: the salutation (1:1–2), the thanksgiving (1:3–23), the letter body

(1:24–4:9) with body-opening (1:24–2:5), body-middle (2:6–4:6), and body-closing (4:7–9), and letter closing (4:10–18) (Lincoln 2000: 556). Although scholars vary little from this basic analysis, one scholar identifies Colossians as a paraenetic letter and then divides it into paraenetic affirmation (1:3–2:7), paraenetic correction (2:8–23), and paraenetic exhortation (3:1–4:6) (Wilson 1997).

## Rhetorical Analysis

Slightly before the appearance of H. D. Betz's monumental rhetorical work on Galatians (1979), Bujard investigated various rhetorical figures and strategies in Colossians (Bujard 1973: 130–214). The majority of the rhetorical work on Colossians, however, follows Betz's approach to rhetorical analysis. Scholars primarily place Colossians in the rhetorical species of deliberative rhetoric (Aletti 1993: 39; Lincoln 2000: 557) without denying elements of the epideictic and forensic rhetorical species (Olbricht 1996: 310–11). The purpose of the letter is rarely discussed in terms of a rhetorical exigence (Lincoln 2000: 557). Aletti (1993: 39; cf. Lincoln 2000: 557–60) presents a complete rhetorical analysis in an epistolary frame: epistolary frame-salutation (1:1–2), *exordium* (1:3–23) with a concluding *partitio* (1:21–3), *probatio* (1:24–4:1), *exhortatio* (4:2–6) functioning as a *peroratio*, and resumption of the epistolary frame (4:7–18). Rhetorical analysis is in some tension with epistolary analysis, and some opponents of the rhetorical approach hold that analyzing a Pauline letter according to the categories of a speech is at best imprecise and at worst simply not applicable or completely wrong (Classen 2002: 95–113).

## Bibliography

Abbott, T. K. *The Epistles to the Ephesians and to the Colossians*. International Critical Commentary. Edinburgh: T. & T. Clark, 1897.

Aletti, J. N. *St. Paul, Épitre aux Colossiens*. Études bibliques. Paris: Gabalda, 1993.

Arnold, C. E. "Colossae." *Anchor Bible Dictionary* 1, 1089–90.

Arnold, C. E. *The Colossian Syncretism*. Wissenschaftliche Untersuchungen zum Neuen Testament, 2.77. Tübingen: Mohr Siebeck, 1995.

Attridge, H. W. "On Becoming an Angel: Rival Baptismal Theologies at Colossae." Pp. 81–98 in *Religious Propaganda and Missionary Competition in the New Testament World: Essays Honoring Dieter Georgi*. Edited by Lukas Bornmann et al. Leiden: E. J. Brill, 1994.

Aune, D. E. *The New Testament in its Literary Environment*. Library of Early Christianity, ed. W. A. Meeks. Philadelphia: Westminster Press, 1987.

Aune, D. E. "Colossians, Paul's Letter to the." Pp. 103–7 in *The Westminster Dictionary of New Testament and Early Christian Literature and Rhetoric*. Louisville, KY: Westminster John Knox Press, 2003.

Bandstra, A. J. *The Law and the Elements of the World: An Exegetical Study in Aspects of Paul's Teaching*. Kampen: Kok, 1964.

Barclay, J. M. G. *Colossians and Philemon*. New Testament Guides, ed. A. T. Lincoln. Sheffield: Sheffield Academic Press, 1997.

Barth, M. and H. Blanke. *Colossians: A New Translation with Introduction and Commentary*. Trans. A. B. Beck. Anchor Bible, 34. New York: Doubleday, 1994.

Beetham, C. A. *Echoes of Scripture in the Letter of Paul to the Colossians*. Biblical Interpretation Series, 96. Leiden and Boston: Brill, 2008.

Best, E. "Who Used Whom? The Relationship of Ephesians and Colossians," *New Testament Studies* 43 (1997), 72–96.

Best, E. *Ephesians*. International Critical Commentary. Edinburgh: T. & T. Clark, 1998.

Betz, H. D. *Galatians*. Hermeneia. Philadelphia: Fortress Press, 1979.

Bevere, A. R. *Sharing in the Inheritance: Identity and the Moral Life in Colossians*. *Journal for the Study of the New Testament* Supplementary Series, 226. London: Sheffield Academic Press, 2003.

Blinzler, J. "Lexikalisches zu dem Terminus τὰ στοικεία τοῦ κόσμου bei Paulus," *Analecta biblica* 18 (1961), 429–42.

Bowen, C. R. "The Original Form of Paul's Letter to the Colossians," *Journal of Biblical Literature* 43 (1924), 177–206.

Brown, R. E. *An Introduction to the New Testament*. New York: Doubleday, 1997.

Bruce, F. F. *The Epistles to the Colossians, to Philemon and to Ephesians*. New International Commentary on the New Testament. Grand Rapids: Eerdmans, 1984.

Bujard, W. *Stilanalytische Untersuchungen zum Kolosserbrief als Beitrag zur Methodik von Sprachvergleichen*. Göttingen: Vandenhoeck & Ruprecht, 1973.

Burney, C. F. "Christ as the ARXH of Creation (Prov. 8:22; Col. 1:15–18; Rev. 3:14)," *Journal of Theological Studies* 27 (1925–6), 160–77.

Caird, G. B. *Paul's Letters from Prison*. Oxford: Oxford University Press, 1976.

Campbell, D. A. "The Scythian Perspective in Col. 3:11: A Response to Troy Martin," *Novum Testamentum* 39 (1997), 81–4.

Campbell, D. A. "Unravelling Colossians 3:11b." *New Testament Studies* 42 (1996), 120–32.

Cannon, G. E. *The Use of Traditional Materials in Colossians*. Macon, GA.: Mercer, 1983.

Carr, W. *Angels and Principalities*. SNTS Monograph Series, 42. Cambridge: Cambridge University Press, 1981.

Classen, C. J. "St. Paul's Epistles and Ancient Greek and Roman Rhetoric." Pp. 95–113 in *The Galatians Debate: Contemporary Issues in Rhetorical and Historical Interpretation*. Edited by M. D. Nanos. Peabody, MA: Hendrickson, 2002.

Clifford, R. J. "The Bible and the Environment." Pp. 1–26 in *Preserving the Creation*. Edited by K. W. Irwin and E. D. Pellegrino. Washington, DC: Georgetown University Press, 1994.

Crouch, J. E. *The Origin and Intention of the Colossian Haustafel*. Forschungen zur Religion und Literatur des Alten und Neuen Testaments, 109. Göttingen: Vandenhoeck & Ruprecht, 1972.

Davis, J. J. "Ecological 'Blind Spots' in the Structure and Content of Recent Evangelical Systematic Theologies," *Journal of the Evangelical Theological Society* 43 (2000), 273–86.

DeMaris, R. E. *The Colossian Controversy*. *Journal for the Study of the New Testament* Supplementary Series, 96. Sheffield: JSOT, 1994.

Dibelius, M. "The Isis Initiation in Apuleius and Related Initiatory Rites." Pp. 61–121 in *Conflict at Colossae*. Rev. edn. Edited by F. O. Francis and W. A. Meeks. SBL Sources for Biblical Study, 4. Missoula, MT: Scholars Press, 1975.

Donelson, L. R. *Colossians, Ephesians, 1 and 2 Timothy, and Titus*. Westminster Bible Companion. Louisville, KY: Westminster/John Knox Press, 1996.

Dunn, J. D. G. "The Colossian Philosophy: A Confident Jewish Apologia," *Biblica* 76 (1995), 153–81.

Dunn, J. D. G. *The Epistles to the Colossians and Philemon*. New International Greek Testament Commentary. Grand Rapids: Eerdmans; Carlisle: Paternoster, 1996.

Evans, C. A. "*The Colossian Mystics*," *Biblica* 63 (1982), 188–205.

Fitzgerald, J. T. "Vice/Virtue Lists." *Anchor Bible Dictionary* 6, 857–9.

Fowl, S. E. *The Story of Christ in the Ethics of Paul: An Analysis of the Hymnic Material in the Pauline Corpus*. Journal for the Study of the New Testament Supplementary Series, 36. Sheffield: JSOT, 1990.

Francis, F. O. "Humility and Angelic Worship in Colossae." Pp. 163–95 in *Conflict at Colossae*. Rev. edn. Edited by F. O. Francis and W. A. Meeks. SBL Sources for Biblical Study, 4. Missoula, MT: Scholars Press, 1975.

Francis, F. O. and W. A. Meeks (eds.). *Conflict at Colossae*. Rev. edn. SBL Sources for Biblical Study, 4. Missoula, MT: Scholars Press, 1975.

Furnish, V. P. "Colossians." *Anchor Bible Dictionary* 1, 1090–6.

Furnish, V. P. "Ephesians." *Anchor Bible Dictionary* 2, 535–42.

Garland, D. E. *Colossians and Philemon*. The NIV Application Commentary. Grand Rapids: Zondervan, 1998.

Gunther, J. J. *St. Paul's Opponents and their Background*. Supplements to Novum Testamentum, 35. Leiden: E. J. Brill, 1973.

Hartman, L. "Humble and Confident: On the So-Called Philosophers in Colossae." Pp. 25–39 in *Mighty Minorities: Minorities in Early Christianity – Positions and Strategies*. Edited by D. Hellholm et al. Oslo: Scandinavian University Press, 1995.

Hay, D. *Glory at the Right Hand: Psalm 110 in Early Christianity*. SBL Monograph Series, 18. Nashville: Abingdon, 1973.

Hay, D. M. *Colossians*. Abingdon New Testament Commentaries. Nashville: Abingdon, 2000.

Head, B. V. (ed.). *Catalogue of the Greek Coins of Phrygia in the British Museum*. London: British Museum, 1906.

Héring, J. P. *The Colossian and Ephesian Haustafeln in Theological Context: An Analysis of their Origins, Relationship, and Message*. New York: Peter Lang, 2007.

Holtzmann, H. J. *Kritik der Epheser- und Kolosserbriefe auf Grund einer Analyse ihres Verwandtschaftsverhältnisses*. Leipzig: Wilhelm Engelmann, 1872.

Hooker, M. D. "Were There False Teachers in Colossae?" Pp. 315–31 in *Christ and the Spirit in the New Testament*. Edited by B. Lindars and S. Smalley. Cambridge: Cambridge University Press, 1973.

Hübner, H. *An Philemon. An die Kolosser, An die Epheser*. Handbuch zum Neuen Testament, 12. Tübingen: Mohr Siebeck, 1997.

Hübner, H. "*Der Diskussion um die deuteropaulinischen Briefe seit 1970: Der Kolosserbrief I*," Theologische Rundschau 68 (2003), 263–85.

Karris, R. J. *A Symphony of New Testament Hymns: Commentary on Philippians 2:5–11, Colossians 1:15–20, Ephesians 2:14–16, 1 Timothy 3:16, Titus 3:4–7, 1 Peter 3:18–22, and 2 Timothy 2:11–13*. Collegeville, MN: Liturgical Press, 1996.

Käsemann, E. "A Primitive Christian Baptismal Liturgy." Pp. 149–68 in *Essays on New Testament Themes*. Trans. W. J. Montague. Philadelphia: Fortress Press, 1982.

Kiley, M. *Colossians as Pseudepigraphy*. Sheffield: JSOT, 1986.

Knox, J. *Philemon among the Letters of Paul*. Rev. edn. New York and Nashville: Abingdon Press, 1959.

Kümmel, W. G. *Introduction to the New Testament*. Rev. edn. Trans. H. C. Kee. Nashville: Abingdon, 1975.

Lähnemann, J. *Der Kolosserbrief: Komposition, Situation und Argumentation*. Studien zum Neuen Testament, 3. Gütersloh: Gerd Mohn, 1971.

Leppä, O. *The Making of Colossians: A Study in the Formation and Purpose of a Deutero-Pauline Letter*. Publications of the Finnish Exegetical Society 86. Göttingen and Helsinki: Vandenhoeck & Ruprecht/Finnish Exegetical Society, 2003.

Lightfoot, J. B. *St. Paul's Epistles to Colossians and Philemon.* Peabody, MA: Hendrickson, 1995 (org. 1875).

Lincoln, A. T. *Ephesians.* Word Biblical Commentary, 42. Dallas: Word Books, 1990.

Lincoln, A. T. "The Household Code and Wisdom Mode of Colossians," *JSNT* 74 (1999), 93–112.

Lincoln, A. T. *Colossians.* New Interpreter's Bible, 11. Nashville: Abingdon Press, 2000.

Lindemann, A. "Die Gemeinde von 'Kolossä.' Erwägungen zum 'Sitz im Leben' eines deutero-paulinischen Briefes," *Wort und Dienst* 16 (1981), 11–34.

Lohse, E. *Colossians and Philemon.* Trans. W. R. Poehlmann and R. J. Karris. Hermeneia. Philadelphia: Fortress Press, 1971.

MacDonald, M. Y. *Colossians and Ephesians.* Sacra Pagina, 17. Collegeville, MN: Liturgical Press, 2000.

Martin, R. P. *Colossians and Philemon.* New Century Bible. London: Oliphants, 1974.

Martin, T. W. "But Let Everyone Discern the Body of Christ (Colossians 2:17)," *Journal of Biblical Literature* 114 (1995a), 249–55.

Martin, T. W. "The Scythian Perspective in Col. 3:11," *Novum Testamentum* 37 (1995b), 249–61.

Martin, T. W. *By Philosophy and Empty Deceit: Colossians as Response to a Cynic Critique. Journal for the Study of the New Testament* Supplementary Series, 118. Sheffield: Sheffield Academic Press, 1996a.

Martin, T. W. "Pagan and Judeo-Christian Time-Keeping Schemes in Gal 4.10 and Col. 2.16," *New Testament Studies* 42 (1996b), 105–19.

Martin, T. W. "Scythian Perspective or Elusive Chiasm: A Reply to Douglas A. Campbell." *Novum Testamentum* 41 (1999), 256–64.

Martyn, J. L. *Galatians.* Anchor Bible, 33A. New York: Doubleday, 1997.

Mayerhoff, E. T. *Der Brief an die Colosser, mit vornehmlicher Berücksichtigung der drei Pastoralbriefe kritisch geprüft.* Berlin: H. Schultze, 1838.

McGuire, A. "Equality and Subordination in Christ: Displacing the Powers of the Household Code in Colossians." Pp. 65–85 in *Religion and Economic Ethics.* Edited by J. F. Gower. Lanham, MD: University Press of America, 1990.

Meeks, W. A. "To Walk Worthily of the Lord': Moral Formation in the Pauline School Exemplified by the Letter to Colossians." Pp. 37–58 in *Hermes and Athena.* Edited by E. Stump and T. P. Flint. Notre Dame: University of Notre Dame Press, 1993.

Meeks, W. A. "The 'Haustafeln' and American Slavery: A Hermeneutical Challenge." Pp. 232–53 in *Theology and Ethics in Paul and his Interpreters.* Edited by E. H. Lovering, Jr. and J. L. Sumney. Nashville: Abingdon, 1996.

Merklein, H. *Studien zu Jesus und Paulus.* Tübingen: Mohr Siebeck, 1987.

Mitton, C. L. *Ephesians.* London: Oliphants, 1976.

Moule, C. F. D. *The Epistles to the Colossians and to Philemon.* Cambridge Greek Testament Commentary. Cambridge: Cambridge University Press, 1957.

Muddiman, J. *A Commentary on the Epistle to the Ephesians.* Black's New Testament Commentaries. London and New York: Continuum, 2001.

Müller, K. "Die Haustafel des Kolosserbriefes und das antike Frauenthema: Eine kritische Rückschau auf alte Ergebnisse." Pp. 263–319 in *Die Frau im Urchristentum.* Quaestiones Disputatae, 95. Edited by G. Dautzenberg et al. Freiburg: Herder, 1983.

Müller, P. *Anfänge der Paulusschule: Dargestellt am zweiten Thessalonicherbrief und am Kolosserbrief.* Abhandlungen zur Theologie des Alten und Neuen Testaments 74. Zurich: Theologischer Verlag, 1988.

Mullins, T. Y. "The Thanksgivings of Philemon and Colossians," *New Testament Studies* 30 (1984), 288–93.

Munro, W. "Col. III.18–IV.1 and Eph. V.21–VI.9: Evidence of a Late Literary Stratum?" *New Testament Studies* 18 (1972), 434–47.

Murphy-O'Connor, Jerome. *Paul: A Critical Life*. Oxford: Oxford University Press, 1997.

O'Brien, P. T. *Colossians, Philemon*. Word Biblical Commentary, 44. Waco: Word Books, 1982.

Olbricht, T. H. "The Stoicheia and the Rhetoric of Colossians: Then and Now." Pp. 308–28 in *Rhetoric, Scripture and Theology: Essays from the 1994 Pretoria Conference*. Edited by S. E. Porter and T. H. Olbricht. Sheffield: Sheffield Academic Press, 1996.

Percy, E. *Die Probleme der Kolosser- und Epheserbriefe*. Skrifter Utgivna Av Kungl. Humanistika Vetenskapssamfundet i Lund 36. Lund: Gleerup, 1946.

Pizzuto, V. A. *A Cosmic Leap of Faith: An Authorial, Structural, and Theological Investigation of the Cosmic Christology in Col. 1:15–20*. Contributions to Biblical Exegesis and Theology, 41. Leuven: Peeters, 2006.

Pokorný, P. *Colossians*. Trans. S. S. Schatzmann. Peabody, MA: Hendrickson, 1991.

Polhill, J. B. "The Relationship between Ephesians and Colossians." *Review and Expositor* 70 (1973), 439–50.

Porter, S. E. and K. D. Clark. "Canonical-Critical Perspective and the Relationship of Colossians and Ephesians," *Biblica* 78 (1997), 57–86.

Reicke, B. "Caesarea, Rome and the Captivity Letters." Pp. 277–86 in *Apostolic History and the Gospel: Biblical and Historical Essays presented to F. F. Bruce on his 60th Birthday*. Edited by W. W. Gasque and R. P. Martin. Exeter: Paternoster, 1970.

Reicke, B. "The Historical Setting of Colossians," *Review and Expositor* 70 (1973), 429–38.

Reuter, R. *Synopse zu den Briefen des Neuen Testaments/Synopsis of the New Testament Letters. Teil 1: Kolosser-, Epheserbrief, vol. 1: Colossians, Ephesians*. Studies in the Religion and History of Early Christianity 5. Frankfurt am Main: Peter Lang, 1997.

Rusam, D. "Neue Belege zu den stoicei'a tou' kovsmou (Gal. 4,3.9, Kol. 2,8.20)," *Zeitschrift für die neutestamentliche Wissenschaft* 83 (1992), 119–25.

Sanders, E. P. "Literary Dependence in Colossians," *Journal of Biblical Literature* 85 (1966), 28–45.

Sappington, T. J. *Revelation and Redemption at Colossae*. Journal for the Study of the New Testament Supplementary Series, 53. Sheffield: JSOT, 1991.

Schenk, W. "Der Kolosserbrief in der neueren Forschung (1945–1985)." *ANRW II Principat* 25.4 (1987), 3327–64.

Schille, G. *Frühchristliche Hymnen*. 2nd edn. Berlin: Evangelische Verlagsanstalt, 1965.

Schmithals, W. "Literarkritische Analyse des Kolosserbriefs." Pp. 149–70 in *Paulus, Apostel Jesu Christi: Festschrift für Günter Klein zum 70. Geburtstag*. Edited by M. Trowitzsch. Tübingen: Mohr Siebeck, 1998.

Schweizer, E. "Letter to the Colossians Neither Pauline nor Post-Pauline." Pp. 3–16 in *Pluralisme et Oecumenisme en Recherches Théologiques*. Edited by Y. Congareral. Paris: Duculot, 1976.

Schweizer, E. *The Letter to the Colossians*. Minneapolis: Augsburg, 1982.

Schweizer, E. "Slaves of the Elements and Worshippers of Angels: Gal. 4,3.9 and Col. 2,8.18.20," *Journal of Biblical Literature* 107 (1988), 455–68.

Smith, I. K. *Heavenly Perspective: A Study of the Apostle Paul's Response to a Jewish Mystical Movement at Colossae*. Library of New Testament Studies, 326. London and New York: T. & T. Clark, 2006.

Standhartinger, A. *Studien zur Entstehungsgeschichte und Intention des Kolosserbriefs*. Supplements to Novum Testamentum, 94. Leiden: Brill, 1999.

Standhartinger, A. "The Origin and Intention of the Household Code in the Letter to the Colossians," *JSNT* 79 (2000), 117–30.

Stettler, C. *Der Kolosserhymnus: Untersuchungen zu Form, traditionsgeschichtlichen Hintergrund und Aussage von Kol 1,15–20.* Wissenschaftliche Untersuchungen zum Neuen Testament, 2.131. Tübingen: Mohr Siebeck, 2000.

Still, T. D. "Eschatology in Colossians: How Realized Is It?" *New Testament Studies* 50 (2004), 125–38.

Sumney, J. L. "Those Who 'Pass Judgment': The Identity of the Opponents in Colossians," *Biblica* 74 (1993), 366–88.

Sumney, J. L. *Colossians.* New Testament Library. Louisville, KY and London: Westminster John Knox, 2008.

Tachau, P. *"Einst" und "Jetzt" im Neuen Testament: Beobachtungen zu einem urchistlichen Predigtschema in der neutestamentlichen Briefliteratur und zu seiner Vorgeschichte.* Forschungen zur Religion und Literatur des Alten und Neuen Testaments, 105. Göttingen: Vandenhoeck & Ruprecht, 1972.

Thurston, B. B. *Reading Colossians, Ephesians and 2 Thessalonians: A Literary and Theological Commentary.* Macon, GA: Smyth & Helwys, 1995.

Wilson, R. McL. *Colossians and Philemon.* International Critical Commentary. London and New York: T. & T. Clark, 2005.

Wilson, W. T. *The Hope of Glory: Education and Exhortation in the Epistle to the Colossians.* Supplements to Novum Testamentum, 88. Leiden: Brill, 1997.

Wolter, M. *Der Brief an die Kolosser. Der Brief an Philemon.* Ökumenischer Taschenbuch-Kommentar zum Neuen Testament 12. Gütersloh: Mohn, 1993.

Wright, N. T. *Colossians and Philemon.* Tyndale New Testament Commentaries. Leicester and Grand Rapids: InterVarsity Press/Eerdmans, 1986.

Wright, N. T. "Poetry and Theology in Colossians 1:15–20," *New Testament Studies* 36 (1990), 444–68.

# CHAPTER 28

# 1 Thessalonians

## Karl P. Donfried

## Major Issues in Recent Study

1 Thessalonians is the earliest extant Pauline letter and, therefore, the earliest extant document of the early Christian movement. Recent scholarship has allowed it to emerge from the shadow of Romans so that it can be viewed in its own right as an important Pauline document, thereby shedding valuable light on the initial period of his apostolic activity. Although 1 Thessalonians is increasingly being freed from the hitherto controlling paradigm of Galatians and Romans, it has not yet been fully understood in terms of the theology and concerns of the early Paul, particularly the Jewish context that shaped the apostle's life and thinking.

Perhaps the most significant issue that needs to be resolved is the dating of 1 Thessalonians. The traditional dating of ca. 50–52 CE is heavily dependent on a non-critical reading of Lucan chronology according to the book of Acts. Some have argued for a date in the early 40s. While this early dating is resisted since it would alter traditional Pauline chronology, to place 1 Thessalonians earlier would allow for a far broader understanding of the development and growth in Paul's articulation of the gospel in vastly different situations over a longer period of time. Also at the forefront of the current discussion is the purpose or purposes of this letter as well as whether epistolary or rhetorical analysis, or a combination of both, best manifest Paul's intention in writing to the Thessalonian Christians.

## Date and Place of Composition

Paul, Timothy, and Silvanus are listed as the co-authors of this letter to the Christian community at Thessalonica, a fact that is at least partially supported by the predominant use of the first person plural ("we"), although it is Paul who is the primary author. Paul and his co-workers arrived in the city after having experienced much conflict in Philippi (Acts 16:11–40; 1 Thess. 2:2). Thessalonica, so named by Cassander, one of Alexander's generals, after his wife who was the daughter of Philip and the half-sister of Alexander the Great, was founded about 316 BCE. When Macedonia became a Roman province in 146 BCE, Thessalonica became the most important city of the province and the center of Roman administration. According to the account in Acts 17:1–15, Paul and his co-workers (Timothy and Silvanus/Silas), encountered strong resistance and were eventually forced to leave Thessalonica. Paul sent Timothy to visit the fledgling congregation and eventually they met each other again in Corinth (Acts 18:5). Upon Timothy's return he shared with Paul the "good news of your faith and love" (3:6) but also the fact that something was "lacking" in their faith (1 Thess. 3:10). This narrative provides the occasion for the apostle's letter to the church at Thessalonica.

If one understands Philippians 4:15 with its reference to "the beginning of the gospel" (RSV; NRSV: "the early days of the gospel") as referring to the beginning of Paul's independent missionary work in Philippi, then 1 Thessalonians 3:1 might well describe Paul's continuing work during this early period in Thessalonica, Athens, and Corinth. If this is a possible interpretation, then the traditional dating, relying heavily on the chronology of Acts, seems to be very late. A date of 50 CE or later does not best fit Paul's thought patterns in 1 Thessalonians, a matter that will be given attention further on. The general argument for this late dating is that Paul appeared before Gallio, proconsul of Achaia (of which Corinth is a part), ca. 52 CE and that Paul would have written 1 Thessalonians somewhat earlier, perhaps in 51 CE. This approach assumes that Acts 18, in fact, describes the apostle's *first* visit to Corinth as opposed to a subsequent one even though there is a tendency in Acts to compress all incidents related to a given city in a way that suggests that they all took place during Paul's visit. Several scholars have raised sharp questions about the reliability of the Acts chronology and, instead, place the beginning of Paul's apostolic work in the period between 37 and 40 CE. Based on such a reconstruction, 1 Thessalonians has been dated as early ca. 43 CE. Whether one leans toward the early or late dating, it must be acknowledged that there can be *no absolutely definitive chronology* of the Pauline period of missionary activity based on the sources currently available to us.

## Archaeological Setting

From an archaeological point of view, the cult of Serapis stands at the center of interest. Shortly after the 1917 fire in Thessaloniki a Serapeion was found in the sacred cult area of the city, some 250–300 meters west/northwest of the agora, and in 1939 a small temple of the Roman period was also discovered under the narthex. This significance of this Serapeum as a source of archaeological and epigraphical data is enormous and perhaps only second to that of Delos. Of the thirty-six inscriptions found, most refer to Serapis and Isis. Additionally, a small fragment of the "Hymn to Isis" has also come to light. The rich evidence now at our disposal suggests that not only were the rites of the Nile performed diligently in this temple by a board of some fourteen priests who were referred to as the "priest of the gods," but it may even be possible that the cult of Cabirus, as well as others, also practiced their secret rites in this temple.

The cult of Dionysus is epigraphically attested to beginning in 187 BCE; included in the epigraphic evidence is the famous "testament of a Thessalonican priestess." As one looks at the Dionysian mysteries in general, there are several components that are of particular interest. The hope of a joyous afterlife is central and appears to be symbolized by the phallus. But the sexual symbols of the cult were not mere representations of the hope of a joyous afterlife; they were also sensually provocative. The fact that the god Dionysus was the god of wine and joy often gave allowance for a strong emphasis on noisy revelry of all sorts. It is likely that this emphasis on the phallus and sensuality offers a possible background for the exhortations contained in 1 Thessalonians 4:3–8 and for the difficult problem of interpreting the term *skeous* (verse 4).

Of the other divinities worshiped at Thessalonica we know that Zeus played an important role; additional references include Asclepius, Aphrodite, Demeter, and the cult of Cabirus. At the time that Paul founded a Christian congregation in Thessalonica there can be little doubt about the prominence of this Cabirus cult, whose god promoted fertility and protected sailors. Not to be overlooked is the close connection between Thessalonica and the island of Samothrace and the probable influence of the Samothracian mysteries in general on the city. The earliest preserved record linking the cult of Samothrace with Thessalonica is an inscription listing the names of individuals who visited the island between about 37 BCE and 43 CE. It is likely that the upper classes were attracted to and involved in the cult of the Samothracian gods no later than the reign of Augustus. When we read in Acts 17:4 that Paul's preaching attracted "not a few of the leading women" to his movement, it is likely that, at a minimum, they were familiar with the mysteries of Samothrace, not to mention their acquaintance and possible participation in the other cults of the city.

Certainly a knowledge of the cults in Thessalonica allows us to understand with more precision such references as 1 Thessalonians 1:9, "you turned to God from idols," and 4:5, "not in the passion of lust like heathen who do not know God." Clearly the more detailed knowledge that one can gather about the Christian community's pagan past, the more likely one will be to interpret certain problematic passages such as 1 Thessalonians 4:1–9 against that broader background. This passage is filled with concentrated paraenetic language. The most frequent Pauline use of *peripateō* ("to walk, behave, conduct oneself") is in the Corinthian letters (1 Cor. 3:3; 7:17; 2 Cor. 4:2; 5:7; 10:2; 12:18). The specific reference "to please God" is only found in Romans 8:8. The reference to "instructions" is found here alone in the Pauline letters and the verbal form, other than in the Thessalonian letters themselves, only in 1 Corinthians 7:10 and 11:1. The one other reference to "the will of God" in a specific ethical context of "doing the will of God" is in Romans 12:2. To "disregard" God who gives you the Holy Spirit has no exact parallel in Paul, with the possible exception of Galatians 2:21, where he talks about setting aside the grace of God. Further, Paul does not often use the full title "the Holy Spirit" except for the most solemn occasions such as in Romans 5:5, 9:1, 14:17, and 15:13, 16 and 19, or when he uses the term in a catalogue (2 Cor. 6:4) or in a benediction (2 Cor. 13:14). Finally, the reference to "unchastity" is again found only in the Corinthian correspondence (1 Cor. 5:1; 6:13, 18; 2 Cor. 12:21), except for its use in the catalogue of vices in Galatians 5:19. All of this suggests that Paul is very deliberately dealing with a situation of grave immorality, not too dissimilar to the cultic temptations of Corinth. Thus, Paul's severe warnings in this section, using the weightiest authorities he can marshal, are intended to distinguish the behavior of the

Thessalonian Christians from that of their former pagan life that is still vibrantly alive in the various cults of the city, including the several civic cults.

Given this background and context, what is the meaning of *skeuos* in 1 Thessalonians 4:4? Both Antistius Vetus and Aelianus interpret the term *skeuos* as referring to the *membrum virile*, and given the strong phallic symbolism in the cults of Dionysus, Cabirus, and Samothrace such a reference is hardly surprising. The additional verb *ktaomai* ("obtain," "acquire") that Paul uses here would suggest a meaning for the phrase something like "to gain control over the *skeuos.*" The specific meaning of this term would surely not be lost on a Thessalonian audience nor would its broader meaning of "gaining control over the body with regard to sexual matters." The reference to *pragmati* ("thing," "deed") in 4:6 would then refer back to this intended meaning.

## Historical Context

What were the precise circumstances of the congregation in Thessalonica and in what ways were they "afflicted"? What did Paul intend with the reference to their suffering (2:14), and with the phrase *thlipsei pollēi* ("much affliction") (1:6) as well as similar references found elsewhere in the letter? It has been argued that the primary "afflictions" that the Thessalonian Christians suffered involved some form of *non-systematic* persecution primarily by non-Christians in the city, and that this situation might have led to the premature death of those Christians to whom Paul refers in 1 Thessalonians 4:13–18. It will be useful to compare the translations of the relevant verses in the RSV and the NRSV, the one translation having preceded my essay, "The Cults of Thessalonica" (in Donfried 2002) and the other having followed it. The translations in question are in italics.

**1 Thessalonians 1:6**
RSV: And you became imitators of us and of the Lord, for you received the word in much *affliction*, with joy inspired by the Holy Spirit.
NRSV: And you became imitators of us and of the Lord, for in spite of *persecution* you received the word with joy inspired by the Holy Spirit.

**1 Thessalonians 3:3**
RSV: that no one be moved by these *afflictions*.
NRSV: so that no one would be shaken by these *persecutions*.

**1 Thessalonians 3:4**
RSV: For when we were with you, we told you beforehand that we were to suffer *affliction* ...
NRSV: In fact, when we were with you, we told you beforehand that we were to suffer *persecution* ...

**1 Thessalonians 3:7**
RSV: For this reason, brethren, in all our distress and *affliction* we have been comforted about you through your faith.
NRSV: For this reason, brothers and sisters, during all our distress and *persecution* we have been encouraged about you through your faith.

Even though the NRSV now interprets *thlipsis* as "persecution," in light of the way the term functions within the entire context of 1 Thessalonians there is still considerable dissent from such a translation. Some prefer a situation involving social harassment; others move toward a more psychological interpretation, i.e. the anguish experienced in breaking with one's past. There are other scholars who, in addition to the NRSV Committee itself, agree that the problem the Thessalonian Christians faced involved far more than social harassment, although this was certainly an important component of a far broader hostility generated by political issues as well. Finally, however, such an important question of translation can only be resolved through a closer analysis of the entire letter and especially such passages as 2:1–12 and 2:13–16. These, and other texts, now await further consideration.

## Purpose

Paul's affectionate letter to the church of the Thessalonians begins with his remembering their "work of faith and labor of love and steadfastness of hope in our Lord Jesus Christ" (1:3). This same triadic formulation occurs again in 5:8: "put on the breastplate of faith and love, and for a helmet the hope of salvation." In chapter 3 we learn that Paul, who is probably writing the letter from Corinth, is anxious about the current status of the Thessalonian church. He hopes that they are not "moved by these afflictions" (3:3) and is apprehensive lest "somehow the tempter had tempted you and that our labor would be in vain" (3:5). As a result he sent Timothy from Corinth both to inquire and to encourage. Upon his return to Paul he brought the "good news of your faith and love" (3:6). This section concludes with the apostle's prayer "that we may see you face to face and supply what is lacking in your faith" (3:10). The overall context of 1 Thessalonians, as well as this specific section, suggests that hope is precisely the element that is defective and requires specific attention. Once this is recognized, then the significance of the sustained eschatological emphasis throughout the letter, especially at key transition points, becomes even more conspicuous. One should note especially 1:10, 2:19, 3:13, 4:13–18, and 5:1–10, 23.

Despite Paul's affection and high regard for these Christians whose faith served as "an example to all the believers in Macedonia and in Achaia" (1:7), he must correct and clarify one major area of misunderstanding: the status of those who have already died in Christ since the end has not yet come. In 4:13 Paul shifts from the repetitious "you know" language (1:5; 2:1, 2, 5, 9, 10, 11; 3:3b–4; 4:1, 2, 6, 10, 11; 5:2) to the phrase "we would not have you ignorant. ..." These "you know" phrases are not superfluous rehearsals, but Paul's method of reminding the Christian church that they are *already now* sharing in the new life in Christ, a life that has hope as an essential ingredient. Thus their past and present participation in hope, as well as the integrity of the apostolic office of Paul and his co-workers over against the spurious claims of Paul's real or imagined antagonists, allows him to deal with the key issue in 4:13–18, namely, that the Thessalonian Christians should not grieve as others do who have no hope "concerning those who are asleep." This problem surfaced when some in the community died prior to the eagerly expected imminent *parousia*. In addition, further anxiety may well have been stimulated by those outside the church who mocked what seemed to them the absurdity of the claims, especially eschatological ones, that were being asserted by Paul and his infant congregation. The apostle assures his audience that the dead in Christ will not suffer disadvantage, they will not be disregarded, and that on the last day they, in fact, "will rise first" (1:16). Paul reaffirms the imminence of *parousia* (5:1–3) and then only in 5:10 does he give his final answer concerning the dead in Christ: "our Lord Jesus Christ ... died for us so that whether we wake or sleep we might live with him."

## Purpose in the Context of Language, Style, and Intertextuality

The Greco-Roman context of Thessalonica has already been reviewed as well as the importance of this background for explaining a variety of terms, concepts and images. It is difficult to reconstruct the original Pauline message proclaimed in Thessalonica; all that one can hope for are some reflections of it in the letter. Significant are elements that could be understood or misunderstood in a distinctly political sense. In 2:12 God, according to the apostle, calls the Thessalonian Christians "into his own kingdom"; in 5:3 there is a frontal attack on the *Pax et Securitas* program of the early principate; and in the verses just preceding this attack one finds three terms rich with political connotation: *parousia*, *apantēsis*, and *kurios*. Frequently *parousia* refers to the arrival of Caesar, a king, or an official, and *apantēsis* refers to citizens meeting a dignitary who is about to visit the city. These two terms are used in this way by Josephus (*Antiquities*, 11.327ff.) and also similarly referred to by such Greek writers as Dio Chrysostom. The term *kyrios* ("lord"), especially when used in the same context as the two preceding terms, also has a definite political sense. Further, the eastern Mediterranean applied the term *kyrios* to the Roman emperors from Augustus on, although the first verifiable inscription of *kyrios* used as a *title* in Greece dates to the time of Nero. All of this, coupled with the use of *euangelion* ("good news") and its possible association with the eastern ruler cult, suggests that Paul and his associates could easily be understood as violating the "decrees of Caesar" (Acts 17:7) in the most blatant manner, and this could easily provide a context for ad hoc persecutions.

What is also striking, however, are the number of words, phrases, and concepts that show possible connections with the type of literature contained in the Dead Sea Scrolls. These include: (1) Eschatological/apocalyptic similarities with regard to the intense expectation of the final consummation of history. (2) The election and calling of God, as when Paul writes to the Thessalonian church that "we know, brothers and sisters beloved by God, that he has chosen [*eklogē*] you" in 1:4. (3) Holiness/sanctification as in 1 Thessalonians 4:3, "For this is the will of God, your sanctification" (literally, "holiness," *hagiasmos*). (4) The light/day//night/darkness contrasts and the use of the term "sons of light." In 1 Thessalonians 5:5 Paul writes: "for you are all sons of light and sons of the day; we are not of the night or of darkness." One of the major descriptors of the Qumran community is that they are "sons of light." (5) The wrath/salvation dualism referred to in 1 Thessalonians 5:9, "For God has destined us not for wrath but for obtaining salvation." (6) The phrase "church of God" found in 1 Thessalonians 2:14

that has its direct parallel in the Qumran term *qahal el*. (7) *Ataktos* and the ethical order. It is now quite likely that the "idlers" or "loafers" of 1 Thessalonians 5:14, the *ataktos* in Greek, should, on the basis of parallel texts related to the Dead Sea Scrolls, be translated as those "who are out of order," namely, those who are not following the *serek*, the order of the community as described in 1 Thessalonians 4:1–12. One of the major documents of the Qumran library is *The Community Rule* (1QS), the *serek hayahad*, and it, too, contains admonitions and encouragement to properly follow its order.

It does appear from 1 Thessalonians that Paul is in contact with a tradition sharing similarities with the Qumran community, and this again raises the question of appropriate dating. Further, it is noteworthy that "justification language," used predominantly in Galatians and Romans, is absent from 1 Thessalonians, although Paul does use, as in Romans, the terms "sanctification" and "salvation." In 1 Thessalonians 4:4, 4, 7 and 5:23, sanctification refers to the quality of new life in Christ, which will culminate in salvation (5:8, 9). Specific use of justification language only appears at a later stage in Paul's thought, provoked by an intense battle with judaizing opponents. Yet the theological substructure that this language represents may be implicit in the "election" language found in 1 Thessalonians (cf.1:1; 2:12; 4:7; 5:24). The apostle's latter justification language represents his early emphasis on election, united with his theology of the cross, and applied to a series of polemical confrontations. This would suggest a parallelism between election and sanctification in 1 Thessalonians, on the one hand, and justification and sanctification in Romans, on the other. Learning how to please God and to do his will in 1 Thessalonians 4:1–3 is reflected in the theme of obedience in Romans 6, and Paul's assertion in 1 Thessalonians 5:9 that "God has not destined us for wrath, but to obtain salvation through our Lord Jesus Christ" is reflected in Romans 5:9. What is also constant from 1 Thessalonians through Romans, with different nuances, is Paul's apocalyptic interpretation of the death and resurrection of Jesus in view of the impending triumph of God. And yet 1 Thessalonians and Romans, although deriving from the same generative source, represent quite different stages of development and articulation that surely took more than the handful of years allowed for by the traditional dating of Paul's letters to develop. The impact of the Dead Sea Scrolls for the understanding of 1 Thessalonians reopens with a new urgency the question of an early and late Paul and the relationship between the two.

## Literary Unity

The overwhelming majority of current Pauline interpreters assert the unity of 1 Thessalonians. Periodically it has been suggested that two separate letters were combined to make up what is subsequently referred to as 1 Thessalonians. Others have suggested that certain parts of the letter are not original. With regard to the latter, the one passage that has been most debated is 1 Thessalonians 2:13–16. The arguments for a later interpolation are complex; there are, however, two dominant ones that appear in the scholarly literature: (1) that 2:13–16 does not properly fit into the structure of the letter, and (2) that Paul's *ad hominem* anti-Judaism in verse 15 is inconsistent with his assertions about the Jews in Romans. Yet the majority of interpreters remain convinced that a careful analysis of the entire letter, together with the recognition that Paul incorporates traditional and formulaic material in 2:3–16, does not support interpolation theories either here or elsewhere in 1 Thessalonians.

## Constituent Literary Forms, Genre, and Epistolary and Rhetorical Analysis

These themes, particularly in their relationship with each other, are multifaceted and are actively under discussion by contemporary scholarship. With regard to 1 Thessalonians and the Pauline letters in general, part of the problem in using these descriptors is that such nomenclature as "epistolary analysis" and "rhetorical analysis" are not used in a uniform way. To begin with the term "epistolary analysis" needs further definition, and might conveniently be divided into three subcategories: formal literary analysis, thematic analysis, and form criticism. *Formal literary analysis* is most involved with structure, the detailed examination of the main letter-body and such formulaic features as the opening and closing forms of the letter itself. *Thematic analysis* is engaged with epistolary *topoi* and themes, such as friendship, consolation, or exhortation. *Form-critical analysis* primarily analyzes *oral* forms, such as liturgical and paraenetic formulae, that have been become incorporated in letters as written forms. Based on these tools, some Pauline scholars suggest that the most appropriate epistolary genre from antiquity for 1 Thessalonians is that of a "letter of friendship," much along the lines described by Pseudo-Demetrius, because of the dominance of philophronetic ("friendship") elements in this document. Indications in this direction are given both by the epistolary salutation and closing conventions, as well as by expressions throughout the letter that make evident the close relationship that existed between writer and audience. Not insignificant in this regard is the fact that the apostle addresses his hearers some fourteen times as "brethren." Affectionate language, whether kinship or familial, characterizes the positive tone of the communication.

Similarly when scholars today refer to "rhetorical analysis" they may be using that descriptor in any of three major ways: in terms of "ancient rhetoric," the "new rhetoric," or a hybrid of the two. The most widely practiced form of rhetorical analysis employed by Pauline scholars is what is frequently referred to as "ancient rhetoric," that is, a rhetoric that is derived from the speeches and categories found in the classical rhetorical handbooks and composition. Remarkably, rhetorical and epistolary handbooks do not discuss the rhetorical *dispositio* (arrangement) of letters, no doubt because it was considered not advisable to undertake persuasion by such means. However, in an imaginary dialogue between Antonius and Catulus in *De oratore* 2.49, Cicero represents Catulus as suggesting that letters could take up and employ rhetorical characteristics taken from speeches. The analysis of Demosthenes' *Epistle* 1 by Frank Hughes (1990) confirms that letters could use rhetoric even if the handbooks from antiquity remained silent.

Rhetorical criticism, understood primarily as including "strategies of persuasion," has as its aim the more precise understanding of the author, and especially the author's purpose in wishing to communicate with a particular audience. Thus, rhetorical analysis can be useful in reconstructing the historical provenance of letters. Yet it is important to note that rhetorical analysis cannot move *directly* from the rhetorical text to the historical or social situation of the audience. Serving as an intermediary between the two is the rhetorical situation; historical situation and rhetorical situation are not identical! One must, therefore, recognize the difference between *what a text says* about a situation and *the situation itself.* While rhetorical criticism can assist in determining the social/historical situation of the audience, a comprehensive evaluation of *all* of the determinative factors will require additional and complementary methods of analysis. Rhetorical criticism, as well as epistolary analysis, is one of several methods, and each needs to be correlated with the insights gained from other approaches. Whereas epistolary analysis concentrates on small, formal units and thus has great difficulty in viewing the entire narrative whole, rhetorical analysis can do both. Epistolary analysis can be useful in designating and characterizing the opening and closing formulae as well as the introductory and concluding conventions of the body middle of the Pauline letters. The inability of the epistolary approach to adequately elucidate the body middle and to sufficiently discern that letters are literary productions in their own right is indeed a limitation. While recognizing that rhetorical criticism can be charged with a certain arbitrariness in the identification and interpretation of certain units, it can nevertheless be demonstrated that rhetorical criticism is likely to bring us in closer proximity to the issues that really matter, i.e., intention and strategy as well as meaning and purpose.

The application of the methods referred to as rhetorical and epistolary analysis must be practiced simultaneously; only in such a way can a synthesis occur. Paul, by his absence from Thessalonica, uses the medium of the letter as a form of dialogue that he expects to be publicly read before the church assembled in that city (1 Thess. 5:2, 7). What we have before us as a letter is, in reality, an ongoing conversation between the apostle and the congregation that he founded. Although forged in written words, it is in reality an oral composition both prior to its sending, in the sense that Paul dictated it to a secretary, and as a result of its sending, insofar as its intention is to become an oral act before the gathered congregation.

It has been argued that 1 Thessalonians should be understood as a "speech act" (Collins 1990) which is, in effect, a rhetorical act; in fact, one finds a wide diversity of clues pointing to the orality of 1 Thessalonians. So, for example, Paul can use the verbs "to write" and "to speak" quite interchangeably and synonymously. The former is found in 4:9 and 5:1; the latter is used in 1:8 and 2:2, 4, 16. Noteworthy in this connection is the phrase used to introduce the word of the Lord in 4:15–17: "for this we declare [speak] to you by the word of the Lord." Here, as elsewhere in the letter, the exegete is forced to recognize that Paul *speaks* through and by means of his written word. Precisely because the apostle actually conceives his speech acts as rhetorical exercises does it become essential to discover the rhetorical devices embedded in his letter and to compare them with possible parallel expressions among the ancient rhetoricians.

According to Aristotle's taxonomy, speeches are divided into three genres (deliberative, forensic, and epideictic). Although a given speech may use more than one genre, normally one will be dominant. Given this taxonomy, is there consensus for a rhetorical classification of 1 Thessalonians ? Some have classified 1 Thessalonians as a deliberative speech, while others classify the letter as epideictic. Relying exclusively on Aristotle, but utilizing the flexibility inherent in *Ars Rhetorica* to incorporate other situations, it has been argued that none of the Aristotelian categories fits 1 Thessalonians, and that the use of a new genre, "church rhetoric," is necessary (Olbricht 1990). Given the lack of consensus with regard to epistolary and rhetorical analysis themselves, not to mention their relationship to one another, one is hesitant to offer even a very abbreviated outline of 1 Thessalonians. What follows must be understood as one possible outline (Hughes) using both rhetorical and epistolary analysis, but clearly giving priority to the former:

1  *Exordium* (introduction) (1:1–10)
2  *Narratio* (narrative) (2:1–3:10)
3  *Partitio* (statement of propositions) (3:11–13)
4  *Probatio* (proof) (4:1–5:3)
5  *Peroratio* (epilogue) (5:4–11)
6  Exhortation (5:12–22)
7  Final prayers and greetings (epistolary conclusion) (5:23–8)

Shaped predominantly by epistolary and thematic criteria, Jan Lambrecht offers the following outline of 1 Thessalonians:

1:1: salutation
      a.  1:2–10: thanksgiving
         b.  2:1–12: apologetical report
      a.  2:13–16: thanksgiving
         b.  2:17–3:8: report on the intervening period
      a.  3:9–10: thanksgiving
3:11–13: eschatological wish-prayer
4:1–2: introductory paraenesis
      a.  4:3–12: paraenesis
         b.  4:13–18: final destiny of Christians
      a.  5:1–8: paraenesis
         b.  5:9–11: final destiny of Christians
      a.  5:12–22: paraenesis
5:23–4: eschatological wish-prayer

These quite different analyses of the structure of Paul's first letter are indicative both of the significant renewed attention that is being given to 1 Thessalonians as well as the remaining scholarly work needed so that these new and diverse insights and approaches may be brought into a more coherent whole.

## Annotated Bibliography

Collins, Raymond F. (ed.). *The Thessalonian Correspondence.* Bibliotheca Ephemeridum Theologicarum Lovaniensium, 87; Leuven: University Press/Peeters, 1990. A most significant collecton of essays dealing with all aspects of 1 Thessalonians.

Donfried, Karl P. *Paul, Thessalonica and Early Christianity*. Grand Rapids: Eerdmans, 2002. In-depth studies of many of the themes discussed above.

Donfried, Karl P. and Johannes Beutler. *The Thessalonians Debate: Methodological Discord or Methodological Synthesis?* Grand Rapids: Eerdmans, 2000. A comprehensive set of essays dealing with rhetorical and epistolary analysis and the relationship between them.

Donfried, Karl P. and I. Howard Marshall. *The Theology of the Shorter Pauline Letters*. New Testament Theology. Cambridge: Cambridge University Press, 1993. Interpretive insights into both exegesis and preaching.

Hughes, Frank W. *Early Christian Rhetoric and 2 Thessalonians*. Journal for the Study of the New Testament Supplementary Series, 30; Sheffield: JSOT Press, 1989. A pathbreaking treatment of the analysis of rhetorical criticism in epistolary contexts.

Hughes, Frank W. "The Rhetoric of 1 Thessalonians." Pp. 94–116 in *The Thessalonian Correspondence*. Edited by Raymond F. Collins. Bibliotheca Ephemeridum Theologicarum Lovaniensium, 87; Leuven: University Press/Peeters, 1990. Contains Hughes' detailed rhetorical analysis of 1 Thessalonians.

Lambrecht, Jan. "A Structural Analysis of 1 Thessalonians 4–5." Pp. 163–78 in *The Thessalonians Debate: Methodological Discord or Methodological Synthesis?* Edited by Karl P. Donfried and Johannes Beutler. Grand Rapids: Eerdmans, 2000. The author presents reservations concerning the use of rhetorical criticism in the analysis of 1 Thessalonians and the reasons for his structural analysis given above.

Malherbe, Abraham J. *The Letters to the Thessalonians: A New Translation with Introduction and Commentary*. Anchor Bible, 32B. New York: Doubleday, 2000. A extraordinary commentary representing a lifetime of work on issues related to 1 Thessalonians.

Olbricht, Thomas H. "An Aristotelian Rhetorical Analysis of 1 Thessalonians." Pp. 216–36 in *Greeks, Romans, and Christians*. Edited by David L. Balch, Everett Ferguson, and Wayne A. Meeks. Minneapolis: Fortress Press, 1990. The author argues for a new rhetorical genre, "church rhetoric."

Wanamaker, Charles A. *The Epistle to the Thessalonians: A Commentary on the Greek Text*. New International Greek Testament Commentary. Grand Rapids and Exeter: Eerdmans/Paternoster 1990. An unusually insightful commentary making significant use of both rhetorical criticism and social-critical scholarship.

Weima, Jeffrey A. D. and Stanley Porter. *An Annotated Bibliography of 1 and 2 Thessalonians*. Nederlands Theologisch Tijdschrift Series, 26; Leiden: Brill, 1998. A most helpful tool for further bibliographical references.

CHAPTER 29

# 2 Thessalonians

Edgar Krentz

## Major Issues and Directions in Recent Study

Only Philemon and Titus are shorter than 2 Thessalonians in the Pauline corpus, yet it is unique in many respects, containing a higher percentage of apocalyptic material than any other letter. Its Christology surprises, since it makes no reference to Jesus' death on the cross or his resurrection, (as do 1 Thessalonians and 1 and 2 Corinthians), and no interpretation of his death as a sacrifice (as do Rom. 3:24–6 and 1 Cor. 5:7). It differs from 1 Thessalonians in such matters – though the degree of difference is a matter of debate.

Such differences determine the major issues that scholars address about 2 Thessalonians. They pose a number of questions. Did Paul write both letters? If he did, what happened in Thessalonica that led to such different emphases? Why is the chronology about the return of Jesus so different? What is the relationship between the two letters? Which letter was written first? Is one modeled on the other?

Some scholars analyze letters using classical rhetoric as an aid in determining the writer's purpose and means of persuasion. Others use epistolary analysis. Both methods use ancient texts to validate their conclusions. Very few scholars combine these methods. The analysis of 2 Thessalonians necessarily involves asking about its place in ancient literary and rhetorical theory.

Another recent approach seeks to locate a text in the social, political, and religious milieu in which the writer lived and the nature of the locale in which the readers lived. It is important to note the ethnicity of the recipients addressed in 2 Thessalonians. Are they Jewish Christians or Gentiles? Greeks or Romans? Urban or rural? Educated or not? Some scholars use modern models to analyze ancient society; others protest against it. Does 2 Thessalonians imply a "millenarian" community or not? Such questions determine decisions about this letter. A final complex of issues is concerned with the thought of the letter (its theology). Is the letter truly Pauline in its thought?

# Constituent Literary Forms

## Epistolary genre

2 Thessalonians is clearly a letter in form, as 1:1–2 and 3:16–17 demonstrate, but what type of letter is it? Epistolary analysis makes use of ancient letter genres, as given in Pseudo-Demetrius and Pseudo-Libanius; see Malherbe (1988) for the Greek and English texts. Malherbe (2000: 360–1) points out that 3:6–15, with the use of the verb *par-aggelomen* (3:6; cf. *noutheteite* in 3:15), "has the force of the ancient 'commanding letter' (*parangelmatikē epistolē*)," citing Pseudo-Libanius, *Epistolary Styles*, 62. Wanamaker (1990: 48) classifies it as a "letter of advice," Pseudo-Demetrius, *Epistolary Types*, 11, which he feels would agree with its classification as deliberative rhetoric. Malherbe's conclusion (2000: 361) is sane: "It is preferable not to assign 2 Thessalonians exclusively to one particular epistolary type." It rather belongs to the "mixed type" (Pseudo-Libanius, 45), which uses differing styles.

## Rhetorical analysis

There was a flurry of interest in the rhetorical analysis of the Thessalonian letters between 1986 and 1988. Robert Jewett (1986: 81–7), provided an extensive rhetorical analysis of them. Two dissertations, by Frank W. Hughes (1989) and Glenn S. Holland (1988) written slightly earlier, but published later, provided rhetorical analyses of 2 Thessalonians. Donfried (2002 = 1993b: 50) suggests an emerging consensus that the rhetorical genre is deliberative, that is, that its aim is to help determine future action by the addresses, a view that Jewett, Hughes (1989: 73–4), Kennedy (1984: 144), Holland (1988: 6), and Wanamaker (1990: 48) all hold. Paul writes to change the readers' beliefs about the future and the practices that result from such beliefs. Each presents a detailed analysis of the letter, summarized in Table 29.1.

Wanamaker's division (1990: 49) is quite different. Such analyses assume that the structure of a Greek oration fits a letter, but illustrate the difficulty of applying oratorical structure to a letter. Subsequent commentators on 2 Thessalonians make almost no

**Table 29.1**

| Rhetorical section | Holland (1988: 8–33) | Jewett (1986: 82–5) | Hughes (1989: 68–73) | Wanamaker (1990: 49) |
|---|---|---|---|---|
| *Exordium* | 1:3–4 | 1:1–12 | 1:1–12 | 1:2–10 |
| *Narratio* | 1:5–12 | 2:1–2 | 2:1–2 | 2:1–3:10 |
| (*Partitio*) | | | | |
| [*Transitus*] | | 3:11–13 | | |
| *Probatio* | 2:1–17 | 2:3–3:5 | 2:3–15 | 4:1–5:22 |
| *Exhortatio* | 3:1–13 | 3:6–15 | 3:1–15 | *vacat* |
| *Peroratio* | 3:14–16 | 3:16–18 | 2:16–17 | 5:23–8 |

use of this analysis. Richard (1995) does not discuss rhetoric at all in his commentary, and Malherbe (2000: 359), says that "It is not clear that attempts to understand 2 Thessalonians in light of ancient rhetorical systems gain much over the form-critical approach, although the two methods are not mutually exclusive."

New Testament scholarship has concentrated interest on determining rhetorical genre and analyzing rhetorical structure (see Chapter 11, "Rhetorical Criticism," in this volume). It has paid little attention to the modes of persuasion delineated by Aristotle in his *Ars Rhetorica* (*ethos*, *pathos*, and *logos*), to discussing style in terms of ancient style theory, or to discussing the use of figures of thought (*schēmata dianoias*) and figures of speech (*schēmata lexeos*) in the Pauline corpus. Much still remains to be done before rhetorical analysis will be a mature discipline in New Testament studies.

## Authorship and Date

The date of the letter's origin depends on whether or not Paul wrote it. No one questioned Pauline authorship until the nineteenth century. On the basis of a comprehensive examination of the relationship between the two letters William Wrede (1903: 3–36) questioned Pauline authorship because the similarity of language and outline (1903: 2–14) was too close to argue for authenticity. Literary dependence alone accounted for the similarity. Trilling (1972 and 1980) supports his conclusion by examining the style, the form, and the theology of the letter. Bailey agrees (1979). Others who argue against Pauline authorship include Holland (1988), Hughes (1989), and Richard (1995: 19–24). There are also strong defenders of Pauline authorship to this day: Jewett (1986: 3–18) Wannamaker (1990: 17–28), and Malherbe (2000: 349–75), among recent scholars, hold that Paul wrote 2 Thessalonians.

Four factors raise questions about authorship: the apparent literary dependence of 2 Thessalonians on 1 Thessalonians; apparent differences in eschatology between 2 Thessalonians 2:3–12 and 1 Thessalonians 4:13–5:11; the more formal, less personal tone of 2 Thessalonians; and the references to forgery in 2 Thessalonians 2:2 and 3:17 (Donfried: 1993a: 85; Nicholl: 2004: 3–4; Still 1999: 47–51). Other issues, however, are at least as important, especially (1) the difference in the way the letters describe the roles of Christ and God, and (2) the difficulty of correlating the letter's theological language with that of the authentic Pauline letters.

## Literary Relation of 1 and 2 Thessalonians

2 Thessalonians resembles 1 Thessalonians in structure and content. Each letter falls into three major sections, surrounded by the epistolary opening and conclusion: An opening thanksgiving (1:3–16), the letter-body (2:1–3:5), and the third section, which discusses lifestyle (2 Thess. 6–16). Bailey (1979: 133) presents this similarity (see Table 29.2). Donfried (2002: 51) calls this similarity "the single most important aspect of the discussion" of the letter's authenticity.

The similarity goes beyond structure. Both letters use unique motifs and expressions. They open in similar fashion; the recipients in both cases are "the church of the

**Table 29.2**

|   |   | 2 Thessalonians | 1 Thessalonians |
|---|---|---|---|
| A | Letter opening | 1:1–12 | 1:1–10 |
|   | 1. Prescript | 1:1–2 | 1:1 |
|   | 2. Thanksgiving | 1:3–12 | 1:2–10 |
| B | Letter body | 2:1–16 | 2:1–3:13 |
|   | 1. Thanksgiving in the middle | 2:13 | 2:13 |
|   | 2. Benediction at the end | 2:16 | 3:11–13 |
| C | Letter close | 3:1–18 | 4:1–5:28 |
|   | 1. *Parenesis* | 3:1–15 | 4:1–5:22 |
|   | 2. Peace wish | 3:16 | 5:23–4 |
|   | 3. Greetings | 3:17 | 5:26 |
|   | 4. Benediction | 3:18 | 5:28 |

Thessalonians" (1 Thess. 1:1; 2 Thess. 1:1), naming inhabitants of cities rather than using city names. Both continue with a long thanksgiving (1 Thess. 1:2–10; 2 Thess. 1:3–12) that describes the situation of the addressees. Both conclude their first major section with a second thanksgiving (1 Thess. 3:9–10; 2 Thess. 2:13–17), though Malherbe (2000: 359 and 439) argues that the two thanksgivings in 2 Thessalonians each introduce the subsequent section. Both letters often use the first person plural, not the singular, even when Paul is clearly meant (forty-five times in 1 Thessalonians, seventeen in 2 Thessalonians; cf. 2 Thess. 3:1–5; Malherbe 2000: 86). The volitive optative *sterixai* ("may he [God] establish") with the direct object *hymōn tas kardias* ("your hearts") closes a major section in each letter (1 Thess. 3:13; 2 Thess. 2:17), a combination found nowhere else in Paul. The parenesis in each concludes with the similar request that the "God [Lord] of peace" do something (1 Thess. 5:23–4; 2 Thess. 3:16), again unique. Prayers in each use the optative *kateuthynai* ("may he [God] direct") found only in these two letters, though in different contexts (1 Thess. 3:11; 2 Thess. 3:16). "Now we beseech you" (*erōtōmen [de] hymas*), the introduction to an appeal, occurs in 1 Thessalonians 4:1 and 2 Thessalonians 2:1, and elsewhere only in Philippians 4:3. These are striking similarities.

However there are equally striking differences. 2 Thessalonians lacks some features of Paul's language: parenthetic expressions, play on prepositions (cf. Gal. 1:11, 12; Rom. 11:36), and initial or end rhyme (the only possibility is 2 Thess. 2:17). 1 Thessalonians uses much pictorial language drawn from daily life (Rigaux 1956: 90); 2 Thessalonians has only two examples: "rest" in 1:6 and the Word of the Lord "running" in 3:2, a sure indication of non-authenticity for Trilling (1972: 56).

## Style and Tone

In 1 Thessalonians Paul writes in a highly personal, friendly style. He is emotionally warm (cf. 3:6–10), praising the Thessalonians (1:5–10) and encouraged by them. He feels deprived at not being able to visit them (2:17–20), describing them as his hope, his joy, his wreath of boasting, and his glory. The second letter has a consistently more detached, impersonal, almost official style. In both thanksgivings Paul writes, "we ought to give thanks" (*eucharistein opheilomen*, 1:3, cf. 2:13). Paul uses the term "brothers" (*adelphoi*) eighteen times in 1 Thessalonians, but it occurs in 2 Thessalonians "only when it is part of a structural formula or when it is taken over from 1 Thessalonians" (2 Thess. 1:3; 2:1, 13, 15; 3:1, 6, 13; Collins 1988: 222). 2 Thessalonians 3:6 introduces the parenesis with the verb "we order" (*paraggelomen*; cf. 3:4, 10, 12), not "we beseech" (*parakaloumen*), as in 1 Thessalonians 4:1 (cf. 4:10; 5:11, 14). The relationship between writer and readers differs from that in 1 Thessalonians. Thus 2 Thessalonians is much less warm, more formal, less personal.

The vocabulary of the letter is, as Trilling says, "allgemein paulinisch, von wenigen Besonderheiten abgesehen, die nicht ins Gewicht fallen" ("in general Pauline, disregarding a few special cases, that do not carry any weight," 1980: 21). Some Pauline terms do not occur in 2 Thessalonians: *agapētos, aiōn, hamartia, an, anēr, apothnēskō, apostolos, ginōskō, gnorizō, egeirō, egō, ethnos, zēteō, kalos, keryssō, laleō, mallon, men, nekros, polys, syn, sōma, teknon, tis*. The particles and prepositions are especially important. The vocabulary used is not un-Pauline; the phraseology is often unusual for Paul.

The two letters differ in sentence structure. 1 Thessalonians uses relatively short sentences, while 2 Thessalonians has long sentences (1:3–12; 2:5–12; 3:7–9), formed of elements joined like links in a chain ("kettenartige Verknüpfung": Dobschütz 1909: 42). Schmidt (1990: 384) refutes Jewett's claim that there are similar long sentences in 2 Corinthians 6:3–10 and 11:24–31. Those sentences contain hardship lists, which extend the word count. He also gives lists of unusual "noun strings." 2 Thessalonians frequently repeats terms or expressions in identical form or a slight variant, a mark of the letter's "poverty of expression." Trilling (1972: 62–3) gives a long list that demonstrates this as a distinctive mark of style of 2 Thessalonians. This pleonastic style also leads to the frequent use of parallelism, in 2 Thessalonians, most frequently synonymous, more rarely synthetic, and almost never antithetical. Trilling (1972: 52–3) gives a long list of such passages. Krodel (1978: 82–3) translates part of the list into English and comments that these parallelisms are "all the more important when we recognize their scarcity in 1 Thessalonians." Weiss (1897: 12–13) points out that Paul himself most frequently used antithetical parallelism, a basic element of his theological thought. There is a surprising amount of pleonasm, frequent use of *pas*, "all" (Trilling 1972: 58–9), and the use of synonymous expressions (Trilling 1972: 59–60).

## The references to forgery

2 Thessalonians 2:2 refers to spurious Pauline letters, while 3:17 calls attention to Paul's own handwriting as a mark of authenticity. If the letter is pseudonymous, the reference to Paul's handwriting in 2 Thessalonians 3:17 is based on the earlier references in 1 Corinthians 16:21, Galatians 6:11, and Philemon 19. Supporters of authenticity regard these references as evidence of Pauline authorship. Nowhere else, however, does Paul suggest it as a mark of authenticity; Galatians 6:17 uses it as a mark of his

personal feelings for the addressees. Only 2 Thessalonians 3:17 uses the handwriting to claim authenticity. The word *semeion*, "sign" (2 Thess. 3:17), elsewhere in Paul always refers to miraculous events or to evidence of the Spirit's activity. Bailey (1979: 138) comments that 3:17 "makes more sense as the product of the pseudonymous author who wished by it to allay any suspicions of non-authenticity which his letter might arouse." Collins (1988: 223–4) notes that it is the "necessary proximity of the composition of 2 Thessalonians to 1 Thessalonians in the event of Pauline authorship of both letters which constitutes the problem of 2 Thess 2:2." He notes elsewhere (1990: 455) that "The key passage for understanding the situation is, of course, 2 Thess 2,1–2 where the author quotes the slogan of those who are causing the disturbance: 'the day of the Lord is at hand.'" Thus 2:1–2 points to a problematic eschatology as the occasion for writing the letter. Its proponents claim Pauline documents as warrants for their view that that day of the Lord is at hand. Their claim makes apocalyptic thought necessary. On balance these two references are not conclusive for or against Pauline authorship.

## Historical Setting and Eschatology

Neither letter identifies Paul as an apostle in its prescript, though Paul refers to his apostolicity in 1 Thessalonians 2:7. He never mentions it in 2 Thessalonians. Both letters describe Paul's manual labor in Thessalonica in similar wording (1 Thess. 2:9; 2 Thess. 3:8) and urge the Thessalonians to imitate him in doing manual labor in quietness or tranquility (*hēsychia*, 1 Thess. 4:11; 2 Thess. 3:12). 1 Thessalonians contains much detail about Paul's personal relations with the Thessalonians and his use of Timothy in maintaining close ties. But 2 Thessalonians is reticent about Paul and never mentions his companions after the greeting in 1:1. This personal reticence agrees with the colder tone of the letter.

2 Thessalonians describes the situation of the readers in the context of the opening thanksgiving (2 Thess. 1:4–12). The Thessalonians are suffering at the least social opposition and possibly even active persecution, as are Paul and his companions (2 Thess. 3:2). There are parallels in the first letter: Paul refers to the pressures (*thlipsesin*) on the Thessalonians in 3:3–4, while 2:14–16 implies more severe persecution. (Some regard the latter passage as a later interpolation.) Suffering and persecution lead to apocalyptic comfort and encouragement. Both letters have extensive sections dealing with eschatology (1 Thess. 4:13–5:11; 2 Thess. 1:6–2:12). But they play quite different roles. Paul uses apocalyptic language as a support for his parenesis in 1 Thessalonians 5:1–11, not as a response to suffering. In 2 Thessalonians apocalyptic is the major topic of the letter, dominating the thought of the first two chapters.

2 Thessalonians 2:1–2 suggests that some readers expected the *parousia* very soon or held that it had already arrived. Paul had stressed the nearness of the Lord's *parousia* ("coming, arrival;" the term is used of the advent, arrival, of a ruler) in 1 Thessalonians 4:15, 17 and 5:1–5, while his later letters continued to say "The Lord is at hand" (1 Cor. 7:29, 31; Rom. 13:11–12; Phil. 4:5). Paul expects the return of Jesus before his own death (1 Thess. 4:15). He uses the language of ruler cult in 1 Thessalonians

4:13–18, describing Christians as going to meet and escort Jesus to earth at his *parousia*. Paul plays on Roman ruler-cult language in the first letter.

The apocalyptic of 2 Thessalonians has a different stress to reinforce the urgent need to stand fast and remain faithful (2 Thess. 2:15) to the God who has called the readers through the gospel (2 Thess. 2:14; cf. Krodel 1978: 74–7). Both letters appeal to earlier teaching, 1 Thessalonians 5:1–2 to explicitly reject time speculation, 2 Thessalonians 2:5 to affirm a sequence of events that shows that time must elapse before the eschaton ("end").

The author of 2 Thessalonians is clearly highly indebted to the Old Testament and early Jewish apocalyptic speculation. (Any commentary will give extensive references.) He uses it to urge fidelity and endurance. God's justice (2 Thess. 1:5) makes them worthy of the kingdom (*basileia*). God will condemn their oppressors and vindicate the faithful at the revelation of the Lord Jesus. Jesus will come in power and glory to "execute vengeance on those who do not know God" (2 Thess. 1:8–9). 2 Thessalonians 2:3–12 describes events that must happen before the eschaton, thus combating the view espoused in 2:1–2: persecution will grow worse, the "man of action contrary to the Torah [*anomia*], the son of destruction" must first appear. His *parousia* will be accompanied by lying signs, wonders, and acts of power, which will deceive and ultimately destroy all who "love the truth in order to be saved" (2 Thess. 2:9–10). Apocalyptic urges fidelity in suffering as the way to ultimate salvation (2 Thess. 2:13–14).

This apocalyptic interpretation of suffering is "the traditions you have been taught, whether through oral speech of my letter" (2 Thess. 2:15). The Thessalonians are to take a stand and grasp such traditions. The writer invokes such traditions against people who are idling in the agora (2 Thess. 3:6); they should rather imitate Paul in working "night and day" with their own hands. Thus Paul becomes a part of the tradition they are to observe, a view that never appears in Paul's authentic letters.

This apocalyptic stress shapes the manner in which the letter presents Jesus. Jesus has no past here, only a future role. The writer nowhere mentions Christ's death or resurrection. Christ is the lord, the *Kyrios* (1:1, 7, 8, 12; 2:1, 8 [13?], 14, 16; 3:3, [5?], 6, 12, 16, 18). How he became the Lord is not made clear. There is no allusion to earlier creedal formulae, as in 1 Thessalonians 1:9–10, 4:14, and 5:10, and so no interpretation of Jesus' death as sacrifice (as in 1 Thess. 5:10). There is nothing like "the word of the cross" (cf. 1 Cor. 1:18) in this letter; nor is he Lord because of the resurrection. Jesus is not the one into whom one is baptized. Baptism is not mentioned, while spirit (*pneuma*) occurs only in 2:2, 2:8, and 2:13. In 2:8 it denotes the power by which Jesus destroys the man of lawlessness; only in 2:13 does it approach the normal Pauline usage.

2 Thessalonians uses language of Jesus that Paul reserves for God. The term "Lord," referring to Jesus, occurs where Paul speaks of God. Thus 2 Thessalonians 2:13 speaks of the "beloved of the Lord," 1 Thessalonians 1:4 of the "beloved of God." 2 Thessalonians 2:14 notes the "glory of our Lord Jesus Christ" (cf. 2 Thess. 1:10, 12). Paul ascribes glory only to God (Rom. 1:23; 3:7, 23; 4:20; 5:2; 6:4; 1 Cor. 10:31, etc.); Jesus only reflects God's glory (2 Cor. 3:18; 4:4, 6). Where 1 Thessalonians 5:23 invokes the "God of peace," 2 Thessalonians 3:12 calls on the "Lord of peace." 1 Thessalonians uses the normal Pauline language (Rom. 15:33; 16:20; 1 Cor. 14:33; 2 Cor. 13:11; Phil. 4:9). 2 Thessalonians has a more developed Christology that exalts Jesus more than does Paul.

How the writer presents God also differs from Paul's language. The basic passage is 2:13–17. God, not Jesus, has been the actor in the past. God chose them as the "first fruits toward salvation" (2 Thess. 2:13). So they are the "assembly of God" (*ekklēsia tou theou*), a locution frequent in Paul (Rom. 16:16, 1 Cor. 1:2; 10:32; 11:16; 11:22; 15:9; 2 Cor. 1:1; Gal. 1:13; 1 Thess. 2:14). Their election by God forms the basis of their conviction and the reason they should remain steadfast. God will show his justice in the punishment of their persecutors. Grace (*charis*) occurs twice in stock formulas (2 Thess. 1:2, 12; 3:18). 2 Thessalonians 1:12 relates grace to the *parousia* of the Lord, while 2:16 ties it to God's love and the gift of comfort and hope in the past; it leads to prayer that God exhort and establish them in the present. The familiar Pauline contour is absent.

2 Thessalonians 1:8–10 describes Jesus' *parousia*; he will execute judgment and gather the faithful, described as "the gospel of our Lord Jesus." Yet God is responsible for all that happens: their election (2 Thess. 2:13), their growing faith and love (2 Thess. 1:3), his past love for them (2 Thess. 2:16), the sanctification of the spirit (2 Thess. 2:13), their past comfort and hope (2 Thess. 2:16). So God is responsible for their existence in the past and will repay those who pressure them at the revelation of Jesus from heaven.

## Tradition and Life

When the writer turns to his parenesis, indicated by the use of the word "finally" (*loipon*, 3:1), he first requests their prayers on his own behalf (3:1–5). He then commands action (*parangellomen*, 3:6) over against those living a disorderly life. Paul uses the verb exhort (*parakaleō*) nine times in 1 Thessalonians (2:12; 3:2, 7; 4:1, 10, 18; 5:11, 14) and glosses it with the verbs "encourage" and "testify" (2:12), with "establish" (3:2), and with "ask" (4:1). Paul uses "command" once (4:11), in relation to work. *Parakaleō* occurs twice in 2 Thessalonians (2:17, 3:12, here in parallel with "command"); "command" is used four times (3:4, 6, 10, 12). There is a double standard tied to the commands: tradition(s) which they are holding on to (2:15; 3:6) and Paul's example as worker, which they must (*dei*, 3:7) follow. Paul himself is now a tradition that the letter contains. The author calls for obedience (3:14); non-obedience requires expulsion from the community. Therefore 2 Thessalonians urges readers to act against those "who live [walk] without order" (2 Thess. 3:6, 11).

Prayers in 1 Thessalonians pray for the survival of the readers in the *parousia* (1 Thess. 5:23), since the coming of Christ is the basis for comfort and encouragement (1 Thess. 4:18; 5:11). 2 Thessalonians prays for right action in word and deed (2:16–17), for "love of God and the endurance of Christ" (3:5), for a life lived in peace (3:16). The eschatology determines the content of the prayer. Thus it is not surprising that 2 Thessalonians urges the readers to proper action against those "who live [walk] without order" (2 Thess. 3:6, 11), because of the imminent *parousia* of the Lord Jesus (2 Thess. 2:8). The Thessalonians themselves should not grow tired of doing what is good (2 Thess. 3:13). So the Thessalonians should pray for right action in word and deed (2:16–17), for "love of God and the endurance of Christ" (3:5), and for a life lived in peace (3:16). The eschatology determines the content of the prayer.

# Addressees

To whom was this letter addressed? The prescript calls them Thessalonians. Most scholars assume this is correct and therefore attempt to relate the letter to 1 Thessalonians. However, if the letter is pseudonymous and based on the first letter, the address may be fictitious. The letter contains almost no specifics about the readers. The persecutors are not named or identified ethnically (contrary to 1 Thess. 2:14–16). The letter gives no information about Paul beyond what one can infer from 1 Thessalonians, no indication of Paul's location, and no description of future plans. One could argue that this is a general letter; pseudonymous, written when Christians in the eastern Mediterranean are facing persecution.

Persecution burgeoned at the end of the first century and led to a stress on apocalyptic in Christian literature. Matthew, written about 90 CE, heightens apocalyptic stress beyond Mark. Matthew 24–5 stresses being prudent and watchful as one endures. The Apocalypse of John is written to encourage persecuted Christians about 95 CE. The appeal to an authoritative tradition fits in well in this period. Paul is invoked as an authority (2 Thess. 2:1–2).

Scholars who favor authenticity cite the universal acceptance of Pauline authorship prior to the nineteenth century. Jewett (1986, 161–78) applies a millenarian model to the two Thessalonian letters. Thessalonians misinterpret the first letter and radicalize Paul's position into a realized eschatology. His millenarian interpretation has won little acceptance. Malherbe (2000: 349–64, summarized on 364) suggests that Paul responds to a threat arising from erroneous teaching. He includes a detailed refutation of the non-Pauline authorship (2000: 364–70). A second defense, proposed by T. W. Manson, reverses the order of composition of 1 Thessalonians and 2 Thessalonians, but it also has gained little support, as Malherbe demonstrates (2000: 361–4). Harnack proposed a different solution to the differences: Paul wrote 1 Thessalonians to the Gentile Christians, 2 Thessalonians to the Jewish Christians (cf. Best 1972: 38–9). For more extensive treatment of all these theories see Krentz (1991a: 517–23).

## Annotated Bibliography

Bailey, J. A. "Who Wrote II Thessalonians," *New Testament Studies* 25 (1979), 131–45. Good summary of arguments for non-Pauline authorship. Table on page 518 © Cambridge University Press. Reprinted with permission.

Best, Ernest. *A Commentary on the First and Second Epistles to the Thessalonians*. Black's New Testament Commentaries. London: A. and C. Black, 1972. Original work favoring Pauline authorship.

Bruce, Frederick Fyvie. *1 and 2 Thessalonians*. Word Biblical Commentary. Waco: Word, 1982. Argues for Pauline authorship.

Collins, R. F. "The Second Epistle to the Thessalonians." Pp. 209–41 in *Letters That Paul Did Not Write*. Good News Studies 28. Wilmington: Michael Glazier, 1988. Summary of evidence for non-authenticity.

Collins, Raymond F. (ed.). *The Thessalonian Correspondence*. Bibliotheca Ephemeridum Theologicarum Lovaniensium, 87. Leuven: Peeters, 1990. Papers from a conference on the Thessalonian letters.

Dobschütz, Ernst von. *Die Thessalonicher Briefe*. Kritisch-exegetischer Kommentar über das Neue Testament, 10. 7. Auflage. Göttingen: Vandenhoeck & Ruprecht, 1909 [repr. 1974].

Donfried, Karl. "The Theology of 2 Thessalonians." Pp. 81–113 in *The Theology of the Shorter Pauline Letters*. Edited by Karl P. Donfried and I. Howard Marshall. New Testament Theology. Cambridge: Cambridge University Press, (1993a). Good summary favoring Pauline authorship.

Donfried, Karl. "2 Thessalonians and the Church of Thessalonica." Pp. 128–44 in *Origins and Method: Towards a New Understanding of Judaism and Christianity: Essays in Honour of John C. Hurd*. Edited by Bradley H. McLean. Sheffield: Sheffield Academic Press, 1993b. Repr. in *Paul, Thessalonica and Early Christianity*. Pp. 49–67. Grand Rapids: William B. Eerdmans, 2002. Cited according to this printing. Rhetorical criticism indicates that 2 Thessalonians is deliberative in genre.

Holland, Glen S. *The Tradition You Received from Us: 2 Thessalonians in the Pauline Tradition*. Hermeneutische Untersuchungen zur Theologie 24. Tübingen: Mohr Siebeck, 1988. Interprets the letter as a development of Pauline thought supported by rhetorical analysis.

Hughes, Frank W. *Early Christian Rhetoric and 2 Thessalonians*. Journal for the Study of the New Testament Supp. 30. Sheffield: Journal for the Study of the Old Testament, 1989. Rhetorical analysis used in support of non-authenticity.

Jewett, Robert. *The Thessalonian Correspondence: Pauline Rhetoric and Millenarian Piety*. Foundations and Facets. Philadelphia: Fortress Press, 1986. Argues for authenticity by applying a millenarian model to the letters.

Jewett, Robert. "A Matrix of Grace: The Theology of 2 Thessalonians as a Pauline Letter." Pp. 63–70 in *Pauline Theology I*. Edited by Jouette M. Bassler. Minneapolis: Fortress Press, Minneapolis, 1991. Just what the title says.

Kennedy, George A. *New Testament Interpretation through Rhetorical Criticism*. Chapel Hill: University of North Carolina Press, 1984. Seminal study by a specialist in classical rhetoric.

Krentz, Edgar. "2 Thessalonians." *Anchor Bible Dictionary* vol. 6 (1991a), 517–23. Basic survey of scholarship on 2 Thessalonians.

Krentz, Edgar. "Through a lens: theology and fidelity in 2 Thessalonians." Pp. 52–62 in *Pauline Theology I*. Edited by Jouette M. Bassler. Minneapolis: Fortress Press, 1991b. Summary of 2 Thessalonians' theology assuming non-authenticity.

Krodel, G. "2 Thessalonians." Pp. 73–96 in J. P. Sampley, J. Burgess, G. Krodel, and R. H. Fuller. *Ephesians, Colossians, 2 Thessalonians, The Pastoral Epistles*. Proclamation Commentaries. Philadelphia: Fortress Press, 1978. General introduction arguing for non-authenticity.

Malherbe, Abraham J. *Ancient Epistolary Theorists*. Atlanta: Scholars Press, 1988. Texts and translations of the surviving ancient texts.

Malherbe, Abraham J. *The Letters to the Thessalonians*. Anchor Bible, 32B. New York: Doubleday, 2000. Basic, detailed commentary. Supports Pauline authorship.

Nicholl, Colin R. *From Hope to Despair: Situating 1 and 2 Thessalonians*. Journal for the Study of the New Testament Supplementary Series, 126. Cambridge: Cambridge University Press, 2004. Argues for authenticity; based on examination of situations addressed and eschatological argumentation.

Richard, Earl J. *First and Second Thessalonians*. Sacra Pagina, 11. Collegeville: Liturgical Press, 1995. Writes to reconstruct a different context based on a partition theory of 1 Thessalonians and the Deutero-Pauline authorship of 2 Thessalonians.

Rigaux, Beda. *Saint Paul: Les Épitres aux Thessaloniciens*. Études Bibliques. J. Paris: Gabalda, 1956.

Schmidt, Daryl. "The Syntactical Style of 2 Thessalonians: How Pauline Is It?" Pp. 383–93 in *The Thessalonian Correspondence*. Edited by Raymond F. Collins. Biblotheca Ephemeridum

Theologicarum Lovaniensium, 87. Leuven: Peeters, 1990. Examination of phraseology of the letter.

Still, Todd. D. *Conflict at Thessalonica: A Pauline Church and its Neighbors.* Journal for the Study of the New Testament Supplementary Series, 183. Sheffield Academic Press, Sheffield, 1999. Examines relations between Christians and non-Christians; pro-authenticity.

Trilling, Wolfgang. *Untersuchungen zum zweiten Thessalonicherbrief.* Erfurter theologische Studien, 27. Leipzig: St. Benno, 1972. Made major additions to Wrede's evidence for non-authenticity.

Trilling, Wolfgang. *Der Zweite Brief an die Thessalonicher.* Evangelisch-katholischer Kommenter zum Neuen Testament, 14. Zurich, Cologne, and Neukirechen-Vluyn: Benziger/Einsiedeln/Neukirchener, 1980. Major German commentary; written assuming pseudepigraphy.

Wannamaker, C. A. *The Epistles to the Thessalonians: A Commentary on the Greek Text.* New International Greek Testament Commentary. Grand Rapids: William B. Eerdmans, 1990. Written on the assumption that 2 Thessalonians is the earlier letter; applies rhetorical theory.

Weiss, J. *Beiträge zur Paulinischen Rhetorik.* Göttingen: Vandenhoeck & Ruprecht, 1897. Significant early study of Pauline style and rhetoric.

Wrede, William. *Die Echtheit des zweiten Thessalonicherbriefs.* Texte und Untersuchungen, NS 9. 2. Leipzig: J. C. Hinrichs, 1903. The first convincing demonstration of pseudepigraphic authorship.

# CHAPTER 30

# Paul's Letter to Philemon

## John R. Levison

## Major Issues in the Recent Study of Philemon

### Emancipation or equivocation

Paul's letter to Philemon addresses itself to the explosive issue of the relationship between a Roman master and his slave. Paul's oblique approach to this relationship is a disappointment. Why, simply put, did Paul not denounce the institution of Roman slavery? As J. B. Lightfoot (1890: 321) writes in his commentary, "the word 'emancipation' seems to be trembling on his lips, and yet he does not utter it."

Paul does appear to equivocate. Nowhere does he condemn slavery, despite the baptismal formula in Galatians 3:28, "There is no longer Jew or Greek ... slave or free ... male and female; for all are one in Christ Jesus." The appraisal of slavery that underlies the letter to Philemon rather is aligned with the instructions Paul proffers in 1 Corinthians 7:21–4, where he advises slaves to remain in slavery because "whoever was called in the Lord as a slave is a freed person belonging to the Lord" (7:22) – though in 1 Corinthians, in contrast to Philemon, Paul's instructions are perhaps more palatable because they are based upon the eschatological expectation that conditions would not remain as they were and, thus, slaves would be manumitted, so to speak, by an imminent resurrection. The authors of the household codes – whether Paul himself or protégés who wrote in his name – evince little tension between unity in Christ and the institution of slavery when they opt not to condemn slavery but instead to inhibit the mistreatment of slaves (Col. 3:22–3; 4:1; Eph. 6:5–9; cf. 1 Tim. 6:1–2; Titus 2:9–10).

### The absence of precedent

While those of us who read Paul's letter to Philemon in the twenty-first century could perhaps wish for a more forthright condemnation of the institution of slavery – particularly since the formula which Paul affirms in Galatians 3:28 is so unequivocal – we must take care not to judge Paul too harshly. There was simply no precedent in Paul's world for eschewing slavery.

Paul's own Jewish scriptures, while limiting the harshness of slavery because the Israelites were believed to have had their origins in an exodus from slavery in Egypt (e.g., Exod. 20:1–2; Lev. 25:42–5; Deut. 15:15), by no means abolish slavery. In the so-called Covenant Code, for example, a male Hebrew slave (i.e., not a foreigner) is freed after six years of enslavement, though he may not take, even then, a wife and children whom the master has given him (Exod. 21:1–6). There are inequities as well in the treatment of slaves. An ox that killed a free Israelite could bring the death penalty on its owner, while the death of a slave brought a penalty of thirty silver shekels (Exod. 21:28–32). A similar discrepancy is evident in a prescription according to which the penalty for killing one's slave is grounded in the assumption that a slave is property: "When a slaveowner strikes a male or female slave with a rod and the slave dies immediately, the owner shall be punished. But if the slave survives a day or two, there is no punishment; for the slave is the owner's property" (Exod. 21:20–1).

This legacy of ambiguity continued into the Greco-Roman era. Ben Sira's instructions during the early second-century BCE evince a decided cynicism toward slaves that is consistent with scriptural proverbs, which state that slaves do not respond to verbal discipline (Prov. 29:19) and that pampered slaves will become ungrateful (29:21). For Ben Sira, there exists no tension between his advice to treat slaves well and to torture recalcitrant slaves. Further, a slave should be treated "like a brother," not for the sake of altruism, but because of the cost and productivity of a slave – and the difficulty of tracking down a runaway (Sir. 33:25–33).

Nor do Greek and Roman thinkers provide the logic of liberation. On the contrary, Aristotle delivers the ideological foundation for slavery with his discussion of "natural slavery" (*Politics*, 1). Even one of the most magnanimous views of slaves in Roman literature, Seneca's *Moral Epistles*, 47, while ridiculing greedy slave owners and lauding skilled slaves (2–8), never recommends the manumission of all slaves. Although he acknowledges that one's slave "sprang from the same stock, is smiled upon by the same skies, and on equal terms with yourself breathes, lives, and dies," and although a master can "see in him a free-born man" (10), Seneca prevaricates at the suggestion that he is, with his advice, "offering the liberty-cap [of manumission] to slaves in general and toppling down lords from their high estate, because I bid slaves respect their masters instead of fearing them" (17–18).

Nor is there historical precedent for the rejection of the institution of slavery. Even movements of resistance, such as the famed rebellion in 70 BCE led by Spartacus, were not intended to eradicate slavery. Their aims were more modest – to temper the harsh excesses of slavery.


*Practical considerations*

The absence of Jewish, Greek, and Roman precedent serves in part to explain the ambiguity of Paul's letter toward the abolishing of slavery. So too, writes J. M. G. Barclay (1991: 183), did "practical considerations" lead to the ambiguity of this letter. The manumission of Onesimus, suggests Barclay, would have generated enormous difficulties, such as the loss of slaves who were integral to running Philemon's household, which provided the venue for the Colossian church's meetings (1991: 176). Further, the manumission of Onesimus – especially if he had run away illegally – would have had a devastating impact upon the morale of those obedient slaves whom Philemon had chosen not to manumit.

Therefore, although Paul believed that slave and master were brother and sister in Christ, he could not facilely recommend manumission. Barclay suspects that Paul, caught on the horns of this dilemma between equality in Christ and the practical concerns of manumission, "can do little more than offer a variety of different suggestions, none with the certainty of a clear instruction" (1991: 183).

### The (un)likelihood of manumission

Another unknown is whether Onesimus was destined for a lifetime of slavery or manumission. Rural slaves, who served on farms, typically were slaves for life; they labored with the knowledge that they would probably never be manumitted. Urban household slaves, in contrast, had better chances of manumission; frequently they were educated and literate, and they could often anticipate manumission during their master's lifetime or at their master's death, as a reward for devoted service (Wiedemann 1981: 122–3).

Either scenario helps us to understand Paul's predicament. If Onesimus was an agricultural slave, with virtually no prospect of manumission, the unprecedented nature of a demand for manumission would have been difficult to communicate effectively in a letter from prison. Could Paul have made the unheard-of request or demand that Onesimus be emancipated without befuddling Philemon altogether? More sensibly, as we shall see, he opts instead to lead Philemon carefully – with considerable subtlety – to this conviction.

If, on the other hand, Onesimus was an urban slave with the prospect of manumission, Paul may have avoided pressing Philemon too hard for two reasons. First, Paul may not have wanted to risk alienating Philemon for an earlier date of manumission; the issue was not *whether* Onesimus would be manumitted but *how soon*. Simply put, there may have been too little at stake to motivate Paul to pull rank, so to speak, on Philemon. Second, Paul may have wanted to avoid appearing demanding, aggressive, and avaricious; he was, after all, making a clear request that Philemon give up Onesimus in order for the slave to labor alongside him. Paul's muted tones are, therefore, understandable, for Paul would have appealed to this wealthy Christian leader as a friend and brother, yet he probably would not have risked alienating Philemon for the sake of the apparently self-serving demand that Onesimus be released to work alongside Paul.

### Summary

Many of the introductory issues that concern other Pauline letters lie outside the purview of scholarship on this letter. There are no significant textual variants (eighteen of twenty-five verses are variant-free), no serious question of Pauline authorship, and no indication that the letter is anything but a literary unity. Yet many puzzles concerning this communiqué remain unsolved, perhaps because it is so short – the letter numbers a mere 335 words – and certainly because Paul's request is so indirect.

It appears that Paul could do little by way of mounting support for the freeing of Onesimus, as he lingered, an old man, in prison. Left with no precedent, few resources, and practical considerations about the consequences of manumission, Paul took the familiar route of penning a letter to a slave owner in a Christian community intended to persuade him to relinquish his control over a single slave. The letter, which is ambiguous and oblique, avoids either overwhelming Philemon (if the request is unprecedented) or alienating him (if the request is for an early manumission). Given these considerations, it is difficult to say whether Paul's personal mediation on Onesimus' behalf represents a grand act of cowardice or an exemplar of courage – or, as seems more likely, something in between.

However we may judge Paul's courage or cowardice, the letter seems to have been effective, if Colossians 4:9 provides a window to Christian antiquity: Onesimus – presumably the slave of this letter – has been sent with Tychicus to Colossae and called "a faithful and beloved brother." This is what Paul had anticipated in his letter to Philemon, where he promised that Philemon would have Onesimus back no longer as a slave but as a "beloved brother" (v. 16).

## The Identity of Onesimus

The traditional interpretation of Paul's letter to Philemon, since the days of John Chrysostom, has been that Onesimus, a slave owned by a Colossian church leader, Philemon, had run away from his master (v. 15) after having defrauded or robbed him; the close association of the verbs, "wronged" (ἠδίκησεν) and "owes" (ὀφείλει), in verse 18 is said to suggest this. Onesimus landed in prison with Paul, either by accident or purposefully, where he became a convert to Christianity. Paul, who had experienced Onesimus' services (v. 13), asked Philemon to receive Onesimus back as a brother in Christ and to send him to serve Paul. Paul offered to repay whatever Onesimus had cost Philemon, either due to time lost while away or robbery.

There is, however, no explicit reference in this letter to Onesimus as a fugitive. Moreover, since running away was highly punishable, why is Paul so casual about any wrongdoing? Even the conditional particle, "if" in verse 18 – "*if* he has wronged you" – leaves open the question of culpability altogether. The request for a warm reception with hardly a glance at Onesimus' fugitive status is puzzling. Even more puzzling is a historical question. How could Onesimus, a Roman slave, and Paul, a Roman citizen, have been placed in the same prison cell, for typically they would have been incarcerated in different prisons (Fitzmyer 2000: 13, 84)? Finally, how likely is it that Onesimus, an arrested fugitive slave, met Paul serendipitously in Rome, Caesarea, or Ephesus, even if they shared a prison? All of these issues – no reference to a crime, the problem of different prisons, and the unlikelihood of a chance encounter – make the traditional portrait of Onesimus as a fugitive slave a dubious construal.

If Onesimus was not a fugitive seeking permanent escape, why then did he visit Paul? Several hypotheses have been proposed.

1  Philemon authorized Onesimus to visit Paul, and Paul wanted him to remain. The verbs, ἠδίκησεν and ὀφείλει, do not refer to any wrongdoing but to lost wages that accrued to Philemon while Onesimus was with Paul. The problem with this proposal is that it begs the question of why Paul pleads with Philemon to receive Onesimus back. Would not both principals have assumed that Onesimus would return to Philemon once his task was accomplished?

2  Onesimus was not a slave but Philemon's estranged brother. "The problem ... was not that Onesimus was a real slave (for he was not), nor that Onesimus was not a real brother to Philemon (for he was), but that Onesimus was not a *beloved* brother to Philemon. The emphasis of verse 16b, therefore, is not on *adelphon*, but on *agapeton*" (Callahan 1997: 372). This proposal founders on the statement, "that you may have him back ... no longer as a slave, but as more than a slave ..." (vv. 15–16).

3  Onesimus was the slave, not of Philemon, but of Archippus, whom Paul addresses in Philemon 2 and who is mentioned, alongside Onesimus, in Colossians 4:17. The letter to Philemon is, in fact, "the letter from Laodicea" mentioned in Colossians 4:16, and the *diakonia* Archippus is to fulfill in Colossians 4:16 is to give Onesimus to Paul for the sake of the gospel. Paul is not, therefore, mediating between Archippus and Onesimus; rather, he is asking Archippus to give him Onesimus as co-worker and promising Archippus that he will receive Onesimus back as a brother. This interpretation, tendered by J. Knox (1959) and more recently championed by S. Winter (1987), does not satisfactorily answer the question of why Philemon is mentioned first in the letter if Archippus is the primary recipient.

4  A rift between slave and master prompted Onesimus to seek a mediator. Onesimus, aware of Paul's friendship with Philemon, asked Paul to take on the role of *amicus domini* (master's friend), which Paul did by writing a letter to Philemon on Onesimus' behalf (Fitzmyer 2000: 17–18, 20–3). There is Roman precedent for this proposal. Proclus, a first-century CE jurist whom Justinian quotes in his *Digest* of juridical opinions (21.1.17.4), took on this role. Justinian refers as well to a slave who fled in the hopes that his mother would intercede (*Digest*, 21.1.43.618). Perhaps the closest literary analogue in this regard concerns a freed slave of Sabianus (freedmen tended to rely on former masters), on whose behalf Pliny the Younger interceded by writing a letter intended to convince – but, like Paul, not to coerce – Sabianus to forgo past grievances and to receive the freed slave back with impunity.

In summary, Onesimus has been identified variously as an arrested runaway slave seeking a permanent escape from Philemon, a temporary fugitive in search of an *amicus domini*, an authorized slave of Philemon or Archippus, and Philemon's estranged brother. The intercessory tone of Paul's letter, coupled with the inadequacies of the other hypotheses – the unlikelihood of a chance encounter between Onesimus and Philemon in the same prison (against Chrysostom et al.), the primacy of Philemon in the first line (against Knox), the mention in verse 16 of receiving Onesimus back no longer as a slave (against Callahan) – suggest that Onesimus knew about Philemon's relationship with Paul. He sought out Paul for intercession in some matter that had put him at odds with his master.

## Historical Setting

If we cannot be certain about the identity of Onesimus, we are beset equally by the question of the prison from which Paul penned this letter. Three suggestions are possible, none of which is certain. First, Paul wrote as a prisoner in Ephesus during the mid-50s CE – though there is no clear reference in the New Testament to imprisonment in Ephesus (see 1 Cor. 15:32; 16:9; 2 Cor. 1:8–9; 6:5; 11:23–4). Second, Paul wrote from a prison in Caesarea Maritima, on the eastern Mediterranean coast, during the late 50s CE (Acts 23:35; 24:26–7). Third, Paul wrote under house arrest at Rome probably during the early 60s CE (Acts 28:16, 30).

What commends the Ephesian hypothesis is that the city would have been closer to Colossae than Rome or Caesarea. Onesimus could have traveled to Ephesus in less than a week, and Paul could credibly promise to visit Philemon following his release, as he does in Philemon 22. Nevertheless, since the fourth century, Rome has been considered the letter's place of origin. The Roman hypothesis is supported by the intimate relation of the letters to Philemon and the Colossians, which scholars typically trace to Rome (if Colossians is not a post-Pauline composition), given that the letter to Philemon mentions the same figures as Colossians 4:16–17. Fortunately, the question of which prison Paul occupied does not measurably affect the interpretation of Paul's letter.

## Language and Style

Paul's letter lacks elements that characterize many of his other letters. Paul does not appeal to the Jewish scriptures; in fact, the premise of the letter – returning an escaped slave to a master rather than granting permanent refuge – seems to be an abrogation of Deuteronomy 23:16–17 (Masoretic Text). Nor does Paul incorporate credos and hymns of the church, as he often does elsewhere (e.g., Rom. 1:3–4, 1 Cor. 15:3–8; Gal. 3:27–8, and possibly Phil. 2:5–11). Yet this does not mean that Paul's language and style are thoughtlessly constructed.

Paul's literary skill is apparent in the body of the letter through a particular use of repetition: a word or theme or phrase that is introduced in one sentence reappears in a subsequent sentence, in which a new word or phrase is introduced. That new element is then repeated, while another new element is introduced. The rhetorical effect is like a staircase in which the thought is carried along, word by word, until the reader is led inevitably through a series of connected verbal steps to a clear conclusion. This technique, which D. F. Watson identifies tentatively as transplacement (*Rhetorica ad Herennium*, 4.14.20–1; Quintilian, *De oratore*, 9.3.41–2), begins in verse 7 and continues until verse 13:

In verse 7, Paul introduces two words to depict the source of his joy: Philemon's own love, ἐπὶ τῇ ἀγάπῃ σου, and the seat of emotions which this love touches, τὰ σπλάγχνα τῶν ἁγίων.

In verse 9, Paul repeats the word, love, (τὴν ἀγάπην), to reinforce that the basis of his appeal is love rather than authority. He also introduces a new term that will lead the argument along, "encourage" (παρακαλῶ), to describe the strategy he prefers rather than commanding Philemon. Further, he picks up his initial self-designation (v. 1), "prisoner" (δέσμιος) in anticipation of verse 10.

In verse 10, Paul repeats from verse 9 "encourage" (παρακαλῶ), to reinforce that the basis of his appeal does not lie in his own authority; and a reference to imprisonment (ἐν τοῖς δεσμοῖς) to evoke Philemon's sympathy by underscoring his deplorable situation. Paul also introduces the figure "Onesimus," Ὀνήσιμον, literally "useful," which will provide the basis for the following pun in verse 11.

In verses 11–12, Paul recalls the name, Onesimus, through the paired words, "useless" and "useful" – ἄχρηστον and εὔχρηστον. Onesimus, whose name means "useful," will now be "useful" (εὔχρηστον) rather than "useless" (ἄχρηστον) to Philemon (v. 11). Paul also repeats the word, "heart" (τὰ ἐμὰ σπλάγχνα), which was introduced in verse 7 – this time in reference to Onesimus.

In verse 13, Paul repeats the phrase from verse 10, ἐν τοῖς δεσμοῖς, this time with still another explicit reference to imprisonment for his mission (τοῦ εὐαγγελίου). This prepositional phrase recalls as well Paul's earlier reference to his being a "prisoner" (v. 9).

The subtle development of Paul's thought is evident in this diagram of repeated terms:

verse 7: ἐπὶ τῇ ἀγάπῃ σου – τὰ σπλάγχνα τῶν ἁγίων
verse 9: τὴν ἀγάπην – παρακαλῶ – δέσμιος Χριστοῦ Ἰησοῦ
verse 10: παρακαλῶ – ἐν τοῖς δεσμοῖς – Ὀνήσιμον ("useful")
verses 11–12: ἄχρηστον – εὔχρηστον – τὰ ἐμὰ σπλάγχνα
verse 13: ἐν τοῖς δεσμοῖς

This considered rhetorical structure indicates that this is no sentimental appeal to Philemon written hastily. It is well crafted and careful, as Paul leads Philemon subtly toward Onesimus' release.

This appeal is further cemented by the threefold reference to the seat of emotions in verses 7, 12, and 20. In verse 7, Paul refers to the heartfelt feeling which Philemon's love evokes (τὰ σπλάγχνα τῶν ἁγίων ἀναπέπαυται διὰ σοῦ). In verse 12, Paul's heartfelt feeling is personified by Onesimus (τὰ ἐμὰ σπλάγχνα). In verse 20, Paul asks Philemon to refresh Paul's heartfelt feeling by fulfilling his request (ἀνάπαυσόν μου τὰ σπλάγχνα ἐν Χριστῷ). The repetition of the expression ἀναπαύειν ... τὰ σπλάγχνα, provides a stunning bookmark to Paul's appeal. The heartfelt refreshment which Philemon has given to other Christians (v. 7) he is now asked to give to Paul in a specific demand voluntarily met, in a decisive moment of generosity (v. 20). It is to Philemon's credit – and due in no small measure to Paul's literary skill – that Onesimus would indeed be freed to serve with Paul.

## Rhetorical Analysis

Paul's letter to Philemon is at once intimate and public. The spotlight seems to shine exclusively upon Paul, Philemon, and Onesimus, a slave to which they both lay claim. Yet these three principals also share the spotlight with a coterie of colleagues, male and female, who comprise an audience of sorts that gives cogency to Paul's appeal to Philemon. Many are the recipients alongside Philemon: Apphia, Archippus, and the church in Philemon's house. Further, Paul writes with Timothy – who is also described as a brother (v. 1) – and sends greetings from several others: Epaphras, Mark, Aristarchus, Demas, and Luke. Paul's muted appeal to free Onesimus is more than an individual matter, therefore, since the letter was to be read, as the opening lines indicate, in the context of a church.

Particularly salient, in light of the intimate yet public tone of the letter, is the way in which Paul tends to set aside possible rhetorical appeals to *ethos* (self-presentation that inspires confidence in the hearer) and *logos* (modes of logical argumentation) in favor of *pathos* – stress upon the relationship between speaker and hearer. It is with a capable hand that Paul develops *pathos* as singularly important in his effort to compel Philemon to manumit Onesimus and to send him to work with Paul. Paul expresses such intimacy through relational terms: Paul is Philemon's brother (vv. 7, 20) and Onesimus' father (v. 10); Philemon and Onesimus have the potential to be brothers (v. 16). There are intimate touches as well in this brief letter, such as when Paul describes himself as an "old man" (v. 9) or when he adds, nearly as an afterthought, that Philemon should prepare a guest room (v. 22).

It is these two aspects that set this letter apart from Paul's other letters. Paul's appeal is both public and intimate, and it is deeply rooted in *pathos*.

### Prescript (verses 1–3)

Paul begins naturally by identifying himself and his co-author, Timothy, and the letter's recipients: Philemon, Apphia, Archippus, and the church that meets in (presumably) Philemon's house (v. 1). The preface concludes with a greeting to these recipients (ὑμῖν) that is typical of Paul's own letters, with references to God the father and the Lord Jesus Christ (v. 3).Yet sandwiched between these two elements of communal address, Paul addresses Philemon with the second person singular pronoun, σου (v. 2). This shift from plural (v. 1) to singular (v. 2) to plural (v. 3) sparks a touch of *pathos* between Paul and Philemon without forfeiting the communal pressure which the church can exert upon Philemon to fulfill Paul's request.

### Thanksgiving or exordium (verses 4–7)

This intimacy between Paul and Philemon underlies the letter's thanksgiving, which is dripping with *pathos*. The epistolary camera, so to speak, has left the other personae out of its scope in order to focus exclusively upon Paul's perception of Philemon. Paul claims to thank God always for Philemon in his prayers because he has heard of Philemon's love for all believers and his faith in Jesus – an energizing sort of faith and love that provide encouragement to Paul and many other believers. This thanksgiving appears at first blush to border on the obsequious, for it functions rhetorically as a formal *captatio benevolentiae* intended to secure Philemon's goodwill. Yet the remainder of the letter suggests otherwise; Paul is writing tenderly, if forcefully, to Philemon. The thanksgiving, in fact, introduces key words and ideas that will dominate the body of the letter: love (vv. 5, 7, 9); good (vv. 6, 14); fellowship (vv. 6, 17); and heart (vv. 7, 12, 20). This thanksgiving, therefore, provides Paul with the opportunity to introduce those qualities in Philemon to which he can later appeal, when he urges Philemon to accept Onesimus.

### Body of proof (verses 8–16)

In what would be the proof in a formal speech, Paul delineates what he hopes Philemon will do. Yet Paul's appeal is not principally logical, in the sense of what Roman rhetoricians would have called internal logic, which entails the use of modes of argumentation, such as enthymemes, arguments *a fortiori*, etc. Nor does he appeal to external sources (what rhetoricians called external logic), such as the scriptures, to impel Philemon to release Onesimus for service to Paul's mission. Nor is Paul's appeal based in a bold and credible self-presentation. On the contrary, Paul appears to adopt the rhetorical trope of *antiphrasis* – the abandonment of a cogent argument – in favor of self-deprecation; he refers to himself nowhere in the letter as an apostle or slave of Jesus Christ (perhaps out of sensitivity to Onesimus) but as an old man (v. 9) who exists "in chains" (vv. 10, 13). This approach can pay huge dividends in terms of *pathos*, as John Chrysostom noted: "For who would not receive with open arms a combatant who had been crowned? Who seeing him bound for Christ's sake, would not have granted him ten thousand favors?" (*Homily in Philemon*, 2.2.9).

If the body of this letter is short on *logos* and *ethos*, it is long on *pathos*. Every rhetorical move Paul makes is couched in terms of relationships. Paul expresses deference toward Philemon when he opts to "encourage" him on the basis of love rather than "command" him (vv. 8–9) because he wants to do nothing without Philemon's consent (vv. 13–14). Paul's singular mode of self-presentation is as a father to Onesimus, whom Paul urges Philemon to accept as a "beloved brother."

### Concluding summary or peroration (verses 17–22)

Letters were intended to provide surrogate presence in antiquity, and the beginning of Paul's peroration accomplishes this intention in two ways. First, Paul portrays Onesimus, who perhaps carried this letter, as a surrogate, when he urges Philemon to "receive him as me" (v. 17). He also stresses his promise to repay any debts that have accrued to Onesimus by writing in his own hand (v. 19).

The final lines of this peroration are rich in pathos. Paul leaves behind the legal language of reimbursement (vv. 18–19), adopting instead the familial term, "brother"

(v. 20). When he reiterates his request, he even leaves behind the specter of Onesimus. It is as if Paul has drawn the curtain that isolates him and Philemon in order to request, "Brother ... refresh my deepest feelings in Christ" (v. 20). These words are the mirror image of what Paul had praised Philemon for in the exordium of the letter: "the deepest feelings of the believers have been refreshed through you, brother" (v. 7). Paul is asking Philemon, his brother, to do for him what he had done for the believers – refresh his deepest feelings to an extent that even Paul cannot anticipate (v. 21).

If this direct but intimate request does not tighten the bond between Philemon and Paul, then Paul's next request will, if a bit more obliquely. Paul ends this peroration by asking Philemon to prepare a room in his own house. Paul intends, in other words, to sleep in Philemon's home.

Paul knows that the need for a place to sleep will become a reality through God's response to prayer. Yet – and this shift is vital – Paul unexpectedly peels back the curtain that had isolated Philemon and himself to expose once again the community as a whole. It is not Philemon's prayers alone that will bring the release of Paul but the church's; he writes, "For I hope that through your [ὑμῶν] prayers I will be released to you [ὑμῖν]" (v. 22). The community, in other words, is brought once again front and center into the purview of Paul's letter.

### Postscript (verses 23–5)

The role of the community is evident as well in the greetings Paul passes to the recipients of this letter. Epaphras is called a "co-prisoner," while Mark, Aristarchus, Demas, and Luke he designates "co-workers" (vv. 23–4). Paul's adoption of words that begin with the prefix, co-, (συν-), is not arbitrary. These designations provide a literary bookend to the letter's opening lines, in which Paul designated Philemon himself as a "co-worker" (v. 1: συνεργῷ) and Archippus a "co-soldier" (v. 2: συστρατιώτῃ). This symmetry in the letter continues to its final line, for the letter ends, as it began, with the sending of grace (vv. 3, 25).

### Summary of Paul's rhetoric

If a deep bond of pathos exists between Paul and Philemon, it is not an exclusive bond. If Paul assumes that Philemon, because of his love and faith, will outrun Paul's expectations, it is not an assumption that Paul is willing to make without allowing the church to overhear his request. If Paul is asking Philemon to receive Onesimus as a beloved brother, it is not without the realization that Onesimus will be kin as well to the likes of Timothy their brother and Apphia their sister (vv. 1–2). If Paul prays for Philemon, it is not without the expectation that the entire church will pray for his own release (vv. 4–5, 22). In other words, Paul's letter to Philemon is a mine rich with the coercion that issues from *pathos*, from intimacy within a communal context. Paul has neither managed to surrender Philemon's will to the communal will nor ignored the community in his intimate appeal to Philemon. Paul seems to grasp that Philemon's decision, though it is about his own slave, his personal property, is not entirely his own, that what one does with one's possessions is not entirely a personal matter, that the church provides the community of grace, the co-workers and co-fighters, a network of praying people that inevitably shapes the values of its individuals. Paul writes in a way that permits them a wide berth to overhear a request that may cost Philemon dearly.


## Bibliography and Further Reading

Barclay, J. M. "Paul, Philemon and the Dilemma of Christian Slave-Ownership," *New Testament Studies* 37 (1991), 161–86.
Bartchy, S. S. *MALLON CHRESAI: First Century Slavery and the Interpretation of 1 Cor. 7:21.* Society of Biblical Literature Dissertation Series, 11. Missoula, MT: Scholars Press, 1973.
Bieberstein, S. "Disrupting the Normal Reality of Slavery: A Feminist Reading of the Letter to Philemon," *Journal for the Study of the New Testament* 79 (2000), 105–16.
Callahan, A. D. *Embassy of Onesimus: The Letter of Paul to Philemon.* The New Testament in Context. Valley Forge, PA: Trinity Press International, 1997.
Church, F. F. "Rhetorical Structure and Design in Paul's Letter to Philemon," *Harvard Theological Review* 71 (1978), 17–33.
Fitzmyer, J. A. *The Letter to Philemon.* Anchor Bible 34 C. New York: Doubleday, 2000.
Frilingos, C. " 'For my child, Onesimus': Paul and Domestic Power in Philemon," *Journal of Biblical Literature* 119 (2000), 91–104.
Knox, J. *Philemon among the Letters of Paul: A New View of its Place and Importance.* Rev. edn. Nashville: Abingdon, 1959.
Lightfoot, J. B. *Saint Paul's Epistles to the Colossians and to Philemon: A Revised Text with Introductions, Notes and Dissertations.* 9th edn. London: Macmillan, 1890.
Llewellyn, S. R. "The Government's Pursuit of Runaway Slaves." *New Documents Illustrating Early Christianity* 8 (1997–8), 9–46.
Martin, D. B. *Slavery as Salvation: the Metaphor of Slavery in Pauline Christianity.* New Haven: Yale University Press, 1990.
Nordling, J. G. "Onesimus Fugitivus: A Defense of the Runaway Slave Hypothesis in Philemon," *Journal for the Study of the New Testament* 41 (1991), 97–119.
Petersen, N. R. *Rediscovering Paul: Philemon and the Sociology of Paul's Narrative World.* Philadelphia: Fortress Press, 1985.
Rapske, B. M. "The Prisoner Paul in the Eyes of Onesimus," *New Testament Studies* 37 (1991), 187–203.
Schenk, W. "Der Brief des Paulus an Philemon in der neueren Forschung (1945–1987)," *Aufstieg und Niedergang der römischen Welt* 2 25/4 (1987), 3439–95.
Taylor, N. H. "Onesimus: A Case Study of Slave Conversion in Early Christianity," *Religion and Theology* 3 (1996), 259–81.
Vos, C. de. "Once a Slave, Always a Slave? Slavery, Manumission and Relational Patterns in Paul's Letter to Philemon," *Journal for the Study of the New Testament* 82 (2001), 89–105.
Wiedemann, T. (ed.). *Greek and Roman Slavery.* New York: Routledge, 1981.
Wilson, A. "The Pragmatics of Politeness and Pauline Epistolography: A Case Study of the Letter to Philemon," *Journal for the Study of the New Testament* 48 (1992), 107–19.
Winter, S. C. "Paul's Letter to Philemon," *New Testament Studies* 33 (1987), 1–15.

CHAPTER 31

# Ephesians

## Margaret Y. MacDonald

## Major Issues and Directions in Recent Study

Many believe that Ephesians is the most beautiful of all of the Pauline epistles. Its majestic presentations of major theological themes have had timeless appeal. Its liturgical language and focus on unity make it especially well suited to worship in diverse settings. It has often been suggested that many Bible readers actually view Paul through the lens of Ephesians; the work almost seems to be a deliberate summary of the apostle's thought. But for all of its influence and popularity, scholars have found the work frustratingly elusive – especially from a historical perspective.

Unlike much of Paul's correspondence, Ephesians reveals virtually nothing about its specific context. The document makes almost no references to specific events. In contrast to Colossians and other letters in the Pauline corpus that reflect a network of relationships between Paul and his fellow workers, Ephesians refers only to Tychicus (6:21–2; cf. Col. 4:7–8; 2 Tim. 4:12; Titus 3:12; Acts 20:4). Even the identity of the addressees is unknown. The words "in Ephesus" are missing from the greeting (1:1) in several important textual witnesses and, therefore, many modern translations include the phrase in brackets or as an alternate reading in the notes. While it is often thought that the gap in the address is best explained by the theory that the document is actually a circular letter intended for more than one congregation (cf. 1 Pet. 1:1; Rev. 1:4), this is by no means certain. Moreover, although it has usually been understood as rooted in the context of Asia Minor, there is simply no way to establish conclusively that Ephesians was actually intended for a congregation or congregations in Ephesus. The superscription, "To the Ephesians" was not part of the original work and definite evidence for its use cannot be established before the end of the second century CE. To complicate the problems of historical reconstruction still further, there is uncertainty about the nature of the document itself, with some commentators questioning whether Ephesians is truly an epistle and arguing that it might more closely resemble a sermon, liturgical tract, or even some other type of discourse altogether such as an honorific decree (see "Genre" below).

The interpretive puzzles surrounding Ephesians have been compounded by the debate concerning the authorship of the document. For some scholars the changes in the thought and style of the work in comparison to the undisputed Pauline letters have seemed significant enough to rule out the traditional understanding of Paul as the author. The most frequently noted features leading to this conclusion include the use of words and expressions not found elsewhere in the Pauline epistles (e.g., "the heavenly places" [*ta epourania*]; cf. 1:3, 20; 2:6; 3:10; 6:12), very long sentences that typically amass synonyms, and the fact that Ephesians does not conceive of the church in local terms (all references are to the universal *ekklesia*). Yet by far the most important characteristic that has led to the opinion that the work is pseudonymous is the presence of extensive literary parallels between Ephesians and the other letters in the Pauline corpus, especially Colossians. While a significant number of commentators continue to argue that Ephesians was composed by Paul (Barth 1974; Bruce 1984; O' Brien 1999; Hoehner 2002; Heil 2007), it is probably the case that the majority of commentators today consider the work to be deutero-Pauline (but see charts on authorship in Hoehner 2002: 9–20).

If one seeks to locate major directions in the study of Ephesians in recent times, it is more difficult to arrive at clearly identifiable scholarly trends and significant points of consensus than in the case of many of the letters of Paul. It is clear that there have been several learned and influential commentaries on the work (e.g., Lincoln 1990; Schnackenburg 1991). There have also been important studies on particular aspects of the document such as liturgical influences (e.g., Dahl, 1951, 1976; Kirby 1968), on specific passages such as the teaching on marriage in Ephesians 5:21–33 (e.g., Sampley 1971), or the relationship of Ephesians to the remainder of the Pauline corpus (e.g., Goodspeed 1933; Mitton 1951). But despite many attempts to arrive at broad explanatory theories, there has never been a general consensus as to the overall purpose of the letter to the Ephesians, with many commentators now favoring the view that the work had more than one purpose (e.g., Barth 1974; Lincoln 1990; MacDonald 2000). The dominance of traditional historical-critical methods has in part been responsible for the fact that until quite recently work on Ephesians was becoming hampered by scholarly "dead ends" and, therefore, was subject to comparative neglect in Pauline studies (especially in the English-speaking world). The document simply resists being pinned down to particular historical problems such as a battle with opponents or some community crisis. But the proliferation of new methodologies and theoretical approaches has led the way past some of these dead ends, and exciting new directions in the study of Ephesians are emerging.

The new directions in the study of Ephesians may be broken down into four main categories. First, Ephesians has profited from the growing emphasis in Pauline studies on broader comparative work on religion in the ancient world. Comparison to the Dead Sea Scrolls (e.g., Perkins 1997; Dahl 2000), and to the diverse evidence for magical practices in Asia Minor (Arnold 1989), have proven to be especially promising. Secondly, in keeping with the growing interest in Paul and politics, the points of contact between imperial ideology and Ephesians are of increasing interest to scholars (e.g., Faust 1993; MacDonald 2004). Thirdly, the nature of the patterns of argumentation in Ephesians has been analyzed by means of rhetorical analysis with important conclusions emerging about their impact in community life (Lincoln 1990). Fourthly, social-scientific methodologies have been employed in an effort to understand the social processes and cultural values reflected in the text (MacDonald 1988, 2000). Finally, the presence of the house-hold code (5:21–6:9), including a detailed and symbolically rich exposition of marriage, has led to several feminist analyses of the text (e.g., Tanzer 1994; Osiek 2002).

## Historical Setting and Date

Those scholars who argue that Ephesians was written by Paul usually understand it to have been composed during Paul's imprisonment in Rome (cf. Acts 28:16–31). They generally date the document to late in the apostle's career (the early 60s) in close prox-imity to the composition of Colossians. For those who hold that the work is deutero-Pauline it becomes impossible to identify a specific place of composition, for even if such a location were revealed by the text, any certainty would be ruled out by author's exercise in pseudepigraphy. Moreover, in the case of a pseudepigraphon, it is quite pos-sible that the provenance and the destination of the work would be the same (Muddiman 2001: 35). Because the document has traditionally been associated with Ephesus, is closely related to Colossians, and has a general ethos that is in keeping with Pauline Christianity in the area, scholars have generally opted for the view that the cities of Asia Minor provide the most likely setting. The probable dependence of Ephesians upon Colossians (see below) has also been a major contributing factor to the widely held view that Ephesians was composed in the latter decades of the first century CE – frequently a date of 80–90 has been suggested. In many respects Ephesians appears to reflect the situation of the Pauline community making a transition into a new generation and looking back to its origins (e.g., 2:19–20).

One of the most ambitious attempts to identify the precise community or communi-ties to which Ephesians was addressed in recent times has come from Andrew Lincoln (1990: 3–4). On the basis of grammatical considerations with respect to the address, he has argued that it originally contained two place names (taking up some of the earlier suggestions of A. van Roon). Drawing upon the close relationship between Ephesians and Colossians, he has suggested that these place names were originally Hierapolis and Laodicea (cf. Col. 2:1–3; 4:15–16). In ancient times, the early church figure Marcion actually designated the work as the epistle "To the Laodiceans" – a fact that plays a central role in Muddiman's (2001) proposal that the author of Ephesians used a genuine letter from Paul to the Loadiceans as the basis for his work. But in the end, it must be admitted that the only fact that can be recovered from the document itself with any degree of certainty about the identity of the recipients is that they were (predominantly?) Gentile (2:11–22; cf. 2:1–3; 4:17–19). It has often been suggested that the notion of a Gentile audience receives further support from the tendency to distinguish "we" (Jewish Christians associated with Paul who first came to believe) from "you" (the Gentile addressees who also believed) as in Ephesians 1:12–14. But this distinction is also subject to other possible interpretations, including the fact that it may simply represent a rhetorical strategy for drawing recipients into the discussion (Lincoln 1990: 36–8; MacDonald 2000: 203–4).

The "you/we" contrast does, however, raise questions about the nature of Jewish–Gentile relations reflected in the text. The frequent allusions to Jewish scripture (direct citations are rare), the parallels with the Dead Sea Scrolls (especially in the presentation of the Gentile non-believing world), and the interest in clarifying the relationship between the Gentile audience and Israel (2:11–22) have led to a consensus among commentators that the document reflects Jewish-Christian authorship. This acknowl-edgment of the author's Jewish background has frequently been followed by expres-sions of puzzlement concerning the author's attitude towards the situation of the Gentile community (or communities) vis-à-vis Judaism: While the author of Ephesians clearly has a strong interest in the Jewish origins of the church (2:11–22), he or she seems remarkably unconcerned – especially when one compares Ephesians to the undisputed letters – about *concrete* relations with Jews in or outside of the church (Dahl 2000: 446). But some recent studies suggest that we should avoid taking this first impression at face value. Increasingly commentators are stressing the importance of Jewish material as offering the most important intellectual background for Ephesians (Perkins 1997) and have warned against a tendency to dismiss the presence of Jewish Christians (Muddiman 2001) among the audience (see "Major Themes" below).

## Relation to Colossians

Among the Pauline epistles no two works more closely resemble each other than Colossians and Ephesians. In fact, Ephesians reproduces more than one-third of the words found in Colossians. The most striking parallels include the following: Eph. 1:7/Col. 1:14; Eph. 2:5/Col. 2:13; Eph. 3:2/Col. 1:25; Eph. 3:9/Col. 1:26; Eph. 4:16/Col. 2:19. The majority of commentators have argued in favor of the priority of Colossians, but it has sometimes been suggested that Colossians represents an abridged version of Ephesians. In fact, Ernest Best (1998: 20–36) has questioned some of the main argu-ments in support of the widely held view that the author of Ephesians was familiar with Colossians, noting that in some places the relationship could more easily be explained if the reverse were true. Yet the nature of the extended, almost verbatim agreement between the recommendation of Tychicus in Ephesians 6:21–2 and Colossians 4:7–8 makes more sense if the author of Ephesians worked from the author of Colossians' descriptive list of fellow workers and greetings than the reverse (MacDonald 2000: 353).

The nature of the close relationship between Colossians and Ephesians extends far beyond literary dependence to include major overlaps in theological and ethical content. Both Colossians and Ephesians refer to the expansion and filling up of the universe with divinity with reference to the concept of "filling up" or fullness (*pleroma*; Col. 1:9; 2:9; Eph. 1:10, 23; 3:19; 4:13). The notion of Christ as ruler of the cosmos (cf. Phil. 2:6–11) becomes intertwined with the Pauline symbol of the body of Christ so that a new vision of the body emerges (e.g., Col. 1:18–22; 2:9–10, 19; 3:15; Eph. 1:22–3; 4:14–16; 5:23, 30). The body of Christ becomes the means for describing the cosmic reconciliation that occurs through Christ, so that in Ephesians even the reconciliation of Jew and Gentile takes on cosmic dimensions (2:13–22). It is also important to note that in these works the body is explicitly called the church and Christ becomes the head of the body. Many commentators have sensed a possible correlation between this "vertical" symbolism with the appearance of the hierarchical household codes embracing the believing paterfamilias as head of the family (Col. 3:18–4:1; Eph. 5:21–6:9). Ethics play a central role in Colossians and Ephesians and in both cases the author employs remembrances of baptism to instill appropriate behavior (e.g., Col. 1:12–14; 2:5–9; 3:1–3, 10–11; Eph. 1:11–14; 2:1–6; 4:4–6, 22–4, 30; 5:8–14, 25–7).

In seeking to understand the relation between Colossians and Ephesians, it is also important to note key differences between the two works. Most obviously, there are several texts in Ephesians that are unique to that epistle (e.g., 2:4, 7–11, 17–20, 22; 4:4–5, 7, 9–12, 14, 17, 21, 26–8, 30; 5:21, 26, 28–9, 31–3; 6:2–3, 10–17, 23–4). The detailed treatment of marriage in Ephesians 5:22–33 stands out especially in this regard and represents a marked contrast to the brief mention of marriage in Colossians 3:18–4:1. There are also instances where substantial portions of Colossians have no parallel in Ephesians. Here the description of the false teaching in Colossians 2:8–23 is notable in contrast to the virtual absence of any mention of opponents in Ephesians (see "Purpose" below). Finally, it is important to recognize that sometimes terms do not have exactly the same meaning in Colossians and Ephesians. Stewardship (*oikonomia*), for example, in Colossians refers to Paul's apostolic commission (Col. 1:25), but in Ephesians it is used in conjunction with God's plan for the universe (Eph. 1:10; 3:2, 9).

## Purpose

There have been many different proposals, but no real consensus on the issue of the purpose for which Ephesians was written. Ephesians 2:11–22 has often figured prominently in these proposals. Some have viewed the text as directed to Gentile Christians who were in danger of divorcing themselves from their Jewish origins (e.g., Käsemann 1966). But the main problem with this idea is that Ephesians offers no substantial evidence of tension between groups. In fact, Muddiman (2001: 16–17) has recently argued that even the focus on the Gentiles cannot be immediately adopted as a literal description of the community when one accepts that Ephesians is a pseudepigraphal work. He notes that it is equally possible that Ephesians was intended to comfort Jewish Christians who have too frequently been dismissed by commentators as an intended audience for the work.

Along different lines, the presence of liturgical influences has also figured prominently in attempts to identify the purpose of Ephesians. Arguing that Ephesians 1:3–14 is best understood as a blessing before baptism, Dahl (1951) viewed Ephesians as instructions to Gentile believers on the meaning of baptism, while Kirby (1968) sought to uncover points of contact between Ephesians (reflecting Christian rites, including a Christian celebration of Pentecost) and Jewish liturgical traditions. Generally speaking, theories concerning the liturgical origins of Ephesians have been less popular of late because of their failure to account for many features of the text, including epistolary elements (see "Genre" below). But social-scientific investigations of ritual have allowed for a greater appreciation of the significance of baptism and hymns (cf. 5:18–20) in the development of beliefs and structures for community life (MacDonald 2000).

Given how an awareness of the conversations between Paul and various opponents has illuminated such letters as Galatians and 1 Corinthians, and the centrality of false teaching to the purpose of Colossians, it is not surprising that there have been attempts to read Ephesians against some type of "heresy." While there is clearly great interest in revelation, insight, and mystery throughout Ephesians as highlighted by Michael Goulder (e.g., 1:3–14; 3:2–5, 8–10, 18–19), his theory (1991) that Ephesians responds to Jewish Christian visionaries has not been generally accepted. The notion that Ephesians responds to Gnostic opponents has been more popular (e.g., Schlier 1957; Pokorný 1965). But the presence of general points of contact with later Gnostic works (whose authors sometimes appealed to Ephesians to support their views on such topics as "sacred marriage") does not offer conclusive evidence for specific Gnostic opponents in the first century. Most seriously, any proposal of Ephesians as anti-heretical must deal with the objection that in only one place in the work does the author make a general reference to false teachers (4:14). Attempts to explain the setting and purpose of Ephesians in light of a response to more general aspects of pagan culture have seemed more convincing of late than efforts to identify particular opponents. For example, while it has not escaped criticism as too narrowly focused, one theme (cf. Lincoln 1990: lxxxi), Arnold's (1989) attempt to read the focus on the supremacy of Christ in relation to "principalities and powers" within an Asia Minor context of magical pursuits, has been quite influential.

No discussion of the purpose of Ephesians would be complete without reference to the theory of E. J. Goodspeed (1933) that Ephesians was a preface for an initial collection of Paul's letters (developed further by Mitton 1951). While the specific theory has generally been rejected because its historical foundations are so dubious, it has nevertheless been highly influential as a catalyst for subsequent works which have viewed Ephesians as a summary and interpretation of Paul's teaching for a new generation. For some scholars the "generalizing" tendencies of Ephesians are rooted in a desire to address themes of broad relevance to the church such as "unity" (e.g., Schnackenburg 1991). Others have concentrated more specifically on the potential crisis caused by the death of Paul (e.g., Lincoln 1990), with the nature of the authority of the apostle sometimes highlighted with the aid of social-scientific analysis (MacDonald 1988, 2000). Some have envisioned a "Pauline school" – a circle of Paul's collaborators and their disciples who sought to interpret the Pauline heritage (Best 1998). But it should be noted that among scholars who have emphasized the role of Ephesians in bringing Paul's voice to bear upon new circumstances, the view that the work had more than one purpose is often apparent (e.g., Lincoln 1990; MacDonald 2000).

## Language and Style

Commentators have frequently noted that the language of Ephesians is significantly different from that of the undisputed letters of Paul. Approximately ninety words occur in Ephesians that do not appear in the undisputed epistles and forty words do not appear in the New Testament at all. It is important not to attach too much weight to such statistics, however, as one can easily imagine a word either being left out or included for no reason other than its potential utility at any given moment in a specific context (see Muddiman 2001: 3–4). More revealing is the author's substitution of related expressions or synonyms for usual Pauline expressions. It is possible here only to offer a few examples: Ephesians speaks of "in the heavenly places" (*en tois epouraniois*; 1:3, 20; 2:6; 3:10; 6:12) where Paul simply speaks of "in the heavens" (*en tois ouranois*; 2 Cor. 5:1; Col. 1:16, 20 cf. Phil. 3:20). While Ephesians makes extensive use of the Pauline term "grace" (*charis*; cf. 1:6, 7; 2:5, 7, 8; 4:7, 29), Ephesians 1:6 uses the verb "to grace" (or "to favor"; *charitoō*), a term that is found elsewhere in the New Testament only at Luke 1:28. In keeping with the New Testament literature of the later decades of the first century, the word "devil" (*diabolos*) appears in Ephesians (4:27; 6:11; cf. 1 Tim. 3:7; 2 Tim. 2:26; 1 Pet. 5:8) rather than the word "Satan" as in Paul's letters.

Some of the linguistic features seem to be closely tied to the theological message of the epistle. For example, both the exclusive focus in Ephesians on the universal (not local) *ekklesia* (1:22; 3:10, 21; 5:23, 24, 25, 27, 29, 32) and the particular use of the Pauline concept of "mystery" (3:3–12; 5:32) reveal profound theological interest in the identity of the church (see "Major Themes" below). Sometimes there is a notable absence and/or radical transformation of key Pauline concepts – a fact that seems even more significant given the author of Ephesians' apparently deliberate attempt to summarize Paul's message. In Ephesians 2:5 we hear that "by grace you have been saved" when in the undisputed letters "by grace" (or by faith) is usually used in conjunction with justification language (e.g., Rom. 3:24; 5:1; but see the discussion in Lincoln 1990: 104). In the undisputed letters the opposition between faith and works is used to describe the meaning of life in Christ in relation to the Jewish law. Yet in Ephesians "works" stands for human accomplishment in general – perhaps a sign that disputes concerning the meaning of the Jewish law have subsided (2:8–10). Moreover, believers are described as having been created for "good works," a phrase for which there is no precise parallel in the undisputed epistles (but see 2 Cor. 9:8; 2 Thess. 2:17). In keeping with the interest in ethical conduct, revised Pauline concepts are used to define the ultimate purpose of believers' lives as announcing God's purpose for the world by means of their good works (2:10).

Commentators have also frequently noted that the style of Ephesians is significantly different from that of the undisputed letters of Paul. There are very long single sentences in Greek which are often extended by means of relative clauses (e.g., 1:3–14; 4:11–16). There is also a great deal of repetition and redundancy. This can be seen in the piling up of synonyms such as in the list of terms associated with God's purpose in Ephesians 1:3–14, the placing of similar words with similar meanings side by side (e.g., "wisdom and insight," Eph. 1:8), and detected in such expressions as "the working of his power" (3:7) or "the strength of his might" (6:10). At times the style seems effusive or ornate – designed to arouse listeners – especially when the same word is repeated frequently as in the fourfold reference to peace in Ephesians 2:14–17 or the pervasive use of the term "all" throughout the epistle. Such stylistic features have been linked especially to liturgical influences which are especially evident in the first half of Ephesians (see "Genre" below).

## Intertextuality

Although the author of Ephesians frequently alludes to scripture, the work contains only a few direct scriptural quotations. Psalm 68:18 is cited in Ephesians 4:8–9 in an unusual manner; the changes reflect points of contact with ancient rabbinic tradition that read the psalm as a reference to Moses ascending Mount Sinai (see Lincoln 1990: 242–3). The author of Ephesians understands Christ as the new Moses who gives gifts. Further examples of modified citations are found in Ephesians 6:2–3, which refers to the commandment from the Decalogue (LXX Exod. 20:12; Deut. 5:16) about honoring parents (Lincoln 1990: 397) and Ephesians 1:21–2, where a juxtaposition of Psalm 8:6 and Psalm 110:1 occurs evidently following Paul's lead in 1 Corinthians 15:25, 27 (Lincoln 1990: 66). The reference to Genesis 2:24 in Ephesians 5:31 is more straightforward, but there are questions about its role in informing the teaching on marriage. In particular the relationship between Genesis 2:24 and the reference to the concept of mystery in Ephesians 5:32 – a central concept in Ephesians (cf. 1:9; 3:3, 9; 6:19) and in some Gnostic texts which echo Ephesians (e.g., *Gospel of Philip*, 64; 70; 82) – has given rise to significant debate (MacDonald 2000: 331).

There are many interesting allusions to scripture, including, for example, LXX Isaiah 57:19 and 52:7 in Ephesians 2:17, serving to bolster the fourfold repetition of the term "peace" so pivotal to the presentation of what Christ has accomplished (for other allusions see Eph. 4:25 [Zech. 8:16]; 4:26 [Ps. 4:4]; 5:18 [Prov. 23:31]; 6:14 [Isa. 59:17]; 6:15 [Isa. 52:7]; 6:16 [Wisd. 5:19); 6:17 [Isa. 59:17]). But it is in the teaching on marriage that the allusions to scripture are most pervasive; together with the direct citation of Genesis 2:24 in Ephesians 5:31, these allusions anchor the major theological messages about the relationship between the human and the divine (Eph. 5:26 [Ezek. 16:9]; 5:28 [Lev. 19:18]). The author of Ephesians has transposed the use of marriage as a metaphor for God's relationship with Israel in the book of Hosea and elsewhere to speak about the relationship between Christ and the church.

It is best to think of the author of Ephesians' use of scriptural traditions as part of a more general pattern of reliance on traditional material. That liturgy is central to the traditional elements of the work is made especially clear by the citation of an early Christian hymn in Ephesians 5:14. The weight attached to this traditional element is illustrated by the fact that the same introductory formula ("Therefore it says") is used with respect to the scripture citation in Ephesians 4:8. The author of Ephesians is also deeply influenced by phrases and themes from the Pauline letters. Here it is especially important to consider Colossians (see "Relation to Colossians" above), but the author appears to make use of other letters as well. Texts such as Ephesians 2:11–22 and 4:1–16 offer a summary of Pauline teaching, taking up key themes such as "the unity of Jew and Gentile in one church" and "the many gifts in one body." But within these texts it is also possible to detect direct appeal to Pauline phrases, expressions, and concepts, for example "having no hope" (2:12 [1 Thess. 4:13]), temple imagery (2:20–2 [1 Cor. 3:9–17]), "I beseech you" (4:1 [Rom. 12:1]), "one body, one Spirit" (4:4–6 [1 Cor. 12:13; cf. Rom. 12:5]), "the apostles, the prophets, the evangelists, the pastors and teachers" (4:11 [1 Cor. 12:28]).

## Major Themes

The first three chapters of Ephesians concentrate upon God's purpose for the world. In fact, the author of Ephesians focuses so strongly upon God's gift of salvation to the world that themes of election and predestination (in keeping with concepts seen in the Qumran literature) become central to the work (e.g., 1:3–14). While the notion of future deliverance does not disappear altogether (e.g., 1:13–14; 6:13), the emphasis on present salvation is predominant, with believers being depicted as already seated with Christ in the heavenly places (2:6). It is within this framework that the focus on the identity of the church in Ephesians must be understood. The universal *ekklēsia* exists on account of what God has accomplished in Christ and, as God's creation, it has the power to make God's wisdom known to the spiritual powers in the heavenly places (3:10).

The idea of the church attaining cosmic proportions is reinforced by the manner in which the theme of unity is woven throughout Ephesians. Unity is the most clearly visible product of God's interaction with the world. It characterizes the smallest cell of believers, the family (5:21–6:9), and extends to the life of the house-church community as unity of the Spirit (4:1–16) and ultimately to the universal *ekklēsia* (2:15–22). The theme of unity works in conjunction with the related themes of peace and love to determine the priorities of the *ekklēsia*. The church is the place where the peace accomplished by the blood of the cross – breaking down all barriers including old divisions between Gentiles and Israel – is revealed (2:13–14). Love (see Heil 2007) in imitation of Christ (5:2) shapes the community (4:15–16) and is that which fundamentally characterizes the union between Christ and the church, providing the model for love between husband and wife (5:25–6).

Despite its frequent focus on the heavenly realm, Ephesians places a great deal of emphasis on moral conduct and commitment. This is revealed especially in the ethical exhortations in the final three chapters, but there are also indications of this priority in the first half of the work. Indeed the interrelationships between the doctrinal and ethical segments of the letter are profound. In describing the state of the universe, for example, the author of Ephesians points to spiritual powers that continue to threaten the world (e.g., 2:2; cf. 1:21). But virtue is the armor that will protect them from these menacing forces (6:10–20). The household code (5:21–6:9) includes extensive theological reflection on the meaning of marriage as a reflection of the relationship between Christ and church. This suggests that daily life for believers – even when largely conventional – was infused with meaning for those who belonged to the household of God and were committed to heavenly citizenship (2:19). In fact, Ephesians prepares the way for the type of theological reflection we encounter in 5:21–6:9 with the description of the Father (*pater*) from every family (*patria*) on earth and in heaven takes its name (3:14).

## Outline and Constituent Literary Forms

Ephesians opens with an address and greeting (1:1–2); the address follows Colossians closely and the greeting resembles that found consistently throughout Paul's letters. The main body of the work is usually understood as divided into two major sections, including a doctrinal exposition (1:3–3:21) and ethical exhortations (4:1–6:20). Although it has sometimes been understood as an extended thanksgiving (Sanders 1962; cf. 1 Thess. 1–3), part 1 may actually be broken down into several related parts. It includes a blessing (1:3–14; most likely drawing its origins from the extended blessing of Jewish worship [*berakah*]), and a thanksgiving (1:15–23) which follows the usual form found in Pauline letters (e.g., Philem. 4–5; Col. 1:3–4) and which is closely associated with prayer as in Colossians. The next two sections draw upon themes that are introduced via the thanksgiving. Ephesians 2:1–10 returns to the question of how God's plan works through Christ and its consequences for believers and, with a focus on the unity of Jews and Gentiles, 2:11–22 picks up again on the theme of the universal church introduced in 1:22–3. Ephesians 3:1 introduces a prayer and doxology that is taken up again at 3:14–21 (constituting the second prayer report in the epistle after 1:15–23). In essence, Ephesians 3:1–13 is a digression on the role of the apostle as the interpreter of divine mystery that serves as a bridge between the two major components of the work. It is the apostle who reveals the mystery of Christ (3:4), who has the authority to call believers to lead a life worthy of their calling in Ephesians 4:1–16.

The description of the sons of disobedience and the children of light in Ephesians 4:17–5:20 (involving a long virtue and vice list) continues the emphasis on ethics. Although there is debate about whether Ephesians 5:21 is more closely associated with 4:17–5:20 or 5:22–6:9 (MacDonald 2000: 325–6), there is no doubt that 5:22–6:9 forms a self-contained unit: the household code. This typical form of early Christian discourse (cf. Col. 3:18–4:1; 1 Pet. 2:18–3:7; 1 Tim. 2:8–15; 3:4; 6:1–2; Titus 2:1–10; 3:1; Ignatius, *Polycarp*, 4:1–5:1; Polycarp, *Philippians*, 4:2–6:1) drew its origins from Hellenistic discussions of "household management" among philosophers and moralists from Aristotle onward (e.g., Aristotle, *Politics*, 1.1260a9–14; Dionysius of Halicarnassus, *Roman Antiquities*, 1.9–2.29). The ethical segment concludes with the call to do battle with evil in Ephesians 6:10–20 (see "Rhetorical Analysis" below). Finally, there is a conclusion (6:21–4) involving reference to personal matters (see "Relation to Colossians" above). The conclusion also includes a final blessing that incorporates typical features of the endings of Paul's letters, such as a wish for peace and a bestowal of grace.

## Genre and Epistolary Analysis

For some commentators the liturgical-catechetical style of Ephesians has seemed so pervasive that they have viewed the work as a sermon or liturgical tract simply cast in the form of a letter (e.g., Kirby 1968; Gnilka 1971). Such theories have now generally fallen out of favor. This is out of recognition of the importance of liturgical influences generally in Pauline works (but conversely also the lack of clear-cut evidence concerning Jewish and Christian sermons and liturgies in this era) and because Ephesians exhibits many of the features of a standard Pauline letter. For example, Ephesians includes the typical salutation, conclusion, and thanksgiving for the good conduct of believers. The blessing of Ephesians 1:3–14 finds a parallel in the opening of 2 Corinthians (cf. 1 Pet. 1:3–12; yet of Pauline letters only Ephesians includes both an introductory blessing and a thanksgiving). While it is unquestionably influenced by liturgical forms, Ephesians 1:3–3:21 constitutes a doctrinal section that, as in other letters, is followed by an ethical exposition (e.g., Galatians, Colossians). Yet it is important to note that advances in the formal analysis of ancient letters (to what extent they were governed by epistolary and rhetorical conventions: see Aune 1987; Malherbe

1988) has proven to be important for analysis of Ephesians. For example, the apparent lack of a "body middle" in Ephesians has raised questions about what to make of a work that moves immediately from an opening, to a combined blessing/thanksgiving, to concluding exhortations and a closing (Hendrix 1988: 3). Debate about the genre of Ephesians has by no means completely abated. Noting the density of the language of Ephesians 1–3 and the "public" orientation of the work in general, Holland Hendrix (1988) has argued that in form Ephesians follows the conventions of an honorific decree framed in an epistolary genre. Andrew Lincoln (1990: xl), on the other hand, views it as a "natural extension of the Pauline letter in the direction of an epistolary sermon or homily." David Aune (1987: 18) prefers to categorize it as a "general letter" revealing a more distant relationship between parties and dealing with matters that transcend particular circumstances.

In discussing genre, it is also important to consider the nature of Ephesians as a pseudepigraphal work. For example, in keeping with Jewish pseudepigraphy (Kitchen 1994: 28), Ephesians develops the figure of Paul as an authoritative figure from the past (MacDonald 2000: 268–73; cf. Eph. 3:1–13). The writing of a pseudepigraphal letter should by no means be understood as misrepresentation in the modern sense. Ephesians is rooted in a context where modern notions of copyright simply did not exist and where the literary device of pseudonymity was widespread in the Greco-Roman world (on the writing of pseudepigraphal letters in particular see Donelson 1986). Rooted in Jewish traditions, the author of Ephesians inherited the tendency for disciples and successors to develop the tradition and write in the name of originators or teachers (cf. Wisdom of Solomon, 1 Enoch). The author of Ephesians, however, was by no means devoid of theological creativity. Making use of Pauline materials (especially Colossians), the author presented new theological messages for the end of the first century CE.

## Rhetorical Analysis

The attempt to understand the impact of the Pauline letters as read aloud to congregations has encouraged rhetorical analysis of the works. Lincoln, for example, argues that the first part of Ephesians is largely representative of the epideictic rhetorical genre, intended to bolster adherence to certain values. The extended thanksgiving of Ephesians 1–3 acts as rhetorical strategy by kindling religious emotions (e.g., awe in the face of God) and commitment. It might be broken down into an *exordium* (1:1–23) designed to render the audience receptive, and the *narratio* (2:1–3:21) divulging the circumstances upon which they should base their judgment (e.g., what God has accomplished among the Gentiles). Under normal circumstances, one would expect the *argumentatio* at this point – the centre of most discourses (corresponding to absence of the letter-body; see "Genre" and "Epistolary Analysis" above). But instead part 2 of the letter moves immediately into a long *exhortatio* (4:1–6:9) containing largely deliberative rhetorical elements designed to convince the audience to take up certain actions (e.g., behavior that is consciously distinct from the non-believing world). The letter concludes with a *peroratio* (6:10–24) including a postscript (6:21–4) and a striking final appeal to stand firm in spiritual warfare (6:10–20; Lincoln 1990: xliii–xliv). Lincoln

(1990: 430–60) has argued that this section serves as a summary of the major concerns of the letter as a whole, drawing attention to parallels with the speeches of generals before battle. Increasingly, rhetorical analysis is complementing socio-historical investigation; in this case both methodologies may work together to uncover the nature of Ephesians' response to society and to explore the reasons for its greater encouragement of distinction from the non-believing world in comparison to other Pauline works (MacDonald 2000: 342–50).

## Annotated Bibliography

Arnold, Clinton E. *Ephesians, Power, and Magic: The Concept of Power in Ephesians in Light of its Historical Setting*. Cambridge: Cambridge University Press, 1989. Highlighting the importance of Ephesus as a centre for magical practices, Arnold argues that Ephesians was written because believers felt threatened by the influence of hostile spiritual powers.

Aune, David E. *The New Testament in its Literary Environment*. Philadelphia: Westminster, 1987. This work includes a valuable discussion of ancient letters generally and early Christian letters (including types of letters) in particular.

Barth, Markus. *Ephesians*. 2 vols. Anchor Bible, 34, 34A. Garden City, NY: Doubleday, 1974. This is a major commentary arguing that Paul is the author of Ephesians.

Best, Ernest. *A Critical and Exegetical Commentary on Ephesians*. International Critical Commentary. Edinburgh: T. & T. Clark, 1998. Best questions many of the traditional arguments in support of the idea that the author of Ephesians used Colossians and argues instead that Colossians and Ephesians were both produced independently, at about the same time, within the context of a Pauline school in Ephesus.

Bruce, F. F. *The Epistles to the Colossians, to Philemon, and to the Ephesians*. New International Commentary on the New Testament. Grand Rapids: Eerdmans, 1984. This is a major commentary arguing that Paul is the author of Ephesians.

Dahl, Nils A. "Addresse und Proömium des Epheserbriefes." *Theologische Zeitschrift* 7 (1951), 241–64. This article examines the liturgical influence in the first part of Ephesians.

Dahl, Nils A. "Anamnesis: Memory and Commemoration in the Early Church." Pp. 11–29 in *Jesus in the Memory of the Early Church: Essays*. Minneapolis: Augsburg, 1976. This is an important essay for understanding the impact of liturgical influences on Ephesians.

Dahl, Nils A. *Studies in Ephesians: Introductory Questions, Text- and Edition-Critical Issues, Interpretation of Texts and Themes*. Edited by David Hellholm. Vemund Blomkvist and Tord Fornberg. Tübingen: Mohr Siebeck, 2000. This study considers many questions key to the interpretation of Ephesians, including points of contact with the Dead Sea Scrolls and the relationship between Jews and Gentiles.

Donelson, L. R. *Pseudepigraphy and Ethical Argument in the Pastoral Epistles*. Tübingen: Mohr Siebeck, 1986. This work contains a detailed examination of the pseudepigraphal letter in the Greco-Roman world and in early Christian literature.

Faust, Eberhard. *Pax Christi et Pax Caesaris: Religionsgeschichtliche, traditions-geschichtliche und sozialgeschichtliche Studien zum Epheserbrief*. Freiburg and Göttingen: Universitätsverlag/ Vandenhoeck & Ruprecht, 1993. Concentrating especially on Ephesians 2:11–22, Faust discusses points of contact between Ephesians and Roman imperial ideology and examines the situation in the empire after the Jewish War of 66–70 CE.

Gnilka, Joachim. *Der Epheserbrief*. Freiburg: Herder, 1971. Gnilka viewed Ephesians as a liturgical homily.

Goodspeed, E. J. *The Meaning of Ephesians*. Chicago: University of Chicago Press, 1933. In this highly influential study Goodspeed argued that the author of Ephesians (probably Onesimus, following the suggestion of J. Knox) was inspired by Acts to collect the letters of Paul and wrote Ephesians as a type of covering letter.

Goulder, Michael D. "The visionaries of Laodicea," *Journal for the Study of the New Testament* 43 (1991), 15–39. Goulder argues that Ephesians responds to Jewish Christian visionaries and highlights the importance of visionary phenomena in general for understanding the text.

Heil, John Paul. *Empowerment to Walk in Love for the Unity of All in Christ*. Atlanta: Society of Biblical Literature, 2007. This is mainly a literary study of Ephesians, concentrating on the structures of chiasm. Heil's analysis leads him to highlight the importance of the theme of love for Ephesians.

Hendrix, Holland. "On the Form and Ethos of Ephesians," *Union Seminary Quarterly Review* 42 (1988), 3–15. Highlighting the difficulties raised by Ephesians for epistolary analysis, Hendrix argues that the work constitutes an epistolary decree in which the author proclaims the universal benefactions of God.

Hoehner, Harold W. *Ephesians: An Exegetical Commentary*. Grand Rapids: Baker Academic, 2002. This is one of the most detailed defenses of Pauline authorship in recent times. Hoehner argues that more commentators continue to defend the Pauline authorship of Ephesians than is often realized.

Käsemann, Ernst. "Ephesians and Acts." Pp. 288–97 in *Studies in Luke–Acts*. Edited by Leander E. Keck and J. Louis Martyn. Nashville and New York: Abingdon, 1966. Käsemann argued that Ephesians 2:11–22 was written to warn Gentiles against divorcing themselves from the Jewish roots of the church. He also saw Ephesians as representative of nascent early Catholicism.

Kirby, John C. *Ephesians: Baptism and Pentecost. An Inquiry into the Structure and Purpose of the Epistle to the Ephesians*. London: SPCK, 1968. This is an important work on liturgical background of Ephesians. Kirby was one of many scholars who viewed Ephesians as a sermon cast in the form of a letter.

Kitchen, Martin. *Ephesians*. London and New York: Routledge, 1994. This work contains an especially valuable discussion of the relationship between Ephesians and Jewish pseudepigraphy.

Lincoln, Andrew T. *Ephesians*. Word Biblical Commentary 42. Dallas: Word Books, 1990. This is one of the most complete and important commentaries in recent years. It includes thorough rhetorical analysis of Ephesians.

MacDonald, Margaret Y. *The Pauline Churches: A Socio-Historical Study of Institutionalization in the Pauline and Deutero-Pauline Writings*. Cambridge: Cambridge University Press, 1988. Draws upon insights from the social sciences to investigate how the process of institutionalization affected change in the Pauline movement over time.

MacDonald, Margaret Y. *Colossians and Ephesians*. Edited by Daniel J. Harrington SJ. Sacra Pagina, 17. Collegeville, MN: Liturgical Press, 2000. Draws upon insights from the social sciences to analyze the text, illustrating how ancient cultural values and social processes shape Colossians and Ephesians.

MacDonald, Margaret Y. "The Politics of Identity in Ephesians," *Journal for the Study of the New Testament* 26 (2004), 419–44. In response to some commentators who have contended that the author of Ephesians failed to show interest in contemporary Jews, MacDonald argues that Ephesians 2:11–22 is best understood as reflecting engagement with the fate of the Jewish people. She draws upon recent work on the political framework of the Pauline epistles and compares Ephesians to Josephus, *Against Apion*.

Malherbe, Abraham J. *Ancient Epistolary Theorists*. Atlanta: Scholars, 1988. Malherbe illuminates ancient epistolary theory and considers how rhetorical and philosophical conventions shaped the composition of epistles in the Greco-Roman world.

Mitton, C. Leslie. *The Epistle to the Ephesians*. Oxford: Clarendon Press, 1951. Mitton took up and refined many of the ideas of E. J. Goodspeed concerning the origins of Ephesians.

Muddiman, John. *The Epistle to the Ephesians*. Black's New Testament Commentaries. London and New York: Continuum, 2001. Muddiman argues that a genuine letter from Paul to the Laodiceans (probably written from Ephesus around 54) was used as a source by the author of Ephesians around 90 CE.

O'Brien, Peter T. *The Letter to the Ephesians*. Pillar New Testament Commentaries. Grand Rapids: Eerdmans, 1999. This is one of the most frequently cited commentaries which advocates the traditional view that Ephesians was composed by Paul.

Osiek, Carolyn. "The Bride of Christ (Ephesians 5:22–33): A Problematic Wedding," *Biblical Theology Bulletin* 32 (2002), 29–39. Paying close attention to the function of simile and metaphor, Osiek examines the problematic nature of the passage in Ephesians that compares the union of husband and wife to that of Christ and the church.

Perkins, Pheme. *Ephesians*. Abingdon New Testament Commentaries. Nashville: Abingdon, 1997. This is a concisely written commentary which includes interesting comparisons between Ephesians and the Qumran literature.

Pokorný, Petr. *Der Epheserbrief und die Gnosis*. Berlin: Evangeslische Verlagsanstalt, 1965. Pokorný is one of many scholars who has argued that Ephesians responds to Gnostic tendencies.

Sampley, J. Paul. *"And the Two Shall Become One Flesh": A Study of Traditions in Eph. 5:21–33*. Cambridge: Cambridge University Press, 1971. Sampley traces the influence of Old Testament traditions on Ephesians, especially on the marriage teaching.

Sanders, J. T. "The Transition from Opening Epistolary Thanksgiving to Body in the Letters of the Pauline Corpus," *Journal of Biblical Literature* 81 (1962), 348–62. Sanders argues that the first three chapters of Ephesians may be viewed essentially as one long thanksgiving.

Schlier, Heinrich. *Der Brief an die Epheser*. Dusseldorf: Patmos, 1957. Schlier argued that Ephesians responds to Gnostic opponents. The work includes extensive discussion of the Sacred Marriage traditions in ancient literature.

Schnackenburg, Rudolf. *Ephesians: A Commentary*. Trans. Helen Heron. Edinburgh: T. & T. Clark, 1991. Schnackenburg argues that Ephesians was a circular letter written to address issues of general relevance including the unity of the church and the need to call Christians to engage in behavior that will set them apart their pagan environment.

Tanzer, Sarah. "Ephesians." Pp. 325–47 in *Searching the Scriptures 2: A Feminist Commentary*. Edited by Elisabeth Schüssler Fiorenza. New York: Crossroad, 1994. Tanzer offers a feminist analysis of the letter, arguing that the household code was a later addition to Ephesians.

CHAPTER 32

# The Pastoral Letters:
# 1 and 2 Timothy and Titus

## David E. Aune

## Introduction

The Pastorals constitute a group of three closely related letters that, together with
Philemon, make up a small collection of Pauline letters addressed to individuals rather
than congregations. This small group of letters was designated "Pastoral Letters" in the
early eighteenth century because they were written by a pastor (Paul) with practical
advice for other pastors (Timothy and Titus). Though it is widely assumed that the
Pastorals are the product of a single author and are typically treated as a small corpus,
it is nevertheless important to emphasize the distinctive features that characterize
each letter. The Pastoral Letters are problematic because it is difficult to determine who
wrote them, when they were written, why they were written, and to whom they were
written.

## Major Issues and Directions in Recent Study

The disputed Pauline authorship of the Pastorals continues to dominate the discussion
of these letters, even though by the beginning of the twenty-first century, an estimated
80 to 90 percent of concerned scholars judged them to be pseudepigraphal (Harding
2001; Collins 2002: 4). Arguments for their authenticity are largely made by scholars
whose theological views of biblical inspiration make it difficult for them to accept the
possibility of pseudonymous authorship. The order in which the three letters were
written is another issue on the front burner, with most scholars maintaining that the
canonical order does not represent the order in which the Pastorals were written.
Another issue that continues to be discussed is the nature of the heresy mentioned in
each of the three letters. Even though the identification of "Jewish Christian Gnostics"
as a broad designation for the heresy reflected in the Pastorals is widely held, that rubric
is the result of synthesizing the various, sometimes contradictory, characteristics of the
opponents and is therefore virtually useless historically. The problem of identifying the
heresy or heresies addressed in the Pastorals therefore remains unsolved.

In recent decades, one of the most discussed passages in the Pastorals has been 1 Timothy 2:9–15 and the question of the role of women in ministry. Several have argued that the Pastorals were written to counteract the influence of a group of independent women in the communities addressed (MacDonald 1983). Some have argued that this passage must be read in the context of all the Pastoral Letters and particularly the household codes in 1 Timothy 2:8–3:13 and 5:1–6:2 (Heidebrecht 2004). For Heidebrecht, Paul's instruction for women is part of his concern with the presence of "different teaching" in the church. Women, especially the younger widows, he argues, have been involved in the promotion of this different teaching and Paul tries to prohibit them from continuing to deceive others. One of the current trends in research on the Pastorals maintains that the author makes creative use of the materials he incorporates into the letters, which he transforms into a coherent theological and ethical message (Miller 1997: appendix A). Most commentators on the Pastorals do not address the problem of the literary structure of the letters.

2 Timothy 3:16, with its emphasis on the inspiration of scripture, has functioned as a *crux interpretum* for discussions of that doctrine: "All scripture is inspired by God and is useful for teaching, for reproof, for correction, and for training in righteousness." Several observations are in order (following Marshall 1999: 790–6): (1) The term "scripture" probably refers, not to "the scriptures" generally, but more specifically to a specific passage of scripture, i.e., in the Jewish scriptures. (2) The term "all" is probably distributive, meaning "every passage of scripture" (cf. Collins 2002: 263). (3) The critical term θεόπνευστος ("God-breathed"), a term possibly coined by the author, should be taken in the passive sense meaning that every passage of scripture comes from God.

## Authorship, Date, and Order of Composition

Despite the fact that 1 and 2 Timothy both open with the phrase "Paul, an apostle of Christ Jesus," and Titus opens with "Paul, a servant of God and an apostle of Jesus Christ," the Pauline authorship of the Pastorals has been increasingly in doubt since the beginning of the nineteenth century. The vast majority of all critical New Testament scholars now regard the Pastorals as pseudepigraphal letters. Scholars have been generally agreed, however, that all three letters were probably written by the same unknown individual, though this issue is beginning to be questioned (Herzer 2004).

There are a number of arguments for doubting Pauline authorship: (1) The earliest collection of the Pauline letters survives in the battered papyrus codex P[46], dating to ca. 200 CE. It probably contained ten letters (it now ends with 1 Thess. 5:28); 2 Thessalonians and the Pastorals are missing, but the size of the codex (84 out of 100 leaves have survived) indicates that while 2 Thessalonians was originally included, the Pastorals were not. (2) Marcion of Sinope omitted the Pastorals from his collection of Pauline letters (Tertullian, *Against Marcion*, 5.21), but the reasons for this judgment are unknown. (3) The theological character of the Pastorals has different emphases than the genuine Pauline letters (i.e., Romans, 1–2 Corinthians, Galatians, Philippians, 1 Thessalonians, Philemon). Thus the typical Pauline terms "law," "faith," and "righteousness" also appear in the Pastorals, but with a different meaning. For example, "faith" in Paul is an existential relationship with Christ, but in the Pastorals is a term for the content of faith (Collins 2002: 367). Characteristically Pauline terms like "cross" and "revelation" do not occur at all. Non-Pauline terms or phrases such as "savior," "epiphany," and "the saying is faithful" have become important. (4) *Language*. There are striking differences between the vocabulary and phraseology of the Pastorals when compared with the authentic Pauline letters. The Pastorals have a total word count of 3,484 words with a vocabulary of 901 words, 306 of which are not found in the other Pauline letters (ca. 33 percent), and 335 of which are not found in the rest of the New Testament. Harrison (1921: 16ff.) observes that a larger percentage of the *hapax legomena* (i.e., words occurring just once) in the Pastorals are missing from the Septuagint than the *hapax legomena* from the genuine Pauline letters and also that many of the *hapax legomena* in the Pastorals are not attested in other Greek writings before the end of the first century. (5) *Style*. There is a difference in style between the Pastorals and the authentic Pauline letters; Brox contrasts the "explosive style" of Paul with the "more peaceful" address of the Pastorals (1969: 47). (6) *Historical and geographical references*. Paul's ministry in the Pastorals cannot easily be made to fit Paul's life as narrated in the Acts of the Apostles before his Roman imprisonment in 61–2 CE. (7) *Characteristics of pseudepigraphal letters*: The Pastorals exhibit several features characteristic of pseudepigraphal letters (Bauckham 1988): (a) One way of bridging the gap between the supposed addressee(s) and the real addressee(s) of a pseudepigraphal letter is to make clear that the contents are to be passed on to others in addition to the fictional addressee(s) (1 Tim. 4:6, 11; 6:2; 2 Tim. 2:2, 14; Titus 2:2, 6, 9, 15; 3:1). (b) The testamentary letter form is an ideal vehicle for pseudepigraphal letters since it characteristically addresses a situation after the death of the author. 1 and 2 Timothy both refer to what will occur after Paul's death (1 Tim. 4:1–3; 2 Tim. 3:1–5; 4:3–4), and Timothy is instructed with regard to his own conduct after the death of Paul (2 Tim. 3:5, 10–4:2, 5). (c) Pseudepigraphal letters often set the historical scene of the ostensible recipients a little more fully than would actually be necessary; this is the case with the description of the false teachers in 2 Timothy 2:17–18.

A number scholars have steadfastly maintained the Paul is the actual author of the Pastorals, either personally or through the use of a secretary. There is clear evidence that Paul dictated his letters to an assistant (Rom. 16:22; 1 Cor. 16:21; Gal. 6:11; Philem. 19), though in the case of the Pastorals the issue centers on how much freedom the secretary would have had in terms of vocabulary and phraseology. E. R. Richards (1992) discusses how Greek and Roman letter-writers used secretaries, distinguishing between author-controlled and secretary-controlled composition. Richards (2004: 64–93) suggests that secretaries could vary from mere transcribers taking dictation to contributors to the final composition. Few today would go as far William Foxwell Albright (1891–1971), who held an opinion not easily justified by the extant evidence (quoted in Longenecker 1974: 294):

> Since St. Paul's Greek was dictated to different amanuenses at different times and in difference places, we could not possibly expect uniform quasi-literary style or vocabulary in his letters. For this reason attempts to determine the authorship of the Pauline Epistles by statistical data obtained with the use of computing machines prove little except the kind of literary Greek preferred by different amanuenses.

2 Timothy 1:8 and 2:9 refer to "Paul's" imprisonment, presumably in Rome. If the actual author of the Pastorals is Paul, then they must have been written before his execution in Rome (ca. 62–4 CE; probably 62 CE), and must further be integrated with what is known of Paul's life and travels from his other letters and the Acts of the Apostles. An alternative to regarding the Pastorals as pseudepigraphal places them between the Roman imprisonment narrated in Acts 28:17–31 (ca. 62 CE) and his so-called second Roman imprisonment, known only from the Pastorals. However, if the Pastorals are pseudonymous, as many critical scholars argue, then their date is probably much later than 62 CE, perhaps as late as the beginning of the second century to ca. 125 CE. The Pastorals should probably be dated to the first quarter of the second century, more narrowly from ca. 110–120 CE. Witherington (2006: 23–38) has argued that while apocalypses lend themselves to pseudepigraphy, the situation-specific character of letters does not make pseudepigraphy an easy task, since neither the named author or recipient is real. Thus systematic deception is required to introduce a pseudepigraphal letter into a faith community and the early church tended to reject works that were deceptive when they recognized them as such.

The presumption of pseudonymity, however, has not prevented some from attempting to identify the real author. S. G. Wilson (1979), following Moule (1962: 220–1) and A. Strobel in a 1969 essay, argues that Luke is the actual author of the Pastorals, basing their arguments on language and style. Wilson further emphasizes the common theological perspective shared by Luke and the Pastorals, centering his discussion on eschatology, salvation, Christian citizenship, the church and ministry, Christology, and the place of the law in scripture. Wilson further argues that Luke wrote the Pastorals after the completion of Acts (Wilson 1979: 3). Luke had a few fragments of Pauline writings with which to work, in his view, but did not really understand Paul, though he was sympathetic to him. He wrote these pseudonymous letters to use the authority of Paul to combat heresy in Asia Minor (Wilson 179: 117, 121). Despite similarities between Luke–Acts and the Pastorals, there is little evidence to actually suggest identity of authors. Witherington (2006: 57–62), following Moule, develops a variant of the foregoing hypothesis by suggesting that Luke was Paul's amanuensis for all three Pastoral Letters. Hans F. von Campenhausen (1963) has produced a number of intriguing arguments that Polycarp of Smyrna is the author of the Pastorals, based on the many linguistic similarities between the Pastorals and Polycarp's letter to the Philippians (a view accepted by Hoffmann 1984: 284). A summary of von Campenhausen's views and a brief critique can be found in Hartog (2002: 228–31). Walter Bauer (1971: 224) argued the reverse, namely, that the Pastorals contain allusions to Polycarp, *Philippians*. Methodologically, of course, it is easier to argue that the ostensible author is not in fact the actual author (given a corpus of texts actually written by the author in question) than it is to argue that a specific person not named in the text is the actual author.

While there are many who regard the Pastoral Letters as authentic, there have been various ways of associating these compositions with Paul: (1) The traditional view, which is still in play among conservatives, is that the Pastorals were written in the 50s or 60s of the first century by Paul himself. (2) A modern mediating view is that the Pastorals were written during Paul's lifetime by a member of Paul's circle and sent under Paul's own authority. (3) Another type of modern mediating view is that while not actually written by Paul, the Pastorals contain several authentic fragments of genuine Pauline notes (Harrison 1921, 1964; Miller 1997). (4) A view that takes the pseudepigraphal character of the Pastorals seriously maintains that they were the product of a Pauline school that may have supervised the collection of the Pauline letter corpus and also produced the deutero-Pauline letters Colossians and Ephesians.

The dating of the Pastorals involves two separate but related issues. The first is approximate date when the entire corpus was written, and the second is the problem of the order in which they were written. There are three general time-frames for dating the Pastorals. (1) Those favoring Pauline authorship maintain that the Pastorals originated before the end of the first Christian generation, i.e., before Paul's death ca. 62 CE. (2) Some of those maintaining the pseudepigraphal character of the Pastorals have argued that they originated during the second Christian generation, i.e., between 65 and 90 CE (Collins 2002: 9). (3) Others who maintain that the Pastorals are pseudepigraphal place their origin sometime during the third Christian generation, i.e., from ca. 90 to 130 CE. If Polycarp's letter to the Philippians alludes to the Pastorals (see below, "Reception in the Second Century"), as I think it does, then the date of Polycarp's letter becomes important for dating the Pastorals. Hartog (2002: 169) dates Polycarp's *Philippians* to ca. 115 CE. His arguments are superior to those of Harrison, who argues that Polycarp refers to the heretic Marcion, and dates the final form of the letters to ca. 135 CE.

Most scholars do not regard the canonical order of the Pastorals to be identical with the order in which they were written. The Pastoral Letters first appear in canonical context in Codex Claromontanus in the order 1 Timothy–2 Timothy–Titus, their present canonical order. This arrangement is based on decreasing length (1 Timothy: 1,586 words; 2 Timothy: 1,235 words; Titus: 663 words). In the Muratorian Canon (line 60) and Ambrosiaster, however, they occur in a different order: Titus–1 Timothy–2 Timothy, an order that Quinn (1990: 63–4, 78; see also Quinn and Wacker 2000; Klauck 2006: 324–5) regards as the original order. Quinn argues that the epistolary opening in Titus 1:1–3 provides an appropriate thematic introduction to the entire corpus. Wolter (1988: 21–2), however, argues convincingly for the order 1 Timothy–Titus–2 Timothy, pointing to the importance of 1 Timothy 1:12–17 in presenting the total united image of Paul fostered by the Pastorals. There are also those who have argued that 2 Timothy was the first of the Pastorals to be written, followed by Titus and 1 Timothy (Brown 1997: 675). The order in which the Pastorals were written, then, remains a contested issue.

## Reception in the Second Century

According to *Biblia Patristica* (1975), the Pastorals are quoted or alluded to about 450 times in the second century, though most of these come from the last third of the century. The most recent and detailed discussion of the reception of the Pastorals in the second century is by Carsten Looks (1999). Modern doubts about the Pauline authorship of the Pastorals were not shared by any early Christian author. Looks formulated a spectrum of six categories ranging from *sicher* ("certain") for parallels using quotation formulas with a named author or source, to *ausgeschlossen* ("excluded") when just one or two words are parallel that do not belong to the special vocabulary of the Pastorals. In the corpus of seven authors included in the Apostolic Fathers (*1–2 Clement*, Ignatius, Polycarp to the Philippians, the fragments of Papias, the *Epistle of Barnabas* and the *Shepherd of Hermas*), it is highly probable that *1 Clement* alludes to the Pastorals, which means that they were known in Rome at the end of the first century, cautiously concluding that they were composed ca. 80 CE (Looks 1999: 77–123, 215–16). Looks has identified six passages in *1 Clement* that are very possible to probable allusions (*gut möglich bis wahrscheinlich*), including *1 Clement*, 2:7 (2 Tim. 2:21; Titus 1:3), *1 Clement*, 45:7 (2 Tim. 1:3), *1 Clement*, 1:3 (Titus 2:4–5), *1 Clement*, 7:3 (1 Tim. 2:3), *1 Clement*, 62:1 (Titus 2:12), and *1 Clement*, 60:4–61:2 (1 Tim. 2:1–3). Let us look more closely at one of these passages:

| *1 Clement*, 45:7 | 2 Timothy 1:3 |
|---|---|
| "… those who minister to his name with a clear conscience [ἐν καθαρᾷ συνειδήσει λατρευόντων]." | "I thank God whom I serve with a clear conscience [λατρεύω … ἐν καθαρᾷ συνειδήσει], as did my fathers, when I remember you constantly in my prayers." |

The four Greek words in these two texts occur in tandem only in these two passages in early Christian literature. In Looks' judgment it is more probable that the Pastorals were known and used by Polycarp of Smyrna in his letter to the Philippians (Looks 1999: 153–87, 216–17). Out of a total of twenty-nine possible allusions investigated, Looks finds one that is very probable (*sehr wahrscheinlich*) and six that are very possible to probable (*gut möglich bis wahrscheinlich*). Here is the one double set of allusions that he regards as very probable (Looks 1999: 156–61):

| 1 Timothy 6:10a … 6:7a | Polycarp, *Philippians*, 4:1 |
|---|---|
| "For the love of money is the root of all evils … for we brought nothing into the world, and we cannot take anything out of the world." | "The love of money is the beginning of all difficulties. And so, since we know that [εἰδότες … ὅτι] we brought nothing into the world and can take nothing out of it … ." |

While this parallel has been discounted by Dibelius and Conzelmann (1972: 84–6) who argue that it is based on a common fund of moral exhortations of the time, the arguments for a literary dependence are strong, particularly since the phrase "knowing that" (εἰδότες ὅτι) is a "formulaic introduction" used to introduce traditional material used by Polycarp (Hartog 2002: 179). Berding (1999: 349–50) argues that clusters of allusions to 1 and 2 Timothy in *Philippians* occur after each of the three mentions of the name of Paul (3:2; 9:1; 11:3), suggesting that Polycarp assumed Paul to be their author (the allusion are listed in a chart in Berding 1999: 353–5 and in two graphs on 358). Nevertheless, it this is regarded as a likely allusion to the Pastorals, it would suggest that they antedated the composition of Polycarp's *Philippians*, perhaps written ca. 115 CE. Looks thinks that three passages in Justin Martyr and four in Theophilus of Antioch have "very probable" allusions to the Pastorals. According to Looks, Irenaeus is the earliest author to "certainly" allude to the Pastorals, which he does six times, while Tertullian does so four times (Looks 1999: 323–75).

## Historical Setting and Purpose

The problem of determining the historical setting and purpose or occasion of the Pastoral Letters is largely dependent on the issues of authenticity and date. One feature of the letters is the references to a series of beliefs and practices of which the author disapproves. The "heresy" reflected in the Pastorals has been given the generally broad label of "Jewish Christian Gnosis," a view accepted by many modern scholars (Schmithals 1984: 93–4). Jewish Christian features of the heresy are found in 1 Timothy 1:7 (they desire to be teachers of the law); Titus 1:10 (those belonging to the circumcision party are deceivers); Titus 1:14 (they give heed to Jewish myths); Titus 1:16 (they pretend to know God). On the other hand, passages that seem to reflect a form of Gnosticism proper include 1 Timothy 6:20–1 (Timothy is enjoined to avoid "what is falsely called knowledge); Titus 1:16 ("they profess to know God); 2 Timothy 2:18 (they hold that the resurrection is already past); 1 Timothy 1:4 (they are occupied with myths and genealogies that promote endless speculation; cf. 1 Timothy 4:7; 2 Timothy 4:4; Titus 1:14; 3:9); 1 Timothy 4:3 (they forbid marriage and enjoin abstinence from foods). While there are parallels to each of these "Jewish Christian" and "Gnostic" characteristics (Wolter 1988: 256–61), when all of these varied charges and features are combined they do not produce a consistent profile of any single group of opponents. The supposition that a single heretical group is the object of the polemic in the Pastorals therefore has no support in the letters themselves, but is the creation of those who are driven to read the Pastorals against a consistent historical background. In fact the various beliefs and practices against which the author rails are a pastiche of the author's inventory of beliefs and behaviors opposed in spirit to early Christianity. When viewed as a whole they are vague because the author intended them to be vague so that these classical heretical symptoms would have concrete applications in every time and place. The view that the author of the Pastorals was opposing Marcion, advocated by Harrison (1921), and more recently by Hoffmann (1984), particularly in view of the occurrence of the terms "knowledge" (γνῶσις) and "contradiction" (ἀντίθεσις), despite the fact that "knowledge" is a widely used term and "contradiction" or "antithesis" is a standard term in Greek logic and rhetoric (Gray 2007: 312–13). The views of Harrison and Hoffmann are further examples of supposing that even though the Pastorals are pseudepigraphal, they *must* have a historical setting consistent with the vague and general hints found in the letters. Unlike the historical Paul, the author of the Pastorals does not engage in a theological refutation of the heretics, but rather emphasizes moral behavior as the only real criterion to distinguish true from false belief.

The setting in which 2 Timothy was written has typically been extrapolated from 2 Timothy 4:1–8 (sometimes said to be based on Phil. 2:12–30), whether the setting is historical or fictional. Here the author begins with a final and solemn charge to Timothy, which many have construed as analogous to a final testament or farewell speech (Martin 1997; Marshall 1999: 797, who suggests that it also resembles other genres such as an "ordination charge"). At the conclusion of the passage, "Paul" speaks of himself as on the point of being poured out as a libation (a metaphor for death; cf. Marshall 1999: 805–6), concluding "I have fought the good fight. I have finished the race. I have kept the faith" (2 Tim. 4:7).

# Church Organization

One of the distinctive features of the Pastoral Letters is the fact that they reflect a higher development of local community offices than any other document or set of documents in the New Testament. Several different functions or offices of leadership are mentioned in the Pastoral Letters, though there is no explicit hierarchical relationship between them: (1) bishops (from the Greek term *episcopos*, "overseer, guardian"), (2) deacons (from the Greek word *diakonos*, "servant"), (3) widows (a translation of the Greek word *chēra*, "widow") and (4) elders (from the Greek word *presbyteros*, "elder," the etymological origin of the English word "priest" with similar forms in other Indo-European languages; e.g. French: *prêtre*, Spanish *preste*, German *Priester*, Norwegian *prest*). The requirements for church leaders in the Pastorals are exclusively spiritual and ethical; nothing is said about the actual day-to-day duties and responsibilities of bishops and deacons. Consequently we learn virtually nothing about the relationship between the spiritual leaders' designations in the Pastorals nor about their role in church life. In the late nineteenth and early twentieth centuries, the development of church offices was often conceptualized in terms of an antithesis between charismatics who are bearers of the Spirit (the charismatic and dynamic element) and in consequence lead local communities, over against the selection of office-holders who are bearers of the Spirit in consequence of their institutional role which begins with the laying on of hands, frequently labeled "early Catholicism" by German Protestant scholars.

The office of bishop is referred to twice in the Pastorals (1 Tim. 5:17–19; Titus 1:7–9), each time in the singular, in contrast to the single occurrence of the term in the plural in the authentic Pauline letters (Phil. 1:1) in the epistolary adscript "To all the saints in Christ Jesus who are at Philippi, with the bishops and deacons." Like the western Anatolian Christian communities addressed by Ignatius of Antioch in his letters (ca. 117 CE), each local church envisioned by the Pastorals apparently had single bishop. Titus 1:5–7 suggests that a "bishop" was equivalent to an "elder," perhaps in the sense that all bishops were elders, but not all elders were bishops (though this is speculation). In Acts (written ca. 90 CE, perhaps twenty or twenty-five years earlier than the Pastorals), elders and bishops also appear to be different designations for the same office (Acts 20:17, 28).

The role of deacon is mentioned twice in the Pastorals, in 1 Timothy 3:8–13 and 4:6. In the middle of the discussion of the ethical requirements of a deacon in 1 Timothy 3:8–13 we find this statement: "The women likewise must be serious, no slanderers, but temperate, faithful in all things." This suggests that there were women who functioned as deacons, a point made by this translation of 1 Timothy 3:11: "Women in this office must likewise be dignified, not scandalmongers, but sober, and trustworthy in every way." One of the requirements for a deacon is that he be married only once (1 Tim. 3:12).

Widows (1 Tim. 5:3–16; cf. Titus 2:3–5) are older women who do not remarry (1 Tim. 5:9b; the same requirement is made of bishops and deacons; see 1 Tim. 3:2, 12). Widows are "enrolled" (the Greek term is *katalegō*, "enlist, enroll," which indicates a formalized procedure) at age 60 and older and with no visible means of support (1 Tim. 5:9, 11). This may reflect an Order of Widows (see Ignatius, *Smyrnaeans*, 13:1; Polycarp,

*Philippians*, 4:3 for evidence for such an order in the early second century) whose ministry centered in intercessory prayer (1 Tim. 5:5) and perhaps other types of service.

The position of elder (the same term is also used for an elderly man, cf. 1 Tim. 5:1, and an office in the local church) is discussed briefly in 1 Timothy 5:17–19 and Titus 1:5–9. In the eastern Mediterranean region, it appears that the term "elder" was the basic designation for wise and experienced older men who were thought competent to provide leadership in Christian community. "Apostles and elders" are frequently referred to in Acts as the highest authorities in the church of Jerusalem (Acts 15:2, 4, 6, 22, 23; 16:4; cf. 21:18). In Titus 1:5, "Paul" advises Titus "to appoint elders in each town in accordance with the principles I have laid down." This text indicates that authorities outside the local church were responsible for appointing the primary local official who was regarded as the highest authority in each community. This coheres well with Acts 14:23, where we are told that "they [Paul and Barnabas"] ... appointed elders for them in every church." Since elders and bishops are virtually equivalent terms for the same role (Titus 1:5–7; Acts 20:17, 28), this suggests that individual bishops were apparently named by authorities external to the local church.

## Intertextuality

Each of the Pastorals has been seen in connection with one of the genuine Pauline letters (1 Timothy and 1 Corinthians; 2 Timothy and Philippians; Titus and Galatians). Titus 1:12 contains a quotation of an ethnic slur attributed by scholars to Epimenides of Crete (ca. 600 BCE): "Cretans are always liars, vicious brutes, lazy gluttons." This quotation is introduced with the phrase "one of their own prophets has said" and is followed by the evaluative judgment "this statement is true" (Titus 1:13). This constitutes the so-called "liar paradox" (a logical problem widely known – and derided as a waste of time – in antiquity) discussed in detail by Gray (2007: 303): "If the Cretans are always liars, and if the speaker – usually identified as Epimenides – is a Cretan, then he must be a liar. And if he is a liar, then his 'testimony' cannot be true." Gray argues that the author was fully aware of the paradox he was using, intending to poke fun at himself and at the same time castigate the local population (Gray 2007: 309). Just before the quotation from Epimenides, the author speaks of those who are "idle talkers and deceivers" maintaining that "they must be silenced" (Titus 1:10–11). Similarly, in 2 Timothy 2:14, the author enjoins: "warn them before God that they are to avoid wrangling over words, which does no good but only ruins those who are listening," and 1 Timothy 1:6 mentions those who have wandered off into useless discussions.

## Constituent Literary Forms

Among New Testament letters, the Pastorals make extensive use of various types of preformed traditions. Prominent among this preformed material are the various types of paraenetic lists or catalogues. These include virtue and vice lists and lists of qualifications for church leaders, such as bishops, elders, and deacons (1 Tim. 3:2–4, 8–10,

11–12; 4:12; 6:11, 18; 2 Tim. 2:22–5; 3:10; Titus 1:8; 2:2–10). Household rules, in which a social hierarchy is presumed, are found in 1 Timothy 2:1–15 and 6:1–2, and Titus 2:1–10, and are part of the conception of the church as the Household of God that pervades the Pastorals. The metaphor of the church as a household goes beyond the household rules appropriate for an extended family and includes church officials, such as bishops, deacons, and elders. The Pastorals also contains lists of social obligations for older men (Titus 2:2), older women (Titus 2:3–4); young men (Titus 2:6); young women (Titus 2:4–5), slaves (Titus 2:9–10), and widows (1 Tim. 5:9–14).

The phrase "faithful saying" (πιστὸς ὁ λόγος) occurs five times (1 Tim. 1:15; 3:1; 4:9; 2 Tim. 2:11; Titus 3:8; see Knight 1979), occurring in each of the three Pastoral Letters, but never in the undisputed letters of Paul (outside the Pastorals it occurs just three times: once in Dionysius of Halicarnassus and twice in Dio Chrysostom). Knight (1979: 99–102) refers to this formula as a "quotation-commendation formula," while Collins (2002: 42–3) calls it a "formula of endorsement" of traditional material when it *follows* its referent, though when it *precedes* its referent it is an "invitation to belief." Johnson (2001: 180) proposes that "it serves as a warrant or certification concerning another statement." The formula is sometimes problematic, since its reference is not always clear and occasionally seems to interrupt the flow of the argument (e.g., 1 Tim. 3:1; 4:9). The first occurrence of the formula is in 1 Timothy 1:15 with a clear reference: "The saying is sure and worthy of full acceptance, that Christ Jesus came into the world to save sinners – of whom I am foremost." The reference of the second saying, however, is problematic (1 Tim. 3:1): "The saying is sure: whoever aspires to the office of bishop desires a noble task" (R. A. Campbell: 1994: 74). The same uncertainty occurs with the occurrence of the formula in 1 Timothy 4:9: does it go with 1 Timothy 4:8 or 4:10 (some commentators have preferred the former and some the latter)? The situation is relatively certain in 2 Timothy 2:11, which is followed by a five-line saying (2 Tim. 2:11–13):

> This saying is sure:
> if we have died with him, we will also live with him;
> if we endure, we will also reign with him;
> if we deny him, he will also deny us;
> if we are faithless, he remains faithful –
> for he cannot deny himself.

This quasi-hymnic or creedal unit consists of six lines, five of which contain antithetical statements or distichs, while line 3 is an exception and lacks the antithetical pattern: "if we deny him, he will also deny us," which has the pattern of a pronouncement of sacral law (Aune 1983: 166–8) and has a close parallel in Q 12:9 (= Matt. 10:33): "But whoever denies me before others will be denied before the angels of God." R. A. Campbell (1994: 77–80) has provided a stylistic analysis of the faithful sayings in which he proposes a four-part structure that applies rather neatly to each of the says. I will reproduce only his four-part analysis of Titus 3:8 (R. A. Campbell 1994: 79):

A  Introductory formula:
   *The saying is sure:*

B  Parenthetical reinforcement:
   *I desire that you insist on these things,*

C   The saying:
*so that those who have come to believe in God may be careful to devote themselves to good works;*

D   Further qualification:
*these things are excellent and profitable for everyone.*

1 Timothy 3:16, with its introductory formula, rhythmical style, and unusual vocabulary, has often been thought to be a previously existing Christian hymn inserted by the author into its present epistolary setting (Stenger 1977). The six-line hymn with its introduction is quoted here with a brief statement of the probable meaning of each line in parentheses:

| | |
|---|---|
| Great indeed, we confess, is the mystery of our religion: | |
| He was manifested in the flesh, | (incarnation) |
| vindicated in the Spirit | (resurrection) |
| seen by messengers [ἀγγέλοις], | (apostles as witnesses to resurrection) |
| preached among the nations, | (gospel proclaimed to Gentiles) |
| believed on in the world, | (acceptance of the gospel) |
| taken up in glory. | (ascension of Christ) |

The hymn is introduced with a relative pronoun ("*who* was manifested in the flesh), just like two other early Christian hymns, Philippians 2:6–11 and Colossians 1:15–20. The text is extremely economical, consisting of just eighteen words. Each line begins with a verb in the aorist passive followed by a nominal construction in the dative (Collins 2002: 107). This hymn is frequently divided into two strophes of three lines each, with the first strophe referring to the earthly life of the incarnate Jesus and the second to the exalted Lord. Others divide the hymn into three strophes of two lines each, each strophe containing an alternation between heaven and earth. Ultimately no analysis has proven convincing (see Marshall 1999: 500–4). New Testament hymns, such as John 1:1–18, Philippians 2:6–11, and Colossians 1:15–20, often exhibit a descent/ascent pattern narrating the pre-incarnate, incarnate, and post-incarnate career of Jesus, which is approximately exhibited in 1 Timothy 3:16.

## Genre

Each of the Pastorals presents itself as a letter framed with the typical epistolary conventions used to open and close early Christian letters (see "Epistolary Analysis"), probably modeled on genuine Pauline letters which were in circulation when the Pastorals were written. However, since these letters are pseudepigraphal, they were never actually sent to the named recipients, but in all likelihood rather circulated, at least initially, as a small collection of Pauline letters. 1 Timothy and Titus have been compared to the manuals of church order that appeared from the second through the fourth centuries, including the *Didache* (early second century), the *Didascalia Apostolorum* (third century), and the *Apostolic Constitutions* (fourth century) (see Dibelius and Conzelmann 1972: 5–7). Johnson (2001: 139) and W. A. Richards (2002: 133–6) argue against this classification, but their arguments are not convincing. Since they do not appear to incorporate earlier sources with a church order character, these letters are part of the continued development of manuals of church order that had their beginnings in Paul and *1 Clement*. The official character of these letters is immediately indicated by the author's attribution of authority to Paul as "an apostle of Christ Jesus by the command of God our Savior and of Christ Jesus our hope" (1 Tim. 1:1, 2 Tim. 1:1 and Titus 1:1 contain similar titular variations).

2 Timothy, on the other hand, has the character of a testament or farewell speech (cf. 2 Tim. 4:1–8), and is at the same time a fictitious personal paraenetic letter. In all three letters, the named author, "Paul," of course, is not the real author, nor are the named recipients ("Timothy" and "Titus") the real addressees. "Paul" functions as a respected authority figure, while "Timothy" and "Titus" are paradigms of ideal Christian ministers and who appropriately mediate "Paul's" authority. Relatively loose functional parallels to the Pastoral Letters from the Greco-Roman world are the pseudepigraphic Stoic-Cynic letters purportedly written by such famous philosophers or sages as Anacharsis, Crates, Diogenes, Heraclitus, and Socrates to various fictional followers (Malherbe 1977). Just as the Pastorals are dependent on aspects of the Pauline tradition, so the Stoic-Cynic letters are dependent on the doxographical tradition associated with the sages to whom they are attributed. The closest parallel to the Pastorals in early Christian literature is the letter of Polycarp to the Philippians (in Polycarp, *Philippians*, 5–6, the author addresses injunctions to elders and deacons modeled on the household code).

1 Timothy and Titus are also fictitious official paraenetic letters that are intended for a wider Christian audience than the two individuals to whom they are purportedly addressed. 1 Timothy, as Johnson (2001: 137) observes, makes frequent reference to commands or instructions (1 Tim. 1:3, 5, 18; 4:11; 5:7; 6:13, 14, 17). These instructions are designed to regulate life and worship within the Christian community and involve such matters as aspects of prayer and worship (1 Tim. 2:1–7), the subordinate role of women and their role in worship (1 Tim. 2:8–15), qualifications for bishops and deacons (1 Tim. 3:1–13), the importance of caring for widows (1 Tim. 5:3–16), and appropriate attitudes for the wealthy (1 Tim. 6:17–19). These paraenetic sections are intercalated with advice for Timothy, the addressee of 1 Timothy. Since much of 1 Timothy and Titus consists of moral and behavioral exhortation, it is appropriate to categorize them in a general way as paraenetic letters (Fiore 1986: 3, 101–63). Pseudo-Libanius, *Epistolary Styles*, lists and discusses forty-one types of letter including paraenetic letters (5, 52):

> The paraenetic style is that in which we exhort someone by urging him to pursue some thing. Paraenesis is divided into two parts, encouragement and dissuasion. Some also call it the advisory style, but do so incorrectly, for paraenesis differs from advice. For paraenesis is hortatory speech that does not admit of a counter-statement, for example, if someone should say that we must honor the divine. For nobody contradicts this exhortation were he not mad to begin with.

Johnson (2001: 139–40) proposed that 1 Timothy and Titus exhibit similarities to the broad category of "royal correspondence." He argued that PTeb 703 (third century BCE), a self-described ὑπόμνημα ("memorandum"), is a good example of *mandata principiis* ("commands of a ruler") letters, "a well-attested letter form" that provides a very close generic parallel to 1 Timothy and Titus. Further he suggests that this generic identification is relevant, though not decisive, for arguing the authenticity of the Pastorals and "ought to shift the discussion concerning authenticity decisively" (Johnson 2001: 142). However, Mitchell (2002) has demonstrated that PTeb 703 is *not* a *mandata principiis* letter and its content is not that of *mandata principis*. She concludes that the inflated parallels between PTeb 703 and 1 Timothy contribute little to the issues of the genre and authenticity of 1 Timothy. Witherington (2006: 90–1) makes the same mistake as Johnson (whom he does not cite) in referring to a *mandatum principiis* as a letter, and even compounds the mistake by erroneously referring to PTeb 703 as a letter. This does not mean that 1 Timothy cannot share common features with *mandata principiis*, only that PTeb 703 is not a valid example of the genre.

## Epistolary Analysis

According to A. T. Hanson (1968: 42), "The Pastorals are made up of a miscellaneous collection of material. They have no unifying theme; there is no development of thought." This judgment finds some support in the fact that commentators on the Pastoral Letters rarely propose convincing analyses of these letters. Since the Pastorals are pseudepigraphal letters written ca. 100 CE, the genuine Pauline letters were probably already available in collections of various sizes and served as models for the epistolary features of the Pastorals.

### 1 Timothy

The opening epistolary formulas include an epistolary prescript that mentions Paul as the sender (1:1) and Timothy as the recipient (1:2a) and a salutation (1:2b): "Grace, mercy, and peace from God the Father and Christ Jesus our Lord." While the letter is addressed to "Timothy," the final grace benediction contains a second person plural noun indicating that the recipients are also communities. Unlike most Pauline letters, however, there is no thanksgiving period (as in Galatians) or blessing following (as in 2 Corinthians). The body of the letter (1:3–6:21a) consists of three elements: (1) The first part of Timothy's commission is given in 1:3–3:13. (2) There follows a core of prophetic and hymnic texts relating to the Christian community under the metaphor of the household of God (3:14–4:5), in which the apostolic *parousia* form (the anticipated arrival and present of Paul) in 3:14–16 is adopted in a new form, i.e., Paul is present in the manifold shapes of offices in the post-apostolic period. (3) The body (4:6–6:21a) consists of the second installment of Timothy's commission. Finally, the epistolary ending omits the customary primary and secondary greetings (Miller 1997: 1–2) and consists of an extremely short grace benediction (6:21b): "Grace be with you [ὑμῶν]."

## 2 Timothy

The opening epistolary formulas consist of a prescript with mention of Paul as the sender (1:1), an adscript directed to Timothy (1:2a), and a salutation (1:2b), followed by an unusually long thanksgiving period (1:3–14). The body of the letter is in the form of a testament (2:1–4:8), with similarities to Paul's farewell speech in Acts 20:17–35 and is sandwiched between a description of "Paul's" situation (1:15–18) and arrangements for his associates (4:9–18). The testamentary character of the body of the letter is particularly reflected in "Paul's" awareness of his imminent death (4:1–8). Finally, the concluding epistolary formulas include primary and secondary greetings (4:19–21) and a final grace benediction (4:22).

## Titus

The opening epistolary formulas (Titus 1:1–4) consists of the customary three-part prescript with an extremely long superscription identifying "Paul" in some detail (1:1–3). The recipient is Titus (1–4a), and the salutation is phrased in the common Pauline idiom: "Grace and peace from God the Father and Christ Jesus our Savior" (1:4b), differing slightly from the salutation in 1 Timothy 1:2b and 2 Timothy 1–2b. The body of the letter (1:5–3:11) contains two different types of material: (1) A series of orders to appoint elders and bishops in the towns of Crete, together with a specification of their moral and spiritual qualities (1:5–16). (2) Paraenesis for the entire Christian congregation (2:1–3:11). Finally, the epistolary ending consists of travel arrangements for Paul's associates (3:12–14), a short section containing secondary and primary greetings (3:15a), followed by a concluding grace benediction: "Grace be with you all" (3:15b).

# Rhetorical Analysis

Unlike much of the rest of the Pauline corpus, during the last thirty years the Pastorals have only rarely been subject to rhetorical analysis and the results have, for the most part, not been convincing. Occasionally, stalwarts have attempted to apply the three main ancient rhetorical genres (deliberative, juridical, and epideictic) to the Pastorals, but with little success. B. Campbell (1997), has attempted a rhetorical analysis of 1 Timothy 4, apparently on the assumption that it is a rhetorical unit that is equivalent to a speech (a doubtful assumption, even though scholars have occasionally attempted to provide rhetorical analyses of partial texts in the Pauline literature). Another analysis has been proposed by Harding (1998), who founders on the problem that the Pastorals are not speeches in a sense analogous to Paul's letter to the Galatians, which despite its epistolary form is an assembly of arguments focusing on one problem (must one become a Jew to be a Christian?).

C. J. Classen (1997), a classicist, has proposed a rhetorical reading of Titus that studiously avoids the major rhetorical genres used in antiquity (forensic, deliberative, epideictic), suggesting the following summary outline (Classen 1997: 444):

Salutatio (1:1–4)

Purpose of Titus' mission (1:5–6)
    with justification
    (necessary qualities of an ἐπίσκοπος) (1:7–9)
    with further justification
    (the necessity of these qualities) (1:10–13a)

General orders to Titus (1:13b–14)
    with justification (1:15–16)

Orders with regard to specific groups (2:1)
    to old men (2:2)
    to old women (2:3–4a)
    to young women (2:4b–5)
    to young men (2:6–8)
    to slaves (2:9–10)
    with general justification (2:11–14)

Summary (of 1:13–2:14) (2:15)

Orders with regard to specific aspects (3:1–2)
    with justification (3:3–7)

Summary (of 1:5–3:7) (3:8–11)

Personal instructions (3:12–14)
Greetings (3:15)

Classen defines rhetoric very simply as "the deliberate, calculated use of language for the purpose of communicating information" (Classen 1997: 428). His discussion and outline summary of the rhetoric of Titus resembles the traditional way that New Testament scholars have worked out content outlines of the Pauline letters. Precisely because he does not attempt to shoehorn Titus into a pre-existing rhetorical form, his analysis proves both successful and useful.

## Annotated Bibliography

Aune, David E. *Prophecy in Early Christianity and the Ancient Mediterranean World.* Grand Rapids: Eerdmans, 1983. A comprehensive study of early Christian prophecy and prophetic speech forms in the context of prophecy and oracles in the Old Testament, early Judaism, and the Greco-Roman world.

Bauckham, Richard. "Pseudo-Apostolic Letters," *Journal of Biblical Literature* 107 (1988), 469–94. The author identifies several characteristics of pseudepigraphal letters that apply most directly to 2 Peter and the Pastorals.

Bauer, Walter. *Orthodoxy and Heresy in Earliest Christianity.* Trans. and ed. Robert Kraft and Gerhard Krodel. Philadelphia: Fortress Press, 1971. A classic study emphasizing the early existence of what was later labeled heresy in many Mediterranean centers of early Christianity.

Berding, K. "Polycarp of Smyrna's View of the Authorship of 1 and 2 Timothy," *Vigiliae Christianae* 53 (1999), 349–60.

Brown, Raymond E. *An Introduction to the New Testament.* Anchor Bible Reference Library. New York: Doubleday, 1997. A balanced introduction to the books of the New Testament by one of the more prominent Roman Catholic biblical scholars; Brown died in 1998.

Brox, Norbert. *Die Pastoralbriefe.* 4th edn. Regensburger Neues Testament, 7.2. Regensburg: Putset, 1969. An important commentary on the Pastorals by a Roman Catholic scholar who regards them as pseudepigraphal.

Bush, Peter G. "A Note on the Structure of 1 Timothy," *New Testament Studies* 36 (1990), 152–6.

Campbell, Barth. "Rhetorical Design in 1 Timothy 4," *Bibliotheca Sacra* 154 (1997), 189–204. An attempt to analyze 1 Timothy 4 rhetorically.

Campbell, R. A. "Identifying the Faithful Sayings in the Pastoral Epistles," *Journal for the Study of the New Testament* 54 (1994), 73–86.

Campenhausen, Hans Freiherr von. "Polykarp von Smyrna und die Pastoralbriefe," Pp. 197–252 in *Aus der Frühzeit des Christentums: Studien zur Kirchengeschichte des ersten und zweiten Jarhunderts.* Tübingen: Mohr Siebeck, 1963. Von Campenhausen argues that Polycarp is the probable author of the Pastorals.

Classen, C. Joachim. "A Rhetorical Reading of the Epistle to Titus." Pp. 427–44 in *A Rhetorical Analysis of Scripture: Essays from the 1995 London Conference.* Edited by Stanley E. Porter and Thomas H. Olbricht. *Journal for the Study of the New Testament* Supplementary Series, 146. Sheffield: Sheffield Academic Press, 1997. An important rhetorical approach to Titus by a classical scholar who has specialized in Greco-Roman rhetoric.

Collins, Raymond F. *1 and 2 Timothy and Titus: A Commentary.* New Testament Library. Louisville and London: Westminster John Knox, 2002. An excellent commentary by an American Roman Catholic scholar who regards the Pastorals as pseudepigraphal.

Dibelius, Martin and Hans Conzelmann. *The Pastoral Epistles: A Commentary on the Pastoral Epistles.* Translated by Philip Buttolph and Adela Yarbro Collins. Philadelphia: Fortress Press, 1972.

Donelson, Lewis R. *Pseudepigraphy and Ethical Argument in the Pastoral Epistles.* Hermeneutische Untersuchungen zur Theologie, 22. Tübingen: Mohr Siebeck, 1986.

Fiore, Benjamin. *The Function of Personal Example in the Socratic and Pastoral Epistles.* Rome: Biblical Institute, 1986. The author proposes that the Pastorals arose in a school context, and that literary imitation produced pseudonymous literary production.

Gray, Patrick. "The Liar Paradox and the Epistle to Titus." *Catholic Biblical Quarterly* (2007), 302–14. Gray provides an excellent discussion of ancient evidence and modern discussions of the liar paradox, arguing that the author of Titus was aware of the logical mess created by the paradox in Titus 1:12–13, but intentionally used it.

Hanson, A. T. *Studies in the Pastoral Epistles.* London: SPCK, 1968.

Harding, Mark. *Tradition and Rhetoric in the Pastoral Epistles.* New York: Peter Lang, 1998.

Harding, Mark. *What Are They Saying about the Pastoral Epistles?* New York: Paulist Press, 2001. A competent introduction to current issues in the study of the Pastorals.

Harrison, P. N. *The Problem of the Pastoral Epistles.* Oxford: Oxford University Press, 1921. Classic study that argues on the basis of language and style that the Pastorals are pseudonymous compositions, written either from Rome or Ephesus.

Harrison, P. N. *Paulines and Pastorals.* London: Villiers Publications, 1964. The author's final views on the pseudonymous composition of the Pastorals, including a preference for Ephesus as the place from which they were written and the reign of Trajan or the early reign of Hadrian as the time of composition.

Hartog, Paul. *Polycarp and the New Testament.* Wissenschaftliche Untersuchungen zum Neuen Testament, 2.134. Tübingen: Mohr Siebeck, 2002. The author has convincingly analyzed Polycarp's quotations and allusions to the New Testament.

Heidebrecht, Douglas. "Reading 1 Timothy 2:9–15 in its Literary Context," *Direction* 33 (2004), 171–84.

Herzer, Jens. "Abschied vom Konsens? Die Pseudepigraphie der Pastoralbriefe als Herausforderung an die neutestamentliche Wissenschaft," *Theologische Literaturzeitung* 129 (2004), 1267–82.

Hoffmann, R. Joseph. *Marcion: On the Restitution of Christianity: An Essay on the Development of Radical Paulinist Theology in the Second Century.* Chico: Scholars Press, 1984.

Johnson, Luke Timothy. *Letters to Paul's Delegates: 1 Timothy, 2 Timothy, Titus.* Valley Forge: Trinity Press International, 1996. An excellent commentary on the Pastorals by a Roman Catholic scholar who regards them as authentic Pauline letters.

Johnson, Luke Timothy. *The First and Second Letters to Timothy.* Anchor Bible, 35A. New York: Doubleday, 2001. A more comprehensive and developed commentary than that written by the author in 1996.

Karris, Robert J. "The Background and Significance of the Polemic in the Pastoral Epistles," *Journal of Biblical Literature* 92 (1973), 549–64.

Kelly, J. N. D. *A Commentary on the Pastoral Epistles.* Black's New Testament Commentaries. London: Black, 1963. A competent commentary by an Anglican scholar who regards the Pastorals as authentically Pauline.

Klauck, Hans-Josef. *Ancient Letters and the New Testament: A Guide to Context and Exegesis.* Waco: Baylor University Press, 2006. Currently the most important guide to the form, genre, and structure of ancient epistolary literature and the use of this knowledge for the interpretation of New Testament epistolary literature.

Knight, George W. *The Faithful Sayings in the Pastoral Letters.* Grand Rapids: Baker, 1979.

Knight, George W. *The Pastoral Epistles: A Commentary on the Greek Text.* New International Greek Testament Commentary. Grand Rapids: Eerdmans; Carlisle: Paternoster, 1992.

Longenecker, Richard N. "Ancient Amanuenses and the Pauline Epistles." Pp. 281–97 in *New Dimensions in New Testament Study.* Edited by Richard N. Longenecker and Merrill C. Tenney. Grand Rapids: Zondervan, 1974. A study focusing on Paul's use of secretaries in the writing of his letters, opening the way to regarding them as genuine Pauline productions.

Looks, Carsten. *Das Anvertraute bewahren: Die Rezeption der Pastoralbriefe im 2. Jahrhundert.* Munich: Herbert Utz, 1999. An important monograph on the earliest evidence for the existence and use of the Pastorals in the second-century church.

MacDonald, Dennis R. *The Legend and the Apostle: The Battle for Paul in Story and Canon.* Philadelphia: Westminster, 1983. The author argues that the Pastorals were written to correct the image of Paul depicted in the oral legends behind the *Acts of Paul* (particularly the character of Thecla) and to repress the women who use these legends as justification for their own celibate ministry independent of male authority. The characteristics of the false teachers in the Pastorals, according to MacDonald, resemble those of Paul in the legends.

Malherbe, A. J. (ed.). *The Cynic Epistles.* SBL Sources for Biblical Study, 12. Missoula: Scholars Press, 1977. A collection of pseudepigraphal letters attributed to Cynic heroes of the past, with Greek texts and English translations.

Malherbe, A. J. "Paraenesis in the Epistle to Titus." Pp. 297–300 in *Early Christian Paraenesis in Context.* Edited by James Starr and Troels Engberg Petersen. Berlin and New York: Walter de Gruyter, 2002.

Marshall, I. H. in collaboration with Philip H. Towner. *The Pastoral Epistles*. International Critical Commentary. London and New York: T. & T. Clark International, 1999. An important Evangelical commentary on the Pastorals.

Martin, Seán Charles. *Pauli Testamentum: 2 Timothy and the Last Words of Moses*. Rome: Editrice Pontificia Università Gregoriana, 1997. A study of the testamentary form of 2 Timothy.

Metzger, Wolfgang. *Der Christushymnus 1. Timotheus 3, 16: Fragmente eine Homologie der paulinischen Gemeinden*. Stuttgart: Calwer Verlag, 1979.

Miller, James D. *The Pastoral Letters as Composite Documents*. SNTS Monograph Series, 93. Cambridge: Cambridge University Press, 1997. The author argues that single-author theories, whether Pauline authorship or pseudonymous authorship, do not adequately explain the Pastorals, which he thinks are composite documents assembled by an editor from genuine notes of Paul to his co-workers. The Pastorals contain an amazing number of diverse literary forms and preformed elements, all loosely arranged. The authentic core (or single plausible note) of 1 Timothy consists of 1:1–7, 18–20; 3:14–15; 6:20–1.

Mitchell, M. "PTeb 703 and the Genre of 1 Timothy: The Curious Career of a Ptolemaic Papyrus in Pauline Scholarship." *Novum Testamentum* 44 (2002), 344–70. Mitchell calls attention to the flaws in arguments that PTeb 703 is not in fact an example of the genre *mandata principiis* ("commandments of a ruler"), so that arguments that 1 Timothy is *mandatum principiis* on the basis of PTeb 703 are invalid.

Moule, C. F. D. *The Birth of the New Testament*. New York and Evanston: Harper & Row, 1962. A creative introduction to New Testament origins by an Anglican New Testament scholar. He argues briefly for the Lukan authorship of the Pastorals, inspiring Wilson (1979) to argue the position in detail.

Prior, Michael. *Paul the Letter-Writer and the Second Letter to Timothy. Journal for the Study of the New Testament* Supplementary Series, 23. Sheffield: JSOT Press, 1989. Prior discusses in detail the three options for authorship: authenticity, pseudonymity, and the fragment hypothesis, concluding that the last two options are ultimately untenable. With regard to 2 Timothy itself, the author argues that it was written from Rome during Paul's imprisonment there. He argues that the paraenetic character of 2 Timothy is focused on Timothy himself, who needs to overcome his reluctance and undergo his share of suffering by coming to aid Paul and his mission.

Quinn, Jerome D. *The Letter to Titus: A New Translation with Notes and Commentary and an Introduction to Titus*. Anchor Bible, 35. New York: Doubleday, 1990.

Quinn, Jerome D. and William C. Wacker. *The First and Second Letters to Timothy*. Eerdmans Critical Commentary. Grand Rapids: Eerdmans, 2000. This is an important, detailed study of 1 and 2 Timothy, produced by Wacker after the death of Monsignor Quinn in 1988. The commentary itself, in part because of its posthumous character, focuses on lexical and source-critical issues and therein lies its chief value. Quinn regards the Pastorals as deutero-Pauline, arguing that the author of Luke–Acts wrote them in the mid-80s as an epistolary appendix of Luke–Acts, bringing the narrative up to Paul's death. Nevertheless he is eager to defend the traditional and authentically Pauline character of the doctrinal material in the letters.

Reuter, Rainer. *Synopse zu den Briefen des Neuen Testaments/Synopsis of the New Testament Letters*, vol. 2: *Die Pastoralbriefe/The Pastoral Letters*. Arbeiten zur Geschichte des antiken Judentums und des Urchristientum, 6. Frankfurt: Lang, 1998. A thorough examination of all the parallels between the Pastoral Letters and the other letters of the Pauline corpus, whether authentic or pseudonymous. A useful tool for comparing the Pastorals with the genuine Pauline letters.

Richards, E. R. *The Secretary in the Letters of Paul*. Wissenschaftliche Untersuchungen zum Neuen Testament, 42. Tübingen: Mohr Siebeck, 1992. The author surveys classical literature to discover how ancient letter-writers used secretaries.

Richards, E. R. *Paul and First Century Letter-Writing: Secretaries, Composition and Collection*. Downers Grove: InterVarsity, 2004. A popular version of Richards' 1992 dissertation.

Richards, William A. *Difference and Distance in Post-Pauline Christianity: An Epistolary Analysis of the Pastorals*. New York: Peter Lang, 2002.

Roloff, Jürgen. *Der Erste Brief an Timotheus*. Evangelisch-katholischer Kommentar zum Neuen Testament, 15 Zurich: Benziger; Neukirchen-Vluyn: Neukircher Verlag, 1988.

Schmithals, Walter. *Neues Testament und Gnosis*. Darmstadt: Wissenschaftliche Buchgesellschaft, 1984.

Schröter, Jens. "Kirche im Anschluss an Paulus: Aspekte der Paulusrezeption in der Apostelgeschichte und in den Pastoralbriefen," *Zeitschrift für die neutestamentliche Wissenschaft und die Kunde der alteren Kirche* 98 (2007), 77–104.

Smith, Craig A. "A Study of 2 Timothy 4:1–8: The Contribution of Epistolary Analysis and Rhetorical Criticism," *Tyndale Bulletin* 57 (2006), 151–4.

Stenger, Werner. *Der Christushymnus 1 Tim 3,16: eine strukturanalytische Untersuchung*. Frankfurt am Main: P. Lang, 1977.

Towner, Philip H. *The Goal of Our Instruction: The Structure of Theology and Ethics in the Pastoral Epistles. Journal for the Study of the New Testament Supplementary Series, 34*. Sheffield: Sheffield Academic Press, 1989.

Verner, D. C. *The Household of God: The Social World of the Pastoral Epistles*. Society of Biblical Literature Dissertation Series, 71. Chico: Scholars Press, 1983. The author argues that the Pastorals present the church as the household of God, since the author assumes that the household is the basic unit of the church and the church is a social structure modeled on the household.

Wilson, Stephen G. *Luke and the Pastoral Epistles*. London: SPCK, 1979. The author argues in a careful way that Luke is the author of the Pastorals.

Witherington, Ben. *Letters and Homilies for Hellenized Christians*, vol. 1: *A Socio-Rhetorical Commentary on Titus, 1–2 Timothy and 1–2–3 John*. Downers Grove: InterVarsity Press, 2006. A good commentary by a prolific Evangelical scholar who regards the Pastorals as authentically Pauline.

Wolter, Michael. *Die Pastoralbriefe als Paulustradition*. Forschungen zur Religion und Literatur des Alten und Neuen Testaments, 146. Göttingen: Vandenhoeck & Ruprecht, 1988. For Wolter the Pastorals are pseudepigraphical, and the figure of Paul is presented as the exemplar of all those who come to faith and functions further as "the guarantor of salvation" as well as the norm for its preaching and witness. The major danger addressed by the author of the corpus is that of deserting Paul.

# CHAPTER 33
# The Letter of James

## Paul A. Holloway

### Major Issues and Directions in Recent Study

The past two decades have seen a number of important studies on the letter of James. The perennial issues of authorship and the letter's *prima facie* critique of Paul continue to be discussed with insight (Johnson 1995; Hengel 1988; Bauckham 1999). Fresh work has also been done of the letter's relationship to the Q tradition of the sayings of Jesus (Hartin 1991), and there have been several significant thematic studies: personal speech-ethics (Baker 1995), poverty (Maynard-Reid 1987), and eschatology (Penner 1996). The study of James has also benefited from recent efforts to recover the historical James of Jerusalem and the early traditions associated with him (Pratscher 1987; Painter 1999). Studies emphasizing the diversity within early Christianity have given attention to James as a valuable witness to non-Pauline forms of Christianity (Dunn 1990), and the striking presence of Hellenistic philosophical terms in James has now been expertly discussed (Jackson-McCabe 2001). The theology of James, long ignored, is beginning to be fruitfully studied (Konradt 1999). We will return to some of these issues below. Here we will touch briefly on the traditional issues of authorship and the letter's critique of Paul.

The consensus view that James represents a markedly Hellenized form of Jewish Christianity and is therefore late and pseudepigraphal (Brown 1997; Schnelle 1998; Koester 2000) has recently been challenged on the grounds that Hellenism was already present in Jerusalem in the lifetime of James (Hengel 1988; Johnson 1995; Bauckham 1999). It is of course true that, within limits, Jerusalem was a Hellenistic city in the first century. But it does not follow that the historical James, a Jewish artisan from Nazareth turned leader of the Jerusalem church, was sufficiently Hellenized to write the letter attributed to him. Indeed, on balance one would have to judge that whatever James' native abilities (and they must have been considerable) this remains rather unlikely. It is also unlikely that James of Jerusalem, whose concern that Jewish Christians outside Jerusalem continue to observe Jewish food laws is well documented (Gal. 2:12; cf. Acts 15:20, 29), would have written a letter to just these people urging continued legal observance but omitting any reference to this important point of law. If James 5:7–11 witnesses to a delay of the *parousia* ([second ]"coming [of Christ]"), this too points to a late date for the letter. It also remains a problem that the letter of James was not accorded canonical status until very late, a surprising fact if it did indeed issue from the brother of Jesus. Martin (1988) has proposed that, while the letter of James itself is late and pseudepigraphal, certain traditional elements in the letter go back to James of Jerusalem. This is a reasonable but by no means necessary compromise.

Johnson (1995) has argued that James 2:14–26 was not written in response to Paul's doctrine of justification by faith apart from works of the law, (1) because unlike Paul the author of James never connects works (ἔργα) and law (νόμος), but always conceives works in the general moral sense of deed or effort, and (2) because the initially striking verbal and thematic similarities between Paul and the author of James can be explained by the fact that both were moralists within the same messianic movement. Given the recent work on Paul and the law it is important to revisit traditional assessments of Paul and James, but there are problems with Johnson's analysis (Jackson-McCabe 2001). Regarding Johnson's first objection, it is simply not the case that the author of James never connects works and the law. In 1:25, for example, the one who attends carefully to "the perfect law [νόμος] of freedom" becomes the "doer of a work [ἔργου]." Similarly, the multiple references to "works" (ἔργα) in 2:14–26 are obviously to be interpreted in the context of 2:1–13, where the law, variously described as "the royal law [νόμος]" and "the law [νόμος] of freedom," is in view.

Johnson's second claim that the similarities between the letter of James and Paul do not indicate direct knowledge but merely a common paraenetic tradition is equally problematic. Paul's treatment of justification by faith, and in particular of the Abraham story, is idiosyncratic, and it is precisely this doctrine with its attendant reading of the Abraham story that James rejects. James 2:14–26 is almost certainly a response to Paul (Hengel 1988). It is even likely that the author of James had access to some of Paul's letters (Lüdemann 1989; Tsuji 1997). The objection that James could not be responding to Paul because he misunderstands Paul's position on the law is a *non sequitur*, since scholars still wrestle with Paul's meaning. Indeed, Paul himself complains of being misrepresented on precisely this issue in Romans 3:8. Johnson's desire to rehabilitate the letter of James is commendable, but in the current academic climate the letter's disagreement with Paul is hardly a liability.

## Date and Place of Composition

The questions of when and where the letter of James was written are linked to the question of authorship. The letter claims to be written by "James the slave of God and of the Lord Jesus Christ," which virtually all scholars interpret to be a reference to James of Jerusalem the brother of Jesus. If James was the actual author, then the letter was written from Jerusalem sometime prior to James' execution by Annas the Younger around 62 CE (Josephus, *Jewish Antiquities*, 20.199–203). If, on the other hand, the letter is pseudepigraphal, as it most likely is, then the questions of date and place of composition cannot be determined with any degree of probability, though a Diaspora origin would be indicated on the assumption that a pseudepigraphal letter originates from its purported place of destination. A variety of specific locales within the

572     PAUL A. HOLLOWAY

Mediterranean Diaspora have been suggested. Scholars who see a connection between James and Hermas incline toward Rome as a possible point of origin (Laws 1980). Those who follow Streeter in assigning the synoptic source M (special M[atthew]; see Chapter 15, "The Synoptic Problem," in this volume) to traditions emanating from James incline toward Antioch (Martin 1988; Painter 1999). Egypt, or more specifically Alexandria, has also been reasonably suggested (Paulsen 1987; Schnider 1987). Many scholars think that it is not possible to determine the letter's provenance.

## Historical Setting

James is addressed to "the twelve tribes in the Diaspora" (1:1), which in the larger context of the letter may reasonably be taken to mean Jewish Christians outside Palestine. These readers are assumed to hold regular meetings open to outsiders (2:2) and to have official leaders or "elders of the church" who may be called upon in time of personal crisis (5:14). Also present among the readers are "teachers" (3:1; Zimmermann 1988), in the ranks of whom the author places the letter's fictive writer and perhaps himself (note the use of the first person plural "we" in 3:1).

References to wealth and status characterize much of the letter, which unambiguously sides with the poor and humble against the rich and powerful. We will return to this theme below when we discuss the purpose of James, but for now it should be noted that this emphasis almost certainly reflects actual historical exigencies. Proponents of an early dating of the letter see a reference to the oppression of poor Jewish Christians by the Sadducean oligarchy (Riesner 1998). Schnelle (1998), who dates the letter late, has suggested that these concerns answer to second-generation conditions in which more and more wealthy people are joining the Christian movement (Frankemölle 1994; Popkes 2001; cf. Lampe 1993). Whatever the case, it is clear that the author of James believes his readers to be facing the allurements of wealth and status.

The author's Torah piety is well known. Unlike Paul, and probably in conscious opposition to him, he regards the Jewish law as perfect and liberating (1:25; 2:12; contrast Gal. 5:1), and he enjoins its careful study and observance. However, as we have already noted, he remains strangely silent about the cultic elements of the law such as circumcision and food laws, suggesting a more or less Hellenized form of Jewish Christianity. This is further supported by the letter's effective use of Hellenistic philosophical terms and categories (1:21; 3:6; Jackson-McCabe 2001), along with various rhetorical techniques associated with the schools (e.g., the diatribe). The letter also reveals a passing knowledge of magic (2:19; 4:7) and astronomy (1:17; Laws 1980). The overall cosmopolitanism of James strongly suggests a Diaspora urban setting.

## Purpose

Two groups dominate the rhetoric of James: the poor and the rich. The poor are variously characterized as "the humble brother" (1:9), "orphans and widows in their distress" (1:27), "a poor person in dirty clothes" (2:2), "a brother or sister [who] is naked and lacks daily food" (2:15), the defrauded "laborer" or "harvester" (5:4), or simply "any among you suffering" (5:13). The rich by contrast are those "with gold rings and in fine clothes" (2:2), those "who oppress you ... drag you into court ... blaspheme the excellent name" (2:6–7), those "who [arrogantly] say, 'Today or tomorrow we will go to such and such a place and spend a year there, doing business and making money'" (4:13), those who "have kept back the wages" of the laborer and the harvester (5:4), those who "have condemned and murdered the righteous person, who does not resist" (5:6).

To be sure, "poor" and "rich" in James represent two different economic classes, but they also represent dichotomous ways of life that lead to two very different outcomes in the eschatological justice of God (Maynard-Reid 1987). God has "chosen the poor in the world to be rich in faith and heirs of the kingdom which he has promised to those who love him" (2:5). The rich, on the other hand, can only "weep and wail for the miseries that are coming" (5:1; cf. 1:10–11). They "have laid up treasure in the last days" (5:3), and in so doing they foolishly "have fattened [themselves] in a day of slaughter" (5:5).

The author of James unambiguously envisages his readers to be from the ranks of the poor. He writes to encourage and comfort them with promises of final vindication and reward (Verseput 1998). He is especially concerned to steer them away from the ways of the rich, whom he consistently portrays as outside the community of faith (see especially 2:1–13: "who oppress *you* ... drag *you* into court"). The rich exemplify friendship with the world and enmity with God (4:4); they are presumptuous, avaricious, and oppressive (4:13–5:6); they live by an earthy wisdom that is demonic and contentious (3:14–16). To follow their ways leads one down the path of double-mindedness (4:8; cf. 1:8) and desire (1:13–15; cf. 4:1–5; 5:5), and eventually to the sins of partiality (2:1–13), indifference (2:14–17), strife (3:14–16), and violence (4:1–2; 5:6).

In contrast to the ways of the rich, the author of James idealizes the ways of the poor as the life of simple faith and unwavering obedience to Torah. In Torah one finds one's true self (1:21, 23), and to faithfully follow its precepts no matter how inconvenient leads to wholeness and life (1:21, 25; 2:22–3), and in the end eternal reward (1:12, 21; 2:5). Those who live according to Torah do not need to seek personal wealth, since they will be exalted by God (1:9; 4:10). For the present they are sustained by prayer (1:5; 5:13; cf. 4:3) and by the fellowship of a Torah-observant community (5:14–20), while they await the imminent return of messiah (5:7–11).

One pitfall the author is especially keen for his readers to avoid is *hearing* Torah but not *doing* it (1:22; 4:11), for it is only in doing Torah that one is blessed (1:25). This brings him into explicit conflict with the Pauline doctrine of justification by faith (Hengel 1988; Tsuji 1997), since in his view to seek justification "by faith *only*" (ἐκ πίστεως μόνον; 2:24) is tantamount to being "a hearer *only*" (μόνον ἀκροαταί; 1:22) and not a doer of Torah. It has often been argued, of course, that the author of James has failed to grasp the moral dimension of Paul's teaching. But this argument misses the mark, since strictly speaking Paul's moral instruction flows not from justification by faith but from the believer's mystical participation in Christ (Sanders 1977). Perhaps Paul himself found little ethical inducement in his doctrine. At any rate, James self-consciously rejects Paul's teaching on justification as leading to inaction and indifference, two characteristic sins of the rich (2:14–26).

## Language and Style

The language and style of James bear directly upon the question of authorship and have been repeatedly analyzed (Mayor 1897; Ropes 1916; Schlatter 1932; Turner 1976; Baasland 1988). There is little debate on the correctness and relatively high quality of James' prose. The question is only whether a Jewish artisan from Nazareth, even after serving for a number of years as the head of a messianic sect in Jerusalem, could have produced such a letter.

James is written in simple but good Hellenistic prose. Its generally paratactic style, not uncommon in paraenetic materials, avoids lengthy periods and is frequently asyndetic, often to good effect (e.g., 1:27; 2:13; 4:2; 5:6). Mayor counts 140 sentences without a subordinate verb, forty-two with a single subordinate verb, and only seven with two or more subordinate verbs. Schlatter reckons that seventy-nine of James' sentences begin without a conjunction. Such *brevitas* accords nicely with James' injunction to "bridle the tongue" (3:1–12; cf. 1:26; Johnson 1995).

Brevity notwithstanding, James is rich in figures of speech, including an occasional rhetorical flourish, such as pleonasm (δαμάζεται ... δεδαμάσται; 3:7) and rhyming (ἀνεμιζομένῳ καὶ ῥιπιζομένῳ; 1:6; cf. 1:14; 2:12 and 4:8). Other figures include: *anadiplosis* (e.g., βραδύς ... βραδύς, 1:19; οὕτως ... οὕτως, 2:12; ἐν αὐτῇ ... ἐν αὐτῇ, 3:9; πόθεν ... πόθεν, 4:1; ἄγε νῦν οἱ ... ἄγε νῦν οἱ, 4:13; 5:1), alliteration (initial π 1:2, 3, 11, 17, 22; 3:2; initial δ: 1:1, 6, 21; 2:16; 3:8; κ: 2:3; 4:8; initial λ: 1:4; initial μ: 3:5), *polyptoton* (e.g., πειραζόμενος ... πειράζομαι ... ἀπείραστος ... πειράζει ... πειράζεται; 1:13–14), *paronomasia* (χαίρειν ... χαράν, 1:1–2; ἔργων ... ἀργή, 2:20; ἀδιάκριτος ἀνυπόκριτος, 3:17; φαινομένη ... ἀφαινιζομένη, 4:14), *parechesis* (ἀπελήλυθεν ... ἀπελόθετο; 1:24), and *inclusio* (τί τὸ ὄφελος; 2:14 and 16; cf. 1:2 and 12). The abundance of these figures makes it extremely unlikely that James owes its Greek to a secretary.

Figures of thought are equally abundant and include: irony (1:10), paradox (1:2, 15; 2:5; 3:9–12; 4:10), simile (1:6, 10, 23–4), metaphor (3:6; 4:14), personification (1:14–15; 2:13; 5:4), antithesis (1:20, 22; 4:4), rhetorical question (2:2–7, 14–16, 20–1, 25; 3:11–12; 4:1, 4–5, 12), hyperbole (3:6–8), *synkrisis* (3:15–17), and *exemplum* (2:21–3, 25; 5:10, 11, 17–18). The use of *gradatio* in 1:3–4 (δοκίμιον → ὑπομονή → ἔργον τέλειον) and 1:14–15 (ἐπιθυμίας → ἁμαρτία → θάνατος) is particularly fine. A line of hexameter is quoted in 1:17 (Ropes 1916). It may seem strange in light of the above observations that James contains numerous instances of hiatus (Turner 1976), a flaw to be sure, but one suspects that the author simply did not aspire to this level of style. Ironically, the presence of hiatus argues strongly against the use of a professional secretary, who would have almost certainly corrected this infelicity, and thus for the author's own inherent linguistic competence as reflected in the overall quality of the letter.

The vocabulary of James is rich and at times elevated, but in general reflects the language of the Septuagint (LXX), which is explicitly quoted in 2:8–11, 23, and 4:6. Only thirteen terms in James are not also found in the LXX (Agourides 1963). And several terms cannot be understood without reference to the LXX (Johnson 1995):

προσωπολημψία ("partiality"; 2:1) and προσωπολημπτεῖν ("to show partiality"; 2:9) derives from πρόσωπον λαβεῖν the LXX's translation of the Hebrew phrase נשא פנים, *nasha panim* ("to receive the face").

## Intertextuality

While it is not always possible to show direct literary dependence, the author of James makes extensive use of traditional Jewish and Christian materials. He is perhaps most obviously influenced by the Jesus tradition as represented in the synoptic sayings source Q. It is not clear whether he used some form of the document itself (Hartin 1991) or drew directly from the oral tradition of the sayings of Jesus, or both. (See Penner 1996 for a helpful synopsis of the parallels.) Whatever the case may have been, Bauckham (1999) has shown that the author of James creatively reworks this material so as to effectively make it his own, a technique characteristic of Hellenistic gnomic wisdom (cf. Seneca's reuse of Epicurean maxims in his *Moral Epistles*). Examples include: 1:5 (Matt. 7:7), 1:6 (Matt. 21:21), 2:5 (Luke 6:20), 2:13 (Matt. 5:7), 3:18 (Matt. 5:9), 4:8 (Matt. 5:8), and 5:12 (Matt. 5:34).

The author of James also draws extensively on the Jewish scriptures. His numerous references to "law" (1:25; 2:8, 9, 10, 11, 12; 4:11 [four times]; cf. 4:12 "law giver") are of course references to Torah, which he explicitly quotes at 2:8 (Lev. 19:18), 2:11 (Exod. 20:13, 15), and 2:23 (Gen. 15:6). He also quotes or makes clear verbal allusion to Proverbs 3:34 (in 4:6), 1:12 (5:20), Isaiah 5:9 (5:4), and Jeremiah 12:3 (5:5), and cites the examples of Abraham (2:21–3), Rahab (2:25), the prophets (5:10), Job (5:11), and Elijah (5:17–18). The influence of Ben Sira can be seen at 1:19 (Sir. 5:11) and 3:13 (Sir. 3:17), while an otherwise unknown "scripture" (γραφή) is quoted at 4:5. A number of striking parallels also exist between James and the *Testaments of the Twelve Patriarchs* (Mayor 1897) and 4Q185 (Verseput 1998). The line of hexameter at 1:17 may come from a Jewish oracle.

We have already indicated that author of James had likely read one or more of Paul's letters, especially Romans. The author of James also draws freely on the early Christian hortatory tradition. Here he stands closest to the author of 1 Peter: 1:2 (cf. 1 Pet. 1:6–7); 1:21 (1 Pet. 2:1–2); 4:7 (1 Pet. 5:8); 4:10 (1 Pet. 5:6); 5:9 (1 Pet. 5:10). The claim that friendship with the world is enmity with God finds a parallel in the Johannine writings (John 15:15–18), as does the contrast between loving in word but not in deed (1 John 3:17), and between that which comes from above and from below (John 3:31). Traditional themes such as the righteous sufferer (Painter 1999) and the two ways (Johnson 1995) are also present.

## Literary Genre

The literary genre of James may be discussed independently of its authenticity. James presents itself as a letter sent "to the Twelve Tribes in the Diaspora" (1:1). Whether or not this is a literary fiction (and there is good reason to think that it is), James is thus in form at least a Diaspora letter, that is, a letter from a central religious authority in

Jerusalem addressed to religious adherents elsewhere in the ancient Mediterranean and Near Eastern world. There are a number of examples of this type of letter (Taatz 1991; Tsuji 1997; Niebuhr 1998). Typically, however, letters of this sort were addressed to a specific community regarding a specific problem (e.g., Jer. 29:1–23; *Letter of Jeremiah* (= Baruch 6:1–73); 2 Macc. 1:1–9; 1:10–2:18; *Elephantine Papyri*, 30–2; Cowley 1923). James should therefore be further differentiated as a general encyclical (Strecker 1992; compare *2 Baruch*, 78:1–87:1).

To say that James is an encyclical Diaspora letter, however, does not adequately describe its genre. The book of Revelation, for example, is similarly presented as an encyclical letter (Rev. 1:4, 11), but on the basis of its overall content and structure it is obviously also an apocalypse. On the basis of its overall content and structure James may also be described as wisdom paraenesis – "wisdom" insofar as it draws upon Jewish wisdom traditions, "paraenesis" insofar as it presents those traditions in Hellenistic form. Similar Hellenistic wisdom texts include: the Wisdom of Ben Sira, the *Sentences of Pseudo-Phocylides*, and 4Q185 (Verseput 1998).

James' wisdom is typical for the period in that it draws on both legal and eschatological traditions (Penner 1996; Bauckham 1999). The appropriation of legal material by wisdom is documented as early as Ben Sira (e.g., Sir. 24). An eschatological horizon is found by the turn of the era (Collins 1997; e.g., Wisdom of Solomon; 4Q185). It should also be mentioned that while the wisdom of James may seek to preserve a particular interpretation of Christianity, it is does not represent an uncritical conservatism, since on a number of points it challenges traditional assumptions (such as wealth being the reward for righteousness; Maynard-Reid 1987). The wisdom of James is rightly called apocalyptic in that it presupposes the Great Reversal in which the first in this world (the rich) will be destroyed and the last (the poor) will be exalted.

## Constituent Literary Forms

James contains a variety of constituent literary forms. These have been helpfully discussed by Bauckham (1999), whose analysis is here summarized. The most characteristic literary form in James is the aphorism, the short, self-contained wisdom sentence, which itself takes a variety of forms. The following forms are found in James: macarisms or beatitudes ("Blessed is ..." 1:12, 25; 5:11), "whoever" sayings (2:10, 4:4, 1; 5:20), conditional sayings ("If anyone ..." 1:5, 26; 3:2), antitheses or paradoxes (1:9–10a; 2:5, 18b; 3:7–8a, 15; 4:10), wisdom admonitions (in the imperative mood: 1:19b; 4:8; 5:9a, 12, 16a), wisdom sentences (in the indicative mood: 1:3–4, 15, 20; 2:5, 26; 3:12b, 16; 4:4), and statements of reciprocity (2:13a; 3:6c, 18).

James also contains a number of similitudes or parables. Some of these are short comparisons that could easily be classified as aphorisms. For example: "Just as the body without the spirit is dead, so faith without works is dead" (2:26). Similarly: "The one who doubts is like [ἔοικεν] a wave of the sea driven by the wind and tossed about" (1:6). Others are elaborated with a short narrative: "If anyone is a hearer of the word and not a doer, he is like [ἔοικεν] a man observing his natural face in a mirror. For he observes himself, goes out, and immediately forgets what he looks like" (1:23–34; cf. 1:10b–11).

James 5:1–6 is in the form of a prophetic judgment oracle: "Come now you who are rich; weep and wail for the humiliations that are coming upon you. ... Your gold and your silver are dissolved and their rust will be a witness against you and will devour your flesh" (cf. 1:9–11). A similar oracle – strictly speaking an indictment oracle versus a judgment oracle because it lacks a promise of judgment – is found 4:13–17: "Come now you who say 'Today or tomorrow we will go into such and such city ... and make a profit.' ... Instead, you should say, 'If the Lord wills ...'." The presence of such prophetic forms is indicative of James' eschatological wisdom.

James has often been noted for its use of the diatribe style, which attempts to simulate informal moral instruction in the philosophical schools (Stowers 1981). The diatribe is a conversational style and as such employs a number of subordinate forms and rhetorical devices. At the center of the diatribe is an exchange with an imaginary interlocutor, who poses problems to the teacher, who in turn summarily refutes him. James 2:18–23 is just such an exchange. The interlocutor is introduced in 18a: "But someone will say. ..." The sense of what follows in verses 18b–19 is difficult, and scholars debate when the author starts his response. But the author is clearly speaking in 2:20: "But do you [sing.] not want to know, O empty man, that. ..." The second person plural appears again in 2:24, by which point the dialogue with the interlocutor is over. All of 2:1–26, with its short sentences, rhetorical questions, proof-texting of scripture, illustrative analogies, and exempla, may be classified as diatribal. Elements characteristic of the diatribe style, but not unique to it, occur by themselves elsewhere in James: the second person singular (4:11b–12), rhetorical questions (3:11–12; 4:4–5), questions asked and answered by the author (5:13–14), and maxims and quotations (4:5–6). The topic of moral inconsistency (3:13–14; cf. 3:11–12; 4:4, 12) is also characteristic of the diatribe.

## Epistolary Analysis

The only undisputed epistolary element in James is the prescript: "James, a slave of God and of the Lord Jesus Christ, to the twelve tribes in the Diaspora: Greetings" (1:1). It is perhaps indicative of the letter's Hellenistic flavor that whereas Paul follows a Jewish salutation (e.g., "Grace and peace to you") in all his letters James employs the secular "Greetings" (χαίρειν). A fuller epistolary analysis of James has been attempted by Francis (1970), but few have followed him. Recently, Thurén has argued that the letter contains several epistolary formulas or clichés (e.g., 5:12: πρὸ πάντων), but none of these is unambiguous.

## Rhetorical Analysis

Any discussion of the rhetoric of James must begin with Dibelius' classic Meyer commentary (1988; originally published in 1921) Dibelius classified James as early Christian paraenesis, by which he meant a collection of loosely connected ethical admonitions brought together primarily by means of "catchwords" (Stichwörter). Dibelius allowed that the core of the James consisted of three diatribal "treatises" (Abhandlungen; 2:1–13;

2:14–26; and 3:1–12); but beyond this he found only loosely formed "groups of sayings" (*Spruchgruppen*; e.g., 3:13–17; 4:1–6; 4:13–16), or even more loosely formed "series of sayings" (*Spruchreihen*; e.g., 1–27 and 5:7–20) and individual aphorisms (e.g., 3:18; 4:17).

Dibelius' account of paraenesis in general and of James in particular is now generally rejected. However, the problems he raised for the rhetorical analysis of James remain a major point of study. There is, to be sure, an emerging consensus that James must exhibit some rhetorical structure. But the precise nature of that structure, as well as its general contours, are much debated, largely along the lines first traced by Dibelius.

Three basic approaches may be identified. The first and by far most common approach accepts Dibelius' general thesis but with the qualification that the author of James arranged originally separate paraenetic materials into a more or less coherent whole according to various themes (Martin 1988; Davids 1988; Johnson 1995; Bauckham 1999). Johnson has recently suggested that 1:2–27 functions as an "epitome" introducing the disparate themes taken up in more detail in 2:1ff. (but see Bauckham).

A second approach, which discerns a much greater coherence in James, employs the categories of the Greco-Roman rhetorical handbooks to uncover an overall flow of thought or logic to the text (Wuellner 1978; Baasland 1988; Thurén 1995). Wuellner was one of the first modern scholars to take this approach. He analyzed James as follows: epistolary prescript (1:1), *exordium* (1:2–4), *narratio* (1:5–11), *propositio* (1:12), *argumentatio* (1:13–5:6), and *peroratio* (5:7–20). Baasland has taken a similar approach, though he finds two *propositiones* (1:16–22) and (3:13–18). Thurén, whose rhetorical analysis is perhaps the most comprehensive to date, has helpfully called attention to the repetition of the themes of suffering and endurance in the *exordium* and *peroratio*.

A third approach, which also draws upon Greco-Roman rhetorical culture, but with less ambition, seeks to explain the composition of certain smaller units in James (e.g., 2:1–13; 3:1–12) on the basis of the techniques taught in the secondary grammar schools and preserved in the progymnastic handbooks (Watson, 1993a, 1993b; Wachob 2000).

Whatever approach one eventually takes to James, one must keep in mind that it is characteristic of all paraenetic discourse to preserve more or less the original integrity of the aphoristic materials from which it is composed (Popkes 2001). As a result, whatever structure a parenetic text like James exhibits (and James is a coherent document), this structure will always be loose and capable of a variety of interpretations, which is part of the genre's lasting appeal.

In his famous *Gnomon Novi Testamenti*, first published in 1742, Johannes Albrecht Bengel proposed a classic analysis of James that has largely been passed over in current analyses, but which still has much to recommend it. The following is a slightly modified form of it.

| | | |
|---|---|---|
| 1:1 | I. | Epistolary prescript |
| 1:2–18 | II. | Introduction: On the benefits of endurance; on the nature of "testing" |
| 1:19–5:6 | III. | Body of the letter: |
| 1:19–21 | | A. Proposition: "Be quick to listen, slow to speak, and slow to anger" or "Receive with meekness the implanted word which is able to save your souls" |

| 1:22–2:26 | B | First heading: On being quick to listen: being doers of the word not hearers only |
|---|---|---|
| 3:1–18 | C | Second heading: On being slow to speak: avoid the tongue, show wisdom through deeds |
| 4:1–5:6 | D | Third heading: On being slow to anger: put away the desires that lead to strife |
| 5:7–20 | IV. | Concluding matter: Renewed call to endurance |

## Annotated Bibliography

Agourides, S. C. "The Origin of the Epistle of James," *Greek Orthodox Theological Review* 9 (1963), 67–78.

Baasland, E. "Literarische Form, Thematik und geschichtliche Einordnung des Jakobusbriefes." *Aufstieg und Niedergang der römischen Welt* 2 25/5 (1988), 3646–84. Wide-ranging essay with a number of valuable insights.

Baker, William R. *Personal Speech Ethics in the Epistle of James.* Wissenschaftliche Untersuchungen zum Neuen Testament, 2/68. Tübingen: Mohr Siebeck, 1995. Essential study on this important theme.

Bauckham, Richard. *James: Wisdom of James, Disciple of Jesus the Sage.* New Testament Readings. London and New York: Routledge, 1999. Original observations by an important British scholar.

Brown, Raymond E. *An Introduction to the New Testament.* Anchor Bible Reference Library. New York: Doubleday, 1997. An introduction that focuses on the content of the New Testament writings.

Collins, John J. "Wisdom Reconsidered, in Light of the Scrolls," *Dead Sea Discoveries* 4 (1997), 265–81. Authoritative essay on the development of Jewish wisdom; essential to locating James in an evolving tradition.

Cowley, A. E. *Aramaic Papyri of the Fifth Century B.C.* Oxford: Clarendon Press, 1923. Standard collection.

Davids, Peter H. "The Epistle of James in Modern Discussion." *Aufstieg und Niedergang der römischen Welt* 2 25/5 (1988), 3621–45.

Dibelius, Martin. *James: A Commentary on the Epistle of James.* 11th edn., rev. Heinrich Greeven. Trans. Michael A. Williams. Hermeneia. Philadelphia: Fortress Press, 1988. [This commentary first appeared in German as: Martin Dibelius, *Der Brief des Jakobus.* 7th edn. Kritish-exegetischer Kommentar über das Neue Testament, 20. Göttingen: Vandenhoeck & Ruprecht, 1921.] Classic commentary. Point of departure for all modern study of James.

Dunn, James D. G. *Unity and Diversity in the New Testament.* 2nd edn. London and Philadelphia: SCM Press/Trinity Press International, 1990. Important early study of diversity in early Christianity.

Francis, Fred O. "The Form and Function of the Opening and Closing Paragraphs of James and I John," *Zeitschrift für die neutestamentliche Wissenschaft* 61 (1970), 110–26. Early influential epistolary analysis.

Frankemölle, Hubert. *Der Brief des Jakobus.* Ökumenischer Taschenbuchkommentar zum Neuen Testament, 17/1–2. Gütersloh: Gütersloher Verlagshaus (Gerd Mohn), 1994. Major continental commentary; linguistically sophisticated.

Hartin, Patrick J. *James and the Q Sayings of Jesus. Journal for the Study of the New Testament* Supplementary Series, 47. Sheffield: JSOT Press, 1991. Frequently cited study; argues that author of James knew Q.

Hengel, Martin. "Die Jacobusbrief als antipaulinische Polemik." Pp. 148–78 in *Tradition and Interpretation of the New Testament: Essays in Honor of E. Earle Ellis*. Edited by G. Hawthorne and O. Betz. Grand Rapids: Eerdmans, 1988. Attempts to read James as a comprehensive response to Paul.

Jackson-McCabe, Matt A. *Logos and Law in the Letter of James: The Law of Nature, the Law of Moses, and the Law of Freedom*. Supplements to *Novum Testamentum*, 100. Leiden: Brill, 2001. Original and compelling study of the Hellenistic philosophical assumptions underlying James.

Johnson, Luke Timothy. *The Letter of James: A New Translation with Introduction and Commentary*. Anchor Bible, 37A. New York: Doubleday, 1995. Important American commentary.

Koester, Helmut. *Introduction to the New Testament*. 2 vols. 2nd edn. New York: Walter de Gruyter, 1995, 2000.

Konradt, Matthias, "Theologie in der 'stohernen Epistel': Ein Literaturbericht zu neueren Ansätzen in der Exegese des Jakobriefes," *Verkündigung und Forschung* 44 (1999), 54–78. Helpful survey of recent work on the theology of James.

Lampe, Peter and Ulrich Luz. "Post-Pauline Christianity and Pagan Society." Pp. 242–80 in *Christian Beginnings*. Edited by Jürgen Becker. Trans. Annemarie S. Kidder and Reinhard Krauss. Louisville: Westminster John Knox, 1993. Important discussion of second- and third-generation Christianity; relevant to the social context of James.

Laws, Sophie. *A Commentary on the Epistle of James*. Harper's New Testament Commentaries. San Francisco: Harper & Row, 1980. A popular but fine commentary.

Lüdemann, Gerd. *Opposition to Paul in Jewish Christianity*. Minneapolis: Fortress Press, 1989. Argues convincingly that the author of James had read at least some of Paul's letters.

Martin, Ralph P. *James*. Word Biblical Commentary, 48. Waco, TX: Word, 1988. Major Evangelical commentary; no surprises.

Maynard-Reid, Pedrito U. *Poverty and Wealth in James*. Maryknoll, NY: Orbis, 1987. Very insightful study on this central but until recently neglected theme.

Mayor, Joseph B. *The Epistle of St. James*. London: Macmillan, 1897. Major commentary in its day.

Niebuhr, K. W. "Der Jakobusbrief im Licht frühjüdischer Diasporabriefe," *New Testament Studies* 44 (1998), 420–43. Helpful study of the genre of James.

Painter, John. *Just James: The Brother of Jesus in History and Tradition*. Minneapolis: Fortress Press, 1999. Important study of the historical James and the traditions surrounding him.

Paulsen, Henning. "Jakobusbrief." Pp. 488–95 in *Theologische Realenzyklopädie*. Vol. 17. Edited by G. Krause and G. Müller. Berlin: Walter de Gruyter, 1987.

Penner, Todd. *The Epistle of James and Eschatology: Re-reading an Ancient Christian Letter*. Journal for the Study of the New Testament Supplementary Series, 121. Sheffield: Sheffield Academic Press, 1996. Seeks to read James as a kind of eschatological community instruction.

Popkes, Wiard. *Der Brief des Jakobus*. Theologischer Handkommentar zum Neuen Testament, 14. Leipzig: Evangelische Verlagsanstalt, 2001. Very important continental commentary.

Pratscher, Wilhelm. *Der Herrenbruder Jacobus und die Jacobustradition*. Göttingen: Vandenhoeck & Ruprecht, 1987. Comprehensive study of the historical James and the traditions surrounding him.

Riesner, R. *Paul's Early Period: Chronology, Mission Strategy, Theology*. Grand Rapids: Eerdmans, 1998. Erudite study of Paul's early period; passing relevance to James.

Ropes, James H. *James*. International Critical Commentary. Edinburgh: T. & T. Clark, 1916. Older standard philological commentary.

Sanders, E. P. *Paul and Palestinian Judaism: A Comparison of Patterns of Religion*. Minneapolis: Fortress Press, 1977. The point of departure for all modern studies of Paul. Key to understanding Paul and Torah.

Schlatter, A. *Der Brief des Jakobus*. Stuttgart: Calwer, 1932. Early but still useful commentary.

Schnelle, Udo. *History and Theology of the New Testament Writings*. Trans. M. Eugene Boring. Minneapolis: Augsburg Fortress, 1998.

Schnider, Franz. *Der Jakobusbrief*. Regensburger Neues Testament. Regensburg: Pustet, 1987. Insightful popular continental commentary.

Stowers, Stanley K. *Diatribe and Paul's Letter to the Romans*. Society of Biblical Literature Dissertation Series, 57. Chico, CA: Scholars Press, 1981. Major reassessment of the so-called diatribe style. Relevant to describing diatribal elements in James.

Strecker, Georg. *Literaturgeschichte des Neuen Testament*. Göttingen: Vandenhoeck & Ruprecht, 1992.

Taatz, I. *Frühjüdische Briefe: Die paulinischen Briefe im Rahman der offiziellen religiösen Briefe des Frühjudentums*. Novum Testamentum et Oribis Antiquus, 16. Freiburg and Göttingen: Universitätsverlag/Vandenhoeck & Ruprecht, 1991. Important study of early Jewish letters.

Thurén, Lauri. "Risky Rhetoric in James," *Novum Testamentum* 37 (1995), 262–84. Attempts a thoroughgoing rhetorical analysis of the letter in order to uncover its theology.

Tsuji, Manabu. *Glaube zwischen Vollkommenheit und Verweltlichung: Eine Untersuchung zur literarischen Gestalt und zur inhaltlichen Kohärenz des Jakobusbriefes*. Wissenschaftliche Untersuchungen zum Neuen Testament, 2/93; Tübingen: Mohr Siebeck, 1997. A wide-ranging study that makes a number of insightful observations. Particularly helpful on the letter's anti-Paulinism.

Turner, N. *Style*. In J. H. Moulton, *A Grammar of New Testament Greek*. Vol. 4. Edinburgh: T. & T. Clark, 1976. Contains a competent analysis of the genre and prose style of James (pp. 114–20).

Verseput, Donald J. "Wisdom, 4Q185, and the Epistle of James," *Journal of Biblical Literature* 117 (1998), 691–707. Fits James loosely in a wisdom context.

Wachob, Wesley Hiram. *The Voice of Jesus in the Social Rhetoric of James*. Society for New Testament Studies Monograph Series 106. Cambridge: Cambridge University Press, 2000. Socio-rhetorical analysis of James 2:1–13.

Watson, D. F. "James 2 in Light of Greco-Roman Schemes of Argumentation," *New Testament Studies* 39 (1993a), 94–121. Applies the progymnastic handbooks to James 2.

Watson, D. F. "The Rhetoric of James 3:1–12 and a Classical Pattern of Argumentation," *Novum Testamentum* 35 (1993b), 48–64. Applies the progymnastic handbooks to James 3:1–12.

Wuellner, Wilhelm H. "Der Jakobusbrief im Licht der Rhetorik und Textpragmatik," *Linguistica Biblica* 43 (1978), 5–65. Early theoretical rhetorical analysis of James.

Zimmermann, A. F. *Die urchristlichen Lehrer*. 2nd edn. Tübingen: Mohr Siebeck, 1988. A comprehensive reassessment of the place of the teacher in early Christianity; important for contextualizing James 3:1.

CHAPTER 34

# 1 Peter

Brian Han Gregg

## Major Issues and Directions in Recent Study

A number of specific issues have generated scholarly interest and debate in the last century. Among the more contentious questions are the following. (1) What is the date of 1 Peter's composition? (2) Is the letter's attribution to the apostle Peter trustworthy or is it a pseudonymous work? (3) What role does baptism play in understanding the content and purpose of the letter? (4) What are the cause and nature of the suffering experienced by the letter's addressees? (5) Is the designation "aliens and exiles" (2:11 cf. 1:1) to be understood as a reference to the addressees' social status or does it refer to metaphorical alienation brought on by commitment to Jesus? (6) Does 1 Peter encourage accommodation to Greco-Roman social and moral values in order to alleviate hostility or does it exhort its listeners to maintain a distinctively Christian identity, hoping to convert those who attack the community of faith? (7) What is the meaning of the two enigmatic proclamations, one to the "spirits" (3:18–20), and the other to the "dead" (4:6)? (8) How should a twenty-first-century Westerner approach 1 Peter's advice to "wives"?

## Place of Composition, Date, and Author

Though Antioch in Syria (Boismard 1957) and Asia Minor (Hunzinger 1965) have both been suggested as the letter's place of origin, there is a wide degree of consensus that 1 Peter was written from Rome. Several factors converge to make this the most probable option. (1) The most significant piece of evidence lies in 1 Peter 5:13: "Your sister church in Babylon, chosen together with you sends you greetings." "Babylon" is best understood as a symbolic reference to Rome, as demonstrated by parallel usage in *4 Ezra*, *2 Baruch*, *Sibylline Oracles*, and Revelation. (2) Papias (Eusebius, *Ecclesiastical History*, 2.15.2) explicitly identifies Rome as the place of origin. (3) Later tradition held that Peter and Mark (referred to as his "son" in 5:13) were both known to have ministered in Rome (Ignatius, *Romans*, 4:3; Eusebius, *Ecclesiastical History*, 2.15.2, 2.25.1–

8,3:1.2–3; Irenaeus, *Against Heresies*, 3.1.5; Tertullian, *Against Marcion*, 4.5; *On Baptism*, 4). Even if 1 Peter was not written by the apostle, its reliance on his authority necessitates a locale where he was known to have ministered.

1 Peter claims to have been written by "Peter, an apostle of Jesus Christ" (1:1). This claim was clearly taken at face value by the early church. The relative ease with which 1 Peter found inclusion in the canon (in stark contrast to 2 Peter) attests to the assurance the early church had that Peter was indeed its author. There are, however, potential problems with attributing the letter to Peter. Two in particular are worthy of note. (1) The Greek found in 1 Peter ranks among the best in the New Testament. In addition, the author displays a remarkable facility with the LXX (Septuagint, i.e., the Greek version of the Old Testament), adeptly weaving allusions into the text of his letter. One naturally wonders how Peter, an uneducated Galilean fisherman (see Acts 4:13) could have attained such literary skill. Some have sought to attribute the elegant Greek to an amanuensis or secretary, Silvanus. While this would potentially alleviate the difficulty for Petrine authorship, it is by no means clear that the Greek phrase *dia Silouanou* ("through" or "by Silvanus") in 5:12 should be interpreted to mean that he was functioning as an amanuensis. On the contrary, with one exception (Eusebius, *Ecclesiastical History*, 4.23.11), all of the parallels suggest that Silvanus is acting as a courier for the letter (Richards 2000). (2) The second potential stumbling block to Petrine authorship involves the designation of "Babylon" for Rome. Every document to make such an identification (4 *Ezra*, 2 *Baruch*, *Sibylline Oracles*, and Revelation) does so *after* the destruction of the Second Temple in 70 CE. In fact, Rome may have been referred to as Babylon precisely *because* it had destroyed God's Temple, much like Babylon, a Near Eastern power, had earlier been the agent of God's judgment. If, as the various traditions of the early church argue with a single voice, Peter was martyred in Rome between 64 and 67 CE under Nero, then he cannot have composed 1 Peter after the destruction of the Second Temple. While these two factors do not exclude the possibility of Petrine authorship, they do point to the likelihood that 1 Peter was written pseudonymously, perhaps by a "Petrine group" in Rome (Best 1971; Elliott 1990).

Prior to the mid-1970s the date of 1 Peter was principally determined by connecting its discussions of suffering with persecutions that took place in the reigns of Nero (54–68), Domitian (81–96), or Trajan (98–117). However, fresh analysis of the content of 1 Peter and the suffering passages in particular has effectively reversed this trend, demanding a date which presupposes relatively peaceful relations with Roman authorities. If one holds to Petrine authorship, it is safe to assume that 1 Peter was written after Paul's letter to the Romans in 58 CE (which presumably would have greeted Peter had he been in Rome) and prior to Nero's fateful fire in 64 CE. If one assumes that 1 Peter is pseudonymous, however, the decision becomes more difficult. The reference to Rome as Babylon suggests that 1 Peter was composed sometime after the destruction of the Temple in 70 CE, providing a useful *terminus a quo* ("[earliest] limit from which") the composition of 1 Peter could have occurred. Literary evidence suggests that 1 Peter was used by 1 *Clement*, usually dated ca. 95 CE (Elliott 2000: 138–40). Since Revelation is thought to reflect the turbulent conditions of Domitian's final years in the 90s (see Chapter 37, "The Apocalypse of John," in this volume), it is safe to assume that 1 Peter was written sometime between 70 and 90 CE.

## Historical Setting

1 Peter is addressed to "the exiles of the Dispersion in Pontus, Galatia, Cappadocia, Asia, and Bithynia" (1:1). These four Roman provinces (Pontus and Bithynia were joined into a single province in 65 BCE) incorporated all of Asia Minor north of the Taurus Mountains. Together they formed an enormous tract of land, some 129,000 square miles. Within this space there was naturally a great deal of cultural, historical, economic, geographic, and religious diversity. It is quite likely that the various Christian communities addressed in 1 Peter shared very little in common beyond their devotion to Jesus. It is not surprising, then, that 1 Peter casts its net wide, sticking to common concerns like family, community, empire, righteous living, and the essentials of the faith. Unlike much of the Pauline correspondence, there is nothing to suggest that particular churches and their problems are in view. Hence, there is every indication that 1 Peter should be considered a genuinely "catholic" epistle, written with a broad audience in mind. 1 Peter also appears to address both Jewish and Gentile adherents to the faith. The book is steeped in Old Testament allusions and Jewish nomenclature serves to designate insiders and outsiders (1:1; 2:12; 4:3). At the same time, 1 Peter clearly addresses those who have come out of a pagan background (1:14, 18; 4:3–4).

The recipients of 1 Peter are, however, united through shared experience. A survey of the themes addressed in 1 Peter makes it clear that it was written to communities under duress (1:6; 2:12, 15, 18–20; 3:9, 13–17; 4:1, 4, 6b, 12–14, 16, 19; 5:8–10). They are all experiencing suffering that has resulted from their profession of faith in Jesus. It is this common experience of suffering that generated the letter of 1 Peter.

John Elliott has argued at length that 1 Peter addresses communities of believers that also share a similar social status (Elliott 1990, 2000). They are *paroikoi*, "aliens," and *parepidēmoi*, "strangers" (2:11 cf. 1:1). According to this reading, the letter addresses people who (prior to their conversion) occupied a marginal place in their communities by virtue of their social status as resident aliens or visitors. There are, however, good reasons to question such identification. (1) Metaphors, comparisons, and allusions are all commonplace in 1 Peter (see below). It is not difficult to understand why Abraham (who calls himself an "alien and stranger") might be invoked as a model of living apart from one's "true" home, experiencing alienation because of his choice to follow God (Gen. 23:4). In fact, Hebrews makes a very similar point about Abraham, "For he looked forward to the city that has foundations, whose architect and builder is God" (Heb. 11:10). "All of these died in faith without receiving the promises, but from a distance they saw and greeted them. They confessed that they were strangers and foreigners on the earth" (Heb. 11:13). Likewise, Paul uses the same metaphor when he tells the Philippians that "their citizenship is in heaven" (Phil. 3:20). Such a metaphor also accords well with 1 Peter's overall application of the identity and history of Israel to the Christian communities (see below). (2) The reference to aliens and strangers in 2:11 is introduced with the particle *hōs* ("like, as"). This particle is regularly used in 1 Peter to introduce a metaphor (1:14; 2:2, 5, 16, 25; 5:8). (3) The presumption that the addressees felt marginalized by their neighbors prior to their conversion encounters an obstacle in 4:3–4, which suggests that new believers are slandered because of their new behavior. (4) In light of Pliny's later assertions that there were "many of every rank" and "Roman citizens" among their adherents (*Epistles*, 10.96), it is improbable that Christianity only made headway among this population of alien workers. (5) Furthermore, it seems unlikely that a circular letter which otherwise seems intent on delivering a widely accessible message would speak so specifically to a single social class.

## Purpose

A number of different hypotheses have been generated regarding the purpose of 1 Peter. Two different proposals take as their starting point the references to "baptism" (3:21) and "new birth" (1:3, 23). One argues that an earlier version of 1 Peter originally functioned as a baptismal homily (Perdelwitz 1911; Reicke 1946; Beare 1958; Marxsen 1979). As such, it provided words of instruction and encouragement to new believers who chose to unite themselves with Christ. Another suggests that an earlier version of 1 Peter functioned as a baptismal liturgy with various portions of the text read aloud by the participants in the liturgy (Windisch 1951: 156–60; Cross 1954). Recent scholarship on 1 Peter has raised a number of arguments that render these two hypotheses highly unlikely. (1) Indicators of 1 Peter's composite character (which in turn generated the possibility that a homily or liturgy lay behind the current letter form) have proven unconvincing. (2) There is a paucity of actual references to "baptism." (3) It is unlikely that 1 Peter's "new birth" imagery was intended as an allusion to the liturgical act of baptism (Dalton 1974: 266).

Other proposals focus on the Petrine authorship of 1 Peter. Noting the collaboration of Peter and Silvanus (a co-worker of Paul's) as well as the presence of many potentially "Pauline" themes, Baur suggested that the purpose of 1 Peter was to ease the tensions between "Petrine" and "Pauline" Christianity (Baur 1856). This proposal is far too speculative to merit much consideration. It is built entirely upon a hypothetical reconstruction of the early church rather than the content of the letter itself. A less extreme position suggests that 1 Peter seeks to expand the authority of Peter (Elliott 1980).

Most recent work on 1 Peter has wisely sought a correlation between the purpose of the letter and the ever-present discussion of suffering. Hence, the purpose of 1 Peter was to provide encouragement in the midst of suffering so that communities of believers might not lose sight of either their special identity in Christ (1:1–10, 18–23; 2:4–5, 9–10) or their mission to the world (2:12; 3:2, 15–16). Though this suffering is called a "fiery ordeal" (4:12), it is unlikely that a state-sponsored persecution is in view. There is no mention of violence or threat to life. 1 Peter exhorts its addressees to "accept the authority of every human institution, whether of the emperor supreme, or of the governors" (2:13–14). They are to "Honor the emperor" (2:17). It strains credulity to believe that such advice would be issued in the midst of a state-sponsored persecution. Rather, it would appear that the Christian communities were suffering from pervasive slander, hostility, and ill-will directed at them by their neighbors, those who were suspicious and fearful of this new movement (2:12; 3:16; 4:4, 14).

## Language and Style

The language of 1 Peter represents a fairly refined level of Koine Greek with some remarkable similarities to the vocabulary and style of classical Greek writings (Selwyn 1964: 499–501). The letter includes sixty-one New Testament *hapax legomena* (words unique within the New Testament), a surprisingly large number given 1 Peter's 1,675 total words. Among the semantic fields with a high proportion of occurrences are (1) suffering and abuse, (2) holiness, (3) family, (4) conduct, (5) eschatological realities.

A number of stylistic traits point directly to the letter's paraenetic function. There is a total of fifty-four imperatives found within its five chapters. In addition, it makes use of *oun* ("therefore") at critical junctures to signal that the preceding exhortation should elicit an appropriate response (2:1, 7; 4:1, 7; 5:1, 6). 1 Peter also regularly employs antitheses – often as a means of delineating insiders from outsiders and exhorting insiders to live lives worthy of their calling in Christ (1:14–15, 23; 2:9; 4:6).

Another prominent feature of 1 Peter is its regular application of comparisons (1:1, 3, 7, 14, 23; 2:2, 5, 11, 16, 25; 3:4–5; 5:8). Many of these comparisons are intended to affect the way in which those who have joined the Christian community perceive themselves in relation to Christ and the world around them. Other stylistic traits of 1 Peter include verbal and thematic repetition, parallelism, *Stichwörter* (link-words), and chiasms (Elliott 2000: 41–80).

## Intertextuality

1 Peter uses a host of quotes and allusions from the Old Testament in order to advance its case, adding rich layers of subtext to all those familiar with the Jewish scriptures. In each case the wording is clearly dependent upon the LXX. Thirteen texts are directly cited in 1 Peter: Lev. 19:2 (1:16); Isa. 40:6–8 (1:24–5); Ps. 34:8 (2:3); Isa. 28:16 (2:6); Ps. 118:22 (2:7b); Isa. 8:14 (2:8); Hos. 2:23 (2:10); Isa. 53:9 (2:22); Ps. 34:12–16 (3:10–12); Isa. 8:12 (3:14); Prov. 10:12 (4:8); Prov. 11:31 (4:18); Prov. 3:34 (5:5). Among the more transparent allusions belong: Exod. 24:3–8; 29:21; Lev. 8:30 (1:2); Exod. 12:11 (1:13); Exod. 19:5–6; Isa. 9:2; 43:20–1; (2:9); Gen. 23:4; Ps. 39:12 (2:11); Prov. 24:21 (2:17); Isa. 53:6, 12 (2:23); Isa. 53:4–6, 12; Ezek. 34:4–5, 16 (2:24–5); Gen. 18:12; Prov. 3:25 (3:6); Gen. 6–8 (3:20); Ps. 110:1 (3:22).

The pervasive use of the Old Testament serves two primary purposes. First, it reminds 1 Peter's addressees that their story is part of a much larger one. They are the rightful heirs of the promises of God. They are the true "Israel" of which the scriptures speak. This identification is evident in a number of different passages. (1) They are collectively (both Jew *and* Gentile) referred to as "the exiles of the Dispersion" (1:2), evoking the challenge confronting Israel to faithfully maintain its identity as the people of God in the midst of exile. (2) Those outside the community of faith are referred to collectively as "Gentiles" (2:12; 4:3). This is the case in spite of the fact that many of those inside the community of faith are *ethnically* Gentiles. (3) The adoption of a new identity as "God's people" is described using a citation from Hosea. "Once you were not a people, but now you are God's people; once you had not received mercy, but now you have received mercy" (1 Pet. 2:10; Hos. 2:23). (4) The community of faith is described in terms of Israel's distinctive identity in relation to God. "You shall be holy as I am holy" (1 Pet. 1:16; Lev. 19:2). "You are a chosen race, a royal priesthood, a holy nation, God's own people" (1 Pet. 2:9; Exod. 19:5–6; Isa. 43:20–1).

Second, the extensive use of scriptural citation and allusion provide authority to the message of 1 Peter. The encouragement and exhortation which the letter seeks to instill find full support in the scriptural voices summoned on their behalf.

Several noteworthy patterns can be discerned concerning 1 Peter's use of the Old Testament. (1) 1 Peter draws extensively upon a specific collection of texts, namely: Genesis, Exodus, Leviticus, Isaiah, Hosea, Psalms, and Proverbs. (2) Many of the passages employed by 1 Peter speak directly to the suffering of the communities being addressed by reinforcing that suffering is nothing new for the people of God. Abraham and Sarah lived as aliens in a foreign land. They were waiting for the land of promise, always aware that their worship of God made them strangers to those around them (Gen. 23:4; 1 Pet. 2:11). The Exodus narrative is consistently alluded to ("sprinkling of blood": 1 Pet. 1:2; Exod. 24:3–8; 29:21; "gird up your loins": 1 Pet. 1:13; Exod. 12:11; "a royal priesthood, a holy nation": 1 Pet. 2:9; Exod. 19:5–6), each time underscoring God's promises for a people experiencing suffering. One sequence of 1 Peter (2:22–5) represents an extended reflection on the suffering servant in Isaiah 53, including a citation from 53:9 (1 Pet. 2:22) and allusions to 53:4–6, 12. The servant, interpreted as Jesus, serves as a reminder for the communities that their savior walked the path of suffering. "But if you endure when you do right and suffer for it, you have God's approval. For to this you have been called, because Christ also suffered for you, leaving you an example, so that you should follow in his steps" (2:20–1). (3) Another constellation of texts bolsters the author's call to righteous and holy living. Prominent among these are the following. "You shall be holy, for I am Holy" (1 Pet. 1:16; Lev. 19:2). "Honor Everyone. Love the family of believers. Fear God. Honor the Emperor" (1 Pet. 2:17; Prov. 24:21). "Those who desire life and desire to see good days, let them keep their tongues from evil and their lips from speaking deceit; let them turn away from evil and do good; let them seek peace and pursue it. For the eyes of the Lord are on the righteous, and his ears are open to their prayer. But the face of the Lord is against those who do evil" (1 Pet. 3:10–12; Ps. 34:12–16). "Above all, maintain constant love for one another, for love covers a multitude of sins" (1 Pet. 4:8; Prov. 10:12). "If it is hard for the righteous to be saved, what will become of the ungodly and the sinners?" (1 Pet. 4:18; Prov. 11:31). "God opposes the proud but gives grace to the humble" (1 Pet. 5:5; Prov. 3:34).

## Unity

1 Peter's unity as a letter has not gone unquestioned. Those who argue for a composite text see an identifiable break in sources between 4:11 and 4:12 (Moule 1956; Fitzmyer 1968; Marxsen 1979). 1 Peter 4:7–10 is understood as a set of concluding remarks that lead to the doxology at the end of 4:11, "To him belong the glory and the power forever and ever. Amen." This initial evidence of a division of the text of 1 Peter has been supplemented by two further arguments. (1) While the suffering addressed in the

first portion of 1 Peter is potential (1:6; 3:13, 14, 17), the "fiery ordeal" addressed in the second portion is presently affecting the communities of faith (4:12, 19). (2) Various literary differences have been posited between the two sections, including distinctive style, form, and content.

Various tradition histories sought to build upon the conclusion that 1 Peter was indeed a composite document. Many of these assumed that the first portion of 1 Peter existed in a non-epistolary form. 1 Peter 1:1–2 and 4:12–5:14 were understood as later additions to an early (usually baptismal) homily or liturgy.

Recent studies on the integrity of 1 Peter have consistently rejected the notion of a composite document. Serious doubts have been raised concerning the evidence for a division in sources between 4:11 and 4:12. Though doxologies can be used to end a document, there are plenty of instances in which they occur within the body of a letter (Rom. 1:25; 9:5; 11:36; Gal. 1:5; Eph. 3:21; 1 Tim. 1:17). The attempt to differentiate between potential and actual suffering simply does not line up with the content of the letter. In each portion of the letter the suffering addressed is "present." Finally, the unity of the letter has been convincingly argued from a literary vantage point as well (Best 1971: 26–8; Combrini 1980). When set alongside the fact that there is no manuscript evidence for an earlier version of 1 Peter, the natural conclusion is that the version of 1 Peter available to us corresponds to the original letter.

## Genre

1 Peter clearly presents itself as a letter. Two kinds of letters emerge as potentially helpful categories for understanding 1 Peter. (1) The letter of 1 Peter explicitly indicates that it is intended as a word of encouragement. "I have written this short letter to encourage you and to testify that this is the true grace of God" (5:12). Such an aim certainly coheres well with the content of the letter. Therefore, one useful category for understanding the genre of 1 Peter is that of a "paraenetic/hortatory letter" (Stowers 1986: 96–7). (2) The letter of 1 Peter is addressed to a large group of people, "To the exiles of the Dispersion in Pontus, Galatia, Cappadocia, Asia, and Bithynia" (1:1). As such, it functions as a "circular letter," a genre not unknown in Jewish and Christian circles (Aune 1987: 180). In fact, the sequence in which the Roman provinces are listed may suggest the order in which the letter was intended to travel. This potentially explains why Pontus and Bithynia are listed separately in spite of their first-century status as a single Roman province. Reading 1 Peter as a circular letter helps explain the general applicability of the letter's content.

## Constituent Literary Forms

Among the constituent literary forms found in 1 Peter are the following: (1) a standard epistolary greeting (1:1–2) and closing (5:12–14); (2) an extended blessing (1:3–12); (3) two doxologies (4:11; 5:11); (4) a household code (2:18–3:7); (5) a catalogue of vices (2:1); (6) a benediction (5:14). We have already noted that attempts to discern an early Christian homily or liturgy (usually baptismal in both instances) embedded in the text of 1 Peter have proven misguided. The literary forms found in 1 Peter are precisely those you would expect to find in a paraenetic/hortatory letter. Several attempts have been made to locate the origins of particular portions of 1 Peter in early Christian confessions or hymns (1 Pet. 1:18–21; 2:21–5; 3:18–22; 5:5–9; Bultmann 1947: 293, 297; Boismard 1961: 60–7; 111–32; Goppelt 1993: 207–10). While 1 Peter almost certainly does draw on traditional Christian material (hymns, catechisms, creeds, liturgy, and prayer), these specific proposals are based on little more than conjecture.

## Epistolary Analysis

Epistolary analysis of 1 Peter is a relatively straightforward process (Achtemeier 1996: 73–4; Michaels 1988: xxxvii). The first two verses comprise a standard epistolary opening, complete with a superscript, "Peter, an apostle of Jesus Christ," an extended adscript, "To the exiles of the Dispersion ... ," and a salutation, "May grace and peace be yours in abundance." The opening is followed by an extended blessing (1:3–12) which sets up many of the themes to be discussed in the body of the letter. The body itself can be separated into three major parts: 1:13–2:10; 2:11–4:11; 4:12–5:11. Divisions are signaled by the new address in 2:11, "beloved," and the doxology in 4:11, "To him belong the glory and the power forever and ever. Amen." Within these three sections of the body further separations can be made on the basis of content and compositional devices. Elliott has identified the following as distinct subunits within the body of 1 Peter: (body opening): 1:13–21; 1:22–2:3; 2:4–10; (body middle): 2:11–12; 2:13–17; 2:18–25; 3:1–7; 3:8–12; 3:13–17; 3:18–22; 4:1–6; 4:7–11; (body closing): 4:12–19; 5:1–5a; 5:5b–11 (Elliott 2000: 80–2). The letter ends with a recommendation of the courier Silvanus, a summary of the letter's aim, greetings, and a final benediction, "Peace to all of you who are in Christ" (5:12–14).

## Rhetorical Analysis

Rhetorical analysis of 1 Peter has by and large produced the same text divisions as epistolary analysis. Thurén (1995: 88–183) lists the divisions in the following manner. (1) The first rhetorical unit (1:1–12) is an *exordium*, and functions as a general motivation. (2) 1:13–2:10 can be variously understood as a continuation of the *exordium* or the beginning of the *argumentatio*. Either way it continues to lay the groundwork for what is to follow. (3) Verses 2:11–3:12 contain the central *argumentatio*, which seeks to win the addressees to the author's perspective. (4) Verses 3:13–4:11 are part of the *expolitio*, clarifying the preceding argument. (5) There is a *recapitulatio* of the *exordium* in 4:12–5:7. (6) Finally, there is a *peroratio* in 5:8–14.

## Theology

1 Peter displays a rich and diverse theology of suffering. (1) Undeserved suffering functions as a test of the "genuineness of faith" (1:6–7; 4:12). (2) Suffering leads to purifica-

tion, "Whoever has suffered in the flesh is finished with sin" (4:1). (3) The suffering of the "household of God" is indicative of God's imminent judgment and holds the promise of hoped-for salvation. Hence, suffering believers should "entrust themselves to the faithful Creator" (4:17–19). (4) Suffering "for the name of Christ" should be counted a blessing because it is evidence that "the spirit of glory, which is the Spirit of God, is resting on you" (4:14). (5) Christ's innocent suffering not only serves as a model for the community of faith (2:21) but it also rescued from sin (2:24; 3:18). (6) Those who unite their sufferings with Christ will be glorified by God with Christ (1:9; 2:4–5; 5:1).

Eschatology plays a primary role in 1 Peter on two levels. First, Christ's suffering, rejection, death, and resurrection are dealt with as eschatological realities. They have fundamentally changed God's relationship with his people and the world (1:2; 2:4–10, 21–5; 3:18–22; 4:13; 5:1). Second, these key events in the life of Christ anticipate his glorious return, that point at which he definitively brings salvation and judgment to the earth (1:5, 7, 17; 2:23; 4:5, 13; 5:1, 4). These twin eschatological emphases are summed up in 1 Peter 1:20–1. "He was destined before the foundation of the world, but was revealed at the end of the ages for your sake. Through him you have come to trust in God, who raised him from the dead and gave him glory, so that your faith and hope are set on God." Not surprisingly, *apokalyptein* ("to reveal") and *apokalypsis* ("revelation") both frequently occur in 1 Peter (three times each; a higher proportional use than any other New Testament document). God has revealed the end of the ages in Christ and that revelation will be brought to completion upon Christ's return.

1 Peter's eschatological emphasis functions in two capacities. On the one hand, it is used to encourage those experiencing suffering. They will be vindicated by their Creator – and they will not have to wait long (1:6; 4:7; 5:10). On the other hand, it provides a basis for exhortation to right living (1:17; 4:1–6, 7–11, 12–19; 5:1–4).

One of 1 Peter's integrative themes is that of the household. One complete section of the letter is devoted to advice pertaining to those who find themselves in specific household roles. This household code addresses slaves (2:18–25), wives (3:1–6), and husbands (3:7). David Balch has argued at length that the code in 1 Peter should be understood in light of its Greco-Roman parallels as an attempt to accommodate to the social and moral values of the surrounding culture. In this manner the suffering experienced by the Christian communities might be assuaged (Balch 1981; cf. Talbert 1986). This might be a reasonable conclusion if the household code were read in isolation, but the rest of the text of 1 Peter makes it difficult to substantiate such a proposition. The community is encouraged to remember and maintain its distinctive identity in the midst of persecution (1:14–15; 2:9–10; 4:3–5, 14–16; 5:8–9). Furthermore, there is every indication that the conversion of outsiders was the hoped-for outcome (2:12; 3:2, 15–16).

Household imagery also plays an important role in describing the community of God. Believers are referred to as "children" (1:14) and "new born babes" (2:2–3). God is their "father" (1:2, 3, 17) and they are to live as "brothers" (and sisters) to one another (1:22–3; 2:17; 3:8; 5:9, 12). Together they constitute a *oikos pneumatikos* or "spiritual household" (2:5). This household provides them with a community, a place of belonging and support which enables them to deal with the alienation they experience from their neighbors. Hence, while the gospel has driven a wedge between them and their former communities, it has also provided them with something greater, a new "family," with God himself as loving father.

The greatest theological puzzle in 1 Peter involves the interpretation of two enigmatic texts which refer to proclamations made to the "spirits" and the "dead." "He was put to death in the flesh, but made alive in the spirit, in which also he went and made proclamation to the spirits in prison, who in former times did not obey, when God waited patiently in the days of Noah" (3:18–20). "For this is the reason the gospel was proclaimed even to the dead, so that, though they had been judged in the flesh as everyone is judged, they might live in the spirit as God does" (4:6).

These two texts have commonly been interpreted in light of one another, with the assumption being that they refer to the same event. The most compelling explanation of each, however, allows for their separate interpretation (Reicke 1946; Dalton 1965). In 1 Peter 3:18–20 the reference to the days of Noah, the use of *pneuma* or "spirit" (the common way of referring to a supernatural being), the qualifier "disobedient," and the mention of imprisonment, suggest that the disobedient "sons of God" of Genesis 6:1–4 are in view. An extensive body of Second Temple literature developed elaborate scenarios concerning these rebellious angels. Variously referred to as "spirits," "sons of heaven," "giants," and "watchers," these supernatural beings were judged in Noah's flood and were thought to be imprisoned until the time of their final judgment (*1 Enoch*, 10:11–12; *Jubilees*, 5:6). In this interpretation, Christ "proclaimed" judgment upon the sons of God after achieving his victory on the cross.

1 Peter 4:6 uses the passive voice to describe proclaiming the gospel to the dead (thus making the agent of the preaching unclear). There are two ways to interpret this proclamation. (1) Those who demonstrated faith in God prior to the advent of Jesus are now saved through the same gospel so that they too might live in the spirit (Horrell 2003; cf. Heb. 11:39–40). (2) Those who accepted the gospel but have passed away before Jesus' glorious return still live in the spirit (Dalton 1965; cf. 1 Thess. 4:13–18).

## Annotated Bibliography

Achtemeier, Paul J. "Newborn Babes and Living Stones: Literal and Figurative in 1 Peter." Pp. 207–36 in *To Touch the Text: Biblical and Related Studies in Honor of Joseph H. Fitzmyer*. Edited by M. Horgan and P. Kobelski. New York: Crossroads; Continuum, 1988. Seeking a means of discerning when a particular designation calls for a literal or figurative reading, Achtemeier identifies 1 Peter's "controlling metaphor" in the following manner. It is the "Christian community as the new People of God constituted by the Christ who suffered (and rose)."

Achtemeier, Paul. J. *1 Peter: A Commentary on First Peter*. Hermeneia. Minneapolis: Fortress Press, 1996. This comprehensive commentary combines a thorough introduction with detailed exegesis and an excellent grasp of secondary literature.

Balch, David L. *Let Wives Be Submissive: The Domestic Code in 1 Peter*. Society of Biblical Literature Monograph Series, 26. Chico, CA: Scholars Press, 1981. Pointing out the many affinities between the household code in 1 Peter and those in Greco-Roman sources, Balch argues that 1 Peter urges its addressees to avert persecution and win respect by accommodating to the moral and social values of their neighbors.

Baur, F. C. "Der erste petrinische Brief, mit besondererBeziehung auf das Werk: Der petrinische Lehrbegriff von Bernhard Weiss." *Theologisches Jahrbuch* 15 (1856), 193–240.

Beare, Francis W. *The First Epistle of Peter: The Greek Text with Introduction and Notes.* Oxford: Blackwell, 1958. Beare is a proponent of the baptismal homily hypothesis. The commentary includes a reasonably full discussion 1 Peter's theology alongside discussion of other introductory issues.

Best, Ernest, *1 Peter.* New Century Bible. London: Marshall, Morgan & Scott, 1971. Best's commentary is relatively brief compared to more recent treatments. The introduction includes a sizable section devoted to the question of authorship and concludes that 1 Peter was the work of a "Petrine school."

Boismard, Marie-Émile. "Une liturgie baptismale dans la *Prima Petri*," *Revue biblique* 63 (1956), 182–208, and 64 (1957), 161–83. These two successive articles argue that 1 Peter was based on an early baptismal liturgy.

Boismard, Marie-Émile. *Quatre hymnes baptismales dans la première épître de Pierre.* Lectio Divina, 30. Paris: Cerf, 1961. In an exploration of early Christian traditions that might lie behind 1 Peter, Boismard argues that four different passages in 1 Peter (1:18–21; 2:21–5; 3:18–22; 5:5–9) reproduce portions of early baptismal hymns.

Bultmann, Rudolph. "Bekenntnis- und Leidfragmente im ersten Petrusbrief." Pp. 1–14 in *In honorem Antonii Fridrichsen sexagenarii edenda curavit Seminarium Neotestamenticum Upsaliense.* Coniectanea Neotestamentica, 11. Lund: C.W.K. Gleerup, 1947.

Casurella, Anthony. *Bibliography of Literature on First Peter.* Leiden: Brill, 1996. This bibliography is divided into ten categories: (1) Commentaries; (2) Dictionary and Encyclopedia Articles; (3) Descent to Hades; (4) Exposition and/or Application of Individual Passages; (5) Exposition of Entire Book; (6) Miscellaneous; (7) Parallels, Relationships, Backgrounds; (8) Peter in the New Testament; (9) Sermons and Preaching; (10) Text of 1 Peter.

Combrini, H. J. B. "The Structure of 1 Peter," *Neotestamentica* 9 (1980), 34–63. Combrini provides an in-depth analysis of 1 Peter's literary structure, demonstrating the overarching unity of the letter.

Cross, Frank L. *1 Peter: A Paschal Liturgy.* London: Mowbray, 1954. Building on the hypothesis that 1 Peter contains an early baptismal liturgy, Cross argues that the liturgy was shaped in part by its emphasis on suffering. In light of its linguistic similarity to Passover (*paschō; pascha*), Cross suggests that the baptismal liturgy had been written in order to initiate new believers on Easter day, the Christian equivalent of a new Passover.

Dalton, William Joseph. *Christ's Proclamation to the Spirits; A Study in 1 Peter 3:18–4:6.* Analecta Biblica, 23. Rome: Pontifical Biblical Institute, 1965. Dalton demonstrates that 1 Peter 3:18–20 need not refer to the same events as 4:6. Furthermore, Dalton argues that Christ's proclamation to the Spirits (1 Pet. 3:18–20) can only adequately be understood in light of the numerous Second Temple traditions that sought to interpret the enigmatic reference to the "sons of God" in Genesis 6.

Dalton, William Joseph. " 'So that your faith may also be your hope in God' (1 Peter 1:21)." Pp. 262–74 in *Reconciliation and Hope: New Testament Essays on Atonement and Eschatology Presented to L. L. Morris on his 60th Birthday.* Edited by R. Banks. Exeter: and Grand Rapids: Paternoster/Eerdmans, 1974. Dalton argues that 1 Peter was written to those suffering in order to remind them of their eschatological hope in Jesus Christ. This is also the correct context within which to understand the new birth imagery used in 1 Peter.

Davids, Peter H. *The First Epistle of Peter.* New International Commentary on the New Testament. Grand Rapids: Eerdmans, 1990. One of the strengths of Davids' commentary is its accessibility to a wide audience. Technical material is consistently reserved for the footnotes. Its layout is easy to follow because it addresses the material in a straightforward verse-by-verse manner. Occasionally, however, this strength becomes a weakness insofar as it masks larger structural elements within the letter.

Elliott, John H. *The Elect and the Holy: An Exegetical Examination of 1 Peter.* Supplements to *Novum Testamentum*, 12. Leiden: Brill, 1966. Elliott argues that 1 Peter 2:4–10 should be understood first and foremost as an exposition on the election of the people of God. Correct exegesis of its constituent parts (particularly the image of priesthood) must take into account this larger argument.

Elliott, John H. "Peter, Silvanus, and Mark in 1 Peter and Acts." Pp. 250–67 in *Wort in der Zeit: Neutestamentlichen Studien: Festgabe für Karl Heinrich Regensdorf zum 75. Geburstag.* Edited by W. Haubeck and M. Bachmann. Leiden: Brill, 1980. Elliott identifies a "Petrine group" as responsible for authoring 1 Peter. It sought to strengthen the church in Asia Minor and to fortify the influence of the Petrine group outside of Rome.

Elliott, John H. *A Home for the Homeless: A Social-Scientific Criticism of 1 Peter, its Situation and Strategy.* 2nd edn. Minneapolis: Fortress Press, 1990. This study focuses on the address "aliens and strangers" (1 Pet. 2:11; cf. 1:1), arguing that the terms are to be taken at face value as descriptions of the previous and current social status of those who have embraced the gospel. They are resident aliens and migratory workers, marginalized by their neighbors. 1 Peter exhorts these aliens and strangers to take comfort in the fact that they now have a home established for them by God. He has provided a "home for the homeless."

Elliott, John H. "Disgraced yet Graced: The Gospel according to 1 Peter in the Key of Honor and Shame," *Biblical Theology Bulletin* 25 (1995), 166–78. This article employs the social-scientific categories of honor and shame in order to shed light on the language, themes, and approach of 1 Peter.

Elliott, John H. *1 Peter.* Anchor Bible, 37B. New York: Doubleday, 2000. Elliott's exhaustive commentary combines a comprehensive introduction with detailed exegesis and a thorough bibliography. Elliott has long been a major figure in the study of 1 Peter. This commentary integrates his many previous contributions to the interpretation of the text.

Fitzmyer, Joseph A. "The First Epistle of Peter." Pp. 362–8 in *The Jerome Biblical Commentary.* Edited by Raymond Brown et al. Englewood Cliffs: Prentice-Hall, 1968.

Furnish, Victor P. "Elect Sojourners in Christ: An Approach to the Theology of 1 Peter," *Perkins Journal* 28 (1975), 1–11. Furnish argues that the major themes of 1 Peter are all laid out in the first twelve verses. 1 Peter speaks of the promises and demands that result from God's election of the addressees, those who must temporarily live as sojourners in the world.

Goppelt, Leonhard. *A Commentary on 1 Peter.* Trans. J. Alsup. Grand Rapids: Eerdmans, 1993. Originally published in 1978, this is the finest German commentary on 1 Peter. Goppelt lays a great deal of emphasis on the alienation experienced by the early Christian community. Living as disciples of Christ in a pagan world naturally led to persecution of various sorts.

Holloway, Paul A. "*Nihil inopinati accidisse* – 'Nothing unexpected has happened': A Cyrenaic Consolatory *Topos* in 1 Pet. 4:12ff.," *New Testament Studies* 48 (2002), 433–48. Calling attention to the use of a Greco-Roman consolatory *topos* in 1 Peter 4:12, Holloway suggests that consolation was one of the major goals of 1 Peter.

Horrell, David G. "Who Are 'the Dead' and When Was the Gospel Preached to Them? The Interpretation of 1 Pet. 4:6," *New Testament Studies* 49 (2003), 70–89. Horrell rejects the hypothesis that the "dead" to whom the gospel is preached in 4:6 should be understood as those who have died since hearing the gospel. Rather, the proclamation is made to the dead of previous generations.

Hunzinger, Claus-Hunno. "Babylon als Deckname für Rom und die Datierung des 1. Petrusbriefes." Pp. 67–77 in *Gottes Wort und Gottes Land: Hans-Wilhelm Hertzberg zum 70. Geburtstag*. Edited by H. Graf Reventlow. Göttingen: Vandenhoeck & Ruprecht, 1965.

Levine, Amy-Jill and M. M. Robbins (eds.). *A Feminist Companion to the Catholic Epistles and Hebrews*. London and New York: T. & T. Clark, 2004. The volume contains a number of essays on key passages in 1 Peter, including the household code, 1 Peter's use of Sarah, and reading 1 Peter in light of feminist theologies of suffering. Essays on 1 Peter include contributions by W. Carter, J. W. Aageson, M. Misset-van de Weg, B. J. Bauman-Martin, C. C. Kroeger, and J. K. Applegate.

Lohse, Eduard, "Paränese und Kerygma im 1 Petrusbrief," *Zeitschrift für die neutestamentliche Wissenschaft und die Kunde der älteren Kirche* 45 (1954), 68–89. Lohse explores the roots of primitive Christian parenesis in 1 Peter, concluding that the confessional and hymnic elements employed in the letter are tied to the early Christian kerygmatic emphasis on following in the way of the suffering Christ.

Marxsen, Willi. "Der Mitälteste und Zeuge der Leiden Christi." Pp. 377–93 in *Theologica Crucis – Signum Crucis; Festschrift für Erich Dinkler zum 70. Geburtstag*. Edited by C. Andersen and G. Klein. Tübingen: Mohr Siebeck, 1979. Marxsen argues that 1 Peter is a composite text containing a baptismal homily.

Michaels, J. Ramsey. *1 Peter*. Word Biblical Commentary 49. Waco: Word, 1988. Though very readable, Michaels' commentary often fails to cite or interact with alternative viewpoints.

Moule, C. F. D. "The Nature and Purpose of 1 Peter," *New Testament Studies* 3 (1956–7), 1–11. Seeing a clear division in sources between 4:11 and 4:12, Moule suggests that 1 Peter contains two different letters. The first letter was written for communities which faced the possibility of undeserved suffering. The second letter addressed those who were already in the midst of suffering.

Perdelwitz, E. Richard. *Die Mysterienreligion und das Problem des 1. Petrusbriefs*. Religionsversuche und Vorarbeiten, 11/3. Geissen: Töpelmann, 1911. Perdelwitz was the first to argue that 1 Peter included a baptismal homily as its primary source.

Reicke, Bo. *The Disobedient Spirits and Christian Baptism*. Acta Seminarii Neotestamentici Upsaliensis, 13. Copenhagen: Munksgaard, 1946. Reicke interprets the enigmatic reference to the disobedient spirits in light of a perceived baptismal context in 1 Peter. He also makes use of relevant Second Temple parallels.

Richards, E. Randolph. "Silvanus Was Not Peter's Secretary: Theological Bias in Interpreting *dia Silouanou ... egrapsa* in 1 Peter 5:12," *Journal of the Evangelical Theological Society* 43 (2000): 417–22. Richards argues against the frequently promulgated view that 1 Peter 5:12 points to Silvanus' role as Peter's amanuensis.

Selwyn, Edward G. *The First Epistle of Peter*. 2nd edn. London: Macmillan, 1964. Arguing that an extensive store of common Christian tradition lay behind 1 Peter, Selwyn's commentary provides a thorough form-critical analysis of the traditions behind the letter. It also includes a long essay on the "descent into Hades." The first edition appeared in 1947.

Stowers, Stanley K. *Letter Writing in Greco-Roman Antiquity*. Philadelphia: Westminster, 1986.

Talbert, Charles H. (ed.). *Perspectives on 1 Peter*. Macon, GA: National Association of Baptist Professors of Religion, 1986. This book contains a number of important essays on 1 Peter. Among them are articles written by John Elliott and David Balch, part of an ongoing dialogue about 1 Peter's approach to those outside the community of faith. Elliott argues for an approach that emphasizes the community's distinctive identity and encourages evangelistic engagement with outsiders. Balch contends that the household code functions as an apologetic for the Christian community, an attempt to convince outsiders that they are socially responsible members of the local community as well as the empire.

Thurén, Lauri. *Argument and Theology in 1 Peter: The Origins of Christian Paraenesis. Journal for the Study of the New Testament*, Supplementary Series, 114. Sheffield: Sheffield Academic Press, 1995. Thurén seeks to identify the motivation behind early Christian Paraenesis. To this end Thurén focuses his attention on the rhetorical function and context of the motivating expressions that lie behind 1 Peter's exhortations.

van Unnik, Willem C. "The Teaching of Good Works in 1 Peter," *New Testament Studies* 1 (1954), 92–110. Van Unnik's work examines the ethical exhortations in 1 Peter, a theme of great importance in the letter.

Wifstrand, Albert. "Stylistic Problems in the Epistles of James and Peter," *Studia Theologica* 1 (1948), 170–82. Wifstrand analyses the Greek language and style of 1 Peter, noting both its higher linguistic standard and its more occasional use of spoken forms.

Windisch, Hans. *Die Katholischen Briefe*. 3rd edn. Rev. and ed. H. Preisker. Handbuch zum Neuen Testament. Tübingen: Mohr Siebeck, 1951. Preisker's additions to this commentary represented the first claim that 1 Peter 1:3–4:11 was originally a baptismal liturgy.

# CHAPTER 35

# 2 Peter and Jude

Kevin B. McCruden

## Major Issues and Directions in Recent Study

Often included within the category of the seven general epistles (Harrington 2003: 162), 2 Peter and Jude frequently elicit reactions ranging from neglect to dismissal among contemporary readers (McKnight and Osborne 2004: 385; Wall 2001: 65). Typically, such reactions pertain to the perceived content and style of these pieces. For example, pointing to a pervasive theme of divine judgment against opponents, many view these texts as inordinately polemical (Kraftchick 2002: 17; Webb 1996: 140). Still others find the argumentation of these letters – especially in the case of Jude's many scriptural and non-scriptural references – frustratingly cryptic; and not a few commentators have complained about 2 Peter's penchant for florid prose (Thurén 1996: 340). And while positive assessments of these letters do abound, one just as frequently encounters a ranking of these texts as theologically marginal as compared to the remainder of the canonical writings of the New Testament (Kraftchick 2002: 71; Meier 1999: 65).

While these negative appraisals merit some attention, one wonders whether they prove adequate as comprehensive indices of the deeper significance of these texts. Certainly the polemical tone of these letters makes their ecumenical appropriation more difficult. However, both 2 Peter and Jude attest to important historical and theological currents within early Christianity that warrant renewed examination. Paramount among these currents would be the shared witness of these texts to the abiding eschatological expectation of early Christianity on the one hand, and the attendant implications of such eschatological anticipation as related to the issue of the Christian ethical life on the other (Charles 2002: 331–43).

Recent study of 2 Peter and Jude has resulted in the virtual abandonment of such earlier interpretive categories as early Catholicism and Gnosticism (Charles 1993: 48–61; Desjardins 1987: 93–5). According to the former, both letters witness to the progressive hierarchical development of the Christian movement discernible in the second century CE. Particularly expressive of such hierarchical progression, it is argued, is the construal of faith as a regulated body of tradition (Jude 3, 17; 2 Pet. 1:1, 3:2) on the one hand, in company with a waning anticipation for the close of the age, on the other (Bauckham 1983: 8).

None of these characteristics, however, really suits the evidence of either letter. For example, neither Jude's reference to the "faith" (*pistis*) that was "once and for all handed down to the saints" (3) nor 2 Peter's reference to "those who have received a faith [*pistis*] equal in honor to our own" (2 Pet. 1:1), necessarily refers to a conception of faith as a fixed deposit of tradition. In the case of Jude, the expression more than likely points to the author's conviction in the sufficiency of salvation available through the Christ event (Kraftchick 2002: 30). In essence, Jude's reference to faith functions to provide pastoral assurance to the community about the disclosure of God's presence to the faithful, both now and in the age to come. It is this providential presence mediated through Christ that renders the community "beloved in God" (Jude 1) and accounts for the "salvation held in common" between the author and the community (Jude 3). A similar pastoral dimension is likely at work in 2 Peter's connection of faith with the gift of divine knowledge (see 2 Pet. 1:2).

However, even if we were to accept the claim that the authors of Jude and 2 Peter are thinking of faith in formulaic terms, such theological activity was in no sense a late hierarchical development: it was integral to primitive Christianity from the start. As early as the 50s of the first century the early Christian missionary Paul could quote highly traditional formulaic statements such as those contained in 1 Corinthians 15:3–8 and Romans 3:24–5 (Harrington 2003: 191–3). As for the contention that 2 Peter and Jude attest to a waning of hope in the dawning age to come, this claim is plainly without evidence. Both letters espouse a thoroughgoing eschatological perspective (Jude 21; 2 Pet. 3:11–13) that looks forward to the community's glorious communion with Christ at the close of the age (Bauckham 1983: 8–9). Indeed, the author of 2 Peter (see 2 Pet. 3:12) confidently looks forward to a dramatic, cataclysmic termination of the cosmos itself (Adams 2005: 122).

Turning to the category of Gnosticism – a term inclusive of various second-century intellectual movements marked by cosmological dualism – compelling evidence for the influence of Gnostic concepts on 2 Peter and Jude seems unlikely (Adams 2005: 109). It is now generally recognized that developed Gnostic doctrines did not exist in the period in which the bulk of the New Testament writings emerged, i.e., the first century CE (Harrington 2003: 181; Brown 1997: 758).[1] Nevertheless, some scholars point to the description of the immoral behavior of the opponents gleaned from the polemical passages of both letters as evidence in support of some form of Gnostic influence on 2 Peter and Jude (see especially Jude 4, 8, 16; 2 Pet. 2:2, 13, 18). They argue that such behavior attests to a profound experience of spiritual freedom on the part of the opponents that manifests itself in a libertine attitude to the material world (Desjardins 1987: 93; Talbert 1966: 141). Apart from the question concerning whether or not such charges of immorality against the opponents accurately reflect circumstances in the community, it is important to remember that Gnosticism was a rather variegated phenomenon. Indeed, certain second-century Gnostics seem to have led very ascetic lives as an expression of their spiritual insight (Desjardins 1987: 93). In other words, there is nothing necessarily Gnostic about immoral behavior. Most importantly, one encounters little of what appears as cosmological dualism in these letters; that is, that conception linking various forms of second-century Gnostic systems wherein the created physical world is viewed as irremediably evil as compared to a transcendent spiritual dimension (Bauckham 1983: 12, 146; Desjardins 1987: 95).

Newer perspectives have emerged in place of the categories described in the previous paragraphs that promise renewed insight into the deeper significance of these texts. These would include: (1) a concern for the role that the categories of honor and shame play in the context of early Christian identity formation (Neyrey 1993: 3–7 ); (2) a deeper appreciation of early Christian creedal formulae that evince theologically exalted claims for the person of Jesus (Callan 2001: 253–64; Starr 2000: 29–31); (3) an increased awareness of the rhetorical sophistication of both 2 Peter and Jude (Watson 1988; Wendland 1994: 193–228); and finally, a sensitivity to the salient pastoral dimension of these texts (Charles 2002: 343).

Complementing these newer perspectives has been an emerging consensus among scholars to concentrate less on the question of the precise historical provenance of 2 Peter and Jude (Gerdmar 2001: 299) and more on the *type* of Christianity discernible in these texts. Although it is impossible to reconstruct the precise provenance of these letters due to the relative scarcity of internal evidence, a persuasive case can be made that each of these texts displays a fundamentally "Jewish kind of Christianity" mediated through a committed faith perspective in Christ (Harrington 2003: 167, 231; Gerdmar 2001: 334; Bauckham 1983: 10). Indeed, viewing 2 Peter and Jude as broadly indebted to the symbols of Jewish apocalyptic (Lyle 1998: 9) seems more profitable than simply dividing these texts rather sharply – and perhaps too simplistically – along the lines of a strongly Jewish/Palestinian outlook for Jude and a strongly Hellenistic/Greek outlook for 2 Peter (Gerdmar 2001: 334). This is not to suggest that 2 Peter and Jude should be interpreted monolithically. The letters do, I think, envision different occasions, with the occasion of 2 Peter being perhaps the more accessible of the two. But as I propose below, the letters may not necessarily stem from different geographic locations as is often proposed in contemporary scholarship.

## Authorship and Provenance of Jude and 2 Peter

Although 2 Peter and Jude are often viewed together due to certain thematic and literary parallels that they share, most commentators in fact see these letters as arising from quite dissimilar historical settings. As previously noted, placing either text within its appropriate historical provenance is an uncertain task. This is due in part to the brevity of these letters and in part to their unique epistolary features. Most examples of letters in the New Testament employ a formal introduction called a prescript that serves to identify *both* the sender and the recipients of the correspondence. Unfortunately, neither Jude nor 2 Peter identifies its recipients in their respective prescripts. Jude is addressed simply to those who are "called, beloved to God the Father and kept safely secured for Jesus Christ" (Jude 1). The prescript of 2 Peter sounds even more general: "Simeon Peter, a servant and apostle of Jesus Christ to those who have obtained a faith equal in honor to our own ..." (2 Pet. 1:1). Both letters conclude, moreover, not with customary epistolary endings but with elaborate doxologies

(Jude 24–5; 2 Pet. 3:18) devoid of personal details that might aid the task of historical reconstruction.

Nevertheless, proposals concerning the provenance of both letters usually begin with decisions concerning the authorship of each text. Although there is no consensus regarding whether the ascribed author of 2 Peter was indeed the apostle Peter, it is certainly accurate to say that the majority of modern commentators see the work as a pseudonymous piece: that is, written in the name of the historical apostle only (Adams 2005: 106 no. 1; Gilmour 2001: 291–2). Various factors make this assessment compelling. Of primary importance is 2 Peter's usage of a distinctive Greek vocabulary (Harrington 2003: 236; Thurén 1996: 339). 2 Peter contains some fifty-seven words not found elsewhere in the entire New Testament and thirty-two of these words do not appear in the Septuagint, the Greek version of the Jewish Bible, either (Bauckham 1983: 135). This linguistic consideration, combined with the author's familiarity with Hellenistic ethical (2 Pet. 1:5–7) and philosophical concepts (2 Pet. 3:10), seems more fitting for a Hellenized Jewish author than Peter the Palestinian apostle (Harrington 2003: 236). In a balanced study that ultimately advocates neither for Petrine authorship nor for pseudonymity, Michael Gilmour summarizes the major factors that militate against authorship by the historical Peter. These factors include: 2 Peter's literary dependence on Jude; 2 Peter's awareness of a collection of the apostle Paul's writings as scripture (2 Pet. 3:15–16); the relatively slow acceptance of the canonical status of 2 Peter by the early church; and finally, the observation that in terms of literary genre 2 Peter seems best to approximate the Jewish genre of a testament (Gilmour 2001: 295). According to the detailed description provided by Richard Bauckham (1983: 131–5), the latter was an established literary form in both Jewish and early Christian circles in which the dying hero bequeaths his legacy and authoritative words to his followers (2 Pet. 1:12–15). Bauckham has demonstrated that the testament genre was customarily received by the intended audience as a literary function (1983: 134).

The strong likelihood that 2 Peter is pseudonymous actually helps little in decisions regarding provenance. For this task, one is dependent upon several ambiguous leads found within the letter itself, and for this reason any proposal as to provenance can be only plausible at best. On the one hand, the author's use of the testament genre, the expectation of an apocalyptic end of the world, and a broad familiarity with stories from the Jewish Bible and Jewish legends (see 2 Pet. 2:4–16), betrays the Jewishness of the text (Harrington 2003: 236). On the other hand, 2 Peter's familiarity with Stoic philosophical vocabulary and cosmological theories (2 Pet. 1:5–6; 3:10) likely indicates a dominant Greco-Roman environment familiar with such ideas (Fornberg 1977: 122–4; Charles 2002: 334–41; Adams 2005: 118 n.58). Although contested by some scholars (Gerdmar 2001: 302–5), Richard Bauckham's reconstruction that argues both for a Roman origin for 2 Peter and a destination for the letter somewhere in Asia Minor makes the best sense of the rather scant evidence available from the text (1983: 159–62).

The following considerations make the Rome proposal attractive. In keeping with the stylized features of the testament genre, 2 Peter 1:13–15 presents the reader with the dramatic image of the apostle Peter as he contemplates his approaching death. According to 1 Clement, 5, Peter was martyred in the imperial capital of Rome. In addition, on the basis of 2 Peter 3:1, the author seems to have knowledge of 1 Peter (Thurén 1996: 344; Kraftchick 2002: 148–9), a letter which was written from Rome to certain early Christian communities in the area of Asia minor (1 Pet. 5:13).[2] As for a possible destination for 2 Peter, the likely reference to 1 Peter in 2 Peter 3:1 makes the proposal for a destination somewhere in Asia Minor plausible, since 1 Peter was addressed to churches in that region (see 1 Pet. 1:1). In addition, 2 Peter's reference to a collection of Paul's letters (2 Pet. 3:16) may point to Asia Minor, since this was a major site of Paul's mission field (Gilmour 2002: 21; Kraftchick 2002: 73). Beyond this, it is very difficult to pinpoint the provenance of 2 Peter.

As is the case with 2 Peter, questions concerning the provenance and authorship of Jude are frequently linked. The author identifies himself in the opening line of the letter (Jude 1) as "Jude, a slave of Jesus Christ and brother of James." Although the name Jude/Judas (*Ioudas*), appears in certain of the gospels and the Acts of the Apostles as one of the twelve apostles (Luke 6:16; John 14:22; Acts 1:13), the reference to a brother called James makes it all but certain that the Jude listed here is meant to have the ancient reader recall the James who was the brother of Jesus and the principal leader of the primitive Christian community in Jerusalem. Hence, the ascribed author is Jude, who is listed fourth in the list of Jesus' siblings (Mark 6:3; Matt. 13:55).

For some scholars a number of factors make it plausible that a Palestinian Jew, for example the historical Jude, is the actual author of the letter. These would include: the ethical seriousness of the letter, Jude's strongly Jewish and apocalyptic tone, and Jude's deep acquaintance with narratives from both the Jewish Bible and the later expansions of these stories in the literature of so-called Second Temple Judaism (Lyle 1998: 9–13; Bauckham 1982: 16). It seems more likely, however, that Jude is a pseudonymous piece (Wall 2001: 64; Neyrey 1993: 31; Harrington 2003: 183; Meier 1999: 66–7). The most compelling evidence is again linguistic. Presumably the historical Jude, like Jesus himself, spoke Aramaic, and not Greek. The Greek of Jude is of good quality, evincing a rather elaborate vocabulary (Harrington 2003: 176). A demonstrated awareness, moreover, of various rhetorical techniques, together with an almost scribal awareness of a broad range of biblical and extra-biblical traditions, also makes it quite unlikely that a Palestinian village artisan is the author of this letter (Neyrey 1993: 31). One of course might object at this point that Hellenistic culture had already made inroads into Palestine by the first century CE (Gerdmar 2001: 303; Thurén 1997: 464), thereby making it possible for a Palestinian Jew to possess both a good command of the Greek language and rhetorical skill. While this is possible, the author's demonstrated facility with Greek still gives one pause, as does Jude's concluding doxology, with its rather exalted portrayal of Christ as the coming Lord (Jude 21).

While eschewing authorship by the historical Jude, other scholars nonetheless find a Palestinian provenance for the letter attractive. On this issue, there is evidence to suggest that Jesus' family, and not just James, had influence in Palestine as early missionaries (see 1 Cor. 9:5). Hence, ascribing a letter to Jude might resonate with a community located somewhere in a Palestinian locale (Brown 1997: 750). Indeed, there is a tradition reported in Eusebius (*Ecclesiastical History*, 3.19–20) that in the mid-second century certain relatives of Jude were respected there (Bauckham 1990: 45–133). Certain thematic elements in the letter also make a Palestinian provenance for the origin of the letter plausible. In addition to a strong familiarity with the scripture of the Jewish Bible, Jude shows a clear knowledge of such extra-biblical texts as *1 Enoch* and the *Testament of Moses*, both of which were representative of the literature of Palestinian Judaism (Bauckham 1983: 7).[3] In addition, Jude's method of explicating Scripture is somewhat comparable to the *pesher* style of exegesis practiced at Qumran (Bauckham 1983: 5; Neyrey 1993: 29). Through this method, discrete passages of scripture were interpreted as applying to the life situation of the community of the Jewish sectarians. A final factor that makes the Palestinian proposal plausible concerns the whole issue of Jude's scriptural allusions. Jude's references to Jewish scripture suggest an acquaintance with the relevant text in Hebrew, rather than the Greek of the Septuagint (Bauckham 1983: 7). If this is accurate, a Palestinian provenance for Jude seems likely, since the Septuagint was the version of the Jewish Bible customarily utilized by early Christian communities who lived outside Palestine.

A possible factor weighing against a Palestinian provenance for Jude, however, is the author's good command of Greek and evident rhetorical craft, which together may point to a Hellenized Jewish author rather than a Palestinian author (Kraftchick 2002: 21; Neyrey 1993: 30). It should also be remembered that familiarity with the stories and traditions of the Jewish Bible was present in Christian communities resident outside of Palestine. Paul's letter to the Romans is a case in point. Much of Paul's argument in that letter seems to presume that the predominantly Gentile Christians in Rome espoused a very Jewish kind of Christianity (Romans 1:18–3:20). Indeed, Jude could have been written in any place in which an appreciation for the Jewish heritage was strong. One immediate candidate that comes to mind – in addition to Palestine – is Rome. To my knowledge, a Roman provenance for Jude is seldom entertained, yet it is interesting to compare Jude with writings such as Hebrews and 1 Peter on this count. Both 1 Peter and Hebrews display a marked preference for Jewish symbols and terminology, and both letters likely stem from a Roman provenance (Brown and Meier 1983: 128–58). Moreover, in my judgment, certain linguistic and thematic parallels between these three letters are at the very least provocative. For example, 1 Peter takes care to ascribe to its addressee the designation, "beloved," which is an epithet suggestive of God's selection of 1 Peter's Gentile audience as the new covenant people of God (1 Pet. 3:12). Jude also applies this epithet to its audience (Jude 3, 17, 20). More significantly, 1 Peter employs the Greek verb *tēreō* ("keep," "preserve") to comment on the glorious inheritance that the faithful will obtain in heaven (1 Pet. 1:4). This verb is a favorite term also for the author of Jude, who uses it no fewer than five times in the brief span of twenty-five verses (Jude 1, 6 (twice), 13, 21). In verses 1 and 21 the author employs this verb to express the close relationship the faithful share with Christ and God, respectively, in a manner that is comparable with 1 Peter's usage. As for connections between Jude and Hebrews, we might point to the attention given to the role of angels in both writings (Heb. 1:1–14; Jude 6) in addition to a similar method of argumentation through a process of scriptural explication followed by pastoral application (Jude 5–11 and Heb. 3:7–4:3). In terms of the latter, it seems significant that both Hebrews and Jude begin their respective sections devoted to scriptural explication by placing the biblical example of Israel's disobedience in the wilderness in a primary position at the head of the scriptural examples (see Jude 5; Heb. 3:7ff.). While such observations are far from establishing a Roman provenance for Jude, they are suggestive enough in my judgment to at least consider the proposal.

## Epistolary, Literary, and Rhetorical Analysis

It is clear that 2 Peter and Jude share some type of literary dependence (Kraftchick 2002: 79). This is evident in the material comprising 2 Peter 2:1–3:3, which closely approximates the polemical statements and scriptural examples found in Jude 4–18. Terrance Callan observes that although the author of 2 Peter seldom quotes Jude directly, he paraphrases Jude extensively and even adopts some of Jude's language in the process of adapting Jude (Callan 2004: 43). Indeed, Callan shows that 2 Peter has copied eighty of the 311 words that constitute Jude 4–18 (Callan 2004: 43). The following verses show the extent of 2 Peter's adaptation of Jude: 2 Pet. 1–3 (Jude 4); 2 Pet. 4 (Jude 6); 2 Pet. 6 (Jude 7); 2 Pet. 10: (Jude 7–8); 2 Pet. 11 (Jude 9); 2 Pet. 12 (Jude 10); 2 Pet. 13 (Jude 12); 2 Pet. 15 (Jude 11); 2 Pet. 17 (Jude 12–13); 2 Pet. 18 (Jude 16); 2 Pet. 3:2 (Jude 17); 2 Pet. 3:3 (Jude 18).

Some scholars explain these parallels either by drawing on the theory that Jude copied 2 Peter (Gerdmar 2001: 123) or that both authors depended on a common literary source. It is more likely, however, that Jude served as a literary template for 2 Peter (Adams 2005: 109; Callan 2004: 42; Wall 2001: 65; Lyle 1998: 15). This is best seen by closely comparing the material in Jude 5–11 with 2 Peter 2:4–16. Jude 5–11 introduces a threefold series of biblical and extra-biblical examples illustrative of the theme of disobedience and God's punishment of disobedience. The series includes: the account of Israel's lack of faith in the wilderness taken from Numbers 14:26–38 (Jude 5); the account of the fallen angels taken from Genesis 6:1–4 (Jude 6); and finally the story of Sodom and Gomorrah (Jude 7) taken from Genesis 19:1–28. Jude then interrupts this pattern of biblical allusions in verse 9, with the extra-biblical account of Michael's contest with the Devil over the corpse of Moses. This latter account likely derives from the lost ending of the *Testament of Moses*. Jude then resumes the threefold pattern in verse 11 by citing three biblical figures who, according to Richard Bauckham (Bauckham 1983: 79–84 ), were notorious in later Jewish legend for their disobedience, namely Cain (Gen. 4:8), Balaam (Num. 31:16ff), and Korah (Num. 16:1–50).

In adapting the above, the author of 2 Peter omits the reference to Israel's lack of faith in the wilderness (Jude 5) and inserts between the account of the fallen angels and the scene of Sodom and Gomorrah an allusion to the flood story taken from Genesis 7:6ff. (2 Pet. 2:4–9). Conspicuous in this editing is the author's clear emphasis on the righteous figures of both Noah and Lot (2 Pet. 2:5–9). Both figures are likely employed by the author of 2 Peter as models of endurance and virtue to be emulated by the community (Charles 2002: 337–8). Lastly, the author of 2 Peter omits Jude's references to Cain and Korah, while retaining the Balaam account alone. As Daniel Harrington notes, the author of 2 Peter therefore recasts Jude's biblical examples in their customary "chronological order" as they appear in the biblical text (see Harrington 2003: 162). 2 Peter also omits Jude's extra- biblical references to the lost ending of the *Testament of Moses* (Jude 8), as well as Jude's later reference to 1 Enoch 1:9 in verse 14. While these last two omissions may hint at apprehensions concerning the authority of these particular texts (Harrington 2003: 163), my own suspicion is that 2 Peter utilizes examples from Torah alone since these texts were likely pivotal for Christian identity-formation in his own community.

In terms of ancient literary categories, 2 Peter and Jude incorporate elements from both Jewish and Greco-Roman forms of letter-writing. Both Jude and 2 Peter, therefore, contain formal prescripts with the following elements that were highly stereotypical for ancient letters: sender, addressee, and opening salutation (Jude 1–2; 2 Pet. 1–2). Although genuine letters, both 2 Peter and Jude depart from the letter format in important ways, however. Neither letter, for example, concludes with a formal farewell section typical of most letters in the New Testament (see 1 Cor. 16:19–20). Instead, one encounters concluding doxologies praising God and Christ. Moreover, much like Hebrews, Jude is replete with various rhetorical devices suggestive of an originally oral, homiletic context (Thurén 1997: 454). For example, the author frequently employs triple expressions and rhetorical patterns of three (Wendland 1994: 215) (see Jude 2, 5–7, 11, 12–13, 3, 17, 20). Jude also makes ample use of catchwords (Charles 1993: 20–42) that serve to the entire letter into a coherent whole: "beloved" (*agapētoi*) (vv. 3, 17, 20); the verb *tēreō* ("keep," "preserve") (vv. 1, 6a, 6b, 13, 21); the Greek word for "impiety" in various forms of speech (vv. 4, 15, 18): *asebeis* (v. 4), *asebeias*, *ēsebēsan*, *aseibeis* (v. 15), *aseibeiōn* (v. 18). Alternating between a pattern of explication of scripture followed by scriptural application and finally pastoral exhortation (see Jude 5–11, 17–23), the main body of Jude functions essentially as a sermon aimed ultimately at exhortation (Charles 1993: 20). Jude, therefore, may best be described as a sermon in the form of a letter (Bauckham 1983: 3). As mentioned earlier in the section dealing with the question of the authorship of 2 Peter, 2 Peter best suits the testament genre.

In addition to employing a full range of rhetorical devices such as assonance, alliteration, and verbal repetition (Starr 2000: 31–46; Kraftchick 2002: 76; Watson 1988: 195–7), the author of 2 Peter also prefers uncommon and unusual words, complex syntax, and generally ornate expressions (Thurén 1996: 339). For all these reasons, the letter's style has frequently been described as particularly solemn and grand, if not artificially noble; and many have argued that this style reflects the so-called Asian or grand style discussed by such ancient rhetorical theorists as Quintilian (Watson 1988: 146; Callan 2003: 203–25). The adoption of this style confirms that the author is primarily trying to appeal to the *pathos* or the emotions of the audience. The solemn tone of the author's prose, therefore, functions to celebrate the power and nobility of the ideas touching upon the gift of Christian existence both in this age and in the age to come (Callan 2003: 223–4). In conjunction with employing the fictive figure of the apostle Peter, the adoption of this solemn style also functions rhetorically to garner respect and a receptive hearing for the author from the audience (Thurén 1996: 345).

Both 2 Peter and Jude can profitably be examined in accordance with Greco-Roman rhetorical categories inclusive of deliberative, forensic, and epideictic oratory. Each of these species of oratory was concerned with the different kinds of persuasive speech requisite for influencing specific audiences. Deliberative oratory, the oratory of politics, concerns itself with the task of persuading a particular audience to adopt a future action. Forensic oratory, the oratory of law courts, seeks to convince an audience of something that has occurred in the past. Lastly, epideictic oratory is the oratory of celebration (Wendland 1994: 201). While elements of each of these categories can be discerned in both letters, Jude most approximates the deliberative style (Watson 1988: 79), since it aims at the pastoral goal of encouraging the faithful to live a certain kind of life (Jude 20–1). 2 Peter contains a subtle balance of both deliberative and epideictic features (Watson 1988: 85–6), since it celebrates the life of virtuous transformation made possible through Christ (2 Pet. 1:3–11) and calls on the faithful to grow more deeply in this transformed life (2 Pet. 3:11–14, 17–18).

## Occasion and Purpose of Jude

2 Peter and Jude address concrete situations facing first-century Christian communities; however, reconstructions of the occasion and purpose of each letter can proceed only tentatively. Both texts clearly envision some form of communal crisis associated with either false teachers (2 Pet. 2:1) or anonymous intruders (Jude 4, 19). In the case of Jude, the opponents seem to be well integrated within the community (see Jude 12). At the risk of oversimplifying matters, the respective occasion of each letter centers mainly on considerations of inappropriate behavior (Jude 16) and inappropriate teaching (2 Pet. 3: 4).

Since portions of Jude served as a literary source for 2 Peter, I will consider the occasion and purpose of Jude first. Clearly, the most evocative language in the letter centers on the proposed immoral behavior of individuals, who have "stealthily slipped into the community" (Jude 4). Broadly slandering these opponents as "impious sinners" (Jude 15) who have exchanged God's grace for "licentious behavior" (Jude 4), the author paints these opponents with stock terms of abuse in keeping with ancient models of rhetorical invective (Harrington 2003: 190). To this end, Jude depicts his opponents as "irrational animals" that function merely by "instinct" (Jude 10); the opponents are devious individuals, whose collective speech serves merely to flatter for personal gain (Jude 16). Collectively depraved, such persons "defile the flesh" (Jude 8) and embody lives that are guided by their disordered "passions" (*epithymias*) (Jude 16, 18).

Accompanying these indictments of the opponents' behavior is the rather enigmatic description of the intruders in verse 8 as "dreamers," who "speak violence against the glorious ones." Interpreting "dreamers" as a reference to ecstatic visionary experiences, Richard Bauckham, among other commentators, views the opponents in Jude as essentially charismatic Christians, who are living lives free of moral restraint (Bauckham 1982: 11; Neyrey 1993: 31–2; Kraftchick 2002: 33). In much the same vein, Daniel Harrington argues that the opponents may best be seen as radical Paulinists. That is, they are Christians who advocate Paul's law-free gospel and revel in an exalted spiritual existence (Jude 19) that enables them to live apart from moral mandates (Harrington 2003: 194). Such an over-developed sense of their own present salvation may also explain the curious description of the opponents in verse 8 as those who speak violence against the "glorious ones." Although some see Jude's reference here to *doxas* "glorious ones" (v. 8) as an allusion to those holding authority in the community (Desjardins 1987: 94), it is more likely that the phrase "glorious ones" refers to angelic beings

(Kraftchick 2002: 42). According to Harrington, this reference to angels may provide evidence of an element of deviant teaching in the opponents' theology, namely the explicit denigration of angels fueled by an over-enthusiastic sense of fully attained salvation.

While it is possible that these charges of immorality may reflect the behavior of the opponents, it is more likely that they are rhetorically motivated, since it was quite common in antiquity to accuse one's opponents of sexual immorality (Thurén 1997: 457). Significantly, although the author accuses the opponents of licentiousness (Jude 4), sexual misconduct (Jude 8), and impiety (Jude 4, 15, 18), the actual content of these charges is never precisely defined. Much the same can be said for the charges of immorality found in 2 Peter 2:1–3:3 (see esp. 2 Pet. 2:2, 9–10, 14, 18; 3:3). The likelihood is strong, therefore, that the charges of immoral behavior in both letters are simply stock and stereotypical, revealing little about the opponents' actual behavior in either letter (Adams 2005: 108–9).

In the case of Jude, however, it may nonetheless be possible to argue for a middle position. While such rhetorical invective reveals little about actual behavior, it may reflect an occasion in which some in the community are repudiating a radical sexual ethic held in common by both the author and the communal majority (Desjardins 1987: 98–9). On this reading, the principled rejection of a rigorous sexual ethic (Jude 8) on the part of the opponents calls forth a rhetorically vehement response accusing the opponents of all sorts of sexual irregularities from the author. With this possibility in mind, it is probably safer to view these moral indictments of the opponents in Jude as rhetorical ploys on the author's part that function to discredit the collective character of the opponents (Thurén 1997: 458–9). Such rhetoric would have been highly effective, since it was aimed at an ancient audience in which the larger group played a stronger role in identity-formation than the individual. Whatever their precise offense may have been, the author sees the opponents as destructive to the community, and this provokes a strong pastoral response in Jude 12–13, in which rhetorical exaggeration (Thurén 1997: 458) plays a critical role:

> These men who fearlessly dine together at your love feasts while all the while shepherding themselves are like hidden reefs. They are waterless clouds carried along by the winds; late autumn trees, fruitless, twice dead, and uprooted; wild waves of the sea casting up their shameful deeds like foam; they are wandering stars for whom the gloom of darkness has been reserved forever.

Crafted for an ancient audience for whom the categories of shame and honor were vitally important (Neyrey 1993: 6), such language functions to strip the opponents of every dimension of honor. Therefore, the author compares the opponents to hidden and destructive reefs (*spilades*) (Jude 12) on which the community may become shipwrecked (Kraftchick 2002: 48–9). The string of nature imagery that follows (Jude 12–13) inclusive of waterless clouds, fruitless trees, storm-tossed seas, and wandering stars, further denigrates the opponents as thoroughly destructive and contrary to all that is natural (Kraftchick 2002: 50–3). This imagery, in tandem with the accusations concerning immorality described above, implicitly casts the opponents in as shameful a light as possible (Thurén 1997: 459). It seems likely that the author of 2 Peter has adapted portions of Jude in 2:1–3:3 for a similar rhetorical effect and that the portrait of the opponents' immoral behavior in 2 Peter 2:1–3:3 is, therefore, likely not historical (Adams 2005: 108).

While Jude's strategy of rhetorical denunciation may seem at first sight to further obscure the occasion and purpose of the letter, it may actually provide clues for the accurate interpretation of the text. While Jude is a letter addressed to a real situation of community discord, its larger purpose is to engage in the pastoral task of community identity-formation. That is, the author is less concerned with the immoral behavior of the opponents than he is with encouraging the faithful members of the community to lead lives of obedience and moral rectitude as they wait for the end of time. In other words, the author of Jude calls on the community to lead a life commensurate with their identity as the beloved people of God.

Integral to this task of identity-formation is an attempt to assure the community of their honorable identity as God's people. To that end, the author designates them as "called" (*klētois*) and assures them that they are "beloved to God" and share with the author a common salvation (Jude 3). The faithful in the community are, moreover, kept secure by Christ and have the assurance of having God's Spirit (Jude 1, 19). All of this functions as theological assurance to the faithful that they can indeed stand blameless before God when the eschatological end of days arrives (Jude 24). In contrast, the deviant members of the community will face judgment on that day, in accordance with the biblical and extra-biblical examples assembled by the author (Jude 5–16). This is why Jude may best be understood as an example of deliberative rhetoric, since the letter utilizes persuasive speech that functions to encourage the readers to live a particular kind of life in the future. Paradoxically, one effective way to carry out such encouragement is to spell out for the faithful the consequences of a life devoid of obedience and moral seriousness.

> But I wish to remind you, although you already know all these things, that after the Lord had once saved a people from the land of Egypt, he later destroyed those who did not believe. And as for the angels who did not preserve their own station but abandoned their particular dwelling, he has kept them in eternal chains under darkness for the judgment of the great day. Just as Sodom and Gomorrah and the cities around them indulged in immorality in the same manner as they and went after the flesh of another, thereby presenting an example when they undergo the punishment of fire.

As we saw above, in this section of the letter the author collects three negative examples illustrative of disobedience. In each of these examples, moreover, the consequences of disobedience are spelled out in terms of the divine judgment that awaits those who disobey God. Two of Jude's examples center on past deeds of sexual sin (Jude 6 and 7) that function to echo and point ahead to the charges of improper sexual activity lodged against the opponents throughout the letter. Verse 8 then explicitly applies these examples and the consequent divine judgment to the opponents. From here until verse 17 the pattern of biblical and extra-biblical examples of disobedience and application to the opponents continues.

Through these examples, the author endeavors to convince the community that divine judgment awaits the opponents just as God punished other sinners in the past. Indeed, the care with which the author has emphasized the certainty of God's judgment on the opponents functions, in part, to evoke from the community a verdict of present judgment against the opponents in its midst (Webb 1996: 148). However, it is equally important to see that both the emphasis on the opponents' sexual impurity and the assured judgment by God function as an implicit call to the faithful to lead lives of sexual purity and overall moral rectitude, for only such a life will render them "without blemish" (Jude 24) at the end of time:

> But you beloved, build yourselves up by means of your holy faith, pray in the Spirit and keep yourselves in the love of God as you patiently await the mercy of our Lord Jesus Christ which leads to eternal life ... To the one who is able to keep you from stumbling and to establish you as blameless before his glory with rejoicing ... .

## The Occasion and Purpose of 2 Peter

Scholarly reflection on the occasion and purpose of 2 Peter frequently dwells on the material found in 2 Peter 3:4–13. In these verses, the author attributes a skeptical position to certain members within the community with respect to the expectation for the end of the world: "And they say, Where is the promise of his coming? From the time that the fathers fell asleep, everything remains the same just as from the beginning of creation" (2 Pet. 3:4). Compared to the rather generalized moral slander borrowed from Jude and found in 2:1–3:3, the language in 2 Peter 3:4–13 sounds rather specific. Such specificity makes it more plausible that in this section of the letter we encounter a relatively accurate portrayal of positions advocated by some in the community (Adams 2005: 108–9). Specifically, it would appear that some in the community are expressing doubt concerning the expected arrival of Jesus as the exalted end-time judge. This same concern was broached earlier in the letter (2 Pet. 1:16–18) when the author pointed to his eyewitness testimony of Jesus' transfiguration as validation for the promise of Christ's *parousia* or end-time arrival (Neyrey 1980b: 504–19).

However, accompanying this skepticism concerning Christ's arrival at the end of time are certain passages in the letter (2 Pet. 3:9, 12) that seem to hint at more generalized misgivings concerning the theoretical possibility of divine intervention at all (Adams 2005: 111). For this reason, numerous scholars have proposed that the purpose of 2 Peter is connected precisely with the refutation of Christians who hold to a kind of principled philosophical rejection of the possibility for divine intervention in the world. Such skepticism was a notable feature especially of first-century Epicurean philosophy (Neyrey 1980a: 407–31; Green 2001: 107–22).

However, Edward Adams has recently challenged this common assessment of the occasion of the letter. Taking the term "fathers" in 2 Peter 3:4 as a reference to Old Testament prophecies relating to the end of the world, Adams argues that the objection in view in 2 Peter 3:4 does not concern the theoretical possibility of divine intervention in the world. Rather, the nature of the skepticism concerns the empirical observation that various Old Testament prophecies envisioning a new creation – such as those found in Isaiah 65:17 (see 2 Pet. 3:13) – are still unfulfilled (Adams 2005: 114). This apparent failure of the prophetic vision invalidates, therefore, both the promises relating to God's dramatic advent into history and the related expectation that Jesus will usher in the conclusion of history as the exalted end-time judge (Adams 2005: 114). Adams argues further that if there is any philosophical component to the eschatological skepticism criticized by the author of 2 Peter it likely has to do with a principled view of the cosmos as stable and unchanging, a view that is inconsistent with both Stoic and Epicurean cosmological reflection (Adams 2005: 116). Therefore, the occasion of 2 Peter centers on a particular type of eschatological skepticism that has been nurtured by the experience of unfulfilled scriptural promises concerning the end of the world, in company with a kind of Platonic conception of reality that views the cosmos as an immutable entity that endures forever without change (2 Pet. 3:4).

Adams' reconstruction presents an insightful new angle from which to view the undeniable eschatological concerns present in 2 Peter. Moreover, this reconstruction of the occasion of the letter accounts nicely for the author's attempt in 3:5–7 and 3:10 to emphasize both the provisional nature of the world and its destiny of destruction by God. Yet it is important to see that such eschatological concerns comprise only one dimension of the letter. One of the most interesting features of 2 Peter is the importance given to the role of virtue in the lives of the faithful (see 2 Pet. 1:5–11; 3:11). To a degree stronger than anything we encounter in Jude, the author of 2 Peter emphasizes the present dimension of salvation in the moral lives of the faithful (Callan 2001: 549–59). Although full salvation lies in the eschatological age to come, the faithful can even now participate in the very excellence that belongs to Christ through the life of virtue (Starr 2000: 43–5). While the author of 2 Peter stops short of the doctrine of the human becoming divine (Starr 2000: 45) the language of participation in the divine (2 Pet. 1:4) as well "entry" into the kingdom of Christ (2 Pet. 1:11) clearly works on the premise that the life of Christian virtue in the present approximates the stability of the eternal kingdom that is the destiny for the faithful (2 Pet. 3:17–18). Indeed, near the conclusion of the letter the theme of the virtuous life is closely connected to the author's eschatological assurances concerning the end of all things (2 Pet. 3:11–14):

> Since everything is to be destroyed in this way, what sorts of persons must you be behaving in a manner befitting holiness and piety as you patiently await and hasten the coming of the day of God, on account of which day the heavens will be destroyed by fire and the elements melt through burning? But according to his promise we patiently wait for new heavens and a new earth in which righteousness dwells. For this reason, beloved, as you wait for these things, hasten to be found by him in peace without spot and blemish.

It seems to me that the question we must address at this point concerns how best to connect these ethical and eschatological aspects of 2 Peter to the larger question with which we began our discussion concerning the letter's occasion and purpose. Here it may be possible to argue along with Charles (2002: 331–43) that certain members of the community addressed in 2 Peter are employing eschatological skepticism as a pretext for leading immoral lives (see 2 Pet. 3:19–20). The virtue of such a proposal is that it helps explain why the author has adopted and adapted the polemical material taken from Jude 4–18. Much like Jude, the author of 2 Peter reviles his opponents in order to evoke from his audience a verdict of shame with respect to the deviant members of the community. However, just as we observed in our discussion of the rhetorical function of denunciatory language in the section on Jude, it seems unwise in the final analysis to view the moral indictments we find in 2 Peter 2:1–3:3 without a good deal of historical suspicion.

In the end, perhaps the best way to think of the occasion and purpose of 2 Peter is to appreciate as deeply as we can the strongly pastoral dimension of the letter. Given the generally negative moral appraisal of the world discernible in the letter (see 2 Pet. 1:4; 3:13), I am inclined to agree with Charles' reconstruction of the community addressed in 2 Peter as a culturally beleaguered group struggling to live lives of almost holy separateness in the midst of a hostile Greco-Roman culture (Charles 2002: 342). Much like Paul does in his pastoral letter addressed to the Thessalonian Christians (see 1 Thess. 5: 1–9), the author of 2 Peter counterbalances his call to the faithful to live out their glorious destiny in the present with a graphic portrait of what awaits the present world and the ungodly within it (2 Pet. 3:7). Unlike Charles, however, I think the author's emphasis in 2 Peter on both moral striving and the certainty of eschatological judgment is addressed more to the community as whole than deviant members *per se*. To this extent, 2 Peter shares much in common with the overall purpose of Jude.

## Notes

1  Dating either Jude or 2 Peter remains speculative. A date in the late first or early second century is plausible.
2  1 Peter 5:13 refers to Babylon, which was a code word for Rome in both Jewish and Christian circles in the late first century.
3  Jude 9 shows an awareness of post-biblical Jewish legends surrounding the death and burial of Moses. It is possible that in verse 9 Jude preserves in some form the lost ending of the so-called Testament of Moses. While the latter was likely composed in the first century CE, it is preserved only in a fifth-century Latin manuscript that breaks off before the account of the end of Moses' life. Jude 14–15 contains an explicit reference to the composite apocalyptic work entitled *1 Enoch*. Jude quotes *1 Enoch*, 1:9, a verse deriving from the oldest section of the work, the *Book of the Watchers*, which dates from the second century BCE.

## Annotated Bibliography

Adams, Edward. " 'Where is the promise of his coming?' The Complaint of the Scoffers in 2 Peter 3:4," *New Testament Studies* 51 (2005), 106–22. An important, recent study challenging the consensus view that 2 Peter 3:4 envisions principled skepticism concerning the premise of divine intervention in the world. Adams argues that the author of 2 Peter opposes a view of the cosmos understood as unchanging and immutable by employing Stoic principles that emphasize the coming dissolution of the cosmos.

Bauckham, Richard, J. *Jude, 2 Peter*. Word Biblical Commentary, 50. Waco: Word Books, 1983. Bauckham's commentary remains one of the best single resources on the background and

exegesis of 2 Peter and Jude. Important emphases include: a detailed treatment of the testament genre as background for explicating the literary genre of 2 Peter; a persuasive argument for situating Jude in a Palestinian provenance; and a solid emphasis on the apocalyptic
worldview of Jude. Bauckham argues for authorship of the letter of Jude by the historical
Jude, one of Jesus' brothers.

Bauckham, Richard, J. *Jude and the Relatives of Jesus in the Early Church*. Edinburgh: T. & T. Clark,
1990. A significant work by Bauckham that reprises in more detail some of the central
aspects of his commentary relating to Jude. In part, a detailed study on the historical question relating to Jesus' relatives, and in part exegetical reflection on the phenomenon of
Palestinian Christianity. Along the way, Bauckham draws attention both to the similarities
between Jude's scriptural interpretation and the exegetical practices at Qumran as well as
to the sophisticated Christological claims emerging from Palestinian Christianity.

Brown, Raymond E. *Introduction to the New Testament*. New York: Doubleday, 1997.

Brown, Raymond E. and John P. Meier. *Antioch and Rome: New Testament Cradles of Catholic
Christianity*. New York: Paulist Press, 1983.

Callan, Terrance. "The Christology of the Second Letter of Peter," *Biblica* 82 (2001), 253–63. In
this piece, Callan contributes to the recent scholarly attention given to exalted Christological
claims in 2 Peter and Jude. Noting that few New Testament texts explicitly identify Jesus as
God, Callan argues that the author of 2 Peter applies the title of "God" to Jesus in 2 Peter 1:1
and thereby works with a theological assessment that sees Jesus as divine. For Callan, 2 Peter
reveals early Christian attempts to employ the title "God" in two ways: one as a "proper" noun
to denote the God of the Jewish Bible, the other as a title for Christ in the form of a "common
noun" to convey Christ's divinity without comprising the essential oneness of the God.

Callan, Terrance. "The Soteriology of the Second Letter of Peter," *Biblica* 82 (2002), 549–59.

Callan, Terrance. "The Style of the Second Letter of Peter," *Biblica* 84 (2003), 202–25. Describing
the literary style of 2 Peter as approximating the "Asian" style of rhetoric, Callan connects
the floridness of the Asian style with the author's desire to appeal to the emotions of the
reader. For Callan, 2 Peter's lofty rhetoric complements the high Christology of the letter
and functions as an emotional appeal to the reader to live a life of virtue.

Callan, Terrance. "The Use of the Letter of Jude by the Second Letter of Peter," *Biblica* 85 (2004),
42–65. A helpful terminological analysis of the literary relationship existing between Jude
4–18 and 2 Peter 2:1–3:3. Accepting the likely dependence of 2 Peter on Jude, Callan
understands this borrowing as running more along the lines of creative adaptation rather
than straightforward copying. In part, this adaptation speaks to the unique occasion of 2
Peter as a letter that addresses a warning to a community to be on guard against opponents
who deny Jesus' return in glory.

Charles, J. Daryl. *Literary Strategy in the Epistle of Jude*. Scranton: University of Pennsylvania,
1993.

Charles, J. Daryl. "The Function of Moral Typology in 2 Peter." Pp. 331–43 in *Character and
Scripture: Moral Formation, Community, and Biblical Interpretation*. Edited by William P.
Brown. Grand Rapids: Eerdmans, 2002.

Desjardins, Michel. "The Portrayal of the Dissidents in 2 Peter and Jude: Does It Tell Us More
about the 'Godly' than the 'Ungodly'?" *Journal for the Study of the New Testament* 30 (1987),
89–102. Desjardins interprets the occasion of Jude as stemming from a strongly eschatological and sectarian community opposed to less rigorous members of the community. The
strong moral categories of Jude point to an ethic of sexual renunciation on the part of the
author of the letter.

Fornberg, Tord. *An Early Church in a Pluralistic Society: A Study of 2 Peter*. Coniectanea biblica,
New Testament, 9. Lund: Gleerup, 1977. An important study arguing for the Hellenistic

setting of 2 Peter. For Fornberg, 2 Peter represents a conscious effort to articulate the significance of the Christ event in conceptual categories relevant for a Gentile community likely living in a strongly Hellenistic urban setting. An influential study for decisions regarding the Hellenistic conceptual provenance of the letter.

Gerdmar, Anders. *Rethinking the Judaism-Hellenism Dichotomy: A Historiographical Case Study of 2 Peter and Jude*. Coniectanea biblica, New Testament, 36. Stockholm: Almqvist & Wiksell, 2001. A very detailed work that places both letters within a Palestinian setting. Gerdmar challenges the consensus view that sees 2 Peter and Jude as texts expressive of a profoundly Hellenistic and Jewish background, respectively. Gerdmar argues that both letters reveal the heritage of Jewish Christianity and should be interpreted in light of the apocalyptic mentality seen in texts like *1 Enoch, 4 Ezra*, and *2 Baruch* on the Jewish side, and the book of Revelation on the Christian side.

Gilmour, Michael J. "Reflections on the Authorship of 2 Peter," *Evangelical Quarterly* 73 (2001), 291–309.

Gilmour, Michael J. *Significance of the Parallels between 2 Peter and Other Early Christian Literature*. Academia Biblica 10. Atlanta: Society of Biblical Literature, 2002.

Green, Gene L. "'As for prophesies, they will come to an end': 2 Peter, Paul and Plutarch on the 'obsolescence of oracles,'" *Journal for the Study of the New Testament* 23–4 (2001), 107–22. Green views 2 Peter within the context of ancient intellectual skepticism over the validity of various forms of divination understood as prophetic messages from the gods relating to future events. 2 Peter witnesses to such skepticism in the letter's depiction of the opponents as denying the promise of the eschatological arrival of Christ at the end of the age.

Harrington, Daniel J. *Jude and 2 Peter*. Sacra Pagina, 15. Minnesota: Collegeville, 2003. Provides a recent and academically informed discussion that is especially attentive to the theological and pastoral dimensions of the scriptural text. Harrington highlights the important witness in these letters to the phenomenon of Jewish Christianity, in particular the heritage of apocalyptic thought.

Kraftchick, Steven J. *Jude/2 Peter*. Abingdon New Testament Commentaries. Nashville: Abingdon, 2002. A recent commentary suitable for advanced undergraduates. Presents in an accessible manner what is argued with more scholarly detail in the commentaries by Bauckham, Neyrey, and Harrington. Kraftchick's comments on the rhetorical dimension of the correspondence are particularly good.

Lyle, Kenneth R. *Ethical Admonition in the Epistle of Jude*. Studies in Biblical Literature 4. New York: Peter Lang, 1998.

McKnight, Scot and Grant R. Osborne. *The Face of New Testament Studies: A Survey of Recent Research*. Grand Rapids: Baker Academic, 2004. Good bibliographic resource of recent studies on Jude and 2 Peter. Treats select major issues in the study of Jude and 2 Peter competently, but in a summary fashion.

Meier, John. "Forming the Canon on the Edge of the Canon," *Mid-Stream* 38 (1999), 65–70.

Neyrey, Jerome H. "The Form and Background of the Polemic in 2 Peter," *Journal of Biblical Literature* 99 (1980a), 407–31. A major essay length treatment dealing with the theme of eschatological skepticism in 2 Peter. Neyrey critiques Käsemann's disparagement of 2 Peter's Christology by noting that the occasion of 2 Peter stems more from concerns relating to theodicy than Christological appraisal. Neyrey's piece has proven influential in terms of reading 2 Peter against the background of Hellenistic and Hellenistic Jewish debates on the possibility of divine judgment.

Neyrey, Jerome H. "The Apologetic Use of the Transfiguration in 2 Peter 1:16–21," *Catholic Biblical Quarterly* 42 (1980b), 504–19.

Neyrey, Jerome H. *2 Peter, Jude*. Anchor Bible, 37C. New York: Doubleday, 1993. Provides an insightful treatment of the letters from the perspective of an established scholar of the social-scientific approach. For Neyrey, the social categories of honor and shame inform an attempt in both letters to shape the communal identity of the original recipients of the letters.

Reese, Ruth Anne. *Writing Jude: The Reader, the Text, and the Author in Constructs of Power and Desire*. Biblical Interpretation Series, 51. Leiden: Brill, 2000.

Starr, James R. *Sharers in Divine Nature: 2 Peter 1:4 in its Hellenistic Context*. Coniectanea biblica, New Testament, 33. Stockholm: Almqvist & Wiksell International, 2000.

Talbert, Charles. "II Peter and the Delay of the Parousia," *Vigiliae Christianae* 20 (1966), 137–45.

Thurén, Lauri. "Style Never Goes out of Fashion: 2 Peter Re-evaluated." In *Rhetoric, Scripture and Theology*. Edited by S. E. Porter and T. H. Olbricht. Sheffield: JSNTSS, 1996.

Thurén, Lauri. "Hey Jude! Asking for the Original Situation and Message of a Catholic Epistle," *New Testament Studies* 43 (1997), 451–65. An important recent essay highlighting the rhetorical function of denunciatory speech in Jude. Jude's excoriation of the opponents' collective moral character functions less as a reliable description of the opponents' actual behavior and more as a rhetorical tool to discredit the opponents in the eyes of Jude's addressees.

Wall, Robert W. "The Canonical Function of 2 Peter," *Biblical Interpretation* 9 (2001), 64–81. Wall addresses the often negative theological appraisal of 2 Peter and argues that the letter affords a valuable theological vision when viewed in tandem with 1 Peter. Taken together, both letters evince a characteristically Petrine emphasis on the important ethical dimension of the Christ event. This theological dimension should be noted quite apart from historical-critical questions concerning the authorship and literary genre of the letter.

Watson, Duane F. *Invention, Arrangement, and Style: Rhetorical Criticism of Jude and 2 Peter*. Society of Biblical Literature Dissertation Series, 104. Atlanta: Scholars, 1988. Fast becoming a standard work that considers 2 Peter and Jude in accordance with the categories of classical rhetoric. While both letters evince rhetorical sophistication, 2 Peter seems better acquainted with rhetorical principles *per se*. Watson's work is indispensable for the debate over the rhetorical dimension of Jude and 2 Peter.

Webb, Robert. "The Eschatology of the Epistle of Jude and its Rhetorical and Social Functions," *Bulletin for Biblical Research* 6 (1996), 139–51. Noting Jude's emphasis on eschatological judgment, Webb argues persuasively for seeing in Jude a rhetorical strategy whereby the author calls on members of the community to pronounce deviant members presently guilty in anticipation of God's future judgment.

Wendland, E. R. "A Comparative Study of 'Rhetorical Criticism', Ancient and Modern with Special Reference to the Larger Structure and Function of the Epistle of Jude," *Neotestamentica* 28/1 (1994), 193–228.

# CHAPTER 36
# Hebrews

## Craig R. Koester

Hebrews is one of early Christianity's most carefully crafted sermons. It addresses readers who have accepted the gospel and experienced conflict with those outside their community, and who now face the challenge of remaining faithful in a context where many in the wider society reject their convictions. The author understands that readers are confronted with the apparent contradiction between the hope of salvation and the dispiriting realities of daily life. His response involves looking to Jesus, who was subjected to abuse and death before being exalted to glory at God's right hand. The implication is that if God brought Jesus through suffering to glory, God will do the same for those who follow Jesus. Presenting Jesus as the heroic pioneer of salvation and merciful high priest, the divine Son of God and an afflicted human being, the author seeks to bolster the confidence of his readers in order that they might hold fast to their confession of faith and continue supporting each other in community.

## Major Issues in the Study of Hebrews

The authorship of Hebrews has long been debated because the book never discloses who wrote it. Three main positions have emerged concerning the author's identity: some maintain that it was written by Paul, others that the author was a companion of Paul, and still others that the author's identity remains unknown. Those who think that Paul wrote Hebrews observe that its concluding verses refer to "our brother Timothy," an expression that Paul sometimes used of his co-worker Timothy (Heb. 13:23; 2 Cor. 1:1; 1 Thess. 3:2; Philem. 1), and include greetings and admonitions like those at the end of Paul's letters. Theologically, Hebrews is similar to Paul's letters in its presentation of the saving work of Christ and its comments about the Jewish law, the new covenant, and faith (Heb. 8:6–13; 11:1–40; 2 Cor. 3:1–18; Rom. 1:17–18). Against Pauline authorship, however, many have noted that the author of Hebrews received the gospel second-hand, whereas Paul claims to have received it from Christ (Heb. 2:3; Gal. 1:11–12), and they note that Hebrews has a distinctive style and non-Pauline themes, such as the priesthood of Christ. Today, few think that Paul wrote Hebrews. Alternatively, the proposal that Hebrews was written by one of Paul's companions would account for the affinities between Paul's letters and Hebrews, while recognizing Hebrews' unique style and content. Paul's co-workers Barnabas, Apollos, Silas, and Priscilla have all been suggested as possible authors, but since Hebrews makes no clear reference to any of them, most interpreters now concede that the author's identity remains unknown.

The intended readership of Hebrews has been construed in different ways. The traditional title, "To the Hebrews," was affixed to the book by the end of the second century CE, and many have assumed that its contents show that it was originally written for Jewish or "Hebrew" Christians. The book mentions figures from Israel's history, such as Abraham, Sarah, Melchizedek, Moses, Aaron, and many more. There are contrasts between the old and new covenants, the Levitical priesthood and Christ's priesthood, and Mount Sinai and the heavenly Jerusalem, all of which would have been of interest to Jewish Christian readers. Others, however, have proposed that the book addressed Gentile Christians, since the readers entered the Christian community by turning from "dead works" and being "enlightened" – expressions that sometimes meant conversion from paganism (Heb. 6:1–4). They also note that one cannot assume that only Jewish Christians would have been interested in Old Testament imagery since Paul makes extensive use of the Old Testament in his letter to the Galatian Christians, who were Gentiles. In the end Hebrews does not provide enough information to determine whether the intended readers were Jewish or Gentile Christians, and the group may well have included people from both types of backgrounds.

A traditional way to read Hebrews has been to assume that it shows the superiority of Christ over the institutions of Old Testament Israel. The chapter divisions found in most Bibles emphasize the points at which the book compares Jesus to Moses (3:1), Aaron (5:1), and Melchizedek (7:1), and Christ's sacrifice to the sacrificial system established by the Mosaic law (9:1; 10:1). Interpreting the structure of Hebrews this way fits the theory that it was written to dissuade the readers from leaving the Christian faith and returning to Judaism. An alternative was developed by Albert Vanhoye, who divided Hebrews into five concentric sections that are arranged around the central theme of Christ's priesthood, which he took to be the main point of the book (8:1). Forms of his five-part outline appear in many commentaries and studies of Hebrews. Yet another approach, which has been especially popular among German scholars, has been to stress that Hebrews is not so much a treatise on the superiority of Christ or a presentation of Christ's high priesthood as it is a "word of exhortation" that is designed to renew the faith of its readers (13:22). They often divide Hebrews into three sections that are marked by the calls to hold fast to the community's confession of faith (4:14–16; 10:19–25). Although this approach has not been entirely successful in showing how each section relates to the other parts of the book, it points in a promising direction by emphasizing the role of Hebrews as a form of persuasive speech that could have addressed the dispiriting circumstances of an early Christian community. The outline of Hebrews given below will draw on aspects of these various proposals while showing that the work's structure follows the flow of Greco-Roman speeches.

The distinctive form and the unique themes of Hebrews make it challenging to determine where Hebrews fits within the varied currents of early Christian theology and practice. Most modern bibles follow the tradition of placing Hebrews between the thirteen letters that bear Paul's name and the epistles of James, Peter, John, and Jude. This position in the New Testament accurately reflects the sense that Hebrews' theology has affinities with that of Paul and other early Christian writers, even though it does not fit neatly into just one theological tradition. Like Paul, Hebrews speaks of the preexistent Son of God becoming human in obedience to God and shedding his blood to provide atonement for human sins, then being exalted to heavenly glory (Heb. 1:1–4; 2:14–17; 9:11–14; Phil. 2:5–11; Rom. 3:21–6). Both Hebrews and Paul quote Habbakuk 2:4 – "the righteous one will live by faith" – when discussing faith (Heb. 10:38; Gal. 3:11; Rom. 1:17). Both connect the reference to the lord sitting at God's right hand until his enemies are made his footstool from Psalm 110:1 with the portion of Psalm 8:6 that tells of God putting all things under the feet of the Son of Man (Heb. 1:13; 2:5–8; 1 Cor. 15:25–7). Both also invoke Abraham as an example of faith (Heb. 11:8–19; Gal. 3:6–9; Rom. 4:1–25). At the same time, Hebrews is like 1 Peter in that it emphasizes Christ's death "once for all" as a sinless victim (Heb. 7:26–7; 1 Pet. 2:22; 3:18) and depicts the faithful as members of God's household, who live as strangers and sojourners on the earth (Heb. 3:2–6; 11:8–16; 13:14; 1 Pet. 2:5, 11). These and other affinities with various early Christian writings suggest that Hebrews was composed in a context where multiple streams of Christian tradition intersected and enriched each other.

Studies of Hebrews often debate whether the book works with a philosophical world-view. Many have noted that Hebrews distinguishes the transcendent world above from the visible world below in a manner similar to Plato and the Jewish writer Philo, who interpreted the biblical tradition in Platonic categories. Plato maintained that people on earth could perceive the visible "shadows" of transcendent realities, but not the realities themselves (*Republic*, 514A–515D). Hebrews uses similar expressions when contrasting the "true" heavenly sanctuary with its earthly "shadow" (Heb. 8:1–5). Those who highlight the similarities between Hebrews and philosophical texts some-times note that many Christian theologians of the second through the fifth centuries CE worked within a Platonic philosophical framework, and suggest that Hebrews may have been one of the earliest texts to present the Christian message in a philosophical form to the Greco-Roman world. Nevertheless, Hebrews lacks key Platonic language, such as the distinction between the higher "intelligible" and the lower "perceptible" worlds, and the idea that visible things are "copies" of heavenly archetypes. Moreover, in Platonism one relates to the transcendent order by the power of the mind, whereas in Hebrews the connection occurs through faith. Hebrews' complex relationship to its Greco-Roman cultural context can best be discerned by taking the circumstances of its composition into account.

## Date and Place of Composition

Hebrews was probably composed between 60 and 90 CE. On the one hand, it is unlikely that Hebrews was written before the middle of the first century CE. The readers were not eyewitnesses of Jesus' ministry but received the gospel secondhand from "those who heard" (2:3). The author implies that the evangelists who brought the message belonged to the first Christian generation without necessarily claiming that they personally heard Jesus preach. Much of the evangelistic work of this generation took place in the 40s and 50s of the first century, and Hebrews writes about the founding and subsequent history of the readers' community as if those early experiences were some time in the past. The vivid experience of a persecution, for example, is something that belongs to the readers' memories rather than to their present experience (10:32–4). Accordingly, it seems unlikely that Hebrews was written before about 60 CE. On the other hand, Hebrews was probably composed before the first century ended. The conclusion refers to an upcoming visit of Timothy, who worked alongside Paul during the 50s. Assuming that this is a genuine reference to Paul's co-worker, it seems unlikely that Timothy would be traveling in the second century CE. Moreover, material from Hebrews was used in the early Christian letter known as *1 Clement*, which was probably composed at Rome in the last decade of the first century. Therefore, there is little reason to think that Hebrews was written after 90 CE.

A more precise date is difficult to determine because it is not clear whether Hebrews was written before or after the Jerusalem temple was destroyed in 70 CE. Despite Hebrews' interest in Israel's priesthood and sanctuary, the book never refers to the Jerusalem temple. The only sanctuary mentioned is the tabernacle of Moses' time, which is described in the book of Exodus. Some assume that Hebrews' references to the ancient tabernacle actually pertain to the temple that stood in Jerusalem in New Testament times, and argue that since Hebrews assumed that sacrifices were still being offered, the temple must have been standing (7:27–8; 8:3–5; 9:6–7; 10:1–3, 8). This would mean that Hebrews was written before 70 CE. Nevertheless, decades after the temple was destroyed some Jewish and Christian authors wrote as if sacrifices were still being offered and priests were continuing to carry out their ministry (Josephus, *Against Apion*, 2.77; *1 Clement*, 40–1; *Epistle of Diognetus*, 3). Hebrews could have done the same. The way Hebrews develops its arguments using only the biblical descriptions of the tabernacle, without referring to the temple, leaves open the possibility that the book was composed either before or after 70 CE. Attempts to determine a more specific date by identifying the persecution mentioned in Hebrews 10:32–4 have also been unsuccessful because the kind of violence described by the author occurred at various times and places. It is best to place the book within the years 60–90 CE without making interpretation dependent on a more precise date.

The Christians addressed by Hebrews were probably located in Italy. This is suggested by the comment, "Those from Italy send you greetings" (13:24). Although some assume that the author wrote the book in Italy, most now take those "from Italy" to be people who had traveled from Italy to another location in the Roman empire and who wanted to send greetings to those back home. There were Christian congregations in the Italian cities of Puteoli and Rome by the middle of the first century (Acts 28:13–15; Rom. 16:1–16), and the earliest known authors to have made use of Hebrews were located in Rome. One was the writer of *1 Clement*, who wrote of Christ the high priest in language reminiscent of Hebrews 1, and the other was the author of the *Shepherd of Hermas*, who discussed whether apostate Christians could repent, an issue raised in Hebrews 6:4–6.

The main alternative to a Roman destination is to suggest that the readers were in Jerusalem and that the author wrote to them from Italy. The chief reason for this view is that Hebrews' discussion of the priesthood and sanctuary would have been of interest to people in Jerusalem where the temple was located. Nevertheless, it seems unlikely that the author would have written to people in Jerusalem using an elegant Greek style and basing his arguments on the Septuagint, the Greek translation of Israel's scriptures, rather than on the Hebrew text. Moreover, Hebrews never mentions the Jerusalem temple, speaking only of the tabernacle as depicted in Exodus. Finally, the persecution mentioned in Hebrews 10:32–4 does not seem to have resulted in any deaths, whereas persecutions in Jerusalem led to the deaths of Stephen and James (Acts 7:58–8:3; 12:1–2). The mention of Italy in Hebrews 13:24 and the use of Hebrews by Christians in Rome in the late first and early second centuries suggest that the book was written for readers living in Italy. The author's location, however, is unknown.

## Historical Setting

Hebrews addressed Christians who were experiencing a sense of discouragement and a decline in community life. Their circumstances can best be understood by looking at the way their community developed over time. The author refers to the history of the group at several points, allowing us to discern three phases.

Phase 1 centered on the readers' initial hearing of the gospel and their acceptance of the Christian faith. The author recalls that the community was formed when the message that Jesus proclaimed "was attested to us by those who heard," while "God added his testimony by signs and wonders and various miracles and by gifts of the Holy Spirit, distributed according to his will" (2:3–4). Hebrews refers to those who brought the gospel message by using the plural, which suggests that two or more evangelists worked together. Their message focused on "salvation" (2:2), which probably meant deliverance from divine judgment and from powers of evil for life in God's kingdom. The miraculous signs and wonders that the evangelists performed to validate their message may have been healings or exorcisms (cf. Acts 14:8–18; 16:16–18; 19:11–12). Through the work of the evangelists, the readers experienced a vivid sense of the working of the Holy Spirit. They were moved to repent of sin, to profess their faith in God, and to be baptized (Heb. 6:1–2).

Belief and experience reinforced each other in a positive way during this initial phase of the community's life. The message brought by the evangelists awakened hopes that the readers would obtain a place in the kingdom of God (1:14). Miracles and a vivid sense of the Spirit's activity confirmed the message experientially. At the same time, conversion apparently planted the seeds of conflict between the Christian community and the wider society. Hebrews twice calls their conversion "enlightenment," which implies that the unconverted remain in darkness, with its connotations of sin, ignorance, and death (6:4; 10:32). By turning away from their previous patterns of belief, the readers made at least an implicitly negative judgment on the beliefs and values of those who did not share their same faith, and this seems to have generated tensions between the newly established Christian community and the wider society.

Phase 2 was marked by open conflict with those outside the community and solidarity among those inside the community. The author recalls that in "those earlier days," after "you had been enlightened, you endured a hard struggle with sufferings, sometimes being publicly exposed to abuse and persecution, and sometimes being partners with those so treated." Nevertheless, "you had compassion for those who were in prison, and you cheerfully accepted the plundering of your possessions, knowing that you yourselves possessed something better and more lasting" (10:32–4). The passage suggests that members of the local populace denounced Christians to the civic authorities, who imprisoned some of them (Acts 16:19–25). There is little evidence that Roman authorities carried out systematic persecutions of Christians in the first century. Although Nero became notorious for arresting and executing Christians after the great fire in Rome in 64 CE, persecutions were generally local affairs initiated by residents of a town or city. Denunciations often depicted Christians as a threat to the social order, which prompted officials to take action against them (16:20–1; 17:7). The physical abuse could have been carried out either by a mob (18:17) or by the authorities, who could beat people when gathering evidence or punishing them (16:22–3). Since there is little evidence that there were legal grounds for confiscating Christian property, it was probably seized without authorization.

The actions taken against Christians were presumably intended to pressure them into giving up their beliefs, to marginalize those who refused to do so, and to dissuade others from joining the Christian group. Tactics like public denunciation deprived people of honor and dignity in the eyes of others. Abuse and loss of property were physically and emotionally painful, and prison conditions were harsh and degrading. Nevertheless, Hebrews indicates that the persecution actually had the reverse effect, fostering a deeper sense of solidarity within the Christian community. Rather than weakening the bonds of the Christians, the attacks by outsiders defined and deepened Christian loyalties, at least for a time.

Phase 3 was characterized by ongoing, but less intense, friction between Christians and non-Christians, and an increasing sense of discouragement among the Christians. This is the phase in which Hebrews was written. The author assumed that verbal attacks against the community would continue and that some people would remain in prison (Heb. 13:3, 13). In practical terms supporting prisoners over a period of time was discouraging to those who awaited their release, and associating with prisoners brought both a social stigma and the possibility of losing one's own freedom. Some Christians continued the practice of caring for others (6:10; 13:1), but others showed signs of malaise. The author cautions against "drift," a term that suggests a gradual and perhaps unthinking movement away from the faith (2:1). He points to the danger of neglecting the Christian faith and community (2:3; 10:25), and reproves his listeners for their sluggishness (5:11; 6:12).

The author recognized that one way to deal with ongoing reproach would be to "shrink back" from the Christian community in order to obtain a more favorable judgment from society (10:39). If confessing faith in Christ meant losing possessions, one might seek greater economic security by abandoning one's confession. If meeting with Christians meant being treated with contempt, one might hope for more honorable treatment by leaving the Christian community (10:25). Although apostasy could conceivably be the culmination of these tendencies (6:4–6), the author's call to "hold fast" the confession shows that the readers have not yet abandoned the faith altogether (3:6; 4:14; 10:23). The challenge facing the author was to give readers an incentive to persevere.

## Purpose

Hebrews was written to encourage readers to remain faithful to God, Christ, and the Christian community. In the face of dispiriting circumstances, the author reminds readers of what God has already done in the past, underscores the promise of what God will do in the future, and thereby gives readers reason to remain faithful in the present. The grand portrait of Christ in glory and the reminder of the readers' hope of salvation culminate in an exhortation not to drift away from the Christian message (1:1–2:4). The depiction of Christ as the pioneer of salvation, who has liberated people from bondage to the fear of death, together with the negative example of Moses' generation falling into unbelief and the positive announcement of God's promise of rest, issue into an exhortation to strive in hope of entering God's rest (2:10–4:11). Christ's priesthood and self-sacrifice are identified as the means by which God provides atonement and establishes a new covenant, which means that readers have good reason to approach God with confidence, to hold fast their confession of faith, and to continue meeting with other Christians (10:19–25). The stories of people from Abel to the Maccabean martyrs, who lived by faith in difficult situations, encourage the readers to run their own race of faith with perseverance (11:1–12:2). Given all that God has done, readers are to show their gratitude to God by lives that offer praise to him and service to others (12:28–13:21).

## Language and Style

Hebrews uses vivid language and bold imagery to convey its message. Ancient writers understood that ideas often find their most powerful expression when "you seem to see what you describe and bring it vividly before the eyes of your audience" so that "attention is drawn from the reasoning to the enthralling effect of the imagination" (Longinus, *On the Sublime*, 15.1.11). Hebrews follows this practice masterfully. When speaking about Christ's incarnation, crucifixion, and resurrection, the author depicts Christ in heroic terms as one who entered the realm of death in order to do battle with evil and liberate the people who have been held captive by fear (Heb. 2:10–15). Instead of dealing abstractly with the atoning significance of Christ's death, the author paints a picture of the ancient tabernacle with its forecourt, inner court, and furnishings, and then describes Christ's entry into the inner chamber of the sanctuary through the blood that he shed for others (9:1–14). The author defines faith as "the assurance of things hoped for, the conviction of things not seen" in 11:1, but instead of discussing faith as a concept, he shows readers the dynamics of faith by tracing the journeys of Abraham and his descendants, by telling of Moses' conflict with the king of Egypt and Israel's passage through the sea, and by cataloging the sufferings of the martyrs (Heb. 11:4–40).

The author employs a range of Greek styles in order to communicate various types of subject matter. An elevated style is used for elevated subjects. The opening sentence on God's manner of speaking is an elaborate sentence that includes all of 1:1–4. It is marked by vivid vocabulary like "reflection of God's glory" and "exact imprint of God's very being," and it uses the paraphrase "the Majesty on high" for God. Nearly half the words in 1:1 begin with the letter *p*, a use of alliteration that would have helped catch a listener's ear. Later sections of Hebrews sometimes conclude with complex sentences or "periods" that are crafted with an elegant symmetry. For example, one period begins by announcing that God's word (*logos*) scrutinizes human hearts, and it ends by reminding readers that all people must render account (*logos*) to God (4:12–13).

The author can also use a simple and direct style to impress points upon readers. After telling of the wilderness generation's penchant for testing God, the author addresses a forceful battery of questions to the readers in order to drive home the dire consequences of unbelief: "Now who were they who heard and yet were rebellious? Was it not all those who left Egypt under the leadership of Moses? But with whom was he angry forty years? Was it not those who sinned ...?" (3:16–18). Similarly, the exhortations at the conclusion of Hebrews are stated directly since they call for obedience, not contemplation: "Let mutual love continue. Do not neglect to show hospitality to strangers ... Remember those who are in prison" (13:1–3).

Hebrews' use of language enhances the effectiveness of its argument. Its metaphors are engaging. To underscore the surety of Christian hope, the author calls it an "anchor of the soul" (6:19). By referring to basic Christian teaching as milk, in contrast to the solid food taken by adults, Hebrews presses readers to see their dullness as a mark of immaturity that they will want to overcome (5:12–14). By depicting the life of faith as a footrace, the author helps readers see themselves not as victims of social reproach but as athletes engaged in a noble struggle (12:1–3). The technique of anaphora, the repeating of a key word, is most fully developed in chapter 11, where the author says repeatedly that the people of God must live "by faith." Sometimes the author rapidly lists a number of items, giving the impression that many more could be added. For example, he speaks of "Gideon, Barak, Samson, Jephthah, David and Samuel and the prophets" who through faith "conquered kingdoms, administered justice, obtained promises, shut the mouths of lions, quenched raging fire" – and the list goes on, giving readers a vivid sense of the magnitude of faith's powers (11:32–4). The author uses an expansive vocabulary and even combines familiar components to coin new words, such as *agenealogētos* ("without genealogy," 7:3) and *haimatekchysia* ("outpouring of blood," 9:22).

## Intertextuality

The author of Hebrews develops his argument by engaging many texts from Israel's scriptures. Much of the material comes from books that are included in all Jewish and Christian bibles, but the author also knows the stories of the martyrs that appear in the deuterocanonical books of the Maccabees (11:35–8) and probably the tradition that Isaiah was killed by being sawn in two, which is found in various non-canonical writings (11:37). Hebrews relies on the Septuagint, the ancient Greek translation of the Old

Testament. This is most evident at the points where the author quotes scripture in a form that corresponds to the Septuagint but differs from standard Hebrew texts. For example, the quotation of Psalm 40:7 in Hebrews 10:5 reads "a body you have prepared," which corresponds to the Greek version of the Psalm, rather than "ears you have dug," which is the way the passage reads in Hebrew. The reference to Genesis 47:31 in Hebrews 11:21 refers to "staff" rather than "bed." The idea that the son of man was made lower than the angels "for a little while" (2:7) depends on the Greek version of Psalm 8:5, since the Hebrew text of the psalm uses a word that means "a little lower" in degree.

A brief survey of Hebrews, beginning with its first chapter, shows how the author makes use of the Old Testament. Hebrews opens by announcing that God, who previously spoke by Israel's prophets, has now spoken by a Son. To reinforce this claim, the author quotes a series of Old Testament passages almost without comment. Passages from the Psalms, 2 Samuel 7, and Deuteronomy 32 enable readers to hear God address a royal figure as his Son, who is superior to the angels. Other psalm texts show God celebrating the righteous rule of his anointed one, who is addressed as "God" (Heb. 1:5–14). The key text is Psalm 110:1, which tells of God giving his chosen one a place at his right hand. Early Christians regularly interpreted this passage as a commentary on Jesus' resurrection and ascension to heavenly glory (Matt. 22:44; Mark 12:36; Luke 20:42; Acts 2:34), and by joining other biblical passages to this psalm the author of Hebrews allows the quotations to give readers an impression of the grandeur of the exalted Son of God.

This pattern of usage shows that the author understands the Old Testament in light of Christ and Christ in light of the Old Testament. The two are taken together. When read in their original contexts many of the Old Testament passages quoted refer either to God or to the king of Israel, but the author of Hebrews reads the texts retrospectively in light of Jesus' exaltation. The author interprets the Old Testament in light of Christ because he understands that Christ's crucifixion and exaltation are God's definitive means of communication, and he takes the Old Testament writings to foreshadow these events. At the same time, the author does not have unmediated access to the heavenly throne room and cannot gaze upon the exalted Christ with the unaided eye. Therefore, he seeks to discern something about the exalted Son of God by looking at the scriptures that anticipate his coming. The author finds the righteous rule of the ascended Son of God reflected in the royal psalms, which speak of the glory of God's anointed king.

Hebrews 2–4 includes quotations of biblical texts followed by interpretations. In 2:5–9 the author quotes from Psalm 8, which tells of God creating human beings for glory and honor. The interpretation of the psalm raises the objection that people do not necessarily see God's glorious intentions realized in their own experiences, which often fall short of glory. In response to this objection, the author directs readers to the story of Jesus, who suffered and died but was later raised to heavenly glory. Since Jesus suffered and was glorified, readers can be confident that even though they suffer, they too have the hope of future glory with God. The argument continues with a quotation and interpretation of Psalm 95:9–11 in Hebrews 3–4. The psalm recalls how Moses' generation tested God in the wilderness and failed to enter God's rest in the promised land, and it exhorts its readers not to harden their hearts in the same way. Hebrews first interprets the psalm as a sharp warning about the consequences of unfaithfulness (3:12–19), then the author interprets the psalm as a word of promise, since it gives assurance that those who do not harden their hearts will enter God's rest (4:1–10).

Using one passage of scripture to interpret another is one of the techniques that Hebrews employs. To show what the psalm means when it extends the hope of entering God's "rest," Hebrews refers readers to Genesis 2:2, which speaks of the "rest" that God enjoyed on the seventh day of the Creation. By reading Genesis 2 and Psalm 95 together, the author gives readers encouragement to hope that God's purposes will culminate in the faithful entering the rest that God himself enjoys. A similar interpretive strategy shapes Hebrews' intriguing discussion of Melchizedek, the priest and king of Salem who is briefly mentioned in connection with Abraham in Genesis 14:18–20. After summarizing the passage from Genesis, Hebrews says that Melchizedek has "neither beginning of days nor end of life, but resembling the Son of God, he remains a priest forever" (Heb. 7:3). This astonishing claim arises in part from the way the author reads Genesis in light of Psalm 110:4, the only other text to mention Melchizedek: "You are a priest forever according to the order of Melchizedek." Since the psalm speaks of Melchizedek's everlasting priesthood, the author of Hebrews assumes that Genesis 14 reflects it as well.

The central section of Hebrews combines elements from three major Old Testament passages to convey the significance of Christ's death. One text is Jeremiah 31:31–4, where God declares that he will make a new covenant under which he will show mercy toward iniquity and offer definitive forgiveness for sins. The passage is quoted in Hebrews 8:8–12. Although Jeremiah's oracle promises a new covenant, the prophet does not specify how God will bring the covenant about. Therefore, the second text that Hebrews invokes is Exodus 24:3–8, which relates that Moses established the first covenant by means of a sacrifice at Mount Sinai. Since the Sinai covenant was inaugurated with a sacrifice, Hebrews infers that the new covenant must also involve a sacrifice, the self-sacrifice Christ made through his crucifixion (Heb. 9:18–22). The author reinforces the idea that Jesus' covenant-making sacrifice is an atoning sacrifice by drawing on a third passage, the biblical stipulations for the Day of Atonement in Leviticus 16:1–22. That passage tells of the high priest offering a sacrifice in the outer court of the sanctuary before entering its inner court to complete the work of atonement. Hebrews likens this to the work of Christ, who made his self-sacrifice on earth before being exalted to God's presence in heaven, where he has become a source of eternal redemption for people (Heb. 9:1–14). When taken together these three texts show how the notions of covenant, sacrifice, and forgiveness are interrelated ideas that convey the significance of Christ's death.

The final section of Hebrews summarizes much of the biblical story, from the Creation to the Maccabean martyrs of the second century BCE, to show that in every generation the people of God have had to live by faith (11:1–40). The author's interpretive lens is Habakkuk 2:4, "The righteous one will live by faith," which is quoted in Hebrews 10:38. The relationship between this quotation and the summary of biblical history that follows it in Hebrews 11 is twofold. On the one hand, righteous figures like Abel, Enoch, Noah, and others provide examples of what Habakkuk means when he speaks of living by faith. On the other hand, Habakkuk's words provide a way of understanding the biblical story as a whole, enabling readers to discern that faith is what empowers biblical figures to live in the face of disappointment and conflict, even though a particular Old Testament story might not make the role of faith explicit.

## Unity

Hebrews can best be understood as a unified composition. A consistent, well-developed Greek style is used throughout, and the sections of its argument are connected to each other without obvious seams or signs of editing. The text flows well from the elevated opening paragraph about God speaking through the prophets and the Son in 1:1–4 to the benediction and "Amen" in 13:20–1. Questions about its unity do, however, arise in relation relate to the epistolary conclusion in 13:22–5. Some have wondered whether these verses might have been appended to a previously complete composition, either by the author or by someone else. They point out that neither the opening nor the body of Hebrews has the features of a letter, whereas the concluding verses follow the usual conventions for the conclusions of letters. Elsewhere the author commonly refers to what is being "said" rather than what is being "written," and rarely uses the first-person-singular "I," whereas the conclusion refers to writing and repeatedly uses the first person singular. Since Paul's companion Timothy is mentioned in 13:23, some propose that the postscript was added to give the impression that Hebrews was a Pauline letter.

There are good reasons, however, for assuming that the concluding verses are an integral part of Hebrews. Early Christian letter closings included requests for prayer, comments about future visits, and benedictions like those in 13:18–21, along with the personal notes and greetings that appear in 13:22–5. The author shifted to the first-person "I" in 13:19 so that 13:22–5 simply continues the pattern. Moreover, someone intending to give the impression that Hebrews was a Pauline letter almost certainly would have created for Hebrews an epistolary opening similar to that of Paul's letters, and would probably have mentioned Paul's name, rather than merely implying a connection by referring to Timothy. Hebrews can best be understood as a unified composition by one author.

## Genre

Hebrews has characteristics of both a letter and a speech. For centuries Hebrews was regarded as a letter because it concludes like many other early Christian letters with a section that includes brief personal notes, greetings, and a final "Grace be with all of you" (13:22–5). Although Hebrews lacks the usual epistolary introduction, which names the sender and addressees and gave greetings, interpreters have sometimes speculated that the author might have omitted it from the original composition or that it might have been lost or omitted when the manuscript was copied.

Today it is more common to see Hebrews as a speech that was given a short epistolary conclusion. Hebrews calls itself "a word of exhortation," an expression that was sometimes used for sermons (13:22). For example, the book of Acts says that when Paul and his companions were in a synagogue, the officials invited Paul to give a "word of exhortation" after passages were read from the law and the prophets (Acts 13:15). In the sermon that follows, Paul expounds the meaning of Jesus' death and resurrection in light of the Jewish scriptures, which Hebrews also does. Identifying Hebrews as an early Christian sermon or speech is also helpful because the author often refers to speaking rather than to writing (Heb. 2:5; 5:11; 6:9) and follows patterns of classical rhetoric, as will be noted below.

Hebrews has affinities with different types of speeches and cannot be neatly placed in one distinct category. Ancient rhetorical handbooks called speeches that counseled people to follow a certain course of action in the future "deliberative," and since Hebrews summons readers to pursue the path of faithfulness in the hope of inheriting a place in God's heavenly city, the book is to some extent a deliberative speech. Alternatively, speeches that seek to reinforce values that people already hold, by commending what is praiseworthy and condemning what is shameful, are called "epideictic." Since Hebrews calls readers to hold fast the faith they already profess, the book also has some of the traits of an epideictic speech. Trying to place Hebrews in one category or the other is not helpful because the handbooks recognize that both types of rhetoric can occur in the same speech, as they do in Hebrews.

## Structure

Hebrews is structured according to the patterns of ancient speeches. Rhetorical handbooks indicated that speeches were to include several standard elements, although they also recognized that speakers could show considerable freedom in adapting typical patterns to specific situations. The usual features of a speech are as follows: The introduction or *exordium* is to prepare listeners to give proper attention to the speaker. A narration of facts pertaining to the topic may follow the introduction, but it is not essential. The next main elements are the proposition or thesis, which defines the issue to be addressed, and the arguments that support the speaker's position. The final component is the conclusion or peroration that brings the speech to a close. Hebrews includes all of these elements except the optional section on narrating the facts.

The author makes transitions between major sections by digressions in which he departs from the main line of argument to appeal for attention and warn about the dangers of neglecting or spurning the word of God (2:1–4; 5:11–6:20; 10:26–39; 12:25–7). The digressions are important because they help to regain the readers' attention before the author begins a new section of his speech. Short digressions, which contrast the way that God spoke in the past at Sinai with the way God now addresses the listeners, make the transition from the introduction to the proposition (2:1–4) and from the final series of arguments to the conclusion (12:25–7). Longer digressions create transitions between major sections of the argument by warning about apostasy, recalling the listeners' faithfulness, and encouraging perseverance (5:11–6:20; 10:26–39). Hebrews can be outlined as follows:

Introduction (1:1–2:4)
Proposition (2:5–9)
Arguments (2:10–12:27)
A   First Series (2:10–6:20)
    1   Argument: Jesus received glory through faithful suffering – a way that others are called to follow (2:10–5:10)
    2   Transitional Digression (5:11–6:20)
B   Second Series (7:1–10:39)
    1   Argument: Jesus' suffering is the high-priestly sacrifice that allows others to approach God (7:1–10:25)
    2   Transitional Digression (10:26–39)
C   Third Series (11:1–12:27)
    1   Arguments: People persevere through suffering to glory by faith (11:1–12:24)
    2   Transitional Digression (12:25–7)
Conclusion (12:28–13:21)
Epistolary Postscript 13:22–5

The introduction (1:1–2:4) is framed by complex sentences that deal with God's manner of speaking in the past through prophets and angels, and in the present through his Son (1:1–4; 2:2–4). The first paragraph of the introduction presents the Son as the heir and creator of all things, who is seated at God's right hand (1:1–4), and the paragraph that follows cites a series of Old Testament passages to provide support for these claims (1:5–14). The final paragraph calls for the readers to give their full attention to what is being said and warns about the consequences of neglecting the Christian message (2:1–4).

The proposition (2:5–9) is a pivotal section, consisting of a quotation of Psalm 8:4–6 followed by a brief exposition of the text. It is located between two other sections of the speech, each of which is neatly framed. In content, the proposition is situated precisely at the point where attention turns from the glory of the exalted Christ to the significance of his suffering. In the span of a few verses, the author states the themes that will be developed in the remainder of the speech: Christ's movement from suffering to glory, his suffering on behalf of others, and the idea that one can "see" the fulfillment of God's promises in Christ, despite their apparent non-realization in human experience.

The first series of arguments (2:10–5:10) is framed by statements that Christ was "made complete through suffering," so that he has become the pioneer or source of salvation for others (2:10; 5:8–10). Before this section the author focused on the glory of the ascended Christ, whereas these arguments emphasize the suffering that preceded Christ's exaltation. Paragraphs comparing Christ's glory to that of Moses and Aaron, together with images from the exodus and wilderness wanderings, help to unify the section. A lengthy and carefully crafted sentence that summarizes Christ's suffering and exaltation brings the first series of arguments to a close (5:5–10). The digression that follows this section turns aside from the main argument to reprove the listeners for their lack of learning (5:11–6:20) in contrast to Christ's way of learning through suffering (5:8). The author lets his readers know that he is returning to the main argument by restating the point he made just before the digression, namely, that Christ is a priest forever (5:10; 6:20).

The second series of arguments (7:1–10:25) shows that Christ the high priest suffered in order to make the sacrifice that allows his followers to enter God's presence. Successive comparisons of the Levitical priesthood and Christ's priesthood, the old and new covenants, animal sacrifices and Christ's self-sacrifice, integrate the section. In the previous series of arguments, the author showed the similarities between the priesthood of Aaron and Jesus, but here he stresses the differences between the Levitical priestly service and Christ's priestly service. Formally, this segment concludes with an intricate and lengthy sentence that draws together the main themes and invites listeners to draw near to God as the Day of the Lord draws near to them (10:19–25). A digression, which echoes earlier warnings about the dangers of turning from God and encourages listeners to remain faithful, makes the transition into the final series of arguments (10:26–39).

The third series of arguments (11:1–12:24) begins and ends with comments about the blood of Abel (11:4; 12:24). The section traces the journeys of the righteous who endured conflict, disappointment, and death on earth, culminating with the spirits of the righteous being made complete in God's heavenly city (12:22–4). Abraham lived as a foreigner on earth in the hope of life in God's city (11:10, 16), Moses gave up wealth in Egypt for a future reward (11:26–7), and the martyrs accepted death in the hope of resurrection (11:35). The depiction of the faithful in the heavenly Jerusalem shows that they did not persevere in vain, for God will be faithful to his promises (12:22–4). A short digression urging listeners to heed the one who is speaking concludes the section (12:25–7).

The conclusion (12:28–13:21) refers to service "pleasing" to God in its opening statement (12:28) and final benediction (13:21). The first and last paragraphs of the conclusion deal with the importance of offering service or sacrifice to God, serving other people, and remembering one's leaders. The central paragraph creatively fuses themes of Christ's priestly sacrifice and the hope of entering the city of God in order to shape and support this view of Christian discipleship. The epistolary postscript (13:22–5) begins after the final benediction and includes many features typical of conclusions on early Christian letters: a comment about what has been written, sharing of personal information and mention of a future visit, an extension of greetings, and a parting wish.

## Rhetorical Analysis

Speakers in antiquity understood that persuasion comes from the interplay of three things: the content of a speech (*logos*), appeals to emotion (*pathos*), and the character of the presenter (*ethos*). Considering each category in turn can help to show the multidimensional way in which Hebrews seeks to move its readers to a renewed sense of commitment to God, Christ, and the Christian community.

First we can consider the content of Hebrews. The introduction leads into the subject of the speech indirectly. Rather than stating the main theme, the introduction's presentation of Christ in glory helps establish rapport with readers by affirming some elements of the Christian tradition that they already hold to be true. Only in 2:5–9 does the author define the issue facing his readers. It seems likely that the causes of the dispiriting situation addressed by Hebrews were complex and that the author could not assume that everyone would have understood the reasons for the community's decline in the same way. Therefore, he defines the problem as the apparent contradiction between the glory that God has promised people and the fact that they do not "see" this promise realized in their own experience. For them, being marginalized socially seems to call God's promises into question.

The arguments in Hebrews are designed to overcome this apparent contradiction between the claims of faith and social experiences of the readers. In chapters 2–6 the author acknowledges that God's people may not see God's promises of glory, honor, and salvation fulfilled in their own experiences, but they can persevere by considering the experience of Jesus, who willingly identified with suffering human beings and who suffered himself before being exalted to heavenly glory. Since God brought Jesus through suffering to glory, those who follow Jesus can be confident that God will also bring them to the glory he has promised. In chapters 7–10 the author shows that Jesus can be considered a priest, whose self-offering provides a complete sacrifice for sins and establishes a new covenant. Therefore, those who trust him may draw near to God with confidence. In chapters 11–12 the author gives examples of previous generations of God's people, who steadfastly endured disappointment, conflict, and death. The listeners, too, are called to persevere in faith by looking toward a future in God's heavenly city and a glory that is not evident to the eye, but which can be perceived by faith in the promises of God. The concluding exhortations in chapter 13 relate the service that Christ performed for the readers to the ongoing service that they are to perform in their own communities.

Comparison and contrast sharpen the arguments. Comparison is a way for an author to praise someone by showing that the person is greater than other illustrious figures. Hebrews makes use of comparison when showing that Christ is superior to angels, Moses, and Levitical priests (1:1–14; 3:1–6; 7:1–28). All of these are worthy of honor, while Christ is worthy of even greater honor. Sometimes the author makes comparisons to enhance his warnings. For example, if transgressions of the Mosaic law warrant punishment, then spurning the grace Christ offers will bring even greater punishment (2:1–4; 10:26–31). A related technique is to create antitheses to give a clearer sense of the superiority of Christ and the benefits he provides. In chapters 8–10 the author uses antitheses to heighten the differences between the old and new covenants and between Levitical sacrifices and Christ's self-sacrifice.

Examples enhance the appeal of Hebrews. Speakers and writers in antiquity valued the way examples could make points vividly to their audiences. Although insisting that logic is important, they recognized that logic alone often failed to persuade people. A good example, however, could demonstrate a point so vividly that readers would be drawn to the author's point of view. In Hebrews, the wilderness generation offers a vivid example of the consequences of unfaithfulness. Those who consider the way the people of Moses' time died in the wilderness will want to avoid following their pattern of unbelief (3:7–19). Conversely, the stories of Abraham, Sarah, and their descendants living as strangers in the promised land, of Moses leading the people out of slavery, and of the martyrs suffering torture and death show readers the power of faith in the face of difficulty. By listing example after example in chapter 11, the author creates a kind of momentum that can make readers want to join the company of the faithful.

A second dimension is appeal to emotion. As the author of Hebrews presents his argument, he develops the interplay between the positive feelings of confidence and sympathy, which he uses to draw people to faithfulness, and the negative feelings of fear and shame, which he uses to create an aversion to unfaithfulness. On the one hand, the author gives readers reason to feel confident because help is available from God (4:14–16; 13:6), Christ cleanses their consciences (9:15), and they are encircled by a great cloud of faithful witnesses (12:1). On the other hand, readers may be inclined to abandon their faith because they fear it might lead to social conflict, but the author warns that it is more "terrifying to fall into the hands of the living God" (10:31), whose fiery judgment upon the faithless is fearsome (6:4–8; 10:27; 12:29). Again, the community addressed by Hebrews had been treated with contempt by nonbelievers, but the author of Hebrews insists that to follow Jesus is to "despise the shame" of society (12:2) in the confidence that God and Christ are not ashamed of them (2:11; 11:16). Finally, the author appeals to the readers' sympathy when telling of the way Jesus suffered, even though he was innocent, because he identified with human beings in need (2:11–14; 4:15). Such reminders of the manner of Jesus' suffering reinforce the listeners' faith by awakening sympathy for one who suffered unjustly, as well as by eliciting gratitude for his suffering on their behalf.

A third dimension of persuasion comes from the character of the presenter. Readers or listeners are more likely to be persuaded by someone they trust than by someone they do not trust. Therefore, speakers developed ways to help make the audience well disposed. Accordingly, the author of Hebrews begins by focusing on God rather than on himself. He tells of the way God spoke in the past through the prophets and now by a Son, and instead of offering his own reflections on these points he offers readers a rapid series of biblical quotations in which God is identified as the speaker. Identifying God as the principal speaker in the introduction and elsewhere helps make the author's case persuasive because listeners are expected to recognize the integrity of God's character (6:18). The implication is that those who relinquish their faith in God's promises in effect deny the integrity of God's character.

The author's own character also plays a role, even though the author's name is never given. The author identifies himself with his audience by using the first person plural, so that his readers know that he too is addressed by the word of God (1:2; 2:3; 4:2) and shares their confession of faith (3:1; 4:14; 10:23). Like them, he must reckon with divine judgment (2:3; 4:13; 10:26), trust in divine mercy (4:15–16; 9:14), and strive in faith (4:11; 10:24; 11:39; 12:1). The author demonstrates his familiarity with scripture by frequent citation of texts, so that readers can be confident that he knows the tradition. Finally, he is bold in his confession (1:1–4) and direct in his exhortations, so that when he urges his readers to bold in their confession (3:6; 4:16; 10:19; 10:35) and to exhort one another (3:13; 10:24), his directives have integrity, since they are to do what he is already doing.

## Theological Issues and Themes

Hebrews offers a rich and multifaceted portrayal of Jesus Christ. The opening chapter identifies Christ as the Son of God, who bears the radiance of God's glory and the imprint of God's being. According to Israel's tradition, God created the world by his word. Hebrews in turn identifies the word of God with the Son of God, declaring that God spoke through the Son through whom he created the world (1:2). The divine Son, who is addressed as "God," reigns forever in righteousness (1:8). The created order will pass away, but the Son will not. Readers may be discouraged because of conflict and injustice in the world around them, but the world is transient; the Son remains forever. Therefore, readers are to place their trust in the everlasting Son of God rather than being moved to unbelief by changing conditions of this world.

Jesus' humanity and ministry on earth also play important roles in Hebrews. The Son of God identified with human beings by taking on their flesh and blood and suffering death (2:11–15). Recalling the traditions of Christ's passion, the author tells of Jesus offering prayers to God with loud cries and tears, enduring the shame of the cross, and suffering abuse at the hands of his opponents (5:7; 12:2; 13:12). The author assures readers that Jesus can sympathize with them because he suffered and was tested in the same ways as other human beings, except that he was without sin (2:18; 4:15). Since Jesus was human and proved faithful through suffering, he can also serve as an example for other people to follow in their own lives (12:3; 13:13). Finally, Jesus' suffering in the flesh gives integrity to Hebrews' theology of the atonement. The author affirms that without an outpouring of blood there is no forgiveness of sins, arguing that Jesus' death entailed the effusion of blood that fulfills what is required for an authentic sacrifice (9:12, 14, 22).

Jesus' high priesthood is a hallmark of Hebrews' Christology. The priests of Israel were to offer sacrifices for sin and thereby offer grace and forgiveness to those in need, and Hebrews argues that Christ offers grace in a definitive way to people through his self-sacrifice (4:14–5:4). Most distinctive in Hebrews, however, is that Jesus is a priest according to the order of Melchizedek (5:6). The basis for making this identification is fairly simple. Early Christians accepted that Jesus' resurrection and ascension to glory at God's right hand fulfilled Psalm 110:1: "The Lord said to my lord, 'Sit at my right hand until I make your enemies your footstool.'" Hebrews notes that Psalm 110:4 calls this same royal figure "a priest forever according to the order of Melchizedek." If Psalm 110:1 applies to Christ, the author assumes that 110:4 does as well. In Israel's tradition the roles of priest and king were ordinarily separated, but Melchizedek was both a king and a priest, setting a precedent for ascribing both royal and priestly functions to Jesus. Moreover, Psalm 110:4 speaks of one who will serve as a priest forever, and Hebrews points out that Jesus is uniquely qualified to be such a priest because he has now risen from the dead and lives eternally – something that cannot be said of any other priest (Heb. 7:15–28). By depicting Jesus as the consummate high priest, Hebrews establishes a basis for understanding Jesus' death as a sacrifice of atonement and his current work in heaven as intercession (7:25; 9:11–14).

Hebrews' understanding of God's saving work is related to the themes of promise and covenant. The promises made to Abraham establish God's intentions for people.

God promised to bless Abraham and to give him land and descendants (6:14; 11:9, 12). Abraham received the fulfillment of the promises in a limited way when he was blessed by Melchizedek, when his son Isaac was born, and when he sojourned in the land of Canaan, but neither Abraham nor the generations that followed received fulfillment of the promises in the full and final sense. Hebrews insists that this does not mean that God is unreliable, but that the promises point to realities that are future rather than past and heavenly rather than earthly.

Sin, which involves unbelief and the actions that proceed from unbelief, constitutes a barrier to the fulfillment of God's promises because sin separates people from God. As a way of dealing with sin, the covenant of Moses' time prescribed sacrifices, a priesthood, and sanctuary by which atonement could be made, but the sacrifices cleansed only the flesh, the priests were subject to sin and death, and the sanctuary was earthly. Therefore God appointed Jesus to serve as the sinless high priest in the heavenly sanctuary and to establish a new covenant that would cleanse the human conscience and thereby bring people into a right relationship with God. The establishment of the new covenant fulfills the promise of mercy God made in Jeremiah 31:31–4, and it serves as the harbinger of the fulfillment of all God's promises, including everlasting life in God's kingdom (Heb. 8:1–10:18). There is constancy in God's promise of blessing but change in the covenants by which God overcomes the promise of human sin in order to bring his promises to their fulfillment.

Hebrews uses the term "perfect" for the accomplishment of God's purposes. The Greek words that are usually translated "perfect" are based on the root *tel-*, which has to do with reaching a goal. Jesus is made perfect through his death and exaltation to heavenly glory so that he now serves as high priest at God's right hand (5:9). Others are made perfect when they go where Jesus has gone, following their forerunner into the presence of God. The arguments in Hebrews begin by saying that God brought Jesus to perfection in order that many others might also share in glory (2:10), and they culminate in the heavenly Jerusalem, where the faithful are made perfect by receiving the blessings that God has promised in the company of angels (12:22–4).

## Annotated Bibliography

Attridge, Harold W. *Hebrews*. Hermeneia. Philadelphia: Fortress Press, 1989. A balanced historical-critical commentary.

Croy, N. Clayton. *Endurance in Suffering: Hebrews 12:1–13 in its Rhetorical, Religious and Philosophical Context*. Society for New Testament Studies Monograph Series, 98. Cambridge: Cambridge University Press, 1998.

DeSilva, David A. *Perseverance in Gratitude: A Socio-Rhetorical Commentary on the Epistle "to the Hebrews."* Grand Rapids: Eerdmans, 2000. A commentary that explores the rhetorical dimensions and social setting of Hebrews with special attention to the place of honor, shame, and gratitude.

Eisenbaum, Pamela Michelle. *The Jewish Heroes of Christian History: Hebrews 11 in Literary Context*. Society of Biblical Literature Dissertation Series, 156. Atlanta: Scholars Press, 1997. Studies the use of examples in Greco-Roman and Jewish sources, and the way Hebrews 11 tells the story Israel to bolster Christian claims.

Ellingworth, Paul. *The Epistle to the Hebrews*. New International Greek Testament Commentary. Grand Rapids: Eerdmans and Carlisle: Paternoster, 1993. A detailed commentary on the Greek text.

Guthrie, George H. *The Structure of Hebrews: A Textlinguistic Analysis*. Supplements to *Novum Testamentum*, 73. Leiden: Brill, 1994. A survey of proposals and a new approach to the structure of Hebrews.

Horton, Fred L., Jr. *The Melchizedek Tradition: Through the First Five Centuries of the Christian Era and in the Epistle to the Hebrews*. Society for New Testament Studies Monograph Series, 30. Cambridge: Cambridge University Press, 1976.

Hurst, Lincoln D. *The Epistle to the Hebrews: Its Background of Thought*. Society for New Testament Studies Monograph Series, 65. Cambridge: Cambridge University Press, 1990. Seeks to show that Hebrews does not work with a Platonic philosophical worldview, but is more closely tied to the apocalyptic tradition and currents in early Christianity.

Isaacs, Marie E. *Sacred Space: An Approach to the Epistle to the Hebrews. Journal for the Study of the New Testament* Supplementary Series, 73. Sheffield: Sheffield Academic Press, 1992. Focuses on the way Hebrews envisions salvation in spatial terms as entering God's rest, the sanctuary, and Mount Zion, and interprets Hebrews as a response to concerns about gaining access to God.

Koester, Craig R. *Hebrews: A New Translation with Introduction and Commentary*. Anchor Bible, 36. New York: Doubleday, 2001. A comprehensive commentary that surveys the history of interpretation of Hebrews, its social setting, formal and rhetorical aspects, and key theological issues. Attention is given to a wide range of ancient and modern sources.

Lane, William L. *Hebrews*. 2 vols. Word Biblical Commentary, 47. Dallas: Word Books, 1991. A detailed commentary that stresses the differences between Hebrews and Greco-Roman philosophy.

Lindars, Barnabas. *The Theology of the Letter to the Hebrews*. Cambridge: Cambridge University Press, 1991. Gives special attention to Hebrews' message of the priesthood and sacrifice of Jesus, which meet the intended readers' need for the assurance of forgiveness.

Peterson, David. *Hebrews and Perfection: An Examination of the Concept of Perfection in the Epistle to the Hebrews*. Society for New Testament Studies Monograph Series, 47. Cambridge: Cambridge University Press, 1982.

Thompson, James W. *The Beginnings of Christian Philosophy: The Epistle to the Hebrews. Catholic Biblical Quarterly* Monograph Series, 13. Washington, DC: Catholic Biblical Association, 1982. Maintains that Hebrews presents the Christian message by drawing on the philosophical categories.

Vanhoye, Albert. *Structure and Message of the Epistle to the Hebrews*. Rome: Biblical Institute, 1989. A brief presentation of Vanhoye's influential interpretation of the structure of Hebrews.

# CHAPTER 37

# The Apocalypse of John

## David L. Barr

## Perspectives on the Apocalypse

We do not know how the earliest audience of the Apocalypse interpreted it – they left us no records – though we can make some inferences by looking at other similar writings (see "Literary Analysis" below). We do know that several interpreters in the second century understood it as predicting the return of Jesus to this earth and the setting up of the kingdom of God; these interpreters included Papias of Hierapolis, Justin Martyr, and Irenaeus. But we also know that the second century was a time of intense prophetic activity that produced a variety of millenarian movements. It is hard to decide whether the Apocalypse was stimulating the prophetic movements or if these new prophets were shaping the Apocalypse to their own vision.

Others took a different view, protesting that the Apocalypse was written in "mystical and symbolic language" not meant to be taken materialistically (Eusebius, *Ecclesiastical History*, 3.39.11–13). While this view can be traced back to the second century, it came to the fore in the early fourth century with the triumph of Christianity. When Christians controlled Rome it was no longer reasonable to suppose that Rome was the beast in service to the dragon; other meanings must be sought.

This other view was most fully articulated by Augustine; it came to be the common view for nearly a thousand years. Augustine understood the Apocalypse symbolically and taught that it referred to the present experience of God's rule in the world, for God's rule appears anytime men and women are converted to Christian faith. The New Jerusalem descends from heaven whenever grace is experienced. The City of God is not a place but an experience; it represents those who submit to God's rule. Babylon, by contrast, represents those who refuse (*City of God*, 20.6–19). While the details shifted and interest in the Apocalypse waxed and waned, this symbolic view characterized most medieval interpreters.

In the social upheavals of the waning of the Middle Ages, characterized by the crusades, divisions in the church, conflicts between pope and emperor, and natural disasters like the Black Death, a new view of the Apocalypse emerged. The impetus behind this new view was a remarkable man by the name of Joachim of Fiore (d. 1202).

Joachim accepted Augustine's view that the rule of God already exists in the world, but he made a radical shift that resulted in a rebirth of millennial expectation. At the heart of his teaching is the claim that there are three ages to the world: the Age of the Father (seen in the Old Testament), the Age of the Son (seen in the New Testament and the church), and the Age of the Spirit (just dawning in his own time). Efforts to delineate this new age led interpreters to probe the Apocalypse for "signs of the times," imagining that historical events were somehow predicted in the Apocalypse.

This view that a new age was dawning, that its signs could be traced by correlating historical events with scenes in the Apocalypse, and that this new age included the overthrow of Rome proved very useful to those who would reform the church. Beginning already in the fourteenth century this new way of interpreting the Apocalypse eventually became the established Protestant view. Each new disaster – natural or political – was seen as the harbinger of the final days.

As the world stubbornly refused to end, many interpreters returned to a more symbolic interpretation. Echoing Augustine's view that the millennium was already appearing on earth, they saw it as the work of Christians to bring about the gradual improvement of society. This was the view of Jonathan Edwards (d. 1803), and was one of the motivations for the great missionary outreach of the nineteenth century.

A less optimistic view emerged in the mid-nineteenth century, one that saw the world getting worse not better. Two new ideas emerged. The first is called Dispensationalism, the idea that God's activity in the world is divided into seven distinct epochs (dispensations). The Apocalypse was seen as an outline the events of the final dispensation, and by closely observing world events one could deduce when the end will come. A second innovation was the idea that Christians would be removed from the world before the final age of evil. This idea, soon to be known as the Rapture, emerged from sectarian groups in England but soon spread to the United States, where it has flourished. The first explicit use of the term Rapture was in the June 1830 edition of *The Morning Watch*, a prophecy journal published in London. The editors of the journal thought they had hit upon a doctrine "hidden" in scripture – a mystery kept secret from the church until the end time.

This brief overview of the ways the Apocalypse has been viewed demonstrates how adaptable the book is to basic shifts in worldview. What follows is an exploration of how the book appears in the work of modern scholarship, embedded (but not trapped) in a post-Enlightenment worldview that seeks to explain the Apocalypse in terms of its historical context, literary forms, and social significance.

## Major Issues and Directions in Recent Study

There has been a dramatic increase in publications on the Apocalypse in the last two decades, with a corresponding diversity of approaches. The older approaches of discussing the theology and historical context of the work continue to be pursued, but newer approaches have emerged. These range from narrative criticism and sociological analysis to feminist and postmodernist critiques. Major issues addressed by a variety of approaches include the following.

## Persecution

There has been a strong shift away from the hypothesis that Revelation was written during a time of persecution (see "Historical Setting and Purpose" below). A few scholars still advocate the older view, but most have either abandoned it entirely or seriously modified it. Some, for example, argue that while there was no real crisis in Asia Minor, there was a "perceived crisis" – that is, John and his communities felt threatened by Roman oppression. This topic is still debated, but the great majority of recent analysis concludes that there was no official or widespread persecution in John's time; it was an era of relative peace and prosperity.

## Emperor worship

If the context of Revelation is not persecution, then we need to take a broader and more critical look at the imperial cult. There is a strong move away from viewing the imperial cult as some kind of special development of some particular emperor or as an anti-Christian institution to viewing it as a normal aspect of life in the empire. It was not something forced on resistant subjects from the imperial center but something freely offered – even sought – by provincial elites who benefited from the status and economic advantages connected with it. (For more details see "Historical Setting" below.)

## Community conflict

Scholars have always recognized an element of polemic against other community leaders in the Apocalypse, but today this is often seen as one of the major purposes of the work. These conflicts are commonly seen as based as much in socio-economic realities as in doctrinal difference, with John's opponents allied with the wealthier members of the community who need ways to participate more fully in their culture. These other leaders advocate eating meat offered to idols, for example, because this allows them to eat in the homes of their pagan associates (as Paul permitted, 1 Cor. 8–10). For John such involvement is spiritual fornication.

This hostility to culture has also been suggested as the root of John's hostility to Asian Jews, whom he calls a "synagogue of Satan" (2:9; 3:9). Earlier scholars attributed this hostility to supposed Jewish hostility, imagining that they denounced Christians to the persecuting Romans. Again, if persecution is not the issue, this hypothesis loses some of its cogency. An alternative view is that John sees these Jews as too fully embedded in Roman culture: they have joined the other side.

## Ethics and violence

Some have always been offended by the portrayal of extreme violence in the Apocalypse, while others have justified it as an appropriate response to the violence against Christians. The conclusion that persecution is not a likely context (see "Historical Setting") has made the issue even more problematic. There has emerged no completely satisfactory solution. The problem is not only the amount and extremity of the violence (e.g., the lake of fire) but that the violence forms one of the basic metaphorical structures of the work, in the idea of a holy war (see "Literary Analysis" below). Thus power and coercion seem to be the ultimate values of its universe, hardly the usual Christian virtues.

Thus some have judged the work to advocate an immoral worldview, condemning especially its images of violence against women (e.g., 17:16). Others see the form of the Apocalypse (as a war narrative, for example) as a problem, but not the content, which they argue is about faithful suffering not about vengeance. John consciously transforms the symbol of a holy war into a statement of conquest through suffering (12:11). Others argue that the portrayal of violence in the story is meant to have a cathartic effect on the audience, purging them of their vengeful emotions. These are issues that have only begun to be addressed.

## Myth

Everyone recognizes mythic elements in the Apocalypse: dragon, land and sea beasts, threatened births, wicked kings, and avenging knights. The question is what to make of such themes. Is the Apocalypse to be understood as a myth – not in the crude sense of a made-up story but in the substantial sense of a charter story? A story not about the past or the future, but about the present, about what life is truly like.

Even in scholarship, myth is not a precise category. While it was quite common in the nineteenth century to view the Apocalypse as myth, few scholars today use the category. In popular speech "myth" has come to mean something that is untrue, and even in scholarship there has been a strong tendency, most notably in the work of Rudolf Bultmann, to view myth as a primitive, unscientific, and inferior way of thinking. It is, however, a valuable category commonly used in the study of religion today. Whatever our own proclivities, the ancients apprehended the world in myth.

Viewed as a myth, the creation story is not about what happened at the beginning of time; rather, it seeks to answer basic questions about human existence (What is the meaning of being human? Why is innocence always lost? Why is life so hard?). Viewed as myth, the Apocalypse is not about what will happen at the end of time; rather, it seeks to answer basic human questions: How do we overcome evil in the world? Why do things always go wrong? Is might the final arbiter of the good? These questions are impossible to answer, but myth provides a group with a shared vision, a sense of common meaning. (See also the discussion below of myth as one of the constituent literary forms of the Apocalypse.)

## Orality

The last two decades have produced a wealth of studies on primary and secondary orality in the Greco-Roman world. In studies of early Christianity, much of this interest has been in Jesus as an oral teacher (primary orality) and in the gospels as instances of oral teaching transposed to writing that are then enunciated in oral performance (sec-ondary orality). Clearly the Apocalypse is also an instance of secondary orality in which a reader "sounds again" the words written on the page (1:3).

As an oral performance the meaning of the Apocalypse is not simply in its words but also in the experience it provided to the audience. In this experience one hears the voice of John re-presented in the voice of the reader and, more significantly, one hears the voice of Jesus re-presented in the voice of John. ("I John," 1:9; "I Jesus," 22:16). Viewed this way the purpose of the Apocalypse is not just to communicate information; it intends to make Jesus present to the assembly.

### Social construction of reality

Drawing on ideas from the sociology of knowledge, many recent studies of the Apocalypse have explored the ways the images, ideas, and actions presented function to construct a new view of the world. Reality is never just the world as it exists; it is the world as it is experienced through the lenses of social perception. The world viewed through Roman eyes sees the emperor as the savior and benefactor of the world; John sought to create another reality. He teaches his audience to live in a world where the emperor is in league with Satan and the true savior and benefactor of the world was killed by Roman power – and yet stands.

In the social reality constructed by the Apocalypse all values are reversed. Those who seem to have power do not; those who seem to be powerless nevertheless control the destiny of the world. The Roman propaganda spoke of the peace established by the emperor, but John portrays Rome as the beast in the service of the dragon that launches war on those who follow the word of God and the testimony of Jesus (Rev. 12–13).

## Date and Place of Composition

Since all connections between the Apocalypse and actual events of its time are hidden in symbolic statements (such as the identity of the beast as 666: surely a reference to the Roman emperor, but which one?) there can be no definitive answer as to the date of the work. The strong majority of scholars argue for a date late in the first century, perhaps around 95 CE. The main arguments in favor of this date include the external testimony of Irenaeus (d. about 202 CE) that it was written in the time of Domitian (d. 96 CE; see *Against the Heretics*, 5.30.3). We do not, however, know on what basis Irenaeus made this judgment. The case needs to be argued on internal evidence, but such evidence is equivocal.

Some attempt to use the numerical reference to the "seven rulers" in 17:9–11 to establish when John wrote, with various schemes to count the emperors, but given the highly symbolic way John uses numbers this seems a dubious undertaking. The same may be said for other arguments based on the circumstances in the seven churches (2–3) or the highly developed state of the imperial cult, for these conditions existed throughout the first century. It used to be common to date the Apocalypse to the time of Domitian based on allegations that Domitian launched a major persecution of Christians reflected in the book. This is doubtful on two counts: there is little evidence of imperial persecution under Domitian and the Apocalypse does not report persecution as a present experience so much as anticipate it in the future (see also "Historical Setting" below).

The main argument in favor of a late first-century date is the use of the figure "Babylon" for Rome, for that implies a time after Rome (like Babylon of old) destroyed Jerusalem (thus some years post-70). The main argument in favor of a mid-first-century date is that the reference to the temple in 11:1–13 seems to assume that the temple is still standing (thus pre-70).

All this data can be accounted for if we imagine that John has edited visions experienced over the course of several decades into the current Apocalypse late in the first century. Further reasons for seeing this work as composed over time are discussed under the heading of "Unity" below.

The place of composition is not debated, as John makes a clear statement that he is on an island off the coast of Asia Minor somewhat south of Ephesus, Patmos by name (1:9). More obscure is his reason for being there. He says simply that he is there "for the word of God and the testimony of Jesus." This is usually understood to mean he has been banished there because of his proselytizing work. This theory was developed when it was assumed that the Apocalypse was written during a time of persecution and commentators regularly referred to Patmos as a penal colony. It was not. Nor is it easy to imagine how a man of John's social status would be banished (more technically, relegated) to an island, as this was a device to deal with wealthy and powerful figures who needed to be isolated. There are two other possible interpretations to John's words. Perhaps he has gone to Patmos as part of his evangelical mission, to bring them the word of God and testimony of Jesus. Or perhaps he has gone to Patmos precisely to put this visionary material into writing, that is, to assemble the word of God and testimony of Jesus.

Whatever his reason for being absent from his communities, we should read the Apocalypse as the voice of the absent John, now made present by the voice of the public reader before the assembled congregation (1:3). In like manner, John has become the voice for the absent Jesus (1:10–11).

Equally important as where the Apocalypse was written is where it was read. While the number of churches (seven) must be taken to represent all the churches, John names seven specific communities. They were among the most important cities of Asia Minor, six of them being capitals of their regions. The grandeur of these cities, still evident in the ruins of Ephesus, Pergamum, and Sardis, is astonishing. Pergamum boasted a magnificent library, second only to that at Alexandria. They were in the first century experiencing a time of prosperity and a remarkable increase in public buildings, many of them subsidized by Rome.

## Historical Setting

The Emperor Nero had launched a bitter vendetta against Christians in Rome, blaming them for the fire of 64 CE. That turmoil ended with Nero's death in 68 CE, and there is no evidence that subsequent emperors maintained the hostility and no evidence that it spread beyond Rome even in Nero's time. The infamous persecutions occurred in the third century not the first. There is no evidence of systematic, official, or even widespread persecution at the time the Apocalypse was written.

This is not to say there was no suffering at all. We see from Pliny's correspondence with Trajan in the early second century that Christians could be indicted and even killed when they refused to obey the government. Pliny, it seems, had published a decree forbidding secret assemblies and was informed that these Christians persisted in their night-time assemblies (see Pliny, *Letters*, 10.96 and 10.97). His interrogations, torture, and executions are justified by his conception of the totalitarian power of Rome. John anticipates a violent struggle between those who hold the testimony of Jesus and those who give their allegiance to Rome, but he only knows the name of one person who has died in the struggle, Antipas of Pergamum (2:13).

We must not underestimate the tenuous position of Christians – indeed of all minority communities – in an empire premised on the absolute power of the emperor. And the line between honoring the emperor and worshiping the emperor was often indistinct. John's purpose was to make that line ever more vivid (see "Purpose" below).

The imperial cult was a complex social institution about which there is much misunderstanding. Ordinary people would rarely be required to participate in it, though they might choose to for the benefits (festivals with free food, loyalty to one's city, social status). Having an imperial liturgy was a great honor – and three of John's cities had major temples to Roma and the emperor, Ephesus, Pergamum, and Smyrna. Only the wealthiest citizens could aspire to hold office in the imperial cult, but many more could participate. There were trained choirs, a variety of functionaries, and incorporation of the emperor into other cults, especially of civic gods and goddesses but even in family piety. Imperial worship had become a pervasive facet of life in these cities.

To understand what it meant to worship the emperor requires some familiarity with the role of religion in the Greco-Roman world. For the Greeks and Romans, one needed to express the appropriate amount of reverence for all those higher on the social scale. Those who did so could be said to exhibit piety (Latin *pietas*, Greek *eusebeia*); those who fell short were impious and those who were excessively servile were superstitious.

Of course the proper amount of reverence depends on how one regards the emperor. In imperial propaganda the emperor was portrayed at the apex of the hierarchy, with only Providence above him. The emperor was thus the benefactor of the whole world, its supreme guide, lord, and savior. It was only fitting that holidays, rituals, songs, prayers, and sacrifices should be devoted to him. Clearly some of these were beyond what a Christian could accept; but were they all?

Christians disagreed with each other as to their duty toward the emperor. The author of 1 Peter thought it appropriate to "honor the emperor" (2:17) and Paul thought all should be subject to rulers (Rom. 13:1–7). Surely some in Asia Minor pursued a similar path, but not John. John saw the emperor and the whole imperial system as demonic (e.g., 17:9–14) and advocated withdrawal (e.g., 18:1–5). In fact, John saw the problem as extending far beyond the imperial cult.

Piety pervaded every area of life, for in each arena one should give proper reverence to the powers that be. Thus every theatrical performance began with a sacrifice to Dionysus, god of song; every trade guild would be devoted to a patron deity and would begin meetings with an invocation and small sacrifice of wine; education was devoted to learning the stories of the gods, with Homer's *Iliad* providing the basic text; sporting events were devoted to a particular god or goddess; public festivals (a source of meat in diets scarce in meat) were devoted to various gods; even the very coins one used in the marketplace were marked by an image of a god. Thus, according to John, one could not buy or sell without staining one's hand with the mark of the beast (13:16–17).

Unlike Paul, who had earlier allowed his followers to eat sacrificial meat bought in the market or served in private homes (1 Cor. 8–10), John completely rejected such participation, condemning those who permitted it (2:12–17, 18–28). But this particular practice is only indicative of the broader issue: how does one keep the testimony of Jesus and follow the word of God in a culture entirely devoted to other gods?

## Purpose

Perhaps the most dramatic shift in understanding the Apocalypse is how scholars evaluate the purpose of the work. The older view was that it was written to give comfort and courage to communities undergoing persecution. The newer view is almost the opposite: it was written to convince communities all too comfortable with Rome to pull back and separate themselves from Roman cultural life.

There is no doubt that Rome is portrayed in a radically negative fashion: as beast (13:1–4), as prostitute (17:1–5), and as Satan's dupe (13:4). Her downfall is imaged as burning (18:7–9), as desolation (18:2), and as drowning (18:21), and the wealthy and powerful lament her passing (18). The question is why? When the historical context was seen as Roman persecution, scholars concluded that John was trying to give the persecuted a reason to remain faithful, namely, that Rome would soon be destroyed. But scholars have largely rejected the historical reconstruction of the period as a time of persecution (see "Historical Setting" above).

The very fact that John worked so hard to show Rome as evil argues against the thesis of persecution; if persecution were routine, Rome's evil would be obvious. Rather, John sees these nascent Christian communities being seduced by the power, prosperity, and beauty of Rome. He sees the great danger to be compromise, to accommodate even to assimilate to Roman culture. Thus he portrays his chief rival, a woman prophet from Thyatira who permits the eating of sacrificial meat, as Jezebel (2:20), the ancient queen of Israel who supported the worship of Baal (1 Kgs 18–19). And he calls her male associate Balaam, the ancient prophet who advised the Canaanites that the best way to defeat the invading Israelites was to intermarry and assimilate (Num. 22–4).

This may also explain John's hostility to the Jewish community, whom he calls "a synagogue of Satan" (2:9; 3:9). Again, when persecution was seen as the context, these references were explained as stemming from Jewish hostility; the usual scenario envisioned Jews denouncing Christians to the Roman authorities. The more likely scenario is that John saw in the synagogue what he feared most in his own community: integration into Roman culture. Many of the Jewish communities of Asia Minor were old, established communities who had long ago worked out various compromises that allowed them to participate in trade, hold public office, even attend the theater and other cultural events. They had, in John's view, joined the other side. They were a synagogue of Satan (This is not unlike Jesus' rebuke to Peter in Mark 8:31–3.)

John's vision of the community as separate and holy put him in competition with others in the community who advocated various forms of compromise (for example, eating sacrificial food) and he expends considerable effort undermining their authority. He disparagingly labels them Jezebel, Balaam, Nicolaitans (Rev. 2–3). The purpose of John's Apocalypse was to reveal what was really going on behind the scenes, to see the beast behind the beauty of Roman culture (see "Genre" below).

## Language and Style

There are many irregularities of language and style in this writing. The case endings of nouns are sometimes wrong – especially after prepositions; agreement between subjects and verbs are not always correct; gender agreements between nouns and pronouns are not always correct. Three explanations have been offered for these peculiarities: the influence of common speech, the influence of the Greek translations of the Hebrew scriptures, and the likelihood that the author was not a native Greek speaker. Probably all three are at work, but the most important is the last: the author seems to be thinking in a Semitic language (probably Aramaic) and transposing his thoughts into Greek. At other times the author draws on the Hebrew scriptures for inspiration and some of the Hebrew way of speaking carries over into Greek.

There is another possibility also, namely that the author consciously employed a diction that sounded "biblical" on the one hand and "ecstatic" on the other. Such a diction would reinforce the audience's impression that this writing is not simply John's; it came to him "in the spirit." One consequence of this (mis)use of Greek was the tendency of various scribes to fix it, giving us a great variety of textual emendations over the centuries and making the effort to establish the original reading very complex.

Another aspect of John's language is its liturgical nature. Not only are there extensive descriptions of the liturgy around the divine throne, the text provides the actual words of hymns (e.g., 4:8–11; 5:9–13; 7:10–11) and specific liturgical statements (e.g., "blessed are the ones who … ," 1:3; 14:13). And, in fact, the whole vision is said to have occurred "on the Lord's day" (1:10). This liturgical language is not just window-dressing, for a central theme of the Apocalypse is the proper worship of God (22:9; contrast 13:4).

## Intertextuality

Intertextuality refers not just to the relationship of one text to another, but to their ongoing mutual influence. Thus John's use of the Hebrew scriptures must be viewed not only as their having an influence on him, but also as his having an influence on them. Having taken up Daniel's Son of Man (Dan. 7:13), John changes the way Daniel is read by identifying this Son of Man with the Risen Jesus (Rev. 1:13; in Daniel it was a corporate image for Israel, Dan. 7:18). And, of course, by reappropriating this corporate image, the reader of the Apocalypse might develop new insights into John's characterization of Jesus. It is an ongoing dialectical process. And it is not just Daniel.

While the author never quotes from the scriptures, never uses a stylized expression like "it is written" or a fulfillment formula, he constantly uses the words and images of the Bible, especially of Daniel, Ezekiel, and Isaiah, but also from Zechariah, Joel, and the Psalms. This phenomenon can be clearly seen by comparing Revelation 4 with Ezekiel 1; Revelation 13 with Daniel 7; and Revelation 21–2 with Ezekiel 40–8. It is not that John simply copies from the source-text; rather, it is as if he read the source-text and then experienced his own revelation that he casts in the images and themes of the original. Thus the four-faced creatures of Ezekiel (1:10) become four separate creatures around the heavenly throne (4:7; see also "Constituent Literary Forms" below). John uses, transforms, and is transformed by earlier scriptures.

Many have wondered whether John intended to recall not just the words of scripture but the context and significance of the original. And there is the additional difficulty of how familiar his audience could be expected to be with his source-texts. Neither question can be answered with any assurance, and, in fact, it seems that sometimes John intended the broader context and other times he did not. It is also likely that some in the audience would have benefited by their prior knowledge of his sources while others would have known nothing of them. There is nothing that John says that is unintelligible without the prior knowledge, but much that can be learned by comparing his text with the earlier texts.

## Unity

The question of the unity of the Apocalypse can be asked in two ways, the first having to do with the use of pre-existing sources, the second having to do with the unity of the story told. In the first case we are asking whether all the material in the Apocalypse is John's own composition or whether he wove material already in existence into his own composition. Such analysis, often called source criticism, was very common in the nineteenth century but has receded into the background today. A few scholars continue to raise important points; for while this is a very difficult question to answer with any confidence, since none of these earlier sources has survived independently, there are several elements of the Apocalypse that seem to stem from an earlier time and a different context. There are numerous scenes whose characters and actions are unique and relatively self-contained, that is, the characters do not appear in other scenes and the actions do not have any impact on the general narrative. There are perhaps a dozen such scenes, including such well-known incidents as the sealing of the 144,000 (7:1–17), the woman in the wilderness (12:1–18), and the rider on the white horse (19:11–16). These may well be visions from an earlier time, either John's own earlier work or that of other visionaries that he has incorporated into his work.

In addition to this question of the unity of the materials is the question of the unity of the composition; that is, whatever the source of the material, has the author woven it into a unified story? Here too there are problems, manifest, for example, in the radically divergent ways in which various commentators present the structure of the work.

Many have been fascinated by the reappearing sequences of seven elements and have tried to organize the whole work in this manner – adding "unnumbered" series of sevens where John does not consciously number them. Others divide the work into two major segments: the messages to the seven churches (1–3) and the apocalyptic vision that begins with John's ascent into heaven (4–22). Others divide this last segment in various ways, some into two segments (most often 4–11 and 12–22); some into three (typically 4–11; 12:1–19:10; and 19:11–22:21, but others suggest 4–16; 17–20; and 21–2); and some into more, usually on the basis of similar content (for example, 4:1–8:1; 8:2–11:19; 12:1–14:20; 15:1–16:21; 17:1–19:10; and 19:11–22:21). Clearly there is no scholarly agreement on this basic question; just as clearly, the answer depends on how you phrase the question. Another way to ask the question is to ask after the plot of the narrative (discussed below under "Literary Analysis").

Most scholars agree that the Apocalypse contains divergent material and that this material is not completely integrated. There are many unconnected elements that the reader is left to integrate into the overall story. Two common strategies for harmonizing this divergent material are the concepts of interludes and recapitulation. An interlude is a segment of material inserted into some larger unit; for example, the scene of the sealing of the 144,000 is inserted into the sequence of seven seals, between seal six and seal seven (7:1–17; see also the segment in 10:1–11:14 that comes between the sixth and seventh trumpets). We can think of them as embedded narratives that interact with the larger narrative.

Recapitulation is a way of describing various kinds of repetition in the story; for example, the series of seven bowls closely parallels the series of seven trumpets (compare 8:7–11:15 with 16:2–17). Those who speak of recapitulation see such repetition as a going over the same ground again with some added perspective. Thus the events of the story are not a linear sequence but a circling spiral.

## Genre: Prophecy or Apocalypse?

Prophecy and apocalypse are distinct but overlapping genres. Both forms claim to present a revelation from God about some pressing historical or social problem, but they differ in their manner of reception, their mode of presentation, their typical traits, and their basic worldviews.

Prophets typically claim to have encountered the divine in a visionary state (e.g., Isa. 6, Jer. 1, Ezek. 1). John too makes such a claim (1:9–11). Writers of apocalypses typically make two additional claims: that they have received their revelations in night-time dreams (as Dan. 7–12) or that they have journeyed to heaven (as *2 Enoch*, 3:1–4:1; *Ascension of Isaiah*, 7). John also claims to have made such a journey (4:1–2).

More divergent still are their modes of presentation. The prophets were oral performers who resorted to writing as a secondary mode (see Jer. 36); apocalypses are in the first instance written texts presented in a secondary mode of orality. This is in part due to a striking feature of apocalypses: they are pseudonymous works that claim to be written by prophets long dead and just now made public (e.g., Dan. 12:4, 9). Now clearly John's work is in the first instance a written work, for the command is repeatedly made to write (e.g., 1:11, 19; 2:1; 14:13; 19:19) and it concludes with a curse intended to fix the written form of the text (22:18–19). It does not, however seem to be pseudonymous. It makes the plain presumption that the audience knows the author (e.g., 1:9) and in fact is presented as a letter (1:4), a form that presupposes a known author. There is, of course, the ambiguity that John presents it as the "apocalypse of Jesus Christ, which God gave him" (1:1) and even allows himself to speak in Jesus' voice: "I Jesus" (22:16). Still, the real author, John, never disappears, as is the case in all other apocalypses. Nevertheless, in the emphasis on writing, John is closer to the apocalyptic mode than the prophetic.

The distance becomes even greater when we look at the typical traits and devices used in the two genres. While both engage in extensive symbolic statements and actions, apocalypse tends toward the unusual – one might even say the bizarre. Stylized use of colors, numbers, and animals is common, with the animals portrayed in mythic terms (multiple heads, various numbers and sizes of horns, composite bodies of various species). Were we to construe John's work on a continuum of writings from prophetic to apocalyptic, it would be far closer to the apocalyptic.

Still, John calls his own work "words of prophecy" (1:3; 22:7, 10, 18), and it is useful to ask what that might have meant. The primary forms of prophecy were oracles of judgment and oracles of salvation. The former exhorted the audience to change their behavior; the latter exhorted them to persevere in times of trial. Both these modes are evident in the seven messages to the churches (2–3) and in the closing narrative (22), though they are little evident in the main section of the book. Like other apocalypses, John's Revelation is largely dualistic: there are good folk and there are evil folk. In the coming eschatological climax the former will be rewarded and the latter condemned. Prophecy is more ambiguous: the evil can repent and the good sin. John incorporates this larger prophetic vision into his apocalypse.

There is great diversity in the way the terms apocalyptic and apocalypse have been used in scholarly writing, but scholars today tend to use the words with more precision. Apocalyptic is generally used to designate a dualistic worldview that sees the present age as a time of evil, ruled by Satan. This is a radical shift from the worldview of the religion of Israel at the time of the classical prophets, who saw the world as ruled by God alone. An apocalypse generally incorporates this apocalyptic worldview, but is more especially a literary designation. The most widely accepted definition today sees it as a subtype of revelatory literature involving the following aspects: a narrative framework, angelic intermediaries, disclosure of the real (heavenly) world, and a vision of the final salvation of the human world.

Thus an apocalyptic worldview presumes that there is much going on behind the scenes; things are not as they appear. An apocalypse is written to let us peer behind the scenes. Literally, the word means to remove the veil. An apocalypse is written to allow its audience to see the cosmic struggle between the forces of good and evil that is being waged on the spiritual level so that they might better understand their present situation, and to motivate them to cooperate with the (hidden) forces of good. John aims to unmask the seeming benevolence of Rome and the lure of Greco-Roman culture and so motivate his audience to resist assimilation (see "Purpose" above).

## Constituent Literary Forms

Within the general form of an apocalypse, somewhat modified by John's prophetic call to repentance, John uses a variety of literary forms, some of them common to apocalypses and some of them unique to this work.

The most common mode of any apocalypse, deriving from prophecy, is the symbolic vision report. Here the prophet describes what he saw while in an altered state of consciousness, either a dream (Dan. 7:1) or a trance (John 1:10; 4:2; 17:3; 21:10). John's report is often dual, reporting both what he saw and what he heard. Further, there is often tension between the two modes, with one reinterpreting the other. For example in chapter 5, John hears that the "lion of the tribe of Judah" has conquered, but what he sees is a "lamb standing as though it had been slaughtered." (5:5–6). In this case the vision reinterprets the audition. At other times it works the other way. In chapter 12 the vision of heavenly warfare is reinterpreted by what John heard, namely that it was the death of the lamb and his followers that won this war (12:10–11). The meaning of John's report is often not simply the vision or the audition, but the creative tension between them.

Closely connected to the vision report is the autobiographical narrative. At certain key points in the story John highlights his own presence in the story. This happens at the beginning ("I, John ... was on the island called Patmos ... ," 1:9) and at the ending ("I, John, am the one who heard and saw these things ... ," 21:8). These two incidents form a real-world frame around the ever more fantastic stories in between. While he constantly reminds the audience that he witnessed these things ("I saw"/"I heard"), there are only four other places where he narrates a story in which he appears, that is, the story is about him. He describes his ascent into heaven and experience before the heavenly throne (see 4:1; 5:4); he tells a story about an angel giving him first a scroll to eat and then a measuring rod to measure the temple (10: 8–11:3); he tells of an angel who transports him to places where he sees two contrasting women, a debauched woman and a virgin bride (17, esp. 1–8 and 21:9–10); and he twice shows his mistaken attempt to worship an angel (19:10; 22:8–9). These scenes are not as random as they might appear; the first two anticipate major segments of his apocalypse: the visions in heaven (4–11) and the vision of cosmic war (12–22). The last two focus on the major theme of the work: the proper recipient of reverence.

Prior to the autobiographical narrative, John presents the audience with another form, the letter (1:4), a form he returns to in the closing (22:21, compare the endings of Paul's letters, for example, Gal. 6:18 or 1 Cor. 16:23). However, between these two points there are no other indicators of the letter form. Even the individual messages to the seven churches (2–3) take more the form of an imperial decree than of a letter. Still, John apparently wants the audience to think of this communication as a letter. It is the only known apocalypse to be cast in the form of a letter. Two reasons have been suggested for this: it enabled John to abandon the pseudepigraphical aspect of apocalypses in favor of direct communication between himself and his audience and it was a form that people were accustomed to having read in the worship assembly.

And it is clear that John expected his apocalypse to be read aloud, for he includes the form of an oral performance, explicitly indicating the roles of the public reader and the audience (1:3). As an oral performance, the Apocalypse would be primarily an experience rather than a source of information. Our way of silently studying and comparing various aspects of the word would be quite different from that of the original audience. This orality provides the broadest literary context of the Apocalypse. Thus we can see something of the complexity of John's apocalypse: a series of symbolic vision reports, set within the context of an autobiographical narrative, set within the context of a letter, set within the context of an oral performance.

Three other constituent forms deserve mention, each of which is both a means of presentation and a mode of reception. The first I will call "scripture reused." In a situation where scripture was regarded as the words of God, many interpreters thought they could look therein and discover new meanings. Sometimes interpreters made formal comments on the scriptural text, often with a formula like "this was to fulfill what was spoken by the prophet" or "interpreted this means." Another technique, widely used in apocalypses, is to take up the scriptural words and images and use them in a new vision. This technique is evident throughout the Apocalypse, as, for example, when the author uses the scriptural description of the Son of Man from Daniel 7–10 to describe the heavenly Christ (1:14–16). Some scenes are lifted rather directly (compare Rev. 10:8–10 with Ezek. 3:1–3) but scriptural allusions occur on every page. (See "Intertextuality" above.)

A second form can be called "astral interpretation," discerning the divine will by looking at the stars. The most dramatic instance of this is John's allusions to the zodiac in 12:1–6. This is related to astrology, but whereas ancient Gentiles believed the stars controlled human destiny, ancient Jews (and Christians) believed God controlled destiny, but used the stars to do it. At the least, one could read the divine will in the constellations.

A third form of major importance in the Apocalypse is myth, primal stories about the spiritual world. John uses a number of discrete myths (such as the stories of the Queen of Heaven and the threatened birth in chapter 12) but one myth pervades his story. John's whole work, but especially the last half (12–22) is built on the combat myth. This myth goes back at least to the Babylonian Creation story (the *Enuma Elish*) but was equally important to the imperial cult. It saw the world as a battleground between the forces of good and the forces of evil. This mythic dimension provides much of the structure of John's work (see "Literary Analysis" below).

Two aspects of John's mythological traditions are important. First, he uses myth to interpret and categorize contemporary historical experience. His enemies are "Jezebel" and "Balaam" not just rival first-century prophets; the Jewish community is a "synagogue of Satan" not just other Jews who take a different attitude toward Rome; and Rome itself is a dupe of Satan, ruling only by his magic. This leads to a second important observation: John uses and reverses imperial mythology. In the imperial myth the emperor is the savior, the warrior who defeats the chaos monster, and brings peace and prosperity to the world – Pax Romana. In John's story, the emperor is the chaos monster who must be destroyed by the heavenly warrior Jesus.

## Epistolary Analysis

Revelation is unique among apocalypses in being cast in the form of a letter, and the significance of this fact is disputed. The epistolary features are limited to the opening and closing (1:4–5; 22:21), with the body of the work showing little evidence of composition as a letter. Most conclude that these epistolary features are secondary, formal, traits added to an existing work to make it appear more like a letter. A partial parallel can be found in Hebrews, which ends like a letter (Heb. 13:22–5), and in Barnabas, which begins like a letter (1:1–5). In neither case does the letter element have much significance for interpreting the work. Most conclude the same regarding Revelation.

There are, however, two possible reasons for casting the Apocalypse in the form of a letter. First, the specific wording used is reminiscent of the Pauline letter, and the Apocalypse was written in a geographical area where Paul's influence was important. Such letters were regularly read in the worship assemblies and would thus provide some precedent for John's instruction to have this letter read aloud (1:3). Second, unlike all other apocalypses this one is not pseudonymous. Clearly the audience knows the author, and part of his authority rests on this relationship. The letter form helps John bend the apocalyptic genre to his own purposes. Additionally, this is a prophetic letter, that is, one for which John is meant to be seen as the scribe and not the author (see, e.g., Jer. 29:3–23). Twelve times John is told to write what he sees and hears. This idea that John is merely conveying a message from the divine fits nicely with the underlying notion of an apocalypse as an unveiling of the divine world (see "Genre" above). Thus the letter form strengthens John's message both by making it fit what is ordinarily read during worship and by signaling that John is merely the messenger for a message that originates above.

## Rhetorical Analysis

Rhetoric is the art of persuasion, and clearly the Apocalypse seeks to persuade its audience to think and act in different ways. Rhetorical analysis asks how it seeks to achieve this goal. At the most basic level scholars examine the rhetorical techniques employed. A great variety of techniques are pointed to, from name-calling, sarcasm, and innuendo to claims to secret knowledge and direct contact with Jesus. Much of the rhetoric of the Apocalypse aims to establish the authority of the author.

At a more complex level, there has been some analysis of John's narrative rhetoric, that is, how the story as story seeks to persuade. Such analysis asks how the basic elements of the story (point of view, nature of the narrator, story setting, characterization, and such) work behind the scenes to influence how the audience is persuaded by the story. One aspect of this narrative rhetoric speaks of the implied rhetorical situation. The degree to which an author is successful rhetorically depends on the degree to which that author makes contact with the audience. Thus an analysis of John's rhetorical purpose will reveal something about the actual audience of the work (or at least of John's perception of that audience).

Finally, one can speak of the rhetorical analysis of the Apocalypse not simply as a method for discovering an original meaning but also as a practice of producing new meanings by interacting with the text. Here the interpreter seeks to understand the rhetorical practice of the Apocalypse itself, its political and public rhetorical situation, and to create a similar rhetorical practice in the process of interpretation.

## Literary Analysis

Scholars generally agree that apocalypses, including John's Apocalypse, are narratives, but only recently has there been much attention to the specifically narrative aspects of the writing. These narrative aspects include plot (the relationship between the incidents of a story), characterization (the presentation of the actors), point of view (how the story is focused), and temporal distortions (such as anachronisms, repetition, foreshadowing, and duration), among others.

It is too early for there to be much scholarly consensus on these issues, but there has been enough analysis to indicate the importance of literary topics. For example, John seems deliberate in the way he characterizes the actors. John's opponent, whom he calls Jezebel, is characterized with the same motifs as the debauched woman who represents Roman rule: both are mothers, sexually impure, tainted by impure food, named by allusion to Israel's past corruption, and destined for destruction. Jesus is characterized first as a grand heavenly human being (1:12–16), then as a slaughtered lamb standing in the midst of God's throne (5:6), and finally as a heavenly warrior mounted on a white horse (19:11).

The plot of John's story is not obvious, as the great variety of ways scholars see the structure of the work make plain. The primary indicators of plot are continuity of action, changes in scene, and underlying paradigm (or plot type). Thus Aristotle demanded that a plot have a beginning, a middle, and an end: its first action must be self-evident and it must lead through a series of logical steps to a fitting conclusion. John's story starts in just such a logical way. He reports an unusual incident he experienced on Patmos in which a heavenly human being appears to him and dictates letters. But when the letters end, John ascends to heaven. There is no logical connection between the letters and this ascent, and the letters are never again referred to. The reader is left to imagine the connection between these two sequences.

The sequence of events initiated by John's ascent is also easy to trace, at least up to the end of chapter 11, where John's peering into the heavenly temple seems to initiate a new sequence, dominated by the dragon and his two henchmen, who make war on the heavenly woman and her children.

Viewed this way, and that is only one way in which the reader might construe the plot, John's story consists of three interrelated stories: The writing of the letters, the witness of the heavenly court, and the vision of the cosmic war and its aftermath. These three stories are not necessarily sequential, especially since the end of the second story already proclaims that "the kingdoms of this world have become the kingdom of our Lord and his messiah" (11:15). They may, in fact, be three ways of telling the same story of how God's kingdom comes, the first showing the action within the churches, the second portraying the heavenly reality, and the third portraying the social and political reality.

Whether this is the best way to view the plot is less important than the questions it raises and the promise of new insights that such literary analysis provides.

## Theological Issues and Themes

If theology is the systematic reflection on, and explanation of, religious experience, we should not speak of the theology of the Apocalypse, for it is a portrayal of experience not a reflection on it. It does, however, raise important issues that theology seeks to deal with. Chief among these are the issues of eschatology, ecclesiology, and Christology. It also raises many other themes, such as the meaning of God's sovereignty, the nature of evil, and the role of humans in establishing God's rule in the world. In each of these cases the Apocalypse does not so much teach a doctrine as tell the story in a way that implies certain conclusions.

Thus the image of God on the heavenly throne (Rev. 4), the assertion that God "was, is, and is to come" (1:4; 1:8; 4:8), as well as the repeated appellation "the almighty" (1:8; 4:8; 11:7; 15:3, etc.) clearly imply divine sovereignty. At the same time, the inclusion of the witness of the martyrs along with the blood of Jesus (12:11), the role of the innocent lives under the altar (6:11), and the cosmic significance assigned to the prayers of the saints (8:3–5), all imply that humans play a central role in the drama. Evil clearly originates with Satan (12:9, 12), but just as clearly it is focused through Roman political and economic exploitation (13; 18), and manifests itself in human action (19:19), even within the church (2–3). Theology may wish to explain and resolve these tensions; John never does. Nor are the major issues entirely clear.

### Eschatology

Apocalypses generally imagine that the end of the age is at hand and that some decisive divine act will shortly bring the era of evil to a close. It is generally assumed that John both shares this view and that he sees the coming divine act as the Second Coming of Jesus. Certain scenes seem to support these conclusions: the rider on the white horse (19:11–21) clearly represents Jesus, and Jesus' coming is said to be soon (1:1; 3:11; 22:6–7). At the same time John can speak of the rule of God and Christ as already complete (11:15). And whenever there is a claim that Jesus conquers evil, it is always through an image of his life and death (e.g., 5:5–6; 12:12; even 19:15). The decisive divine act that overthrows evil has already occurred in the life and death of Jesus, even if the working out of this victory remains for the future.

### Christology

The story announces itself as "the revelation of Jesus Christ" (1:1) and in one sense the whole of it aims to reveal Jesus. Still we are told surprisingly little about him: none of the teachings of Jesus appears and none of his deeds is rehearsed except his death and exaltation. Of the three main images of him, the image of the slain-yet-standing Lamb far overshadows the image of the heavenly human (1:13ff.) and the image of the divine warrior (19:11ff.). The lamb first appears at 5:6 but is portrayed in a dozen scenes, with thirty explicit references. The most important characteristic of John's Jesus is his death, and the function of that death is to overthrow the powers of evil (e.g., 12:11).

Scholars generally agree that the Apocalypse has a high Christology, regarding the Christ as a divine and pre-existent figure. He is called "the first and the last" (1:17) and the "origin [*arche*] of God's creation" (3:14). More importantly, he shares the throne of God (3:21) and receives worship (5:7–14). Sometimes the same words are used to describe both ("alpha and omega," 1:8; 22:13). Still, very little attention is given to either Jesus' status or his pre-existence; the focus of the story is on his present activity in the life of the community, through the spirit and, especially, through the voice of his prophets.

*Ecclesiology*

The Apocalypse contains extensive liturgical material, so much so that some have suggested it derived from the actual liturgy of the late first century. This is unlikely. Still, a considerable amount of the text deals with what happens in church: not only the seven messages (1–3), but also the narrative framework of the scene in heaven which involves a kind of divine liturgy (4–11). It has been observed that this liturgical portrayal of God's rule precedes the dramatic presentation of that rule in scenes of holy war. This suggests a central role for the church in John's vision.

One aspect of the central role of the church is the inherent connection between story and ritual; ritual really is the acting out of the vital story of the group. The Christian story, and thus Christian ritual, centers on the death and resurrection of the Christ. This is the fundamental story of the Apocalypse. Some have suggested that the Apocalypse really is the dramatization of the Lord's Prayer: "Our Father, who art in heaven, hallowed be thy name; thy kingdom come; thy will be done on earth as it is in heaven ... ."

It is this inherent connection between worship, story, and kingdom that explains the tensions between John's community and the Roman government. It is not incidental that the heavenly worship portrays God on a throne – an inherently political image.

A second aspect of the centrality of the church involves the question of how one ought to live in society, an issue at the heart of the tensions within John's community. There were some leaders who advocated a more moderate stance toward Rome. They, like Paul in an earlier generation, thought some accommodation was possible so that they could participate in the civic and economic life of the cities. They probably represented the more affluent members of the community, those engaged in trade, members of the guilds, active in civic life. John saw these leaders as betraying the faith and named them after ancient villains who had been responsible for tainting Israel's worship of the one true God with elements of other religions: Balaam and Jezebel.

John's Apocalypse sought nothing less than the redefinition of the church achieved through a redefinition of reality. Reality is now defined not by Roman power but by the redemptive death of Jesus and the suffering of his faithful followers.

## Annotated Bibliography

Aune, David E. *The Cultic Setting of Realized Eschatology in Early Christianity*. Leiden: E. J. Brill, 1972. Still an indispensable book for understanding the liturgical locus of apocalyptic writings.

Aune, David E. *Revelation*. 3 vols. Word Biblical Commentary. Nashville: Thomas Nelson, 1997–8. The best commentary currently available, providing a comprehensive treatment of major issues with splendid bibliographies. Detailed exposition of the text in conversation with leading interpreters.

Barr, David L. *Tales of the End: A Narrative Commentary on the Book of Revelation*. The Storytellers Bible, 1. Santa Rosa, CA: Polebridge Press, 1998. A serious treatment of the narrative elements of the Apocalypse, including plot, characterization, focalization, temporal distortion, and myth.

Collins, Adela Yarbro. *The Combat Myth in the Book of Revelation*. Chico: Scholars Press, 1976. Classic presentation of the origin, scope, and use of the combat myth.

Collins, Adela Yarbro. *Crisis and Catharsis: The Power of the Apocalypse*. Philadelphia: Westminster Press, 1984. Best treatment of the context of the Apocalypse as relative deprivation along with sensible discussions of date, authorship, and dramatic effect.

Collins, John J. *The Apocalyptic Imagination: An Introduction to the Jewish Matrix of Christianity*. Los Angeles: Crossroad, 1984. Best introduction to apocalyptic as a way of thinking, including an excellent discussion of genre and a survey of most surviving apocalyptic writings.

Duff, Paul Brooks. *Who Rides the Beast? Prophetic Rivalry and the Rhetoric of Crisis in the Churches of the Apocalypse*. Oxford: Oxford University Press, 2001. A clear statement of the evidence of intra-Christian conflict in the setting of the Apocalypse.

Friesen, Steven J. *Imperial Cults and the Apocalypse of John: Reading Revelation in the Ruins*. Oxford: Oxford University Press, 2001. A masterful presentation of the workings of the imperial cult as the context of John's Apocalypse.

Kovacs, Judith L. and Christopher Rowland. *Revelation: The Apocalypse of Jesus Christ*. Oxford: Blackwell Publishing, 2004. The commentary provides a helpful survey of interpretations of the Apocalypse in scholarly, traditional, and artistic venues.

Kraybill, J. Nelson. *Imperial Cult and Commerce in John's Apocalypse*. Sheffield: Sheffield Academic Press, 1996. Excellent discussion of trade, the guild system, and the economy of Asia Minor under Roman rule as a context for John's resistance to cultural accommodation.

Muse, Robert L. *The Book of Revelation: An Annotated Bibliography*. Books of the Bible, 2. New York: Garland Publishing, 1996. A comprehensive bibliography divided by topics. Includes works in English primarily, but includes some attention to German, French, and Italian scholarship through about 1990.

Pippin, Tina. *Apocalyptic Bodies: The Biblical End of the World in Text and Image*. London: Routledge, 1999. Important contribution to a feminist counter-reading of the Apocalypse.

Reddish, Mitchell. *Apocalyptic Literature: A Reader*. Peabody MA: Hendrickson, 1990; repr. 1995. Useful collection of major apocalyptic texts.

Schüssler Fiorenza, Elisabeth. *Revelation: Vision of a Just World*. Minneapolis: Fortress Press, 1991. An important contribution to feminist, liberationist readings of the Apocalypse; one of the few commentaries that attempt to go beyond an historical-critical methodology.

Schüssler Fiorenza, Elisabeth. *The Book of Revelation: Justice and Judgment*. 2nd edn. Minneapolis: Fortress Press, 1998. Pioneering work on social and political reading of the Apocalypse through feminist and liberationist methods.

Sweet, J. P. M. *Revelation*. Philadelphia: Westminster Press, 1979; repr. Philadelphia: Trinity Press International, 1990. One of the best historical commentaries with sensible discussions of major issues.

Thompson, Leonard L. *The Book of Revelation: Apocalypse and Empire*. Oxford: Oxford University Press, 1990. Important evaluation of the social and historical context of the Apocalypse, showing that Roman persecution is not a likely hypothesis.

Thompson, Steven. *Apocalypse and Semitic Syntax*. Society for New Testament Studies Monograph Series, 52. Cambridge: Cambridge University Press, 1985. Careful discussion of the linguistic peculiarities of the Apocalypse.

Wainwright, Arthur. *Mysterious Apocalypse: Interpreting the Book of Revelation*. Nashville: Abingdon Press, 1993. Valuable history of the interpretation of the Apocalypse from earliest times.

CHAPTER 38

# New Testament Apocrypha

## Petra Heldt

The term "New Testament Apocrypha" (NTA) has traditionally been used to denote various ancient writings that concern the very origins of Christianity, but which were not received into the canon of the New Testament. In recent decades there has been much debate about what writings belong to this category, how it should be defined, and even whether the term should continue to be used. Thus it is appropriate to indicate the main lines of that debate before discussing a selection from the individual writings themselves.

## Questions of Principle

Contemporary scholars are often hesitant to employ the term NTA at all, since they believe that the study of these writings should not be prejudiced by any value judgment implied by the absence of canonical status. They are also unsure about what writings should count as NTA. Thus Elliott (1993: xi), called them an "amorphous and wide-ranging group" of texts, neither comprising an agreed corpus of writings nor created within a defined time range, but often revised later and adjusted to new circumstances. Also the term "apocrypha" for these texts is sometimes regarded as arbitrary because few were "secret" writings for an inner circle (the *Apocalypse of Paul?*) or "fictitious" (the *Acts of John?*) or even "heretical" (the *Gospel of Thomas?*). Nor can they all easily be classified under the New Testament genres as gospels, acts, epistles, and apocalypses.

   On the other hand, from very early times such writings were compared and contrasted with what became the canonical New Testament. According to the research of Christoph Markschies (Markschies 2001), the inventories of ancient Christian libraries on papyrus already imply judgments about the status of such writings from the second century on. By the start of the third century, lists of non-canonical writings had emerged. Origen (ca. 200 CE), for instance, listed four apocryphal works: the *Gospel of the Egyptians*, the *Gospel of the Twelve*, the *Second Epistle of Peter*, and the *Shepherd of Hermas*. In the sixth century, the so-called *Decretum Gelasianum* presented a standard list of some thirty apocryphal writings, basically clustered according to the genres of the New Testament. They were the *Shepherd of Hermas*, the *Clementine Recognitions*, four acts (Andrew, Thomas, Peter, Philip), nine gospels (Matthias, Barnabas, James the younger, Peter, Thomas, Bartholomew, Andrew, Lucia, Hesychius), eleven books (*the Infant Savior, the Birth of the Savior, the Shepherd, Leucius, Fundaments, Thesaurus, the Daughters of Adam Leptogeneseos, the Cento on Christ put together in Virgilian verses, Acts of Paul and Thecla*, the book which is called *Nepos's*, and the books of *Proverbs* written by heretics and prefixed with the name of holy Sixtus), three revelations (Paul, Thomas, Stephen), and many others.

From late antiquity on, the NTA were instrumental in fashioning Christian culture at all levels. Icons presented the narrative of Jesus according to the *Protevangelium of James*, images of piety were promoted by the *Acts of Paul and Thecla* and the books on the assumption of Mary, and notions of hell and purgatory reflected the account of the *Descent of Christ to the World Below*. The *Legenda Aurea* (*Golden Legends*), containing reworked versions of a wide range of apocrypha, disseminated this material amongst the populace at large. Preachers prepared collections of apocryphal texts for preaching purposes (Irena Backhus [1998], on Christoph Scheurl's collection from 1506). Maire Herbert and Martin McNamara's *Irish Biblical Apocrypha* (1989) exemplifies how such collections could emerge from regional interests.

The emergence of printed books reinforced the impression that there existed a fixed corpus of NTA, forming a kind of alternative New Testament. Especially influential in this respect was the three-volume edition of Johann Albert Fabricius, *Codex Apocryphus Novi Testamenti* (1703). His selection, classification, and arrangement of texts created a trend whereby these documents, for some 300 years, enjoyed a semi-official status, as if they formed a definite corpus of written material. Volume 1 contained five apocryphal gospels, fragments of gospels, sayings of Christ, and two epistles of Pilate. Volume 2 comprised ten books of acts of various apostles, six apocryphal epistles, fragments of epistles, eleven apocryphal apocalypses, Revelations of the Patriarchs and Prophets, and ascensions. Volume 3 added liturgies and *varia*.

Besides his celebrated critical editions of the New Testament (from 1841 on), Tischendorf also produced an influential critical edition of the Greek and Latin NTA. Volume 1 (1851) contained acts, volume 2 (1852) gospels, and volume 3 (1866) apocalypses. A second edition was issued by Lipsius and Bonnet (1891–1903). For the apocryphal gospels, a modestly priced collection of the major Greek and Latin texts, with Spanish translations and extensive notes and bibliography, has been published by Aurelio de Santos Otero in successive editions from 1956 on.

A comprehensive critical edition, including the different oriental and other languages, is currently appearing (it began in 1981) under the general editorship of Francis Bovon as *Corpus Christianorum Series Apocryphorum* (*CCSA*). The editors of this series replaced the conventional name New Testament apocrypha with "Christian apocryphal literature," indicating that the writings concerned are treated in their own right, independent of the question of canonicity. *CCSA* includes the *Clavis Apocryphorum Novi Testamenti* of M. Geerard (1992), which lists some 346 apocryphal books, often in more than one revision, version, or edition. They are organized under nine categories: (1) apocrypha about the public life of Jesus (48, including 17 gospel fragments);

(2) apocrypha about the nativity and the infancy of Jesus (10); (3) gospels concerning the death and resurrection of Jesus (24); (4) legend(s) of Abgar, king of Edessa; (5) apocrypha about the Virgin Mary; (6) apocrypha about John the Baptist; (7) apocryphal acts of the apostles; (8) epistles; (9) apocalypses.

There are several collections of NTA in English translation. The most recent standard editions are J. K. Elliott, *The Apocryphal New Testament* (1993), including apocryphal gospels, acts, epistles, and apocalypses in one volume, and R. McL. Wilson, *New Testament Apocrypha*, in two volumes: I: *Gospels and Related Writings* (1991) and II: *Apostolic and Early Church Writings* (1993). Wilson's version is translated from the fifth German edition of Wilhelm Schneemelcher, *Neutestamentliche Apocryphen, I: Evangelien* (1987, corrected 6th edn. 1990) and *II: Apostolisches, Apokalypsen und Verwandtes* (1989; corrected 6th edn. 1997).

Current research on the NTA has been enriched by the discovery of large caches of other documents in recent decades. These include the Oxyrhynchus papyri, the Nag Hammadi codices and the Fayyum Fragment, but also rediscovered texts of writings disputed in the works of the Church Fathers, as well as collections of early church writers in libraries in Europe and the Middle East. (The scrolls from Qumran also offer insights for the study of NTA.) Those finds bear witness to a fascination with the NTA in the east, where the texts were rendered in such languages as Ethiopic (Geez), Coptic, Syriac, and Armenian, sometimes preserving earlier versions or readings than those available in Greek or Latin.

In view of the debate about the term NTA, Schneemelcher (1990) suggested dividing the apocryphal writings into three chronological categories: those contemporary with the writings that were later canonized (until ca. 100 CE) those composed when the canon was in formation (until ca. 200 CE), and those written after the fixation of the canon. An example of the third group is the *Acts of Pilate*, which may date from the fifth century but preserves earlier accounts. The problem with this classification, however, is that precisely the dates of these writings are often a matter of surmise. A new edition of Schneemelcher is currently being prepared under the editorship of Christoph Markschies (Markschies 1998).

New proposals for how to read the NTA have also emerged in recent decades. Notably Helmut Koester, *Introduction to the New Testament* (1982), sought to free the NTA from being judged by the canon of the church and to place the apocryphal material in its historical context. Likewise, Koester's *Ancient Christian Gospels: Their History and Development* (1990) employed apocryphal writings for insights into the earliest stages of the development of the gospel tradition. He suggested that the first phase of the history of the gospel literature comprised six "apocryphal" documents: the sayings source (Q), the *Gospel of Thomas*, the *Dialogue of the Savior*, the *Unknown Gospel* of Papyrus Egerton 2, the *Apocryphon of James*, and the *Gospel of Peter*.

Currently, research focuses on the historical circumstances of any and all apocryphal compositions and their witness to cultural, political, and sociological factors in their period. A prime example of this approach is the annual edited by Pierre Geoltrain, Jean-Claude Picard, and Alain Desreumaux. Originally entitled *Apocrypha: Le Champ des Apocryphes* (volume 1, 1990), since volume 3 (1992) it has appeared as *Apocrypha: Revue Internationale des Littératures Apocryphes / International Journal of*

*Apocryphal Literatures.* In their manifesto (*Apocrypha* 1, 1990), the editors declared their intention "to offer a forum for expression, exchange and confrontation for all those wishing to transform the old object of erudition into a new subject for historical reconstruction."

Although the older scholarly consensus on the NTA is now often challenged, a new consensus has not yet emerged. To quote A. F. J. Klijn (1988): "It appears, however, that it has become more and more difficult to find an adequate definition of what is supposed to be 'apocryphal.'" Klijn attributed the lack of clarity to "a great number of writings among the Nag Hammadi discoveries which are supposed to be of an apocryphal nature." Similarly, James Charlesworth (1987), and Christoph Markschies (1998) emphasized the need to find criteria for defining apocrypha and distinguishing them from legends, martyrdoms, and homilies.

In the context of the present book, it is important to note those questions of principle, but not to dwell on them. Rather, it will suffice to concentrate on those compositions which are arguably closest to the canonical New Testament in date and character or which exercised a significant influence on the history of the church from an early period on. That is, the present discussion can confine itself to approximately the traditional scope of the term NTA, but without ascribing to this term dogmatic or other ideological implications. Thus there are apocryphal gospels, apocryphal acts, apocryphal epistles, and apocryphal apocalypses. Some other early compositions of interest can also be included under those subdivisions, although they do not fit into them so obviously. Also there are some works that have survived in full, though sometimes in markedly distinct versions, while others are known only from manuscript fragments or from occasional quotations by other authors.

## Apocryphal Gospels

The genre of "gospel" is not limited to a narrative account of traditions, as found in the four canonical gospels, but includes also collections of sayings of Jesus, like the Coptic *Gospel of Thomas*, and even the Sethian revelation (bearing little resemblance to the story of the earthly Jesus) found in the *Gospel of the Egyptians*, also known as the *Holy Book of the Great Invisible Spirit*. A gospel may also comprise dialogues of the resurrected Jesus with the disciples, as in the *Epistula Apostolorum*, or it could contain just parts of the life of Jesus, such as his infancy or his death and resurrection.

Schneemelcher (1990) distinguished between three kinds of apocryphal gospels: those connected with the canonical gospels, those expressing forms of Gnosis, and those which are gospels only in name, since their content belongs to a different genre, such as various Nag Hammadi texts. A borderline case is the *Epistula Apostolorum*, which utilizes gospel material alongside church regulations and homiletic traditions. The *Clavis* of *CCSA* prefers to divide its gospels mainly into three chronological categories referring to the life of Jesus, as noted above, while adding the legend(s) of Abgar as a fourth category. This classification will be followed here. The discussion will focus on salient examples in each category.

## The public life of Jesus

*Fragments*    Amongst the seventeen fragments extant, the *Gospel of Peter* takes an eminent place. It is known from one eighth- or ninth-century Greek manuscript found at Akhmim in Upper Egypt. This fragment begins: "But of the Jews none washed the hands, neither Herod nor his judges," upon which Pilate handed Jesus over to them. It goes on to relate the passion story and the empty tomb, with a "young man" announcing the resurrection. It breaks off with "I, Peter" back in Galilee fishing, that is, presumably about to meet the risen Christ – but for the *first* time – in a situation like chapter 21 of John's Gospel. It is widely agreed today that the Akhmim manuscript belongs to the *Gospel of Peter* mentioned by Serapion of Antioch (end of the second century) in a letter quoted by Eusebius (*Ecclesiastical History*, 6:12.1–6).

There have been many attempts to account for the evident similarities to and differences from the canonical gospels. Thus Koester (1990) granted the *Gospel of Peter* pre-eminence over the canonical gospels, arguing that the latter drew from the same epiphany account as a common source. Schneemelcher (1990) regarded the *Gospel of Peter* as belonging to the tradition of anti-Jewish polemics, claiming that it gives Herod a more prominent role than Pilate and noting that Jews, not Roman soldiers, mock Jesus and put him to death. Malcolm Lowe (1981), however, pointed out that the *Gospel of Peter* is obviously *less* anti-Jewish than the synoptic gospels, since – like John's Gospel – there is no mention of "crowds" or "all the people" when Jesus is condemned, but only of a handful of local leaders and their officers.

Another notable fragment, but shorter, is Papyrus Egerton 2 (PEg2), dated by scholars variously to 150–200. It consists of four pericopes from an unidentified gospel: a dispute between Jesus and the teachers of law (*nomikoi* instead of *grammateis*); an attempt to stone Jesus and the healing of a leper; questions about taxes; and, unparalleled in the canonical gospels, a miracle by Jesus at the river Jordan. Koester (1982) ascribed the contents to Jewish-Christian circles and argued for an origin in time similar to the synoptic gospels and before John's Gospel. Whereas Kurt Erlemann (1996) argues that the document came into existence independently from the synoptic gospels, Schneemelcher (1990) believed that the author of PEg2 knew all four canonical gospels, although referring to them without working from a written version.

*Agrapha*    By *agrapha* is meant sayings of Jesus not found in the canonical gospels. Examples occur in Acts 20:35 and in such manuscript variants of the canonical gospels as Luke 6:4 in the version of Codex Bezae. Hofius (1983) accepted seven such sayings, down from almost 200 in Resch's compilation (1889).

In this respect, the Nag Hammadi Coptic *Gospel of Thomas* is of particular interest. It contains 114 largely unconnected brief items, of which at least some might be referred to Jesus, but all of which may have been in circulation in the second century. A *Gospel of Thomas* is mentioned by Origen and Cyril of Jerusalem (*Catecheses*, 4:36; 6:31), but it remains unclear whether this was the *Gospel of Thomas* or the *Infancy Gospel of Thomas* (see below) or something else. Among many speculations about the origins of the *Gospel of Peter*, Blatz in Schneemelcher (1990) argued that it is a fourth-century rendition of an earlier Coptic text, whereas Quispel (1969) and Koester (1990) assumed a Greek antecedent of the Coptic version, antedating the canonical gospels. The ascetic and

Gnostic features in the *Gospel of Thomas* provide an early witness to the transmission of the sayings of Jesus in encratite and Gnostic circles, perhaps also in Manichaean settings (Blatz).

*Jewish-Christian Gospels*    References to a Jewish-Christian gospel, the *Gospel of the Hebrews*, are found early in Irenaeus, Clement of Alexandria, and Origen, as well as in Eusebius. Origen also mentioned the *Gospel of the Twelve*, but Jerome identified the latter with the *Gospel of the Hebrews*. Jerome himself speaks of the *Gospel of the Nazarenes* and Epiphanius of the *Gospel of the Ebionites*. Whether these were four distinct gospels, or only three or even two going under different names, has been disputed by such scholars as Klostermann, Waitz, and Dibelius. The language, or the original language, of the various gospels (Greek, Hebrew, or Aramaic) is also uncertain.

According to the ancient mentions, the *Gospel of the Hebrews* contained wisdom traditions, referred to Mount Tabor, and described appearances of Jesus after the resurrection to James, Peter, and the apostles; the *Gospel of the Nazarenes* told of the rich young man and of the master with the three servants; and the *Gospel of the Ebionites* included the baptism, the Last Supper, and the passion, with a brief reference to the resurrection. Origen says nothing about the content of the *Gospel of the Twelve*.

*Dialogues with the savior*    Of the seven such dialogues listed by the *Clavis*, the *Epistula Apostolorum* is often seen as a singular non-Gnostic example of this category. It may have been composed in Greek in the late second century (Elliott 1993), but it is extant today in five diverse complete Ethiopic manuscripts and a number of diverse Coptic fragments. It begins as an epistle of the council of the apostles to the Catholics in the world to ensure the teaching of the complete unity of God and Son of God in the savior who suffered, died and rose again, contrary to the docetic teaching of Cerinthus and Simon. Accordingly, Montague Rhodes James (1953) and Elliott (1993) classified it under "apocryphal epistles."

The account then shifts to a dialogue with the savior, or rather to instructions and revelations of Jesus to the three women at the tomb and then to the disciples, relating how in heaven Jesus had at his disposal the wisdom and power of the Father. He was made like the angels in his descent to Mary and remained unrecognized. The text stresses the resurrection of the flesh together with the soul and the spirit before the judgment. Paul is confirmed as a preacher and an apostle. The work ends with the ascension of Jesus after having described, like an apocalypse, terrors of the end time, the deliverance of the apostles, and the faithful won by them.

*Gnostic gospels*    According to Puech (in the third German edition [1959] of Schneemelcher 1990), the Gnostic type of gospel is typically one in which the risen Christ reveals an esoteric teaching to his disciples in response to their questions. That definition can still stand, even after all the more recent work evaluating Nag Hammadi manuscripts and studying the complex subject of the literary genres of Gnostic gospels.

The *Clavis* lists seven Gnostic gospels. The most notable is the *Pistis Sophia*. It is found in a Coptic Gnostic document from about the third century, known as the Codex Askewianus after the man who discovered it in 1792. It has now been republished in the Nag Hammadi Studies series. Following Koestlin (1854), Schmidt and MacDermot (1978) observed that Codex Askewianus is a compilation of texts which appear as two parts in four books.

The first part, the *Pistis Sophia* proper, comprises Book 1 and most of Book 2. It surveys the post-resurrection teaching of Jesus, including the order to Philip, Matthew, and Thomas to relate his speeches in a written form after his resurrection (*Pistis Sophia*, 42–3). The account is not an ongoing narrative, but certain issues recur. One is the element of light: the light-power by which Jesus ascends and descends on the Mount of Olives; the garments of light by which he rises through the aeons that rebel against the light; the light of Jesus who rescues *Pistis Sophia* from the Chaos to a higher place, where it receives the crown of light. The meeting of the two light powers, Jesus and *Pistis Sophia*, results in the great outpouring of light. Michael and Gabriel take some of this light to the Chaos. Mary the Mother of Jesus, another Mary and various apostles offer their interpretations of those events.

The second part of Codex Askewianus bears the title *A Part of the Books of the Savior*. It consists of teachings of the savior given to the disciples as answers to their questions. Issues include the effectiveness of mysteries in general and their efficiency in the forgiveness of sins in particular, the outer darkness and places of punishment and the dragon, and the souls of the patriarchs and prophets. There is a ritual prayer of Jesus after his resurrection in the presence of the disciples and a number of discourses by the savior, such as on the separation of the archons, the purification of souls, and the mysteries of baptism of fire, water, and spirit. Most questions come from Mary Magdalene, but many also come from Mary, Salome, Peter, Andrew, Thomas, Bartholomew, and John.

In both of its parts, as Kurt Rudolph has pointed out (1983), the text reads as if it presupposes the authority of the canonical books of the Old Testament, the New Testament gospels, and the epistles of Paul, but expands their account in the name of a superior revelation. Some recent scholars have surmised that such speculations were not seen as "heretical" in their time, despite their Gnostic character. Rather, as Christoph Markschies (2001) suggests, those responsible for writing and compiling such books were employing the current scholarly standards and methods of philosophical schools in order to interpret a canonical text esoterically.

## Nativity and infancy stories

Amongst the *Clavis* list of ten gospels about the nativity and infancy of Jesus, the *Protevangelium of James* (PJ) was particularly influential. Extant in 140 Greek manuscripts from the third century CE on, and in translations into major oriental languages, its author claims to be James the brother of Jesus. Specifically, James is a son of the aged Joseph by his deceased first wife.

Besides the typical Greek version, two others are found in a few Greek manuscripts. Lowe (1981), however, has shown that the Ethiopic version contains readings antecedent to all three Greek versions. An example is *PJ* 17:2 in the Ethiopic: Mary smiles as she tells Joseph that she is gripped by labor pains; they therefore start making preparations for the birth. All the Greek versions ingeniously evade the imputation of birth pangs, Eve's punishment (Gen. 3:16), to Mary. Instead, Joseph sees Mary first sad and then smiling and *supposes* that she is suffering some pain from the unborn child, but is corrected when Mary explains that she has seen two people, one lamenting and one rejoicing. The inspiration for this editorial correction may come from Luke 2: 34 ("the fall and rise of many in Israel").

Another example is Ethiopic *PJ* 17:1: King Herod orders a census of the inhabitants of Bethlehem. In the Greek manuscripts, the order comes from "King Augustus" (in Greek the Roman emperor is commonly termed *basileus*, lit. "king") or from Caesar Augustus or from Herod and Augustus jointly, yet concerns only Bethlehem. Luke's Gospel, of course, makes it a census of the whole world, "when Quirinius was governor of Syria," but that is known to be chronologically impossible. Indeed, only the version of the Ethiopic *PJ* has any historical plausibility, since Herod is known to have hunted out and killed putative rivals of Davidic or Hasmonean ancestry. Such examples show how some apocrypha may cast unexpected light on the canonical accounts.

The *Protevangelium of James* was probably known to Justin Martyr (*Dialogue with Trypho*, 78.5) and Clement of Alexandria (*Stromata*, 7.93.7) and certainly to Origen (*Commentary on the Gospel of Matthew*, 10.17). The name *Protevangelium of James* itself was made current by Tischendorf. In the manuscripts it bears various names, often referring to Mary instead of Jesus. Indeed, the whole book concerns rather the infancy of Mary, leading up to the birth of Jesus.

According to the story, Mary is the only child of her parents, Joachim and Anne. Like Samuel, she was born miraculously in their old age and dedicated to live in the temple. Approaching puberty, she is espoused by lot, again miraculously, to Joseph, an architect and aged widower with children. The priests expect Joseph to behave as a guardian rather than as a husband, but while he is absent on a building project Mary accepts the annunciation that she will bear Jesus. She convinces Joseph that her pregnancy is due to divine action, but fails to do so with the temple priests, who therefore condemn both to drink of the water of the ordeal. When they survive the ordeal, however, the priest absolves them: "If the Lord has not manifested your sins, neither do I condemn you." Mary gives birth to Jesus in a cave outside Bethlehem. Supernatural events confirm both the virginity and the cosmic significance of the birth. Besides Herod's slaughter of the innocents and other events mentioned in the canonical accounts, the narrative concludes with the hiding of Elizabeth and her son John in a mountain, which opens up to receive them, and the murder of John's priestly father Zechariah in vestibule of the Temple, near the altar (cf. Luke 11:51).

Although never included in lists or collections of canonical texts, the contents of the *PJ* were accepted as genuine tradition in the churches of the East and the West alike (see the notes in Santos Otero 1999). More than any other text, it determined both the iconography and the sacred geography of the infant Jesus and his mother, even in contradiction to some details of the canonical accounts (for example, the birth of Jesus in a cave). It also influenced hymns, liturgies, and poetry. Churches were later built on places that it mentions: St. Anne's in Jerusalem, the Kathisma on the way from Jerusalem to Bethlehem, the Milk Grotto in Bethlehem, and Elizabeth's hiding place in a cleft mountain in Ein Karem near Jerusalem. The work is the principal source for the traditional veneration of Mary, including the Feast of the Presentation of Mary in the temple, and the devotion to St. Anne.

A number of childhood events (*paidika*) of Jesus have been preserved in many versions (in Greek, Latin, and oriental languages) of an *Infancy Gospel of Thomas* (wholly distinct from the Nag Hammadi Coptic *Gospel of Thomas*). They fill a gap, as it were, between the birth of Jesus and his youthful visit to the temple (Luke 2:41–51), but these popular tales could not win the blessing of the church: Jesus plays miraculous nasty tricks on people, like a childhood enemy and a bothersome schoolmaster, even making them drop dead in some versions! Besides giving a conspectus of the multiple pericope orders in the many versions, Lowe (1981) showed that their chronology can be illuminated by the progressive multiplication of the term *Ioudaios* as the tradition evolved: the editors of later versions tended to turn "a man" or "they" in earlier versions into a *Ioudaios* or *hoi Ioudaioi*, that is, they increasingly identified the adversaries of the boy Jesus as Jews.

### Death and resurrection accounts

Of the twenty-four gospels of this kind in the *Clavis*, the *Gospel of Nicodemus* and its predecessors are the most notable. In the medieval period, this gospel was authoritative for portrayals of Jesus' death and resurrection in art and literature. The legends of Joseph of Arimathea, the Holy Grail, and the Harrowing of Hell derive from it. The predecessors of the *Gospel of Nicodemus* were two originally independent documents, the *Acts of Pilate* and the *Descent of Christ to the World Below*. They were subsequently compiled to form the first and second parts of what is now commonly called the *Gospel of Nicodemus*, though this title for the work does not appear before the thirteenth century.

There are two Greek versions and one Latin version of the *Acts of Pilate*. It is the scholarly consensus that Greek version A is the oldest one, produced in 425, according to its prologue, as a revision of a version used by Ephiphanius when writing against the Quartodecimans in 375 or 376. Indeed, Epiphanius himself (*Against Heresies*, 50.1) reports details of matters found in Greek A. This text is not as long as the *Descent* and is in this form also known in Coptic, Syriac, Armenian, Latin, and old Slavic versions. Greek version B calls the mother of Jesus *theotokos* and thus it is unlikely to have existed before the *theotokos* controversy of the early fourth century and may be much later. It adds to Greek manuscript A details of the canonical accounts, especially where it deals with the crucifixion and death of Jesus. Some medieval Latin manuscripts radically shorten the last chapter of Greek A and add the text of the previously independent *Descent*. Those three versions of the *Acts of Pilate* are assumed to be the fifth- or sixth-century result of the growth of a much earlier narrative that was referred to, in some shape and form, by Justin (*First Apology*, 35 and 48) and Eusebius (*Ecclesiastical History*, 9.5.1).

The first section (chapters 1–11) of the *Acts of Pilate* is an account of the trial, crucifixion, and burial of Jesus. It recounts the admiration for Jesus shown by Pilate's runner, standard-bearers, and wife, besides discussions about the legitimate birth of Jesus and whether he is a king or God. The woman asking Jesus for a miracle is called Bernice (Latin: Veronica), the two malefactors condemned with Jesus are called Dysmas and Gestas, and the soldier piercing the side of Jesus is called Longinus. All these names became part of the popular passion story. The second section (chapters 12–16) is an addition describing the discussions in the Sanhedrin about the resurrection of Jesus, while Joseph of Arimathea is arrested, miraculously disappears, but is found again and testifies to the Sanhedrin. The penitent Sanhedrin eventually believes witnesses from

Galilee to the resurrection of Jesus and his ascension. The latter takes place near Jerusalem in Greek B, but evidently in Galilee in the other versions.

The *Descent of Christ to the World Below*, which exists in one Greek and two Latin versions, purports to be the account of Christ's descent to hell by the two witnesses Leucius and Charinus, the sons of Simeon, who have risen from the dead with Jesus. Their testimony contains reports about hell by Adam, Isaiah, Simeon, and John the Baptist, all confirmed by Seth, with further reports from David, Habakkuk, Michaeas, Enoch, and Elias; it also presents discussions between Satan and Hell about Jesus.

### Legend(s) of Abgar

The original *Legend of Abgar*, from about the second century, is based on an assumed conversation between Jesus and Abgar V, the king of Edessa (9–46 CE). In the fourth century, Eusebius (*Ecclesiastical History*, 1.13) and the *Doctrine of Addai* added to the basic story.

Eusebius asserted that the report derived from correspondence between the king and Jesus and was kept in the archives of Edessa. In her famous pilgrim diary, Egeria (ca. 375) claimed to have seen Jesus' letter. According to Eusebius, the correspondence dealt with the king's request to be healed. Jesus replied that he would send a disciple; later Thaddaeus (Addai in the Syriac version) healed the king and converted Edessa to Christianity. The *Doctrine of Addai* does not mention a letter of Jesus to Abgar, but it names Ananias as the painter of a portrait of Jesus. It also recounts details of fourth-century Christian worship in Jerusalem and Edessa. Renderings in Syriac, Greek, Latin, Armenian, Arabic, Coptic, and Slavonic versions testify to the popularity of both apocryphal accounts.

## Apocryphal Acts

The *Clavis* counts twenty-four apocryphal books of acts in more than 113 documents. Such a book generally goes under the name of a single apostle, unlike the canonical Acts of the Apostles. Five of those books, already linked in ancient times, will be the main focus here. Finally, books about the assumption of Mary also relate to the apostolic age, although the *Clavis* and others treat them as a distinct category.

A corpus of five apocryphal apostolic Acts is defined in the Coptic *Manichaean Psalm-Book* from ca. 340, namely the *Acts of John*, the *Acts of Peter*, the *Acts of Paul*, the *Acts of Andrew*, and the *Acts of Thomas*. The same group of five books is mentioned by Eusebius (*Ecclesiastical History*, 3.1) and by Faustus of Mileve (Augustine, *Against Faustus*, 30.4). This corpus was still available ca. 850 to the Greek compiler Photius (*Bibliotheca*, Cod. 114). Surviving today in a rather fragmentary state, these various acts probably originated in the second and third centuries. The Manichaeans, followed by Augustine (*Against Faustus*, 2.6) and Photius (*Bibliotheca*, Cod. 114), name the author of the corpus as Leucius or Leucius Charinus, but these names themselves originated in apocryphal writings (only Epiphanius defines Leucius as the companion of John the Apostle). Also the five books, though interrelated, are not homogeneous.

Today, consequently, it is believed that each book was composed by a different unknown author, including the *Acts of John* (the only book claiming Leucius for its author).

Lipsius (1883) held that these apocryphal acts were of Gnostic origin, but this is now doubted. Such discoveries as the manuscripts from Nag Hammadi have so much changed the perception of Gnosis that even to speak of "Gnostic influences" in those acts means little. Walter Bauer (1971) has shown that the boundaries between different schools of thinking in the second and third centuries were flexible, making it difficult to ascribe any theological product to a single school. Each of these documents, too, reflects a variety of influences.

As to the literary genre of these acts, Schneemelcher (1997) noted five principal features linking them to Hellenistic literature: the travel theme, the marvelous characteristics of the hero, encounters with wonders (talking animals, cannibals), didactic speeches, and the erotic theme (whether in love tales or in ascetic and encratite features). David Pao (1995) likened especially the *Acts of Andrew* to the biographies of philosophers. Many scholars classify the acts with Hellenistic popular novels, which were designed for edification alongside entertainment. They are, perhaps, "the most important witnesses to the religious ideals" of many Christians, "ideals which did not always follow the paths which were later considered acceptable to the Christian Church" (Schneemelcher, 1997).

## The Acts of John

This book depicts the activities of the apostle John in Asia Minor, although showing little knowledge of the area and giving the wrong date for the destruction of the temple of Artemis in Ephesus. Its provenance has been seen as Egyptian (Junod and Kaestli 1983) or East Syrian (Schaeferdieck in Schneemelcher, 1997). Some of its exoteric traditions were known to Clement of Alexandria (*Adumbrations* on 1 John 1:1), but the earliest clear evidence for its existence is its condemnation by Eusebius (*Ecclesiastical History*, 3.25.6). Epiphanius (*Pan*, 47.1.5) mentioned encratite use of the *Acts of Andrew, Thomas,* and *John*.

The Second Council of Nicea in 787 condemned the *Acts of John* to be burned (Mansi 1758–98: XIII, 176A), but parts have survived in Greek, Syriac, Coptic, Armenian, Georgian, Arabic, Slavonic, and Ethiopic as chapters 18–115, together with a few lines of the fourth-century Latin version. Elliott (1993) saw in the remnants three parts of an early version; his approach is followed here (Schneemelcher 1997, arranged the material differently).

The first part covers John's first and second stays in Ephesus (chs. 18–55 and 58–86). Prompted by a vision (ch. 18), he travels from Miletus to Ephesus, where he raises Lycomedes and his wife Cleopatra from the dead. After a friend of Lycomedes paints a portrait of John, there is a discussion about the value of such an icon for worshiping God, followed by a sermon given by John in a theater and the public healing of a sick woman (chs. 19–36). The first stay ends with the destruction of the temple of Artemis by John and the conversion of the goddess's followers; John raises the priest of Artemis from the dead and changes a parricide for the better (chs. 37–55). The second stay in

Ephesus (chs. 58–61) focuses on the encratite story of the beautiful Drusiana, who prefers to die rather than be the cause of temptation for Calimachus. John raises Drusiana and Calimachus to life, ending with the breaking of bread and a prayer of thanksgiving (chs. 62–86).

The other two parts also circulated independently. Part 2 is a gospel of John (chs. 87–105), containing a sermon on the polymorphous nature of Christ (chs. 88–93), the Hymn of Christ (which was set to music in 1917 by the British composer Gustav Holst), and a revelation on the mystery of the cross. The third part, the Metastasis (chs. 106– 115), consists of John's last act of worship, prayer, the breaking of bread and prayer of thanksgiving, then his death in Ephesus. It is notable that, although the eucharistic prayer is said twice, only bread is mentioned each time. This recalls a peculiarity of John's Gospel: the Last Supper is not a eucharist but instead both eating the flesh and drinking the blood of Jesus are related to eating bread alone and not to wine (ch. 6). Also encratite circles in Syria and Asia Minor are known to have celebrated the eucharist with bread as the focal point, and water, as in the *Acts of Thomas* (chs. 27, 29 et seq.).

## The Acts of Peter

The first direct evidence for this book comes from its rejection by Eusebius (*Ecclesiastical History*, 3.3.2). A reference in Tertullian implies he employed the original Greek version, thus it must have originated before ca. 190. Unsuccessful attempts have been made to establish a literary dependency upon the *Acts of John* or an interrelation with the Pseudo-Clementine literature (the latter is now dated later, ca. 260). Carl Schmidt (1903) and Léon Vouaux (1922) argued that the author of the *Didascalia* (early third century) may have employed the *Acts of Peter*. Regarding its origins, some scholars have sought to find earlier sources in it, while others emphasize the element of free creation or oral production. Christine M. Thomas (1992) argued for a coexistence of oral and written traditions and for two written sources combined by two different redactors: one collected the stories of Marcellus, the struggle between Peter and Simon, and the martyrdom; the other combined the themes of apostasy and repentance.

Of the original Greek version only the martyrdom, which circulated independently (also in oriental languages), has survived intact; there is also a small Oxyrhynchus fragment. A Coptic papyrus remnant of the probable beginning of the book contains the story of Peter's daughter. The sixth- to seventh-century Vercelli Manuscript, a Latin translation from somewhat earlier Greek, contains the healing of the gardener's daughter by Peter, an episode also known to Augustine (*Against Adimantus*, 17.5). Another Latin version occurs in the *Vita Abercii* (fourth century), reporting speeches of Peter and Paul. Judging from the description of the work in the *Stichometry* of Nicephorus (ca. 850), about two-thirds of the work has survived. The missing third is assumed to have contained stories about Peter and Paul in Jerusalem.

Taking place in Jerusalem and Rome, the *Acts of Peter* focuses on three topics. One is the encratite sympathies manifested in the two parallel stories of Peter's daughter and the gardener's daughter, intimating that suffering or death is a gift from God if virginity is thereby preserved. Another topic is the contest with Simon Magus; this is not a polemical discussion of Simonian Gnosticism but a contest between God and the Devil. The third topic is the martyrdom, which circulated widely as an extract. It starts with Simon's fatal attempt to ascend to heaven and contains the famous conversation between Peter and Jesus. Fleeing from Rome, Peter meets Jesus on the way and asks him where he is going (*Quo vadis?*). Jesus answers, "To Rome, to be crucified again." Thereupon Peter turns back to Rome to die. The story ends with a vision that frightens Nero into stopping the persecution of Christians.

## The Acts of Paul

This work is already attested by Tertullian (ca. 190 CE), who rejected it as the pious attempt of an unnamed presbyter from the province of Asia to add to the apostle's fame "out of love for Paul" (*On Baptism*, 17). Other early authors, however, approved of it: Hippolytus (204) saw it as authentic (*Commentary on Daniel*, 3:29) and Origen (ca. 227) appreciated it (*Commentary on the Gospel of John*, 20.12). Eusebius calls it disputed (*Ecclesiastical History*, 3.3.5). After Jerome, who followed Tertullian, the work was often considered inauthentic. No single manuscript preserves the whole work, but there are substantial Greek and Coptic fragments. One contains a story often depicted in art: Paul is confronted with a lion in the arena of Ephesus, but it is the lion previously baptized by Paul. The two politely converse until both can make their escape, since a miraculous hailstorm kills the other wild animals and many eager spectators, putting the rest to flight.

Three major parts of the work circulated separately. One is the *Acts of Paul and Thecla*. Thecla hears Paul preaching and follows him as an assistant, abandoning her family and her engagement. Braving persecution and miraculously surviving the punishment of fighting with wild beasts, Thecla baptizes herself. This popular story is assumed to be fictional in spite of its mentioning the historic figure of Queen Tryphoena of Pisidian Antioch. The narrative might have served as an example for women to claim authority to teach and to baptize; this is probably why Tertullian rejected it.

A second part, Paul's *Third Epistle to the Corinthians*, probably comes from the second century, independent of the *Acts of Paul* in authorship and circulation. For a time it became part of the Armenian and Syriac canons. It notes that two presbyters of the Corinthians had written to Paul in prison in Philippi, seeking his response to the teaching of Simon and Cleobius. These two had claimed that "one must not appeal to the prophets," that "God is not almighty," that "there is no resurrection of the body," that "man has not been made by God," that "Christ has neither come in the flesh, nor was he born of Mary," and that "the world is not the work of God but of angels" (1.10–15). The apostle answers confirming the authority of the prophets and of God and the bodily resurrection through the salvation and resurrection of the Jesus who was born of Mary.

Thirdly, the *Martyrdom of Paul* reports Paul's activities in Rome and Nero's persecution of Christians under Nero. It says that when Paul was beheaded, not blood but milk flowed from his neck onto the clothes of the executioner. On the basis of the Coptic Heidelberg papyrus (ca. sixth century), Elliott (1993) argued that these three sections were incorporated in a larger work and that Paul's travel sequence could be reconstructed: a journey from Damascus to Jerusalem, then Paul in Antioch, Myra, Sidon, Tyre, Corinth, and Puteoli.

The Greek Hamburg papyrus (ca. 300) contains additional information about Paul in Ephesus and Corinth, then about the journey from Corinth to Italy. Whereas Carl Schmidt (1936) claimed that the book must depend on the canonical Acts of the Apostles, the discovery of the early Hamburg papyrus enabled W. Rordorf (1988) and Schneemelcher (1997) to argue for literary independence, though Schneemelcher assumed that the author had knowledge of the canonical Acts.

## The Acts of Andrew

Almost everywhere from Armenia to Spain this book was particularly popular between the third and ninth centuries. Yet its first mention, by Eusebius (*Ecclesiastical History*, 3.25.6), is negative, and Hippolytus (*Against Heresies*, 2.47.1, etc.) comments that it was employed by ascetic and encratite groups. Having become an object of condemnation, its text was reworked several times.

The original Greek text is not extant. Schneemelcher (1997) places its composition closer to 150 than to 200, perhaps in Alexandria. The book of Gregory of Tours, *Liber de Miraculis Beati Andreae Apostoli* (sixth century), is seen as the best authority for the general shape of the *Acts of Andrew*, except that it has reduced the martyrdom of Andrew to a short note about the circumstances. The epitome remarks that it has eliminated the work's long-windedness and selected only the miracles. The work was not included in the *Stichometry* of Nicephoprus, however, thus its length is unstated there. Schneemelcher (1997), partially reconstructed the original *Acts of Andrew* on the basis of Gregory of Tours, the Coptic papyrus Utrecht 1 (fourth century), the Armenian martyrdom, and five Greek versions of the martyrdom, besides excerpts from the book found in Greek reworkings.

The chapters of Gregory's work are held to follow the structure of his source. If so, the *Acts of Andrew* began with the journey of Andrew from Pontus to Patras in Greece (chs. 2–21). He went first by way of Amasia, Sinope, Nicaea, Nicomedia, and Byzantium, variously preaching, performing miracles and overcoming demons and storms, all of which stimulated mass conversions. Advised by an angel, he entered a ship in Perinthus and converted the crew. More of the same followed in Philippi and Thessalonica, where Andrew had a vision of his martyrdom in Patras. Arriving in Patras (chs. 22–4), he healed the Proconsul Lisbios and revived the latter's concubine and his wife, besides forty corpses from a shipwreck at the beach. Next he made a trip to Achaia (chs. 25–9) for miracles and conversions there. Back in Patras (chs. 30–5), he healed Maximilla, wife of the Proconsul Aegeates, among others. Then, however, the ire of Aegeates was roused against Andrew and other Christians when Maximilla converted and turned encratite.

Gregory describes only briefly the subsequent crucifixion of Andrew on the orders of Aegeates, the burial of Andrew by Maximilla, and a miracle by the grave (chs. 36–7), remarking that there exists a separate work describing Andrew's martyrdom. In fact, several accounts of the martyrdom are available. The Armenian version of the sixth or seventh century is the most reliable source for Andrew's speech before his crucifixion, explaining that he and the cross, being of the same nature, are in the process of being unified, and that the cross reveals only partly the secret that it bears.

Elliott (1993) believes that the *Acts of Andrew* belongs to a broader Andrew cycle embracing three further apocryphal writings. One of them, the *Acts of Andrew and Matthias*, was set amongst cannibals and contained the legends located in Scythia. MacDonald (1983, 1990) revived the earlier assumption that the account of the *Acts of Andrew and Matthias* was to some extent part of the original *Acts of Andrew*, but Schneemelcher (1997) continued to separate the former from the latter. The other two writings are the Greek and Slavonic *Acts of Peter and Andrew*, as a sequel to the *Acts of Andrew and Matthias*, and the Coptic Acts of *Andrew and Paul* (eighth or ninth century).

## The Acts of Thomas

This book was known to Epiphanius (*Against Heresies*, 2.47.1), who commented on its encratite nature, and to Augustine (*Sermon on the Mount*, 1.20.65), who noted its Manichaean tendencies. Scholars have assigned its origin to East Syria at the beginning of the third century. Both encratism and Manichaeism were known tendencies in that area and time. Of the five major books of acts this is the only one to have survived in its entirety. There is a Syriac manuscript from the seventh century and a fragmentary one from the fifth or sixth century. A Greek version exists, which is a translation of a Syriac antecedent of the fragmentary text. It is thought that this Greek translation generally preserves the earliest form, except for the Hymn of the Pearl (see below). Paul-Huber Poirier (1996) has examined the specific contribution of the *Acts of Thomas*, the *Gospel of Thomas*, and the *Book of Thomas* to the construction of the Thomas tradition.

This apocryphal composition reflects the Syriac tradition that identified the apostle Thomas Didymus ("the twin") of John's Gospel as Jude, the twin brother of Jesus and author of the New Testament epistle. Thus Thomas looks like Jesus (chs. 11, 34), shares in the redeeming work (chs. 31, 39), and is the recipient and mediator of secret revelations (ch. 39). The book is also the earliest witness for two traditions. First, that Thomas was the apostle of India, with references to the historical figure of King Gundaphorus (first century) and to the active cultural and commercial relations between North India and Syria. Second, how Thomas met martyrdom and how his bones were brought to Edessa. Also the *Legend of Abgar* (see above) traced the evangelization of Edessa back to Thaddaeus (often identified with Jude), while Origen referred to Thomas as the apostle of Parthia.

Earlier scholars, such as Günther Bornkamm (1933), held that the book presented the mystery of redemption in Gnostic garb. More recently, Elliott (1993) and others have read the narrative as a fictional romance of conversion whose themes include orthodox views of incarnation (chs. 79, 80, 143) and of redemption through Christ's suffering (ch. 72). A notable feature is the sacramental ceremonies, included anointing with oil and the eucharist as a communion in bread only (chs. 27, 29, 49f., 133). Nearly all the stories of conversion conclude with an atoning ritual consisting of sealing the new converts with oil and an associated eucharist (e.g., chs. 26f., 49f., 121, 133, 157). The relationship between the unction and baptism with water is not altogether clear.

The book consists of thirteen *praxeis* ("acts"), leading up to the martyrdom. The first part of the book (*praxeis* 1–6) recounts how Thomas received the lot from amongst the apostles to go to India and, in stories full of symbolism and typology, how the apostle arrived at the court of King Gundaphorus and had dealings with him. The second part (*praxeis* 7–13) focuses on the conversion of all the people at the court of King Misdai. The king put Thomas to death (like Andrew) on account of a noble woman who turned encratite.

In the second *praxis* (chs. 17–29), Thomas is commissioned by King Gundaphorus to build a royal palace. He spends the money sent him by the king on the poor and sick. Officials come to inspect the project, but he convinces them that an invisible building is rising up, only more money is needed to complete it. Eventually the king himself comes, reacting furiously to Thomas' claim to have built a palace in heaven for the king. Thomas escapes a horrid death only by curing the king's sick brother Gad. The motif of an expensive, invisible project recurred later in the legend of Barlaam and Josaphat, in the Eulenspiegel saga, and in Hans Andersen's tale of the emperor's new clothes.

Earlier scholarship accepted that Gad and Abban the merchant were real people, and regarded the account as historical. Although J. N. Farquhar (1927) thought that the account was fictional, he also accepted that Thomas indeed evangelized India. Contemporary scholars such as Elliott (1993), however, have reservations about the historicity of the Thomas story.

The book contains two celebrated oriental hymns. The Wedding Hymn (chs. 6–7) praises the beauty of the bride who is "the daughter of the Light," the pride of the king, fed by ambrosia, served by twelve men, who praise the groom. According to the book, Thomas sang the Hymn in his mother tongue Hebrew and the flautist was a Hebrew woman. The poem can be read literally or metaphorically (a Syriac tradition calls the bride "church").

The Hymn of the Pearl (chs. 108–13) is of unknown origin. Most scholars presume that it existed before the book itself. The text is extant in a tenth-century Syriac manuscript and, with a different wording, in an eleventh-century Greek manuscript; these are generally assumed to represent two separate text transmissions. The original language may have been Syriac. Identifying Iranian words in the hymn, some scholars have assumed a Parthian origin. In the hymn a prince from the East, leaving his garment of light behind, is sent to Egypt to get a pearl in the possession of a dragon. Living with the people of the land, the prince forgets his origin. A letter from the king reminds him of his identity and task. The prince conquers the dragon and returns with the pearl to the East, to be dressed with the garment of light.

Scholars have proposed various readings of the allegory. If the child signifies the human soul, then the story tells of the soul's human incarnation, disengagement from the body, and reunion with God, implying an appeal for conversion. Others see a Gnostic myth in which donning a garment signifies the acquisition of self-knowledge. Yet others see a redeemer myth, with the son signifying Christ. Jacques E. Ménard (1968) researched the layers of the narrative, seeing in it a Manichaean version based on a Gnostic reworking of an original Jewish-Christian work.

*The Assumption of Mary*

The *Clavis* lists on twenty-one pages, organized in ten language groups, the large number of texts recounting the *transitus* (obsequies) of Mary, that is, what other authors call her assumption or dormition ("falling asleep," "passing away"). Tischendorf (1876) edited the two standard texts of the *transitus*, attributing the Greek account to John the Theologian (John the Apostle) and the Latin one to Melito of Sardis (late second century). By the fifth century, at any rate, there was a church in Jerusalem with an empty tomb commemorating the event.

The Italian edition by Erbetta (1981) contains the largest collection of such texts. They are found in Greek, Latin, and most Middle Eastern languages. Mary Clayton (1999) has argued for a Syriac source of the various Ethiopic, Armenian, and Arabic accounts, even for the Irish tradition, whereas James (1953) assumed that these legends originated in Egypt and gave prominence to Coptic material. The basic narrative tells of an angel announcing that the death of Mary in Jerusalem is immanent, whereupon the apostles gather from all over and witness Mary's corporeal assumption. The Syriac rendition hints at Mary's fear of death and describes her assumption to a paradise separate from heaven.

# Apocryphal Epistles

The genre of apocryphal epistles is somewhat amorphous. Schneemelcher (1997) does not use the term at all, preferring to classify anything of the kind under other headings. Elliott (1993) includes under apocryphal epistles the *Legend of Abgar* and the *Epistula Apostolorum* (both classified otherwise in the *Clavis*, see above), besides the *Epistle to the Alexandrians*, known only from its mention in the Muratorian Fragment, where it is rejected as Marcionite. To these he adds three epistles or groups of epistles: the *Epistle of Lentulus* (Latin, thirteenth century) claims to be written by a Roman official Lentulus at the time of Tiberius, describing Jesus' physical appearance; the *Epistle of Paul to the Laodiceans* (originally Latin? fourth century?) claims to be the letter referred to by Paul (Col. 4:16); the *Correspondence between Paul and Seneca* comprises fourteen letters, really composed over a period of several hundred years.

These last three items are classified as epistles also by the *Clavis*, which adds four more: *Pseudo-Titus* (Latin, fourth or fifth century) is a treatise on celibacy (Elliott places it under apocryphal acts); the *Epistle of James to Quadratus* (extant in Syriac), which is classified by Mario Erbetta (1981) as the last of the seven documents of the Pilate Cycle; the *Epistles of Longinus, Augustus, Ursinus and Patrophilus* (Syriac, sixth century?), see Nicole Zeegers-Vander Vorst (1980); the *Epistle from Heaven on the Observance of the Lord's Day* (Latin, sixth century), originating in Spain and widespread in East and West, see Erbetta (1981). The *Clavis* further groups four epistle-like items under the Pilate Cycle: *Pilate to Claudius; Paul's Anaphora and Tiberius' Response; Paul's Anaphora and Paradosis; Pilate to Herod.*

# Apocryphal Apocalypses

The last book of the New Testament explicitly announces itself as an "apocalypse." As a literary genre, the apocalypse had already existed for three centuries in Jewish circles. The term covers a vast area, including prophecy, oracles, journeys to heavenly realms, and visions of the world to come. Yet John J. Collins' broad definition (1979) of an apocalypse has gained currency: "a genre of revelatory literature with a narrative framework, in which a revelation is mediated by an otherworldly being to a human recipient, disclosing a transcendent reality that is both temporal, insofar as it envisages eschatological salvation, and spatial, insofar as it involves another supernatural world."

Martha Himmelfarb (1983) pointed out that Jewish and Christian apocalypses share an interest in "tours of hell." Richard J. Bauckham (1990) discerned three stages in the development of such tours. First are cosmic tours, such as *1 Enoch*, which concentrate on the fate of the dead. When a belief emerged in the after-death punishment of the wicked, the tour could include a look at the miseries of hell, as in the *Apocalypse of Peter* or in the *Apocalypse of Elijah*. Second, the genre of tours of "the seven heavens" could add visits to paradise and hell, as in *3 Baruch*. Third come apocalypses that have a tour element, but their only interest is in the fate of the dead, such as the *Apocalypse of Zephaniah* and the *Apocalypse of Paul*. In the latter, the dead, righteous and wicked alike, are first taken up to the throne of God for judgment, then sent to paradise or hell (*Apocalypse of Paul*, 14–18). Such a scheme, Bauckham argued, may well have developed from the pattern of *3 Baruch*: ascent through the heavens, visit to paradise, visit to hell.

The *Clavis* lists thirty-two apocalypses, including two from Nag Hammadi. Elliott (1993) presents six apocalypses in detail and nine briefly. Schneemelcher (1997) offers nine apocalypses in three chronological categories: Apocalyptic of Primitive Christianity, comprising the *Ascension of Isaiah* and the *Apocalypse of Peter*; Apocalyptic Prophecy of the Early Church, comprising *5 Ezra*, *6 Ezra*, the *Sibylline Oracles*, and *Elchasai*; (3) Later Apocalypses, namely, the Coptic *Apocalypse of Paul* and *Apocalypse of Peter* (both from Nag Hammadi), the Greek *Apocalypse of Paul* and the *Apocalypse of Thomas*. Two historically influential Greek apocalypses will be discussed here.

## *The* Apocalypse of Peter

It was Bauckham (1988) who, after some sixty years, reopened research on this work (completely different from the *Apocalypse of Peter* from Nag Hammadi). According to Bauckham (1994), it seems to have been composed in Greek at the time of Bar Kokhba (ca. 132). It became extremely popular in history, being frequently quoted in Christian literature from Clement of Alexandria (*Ecloge*, 41, etc.) and Methodius (*Symposium* 2.6) on. Besides painting vivid pictures of heaven and hell and of the punishment of the wicked, the book turns the Old Testament patriarchs into high priests of the church.

The text is extant in its entirety in an Ethiopic version; there are also three Greek fragments of a less full version. Material shared by both sometimes follows a different order or employs a different manner of expression. For instance, the revelation of the punishments of hell takes the form of a vision given to Peter in the Greek, but in the Ethiopic they are put in the future tense as a prophecy. Bauckham followed James (1911), who argued that the Ethiopian manuscript reflects the Greek original apart from minor details; the Akhmim manuscript is a secondary edited Greek version (cf. Lowe [1981], above, on the Ethiopic *PJ*). James explained it "as an adaptation of the Apocalypse of Peter by the author of the Gospel of Peter who thus made it part of his Gospel."

## *The* Apocalypse of Paul (Visio Pauli)

Since the introduction to this book says that Paul's vision was hidden until the consulate of Theodosius and Cynegius (388), Elliott (1993) assumes that it was written then, possibly in Greek. There exist a short Greek form and translations into Latin and oriental and Slavic languages.

The author may have employed material from earlier apocalypses for the descriptions of punishments. Besides the cosmic tour, the *Apocalypse of Paul* features a dialogue between the creation and God: the creation complains about sinful man, but God responds that there is both divine hope for man's repentance and divine patience. The book was employed by authors of the fourth and fifth centuries (Prudentius, Augustine, Sozomen) and stimulated similar works, such as Epiphanius' *Ascent of Paul*. It also inspired popular accounts of heaven and hell, including Dante's *Inferno*.

## Annotated Bibliography

### *Editions, old and new*

Bovon, F., P. Geoltrain, and F. Schmidt (eds.). *Corpus Christianorum Series Apocryphorum (CCSA)*. 15 vols. Turnhout: Brepols, 1983 to date. Comprehensive critical edition with a French translation; gradually replacing the former standard edition of Lipsius-Bonnet.

Dubois, J.-D. "'The New *Series Apocryphorum* of the *Corpus Christianorum*." *The Second Century* 4/1 (1984), 29–36. This book review explains the purpose, structure, and intention of *CCSA*.

Erbetta, M. *Gli Apocrifi del Nuovo Testamento.* I/1: *Vangeli: infanzia e passione di Cristo, assunzione di Maria: versione e commento.* 2nd edn. Torino: Marietti Editori, 1981. I/2: *Aneddotica dell'infanzia e della passione; scritti assunzionistici.* Torino: Marietti Editori, 1983. II: *Atti e leggende: versione e commento.* Torino: Marietti Editori, 1966. III: *Lettere e apocalissi: versione e commento.* Torino: Marietti Editori, 1969. This Italian edition contains a very large collection of texts of the assumption of Mary.

Geerard, M. (ed.). *Clavis Apocryphorum Novi Testamenti. CCSA.* Turnhout: Brepols, 1992. The first *clavis* for NTA in modern times, listing some 346 apocryphal books, often in more than one revision, version, or edition.

Lipsius, R. A. and M. Bonnet. *Acta Apostolorum. Apocrypha.* 3 vols. Leipzig: Hermann Mendelssohn, 1891, 1898, 1903; repr. Hildsheim, 1959. The three volumes of Lipsius and Bonnet serve as a second edition of Tischendorf's edition. Tischendorf remains to be an influential version of the Greek and Latin NTA. While still being an important text edition, Lipsius and Bonnet is gradually replaced by the now main edition of *Corpus Christianorum Series Apocryphorum*.

Santos Otero, A. de. *Los Evangelios Apocrifos. Biblioteca de Autores Cristianos*, sect. I. Sagradas Escrituras, 148. Madrid: La Editorial Catolica, 1999. Successive editions. published most recently as vol. 22 in the series Estudios y Ensayos, Madrid, 2004. A modestly priced collection of the major Greek and Latin texts, with Spanish translations and extensive notes and bibliography.

Tischendorf, C. Von. *Acta Apostolorum*. Vol. 1: *Apocrypha*. Leipzig: Avenarius & Mendelssohn, 1851. Vol. 2: *Evangelia Apocrypha*. Leipzig: Hermann Mendelssohn, 1852; repr. Hildesheim, 1966 and 1987. Vol. 3: *Apocalypses Apocryphae*. Leipzig: Hermann Mendelssohn, 1866; repr. Hildesheim, 1966.

## Modern translations

Elliott, J. K. (ed.). *The Apocryphal New Testament: A Collection of Apocryphal Christian Literature in an English Translation based on M. R. James*. Oxford: Clarendon Press, 1993. This one-volume edition represents a thorough revision of James' *Apocryphal New Testament* and replaces the former as standard edition.

Herbert M. and M. McNamara (eds.). *Irish Biblical Apocrypha: Selected Texts in Translation*. Edinburgh: T. & T. Clark, 1989. English translation with annotations of the most important Irish apocryphal literature.

James, M. R. (ed.). *The Apocryphal New Testament*. Oxford: Clarendon Press, 1924; corrected edn, 1953. This formerly standard English collection of apocryphal material on the New Testament, complete with translations and comments, is still widely employed, but now replaced by the revised edition edited by Elliott.

Schneemelcher, Wilhelm (ed.). *Neutestamentliche Apocryphen in deutscher Übersetzung*, vol. 1: *Evangelien*. 6th edn. Tübingen: Mohr Siebeck, 1990; vol. 2: *Apostolisches, Apokalypsen und Verwandtes*. 6th edn. Tübingen: Mohr Siebeck, 1997. These two volumes contain a large selection of NTA, including valuable commentaries.

Wilson, R. L. (trans.). *New Testament Apocrypha*. Vol. 1: *Gospels and Related Writings*. Cambridge and Louisville: James Clarke/Westminster/John Knox Press, 1991. Vol. 2: *Apostolic and Early Church Writings*. Cambridge and Louisville: James Clarke/Westminster/John Knox Press, 1993. This version is the English rendition of Schneemelcher 1989 and 1990.

## Reference works

Allberry, C. R. C. (ed.). *A Manichaean Psalm-Book*. Part II. Stuttgart: W. Kohlhammer, 1938. A bilingual Coptic–English edition of 289 numbered and groups of unnumbered psalms of the ca. fourth-century Coptic Manichaean papyri of 3,500 pages, found in Egypt in 1930.

Henry, R. (ed. and trans.). *Photius. Bibliothèque*. 8 vols. Paris: Société d'Édition Les Belles Lettres, 1959–77. Bilingual French–Greek edition of the extensive library of the Patriarchate in Constantinople as reported and annotated by Patriarch Photius (d. ca. 895). Numerous references to NTA. A useful addition is Jacques Schamp (ed.). *Photius. Bibliothèque*. Vol. 9: *Index*. Paris: Les Belles Lettres, 1990.

Robinson, J. M. (ed.). *The Nag Hammadi Library in English: Translated and Introduced*. 3rd, completely revised, edn. Leiden: E. J. Brill, 1988. This one-volume edition contains the fourth-century papyrus texts of the Coptic Gnostic Library as it is known now, found in 1945. The texts are relevant for the study of NTA.

Robinson, J. M. (ed.). *The Coptic Gnostic Library: A Complete Edition of the Nag Hammadi Codices. Edited with English Translation, Introduction and Notes*. 5 vols. Leiden: Brill, 2000. Bilingual Coptic–English standard version of the Coptic Gnostic Library.

## Popular historic literary use of New Testament apocrypha

Backhus, I. "Christoph Scheurl and his Anthology of 'New Testament Apocrypha' (1506, 1513, 1515)." *Apocrypha* 9 (1998), 133–56. For edifying purposes, Scheurl (d. 1542) collected material of the NTA.

Fleith, B. "Die *Legenda Aurea* und ihre dominikanischen Bruderlegendare – Aspekte der Quellenverhältnisse apokryphen Gedankenguts." *Apokrypha* 7 (1996), 167–91. Fleith analyses the apocryphal source material employed in the compilation of the *Legenda Aurea* (c. twelfth entury).

McNamara, M. (ed.). *The Apocrypha in the Irish Church*. Dublin: Institute for Advanced Studies, 1975; corrected repr. 1984. A historic survey of the apocrypha of both the Old and the New Testaments as preserved in the Irish Church.

## General introduction

### Status of research

Geoltrain, P., J.-P. Claude Picard, and A. Desreumaux (eds.). *Apocrypha: Le Champ des Apocryphes.* Vols. 1 and 2. Turnhout: Brepols, 1990. Vols. 3–10: *Apocrypha: Revue Internationale des Littératures Apocryphes / International Journal of Apocryphal Literatures.* Edited by Albert Frey and Jean-Daniel Kaestli. (1992– ). From vol. 11 onwards (2004), this has been edited by Jean-Daniel Dubois and Marie-Jo Pierre. One volume per annum is published under changing editorship; it is currently the most influential international revue for NTA research.

Charlesworth, J. H. with J. R. Mueller, assisted by many. *The New Testament Apocrypha and Pseudepigrapha: A Guide to Publications, With Excursuses on Apocalypses.* Atla Bibliography Series, 17. Metchen, NJ and London: American Theological Library Association/Scarecrow Press, 1987. A guide to the study of the NTA.

Markschies, C. "'Neutestamentliche Apokryphen'. Bemerkungen zu Geschichte und Zukunft einer von Edgar Hennecke im Jahr 1904 begründeten Quellensammlung." *Apocrypha* 9 (1998), 97–132. Reporting about the conception and structure of Schneemelcher's NTA revision in progress; the new edition will be edited by Christoph Markschies, programmatically called "Antike Christliche Apokryphen in deutscher Übersetzung."

## Relationship between the New Testament canon and the New Testament apocrypha

Elliott, J. K. "The Influence of the Apocrypha on Manuscripts of the New Testament." *Apocrypha* 8 (1997), 265–71. The author suggests that apocryphal texts had no scribal influence on the New Testament.

Jacobs, A. A. "The Disorder of Books: Priscillian's Canonical Defense of Apocrypha." *Harvard Theological Review* 93/2 (2000), 135–59. Jacobs juxtaposes Athanasius' canon and Priscillian's apocrypha and discovers a contest over scriptural exegesis.

Markschies, C. "Neuere Forschungen zur Kanonisierung des Neuen Testaments." *Apocrypha* 12 (2001), 237–62. Markschies shows that the length of the New Testament canon varies depending on the context of the institution that employs the canon.

## Relationship between the New Testament apocrypha and early Christian orthodoxy

Bauer, W. *Orthodoxy and Heresy in Earliest Christianity.* Trans. from German, rev. and expanded R. A. Kraft and G. Krodel. Philadelphia: Fortress Press, 1971; London: SCM, 1972.

Harrington, D. J. "The Reception of Walter Bauer's *Orthodoxy and Heresy in Earliest Christianity* during the Last Decade." *Harvard Theological Review* 73 (1980), 289–98. In addition to reporting on the reception of Bauer's book in modern reviews and to pointing to articles that criticize aspects of Bauer's argument, Harrington presents a summary and a critique of that German scholar's influential thesis, namely: the part of Bauer's argument about early Christian diversity is well received but not the part about the reconstruction of how orthodoxy triumphed.

## Apocryphal gospels

Erlemann, K. "Papyrus Egerton 2: 'Missing Link' zwischen synoptischer und johanneischer Tradition." *New Testament Studies* 42/1 (1996), 12–34. The author interprets the important Papyrus Egerton 2 as a historic and literary link between the synoptic gospels and the Gospel of John.

Evans, C. A. "The Interpretation of Scripture in the New Testament Apocrypha and Gnostic Writings." Pp. 430–56 in *A History of Biblical Interpretation*, vol. 1: *The Ancient Period.* Edited by Alan J. Hauser and Duane F. Watson. Grand Rapids: William B. Eerdmans, 2003. Evans introduces exegetical data found in the apocryphal gospels; contains a valuable bibliography on NTA, Gnosis, and Gnosticism.

Gero, S., "Apocryphal Gospels: A Survey of Textual and Literary Problems." *Aufstieg und Niedergang der römischen Welt* 2.25/5 (1988), 3969–96. A significant addition to standard NTA handbooks, concentrating on material either excluded from regular NTA editions or made accessible only recently.

Klauck, Hans-Joseph. *Apocryphal Gospels: An Introduction.* London and New York: T. & T. Clark International, 2003. First published as *Apokryphe Evangelien: Eine Einführung*, Stuttgart: Katholisches Bibelwerk, 2002. The book provides a helpful classification of a wide range of apocryphal gospel material, including the Toledoth Yeshu as an anti-gospel.

Koester, H. *Ancient Christian Gospels: Their History and Development.* Philadelphia and London: Trinity Press International/SCM Press, 1990. Koester employs apocryphal writings for insights into the earliest stages of the development of the gospel tradition.

Lowe, M. "*Ioudaios* of the Apocrypha: A Fresh Approach to the Gospels of James, Pseudo-Thomas, Peter and Nicodemus." *Novum Testamentum* 23/1 (1981), 56–90. The evolving usage of terms of nationality provides a fertile tool for elucidating textual and text-historical issues in these apocrypha.

Poirier, P.-H. "Evangile de Thomas. Livre de Thomas. Une tradition et ses transformations." *Apocrypha* 7 (1996), 9–26. The article is a prominent contribution to the construction of the Thomas tradition.

## Apocryphal acts

Clayton, M. "The *Transitus Mariae*: The Tradition and its Origins." *Apocrypha* 10 (1999), 74–98. For determining the origin of the early text of the *Transitus*, the Syriac *Obsequis* is crucial.

Pao, D. W. "The Genre of the *Acts of Andrew*," *Apocrypha* 6 (1995), 179–202. Discussion of genre;
arguing that this text employs rather the genre of biographies of philosophers than that of
novels.

Plümacher, E. "Apocryphe Apostelakten." PRE Supp. XV, Hans Gärtner (Hg.), *Acilius bis Zoilos*.
Cols. 12–70. Munich: Alfred Druckenmüller, 1978. This is the standard article on the
subject, full of valuable indications to the literary style and genre employed from the Greco-
Roman world.

Thomas, C. M. "Word and Deed: The *Acts of Peter* and Orality," *Apocrypha* 3 (1992), 125–64.
The author seeks to describe the interaction between written and oral modes in antiquity.

## Apocryphal apocalypses

Bauckham, R. "The *Apocalypse of Peter*: A Jewish Christian Apocalypse from the Time of Bar
Kokhba," *Apocrypha* 5 (1994), 7–111. The most thorough scholarly analysis of that apocalypse to date, placing the book in close historic proximity to the Jewish Bar Kokhba revolt
(ca. 134 CE).

Frankfurter, D. "Early Christian Apocalypticism: Literature and Social World." Pp. 415–53 in
*Encyclopedia of Apocalypticism*, vol. 1: *The Origins of Apocalypticism in Judaism and Christianity*.
Edited by John J. Collins. New York and London: Continuum, 2003. Frankfurter examines
apocryphal apocalypses of the first three centuries CE showing their readers' attraction to
heavenly revelation as a mode of authority.

Himmelfarb, Martha. *Tours of Hell: An Apocalyptic Form in Jewish and Christian Literature*.
Philadelpia: University of Pennsylvania Press, 1983. The study traces the genre of the tour
apocalypse back to the Jewish third-century BCE *Book of the Watchers*; the Christian
*Apocalypse of Peter* is linked with later Jewish tours of hell; the combination of sin and pun-
ishment, common to Jewish and Christian tour apocalypses, is traced to a common, if lost,
Jewish source. The author employs a similar analytical approach for examining the
apocalyptic theme of the ascent to heaven in her *Ascent to Heaven in Jewish and Christian
Apocalypses*. Oxford: Oxford University Press, 1993.

Yarbro Collins, A. "Early Christian Apocalyptic Literature." *Aufstieg und Niedergang der römischen
Welt*. 2. 25/6 (1988), 4665–711. Influential article, defines important criteria by which to
identify the apocalypse as a literary genre.

## References

Bauckham, Richard J. "Early Jewish Visions of Hell," *Journal of Theological Studies* 41 (1990),
355–85.

Bornkamm, Günther. *Mythos und Legende in den apokryphen Thomasakten. Beiträge zur
Geschichte der Gnosis und zur Vorgeschichte des Manichäismus*. Forschungen zur Religion
und Literatur des Alten und Neuen Testaments, Heft 31. Göttingen: Vandenhoeck &
Ruprecht, 1933.

Collins, John. J. "Introduction: Toward the Morphology of a Genre." Pp. 1–20 in *Apocalypse: The
Morphology of a Genre*. Edited by John J. Collins. Semeia, 14. Chico, CA: Scholars Press, 1979.

Farquhar, J. N. "The Apostle Thomas in North India," *Bulletin of the John Rylands Library* 10
(1926/7), 80–111.

Hofius, Otfried. "Unbekannte Jesusworte." Pp. 355–82 in *Evangelium und die Evangelien: Vorträge vom Tübinger Symposium 1982*. Edited by Peter Stuhlmacher. Tübingen: Mohr Siebeck, 1983.

James, M. R. "A New Text of the Apocalypse of Peter," *Journal of Theological Studies* 12 (1911), 362–83.

Junod, Eric and Jean-Daniel Kaestli (eds.). *Acta Iohannis*. 2 vols. Corpus Christianorum. Series Apocryphorum, 1–2. Turnhout: Brepols, 1983.

Klijn, A. F. J. Review of *Neutestamentliche Apokryphen in deutscher Übersetzung* by Wilhelm Schneemelcher, *Vigiliae Christianae* 42 (1966), 504–5.

Koester, Helmut. *Introduction to the New Testament*. Philadelphia: Fortress Press, 1982.

Koestlin, Karl Reinhold. "Das gnostische System des Buches Pistis Sophia." Vol. 1, pp. 1–104; vol. 2, pp. 137–96 in *Theologische Jahrbücher 13*. Tübingen: Ludwig Friedrich Fues, 1854.

Lipsius, R. A. *Die Apokryphen Apostelgeschichten und Apostellegenden: Ein Beitrag zur altchristlichen Literaturgeschichte*. Braunschweig: C. A. Schwetschke und Sohn, 1883.

MacDonald, Dennis Ronald. *The Legend and the Apostle: The Battle for Paul in Story and Canon*. Philadelphia: Westminster Press, 1983.

MacDonald, Dennis Ronand. *The Acts of Andrew and the Acts of Andrew and Matthias in the City of the Cannibals*. Texts and Translations, 33. Christian Apocrypha 1. Atlanta: Scholars Press, 1990.

Mansi, Gian Domenico. *Sacrorum Conciliorum nova et amplissima collectio*. 31 vols. Florence and Venice, 1758–98.

Ménard, Jacques E. "Les Origines de la gnose," *Revue des sciences religieuses* 42 (1968), 24–38

Quispel, Gilles. "Latin Tatian or the Gospel of Thomas in Limburg," *Journal of Biblical Literature* 88 (1969), 321–30.

Resch, Alfred. *Agrapha: aussercanonische Evangelienfragmente gesammelt und untersucht*. Leipzig: J. C. Hinrichs, 1889.

Rordorf, Willy. "Les Actes de Paul sur papyrus: Problèmes liés aux PMich inv 1317 et 3788." Pp. 453–61 in *Proceedings of the XVIII International Congress of Papyrology, Athens, 25–31 May 1986*, vol. 1. Athens: Greek Papyrological Society, 1988.

Rudolph, Kurt. *Gnosis: The Nature and History of Gnosticism*. Trans. and ed. Robert McLachlan Wilson. San Francisco: Harper & Row, 1983.

Schmidt, Carl. *Die alten Petrusakten im Zusammenhang der apokryphen Apostellitteratur nebst einem neuentdeckten Fragment*. Texte und Untersuchungen, 24. Leipzig: J. C. Hinrichs, 1903.

Schmidt, Carl unter Mitarbeit von W. Schubart. Πραξεις Παυλου, *Acta Pauli. Nach dem Papyrus der Hamburger Staats- und Universitäts-Bibliothek*. Glückstadt and Hamburg, 1936.

Schmidt, Carl (ed.) and Violet Macdermot (trans.). *Pistis Sophia*. Nag Hammadi Studies, 9. Leiden: E. J. Brill, 1978.

Tischendorf, Constantin von. *Evangelia Apocrypha: Adhibitis plurimis codicibus graecis et latinis maximam partem nunc primum consultis atque ineditorum copia insignibus*. 2nd edn. Leipzig: Hermann Mendelssohn, 1876.

Vouaux, Léon. *Les Actes de Pierre. Introduction, Textes, Traduction et Commentaires*. Paris: Letouzey & Ané, 1922.

Zeegers-Vander Vorst, Nicole. "Quatre Pièces apocryphes néotestamentaires en version syriaque." Pp. 65–77 in *Symposium Syriacum 1980*. Rome: Pontificum Institutum Studiorum Orientalium / Pontificio Istituto Orientale, 1983.

# Index

CPSIA information can be obtained
at www.ICGtesting.com
Printed in the USA
BVOW09*0452121217

502544BV00012B/142/P